Praise for *Hands-On Machine Learning with Scikit-Learn and PyTorch*

This book is an excellent starting point for beginners looking to understand the essential history and foundational concepts of machine learning. With well-structured code sections and practical examples, it takes readers from the basics to cutting-edge machine learning and deep learning techniques, leveraging PyTorch and Scikit-Learn for hands-on implementation.

—*Louis-François Bouchard, educator and cofounder and CTO at Towards AI*

Géron strikes the sweet spot: practical Scikit-Learn and PyTorch implementations that teach concepts, balanced with theory that clarifies rather than overwhelms. From first principles to state-of-the-art methods, this hands-on approach gets you productive quickly. This is the book I recommend for getting started in ML.

—*Ulf Bissbort, cofounder and CTO at ZefHub*

This book is your ultimate map for navigating the uncharted world of machine learning. Keep it within reach.

—*Haesun Park, Microsoft AI MVP, Google Cloud Champion Innovator*

This book launched a generation of ML practitioners. Brilliantly updated to cover PyTorch, it is once again the definitive hands-on guide to the field.

—*Tarun Narayanan, machine learning engineer, Amazon AGI*

A true bible for beginners in machine learning, this book not only provides clear explanations and hands-on examples but also uses thoughtfully designedfigures to simplify complex concepts, making it an indispensable resource for building a strong foundation.

—Meetu Malhotra,
Harrisburg University of Science and Technology, PA USA

Hands-On Machine Learning with Scikit-Learn and PyTorch

Concepts, Tools, and Techniques to Build Intelligent Systems

Aurélien Geron

Hands-On Machine Learning with Scikit-Learn and PyTorch
by Aurélien Geron

Published by O'Reilly Media, Inc., 141 Stony Circle, Suite 195, Santa Rosa, CA 95401.

O'Reilly books may be purchased for educational, business, or sales promotional use. Online editions are also available for most titles (*https://oreilly.com*). For more information, contact our corporate/institutional sales department: 800-998-9938 or *corporate@oreilly.com*.

Acquisitions Editor: Nicole Butterfield
Develeopment Editor: Michele Cronin
Production Editor: Beth Kelly
Copyeditor: Sonia Saruba
Proofreader: Kim Cofer
Indexer: Potomac Indexing LLC
Cover Designer: Susan Brown
Cover Illustrator: José Marzan Jr.
Interior Designer: David Futato
Interior Illustrator: Kate Dullea

October 2025: First Edition

Revision History for the First Edition
2025-10-22: First Release

See *https://oreilly.com/catalog/errata.csp?isbn=9798341607989* for release details.

979-8-341-60798-9

[LSI]

Table of Contents

Part II. Neural Networks and Deep Learning

Preface

In 2006, Geoffrey Hinton et al. published a paper (*https://homl.info/hinton2006*)[1] showing how to train a deep neural network capable of recognizing handwritten digits with state-of-the-art precision (>98%). They branded this technique "deep learning". A deep neural network is a (very) simplified model of our cerebral cortex, composed of a stack of layers of artificial neurons. Training a deep neural net was widely considered impossible at the time,[2] and most researchers had abandoned the idea in the late 1990s. This paper revived the interest of the scientific community, and before long many new papers demonstrated that deep learning was not only possible, but capable of mind-blowing achievements that no other machine learning (ML) technique could hope to match (with the help of tremendous computing power and great amounts of data). This enthusiasm soon extended to many other areas of machine learning.

A decade later, machine learning had already conquered many industries, ranking web results, recommending videos to watch and products to buy, sorting items on production lines, sometimes even driving cars. Machine learning often made the headlines, for example when DeepMind's AlphaFold machine learning system solved a long-standing protein-folding problem that had stomped researchers for decades. But most of the time, machine learning was just working discretely in the background. However, another decade later came the rise of AI assistants: from ChatGPT in 2022, Gemini, Claude, and Grok in 2023, and many others since then.

1 Geoffrey E. Hinton et al., "A Fast Learning Algorithm for Deep Belief Nets", *Neural Computation* 18 (2006): 1527–1554.

2 Despite the fact that Yann LeCun's deep convolutional neural networks had worked well for image recognition since the 1990s, although they were not as general-purpose.

AI has now truly taken off and it is rapidly transforming every single industry: what used to be sci-fi is now very real.[3]

Machine Learning in Your Projects

So, naturally you are excited about machine learning and would love to join the party! Perhaps you would like to give your homemade robot a brain of its own? Make it recognize faces? Or learn to walk around?

Or maybe your company has tons of data (user logs, financial data, production data, machine sensor data, hotline stats, HR reports, etc.), and more than likely you could unearth some hidden gems if you just knew where to look. With machine learning, you could accomplish the following and much more (*https://homl.info/usecases*):

- Segment customers and find the best marketing strategy for each group.
- Recommend products for each client based on what similar clients bought.
- Detect which transactions are likely to be fraudulent.
- Forecast next year's revenue.
- Predict peak workloads and suggest optimal staffing levels.
- Build a chatbot to assist your customers.

Whatever the reason, you have decided to learn machine learning and implement it in your projects. Great idea!

Objective and Approach

This book assumes that you know close to nothing about machine learning. Its goal is to give you the concepts, tools, and intuition you need to implement programs capable of *learning from data*.

We will cover a large number of techniques, from the simplest and most commonly used (such as linear regression) to some of the deep learning techniques that regularly win competitions. For this, we will be using Python—the leading language for data science and machine learning—as well as open source and production-ready Python frameworks:

3 Geoffrey Hinton was awarded the 2018 Turing Award (with Yann LeCun and Yoshua Bengio) and the 2024 Nobel Prize in Physics (with John Hopfield) for early work on neural networks back in the 1980s. DeepMind's founder and CEO Demis Hassabis and director John Jumper were awarded the 2024 Nobel Prize in Chemistry for their work on AlphaFold. They shared this Nobel Prize with another protein researcher, David Baker.

- Scikit-Learn (*https://scikit-learn.org*) is very easy to use, yet it implements many machine learning algorithms efficiently, so it makes for a great entry point to learning machine learning. It was created by David Cournapeau in 2007, then led by a team of researchers at the French Institute for Research in Computer Science and Automation (Inria), and recently Probabl.ai.
- PyTorch (*https://pytorch.org*) is a powerful and flexible library for deep learning. It makes it possible to train and run all sorts of neural networks efficiently, and it can distribute the computations across multiple GPUs (graphics processing units). PyTorch (PT) was developed by Facebook's AI Research lab (FAIR) and first released in 2016. It evolved from Torch, an older framework coded in Lua. In 2022, PyTorch was transitioned to the PyTorch Foundation, under the Linux Foundation, to promote community-driven development.

We will also use these open source machine learning libraries along the way:

- XGBoost (*https://xgboost.readthedocs.io*) in Chapter 6 to implement a powerful technique called *gradient boosting*.
- Hugging Face (*https://huggingface.co*) libraries in Chapters 13 and 15 to download datasets and pretrained models, including transformer models. Transformers are incredibly powerful and versatile, and they are the main building block of virtually all AI assistants today.
- Gymnasium (*https://gymnasium.farama.org*) in Chapter 19 for reinforcement learning (i.e., training autonomous agents).

The book favors a hands-on approach, growing an intuitive understanding of machine learning through concrete working examples and just a little bit of theory.

While you can read this book without picking up your laptop, I highly recommend you experiment with the code examples.

Code Examples

All the code examples in this book are open source and available online at *https://github.com/ageron/handson-mlp*, as Jupyter notebooks. These are interactive documents containing text, images, and executable code snippets (Python in our case). The easiest and quickest way to get started is to run these notebooks using Google Colab: this is a free service that allows you to run any Jupyter notebook directly online without having to install anything on your machine. All you need is a web browser and a Google account.

In this book, I will assume that you are using Google Colab, but I have also tested the notebooks on other online platforms such as Kaggle and Binder, so you can use those if you prefer. Alternatively, you can install the required libraries and tools (or the Docker image for this book) and run the notebooks directly on your own machine. See the instructions at *https://homl.info/install-p*.

This book is here to help you get your job done. If you wish to use additional content beyond the code examples, and that use falls outside the scope of fair use guidelines, (such as selling or distributing content from O'Reilly books, or incorporating a significant amount of material from this book into your product's documentation), please reach out to O'Reilly for permission, at *permissions@oreilly.com*.

We appreciate, but generally do not require, attribution. An attribution usually includes the title, author, publisher, and ISBN. For example: "*Hands-On Machine Learning with Scikit-Learn and PyTorch* by Aurélien Geron. Copyright 2026 Aurélien Geron, 979-8-341-60798-9."

Prerequisites

This book assumes that you have some Python programming experience. If you don't know Python yet, *https://learnpython.org* is a great place to start. The official tutorial on Python.org (*https://docs.python.org/3/tutorial*) is also quite good.

This book also assumes that you are familiar with Python's main scientific libraries—in particular, NumPy (*https://numpy.org*), pandas (*https://pandas.pydata.org*), and Matplotlib (*https://matplotlib.org*). If you have never used these libraries, don't worry; they're easy to learn, and I've created a tutorial for each of them. You can access them online at *https://homl.info/tutorials-p*.

Moreover, if you want to fully understand how the machine learning algorithms work (not just how to use them), then you should have at least a basic understanding of a few math concepts, especially linear algebra. Specifically, you should know what vectors and matrices are, and how to perform some simple operations like adding vectors, or transposing and multiplying matrices. If you need a quick introduction to linear algebra (it's really not rocket science!), I provide a tutorial at *https://homl.info/tutorials-p*. You will also find a tutorial on differential calculus, which may be helpful to understand how neural networks are trained, but it's not entirely essential to grasp the important concepts. This book also uses other mathematical concepts occasionally, such as exponentials and logarithms, a bit of probability theory, and some basic concepts from statistics, but nothing too advanced. If you need help on any of these, please check out *https://khanacademy.org*, which offers many excellent and free math courses online.

Roadmap

This book is organized in two parts. Part I, "The Fundamentals of Machine Learning", covers the following topics:

- What machine learning is, what problems it tries to solve, and the main categories and fundamental concepts of its systems
- The steps in a typical machine learning project
- Learning by fitting a model to data
- Minimizing a cost function (i.e., a measure of prediction errors)
- Handling, cleaning, and preparing data
- Selecting and engineering features (i.e., data fields)
- Selecting a model and tuning hyperparameters using cross-validation (e.g., training many model variants and choosing the one that performs best on data it didn't see during training)
- The challenges of machine learning, in particular underfitting and overfitting (the bias/variance trade-off)
- The most common learning algorithms: linear and polynomial regression, logistic regression, *k*-nearest neighbors, decision trees, random forests, and ensemble methods
- Reducing the dimensionality of the training data to fight the "curse of dimensionality"
- Other unsupervised learning techniques, including clustering, density estimation, and anomaly detection

Part II, "Neural Networks and Deep Learning", covers the following topics:

- What neural nets are and what they're good for
- Building and training deep neural nets using PyTorch
- The most important neural net architectures: feedforward neural nets for tabular data; convolutional nets for computer vision; recurrent nets and long short-term memory (LSTM) nets for sequence processing; encoder-decoders, transformers, state space models (SSMs), and hybrid architectures for natural language processing, vision, and more; autoencoders, generative adversarial networks (GANs), and diffusion models for generative learning
- How to build an agent (e.g., a bot in a game) that can learn good strategies through trial and error, using reinforcement learning
- Loading and preprocessing large amounts of data efficiently

The first part is based mostly on Scikit-Learn; the second part uses mostly PyTorch.

Don't jump into deep waters too hastily: deep learning is no doubt one of the most exciting areas in machine learning, but you should master the fundamentals first. Moreover, many problems can be solved quite well using simpler techniques such as random forests and ensemble methods (discussed in Part I). Deep learning is best suited for complex problems such as image recognition, speech recognition, or natural language processing, and it often requires a lot of data, computing power, and patience (unless you can leverage a pretrained neural network, as you will see).

If you are particularly interested in one topic and want to reach it as quickly as possible, Figure P-1 will show you which chapters you must read first, and which ones you can safely skip.

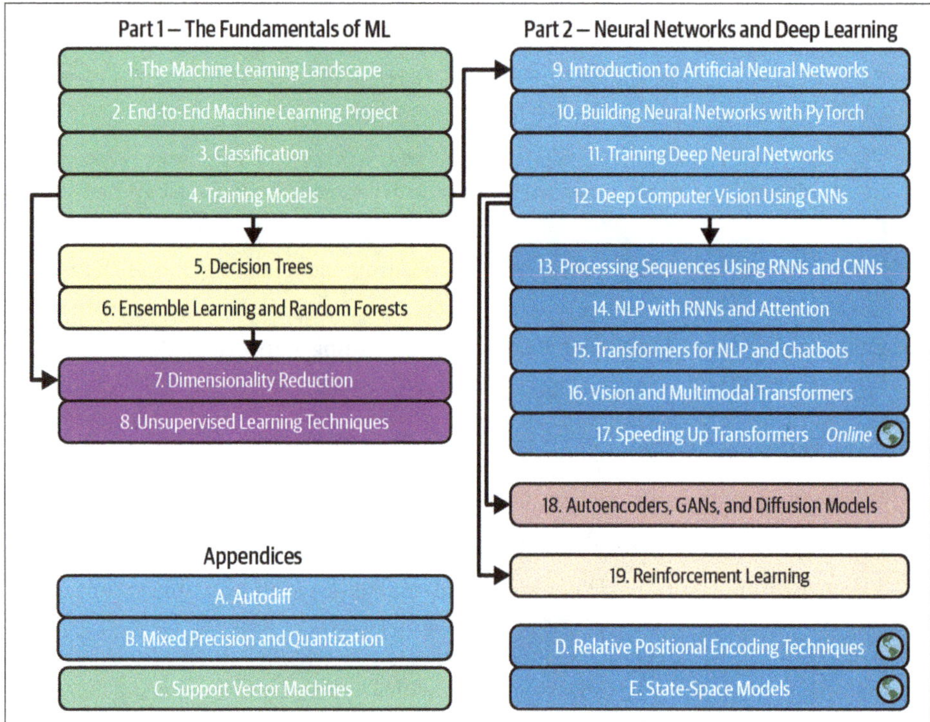

Figure P-1. Chapter dependencies

Changes Between the TensorFlow and PyTorch Versions

I wrote three TensorFlow (TF) editions of this book, published by O'Reilly in 2017, 2019, and 2022. TF was the leading deep learning library for many years, used internally by Google and therefore optimized for production at scale. But PyTorch has gradually taken the lead, owing to its simplicity, flexibility and openness: it now dominates research papers and open source projects, which means that most new models are available in PyTorch first. As a result, the industry has also gradually shifted toward PyTorch.

In recent years, Google has reduced its investments in TensorFlow, and focused more on JAX, another excellent deep learning library with a great mix of qualities for both research and production. However, its adoption is still low compared to PyTorch.

This is why I chose to use PyTorch this time around! O'Reilly and I decided to make it the first edition of a new PyTorch series rather than the fourth edition of the original series. This leaves the door open for a JAX series or perhaps a new edition for the TF series (time will tell if either are needed).

If you have already read the latest TensorFlow version of this book, here are the main changes you will find in this book (see *https://homl.info/changes-p* for more details):

- All the code in the book was updated to recent library versions.
- All the code in Part II was migrated from TensorFlow and Keras to PyTorch. There were significant changes in all of these chapters.
- TensorFlow-specific content was removed, including former Chapters 12 and 13, and former Appendices C and D.
- Chapter 10 now introduces PyTorch.
- I also added three new chapters on transformers:
  - Chapter 15 covers transformers for natural language processing, including how to build a chatbot.
  - Chapter 16 presents vision transformers and multimodal transformers.
  - Chapter 17, available online at *https://homl.info/*, discusses several advanced techniques to speed up and scale up transformers. This includes FlashAttention, mixture of experts (MoE), low-rank adaptation (LoRA), and many more.
- There are also three new appendices: Appendix B explains how to shrink models so they can run faster and fit on smaller devices, "Relative Positional Encoding" discusses advanced positional encoding techniques for transformers, and "State-Space Models (SSMs)" presents state-space models.

- To make room for the newer content, the chapter on support vector machines (SVMs) was moved online (*https://homl.info*) and renamed "Support Vector Machines"; the last two appendices are also online at the same URL, and the deployment chapter was partially merged into Chapter 10.

The three editions of the TensorFlow/Keras version of this book are nicknamed homl1, homl2, and homl3. This book, which is the first edition of the PyTorch version, is nicknamed homlp. Try saying that three times in a row.

Most of the changes compared to the latest TensorFlow edition are in the second part of the book. If you have read homl3, then don't expect big changes in the first part of the book: the fundamental concepts of machine learning haven't changed since 2022.

Other Resources

Many excellent resources are available to learn about machine learning. For example, Andrew Ng's ML course on Coursera (*https://homl.info/ngcourse*) is amazing, although it requires a significant time investment.

There are also many interesting websites about machine learning, including Scikit-Learn's exceptional User Guide (*https://homl.info/skdoc*). You may also enjoy Dataquest (*https://dataquest.io*), which provides very nice interactive tutorials, and countless ML blogs and YouTube channels.

There are many other introductory books about machine learning. In particular:

- Joel Grus's *Data Science from Scratch*, 2nd edition (O'Reilly), presents the fundamentals of machine learning and implements some of the main algorithms in pure Python (from scratch, as the name suggests).
- Stephen Marsland's *Machine Learning: An Algorithmic Perspective*, 2nd edition (Chapman & Hall), is a great introduction to machine learning, covering a wide range of topics in depth with code examples in Python (also from scratch, but using NumPy).
- Sebastian Raschka's *Machine Learning with PyTorch and Scikit-Learn*, 1st edition (Packt Publishing), is also a great introduction to machine learning using Scikit-Learn and PyTorch.
- François Chollet's *Deep Learning with Python*, 3rd edition (Manning), is a very practical book that covers a large range of topics in a clear and concise way, as you might expect from the author of the excellent Keras library. It favors code examples over mathematical theory.

- Andriy Burkov's *The Hundred-Page Machine Learning Book* (*https://themlbook.com*) (self-published) is very short but covers an impressive range of topics, introducing them in approachable terms without shying away from the math equations.
- Yaser S. Abu-Mostafa, Malik Magdon-Ismail, and Hsuan-Tien Lin's *Learning from Data* (AMLBook) is a more theoretical approach to ML that provides deep insights, in particular on the bias/variance trade-off (see Chapter 4).
- Stuart Russell and Peter Norvig's *Artificial Intelligence: A Modern Approach*, 4th edition (Pearson), is a great (and huge) book covering an incredible amount of topics, including machine learning. It helps put ML into perspective.
- Jeremy Howard and Sylvain Gugger's *Deep Learning for Coders with fastai and PyTorch* (O'Reilly) provides a wonderfully clear and practical introduction to deep learning using the fastai and PyTorch libraries.
- Andrew Ng's *Machine Learning Yearning* is a free ebook that provides a thoughtful exploration of machine learning, focusing on the practical considerations of building and deploying models, including data quality and long-term maintenance.
- Lewis Tunstall, Leandro von Werra, and Thomas Wolf's *Natural Language Processing with Transformers: Building Language Applications with Hugging Face* (O'Reilly) is a great practical dive into transformers using popular libraries by Hugging Face.
- Jay Alammar and Maarten Grootendorst's *Hands-On Large Language Models* is a beautifully illustrated book on LLMs, covering everything you need to know to understand, train, fine-tune, and use LLMs across a wide variety of tasks.

Finally, joining ML competition websites such as Kaggle.com will allow you to practice your skills on real-world problems, with help and insights from some of the best ML professionals out there.

Conventions Used in This Book

The following typographical conventions are used in this book:

Italic
: Indicates new terms, URLs, email addresses, filenames, and file extensions.

`Constant width`
: Used for program listings, as well as within paragraphs to refer to program elements such as variable or function names, databases, data types, environment variables, statements, and keywords.

`Constant width bold`
: Shows commands or other text that should be typed literally by the user.

`Constant width italic`
: Shows text that should be replaced with user-supplied values or by values determined by context.

Punctuation
: To avoid any confusion, punctuation appears outside of quotes throughout the book. My apologies to the purists.

This element signifies a tip or suggestion.

This element signifies a general note.

This element indicates a warning or caution.

O'Reilly Online Learning

For more than 40 years, *O'Reilly Media* has provided technology and business training, knowledge, and insight to help companies succeed.

Our unique network of experts and innovators share their knowledge and expertise through books, articles, and our online learning platform. O'Reilly's online learning platform gives you on-demand access to live training courses, in-depth learning paths, interactive coding environments, and a vast collection of text and video from O'Reilly and 200+ other publishers. For more information, visit *https://oreilly.com*.

How to Contact Us

Please address comments and questions concerning this book to the publisher:

O'Reilly Media, Inc.
141 Stony Circle, Suite 195
Santa Rosa, CA 95401
800-889-8969 (in the United States or Canada)
707-827-7019 (international or local)
707-829-0104 (fax)
support@oreilly.com
https://oreilly.com/about/contact.html

We have a web page for this book, where we list errata, examples, and any additional information. You can access this page at *https://oreil.ly/hands-on-machine-learning*.

For news and information about our books and courses, visit *https://oreilly.com*.

Find us on LinkedIn: *https://linkedin.com/company/oreilly-media*

Watch us on YouTube: *https://youtube.com/oreillymedia*

Acknowledgments

Never in my wildest dreams did I imagine that the three TensorFlow editions of this book would reach such a large audience. I received so many messages from readers, many asking questions, some kindly pointing out errata, and most sending me encouraging words. I cannot express how grateful I am to all these readers for their tremendous support. Thank you all so very much! Please do not hesitate to file issues on GitHub (*https://homl.info/issues-p*) if you find errors in the code examples (or just to ask questions), or to submit errata (*https://homl.info/errata-p*) if you find errors in the text. Some readers also shared how this book helped them get their first job, or how it helped them solve a concrete problem they were working on. I find such feedback incredibly motivating. If you find this book helpful, I would love it if you could share your story with me, either privately (e.g., via LinkedIn (*https://linkedin.com/in/aurelien-geron*)) or publicly (e.g., tweet me at @aureliengeron or write an Amazon review (*https://homl.info/amazon-p*)).

Huge thanks as well to all the generous people who offered their time and expertise to review this book, correcting errors and making countless suggestions. They made this book so much better: Jeremy Howard, Haesun Park, Omar Sanseviero, Lewis Tunstall, Leandro Von Werra, and Sam Witteveen reviewed the table of contents and helped me refine the scope of the book. Hesam Hassani, Ashu Jha, Meetu Malhotra, and Ammar Mohanna reviewed the first part, while Ulf Bissbort, Louis-Francois Bouchard, Luba Elliot, Thomas Lacombe, Tarun Narayanan, Marco Tabor, and my dear brother Sylvain reviewed the second part. Special thanks to Haesun Park, who reviewed every single chapter. You are all amazing!

Of course, this book would not exist without the fantastic staff at O'Reilly. I am especially indebted to Michele Cronin, who reviewed every chapter and supported me weekly for a whole year. I am also deeply grateful to Nicole Butterfield for leading this project and helping refine the book's scope, and to the production team—particularly Beth Kelly and Kristen Brown—who did a remarkable job. I want to acknowledge Sonia Saruba for her countless careful copyedits, Kate Dullea for making my diagrams much prettier, and Susan Thompson for the beautiful orangutan on the cover.

Last but not least, I am infinitely grateful to my beloved wife, Emmanuelle, and to our three wonderful children—Alexandre, Rémi, and Gabrielle—for encouraging me to work so hard on this book. Their insatiable curiosity was priceless: explaining some of the most difficult concepts in this book to my wife and children helped me clarify my own thoughts and directly improved many parts of it. Plus, they kept bringing me cookies and coffee. Who could ask for more?

PART I

The Fundamentals of Machine Learning

CHAPTER 1

The Machine Learning Landscape

Not so long ago, if you had picked up your phone and asked it to tell you the way home, it would have ignored you—and people would have questioned your sanity. But machine learning is no longer science fiction: billions of people use it every day. And the truth is it has actually been around for decades in some specialized applications, such as optical character recognition (OCR). The first ML application that really became mainstream, improving the lives of hundreds of millions of people, discretely took over the world back in the 1990s: the *spam filter*. It's not exactly a self-aware robot, but it does technically qualify as machine learning: it has actually learned so well that you seldom need to flag an email as spam anymore. Then thanks to big data, hardware improvements, and a few algorithmic innovations, hundreds of ML applications followed and now quietly power hundreds of products and features that you use regularly: voice prompts, automatic translation, image search, product recommendations, and many more. And finally came ChatGPT, Gemini (formerly Bard), Claude, Perplexity, and many other chatbots: AI is no longer just powering services in the background, it *is* the service itself.

Where does machine learning start and where does it end? What exactly does it mean for a machine to *learn* something? If I download a copy of all Wikipedia articles, has my computer really learned something? Is it suddenly smarter? In this chapter I will start by clarifying what machine learning is and why you may want to use it.

Then, before we set out to explore the machine learning continent, we will take a look at the map and learn about the main regions and the most notable landmarks: supervised versus unsupervised learning and their variants, online versus batch learning, instance-based versus model-based learning. Then we will look at the workflow of a typical ML project, discuss the main challenges you may face, and cover how to evaluate and fine-tune a machine learning system.

This chapter introduces a lot of fundamental concepts (and jargon) that every data scientist should know by heart. It will be a high-level overview (it's the only chapter without much code), all rather simple, but my goal is to ensure everything is crystal clear to you before we continue on to the rest of the book. So grab a coffee and let's get started!

If you are already familiar with machine learning basics, you may want to skip directly to Chapter 2. If you are not sure, try to answer all the questions listed at the end of the chapter before moving on.

What Is Machine Learning?

Machine learning is the science (and art) of programming computers so they can *learn from data*.

Here is a slightly more general definition:

> [Machine learning is the] field of study that gives computers the ability to learn without being explicitly programmed.
>
> —Arthur Samuel, 1959

And a more engineering-oriented one:

> A computer program is said to learn from experience *E* with respect to some task *T* and some performance measure *P*, if its performance on *T*, as measured by *P*, improves with experience *E*.
>
> —Tom Mitchell, 1997

Your spam filter is a machine learning program that, given examples of spam emails (flagged by users) and examples of regular emails (nonspam, also called "ham"), can learn to flag spam. The examples that the system uses to learn are called the *training set*. Each training example is called a *training instance* (or *sample*). The part of a machine learning system that learns and makes predictions is called a *model*. Neural networks and random forests are examples of models.

In this case, the task *T* is to flag spam for new emails, the experience *E* is the *training data*, and the performance measure *P* needs to be defined; for example, you can use the ratio of correctly classified emails. This particular performance measure is called *accuracy*, and it is often used in classification tasks (we will discuss several others in Chapter 3).

If you just download a copy of all Wikipedia articles, your computer has a lot more data, but it is not suddenly better at any task. This is not machine learning.

Why Use Machine Learning?

Consider how you would write a spam filter using traditional programming techniques (Figure 1-1):

1. First you would examine what spam typically looks like. You might notice that some words or phrases (such as "4U", "credit card", "free", and "amazing") tend to come up a lot in the subject line. Perhaps you would also notice a few other patterns in the sender's name, the email's body, and other parts of the email.
2. You would write a detection algorithm for each of the patterns that you noticed, and your program would flag emails as spam if a number of these patterns were detected.
3. You would test your program and repeat steps 1 and 2 until it was good enough to launch.

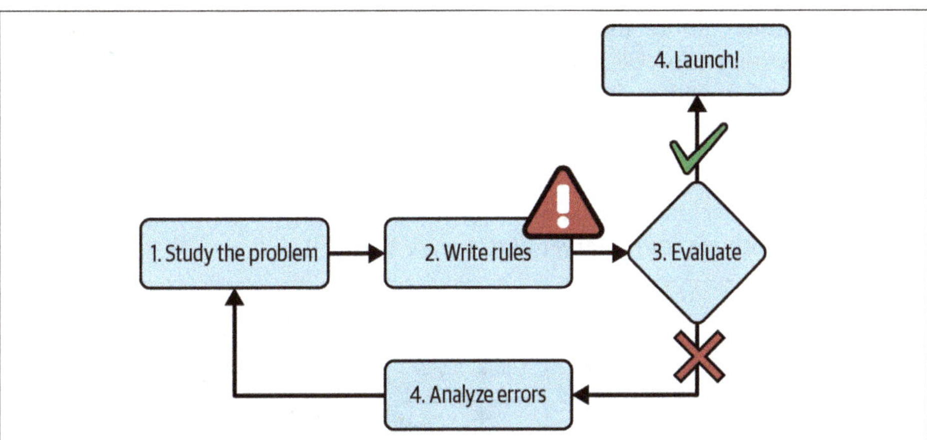

Figure 1-1. The traditional approach

Since the problem is difficult, your program will likely become a long list of complex rules—pretty hard to maintain.

In contrast, a spam filter based on machine learning techniques automatically learns which words and phrases are good predictors of spam by detecting unusually frequent patterns of words in the spam examples compared to the ham examples (Figure 1-2). The program is much shorter, easier to maintain, and most likely more accurate.

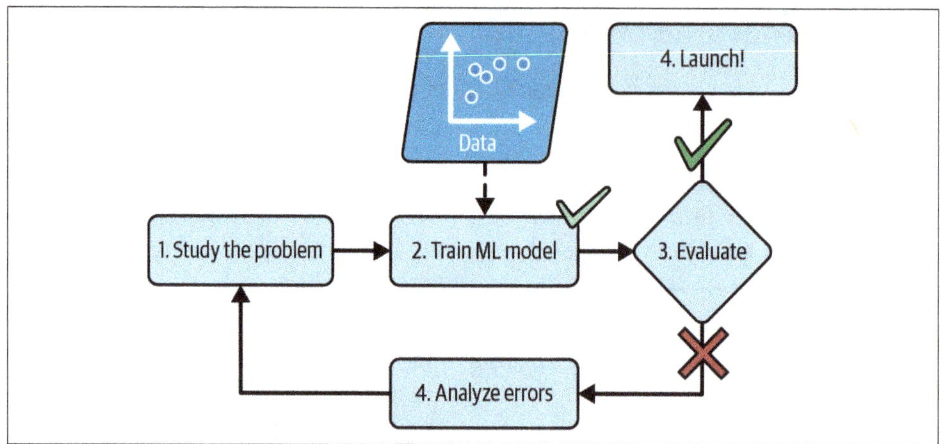

Figure 1-2. The machine learning approach

What if spammers notice that all their emails containing "4U" are blocked? They might start writing "For U" instead. A spam filter using traditional programming techniques would need to be updated to flag "For U" emails. If spammers keep working around your spam filter, you will need to keep writing new rules forever.

In contrast, a spam filter based on machine learning techniques automatically notices that "For U" has become unusually frequent in spam flagged by users, and it starts flagging them without your intervention (Figure 1-3).

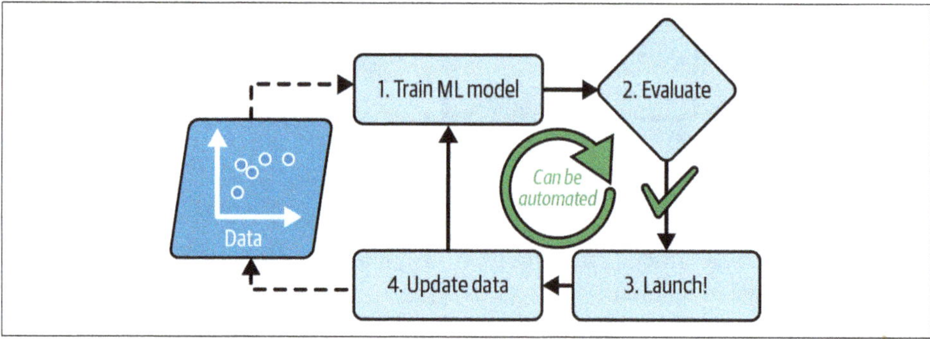

Figure 1-3. Automatically adapting to change

Another area where machine learning shines is for problems that either are too complex for traditional approaches or have no known algorithm. For example, consider speech recognition. Say you want to start simple and write a program capable of distinguishing the words "one" and "two". You might notice that the word "two" starts with a high-pitch sound ("T"), so you could hardcode an algorithm that measures high-pitch sound intensity and use that to distinguish ones and twos—but obviously this technique will not scale to thousands of words spoken by millions of very different people in noisy environments and in dozens of languages. The best solution (at least today) is to write an algorithm that learns by itself, given many example recordings for each word.

Finally, machine learning can help humans learn (Figure 1-4). ML models can be inspected to see what they have learned (although for some models this can be tricky). For instance, once a spam filter has been trained on enough spam, it can easily be inspected to reveal the list of words and combinations of words that it believes are the best predictors of spam. Sometimes this will reveal unsuspected correlations or new trends, and thereby lead to a better understanding of the problem. Digging into large amounts of data to discover hidden patterns is called *data mining*, and machine learning excels at it.

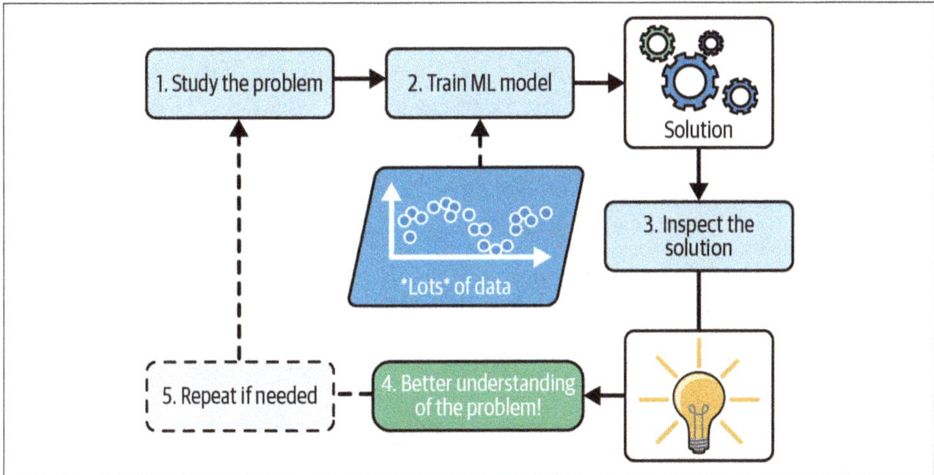

Figure 1-4. Machine learning can help humans learn

To summarize, machine learning is great for:

- Problems for which existing solutions require a lot of work and maintenance, such as long lists of rules (a machine learning model can often simplify code and perform better than the traditional approach)
- Complex problems for which using a traditional approach yields no good solution (the best machine learning techniques can perhaps find a solution)
- Fluctuating environments (a machine learning system can easily be retrained on new data, always keeping it up to date)
- Getting insights about complex problems and large amounts of data

Examples of Applications

Let's look at some concrete examples of machine learning tasks, along with the techniques that can tackle them:

Analyzing images of products on a production line to automatically classify them
: This is image classification, typically performed using convolutional neural networks (CNNs; see Chapter 12) or vision transformers (see Chapter 16).

Detecting tumors in brain scans
: This is semantic image segmentation, where each pixel in the image is classified (as we want to determine the exact location and shape of tumors), typically using CNNs or vision transformers.

Automatically classifying news articles
: This is natural language processing (NLP), and more specifically text classification, which can be tackled using recurrent neural networks (RNNs) and CNNs, but transformers work even better (see Chapter 15).

Automatically flagging offensive comments on discussion forums
: This is also text classification, using the same NLP tools.

Summarizing long documents automatically
: This is a branch of NLP called text summarization, again using the same tools.

Estimating a person's genetic risk for a given disease by analyzing a very long DNA sequence
: Such a task requires discovering spread out patterns across very long sequences, which is where state space models (SSMs) particularly shine (see "State-Space Models (SSMs)" at *https://homl.info*).

Creating a chatbot or a personal assistant
: This involves many NLP components, including natural language understanding (NLU) and question-answering modules.

Forecasting your company's revenue next year, based on many performance metrics
: This is a regression task (i.e., predicting values) that may be tackled using any regression model, such as a linear regression or polynomial regression model (see Chapter 4), a regression support vector machine (see the online appendix on SVMs at *https://homl.info*), a regression random forest (see Chapter 6), or an artificial neural network (see Chapter 9). If you want to take into account sequences of past performance metrics, you may want to use RNNs, CNNs, or transformers (see Chapters 13 to 15).

Making your app react to voice commands
: This is speech recognition, which requires processing audio samples. Since they are long and complex sequences, they are typically processed using RNNs, CNNs, or transformers (see Chapters 13 to 15).

Detecting credit card fraud
: This is anomaly detection, which can be tackled using isolation forests, Gaussian mixture models (see Chapter 8), or autoencoders (see Chapter 18).

Segmenting clients based on their purchases so that you can design a different marketing strategy for each segment
: This is clustering, which can be achieved using *k*-means, DBSCAN, and more (see Chapter 8).

Representing a complex, high-dimensional dataset in a clear and insightful diagram
: This is data visualization, often involving dimensionality reduction techniques (see Chapter 7).

Recommending a product that a client may be interested in, based on past purchases
: This is a recommender system. One approach is to feed past purchases (and other information about the client) to an artificial neural network (see Chapter 9), and get it to output the most likely next purchase. This neural net would typically be trained on past sequences of purchases across all clients.

Building an intelligent bot for a game
: This is often tackled using reinforcement learning (RL; see Chapter 19), which is a branch of machine learning that trains agents (such as bots) to pick the actions that will maximize their rewards over time (e.g., a bot may get a reward every time the player loses some life points), within a given environment (such as the game). The famous AlphaGo program that beat the world champion at the game of Go was built using RL.

This list could go on and on, but hopefully it gives you a sense of the incredible breadth and complexity of the tasks that machine learning can tackle, and the types of techniques that you would use for each task.

Types of Machine Learning Systems

There are so many different types of machine learning systems that it is useful to classify them in broad categories, based on the following criteria:

- How they are guided during training (supervised, unsupervised, semi-supervised, self-supervised, and others)
- Whether or not they can learn incrementally on the fly (online versus batch learning)

- Whether they work by simply comparing new data points to known data points, or instead by detecting patterns in the training data and building a predictive model, much like scientists do (instance-based versus model-based learning)

These criteria are not exclusive; you can combine them in any way you like. For example, a state-of-the-art spam filter may learn on the fly using a deep neural network model trained using human-provided examples of spam and ham; this makes it an online, model-based, supervised learning system.

Let's look at each of these criteria a bit more closely.

Training Supervision

ML systems can be classified according to the amount and type of supervision they get during training. There are many categories, but we'll discuss the main ones: supervised learning, unsupervised learning, self-supervised learning, semi-supervised learning, and reinforcement learning.

Supervised learning

In *supervised learning*, the training set you feed to the algorithm includes the desired solutions, called *labels* (Figure 1-5).

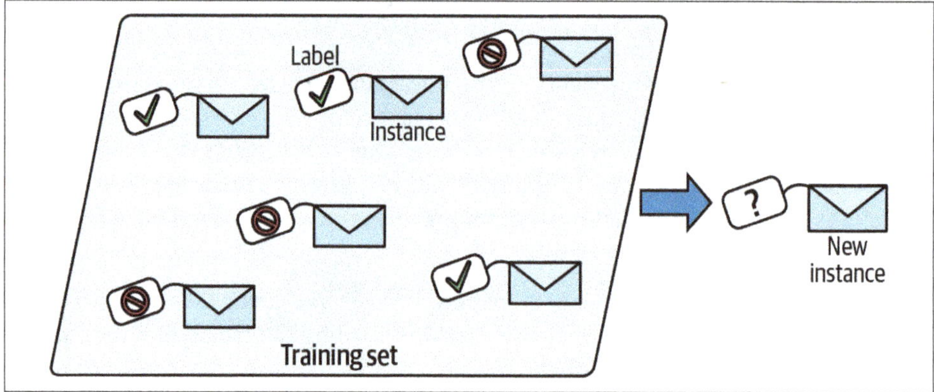

Figure 1-5. A labeled training set for spam classification (an example of supervised learning)

A typical supervised learning task is *classification*. The spam filter is a good example of this: it is trained with many example emails along with their *class* (spam or ham), and it must learn how to classify new emails.

Another typical task is to predict a *target* numeric value, such as the price of a car, given a set of *features* (mileage, age, brand, etc.). This sort of task is called *regression* (Figure 1-6).[1] To train the system, you need to give it many examples of cars, including both their features and their targets (i.e., their prices).

Note that some regression models can be used for classification as well, and vice versa. For example, *logistic regression* is commonly used for classification, as it can output a value that corresponds to the probability of belonging to a given class (e.g., 20% chance of being spam).

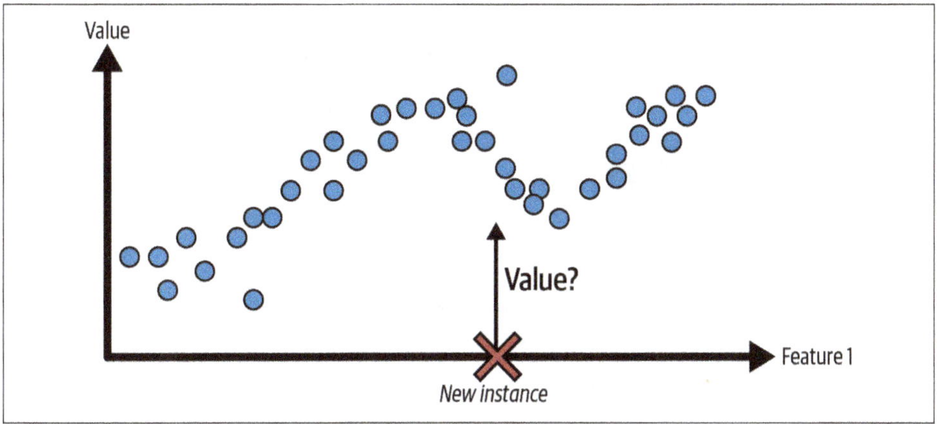

Figure 1-6. A regression problem: predict a value, given an input feature (there are usually multiple input features, and sometimes multiple output values)

The words *target* and *label* are generally treated as synonyms in supervised learning, but *target* is more common in regression tasks and *label* is more common in classification tasks. Moreover, *features* are sometimes called *predictors* or *attributes*. These terms may refer to individual samples (e.g., "this car's mileage feature is equal to 15,000") or to all samples (e.g., "the mileage feature is strongly correlated with price").

Unsupervised learning

In *unsupervised learning*, as you might guess, the training data is unlabeled. The system tries to learn without a teacher.

For example, say you have a lot of data about your blog's visitors. You may want to run a *clustering* algorithm to try to detect groups of similar visitors (Figure 1-7). The features may include the user's age group, their region, their interests, the duration of

1 Fun fact: this odd-sounding name is a statistics term introduced by Francis Galton while he was studying the fact that the children of tall people tend to be shorter than their parents. Since the children were shorter, he called this *regression to the mean*. This name was then applied to the methods he used to analyze correlations between variables.

their sessions, and so on. At no point do you tell the algorithm which group a visitor belongs to: it finds those connections without your help. For example, it might notice that 40% of your visitors are teenagers who love comic books and generally read your blog after school, while 20% are adults who enjoy sci-fi and who visit during the weekends. If you use a *hierarchical clustering* algorithm, it may also subdivide each group into smaller groups. This may help you target your posts for each group.

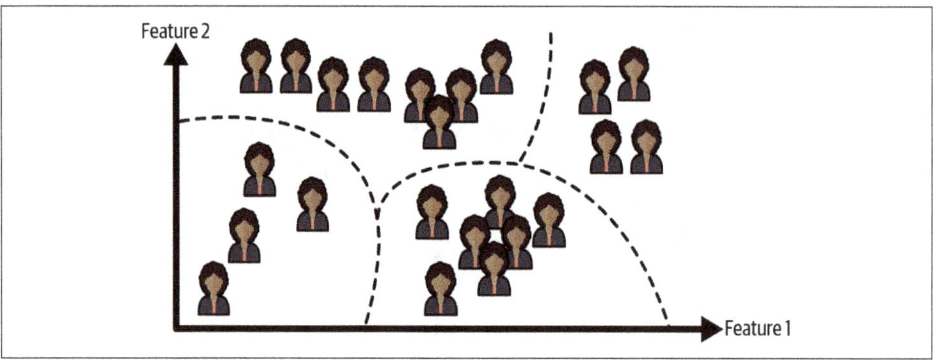

Figure 1-7. Clustering

Visualization algorithms are also good examples of unsupervised learning: you feed them a lot of complex and unlabeled data, and they output a 2D or 3D representation of your data that can easily be plotted (Figure 1-8). These algorithms try to preserve as much structure as they can (e.g., trying to keep separate clusters in the input space from overlapping in the visualization) so that you can understand how the data is organized and perhaps identify unsuspected patterns.

A related task is *dimensionality reduction*, in which the goal is to simplify the data without losing too much information. One way to do this is to merge several correlated features into one. For example, a car's mileage may be strongly correlated with its age, so the dimensionality reduction algorithm will merge them into one feature that represents the car's wear and tear. This is called *feature extraction*.

It is often a good idea to try to reduce the number of dimensions in your training data using a dimensionality reduction algorithm before you feed it to another machine learning algorithm (such as a supervised learning algorithm). It will run much faster, the data will take up less disk and memory space, and in some cases it may also perform better.

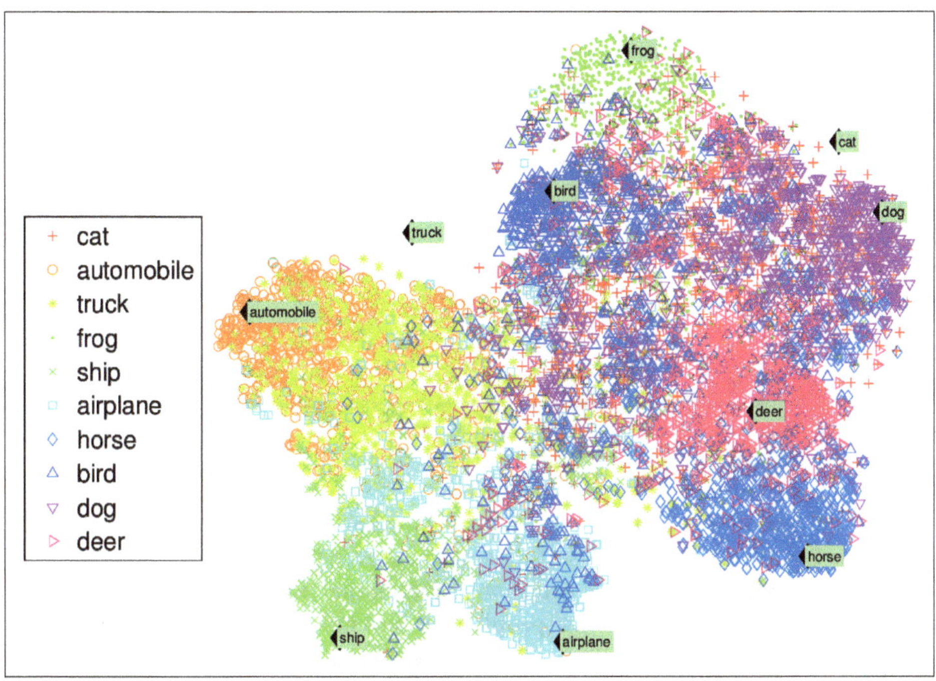

Figure 1-8. Example of a t-SNE visualization highlighting semantic clusters[2]

Yet another important unsupervised task is *anomaly detection*—for example, detecting unusual credit card transactions to prevent fraud, catching manufacturing defects, or automatically removing outliers from a dataset before feeding it to another learning algorithm. The system is shown mostly normal instances during training, so it learns to recognize them; then, when it sees a new instance, it can tell whether it looks like a normal one or whether it is likely an anomaly (see Figure 1-9). The features may include distance from home, time of day, day of the week, amount withdrawn, merchant category, transaction frequency, etc. A very similar task is *novelty detection*: it aims to detect new instances that look different from all instances in the training set. This requires having a very "clean" training set, devoid of any instance that you would like the algorithm to detect. For example, if you have thousands of pictures of dogs, and 1% of these pictures represent Chihuahuas, then a novelty detection algorithm should not treat new pictures of Chihuahuas as novelties. On the other hand, anomaly detection algorithms may consider these dogs as so rare and so different

2 Notice how animals are rather well separated from vehicles and how horses are close to deer but far from birds. Figure reproduced with permission from Richard Socher et al., "Zero-Shot Learning Through Cross-Modal Transfer", *Proceedings of the 26th International Conference on Neural Information Processing Systems* 1 (2013): 935–943.

from other dogs that they would likely classify them as anomalies (no offense to Chihuahuas).

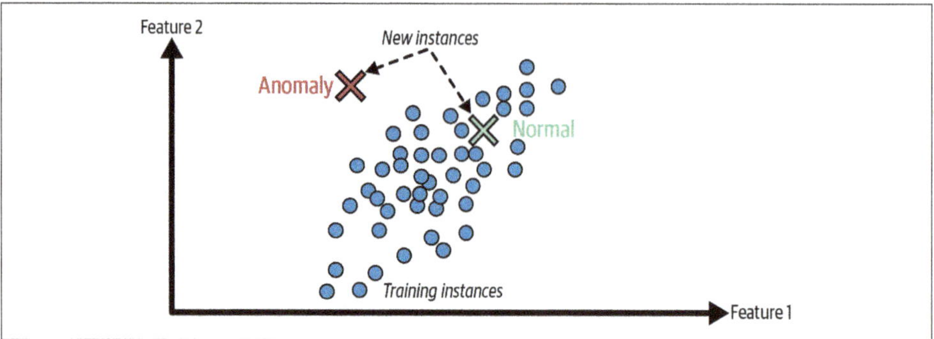

Figure 1-9. Anomaly detection

Finally, another common unsupervised task is *association rule learning*, in which the goal is to dig into large amounts of data and discover interesting relations between attributes. For example, suppose you own a supermarket. Running an association rule on your sales logs may reveal that people who purchase barbecue sauce and potato chips also tend to buy steak. Thus, you may want to place these items close to one another.

Semi-supervised learning

Since labeling data is usually time-consuming and costly, you will often have plenty of unlabeled instances, and few labeled instances. Some algorithms can deal with data that's partially labeled. This is called *semi-supervised learning* (Figure 1-10).

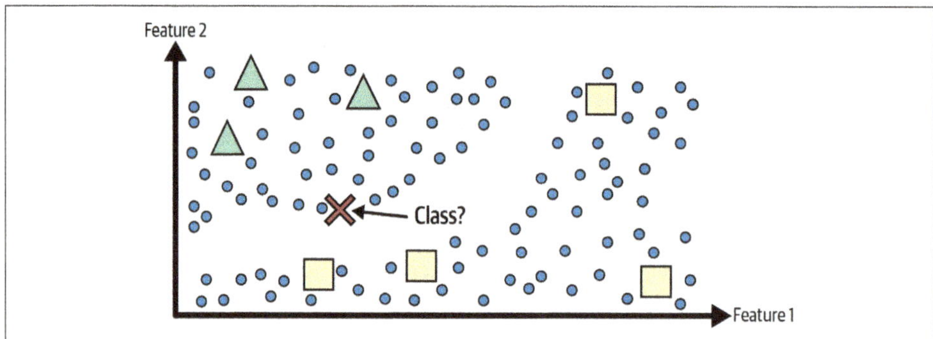

Figure 1-10. Semi-supervised learning with two classes (triangles and squares): the unlabeled examples (circles) help classify a new instance (the cross) into the triangle class rather than the square class, even though it is closer to the labeled squares

Some photo-hosting services, such as Google Photos, are good examples of this. Once you upload all your family photos to the service, it automatically recognizes that the same person A shows up in photos 1, 5, and 11, while another person B shows up in photos 2, 5, and 7. This is the unsupervised part of the algorithm (clustering). Now all the system needs is for you to tell it who these people are. Just add one label per person[3] and it is able to name everyone in every photo, which is useful for searching photos.

Most semi-supervised learning algorithms are combinations of unsupervised and supervised algorithms. For example, a clustering algorithm may be used to group similar instances together, and then every unlabeled instance can be labeled with the most common label in its cluster. Once the whole dataset is labeled, it is possible to use any supervised learning algorithm.

Self-supervised learning

Another approach to machine learning involves actually generating a fully labeled dataset from a fully unlabeled one. Again, once the whole dataset is labeled, any supervised learning algorithm can be used. This approach is called *self-supervised learning*.

For example, if you have a large dataset of unlabeled images, you can randomly mask a small part of each image and then train a model to recover the original image (Figure 1-11). During training, the masked images are used as the inputs to the model, and the original images are used as the labels.

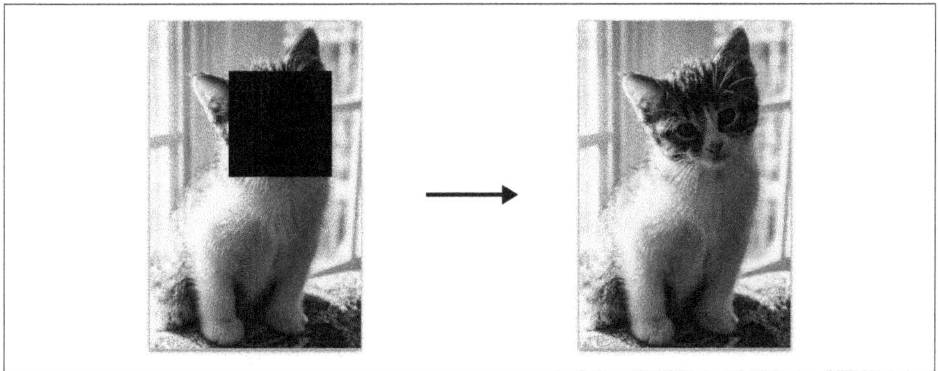

Figure 1-11. Self-supervised learning example: input (left) and target (right)

3 That's when the system works perfectly. In practice it often creates a few clusters per person, and sometimes mixes up two people who look alike, so you may need to provide a few labels per person and manually clean up some clusters.

The resulting model may be quite useful in itself—for example, to repair damaged images or to erase unwanted objects from pictures. But more often than not, a model trained using self-supervised learning is not the final goal. You'll usually want to tweak and fine-tune the model for a slightly different task—one that you actually care about.

For example, suppose that what you really want is to have a pet classification model: given a picture of any pet, it will tell you what species it belongs to. If you have a large dataset of unlabeled photos of pets, you can start by training an image-repairing model using self-supervised learning. Once it's performing well, it should be able to distinguish different pet species: when it repairs an image of a cat whose face is masked, it must know not to add a dog's face. Assuming your model's architecture allows it (and most neural network architectures do), it is then possible to tweak the model so that it predicts pet species instead of repairing images. The final step consists of fine-tuning the model on a labeled dataset: the model already knows what cats, dogs, and other pet species look like, so this step is only needed so the model can learn the mapping between the species it already knows and the labels we expect from it.

Transferring knowledge from one task to another is called *transfer learning*, and it's one of the most important techniques in machine learning today, especially when using *deep neural networks* (i.e., neural networks composed of many layers of neurons). We will discuss this in detail in Part II.

As we will see in Chapter 15, large language models (LLMs) are trained in a very similar way, by masking random words in a huge text corpus and training the model to predict the missing words. This large pretrained model can then be fine-tuned for various applications, from sentiment analysis to chatbots.

Some people consider self-supervised learning to be a part of unsupervised learning, since it deals with fully unlabeled datasets. But self-supervised learning uses (generated) labels during training, so in that regard it's closer to supervised learning. And the term "unsupervised learning" is generally used when dealing with tasks like clustering, dimensionality reduction, or anomaly detection, whereas self-supervised learning focuses on the same tasks as supervised learning: mainly classification and regression. In short, it's best to treat self-supervised learning as its own category.

Reinforcement learning

Reinforcement learning is a very different beast. The learning system, called an *agent* in this context, can observe the environment, select and perform actions, and get *rewards* in return (or *penalties* in the form of negative rewards, as shown in Figure 1-12). It must then learn by itself what is the best strategy, called a *policy*, to get the most reward over time. A policy defines what action the agent should choose when it is in a given situation.

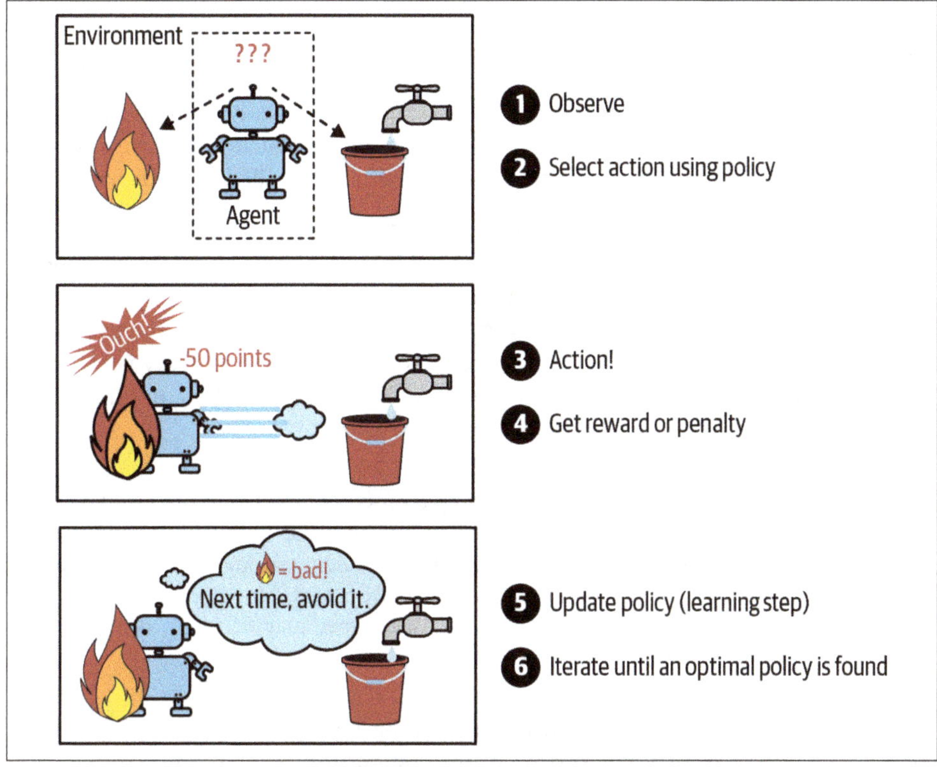

Figure 1-12. Reinforcement learning

For example, many robots implement reinforcement learning algorithms to learn how to walk. DeepMind's AlphaGo program is also a good example of reinforcement learning: it made the headlines in May 2017 when it beat Ke Jie, the number one ranked player in the world at the time, at the game of Go. It learned its winning policy by analyzing millions of games, and then playing many games against itself. Note that learning was turned off during the games against the champion; AlphaGo was just applying the policy it had learned. As you will see in the next section, this is called *offline learning*.

Batch Versus Online Learning

Another criterion used to classify machine learning systems is whether the system can learn incrementally from a stream of incoming data. For example, random forests (see Chapter 6) can only be trained from scratch on the full dataset—this is called batch learning—while other models can be trained one batch of data at a time, for example, using *gradient descent* (see Chapter 4)—this is called online learning.

Batch learning

In *batch learning*, the system must be trained using all the available data. This will generally take a lot of time and computing resources, so it is typically done offline. First the system is trained, and then it is launched into production and runs without learning anymore; it just applies what it has learned. This is called *offline learning*.

Unfortunately, a model's performance tends to decay slowly over time, simply because the world continues to evolve while the model remains unchanged. This phenomenon is often called *data drift* (or *model rot*). The solution is to regularly retrain the model on up-to-date data. How often you need to do that depends on the use case: if the model classifies pictures of cats and dogs, its performance will decay very slowly, but if the model deals with fast-evolving systems, for example making predictions on the financial market, then it is likely to decay quite fast.

Even a model trained to classify pictures of cats and dogs may need to be retrained regularly, not because cats and dogs will mutate overnight, but because cameras keep changing, along with image formats, sharpness, brightness, and size ratios. Moreover, people may love different breeds next year, or they may decide to dress their pets with tiny hats—who knows?

If you want a batch learning system to know about new data (such as a new type of spam), you need to train a new version of the system from scratch on the full dataset (not just the new data, but also the old data), then replace the old model with the new one. Fortunately, the whole process of training, evaluating, and launching a machine learning system can be automated (as we saw in Figure 1-3), so even a batch learning system can adapt to change. Simply update the data and train a new version of the system from scratch as often as needed.

This solution is simple and often works fine, but training using the full set of data can take many hours, so you would typically train a new system only every 24 hours or even just weekly. If your system needs to adapt to rapidly changing data (e.g., to predict stock prices), then you need a more reactive solution.

Also, training on the full set of data requires a lot of computing resources (CPU, memory space, disk space, disk I/O, network I/O, etc.). If you have a lot of data and you automate your system to train from scratch every day, it will end up costing you a lot of money. If the amount of data is huge and your system must always be up to date, it may even be impossible to use batch learning.

Finally, if your system needs to be able to learn autonomously and it has limited resources (e.g., a smartphone application or a rover on Mars), then carrying around large amounts of training data and taking up a lot of resources to train for hours every day is a showstopper.

A better option in all these scenarios is to use algorithms that are capable of learning incrementally.

Online learning

In *online learning*, you train the system incrementally by feeding it data instances sequentially, either individually or in small groups called *mini-batches*. Each learning step is fast and cheap, so the system can learn about new data on the fly, as it arrives (see Figure 1-13). The most common online algorithm by far is gradient descent, but there are a few others.

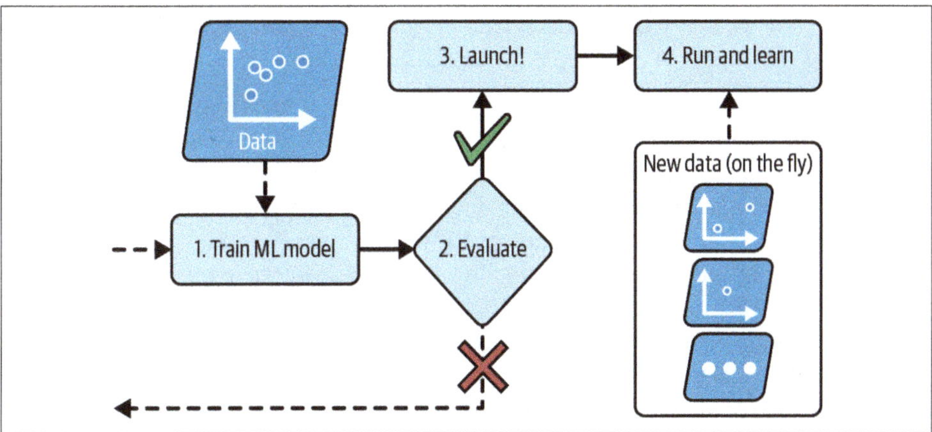

Figure 1-13. In online learning, a model is trained and launched into production, and then it keeps learning as new data comes in

Online learning is useful for systems that need to adapt to change extremely rapidly (e.g., to detect new patterns in the stock market). It is also a good option if you have limited computing resources; for example, if the model is trained on a mobile device.

Most importantly, online learning algorithms can be used to train models on huge datasets that cannot fit in one machine's memory (this is called *out-of-core* learning). The algorithm loads part of the data, runs a training step on that data, and repeats the process until it has run on all of the data (see Figure 1-14).

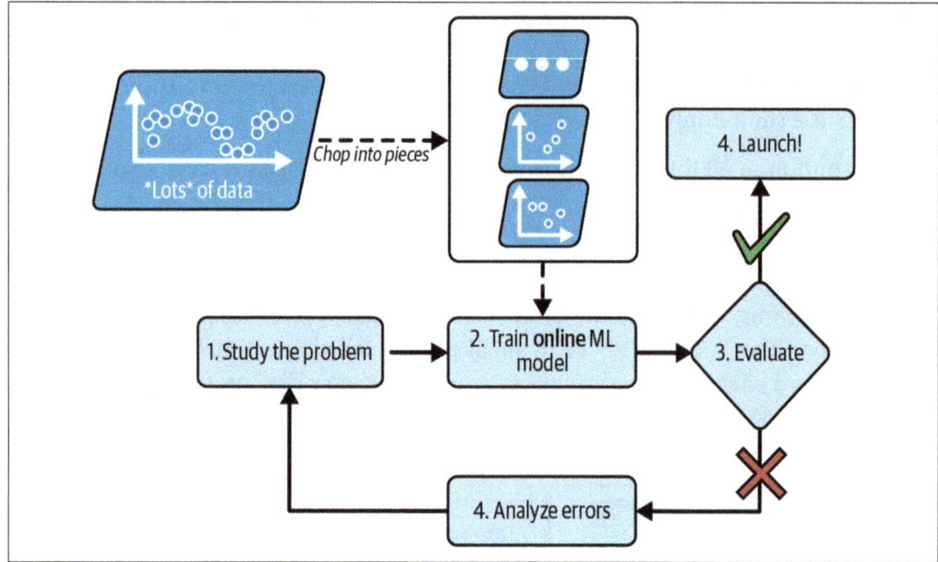

Figure 1-14. Using online learning to handle huge datasets

One important parameter of online learning systems is how fast they should adapt to changing data: this is called the *learning rate*. If you set a high learning rate, then your system will rapidly adapt to new data, but it will also tend to quickly forget the old data: this is called *catastrophic forgetting* (or *catastrophic interference*). You don't want a spam filter to flag only the latest kinds of spam it was shown! Conversely, if you set a low learning rate, the system will have more inertia; that is, it will learn more slowly, but it will also be less sensitive to noise in the new data or to sequences of nonrepresentative data points (outliers).

Out-of-core learning is usually done offline (i.e., not on the live system), so *online learning* can be a confusing name. Think of it as *incremental learning*. Moreover, mini-batches are often just called "batches", so *batch learning* is also a confusing name. Think of it as learning from scratch on the full dataset.

A big challenge with online learning is that if bad data is fed to the system, the system's performance will decline, possibly quickly (depending on the data quality and learning rate). If it's a live system, your clients will notice. For example, bad data could come from a bug (e.g., a malfunctioning sensor on a robot), or it could come from someone trying to game the system (e.g., spamming a search engine to try to rank high in search results). To reduce this risk, you need to monitor your system closely and promptly switch learning off (and possibly revert to a previously working state) if you detect a drop in performance. You may also want to monitor the input data and react to abnormal data; for example, using an anomaly detection algorithm (see Chapter 8).

Instance-Based Versus Model-Based Learning

One more way to categorize machine learning systems is by how they *generalize*. Most machine learning tasks are about making predictions. This means that given a number of training examples, the system needs to be able to make good predictions for (generalize to) examples it has never seen before. Having a good performance measure on the training data is good, but insufficient; the true goal is to perform well on new instances.

There are two main approaches to generalization: instance-based learning and model-based learning.

Instance-based learning

Possibly the most trivial form of learning is simply to learn by heart. If you were to create a spam filter this way, it would just flag all emails that are identical to emails that have already been flagged by users—not the worst solution, but certainly not the best.

Instead of just flagging emails that are identical to known spam emails, your spam filter could be programmed to also flag emails that are very similar to known spam emails. This requires a *measure of similarity* between two emails. A (very basic) similarity measure between two emails could be to count the number of words they have in common. The system would flag an email as spam if it has many words in common with a known spam email.

This is called *instance-based learning*: the system learns the examples by heart, then generalizes to new cases by using a similarity measure to compare them to the learned examples (or a subset of them). For example, in Figure 1-15 the new instance would be classified as a triangle because the majority of the most similar instances belong to that class.

Instance-based learning often shines with small datasets, especially if the data keeps changing, but it does not scale very well: it requires deploying a whole copy of the training set to production; making predictions requires searching for similar instances, which can be quite slow; and it doesn't work well with high-dimensional data such as images.

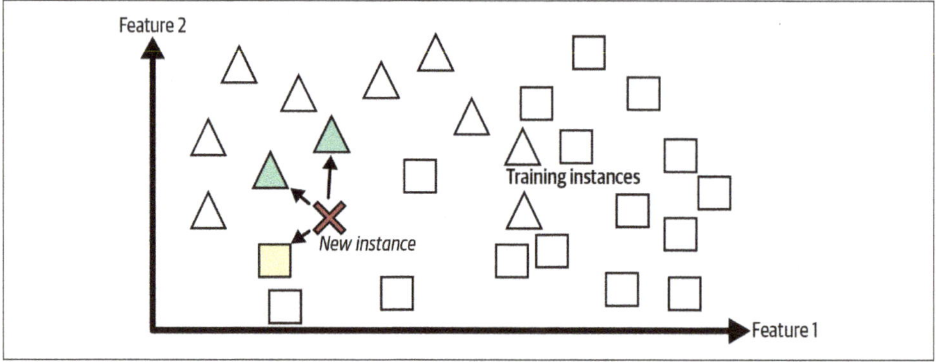

Figure 1-15. Instance-based learning: in this example we consider the class of the three nearest neighbors in the training set

Model-based learning and a typical machine learning workflow

Another way to generalize from a set of examples is to build a model of these examples and then use that model to make *predictions*. This is called *model-based learning* (Figure 1-16).

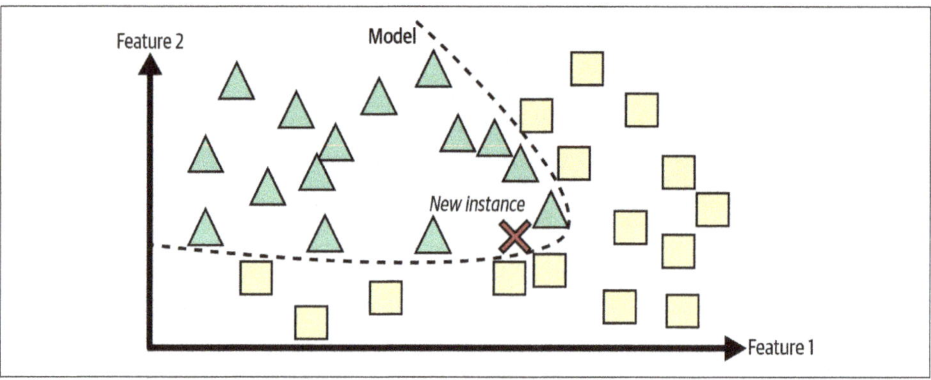

Figure 1-16. Model-based learning

For example, suppose you want to know if money makes people happy, so you download the Better Life Index data from the OECD's website (*https://www.oecdbetterlifeindex.org*), and World Bank stats (*https://ourworldindata.org*) about gross domestic product (GDP) per capita. Then you join the tables and sort by GDP per capita. Table 1-1 shows an excerpt of what you get.

Table 1-1. Does money make people happier?

Country	GDP per capita (USD)	Life satisfaction
Turkey	28,384	5.5
Hungary	31,008	5.6
France	42,026	6.5
United States	60,236	6.9
New Zealand	42,404	7.3
Australia	48,698	7.3
Denmark	55,938	7.6

Let's plot the data for these countries (Figure 1-17).

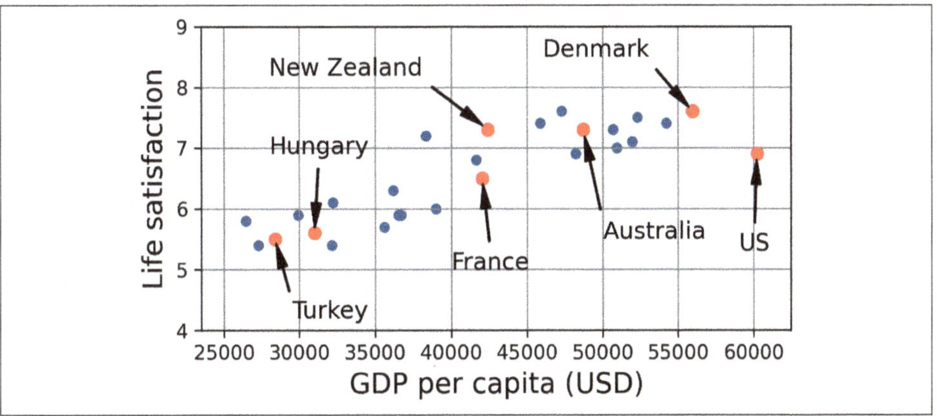

Figure 1-17. Do you see a trend here?

There does seem to be a trend here! Although the data is *noisy* (i.e., partly random), it looks like life satisfaction goes up more or less linearly as the country's GDP per capita increases. So you decide to model life satisfaction as a linear function of GDP per capita (you assume that any deviation from that line is just random noise). This step is called *model selection*: you selected a *linear model* of life satisfaction with just one attribute, GDP per capita (Equation 1-1).

Equation 1-1. A simple linear model

$$\text{life\_satisfaction} = \theta_0 + \theta_1 \times \text{GDP\_per\_capita}$$

This model has two *model parameters*, θ_0 and θ_1.[4] By tweaking these parameters, you can make your model represent any linear function, as shown in Figure 1-18.

4 By convention, the Greek letter θ (theta) is frequently used to represent model parameters.

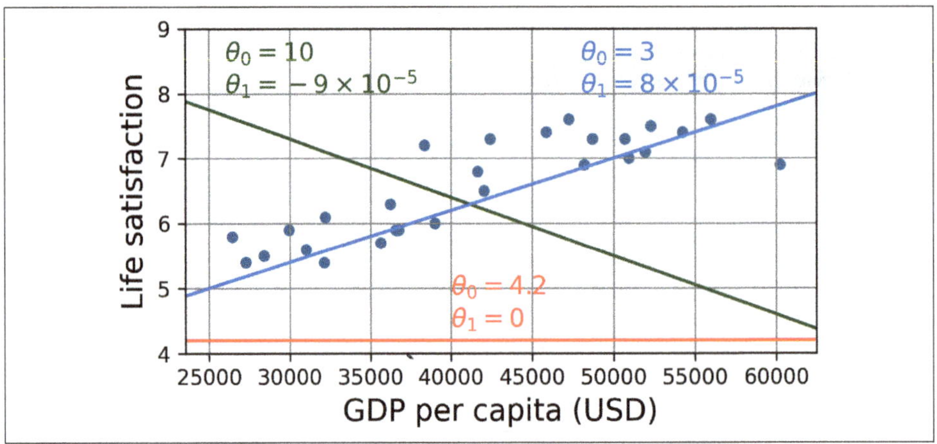

Figure 1-18. A few possible linear models

Before you can use your model, you need to define the parameter values θ_0 and θ_1. How can you know which values will make your model perform best? To answer this question, you need to specify a performance measure. You can either define a *utility function* (or *fitness function*) that measures how *good* your model is, or you can define a *cost function* (a.k.a., *loss function*) that measures how *bad* it is. For linear regression problems, people typically use a cost function that measures the distance between the linear model's predictions and the training examples; the objective is to minimize this distance.

This is where the linear regression algorithm comes in: you feed it your training examples, and it finds the parameters that make the linear model fit best to your data. This is called *training* the model. In our case, the algorithm finds that the optimal parameter values are $\theta_0 = 3.75$ and $\theta_1 = 6.78 \times 10^{-5}$.

Confusingly, the word "model" can refer to a *type of model* (e.g., linear regression), to a *fully specified model architecture* (e.g., linear regression with one input and one output), or to the *final trained model* ready to be used for predictions (e.g., linear regression with one input and one output, using $\theta_0 = 3.75$ and $\theta_1 = 6.78 \times 10^{-5}$). Model selection consists in choosing the type of model and fully specifying its architecture. Training a model means running an algorithm to find the model parameters that will make it best fit the training data, and hopefully make good predictions on new data.

Now the model fits the training data as closely as possible (for a linear model), as you can see in Figure 1-19.

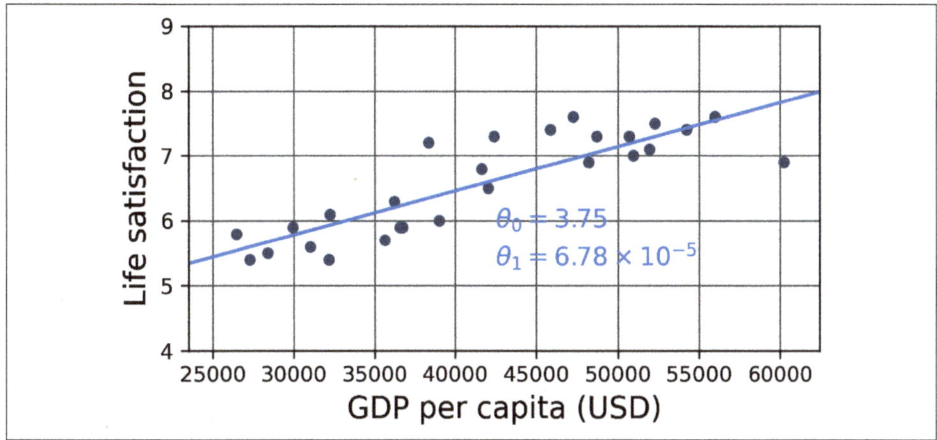

Figure 1-19. The linear model that fits the training data best

You are finally ready to run the model to make predictions. For example, say you want to know how happy Puerto Ricans are, and the OECD data does not have the answer. Fortunately, you can use your model to make a good prediction: you look up Puerto Rico's GDP per capita, find \$33,442, and then apply your model and find that life satisfaction is likely to be somewhere around $3.75 + 33{,}442 \times 6.78 \times 10^{-5} = 6.02$.

To whet your appetite, Example 1-1 shows the Python code that loads the data, separates the inputs `X` from the labels `y`, creates a scatterplot for visualization, and then trains a linear model and makes a prediction.[5]

Example 1-1. Training and running a linear model using Scikit-Learn

```
import matplotlib.pyplot as plt
import numpy as np
import pandas as pd
from sklearn.linear_model import LinearRegression

# Download and prepare the data
data_root = "https://github.com/ageron/data/raw/main/"
lifesat = pd.read_csv(data_root + "lifesat/lifesat.csv")
X = lifesat[["GDP per capita (USD)"]].values
y = lifesat[["Life satisfaction"]].values

# Visualize the data
lifesat.plot(kind='scatter', grid=True,
             x="GDP per capita (USD)", y="Life satisfaction")
plt.axis([23_500, 62_500, 4, 9])
plt.show()
```

5 It's OK if you don't understand all the code yet; I will present Scikit-Learn in the following chapters.

```
# Select a linear model
model = LinearRegression()

# Train the model
model.fit(X, y)

# Make a prediction for Puerto Rico
X_new = [[33_442.8]]  # Puerto Rico' GDP per capita in 2020
print(model.predict(X_new)) # outputs [[6.01610329]]
```

If you had used an instance-based learning algorithm instead, you would have found that Poland has the closest GDP per capita to that of Puerto Rico ($32,238), and since the OECD data tells us that Poles' life satisfaction is 6.1, you would have predicted a life satisfaction of 6.1 as well for Puerto Rico. If you zoom out a bit and look at the next two closest countries, you will find Portugal with a life satisfaction of 5.4, and Estonia with a life satisfaction of 5.7. Averaging these three values, you get 5.73, which is a bit below your model-based prediction. This simple algorithm is called *k-nearest neighbors* regression (in this example, $k = 3$).

Replacing the linear regression model with k-nearest neighbors regression in the previous code is as easy as replacing these lines:

```
from sklearn.linear_model import LinearRegression
model = LinearRegression()
```

with these two:

```
from sklearn.neighbors import KNeighborsRegressor
model = KNeighborsRegressor(n_neighbors=3)
```

If all went well, your model will make good predictions. If not, you may need to use more attributes (employment rate, health, air pollution, etc.), get more or better-quality training data, or perhaps select a more powerful model (e.g., a polynomial regression model).

In summary:

- You studied the data.
- You selected a model.
- You trained it on the training data (i.e., the learning algorithm searched for the model parameter values that minimize a cost function).
- Finally, you applied the model to make predictions on new cases (this is called *inference*), hoping that this model will generalize well.

This is what a typical machine learning project looks like. In Chapter 2 you will experience this firsthand by going through a project end to end.

We discussed quite a few categories of ML systems, but this field has more! For example, *ensemble learning* involves training multiple models and combining their individual predictions into improved predictions (see Chapter 6); *federated learning* is a decentralized approach where models are trained across multiple devices (e.g., smartphones) and adapted to each user without exchanging raw data, thereby protecting the user's privacy; *meta-learning* is a learning-to-learn approach where models learn how to learn new tasks quickly with minimal data. And the list goes on! Figure 1-20 summarizes the various classifications of ML systems we have discussed so far.

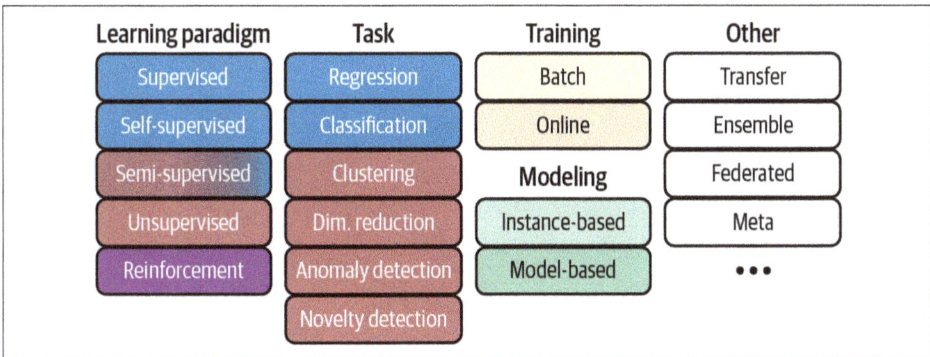

Figure 1-20. Overview of ML categories

We have covered a lot of ground so far: you now know what machine learning is really about, why it is useful, what some of the most common categories of ML systems are, and what a typical project workflow looks like. Now let's look at what can go wrong in learning and prevent you from making accurate predictions.

Main Challenges of Machine Learning

In short, since your main task is to select a model and train it on some data, the two things that can go wrong are "bad model" and "bad data". Let's start with examples of bad data.

Insufficient Quantity of Training Data

For a toddler to learn what an apple is, all it takes is for you to point to an apple and say "apple" (possibly repeating this procedure a few times). Now the child is able to recognize apples in all sorts of colors and shapes. Genius.

Machine learning is not quite there yet; it takes a lot of data for most machine learning algorithms to work properly. Even for very simple problems you typically need thousands of examples, and for complex problems such as image or speech recognition you may need millions of examples (unless you can reuse parts of an existing model, i.e., transfer learning).

The Unreasonable Effectiveness of Data

In a famous paper (*https://homl.info/6*) published in 2001, Microsoft researchers Michele Banko and Eric Brill showed that very different machine learning algorithms, including fairly simple ones, performed almost identically well on a complex problem of natural language disambiguation[6] once they were given enough data (as you can see in Figure 1-21).

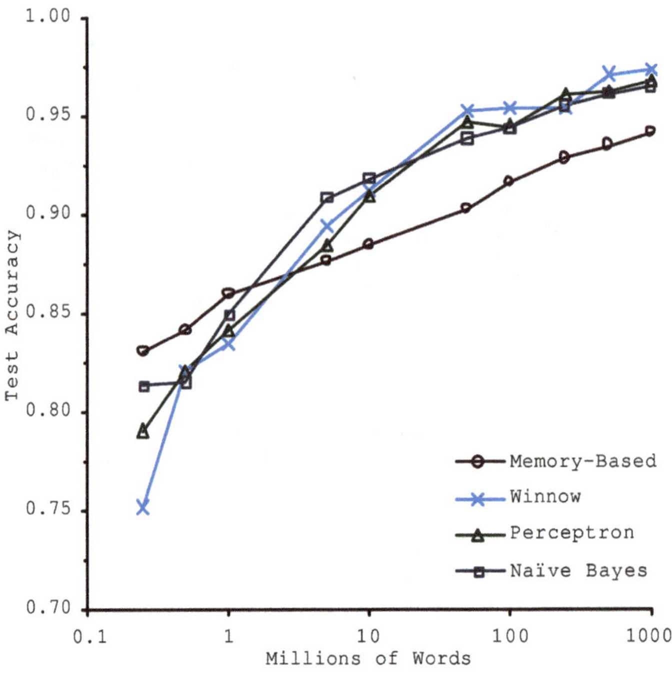

Figure 1-21. The importance of data versus algorithms[7]

6 For example, knowing whether to write "to", "two", or "too", depending on the context.

7 Figure reproduced with permission from Michele Banko and Eric Brill, "Scaling to Very Very Large Corpora for Natural Language Disambiguation", *Proceedings of the 39th Annual Meeting of the Association for Computational Linguistics* (2001): 26–33.

As the authors put it, "these results suggest that we may want to reconsider the trade-off between spending time and money on algorithm development versus spending it on corpus development".

The idea that data matters more than algorithms for complex problems was further popularized by Peter Norvig et al. in a paper titled "The Unreasonable Effectiveness of Data" (*https://homl.info/7*), published in 2009.[8] It should be noted, however, that small and medium-sized datasets are still very common, and it is not always easy or cheap to get extra training data—so don't abandon algorithms just yet.

Nonrepresentative Training Data

In order to generalize well, it is crucial that your training data be representative of the new cases you want to generalize to. This is true whether you use instance-based learning or model-based learning.

For example, the set of countries you used earlier for training the linear model was not perfectly representative; it did not contain any country with a GDP per capita lower than $23,500 or higher than $62,500. Figure 1-22 shows what the data looks like when you add such countries.

If you train a linear model on this data, you get the solid line, while the old model is represented by the dotted line. As you can see, not only does adding a few missing countries significantly alter the model, but it makes it clear that such a simple linear model is probably never going to work well. It seems that very rich countries are not happier than moderately rich countries (in fact, they seem slightly unhappier!), and conversely some poor countries seem happier than many rich countries.

By using a nonrepresentative training set, you trained a model that is unlikely to make accurate predictions, especially for very poor and very rich countries.

It is crucial to use a training set that is representative of the cases you want to generalize to. This is often harder than it sounds: if the sample is too small, you will have *sampling noise* (i.e., nonrepresentative data as a result of chance), but even very large samples can be nonrepresentative if the sampling method is flawed. This is called *sampling bias*.

8 Peter Norvig et al., "The Unreasonable Effectiveness of Data", *IEEE Intelligent Systems* 24, no. 2 (2009): 8–12.

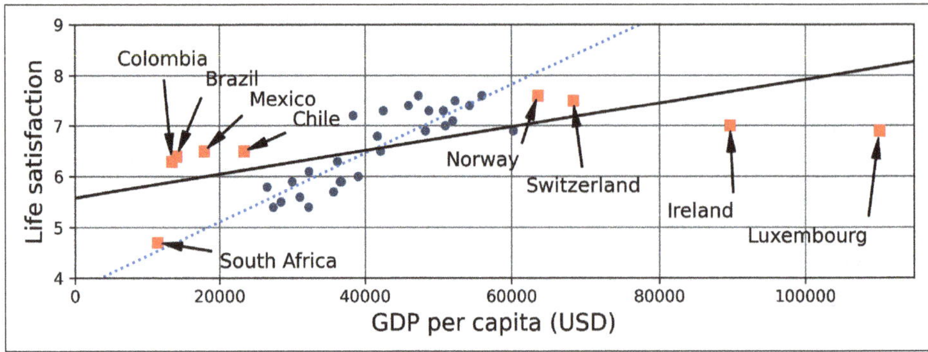

Figure 1-22. A more representative training sample

Examples of Sampling Bias

Perhaps the most famous example of sampling bias happened during the US presidential election in 1936, which pitted Landon against Roosevelt: the *Literary Digest* conducted a very large poll, sending mail to about 10 million people. It got 2.4 million answers, and predicted with high confidence that Landon would get 57% of the votes. Instead, Roosevelt won with 62% of the votes. The flaw was in the *Literary Digest*'s sampling method:

- First, to obtain the addresses to send the polls to, the *Literary Digest* used telephone directories, lists of magazine subscribers, club membership lists, and the like. All of these lists tended to favor wealthier people, who were more likely to vote Republican (hence Landon).
- Second, less than 25% of the people who were polled answered. Again this introduced a sampling bias, by potentially ruling out people who didn't care much about politics, people who didn't like the *Literary Digest*, and other key groups. This is a special type of sampling bias called *nonresponse bias*.

Here is another example: say you want to build a system to recognize funk music videos. One way to build your training set is to search for "funk music" on YouTube and use the resulting videos. But this assumes that YouTube's search engine returns a set of videos that are representative of all the funk music videos on YouTube. In reality, the search results are likely to be biased toward popular artists (and if you live in Brazil you will get a lot of "funk carioca" videos, which sound nothing like James Brown). On the other hand, how else can you get a large training set?

Poor-Quality Data

Obviously, if your training data is full of errors, outliers, and noise (e.g., due to poor-quality measurements), it will make it harder for the system to detect the underlying patterns, so your system is less likely to perform well. It is often well worth the effort to spend time cleaning up your training data. The truth is, most data scientists spend a significant part of their time doing just that. The following are a couple examples of when you'd want to clean up training data:

- If some instances are clearly outliers, it may help to simply discard them or try to fix the errors manually.
- If some instances are missing a few features (e.g., 5% of your customers did not specify their age), you must decide whether you want to ignore this attribute altogether, ignore these instances, fill in the missing values (e.g., with the median age), or train one model with the feature and one model without it.

Irrelevant Features

As the saying goes: garbage in, garbage out. Your system will only be capable of learning if the training data contains enough relevant features and not too many irrelevant ones. A critical part of the success of a machine learning project is coming up with a good set of features to train on. This process, called *feature engineering*, involves the following steps:

- *Feature selection* (selecting the most useful features to train on among existing features)
- *Feature extraction* (combining existing features to produce a more useful one—as we saw earlier, dimensionality reduction algorithms can help)
- Creating new features by gathering new data

Now that we have looked at many examples of bad data, let's look at a couple examples of bad algorithms.

Overfitting the Training Data

Say you are visiting a foreign country and the taxi driver rips you off. You might be tempted to say that *all* taxi drivers in that country are thieves. Overgeneralizing is something that we humans do all too often, and unfortunately machines can fall into the same trap if we are not careful. In machine learning this is called *overfitting*: it means that the model performs well on the training data, but it does not generalize well.

Figure 1-23 shows an example of a high-degree polynomial life satisfaction model that strongly overfits the training data. Even though it performs much better on the training data than the simple linear model, would you really trust its predictions?

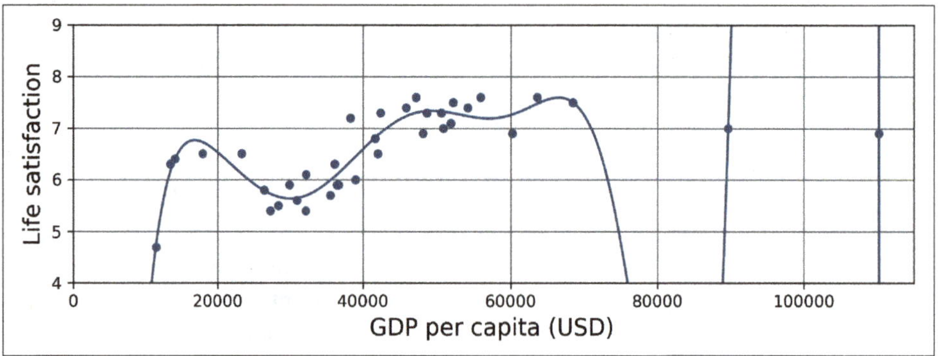

Figure 1-23. Overfitting the training data

Complex models such as deep neural networks can detect subtle patterns in the data, but if the training set is noisy, or if it is too small, which introduces sampling noise, then the model is likely to detect patterns in the noise itself (as in the taxi driver example). Obviously these patterns will not generalize to new instances. For example, say you feed your life satisfaction model many more attributes, including uninformative ones such as the country's name. In that case, a complex model may detect patterns like the fact that all countries in the training data with a *w* in their name have a life satisfaction greater than 7: New Zealand (7.3), Norway (7.6), Sweden (7.3), and Switzerland (7.5). How confident are you that the *w*-satisfaction rule generalizes to Rwanda or Zimbabwe? Obviously this pattern occurred in the training data by pure chance, but the model has no way to tell whether a pattern is real or simply the result of noise in the data.

Overfitting happens when the model is too complex relative to the amount and noisiness of the training data, so it starts to learn random patterns in the training data. Here are possible solutions:

- Simplify the model by selecting one with fewer parameters (e.g., a linear model rather than a high-degree polynomial model), by reducing the number of attributes in the training data, or by constraining the model.
- Gather more training data.
- Reduce the noise in the training data (e.g., fix data errors and remove outliers).

Constraining a model to make it simpler and reduce the risk of overfitting is called *regularization*. For example, the linear model we defined earlier has two parameters, θ_0 and θ_1. This gives the learning algorithm two *degrees of freedom* to adapt the model to the training data: it can tweak both the height (θ_0) and the slope (θ_1) of the line. If we forced $\theta_1 = 0$, the algorithm would have only one degree of freedom and would have a much harder time fitting the data properly: all it could do is move the line up or down to get as close as possible to the training instances, so it would end up around the mean. A very simple model indeed! If we allow the algorithm to modify θ_1 but we force it to keep it small, then the learning algorithm will effectively have somewhere in between one and two degrees of freedom. It will produce a model that's simpler than one with two degrees of freedom, but more complex than one with just one. You want to find the right balance between fitting the training data perfectly and keeping the model simple enough to ensure that it will generalize well.

Figure 1-24 shows three models. The dotted line represents the original model that was trained on the countries represented as circles (without the countries represented as squares), the solid line is our second model trained with all countries (circles and squares), and the dashed line is a model trained with the same data as the first model but with a regularization constraint. You can see that regularization forced the model to have a smaller slope: this model does not fit the training data (circles) as well as the first model, but it actually generalizes better to new examples that it did not see during training (squares).

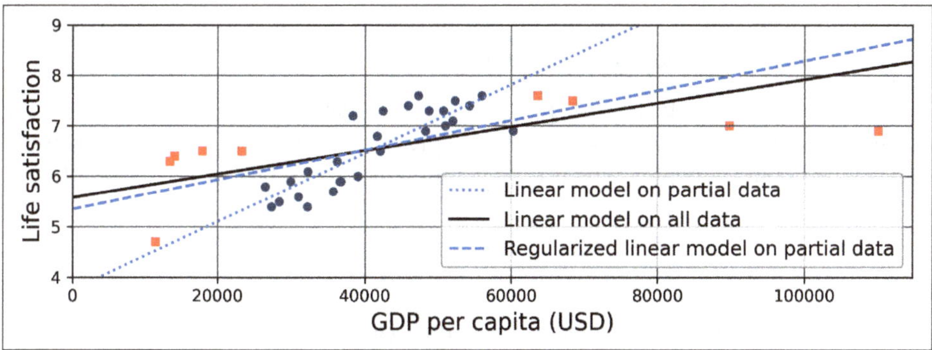

Figure 1-24. Regularization reduces the risk of overfitting

The amount of regularization to apply during learning can be controlled by a *hyperparameter*. A hyperparameter is a parameter of a learning algorithm (not of the model). As such, it is not affected by the learning algorithm itself; it must be set prior to training and remains constant during training. If you set the regularization hyperparameter to a very large value, you will get an almost flat model (a slope close to zero); the learning algorithm will almost certainly not overfit the training data, but it will be less likely to find a good solution. Tuning hyperparameters is an important part of building a machine learning system (you will see a detailed example in the next chapter).

Underfitting the Training Data

As you might guess, *underfitting* is the opposite of overfitting: it occurs when your model is too simple to learn the underlying structure of the data. For example, a linear model of life satisfaction is prone to underfit; reality is just more complex than the model, so its predictions are bound to be inaccurate, even on the training examples.

Here are the main options for fixing this problem:

- Select a more powerful model, with more parameters.
- Feed better features to the learning algorithm (feature engineering).
- Reduce the constraints on the model (for example by reducing the regularization hyperparameter).

Deployment Issues

Even if you have a large and clean dataset and you manage to train a beautiful model that neither underfits nor overfits the data, you may still run into issues during deployment: for example, the model may be too complex to maintain, or too large to fit in memory, or too slow, or it may not scale properly, it may have security vulnerabilities, it may become outdated if you don't update it often enough, etc.

In short, there's more to an ML project than just data and models. However, the skillset required to handle these operational problems are fairly different from those required for data modeling, which is why companies often have a dedicated MLOps team (ML operations) to handle this.

Stepping Back

By now you know a lot about machine learning. However, we went through so many concepts that you may be feeling a little lost, so let's step back and look at the big picture:

- Machine learning is about making machines get better at some task by learning from data, instead of having to explicitly code rules.
- There are many different types of ML systems: supervised or not, batch or online, instance-based or model-based.
- In an ML project you gather data in a training set, and you feed the training set to a learning algorithm. If the algorithm is model-based, it tunes some parameters to fit the model to the training set (i.e., to make good predictions on the training

set itself), and then hopefully it will be able to make good predictions on new cases as well. If the algorithm is instance-based, it just learns the examples by heart and generalizes to new instances by using a similarity measure to compare them to the learned instances.

- The system will not perform well if your training set is too small, or if the data is not representative, is noisy, or is polluted with irrelevant features (garbage in, garbage out). Your model needs to be neither too simple (in which case it will underfit) nor too complex (in which case it will overfit). Lastly, you must think carefully about deployment constraints.

There's just one last important topic to cover: once you have trained a model, you don't want to just "hope" it generalizes to new cases. You want to evaluate it and fine-tune it if necessary. Let's see how to do that.

Testing and Validating

The only way to know how well a model will generalize to new cases is to actually try it out on new cases. One way to do that is to put your model in production and monitor how well it performs. This works well, but if your model is horribly bad, your users will complain—not the best idea.

A better option is to split your data into two sets: the *training set* and the *test set*. As these names imply, you train your model using the training set, and you test it using the test set. The error rate on new cases is called the *generalization error* (or *out-of-sample error*), and by evaluating your model on the test set, you get an estimate of this error. This value tells you how well your model will perform on instances it has never seen before.

If the training error is low (i.e., your model makes few mistakes on the training set) but the generalization error is high, it means that your model is overfitting the training data.

It is common to use 80% of the data for training and *hold out* 20% for testing. However, this depends on the size of the dataset: if it contains 10 million instances, then holding out 1% means your test set will contain 100,000 instances, probably more than enough to get a good estimate of the generalization error.

Hyperparameter Tuning and Model Selection

Evaluating a model is simple enough: just use a test set. But suppose you are hesitating between two types of models (say, a linear model and a polynomial model): how can you decide between them? One option is to train both and compare how well they generalize using the test set.

Now suppose that the linear model generalizes better, but you want to apply some regularization to avoid overfitting. The question is, how do you choose the value of the regularization hyperparameter? One option is to train 100 different models using 100 different values for this hyperparameter. Suppose you find the best hyperparameter value that produces a model with the lowest generalization error—say, just 5% error. You launch this model into production, but unfortunately it does not perform as well as expected and produces 15% errors. What just happened?

The problem is that you measured the generalization error multiple times on the test set, and you adapted the model and hyperparameters to produce the best model *for that particular set*. This means the model is unlikely to perform as well on new data.

A common solution to this problem is called *holdout validation* (Figure 1-25): you simply hold out part of the training set to evaluate several candidate models and select the best one. The new held-out set is called the *validation set* (or the *development set*, or *dev set*). More specifically, you train multiple models with various hyperparameters on the reduced training set (i.e., the full training set minus the validation set), and you select the model that performs best on the validation set. After this holdout validation process, you train the best model on the full training set (including the validation set), and this gives you the final model. Lastly, you evaluate this final model on the test set to get an estimate of the generalization error.

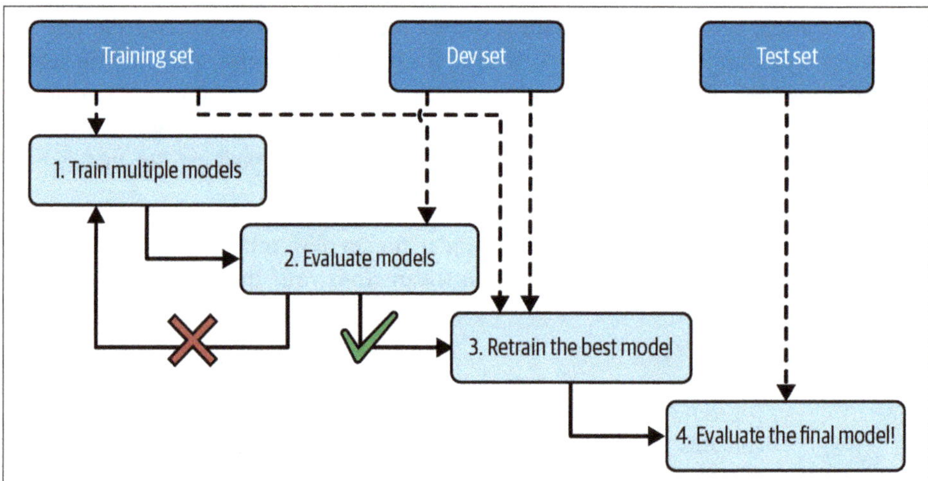

Figure 1-25. Model selection using holdout validation

This solution usually works quite well. However, if the validation set is too small, then the model evaluations will be imprecise: you may end up selecting a suboptimal model by mistake. Conversely, if the validation set is too large, then the remaining training set will be much smaller than the full training set. Why is this bad? Well, since the final model will be trained on the full training set, it is not ideal to compare candidate models trained on a much smaller training set. It would be like selecting the fastest sprinter to participate in a marathon. One way to solve this problem is to perform repeated *cross-validation*, using many small validation sets. Each model is evaluated once per validation set after it is trained on the rest of the data. By averaging out all the evaluations of a model, you get a much more accurate measure of its performance. There is a drawback, however: the training time is multiplied by the number of validation sets.

Data Mismatch

In some cases, it's easy to get a large amount of data for training, but this data probably won't be perfectly representative of the data that will be used in production. For example, suppose you want to create a mobile app to take pictures of flowers and automatically determine their species. You can easily download millions of pictures of flowers on the web, but they won't be perfectly representative of the pictures that will actually be taken using the app on a mobile device. Perhaps you only have 1,000 representative pictures (i.e., actually taken with the app).

In this case, the most important rule to remember is that both the validation set and the test set must be as representative as possible of the data you expect to use in production, so they should be composed exclusively of representative pictures: you can shuffle them and put half in the validation set and half in the test set (making sure that no duplicates or near-duplicates end up in both sets). After training your model on the web pictures, if you observe that the performance of the model on the validation set is disappointing, you will not know whether this is because your model has overfit the training set, or whether this is just due to the mismatch between the web pictures and the mobile app pictures.

One solution is to hold out some of the training pictures (from the web) in yet another set that Andrew Ng dubbed the *train-dev set* (Figure 1-26). After the model is trained (on the training set, *not* on the train-dev set), you can evaluate it on the train-dev set. If the model performs poorly, then it must have overfit the training set, so you should try to simplify or regularize the model, get more training data, and clean up the training data. But if it performs well on the train-dev set, then you can evaluate the model on the dev set. If it performs poorly, then the problem must be coming from the data mismatch. You can try to tackle this problem by preprocessing the web images to make them look more like the pictures that will be taken by the mobile app, and then retraining the model. Once you have a model that performs well on both the train-dev set and the dev set, you can evaluate it one last time on the test set to know how well it is likely to perform in production.

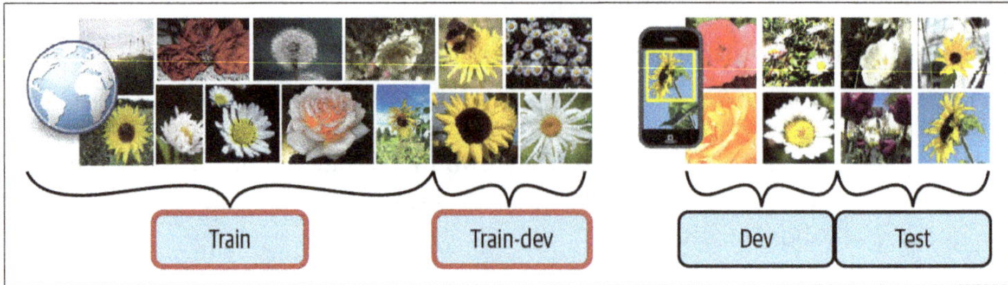

Figure 1-26. When real data is scarce (right), you may use similar abundant data (left) for training and hold out some of it in a train-dev set to evaluate overfitting; the real data is then used to evaluate data mismatch (dev set) and to evaluate the final model's performance (test set)

No Free Lunch Theorem

A model is a simplified representation of the data. The simplifications are meant to discard the superfluous details that are unlikely to generalize to new instances. When you select a particular type of model, you are implicitly making *assumptions* about the data. For example, if you choose a linear model, you are implicitly assuming that the data is fundamentally linear and that the distance between the instances and the straight line is just noise, which can safely be ignored.

In a famous 1996 paper (*https://homl.info/8*),[9] David Wolpert demonstrated that if you make absolutely no assumption about the data, then there is no reason to prefer one model over any other. This is called the *No Free Lunch* (NFL) theorem. For some datasets the best model is a linear model, while for other datasets it is a neural network. There is no model that is *a priori* guaranteed to work better (hence the name of the theorem). The only way to know for sure which model is best is to evaluate them all. Since this is not possible, in practice you make some reasonable assumptions about the data and evaluate only a few reasonable models. For example, for simple tasks you may evaluate linear models with various levels of regularization, and for a complex problem you may evaluate various neural networks.

9 David Wolpert, "The Lack of A Priori Distinctions Between Learning Algorithms", *Neural Computation* 8, no. 7 (1996): 1341–1390.

Exercises

In this chapter we have covered some of the most important concepts in machine learning. In the next chapters we will dive deeper and write more code, but before we do, make sure you can answer the following questions:

1. How would you define machine learning?
2. Can you name four types of applications where it shines?
3. What is a labeled training set?
4. What are the two most common supervised tasks?
5. Can you name four common unsupervised tasks?
6. What type of algorithm would you use to allow a robot to walk in various unknown terrains?
7. What type of algorithm would you use to segment your customers into multiple groups?
8. Would you frame the problem of spam detection as a supervised learning problem or an unsupervised learning problem?
9. What is an online learning system?
10. What is out-of-core learning?
11. What type of algorithm relies on a similarity measure to make predictions?
12. What is the difference between a model parameter and a model hyperparameter?
13. What do model-based algorithms search for? What is the most common strategy they use to succeed? How do they make predictions?
14. Can you name four of the main challenges in machine learning?
15. If your model performs great on the training data but generalizes poorly to new instances, what is happening? Can you name three possible solutions?
16. What is a test set, and why would you want to use it?
17. What is the purpose of a validation set?
18. What is the train-dev set, when do you need it, and how do you use it?
19. What can go wrong if you tune hyperparameters using the test set?

Solutions to these exercises are available at the end of this chapter's notebook, at *https://homl.info/colab-p*.

CHAPTER 2

End-to-End Machine Learning Project

In this chapter you will work through an example project end to end, pretending to be a recently hired data scientist at a real estate company. This example is fictitious; the goal is to illustrate the main steps of a machine learning project, not to learn anything about the real estate business. Here are the main steps we will walk through:

1. Look at the big picture.
2. Get the data.
3. Explore and visualize the data to gain insights.
4. Prepare the data for machine learning algorithms.
5. Select a model and train it.
6. Fine-tune your model.
7. Present your solution.
8. Launch, monitor, and maintain your system.

Working with Real Data

When you are learning about machine learning, it is best to experiment with real-world data, not artificial datasets. Fortunately, there are thousands of open datasets to choose from, ranging across all sorts of domains. Here are a few popular open data repositories you can use to get data:

- Google Datasets Search (*https://datasetsearch.research.google.com*)
- Hugging Face Datasets (*https://huggingface.co/docs/datasets*)
- OpenML.org (*https://openml.org*)

- Kaggle.com (*https://kaggle.com/datasets*)
- UC Irvine Machine Learning Repository (*https://archive.ics.uci.edu*)
- Stanford Large Network Dataset Collection (*https://snap.stanford.edu/data*)
- Amazon's AWS datasets (*https://registry.opendata.aws*)
- U.S. Government's Open Data (*https://data.gov*)
- DataPortals.org (*https://dataportals.org*)
- Wikipedia's list of machine learning datasets (*https://homl.info/9*)

In this chapter we'll use the California Housing Prices dataset from the StatLib repository[1] (see Figure 2-1). This dataset is based on data from the 1990 California census. It is not exactly recent (a nice house in the Bay Area was still affordable at the time), but it has many qualities for learning, so we will pretend it is recent data. For teaching purposes I've added a categorical attribute and removed a few features.

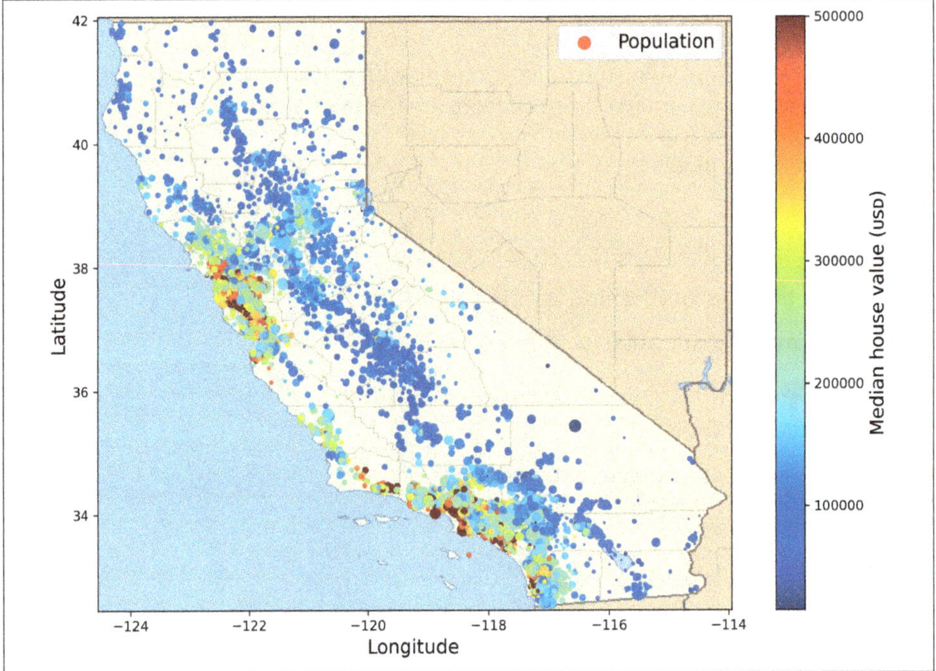

Figure 2-1. California housing prices

1 The original dataset appeared in R. Kelley Pace and Ronald Barry, "Sparse Spatial Autoregressions", *Statistics & Probability Letters* 33, no. 3 (1997): 291–297.

Look at the Big Picture

Welcome to the Machine Learning Housing Corporation! Your first task is to use California census data to build a model of housing prices in the state. This data includes metrics such as the population, median income, and median housing price for each block group in California. Block groups are the smallest geographical unit for which the US Census Bureau publishes sample data (a block group typically has a population of 600 to 3,000 people). I will call them "districts" for short.

Your model should learn from this data and be able to predict the median housing price in any district, given all the other metrics.

Since you are a well-organized data scientist, the first thing you should do is pull out your machine learning project checklist. You can start with the one at *https://homl.info/checklist*; it should work reasonably well for most machine learning projects, but make sure to adapt it to your needs. In this chapter we will go through many checklist items, but we will also skip a few, either because they are self-explanatory or because they will be discussed in later chapters.

Frame the Problem

The first question to ask your boss is what exactly the business objective is. Building a model is probably not the end goal. How does the company expect to use and benefit from this model? Knowing the objective is important because it will determine how you frame the problem, which algorithms you will select, which performance measure you will use to evaluate your model, and how much effort you will spend tweaking it.

Your boss answers that your model's output (a prediction of a district's median housing price) will be essential to determine whether it is worth investing in a given area. More specifically, your model's output will be fed to another machine learning system (see Figure 2-2), along with some other signals.[2] So it's important to make our housing price model as accurate as we can.

The next question to ask your boss is what the current solution looks like (if any). The current situation will often give you a reference for performance, as well as insights on how to solve the problem. Your boss answers that the district housing prices are currently estimated manually by experts: a team gathers up-to-date

2 A piece of information fed to a machine learning system is often called a *signal*, in reference to Claude Shannon's information theory, which he developed at Bell Labs to improve telecommunications. His theory: you want a high signal-to-noise ratio.

information about a district, and when they cannot get the median housing price, they estimate it using complex rules.

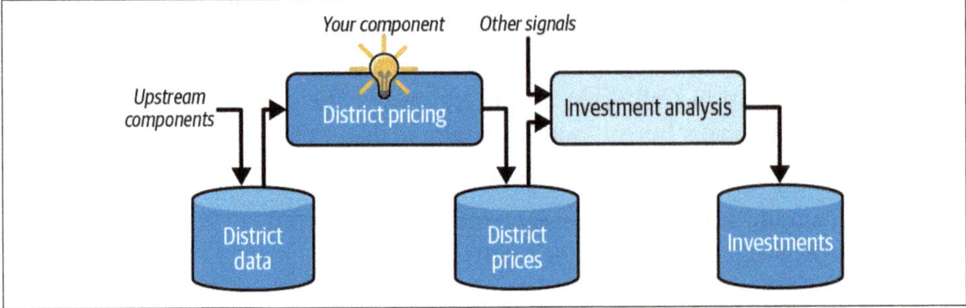

Figure 2-2. A machine learning pipeline for real estate investments

This is costly and time-consuming, and their estimates are not great; in cases where they manage to find out the actual median housing price, they often realize that their estimates were off by more than 30%. This is why the company thinks that it would be useful to train a model to predict a district's median housing price, given other data about that district. The census data looks like a great dataset to exploit for this purpose, since it includes the median housing prices of thousands of districts, as well as other data.

Pipelines

A sequence of data processing components is called a data *pipeline*. Pipelines are very common in machine learning systems, since there is a lot of data to manipulate and many data transformations to apply.

Components typically run asynchronously. Each component pulls in a large amount of data, processes it, and spits out the result in another data store. Then, some time later, the next component in the pipeline pulls in this data and spits out its own output. Each component is fairly self-contained: the interface between components is simply the data store. This makes the system simple to grasp (with the help of a data flow graph), and different teams can focus on different components. Moreover, if a component breaks down, the downstream components can often continue to run normally (at least for a while) by just using the last output from the broken component. This makes the architecture quite robust.

On the other hand, a broken component can go unnoticed for some time if proper monitoring is not implemented. The data gets stale and the overall system's performance drops.

With all this information, you are now ready to start designing your system. First, determine what kind of training supervision the model will need: is it a supervised, unsupervised, semi-supervised, self-supervised, or reinforcement learning task? And is it a classification task, a regression task, or something else? Should you use batch learning or online learning techniques? Before you read on, pause and try to answer these questions for yourself.

Have you found the answers? Let's see. This is clearly a typical supervised learning task, since the model can be trained with *labeled* examples (each instance comes with the expected output, i.e., the district's median housing price). It is a typical regression task, since the model will be asked to predict a value. More specifically, this is a *multiple regression* problem, since the system will use multiple features to make a prediction (the district's population, the median income, etc.). It is also a *univariate regression* problem, since we are only trying to predict a single value for each district. If we were trying to predict multiple values per district, it would be a *multivariate regression* problem. Finally, there is no continuous flow of data coming into the system, there is no particular need to adjust to changing data rapidly, and the data is small enough to fit in memory, so plain batch learning should do just fine.

If the data were huge, you could either split your batch learning work across multiple servers (using the MapReduce technique) or use an online learning technique.

Select a Performance Measure

Your next step is to select a performance measure. A typical performance measure for regression problems is the *root mean squared error* (RMSE). It gives an idea of how much error the system typically makes in its predictions, with a higher weight given to large errors. Equation 2-1 shows the mathematical formula to compute the RMSE.

Equation 2-1. Root mean squared error (RMSE)

$$\mathrm{RMSE}(\mathbf{X},\mathbf{y},h) = \sqrt{\frac{1}{m}\sum_{i=1}^{m}\left(h\left(\mathbf{x}^{(i)}\right) - y^{(i)}\right)^2}$$

Notations

This equation introduces several very common machine learning notations that I will use throughout this book:

- m is the number of instances in the dataset you are measuring the RMSE on.
  - For example, if you are evaluating the RMSE on a validation set of 2,000 districts, then m = 2,000.

- $\mathbf{x}^{(i)}$ is a vector of all the feature values (excluding the label) of the ith instance in the dataset, and $y^{(i)}$ is its label (the desired output value for that instance). $\mathbf{y}$ is a vector containing the labels of all the instances in the dataset.
  - For example, if the first district in the dataset is located at longitude –118.29°, latitude 33.91°, and it has 1,416 inhabitants with a median income of $38,372, and the median house value is $156,400 (ignoring other features for now), then:

$$\mathbf{x}^{(1)} = \begin{pmatrix} -118.29 \\ 33.91 \\ 1{,}416 \\ 38{,}372 \end{pmatrix}$$

    and:

$$y^{(1)} = 156{,}400$$

- $\mathbf{X}$ is a matrix containing all the feature values (excluding labels) of all instances in the dataset. There is one row per instance, and the ith row is equal to the transpose of $\mathbf{x}^{(i)}$, denoted $(\mathbf{x}^{(i)})^\intercal$.[3]
  - For example, if the first district is as just described, then the matrix $\mathbf{X}$ looks like this:

$$\mathbf{X} = \begin{pmatrix} \left(\mathbf{x}^{(1)}\right)^\intercal \\ \left(\mathbf{x}^{(2)}\right)^\intercal \\ \vdots \\ \left(\mathbf{x}^{(1999)}\right)^\intercal \\ \left(\mathbf{x}^{(2000)}\right)^\intercal \end{pmatrix} = \begin{pmatrix} -118.29 & 33.91 & 1{,}416 & 38{,}372 \\ \vdots & \vdots & \vdots & \vdots \end{pmatrix}$$

- h is your system's prediction function, also called a *hypothesis*. When your system is given an instance's feature vector $\mathbf{x}^{(i)}$, it outputs a predicted value $\hat{y}^{(i)} = h(\mathbf{x}^{(i)})$ for that instance ($\hat{y}$ is pronounced "y-hat").
  - For example, if your system predicts that the median housing price in the first district is $158,400, then $\hat{y}^{(1)} = h(\mathbf{x}^{(1)}) = 158{,}400$. The prediction error for this district is $\hat{y}^{(1)} - y^{(1)} = 2{,}000$.

3 Recall that the transpose operator flips a column vector into a row vector (and vice versa).

- RMSE($\mathbf{X}$,y,h) is the cost function measured on the set of examples using your hypothesis h.

We use lowercase italic font for scalar values (such as m or $y^{(i)}$) and function names (such as h), lowercase bold font for vectors (such as $\mathbf{x}^{(i)}$), and uppercase bold font for matrices (such as $\mathbf{X}$).

Although the RMSE is generally the preferred performance measure for regression tasks, in some contexts you may prefer to use another function, especially when there are many outliers in the data, as the RMSE is quite sensitive to them. In that case, you may consider using the *mean absolute error* (MAE, also called the *average absolute deviation*), shown in Equation 2-2:

Equation 2-2. Mean absolute error (MAE)

$$\text{MAE}(\mathbf{X},\mathbf{y},h) = \frac{1}{m}\sum_{i=1}^{m}\left|h\left(\mathbf{x}^{(i)}\right) - y^{(i)}\right|$$

Both the RMSE and the MAE are ways to measure the distance between two vectors: the vector of predictions and the vector of target values. Various distance measures, or *norms*, are possible:

- Computing the root of a sum of squares (RMSE) corresponds to the *Euclidean norm*: this is the notion of distance we are all familiar with. It is also called the ℓ_2 *norm*, denoted $\|\cdot\|_2$ (or just $\|\cdot\|$).
- Computing the sum of absolutes (MAE) corresponds to the ℓ_1 *norm*, denoted $\|\cdot\|_1$. This is sometimes called the *Manhattan norm* because it measures the distance between two points in a city if you can only travel along orthogonal city blocks.
- More generally, the ℓ_k *norm* of a vector $\mathbf{v}$ containing n elements is defined as $\|\mathbf{v}\|_k = (|v_1|^k + |v_2|^k + ... + |v_n|^k)^{1/k}$. ℓ_0 gives the number of nonzero elements in the vector, and ℓ_∞ gives the maximum absolute value in the vector.

The higher the norm index, the more it focuses on large values and neglects small ones. This is why the RMSE is more sensitive to outliers than the MAE. But when outliers are exponentially rare (like in a bell-shaped curve), the RMSE performs very well and is generally preferred.

Check the Assumptions

Lastly, it is good practice to list and verify the assumptions that have been made so far (by you or others); this can help you catch serious issues early on. For example, the district prices that your system outputs are going to be fed into a downstream machine learning system, and you assume that these prices are going to be used as such. But what if the downstream system converts the prices into categories (e.g., "cheap", "medium", or "expensive") and then uses those categories instead of the prices themselves? In this case, getting the price perfectly right is not important at all; your system just needs to get the category right. If that's so, then the problem should have been framed as a classification task, not a regression task. You don't want to find this out after working on a regression system for months.

Fortunately, after talking with the team in charge of the downstream system, you are confident that they do indeed need the actual prices, not just categories. Great! You're all set, the lights are green, and you can start coding now!

Get the Data

It's time to get your hands dirty. Don't hesitate to pick up your laptop and walk through the code examples. As I mentioned in the preface, all the code examples in this book are open source and available online (*https://github.com/ageron/handson-mlp*) as Jupyter notebooks, which are interactive documents containing text, images, and executable code snippets (Python in our case). In this book I will assume you are running these notebooks on Google Colab, a free service that lets you run any Jupyter notebook directly online, without having to install anything on your machine. If you want to use another online platform (e.g., Kaggle) or if you want to install everything locally on your own machine, please see the instructions on the book's GitHub page.

Running the Code Examples Using Google Colab

First, open a web browser and visit *https://homl.info/colab-p*: this will lead you to Google Colab, and it will display the list of Jupyter notebooks for this book (see Figure 2-3). You will find one notebook per chapter, plus a few extra notebooks and tutorials for NumPy, Matplotlib, Pandas, linear algebra, and differential calculus. For example, if you click *02_end_to_end_machine_learning_project.ipynb*, the notebook from Chapter 2 will open up in Google Colab (see Figure 2-4).

A Jupyter notebook is composed of a list of cells. Each cell contains either executable code or text. Try double-clicking the first text cell (which contains the sentence "Welcome to Machine Learning Housing Corp.!"). This will open the cell for editing. Notice that Jupyter notebooks use Markdown syntax for formatting (e.g., `**bold**`, `*italics*`, `# Title`, `[url](link text)`, and so on). Try modifying this text, then press Shift-Enter to see the result.

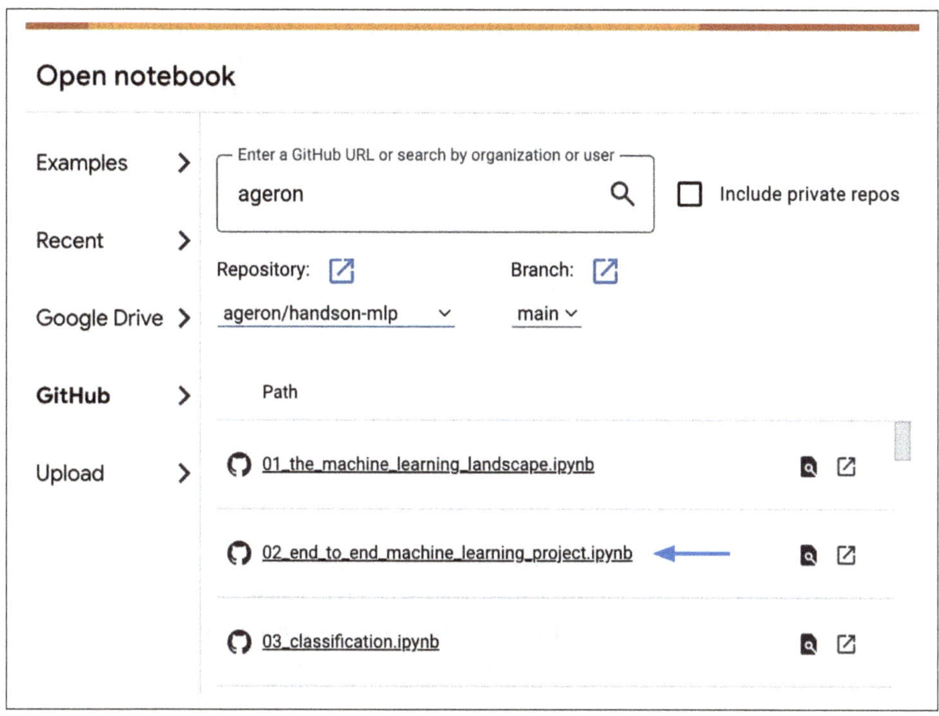

Figure 2-3. List of notebooks in Google Colab

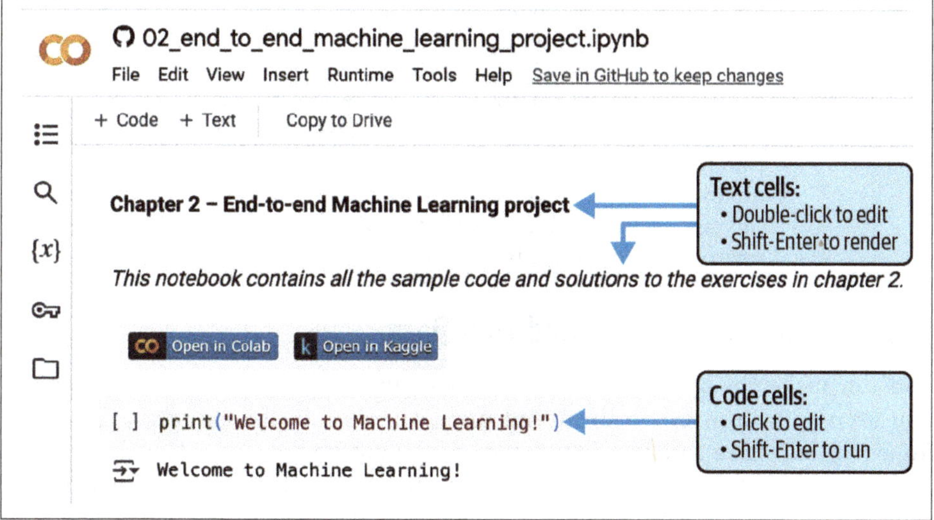

Figure 2-4. Your notebook in Google Colab

Next, create a new code cell by selecting Insert → "Code cell" from the menu. Alternatively, you can click the + Code button in the toolbar, or hover your mouse over the bottom of a cell until you see + Code and + Text appear, then click + Code. In the new code cell, type some Python code, such as `print("Hello World")`, then press Shift-Enter to run this code (or click the ▷ button on the left side of the cell).

If you're not logged in to your Google account, you'll be asked to log in now (if you don't already have a Google account, you'll need to create one). Once you are logged in, when you try to run the code you'll see a security warning telling you that this notebook was not authored by Google. A malicious person could create a notebook that tries to trick you into entering your Google credentials so they can access your personal data, so before you run a notebook, always make sure you trust its author (or double-check what each code cell will do before running it). Assuming you trust me (or you plan to check every code cell), you can now click "Run anyway".

Colab will then allocate a new *runtime* for you: this is a free virtual machine located on Google's servers that contains a bunch of tools and Python libraries, including everything you'll need for most chapters (in some chapters, you'll need to run a command to install additional libraries). This will take a few seconds. Next, Colab will automatically connect to this runtime and use it to execute your new code cell. Importantly, the code runs on the runtime, *not* on your machine. The code's output will be displayed under the cell. Congrats, you've run some Python code on Colab!

To insert a new code cell, you can also type Ctrl-M (or Cmd-M on macOS) followed by A (to insert above the active cell) or B (to insert below). There are many other keyboard shortcuts available: you can view and edit them by typing Ctrl-M (or Cmd-M) then H. If you choose to run the notebooks on Kaggle or on your own machine using JupyterLab or an IDE such as Visual Studio Code with the Jupyter extension, you will see some minor differences—runtimes are called *kernels*, the user interface and keyboard shortcuts are slightly different, etc.—but switching from one Jupyter environment to another is not too hard.

Saving Your Code Changes and Your Data

You can make changes to a Colab notebook, and they will persist for as long as you keep your browser tab open. But once you close it, the changes will be lost. To avoid this, make sure you save a copy of the notebook to your Google Drive by selecting File → "Save a copy in Drive". Alternatively, you can download the notebook to your computer by selecting File → Download → "Download .ipynb". Then you can later visit *https://colab.research.google.com* and open the notebook again (either from Google Drive or by uploading it from your computer).

Google Colab is meant only for interactive use: you can play around in the notebooks and tweak the code as you like, but you cannot let the notebooks run unattended for a long period of time, or else the runtime will be shut down and all of its data will be lost.

If the notebook generates data that you care about, make sure you download this data before the runtime shuts down. To do this, click the Files icon (see step 1 in Figure 2-5), find the file you want to download, click the vertical dots next to it (step 2), and click Download (step 3). Alternatively, you can mount your Google Drive on the runtime, allowing the notebook to read and write files directly to Google Drive as if it were a local directory. For this, click the Files icon (step 1), then click the Google Drive icon (circled in Figure 2-5) and follow the on-screen instructions.

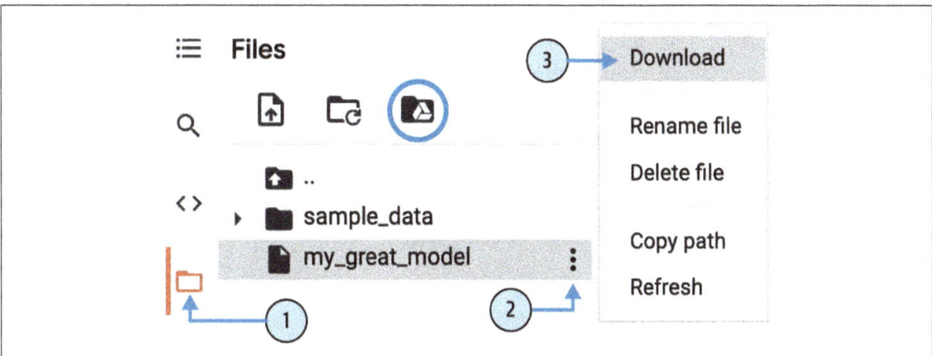

Figure 2-5. Downloading a file from a Google Colab runtime (steps 1 to 3), or mounting your Google Drive (circled icon)

By default, your Google Drive will be mounted at */content/drive/MyDrive*. If you want to back up a data file, simply copy it to this directory by running `!cp [.keep-together]#/content/my_great_model /content/drive/MyDrive.#` Any command starting with a bang (`!`) is treated as a shell command, not as Python code: `cp` is the Linux shell command to copy a file from one path to another. Note that Colab runtimes run on Linux (specifically, Ubuntu).

The Power and Danger of Interactivity

Jupyter notebooks are interactive, and that's a great thing: you can run each cell one by one, stop at any point, insert a cell, play with the code, go back and run the same cell again, etc., and I highly encourage you to do so. If you just run the cells one by one without ever playing around with them, you won't learn as fast. However, this flexibility comes at a price: it's very easy to run cells in the wrong order, or to forget to run a cell. If this happens, the subsequent code cells are likely to fail. For example, the very first code cell in each notebook contains setup code (such as imports), so make sure you run it first, or else nothing will work.

If you ever run into a weird error, try restarting the runtime (by selecting Runtime → "Restart runtime" from the menu) and then run all the cells again from the beginning of the notebook. This often solves the problem. If not, it's likely that one of the changes you made broke the notebook: just revert to the original notebook and try again. If it still fails, please file an issue on GitHub.

Book Code Versus Notebook Code

You may sometimes notice some little differences between the code in this book and the code in the notebooks. This may happen for several reasons:

- A library may have changed slightly by the time you read these lines, or perhaps despite my best efforts I made an error in the book. Sadly, I cannot magically fix the code in your copy of this book (unless you are reading an electronic copy and you can download the latest version), but I *can* fix the notebooks. So, if you run into an error after copying code from this book, please look for the fixed code in the notebooks: I will strive to keep them error-free and up-to-date with the latest library versions.
- The notebooks contain some extra code to beautify the figures (adding labels, setting font sizes, etc.) and to save them in high resolution for this book. You can safely ignore this extra code if you want.

I optimized the code for readability and simplicity: I made it as linear and flat as possible, defining very few functions or classes. The goal is to ensure that the code you are running is generally right in front of you, and not nested within several layers of abstractions that you have to search through. This also makes it easier for you to play with the code. For simplicity, there's limited error handling, and I placed some of the least common imports right where they are needed (instead of placing them at the top of the file, as is recommended by the PEP 8 Python style guide). That said, your production code will not be very different: just a bit more modular, and with additional tests and error handling.

OK! Once you're comfortable with Colab, you're ready to download the data.

Download the Data

In typical environments your data would be available in a relational database or some other common data store, and spread across multiple tables/documents/files. To access it, you would first need to get your credentials and access authorizations and familiarize yourself with the data schema.[4] In this project, however, things are much simpler: you will just download a single compressed file, *housing.tgz*, which contains a comma-separated values (CSV) file called *housing.csv* with all the data.

Rather than manually downloading and decompressing the data, it's usually preferable to write a function that does it for you. This is useful in particular if the data changes regularly: you can write a small script that uses the function to fetch the latest data (or you can set up a scheduled job to do that automatically at regular intervals). Automating the process of fetching the data is also useful if you need to install the dataset on multiple machines.

Here is the function to fetch and load the data:

```
from pathlib import Path
import pandas as pd
import tarfile
import urllib.request

def load_housing_data():
    tarball_path = Path("datasets/housing.tgz")
    if not tarball_path.is_file():
        Path("datasets").mkdir(parents=True, exist_ok=True)
        url = "https://github.com/ageron/data/raw/main/housing.tgz"
        urllib.request.urlretrieve(url, tarball_path)
        with tarfile.open(tarball_path) as housing_tarball:
            housing_tarball.extractall(path="datasets", filter="data")
    return pd.read_csv(Path("datasets/housing/housing.csv"))

housing_full = load_housing_data()
```

If you get an SSL `CERTIFICATE_VERIFY_FAILED` error on macOS, then you most likely need to install the `certifi` package, as explained at *https://homl.info/sslerror*.

When `load_housing_data()` is called, it looks for the *datasets/housing.tgz* file. If it does not find it, it creates the *datasets* directory inside the current directory (which is */content* by default, in Colab), downloads the *housing.tgz* file from the *ageron/data* GitHub repository, and extracts its content into the *datasets* directory; this creates the *datasets/housing* directory with the *housing.csv* file inside it. Lastly, the function loads this CSV file into a Pandas DataFrame object containing all the data, and returns it.

4 You might also need to check legal constraints, such as private fields that should never be copied to unsafe data stores.

If you are using Python 3.12 or 3.13, you should add `filter='data'` to the `extractall()` method's arguments: this limits what the extraction algorithm can do and improves security (see the documentation for more details).

Take a Quick Look at the Data Structure

You start by looking at the top five rows of data using the DataFrame's `head()` method (see Figure 2-6).

```
housing.head()
```

	longitude	latitude	housing_median_age	median_income	ocean_proximity	median_house_value
0	-122.23	37.88	41.0	8.3252	NEAR BAY	452600.0
1	-122.22	37.86	21.0	8.3014	NEAR BAY	358500.0
2	-122.24	37.85	52.0	7.2574	NEAR BAY	352100.0
3	-122.25	37.85	52.0	5.6431	NEAR BAY	341300.0
4	-122.25	37.85	52.0	3.8462	NEAR BAY	342200.0

Figure 2-6. Top five rows in the dataset

Each row represents one district. There are 10 attributes (they are not all shown in the screenshot): `longitude`, `latitude`, `housing_median_age`, `total_rooms`, `total_bedrooms`, `population`, `households`, `median_income`, `median_house_value`, and `ocean_proximity`.

The `info()` method is useful to get a quick description of the data, in particular the total number of rows, each attribute's type, and the number of non-null values:

```
>>> housing_full.info()
<class 'pandas.core.frame.DataFrame'>
RangeIndex: 20640 entries, 0 to 20639
Data columns (total 10 columns):
 #   Column              Non-Null Count  Dtype
---  ------              --------------  -----
 0   longitude           20640 non-null  float64
 1   latitude            20640 non-null  float64
 2   housing_median_age  20640 non-null  float64
 3   total_rooms         20640 non-null  float64
 4   total_bedrooms      20433 non-null  float64
 5   population          20640 non-null  float64
 6   households          20640 non-null  float64
 7   median_income       20640 non-null  float64
 8   median_house_value  20640 non-null  float64
 9   ocean_proximity     20640 non-null  object
dtypes: float64(9), object(1)
memory usage: 1.6+ MB
```

In this book, when a code example contains a mix of code and outputs, as is the case here, it is formatted like in the Python interpreter for better readability: the code lines are prefixed with `>>>` (or `...` for indented blocks), and the outputs have no prefix.

There are 20,640 instances in the dataset, which means that it is fairly small by machine learning standards, but it's perfect to get started. You notice that the `total_bedrooms` attribute has only 20,433 non-null values, meaning that 207 districts are missing this feature. You will need to take care of this later.

All attributes are numerical, except for `ocean_proximity`. Its type is `object`, so it could hold any kind of Python object. But since you loaded this data from a CSV file, you know that it must be a text attribute. When you looked at the top five rows, you probably noticed that the values in the `ocean_proximity` column were repetitive, which means that it is probably a categorical attribute. You can find out what categories exist and how many districts belong to each category by using the `value_counts()` method:

```
>>> housing_full["ocean_proximity"].value_counts()
ocean_proximity
<1H OCEAN     9136
INLAND        6551
NEAR OCEAN    2658
NEAR BAY      2290
ISLAND           5
Name: count, dtype: int64
```

Let's look at the other fields. The `describe()` method shows a summary of the numerical attributes (Figure 2-7).

```
housing.describe()
```

	longitude	latitude	housing_median_age	total_rooms	total_bedrooms	median_house_value
count	20640.000000	20640.000000	20640.000000	20640.000000	20433.000000	20640.000000
mean	-119.569704	35.631861	28.639486	2635.763081	537.870553	206855.816909
std	2.003532	2.135952	12.585558	2181.615252	421.385070	115395.615874
min	-124.350000	32.540000	1.000000	2.000000	1.000000	14999.000000
25%	-121.800000	33.930000	18.000000	1447.750000	296.000000	119600.000000
50%	-118.490000	34.260000	29.000000	2127.000000	435.000000	179700.000000
75%	-118.010000	37.710000	37.000000	3148.000000	647.000000	264725.000000
max	-114.310000	41.950000	52.000000	39320.000000	6445.000000	500001.000000

Figure 2-7. Summary of each numerical attribute

The count, mean, min, and max rows are self-explanatory. Note that the null values are ignored (so, for example, the count of total_bedrooms is 20,433, not 20,640). The std row shows the *standard deviation*, which measures how dispersed the values are.[5] The 25%, 50%, and 75% rows show the corresponding *percentiles*: a percentile indicates the value below which a given percentage of observations in a group of observations fall. For example, 25% of the districts have a housing_median_age lower than 18, while 50% are lower than 29, and 75% are lower than 37. These are often called the 25th percentile (or first *quartile*), the median, and the 75th percentile (or third quartile).

Another quick way to get a feel of the type of data you are dealing with is to plot a histogram for each numerical attribute. A histogram shows the number of instances (on the vertical axis) that have a given value range (on the horizontal axis). You can either plot this one attribute at a time, or you can call the hist() method on the whole dataset (as shown in the following code example), and it will plot a histogram for each numerical attribute (see Figure 2-8).

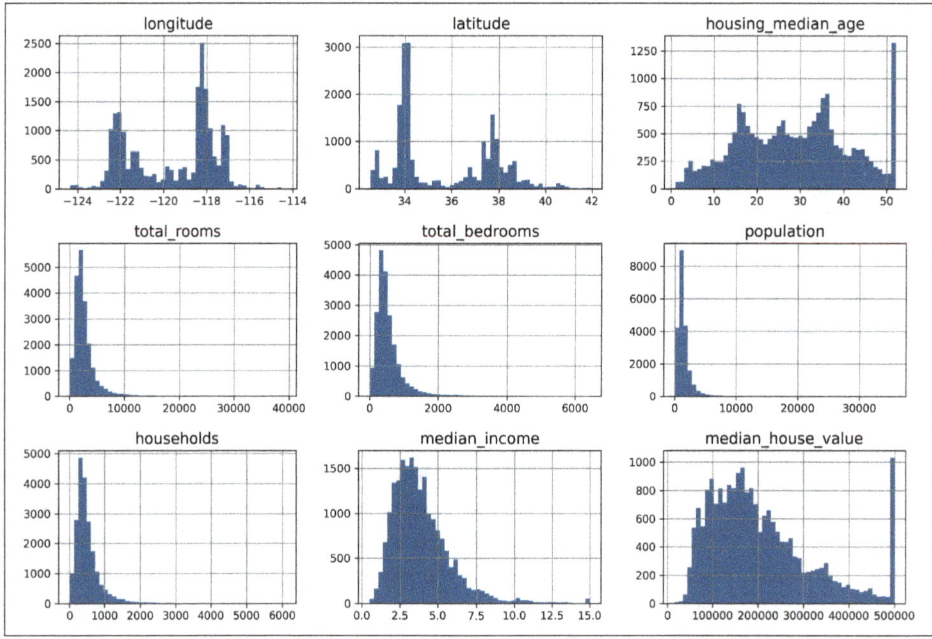

Figure 2-8. A histogram for each numerical attribute

5 The standard deviation is generally denoted σ (the Greek letter sigma), and it is the square root of the *variance*, which is the average of the squared deviation from the mean. When a feature has a bell-shaped *normal distribution* (also called a *Gaussian distribution*), which is very common, the "68-95-99.7" rule applies: about 68% of the values fall within 1σ of the mean, 95% within 2σ, and 99.7% within 3σ.

The number of value ranges can be adjusted using the `bins` argument (try playing with it to see how it affects the histograms):

```
import matplotlib.pyplot as plt

housing_full.hist(bins=50, figsize=(12, 8))
plt.show()
```

Looking at these histograms, you notice a few things:

- First, the median income attribute does not look like it is expressed in US dollars (USD). After checking with the team that collected the data, you are told that the data has been scaled and capped at 15 (actually, 15.0001) for higher median incomes, and at 0.5 (actually, 0.4999) for lower median incomes. The numbers represent roughly tens of thousands of dollars (e.g., 3 actually means about $30,000). Working with preprocessed attributes is common in machine learning, and it is not necessarily a problem, but you should try to understand how the data was computed.
- The housing median age and the median house value were also capped. The latter may be a serious problem since it is your target attribute (your labels). Your machine learning algorithms may learn that prices never go beyond that limit. You need to check with your client team (the team that will use your system's output) to see if this is a problem or not. If they tell you that they need precise predictions even beyond $500,000, then you have two options:
  - Collect proper labels for the districts whose labels were capped.
  - Remove those districts from the training set (and also from the test set, since your system should not be evaluated poorly if it predicts values beyond $500,000).
- These attributes have very different scales. We will discuss this later in this chapter when we explore feature scaling.
- Finally, many histograms are *skewed right*: they extend much farther to the right of the median than to the left. This may make it a bit harder for some machine learning algorithms to detect patterns. Later, you'll try transforming these attributes to have more symmetrical and bell-shaped distributions.

You should now have a better understanding of the kind of data you're dealing with.

Create a Test Set

Before you look at the data any further, you need to create a test set, put it aside, and never look at it. It may seem strange to voluntarily set aside part of the data at this stage. After all, you have only taken a quick glance at the data, and surely you should learn a whole lot more about it before you decide what algorithms to use, right? This is true, but your brain is an amazing pattern detection system, which also means that it is highly prone to overfitting: if you look at the test set, you may stumble upon some seemingly interesting pattern in the test data that leads you to select a particular kind of machine learning model. When you estimate the generalization error using the test set, your estimate will be too optimistic, and you will launch a system that will not perform as well as expected. This is called *data snooping* bias.

Creating a test set is theoretically simple; pick some instances randomly, typically 20% of the dataset (or less if your dataset is very large), and set them aside:

```
import numpy as np

def shuffle_and_split_data(data, test_ratio, rng):
    shuffled_indices = rng.permutation(len(data))
    test_set_size = int(len(data) * test_ratio)
    test_indices = shuffled_indices[:test_set_size]
    train_indices = shuffled_indices[test_set_size:]
    return data.iloc[train_indices], data.iloc[test_indices]
```

You can then use this function like this:

```
>>> rng = np.random.default_rng()  # default random number generator
>>> train_set, test_set = shuffle_and_split_data(housing_full, 0.2, rng)
>>> len(train_set)
16512
>>> len(test_set)
4128
```

Well, this works, but it is not perfect: if you run the program again, it will generate a different test set! Over time, you (or your machine learning algorithms) will get to see the whole dataset, which is what you want to avoid.

One solution is to save the test set on the first run and then load it in subsequent runs. Another option is to set the random number generator's seed (e.g., by passing `seed=42` to the `default_rng()` function)[6] to ensure it always generates the same sequence of random numbers every time you run the program.

However, both these solutions will break the next time you fetch an updated dataset. To have a stable train/test split even after updating the dataset, a common solution is to use each instance's identifier to decide whether it should go in the test set (assuming instances have unique and immutable identifiers). For example, you could compute a hash of each instance's identifier and put that instance in the test set if the hash is lower than or equal to 20% of the maximum hash value. This ensures that the test set will remain consistent across multiple runs, even if you refresh the dataset.

6 You will often see people set the random seed to 42. This number has no special property, other than being the Answer to the Ultimate Question of Life, the Universe, and Everything.

The new test set will contain 20% of the new instances, but it will not contain any instance that was previously in the training set.

Here is a possible implementation:

```
from zlib import crc32

def is_id_in_test_set(identifier, test_ratio):
    return crc32(np.int64(identifier)) < test_ratio * 2**32

def split_data_with_id_hash(data, test_ratio, id_column):
    ids = data[id_column]
    in_test_set = ids.apply(lambda id_: is_id_in_test_set(id_, test_ratio))
    return data.loc[~in_test_set], data.loc[in_test_set]
```

Unfortunately, the housing dataset does not have an identifier column. The simplest solution is to use the row index as the ID:

```
housing_with_id = housing_full.reset_index()  # adds an `index` column
train_set, test_set = split_data_with_id_hash(housing_with_id, 0.2, "index")
```

If you use the row index as a unique identifier, you need to make sure that new data gets appended to the end of the dataset and that no row ever gets deleted. If this is not possible, then you can try to use the most stable features to build a unique identifier. For example, a district's latitude and longitude are guaranteed to be stable for a few million years, so you could combine them into an ID like so:[7]

```
housing_with_id["id"] = (housing_full["longitude"] * 1000
                         + housing_full["latitude"])
train_set, test_set = split_data_with_id_hash(housing_with_id, 0.2, "id")
```

Scikit-Learn provides a few functions to split datasets into multiple subsets in various ways. The simplest function is `train_test_split()`, which does pretty much the same thing as the `shuffle_and_split_data()` function we defined earlier, with a couple of additional features. First, there is a `random_state` parameter that allows you to set the random generator seed. Second, you can pass it multiple datasets with an identical number of rows, and it will split them on the same indices (this is very useful, for example, if you have a separate DataFrame for labels):

```
from sklearn.model_selection import train_test_split

train_set, test_set = train_test_split(housing_full, test_size=0.2,
                                       random_state=42)
```

So far we have considered purely random sampling methods. This is generally fine if your dataset is large enough (especially relative to the number of attributes), but if it is not, you run the risk of introducing a significant sampling bias. When employees at

7 The location information is actually quite coarse, and as a result many districts will have the exact same ID, so they will end up in the same set (test or train). This introduces some unfortunate sampling bias.

a survey company decide to call 1,000 people to ask them a few questions, they don't just pick 1,000 people randomly in a phone book. They try to ensure that these 1,000 people are representative of the whole population, with regard to the questions they want to ask. For example, according to the US Census Bureau, 51.6% of citizens of voting age are female, while 48.4% are male, so a well-conducted survey in the US would try to maintain this ratio in the sample: 516 females and 484 males (at least if it seems likely that the answers may vary across genders). This is called *stratified sampling*: the population is divided into homogeneous subgroups called *strata*, and the right number of instances are sampled from each stratum to guarantee that the test set is representative of the overall population. If the people running the survey used purely random sampling, there would be over 10% chance of sampling a skewed test set with less than 49% female or more than 54% female participants. Either way, the survey results would likely be quite biased.

Suppose you've chatted with some experts who told you that the median income is a very important attribute to predict median housing prices. You may want to ensure that the test set is representative of the various categories of incomes in the whole dataset. Since the median income is a continuous numerical attribute, you first need to create an income category attribute. Let's look at the median income histogram more closely (back in Figure 2-8): most median income values are clustered around 1.5 to 6 (i.e., $15,000–$60,000), but some median incomes go far beyond 6. It is important to have a sufficient number of instances in your dataset for each stratum, or else the estimate of a stratum's importance may be biased. This means that you should not have too many strata, and each stratum should be large enough. The following code uses the `pd.cut()` function to create an income category attribute with five categories (labeled from 1 to 5); category 1 ranges from 0 to 1.5 (i.e., less than $15,000), category 2 from 1.5 to 3, and so on:

```
housing_full["income_cat"] = pd.cut(housing_full["median_income"],
                                    bins=[0., 1.5, 3.0, 4.5, 6., np.inf],
                                    labels=[1, 2, 3, 4, 5])
```

These income categories are represented in Figure 2-9:

```
cat_counts = housing_full["income_cat"].value_counts().sort_index()
cat_counts.plot.bar(rot=0, grid=True)
plt.xlabel("Income category")
plt.ylabel("Number of districts")
plt.show()
```

Now you are ready to do stratified sampling based on the income category. Scikit-Learn provides a number of splitter classes in the `sklearn.model_selection` package that implement various strategies to split your dataset into a training set and a test set. Each splitter has a `split()` method that returns an iterator over different training/test splits of the same data.

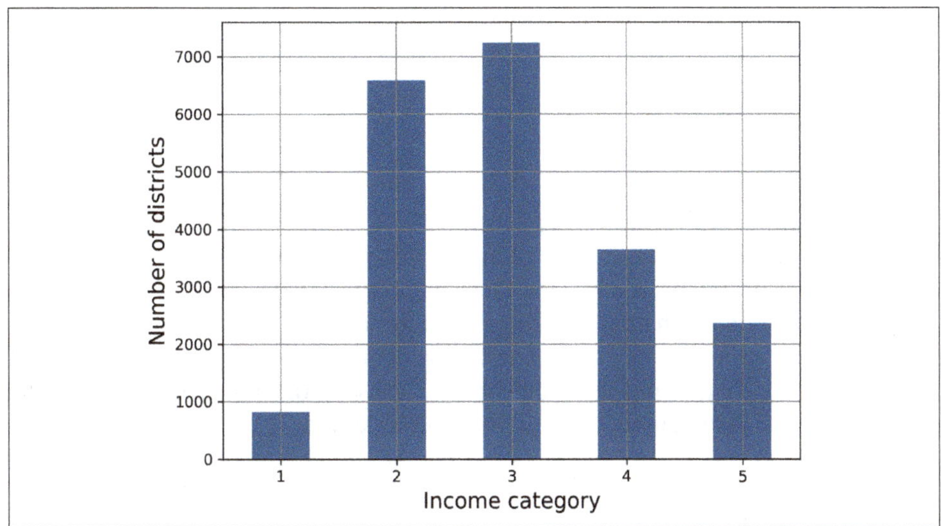

Figure 2-9. Histogram of income categories

To be precise, the `split()` method yields the training and test *indices*, not the data itself. Having multiple splits can be useful if you want to better estimate the performance of your model, as you will see when we discuss cross-validation later in this chapter. For example, the following code generates 10 different stratified splits of the same dataset:

```
from sklearn.model_selection import StratifiedShuffleSplit

splitter = StratifiedShuffleSplit(n_splits=10, test_size=0.2, random_state=42)
strat_splits = []
for train_index, test_index in splitter.split(housing_full,
                                              housing_full["income_cat"]):
    strat_train_set_n = housing_full.iloc[train_index]
    strat_test_set_n = housing_full.iloc[test_index]
    strat_splits.append([strat_train_set_n, strat_test_set_n])
```

For now, you can just use the first split:

```
strat_train_set, strat_test_set = strat_splits[0]
```

Or, since stratified sampling is fairly common, there's a shorter way to get a single split using the `train_test_split()` function with the `stratify` argument:

```
strat_train_set, strat_test_set = train_test_split(
    housing_full, test_size=0.2, stratify=housing_full["income_cat"],
    random_state=42)
```

Let's see if this worked as expected. You can start by looking at the income category proportions in the test set:

```
>>> strat_test_set["income_cat"].value_counts() / len(strat_test_set)
income_cat
3    0.350533
2    0.318798
4    0.176357
5    0.114341
1    0.039971
Name: count, dtype: float64
```

With similar code you can measure the income category proportions in the full dataset. Figure 2-10 compares the income category proportions in the overall dataset, in the test set generated with stratified sampling, and in a test set generated using purely random sampling. As you can see, the test set generated using stratified sampling has income category proportions almost identical to those in the full dataset, whereas the test set generated using purely random sampling is skewed.

Income Category	Overall %	Stratified %	Random %	Strat. Error %	Rand. Error %
1	3.98	4.00	4.24	0.36	6.45
2	31.88	31.88	30.74	-0.02	-3.59
3	35.06	35.05	34.52	-0.01	-1.53
4	17.63	17.64	18.41	0.03	4.42
5	11.44	11.43	12.09	-0.08	5.63

Figure 2-10. Sampling bias comparison of stratified versus purely random sampling

You won't use the `income_cat` column again, so you might as well drop it, reverting the data back to its original state:

```
for set_ in (strat_train_set, strat_test_set):
    set_.drop("income_cat", axis=1, inplace=True)
```

We spent quite a bit of time on test set generation for a good reason: this is an often neglected but critical part of a machine learning project. Moreover, many of these ideas will be useful later when we discuss cross-validation. Now it's time to move on to the next stage: exploring the data.

Explore and Visualize the Data to Gain Insights

So far you have only taken a quick glance at the data to get a general understanding of the kind of data you are manipulating. Now the goal is to go into a little more depth.

First, make sure you have put the test set aside and you are only exploring the training set. Also, if the training set is very large, you may want to sample an exploration set, to make manipulations easy and fast during the exploration phase. In this case, the training set is quite small, so you can just work directly on the full set. Since you're going to experiment with various transformations of the full training set, you should make a copy of the original so you can revert to it afterwards:

```
housing = strat_train_set.copy()
```

Visualizing Geographical Data

Because the dataset includes geographical information (latitude and longitude), it is a good idea to create a scatterplot of all the districts to visualize the data (Figure 2-11):

```
housing.plot(kind="scatter", x="longitude", y="latitude", grid=True)
plt.show()
```

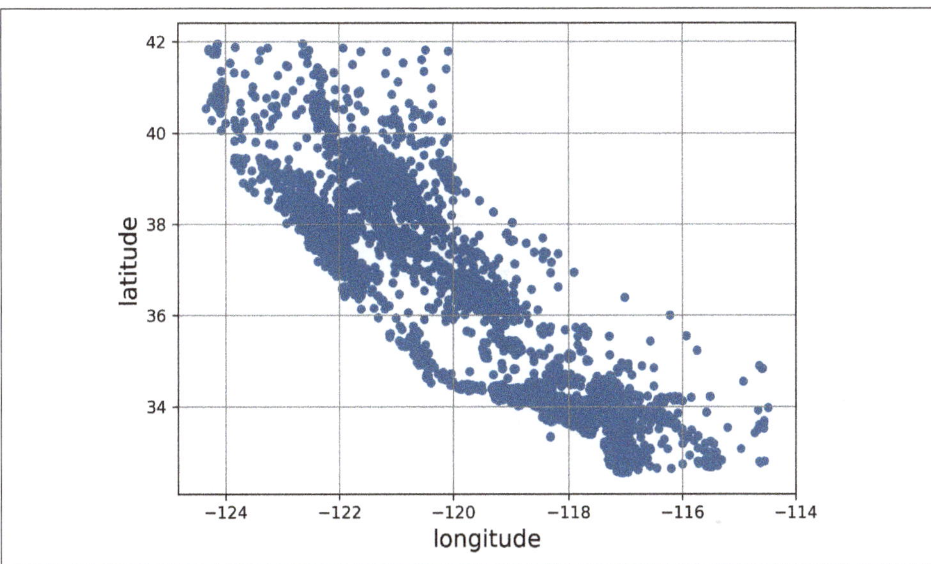

Figure 2-11. A geographical scatterplot of the data

This looks like California all right, but other than that it is hard to see any particular pattern. Setting the `alpha` option to `0.2` makes it much easier to visualize the places where there is a high density of data points (Figure 2-12):

```
housing.plot(kind="scatter", x="longitude", y="latitude", grid=True, alpha=0.2)
plt.show()
```

Now that's much better: you can clearly see the high-density areas, namely the Bay Area and around Los Angeles and San Diego, plus a long line of fairly high-density areas in the Central Valley (in particular, around Sacramento and Fresno).

Our brains are very good at spotting patterns in pictures, but you may need to play around with visualization parameters to make the patterns stand out.

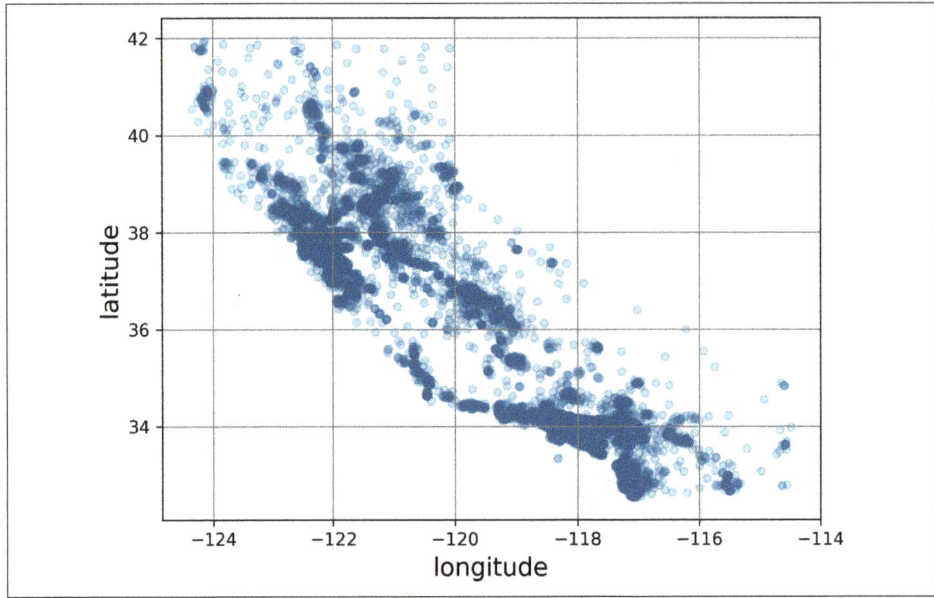

Figure 2-12. A better visualization that highlights high-density areas

Next, you look at the housing prices (Figure 2-13). The radius of each circle represents the district's population (option `s`), and the color represents the price (option `c`). Here you use a predefined color map (option `cmap`) called `jet`, which ranges from blue (low values) to red (high prices):[8]

```
housing.plot(kind="scatter", x="longitude", y="latitude", grid=True,
             s=housing["population"] / 100, label="population",
             c="median_house_value", cmap="jet", colorbar=True,
             legend=True, sharex=False, figsize=(10, 7))
plt.show()
```

This image tells you that the housing prices are very much related to the location (e.g., close to the ocean) and to the population density, as you probably knew already. A clustering algorithm should be useful for detecting the main cluster and for adding new features that measure the proximity to the cluster centers. The ocean proximity attribute may be useful as well, although in Northern California the housing prices in coastal districts are not too high, so it is not a simple rule.

8 If you are reading this in grayscale, grab a red pen and scribble over most of the coastline from the Bay Area down to San Diego (as you might expect). You can add a patch of yellow around Sacramento as well.

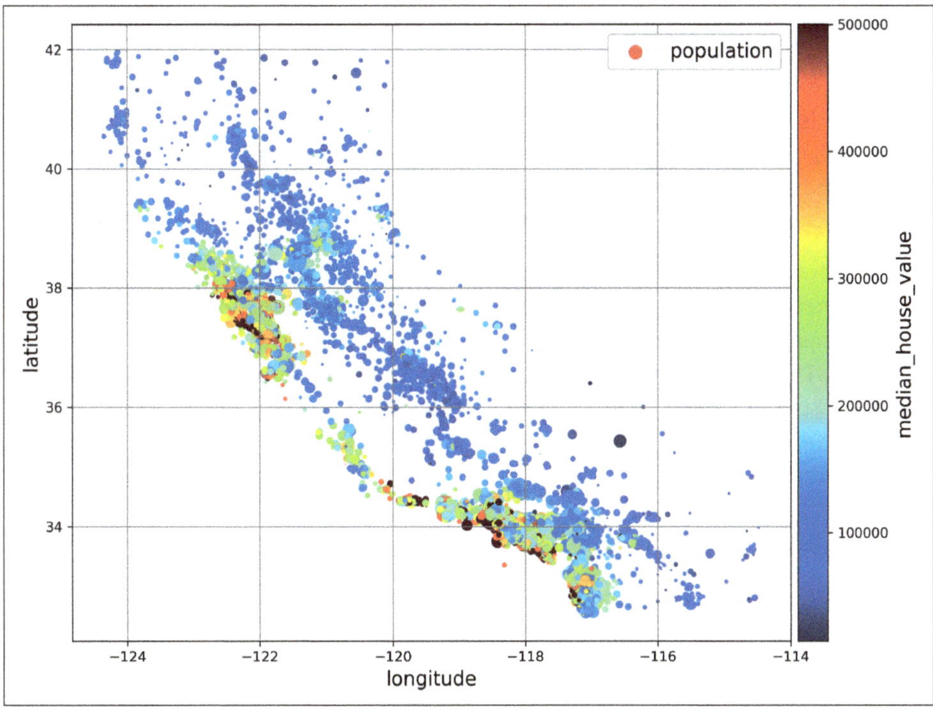

Figure 2-13. California housing prices: red is expensive, blue is cheap, larger circles indicate areas with a larger population

Look for Correlations

Since the dataset is not too large, you can easily compute the *standard correlation coefficient* (also called *Pearson's r*) between every pair of numerical attributes using the `corr()` method:

```
corr_matrix = housing.corr(numeric_only=True)
```

Now you can look at how much each attribute correlates with the median house value:

```
>>> corr_matrix["median_house_value"].sort_values(ascending=False)
median_house_value    1.000000
median_income         0.688380
total_rooms           0.137455
housing_median_age    0.102175
households            0.071426
total_bedrooms        0.054635
population           -0.020153
longitude            -0.050859
latitude             -0.139584
Name: median_house_value, dtype: float64
```

The correlation coefficient ranges from –1 to 1. When it is close to 1, it means that there is a strong positive correlation; for example, the median house value tends to go up when the median income goes up. When the coefficient is close to –1, it means that there is a strong negative correlation; you can see a small negative correlation between the latitude and the median house value (i.e., prices have a slight tendency to go down when you go north). Finally, coefficients close to 0 mean that there is no linear correlation.

Another way to check for correlation between attributes is to use the Pandas `scatter_matrix()` function, which plots every numerical attribute against every other numerical attribute. Since there are now 9 numerical attributes, you would get 9^2 = 81 plots, which would not fit on a page—so you decide to focus on a few promising attributes that seem most correlated with the median housing value (Figure 2-14):

```
from pandas.plotting import scatter_matrix

attributes = ["median_house_value", "median_income", "total_rooms",
              "housing_median_age"]
scatter_matrix(housing[attributes], figsize=(12, 8))
plt.show()
```

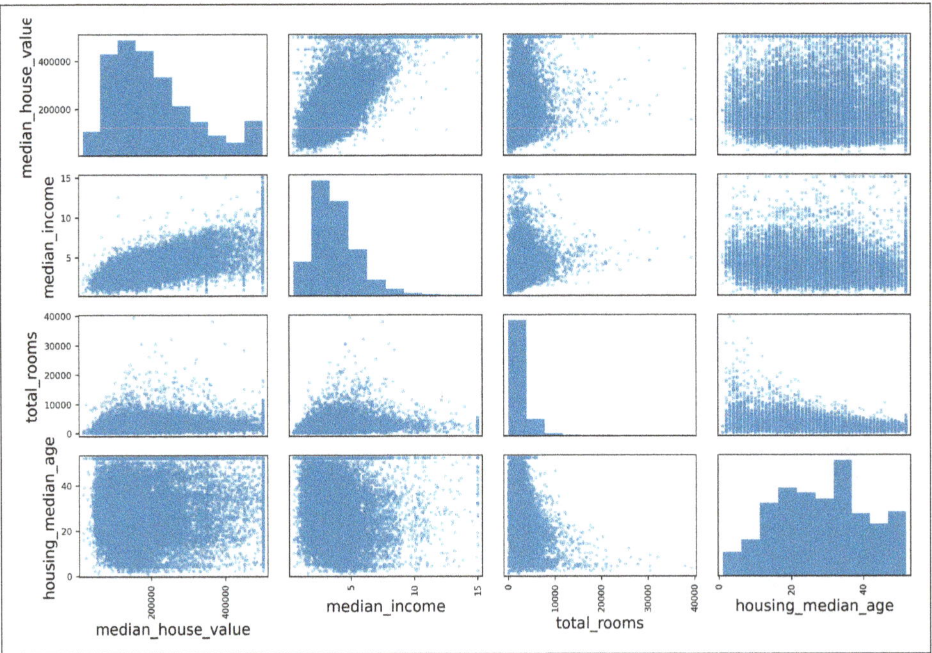

Figure 2-14. This scatter matrix plots every numerical attribute against every other numerical attribute, plus a histogram of each numerical attribute's values on the main diagonal (top left to bottom right)

The main diagonal would be full of straight lines if Pandas plotted each variable against itself, which would not be very useful. So instead, the Pandas displays a histogram of each attribute (other options are available; see the Pandas documentation for more details).

Looking at the correlation scatterplots, it seems like the most promising attribute to predict the median house value is the median income, so you zoom in on that scatterplot (Figure 2-15):

```
housing.plot(kind="scatter", x="median_income", y="median_house_value",
             alpha=0.1, grid=True)
plt.show()
```

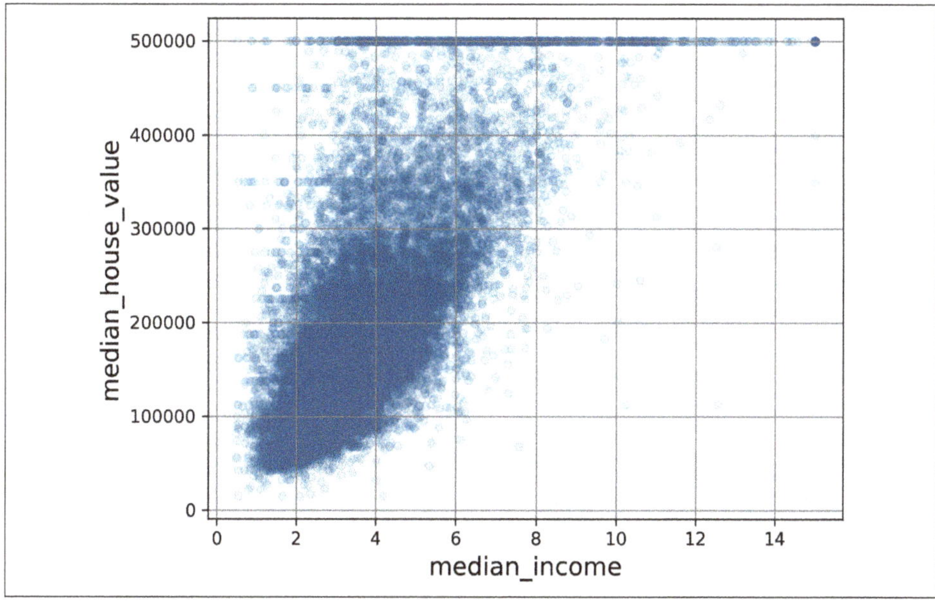

Figure 2-15. Median income versus median house value

This plot reveals a few things. First, the correlation is indeed quite strong; you can clearly see the upward trend, although the data is noisy. Second, the price cap you noticed earlier is clearly visible as a horizontal line at $500,000. But the plot also reveals other less obvious straight lines: a horizontal line around $450,000, another around $350,000, perhaps one around $280,000, and a few more below that. You may want to try removing the corresponding districts to prevent your algorithms from learning to reproduce these data quirks.

Note that the correlation coefficient only measures linear correlations ("as *x* goes up, *y* generally goes up/down"). It may completely miss out on nonlinear relationships (e.g., "as *x* approaches 0, *y* generally goes up"). Figure 2-16 shows a variety of datasets along with their correlation coefficient. Note how all the plots of the bottom row have a correlation coefficient equal to 0, despite the fact that their axes are clearly *not* independent: these are examples of nonlinear relationships. Also, the second row shows examples where the correlation coefficient is equal to 1 or –1; notice that this has nothing to do with the slope. For example, your height in inches has a correlation coefficient of 1 with your height in feet or in nanometers.

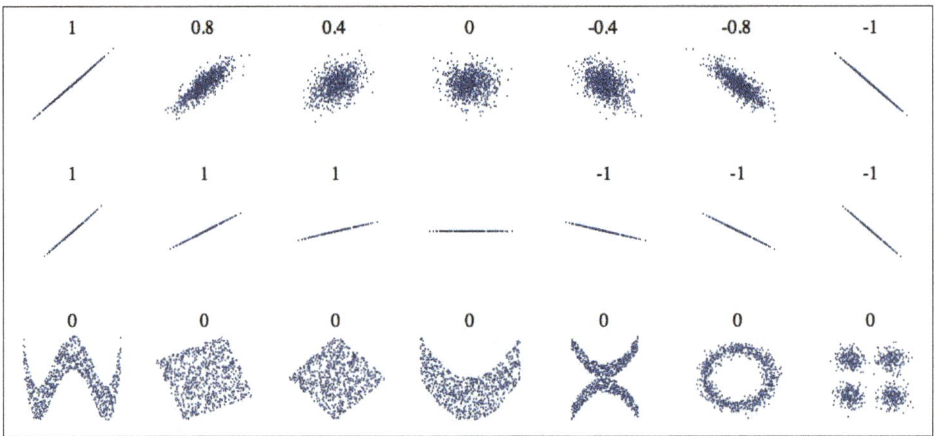

Figure 2-16. Standard correlation coefficient of various datasets (source: Wikipedia; public domain image)

Experiment with Attribute Combinations

Hopefully the previous sections gave you an idea of a few ways you can explore the data and gain insights. You identified a few data quirks that you may want to clean up before feeding the data to a machine learning algorithm, and you found interesting correlations between attributes, in particular with the target attribute. You also noticed that some attributes have a skewed-right distribution, so you may want to transform them (e.g., by computing their logarithm or square root). Of course, your mileage will vary considerably with each project, but the general ideas are similar.

One last thing you may want to do before preparing the data for machine learning algorithms is to try out various attribute combinations. For example, the total number of rooms in a district is not very useful if you don't know how many households there are. What you really want is the number of rooms per household. Similarly, the total number of bedrooms by itself is not very useful: you probably want to compare it to the total number of rooms. And the population per household also seems like an interesting attribute combination to look at. You create these new attributes as follows:

```
housing["rooms_per_house"] = housing["total_rooms"] / housing["households"]
housing["bedrooms_ratio"] = housing["total_bedrooms"] / housing["total_rooms"]
housing["people_per_house"] = housing["population"] / housing["households"]
```

And then you look at the correlation matrix again:

```
>>> corr_matrix = housing.corr(numeric_only=True)
>>> corr_matrix["median_house_value"].sort_values(ascending=False)
median_house_value    1.000000
median_income         0.688380
rooms_per_house       0.143663
total_rooms           0.137455
housing_median_age    0.102175
households            0.071426
total_bedrooms        0.054635
population           -0.020153
people_per_house     -0.038224
longitude            -0.050859
latitude             -0.139584
bedrooms_ratio       -0.256397
Name: median_house_value, dtype: float64
```

Hey, not bad! The new `bedrooms_ratio` attribute is much more correlated with the median house value than the total number of rooms or bedrooms. It's a strong negative correlation, so it looks like houses with a lower bedroom/room ratio tend to be more expensive. The number of rooms per household is also more informative than the total number of rooms in a district—obviously the larger the houses, the more expensive they are.

When creating new combined features, make sure they are not too linearly correlated with existing features: *collinearity* can cause issues with some models, such as linear regression. In particular, avoid simple weighted sums of existing features.

This round of exploration does not have to be absolutely thorough; the point is to start off on the right foot and quickly gain insights that will help you get a first reasonably good prototype. But this is an iterative process: once you get a prototype up and running, you can analyze its output to gain more insights and come back to this exploration step.

Prepare the Data for Machine Learning Algorithms

It's time to prepare the data for your machine learning algorithms. Instead of doing this manually, you should write functions for this purpose, for several good reasons:

- This will allow you to reproduce these transformations easily on any dataset (e.g., the next time you get a fresh dataset).
- You will gradually build a library of transformation functions that you can reuse in future projects.

- You can use these functions in your live system to transform the new data before feeding it to your algorithms.
- This will make it possible for you to easily try various transformations and see which combination of transformations works best.

But first, revert to a clean training set (by copying `strat_train_set` once again). You should also separate the predictors and the labels, since you don't necessarily want to apply the same transformations to the predictors and the target values (note that `drop()` creates a copy of the data and does not affect `strat_train_set`):

```
housing = strat_train_set.drop("median_house_value", axis=1)
housing_labels = strat_train_set["median_house_value"].copy()
```

Clean the Data

Most machine learning algorithms cannot work with missing features, so you'll need to take care of these. For example, you noticed earlier that the `total_bedrooms` attribute has some missing values. You have three options to fix this:

1. Get rid of the corresponding districts.
2. Get rid of the whole attribute.
3. Set the missing values to some value (zero, the mean, the median, etc.). This is called *imputation*.

You can accomplish these easily using the Pandas DataFrame's `dropna()`, `drop()`, and `fillna()` methods:

```
housing.dropna(subset=["total_bedrooms"], inplace=True)  # option 1

housing.drop("total_bedrooms", axis=1, inplace=True)  # option 2

median = housing["total_bedrooms"].median()  # option 3
housing["total_bedrooms"] = housing["total_bedrooms"].fillna(median)
```

You decide to go for option 3 since it is the least destructive, but instead of the preceding code, you will use a handy Scikit-Learn class: `SimpleImputer`. The benefit is that it will store the median value of each feature: this will make it possible to impute missing values not only on the training set, but also on the validation set, the test set, and any new data fed to the model. To use it, first you need to create a `SimpleImputer` instance, specifying that you want to replace each attribute's missing values with the median of that attribute:

```
from sklearn.impute import SimpleImputer

imputer = SimpleImputer(strategy="median")
```

Since the median can only be computed on numerical attributes, you then need to create a copy of the data with only the numerical attributes (this will exclude the text attribute `ocean_proximity`):

```
housing_num = housing.select_dtypes(include=[np.number])
```

Now you can fit the `imputer` instance to the training data using the `fit()` method:

```
imputer.fit(housing_num)
```

The `imputer` has simply computed the median of each attribute and stored the result in its `statistics_` instance variable. Only the `total_bedrooms` attribute had missing values, but you cannot be sure that there won't be any missing values in new data after the system goes live, so it is safer to apply the `imputer` to all the numerical attributes:

```
>>> imputer.statistics_
array([-118.51 , 34.26 , 29. , 2125. , 434. , 1167. , 408. , 3.5385])
>>> housing_num.median().values
array([-118.51 , 34.26 , 29. , 2125. , 434. , 1167. , 408. , 3.5385])
```

Now you can use this "trained" `imputer` to transform the training set by replacing missing values with the learned medians:

```
X = imputer.transform(housing_num)
```

Missing values can also be replaced with the mean value (`strategy="mean"`), or with the most frequent value (`strategy="most_frequent"`), or with a constant value (`strategy="constant", fill_value=`...). The last two strategies support non-numerical data.

There are also more powerful imputers available in the `sklearn.impute` package (both for numerical features only):

- `KNNImputer` replaces each missing value with the mean of the *k*-nearest neighbors' values for that feature. The distance is based on all the available features.
- `IterativeImputer` trains a regression model per feature to predict the missing values based on all the other available features. It then trains the model again on the updated data, and repeats the process several times, improving the models and the replacement values at each iteration.

Scikit-Learn Design

Scikit-Learn's API is remarkably well designed. These are the main design principles (*https://homl.info/11*):[9]

Consistency
: All objects share a consistent and simple interface:

Estimators
: Any object that can estimate some parameters based on a dataset is called an *estimator* (e.g., a `SimpleImputer` is an estimator). The estimation itself is performed by the `fit()` method, and it takes a dataset as a parameter, or two for supervised learning algorithms—the second dataset contains the labels. Any other parameter needed to guide the estimation process is considered a hyperparameter (such as a `SimpleImputer`'s `strategy`), and it must be set as an instance variable (generally via a constructor parameter).

Transformers
: Some estimators (such as a `SimpleImputer`) can also transform a dataset; these are called *transformers*. Once again, the API is simple: the transformation is performed by the `transform()` method with the dataset to transform as a parameter. It returns the transformed dataset. This transformation generally relies on the learned parameters, as is the case for a `SimpleImputer`. All transformers also have a convenience method called `fit_transform()`, which is equivalent to calling `fit()` and then `transform()` (but sometimes `fit_transform()` is optimized and runs much faster).

Predictors
: Finally, some estimators, given a dataset, are capable of making predictions; they are called *predictors*. For example, the `LinearRegression` model in the previous chapter was a predictor: given a country's GDP per capita, it predicted life satisfaction. A predictor has a `predict()` method that takes a dataset of new instances and returns a dataset of corresponding predictions. It also has a `score()` method that measures the quality of the predictions, given a test set (and the corresponding labels, in the case of supervised learning algorithms).[10]

Inspection
: All the estimator's hyperparameters are accessible directly via public instance variables (e.g., `imputer.strategy`), and all the estimator's learned parameters

9 For more details on the design principles, see Lars Buitinck et al., "API Design for Machine Learning Software: Experiences from the Scikit-Learn Project", arXiv preprint arXiv:1309.0238 (2013).

10 Some predictors also provide methods to measure the confidence of their predictions.

are accessible via public instance variables with an underscore suffix (e.g., `imputer.statistics_`).

Nonproliferation of classes
Datasets are represented as NumPy arrays or SciPy sparse matrices, instead of homemade classes. Hyperparameters are just regular Python strings or numbers.

Composition
Existing building blocks are reused as much as possible. For example, it is easy to create a `Pipeline` estimator from an arbitrary sequence of transformers followed by a final estimator, as you will see.

Sensible defaults
Scikit-Learn provides reasonable default values for most parameters, making it easy to quickly create a baseline working system.

Scikit-Learn transformers output NumPy arrays (or sometimes SciPy sparse matrices) even when they are fed Pandas DataFrames as input.[11] So, the output of `imputer.transform(housing_num)` is a NumPy array: `X` has neither column names nor index. Luckily, it's not too hard to wrap `X` in a DataFrame and recover the column names and index from `housing_num`:

```
housing_tr = pd.DataFrame(X, columns=housing_num.columns,
                          index=housing_num.index)
```

Handling Text and Categorical Attributes

So far we have only dealt with numerical attributes, but your data may also contain text attributes. In this dataset, there is just one: the `ocean_proximity` attribute. Let's look at its value for the first few instances:

```
>>> housing_cat = housing[["ocean_proximity"]]
>>> housing_cat.head(8)
      ocean_proximity
13096        NEAR BAY
14973       <1H OCEAN
3785           INLAND
14689          INLAND
20507      NEAR OCEAN
1286           INLAND
18078       <1H OCEAN
4396         NEAR BAY
```

11 If you run `sklearn.set_config(transform_output="pandas")`, all transformers will output Pandas DataFrames when they receive a DataFrame as input: Pandas in, Pandas out.

It's not arbitrary text: there are a limited number of possible values, each of which represents a category. So this attribute is a categorical attribute. Most machine learning algorithms prefer to work with numbers, so let's convert these categories from text to numbers. For this, we can use Scikit-Learn's `OrdinalEncoder` class:

```
from sklearn.preprocessing import OrdinalEncoder

ordinal_encoder = OrdinalEncoder()
housing_cat_encoded = ordinal_encoder.fit_transform(housing_cat)
```

Here's what the first few encoded values in `housing_cat_encoded` look like:

```
>>> housing_cat_encoded[:8]
array([[3.],
       [0.],
       [1.],
       [1.],
       [4.],
       [1.],
       [0.],
       [3.]])
```

You can get the list of categories using the `categories_` instance variable. It is a list containing a 1D array of categories for each categorical attribute (in this case, a list containing a single array since there is just one categorical attribute):

```
>>> ordinal_encoder.categories_
[array(['<1H OCEAN', 'INLAND', 'ISLAND', 'NEAR BAY', 'NEAR OCEAN'],
       dtype=object)]
```

One issue with this representation is that ML algorithms will assume that two nearby values are more similar than two distant values. This may be fine in some cases (e.g., for ordered categories such as "bad", "average", "good", and "excellent"), but it is obviously not the case for the `ocean_proximity` column (for example, categories 0 and 4 are clearly more similar than categories 0 and 1). To fix this issue, a common solution is to create one binary attribute per category: one attribute equal to 1 when the category is `"<1H OCEAN"` (and 0 otherwise), another attribute equal to 1 when the category is `"INLAND"` (and 0 otherwise), and so on. This is called *one-hot encoding*, because only one attribute will be equal to 1 (hot), while the others will be 0 (cold). The new attributes are sometimes called *dummy* attributes. Scikit-Learn provides a `OneHotEncoder` class to convert categorical values into one-hot vectors:

```
from sklearn.preprocessing import OneHotEncoder

cat_encoder = OneHotEncoder()
housing_cat_1hot = cat_encoder.fit_transform(housing_cat)
```

By default, the output of a `OneHotEncoder` is a SciPy *sparse matrix*, instead of a NumPy array:

```
>>> housing_cat_1hot
<Compressed Sparse Row sparse matrix of dtype 'float64'
 with 16512 stored elements and shape (16512, 5)>
```

A sparse matrix is a very efficient representation for matrices that contain mostly zeros. Indeed, internally it only stores the nonzero values and their positions. When a categorical attribute has hundreds or thousands of categories, one-hot encoding it results in a very large matrix full of 0s except for a single 1 per row. In this case, a sparse matrix is exactly what you need: it will save plenty of memory and speed up computations. You can use a sparse matrix mostly like a normal 2D array,[12] but if you want to convert it to a (dense) NumPy array, just call the `toarray()` method:

```
>>> housing_cat_1hot.toarray()
array([[0., 0., 0., 1., 0.],
       [1., 0., 0., 0., 0.],
       [0., 1., 0., 0., 0.],
       ...,
       [0., 0., 0., 0., 1.],
       [1., 0., 0., 0., 0.],
       [0., 0., 0., 0., 1.]], shape=(16512, 5))
```

Alternatively, you can set `sparse_output=False` when creating the `OneHotEncoder`, in which case the `transform()` method will return a regular (dense) NumPy array directly:

```
cat_encoder = OneHotEncoder(sparse_output=False)
housing_cat_1hot = cat_encoder.fit_transform(housing_cat)  # now a dense array
```

As with the `OrdinalEncoder`, you can get the list of categories using the encoder's `categories_` instance variable:

```
>>> cat_encoder.categories_
[array(['<1H OCEAN', 'INLAND', 'ISLAND', 'NEAR BAY', 'NEAR OCEAN'],
       dtype=object)]
```

Pandas has a function called `get_dummies()`, which also converts each categorical feature into a one-hot representation, with one binary feature per category:

```
>>> df_test = pd.DataFrame({"ocean_proximity": ["INLAND", "NEAR BAY"]})
>>> pd.get_dummies(df_test)
ocean_proximity_INLAND  ocean_proximity_NEAR      BAY
0                       True                      False
1                       False                     True
```

12 See SciPy's documentation for more details.

It looks nice and simple, so why not use it instead of `OneHotEncoder`? Well, the advantage of `OneHotEncoder` is that it remembers which categories it was trained on. This is very important because once your model is in production, it should be fed exactly the same features as during training: no more, no less. Look what our trained `cat_encoder` outputs when we make it transform the same `df_test` (using `transform()`, not `fit_transform()`):

```
>>> cat_encoder.transform(df_test)
array([[0., 1., 0., 0., 0.],
       [0., 0., 0., 1., 0.]])
```

See the difference? `get_dummies()` saw only two categories, so it output two columns, whereas `OneHotEncoder` output one column per learned category, in the right order. Moreover, if you feed `get_dummies()` a DataFrame containing an unknown category (e.g., `"<2H OCEAN"`), it will happily generate a column for it:

```
>>> df_test_unknown = pd.DataFrame({"ocean_proximity": ["<2H OCEAN", "ISLAND"]})
>>> pd.get_dummies(df_test_unknown)
   ocean_proximity_<2H OCEAN  ocean_proximity_ISLAND
0                       True                   False
1                      False                    True
```

But `OneHotEncoder` is smarter: it will detect the unknown category and raise an exception. If you prefer, you can set the `handle_unknown` hyperparameter to `"ignore"`, in which case it will just represent the unknown category with zeros:

```
>>> cat_encoder.handle_unknown = "ignore"
>>> cat_encoder.transform(df_test_unknown)
array([[0., 0., 0., 0., 0.],
       [0., 0., 1., 0., 0.]])
```

If a categorical attribute has a large number of possible categories (e.g., country code, profession, species), then one-hot encoding will result in a large number of input features. This may slow down training and degrade performance. If this happens, you may want to replace the categorical input with useful numerical features related to the categories: for example, you could replace the `ocean_proximity` feature with the distance to the ocean (similarly, a country code could be replaced with the country's population and GDP per capita). Alternatively, you can use one of the encoders provided by the `category_encoders` package on GitHub (*https://github.com/scikit-learn-contrib/category_encoders*). Or, when dealing with neural networks, you can replace each category with a learnable, low-dimensional vector called an *embedding* (see Chapter 14). This is an example of *representation learning* (we will see more examples in Chapter 18).

When you fit any Scikit-Learn estimator using a DataFrame, the estimator stores the column names in the `feature_names_in_` attribute. Scikit-Learn then ensures that any DataFrame fed to this estimator after that (e.g., to `transform()` or `predict()`) has the same column names. Transformers also provide a `get_feature_names_out()` method that you can use to build a DataFrame around the transformer's output:

```
>>> cat_encoder.feature_names_in_
array(['ocean_proximity'], dtype=object)
>>> cat_encoder.get_feature_names_out()
array(['ocean_proximity_<1H OCEAN', 'ocean_proximity_INLAND',
       'ocean_proximity_ISLAND', 'ocean_proximity_NEAR BAY',
       'ocean_proximity_NEAR OCEAN'], dtype=object)
>>> df_output = pd.DataFrame(cat_encoder.transform(df_test_unknown),
...                          columns=cat_encoder.get_feature_names_out(),
...                          index=df_test_unknown.index)
...
```

This feature helps avoid column mismatches, and it's also quite useful when debugging.

Feature Scaling and Transformation

One of the most important transformations you need to apply to your data is *feature scaling*. With few exceptions, machine learning algorithms don't perform well when the input numerical attributes have very different scales. This is the case for the housing data: the total number of rooms ranges from about 6 to 39,320, while the median incomes only range from 0 to 15. Without any scaling, most models will be biased toward ignoring the median income and focusing more on the number of rooms.

There are two common ways to get all attributes to have the same scale: *min-max scaling* and *standardization*.

As with all estimators, it is important to fit the scalers to the training data only: never use `fit()` or `fit_transform()` for anything else than the training set. Once you have a trained scaler, you can then use it to `transform()` any other set, including the validation set, the test set, and new data. Note that while the training set values will always be scaled to the specified range, if new data contains outliers, these may end up scaled outside the range. If you want to avoid this, just set the `clip` hyperparameter to `True`.

Min-max scaling (many people call this *normalization*) is the simplest: for each attribute, the values are shifted and rescaled so that they end up ranging from 0 to 1. This is performed by subtracting the min value from all values, and dividing the results by the difference between the min and the max. Scikit-Learn provides a transformer called `MinMaxScaler` for this. It has a `feature_range` hyperparameter that lets you change the range if, for some reason, you don't want 0–1 (e.g., neural networks work best with zero-mean inputs, so a range of –1 to 1 is preferable). It's quite easy to use:

```
from sklearn.preprocessing import MinMaxScaler

min_max_scaler = MinMaxScaler(feature_range=(-1, 1))
housing_num_min_max_scaled = min_max_scaler.fit_transform(housing_num)
```

Standardization is different: first it subtracts the mean value (so standardized values have a zero mean), then it divides the result by the standard deviation (so standardized values have a standard deviation equal to 1). Unlike min-max scaling, standardization does not restrict values to a specific range. However, standardization is much less affected by outliers. For example, suppose a district has a median income equal to 100 (by mistake), instead of the usual 0–15. Min-max scaling to the 0–1 range would map this outlier down to 1 and it would crush all the other values down to 0–0.15, whereas standardization would not be much affected. Scikit-Learn provides a transformer called `StandardScaler` for standardization:

```
from sklearn.preprocessing import StandardScaler

std_scaler = StandardScaler()
housing_num_std_scaled = std_scaler.fit_transform(housing_num)
```

If you want to scale a sparse matrix without converting it to a dense matrix first, you can use a `StandardScaler` with its `with_mean` hyperparameter set to `False`: it will only divide the data by the standard deviation, without subtracting the mean (as this would break sparsity).

When a feature's distribution has a *heavy tail* (i.e., when values far from the mean are not exponentially rare), both min-max scaling and standardization will squash most values into a small range. Machine learning models generally don't like this at all, as you will see in Chapter 4. So *before* you scale the feature, you should first transform it to shrink the heavy tail, and if possible to make the distribution roughly symmetrical. For example, a common way to do this for positive features with a heavy tail to the right is to replace the feature with its square root (or raise the feature to a power between 0 and 1). If the feature has a really long and heavy tail, such as a *power law distribution*, then replacing the feature with its logarithm may help. For example, the `population` feature roughly follows a power law: districts with 10,000 inhabitants are only 10 times less frequent than districts with 1,000 inhabitants, not exponentially less frequent. Figure 2-17 shows how much better this feature looks when you compute its log: it's very close to a Gaussian distribution (i.e., bell-shaped).

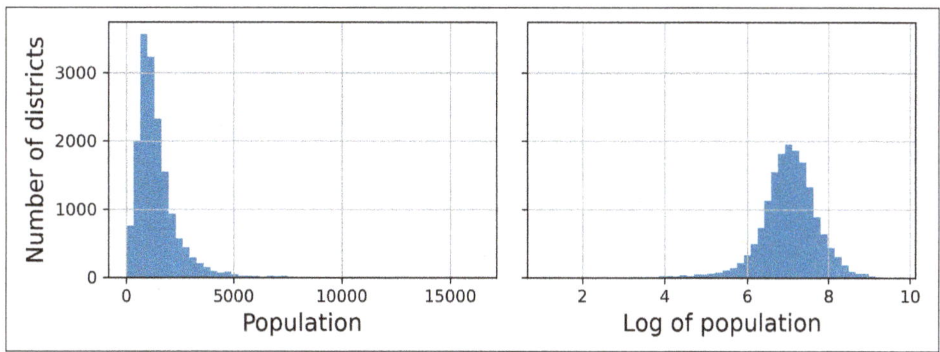

Figure 2-17. Transforming a feature to make it closer to a Gaussian distribution

Another approach to handle heavy-tailed features consists in *bucketizing* the feature. This means chopping its distribution into roughly equal-sized buckets, and replacing each feature value with the index of the bucket it belongs to, much like we did to create the `income_cat` feature (although we only used it for stratified sampling). For example, you could replace each value with its percentile. Bucketizing with equal-sized buckets results in a feature with an almost uniform distribution, so there's no need for further scaling, or you can just divide by the number of buckets to force the values to the 0–1 range.

When a feature has a multimodal distribution (i.e., with two or more clear peaks, called *modes*), such as the `housing_median_age` feature, it can also be helpful to bucketize it, but this time treating the bucket IDs as categories, rather than as numerical values. This means that the bucket indices must be encoded, for example using a `OneHotEncoder` (so you usually don't want to use too many buckets). This approach will allow the regression model to more easily learn different rules for different ranges of this feature value. For example, perhaps houses built around 35 years ago have a peculiar style that fell out of fashion, and therefore they're cheaper than their age alone would suggest.

Another approach to transforming multimodal distributions is to add a feature for each of the modes (at least the main ones), representing the similarity between the housing median age and that particular mode. The similarity measure is typically computed using a *radial basis function* (RBF)—any function that depends only on the distance between the input value and a fixed point. The most commonly used RBF is the Gaussian RBF, whose output value decays exponentially as the input value moves away from the fixed point. For example, the Gaussian RBF similarity between the housing age x and 35 is given by the equation $\exp(-\gamma(x - 35)^2)$. The hyperparameter γ (gamma) determines how quickly the similarity measure decays as x moves away from 35. Using Scikit-Learn's `rbf_kernel()` function, you can create a new Gaussian RBF feature measuring the similarity between the housing median age and 35:

```
from sklearn.metrics.pairwise import rbf_kernel

age_simil_35 = rbf_kernel(housing[["housing_median_age"]], [[35]], gamma=0.1)
```

Figure 2-18 shows this new feature as a function of the housing median age (solid line). It also shows what the feature would look like if you used a smaller `gamma` value. As the chart shows, the new age similarity feature peaks at 35, right around the spike in the housing median age distribution: if this particular age group is well correlated with lower prices, there's a good chance that this new feature will help.

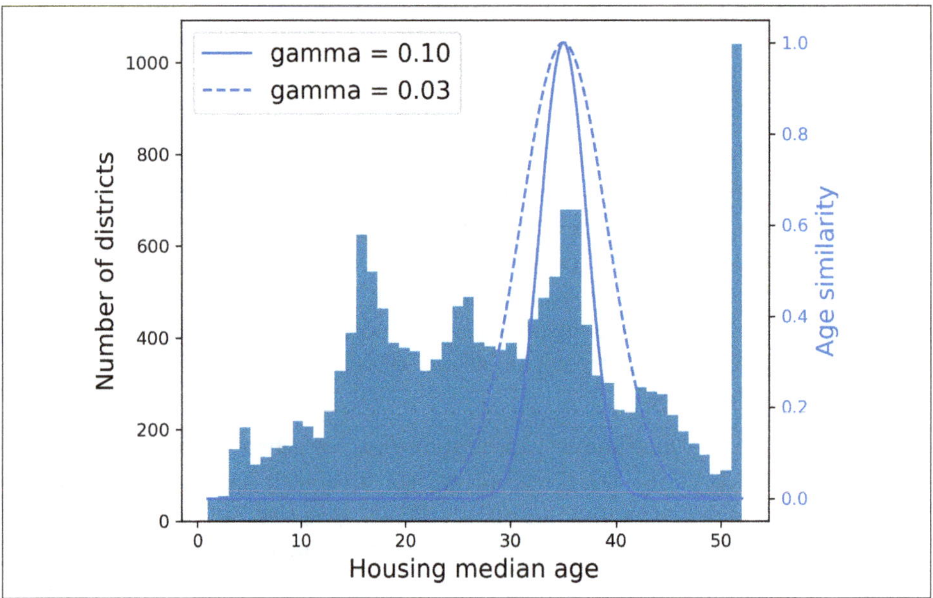

Figure 2-18. Gaussian RBF feature measuring the similarity between the housing median age and 35

So far we've only looked at the input features, but the target values may also need to be transformed. For example, if the target distribution has a heavy tail, you may choose to replace the target with its logarithm. But if you do, the regression model will now predict the *log* of the median house value, not the median house value itself. You will need to compute the exponential of the model's prediction if you want the predicted median house value.

Luckily, most of Scikit-Learn's transformers have an `inverse_transform()` method, making it easy to compute the inverse of their transformations. For example, the following code example shows how to scale the labels using a `StandardScaler` (just like we did for inputs), then train a simple linear regression model on the resulting scaled labels and use it to make predictions on some new data, which we transform back to the original scale using the trained scaler's `inverse_transform()` method.

Note that we convert the labels from a Pandas Series to a DataFrame, since the `StandardScaler` expects 2D inputs. Also, in this example we just train the model on a single raw input feature (median income), for simplicity:

```
from sklearn.linear_model import LinearRegression

target_scaler = StandardScaler()
scaled_labels = target_scaler.fit_transform(housing_labels.to_frame())

model = LinearRegression()
model.fit(housing[["median_income"]], scaled_labels)
some_new_data = housing[["median_income"]].iloc[:5]  # pretend this is new data

scaled_predictions = model.predict(some_new_data)
predictions = target_scaler.inverse_transform(scaled_predictions)
```

This works fine, but it's simpler and less error-prone to use a `TransformedTargetRegressor`, avoiding potential scaling mismatches. We just need to construct it, giving it the regression model and the label transformer, then fit it on the training set, using the original unscaled labels. It will automatically use the transformer to scale the labels and train the regression model on the resulting scaled labels, just like we did previously. Then, when we want to make a prediction, it will call the regression model's `predict()` method and use the scaler's `inverse_transform()` method to produce the prediction:

```
from sklearn.compose import TransformedTargetRegressor

model = TransformedTargetRegressor(LinearRegression(),
                                   transformer=StandardScaler())
model.fit(housing[["median_income"]], housing_labels)
predictions = model.predict(some_new_data)
```

Custom Transformers

Although Scikit-Learn provides many useful transformers, you will occasionally need to write your own for tasks such as custom transformations, cleanup operations, or combining specific attributes.

For transformations that don't require any training, you can just write a function that takes a NumPy array as input and outputs the transformed array. For example, as discussed in the previous section, it's often a good idea to transform features with heavy-tailed distributions by replacing them with their logarithm (assuming the feature is positive and the tail is on the right). Let's create a log-transformer and apply it to the `population` feature:

```
from sklearn.preprocessing import FunctionTransformer

log_transformer = FunctionTransformer(np.log, inverse_func=np.exp)
log_pop = log_transformer.transform(housing[["population"]])
```

The `inverse_func` argument is optional. It lets you specify an inverse transform function, e.g., if you plan to use your transformer in a `TransformedTargetRegressor`.

Your transformation function can take hyperparameters as additional arguments. For example, here's how to create a transformer that computes the same Gaussian RBF similarity measure as earlier:

```
rbf_transformer = FunctionTransformer(rbf_kernel,
                                      kw_args=dict(Y=[[35.]], gamma=0.1))
age_simil_35 = rbf_transformer.transform(housing[["housing_median_age"]])
```

Note that there's no inverse function for the RBF kernel, since there are always two values at a given distance from a fixed point (except at distance 0). Also note that `rbf_kernel()` does not treat the features separately. If you pass it an array with two features, it will measure the 2D distance (Euclidean) to measure similarity. For example, here's how to add a feature that will measure the geographic similarity between each district and San Francisco:

```
sf_coords = 37.7749, -122.41
sf_transformer = FunctionTransformer(rbf_kernel,
                                     kw_args=dict(Y=[sf_coords], gamma=0.1))
sf_simil = sf_transformer.transform(housing[["latitude", "longitude"]])
```

Custom transformers are also useful to combine features. For example, here's a `FunctionTransformer` that computes the ratio between the input features 0 and 1:

```
>>> ratio_transformer = FunctionTransformer(lambda X: X[:, [0]] / X[:, [1]])
>>> ratio_transformer.transform(np.array([[1., 2.], [3., 4.]]))
array([[0.5 ],
       [0.75]])
```

`FunctionTransformer` is very handy, but what if you would like your transformer to be trainable, learning some parameters in the `fit()` method and using them later in the `transform()` method? For this, you need to write a custom class.

The rest of this section shows how to define custom transformer classes. In particular, it defines a custom transformer that groups districts into 10 geographical clusters, then measures the distance between each district and the center of each cluster, adding 10 corresponding RBF similarity features to the data. Since defining custom transformer classes is somewhat advanced, please feel free to skip to the next section and come back whenever needed.

Scikit-Learn relies on duck typing,[13] so custom transformer classes do not have to inherit from any particular base class. All they need is three methods: `fit()` (which must return `self`), `transform()`, and `fit_transform()`. You can get `fit_transform()` for free by simply adding `TransformerMixin` as a base class: the default implementation will just call `fit()` and then `transform()`. If you add `BaseEstimator` as a base class (and avoid using `*args` and `**kwargs` in your constructor), you will also get two extra methods: `get_params()` and `set_params()`. These will be useful for automatic hyperparameter tuning.

For example, here's a custom transformer that acts much like the `StandardScaler`:

```
from sklearn.base import BaseEstimator, TransformerMixin
from sklearn.utils.validation import check_array, check_is_fitted

class StandardScalerClone(BaseEstimator, TransformerMixin):
    def __init__(self, with_mean=True):  # no *args or **kwargs!
        self.with_mean = with_mean

    def fit(self, X, y=None):  # y is required even though we don't use it
        X = check_array(X)  # checks that X is an array with finite float values
        self.mean_ = X.mean(axis=0)
        self.scale_ = X.std(axis=0)
        self.n_features_in_ = X.shape[1]  # every estimator stores this in fit()
        return self  # always return self!

    def transform(self, X):
        check_is_fitted(self)  # looks for learned attributes (with trailing _)
        X = check_array(X)
        assert self.n_features_in_ == X.shape[1]
        if self.with_mean:
            X = X - self.mean_
        return X / self.scale_
```

Here are a few things to note:

- The `sklearn.utils.validation` package contains several functions we can use to validate the inputs. For simplicity, we will skip such tests in the rest of this book, but production code should have them.
- Scikit-Learn pipelines require the `fit()` method to have two arguments `X` and `y`, which is why we need the `y=None` argument even though we don't use `y`.
- All Scikit-Learn estimators set `n_features_in_` in the `fit()` method, and they ensure that the data passed to `transform()` or `predict()` has this number of features.

13 With duck typing, an object's methods and behavior are what matters, not its type: "if it looks like a duck and quacks like a duck, it must be a duck".

- The `fit()` method must return `self`.
- This implementation is not 100% complete: all estimators should set `feature_names_in_` in the `fit()` method when they are passed a DataFrame. Moreover, all transformers should provide a `get_feature_names_out()` method, as well as an `inverse_transform()` method when their transformation can be reversed. See the last exercise at the end of this chapter for more details.

A custom transformer can (and often does) use other estimators in its implementation. For example, the following code demonstrates a custom transformer that uses a `KMeans` clusterer in the `fit()` method to identify the main clusters in the training data, and then uses `rbf_kernel()` in the `transform()` method to measure how similar each sample is to each cluster center:

```
from sklearn.cluster import KMeans

class ClusterSimilarity(BaseEstimator, TransformerMixin):
    def __init__(self, n_clusters=10, gamma=1.0, random_state=None):
        self.n_clusters = n_clusters
        self.gamma = gamma
        self.random_state = random_state

    def fit(self, X, y=None, sample_weight=None):
        self.kmeans_ = KMeans(self.n_clusters, random_state=self.random_state)
        self.kmeans_.fit(X, sample_weight=sample_weight)
        return self  # always return self!

    def transform(self, X):
        return rbf_kernel(X, self.kmeans_.cluster_centers_, gamma=self.gamma)

    def get_feature_names_out(self, names=None):
        return [f"Cluster {i} similarity" for i in range(self.n_clusters)]
```

You can check whether your custom estimator respects Scikit-Learn's API by passing an instance to `check_estimator()` from the `sklearn.utils.estimator_checks` package. For the full API, check out *https://scikit-learn.org/stable/developers*.

As you will see in Chapter 8, *k*-means is a clustering algorithm that locates clusters in the data. For example, we can use it to find the most populated regions in California. How many clusters *k*-means searches for is controlled by the `n_clusters` hyperparameter. The `fit()` method of `KMeans` supports an optional argument `sample_weight`, which lets the user specify the relative weights of the samples. For example, we could pass it the median income if we wanted the clusters to be biased toward wealthy districts. After training, the cluster centers are available via the `cluster_centers_` attribute. *k*-means is a stochastic algorithm, meaning that it relies on randomness to locate the clusters, so if you want reproducible results, you must set the `random_state` parameter. As you can see, despite the complexity of the task, the code is fairly straightforward. Now let's use this custom transformer:

```
cluster_simil = ClusterSimilarity(n_clusters=10, gamma=1., random_state=42)
similarities = cluster_simil.fit_transform(housing[["latitude", "longitude"]])
```

This code creates a `ClusterSimilarity` transformer, setting the number of clusters to 10. Then it calls `fit_transform()` with the latitude and longitude of every district in the training set (you can try weighting each district by its median income to see how that affects the clusters). The transformer uses *k*-means to locate the clusters, then measures the Gaussian RBF similarity between each district and all 10 cluster centers. The result is a matrix with one row per district, and one column per cluster. Let's look at the first three rows, rounding to two decimal places:

```
>>> similarities[:3].round(2)
array([[0.46, 0.  , 0.08, 0.  , 0.  , 0.  , 0.  , 0.98, 0.  , 0.  ],
       [0.  , 0.96, 0.  , 0.03, 0.04, 0.  , 0.  , 0.  , 0.11, 0.35],
       [0.34, 0.  , 0.45, 0.  , 0.  , 0.  , 0.01, 0.73, 0.  , 0.  ]])
```

Figure 2-19 shows the 10 cluster centers found by *k*-means. The districts are colored according to their geographic similarity to their closest cluster center. Notice that most clusters are located in highly populated areas.

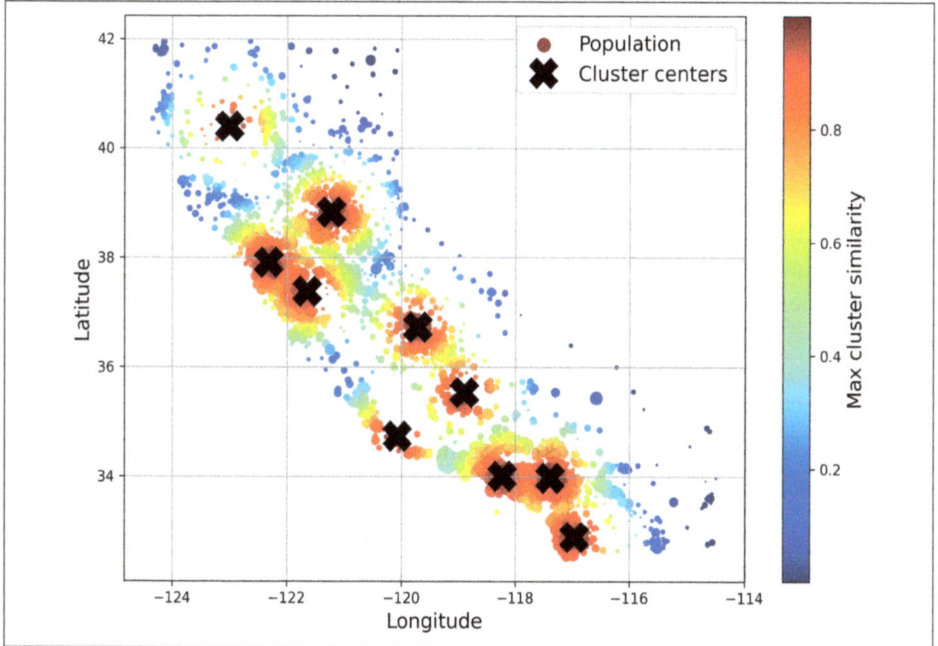

Figure 2-19. Gaussian RBF similarity to the nearest cluster center

Transformation Pipelines

As you can see, there are many data transformation steps that need to be executed in the right order. Fortunately, Scikit-Learn provides the `Pipeline` class to help with such sequences of transformations. Here is a small pipeline for numerical attributes, which will first impute then scale the input features:

```
from sklearn.pipeline import Pipeline

num_pipeline = Pipeline([
    ("impute", SimpleImputer(strategy="median")),
    ("standardize", StandardScaler()),
])
```

The `Pipeline` constructor takes a list of name/estimator pairs (2-tuples) defining a sequence of steps. The names can be anything you like, as long as they are unique and don't contain double underscores (`__`). They will be useful later, when we discuss hyperparameter tuning. The estimators must all be transformers (i.e., they must have a `fit_transform()` method), except for the last one, which can be anything: a transformer, a predictor, or any other type of estimator.

In a Jupyter notebook, if you `import sklearn` and run `sklearn.set_config(display="diagram")`, all Scikit-Learn estimators will be rendered as interactive diagrams. This is particularly useful for visualizing pipelines. To visualize `num_pipeline`, run a cell with `num_pipeline` as the last line. Clicking an estimator will show more details.

If you don't want to have to name the transformers, you can use the convenient `make_pipeline()` function instead; it takes transformers as positional arguments and creates a `Pipeline` using the names of the transformers' classes, in lowercase and without underscores (e.g., `"simpleimputer"`):

```
from sklearn.pipeline import make_pipeline

num_pipeline = make_pipeline(SimpleImputer(strategy="median"), StandardScaler())
```

If multiple transformers have the same name, an index is appended to their names (e.g., `"foo-1"`, `"foo-2"`, etc.).

When you call the pipeline's `fit()` method, it calls `fit_transform()` sequentially on all the transformers, passing the output of each call as the parameter to the next call until it reaches the final estimator, for which it just calls the `fit()` method.

The pipeline exposes the same methods as the final estimator. In this example the last estimator is a `StandardScaler`, which is a transformer, so the pipeline also acts like a transformer. If you call the pipeline's `transform()` method, it will sequentially apply all the transformations to the data. If the last estimator were a predictor instead of a transformer, then the pipeline would have a `predict()` method rather than a `transform()` method. Calling it would sequentially apply all the transformations to the data and pass the result to the predictor's `predict()` method.

Let's call the pipeline's `fit_transform()` method and look at the output's first two rows, rounded to two decimal places:

```
>>> housing_num_prepared = num_pipeline.fit_transform(housing_num)
>>> housing_num_prepared[:2].round(2)
array([[-1.42,  1.01,  1.86,  0.31,  1.37,  0.14,  1.39, -0.94],
       [ 0.6 , -0.7 ,  0.91, -0.31, -0.44, -0.69, -0.37,  1.17]])
```

As you saw earlier, if you want to recover a nice DataFrame, you can use the pipeline's `get_feature_names_out()` method:

```
df_housing_num_prepared = pd.DataFrame(
    housing_num_prepared, columns=num_pipeline.get_feature_names_out(),
    index=housing_num.index)
```

Pipelines support indexing; for example, `pipeline[1]` returns the second estimator in the pipeline, and `pipeline[:-1]` returns a `Pipeline` object containing all but the last estimator. You can also access the estimators via the `steps` attribute, which is a list of name/estimator pairs, or via the `named_steps` dictionary attribute, which maps the names to the estimators. For example, `num_pipeline["simpleimputer"]` returns the estimator named `"simpleimputer"`.

So far, we have handled the categorical columns and the numerical columns separately. It would be more convenient to have a single transformer capable of handling all columns, applying the appropriate transformations to each column. For this, you can use a `ColumnTransformer`. For example, the following `ColumnTransformer` will apply `num_pipeline` (the one we just defined) to the numerical attributes, and `cat_pipeline` to the categorical attribute:

```
from sklearn.compose import ColumnTransformer

num_attribs = ["longitude", "latitude", "housing_median_age", "total_rooms",
               "total_bedrooms", "population", "households", "median_income"]
cat_attribs = ["ocean_proximity"]

cat_pipeline = make_pipeline(
    SimpleImputer(strategy="most_frequent"),
    OneHotEncoder(handle_unknown="ignore"))

preprocessing = ColumnTransformer([
    ("num", num_pipeline, num_attribs),
    ("cat", cat_pipeline, cat_attribs),
])
```

First we import the `ColumnTransformer` class, then we define the list of numerical and categorical column names and construct a simple pipeline for categorical attributes. Lastly, we construct a `ColumnTransformer`. Its constructor requires a list of triplets (3-tuples), each containing a name (which must be unique and not contain double underscores), a transformer, and a list of names (or indices) of columns that the transformer should be applied to.

Instead of using a transformer, you can specify the string `"drop"` if you want the columns to be dropped, or you can specify `"passthrough"` if you want the columns to be left untouched. By default, the remaining columns (i.e., the ones that were not listed) will be dropped, but you can set the `remainder` hyperparameter to any transformer (or to `"passthrough"`) if you want these columns to be handled differently.

Since listing all the column names is not very convenient, Scikit-Learn provides a `make_column_selector` class that you can use to automatically select all the features of a given type, such as numerical or categorical. You can pass a selector to the `ColumnTransformer` instead of column names or indices. Moreover, if you don't care about naming the transformers, you can use `make_column_transformer()`, which chooses the names for you, just like `make_pipeline()` does. For example, the following code creates the same `ColumnTransformer` as earlier, except the transformers are automatically named `"pipeline-1"` and `"pipeline-2"` instead of `"num"` and `"cat"`:

```
from sklearn.compose import make_column_selector, make_column_transformer

preprocessing = make_column_transformer(
    (num_pipeline, make_column_selector(dtype_include=np.number)),
    (cat_pipeline, make_column_selector(dtype_include=object)),
)
```

Now we're ready to apply this `ColumnTransformer` to the housing data:

```
housing_prepared = preprocessing.fit_transform(housing)
```

Great! We have a preprocessing pipeline that takes the entire training dataset and applies each transformer to the appropriate columns, then concatenates the transformed columns horizontally (transformers must never change the number of rows). Once again this returns a NumPy array, but you can get the column names using `preprocessing.get_feature_names_out()` and wrap the data in a nice DataFrame as we did before.

The OneHotEncoder returns a sparse matrix and the num_pipeline returns a dense matrix. When there is such a mix of sparse and dense matrices, the ColumnTransformer estimates the density of the final matrix (i.e., the ratio of nonzero cells), and it returns a sparse matrix if the density is lower than a given threshold (by default, sparse_threshold=0.3). In this example, it returns a dense matrix.

Your project is going really well and you're almost ready to train some models! You now want to create a single pipeline that will perform all the transformations you've experimented with up to now. Let's recap what the pipeline will do and why:

- Missing values in numerical features will be imputed by replacing them with the median, as most ML algorithms don't expect missing values. In categorical features, missing values will be replaced by the most frequent category.
- The categorical feature will be one-hot encoded, as most ML algorithms only accept numerical inputs.
- A few ratio features will be computed and added: bedrooms_ratio, rooms_per_house, and people_per_house. Hopefully these will better correlate with the median house value, and thereby help the ML models.
- A few cluster similarity features will also be added. These will likely be more useful to the model than latitude and longitude.
- Features with a long tail will be replaced by their logarithm, as most models prefer features with roughly uniform or Gaussian distributions.
- All numerical features will be standardized, as most ML algorithms prefer when all features have roughly the same scale.

The code that builds the pipeline to do all of this should look familiar to you by now:

```
def column_ratio(X):
    return X[:, [0]] / X[:, [1]]

def ratio_name(function_transformer, feature_names_in):
    return ["ratio"]  # feature names out

def ratio_pipeline():
    return make_pipeline(
        SimpleImputer(strategy="median"),
        FunctionTransformer(column_ratio, feature_names_out=ratio_name),
        StandardScaler())

log_pipeline = make_pipeline(
    SimpleImputer(strategy="median"),
    FunctionTransformer(np.log, feature_names_out="one-to-one"),
    StandardScaler())
cluster_simil = ClusterSimilarity(n_clusters=10, gamma=1., random_state=42)
```

```python
default_num_pipeline = make_pipeline(SimpleImputer(strategy="median"),
                                     StandardScaler())
preprocessing = ColumnTransformer([
        ("bedrooms", ratio_pipeline(), ["total_bedrooms", "total_rooms"]),
        ("rooms_per_house", ratio_pipeline(), ["total_rooms", "households"]),
        ("people_per_house", ratio_pipeline(), ["population", "households"]),
        ("log", log_pipeline, ["total_bedrooms", "total_rooms", "population",
                               "households", "median_income"]),
        ("geo", cluster_simil, ["latitude", "longitude"]),
        ("cat", cat_pipeline, make_column_selector(dtype_include=object)),
    ],
    remainder=default_num_pipeline)  # one column remaining: housing_median_age
```

If you run this ColumnTransformer, it performs all the transformations and outputs a NumPy array with 24 features:

```python
>>> housing_prepared = preprocessing.fit_transform(housing)
>>> housing_prepared.shape
(16512, 24)
>>> preprocessing.get_feature_names_out()
array(['bedrooms__ratio', 'rooms_per_house__ratio',
       'people_per_house__ratio', 'log__total_bedrooms',
       'log__total_rooms', 'log__population', 'log__households',
       'log__median_income', 'geo__Cluster 0 similarity', [...],
       'geo__Cluster 9 similarity', 'cat__ocean_proximity_<1H OCEAN',
       'cat__ocean_proximity_INLAND', 'cat__ocean_proximity_ISLAND',
       'cat__ocean_proximity_NEAR BAY', 'cat__ocean_proximity_NEAR OCEAN',
       'remainder__housing_median_age'], dtype=object)
```

Select and Train a Model

At last! You framed the problem, you got the data and explored it, you sampled a training set and a test set, and you wrote a preprocessing pipeline to automatically clean up and prepare your data for machine learning algorithms. You are now ready to select and train a machine learning model.

Train and Evaluate on the Training Set

The good news is that thanks to all these previous steps, things are now going to be easy! You decide to train a very basic linear regression model to get started:

```python
from sklearn.linear_model import LinearRegression

lin_reg = make_pipeline(preprocessing, LinearRegression())
lin_reg.fit(housing, housing_labels)
```

Done! You now have a working linear regression model. You try it out on the training set, looking at the first five predictions and comparing them to the labels:

```python
>>> housing_predictions = lin_reg.predict(housing)
>>> housing_predictions[:5].round(-2)  # -2 = rounded to the nearest hundred
```

```
array([246000., 372700., 135700.,  91400., 330900.])
>>> housing_labels.iloc[:5].values
array([458300., 483800., 101700.,  96100., 361800.])
```

Well, it works, but not always: the first prediction is way off (by over $200,000!), while the other predictions are better: two are off by about 25%, and two are off by less than 10%. Remember that you chose to use the RMSE as your performance measure, so you want to measure this regression model's RMSE on the whole training set using Scikit-Learn's `root_mean_squared_error()` function:

```
>>> from sklearn.metrics import root_mean_squared_error
>>> lin_rmse = root_mean_squared_error(housing_labels, housing_predictions)
>>> lin_rmse
68972.88910758484
```

We're not using the `score()` method here because it returns the R^2 *coefficient of determination* instead of the RMSE. This coefficient represents the ratio of the variance in the data that the model can explain: the closer to 1 (which is the max value), the better. If the model simply predicts the mean all the time, it does not explain any part of the variance, so the model's R^2 score is 0. And if the model does even worse than that, then its R^2 score can be negative, and indeed arbitrarily low.

This is better than nothing, but clearly not a great score: the `median_housing_values` of most districts range between $120,000 and $265,000, so a typical prediction error of $68,973 is really not very satisfying. This is an example of a model underfitting the training data. When this happens it can mean that the features do not provide enough information to make good predictions, or that the model is not powerful enough. As we saw in the previous chapter, the main ways to fix underfitting are to select a more powerful model, to feed the training algorithm with better features, or to reduce the constraints on the model. This model is not regularized, which rules out the last option. You could try to add more features, but first you want to try a more complex model to see how it does.

You decide to try a `DecisionTreeRegressor`, as this is a fairly powerful model capable of finding complex nonlinear relationships in the data (decision trees are presented in more detail in Chapter 5):

```
from sklearn.tree import DecisionTreeRegressor

tree_reg = make_pipeline(preprocessing, DecisionTreeRegressor(random_state=42))
tree_reg.fit(housing, housing_labels)
```

Now that the model is trained, you evaluate it on the training set:

```
>>> housing_predictions = tree_reg.predict(housing)
>>> tree_rmse = root_mean_squared_error(housing_labels, housing_predictions)
```

```
>>> tree_rmse
0.0
```

Wait, what!? No error at all? Could this model really be absolutely perfect? Of course, it is much more likely that the model has badly overfit the data. How can you be sure? As you saw earlier, you don't want to touch the test set until you are ready to launch a model you are confident about, so you need to use part of the training set for training and part of it for model validation.

Better Evaluation Using Cross-Validation

One way to evaluate the decision tree model would be to use the `train_test_split()` function to split the training set into a smaller training set and a validation set, then train your models against the smaller training set and evaluate them against the validation set. It's a bit of effort, but nothing too difficult, and it would work fairly well.

A great alternative is to use Scikit-Learn's *k-fold cross-validation* feature. You split the training set into *k* nonoverlapping subsets called *folds*, then you train and evaluate your model *k* times, picking a different fold for evaluation every time (i.e., the validation fold) and using the other *k* – 1 folds for training. This process produces *k* evaluation scores (see Figure 2-20).

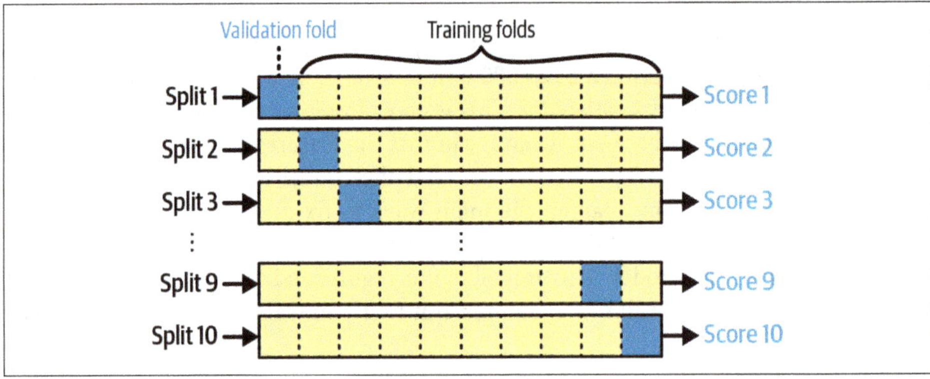

Figure 2-20. k-fold cross-validation, with k = 10

Scikit-Learn provides a convenient `cross_val_score()` function that does just that, and it returns an array containing the *k* evaluation scores. For example, let's use it to evaluate our tree regressor, using *k* = 10:

```
from sklearn.model_selection import cross_val_score

tree_rmses = -cross_val_score(tree_reg, housing, housing_labels,
                              scoring="neg_root_mean_squared_error", cv=10)
```

Scikit-Learn's cross-validation features expect a utility function (greater is better) rather than a cost function (lower is better), so the scoring function is actually the opposite of the RMSE. It's a negative value, so you need to switch the sign of the output to get the RMSE scores.

Let's look at the results:

```
>>> pd.Series(tree_rmses).describe()
count       10.000000
mean     66573.734600
std       1103.402323
min      64607.896046
25%      66204.731788
50%      66388.272499
75%      66826.257468
max      68532.210664
dtype: float64
```

Now the decision tree doesn't look as good as it did earlier. In fact, it seems to perform almost as poorly as the linear regression model! Notice that cross-validation allows you to get not only an estimate of the performance of your model, but also a measure of how precise this estimate is (i.e., its standard deviation). The decision tree has an RMSE of about 66,574, with a standard deviation of about 1,103. You would not have this information if you just used one validation set. But cross-validation comes at the cost of training the model several times, so it is not always feasible.

If you compute the same metric for the linear regression model, you will find that the mean RMSE is 70,003 and the standard deviation is 4,182. So the decision tree model seems to perform very slightly better than the linear model, but the difference is minimal due to severe overfitting. We know there's an overfitting problem because the training error is low (actually zero) while the validation error is high.

Let's try one last model now: the `RandomForestRegressor`. As you will see in Chapter 6, random forests work by training many decision trees on random subsets of the features, then averaging out their predictions. Such models composed of many other models are called *ensembles*: if the underlying models are very diverse, then their errors will not be very correlated, and therefore averaging out the predictions will smooth out the errors, reduce overfitting, and improve the overall performance. The code is much the same as earlier:

```
from sklearn.ensemble import RandomForestRegressor

forest_reg = make_pipeline(preprocessing,
                           RandomForestRegressor(random_state=42))
forest_rmses = -cross_val_score(forest_reg, housing, housing_labels,
                                scoring="neg_root_mean_squared_error", cv=10)
```

Let's look at the scores:

```
>>> pd.Series(forest_rmses).describe()
count       10.000000
mean     47038.092799
std       1021.491757
min      45495.976649
25%      46510.418013
50%      47118.719249
75%      47480.519175
max      49140.832210
dtype: float64
```

Wow, this is much better: random forests really look very promising for this task! However, if you train a `RandomForestRegressor` and measure the RMSE on the training set, you will find roughly 17,551: that's much lower, meaning that there's still quite a lot of overfitting going on. Possible solutions are to simplify the model, constrain it (i.e., regularize it), or get a lot more training data. Before you dive much deeper into random forests, however, you should try out many other models from various categories of machine learning algorithms (e.g., several support vector machines with different kernels, and possibly a neural network), without spending too much time tweaking the hyperparameters. The goal is to shortlist a few (two to five) promising models.

Fine-Tune Your Model

Let's assume that you now have a shortlist of promising models. You now need to fine-tune them. Let's look at a few ways you can do that.

Grid Search

One option would be to fiddle with the hyperparameters manually, until you find a great combination of hyperparameter values. This would be very tedious work, and you may not have time to explore many combinations.

Instead, you can use Scikit-Learn's `GridSearchCV` class to search for you. All you need to do is tell it which hyperparameters you want it to experiment with and what values to try out, and it will use cross-validation to evaluate all the possible combinations of hyperparameter values. For example, the following code searches for the best combination of hyperparameter values for the `RandomForestRegressor`:

```
from sklearn.model_selection import GridSearchCV

full_pipeline = Pipeline([
    ("preprocessing", preprocessing),
    ("random_forest", RandomForestRegressor(random_state=42)),
])
```

```
param_grid = [
    {'preprocessing__geo__n_clusters': [5, 8, 10],
     'random_forest__max_features': [4, 6, 8]},
    {'preprocessing__geo__n_clusters': [10, 15],
     'random_forest__max_features': [6, 8, 10]},
]
grid_search = GridSearchCV(full_pipeline, param_grid, cv=3,
                           scoring='neg_root_mean_squared_error')
grid_search.fit(housing, housing_labels)
```

Notice that you can refer to any hyperparameter of any estimator in a pipeline, even if this estimator is nested deep inside several pipelines and column transformers. For example, when Scikit-Learn sees `"preprocessing__geo__n_clusters"`, it splits this string at the double underscores, then it looks for an estimator named `"preprocessing"` in the pipeline and finds the preprocessing `ColumnTransformer`. Next, it looks for a transformer named `"geo"` inside this `ColumnTransformer` and finds the `ClusterSimilarity` transformer we used on the latitude and longitude attributes. Then it finds this transformer's `n_clusters` hyperparameter. Similarly, `random_forest__max_features` refers to the `max_features` hyperparameter of the estimator named `"random_forest"`, which is of course the `RandomForestRegressor` model (the `max_features` hyperparameter will be explained in Chapter 6).

Wrapping preprocessing steps in a Scikit-Learn pipeline allows you to tune the preprocessing hyperparameters along with the model hyperparameters. This is a good thing since they often interact. For example, perhaps increasing `n_clusters` requires increasing `max_features` as well. If fitting the pipeline transformers is computationally expensive, you can set the pipeline's `memory` parameter to the path of a caching directory: when you first fit the pipeline, Scikit-Learn will save the fitted transformers to this directory. If you then fit the pipeline again with the same hyperparameters, Scikit-Learn will just load the cached transformers.

There are two dictionaries in this `param_grid`, so `GridSearchCV` will first evaluate all 3 × 3 = 9 combinations of `n_clusters` and `max_features` hyperparameter values specified in the first `dict`, then it will try all 2 × 3 = 6 combinations of hyperparameter values in the second `dict`. So in total the grid search will explore 9 + 6 = 15 combinations of hyperparameter values, and it will train the pipeline 3 times per combination, since we are using 3-fold cross validation. This means there will be a grand total of 15 × 3 = 45 rounds of training! It may take a while, but when it is done you can get the best combination of parameters like this:

```
>>> grid_search.best_params_
{'preprocessing__geo__n_clusters': 15, 'random_forest__max_features': 6}
```

In this example, the best model is obtained by setting `n_clusters` to 15 and setting `max_features` to 6.

Since 15 is the maximum value that was evaluated for `n_clusters`, you should probably try searching again with higher values; the score may continue to improve.

You can access the best estimator using `grid_search.best_estimator_`. If `GridSearchCV` is initialized with `refit=True` (which is the default), then once it finds the best estimator using cross-validation, it retrains it on the whole training set. This is usually a good idea, since feeding it more data will likely improve its performance.

The evaluation scores are available using `grid_search.cv_results_`. This is a dictionary, but if you wrap it in a DataFrame you get a nice list of all the test scores for each combination of hyperparameters and for each cross-validation split, as well as the mean test score across all splits:

```
>>> cv_res = pd.DataFrame(grid_search.cv_results_)
>>> cv_res.sort_values(by="mean_test_score", ascending=False, inplace=True)
>>> [...]  # change column names to fit on this page, and show rmse = -score
>>> cv_res.head()  # note: the 1st column is the row ID
    n_clusters  max_features  split0  split1  split2  mean_test_rmse
12          15             6   42725   43708   44335           43590
13          15             8   43486   43820   44900           44069
6           10             4   43798   44036   44961           44265
9           10             6   43710   44163   44967           44280
7           10             6   43710   44163   44967           44280
```

The mean test RMSE score for the best model is 43,590, which is better than the score you got earlier using the default hyperparameter values (which was 47,038). Congratulations, you have successfully fine-tuned your best model!

Randomized Search

The grid search approach is fine when you are exploring relatively few combinations, like in the previous example, but `RandomizedSearchCV` is often preferable, especially when the hyperparameter search space is large. This class can be used in much the same way as the `GridSearchCV` class, but instead of trying out all possible combinations it evaluates a fixed number of combinations, selecting a random value for each hyperparameter at every iteration. This may sound surprising, but this approach has several benefits:

- If some of your hyperparameters are continuous (or discrete but with many possible values), and you let randomized search run for, say, 1,000 iterations, then it will explore 1,000 different values for each of these hyperparameters, whereas grid search would only explore the few values you listed for each one.

- Suppose a hyperparameter does not actually make much difference, but you don't know it yet. If it has 10 possible values and you add it to your grid search, then training will take 10 times longer. But if you add it to a random search, it will not make any difference.
- If there are 6 hyperparameters to explore, each with 10 possible values, then grid search offers no other choice than training the model a million times, whereas random search can always run for any number of iterations you choose.

For each hyperparameter, you must provide either a list of possible values, or a probability distribution:

```
from sklearn.model_selection import RandomizedSearchCV
from scipy.stats import randint

param_distribs = {'preprocessing__geo__n_clusters': randint(low=3, high=50),
                  'random_forest__max_features': randint(low=2, high=20)}

rnd_search = RandomizedSearchCV(
    full_pipeline, param_distributions=param_distribs, n_iter=10, cv=3,
    scoring='neg_root_mean_squared_error', random_state=42)

rnd_search.fit(housing, housing_labels)
```

Scikit-Learn also has `HalvingRandomSearchCV` and `HalvingGridSearchCV` hyperparameter search classes. Their goal is to use the computational resources more efficiently, either to train faster or to explore a larger hyperparameter space. Here's how they work: in the first round, many hyperparameter combinations (called "candidates") are generated using either the grid approach or the random approach. These candidates are then used to train models that are evaluated using cross-validation, as usual. However, training uses limited resources, which speeds up this first round considerably. By default, "limited resources" means that the models are trained on a small part of the training set. However, other limitations are possible, such as reducing the number of training iterations if the model has a hyperparameter to set it. Once every candidate has been evaluated, only the best ones go on to the second round, where they are allowed more resources to compete. After several rounds, the final candidates are evaluated using full resources. This may save you some time tuning hyperparameters.

Ensemble Methods

Another way to fine-tune your system is to try to combine the models that perform best. The group (or "ensemble") will often perform better than the best individual model—just like random forests perform better than the individual decision trees they rely on—especially if the individual models make very different types of errors. For example, you could train and fine-tune a *k*-nearest neighbors model, then create an ensemble model that just predicts the mean of the random forest prediction and that model's prediction. We will cover this topic in more detail in Chapter 6.

Analyzing the Best Models and Their Errors

You will often gain good insights on the problem by inspecting the best models. For example, the `RandomForestRegressor` can indicate the relative importance of each attribute for making accurate predictions:

```
>>> final_model = rnd_search.best_estimator_  # includes preprocessing
>>> feature_importances = final_model["random_forest"].feature_importances_
>>> feature_importances.round(2)
array([0.07, 0.05, 0.05, 0.01, 0.01, 0.01, 0.01, 0.19, [...], 0.  , 0.01])
```

Let's sort these importance scores in descending order and display them next to their corresponding attribute names:

```
>>> sorted(zip(feature_importances,
...            final_model["preprocessing"].get_feature_names_out()),
...        reverse=True)
...
[(np.float64(0.18599734460509476), 'log__median_income'),
 (np.float64(0.07338850855844489), 'cat__ocean_proximity_INLAND'),
 (np.float64(0.06556941990883976), 'bedrooms__ratio'),
 (np.float64(0.053648710076725316), 'rooms_per_house__ratio'),
 (np.float64(0.04598870861894749), 'people_per_house__ratio'),
 (np.float64(0.04175269214442519), 'geo__Cluster 30 similarity'),
 (np.float64(0.025976797232869678), 'geo__Cluster 25 similarity'),
 (np.float64(0.023595895886342255), 'geo__Cluster 36 similarity'),
 [...]
 (np.float64(0.0004325970342247361), 'cat__ocean_proximity_NEAR BAY'),
 (np.float64(3.0190221102670295e-05), 'cat__ocean_proximity_ISLAND')]
```

With this information, you may want to try dropping some of the less useful features (e.g., apparently only one `ocean_proximity` category is really useful, so you could try dropping the others).

The `sklearn.feature_selection.SelectFromModel` transformer can automatically drop the least useful features for you: when you fit it, it trains a model (typically a random forest), looks at its `feature_importances_` attribute, and selects the most useful features. Then when you call `transform()`, it drops the other features.

You should also look at the specific errors that your system makes, then try to understand why it makes them and what could fix the problem: adding extra features or getting rid of uninformative ones, cleaning up outliers, etc.

Now is also a good time to check *model fairness*: it should not only work well on average, but also on various categories of districts, whether they're rural or urban, rich or poor, northern or southern, minority or not, etc. This requires a detailed *bias analysis*: creating subsets of your validation set for each category, and analyzing your model's performance on them. That's a lot of work, but it's important: if your model performs poorly on a whole category of districts, then it should probably not be deployed until the issue is resolved, or at least it should not be used to make predictions for that category, as it may do more harm than good.

Evaluate Your System on the Test Set

After tweaking your models for a while, you eventually have a system that performs sufficiently well. You are ready to evaluate the final model on the test set. There is nothing special about this process; just get the predictors and the labels from your test set and run your `final_model` to transform the data and make predictions, then evaluate these predictions:

```
X_test = strat_test_set.drop("median_house_value", axis=1)
y_test = strat_test_set["median_house_value"].copy()

final_predictions = final_model.predict(X_test)

final_rmse = root_mean_squared_error(y_test, final_predictions)
print(final_rmse)  # prints 41445.533268606625
```

In some cases, such a point estimate of the generalization error will not be quite enough to convince you to launch: what if it is just 0.1% better than the model currently in production? You might want to have an idea of how precise this estimate is. For this, you can compute a 95% *confidence interval* for the generalization error using `scipy.stats.bootstrap()`. You get a fairly large interval from 39,521 to 43,702, and your previous point estimate of 41,445 is roughly in the middle of it:

```
from scipy import stats

def rmse(squared_errors):
    return np.sqrt(np.mean(squared_errors))

confidence = 0.95
squared_errors = (final_predictions - y_test) ** 2
boot_result = stats.bootstrap([squared_errors], rmse,
                              confidence_level=confidence, random_state=42)
rmse_lower, rmse_upper = boot_result.confidence_interval
```

If you do a lot of hyperparameter tuning, the performance will usually be slightly worse than what you measured using cross-validation. That's because your system ends up fine-tuned to perform well on the validation data and will likely not perform as well on unknown datasets. That's not the case in this example since the test RMSE is lower than the validation RMSE, but when it happens you must resist the temptation to tweak the hyperparameters to make the numbers look good on the test set; the improvements would be unlikely to generalize to new data.

Now comes the project prelaunch phase. Presenting your solution effectively is what sets great data scientists apart from good ones. You should create concise reports (Markdown, PDFs, slides), visualize key insights (e.g., using Matplotlib or other tools such as SeaBorn or Tableau), and tailor your message to the audience: technical for peers, high-level for stakeholders. Provide impactful and easy-to-remember statements (e.g., "the median income is the number one predictor of housing prices"). Highlight what you have learned, what worked and what did not, what assumptions were made, and what your system's limitations are.

Your results should be reproducible (as much as possible): make the code accessible to your team (e.g., via GitHub), add a structured *README* file to guide a technical person through the installation steps. Provide clear notebooks (e.g., Jupyter) with code, explanations, and results, writing clean, well-commented code. Define a *requirements.txt* or *environment.yml* file containing all the required libraries along with their precise versions (or create a Docker image). Set seeds for random generators, and remove any other source of variability.

In this California housing example, the final performance of the system is not much better than the experts' price estimates, which were often off by 30%, but it may still be a good idea to launch it, especially if this frees up some time for the experts so they can work on more interesting and productive tasks.

Launch, Monitor, and Maintain Your System

Perfect, you got approval to launch! You now need to get your solution ready for production (e.g., polish the code, write documentation and tests, and so on). Then you can deploy your model to your production environment. The most basic way to do this is just to save the best model you trained, transfer the file to your production environment, and load it. To save the model, you can use the `joblib` library like this:

```
import joblib

joblib.dump(final_model, "my_california_housing_model.pkl")
```

It's often a good idea to save every model you experiment with so that you can come back easily to any model you want. You may also save the cross-validation scores and perhaps the actual predictions on the validation set. This will allow you to easily compare scores across model types, and compare the types of errors they make.

Once your model is transferred to production, you can load it and use it. For this you must first import any custom classes and functions the model relies on (which means transferring the code to production), then load the model using `joblib` and use it to make predictions:

```
import joblib
[...]  # import KMeans, BaseEstimator, TransformerMixin, rbf_kernel, etc.

def column_ratio(X): [...]
def ratio_name(function_transformer, feature_names_in): [...]
class ClusterSimilarity(BaseEstimator, TransformerMixin): [...]

final_model_reloaded = joblib.load("my_california_housing_model.pkl")

new_data = [...]  # some new districts to make predictions for
predictions = final_model_reloaded.predict(new_data)
```

For example, perhaps the model will be used within a website: the user will type in some data about a new district and click the Estimate Price button. This will send a query containing the data to the web server, which will forward it to your web application, and finally your code will simply call the model's `predict()` method (you want to load the model upon server startup, rather than every time the model is used). Alternatively, you can wrap the model within a dedicated web service that your web application can query through a REST API[14] (see Figure 2-21). This makes it easier to upgrade your model to new versions without interrupting the main application. It also simplifies scaling, since you can start as many web services as needed and load-balance the requests coming from your web application across these web services. Moreover, it allows your web application to use any programming language, not just Python.

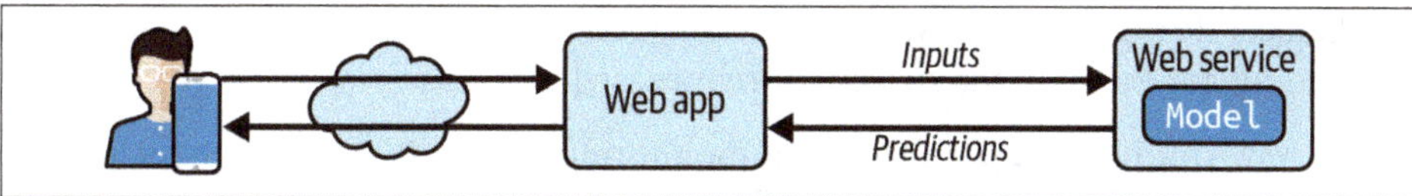

Figure 2-21. A model deployed as a web service and used by a web application

Another popular strategy is to deploy your model to the cloud, for example on Google's Vertex AI (formerly Google Cloud AI Platform and Google Cloud ML Engine): just save your model using `joblib` and upload it to Google Cloud Storage (GCS), then go to Vertex AI and create a new model version, pointing it to the GCS file. That's it! This gives you a simple web service that takes care of load balancing and

14 In a nutshell, a REST (or RESTful) API is an HTTP-based API that follows some conventions, such as using standard HTTP verbs to read, update, create, or delete resources (GET, POST, PUT, and DELETE) and using JSON for the inputs and outputs.

scaling for you. It takes JSON requests containing the input data (e.g., of a district) and returns JSON responses containing the predictions. You can then use this web service in your website (or whatever production environment you are using).

But deployment is not the end of the story. You also need to write monitoring code to check your system's live performance at regular intervals and trigger alerts when it drops. It may drop very quickly, for example if a component breaks in your infrastructure, but be aware that it could also decay very slowly, which can easily go unnoticed for a long time. This is quite common because of data drift: if the model was trained with last year's data, it may not be adapted to today's data.

So, you need to monitor your model's live performance. But how do you do that? Well, it depends. In some cases, the model's performance can be inferred from downstream metrics. For example, if your model is part of a recommender system and it suggests products that the users may be interested in, then it's easy to monitor the number of recommended products sold each day. If this number drops (compared to nonrecommended products), then the prime suspect is the model. This may be because the data pipeline is broken, or perhaps the model needs to be retrained on fresh data (as we will discuss shortly).

However, you may also need human analysis to assess the model's performance. For example, suppose you trained an image classification model (we'll look at these in Chapter 3) to detect various product defects on a production line. How can you get an alert if the model's performance drops, before thousands of defective products get shipped to your clients? One solution is to send to human raters a sample of all the pictures that the model classified (especially pictures that the model wasn't so sure about). Depending on the task, the raters may need to be experts, or they could be nonspecialists, such as workers on a crowdsourcing platform (e.g., Amazon Mechanical Turk). In some applications they could even be the users themselves, responding, for example, via surveys or repurposed captchas.[15]

Either way, you need to put in place a monitoring system (with or without human raters to evaluate the live model), as well as all the relevant processes to define what to do in case of failures and how to prepare for them. Unfortunately, this can be a lot of work. In fact, it is often much more work than building and training a model.

If the data keeps evolving, you will need to update your datasets and retrain your model regularly. You should probably automate the whole process as much as possible. Here are a few things you can automate:

15 A captcha is a test to ensure a user is not a robot. These tests have often been used as a cheap way to label training data.

- Collect fresh data regularly and label it (e.g., using human raters).
- Write a script to train the model and fine-tune the hyperparameters automatically. This script could run automatically, for example every day or every week, depending on your needs.
- Write another script that will evaluate both the new model and the previous model on the updated test set, and deploy the model to production if the performance has not decreased (if it did, make sure you investigate why). The script should probably test the performance of your model on various subsets of the test set, such as poor or rich districts, rural or urban districts, etc.

You should also make sure you evaluate the model's input data quality. Sometimes performance will degrade slightly because of a poor-quality signal (e.g., a malfunctioning sensor sending random values, or another team's output becoming stale), but it may take a while before your system's performance degrades enough to trigger an alert. If you monitor your model's inputs, you may catch this earlier. For example, you could trigger an alert if more and more inputs are missing a feature, or the mean or standard deviation drifts too far from the training set, or a categorical feature starts containing new categories.

Finally, make sure you keep backups of every model you create and have the process and tools in place to roll back to a previous model quickly, in case the new model starts failing badly for some reason. Having backups also makes it possible to easily compare new models with previous ones. Similarly, you should keep backups of every version of your datasets so that you can roll back to a previous dataset if the new one ever gets corrupted (e.g., if the fresh data that gets added to it turns out to be full of outliers). Having backups of your datasets also allows you to evaluate any model against any previous dataset.

As you can see, machine learning involves quite a lot of infrastructure. This is a very broad topic called *ML Operations* (MLOps), which deserves its own book. So don't be surprised if your first ML project takes a lot of effort and time to build and deploy to production. Fortunately, once all the infrastructure is in place, going from idea to production will be much faster.

Try It Out!

Hopefully this chapter gave you a good idea of what a machine learning project looks like as well as showing you some of the tools you can use to train a great system. As you can see, much of the work is in the data preparation step: building monitoring tools, setting up human evaluation pipelines, and automating regular model training. The machine learning algorithms are important, of course, but it is probably preferable to be comfortable with the overall process and know three or four algorithms well rather than to spend all your time exploring advanced algorithms.

So, if you have not already done so, now is a good time to pick up a laptop, select a dataset that you are interested in, and try to go through the whole process from A to Z. A good place to start is on a competition website such as Kaggle (*https://kaggle.com*): you will have a dataset to play with, a clear goal, and people to share the experience with. Have fun!

Exercises

The following exercises are based on this chapter's housing dataset:

1. Try a support vector machine regressor (`sklearn.svm.SVR`) with various hyperparameters, such as `kernel="linear"` (with various values for the `C` hyperparameter) or `kernel="rbf"` (with various values for the `C` and `gamma` hyperparameters). Note that support vector machines don't scale well to large datasets, so you should probably train your model on just the first 5,000 instances of the training set and use only 3-fold cross-validation, or else it will take hours. Don't worry about what the hyperparameters mean for now; these are explained in the online chapter on SVMs at *https://homl.info/*. How does the best `SVR` predictor perform?
2. Try replacing the `GridSearchCV` with a `RandomizedSearchCV`.
3. Try adding a `SelectFromModel` transformer in the preparation pipeline to select only the most important attributes.
4. Try creating a custom transformer that trains a *k*-nearest neighbors regressor (`sklearn.neighbors.KNeighborsRegressor`) in its `fit()` method, and outputs the model's predictions in its `transform()` method. The KNN regressor should use only the latitude and longitude as input and predict the median income. Next, add this new transformer to the preprocessing pipeline. This will add a feature representing the smoothed median income over the nearby districts.
5. Automatically explore some preparation options using `RandomizedSearchCV`.
6. Try to implement the `StandardScalerClone` class again from scratch, then add support for the `inverse_transform()` method: executing `scaler.inverse_transform(scaler.fit_transform(X))` should return an array very close to `X`. Then add support for feature names: set `feature_names_in_` in the `fit()` method if the input is a DataFrame. This attribute should be a NumPy array of column names. Lastly, implement the `get_feature_names_out()` method: it should have one optional `input_features=None` argument. If passed, the method should check that its length matches `n_features_in_`, and it should match `feature_names_in_` if it is defined; then `input_features` should be returned. If `input_features` is `None`, then the method should either return

`feature_names_in_` if it is defined or `np.array(["x0", "x1", ...])` with length `n_features_in_` otherwise.

7. Tackle a regression task of your choice by following the process you learned in this chapter. For example, you can try tackling the Vehicle dataset (*https://homl.info/usedcars*), where the goal is to predict the selling price of a used car, based on its age, the number of kilometers it has driven, its make and model, and more. Another good dataset to try is the Bike Sharing dataset (*https://homl.info/bikes*): the objective is to predict the number of bikes rented within a period of time (column `cnt`), based on the day of the week, the time, and the weather conditions.

Solutions to these exercises are available at the end of this chapter's notebook, at *https://homl.info/colab-p*.

CHAPTER 3
Classification

In Chapter 1 I mentioned that the most common supervised learning tasks are regression (predicting values) and classification (predicting classes). In Chapter 2 we explored a regression task, predicting housing values, using various algorithms such as linear regression, decision trees, and random forests (which will be explained in further detail in later chapters). Now we will turn our attention to classification systems.

MNIST

In this chapter we will be using the MNIST dataset, which is a set of 70,000 small images of digits handwritten by high school students and employees of the US Census Bureau. Each image is labeled with the digit it represents. This set has been studied so much that it is often called the "hello world" of machine learning: whenever people come up with a new classification algorithm they are curious to see how it will perform on MNIST, and anyone who learns machine learning tackles this dataset sooner or later.

Scikit-Learn provides many helper functions to download popular datasets. MNIST is one of them. The following code fetches the MNIST dataset from OpenML.org:[1]

```
from sklearn.datasets import fetch_openml

mnist = fetch_openml('mnist_784', as_frame=False)
```

1 By default Scikit-Learn caches downloaded datasets in a directory called *scikit_learn_data* in your home directory.

The sklearn.datasets package contains mostly three types of functions: fetch_* functions such as fetch_openml() to download real-life datasets, load_* functions to load small toy datasets bundled with Scikit-Learn (so they don't need to be downloaded over the internet), and make_* functions to generate fake datasets, useful for tests. Generated datasets are usually returned as an (X, y) tuple containing the input data and the targets, both as NumPy arrays. Other datasets are returned as sklearn.utils.Bunch objects, which are dictionaries whose entries can also be accessed as attributes. They generally contain the following entries:

"DESCR"
: A description of the dataset

"data"
: The input data, usually as a 2D NumPy array

"target"
: The labels, usually as a 1D NumPy array

The fetch_openml() function is a bit unusual since by default it returns the inputs as a Pandas DataFrame and the labels as a Pandas Series (unless the dataset is sparse). But the MNIST dataset contains images, and DataFrames aren't ideal for that, so it's preferable to set as_frame=False to get the data as NumPy arrays instead. Let's look at these arrays:

```
>>> X, y = mnist.data, mnist.target
>>> X
array([[0, 0, 0, ..., 0, 0, 0],
       [0, 0, 0, ..., 0, 0, 0],
       [0, 0, 0, ..., 0, 0, 0],
       ...,
       [0, 0, 0, ..., 0, 0, 0],
       [0, 0, 0, ..., 0, 0, 0],
       [0, 0, 0, ..., 0, 0, 0]])
>>> X.shape
(70000, 784)
>>> y
array(['5', '0', '4', ..., '4', '5', '6'], dtype=object)
>>> y.shape
(70000,)
```

There are 70,000 images, and each image has 784 features. This is because each image is 28 × 28 pixels, and each feature simply represents one pixel's intensity, from 0 (white) to 255 (black). Let's take a peek at one digit from the dataset (Figure 3-1). All we need to do is grab an instance's feature vector, reshape it to a 28 × 28 array, and display it using Matplotlib's imshow() function. We use cmap="binary" to get a grayscale color map where 0 is white and 255 is black:

```
import matplotlib.pyplot as plt

def plot_digit(image_data):
    image = image_data.reshape(28, 28)
    plt.imshow(image, cmap="binary")
    plt.axis("off")

some_digit = X[0]
plot_digit(some_digit)
plt.show()
```

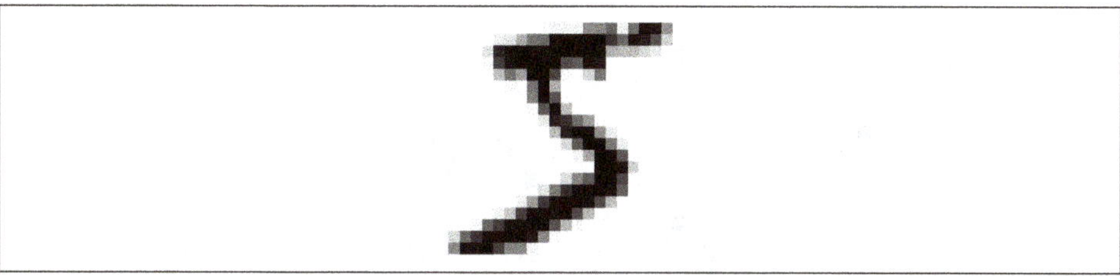

Figure 3-1. Example of an MNIST image

This looks like a 5, and indeed that's what the label tells us:

```
>>> y[0]
'5'
```

To give you a feel for the complexity of the classification task, Figure 3-2 shows a few more images from the MNIST dataset. There's quite a large variety of digit shapes. That said, the images are clean, well centered, not too rotated, and the digits all have roughly the same size: this dataset will not require much preprocessing (real-world datasets aren't usually that friendly).

But wait! You should always create a test set and set it aside before inspecting the data closely. The MNIST dataset returned by `fetch_openml()` is actually already split into a training set (the first 60,000 images) and a test set (the last 10,000 images):[2]

```
X_train, X_test, y_train, y_test = X[:60000], X[60000:], y[:60000], y[60000:]
```

The training set is already shuffled for us, which is good because this guarantees that all cross-validation folds will be similar (we don't want one fold to be missing some digits). Moreover, some learning algorithms are sensitive to the order of the training instances, and they perform poorly if they get many similar instances in a row. Shuffling the dataset ensures that this won't happen.[3]

2 Datasets returned by `fetch_openml()` are not always shuffled or split.

3 Shuffling may be a bad idea in some contexts—for example, if you are working on time series data (such as stock market prices or weather conditions). We will explore this in Chapter 13.

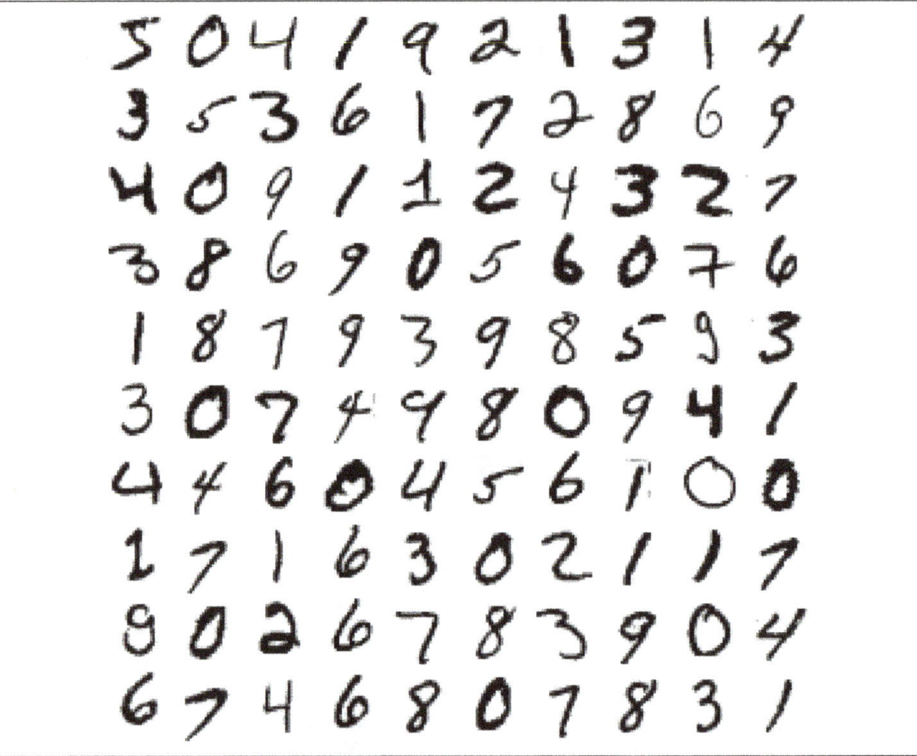

Figure 3-2. Digits from the MNIST dataset

Training a Binary Classifier

Let's simplify the problem for now and only try to identify one digit—for example, the number 5. This "5-detector" will be an example of a *binary classifier*, capable of distinguishing between just two classes, 5 and non-5. First we'll create the target vectors for this classification task:

```
y_train_5 = (y_train == '5')  # True for all 5s, False for all other digits
y_test_5 = (y_test == '5')
```

Now let's pick a classifier and train it. A good place to start is with a *stochastic gradient descent* (SGD, or stochastic GD) classifier, using Scikit-Learn's `SGDClassifier` class. This classifier is capable of handling very large datasets efficiently. This is in part because SGD deals with training instances independently, one at a time, which also makes SGD well suited for online learning, as you will see later. Let's create an `SGDClassifier` and train it on the whole training set:

```
from sklearn.linear_model import SGDClassifier
```

```
sgd_clf = SGDClassifier(random_state=42)
sgd_clf.fit(X_train, y_train_5)
```

Now we can use it to detect images of the number 5:

```
>>> sgd_clf.predict([some_digit])
array([ True])
```

The classifier guesses that this image represents a 5 (`True`). Looks like it guessed right in this particular case! Now, let's evaluate this model's performance.

Performance Measures

Evaluating a classifier is often significantly trickier than evaluating a regressor, so we will spend a large part of this chapter on this topic. There are many performance measures available, so grab another coffee and get ready to learn a bunch of new concepts and acronyms!

Measuring Accuracy Using Cross-Validation

A good way to evaluate a model is to use cross-validation, just as you did in Chapter 2. Let's use the `cross_val_score()` function to evaluate our `SGDClassifier` model, using *k*-fold cross-validation with three folds. Remember that *k*-fold cross-validation means splitting the training set into *k* folds (in this case, three), then training the model *k* times, holding out a different fold each time for evaluation (see Chapter 2):

```
>>> from sklearn.model_selection import cross_val_score
>>> cross_val_score(sgd_clf, X_train, y_train_5, cv=3, scoring="accuracy")
array([0.95035, 0.96035, 0.9604 ])
```

Wow! Above 95% accuracy (ratio of correct predictions) on all cross-validation folds? This looks amazing, doesn't it? Well, before you get too excited, let's look at a dummy classifier that just classifies every single image in the most frequent class, which in this case is the negative class (i.e., *non*-5):

```
from sklearn.dummy import DummyClassifier

dummy_clf = DummyClassifier()
dummy_clf.fit(X_train, y_train_5)
print(any(dummy_clf.predict(X_train)))  # prints False: no 5s detected
```

Can you guess this model's accuracy? Let's find out:

```
>>> cross_val_score(dummy_clf, X_train, y_train_5, cv=3, scoring="accuracy")
array([0.90965, 0.90965, 0.90965])
```

That's right, it has over 90% accuracy! This is simply because only about 10% of the images are 5s, so if you always guess that an image is *not* a 5, you will be right about 90% of the time. Beats Nostradamus.

This demonstrates why accuracy is generally not the preferred performance measure for classifiers, especially when you are dealing with *skewed datasets* (i.e., when some classes are much more frequent than others). A much better way to evaluate the performance of a classifier is to look at the *confusion matrix* (CM).

Implementing Cross-Validation

Occasionally you will need more control over the cross-validation process than what Scikit-Learn provides off the shelf. In these cases, you can implement cross-validation yourself. The following code does roughly the same thing as Scikit-Learn's `cross_val_score()` function, and it prints the same result:

```
from sklearn.model_selection import StratifiedKFold
from sklearn.base import clone

skfolds = StratifiedKFold(n_splits=3)  # add shuffle=True if the dataset is
                                       # not already shuffled
for train_index, test_index in skfolds.split(X_train, y_train_5):
    clone_clf = clone(sgd_clf)
    X_train_folds = X_train[train_index]
    y_train_folds = y_train_5[train_index]
    X_test_fold = X_train[test_index]
    y_test_fold = y_train_5[test_index]

    clone_clf.fit(X_train_folds, y_train_folds)
    y_pred = clone_clf.predict(X_test_fold)
    n_correct = sum(y_pred == y_test_fold)
    print(n_correct / len(y_pred))  # prints 0.95035, 0.96035, and 0.9604
```

The `StratifiedKFold` class performs stratified sampling (as explained in Chapter 2) to produce folds that contain a representative ratio of each class. At each iteration the code creates a clone of the classifier, trains that clone on the training folds, and makes predictions on the test fold. Then it counts the number of correct predictions and outputs the ratio of correct predictions.

Confusion Matrices

The general idea of a confusion matrix is to count the number of times instances of class A are classified as class B, for all A/B pairs. For example, to know the number of times the classifier confused images of 8s with 0s, you would look at row #8, column #0 of the confusion matrix.

To compute the confusion matrix, you first need to have a set of predictions so that they can be compared to the actual targets. You could make predictions on the test set, but it's best to keep that untouched for now (remember that you want to use the test set only at the very end of your project, once you have a classifier that you are ready to launch). Instead, you can use the `cross_val_predict()` function:

```python
from sklearn.model_selection import cross_val_predict

y_train_pred = cross_val_predict(sgd_clf, X_train, y_train_5, cv=3)
```

Just like the `cross_val_score()` function, `cross_val_predict()` performs *k*-fold cross-validation, but instead of returning the evaluation scores, it returns the predictions made on each test fold. This means that you get a clean prediction for each instance in the training set (by "clean" I mean "out-of-sample": the model makes predictions on data that it never saw during training).

Now you are ready to get the confusion matrix using the `confusion_matrix()` function. Just pass it the target classes (`y_train_5`) and the predicted classes (`y_train_pred`):

```python
>>> from sklearn.metrics import confusion_matrix
>>> cm = confusion_matrix(y_train_5, y_train_pred)
>>> cm
array([[53892,   687],
       [ 1891,  3530]])
```

Each row in a confusion matrix represents an *actual class*, while each column represents a *predicted class*. The first row of this matrix considers non-5 images (the *negative class*): 53,892 of them were correctly classified as non-5s (they are called *true negatives*), while the remaining 687 were wrongly classified as 5s (*false positives*, also called *type I errors*). The second row considers the images of 5s (the *positive class*): 1,891 were wrongly classified as non-5s (*false negatives*, also called *type II errors*), while the remaining 3,530 were correctly classified as 5s (*true positives*). A perfect classifier would only have true positives and true negatives, so its confusion matrix would have nonzero values only on its main diagonal (top left to bottom right):

```python
>>> y_train_perfect_predictions = y_train_5  # pretend we reached perfection
>>> confusion_matrix(y_train_5, y_train_perfect_predictions)
array([[54579,     0],
       [    0,  5421]])
```

The confusion matrix gives you a lot of information, but sometimes you may prefer a more concise metric. An interesting one to look at is the accuracy of the positive predictions; this is called the *precision* of the classifier (Equation 3-1).

Equation 3-1. Precision

$$\text{precision} = \frac{TP}{TP + FP}$$

TP is the number of true positives, and *FP* is the number of false positives.

Now consider a model that only makes positive predictions when it's extremely confident. Let's push this to the extreme and suppose that it always makes negative predictions, except for a single positive prediction on the instance it's most confident about. If this one prediction is correct, then the classifier has 100% precision (precision = 1/1 = 100%). Obviously, such a classifier would not be very useful, since it would ignore all but one positive instance. For this reason, precision is typically used along with another metric named *recall*, also called *sensitivity* or the *true positive rate* (TPR): this is the ratio of positive instances that are correctly detected by the classifier (Equation 3-2).

Equation 3-2. Recall

$$\text{recall} = \frac{TP}{TP + FN}$$

FN is, of course, the number of false negatives.

If you are confused about the confusion matrix, Figure 3-3 may help.

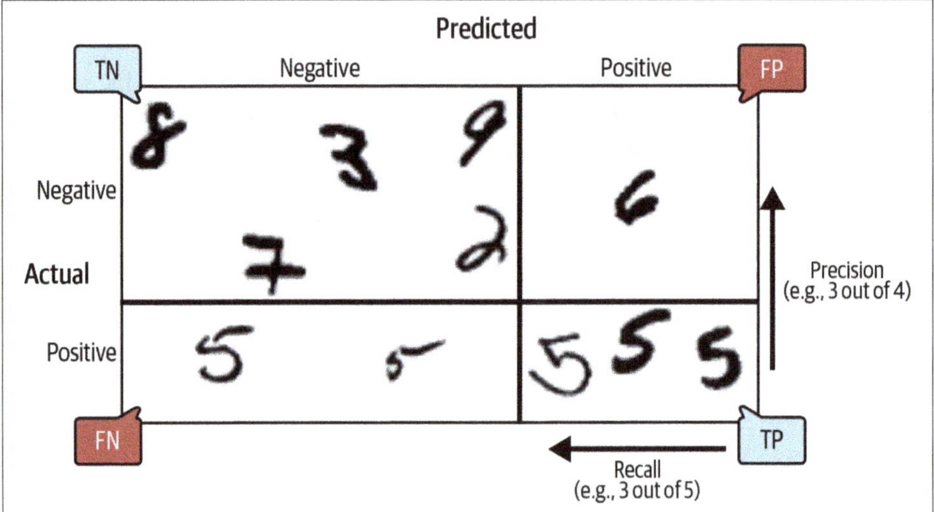

Figure 3-3. An illustrated confusion matrix showing examples of true negatives (top left), false positives (top right), false negatives (lower left), and true positives (lower right)

Precision and Recall

Scikit-Learn provides several functions to compute classifier metrics, including precision and recall:

```
>>> from sklearn.metrics import precision_score, recall_score
>>> precision_score(y_train_5, y_train_pred)  # == 3530 / (687 + 3530)
np.float64(0.8370879772350012)
>>> recall_score(y_train_5, y_train_pred)  # == 3530 / (1891 + 3530)
np.float64(0.6511713705958311)
```

Now our 5-detector does not look as shiny as it did when we looked at its accuracy. When it claims an image represents a 5, it is correct only 83.7% of the time. Moreover, it only detects 65.1% of the 5s.

It is often convenient to combine precision and recall into a single metric called the *F_1 score*, especially when you need a single metric to compare two classifiers. The F_1 score is the *harmonic mean* of precision and recall (Equation 3-3). Whereas the regular mean treats all values equally, the harmonic mean gives much more weight to low values. As a result, the classifier will only get a high F_1 score if both recall and precision are high.

Equation 3-3. F_1 score

$$F_1 = \frac{2}{\frac{1}{\text{precision}} + \frac{1}{\text{recall}}} = 2 \times \frac{\text{precision} \times \text{recall}}{\text{precision} + \text{recall}} = \frac{TP}{TP + \frac{FN + FP}{2}}$$

To compute the F_1 score, simply call the `f1_score()` function:

```
>>> from sklearn.metrics import f1_score
>>> f1_score(y_train_5, y_train_pred)
0.7325171197343846
```

The F_1 score favors classifiers that have similar precision and recall. This is not always what you want: in some contexts you mostly care about precision, and in other contexts you really care about recall. For example, if you trained a classifier to detect videos that are safe for kids, you would probably prefer a classifier that rejects many good videos (low recall) but keeps only safe ones (high precision), rather than a classifier that has a much higher recall but lets a few really bad videos show up in your product (in such cases, you may even want to add a human pipeline to check the classifier's video selection). On the other hand, suppose you train a classifier to detect shoplifters in surveillance images: it is probably fine if your classifier only has 30% precision as long as it has 99% recall. Sure, the security guards will get a few false alerts, but almost all shoplifters will get caught. Similarly, medical diagnosis usually requires a high recall to avoid missing anything important. False positives can be ruled out by follow-up medical tests.

Unfortunately, you can't have it both ways: increasing precision reduces recall, and vice versa. This is called the *precision/recall trade-off*.

The Precision/Recall Trade-Off

To understand this trade-off, let's look at how the `SGDClassifier` makes its classification decisions. For each instance, it computes a score based on a *decision function*. If that score is greater than a threshold, it assigns the instance to the positive class; otherwise it assigns it to the negative class. Figure 3-4 shows a few digits positioned from the lowest score on the left to the highest score on the right. Suppose the *decision threshold* is positioned at the central arrow (between the two 5s): you will find 4 true positives (actual 5s) on the right of that threshold, and 1 false positive (actually a 6). Therefore, with that threshold, the precision is 80% (4 out of 5). But out of 6 actual 5s, the classifier only detects 4, so the recall is 67% (4 out of 6). If you raise the threshold (move it to the arrow on the right), the false positive (the 6) becomes a true negative, thereby increasing the precision (up to 100% in this case), but one true positive becomes a false negative, decreasing recall down to 50%. Conversely, lowering the threshold increases recall and reduces precision.

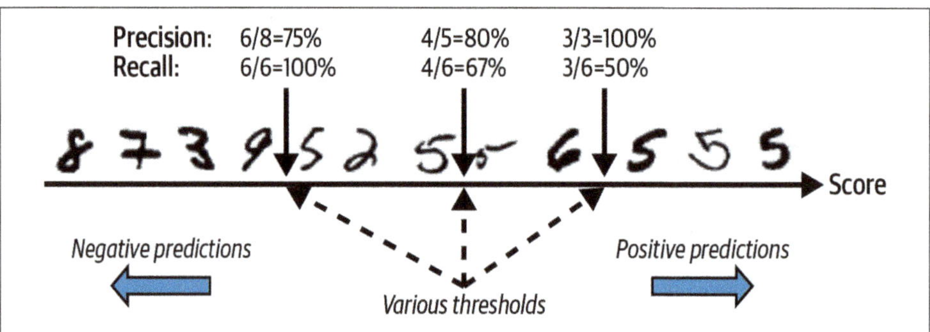

Figure 3-4. The precision/recall trade-off: images are ranked by their classifier score, and those above the chosen decision threshold are considered positive; the higher the threshold, the lower the recall, but (in general) the higher the precision

Instead of calling the classifier's `predict()` method, you can call its `decision_function()` method, which returns a score for each instance. You can then use any threshold you want to make predictions based on those scores:

```
>>> y_scores = sgd_clf.decision_function([some_digit])
>>> y_scores
array([2164.22030239])
>>> threshold = 0
>>> y_some_digit_pred = (y_scores > threshold)
>>> y_some_digit_pred
array([ True])
```

The `SGDClassifier` uses a threshold equal to 0, so the preceding code returns the same result as the `predict()` method (i.e., `True`). Let's raise the threshold:

```
>>> threshold = 3000
>>> y_some_digit_pred = (y_scores > threshold)
>>> y_some_digit_pred
array([False])
```

This confirms that raising the threshold decreases recall. The image actually represents a 5, and the classifier detects it when the threshold is 0, but it misses it when the threshold is increased to 3,000.

How do you decide which threshold to use? One option is to use the `cross_val_predict()` function to get the scores of all instances in the training set, but this time specify that you want to return decision scores instead of predictions:

```
y_scores = cross_val_predict(sgd_clf, X_train, y_train_5, cv=3,
                             method="decision_function")
```

With these scores, use the `precision_recall_curve()` function to compute precision and recall for all possible thresholds (the function adds a last precision of 1 and a last recall of 0, corresponding to an infinite threshold):

```
from sklearn.metrics import precision_recall_curve

precisions, recalls, thresholds = precision_recall_curve(y_train_5, y_scores)
```

Finally, use Matplotlib to plot precision and recall as functions of the threshold value (Figure 3-5). Let's show the threshold of 3,000 we selected:

```
plt.plot(thresholds, precisions[:-1], "b--", label="Precision", linewidth=2)
plt.plot(thresholds, recalls[:-1], "g-", label="Recall", linewidth=2)
plt.vlines(threshold, 0, 1.0, "k", "dotted", label="threshold")
[...]  # beautify the figure: add grid, legend, axis, labels, and circles
plt.show()
```

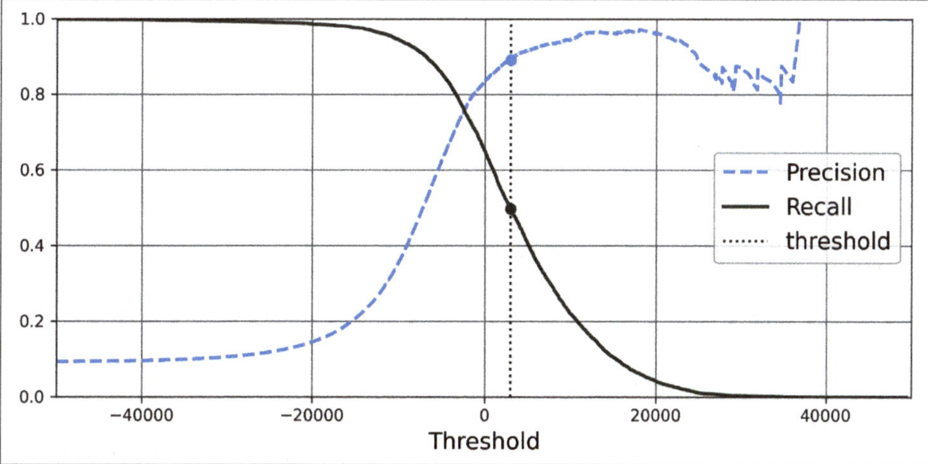

Figure 3-5. Precision and recall versus the decision threshold

You may wonder why the precision curve is bumpier than the recall curve in Figure 3-5. The reason is that precision may sometimes go down when you raise the threshold (although in general it will go up). To understand why, look back at Figure 3-4 and notice what happens when you start from the central threshold and move it just one digit to the right: precision goes from 4/5 (80%) down to 3/4 (75%). On the other hand, recall can only go down when the threshold is increased, which explains why its curve looks smooth.

At this threshold value, precision is near 90% and recall is around 50%. Another way to select a good precision/recall trade-off is to plot precision directly against recall, as shown in Figure 3-6 (the same threshold is shown):

```
plt.plot(recalls, precisions, linewidth=2, label="Precision/Recall curve")
[...]  # beautify the figure: add labels, grid, legend, arrow, and text
plt.show()
```

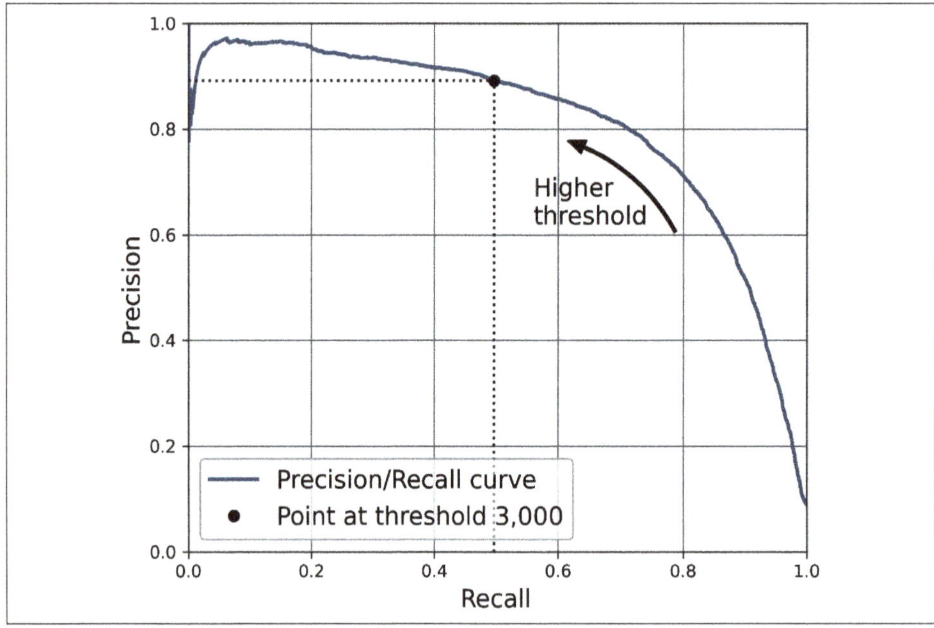

Figure 3-6. Precision versus recall

You can see that precision really starts to fall sharply at around 80% recall. You will probably want to select a precision/recall trade-off just before that drop—for example, at around 60% recall. But of course, the choice depends on your project.

Suppose you decide to aim for 90% precision. You could use the first plot to find the threshold you need to use, but that's not very precise. Alternatively, you can search for the lowest threshold that gives you at least 90% precision. For this, you can use the

NumPy array's `argmax()` method. This returns the first index of the maximum value, which in this case means the first `True` value:

```
>>> idx_for_90_precision = (precisions >= 0.90).argmax()
>>> threshold_for_90_precision = thresholds[idx_for_90_precision]
>>> threshold_for_90_precision
np.float64(3370.0194991439557)
```

To make predictions (on the training set for now), instead of calling the classifier's `predict()` method, you can run this code:

```
y_train_pred_90 = (y_scores >= threshold_for_90_precision)
```

Let's check these predictions' precision and recall:

```
>>> precision_score(y_train_5, y_train_pred_90)
0.9000345901072293
>>> recall_at_90_precision = recall_score(y_train_5, y_train_pred_90)
>>> recall_at_90_precision
0.4799852425751706
```

Great, you have a 90% precision classifier! As you can see, it is fairly easy to create a classifier with virtually any precision you want: just set a high enough threshold, and you're done. But wait, not so fast: a high-precision classifier is not very useful if its recall is too low! For many applications, 48% recall wouldn't be great at all.

If someone says, "Let's reach 99% precision", you should ask, "At what recall?"

Since Scikit-Learn 1.5, there are two new classes you can use to more easily adjust the decision threshold:

- The `FixedThresholdClassifier` class lets you wrap a binary classifier and set the desired threshold manually. If the underlying classifier has a `predict_proba()` method, then the threshold should be a value between 0 and 1 (the default is 0.5). Otherwise, it should be a decision score, comparable to the output of the model's `decision_function()` (the default is 0).
- The `TunedThresholdClassifierCV` class uses *k*-fold cross-validation to automatically find the optimal threshold for a given metric. By default, it tries to find the threshold that maximizes the model's *balanced accuracy*: that's the average of each class's recall. However, you can select another metric to optimize for (see the documentation for the full list of options).

The ROC Curve

The *receiver operating characteristic* (ROC) curve is another common tool used with binary classifiers. It is very similar to the precision/recall curve, but instead of plotting precision versus recall, the ROC curve plots the *true positive rate* (another name for recall) against the *false positive rate* (FPR). The FPR (also called the *fall-out*) is the ratio of negative instances that are incorrectly classified as positive. It is equal to 1 – the *true negative rate* (TNR), which is the ratio of negative instances that are correctly classified as negative. The TNR is also called *specificity*. Hence, the ROC curve plots *sensitivity* (recall) versus 1 – *specificity*.

To plot the ROC curve, you first use the `roc_curve()` function to compute the TPR and FPR for various threshold values:

```
from sklearn.metrics import roc_curve

fpr, tpr, thresholds = roc_curve(y_train_5, y_scores)
```

Then you can plot the FPR against the TPR using Matplotlib. The following code produces the plot in Figure 3-7. To find the point that corresponds to 90% precision, we need to look for the index of the desired threshold. Since thresholds are listed in decreasing order in this case, we use <= instead of >= on the first line:

```
idx_for_threshold_at_90 = (thresholds <= threshold_for_90_precision).argmax()
tpr_90, fpr_90 = tpr[idx_for_threshold_at_90], fpr[idx_for_threshold_at_90]

plt.plot(fpr, tpr, linewidth=2, label="ROC curve")
plt.plot([0, 1], [0, 1], 'k:', label="Random classifier's ROC curve")
plt.plot([fpr_90], [tpr_90], "ko", label="Threshold for 90% precision")
[...]  # beautify the figure: add labels, grid, legend, arrow, and text
plt.show()
```

Once again there is a trade-off: the higher the recall (TPR), the more false positives (FPR) the classifier produces. The dotted line represents the ROC curve of a purely random classifier; a good classifier stays as far away from that line as possible (toward the top-left corner).

One way to compare classifiers is to measure the *area under the curve* (AUC). A perfect classifier will have a ROC AUC equal to 1, whereas a purely random classifier will have a ROC AUC equal to 0.5. Scikit-Learn provides a function to estimate the ROC AUC:

```
>>> from sklearn.metrics import roc_auc_score
>>> roc_auc_score(y_train_5, y_scores)
np.float64(0.9604938554008616)
```

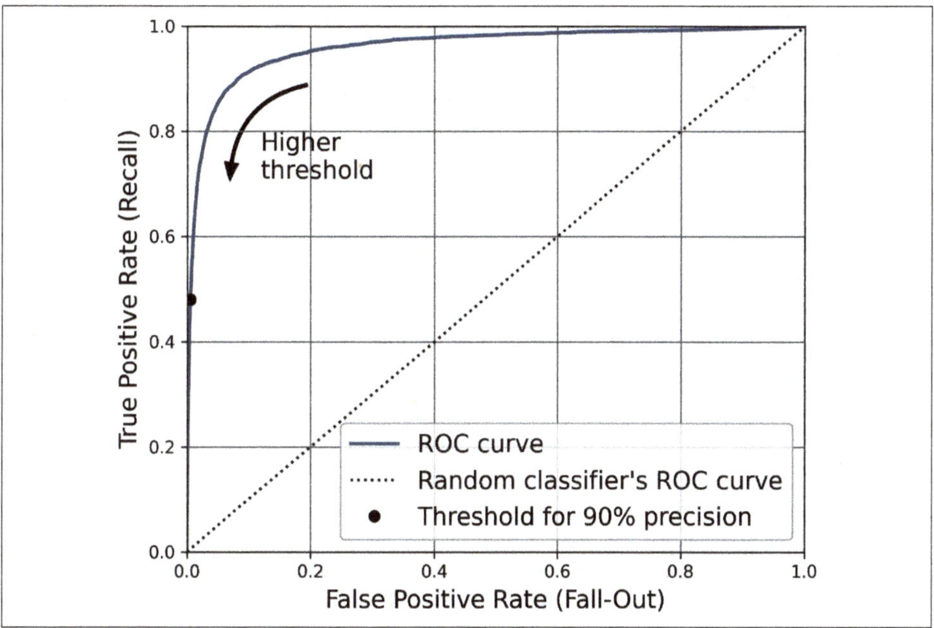

Figure 3-7. A ROC curve plotting the false positive rate against the true positive rate for all possible thresholds; the black circle highlights the chosen ratio (at 90% precision and 48% recall)

Since the ROC curve is so similar to the precision/recall (PR) curve, you may wonder how to decide which one to use. As a rule of thumb, you should prefer the PR curve whenever the positive class is rare or when you care more about the false positives than the false negatives. Otherwise, use the ROC curve. For example, looking at the previous ROC curve (and the ROC AUC score), you may think that the classifier is really good. But this is mostly because there are few positives (5s) compared to the negatives (non-5s). In contrast, the PR curve makes it clear that the classifier has room for improvement: the curve could really be closer to the top-right corner (see Figure 3-6 again).

Let's now create a `RandomForestClassifier`, whose PR curve and F_1 score we can compare to those of the `SGDClassifier`:

```
from sklearn.ensemble import RandomForestClassifier

forest_clf = RandomForestClassifier(random_state=42)
```

The `precision_recall_curve()` function expects labels and scores for each instance, so we need to train the random forest classifier and make it assign a score to each instance. But the RandomForestClassifier class does not have a decision_function() method, due to the way it works (we will cover this in Chapter 6). Luckily, it has a predict_proba() method that returns estimated class probabilities for each instance, and we can just use the probability of the positive class as a score, so precision_recall_curve() will work.[4] We can call the cross_val_predict() function to train the RandomForestClassifier using cross-validation and make it predict class probabilities for every image as follows:

```
y_probas_forest = cross_val_predict(forest_clf, X_train, y_train_5, cv=3,
                                    method="predict_proba")
```

Let's look at the estimated class probabilities for the first two images in the training set:

```
>>> y_probas_forest[:2]
array([[0.11, 0.89],
       [0.99, 0.01]])
```

The model predicts that the first image is positive with 89% probability, and it predicts that the second image is negative with 99% probability. Since each image is either positive or negative, the estimated probabilities in each row add up to 100%.

These are *estimated* probabilities, not actual probabilities. For example, if you look at all the images that the model classified as positive with an estimated probability between 50% and 60%, roughly 94% of them are actually positive. So, the model's estimated probabilities were much too low in this case—but models can be overconfident as well. The CalibratedClassifierCV class from the sklearn.calibration package can calibrate the estimated probabilities using cross-validation, making them much closer to actual probabilities (see the notebook for a code example). This is important in some scenarios, such as medical diagnosis, financial risk assessment, or fraud detection.

The second column contains the estimated probabilities for the positive class, so let's pass them to the precision_recall_curve() function:

```
y_scores_forest = y_probas_forest[:, 1]
precisions_forest, recalls_forest, thresholds_forest = precision_recall_curve(
    y_train_5, y_scores_forest)
```

Now we're ready to plot the PR curve. It is useful to plot the first PR curve as well to see how they compare (Figure 3-8):

4 Scikit-Learn classifiers always have either a decision_function() method or a predict_proba() method, or sometimes both.

```
plt.plot(recalls_forest, precisions_forest, "b-", linewidth=2,
         label="Random Forest")
plt.plot(recalls, precisions, "--", linewidth=2, label="SGD")
[...]  # beautify the figure: add labels, grid, and legend
plt.show()
```

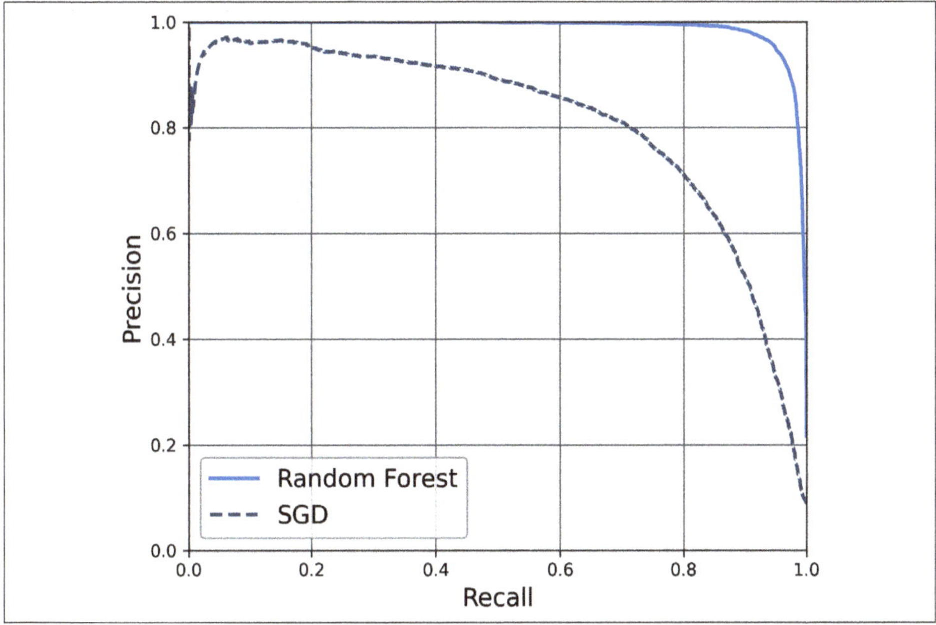

Figure 3-8. Comparing PR curves: the random forest classifier is superior to the SGD classifier because its PR curve is much closer to the top-right corner, and it has a greater AUC

As you can see in Figure 3-8, the `RandomForestClassifier`'s PR curve looks much better than the `SGDClassifier`'s: it comes much closer to the top-right corner. Its F_1 score and ROC AUC score are also significantly better:

```
>>> y_train_pred_forest = y_probas_forest[:, 1] >= 0.5  # positive proba ≥ 50%
>>> f1_score(y_train_5, y_train_pred_forest)
0.9274509803921569
>>> roc_auc_score(y_train_5, y_scores_forest)
0.9983436731328145
```

Try measuring the precision and recall scores: you should find about 99.0% precision and 87.3% recall. Not too bad!

You now know how to train binary classifiers, choose the appropriate metric for your task, evaluate your classifiers using cross-validation, select the precision/recall trade-off that fits your needs, and use several metrics and curves to compare various models. You're ready to try to detect more than just the 5s.

Multiclass Classification

Whereas binary classifiers distinguish between two classes, *multiclass classifiers* (also called *multinomial classifiers*) can distinguish between more than two classes.

Some Scikit-Learn classifiers (e.g., `LogisticRegression`, `RandomForestClassifier`, and `GaussianNB`) are capable of handling multiple classes natively. Others are strictly binary classifiers (e.g., `SGDClassifier` and `SVC`). However, there are various strategies that you can use to perform multiclass classification with multiple binary classifiers.

One way to create a system that can classify the digit images into 10 classes (from 0 to 9) is to train 10 binary classifiers, one for each digit (a 0-detector, a 1-detector, a 2-detector, and so on). Then when you want to classify an image, you get the decision score from each classifier for that image and you select the class whose classifier outputs the highest score. This is called the *one-versus-the-rest* (OvR) strategy, or sometimes *one-versus-all* (OvA).

Another strategy is to train a binary classifier for every pair of digits: one to distinguish 0s and 1s, another to distinguish 0s and 2s, another for 1s and 2s, and so on. This is called the *one-versus-one* (OvO) strategy. If there are N classes, you need to train $N \times (N - 1) / 2$ classifiers. For the MNIST problem, this means training 45 binary classifiers! When you want to classify an image, you have to run the image through all 45 classifiers and see which class wins the most duels. The main advantage of OvO is that each classifier only needs to be trained on the part of the training set containing the two classes that it must distinguish.

Some algorithms (such as support vector machine classifiers) scale poorly with the size of the training set. For these algorithms OvO is preferred because it is faster to train many classifiers on small training sets than to train few classifiers on large training sets. For most binary classification algorithms, however, OvR is preferred.

Scikit-Learn detects when you try to use a binary classification algorithm for a multiclass classification task, and it automatically runs OvR or OvO, depending on the algorithm. Let's try this with a support vector machine classifier using the `sklearn.svm.SVC` class (see the online chapter on SVMs at *https://homl.info*). We'll only train on the first 2,000 images, or else it will take a very long time:

```
from sklearn.svm import SVC

svm_clf = SVC(random_state=42)
svm_clf.fit(X_train[:2000], y_train[:2000])  # y_train, not y_train_5
```

That was easy! We trained the `SVC` using the original target classes from 0 to 9 (`y_train`), instead of the 5-versus-the-rest target classes (`y_train_5`). Since there are 10 classes (i.e., more than 2), Scikit-Learn used the OvO strategy and trained 45 binary classifiers. Now let's make a prediction on an image:

```
>>> svm_clf.predict([some_digit])
array(['5'], dtype=object)
```

That's correct! This code actually made 45 predictions—one per pair of classes—and it selected the class that won the most duels.[5] If you call the `decision_function()` method, you will see that it returns 10 scores per instance: one per class. Each class gets a score equal to the number of won duels plus or minus a small tweak (max ±0.33) to break ties, based on the classifier scores:

```
>>> some_digit_scores = svm_clf.decision_function([some_digit])
>>> some_digit_scores.round(2)
array([[ 3.79,  0.73,  6.06,  8.3 , -0.29,  9.3 ,  1.75,  2.77,  7.21,
         4.82]])
```

The highest score is 9.3, and it's indeed the one corresponding to class 5:

```
>>> class_id = some_digit_scores.argmax()
>>> class_id
np.int64(5)
```

When a classifier is trained, it stores the list of target classes in its `classes_` attribute, ordered by value. In the case of MNIST, the index of each class in the `classes_` array conveniently matches the class itself (e.g., the class at index 5 happens to be class `'5'`), but in general you won't be so lucky; you will need to look up the class label like this:

```
>>> svm_clf.classes_
array(['0', '1', '2', '3', '4', '5', '6', '7', '8', '9'], dtype=object)
>>> svm_clf.classes_[class_id]
'5'
```

If you want to force Scikit-Learn to use one-versus-one or one-versus-the-rest, you can use the `OneVsOneClassifier` or `OneVsRestClassifier` classes. Simply create an instance and pass a classifier to its constructor (it doesn't even have to be a binary classifier). For example, this code creates a multiclass classifier using the OvR strategy, based on an `SVC`:

```
from sklearn.multiclass import OneVsRestClassifier

ovr_clf = OneVsRestClassifier(SVC(random_state=42))
ovr_clf.fit(X_train[:2000], y_train[:2000])
```

Let's make a prediction, and check the number of trained classifiers:

```
>>> ovr_clf.predict([some_digit])
array(['5'], dtype='<U1')
>>> len(ovr_clf.estimators_)
10
```

5 In case of a tie, the first class is selected, unless you set the `break_ties` hyperparameters to `True`, in which case ties are broken using the output of the `decision_function()`.

Training an SGDClassifier on a multiclass dataset and using it to make predictions is just as easy:

```
>>> sgd_clf = SGDClassifier(random_state=42)
>>> sgd_clf.fit(X_train, y_train)
>>> sgd_clf.predict([some_digit])
array(['3'], dtype='<U1')
```

Oops, that's incorrect. Prediction errors do happen! This time Scikit-Learn used the OvR strategy under the hood: since there are 10 classes, it trained 10 binary classifiers. The decision_function() method now returns one value per class. Let's look at the scores that the SGD classifier assigned to each class:

```
>>> sgd_clf.decision_function([some_digit]).round()
array([[-31893., -34420.,  -9531.,   1824., -22320.,  -1386., -26189.,
        -16148.,  -4604., -12051.]])
```

You can see that the classifier is not very confident about its prediction: almost all scores are very negative, while class 3 has a score of +1,824, and class 5 is not too far behind at –1,386. Of course, you'll want to evaluate this classifier on more than one image. Since there are roughly the same number of images in each class, the accuracy metric is fine. As usual, you can use the cross_val_score() function to evaluate the model:

```
>>> cross_val_score(sgd_clf, X_train, y_train, cv=3, scoring="accuracy")
array([0.87365, 0.85835, 0.8689 ])
```

It gets over 85.8% on all test folds. If you used a random classifier, you would get 10% accuracy, so this is not such a bad score, but you can still do much better. Simply scaling the inputs (as discussed in Chapter 2) increases accuracy above 89.1%:

```
>>> from sklearn.preprocessing import StandardScaler
>>> scaler = StandardScaler()
>>> X_train_scaled = scaler.fit_transform(X_train.astype("float64"))
>>> cross_val_score(sgd_clf, X_train_scaled, y_train, cv=3, scoring="accuracy")
array([0.8983, 0.891 , 0.9018])
```

Error Analysis

If this were a real project, you would now follow the steps in your machine learning project checklist (see *https://homl.info/checklist*). You'd explore data preparation options, try out multiple models, shortlist the best ones, fine-tune their hyperparameters using GridSearchCV, and automate as much as possible. Here, we will assume that you have found a promising model and you want to find ways to improve it. One way to do this is to analyze the types of errors it makes.

First, look at the confusion matrix. For this, you first need to make predictions using the `cross_val_predict()` function; then you can pass the labels and predictions to the `confusion_matrix()` function, just like you did earlier. However, since there are now 10 classes instead of 2, the confusion matrix will contain quite a lot of numbers, and it may be hard to read.

A colored diagram of the confusion matrix is much easier to analyze. To plot such a diagram, use the `ConfusionMatrixDisplay.from_predictions()` function like this:

```
from sklearn.metrics import ConfusionMatrixDisplay

y_train_pred = cross_val_predict(sgd_clf, X_train_scaled, y_train, cv=3)
ConfusionMatrixDisplay.from_predictions(y_train, y_train_pred)
plt.show()
```

This produces the left diagram in Figure 3-9. This confusion matrix looks pretty good: most images are on the main diagonal, which means that they were classified correctly. Notice that the cell on the diagonal in row #5 and column #5 looks slightly darker than the other digits. This could be because the model made more errors on 5s, or because there are fewer 5s in the dataset than the other digits. That's why it's important to normalize the confusion matrix by dividing each value by the total number of images in the corresponding (true) class (i.e., divide by the row's sum). This can be done simply by setting `normalize="true"`. We can also specify the `values_format=".0%"` argument to show percentages with no decimals. The following code produces the diagram on the right in Figure 3-9:

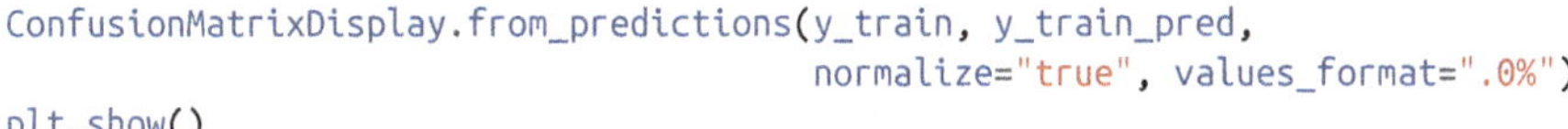

```
ConfusionMatrixDisplay.from_predictions(y_train, y_train_pred,
                                        normalize="true", values_format=".0%")
plt.show()
```

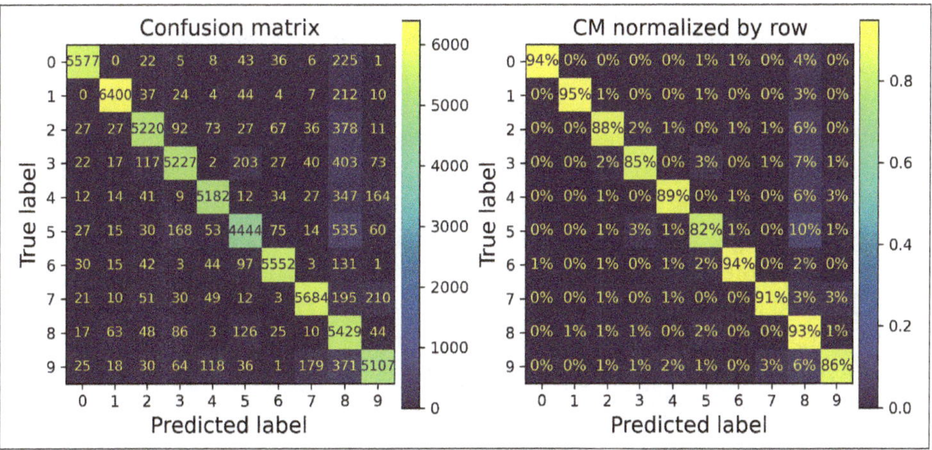

Figure 3-9. Confusion matrix (left) and the same CM normalized by row (right)

Now we can easily see that only 82% of the images of 5s were classified correctly. The most common error the model made with images of 5s was to misclassify them as 8s: this happened for 10% of all 5s. But only 2% of 8s got misclassified as 5s; confusion matrices are generally not symmetrical! If you look carefully, you will notice that many digits have been misclassified as 8s, but this is not immediately obvious from this diagram. If you want to make the errors stand out more, you can try putting zero weight on the correct predictions. The following code does just that and produces the diagram on the left in Figure 3-10:

```
sample_weight = (y_train_pred != y_train)
ConfusionMatrixDisplay.from_predictions(y_train, y_train_pred,
                                        sample_weight=sample_weight,
                                        normalize="true", values_format=".0%")
plt.show()
```

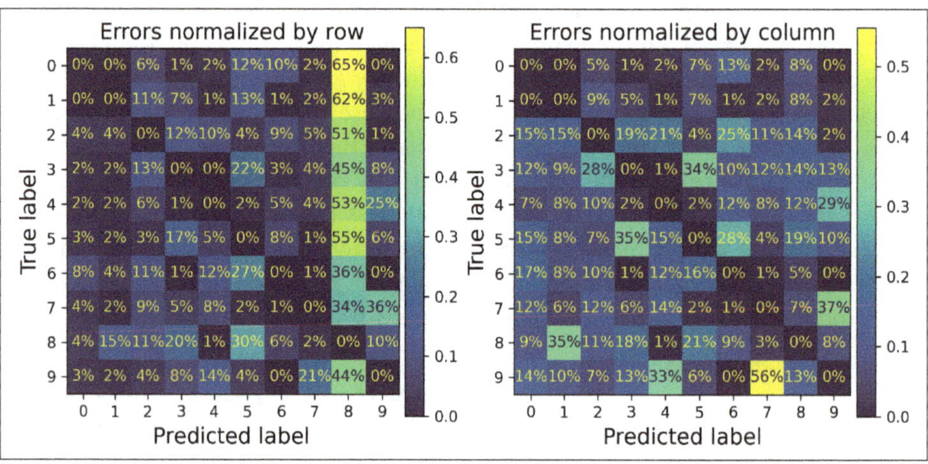

Figure 3-10. Confusion matrix with errors only, normalized by row (left) and by column (right)

Now you can see much more clearly the kinds of errors the classifier makes. The column for class 8 is now really bright, which confirms that many images got misclassified as 8s. In fact this is the most common misclassification for almost all classes. But be careful how you interpret the percentages in this diagram: remember that we've excluded the correct predictions. For example, the 36% in row #7, column #9 in the left grid does *not* mean that 36% of all images of 7s were misclassified as 9s. It means that 36% of the *errors* the model made on images of 7s were misclassifications as 9s. In reality, only 3% of images of 7s were misclassified as 9s, as you can see in the diagram on the right in Figure 3-9.

It is also possible to normalize the confusion matrix by column rather than by row: if you set `normalize="pred"`, you get the diagram on the right in Figure 3-10. For example, you can see that 56% of misclassified 7s are actually 9s.

Analyzing the confusion matrix often gives you insights into ways to improve your classifier. Looking at these plots, it seems that your efforts should be spent on reducing the false 8s. For example, you could try to gather more training data for digits that look like 8s (but are not) so that the classifier can learn to distinguish them from real 8s. Or you could engineer new features that would help the classifier—for example, writing an algorithm to count the number of closed loops (e.g., 8 has two, 6 has one, 5 has none). Or you could preprocess the images (e.g., using Scikit-Image, Pillow, or OpenCV) to make some patterns, such as closed loops, stand out more.

Analyzing individual errors can also be a good way to gain insights into what your classifier is doing and why it is failing. For example, let's plot examples of 3s and 5s in a confusion matrix style (Figure 3-11):

```
cl_a, cl_b = '3', '5'
X_aa = X_train[(y_train == cl_a) & (y_train_pred == cl_a)]
X_ab = X_train[(y_train == cl_a) & (y_train_pred == cl_b)]
X_ba = X_train[(y_train == cl_b) & (y_train_pred == cl_a)]
X_bb = X_train[(y_train == cl_b) & (y_train_pred == cl_b)]
[...]  # plot all images in X_aa, X_ab, X_ba, X_bb in a confusion matrix style
```

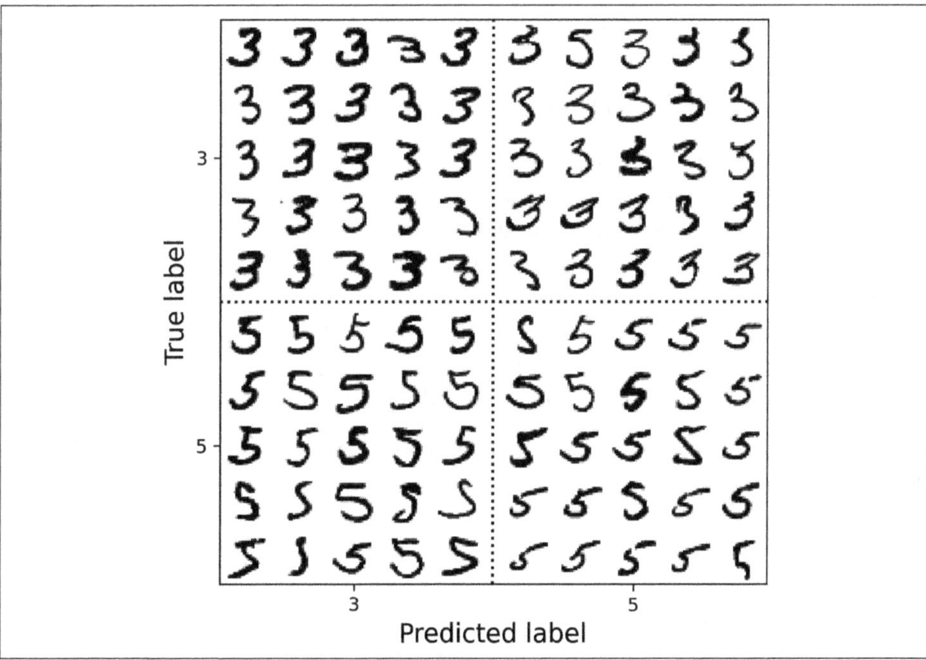

Figure 3-11. Some images of 3s and 5s organized like a confusion matrix

As you can see, some of the digits that the classifier gets wrong (i.e., in the bottom-left and top-right blocks) are so badly written that even a human would have trouble classifying them. However, most misclassified images seem like obvious errors to us.

It may be hard to understand why the classifier made the mistakes it did, but remember that the human brain is a fantastic pattern recognition system, and our visual system does a lot of complex preprocessing before any information even reaches our consciousness. So, the fact that this task feels simple does not mean that it is. Recall that we used a simple `SGDClassifier`, which is just a linear model: all it does is assign a weight per class to each pixel, and when it sees a new image it just sums up the weighted pixel intensities to get a score for each class. Since 3s and 5s differ by only a few pixels, this model will easily confuse them.

The main difference between 3s and 5s is the position of the small line that joins the top line to the bottom arc. If you draw a 3 with the junction slightly shifted to the left, the classifier might classify it as a 5, and vice versa. In other words, this classifier is quite sensitive to image shifting and rotation. One way to reduce the 3/5 confusion is to preprocess the images to ensure that they are well centered and not too rotated. However, this may not be easy since it requires predicting the correct rotation of each image. A much simpler approach consists of augmenting the training set with slightly shifted and rotated variants of the training images. This will force the model to learn to be more tolerant to such variations. This is called *data augmentation* (we'll cover this in Chapter 12; also see exercise 2 at the end of this chapter).

Multilabel Classification

Until now, each instance has always been assigned to just one class. But in some cases you may want your classifier to output multiple classes for each instance. Consider a face-recognition classifier: what should it do if it recognizes several people in the same picture? It should attach one tag per person it recognizes. Say the classifier has been trained to recognize three faces: Alice, Bob, and Charlie. Then when the classifier is shown a picture of Alice and Charlie, it should output `[True, False, True]` (meaning "Alice yes, Bob no, Charlie yes"). Such a classification system that outputs multiple binary tags is called a *multilabel classification* system.

We won't go into face recognition just yet, but let's look at a simpler example, just for illustration purposes:

```
import numpy as np
from sklearn.neighbors import KNeighborsClassifier

y_train_large = (y_train >= '7')
y_train_odd = (y_train.astype('int8') % 2 == 1)
y_multilabel = np.c_[y_train_large, y_train_odd]

knn_clf = KNeighborsClassifier()
knn_clf.fit(X_train, y_multilabel)
```

This code creates a `y_multilabel` array containing two target labels for each digit image: the first indicates whether the digit is large (7, 8, or 9), and the second indicates whether it is odd. Then the code creates a KNeighborsClassifier instance, which supports multilabel classification (not all classifiers do), and trains this model using the multiple targets array. Now you can make a prediction, and notice that it outputs two labels:

```
>>> knn_clf.predict([some_digit])
array([[False,  True]])
```

And it gets it right! The digit 5 is indeed not large (False) and odd (True).

There are many ways to evaluate a multilabel classifier, and selecting the right metric really depends on your project. One approach is to measure the F_1 score for each individual label (or any other binary classifier metric discussed earlier), then simply compute the average score. The following code computes the average F_1 score across all labels:

```
>>> y_train_knn_pred = cross_val_predict(knn_clf, X_train, y_multilabel, cv=3)
>>> f1_score(y_multilabel, y_train_knn_pred, average="macro")
0.976410265560605
```

This approach assumes that all labels are equally important, which may not be the case. In particular, if you have many more pictures of Alice than of Bob or Charlie, you may want to give more weight to the classifier's score on pictures of Alice. One simple option is to give each label a weight equal to its *support* (i.e., the number of instances with that target label). To do this, simply set average="weighted" when calling the f1_score() function.[6]

If you wish to use a classifier that does not natively support multilabel classification, such as SVC, one possible strategy is to train one model per label. However, this strategy may have a hard time capturing the dependencies between the labels. For example, a large digit (7, 8, or 9) is twice more likely to be odd than even, but the classifier for the "odd" label does not know what the classifier for the "large" label predicted. To solve this issue, the models can be organized in a chain: when a model makes a prediction, it uses the input features plus all the predictions of the models that come before it in the chain.

The good news is that Scikit-Learn has a class called ClassifierChain that does just that! By default it will use the true labels for training, feeding each model the appropriate labels depending on their position in the chain. But if you set the cv hyperparameter, it will use cross-validation to get "clean" (out-of-sample) predictions from each trained model for every instance in the training set, and these predictions will then be used to train all the models later in the chain. Note that the order of the classifiers in the chain may affect the final performance. Here's an example showing

6 Scikit-Learn offers a few other averaging options and multilabel classifier metrics; see the documentation for more details.

how to create and train a `ClassifierChain` using the cross-validation strategy. As earlier, we'll just use the first 2,000 images in the training set to speed things up:

```
from sklearn.multioutput import ClassifierChain

chain_clf = ClassifierChain(SVC(), cv=3, random_state=42)
chain_clf.fit(X_train[:2000], y_multilabel[:2000])
```

Now we can use this `ClassifierChain` to make predictions:

```
>>> chain_clf.predict([some_digit])
array([[0., 1.]])
```

Multioutput Classification

The last type of classification task we'll discuss here is called *multioutput–multiclass classification* (or just *multioutput classification*). It is a generalization of multilabel classification where each label can be multiclass (i.e., it can have more than two possible values).

To illustrate this, let's build a system that removes noise from images. It will take as input a noisy digit image, and it will (hopefully) output a clean digit image, represented as an array of pixel intensities, just like the MNIST images. Notice that the classifier's output is multilabel (one label per pixel) and each label can have multiple values (pixel intensity ranges from 0 to 255). This is thus an example of a multioutput classification system.

The line between classification and regression is sometimes blurry, such as in this example. Arguably, predicting pixel intensity is more akin to regression than to classification. Moreover, multioutput systems are not limited to classification tasks; you could even have a system that outputs multiple labels per instance, including both class labels and value labels.

Let's start by creating the training and test sets by taking the MNIST images and adding noise to their pixel intensities, using a random number generator's `integers()` method. The target images will be the original images:

```
rng = np.random.default_rng(seed=42)
noise_train = rng.integers(0, 100, (len(X_train), 784))
X_train_mod = X_train + noise_train
noise_test = rng.integers(0, 100, (len(X_test), 784))
X_test_mod = X_test + noise_test
y_train_mod = X_train
y_test_mod = X_test
```

Let's take a peek at the first image from the test set (Figure 3-12). Yes, we're snooping on the test data, so you should be frowning right now.

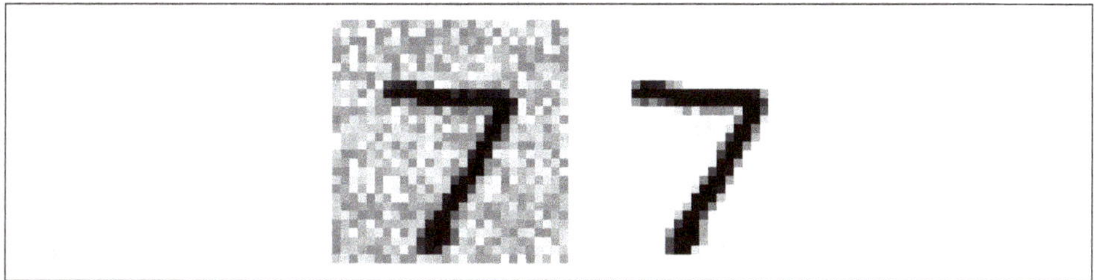

Figure 3-12. A noisy image (left) and the target clean image (right)

On the left is the noisy input image, and on the right is the clean target image. Now let's train the classifier and make it clean up this image (Figure 3-13):

```
knn_clf = KNeighborsClassifier()
knn_clf.fit(X_train_mod, y_train_mod)
clean_digit = knn_clf.predict([X_test_mod[0]])
plot_digit(clean_digit)
plt.show()
```

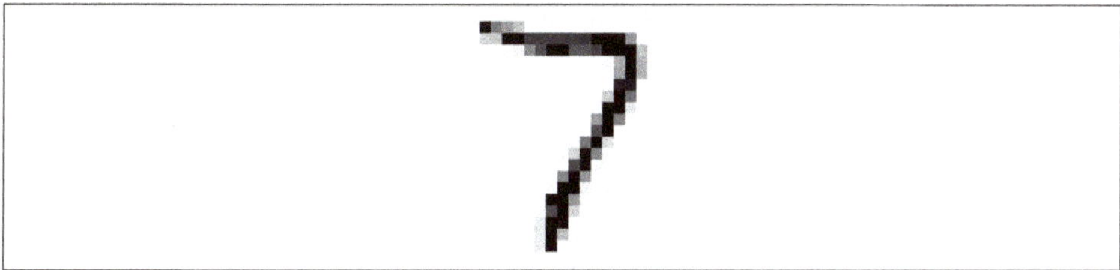

Figure 3-13. The cleaned-up image

Looks close enough to the target! This concludes our tour of classification. You now know how to select good metrics for classification tasks, pick the appropriate precision/recall trade-off, compare classifiers, and more generally build good classification systems for a variety of tasks. In the next chapters, you'll learn how all these machine learning models you've been using actually work.

Exercises

1. Try to build a classifier for the MNIST dataset that achieves over 97% accuracy on the test set. Hint: the `KNeighborsClassifier` works quite well for this task; you just need to find good hyperparameter values (try a grid search on the `weights` and `n_neighbors` hyperparameters).

2. Write a function that can shift an MNIST image in any direction (left, right, up, or down) by one pixel.[7] Then, for each image in the training set, create four shifted copies (one per direction) and add them to the training set. Finally, train your best model on this expanded training set and measure its accuracy on the test set. You should observe that your model performs even better now! This technique of artificially growing the training set is called *data augmentation* or *training set expansion*.

3. Tackle the Titanic dataset. A great place to start is on Kaggle (*https://kaggle.com/c/titanic*). Alternatively, you can download the data from *https://homl.info/titanic.tgz* and unzip this tarball like you did for the housing data in Chapter 2. This will give you two CSV files, *train.csv* and *test.csv*, which you can load using `pandas.read_csv()`. The goal is to train a classifier that can predict the `Survived` column based on the other columns.

4. Build a spam classifier (a more challenging exercise):

   a. Download examples of spam and ham from Apache SpamAssassin's public datasets (*https://homl.info/spamassassin*).

   b. Unzip the datasets and familiarize yourself with the data format.

   c. Split the data into a training set and a test set.

   d. Write a data preparation pipeline to convert each email into a feature vector. Your preparation pipeline should transform an email into a (sparse) vector that indicates the presence or absence of each possible word. For example, if all emails only ever contain four words, "Hello", "how", "are", "you", then the email "Hello you Hello Hello you" would be converted into a vector [1, 0, 0, 1] (meaning ["Hello" is present, "how" is absent, "are" is absent, "you" is present]), or [3, 0, 0, 2] if you prefer to count the number of occurrences of each word.

      You may want to add hyperparameters to your preparation pipeline to control whether to strip off email headers, convert each email to lowercase, remove punctuation, replace all URLs with "URL", replace all numbers with "NUMBER", or even perform *stemming* (i.e., trim off word endings; there are Python libraries available to do this).

   e. Finally, try out several classifiers and see if you can build a great spam classifier, with both high recall and high precision.

Solutions to these exercises are available at the end of this chapter's notebook, at *https://homl.info/colab-p*.

---

7 You can use the `shift()` function from the `scipy.ndimage.interpolation` module. For example, `shift(image, [2, 1], cval=0)` shifts the image two pixels down and one pixel to the right.

CHAPTER 4

Training Models

So far we have treated machine learning models and their training algorithms mostly like black boxes. If you went through some of the exercises in the previous chapters, you may have been surprised by how much you can get done without knowing anything about what's under the hood: you optimized a regression system, you improved a digit image classifier, and you even built a spam classifier from scratch, all without knowing how they actually work. Indeed, in many situations you don't really need to know the implementation details.

However, having a good understanding of how things work can help you quickly home in on the appropriate model, the right training algorithm to use, and a good set of hyperparameters for your task. Understanding what's under the hood will also help you debug issues and perform error analysis more efficiently. Lastly, most of the topics discussed in this chapter will be essential in understanding, building, and training neural networks (discussed in Part II of this book).

In this chapter we will start by looking at the linear regression model, one of the simplest models there is. We will discuss two very different ways to train it:

- Using a "closed-form" equation[1] that directly computes the model parameters that best fit the model to the training set (i.e., the model parameters that minimize the cost function over the training set).
- Using an iterative optimization approach called gradient descent (GD) that gradually tweaks the model parameters to minimize the cost function over the training set, eventually converging to the same set of parameters as the first method. We will look at a few variants of gradient descent that we will use again and

1 A closed-form equation is only composed of a finite number of constants, variables, and standard operations: for example, $a = \sin(b - c)$. No infinite sums, no limits, no integrals, etc.

again when we study neural networks in Part II: batch GD, mini-batch GD, and stochastic GD.

Next we will look at polynomial regression, a more complex model that can fit nonlinear datasets. Since this model has more parameters than linear regression, it is more prone to overfitting the training data. We will explore how to detect whether this is the case using learning curves, and then we will look at several regularization techniques that can reduce the risk of overfitting the training set.

Finally, we will examine two more models that are commonly used for classification tasks: logistic regression and softmax regression.

There will be quite a few math equations in this chapter using basic concepts of linear algebra and calculus. To understand these equations, you need to be familiar with vectors and matrices—how to transpose them, multiply them, and invert them—as well as partial derivatives. If these concepts are unfamiliar, please review the introductory Jupyter notebooks on linear algebra and calculus provided in the online supplemental material (*https://github.com/ageron/handson-mlp*). If you are truly allergic to math, you can just skip the equations; the text should still help you grasp most of the concepts. That said, learning the mathematical formalism is extremely useful, as it will allow you to read ML papers. Although it may seem daunting at first, it's actually not that hard, and this chapter includes code that should help you make sense of the equations.

Linear Regression

In Chapter 1 we looked at a simple linear model of life satisfaction (Equation 4-1).

Equation 4-1. A simple linear model of life satisfaction

$$\text{life\_satisfaction} = \theta_0 + \theta_1 \times \text{GDP\_per\_capita}$$

This model is just a linear function of the input feature `GDP_per_capita`. θ_0 and θ_1 are the model's parameters.

More generally, a linear model makes a prediction by simply computing a weighted sum of the input features, plus a constant called the *bias term* (also called the *intercept term*), as shown in Equation 4-2.

Equation 4-2. Linear regression model prediction

$$\hat{y} = \theta_0 + \theta_1 x_1 + \theta_2 x_2 + \cdots + \theta_n x_n$$

In this equation:

- $\hat{y}$ is the predicted value.
- n is the number of features.
- x_i is the ith feature value.
- θ_j is the jth model parameter, including the bias term θ_0 and the feature weights θ_1, θ_2, $\cdots$, θ_n.

This can be written much more concisely using a vectorized form, as shown in Equation 4-3.

Equation 4-3. Linear regression model prediction (vectorized form)

$$\hat{y} = h_{\boldsymbol{\theta}}(\mathbf{x}) = \boldsymbol{\theta} \cdot \mathbf{x}$$

In this equation:

- $h_{\boldsymbol{\theta}}$ is the hypothesis function, using the model parameters $\boldsymbol{\theta}$.
- $\boldsymbol{\theta}$ is the model's *parameter vector*, containing the bias term θ_0 and the feature weights θ_1 to θ_n.
- $\mathbf{x}$ is the instance's *feature vector*, containing x_0 to x_n, with x_0 always equal to 1.
- $\boldsymbol{\theta} \cdot \mathbf{x}$ is the dot product of the vectors $\boldsymbol{\theta}$ and $\mathbf{x}$, which is equal to $\theta_0 x_0 + \theta_1 x_1 + \theta_2 x_2 + \ldots + \theta_n x_n$.

In machine learning, vectors are often represented as *column vectors*, which are 2D arrays with a single column. If $\boldsymbol{\theta}$ and $\mathbf{x}$ are column vectors, then the prediction is $\hat{y} = \boldsymbol{\theta}^\mathsf{T}\mathbf{x}$, where $\boldsymbol{\theta}^\mathsf{T}$ is the *transpose* of $\boldsymbol{\theta}$ (a row vector instead of a column vector) and $\boldsymbol{\theta}^\mathsf{T}\mathbf{x}$ is the matrix multiplication of $\boldsymbol{\theta}^\mathsf{T}$ and $\mathbf{x}$. It is of course the same prediction, except that it is now represented as a single-cell matrix rather than a scalar value. In this book I will use this notation to avoid switching between dot products and matrix multiplications.

OK, that's the linear regression model—but how do we train it? Well, recall that training a model means setting its parameters so that the model best fits the training set. For this purpose, we first need a measure of how well (or poorly) the model fits the training data. In Chapter 2 we saw that the most common performance measure of a regression model is the root mean squared error (Equation 2-1). Therefore, to train a linear regression model, we need to find the value of $\boldsymbol{\theta}$ that minimizes the RMSE. In practice, it is simpler to minimize the mean squared error (MSE) than the

RMSE, and it leads to the same result (because the value that minimizes a positive function also minimizes its square root).

Learning algorithms will often optimize a different loss function during training than the performance measure used to evaluate the final model. This is generally because the function is easier to optimize and/or because it has extra terms needed during training only (e.g., for regularization). A good performance metric is as close as possible to the final business objective. A good training loss is easy to optimize and strongly correlated with the metric. For example, classifiers are often trained using a cost function such as the log loss (as you will see later in this chapter) but evaluated using precision/recall. The log loss is easy to minimize, and doing so will usually improve precision/recall.

The MSE of a linear regression hypothesis $h_{\boldsymbol{\theta}}$ on a training set $\mathbf{X}$ is calculated using Equation 4-4.

Equation 4-4. MSE cost function for a linear regression model

$$\text{MSE}(\mathbf{X},\mathbf{y},h_{\boldsymbol{\theta}}) = \frac{1}{m}\sum_{i=1}^{m}\left(\boldsymbol{\theta}^{\intercal}\mathbf{x}^{(i)} - y^{(i)}\right)^2$$

Most of these notations were presented in Chapter 2 (see "Notations" on page 45). The only difference is that we write $h_{\boldsymbol{\theta}}$ instead of just h to make it clear that the model is parametrized by the vector $\boldsymbol{\theta}$. To simplify notations, we will just write MSE($\boldsymbol{\theta}$) instead of MSE($\mathbf{X}$, $h_{\boldsymbol{\theta}}$).

The Normal Equation

To find the value of $\boldsymbol{\theta}$ that minimizes the MSE, there exists a *closed-form solution*—in other words, a mathematical equation that gives the result directly. This is called the *normal equation* (Equation 4-5).

Equation 4-5. Normal equation

$$\hat{\boldsymbol{\theta}} = \left(\mathbf{X}^{\intercal}\mathbf{X}\right)^{-1}\mathbf{X}^{\intercal}\mathbf{y}$$

In this equation:

- $\hat{\boldsymbol{\theta}}$ is the value of $\boldsymbol{\theta}$ that minimizes the cost function.
- $\mathbf{y}$ is the vector of target values containing $y^{(1)}$ to $y^{(m)}$.

Let's generate some linear-looking data to test this equation on (Figure 4-1):

```
import numpy as np

rng = np.random.default_rng(seed=42)
m = 200  # number of instances
X = 2 * rng.random((m, 1))  # column vector
y = 4 + 3 * X + rng.standard_normal((m, 1))  # column vector
```

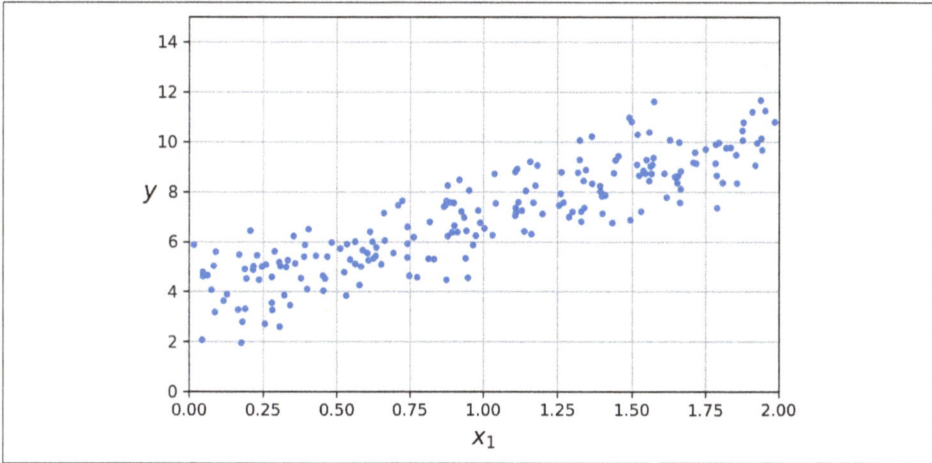

Figure 4-1. A randomly generated linear dataset

Now let's compute $\widehat{\theta}$ using the normal equation. We will use the `inv()` function from NumPy's linear algebra module (`np.linalg`) to compute the inverse of a matrix, and the `@` operator for matrix multiplication:

```
from sklearn.preprocessing import add_dummy_feature

X_b = add_dummy_feature(X)  # add x0 = 1 to each instance
theta_best = np.linalg.inv(X_b.T @ X_b) @ X_b.T @ y
```

The `@` operator performs matrix multiplication. If `A` and `B` are NumPy arrays, then `A @ B` is equivalent to `np.matmul(A, B)`. Many other libraries, like TensorFlow, PyTorch, and JAX, support the `@` operator as well. However, you cannot use `@` on pure Python arrays (i.e., lists of lists).

The function that we used to generate the data is $y = 4 + 3x_1$ + Gaussian noise. Let's see what the equation found:

```
>>> theta_best
array([[3.69084138],
       [3.32960458]])
```

We would have hoped for $\theta_0 = 4$ and $\theta_1 = 3$ instead of $\theta_0 = 3.6908$ and $\theta_1 = 3.3296$. Close enough, but the noise made it impossible to recover the exact parameters of the original function. The smaller and noisier the dataset, the harder it gets.

Now we can make predictions using $\widehat{\boldsymbol{\theta}}$:

```
>>> X_new = np.array([[0], [2]])
>>> X_new_b = add_dummy_feature(X_new)  # add x0 = 1 to each instance
>>> y_predict = X_new_b @ theta_best
>>> y_predict
array([[ 3.69084138],
       [10.35005055]])
```

Let's plot this model's predictions (Figure 4-2):

```
import matplotlib.pyplot as plt

plt.plot(X_new, y_predict, "r-", label="Predictions")
plt.plot(X, y, "b.")
[...]  # beautify the figure: add labels, axis, grid, and legend
plt.show()
```

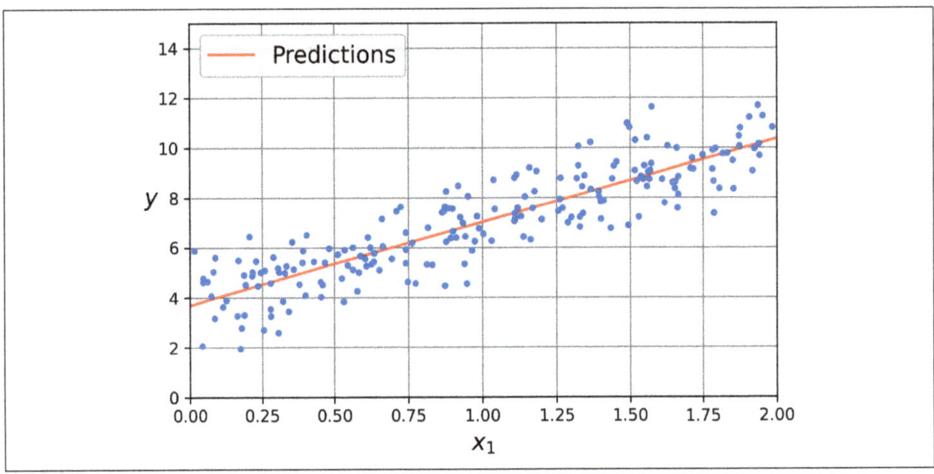

Figure 4-2. Linear regression model predictions

Performing linear regression using Scikit-Learn is relatively straightforward:

```
>>> from sklearn.linear_model import LinearRegression
>>> lin_reg = LinearRegression()
>>> lin_reg.fit(X, y)
>>> lin_reg.intercept_, lin_reg.coef_
(array([3.69084138]), array([[3.32960458]]))
>>> lin_reg.predict(X_new)
array([[ 3.69084138],
       [10.35005055]])
```

Notice that Scikit-Learn separates the bias term (`intercept_`) from the feature weights (`coef_`). The `LinearRegression` class is based on the `scipy.linalg.lstsq()` function (the name stands for "least squares"), which you could call directly:

```
>>> theta_best_svd, residuals, rank, s = np.linalg.lstsq(X_b, y, rcond=1e-6)
>>> theta_best_svd
array([[3.69084138],
       [3.32960458]])
```

This function computes $\hat{\boldsymbol{\theta}} = \mathbf{X}^{+}\mathbf{y}$, where $\mathbf{X}^{+}$ is the *pseudoinverse* of $\mathbf{X}$ (specifically, the Moore–Penrose inverse). You can use `np.linalg.pinv()` to compute the pseudoinverse directly:

```
>>> np.linalg.pinv(X_b) @ y
array([[3.69084138],
       [3.32960458]])
```

The pseudoinverse itself is computed using a standard matrix factorization technique called *singular value decomposition* (SVD) that can decompose the training set matrix $\mathbf{X}$ into the matrix multiplication of three matrices $\mathbf{U}\ \boldsymbol{\Sigma}\ \mathbf{V}^{\intercal}$ (see `numpy.linalg.svd()`). The pseudoinverse is computed as $\mathbf{X}^{+} = \mathbf{V}\boldsymbol{\Sigma}^{+}\mathbf{U}^{\intercal}$. To compute the matrix $\boldsymbol{\Sigma}^{+}$, the algorithm takes $\boldsymbol{\Sigma}$ and sets to zero all values smaller than a tiny threshold value, then it replaces all the nonzero values with their inverse, and finally it transposes the resulting matrix. This approach is more efficient than computing the normal equation, plus it handles edge cases nicely: indeed, the normal equation may not work if the matrix $\mathbf{X}^{\intercal}\mathbf{X}$ is not invertible (i.e., singular), such as if $m < n$ or if some features are redundant, but the pseudoinverse is always defined.

Computational Complexity

The normal equation computes the inverse of $\mathbf{X}^{\intercal}\ \mathbf{X}$, which is an $(n + 1) \times (n + 1)$ matrix (where n is the number of features). The *computational complexity* of inverting such a matrix is typically about $O(n^{2.4})$ to $O(n^3)$, depending on the implementation. In other words, if you double the number of features, you multiply the computation time by roughly $2^{2.4} = 5.3$ to $2^3 = 8$.

The SVD approach used by Scikit-Learn's `LinearRegression` class is about $O(n^2)$. If you double the number of features, you multiply the computation time by roughly 4.

Both the normal equation and the SVD approach get very slow when the number of features grows large (e.g., 100,000). On the positive side, both are linear with regard to the number of instances in the training set (they are $O(m)$), so they handle large training sets efficiently, provided they can fit in memory.

Also, once you have trained your linear regression model (using the normal equation or any other algorithm), predictions are very fast: the computational complexity is linear with regard to both the number of instances you want to make predictions on and the number of features. In other words, making predictions on twice as many instances (or twice as many features) will take roughly twice as much time.

Now we will look at a very different way to train a linear regression model, which is better suited for cases where there are a large number of features or too many training instances to fit in memory.

Gradient Descent

Gradient descent is a generic optimization algorithm capable of finding optimal solutions to a wide range of problems. The general idea of gradient descent is to tweak parameters iteratively in order to minimize a cost function.

Suppose you are lost in the mountains in a dense fog, and you can only feel the slope of the ground below your feet. A good strategy to get to the bottom of the valley quickly is to go downhill in the direction of the steepest slope. This is exactly what gradient descent does: it measures the local gradient of the error function with regard to the parameter vector $\boldsymbol{\theta}$, and it goes in the direction of descending gradient. Once the gradient is zero, you have reached a minimum!

In practice, you start by filling $\boldsymbol{\theta}$ with random values (this is called *random initialization*). Then you improve it gradually, taking one baby step at a time, each step attempting to decrease the cost function (e.g., the MSE), until the algorithm *converges* to a minimum (see Figure 4-3).

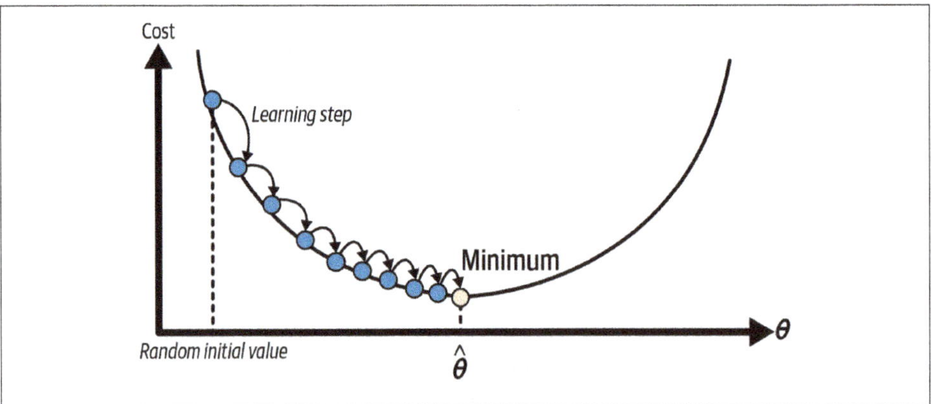

Figure 4-3. In this depiction of gradient descent, the model parameters are initialized randomly and get tweaked repeatedly to minimize the cost function; the learning step size is proportional to the slope of the cost function, so the steps gradually get smaller as the cost approaches the minimum

An important parameter in gradient descent is the size of the steps, determined by the *learning rate* hyperparameter. If the learning rate is too small, then the algorithm will have to go through many iterations to converge, which will take a long time (see Figure 4-4).

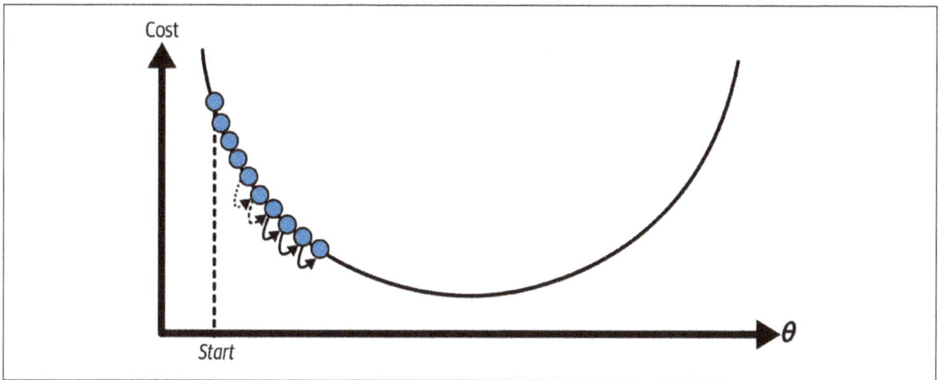

Figure 4-4. Learning rate too small

On the other hand, if the learning rate is too high, you might jump across the valley and end up on the other side, possibly even higher up than you were before. This might make the algorithm diverge, with larger and larger values, failing to find a good solution (see Figure 4-5).

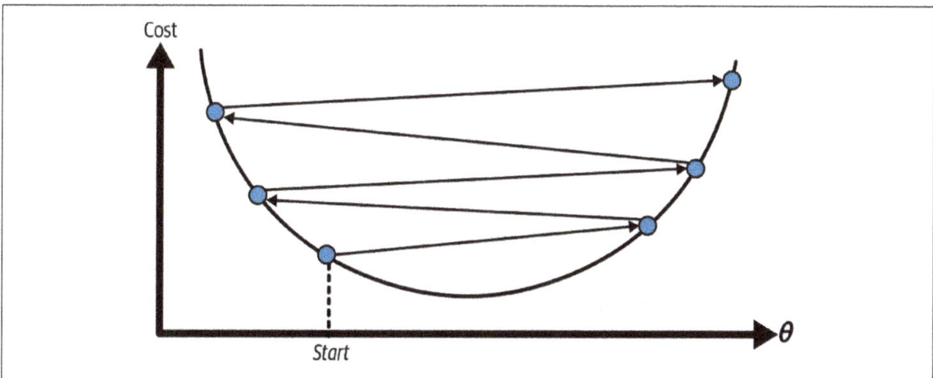

Figure 4-5. Learning rate too high

Additionally, not all cost functions look like nice, regular bowls. There may be holes, ridges, plateaus, and all sorts of irregular terrain, making convergence to the minimum difficult. Figure 4-6 shows the two main challenges with gradient descent. If the random initialization starts the algorithm on the left, then it will converge to a *local minimum*, which is not as good as the *global minimum*. If it starts on the right, then it will take a very long time to cross the plateau. And if you stop too early, you will never reach the global minimum.

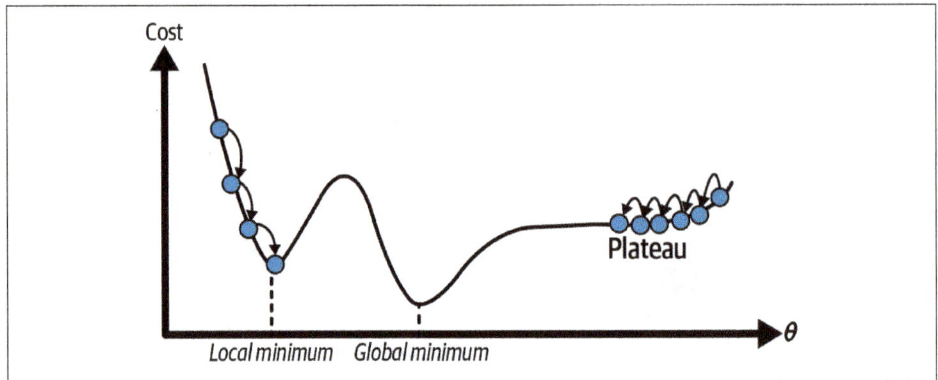

Figure 4-6. Gradient descent pitfalls

Fortunately, the MSE cost function for a linear regression model happens to be a *convex function*, which means that if you pick any two points on the curve, the line segment joining them is never below the curve. This implies that there are no local minima, just one global minimum. It is also a continuous function with a slope that never changes abruptly.[2] These two facts have a great consequence: gradient descent is guaranteed to approach arbitrarily closely the global minimum (if you wait long enough and if the learning rate is not too high).

While the cost function has the shape of a bowl, it can be an elongated bowl if the features have very different scales. Figure 4-7 shows gradient descent on a training set where features 1 and 2 have the same scale (on the left), and on a training set where feature 1 has much smaller values than feature 2 (on the right).[3]

As you can see, on the left the gradient descent algorithm goes straight toward the minimum, thereby reaching it quickly, whereas on the right it first goes in a direction almost orthogonal to the direction of the global minimum, and it ends with a long march down an almost flat valley. It will eventually reach the minimum, but it will take a long time.

This diagram also illustrates the fact that training a model means searching for a combination of model parameters that minimizes a cost function (over the training set). It is a search in the model's *parameter space*. The more parameters a model has, the more dimensions this space has, and the harder the search is: searching

2 Technically speaking, its derivative is *Lipschitz continuous*.

3 Since feature 1 is smaller, it takes a larger change in θ_1 to affect the cost function, which is why the bowl is elongated along the θ_1 axis.

for a needle in a 300-dimensional haystack is much trickier than in 3 dimensions. Fortunately, since the cost function is convex in the case of linear regression, the needle is simply at the bottom of the bowl.

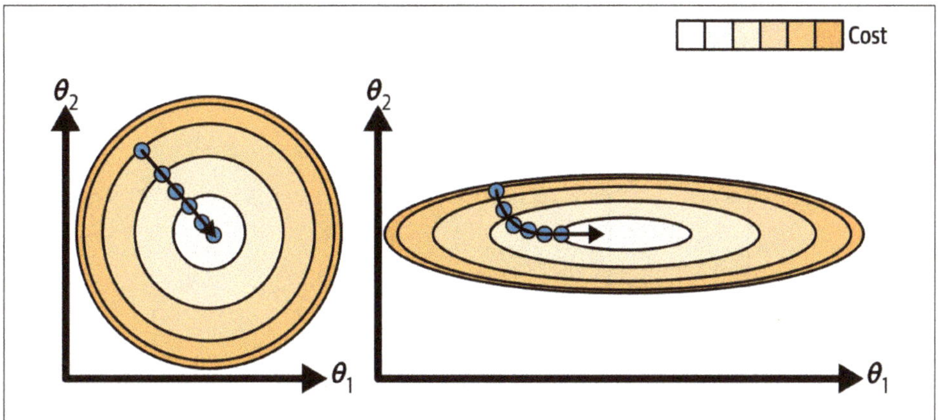

Figure 4-7. Gradient descent with (left) and without (right) feature scaling

When using gradient descent, you should ensure that all features have a similar scale (e.g., using Scikit-Learn's `StandardScaler` class), or else it will take much longer to converge.

Batch Gradient Descent

Most models have more than one model parameter. Therefore, to implement gradient descent, you need to compute the gradient of the cost function with regard to each model parameter θ_j. In other words, you need to calculate how much the cost function will change if you change θ_j just a little bit. This is called a *partial derivative*. It is like asking, "What is the slope of the mountain toward the east?" and then asking the same question facing north (and so on for all other dimensions, if you can imagine a universe with more than three dimensions). Equation 4-6 computes the partial derivative of the MSE with regard to parameter θ_j, denoted ∂ MSE($\boldsymbol{\theta}$) / $\partial\theta_j$.

Equation 4-6. Partial derivatives of the cost function

$$\frac{\partial}{\partial\theta_j}\text{MSE}(\boldsymbol{\theta}) = \frac{2}{m}\sum_{i=1}^{m}\left(\boldsymbol{\theta}^\intercal\mathbf{x}^{(i)} - y^{(i)}\right)x_j^{(i)}$$

Instead of computing these partial derivatives individually, you can use Equation 4-7 to compute them all in one go. The gradient vector, denoted $\nabla_{\boldsymbol{\theta}}\text{MSE}(\boldsymbol{\theta})$, contains all the partial derivatives of the cost function (one for each model parameter).

Equation 4-7. Gradient vector of the cost function

$$\nabla_{\boldsymbol{\theta}}\,\text{MSE}(\boldsymbol{\theta}) = \begin{pmatrix} \frac{\partial}{\partial \theta_0}\text{MSE}(\boldsymbol{\theta}) \\ \frac{\partial}{\partial \theta_1}\text{MSE}(\boldsymbol{\theta}) \\ \vdots \\ \frac{\partial}{\partial \theta_n}\text{MSE}(\boldsymbol{\theta}) \end{pmatrix} = \frac{2}{m}\mathbf{X}^\intercal(\mathbf{X}\boldsymbol{\theta} - \mathbf{y})$$

Notice that this formula involves calculations over the full training set **X**, at each gradient descent step! This is why the algorithm is called *batch gradient descent*: it uses the whole batch of training data at every step (actually, *full gradient descent* would probably be a better name). As a result, it is terribly slow on very large training sets (we will look at some much faster gradient descent algorithms shortly). However, gradient descent scales well with the number of features; training a linear regression model when there are hundreds of thousands of features is much faster using gradient descent than using the normal equation or SVD decomposition.

Once you have the gradient vector, which points uphill, just go in the opposite direction to go downhill. This means subtracting $\nabla_{\boldsymbol{\theta}}\text{MSE}(\boldsymbol{\theta})$ from $\boldsymbol{\theta}$. This is where the learning rate η comes into play:[4] multiply the gradient vector by η to determine the size of the downhill step (Equation 4-8).

Equation 4-8. Gradient descent step

$$\boldsymbol{\theta}^{(\text{next step})} = \boldsymbol{\theta} - \eta \nabla_{\boldsymbol{\theta}}\,\text{MSE}(\boldsymbol{\theta})$$

Let's look at a quick implementation of this algorithm:

```
eta = 0.1  # learning rate
n_epochs = 1000
m = len(X_b)  # number of instances

rng = np.random.default_rng(seed=42)
theta = rng.standard_normal((2, 1))  # randomly initialized model parameters
```

4 Eta (η) is the seventh letter of the Greek alphabet.

```
for epoch in range(n_epochs):
    gradients = 2 / m * X_b.T @ (X_b @ theta - y)
    theta = theta - eta * gradients
```

That wasn't too hard! Each iteration over the training set is called an *epoch*. Let's look at the resulting `theta`:

```
>>> theta
array([[3.69084138],
       [3.32960458]])
```

Hey, that's exactly what the normal equation found! Gradient descent worked perfectly. But what if you had used a different learning rate (`eta`)? Figure 4-8 shows the first 20 steps of gradient descent using three different learning rates. The line at the bottom of each plot represents the random starting point, then each epoch is represented by a darker and darker line.

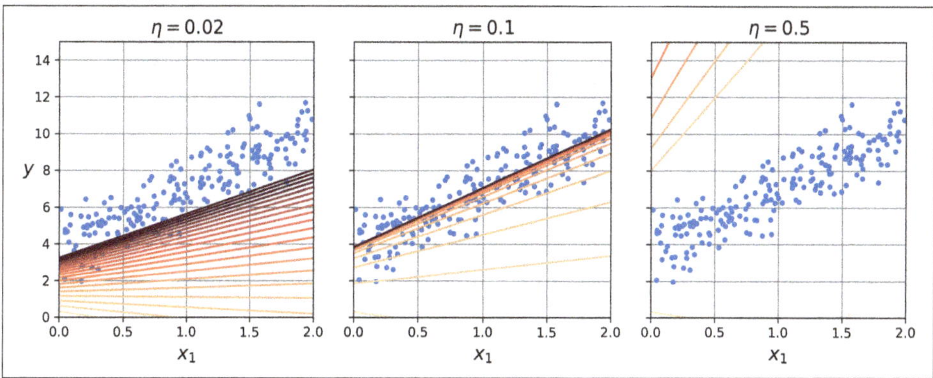

Figure 4-8. Gradient descent with various learning rates

On the left, the learning rate is too low: the algorithm will eventually reach the solution, but it will take a long time. In the middle, the learning rate looks pretty good: in just a few epochs, it has already converged to the solution. On the right, the learning rate is too high: the algorithm diverges, jumping all over the place and actually getting further and further away from the solution at every step.

To find a good learning rate, you can use grid search (see Chapter 2). However, you may want to limit the number of epochs so that grid search can eliminate models that take too long to converge.

You may wonder how to set the number of epochs. If it is too low, you will still be far away from the optimal solution when the algorithm stops; but if it is too high, you will waste time while the model parameters do not change anymore. A simple solution is to set a very large number of epochs but to interrupt the algorithm when the gradient vector becomes tiny—that is, when its norm becomes smaller than a tiny number ε (called the *tolerance*)—because this happens when gradient descent has (almost) reached the minimum.

Convergence Rate

When the cost function is convex and its slope does not change abruptly (as is the case for the MSE cost function), batch gradient descent with a fixed learning rate will eventually converge to the optimal solution, but you may have to wait a while: it can take $O(1/\varepsilon)$ iterations to reach the optimum within a range of ε, depending on the shape of the cost function. If you divide the tolerance by 10 to have a more precise solution, then the algorithm may have to run about 10 times longer.

Stochastic Gradient Descent

The main problem with batch gradient descent is the fact that it uses the whole training set to compute the gradients at every step, which makes it very slow when the training set is large. At the opposite extreme, *stochastic gradient descent* picks a random instance in the training set at every step and computes the gradients based only on that single instance. Obviously, working on a single instance at a time makes the algorithm much faster because it has very little data to manipulate at every iteration. It also makes it possible to train on huge training sets, since only one instance needs to be in memory at each iteration (stochastic GD can be implemented as an out-of-core algorithm; see Chapter 1).

On the other hand, due to its stochastic (i.e., random) nature, this algorithm is much less regular than batch gradient descent: instead of gently decreasing until it reaches the minimum, the cost function will bounce up and down, decreasing only on average. Over time it will end up very close to the minimum, but once it gets there it will continue to bounce around, never settling down (see Figure 4-9). Once the algorithm stops, the final parameter values will be good, but not optimal.

When the cost function is very irregular (as in Figure 4-6), this can actually help the algorithm jump out of local minima, so stochastic gradient descent has a better chance of finding the global minimum than batch gradient descent does.

Therefore, randomness is good to escape from local optima, but bad because it means that the algorithm can never settle at the minimum. One solution to this dilemma is to gradually reduce the learning rate. The steps start out large (which helps make quick progress and escape local minima), then get smaller and smaller, allowing the algorithm to settle at the global minimum. This process is akin to *simulated annealing*, an algorithm inspired by the process in metallurgy of annealing, where molten metal is slowly cooled down. The function that determines the learning rate at each iteration is called the *learning schedule*. If the learning rate is reduced too quickly, you may get stuck in a local minimum, or even end up frozen halfway to the minimum. If the learning rate is reduced too slowly, you may jump around the minimum for a long time and end up with a suboptimal solution if you halt training too early.

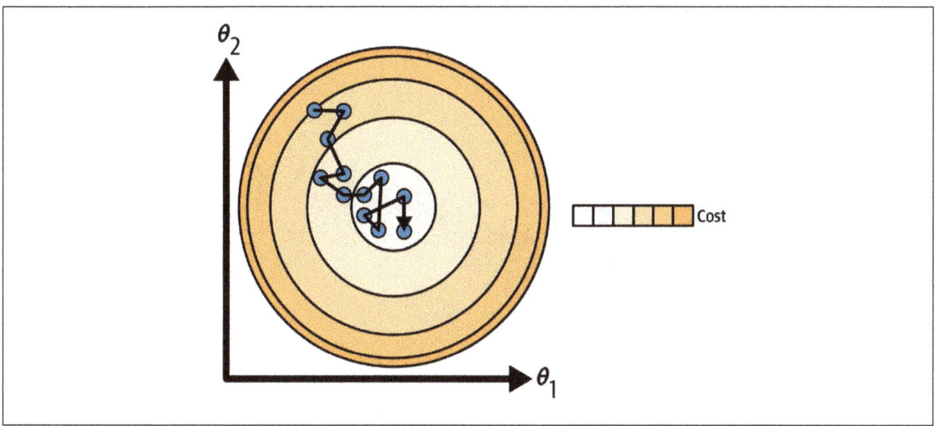

Figure 4-9. With stochastic gradient descent, each training step is much faster but also much more stochastic than when using batch gradient descent

This code implements stochastic gradient descent using a simple learning schedule:

```
n_epochs = 50
t0, t1 = 5, 50  # learning schedule hyperparameters

def learning_schedule(t):
    return t0 / (t + t1)

rng = np.random.default_rng(seed=42)
theta = rng.standard_normal((2, 1))  # randomly initialized model parameters

for epoch in range(n_epochs):
    for iteration in range(m):
        random_index = rng.integers(m)
        xi = X_b[random_index : random_index + 1]
        yi = y[random_index : random_index + 1]
        gradients = 2 * xi.T @ (xi @ theta - yi)  # for SGD, do not divide by m
        eta = learning_schedule(epoch * m + iteration)
        theta = theta - eta * gradients
```

By convention we iterate by rounds of *m* iterations; each round is called an *epoch*, as earlier. While the batch gradient descent code iterated 1,000 times through the whole training set, this code goes through the training set only 50 times and reaches a pretty good solution:

```
>>> theta
array([[3.69826475],
       [3.30748311]])
```

Figure 4-10 shows the first 20 steps of training (notice how irregular the steps are).

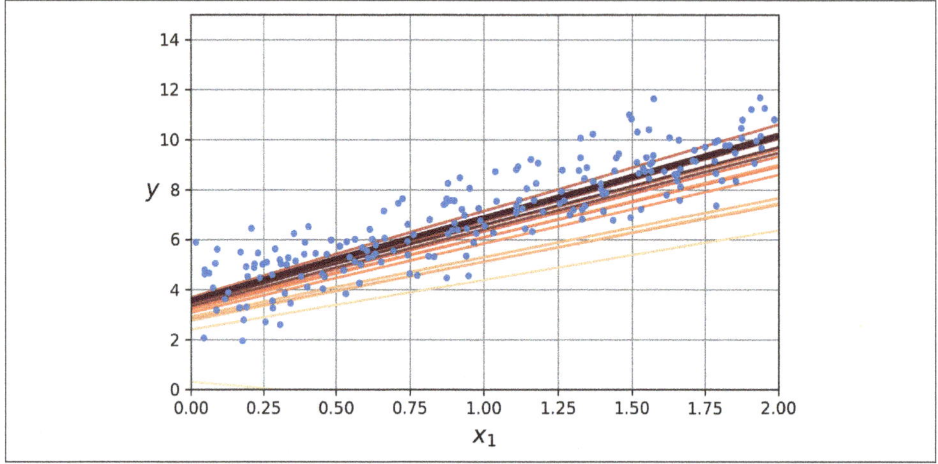

Figure 4-10. The first 20 steps of stochastic gradient descent

Note that since instances are picked randomly, some instances may be picked several times per epoch, while others may not be picked at all. If you want to be sure that the algorithm goes through every instance at each epoch, another approach is to shuffle the training set (making sure to shuffle the input features and the labels jointly), then go through it instance by instance, then shuffle it again, and so on. However, this approach is more complex, and it generally does not improve the result.

When using stochastic gradient descent, the training instances must be independent and identically distributed (IID) to ensure that the parameters get pulled toward the global optimum, on average. A simple way to ensure this is to shuffle the instances during training (e.g., pick each instance randomly, or shuffle the training set at the beginning of each epoch). If you do not shuffle the instances—for example, if the instances are sorted by label—then SGD will start by optimizing for one label, then the next, and so on, and it will not settle close to the global minimum.

To perform linear regression using stochastic GD with Scikit-Learn, you can use the `SGDRegressor` class, which defaults to optimizing the MSE cost function. The following code runs for a maximum of 1,000 epochs (`max_iter`) or until the loss drops by less than 10^{-5} (`tol`) during 100 epochs (`n_iter_no_change`). It starts with a learning rate of 0.01 (`eta0`), using the default learning schedule (different from the one we used). Lastly, it does not use any regularization (penalty=None; more details on this shortly):

```
from sklearn.linear_model import SGDRegressor

sgd_reg = SGDRegressor(max_iter=1000, tol=1e-5, penalty=None, eta0=0.01,
                       n_iter_no_change=100, random_state=42)
sgd_reg.fit(X, y.ravel())  # y.ravel() because fit() expects 1D targets
```

Once again, you find a solution quite close to the one returned by the normal equation:

```
>>> sgd_reg.intercept_, sgd_reg.coef_
(array([3.68899733]), array([3.33054574]))
```

All Scikit-Learn estimators can be trained using the `fit()` method, but some estimators also have a `partial_fit()` method that you can call to run a single round of training on one or more instances (it ignores hyperparameters like `max_iter` or `tol`). Repeatedly calling `partial_fit()` will gradually train the model. This is useful when you need more control over the training process. Other models have a `warm_start` hyperparameter instead (and some have both): if you set `warm_start=True`, calling the `fit()` method on a trained model will not reset the model; it will just continue training where it left off, respecting hyperparameters like `max_iter` and `tol`. Note that `fit()` resets the iteration counter used by the learning schedule, while `partial_fit()` does not.

Mini-Batch Gradient Descent

The last gradient descent algorithm we will look at is called *mini-batch gradient descent*. It is straightforward once you know batch and stochastic gradient descent: at each step, instead of computing the gradients based on the full training set (as in batch GD) or based on just one instance (as in stochastic GD), mini-batch GD computes the gradients on small random sets of instances called *mini-batches*. The main advantage of mini-batch GD over stochastic GD is that you can get a performance boost from hardware acceleration of matrix operations, especially when using *graphical processing units* (GPUs).

The algorithm's progress in parameter space is less erratic than with stochastic GD, especially with fairly large mini-batches. As a result, mini-batch GD will end up walking around a bit closer to the minimum than stochastic GD—but it may be harder for it to escape from local minima (in the case of problems that suffer from local minima, unlike linear regression with the MSE cost function). Figure 4-11 shows the paths taken by the three gradient descent algorithms in parameter space during training. They all end up near the minimum, but batch GD's path actually stops at the minimum, while both stochastic GD and mini-batch GD continue to walk around. However, don't forget that batch GD takes a lot of time to take each step, and stochastic GD and mini-batch GD would also reach the minimum if you used a good learning schedule.

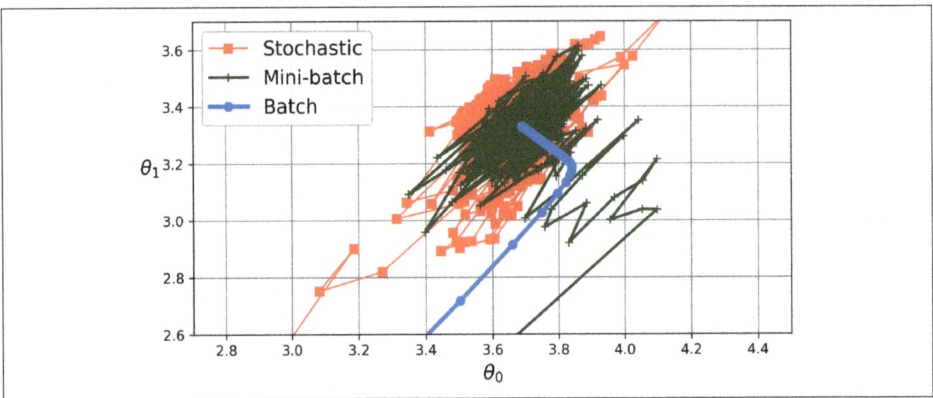

Figure 4-11. Gradient descent paths in parameter space

Table 4-1 compares the algorithms we've discussed so far for linear regression[5] (recall that *m* is the number of training instances and *n* is the number of features).

Table 4-1. Comparison of algorithms for linear regression

Algorithm	Large *m*	Out-of-core support	Large *n*	Hyperparams	Scaling required	Scikit-Learn
Normal equation	Fast	No	Slow	0	No	N/A
SVD	Fast	No	Slow	0	No	`LinearRegression`
Batch GD	Slow	No	Fast	2	Yes	N/A
Stochastic GD	Fast	Yes	Fast	≥2	Yes	`SGDRegressor`
Mini-batch GD	Fast	Yes	Fast	≥2	Yes	N/A

There is almost no difference after training: all these algorithms end up with very similar models and make predictions in exactly the same way.

5 While the normal equation can only perform linear regression, the gradient descent algorithms can be used to train many other models, as you'll see.

Polynomial Regression

What if your data is more complex than a straight line? Surprisingly, you can use a linear model to fit nonlinear data. A simple way to do this is to add powers of each feature as new features, then train a linear model on this extended set of features. This technique is called *polynomial regression*.

Let's look at an example. First, we'll generate some nonlinear data (see Figure 4-12), based on a simple *quadratic equation*—that's an equation of the form $y = ax^2 + bx + c$—plus some noise:

```
rng = np.random.default_rng(seed=42)
m = 200  # number of instances
X = 6 * rng.random((m, 1)) - 3
y = 0.5 * X ** 2 + X + 2 + rng.standard_normal((m, 1))
```

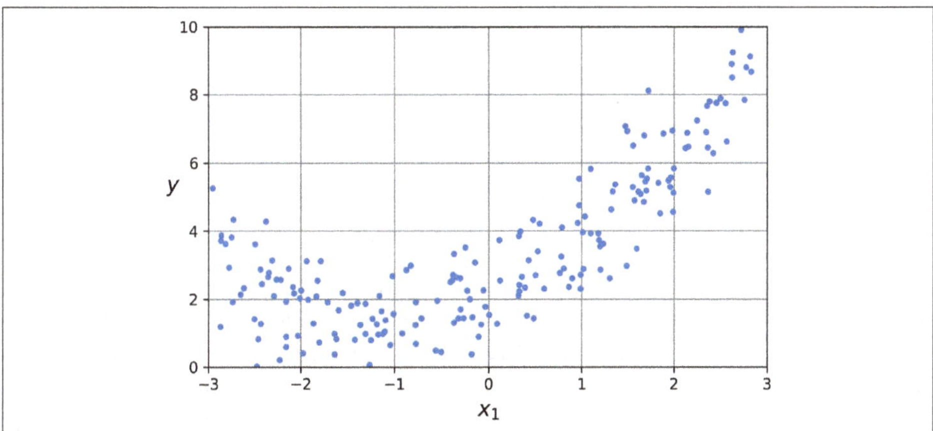

Figure 4-12. Generated nonlinear and noisy dataset

Clearly, a straight line will never fit this data properly. So let's use Scikit-Learn's `PolynomialFeatures` class to transform our training data, adding the square (second-degree polynomial) of each feature in the training set as a new feature (in this case there is just one feature):

```
>>> from sklearn.preprocessing import PolynomialFeatures
>>> poly_features = PolynomialFeatures(degree=2, include_bias=False)
>>> X_poly = poly_features.fit_transform(X)
>>> X[0]
array([1.64373629])
>>> X_poly[0]
array([1.64373629, 2.701869  ])
```

`X_poly` now contains the original feature of `X` plus the square of this feature. Now we can fit a `LinearRegression` model to this extended training data (Figure 4-13):

```
>>> lin_reg = LinearRegression()
>>> lin_reg.fit(X_poly, y)
>>> lin_reg.intercept_, lin_reg.coef_
(array([2.00540719]), array([[1.11022126, 0.50526985]]))
```

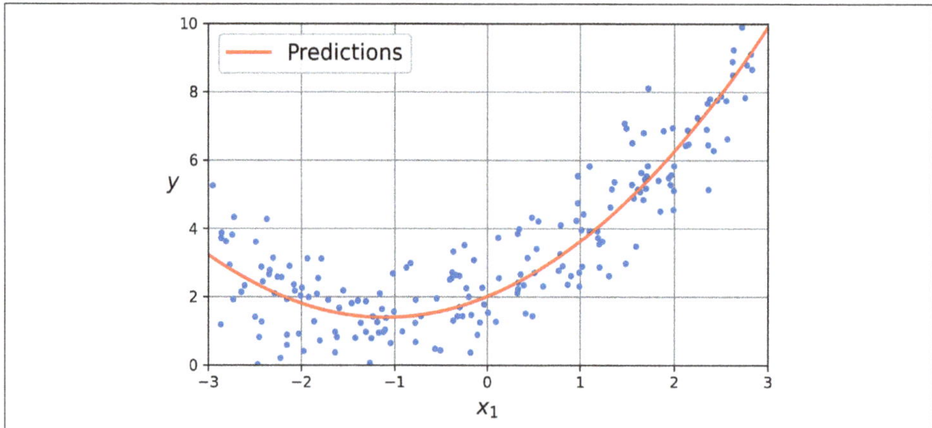

Figure 4-13. Polynomial regression model predictions

Not bad: the model estimates $\hat{y} = 0.56{x_1}^2 + 0.93x_1 + 1.78$ when in fact the original function was $y = 0.5{x_1}^2 + 1.0x_1 + 2.0$ + Gaussian noise.

Note that when there are multiple features, polynomial regression is capable of finding relationships between features, which is something a plain linear regression model cannot do. This is made possible by the fact that `PolynomialFeatures` also adds all combinations of features up to the given degree. For example, if there were two features *a* and *b*, `PolynomialFeatures` with `degree=3` would not only add the features a^2, a^3, b^2, and b^3, but also the combinations ab, a^2b, and ab^2.

`PolynomialFeatures(degree=`*`d`*`)` transforms an array containing *n* features into an array containing $(n + d)! / d!n!$ features, where $n!$ is the *factorial* of *n*, equal to $1 \times 2 \times 3 \times \cdots \times n$. Beware of the combinatorial explosion of the number of features!

Learning Curves

If you perform high-degree polynomial regression, you will likely fit the training data much better than with plain linear regression. For example, Figure 4-14 applies a 300-degree polynomial model to the preceding training data, and compares the result with a pure linear model and a quadratic model (second-degree polynomial). Notice how the 300-degree polynomial model wiggles around to get as close as possible to the training instances.

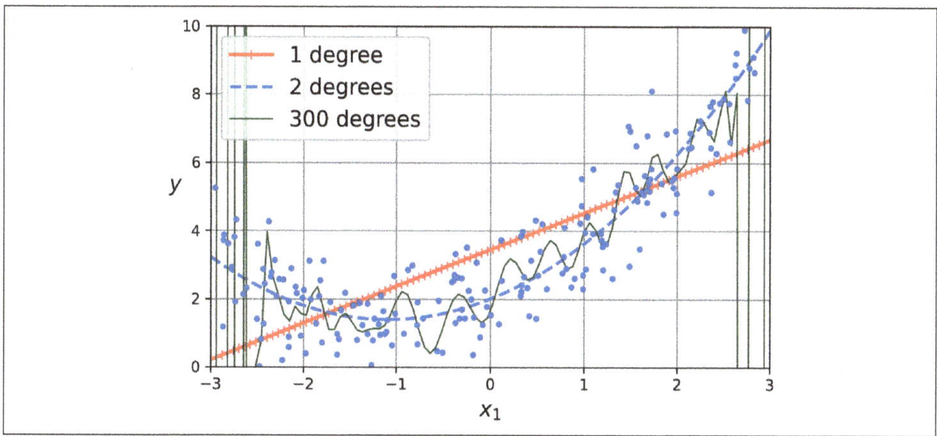

Figure 4-14. High-degree polynomial regression

This high-degree polynomial regression model is severely overfitting the training data, while the linear model is underfitting it. The model that will generalize best in this case is the quadratic model, which makes sense because the data was generated using a quadratic model. But in general you won't know what function generated the data, so how can you decide how complex your model should be? How can you tell that your model is overfitting or underfitting the data?

In Chapter 2 you used cross-validation to get an estimate of a model's generalization performance. If a model performs well on the training data but generalizes poorly according to the cross-validation metrics, then your model is overfitting. If it performs poorly on both, then it is underfitting. This is one way to tell when a model is too simple or too complex.

Another way to tell is to look at the *learning curves*, which are plots of the model's training error and validation error as a function of the training iteration: just evaluate the model at regular intervals during training on both the training set and the validation set, and plot the results. If the model cannot be trained incrementally (i.e., if it does not support `partial_fit()` or `warm_start`), then you must train it several times on gradually larger subsets of the training set.

Scikit-Learn has a useful `learning_curve()` function to help with this: it trains and evaluates the model using cross-validation. By default it retrains the model on growing subsets of the training set, but if the model supports incremental learning you can set `exploit_incremental_learning=True` when calling `learning_curve()` and it will train the model incrementally instead. The function returns the training set sizes at which it evaluated the model, and the training and validation scores it measured for each size and for each cross-validation fold. Let's use this function to look at the learning curves of the plain linear regression model (see Figure 4-15):

```
from sklearn.model_selection import learning_curve

train_sizes, train_scores, valid_scores = learning_curve(
    LinearRegression(), X, y, train_sizes=np.linspace(0.01, 1.0, 40), cv=5,
    scoring="neg_root_mean_squared_error")
train_errors = -train_scores.mean(axis=1)
valid_errors = -valid_scores.mean(axis=1)

plt.plot(train_sizes, train_errors, "r-+", linewidth=2, label="train")
plt.plot(train_sizes, valid_errors, "b-", linewidth=3, label="valid")
[...]  # beautify the figure: add labels, axis, grid, and legend
plt.show()
```

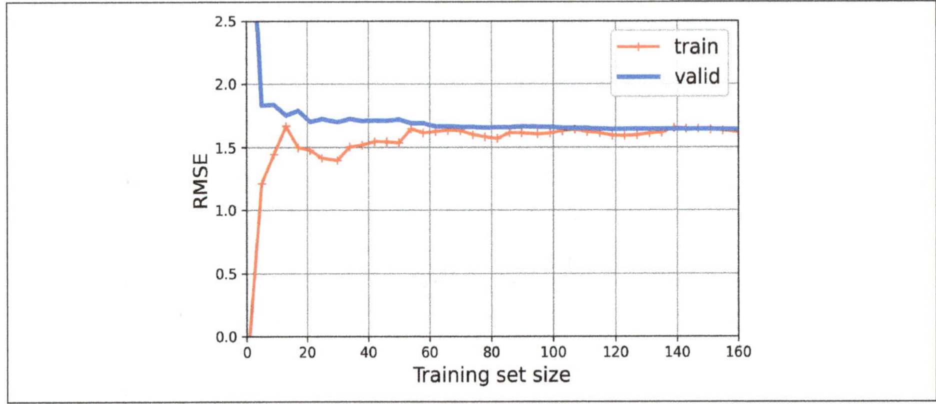

Figure 4-15. Learning curves

This model is underfitting, it's too simple for the data. How can we tell? Well, let's look at the training error. When there are just one or two instances in the training set, the model can fit them perfectly, which is why the curve starts at zero. But as new instances are added to the training set, it becomes impossible for the model to fit the training data perfectly, both because the data is noisy and because it is not linear at all. So the error on the training data goes up until it reaches a plateau, at which point adding new instances to the training set doesn't make the average error much better or worse. Now let's look at the validation error. When the model is trained on very few training instances, it is incapable of generalizing properly, which is why the validation error is initially quite large. Then, as the model is shown more training examples, it learns, and thus the validation error slowly goes down. However, once again a straight line cannot do a good job of modeling the data, so the error ends up at a plateau, very close to the other curve.

These learning curves are typical of a model that's underfitting. Both curves have reached a plateau; they are close and fairly high.

If your model is underfitting the training data, adding more training examples will not help. You need to use a better model or come up with better features.

Now let's look at the learning curves of a 10th-degree polynomial model on the same data (Figure 4-16):

```
from sklearn.pipeline import make_pipeline

polynomial_regression = make_pipeline(
    PolynomialFeatures(degree=10, include_bias=False),
    LinearRegression())

train_sizes, train_scores, valid_scores = learning_curve(
    polynomial_regression, X, y, train_sizes=np.linspace(0.01, 1.0, 40), cv=5,
    scoring="neg_root_mean_squared_error")
[...]  # same as earlier
```

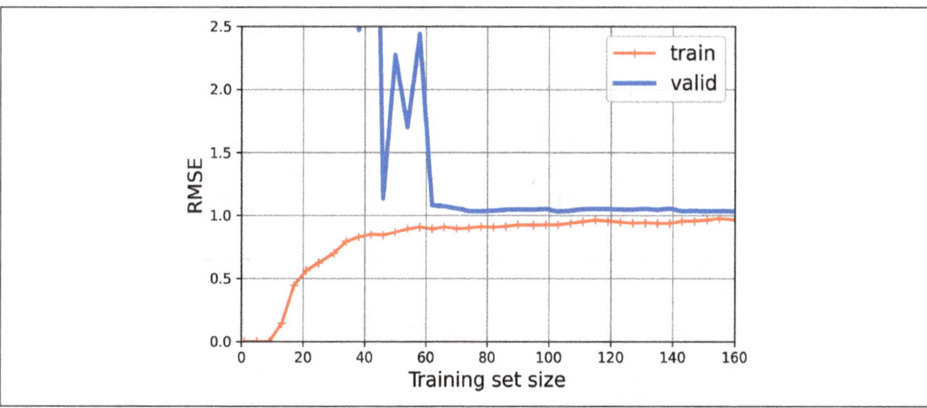

Figure 4-16. Learning curves for the 10th-degree polynomial model

These learning curves look a bit like the previous ones, but there are two very important differences:

- The error on the training data is much lower than before.
- There is a gap between the curves. This means that the model performs better on the training data than on the validation data, which is the hallmark of an overfitting model. If you used a much larger training set, however, the two curves would continue to get closer.

The Bias/Variance Trade-Off

An important theoretical result of statistics and machine learning is the fact that a model's generalization error can be expressed as the sum of three very different errors:

Bias
: This part of the generalization error is due to wrong assumptions, such as assuming that the data is linear when it is actually quadratic. A high-bias model is most likely to underfit the training data.[6]

Variance
: This part is due to the model's excessive sensitivity to small variations in the training data. A model with many degrees of freedom (such as a high-degree polynomial model) is likely to have high variance and thus overfit the training data.

Irreducible error
: This part is due to the noisiness of the data itself. The only way to reduce this part of the error is to clean up the data (e.g., fix the data sources, such as broken sensors, or detect and remove outliers).

Increasing a model's complexity will typically increase its variance and reduce its bias. Conversely, reducing a model's complexity (or increasing regularization) increases its bias and reduces its variance (see Figure 4-17). This is why it is called a trade-off.

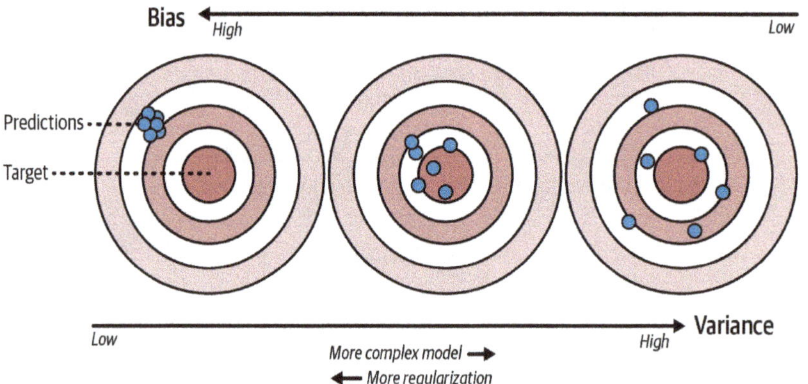

Figure 4-17. Bias/variance trade-off

6 This notion of bias is not to be confused with the bias term of linear models.

One way to improve an overfitting model is to feed it more training data until the validation error gets close enough to the training error.

Regularized Linear Models

As you saw in Chapters 1 and 2, a good way to reduce overfitting is to regularize the model (i.e., to constrain it): the fewer degrees of freedom it has, the harder it will be for it to overfit the data. A simple way to regularize a polynomial model is to reduce the number of polynomial degrees.

What about linear models? Can we regularize them too? You may wonder why we may want to do that: aren't linear models constrained enough already? Well, linear regression makes a few assumptions, including the fact that the true relationship between the inputs and the outputs is linear, the noise has zero mean, constant variance, and is independent of the inputs, plus the input matrix has full rank, meaning that the inputs are not colinear[7] and there at least as many samples as parameters. In practice, some assumptions don't hold perfectly. For example, some inputs may be close to colinear, which makes linear regression numerically unstable, meaning that very small differences in the training set can have a big impact on the trained model. Regularization can stabilize linear models and make them more accurate.

So how can we regularize a linear model? This is usually done by constraining its weights. In this section, we will discuss ridge regression, lasso regression, and elastic net regression, which implement three different ways to do that.

Ridge Regression

Ridge regression (also called *Tikhonov regularization*) is a regularized version of linear regression: a *regularization term* equal to $\frac{\alpha}{m}\sum_{i=1}^{n}\theta_i^2$ is added to the MSE. This forces the learning algorithm to not only fit the data but also keep the model weights as small as possible. This constraint makes the model less flexible, preventing it from stretching itself too much to fit every data point: this reduces the risk of overfitting. Note that the regularization term should only be added to the cost function during training. Once the model is trained, you want to use the unregularized MSE (or the RMSE) to evaluate the model's performance.

7 Inputs are colinear when one input is equal to a linear combination of some other inputs. For example, the temperature in Celsius degrees is colinear with the temperature in Fahrenheit degrees.

The hyperparameter α controls how much you want to regularize the model. If α = 0, then ridge regression is just linear regression. If α is very large, then all weights end up very close to zero and the result is a flat line going through the data's mean. Equation 4-9 presents the ridge regression cost function.[8]

Equation 4-9. Ridge regression cost function

$$J(\boldsymbol{\theta}) = \text{MSE}(\boldsymbol{\theta}) + \frac{\alpha}{m}\sum_{i=1}^{n}\theta_i^2$$

Note that the bias term θ_0 is not regularized (the sum starts at i = 1, not 0). If we define **w** as the vector of feature weights (θ_1 to θ_n), then the regularization term is equal to $\alpha(\|\mathbf{w}\|_2)^2 / m$, where $\|\mathbf{w}\|_2$ represents the ℓ_2 norm of the weight vector.[9] For batch gradient descent, just add $2\alpha\mathbf{w} / m$ to the part of the MSE gradient vector that corresponds to the feature weights, without adding anything to the gradient of the bias term (see Equation 4-7).

It is important to scale the data (e.g., using a `StandardScaler`) before performing ridge regression, as it is sensitive to the scale of the input features. This is true of most regularized models.

Figure 4-18 shows several ridge models that were trained on some very noisy linear data using different α values. On the left, plain ridge models are used, leading to linear predictions. On the right, the data is first expanded using `PolynomialFeatures(degree=10)`, then it is scaled using a `StandardScaler`, and finally the ridge models are applied to the resulting features: this is polynomial regression with ridge regularization. Note how increasing α leads to flatter (i.e., less extreme, more reasonable) predictions, thus reducing the model's variance but increasing its bias.

8 It is common to use the notation $J(\boldsymbol{\theta})$ for cost functions that don't have a short name; I'll often use this notation throughout the rest of this book. The context will make it clear which cost function is being discussed.

9 Norms are discussed in Chapter 2.

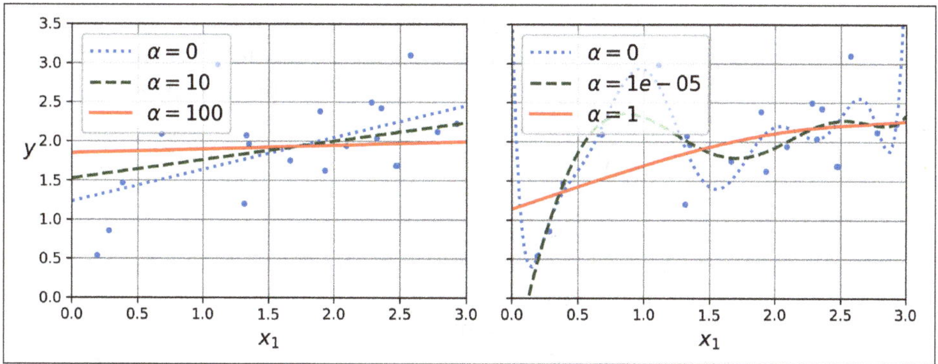

Figure 4-18. Linear (left) and polynomial (right) models, both with various levels of ridge regularization

As with linear regression, we can perform ridge regression either by computing a closed-form equation or by performing gradient descent. The pros and cons are the same. Equation 4-10 shows the closed-form solution, where **A** is the $(n + 1) \times (n + 1)$ *identity matrix*,[10] except with a 0 in the top-left cell, corresponding to the bias term.

Equation 4-10. Ridge regression closed-form solution

$$\hat{\boldsymbol{\theta}} = \left(\mathbf{X}^\top \mathbf{X} + \alpha \mathbf{A}\right)^{-1} \mathbf{X}^\top \mathbf{y}$$

Here is how to perform ridge regression with Scikit-Learn using a closed-form solution (a variant of Equation 4-10 that uses a matrix factorization technique by André-Louis Cholesky):

```
>>> from sklearn.linear_model import Ridge
>>> ridge_reg = Ridge(alpha=0.1, solver="cholesky")
>>> ridge_reg.fit(X, y)
>>> ridge_reg.predict([[1.5]])
array([1.84414523])
```

And using stochastic gradient descent:[11]

```
>>> sgd_reg = SGDRegressor(penalty="l2", alpha=0.1 / m, tol=None,
...                        max_iter=1000, eta0=0.01, random_state=42)
...
>>> sgd_reg.fit(X, y.ravel())  # y.ravel() because fit() expects 1D targets
>>> sgd_reg.predict([[1.5]])
array([1.83659707])
```

10 A square matrix full of 0s except for 1s on the main diagonal (top left to bottom right).

11 Alternatively, you can use the `Ridge` class with the `"sag"` solver. Stochastic average GD is a variant of stochastic GD. For more details, see the presentation "Minimizing Finite Sums with the Stochastic Average Gradient Algorithm" (*https://homl.info/12*) by Mark Schmidt et al. from the University of British Columbia.

The `penalty` hyperparameter sets the type of regularization term to use. Specifying `"l2"` indicates that you want SGD to add a regularization term to the MSE cost function equal to `alpha` times the square of the ℓ_2 norm of the weight vector. This is just like ridge regression, except there's no division by m in this case; that's why we passed `alpha=0.1 / m`, to get the same result as `Ridge(alpha=0.1)`.

The `RidgeCV` class also performs ridge regression, but it automatically tunes hyperparameters using cross-validation. It's roughly equivalent to using `GridSearchCV`, but it's optimized for ridge regression and runs *much* faster. Several other estimators (mostly linear) also have efficient CV variants, such as `LassoCV` and `ElasticNetCV`.

Lasso Regression

Least absolute shrinkage and selection operator regression (usually simply called *lasso regression*) is another regularized version of linear regression: just like ridge regression, it adds a regularization term to the cost function, but it uses the ℓ_1 norm of the weight vector instead of the square of the ℓ_2 norm (see Equation 4-11). Notice that the ℓ_1 norm is multiplied by 2α, whereas the ℓ_2 norm was multiplied by α / m in ridge regression. These factors were chosen to ensure that the optimal α value is independent from the training set size: different norms lead to different factors (see Scikit-Learn issue #15657 (*https://github.com/scikit-learn/scikit-learn/issues/15657*) for more details).

Equation 4-11. Lasso regression cost function

$$J(\boldsymbol{\theta}) = \text{MSE}(\boldsymbol{\theta}) + 2\alpha \sum_{i=1}^{n} |\theta_i|$$

Figure 4-19 shows the same thing as Figure 4-18 but replaces the ridge models with lasso models and uses different α values.

An important characteristic of lasso regression is that it tends to eliminate the weights of the least important features (i.e., set them to zero). For example, the dashed line in the righthand plot in Figure 4-19 (with $\alpha = 0.01$) looks roughly cubic: all the weights for the high-degree polynomial features are equal to zero. In other words, lasso regression automatically performs feature selection and outputs a *sparse model* with few nonzero feature weights. Of course, there's a trade-off: if you increase α too much, the model will be very sparse, but its performance will plummet.

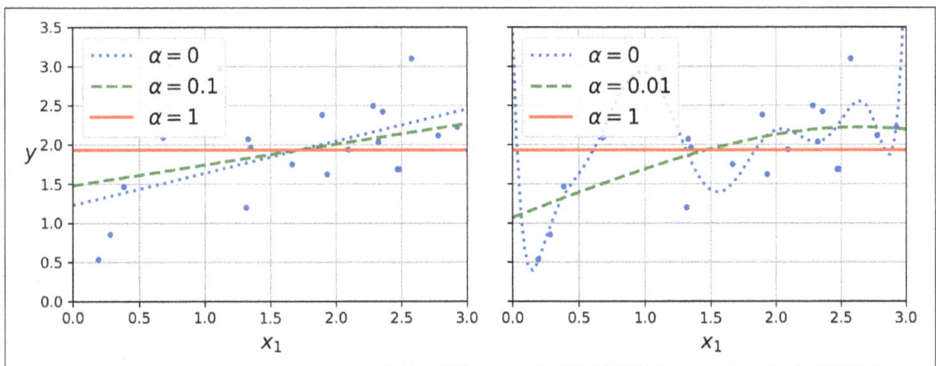

Figure 4-19. Linear (left) and polynomial (right) models, both using various levels of lasso regularization

You can get a sense of why the ℓ_1 norm induces sparsity by looking at Figure 4-20: the axes represent two model parameters, and the background contours represent different loss functions. In the top-left plot, the contours represent the ℓ_1 loss ($|\theta_1| + |\theta_2|$), which drops linearly as you get closer to any axis. For example, if you initialize the model parameters to $\theta_1 = 2$ and $\theta_2 = 0.5$, running gradient descent will decrement both parameters equally (as represented by the dashed yellow line); therefore θ_2 will reach 0 first (since it was closer to 0 to begin with). After that, gradient descent will roll down the gutter until it reaches $\theta_1 = 0$ (with a bit of bouncing around, since the gradients of ℓ_1 never get close to 0: they are either –1 or 1 for each parameter). In the top-right plot, the contours represent lasso regression's cost function (i.e., an MSE cost function plus an ℓ_1 loss). The small white circles show the path that gradient descent takes to optimize some model parameters that were initialized around $\theta_1 = 0.25$ and $\theta_2 = -1$: notice again how the path quickly reaches $\theta_2 = 0$, then rolls down the gutter and ends up bouncing around the global optimum (represented by the red square). If we increased α, the global optimum would move left along the dashed yellow line, while if we decreased α, the global optimum would move right (in this example, the optimal parameters for the unregularized MSE are $\theta_1 = 2$ and $\theta_2 = 0.5$).

The two bottom plots show the same thing but with an ℓ_2 penalty instead. In the bottom-left plot, you can see that the ℓ_2 loss decreases as we get closer to the origin, so gradient descent just takes a straight path toward that point. In the bottom-right plot, the contours represent ridge regression's cost function (i.e., an MSE cost function plus an ℓ_2 loss). As you can see, the gradients get smaller as the parameters approach the global optimum, so gradient descent naturally slows down. This limits the bouncing around, which helps ridge converge faster than lasso regression. Also note that the optimal parameters (represented by the red square) get closer and closer to the origin when you increase α, but they never get eliminated entirely.

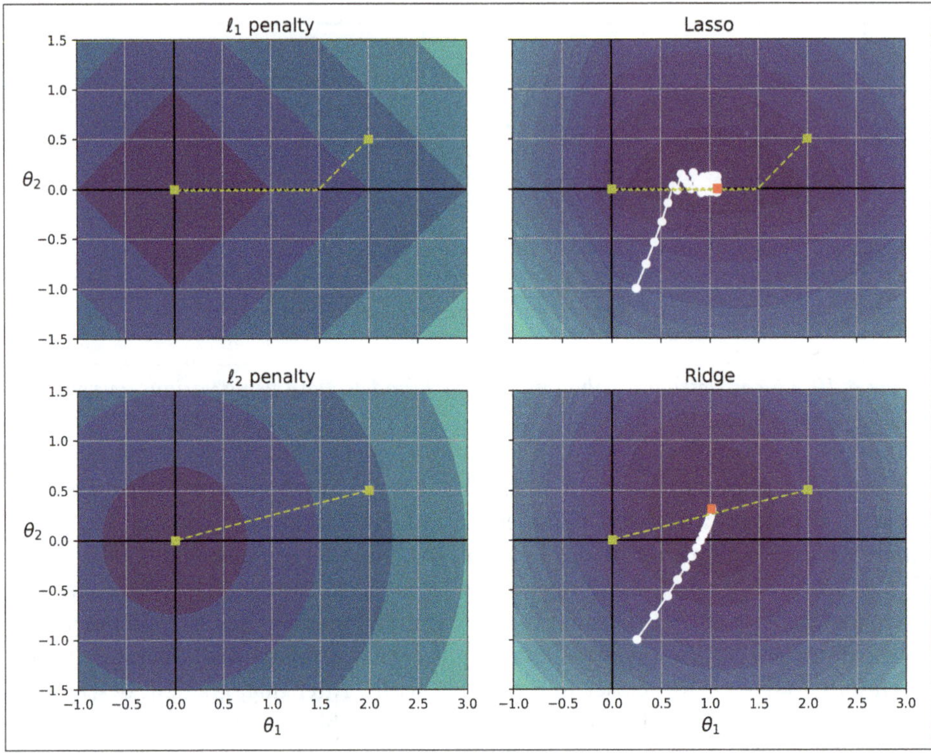

Figure 4-20. Lasso versus ridge regularization

To keep gradient descent from bouncing around the optimum at the end when using lasso regression, you need to gradually reduce the learning rate during training. It will still bounce around the optimum, but the steps will get smaller and smaller, so it will converge.

The lasso cost function is not differentiable at $\theta_i = 0$ (for $i = 1, 2, \cdots, n$), but gradient descent still works if you use a *subgradient vector* **g**[12] instead when any $\theta_i = 0$. Equation 4-12 shows a subgradient vector equation you can use for gradient descent with the lasso cost function.

12 You can think of a subgradient vector at a nondifferentiable point as an intermediate vector between the gradient vectors around that point.

Equation 4-12. Lasso regression subgradient vector

$$g(\mathbf{\theta}) = \nabla_{\mathbf{\theta}} \mathrm{MSE}(\mathbf{\theta}) + 2\alpha \begin{pmatrix} \mathrm{sign}(\theta_1) \\ \mathrm{sign}(\theta_2) \\ \vdots \\ \mathrm{sign}(\theta_n) \end{pmatrix} \quad \text{where } \mathrm{sign}(\theta_i) = \begin{cases} -1 & \text{if } \theta_i < 0 \\ 0 & \text{if } \theta_i = 0 \\ +1 & \text{if } \theta_i > 0 \end{cases}$$

Here is a small Scikit-Learn example using the `Lasso` class:

```
>>> from sklearn.linear_model import Lasso
>>> lasso_reg = Lasso(alpha=0.1)
>>> lasso_reg.fit(X, y)
>>> lasso_reg.predict([[1.5]])
array([1.87550211])
```

Note that you could instead use `SGDRegressor(penalty="l1", alpha=0.1)`.

Elastic Net Regression

Elastic net regression is a middle ground between ridge regression and lasso regression. The regularization term is a weighted sum of both ridge and lasso's regularization terms, and you can control the mix ratio r. When $r = 0$, elastic net is equivalent to ridge regression, and when $r = 1$, it is equivalent to lasso regression (Equation 4-13).

Equation 4-13. Elastic net cost function

$$J(\mathbf{\theta}) = \mathrm{MSE}(\mathbf{\theta}) + r\left(2\alpha \sum_{i=1}^{n} |\theta_i|\right) + (1 - r)\left(\frac{\alpha}{m} \sum_{i=1}^{n} \theta_i^2\right)$$

So when should you use elastic net regression, or ridge, lasso, or plain linear regression (i.e., without any regularization)? It is almost always preferable to have at least a little bit of regularization, so generally you should avoid plain linear regression. Ridge is a good default, but if you suspect that only a few features are useful, you should prefer lasso or elastic net because they tend to reduce the useless features' weights down to zero, as discussed earlier. In general, elastic net is preferred over lasso because lasso may behave erratically when the number of features is greater than the number of training instances or when several features are strongly correlated.

Here is a short example that uses Scikit-Learn's `ElasticNet` (`l1_ratio` corresponds to the mix ratio r):

```
>>> from sklearn.linear_model import ElasticNet
>>> elastic_net = ElasticNet(alpha=0.1, l1_ratio=0.5)
>>> elastic_net.fit(X, y)
```

```
>>> elastic_net.predict([[1.5]])
array([1.8645014])
```

Early Stopping

A different way to regularize iterative learning algorithms such as gradient descent is to stop training as soon as the validation error reaches a minimum. This popular technique is called *early stopping*. Figure 4-21 shows a complex model (in this case, a high-degree polynomial regression model) being trained with batch gradient descent on the quadratic dataset we used earlier. As the epochs go by, the algorithm learns, and its prediction error (RMSE) on the training set goes down, along with its prediction error on the validation set. After a while, though, the validation error stops decreasing and starts to go back up. This indicates that the model has started to overfit the training data. With early stopping you just stop training as soon as the validation error reaches the minimum. It is such a simple and efficient regularization technique that Geoffrey Hinton called it a "beautiful free lunch".[13] That said, the validation error sometimes comes back down after a while: this is called *double descent*. It's fairly common with large neural networks, and is an area of active research.

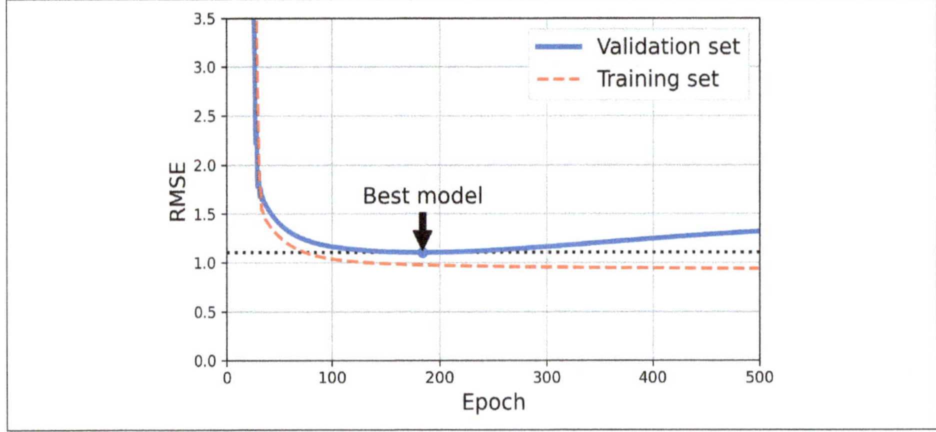

Figure 4-21. Early stopping regularization

With stochastic and mini-batch gradient descent, the curves are not so smooth, and it may be hard to know whether you have reached the minimum or not. One solution is to stop only after the validation error has been above the minimum for some time (when you are confident that the model will not do any better), then roll back the model parameters to the point where the validation error was at a minimum.

13 Slide #63 of the NeurIPS 2015 Deep Learning Tutorial (*https://homl.info/freelunch*).

Here is a basic implementation of early stopping:

```
from copy import deepcopy
from sklearn.metrics import root_mean_squared_error
from sklearn.preprocessing import StandardScaler

X_train, y_train, X_valid, y_valid = [...]  # split the quadratic dataset

preprocessing = make_pipeline(PolynomialFeatures(degree=90, include_bias=False),
                              StandardScaler())
X_train_prep = preprocessing.fit_transform(X_train)
X_valid_prep = preprocessing.transform(X_valid)
sgd_reg = SGDRegressor(penalty=None, eta0=0.002, random_state=42)
n_epochs = 500
best_valid_rmse = float('inf')

for epoch in range(n_epochs):
    sgd_reg.partial_fit(X_train_prep, y_train)
    y_valid_predict = sgd_reg.predict(X_valid_prep)
    val_error = root_mean_squared_error(y_valid, y_valid_predict)
    if val_error < best_valid_rmse:
        best_valid_rmse = val_error
        best_model = deepcopy(sgd_reg)
```

This code first adds the polynomial features and scales all the input features, both for the training set and for the validation set (the code assumes that you have split the original training set into a smaller training set and a validation set). Then it creates an `SGDRegressor` model with no regularization and a small learning rate. In the training loop, it calls `partial_fit()` instead of `fit()`, to perform incremental learning. At each epoch, it measures the RMSE on the validation set. If it is lower than the lowest RMSE seen so far, it saves a copy of the model in the `best_model` variable. This implementation does not actually stop training, but it lets you revert to the best model after training. Note that the model is copied using `copy.deepcopy()`, because it copies both the model's hyperparameters *and* the learned parameters. In contrast, `sklearn.base.clone()` only copies the model's hyperparameters.

Logistic Regression

As discussed in Chapter 1, some regression algorithms can be used for classification (and vice versa). *Logistic regression* (also called *logit regression*) is commonly used to estimate the probability that an instance belongs to a particular class (e.g., what is the probability that this email is spam?). If the estimated probability is greater than a given threshold (typically 50%), then the model predicts that the instance belongs to that class (called the *positive class*, labeled "1"), and otherwise it predicts that it does not (i.e., it belongs to the *negative class*, labeled "0"). This makes it a binary classifier.

Estimating Probabilities

So how does logistic regression work? Just like a linear regression model, a logistic regression model computes a weighted sum of the input features (plus a bias term), but instead of outputting the result directly like the linear regression model does, it outputs the *logistic* of this result (see Equation 4-14).

Equation 4-14. Logistic regression model estimated probability (vectorized form)

$$\hat{p} = h_{\boldsymbol{\theta}}(\mathbf{x}) = \sigma\left(\boldsymbol{\theta}^\intercal \mathbf{x}\right)$$

The logistic—denoted $\sigma(\cdot)$—is a *sigmoid function* (i.e., *S*-shaped) that outputs a number between 0 and 1. It is defined as shown in Equation 4-15 and Figure 4-22.

Equation 4-15. Logistic function

$$\sigma(t) = \frac{1}{1 + \exp(-t)}$$

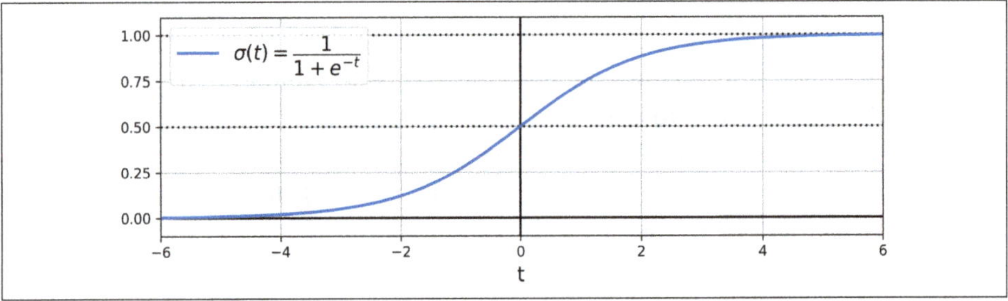

Figure 4-22. Logistic function

Once the logistic regression model has estimated the probability $\hat{p} = h_{\boldsymbol{\theta}}(\mathbf{x})$ that an instance $\mathbf{x}$ belongs to the positive class, it can make its prediction $\hat{y}$ easily (see Equation 4-16).

Equation 4-16. Logistic regression model prediction using a 50% threshold probability

$$\hat{y} = \begin{cases} 0 & \text{if } \hat{p} < 0.5 \\ 1 & \text{if } \hat{p} \geq 0.5 \end{cases}$$

Notice that $\sigma(t) < 0.5$ when $t < 0$, and $\sigma(t) \geq 0.5$ when $t \geq 0$, so a logistic regression model using the default threshold of 50% probability predicts 1 if $\boldsymbol{\theta}^\intercal \mathbf{x}$ is positive and 0 if it is negative.

The score t is often called the *logit*. The name comes from the fact that the logit function, defined as $\text{logit}(p) = \log(p / (1 - p))$, is the inverse of the logistic function. Indeed, if you compute the logit of the estimated probability p, you will find that the result is t. The logit is also called the *log-odds*, since it is the log of the ratio between the estimated probability for the positive class and the estimated probability for the negative class.

Training and Cost Function

Now you know how a logistic regression model estimates probabilities and makes predictions. But how is it trained? The objective of training is to set the parameter vector $\boldsymbol{\theta}$ so that the model estimates high probabilities for positive instances ($y = 1$) and low probabilities for negative instances ($y = 0$). This idea is captured by the cost function shown in Equation 4-17 for a single training instance $\mathbf{x}$.

Equation 4-17. Cost function of a single training instance

$$c(\boldsymbol{\theta}) = \begin{cases} -\log(\hat{p}) & \text{if } y = 1 \\ -\log(1 - \hat{p}) & \text{if } y = 0 \end{cases}$$

This cost function makes sense because $-\log(t)$ grows very large when t approaches 0, so the cost will be large if the model estimates a probability close to 0 for a positive instance, and it will also be large if the model estimates a probability close to 1 for a negative instance. On the other hand, $-\log(t)$ is close to 0 when t is close to 1, so the cost will be close to 0 if the estimated probability is close to 0 for a negative instance or close to 1 for a positive instance, which is precisely what we want.

The cost function over the whole training set is the average cost over all training instances. It can be written in a single expression called the *log loss*, shown in Equation 4-18.

Equation 4-18. Logistic regression cost function (log loss)

$$J(\boldsymbol{\theta}) = -\frac{1}{m}\sum_{i=1}^{m}\left[y^{(i)} log\left(\hat{p}^{(i)}\right) + \left(1 - y^{(i)}\right) log\left(1 - \hat{p}^{(i)}\right)\right]$$

The log loss was not just pulled out of a hat. It can be shown mathematically (using Bayesian inference) that minimizing this loss will result in the model with the *maximum likelihood* of being optimal, assuming that the instances follow a Gaussian distribution around the mean of their class. When you use the log loss, this is the implicit assumption you are making. The more wrong this assumption is, the more biased the model will be. Similarly, when we used the MSE to train linear regression models, we were implicitly assuming that the data was purely linear, plus some Gaussian noise. So, if the data is not linear (e.g., if it's quadratic) or if the noise is not Gaussian (e.g., if outliers are not exponentially rare), then the model will be biased.

The bad news is that there is no known closed-form equation to compute the value of $\boldsymbol{\theta}$ that minimizes this cost function (there is no equivalent of the normal equation). But the good news is that this cost function is convex, so gradient descent (or any other optimization algorithm) is guaranteed to find the global minimum (if the learning rate is not too large and you wait long enough). The partial derivatives of the cost function with regard to the jth model parameter θ_j are given by Equation 4-19.

Equation 4-19. Logistic cost function partial derivatives

$$\frac{\partial}{\partial \theta_j} \text{J}(\boldsymbol{\theta}) = \frac{1}{m} \sum_{i=1}^{m} \left(\sigma\left(\boldsymbol{\theta}^\intercal \mathbf{x}^{(i)} \right) - y^{(i)} \right) x_j^{(i)}$$

This equation looks very much like Equation 4-6: for each instance it computes the prediction error and multiplies it by the jth feature value, and then it computes the average over all training instances. Once you have the gradient vector containing all the partial derivatives, you can use it in the batch gradient descent algorithm. That's it: you now know how to train a logistic regression model. For stochastic GD you would take one instance at a time, and for mini-batch GD you would use a mini-batch at a time.

Decision Boundaries

We can use the iris dataset to illustrate logistic regression. This is a famous dataset that contains the sepal and petal length and width of 150 iris flowers of three different species: *Iris setosa*, *Iris versicolor*, and *Iris virginica* (see Figure 4-23).

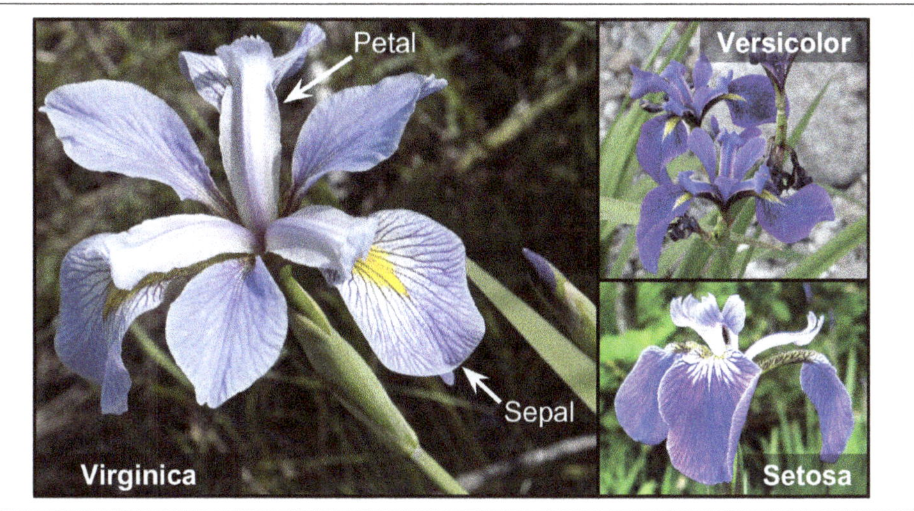

Figure 4-23. Flowers of three iris plant species[14]

Let's try to build a classifier to detect the *Iris virginica* type based only on the petal width feature. The first step is to load the data and take a quick peek:

```
>>> from sklearn.datasets import load_iris
>>> iris = load_iris(as_frame=True)
>>> list(iris)
['data', 'target', 'frame', 'target_names', 'DESCR', 'feature_names',
 'filename', 'data_module']
>>> iris.data.head(3)
   sepal length (cm)  sepal width (cm)  petal length (cm)  petal width (cm)
0                5.1               3.5                1.4               0.2
1                4.9               3.0                1.4               0.2
2                4.7               3.2                1.3               0.2
>>> iris.target.head(3)  # note that the instances are not shuffled
0    0
1    0
2    0
Name: target, dtype: int64
>>> iris.target_names
array(['setosa', 'versicolor', 'virginica'], dtype='<U10')
```

Next we'll split the data and train a logistic regression model on the training set:

```
from sklearn.linear_model import LogisticRegression
from sklearn.model_selection import train_test_split
```

14 Photos reproduced from the corresponding Wikipedia pages. *Iris virginica* photo by Frank Mayfield (Creative Commons BY-SA 2.0 (*https://oreil.ly/O2fAq*)), *Iris versicolor* photo by D. Gordon E. Robertson (Creative Commons BY-SA 3.0 (*https://oreil.ly/pMbrK*)), *Iris setosa* photo public domain.

```
X = iris.data[["petal width (cm)"]].values
y = iris.target_names[iris.target] == 'virginica'
X_train, X_test, y_train, y_test = train_test_split(X, y, random_state=42)

log_reg = LogisticRegression(random_state=42)
log_reg.fit(X_train, y_train)
```

Let's look at the model's estimated probabilities for flowers with petal widths varying from 0 cm to 3 cm (Figure 4-24):[15]

```
X_new = np.linspace(0, 3, 1000).reshape(-1, 1)  # reshape to get a column vector
y_proba = log_reg.predict_proba(X_new)
decision_boundary = X_new[y_proba[:, 1] >= 0.5][0, 0]

plt.plot(X_new, y_proba[:, 0], "b--", linewidth=2,
         label="Not Iris virginica proba")
plt.plot(X_new, y_proba[:, 1], "g-", linewidth=2, label="Iris virginica proba")
plt.plot([decision_boundary, decision_boundary], [0, 1], "k:", linewidth=2,
         label="Decision boundary")
[...] # beautify the figure: add grid, labels, axis, legend, arrows, and samples
plt.show()
```

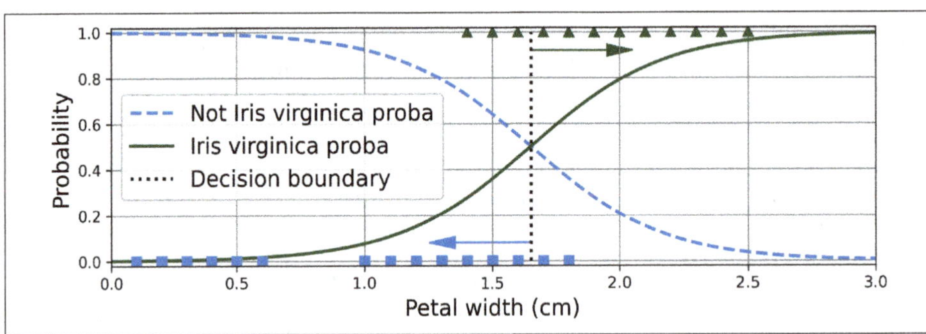

Figure 4-24. Estimated probabilities and decision boundary

The petal width of *Iris virginica* flowers (represented as triangles) ranges from 1.4 cm to 2.5 cm, while the other iris flowers (represented by squares) generally have a smaller petal width, ranging from 0.1 cm to 1.8 cm. Notice that there is a bit of overlap. Above about 2 cm the classifier is highly confident that the flower is an *Iris virginica* (it outputs a high probability for that class), while below 1 cm it is highly confident that it is not an *Iris virginica* (high probability for the "Not Iris virginica" class). In between these extremes, the classifier is unsure. However, if you ask it to predict the class (using the `predict()` method rather than the `predict_proba()` method), it will return whichever class is the most likely. Therefore, there is a *decision boundary* at around 1.6 cm where both probabilities are equal to 50%: if the petal

15 NumPy's `reshape()` function allows one dimension to be –1, which means "automatic": the value is inferred from the length of the array and the remaining dimensions.

width is greater than 1.6 cm the classifier will predict that the flower is an *Iris virginica*, and otherwise it will predict that it is not (even if it is not very confident):

```
>>> decision_boundary
np.float64(1.6516516516516517)
>>> log_reg.predict([[1.7], [1.5]])
array([ True, False])
```

Figure 4-25 shows the same dataset, but this time displaying two features: petal width and length. Once trained, the logistic regression classifier can, based on these two features, estimate the probability that a new flower is an *Iris virginica*. The dashed line represents the points where the model estimates a 50% probability: this is the model's decision boundary. Note that it is a linear boundary.[16] Each parallel line represents the points where the model outputs a specific probability, from 15% (bottom left) to 90% (top right). All the flowers beyond the top-right line have over a 90% chance of being *Iris virginica*, according to the model.

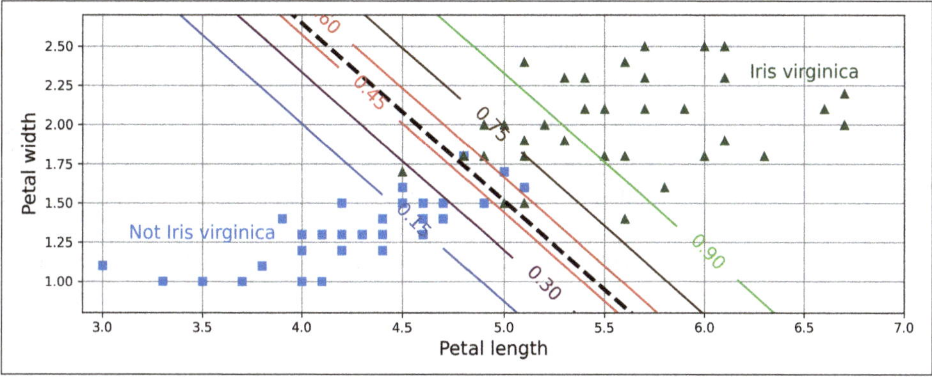

Figure 4-25. Linear decision boundary

The hyperparameter controlling the regularization strength of a Scikit-Learn `LogisticRegression` model is not `alpha` (as in other linear models), but its inverse: `C`. The higher the value of `C`, the *less* the model is regularized.

Just like the other linear models, logistic regression models can be regularized using ℓ_1 or ℓ_2 penalties. Scikit-Learn actually adds an ℓ_2 penalty by default.

16 It is the set of points $\mathbf{x}$ such that $\theta_0 + \theta_1 x_1 + \theta_2 x_2 = 0$, which defines a straight line.

Softmax Regression

The logistic regression model can be generalized to support multiple classes directly, without having to train and combine multiple binary classifiers (as discussed in Chapter 3). This is called *softmax regression*, or *multinomial logistic regression*.

The idea is simple: when given an instance $\mathbf{x}$, the softmax regression model first computes a score $s_k(\mathbf{x})$ for each class k, then estimates the probability of each class by applying the *softmax function* (also called the *normalized exponential*) to the scores. The equation to compute $s_k(\mathbf{x})$ should look familiar, as it is just like the equation for linear regression prediction (see Equation 4-20).

Equation 4-20. Softmax score for class k

$$s_k(\mathbf{x}) = \left(\boldsymbol{\theta}^{(k)}\right)^\intercal \mathbf{x}$$

Note that each class has its own dedicated parameter vector $\boldsymbol{\theta}^{(k)}$. All these vectors are typically stored as rows in a *parameter matrix* $\boldsymbol{\Theta}$.

Once you have computed the score of every class for the instance $\mathbf{x}$, you can estimate the probability $\hat{p}_k$ that the instance belongs to class k by running the scores through the softmax function (Equation 4-21). The function computes the exponential of every score, then normalizes them (dividing by the sum of all the exponentials). The scores are generally called logits or log-odds (although they are actually unnormalized log-odds).

Equation 4-21. Softmax function

$$\hat{p}_k = \sigma(\mathbf{s}(\mathbf{x}))_k = \frac{\exp\left(s_k(\mathbf{x})\right)}{\sum_{j=1}^{K} \exp\left(s_j(\mathbf{x})\right)}$$

In this equation:

- K is the number of classes.
- $\mathbf{s}(\mathbf{x})$ is a vector containing the scores of each class for the instance $\mathbf{x}$.
- $\sigma(\mathbf{s}(\mathbf{x}))_k$ is the estimated probability that the instance $\mathbf{x}$ belongs to class k, given the scores of each class for that instance.

Just like the logistic regression classifier, by default the softmax regression classifier predicts the class with the highest estimated probability (which is simply the class with the highest score), as shown in Equation 4-22.

Equation 4-22. Softmax regression classifier prediction

$$\hat{y} = \underset{k}{\text{argmax}}\ \sigma(\mathbf{s}(\mathbf{x}))_k = \underset{k}{\text{argmax}}\ s_k(\mathbf{x}) = \underset{k}{\text{argmax}}\ \left(\left(\boldsymbol{\theta}^{(k)}\right)^\intercal \mathbf{x}\right)$$

The *argmax* operator returns the value of a variable that maximizes a function. In this equation, it returns the value of k that maximizes the estimated probability $\sigma(\mathbf{s}(\mathbf{x}))_k$.

The softmax regression classifier predicts only one class at a time (i.e., it is multiclass, not multioutput), so it should be used only with mutually exclusive classes, such as different species of plants. You cannot use it to recognize multiple people in one picture.

Now that you know how the model estimates probabilities and makes predictions, let's take a look at training. The objective is to have a model that estimates a high probability for the target class (and consequently a low probability for the other classes). Minimizing the cost function shown in Equation 4-23, called the *cross entropy*, should lead to this objective because it penalizes the model when it estimates a low probability for a target class. Cross entropy is frequently used to measure how well a set of estimated class probabilities matches the target classes.

Equation 4-23. Cross entropy cost function

$$J(\boldsymbol{\Theta}) = -\frac{1}{m}\sum_{i=1}^{m}\sum_{k=1}^{K} y_k^{(i)} \log\left(\hat{p}_k^{(i)}\right)$$

In this equation, $y_k^{(i)}$ is the target probability that the ith instance belongs to class k. In general, it is either equal to 1 or 0, depending on whether the instance belongs to the class or not.

Notice that when there are just two classes ($K = 2$), this cost function is equivalent to the logistic regression cost function (log loss; see Equation 4-18).

Cross Entropy

Cross entropy originated from Claude Shannon's *information theory*. Suppose you want to efficiently transmit information about the weather every day. If there are eight options (sunny, rainy, etc.), you could encode each option using 3 bits, because $2^3 = 8$. However, if you think it will be sunny almost every day, it would be much more efficient to code "sunny" on just one bit (0) and the other seven options on four bits (starting with a 1). Cross entropy measures the average number of bits you actually send per option. If your assumption about the weather is perfect, cross entropy will be equal to the entropy of the weather itself (i.e., its intrinsic unpredictability). But if your assumption is wrong (e.g., if it rains often), cross entropy will be greater by an amount called the *Kullback–Leibler (KL) divergence*.

The cross entropy between two probability distributions p and q is defined as $H(p,q) = -\Sigma_x \, p(x) \log q(x)$ (at least when the distributions are discrete). For more details, check out my video on the subject (*https://homl.info/xentropy*).

The gradient vector of this cost function with regard to $\boldsymbol{\theta}^{(k)}$ is given by Equation 4-24.

Equation 4-24. Cross entropy gradient vector for class k

$$\nabla_{\boldsymbol{\theta}^{(k)}} J(\boldsymbol{\Theta}) = \frac{1}{m} \sum_{i=1}^{m} \left(\hat{p}_k^{(i)} - y_k^{(i)} \right) \mathbf{x}^{(i)}$$

Now you can compute the gradient vector for every class, then use gradient descent (or any other optimization algorithm) to find the parameter matrix $\boldsymbol{\Theta}$ that minimizes the cost function.

Let's use softmax regression to classify the iris plants into all three classes. Scikit-Learn's `LogisticRegression` classifier uses softmax regression automatically when you train it on more than two classes (assuming you use `solver="lbfgs"`, which is the default). It also applies ℓ_2 regularization by default, which you can control using the hyperparameter `C`: decrease `C` to increase regularization, as mentioned earlier.

```
X = iris.data[["petal length (cm)", "petal width (cm)"]].values
y = iris["target"]
X_train, X_test, y_train, y_test = train_test_split(X, y, random_state=42)

softmax_reg = LogisticRegression(C=30, random_state=42)
softmax_reg.fit(X_train, y_train)
```

So the next time you find an iris with petals that are 5 cm long and 2 cm wide, you can ask your model to tell you what type of iris it is, and it will answer *Iris virginica* (class 2) with 96% probability (or *Iris versicolor* with 4% probability):

```
>>> softmax_reg.predict([[5, 2]])
array([2])
>>> softmax_reg.predict_proba([[5, 2]]).round(2)
array([[0.  , 0.04, 0.96]])
```

Figure 4-26 shows the resulting decision boundaries, represented by the background colors. Notice that the decision boundaries between any two classes are linear. The figure also shows the probabilities for the *Iris versicolor* class, represented by the curved lines (e.g., the line labeled with 0.30 represents the 30% probability boundary). Notice that the model can predict a class that has an estimated probability below 50%. For example, at the point where all decision boundaries meet, all classes have an equal estimated probability of 33%.

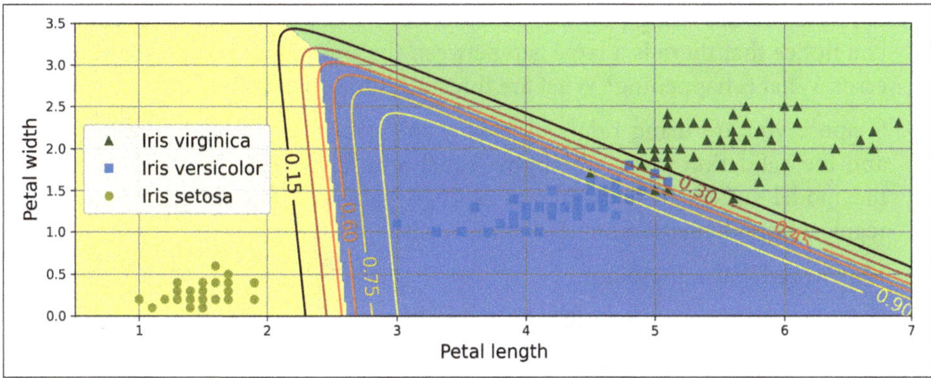

Figure 4-26. Softmax regression decision boundaries

In this chapter, you learned various ways to train linear models, both for regression and for classification. You used a closed-form equation to solve linear regression, as well as gradient descent, and you learned how various penalties can be added to the cost function during training to regularize the model. Along the way, you also learned how to plot learning curves and analyze them, and how to implement early stopping. Finally, you learned how logistic regression and softmax regression work. We've opened up the first machine learning black boxes! In the next chapters we will open many more, starting with support vector machines.

Exercises

1. Which linear regression training algorithm can you use if you have a training set with millions of features?
2. Suppose the features in your training set have very different scales. Which algorithms might suffer from this, and how? What can you do about it?
3. Can gradient descent get stuck in a local minimum when training a logistic regression model?
4. Do all gradient descent algorithms lead to the same model, provided you let them run long enough?
5. Suppose you use batch gradient descent and you plot the validation error at every epoch. If you notice that the validation error consistently goes up, what is likely going on? How can you fix this?
6. Is it a good idea to stop mini-batch gradient descent immediately when the validation error goes up?
7. Which gradient descent algorithm (among those we discussed) will reach the vicinity of the optimal solution the fastest? Which will actually converge? How can you make the others converge as well?

8. Suppose you are using polynomial regression. You plot the learning curves and you notice that there is a large gap between the training error and the validation error. What is happening? What are three ways to solve this?
9. Suppose you are using ridge regression and you notice that the training error and the validation error are almost equal and fairly high. Would you say that the model suffers from high bias or high variance? Should you increase the regularization hyperparameter α or reduce it?
10. Why would you want to use:
    a. Ridge regression instead of plain linear regression (i.e., without any regularization)?
    b. Lasso instead of ridge regression?
    c. Elastic net instead of lasso regression?
11. Suppose you want to classify pictures as outdoor/indoor and daytime/nighttime. Should you implement two logistic regression classifiers or one softmax regression classifier?
12. Implement batch gradient descent with early stopping for softmax regression without using Scikit-Learn, only NumPy. Use it on a classification task such as the iris dataset.

Solutions to these exercises are available at the end of this chapter's notebook, at *https://homl.info/colab-p*.

CHAPTER 5
Decision Trees

Decision trees are versatile machine learning algorithms that can perform both classification and regression tasks, and even multioutput tasks. They are powerful algorithms, capable of fitting complex datasets. For example, in Chapter 2 you trained a `DecisionTreeRegressor` model on the California housing dataset, fitting it perfectly (actually, overfitting it).

Decision trees are also the fundamental components of random forests (see Chapter 6), which are among the most powerful machine learning algorithms available today.

In this chapter we will start by discussing how to train, visualize, and make predictions with decision trees. Then we will go through the CART training algorithm used by Scikit-Learn, and we will explore how to regularize trees and use them for regression tasks. Finally, we will discuss some of the limitations of decision trees.

Training and Visualizing a Decision Tree

To understand decision trees, let's build one and take a look at how it makes predictions. The following code trains a `DecisionTreeClassifier` on the iris dataset (see Chapter 4):

```
from sklearn.datasets import load_iris
from sklearn.tree import DecisionTreeClassifier

iris = load_iris(as_frame=True)
X_iris = iris.data[["petal length (cm)", "petal width (cm)"]].values
y_iris = iris.target

tree_clf = DecisionTreeClassifier(max_depth=2, random_state=42)
tree_clf.fit(X_iris, y_iris)
```

You can visualize the trained decision tree by first using the `export_graphviz()` function to output a graph definition file called *iris_tree.dot*:

```
from sklearn.tree import export_graphviz

export_graphviz(
        tree_clf,
        out_file="iris_tree.dot",
        feature_names=["petal length (cm)", "petal width (cm)"],
        class_names=iris.target_names,
        rounded=True,
        filled=True
    )
```

Then you can use `graphviz.Source.from_file()` to load and display the file in a Jupyter notebook:

```
from graphviz import Source

Source.from_file("iris_tree.dot")
```

Graphviz (*https://graphviz.org*) is an open source graph visualization software package. It also includes a `dot` command-line tool to convert *.dot* files to a variety of formats, such as PDF or PNG.

Your first decision tree looks like Figure 5-1.

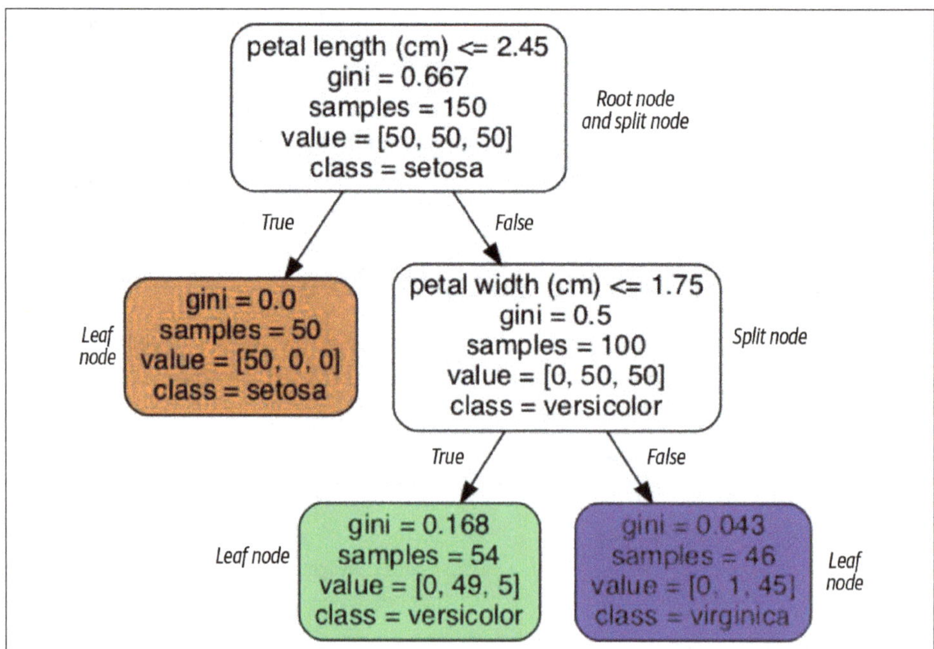

Figure 5-1. Iris decision tree

Making Predictions

Let's see how the tree represented in Figure 5-1 makes predictions. Suppose you find an iris flower and you want to classify it based on its petals. You start at the *root node* (depth 0, at the top): this node asks whether the flower's petal length is smaller than 2.45 cm. If it is, then you move down to the root's left child node (depth 1, left). In this case, it is a *leaf node* (i.e., it does not have any child nodes), so it does not ask any questions: simply look at the predicted class for that node, and the decision tree predicts that your flower is an *Iris setosa* (`class=setosa`).

Now suppose you find another flower, and this time the petal length is greater than 2.45 cm. You again start at the root but now move down to its right child node (depth 1, right). This is not a leaf node, it's a *split node*, so it asks another question: is the petal width smaller than 1.75 cm? If it is, then your flower is most likely an *Iris versicolor* (depth 2, left). If not, it is likely an *Iris virginica* (depth 2, right). It's really that simple.

One of the many qualities of decision trees is that they require very little data preparation. In fact, they don't require feature scaling or centering at all.

A node's `samples` attribute counts how many training instances it applies to. For example, 100 training instances have a petal length greater than 2.45 cm (depth 1, right), and of those 100, 54 have a petal width smaller than 1.75 cm (depth 2, left). A node's `value` attribute tells you how many training instances of each class this node applies to: for example, the bottom-right node applies to 0 *Iris setosa*, 1 *Iris versicolor*, and 45 *Iris virginica*. Finally, a node's `gini` attribute measures its *Gini impurity*: a node is "pure" (`gini=0`) if all training instances it applies to belong to the same class. For example, since the depth-1 left node applies only to *Iris setosa* training instances, its Gini impurity is 0. Conversely, the other nodes all apply to instances of multiple classes, so they are "impure". Equation 5-1 shows how the training algorithm computes the Gini impurity G_i of the ith node. The more classes and the more mixed they are, the larger the impurity. For example, the depth-2 left node has a Gini impurity equal to $1 - (0/54)^2 - (49/54)^2 - (5/54)^2 \approx 0.168$.

Equation 5-1. Gini impurity

$$G_i = 1 - \sum_{k=1}^{n} {p_{i,k}}^2$$

In this equation:

- G_i is the Gini impurity of the ith node.
- $p_{i,k}$ is the ratio of class k instances among the training instances in the ith node.

Scikit-Learn uses the CART algorithm (discussed shortly), which produces only *binary trees*, meaning trees where split nodes always have exactly two children (i.e., questions only have yes/no answers). However, other algorithms, such as ID3, can produce decision trees with nodes that have more than two children.

Figure 5-2 shows this decision tree's decision boundaries. The thick vertical line represents the decision boundary of the root node (depth 0): petal length = 2.45 cm. Since the lefthand area is pure (only *Iris setosa*), it cannot be split any further. However, the righthand area is impure, so the depth-1 right node splits it at petal width = 1.75 cm (represented by the dashed line). Since `max_depth` was set to 2, the decision tree stops right there. If you set `max_depth` to 3, then the two depth-2 nodes would each add another decision boundary (represented by the two vertical dotted lines).

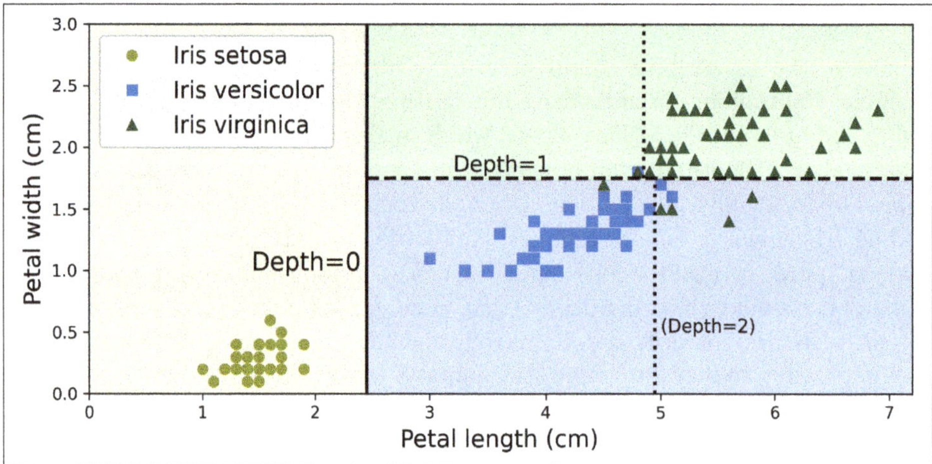

Figure 5-2. Decision tree decision boundaries

The tree structure, including all the information shown in Figure 5-1, is available via the classifier's `tree_` attribute. Type **`help(tree_clf.tree_)`** for details, and see this chapter's notebook (*https://homl.info/colab-p*) for an example.

Model Interpretation: White Box Versus Black Box

Decision trees are intuitive, and their decisions are easy to interpret. Such models are often called *white box models*. In contrast, as you will see, random forests and neural networks are generally considered *black box models*. They make great predictions, and you can easily check the calculations that they performed to make these predictions; nevertheless, it is usually hard to explain in simple terms why the predictions were made. For example, if a neural network says that a particular person appears in a picture, it is hard to know what contributed to this prediction: Did the model recognize that person's eyes? Their mouth? Their nose? Their shoes? Or even the couch that they were sitting on? Conversely, decision trees provide nice, simple classification rules that can even be applied manually if need be (e.g., for flower classification). The field of *interpretable ML* aims at creating ML systems that can explain their decisions in a way humans can understand. This is important in many domains, for example in healthcare, to let a doctor review the diagnosis; in finance, to let analysts understand the risks; in a judicial system, to let a human make the final call; or in human resources, to ensure decisions aren't biased.

Estimating Class Probabilities

A decision tree can also estimate the probability that an instance belongs to a particular class *k*. First it traverses the tree to find the leaf node for this instance, and then it returns the proportion of instances of class *k* among the training instances that would also reach this leaf node. For example, suppose you have found a flower whose petals are 5 cm long and 1.5 cm wide. The corresponding leaf node is the depth-2 left node, so the decision tree outputs the following probabilities: 0% for *Iris setosa* (0/54), 90.7% for *Iris versicolor* (49/54), and 9.3% for *Iris virginica* (5/54). And if you ask it to predict the class, it outputs *Iris versicolor* (class 1) because it has the highest probability. Let's check this:

```
>>> tree_clf.predict_proba([[5, 1.5]]).round(3)
array([[0.    , 0.907, 0.093]])
>>> tree_clf.predict([[5, 1.5]])
array([1])
```

Perfect! Notice that the estimated probabilities would be identical anywhere else in the bottom-right rectangle of Figure 5-2—for example, if the petals were 6 cm long and 1.5 cm wide (even though it seems obvious that it would most likely be an *Iris virginica* in this case).

The CART Training Algorithm

Scikit-Learn uses the *Classification and Regression Tree* (CART) algorithm to train decision trees (also called "growing" trees). The algorithm works by first splitting the training set into two subsets using a single feature k and a threshold t_k (e.g., "petal length ≤ 2.45 cm"). How does it choose k and t_k? It searches for the pair (k, t_k) that produces the purest subsets, weighted by their size. Equation 5-2 gives the cost function that the algorithm tries to minimize.

Equation 5-2. CART cost function for classification

$$J(k,t_k) = \frac{m_{\text{left}}}{m} G_{\text{left}} + \frac{m_{\text{right}}}{m} G_{\text{right}}$$

$$\text{where} \begin{cases} G_{\text{left/right}} \text{ measures the impurity of the left/right subset} \\ m_{\text{left/right}} \text{ is the number of instances in the left/right subset} \\ m = m_{\text{left}} + m_{\text{right}} \end{cases}$$

Once the CART algorithm has successfully split the training set in two, it splits the subsets using the same logic, then the sub-subsets, and so on, recursively. It stops recursing once it reaches the maximum depth (defined by the `max_depth` hyperparameter), or if it cannot find a split that will reduce impurity. A few other hyperparameters (described in a moment) control additional stopping conditions: `min_samples_split`, `min_samples_leaf`, `max_leaf_nodes`, and more.

As you can see, the CART algorithm is a *greedy algorithm*: it greedily searches for an optimum split at the top level, then repeats the process at each subsequent level. It does not check whether the split will lead to the lowest possible impurity several levels down. A greedy algorithm often produces a solution that's reasonably good but not guaranteed to be optimal.

Unfortunately, finding the optimal tree is known to be an *NP-complete* problem.[1] It requires O(exp(m)) time,[2] making the problem intractable even for small training sets. This is why we must settle for a "reasonably good" solution when training decision trees.

1 P is the set of problems that can be solved in *polynomial time* (i.e., a polynomial of the dataset size). NP is the set of problems whose solutions can be verified in polynomial time. An NP-hard problem is a problem that can be reduced to a known NP-hard problem in polynomial time. An NP-complete problem is both NP and NP-hard. A major open mathematical question is whether P = NP. If P ≠ NP (which seems likely), then no polynomial algorithm will ever be found for any NP-complete problem (except perhaps one day on a quantum computer).

2 This *big O notation* means that as m (i.e., the number of training instances) gets larger, the computation time becomes proportional to the exponential of m (it's actually an upper bound, but we make it as small as we can). This tells us how "fast" the computation grows with m, and O(exp(m)) is very fast.

Computational Complexity

Making predictions requires traversing the decision tree from the root to a leaf. Decision trees are generally approximately balanced, so traversing the decision tree requires going through roughly $O(\log_2(m))$ nodes, where m is the number of training instances, and $\log_2(m)$ is the *binary logarithm* of m, equal to $\log(m) / \log(2)$. Since each node only requires checking the value of one feature, the overall prediction complexity is $O(\log_2(m))$, independent of the number of features. So predictions are very fast, even when dealing with large training sets.

By default, the training algorithm compares all features on all samples at each node, which results in a training complexity of $O(n \times m \log_2(m))$.

It's possible to set a maximum tree depth using the `max_depth` hyperparameter, and/or set a maximum number of features to consider at each node (the features are then chosen randomly). Doing so will help speed up training considerably, and it can also reduce the risk of overfitting (but as always, going too far would result in underfitting).

Gini Impurity or Entropy?

By default, the `DecisionTreeClassifier` class uses the Gini impurity measure, but you can select the *entropy* impurity measure instead by setting the `criterion` hyperparameter to `"entropy"`. The concept of entropy originated in thermodynamics as a measure of molecular disorder: entropy approaches zero when molecules are still and well ordered. Entropy later spread to a wide variety of domains, including in Shannon's information theory, where it measures the average information content of a message, as we saw in Chapter 4. Entropy is zero when all messages are identical. In machine learning, entropy is frequently used as an impurity measure: a set's entropy is zero when it contains instances of only one class. Equation 5-3 shows the definition of the entropy of the ith node. For example, the depth-2 left node in Figure 5-1 has an entropy equal to $-(49/54) \log_2 (49/54) - (5/54) \log_2 (5/54) \approx 0.445$.

Equation 5-3. Entropy

$$H_i = - \sum_{\substack{k=1 \\ p_{i,k} \neq 0}}^{n} p_{i,k} \log_2 \left(p_{i,k}\right)$$

So, should you use Gini impurity or entropy? The truth is, most of the time it does not make a big difference: they lead to similar trees. Gini impurity is slightly faster to compute, so it is a good default. However, when they differ, Gini impurity tends to isolate the most frequent class in its own branch of the tree, while entropy tends to produce slightly more balanced trees.[3]

Regularization Hyperparameters

Decision trees make very few assumptions about the training data (as opposed to linear models, which assume that the data is linear, for example). If left unconstrained, the tree structure will adapt itself to the training data, fitting it very closely—indeed, most likely overfitting it. Such a model is often called a *nonparametric model*, not because it does not have any parameters (it often has a lot) but because the number of parameters is not determined prior to training, so the model structure is free to stick closely to the data. In contrast, a *parametric model*, such as a linear model, has a predetermined number of parameters, so its degree of freedom is limited, reducing the risk of overfitting (but increasing the risk of underfitting).

To avoid overfitting the training data, you need to restrict the decision tree's freedom during training. As you know by now, this is called regularization. The regularization hyperparameters depend on the algorithm used, but generally you can at least restrict the maximum depth of the decision tree. In Scikit-Learn, this is controlled by the `max_depth` hyperparameter. The default value is `None`, which means unlimited. Reducing `max_depth` will regularize the model and thus reduce the risk of overfitting.

The `DecisionTreeClassifier` class has a few other parameters that similarly restrict the shape of the decision tree:

`max_features`
: Maximum number of features that are evaluated for splitting at each node

`max_leaf_nodes`
: Maximum number of leaf nodes

`min_samples_split`
: Minimum number of samples a node must have before it can be split

`min_samples_leaf`
: Minimum number of samples a leaf node must have to be created

`min_weight_fraction_leaf`
: Same as `min_samples_leaf` but expressed as a fraction of the total number of weighted instances

`min_impurity_decrease`
: Only split a node if this split results in at least this reduction in impurity

3 See Sebastian Raschka's interesting analysis (*https://homl.info/19*) for more details.

`ccp_alpha`
: Controls *minimal cost-complexity pruning* (MCCP), i.e., pruning subtrees that don't reduce impurity enough compared to their number of leaves; a larger `ccp_alpha` value leads to more pruning, resulting in a smaller tree (the default is 0—no pruning)

To limit the model's complexity and thereby regularize the model, you can increase `min_*` hyperparameters or `ccp_alpha`, or decrease `max_*` hyperparameters. Tuning `max_depth` is usually a good default: it provides effective regularization, and it keeps the tree small and easy to interpret. Setting `min_samples_leaf` is also a good idea, especially for small datasets. And `max_features` is great when working with high-dimensional datasets.

Other algorithms work by first training the decision tree without restrictions, then *pruning* (deleting) unnecessary nodes. A node whose children are all leaf nodes is considered unnecessary if the purity improvement it provides is not statistically significant. Standard statistical tests, such as the χ^2 *test* (chi-squared test), are used to estimate the probability that the improvement is purely the result of chance (which is called the *null hypothesis*). If this probability, called the *p-value*, is higher than a given threshold (typically 5%, controlled by a hyperparameter), then the node is considered unnecessary and its children are deleted. The pruning continues until all unnecessary nodes have been pruned.

Let's test regularization on the moons dataset: this is a toy dataset for binary classification in which the data points are shaped as two interleaving crescent moons (see Figure 5-3). You can generate this dataset using the `make_moons()` function.

We'll train one decision tree without regularization, and another with `min_samples_leaf=5`. Here's the code; Figure 5-3 shows the decision boundaries of each tree:

```
from sklearn.datasets import make_moons

X_moons, y_moons = make_moons(n_samples=150, noise=0.2, random_state=42)

tree_clf1 = DecisionTreeClassifier(random_state=42)
tree_clf2 = DecisionTreeClassifier(min_samples_leaf=5, random_state=42)
tree_clf1.fit(X_moons, y_moons)
tree_clf2.fit(X_moons, y_moons)
```

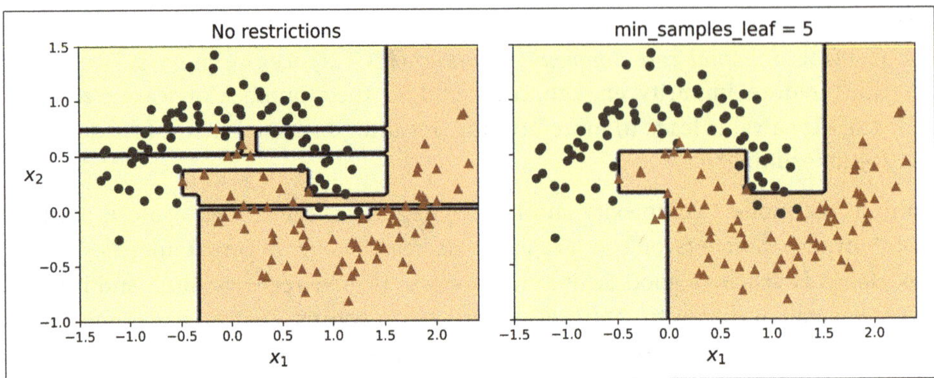

Figure 5-3. Decision boundaries of an unregularized tree (left) and a regularized tree (right)

The unregularized model on the left is clearly overfitting, and the regularized model on the right will probably generalize better. We can verify this by evaluating both trees on a test set generated using a different random seed:

```
>>> X_moons_test, y_moons_test = make_moons(n_samples=1000, noise=0.2,
...                                         random_state=43)
...
>>> tree_clf1.score(X_moons_test, y_moons_test)
0.898
>>> tree_clf2.score(X_moons_test, y_moons_test)
0.92
```

Indeed, the second tree has a better accuracy on the test set.

Regression

Decision trees are also capable of performing regression tasks. While linear regression only works well with linear data, decision trees can fit all sorts of complex datasets. Let's build a regression tree using Scikit-Learn's `DecisionTreeRegressor` class, training it on a noisy quadratic dataset with `max_depth=2`:

```
import numpy as np
from sklearn.tree import DecisionTreeRegressor

rng = np.random.default_rng(seed=42)
X_quad = rng.random((200, 1)) - 0.5  # a single random input feature
y_quad = X_quad ** 2 + 0.025 * rng.standard_normal((200, 1))

tree_reg = DecisionTreeRegressor(max_depth=2, random_state=42)
tree_reg.fit(X_quad, y_quad)
```

The resulting tree is represented in Figure 5-4.

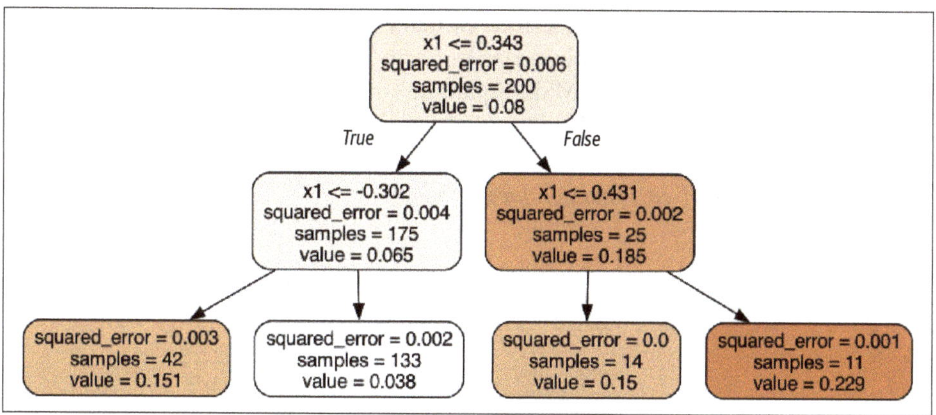

Figure 5-4. A decision tree for regression

This tree looks very similar to the classification tree you built earlier. The main difference is that instead of predicting a class in each node, it predicts a value. For example, suppose you want to make a prediction for a new instance with $x_1 = 0.2$. The root node asks whether $x_1 \leq 0.343$. Since it is, the algorithm goes to the left child node, which asks whether $x_1 \leq -0.302$. Since it is not, the algorithm goes to the right child node. This is a leaf node, and it predicts `value=0.038`. This prediction is the average target value of the 133 training instances associated with this leaf node, and it results in a mean squared error equal to 0.002 over these 133 instances.

This model's predictions are represented on the left in Figure 5-5. If you set `max_depth=3`, you get the predictions represented on the right. Notice how the predicted value for each region is always the average target value of the instances in that region. The algorithm splits each region in a way that makes most training instances as close as possible to that predicted value.

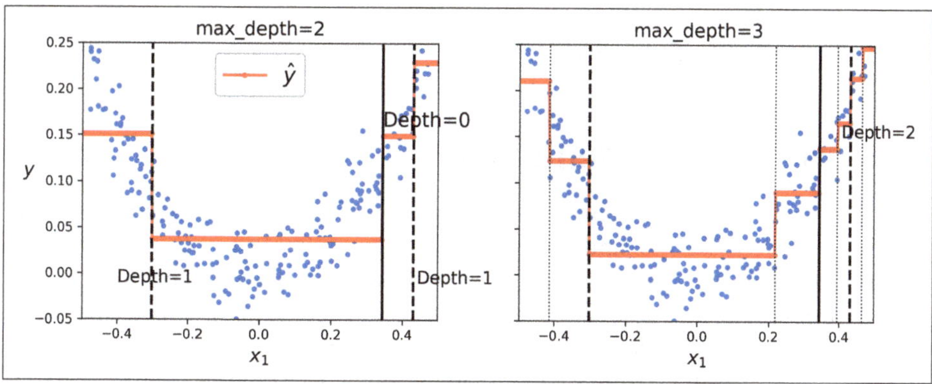

Figure 5-5. Predictions of two decision tree regression models

The CART algorithm works as described earlier, except that instead of trying to split the training set in a way that minimizes impurity, it now tries to split the training set in a way that minimizes the MSE. Equation 5-4 shows the cost function that the algorithm tries to minimize.

Equation 5-4. CART cost function for regression

$$J(k,t_k) = \frac{m_{\text{left}}}{m}\text{MSE}_{\text{left}} + \frac{m_{\text{right}}}{m}\text{MSE}_{\text{right}} \quad \text{where} \begin{cases} \text{MSE}_{\text{node}} = \dfrac{\sum_{i \in \text{node}}\left(\hat{y}_{\text{node}} - y^{(i)}\right)^2}{m_{\text{node}}} \\ \hat{y}_{\text{node}} = \dfrac{\sum_{i \in \text{node}} y^{(i)}}{m_{\text{node}}} \end{cases}$$

Just like for classification tasks, decision trees are prone to overfitting when dealing with regression tasks. Without any regularization (i.e., using the default hyperparameters), you get the predictions on the left in Figure 5-6. These predictions are obviously overfitting the training set very badly. Just setting `min_samples_leaf=10` results in a much more reasonable model, represented on the right in Figure 5-6.

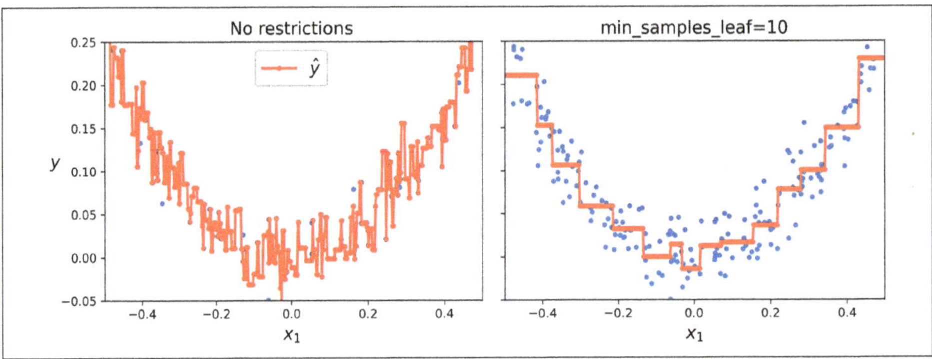

Figure 5-6. Predictions of an unregularized regression tree (left) and a regularized tree (right)

Sensitivity to Axis Orientation

Hopefully by now you are convinced that decision trees have a lot going for them: they are relatively easy to understand and interpret, simple to use, versatile, and powerful. However, they do have a few limitations. First, as you may have noticed, decision trees love orthogonal decision boundaries (all splits are perpendicular to an axis), which makes them sensitive to the data's orientation. For example, Figure 5-7 shows a simple linearly separable dataset: on the left, a decision tree can split it easily, while on the right, after the dataset is rotated by 45°, the decision boundary looks unnecessarily convoluted. Although both decision trees fit the training set perfectly, it is very likely that the model on the right will not generalize well.

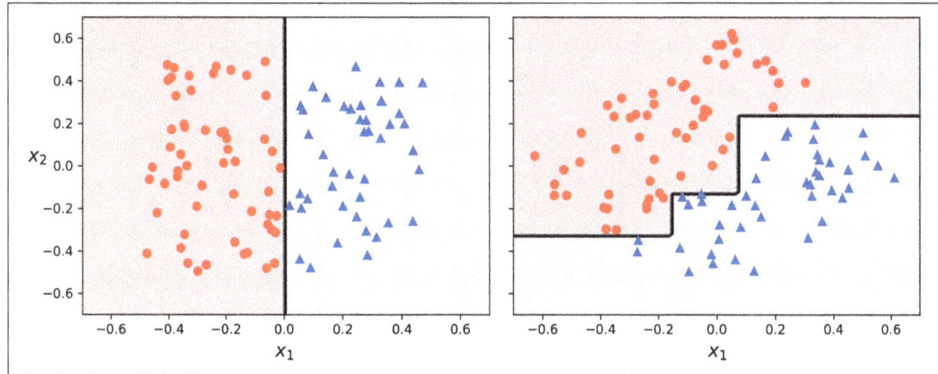

Figure 5-7. Sensitivity to training set rotation

One way to limit this problem is to scale the data, then apply a principal component analysis (PCA) transformation. We will look at PCA in detail in Chapter 7, but for now you only need to know that it rotates the data in a way that reduces the correlation between the features, which often (not always) makes things easier for trees.

Let's create a small pipeline that scales the data and rotates it using PCA, then train a `DecisionTreeClassifier` on that data. Figure 5-8 shows the decision boundaries of that tree: as you can see, the rotation makes it possible to fit the dataset pretty well using only one feature, z_1, which is a linear function of the original petal length and width. Here's the code:

```
from sklearn.decomposition import PCA
from sklearn.pipeline import make_pipeline
from sklearn.preprocessing import StandardScaler

pca_pipeline = make_pipeline(StandardScaler(), PCA())
X_iris_rotated = pca_pipeline.fit_transform(X_iris)
tree_clf_pca = DecisionTreeClassifier(max_depth=2, random_state=42)
tree_clf_pca.fit(X_iris_rotated, y_iris)
```

The `DecisionTreeClassifier` and `DecisionTreeRegressor` classes both support missing values natively, no need for an imputer.

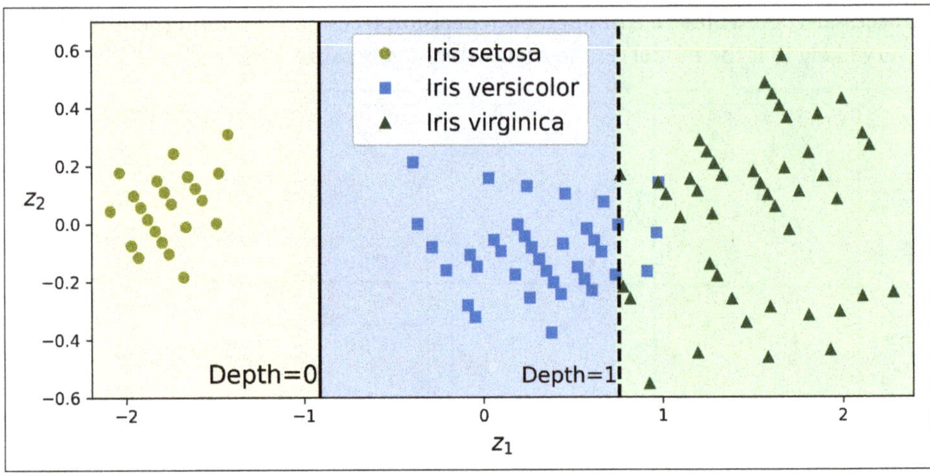

Figure 5-8. A tree's decision boundaries on the scaled and PCA-rotated iris dataset

Decision Trees Have a High Variance

More generally, the main issue with decision trees is that they have quite a high variance: small changes to the hyperparameters or to the data may produce very different models. In fact, since the training algorithm used by Scikit-Learn is stochastic—it randomly selects the set of features to evaluate at each node—even retraining the same decision tree on the exact same data may produce a very different model, such as the one represented in Figure 5-9 (unless you set the `random_state` hyperparameter). As you can see, it looks very different from the previous decision tree (Figure 5-2).

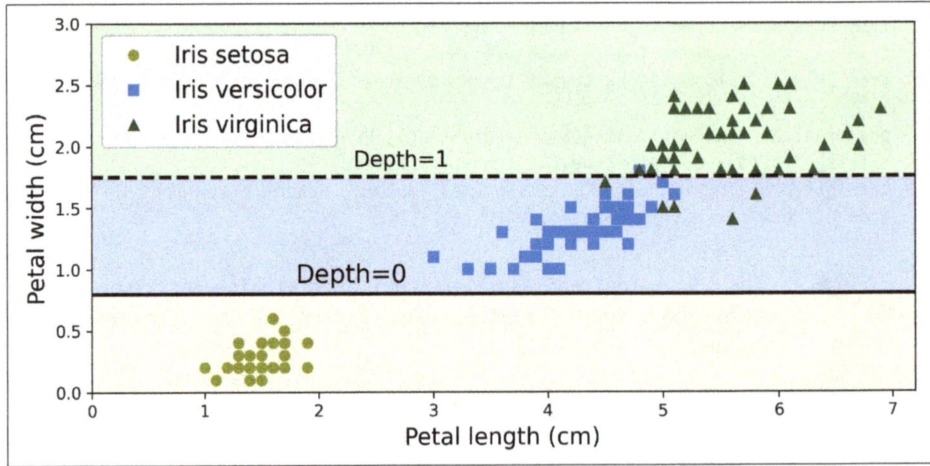

Figure 5-9. Retraining the same model on the same data may produce a very different model

Luckily, by averaging predictions over many trees, it's possible to reduce variance significantly. Such an *ensemble* of trees is called a *random forest*, and it's one of the most powerful types of models available today, as you will see in the next chapter.

Exercises

1. What is the approximate depth of a decision tree trained (without restrictions) on a training set with one million instances?
2. Is a node's Gini impurity generally lower or higher than its parent's? Is it *generally* lower/higher, or *always* lower/higher?
3. If a decision tree is overfitting the training set, is it a good idea to try decreasing `max_depth`?
4. If a decision tree is underfitting the training set, is it a good idea to try scaling the input features?
5. If it takes one hour to train a decision tree on a training set containing one million instances, roughly how much time will it take to train another decision tree on a training set containing ten million instances? Hint: consider the CART algorithm's computational complexity.
6. If it takes one hour to train a decision tree on a given training set, roughly how much time will it take if you double the number of features?
7. Train and fine-tune a decision tree for the moons dataset by following these steps:
   a. Use `make_moons(n_samples=10000, noise=0.4)` to generate a moons dataset.
   b. Use `train_test_split()` to split the dataset into a training set and a test set.
   c. Use grid search with cross-validation (with the help of the `GridSearchCV` class) to find good hyperparameter values for a `DecisionTreeClassifier`. Hint: try various values for `max_leaf_nodes`.
   d. Train it on the full training set using these hyperparameters, and measure your model's performance on the test set. You should get roughly 85% to 87% accuracy.
8. Grow a forest by following these steps:
   a. Continuing the previous exercise, generate 1,000 subsets of the training set, each containing 100 instances selected randomly. Hint: you can use Scikit-Learn's `ShuffleSplit` class for this.
   b. Train one decision tree on each subset, using the best hyperparameter values found in the previous exercise. Evaluate these 1,000 decision trees on the test set. Since they were trained on smaller sets, these decision trees will likely perform worse than the first decision tree, achieving only about 80% accuracy.

c. Now comes the magic. For each test set instance, generate the predictions of the 1,000 decision trees, and keep only the most frequent prediction (you can use SciPy's `mode()` function for this). This approach gives you *majority-vote predictions* over the test set.

d. Evaluate these predictions on the test set: you should obtain a slightly higher accuracy than your first model (about 0.5 to 1.5% higher). Congratulations, you have trained a random forest classifier!

Solutions to these exercises are available at the end of this chapter's notebook, at *https://homl.info/colab-p*.

CHAPTER 6

Ensemble Learning and Random Forests

Suppose you pose a complex question to thousands of random people, then aggregate their answers. In many cases you will find that this aggregated answer is better than an expert's answer. This is called the *wisdom of the crowd*. Similarly, if you aggregate the predictions of a group of predictors (such as classifiers or regressors), you will often get better predictions than with the best individual predictor. A group of predictors is called an *ensemble*; thus, this technique is called *ensemble learning*, and an ensemble learning algorithm is called an *ensemble method*.

As an example of an ensemble method, you can train a group of decision tree classifiers, each on a different random subset of the training set. You can then obtain the predictions of all the individual trees, and the class that gets the most votes is the ensemble's prediction (see the last exercise in Chapter 5). Such an ensemble of decision trees is called a *random forest*, and despite its simplicity, this is one of the most powerful machine learning algorithms available today.

As discussed in Chapter 2, you will often use ensemble methods near the end of a project, once you have already built a few good predictors, to combine them into an even better predictor. In fact, the winning solutions in machine learning competitions often involve several ensemble methods—most famously in the Netflix Prize competition (*https://en.wikipedia.org/wiki/Netflix_Prize*). There are some downsides, however: ensemble learning requires much more computing resources than using a single model (both for training and for inference), it can be more complex to deploy and manage, and the predictions are harder to interpret. But the pros often outweigh the cons.

In this chapter we will examine the most popular ensemble methods, including voting classifiers, bagging and pasting ensembles, random forests, boosting, and stacking ensembles.

Voting Classifiers

Suppose you have trained a few classifiers, each one achieving about 80% accuracy. You may have a logistic regression classifier, an SVM classifier, a random forest classifier, a *k*-nearest neighbors classifier, and perhaps a few more (see Figure 6-1).

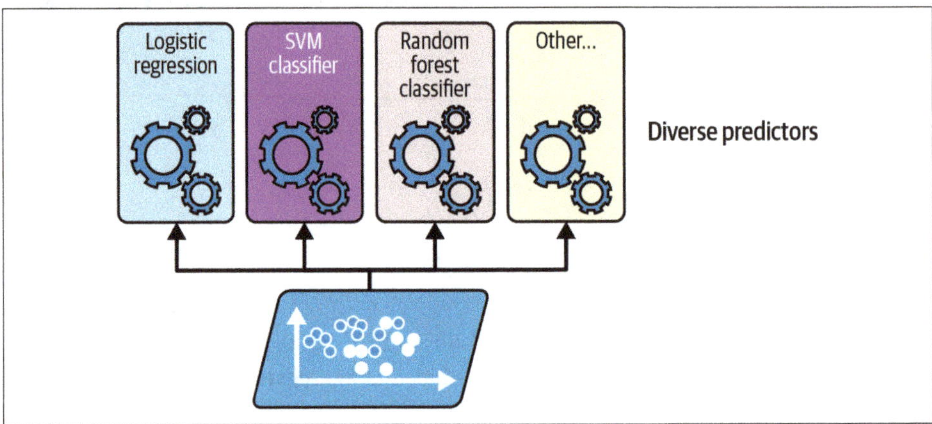

Figure 6-1. Training diverse classifiers

A very simple way to create an even better classifier is to aggregate the predictions of each classifier: the class that gets the most votes is the ensemble's prediction. This majority-vote classifier is called a *hard voting* classifier (see Figure 6-2).

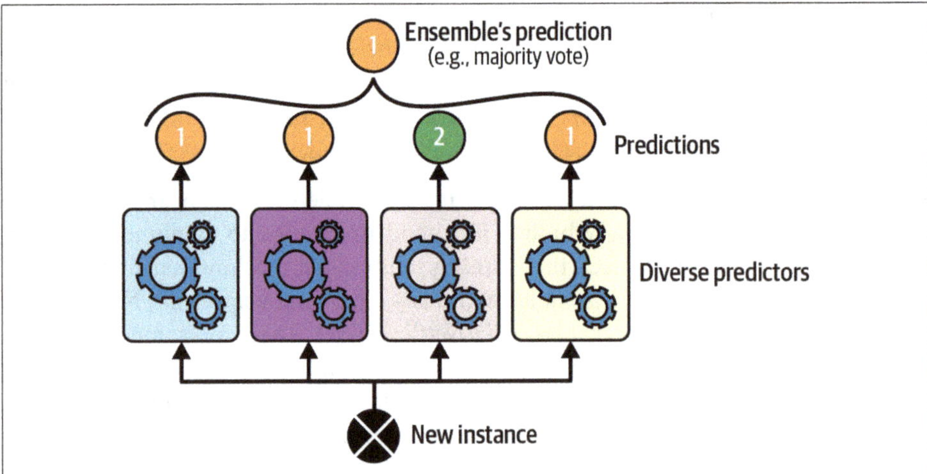

Figure 6-2. Hard voting classifier predictions

Somewhat surprisingly, this voting classifier often achieves a higher accuracy than the best classifier in the ensemble. In fact, even if each classifier is a *weak learner* (meaning it does only slightly better than random guessing), the ensemble can still be a *strong learner* (achieving high accuracy), provided there are a sufficient number of weak learners in the ensemble and they are sufficiently diverse (i.e., if they focus on different aspects of the data and make different kinds of errors).

How is this possible? The following analogy can help shed some light on this mystery. Suppose you have a slightly biased coin that has a 51% chance of coming up heads and 49% chance of coming up tails. If you toss it 1,000 times, you will generally get more or less 510 heads and 490 tails, and hence a majority of heads. If you do the math, you will find that the probability of obtaining a majority of heads after 1,000 tosses is close to 75%. The more you toss the coin, the higher the probability (e.g., with 10,000 tosses, the probability climbs over 97%). This is due to the *law of large numbers*: as you keep tossing the coin, the ratio of heads gets closer and closer to the probability of heads (51%). Figure 6-3 shows 10 series of biased coin tosses. You can see that as the number of tosses increases, the ratio of heads approaches 51%. Eventually all 10 series end up so close to 51% that they are consistently above 50%.

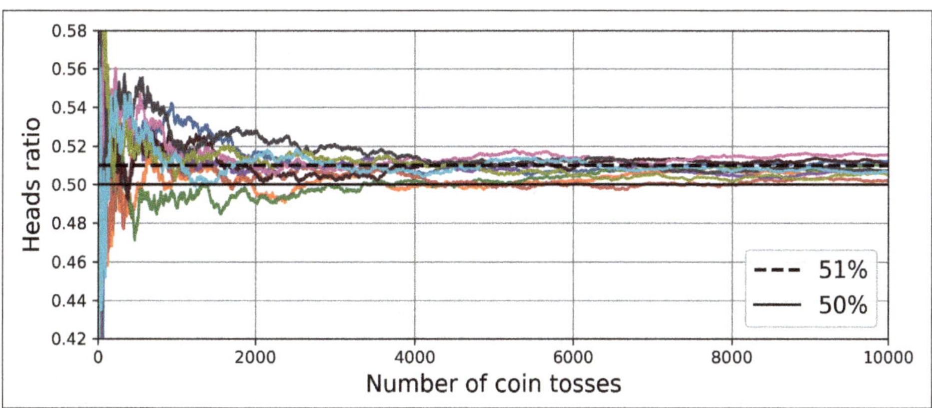

Figure 6-3. The law of large numbers

Similarly, suppose you build an ensemble containing 1,000 classifiers that are individually correct only 51% of the time (barely better than random guessing). If you predict the majority voted class, you can hope for up to 75% accuracy! However, this is only true if all classifiers are perfectly independent, making uncorrelated errors, which is clearly not the case because they are trained on the same data. They are likely to make the same types of errors, so there will be many majority votes for the wrong class, reducing the ensemble's accuracy.

Ensemble methods work best when the predictors are as independent from one another as possible. One way to get diverse classifiers is to train them using very different algorithms. This increases the chance that they will make very different types of errors, improving the ensemble's accuracy. You can also play with the model hyperparameters to get diverse models, or train the models on different subsets of the data, as we will see.

Scikit-Learn provides a `VotingClassifier` class that's quite easy to use: just give it a list of name/predictor pairs, and use it like a normal classifier. Let's try it on the moons dataset (introduced in Chapter 5). We will load and split the moons dataset into a training set and a test set, then we'll create and train a voting classifier composed of three diverse classifiers:

```
from sklearn.datasets import make_moons
from sklearn.ensemble import RandomForestClassifier, VotingClassifier
from sklearn.linear_model import LogisticRegression
from sklearn.model_selection import train_test_split
from sklearn.svm import SVC

X, y = make_moons(n_samples=500, noise=0.30, random_state=42)
X_train, X_test, y_train, y_test = train_test_split(X, y, random_state=42)

voting_clf = VotingClassifier(
    estimators=[
        ('lr', LogisticRegression(random_state=42)),
        ('rf', RandomForestClassifier(random_state=42)),
        ('svc', SVC(random_state=42))
    ]
)
voting_clf.fit(X_train, y_train)
```

When you fit a `VotingClassifier`, it clones every estimator and fits the clones. The original estimators are available via the `estimators` attribute, while the fitted clones are available via the `estimators_` attribute. If you prefer a dict rather than a list, you can use `named_estimators` or `named_estimators_` instead. To begin, let's look at each fitted classifier's accuracy on the test set:

```
>>> for name, clf in voting_clf.named_estimators_.items():
...     print(name, "=", clf.score(X_test, y_test))
...
lr = 0.864
rf = 0.896
svc = 0.896
```

When you call the voting classifier's `predict()` method, it performs hard voting. For example, the voting classifier predicts class 1 for the first instance of the test set, because two out of three classifiers predict that class:

```
>>> voting_clf.predict(X_test[:1])
array([1])
>>> [clf.predict(X_test[:1]) for clf in voting_clf.estimators_]
[array([1]), array([1]), array([0])]
```

Now let's look at the performance of the voting classifier on the test set:

```
>>> voting_clf.score(X_test, y_test)
0.912
```

There you have it! The voting classifier outperforms all the individual classifiers.

If all classifiers are able to estimate class probabilities (i.e., if they all have a `predict_proba()` method), then you should generally tell Scikit-Learn to predict the class with the highest class probability, averaged over all the individual classifiers. This is called *soft voting*. It often achieves higher performance than hard voting because it gives more weight to highly confident votes. All you need to do is set the voting classifier's `voting` hyperparameter to `"soft"`, and ensure that all classifiers can estimate class probabilities. This is not the case for the `SVC` class by default, so you need to set its `probability` hyperparameter to `True` (this will make the `SVC` class use cross-validation to estimate class probabilities, slowing down training, and it will add a `predict_proba()` method). Let's try that:

```
>>> voting_clf.voting = "soft"
>>> voting_clf.named_estimators["svc"].probability = True
>>> voting_clf.fit(X_train, y_train)
>>> voting_clf.score(X_test, y_test)
0.92
```

We reach 92% accuracy simply by using soft voting—not bad!

Soft voting works best when the estimated probabilities are well-calibrated. If they are not, you can use `sklearn.calibration.CalibratedClassifierCV` to calibrate them (see Chapter 3).

Bagging and Pasting

One way to get a diverse set of classifiers is to use very different training algorithms, as just discussed. Another way is to use the same training algorithm for every predictor but train them on different random subsets of the training set. When sampling is performed *with* replacement,[1] this method is called *bagging* (*https://homl.info/20*)[2] (short for *bootstrap aggregating*[3]). When sampling is performed *without* replacement, it is called *pasting* (*https://homl.info/21*).[4]

In other words, both bagging and pasting allow training instances to be sampled several times across multiple predictors, but only bagging allows training instances to be sampled several times for the same predictor. This sampling and training process is represented in Figure 6-4.

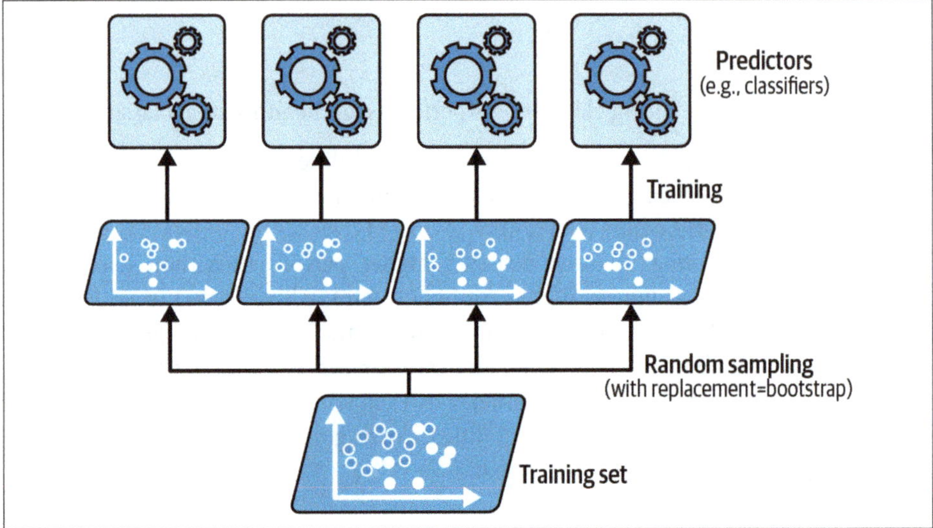

Figure 6-4. Bagging and pasting involve training several predictors on different random samples of the training set

Once all predictors are trained, the ensemble can make a prediction for a new instance by simply aggregating the predictions of all predictors. For classification, the aggregation function is typically the *statistical mode* (i.e., the most frequent prediction, just like with a hard voting classifier), and for regression it's usually just the average. Each individual predictor has a higher bias than if it were trained on the original training set, but aggregation reduces both bias and variance.[5]

---

1 Imagine picking a card randomly from a deck of cards, writing it down, then placing it back in the deck before picking the next card: the same card could be sampled multiple times.

2 Leo Breiman, "Bagging Predictors", *Machine Learning* 24, no. 2 (1996): 123–140.

3 In statistics, resampling with replacement is called *bootstrapping*.

4 Leo Breiman, "Pasting Small Votes for Classification in Large Databases and On-Line", *Machine Learning* 36, no. 1–2 (1999): 85–103.

5 Bias and variance were introduced in Chapter 4. Recall that a high bias means that the average prediction is far off target, while a high variance means that the predictions are very scattered. We want both to be low.

To get an intuition of why this is the case, imagine that you trained two regressors to predict house prices. The first underestimates the prices by $40,000 on average, while the second overestimates them by $50,000 on average. Assuming these regressors are 100% independent and their predictions follow a normal distribution, if you compute the average of the two predictions, the result will overestimate the prices by only (–40,000 + 50,000)/2 = $5,000 on average: that's a much lower bias! Similarly, if both predictors have a $10,000 standard deviation (i.e., a variance of 100,000,000), then the average prediction will have a variance of $(10{,}000^2 + 10{,}000^2)/2^2 = 50{,}000{,}000$ (i.e., the standard deviation will be $7,071). The variance is halved!

In practice, the ensemble often ends up with a similar bias but a lower variance than a single predictor trained on the original training set. Therefore it works best with high-variance and low-bias models (e.g., ensembles of decision trees, not ensembles of linear regressors).

Prefer bagging when your dataset is noisy or your model is prone to overfitting (e.g., deep decision tree). Otherwise, prefer pasting as it avoids redundancy during training, making it a bit more computationally efficient.

As you can see in Figure 6-4, predictors can all be trained in parallel, via different CPU cores or even different servers. Similarly, predictions can be made in parallel. This is one of the reasons bagging and pasting are such popular methods: they scale very well.

Bagging and Pasting in Scikit-Learn

Scikit-Learn offers a simple API for both bagging and pasting: the `BaggingClassifier` class (or `BaggingRegressor` for regression). The following code trains an ensemble of 500 decision tree classifiers:[6] each is trained on 100 training instances randomly sampled from the training set with replacement (this is an example of bagging, but if you want to use pasting instead, just set `bootstrap=False`). The `n_jobs` parameter tells Scikit-Learn the number of CPU cores to use for training and predictions, and `-1` tells Scikit-Learn to use all available cores:

```
from sklearn.ensemble import BaggingClassifier
from sklearn.tree import DecisionTreeClassifier

bag_clf = BaggingClassifier(DecisionTreeClassifier(), n_estimators=500,
                            max_samples=100, n_jobs=-1, random_state=42)
bag_clf.fit(X_train, y_train)
```

6 `max_samples` can alternatively be set to a float between 0.0 and 1.0, in which case the max number of sampled instances is equal to the size of the training set times `max_samples`.

A `BaggingClassifier` automatically performs soft voting instead of hard voting if the base classifier can estimate class probabilities (i.e., if it has a `predict_proba()` method), which is the case with decision tree classifiers.

Figure 6-5 compares the decision boundary of a single decision tree with the decision boundary of a bagging ensemble of 500 trees (from the preceding code), both trained on the moons dataset. As you can see, the ensemble's predictions will likely generalize much better than the single decision tree's predictions: the ensemble has a comparable bias but a smaller variance (it makes roughly the same number of errors on the training set, but the decision boundary is less irregular).

Bagging introduces a bit more diversity in the subsets that each predictor is trained on, so bagging ends up with a slightly higher bias than pasting; but the extra diversity also means that the predictors end up being less correlated, so the ensemble's variance is reduced. Overall, bagging often results in better models, which explains why it's generally preferred. But if you have spare time and CPU power, you can use cross-validation to evaluate both bagging and pasting, and select the one that works best.

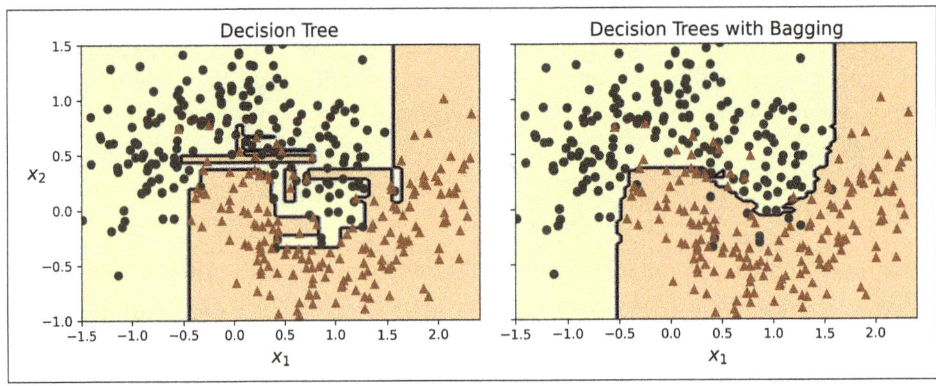

Figure 6-5. A single decision tree (left) versus a bagging ensemble of 500 trees (right)

Out-of-Bag Evaluation

With bagging, some training instances may be sampled several times for any given predictor, while others may not be sampled at all. By default, a `BaggingClassifier` samples *m* training instances with replacement (`bootstrap=True`), where *m* is the size of the training set. With this process, it can be shown mathematically that only about 63% of the training instances are sampled on average for each predictor.[7] The

7 As *m* grows, this ratio approaches 1 – exp(–1) ≈ 63%.

remaining 37% of the training instances that are not sampled are called *out-of-bag* (OOB) instances. Note that they are not the same 37% for all predictors.

A bagging ensemble can be evaluated using OOB instances, without the need for a separate validation set: indeed, if there are enough estimators, then each instance in the training set will likely be an OOB instance of several estimators, so these estimators can be used to make a fair ensemble prediction for that instance. Once you have a prediction for each instance, you can compute the ensemble's prediction accuracy (or any other metric).

In Scikit-Learn, you can set `oob_score=True` when creating a `BaggingClassifier` to request an automatic OOB evaluation after training. The following code demonstrates this. The resulting evaluation score is available in the `oob_score_` attribute:

```
>>> bag_clf = BaggingClassifier(DecisionTreeClassifier(), n_estimators=500,
...                             oob_score=True, n_jobs=-1, random_state=42)
...
>>> bag_clf.fit(X_train, y_train)
>>> bag_clf.oob_score_
0.896
```

According to this OOB evaluation, this `BaggingClassifier` is likely to achieve about 89.6% accuracy on the test set. Let's verify this:

```
>>> from sklearn.metrics import accuracy_score
>>> y_pred = bag_clf.predict(X_test)
>>> accuracy_score(y_test, y_pred)
0.92
```

We get 92.0% accuracy on the test. The OOB evaluation was a bit too pessimistic.

The OOB decision function for each training instance is also available through the `oob_decision_function_` attribute. Since the base estimator has a `predict_proba()` method, the decision function returns the class probabilities for each training instance. For example, the OOB evaluation estimates that the first training instance has a 67.6% probability of belonging to the positive class and a 32.4% probability of belonging to the negative class:

```
>>> bag_clf.oob_decision_function_[:3]  # probas for the first 3 instances
array([[0.32352941, 0.67647059],
       [0.3375    , 0.6625    ],
       [1.        , 0.        ]])
```

Random Patches and Random Subspaces

The `BaggingClassifier` class supports sampling the features as well. Sampling is controlled by two hyperparameters: `max_features` and `bootstrap_features`. They work the same way as `max_samples` and `bootstrap`, but for feature sampling instead of instance sampling. Thus, each predictor will be trained on a random subset of the input features.

This technique is particularly useful when you are dealing with high-dimensional inputs (such as images), as it can considerably speed up training. Sampling both training instances and features is called the *random patches* method (*https://homl.info/22*).[8] Keeping all training instances (by setting `bootstrap=False` and `max_samples=1.0`) but sampling features (by setting `bootstrap_features` to `True` and/or `max_features` to a value smaller than `1.0`) is called the *random subspaces* method (*https://homl.info/23*).[9]

Sampling features results in even more predictor diversity, trading a bit more bias for a lower variance.

Random Forests

As we have discussed, a random forest (*https://homl.info/24*)[10] is an ensemble of decision trees, generally trained via the bagging method (or sometimes pasting), typically with `max_samples` set to the size of the training set. Instead of building a `BaggingClassifier` and passing it a `DecisionTreeClassifier`, you can use the `RandomForestClassifier` class, which is more convenient and optimized for decision trees[11] (similarly, there is a `RandomForestRegressor` class for regression tasks). The following code trains a random forest classifier with 500 trees, each limited to maximum 16 leaf nodes, using all available CPU cores:

```
from sklearn.ensemble import RandomForestClassifier

rnd_clf = RandomForestClassifier(n_estimators=500, max_leaf_nodes=16,
                                 n_jobs=-1, random_state=42)
rnd_clf.fit(X_train, y_train)

y_pred_rf = rnd_clf.predict(X_test)
```

With a few exceptions, a `RandomForestClassifier` has all the hyperparameters of a `DecisionTreeClassifier` (to control how trees are grown), plus all the hyperparameters of a `BaggingClassifier` to control the ensemble itself.

8 Gilles Louppe and Pierre Geurts, "Ensembles on Random Patches", *Lecture Notes in Computer Science* 7523 (2012): 346–361.

9 Tin Kam Ho, "The Random Subspace Method for Constructing Decision Forests", *IEEE Transactions on Pattern Analysis and Machine Intelligence* 20, no. 8 (1998): 832–844.

10 Tin Kam Ho, "Random Decision Forests", *Proceedings of the Third International Conference on Document Analysis and Recognition* 1 (1995): 278.

11 The `BaggingClassifier` class remains useful if you want a bag of something other than decision trees.

The `RandomForestClassifier` class introduces extra randomness when growing trees: instead of searching for the very best feature when splitting a node (see Chapter 5), it searches for the best feature among a random subset of features. By default, it samples $\sqrt{n}$ features (where n is the total number of features). The algorithm results in greater tree diversity, which (again) trades a higher bias for a lower variance, generally yielding an overall better model. So, the following `BaggingClassifier` is equivalent to the previous `RandomForestClassifier`:

```
bag_clf = BaggingClassifier(
    DecisionTreeClassifier(max_features="sqrt", max_leaf_nodes=16),
    n_estimators=500, n_jobs=-1, random_state=42)
```

Extra-Trees

When you are growing a tree in a random forest, at each node only a random subset of the features is considered for splitting (as discussed earlier). It is possible to make trees even more random by also using random thresholds for each feature rather than searching for the best possible thresholds (like regular decision trees do). For this, simply set `splitter="random"` when creating a `DecisionTreeClassifier`.

A forest of such extremely random trees is called an *extremely randomized trees* (*https://homl.info/25*)[12] (or *extra-trees* for short) ensemble. Once again, this technique trades more bias for a lower variance, so they may perform better than regular random forests if you encounter overfitting, especially with noisy and/or high-dimensional datasets. Extra-trees classifiers are also much faster to train than regular random forests, because finding the best possible threshold for each feature at every node is one of the most time-consuming tasks of growing a tree in a random forest.

You can create an extra-trees classifier using Scikit-Learn's `ExtraTreesClassifier` class. Its API is identical to the `RandomForestClassifier` class, except `bootstrap` defaults to `False`. Similarly, the `ExtraTreesRegressor` class has the same API as the `RandomForestRegressor` class, except `bootstrap` defaults to `False`.

Just like decision tree classes, random forest classes and extra-trees classes in recent Scikit-Learn versions support missing values natively, no need for an imputer.

12 Pierre Geurts et al., "Extremely Randomized Trees", *Machine Learning* 63, no. 1 (2006): 3–42.

Feature Importance

Yet another great quality of random forests is that they make it easy to measure the relative importance of each feature. Scikit-Learn measures a feature's importance by looking at how much the tree nodes that use that feature reduce impurity on average, across all trees in the forest. More precisely, it is a weighted average, where each node's weight is equal to the number of training samples that are associated with it (see Chapter 5).

Scikit-Learn computes this score automatically for each feature after training, then it scales the results so that the sum of all importances is equal to 1. You can access the result using the `feature_importances_` variable. For example, the following code trains a `RandomForestClassifier` on the iris dataset (introduced in Chapter 4) and outputs each feature's importance. It seems that the most important features are the petal length (44%) and width (42%), while sepal length and width are rather unimportant in comparison (11% and 2%, respectively):

```
>>> from sklearn.datasets import load_iris
>>> iris = load_iris(as_frame=True)
>>> rnd_clf = RandomForestClassifier(n_estimators=500, random_state=42)
>>> rnd_clf.fit(iris.data, iris.target)
>>> for score, name in zip(rnd_clf.feature_importances_, iris.data.columns):
...     print(round(score, 2), name)
...
0.11 sepal length (cm)
0.02 sepal width (cm)
0.44 petal length (cm)
0.42 petal width (cm)
```

Similarly, if you train a random forest classifier on the MNIST dataset (introduced in Chapter 3) and plot each pixel's importance, you get the image represented in Figure 6-6.

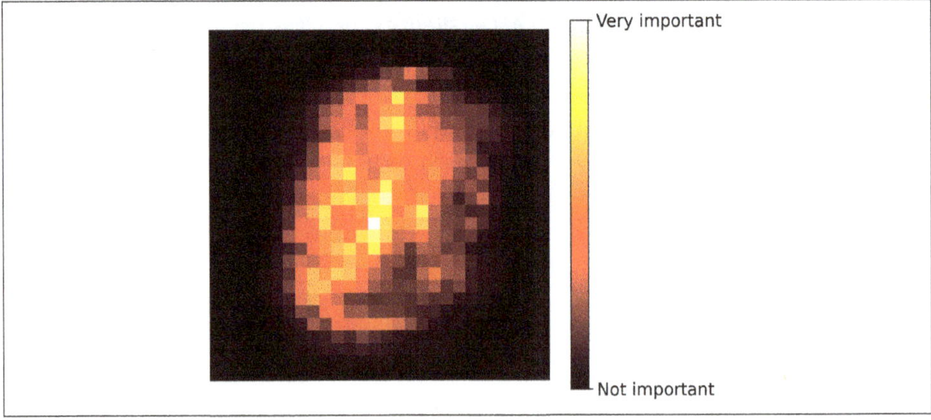

Figure 6-6. MNIST pixel importance (according to a random forest classifier)

Random forests are very handy to get a quick understanding of what features actually matter, in particular if you need to perform feature selection.

Boosting

Boosting (originally called *hypothesis boosting*) refers to any ensemble method that can combine several weak learners into a strong learner. The general idea of most boosting methods is to train predictors sequentially, each trying to correct its predecessor. There are many boosting methods available, but by far the most popular are *AdaBoost* (*https://homl.info/26*)[13] (short for *adaptive boosting*) and *gradient boosting*. Let's start with AdaBoost.

AdaBoost

One way for a new predictor to correct its predecessor is to pay a bit more attention to the training instances that the predecessor underfit. This results in new predictors focusing more and more on the hard cases. This is the technique used by AdaBoost.

For example, when training an AdaBoost classifier, the algorithm first trains a base classifier (such as a decision tree) and uses it to make predictions on the training set. The algorithm then increases the relative weight of misclassified training instances. Then it trains a second classifier, using the updated weights, and again makes predictions on the training set, updates the instance weights, and so on (see Figure 6-7).

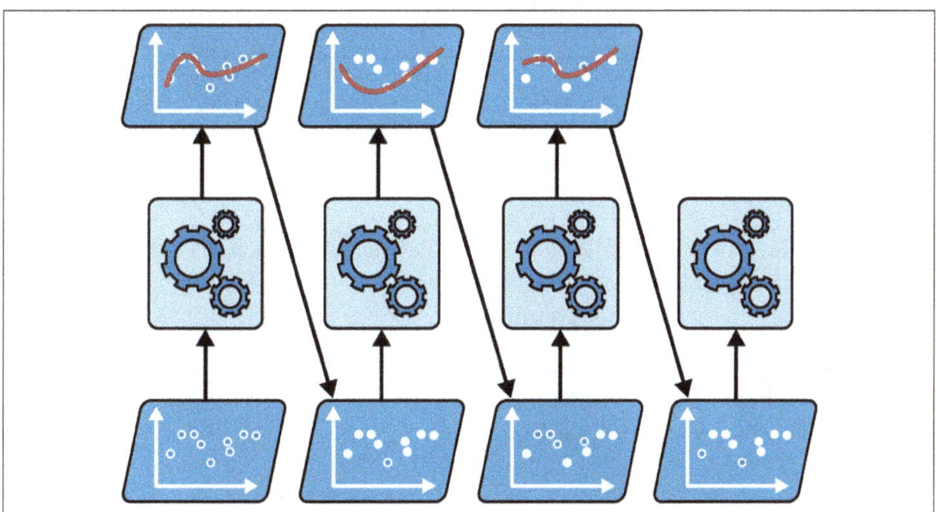

Figure 6-7. AdaBoost sequential training with instance weight updates

13 Yoav Freund and Robert E. Schapire, "A Decision-Theoretic Generalization of On-Line Learning and an Application to Boosting", *Journal of Computer and System Sciences* 55, no. 1 (1997): 119–139.

Figure 6-8 shows the decision boundaries of five consecutive predictors on the moons dataset (in this example, each predictor is a highly regularized SVM classifier with an RBF kernel).[14] The first classifier gets many instances wrong, so their weights get boosted. The second classifier therefore does a better job on these instances, and so on. The plot on the right represents the same sequence of predictors, except that the learning rate is halved (i.e., the misclassified instance weights are boosted much less at every iteration). As you can see, this sequential learning technique has some similarities with gradient descent, except that instead of tweaking a single predictor's parameters to minimize a cost function, AdaBoost adds predictors to the ensemble, gradually making it better.

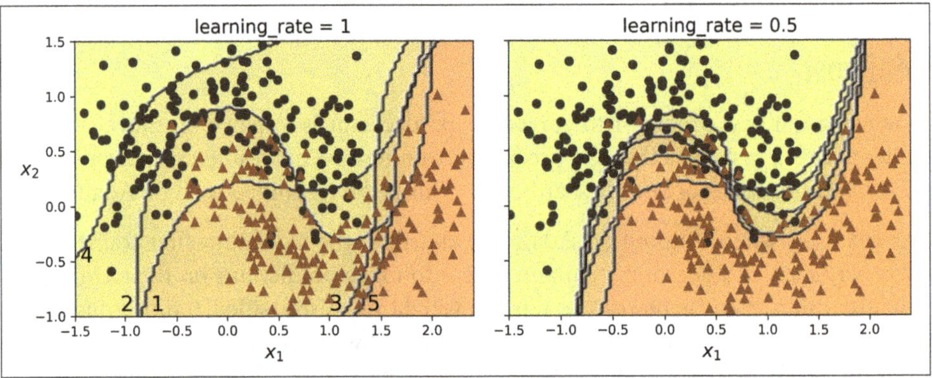

Figure 6-8. Decision boundaries of consecutive predictors

There is one important drawback to this sequential learning technique: training cannot be parallelized since each predictor can only be trained after the previous predictor has been trained and evaluated. As a result, it does not scale as well as bagging or pasting.

Once all predictors are trained, the ensemble makes predictions very much like bagging or pasting, except that predictors have different weights depending on their overall accuracy on the weighted training set.

Let's take a closer look at the AdaBoost algorithm. Each instance weight $w^{(i)}$ is initially set to $1/m$, so their sum is 1. A first predictor is trained, and its weighted error rate r_1 is computed on the training set; see Equation 6-1.

14 This is just for illustrative purposes. SVMs are generally not good base predictors for AdaBoost; they are slow and tend to be unstable with it.

Equation 6-1. Weighted error rate of the jth predictor

$$r_j = \sum_{\substack{i=1 \\ \widehat{y}_j^{(i)} \neq y^{(i)}}}^{m} w^{(i)} \quad \text{where } \widehat{y}_j^{(i)} \text{ is the } j^{\text{th}} \text{ predictor's prediction for the } i^{\text{th}} \text{ instance}$$

The predictor's weight α_j is then computed using Equation 6-2, where η is the learning rate hyperparameter (defaults to 1).[15] The more accurate the predictor is, the higher its weight will be. If it is just guessing randomly, then its weight will be close to zero. However, if it is most often wrong (i.e., less accurate than random guessing), then its weight will be negative.

Equation 6-2. Predictor weight

$$\alpha_j = \eta \log \frac{1 - r_j}{r_j}$$

Next, the AdaBoost algorithm updates the instance weights, using Equation 6-3, which boosts the weights of the misclassified instances and encourages the next predictor to pay more attention to them.

Equation 6-3. Weight update rule

$$\text{for } i = 1, 2, \dots, m$$
$$w^{(i)} \leftarrow \begin{cases} w^{(i)} & \text{if } \widehat{y}^{(i)} = y^{(i)} \\ w^{(i)} \exp(\alpha_j) & \text{if } \widehat{y}^{(i)} \neq y^{(i)} \end{cases}$$

Then all the instance weights are normalized to ensure that their sum is once again 1 (i.e., they are divided by $\sum_{i=1}^{m} w^{(i)}$).

Finally, a new predictor is trained using the updated weights, and the whole process is repeated: the new predictor's weight is computed, the instance weights are updated, then another predictor is trained, and so on. The algorithm stops when the desired number of predictors is reached, or when a perfect predictor is found.

To make predictions, AdaBoost simply computes the predictions of all the predictors and weighs them using the predictor weights α_j. The predicted class is the one that receives the majority of weighted votes (see Equation 6-4).

15 The original AdaBoost algorithm does not use a learning rate hyperparameter.

Equation 6-4. AdaBoost predictions

$$\hat{y}(\mathbf{x}) = \underset{k}{\operatorname{argmax}} \sum_{\substack{j=1 \\ \hat{y}_j(\mathbf{x}) = k}}^{N} \alpha_j \quad \text{where } N \text{ is the number of predictors}$$

Scikit-Learn uses a multiclass version of AdaBoost called *SAMME* (*https://homl.info/27*)[16] (which stands for *Stagewise Additive Modeling using a Multiclass Exponential loss function*). When there are just two classes, SAMME is equivalent to AdaBoost.

The following code trains an AdaBoost classifier based on 30 *decision stumps* using Scikit-Learn's `AdaBoostClassifier` class (as you might expect, there is also an `AdaBoostRegressor` class). A decision stump is a decision tree with `max_depth=1`—in other words, a tree composed of a single decision node plus two leaf nodes. This is the default base estimator for the `AdaBoostClassifier` class:

```
from sklearn.ensemble import AdaBoostClassifier

ada_clf = AdaBoostClassifier(
    DecisionTreeClassifier(max_depth=1), n_estimators=30,
    learning_rate=0.5, random_state=42, algorithm="SAMME")
ada_clf.fit(X_train, y_train)
```

If your AdaBoost ensemble is overfitting the training set, you can try reducing the number of estimators or more strongly regularizing the base estimator.

Gradient Boosting

Another very popular boosting algorithm is *gradient boosting* (*https://homl.info/28*).[17] Just like AdaBoost, gradient boosting works by sequentially adding predictors to an ensemble, each one correcting its predecessor. However, instead of tweaking the instance weights at every iteration like AdaBoost does, this method tries to fit the new predictor to the *residual errors* made by the previous predictor.

Let's go through a simple regression example, using decision trees as the base predictors; this is called *gradient tree boosting*, or *gradient boosted regression trees* (GBRT). First, let's generate a noisy quadratic dataset and fit a `DecisionTreeRegressor` to it:

16 For more details, see Ji Zhu et al., "Multi-Class AdaBoost", *Statistics and Its Interface* 2, no. 3 (2009): 349–360.

17 Gradient boosting was first introduced in Leo Breiman's 1997 paper (*https://homl.info/arcing*) "Arcing the Edge" and was further developed in the 1999 paper (*https://homl.info/gradboost*) "Greedy Function Approximation: A Gradient Boosting Machine" by Jerome H. Friedman.

```python
import numpy as np
from sklearn.tree import DecisionTreeRegressor

m = 100  # number of instances
rng = np.random.default_rng(seed=42)
X = rng.random((m, 1)) - 0.5
noise = 0.05 * rng.standard_normal(m)
y = 3 * X[:, 0] ** 2 + noise  # y = 3x² + Gaussian noise

tree_reg1 = DecisionTreeRegressor(max_depth=2, random_state=42)
tree_reg1.fit(X, y)
```

Next, we'll train a second `DecisionTreeRegressor` on the residual errors made by the first predictor:

```python
y2 = y - tree_reg1.predict(X)
tree_reg2 = DecisionTreeRegressor(max_depth=2, random_state=43)
tree_reg2.fit(X, y2)
```

And then we'll train a third regressor on the residual errors made by the second predictor:

```python
y3 = y2 - tree_reg2.predict(X)
tree_reg3 = DecisionTreeRegressor(max_depth=2, random_state=44)
tree_reg3.fit(X, y3)
```

Now we have an ensemble containing three trees. It can make predictions on a new instance simply by adding up the predictions of all the trees:

```python
>>> X_new = np.array([[-0.4], [0.], [0.5]])
>>> sum(tree.predict(X_new) for tree in (tree_reg1, tree_reg2, tree_reg3))
array([0.57356534, 0.0405142 , 0.66914249])
```

Figure 6-9 represents the predictions of these three trees in the left column, and the ensemble's predictions in the right column. In the first row, the ensemble has just one tree, so its predictions are exactly the same as the first tree's predictions. In the second row, a new tree is trained on the residual errors of the first tree. On the right you can see that the ensemble's predictions are equal to the sum of the predictions of the first two trees. Similarly, in the third row another tree is trained on the residual errors of the second tree. You can see that the ensemble's predictions gradually get better as trees are added to the ensemble.

You can use Scikit-Learn's `GradientBoostingRegressor` class to train GBRT ensembles more easily (there's also a `GradientBoostingClassifier` class for classification). Much like the `RandomForestRegressor` class, it has hyperparameters to control the growth of decision trees (e.g., `max_depth`, `min_samples_leaf`), as well as hyperparameters to control the ensemble training, such as the number of trees (`n_estimators`). The following code creates the same ensemble as the previous one:

```
from sklearn.ensemble import GradientBoostingRegressor

gbrt = GradientBoostingRegressor(max_depth=2, n_estimators=3,
                                 learning_rate=1.0, random_state=42)
gbrt.fit(X, y)
```

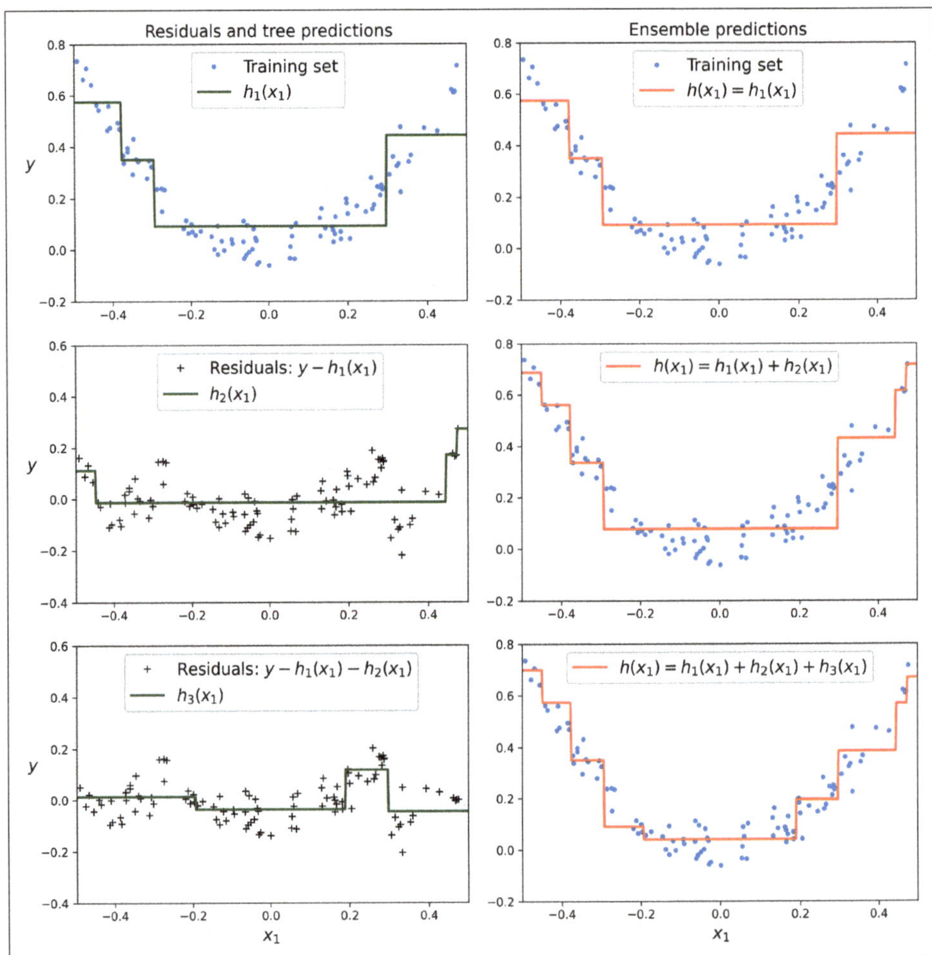

Figure 6-9. In this depiction of gradient boosting, the first predictor (top left) is trained normally, then each consecutive predictor (middle left and lower left) is trained on the previous predictor's residuals; the right column shows the resulting ensemble's predictions

The `learning_rate` hyperparameter scales the contribution of each tree. If you set it to a low value, such as `0.05`, you will need more trees in the ensemble to fit the training set, but the predictions will usually generalize better. This is a regularization technique called *shrinkage*. Figure 6-10 shows two GBRT ensembles trained with different hyperparameters: the one on the left does not have enough trees to fit the training set, while the one on the right has about the right amount. If we added more trees, the GBRT would start to overfit the training set. As usual, you can use cross-validation to find the optimal learning rate, using `GridSearchCV` or `RandomizedSearchCV`.

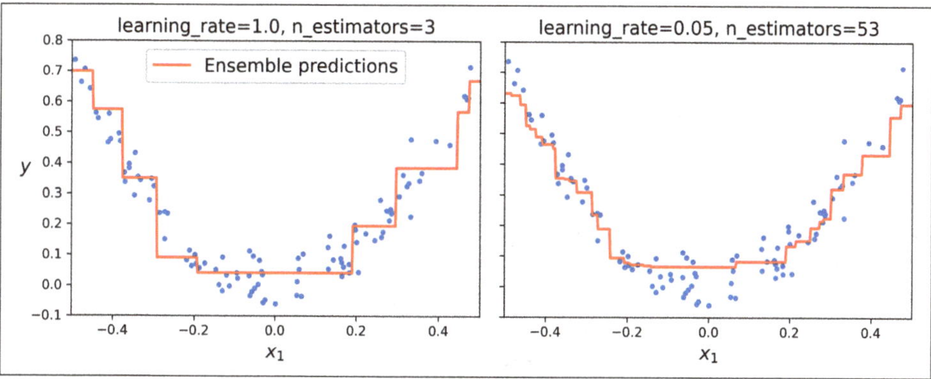

Figure 6-10. GBRT ensembles with not enough predictors (left) and just enough (right)

To find the optimal number of trees, you could also perform cross-validation, but there's a simpler way: if you set the `n_iter_no_change` hyperparameter to an integer value, say 10, then the `GradientBoostingRegressor` will automatically stop adding more trees during training if it sees that the last 10 trees didn't help. This is simply early stopping (introduced in Chapter 4), but with a little bit of patience: it tolerates having no progress for a few iterations before it stops. Let's train the ensemble using early stopping:

```
gbrt_best = GradientBoostingRegressor(
    max_depth=2, learning_rate=0.05, n_estimators=500,
    n_iter_no_change=10, random_state=42)
gbrt_best.fit(X, y)
```

If you set `n_iter_no_change` too low, training may stop too early and the model will underfit. But if you set it too high, it will overfit instead. We also set a fairly small learning rate and a high number of estimators, but the actual number of estimators in the trained ensemble is much lower, thanks to early stopping:

```
>>> gbrt_best.n_estimators_
53
```

When `n_iter_no_change` is set, the `fit()` method automatically splits the training set into a smaller training set and a validation set: this allows it to evaluate the model's performance each time it adds a new tree. The size of the validation set is controlled by the `validation_fraction` hyperparameter, which is 10% by default. The `tol` hyperparameter determines the maximum performance improvement that still counts as negligible. It defaults to 0.0001.

The `GradientBoostingRegressor` class also supports a `subsample` hyperparameter, which specifies the fraction of training instances to be used for training each tree. For example, if `subsample=0.25`, then each tree is trained on 25% of the training instances, selected randomly. As you can probably guess by now, this technique trades a higher bias for a lower variance. It also speeds up training considerably. This is called *stochastic gradient boosting*.

Histogram-Based Gradient Boosting

Scikit-Learn also provides another GBRT implementation, optimized for large datasets: *histogram-based gradient boosting* (HGB). It works by binning the input features, replacing them with integers. The number of bins is controlled by the `max_bins` hyperparameter, which defaults to 255 and cannot be set any higher than this. Binning can greatly reduce the number of possible thresholds that the training algorithm needs to evaluate. Moreover, working with integers makes it possible to use faster and more memory-efficient data structures. And the way the bins are built removes the need for sorting the features when training each tree.

As a result, this implementation has a computational complexity of $O(b \times m)$ instead of $O(n \times m \times \log(m))$, where b is the number of bins, m is the number of training instances, and n is the number of features. In practice, this means that HGB can train hundreds of times faster than regular GBRT on large datasets. However, binning causes a precision loss, which acts as a regularizer: depending on the dataset, this may help reduce overfitting, or it may cause underfitting.

Scikit-Learn provides two classes for HGB: `HistGradientBoostingRegressor` and `HistGradientBoostingClassifier`. They're similar to `GradientBoostingRegressor` and `GradientBoostingClassifier`, with a few notable differences:

- Early stopping is automatically activated if the number of instances is greater than 10,000. You can turn early stopping always on or always off by setting the `early_stopping` hyperparameter to `True` or `False`.
- Subsampling is not supported.
- `n_estimators` is renamed to `max_iter`.
- The only decision tree hyperparameters that can be tweaked are `max_leaf_nodes`, `min_samples_leaf`, `max_depth`, and `max_features`.

The HGB classes support missing values natively, as well as categorical features. This simplifies preprocessing quite a bit. However, the categorical features must be represented as integers ranging from 0 to a number lower than `max_bins`. You can use an `OrdinalEncoder` for this. For example, here's how to build and train a complete pipeline for the California housing dataset introduced in Chapter 2:

```python
from sklearn.pipeline import make_pipeline
from sklearn.compose import make_column_transformer
from sklearn.ensemble import HistGradientBoostingRegressor
from sklearn.preprocessing import OrdinalEncoder

hgb_reg = make_pipeline(
    make_column_transformer((OrdinalEncoder(), ["ocean_proximity"]),
                            remainder="passthrough",
                            force_int_remainder_cols=False),
    HistGradientBoostingRegressor(categorical_features=[0], random_state=42)
)
hgb_reg.fit(housing, housing_labels)
```

The whole pipeline is almost as short as the imports! No need for an imputer, scaler, or a one-hot encoder, it's really convenient. Note that `categorical_features` must be set to the categorical column indices (or a Boolean array). Without any hyperparameter tuning, this model yields an RMSE of about 47,600, which is not too bad.

In short, HGB is a great choice when you have a fairly large dataset, especially when it contains categorical features and missing values: it performs well, doesn't require much preprocessing work, and training is fast. However, it can be a bit less accurate than GBRT, due to the binning, so you might want to try both.

Several other optimized implementations of gradient boosting are available in the Python ML ecosystem: in particular, XGBoost (*https://github.com/dmlc/xgboost*), CatBoost (*https://catboost.ai*), and LightGBM (*https://lightgbm.readthedocs.io*). These libraries have been around for several years. They are all specialized for gradient boosting, their APIs are very similar to Scikit-Learn's, and they provide many additional features, including hardware acceleration using GPUs; you should definitely check them out! Moreover, Yggdrasil Decision Forests (YDF) (*https://ydf.readthedocs.io*) provides optimized implementations of a variety of random forest algorithms.

Stacking

The last ensemble method we will discuss in this chapter is called *stacking* (short for *stacked generalization* (*https://homl.info/29*)).[18] It is based on a simple idea: instead of using trivial functions (such as hard voting) to aggregate the predictions of all predictors in an ensemble, why don't we train a model to perform this aggregation? Figure 6-11 shows such an ensemble performing a regression task on a new instance.

18 David H. Wolpert, "Stacked Generalization", *Neural Networks* 5, no. 2 (1992): 241–259.

Each of the bottom three predictors predicts a different value (3.1, 2.7, and 2.9), and then the final predictor (called a *blender*, or a *meta learner*) takes these predictions as inputs and makes the final prediction (3.0).

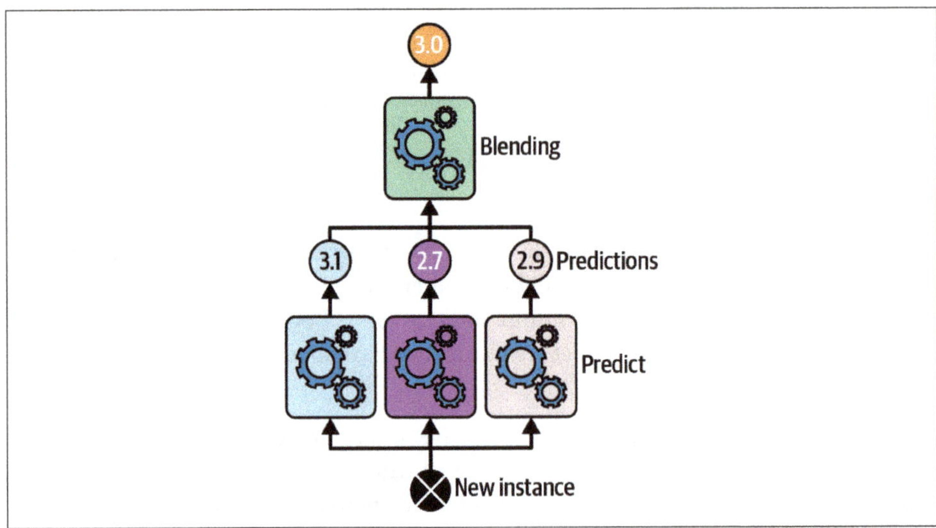

Figure 6-11. Aggregating predictions using a blending predictor

To train the blender, you first need to build the blending training set. You can use `cross_val_predict()` on every predictor in the ensemble to get out-of-sample predictions for each instance in the original training set (Figure 6-12), and use these as the input features to train the blender; the targets can simply be copied from the original training set. Note that regardless of the number of features in the original training set (just one in this example), the blending training set will contain one input feature per predictor (three in this example). Once the blender is trained, the base predictors must be retrained one last time on the full original training set (since `cross_val_predict()` does not give access to the trained estimators).

It is actually possible to train several different blenders this way (e.g., one using linear regression, another using random forest regression) to get a whole layer of blenders, and then add another blender on top of that to produce the final prediction, as shown in Figure 6-13. You may be able to squeeze out a few more drops of performance by doing this, but it will cost you in both training time and system complexity.

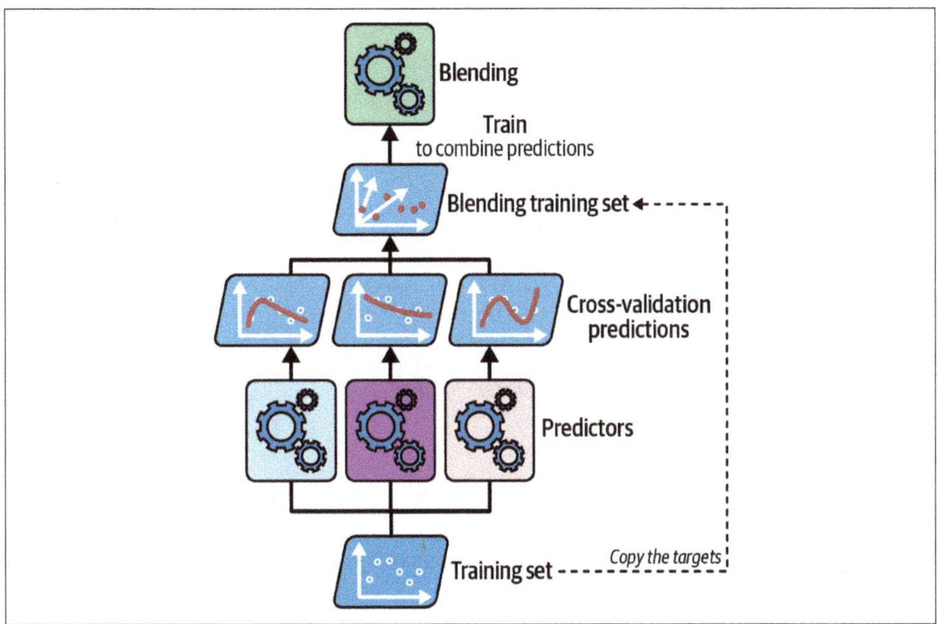

Figure 6-12. Training the blender in a stacking ensemble

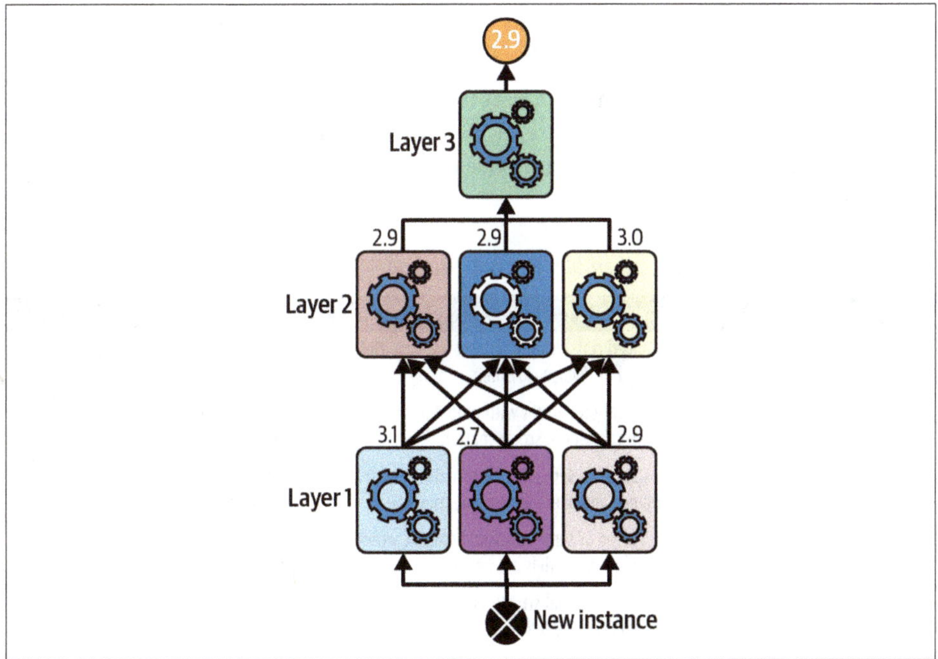

Figure 6-13. Predictions in a multilayer stacking ensemble

Scikit-Learn provides two classes for stacking ensembles: `StackingClassifier` and `StackingRegressor`. For example, we can replace the `VotingClassifier` we used at the beginning of this chapter on the moons dataset with a `StackingClassifier`:

```
from sklearn.ensemble import StackingClassifier

stacking_clf = StackingClassifier(
    estimators=[
        ('lr', LogisticRegression(random_state=42)),
        ('rf', RandomForestClassifier(random_state=42)),
        ('svc', SVC(probability=True, random_state=42))
    ],
    final_estimator=RandomForestClassifier(random_state=43),
    cv=5  # number of cross-validation folds
)
stacking_clf.fit(X_train, y_train)
```

For each predictor, the stacking classifier will call `predict_proba()` if available; if not it will fall back to `decision_function()` or, as a last resort, call `predict()`. If you don't provide a final estimator, `StackingClassifier` will use `LogisticRegression` and `StackingRegressor` will use `RidgeCV`.

If you evaluate this stacking model on the test set, you will find 92.8% accuracy, which is a bit better than the voting classifier using soft voting, which got 92%. Depending on your use case, this may or may not be worth the extra complexity and computational cost (since there's an extra model to run after all the others).

In conclusion, ensemble methods are versatile, powerful, and fairly simple to use. They can overfit if you're not careful, but that's true of every powerful model. Table 6-1 summarizes all the techniques we discussed in this chapter, and when to use each one.

Table 6-1. When to use each ensemble learning method

Ensemble method	When to use it	Example use cases
Hard voting	Balanced classification dataset with multiple strong but diverse classifiers.	Spam detection, sentiment analysis, disease classification
Soft voting	Classification dataset with probabilistic models, where confidence scores matter.	Medical diagnosis, credit risk analysis, fake news detection
Bagging	Structured or semi-structured dataset with high variance and overfitting-prone models.	Financial risk modeling, ecommerce recommendation
Pasting	Structured or semi-structured dataset where more independent models are needed.	Customer segmentation, protein classification
Random forest	High-dimensional structured datasets with potentially noisy features.	Customer churn prediction, genetic data analysis, fraud detection
Extra-trees	Large structured datasets with many features, where speed is critical and reducing variance is important.	Real-time fraud detection, sensor data analysis

Ensemble method	When to use it	Example use cases
AdaBoost	Small to medium-sized, low-noise, structured datasets with weak learners (e.g., decision stumps), where interpretability is helpful.	Credit scoring, anomaly detection, predictive maintenance
Gradient boosting	Medium to large structured datasets where high predictive power is required, even at the cost of extra tuning.	Housing price prediction, risk assessment, demand forecasting
Histogram-based gradient boosting (HGB)	Large structured datasets where training speed and scalability are key.	Click-through rate prediction, ranking algorithms, real-time bidding in advertising
Stacking	Complex, high-dimensional datasets where combining multiple diverse models can maximize accuracy.	Recommendation engines, autonomous vehicle decision-making, Kaggle competitions

Random forests, AdaBoost, GBRT, and HGB are among the first models you should test for most machine learning tasks, particularly with heterogeneous tabular data. Moreover, as they require very little preprocessing, they're great for getting a prototype up and running quickly.

So far, we have looked only at supervised learning techniques. In the next chapter, we will turn to the most common unsupervised learning task: dimensionality reduction.

Exercises

1. If you have trained five different models on the exact same training data, and they all achieve 95% precision, is there any chance that you can combine these models to get better results? If so, how? If not, why?
2. What is the difference between hard and soft voting classifiers?
3. Is it possible to speed up training of a bagging ensemble by distributing it across multiple servers? What about pasting ensembles, boosting ensembles, random forests, or stacking ensembles?
4. What is the benefit of out-of-bag evaluation?
5. What makes extra-trees ensembles more random than regular random forests? How can this extra randomness help? Are extra-trees classifiers slower or faster than regular random forests?
6. If your AdaBoost ensemble underfits the training data, which hyperparameters should you tweak, and how?
7. If your gradient boosting ensemble overfits the training set, should you increase or decrease the learning rate?

8. Load the MNIST dataset (introduced in Chapter 3), and split it into a training set, a validation set, and a test set (e.g., use 50,000 instances for training, 10,000 for validation, and 10,000 for testing). Then train various classifiers, such as a random forest classifier, an extra-trees classifier, and an SVM classifier. Next, try to combine them into an ensemble that outperforms each individual classifier on the validation set, using soft or hard voting. Once you have found one, try it on the test set. How much better does it perform compared to the individual classifiers?

9. Run the individual classifiers from the previous exercise to make predictions on the validation set, and create a new training set with the resulting predictions: each training instance is a vector containing the set of predictions from all your classifiers for an image, and the target is the image's class. Train a classifier on this new training set. Congratulations—you have just trained a blender, and together with the classifiers it forms a stacking ensemble! Now evaluate the ensemble on the test set. For each image in the test set, make predictions with all your classifiers, then feed the predictions to the blender to get the ensemble's predictions. How does it compare to the voting classifier you trained earlier? Now try again using a `StackingClassifier` instead. Do you get better performance? If so, why?

Solutions to these exercises are available at the end of this chapter's notebook, at *https://homl.info/colab-p*.

CHAPTER 7
Dimensionality Reduction

Many machine learning problems involve thousands or even millions of features for each training instance. Not only do all these features make training extremely slow, but they can also make it much harder to find a good solution, as you will see. This problem is often referred to as the *curse of dimensionality*.

Fortunately, in real-world problems, it is often possible to reduce the number of features considerably, turning an intractable problem into a tractable one. For example, consider the MNIST images (introduced in Chapter 3): the pixels on the image borders are almost always white, so you could completely drop these pixels from the training set without losing much information. As we saw in the previous chapter, Figure 6-6 confirms that these pixels are utterly unimportant for the classification task. Additionally, two neighboring pixels are often highly correlated: if you merge them into a single pixel (e.g., by taking the mean of the two pixel intensities), you will not lose much information, removing redundancy and sometimes even noise.

Reducing dimensionality can also drop some useful information, just like compressing an image to JPEG can degrade its quality: it can make your system perform slightly worse, especially if you reduce dimensionality too much. Moreover, some models—such as neural networks—can handle high-dimensional data efficiently and learn to reduce its dimensionality while preserving the useful information for the task at hand. In short, adding an extra preprocessing step for dimensionality reduction will not always help.

Apart from speeding up training and possibly improving your model's performance, dimensionality reduction is also extremely useful for data visualization. Reducing the number of dimensions down to two (or three) makes it possible to plot a condensed view of a high-dimensional training set on a graph and often gain some important insights by visually detecting patterns, such as clusters. Moreover, data visualization is essential to communicate your conclusions to people who are not data scientists—in particular, decision makers who will use your results.

In this chapter we will first discuss the curse of dimensionality and get a sense of what goes on in high-dimensional space. Then we will consider the two main approaches to dimensionality reduction (projection and manifold learning), and we will go through three of the most popular dimensionality reduction techniques: PCA, random projection, and locally linear embedding (LLE).

The Curse of Dimensionality

We are so used to living in three dimensions[1] that our intuition fails us when we try to imagine a high-dimensional space. Even a basic 4D hypercube is incredibly hard to picture in our minds (see Figure 7-1), let alone a 200-dimensional ellipsoid bent in a 1,000-dimensional space.

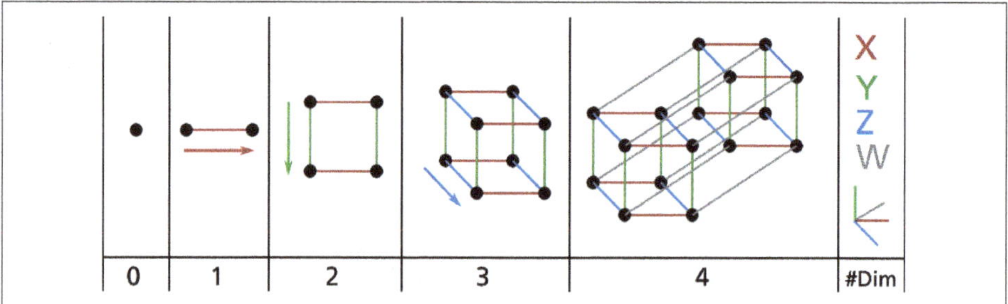

Figure 7-1. Point, segment, square, cube, and tesseract (0D to 4D hypercubes)[2]

It turns out that many things behave very differently in high-dimensional space. For example, if you pick a random point in a unit square (a 1 × 1 square), it will have only about a 0.4% chance of being located less than 0.001 from a border (in other words, it is very unlikely that a random point will be "extreme" along any dimension). But in a 10,000-dimensional unit hypercube, this probability is greater than 99.999999%. Most points in a high-dimensional hypercube are very close to the border.[3]

Here is a more troublesome difference: if you pick two points randomly in a unit square, the distance between these two points will be, on average, roughly 0.52. If

1 Well, four dimensions if you count time, and a few more if you are a string theorist.

2 Watch a rotating tesseract projected into 3D space at *https://homl.info/30*. Image by Wikipedia user NerdBoy1392 (Creative Commons BY-SA 3.0 (*https://oreil.ly/pMbrK*)). Reproduced from *https://en.wikipedia.org/wiki/Tesseract*.

3 Fun fact: anyone you know is probably an extremist in at least one dimension (e.g., how much sugar they put in their coffee), if you consider enough dimensions.

you pick two random points in a 3D unit cube, the average distance will be roughly 0.66. But what about two points picked randomly in a 1,000,000-dimensional unit hypercube? The average distance, believe it or not, will be about 408.25 (roughly $\sqrt{\frac{1,000,000}{6}}$)! This is counterintuitive: how can two points be so far apart when they both lie within the same unit hypercube? Well, there's just plenty of space in high dimensions.

As a result, high-dimensional datasets are often very sparse: most training instances are likely to be far away from each other, so training methods based on distance or similarity (such as *k*-nearest neighbors) will be much less effective. And some types of models will not be usable at all because they scale poorly with the dataset's dimensionality (e.g., SVMs or dense neural networks). And new instances will likely be far away from any training instance, making predictions much less reliable than in lower dimensions since they will be based on much larger extrapolations. Since patterns in the data will become harder to identify, models will tend to fit the noise more frequently than in lower dimensions; regularization will become all the more important. Lastly, models will become even harder to interpret.

In theory, some of these issues can be resolved by increasing the size of the training set to reach a sufficient density of training instances. Unfortunately, in practice, the number of training instances required to reach a given density grows exponentially with the number of dimensions. With just 100 features—significantly fewer than in the MNIST problem—all ranging from 0 to 1, you would need more training instances than atoms in the observable universe in order for training instances to be within 0.1 of each other on average, assuming they were spread out uniformly across all dimensions.

Main Approaches for Dimensionality Reduction

Before diving into specific dimensionality reduction algorithms, let's look at the two main approaches to reducing dimensionality: projection and manifold learning.

Projection

In most real-world problems, training instances are *not* spread out uniformly across all dimensions. Many features are almost constant, while others are highly correlated (as discussed earlier for MNIST). As a result, all training instances lie within (or close to) a much lower-dimensional *subspace* of the high-dimensional space. This sounds abstract, so let's look at an example. In Figure 7-2, a 3D dataset is represented by small spheres (I will refer to this figure several times in the following sections).

Notice that all training instances lie close to a plane: this is a lower-dimensional (2D) subspace of the higher-dimensional (3D) space. If we project every training instance perpendicularly onto this subspace (as represented by the short dashed lines connecting the instances to the plane), we get the new 2D dataset shown in Figure 7-3. Ta-da! We have just reduced the dataset's dimensionality from 3D to 2D. Note that the axes correspond to new features z_1 and z_2: they are the coordinates of the projections on the plane.

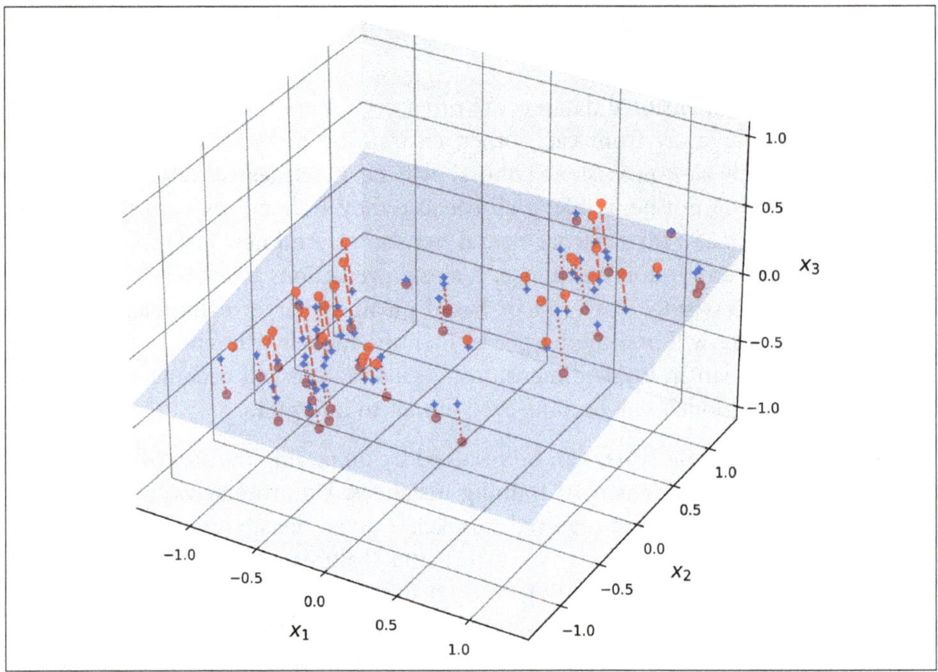

Figure 7-2. A 3D dataset lying close to a 2D subspace

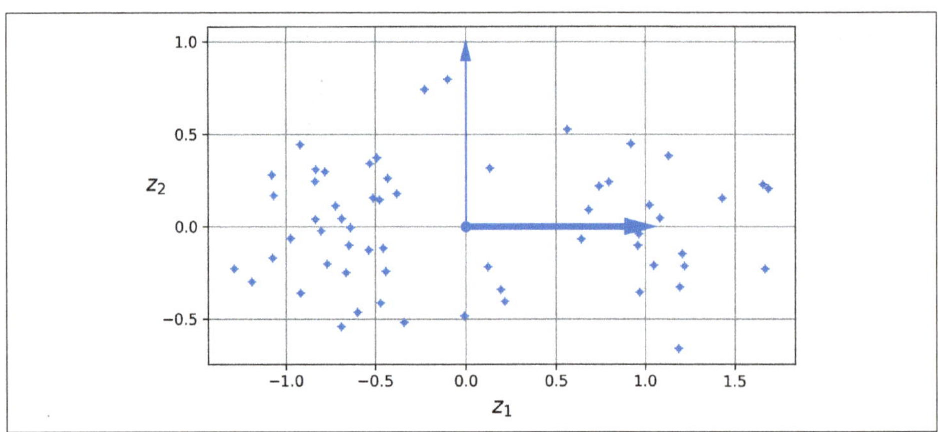

Figure 7-3. The new 2D dataset after projection

Manifold Learning

Although projection is fast and often works well, it's not always the best approach to dimensionality reduction. In many cases the subspace may twist and turn, such as in the Swiss roll dataset represented in Figure 7-4: this is a toy dataset containing 3D points in the shape of a Swiss roll.

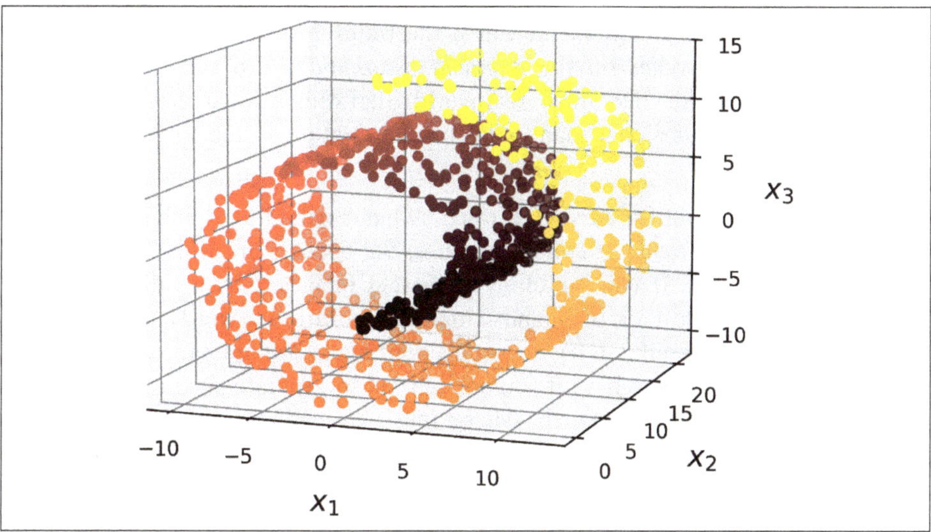

Figure 7-4. Swiss roll dataset

Simply projecting onto a plane (e.g., by dropping x_3) would squash different layers of the Swiss roll together, as shown on the left side of Figure 7-5. What you probably want instead is to unroll the Swiss roll to obtain the 2D dataset on the righthand side of Figure 7-5.

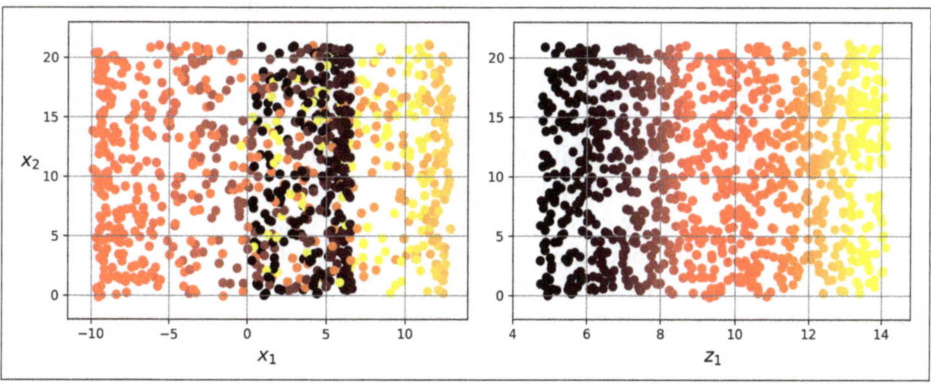

Figure 7-5. Squashing by projecting onto a plane (left) versus unrolling the Swiss roll (right)

The Swiss roll is an example of a 2D *manifold*. Put simply, a 2D manifold is a 2D shape that can be bent and twisted in a higher-dimensional space. More generally, a d-dimensional manifold is a part of an n-dimensional space (where $d < n$) that locally resembles a d-dimensional hyperplane. In the case of the Swiss roll, $d = 2$ and $n = 3$: it locally resembles a 2D plane, but it is rolled in the third dimension.

Many dimensionality reduction algorithms (e.g., LLE, Isomap, t-SNE, or UMAP), work by modeling the manifold on which the training instances lie; this is called *manifold learning*. It relies on the *manifold assumption*, also called the *manifold hypothesis*, which holds that most real-world high-dimensional datasets lie close to a much lower-dimensional manifold. This assumption is very often empirically observed.

Once again, think about the MNIST dataset: all handwritten digit images have some similarities. They are made of connected lines, the borders are white, and they are more or less centered. If you randomly generated images, only a ridiculously tiny fraction of them would look like handwritten digits. In other words, the degrees of freedom available to you if you try to create a digit image are dramatically lower than the degrees of freedom you have if you are allowed to generate any image you want. These constraints tend to squeeze the dataset into a lower-dimensional manifold.

The manifold assumption is often accompanied by another implicit assumption: that the task at hand (e.g., classification or regression) will be simpler if expressed in the lower-dimensional space of the manifold. For example, in the top row of Figure 7-6 the Swiss roll is split into two classes: in the 3D space (on the left) the decision boundary would be fairly complex, but in the 2D unrolled manifold space (on the right) the decision boundary is a straight line.

However, this implicit assumption does not always hold. For example, in the bottom row of Figure 7-6, the decision boundary is located at $x_1 = 5$. This decision boundary looks very simple in the original 3D space (a vertical plane), but it looks more complex in the unrolled manifold (a collection of four independent line segments).

In short, reducing the dimensionality of your training set before training a model will usually speed up training, but it may not always lead to a better or simpler solution; it all depends on the dataset. Dimensionality reduction is typically more effective when the dataset is small relative to the number of features, especially if it's noisy, or many features are highly correlated to one another (i.e., redundant). And if you have domain knowledge about the process that generated the data, and you know it's simple, then the manifold assumption certainly holds, and dimensionality reduction is likely to help.

Hopefully, you now have a good sense of what the curse of dimensionality is and how dimensionality reduction algorithms can fight it, especially when the manifold assumption holds. The rest of this chapter will go through some of the most popular algorithms for dimensionality reduction.

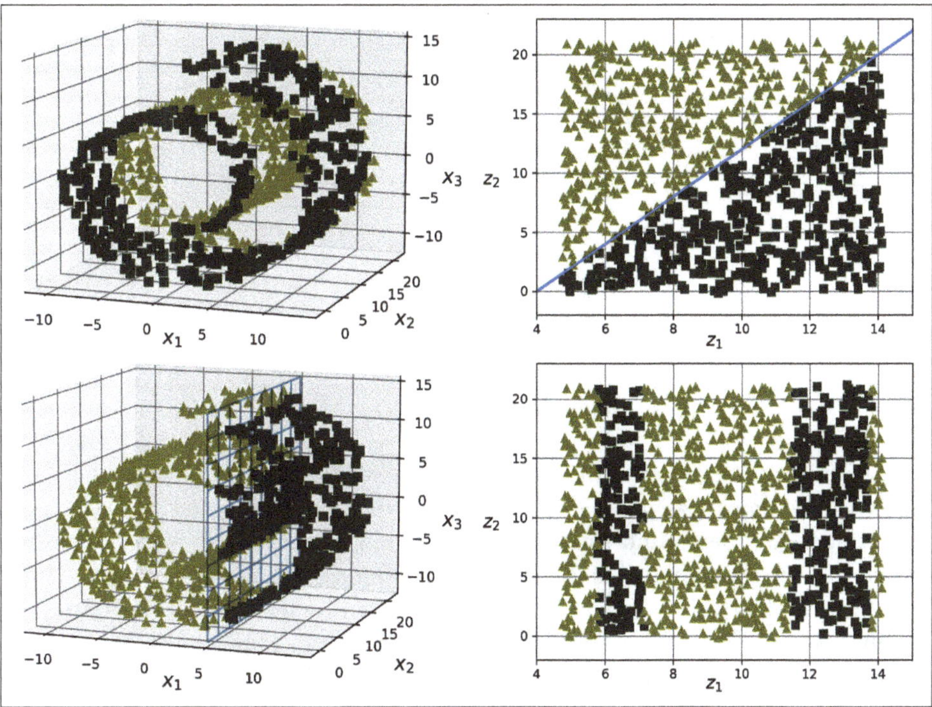

Figure 7-6. The decision boundary may not always be simpler with lower dimensions

PCA

Principal component analysis (PCA) is by far the most popular dimensionality reduction algorithm. First it identifies the hyperplane that lies closest to the data, and then it projects the data onto it, as shown back in Figure 7-2.

Preserving the Variance

Before you can project the training set onto a lower-dimensional hyperplane, you first need to choose the right hyperplane. For example, a simple 2D dataset is represented on the left in Figure 7-7, along with three different axes (i.e., 1D hyperplanes). On the right is the result of the projection of the dataset onto each of these axes. As you can see, the projection onto the solid line preserves the maximum variance (top), while the projection onto the dotted line preserves very little variance (bottom), and the projection onto the dashed line preserves an intermediate amount of variance (middle).

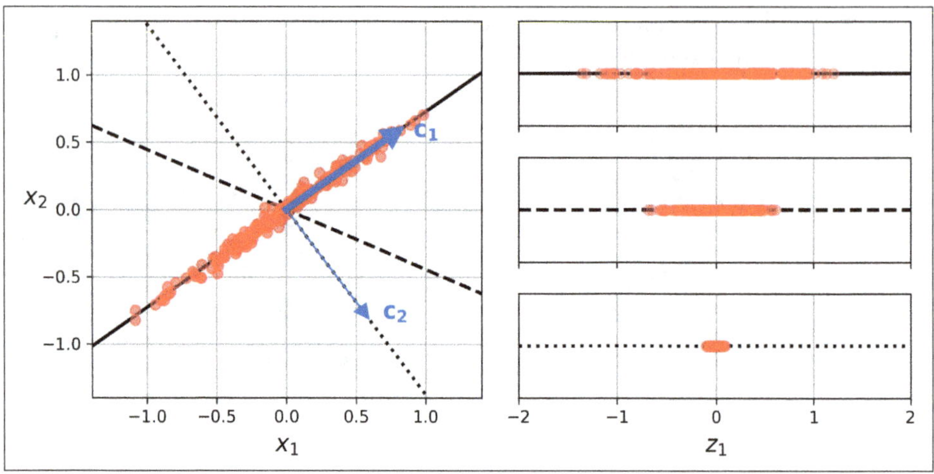

Figure 7-7. Selecting the subspace on which to project

It seems reasonable to select the axis that preserves the maximum amount of variance, as it will most likely lose less information than the other projections. Consider your shadow on the ground when the sun is directly overhead: it's a small blob that doesn't look anything like you. But your shadow on a wall at sunrise is much larger and it *does* look like you. Another way to justify choosing the axis that maximizes the variance is that it is also the axis that minimizes the mean squared distance between the original dataset and its projection onto that axis. This is the rather simple idea behind PCA, introduced way back in 1901 (*https://homl.info/pca*)![4]

Principal Components

PCA identifies the axis that accounts for the largest amount of variance in the training set. In Figure 7-7, it is the solid line. It also finds a second axis, orthogonal to the first one, that accounts for the largest amount of the remaining variance. In this 2D example there is no choice: it is the dotted line. If it were a higher-dimensional dataset, PCA would also find a third axis, orthogonal to both previous axes, and a fourth, a fifth, and so on—as many axes as the number of dimensions in the dataset.

The ith axis is called the ith *principal component* (PC) of the data. In Figure 7-7, the first PC is the axis on which vector $\mathbf{c}_1$ lies, and the second PC is the axis on which vector $\mathbf{c}_2$ lies. In Figure 7-2, the first two PCs are on the projection plane, and the third PC is the axis orthogonal to that plane. After the projection, back in Figure 7-3, the first PC corresponds to the z_1 axis, and the second PC corresponds to the z_2 axis.

4 Karl Pearson, "On Lines and Planes of Closest Fit to Systems of Points in Space", *The London, Edinburgh, and Dublin Philosophical Magazine and Journal of Science* 2, no. 11 (1901): 559–572.

For each principal component, PCA finds a zero-centered unit vector pointing along the direction of the PC. Unfortunately, its direction is not guaranteed: if you perturb the training set slightly and run PCA again, the unit vector may point in the opposite direction. In fact, a pair of unit vectors may even rotate or swap if the variances along these two axes are very close. So if you use PCA as a preprocessing step before a model, make sure you always retrain the model entirely every time you update the PCA transformer: if you don't and if the PCA's output doesn't align with the previous version, the model will be very confused.

So how can you find the principal components of a training set? Luckily, there is a standard matrix factorization technique called *singular value decomposition* (SVD) that can decompose the training set matrix **X** into the product of three matrices **U** **Σ** $\mathbf{V}^\intercal$, where **V** contains the unit vectors that define all the principal components that you are looking for, in the correct order, as shown in Equation 7-1.[5]

Equation 7-1. Principal components matrix

$$\mathbf{V} = \begin{pmatrix} | & | & & | \\ \mathbf{c}_1 & \mathbf{c}_2 & \cdots & \mathbf{c}_n \\ | & | & & | \end{pmatrix}$$

The following Python code uses NumPy's `svd()` function to obtain all the principal components of the 3D training set represented back in Figure 7-2, then it extracts the two unit vectors that define the first two PCs:

```
import numpy as np

X = [...]  # create a small 3D dataset
X_centered = X - X.mean(axis=0)
U, s, Vt = np.linalg.svd(X_centered)
c1 = Vt[0]
c2 = Vt[1]
```

PCA assumes that the dataset is centered around the origin. As you will see, Scikit-Learn's PCA classes take care of centering the data for you. If you implement PCA yourself (as in the preceding example), or if you use other libraries, don't forget to center the data first.

5 The proof that SVD happens to give us exactly the principal components we need for PCA requires some prerequisite math knowledge, such as eigenvectors and covariance matrices. If you are curious, you will find all the details in this 2014 paper by Jonathon Shlens (*https://homl.info/pca2*).

Projecting Down to d Dimensions

Once you have identified all the principal components, you can reduce the dimensionality of the dataset down to *d* dimensions by projecting it onto the hyperplane defined by the first *d* principal components (we will discuss how to choose the number of dimensions *d* shortly). Selecting this hyperplane ensures that the projection will preserve as much variance as possible. For example, in Figure 7-2 the 3D dataset is projected down to the 2D plane defined by the first two principal components, preserving a large part of the dataset's variance. As a result, the 2D projection looks very much like the original 3D dataset.

To project the training set onto the hyperplane and obtain a reduced dataset $\mathbf{X}_{d\text{-proj}}$ of dimensionality *d*, compute the matrix multiplication of the training set matrix **X** by the matrix $\mathbf{W}_d$, defined as the matrix containing the first *d* columns of **V**, as shown in Equation 7-2.

Equation 7-2. Projecting the training set down to d dimensions

$$\mathbf{X}_{d\text{-proj}} = \mathbf{X}\mathbf{W}_d$$

The following Python code projects the training set onto the plane defined by the first two principal components:

```
W2 = Vt[:2].T
X2D = X_centered @ W2
```

There you have it! You now know how to reduce the dimensionality of any dataset by projecting it down to any number of dimensions, while preserving as much variance as possible.

Using Scikit-Learn

Scikit-Learn's `PCA` class uses SVD to implement PCA, just like we did earlier in this chapter. The following code applies PCA to reduce the dimensionality of the dataset down to two dimensions (note that it automatically takes care of centering the data):

```
from sklearn.decomposition import PCA

pca = PCA(n_components=2)
X2D = pca.fit_transform(X)
```

After fitting the `PCA` transformer to the dataset, its `components_` attribute holds the transpose of $\mathbf{W}_d$: it contains one row for each of the first *d* principal components.

Explained Variance Ratio

Another useful piece of information is the *explained variance ratio* of each principal component, available via the explained_variance_ratio_ variable. The ratio indicates the proportion of the dataset's variance that lies along each principal component. For example, let's look at the explained variance ratios of the first two components of the 3D dataset represented in Figure 7-2:

```
>>> pca.explained_variance_ratio_
array([0.82279334, 0.10821224])
```

This output tells us that about 82% of the dataset's variance lies along the first PC, and about 11% lies along the second PC. This leaves about 7% for the third PC, so it is reasonable to assume that the third PC probably carries little information.

Choosing the Right Number of Dimensions

Instead of arbitrarily choosing the number of dimensions to reduce down to, it is simpler to choose the number of dimensions that add up to a sufficiently large portion of the variance—say, 95%. (An exception to this rule, of course, is if you are reducing dimensionality for data visualization, in which case you will want to reduce the dimensionality down to 2 or 3.)

The following code loads and splits the MNIST dataset (introduced in Chapter 3) and performs PCA without reducing dimensionality, then computes the minimum number of dimensions required to preserve 95% of the training set's variance:

```
from sklearn.datasets import fetch_openml

mnist = fetch_openml('mnist_784', as_frame=False)
X_train, y_train = mnist.data[:60_000], mnist.target[:60_000]
X_test, y_test = mnist.data[60_000:], mnist.target[60_000:]

pca = PCA()
pca.fit(X_train)
cumsum = np.cumsum(pca.explained_variance_ratio_)
d = np.argmax(cumsum >= 0.95) + 1  # d equals 154
```

You could then set n_components=d and run PCA again, but there's a better option. Instead of specifying the number of principal components you want to preserve, you can set n_components to be a float between 0.0 and 1.0, indicating the ratio of variance you wish to preserve:

```
pca = PCA(n_components=0.95)
X_reduced = pca.fit_transform(X_train)
```

The actual number of components is determined during training, and it is stored in the n_components_ attribute:

```
>>> pca.n_components_
np.int64(154)
```

Yet another option is to plot the explained variance as a function of the number of dimensions (simply plot cumsum; see Figure 7-8). There will usually be an elbow in the curve, where the explained variance stops growing fast. In this case, you can see that reducing the dimensionality down to about 100 dimensions wouldn't lose too much explained variance.

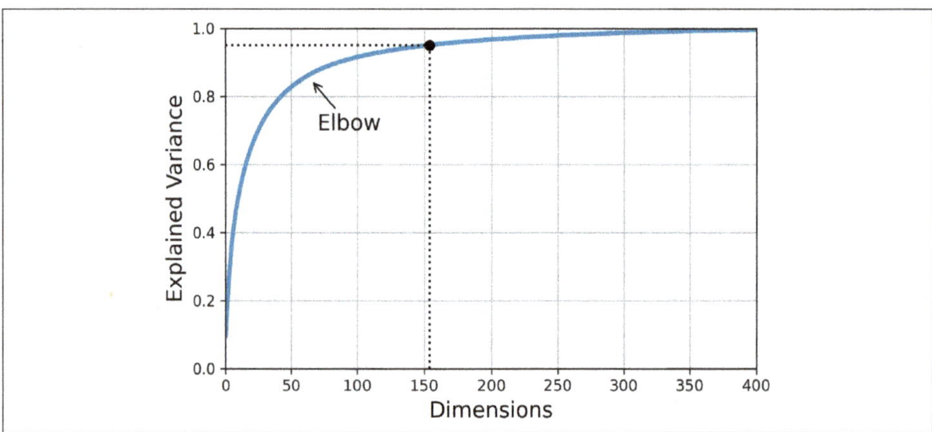

Figure 7-8. Explained variance as a function of the number of dimensions

Alternatively, if you are using dimensionality reduction as a preprocessing step for a supervised learning task (e.g., classification), then you can tune the number of dimensions as you would any other hyperparameter (see Chapter 2). For example, the following code example creates a two-step pipeline, first reducing dimensionality using PCA, then classifying using a random forest. Next, it uses RandomizedSearchCV to find a good combination of hyperparameters for both PCA and the random forest classifier. This example does a quick search, tuning only 2 hyperparameters, training on just 1,000 instances, and running for just 10 iterations, but feel free to do a more thorough search if you have the time:

```
from sklearn.ensemble import RandomForestClassifier
from sklearn.model_selection import RandomizedSearchCV
from sklearn.pipeline import make_pipeline

clf = make_pipeline(PCA(random_state=42),
                    RandomForestClassifier(random_state=42))
param_distrib = {
    "pca__n_components": np.arange(10, 80),
    "randomforestclassifier__n_estimators": np.arange(50, 500)
}
rnd_search = RandomizedSearchCV(clf, param_distrib, n_iter=10, cv=3,
                                random_state=42)
rnd_search.fit(X_train[:1000], y_train[:1000])
```

Let's look at the best hyperparameters found:

```
>>> print(rnd_search.best_params_)
{'randomforestclassifier__n_estimators': np.int64(475),
 'pca__n_components': np.int64(57)}
```

It's interesting to note how low the optimal number of components is: we reduced a 784-dimensional dataset to just 57 dimensions! This is tied to the fact that we used a random forest, which is a pretty powerful model. If we used a linear model instead, such as an `SGDClassifier`, the search would find that we need to preserve more dimensions (about 75).

You may also care about the model's size and speed, not just it's performance. The fewer dimensions, the smaller the model, and the faster training and inference will be. But if you shrink the data too much, then you will lose too much signal and your model will underfit. You need to choose the right balance of speed, size, and performance for your particular use case.

PCA for Compression

After dimensionality reduction, the training set takes up much less space. For example, after applying PCA to the MNIST dataset while preserving 95% of its variance, we are left with 154 features, instead of the original 784 features. So the dataset is now less than 20% of its original size, and we only lost 5% of its variance! This is a reasonable compression ratio, and it's easy to see how such a size reduction would speed up a classification algorithm tremendously.

It is also possible to decompress the reduced dataset back to 784 dimensions by applying the inverse transformation of the PCA projection. This won't give you back the original data, since the projection lost a bit of information (within the 5% variance that was dropped), but it will likely be close to the original data. The mean squared distance between the original data and the reconstructed data (compressed and then decompressed) is called the *reconstruction error*.

The `inverse_transform()` method lets us decompress the reduced MNIST dataset back to 784 dimensions:

```
X_recovered = pca.inverse_transform(X_reduced)
```

Figure 7-9 shows a few digits from the original training set (on the left), and the corresponding digits after compression and decompression. You can see that there is a slight image quality loss, but the digits are still mostly intact.

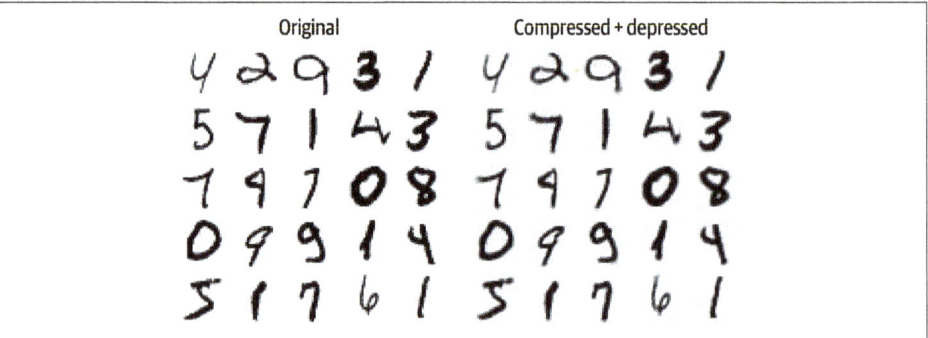

Figure 7-9. MNIST compression that preserves 95% of the variance

The equation for the inverse transformation is shown in Equation 7-3.

Equation 7-3. PCA inverse transformation, back to the original number of dimensions

$$\mathbf{X}_{\text{recovered}} = \mathbf{X}_{d\text{-proj}} \mathbf{W}_d^{\mathsf{T}}$$

Randomized PCA

If you set the `svd_solver` hyperparameter to `"randomized"`, Scikit-Learn uses a stochastic algorithm called *randomized PCA* that quickly finds an approximation of the first d principal components. Its computational complexity is $O(m \times d^2) + O(d^3)$, instead of $O(m \times n^2) + O(n^3)$ for the full SVD approach, so it is dramatically faster than full SVD when d is much smaller than n:

```
rnd_pca = PCA(n_components=154, svd_solver="randomized", random_state=42)
X_reduced = rnd_pca.fit_transform(X_train)
```

By default, `svd_solver` is set to `"auto"`: if the input data has few features (n < 1,000) and at least 10 times more samples ($m > 10n$), then the `"covariance_eigh"` solver is used, which is very fast in these conditions. Otherwise, if max(m, n) > 500 and `n_components` is an integer smaller than 80% of min(m, n), it uses the `"randomized"` solver. In other cases, it uses the full SVD approach. If you want to force Scikit-Learn to use full SVD, trading compute time for a slightly more precise result, you can set `svd_solver="full"`.

Incremental PCA

One problem with the preceding implementations of PCA is that they require the whole training set to fit in memory in order for the algorithm to run. Fortunately, *incremental PCA* (IPCA) algorithms have been developed that allow you to split the training set into mini-batches and feed these in one mini-batch at a time. This is useful for large training sets and for applying PCA online (i.e., on the fly, as new instances arrive).

The following code splits the MNIST training set into 100 mini-batches (using NumPy's `array_split()` function) and feeds them to Scikit-Learn's `IncrementalPCA` class[6] to reduce the dimensionality of the MNIST dataset down to 154 dimensions, just like before. Note that you must call the `partial_fit()` method with each mini-batch, rather than the `fit()` method with the whole training set:

```
from sklearn.decomposition import IncrementalPCA

n_batches = 100
inc_pca = IncrementalPCA(n_components=154)
for X_batch in np.array_split(X_train, n_batches):
    inc_pca.partial_fit(X_batch)

X_reduced = inc_pca.transform(X_train)
```

Alternatively, you can use NumPy's `memmap` class, which allows you to manipulate a large array stored in a binary file on disk as if it were entirely in memory; the class loads only the data it needs in memory, when it needs it. To demonstrate this, let's first create a memory-mapped (memmap) file and copy the MNIST training set to it, then call `flush()` to ensure that any data still in the cache gets saved to disk. In real life, `X_train` would typically not fit in memory, so you would load it chunk by chunk and save each chunk to the right part of the memmap array:

```
filename = "my_mnist.mmap"
X_mmap = np.memmap(filename, dtype='float32', mode='write', shape=X_train.shape)
X_mmap[:] = X_train  # could be a loop instead, saving the data chunk by chunk
X_mmap.flush()
```

Next, we can load the memmap file and use it like a regular NumPy array. Let's use the `IncrementalPCA` class to reduce its dimensionality. Since this algorithm uses only a small part of the array at any given time, memory usage remains under control. This makes it possible to call the usual `fit()` method instead of `partial_fit()`, which is quite convenient:

```
X_mmap = np.memmap(filename, dtype="float32", mode="readonly").reshape(-1, 784)
batch_size = X_mmap.shape[0] // n_batches
inc_pca = IncrementalPCA(n_components=154, batch_size=batch_size)
inc_pca.fit(X_mmap)
```

6 Scikit-Learn uses the algorithm (*https://homl.info/32*) described in David A. Ross et al., "Incremental Learning for Robust Visual Tracking", *International Journal of Computer Vision* 77, no. 1–3 (2008): 125–141.

Only the raw binary data is saved to disk, so you need to specify the data type and shape of the array when you load it. If you omit the shape, `np.memmap()` returns a 1D array.

For very high-dimensional datasets, PCA can be too slow. As you saw earlier, even if you use randomized PCA, its computational complexity is still $O(m \times d^2) + O(d^3)$, so the target number of dimensions d must not be too large. If you are dealing with a dataset with tens of thousands of features or more (e.g., images), then training may become much too slow: in this case, you should consider using random projection instead.

Random Projection

As its name suggests, the random projection algorithm projects the data to a lower-dimensional space using a random linear projection. This may sound crazy, but it turns out that such a random projection is actually very likely to preserve distances fairly well, as was demonstrated mathematically by William B. Johnson and Joram Lindenstrauss in a famous lemma. So, two similar instances will remain similar after the projection, and two very different instances will remain very different.

Obviously, the more dimensions you drop, the more information is lost, and the more distances get distorted. So how can you choose the optimal number of dimensions? Well, Johnson and Lindenstrauss came up with an equation that determines the minimum number of dimensions to preserve in order to ensure—with high probability—that distances won't change by more than a given tolerance. For example, if you have a dataset containing m = 5,000 instances with n = 20,000 features each, and you don't want the squared distance between any two instances to change by more than ε = 10%,[7] then you should project the data down to d dimensions, with $d \geq 4 \log(m) / (\frac{1}{2} \varepsilon^2 - \frac{1}{3} \varepsilon^3)$, which is 7,300 dimensions. That's quite a significant dimensionality reduction! Notice that the equation does not use n, it only relies on m and ε. This equation is implemented by the `johnson_lindenstrauss_min_dim()` function:

```
>>> from sklearn.random_projection import johnson_lindenstrauss_min_dim
>>> m, ε = 5_000, 0.1
>>> d = johnson_lindenstrauss_min_dim(m, eps=ε)
>>> d
7300
```

7 ε is the Greek letter epsilon, often used for tiny values.

Now we can just generate a random matrix **P** of shape [d, n], where each item is sampled randomly from a Gaussian distribution with mean 0 and variance 1 / d, and use it to project a dataset from n dimensions down to d:

```
n = 20_000
rng = np.random.default_rng(seed=42)
P = rng.standard_normal((d, n)) / np.sqrt(d)  # std dev = sqrt(variance)

X = rng.standard_normal((m, n))  # generate a fake dataset
X_reduced = X @ P.T
```

That's all there is to it! It's simple and efficient, and training is almost instantaneous: the only thing the algorithm needs to create the random matrix is the dataset's shape. The data itself is not used at all. This makes random projection particularly well suited for very high-dimensional data such as text or genomics with millions of features, or very sparse data, for which even randomized PCA may take too long to train and require too much memory. At inference time, random projection is just as fast as PCA (i.e., one matrix multiplication). That said, random projection is not a silver bullet: it loses a bit more signal than PCA, so there's a trade-off between training speed and performance.

Scikit-Learn offers a `GaussianRandomProjection` class to do exactly what we just did: when you call its `fit()` method, it uses `johnson_lindenstrauss_min_dim()` to determine the output dimensionality, then it generates a random matrix, which it stores in the `components_` attribute. Then when you call `transform()`, it uses this matrix to perform the projection. When creating the transformer, you can set `eps` to tweak ε (it defaults to 0.1), and `n_components` to force a specific target dimensionality d (you will probably want to fine-tune these hyperparameters using cross-validation). The following code example gives the same result as the preceding code (you can also verify that `gaussian_rnd_proj.components_` is equal to `P`):

```
from sklearn.random_projection import GaussianRandomProjection

gaussian_rnd_proj = GaussianRandomProjection(eps=ε, random_state=42)
X_reduced = gaussian_rnd_proj.fit_transform(X)  # same result as above
```

Scikit-Learn also provides a second random projection transformer, known as `SparseRandomProjection`. It determines the target dimensionality in the same way, generates a random matrix of the same shape, and performs the projection identically. The main difference is that the random matrix is sparse. This means it uses much less memory: about 25 MB instead of almost 1.2 GB in the preceding example! And it's also much faster, both to generate the random matrix and to reduce dimensionality: about 50% faster in this case. Moreover, if the input is sparse, the transformation keeps it sparse (unless you set `dense_output=True`). Lastly, it enjoys the same distance-preserving property as the previous approach, and the quality of the dimensionality reduction is comparable (only very slightly less accurate). In short, it's usually preferable to use this transformer instead of the first one, especially for large or sparse datasets.

The ratio r of nonzero items in the sparse random matrix is called its *density*. By default, it is equal to $\frac{1}{\sqrt{n}}$. With 20,000 features, this means that only 1 in ~141 cells in the random matrix is nonzero: that's quite sparse! You can set the `density` hyperparameter to another value if you prefer. Each cell in the sparse random matrix has a probability r of being nonzero, and each nonzero value is either $-v$ or $+v$ (both equally likely), where $v = \frac{1}{\sqrt{dr}}$.

If you want to perform the inverse transform, you first need to compute the pseudoinverse of the components matrix using SciPy's `pinv()` function, then multiply the reduced data by the transpose of the pseudoinverse:

```
components_pinv = np.linalg.pinv(gaussian_rnd_proj.components_)
X_recovered = X_reduced @ components_pinv.T
```

Computing the pseudoinverse may take a very long time if the components matrix is large, as the computational complexity of `pinv()` is $O(dn^2)$ if $d < n$, or $O(nd^2)$ otherwise.

In summary, random projection is a simple, fast, memory-efficient, and surprisingly powerful dimensionality reduction algorithm that you should keep in mind, especially when you deal with high-dimensional datasets.

Random projection is not always used to reduce the dimensionality of large datasets. For example, a 2017 paper (*https://homl.info/flies*)[8] by Sanjoy Dasgupta et al. showed that the brain of a fruit fly implements an analog of random projection to map dense low-dimensional olfactory inputs to sparse high-dimensional binary outputs: for each odor, only a small fraction of the output neurons get activated, but similar odors activate many of the same neurons. This is similar to a well-known algorithm called *locality sensitive hashing* (LSH), which is typically used in search engines to group similar documents (see Chapter 17).

8 Sanjoy Dasgupta et al., "A neural algorithm for a fundamental computing problem", *Science* 358, no. 6364 (2017): 793–796.

LLE

Locally linear embedding (LLE) (*https://homl.info/lle*)[9] is a *nonlinear dimensionality reduction* (NLDR) technique. It is a manifold learning technique that does not rely on projections, unlike PCA and random projection. In a nutshell, LLE first determines how each training instance linearly relates to its nearest neighbors, then it looks for a low-dimensional representation of the training set where these local relationships are best preserved (more details shortly). This approach makes it particularly good at unrolling twisted manifolds, especially when there is not too much noise. However, it does not scale well so it is mostly for small or medium sized datasets.

The following code makes a Swiss roll, then uses Scikit-Learn's `LocallyLinearEmbedding` class to unroll it:

```
from sklearn.datasets import make_swiss_roll
from sklearn.manifold import LocallyLinearEmbedding

X_swiss, t = make_swiss_roll(n_samples=1000, noise=0.2, random_state=42)
lle = LocallyLinearEmbedding(n_components=2, n_neighbors=10, random_state=42)
X_unrolled = lle.fit_transform(X_swiss)
```

The variable `t` is a 1D NumPy array containing the position of each instance along the rolled axis of the Swiss roll. We don't use it in this example, but it can be used as a target for a nonlinear regression task. The resulting 2D dataset is shown in Figure 7-10.

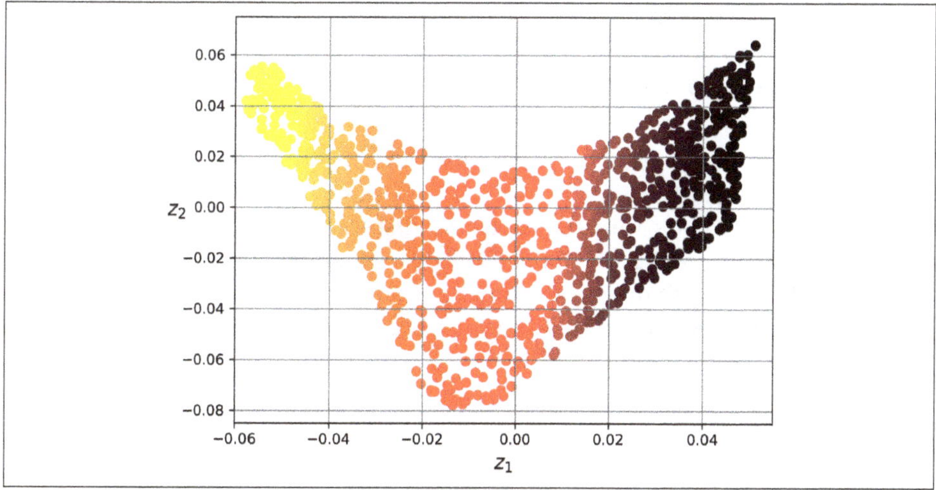

Figure 7-10. Unrolled Swiss roll using LLE

9 Sam T. Roweis and Lawrence K. Saul, "Nonlinear Dimensionality Reduction by Locally Linear Embedding", *Science* 290, no. 5500 (2000): 2323–2326.

As you can see, the Swiss roll is completely unrolled, and the distances between instances are locally well preserved. However, distances are not preserved on a larger scale: the unrolled Swiss roll should be a rectangle, not this kind of stretched and twisted band. Nevertheless, LLE did a pretty good job of modeling the manifold.

Here's how LLE works: for each training instance $\mathbf{x}^{(i)}$, the algorithm identifies its k-nearest neighbors (in the preceding code $k = 10$), then tries to reconstruct $\mathbf{x}^{(i)}$ as a linear function of these neighbors. More specifically, it tries to find the weights $w_{i,j}$ such that the squared distance between $\mathbf{x}^{(i)}$ and $\sum_{j=1}^{m} w_{i,j}\mathbf{x}^{(j)}$ is as small as possible, assuming $w_{i,j} = 0$ if $\mathbf{x}^{(j)}$ is not one of the k-nearest neighbors of $\mathbf{x}^{(i)}$. Thus the first step of LLE is the constrained optimization problem described in Equation 7-4, where $\mathbf{W}$ is the weight matrix containing all the weights $w_{i,j}$. The second constraint simply normalizes the weights for each training instance $\mathbf{x}^{(i)}$.

Equation 7-4. LLE step 1: linearly modeling local relationships

$$\widehat{\mathbf{W}} = \underset{\mathbf{W}}{\operatorname{argmin}} \sum_{i=1}^{m} \left(\mathbf{x}^{(i)} - \sum_{j=1}^{m} w_{i,j} \mathbf{x}^{(j)} \right)^2$$

$$\text{subject to} \begin{cases} w_{i,j} = 0 & \text{if } \mathbf{x}^{(j)} \text{ is not one of the } k \text{ n.n. of } \mathbf{x}^{(i)} \\ \sum_{j=1}^{m} w_{i,j} = 1 \text{ for } i = 1,2,\cdots,m \end{cases}$$

After this step, the weight matrix $\widehat{\mathbf{W}}$ (containing the weights $\widehat{w}_{i,j}$) encodes the local linear relationships between the training instances. The second step is to map the training instances into a d-dimensional space (where $d < n$) while preserving these local relationships as much as possible. If $\mathbf{z}^{(i)}$ is the image of $\mathbf{x}^{(i)}$ in this d-dimensional space, then we want the squared distance between $\mathbf{z}^{(i)}$ and $\sum_{j=1}^{m} \widehat{w}_{i,j}\mathbf{z}^{(j)}$ to be as small as possible. This idea leads to the unconstrained optimization problem described in Equation 7-5. It looks very similar to the first step, but instead of keeping the instances fixed and finding the optimal weights, we are doing the reverse: keeping the weights fixed and finding the optimal position of the instances' images in the low-dimensional space. Note that $\mathbf{Z}$ is the matrix containing all $\mathbf{z}^{(i)}$.

Equation 7-5. LLE step 2: reducing dimensionality while preserving relationships

$$\widehat{\mathbf{Z}} = \underset{\mathbf{Z}}{\operatorname{argmin}} \sum_{i=1}^{m} \left(\mathbf{z}^{(i)} - \sum_{j=1}^{m} \widehat{w}_{i,j} \mathbf{z}^{(j)} \right)^2$$

Scikit-Learn's LLE implementation has the following computational complexity: $O(m \log(m)n \log(k))$ for finding the k-nearest neighbors, $O(mnk^3)$ for optimizing the weights, and $O(dm^2)$ for constructing the low-dimensional representations. Unfortunately, the m^2 in the last term makes this algorithm scale poorly to very large datasets.

As you can see, LLE is quite different from the projection techniques, and it's significantly more complex, but it can also construct much better low-dimensional representations, especially if the data is nonlinear.

Other Dimensionality Reduction Techniques

Before we conclude this chapter, let's take a quick look at a few other popular dimensionality reduction techniques available in Scikit-Learn:

`sklearn.manifold.MDS`
: *Multidimensional scaling* (MDS) reduces dimensionality while trying to preserve the distances between the instances. Random projection does that for high-dimensional data, but it doesn't work well on low-dimensional data.

`sklearn.manifold.Isomap`
: *Isomap* creates a graph by connecting each instance to its nearest neighbors, then reduces dimensionality while trying to preserve the *geodesic distances* between the instances. The geodesic distance between two nodes in a graph is the number of nodes on the shortest path between these nodes. This approach works best when the data lies on a fairly smooth and low-dimensional manifold with a single global structure (e.g., the Swiss roll).

`sklearn.manifold.TSNE`
: *t-distributed stochastic neighbor embedding* (t-SNE) reduces dimensionality while trying to keep similar instances close and dissimilar instances apart. It is mostly used for visualization, in particular to visualize clusters of instances in high-dimensional space. For example, in the exercises at the end of this chapter you will use t-SNE to visualize a 2D map of the MNIST images. However, it is not meant to be used as a preprocessing stage for an ML model.

`sklearn.discriminant_analysis.LinearDiscriminantAnalysis`
: *Linear discriminant analysis* (LDA) is a linear classification algorithm that, during training, learns the most discriminative axes between the classes. These axes can then be used to define a hyperplane onto which to project the data. The benefit of this approach is that the projection will keep classes as far apart as possible, so LDA is a good technique to reduce dimensionality before running another classification algorithm (unless LDA alone is sufficient).

Uniform Manifold Approximation and Projection (UMAP) is another popular dimensionality reduction technique for visualization. While t-SNE is better at preserving the local structure, especially clusters, UMAP tries to preserve both the local and global structures. Moreover, it scales better to large datasets. Sadly, it is not available in Scikit-Learn, but there's a good implementation in the umap-learn package (*https://umap-learn.readthedocs.io*).

Figure 7-11 shows the results of MDS, Isomap, and t-SNE on the Swiss roll. MDS manages to flatten the Swiss roll without losing its global curvature, while Isomap drops it entirely. Depending on the downstream task, preserving the large-scale structure may be good or bad. t-SNE does a reasonable job of flattening the Swiss roll, preserving a bit of curvature, and it also amplifies clusters, tearing the roll apart. Again, this might be good or bad, depending on the downstream task.

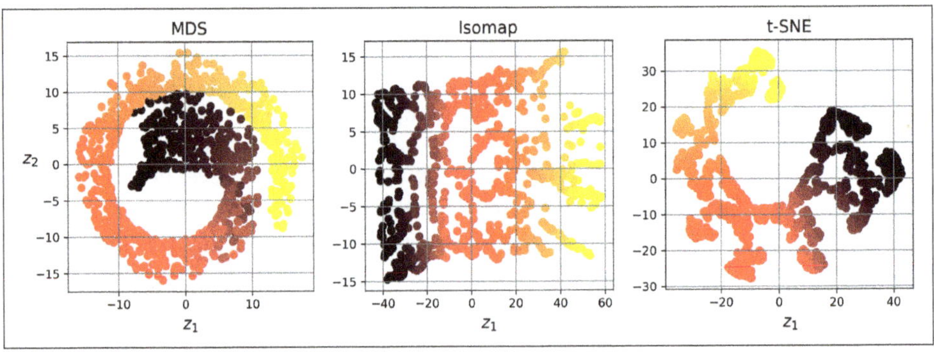

Figure 7-11. Using various techniques to reduce the Swiss roll to 2D

Exercises

1. What are the main motivations for reducing a dataset's dimensionality? What are the main drawbacks?
2. What is the curse of dimensionality?
3. Once a dataset's dimensionality has been reduced, is it possible to reverse the operation? If so, how? If not, why?
4. Can PCA be used to reduce the dimensionality of a highly nonlinear dataset?
5. Suppose you perform PCA on a 1,000-dimensional dataset, setting the explained variance ratio to 95%. How many dimensions will the resulting dataset have?
6. In what cases would you use regular PCA, incremental PCA, randomized PCA, or random projection?
7. How can you evaluate the performance of a dimensionality reduction algorithm on your dataset?

8. Does it make any sense to chain two different dimensionality reduction algorithms?
9. Load the MNIST dataset (introduced in Chapter 3) and split it into a training set and a test set (take the first 60,000 instances for training, and the remaining 10,000 for testing). Train a random forest classifier on the dataset and time how long it takes, then evaluate the resulting model on the test set. Next, use PCA to reduce the dataset's dimensionality, with an explained variance ratio of 95%. Train a new random forest classifier on the reduced dataset and see how long it takes. Was training much faster? Next, evaluate the classifier on the test set. How does it compare to the previous classifier? Try again with an `SGDClassifier`. How much does PCA help now?
10. Use t-SNE to reduce the first 5,000 images of the MNIST dataset down to 2 dimensions and plot the result using Matplotlib. You can use a scatterplot using 10 different colors to represent each image's target class. Alternatively, you can replace each dot in the scatterplot with the corresponding instance's class (a digit from 0 to 9), or even plot scaled-down versions of the digit images themselves (if you plot all digits the visualization will be too cluttered, so you should either draw a random sample or plot an instance only if no other instance has already been plotted at a close distance). You should get a nice visualization with well-separated clusters of digits. Try using other dimensionality reduction algorithms, such as PCA, LLE, or MDS, and compare the resulting visualizations.

Solutions to these exercises are available at the end of this chapter's notebook, at *https://homl.info/colab-p*.

CHAPTER 8

Unsupervised Learning Techniques

Yann LeCun, Turing Award winner and Meta's Chief AI Scientist, famously said that "if intelligence was a cake, unsupervised learning would be the cake, supervised learning would be the icing on the cake, and reinforcement learning would be the cherry on the cake" (NeurIPS 2016). In other words, there is a huge potential in unsupervised learning that we have only barely started to sink our teeth into. Indeed, the vast majority of the available data is unlabeled: we have the input features **X**, but we do not have the labels **y**.

Say you want to create a system that will take a few pictures of each item on a manufacturing production line and detect which items are defective. You can fairly easily create a system that will take pictures automatically, and this might give you thousands of pictures every day. You can then build a reasonably large dataset in just a few weeks. But wait, there are no labels! If you want to train a regular binary classifier that will predict whether an item is defective or not, you will need to label every single picture as "defective" or "normal". This will generally require human experts to sit down and manually go through all the pictures. This is a long, costly, and tedious task, so it will usually only be done on a small subset of the available pictures. As a result, the labeled dataset will be quite small, and the classifier's performance will be disappointing. Moreover, every time the company makes any change to its products, the whole process will need to be started over from scratch. Wouldn't it be great if the algorithm could just exploit the unlabeled data without needing humans to label every picture? Enter unsupervised learning.

In Chapter 7 we looked at the most common unsupervised learning task: dimensionality reduction. In this chapter we will look at a few more unsupervised tasks:

Clustering
The goal is to group similar instances together into *clusters*. Clustering is a great tool for data analysis, customer segmentation, recommender systems, search

engines, image segmentation, semi-supervised learning, dimensionality reduction, and more.

Anomaly detection (also called outlier detection)
: The objective is to learn what "normal" data looks like, and then use that to detect abnormal instances. These instances are called *anomalies*, or *outliers*, while the normal instances are called *inliers*. Anomaly detection is useful in a wide variety of applications, such as fraud detection, detecting defective products in manufacturing, identifying new trends in time series, or removing outliers from a dataset before training another model, which can significantly improve the performance of the resulting model.

Density estimation
: This is the task of estimating the *probability density function* (PDF) of the random process that generated the dataset.[1] Density estimation is commonly used for anomaly detection: instances located in very low-density regions are likely to be anomalies. It is also useful for data analysis and visualization.

Ready for some cake? We will start with two clustering algorithms, *k*-means and DBSCAN, then we'll discuss Gaussian mixture models and see how they can be used for density estimation, clustering, and anomaly detection.

Clustering Algorithms: k-means and DBSCAN

As you enjoy a hike in the mountains, you stumble upon a plant you have never seen before. You look around and you notice a few more. They are not identical, yet they are sufficiently similar for you to know that they most likely belong to the same species (or at least the same genus). You may need a botanist to tell you what species that is, but you certainly don't need an expert to identify groups of similar-looking objects. This is called *clustering*: it is the task of identifying similar instances and assigning them to *clusters*, or groups of similar instances.

Just like in classification, each instance gets assigned to a group. However, unlike classification, clustering is an unsupervised task, there are no labels, so the algorithm needs to figure out on its own how to group instances. Consider Figure 8-1: on the left is the iris dataset (introduced in Chapter 4), where each instance's species (i.e., its class) is represented with a different marker. It is a labeled dataset, for which classification algorithms such as logistic regression, SVMs, or random forest classifiers are well suited. On the right is the same dataset, but without the labels, so you cannot use a classification algorithm anymore. This is where clustering algorithms step in: many of them can easily detect the lower-left cluster. It is also quite easy to see with our own

1 If you are not familiar with probability theory, I highly recommend the free online classes by Khan Academy.

eyes, but it is not so obvious that the upper-right cluster is composed of two distinct subclusters. That said, the dataset has two additional features (sepal length and width) that are not represented here, and clustering algorithms can make good use of all features, so in fact they identify the three clusters fairly well (e.g., using a Gaussian mixture model, only 5 instances out of 150 are assigned to the wrong cluster).

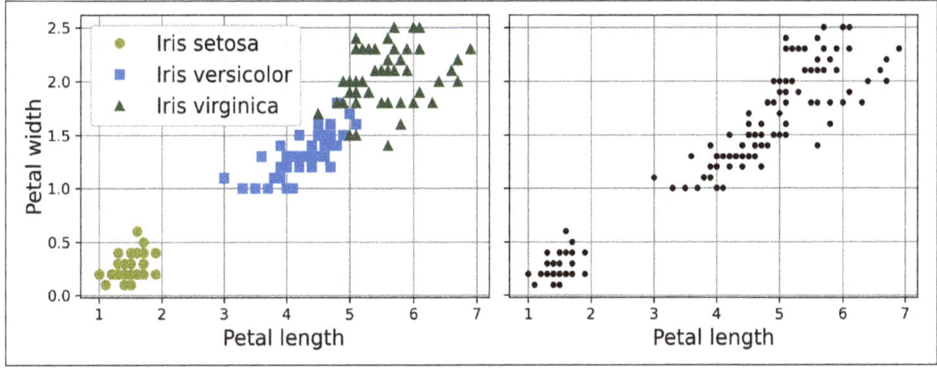

Figure 8-1. Classification (left) versus clustering (right): in clustering, the dataset is unlabeled so the algorithm must identify the clusters without guidance

Clustering is used in a wide variety of applications, including:

Customer segmentation
: You can cluster your customers based on their purchases and their activity on your website. This is useful to understand who your customers are and what they need, so you can adapt your products and marketing campaigns to each segment. For example, customer segmentation can be useful in *recommender systems* to suggest content that other users in the same cluster enjoyed.

Data analysis
: When you analyze a new dataset, it can be helpful to run a clustering algorithm, and then analyze each cluster separately.

Dimensionality reduction
: Once a dataset has been clustered, it is usually possible to measure each instance's *affinity* with each cluster; affinity is any measure of how well an instance fits into a cluster. Each instance's feature vector **x** can then be replaced with the vector of its cluster affinities. If there are *k* clusters, then this vector is *k*-dimensional. The new vector is typically much lower-dimensional than the original feature vector, but it can preserve enough information for further processing.

Feature engineering
: The cluster affinities can often be useful as extra features. For example, we used *k*-means in Chapter 2 to add geographic cluster affinity features to the California housing dataset, and they helped us get better performance.

Anomaly detection (also called outlier detection)
: Any instance that has a low affinity to all the clusters is likely to be an anomaly. For example, if you have clustered the users of your website based on their behavior, you can detect users with unusual behavior, such as an unusual number of requests per second.

Semi-supervised learning
: If you only have a few labels, you could perform clustering and propagate the labels to all the instances in the same cluster. This technique can greatly increase the number of labels available for a subsequent supervised learning algorithm, and thus improve its performance.

Search engines
: Some search engines let you search for images that are similar to a reference image. To build such a system, you would first apply a clustering algorithm to all the images in your database; similar images would end up in the same cluster. Then when a user provides a reference image, all you'd need to do is use the trained clustering model to find this image's cluster, and you could then simply return all the images from this cluster.

Image segmentation
: By clustering pixels according to their color, then replacing each pixel's color with the mean color of its cluster, it is possible to considerably reduce the number of different colors in an image. Image segmentation is used in many object detection and tracking systems, as it makes it easier to detect the contour of each object.

There is no universal definition of what a cluster is: it really depends on the context, and different algorithms will capture different kinds of clusters. Some algorithms look for instances centered around a particular point, called a *centroid*. Others look for continuous regions of densely packed instances: these clusters can take on any shape. Some algorithms are hierarchical, looking for clusters of clusters. And the list goes on.

In this section, we will look at two popular clustering algorithms, *k*-means and DBSCAN, and explore some of their applications, such as nonlinear dimensionality reduction, semi-supervised learning, and anomaly detection.

k-Means Clustering

Consider the unlabeled dataset represented in Figure 8-2: you can clearly see five blobs of instances. The *k*-means algorithm is a simple algorithm capable of clustering this kind of dataset very quickly and efficiently, often in just a few iterations. It was proposed by Stuart Lloyd at Bell Labs in 1957 as a technique for pulse-code modulation, but it was only published (*https://homl.info/36*) outside of the company in 1982.[2] In 1965, Edward W. Forgy had published virtually the same algorithm, so *k*-means is sometimes referred to as the Lloyd–Forgy algorithm.

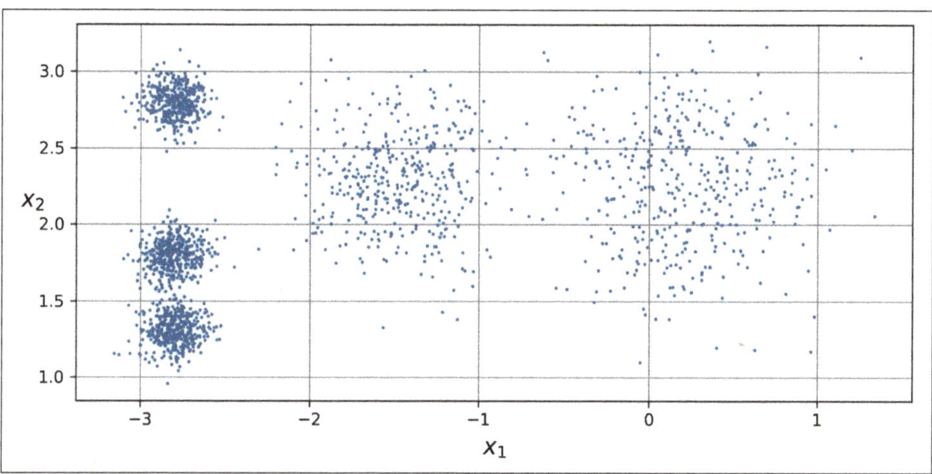

Figure 8-2. An unlabeled dataset composed of five blobs of instances

Let's train a *k*-means clusterer on this dataset. It will try to find each blob's center and assign each instance to the closest blob:

```
from sklearn.cluster import KMeans
from sklearn.datasets import make_blobs

X, y = make_blobs([...])  # make the blobs: y contains the cluster IDs, but we
                          # will not use them; that's what we want to predict
k = 5
kmeans = KMeans(n_clusters=k, random_state=42)
y_pred = kmeans.fit_predict(X)
```

Note that you have to specify the number of clusters *k* that the algorithm must find. In this example, it is pretty obvious from looking at the data that *k* should be set to 5, but in general it is not that easy. We will discuss this shortly.

2 Stuart P. Lloyd, "Least Squares Quantization in PCM", *IEEE Transactions on Information Theory* 28, no. 2 (1982): 129–137.

Each instance will be assigned to one of the five clusters. In the context of clustering, an instance's *label* is the index of the cluster to which the algorithm assigns this instance; this is not to be confused with the class labels in classification, which are used as targets (remember that clustering is an unsupervised learning task). The `KMeans` instance preserves the predicted labels of the instances it was trained on, available via the `labels_` instance variable:

```
>>> y_pred
array([4, 0, 1, ..., 2, 1, 0], dtype=int32)
>>> y_pred is kmeans.labels_
True
```

We can also take a look at the five centroids that the algorithm found:

```
>>> kmeans.cluster_centers_
array([[-2.80389616,  1.80117999],
       [ 0.20876306,  2.25551336],
       [-2.79290307,  2.79641063],
       [-1.46679593,  2.28585348],
       [-2.80037642,  1.30082566]])
```

You can easily assign new instances to the cluster whose centroid is closest:

```
>>> import numpy as np
>>> X_new = np.array([[0, 2], [3, 2], [-3, 3], [-3, 2.5]])
>>> kmeans.predict(X_new)
array([1, 1, 2, 2], dtype=int32)
```

If you plot the cluster's decision boundaries, you get a Voronoi tessellation: see Figure 8-3, where each centroid is represented with an ⊗.

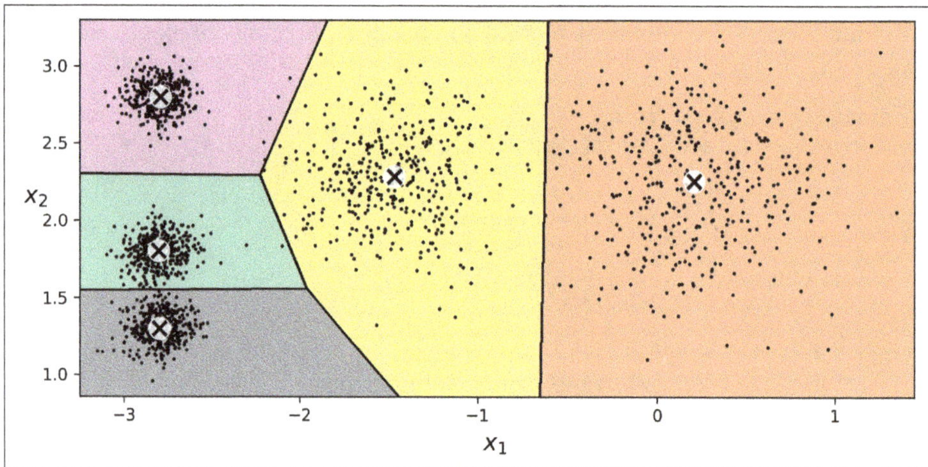

Figure 8-3. k-means decision boundaries (Voronoi tessellation)

The vast majority of the instances were clearly assigned to the appropriate cluster, but a few instances were probably mislabeled, especially near the boundary between the top-left cluster and the central cluster. Indeed, the *k*-means algorithm does not behave very well when the blobs have very different diameters because all it cares about when assigning an instance to a cluster is the distance to the centroid.

Instead of assigning each instance to a single cluster, which is called *hard clustering*, it can be useful to give each instance a score per cluster, which is called *soft clustering*. The score can be the distance between the instance and the centroid or a similarity score (or affinity), such as the Gaussian radial basis function we used in Chapter 2. In the `KMeans` class, the `transform()` method measures the distance from each instance to every centroid:

```
>>> kmeans.transform(X_new).round(2)
array([[2.81, 0.33, 2.9 , 1.49, 2.89],
       [5.81, 2.8 , 5.85, 4.48, 5.84],
       [1.21, 3.29, 0.29, 1.69, 1.71],
       [0.73, 3.22, 0.36, 1.55, 1.22]])
```

In this example, the first instance in `X_new` is located at a distance of about 2.81 from the first centroid, 0.33 from the second centroid, 2.90 from the third centroid, 1.49 from the fourth centroid, and 2.89 from the fifth centroid. If you have a high-dimensional dataset and you transform it this way, you end up with a *k*-dimensional dataset: this transformation can be a very efficient nonlinear dimensionality reduction technique. Alternatively, you can use these distances as extra features to train another model, as in Chapter 2.

The k-means algorithm

So, how does the algorithm work? Well, suppose you were given the centroids. You could easily label all the instances in the dataset by assigning each of them to the cluster whose centroid is closest. Conversely, if you were given all the instance labels, you could easily locate each cluster's centroid by computing the mean of the instances in that cluster. But you are given neither the labels nor the centroids, so how can you proceed? Start by placing the centroids randomly (e.g., by picking *k* instances at random from the dataset and using their locations as centroids). Then label the instances, update the centroids, label the instances, update the centroids, and so on until the centroids stop moving. The algorithm is guaranteed to converge in a finite number of steps (usually quite small). That's because the mean squared distance between the instances and their closest centroids can only go down at each step, and since it cannot be negative, it's guaranteed to converge.

You can see the algorithm in action in Figure 8-4: the centroids are initialized randomly (top left), then the instances are labeled (top right), then the centroids are updated (center left), the instances are relabeled (center right), and so on. As you can see, in just three iterations the algorithm has reached a clustering that seems close to optimal.

The computational complexity of the algorithm is generally linear with regard to the number of instances *m*, the number of clusters *k*, and the number of dimensions *n*. However, this is only true when the data has a clustering structure. If it does not, then in the worst-case scenario the complexity can increase exponentially with the number of instances. In practice, this rarely happens, and *k*-means is generally one of the fastest clustering algorithms.

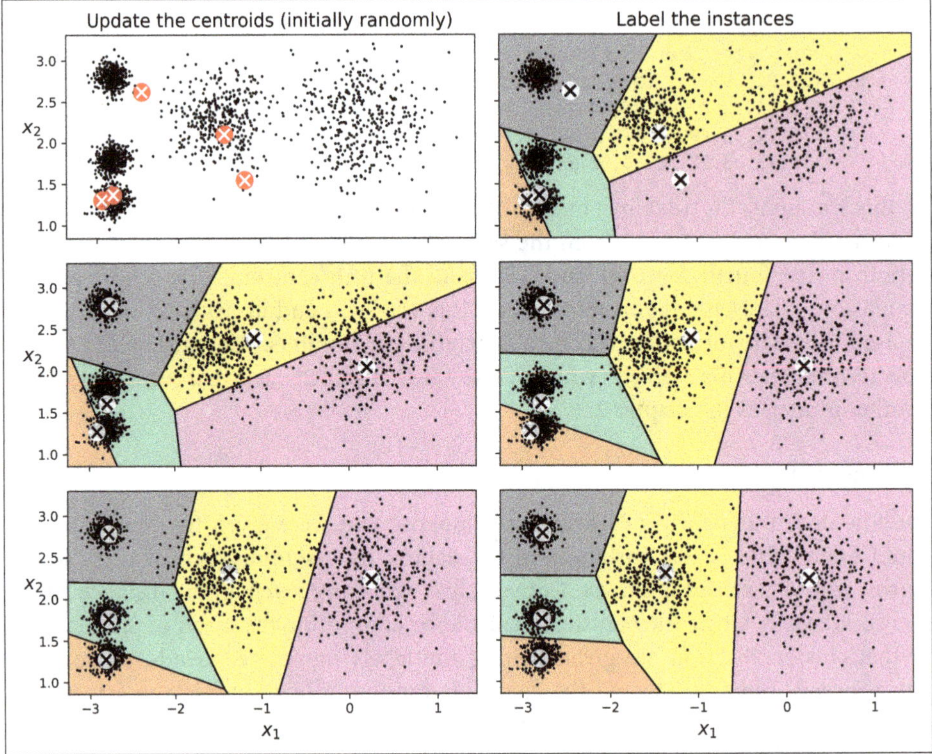

Figure 8-4. The k-means algorithm

Although the algorithm is guaranteed to converge, it may not converge to the right solution (i.e., it may converge to a local optimum): whether it does or not depends on the centroid initialization. Figure 8-5 shows two suboptimal solutions that the algorithm can converge to if you are not lucky with the random initialization step.

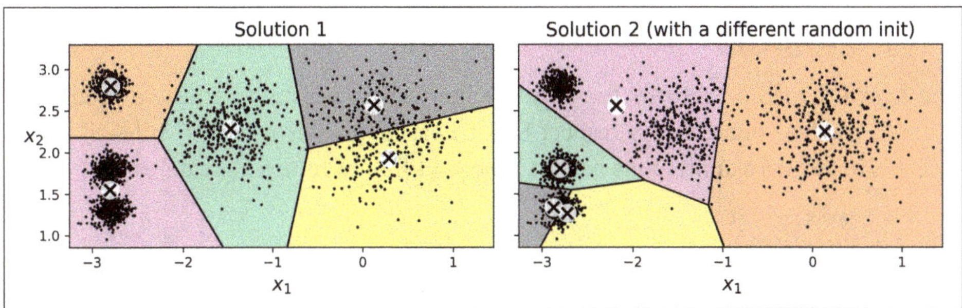

Figure 8-5. Suboptimal solutions due to unlucky centroid initializations

Let's take a look at a few ways you can mitigate this risk by improving the centroid initialization.

Centroid initialization methods

If you happen to know approximately where the centroids should be (e.g., if you ran another clustering algorithm earlier), then you can set the `init` hyperparameter to a NumPy array containing the list of centroids:

```
good_init = np.array([[-3, 3], [-3, 2], [-3, 1], [-1, 2], [0, 2]])
kmeans = KMeans(n_clusters=5, init=good_init, random_state=42)
kmeans.fit(X)
```

Another solution is to run the algorithm multiple times with different random initializations and keep the best solution. The number of random initializations is controlled by the `n_init` hyperparameter: by default it is equal to `10` when using `init="random"`, which means that the whole algorithm described earlier runs 10 times when you call `fit()`, and Scikit-Learn keeps the best solution. But how exactly does it know which solution is the best? It uses a performance metric! That metric is called the model's *inertia*, which is defined in Equation 8-1.

Equation 8-1. A model's inertia is the sum of all squared distances between each instance $\mathbf{x}^{(i)}$ *and the closest centroid* $\mathbf{c}^{(i)}$ *predicted by the model*

$$\text{inertia} = \sum_{i} \| \mathbf{x}^{(i)} - \mathbf{c}^{(i)} \|^2$$

The inertia is roughly equal to 219.6 for the model on the left in Figure 8-5, 600.4 for the model on the right in Figure 8-5, and only 211.6 for the model in Figure 8-3. The `KMeans` class runs the initialization algorithm `n_init` times and keeps the model with the lowest inertia. In this example, the model in Figure 8-3 will be selected (unless we are very unlucky with `n_init` consecutive random initializations). If you are curious, a model's inertia is accessible via the `inertia_` instance variable:

```
>>> kmeans.inertia_
211.59853725816828
```

The `score()` method returns the negative inertia (it's negative because a predictor's `score()` method must always respect Scikit-Learn's "greater is better" rule—if a predictor is better than another, its `score()` method should return a greater score):

```
>>> kmeans.score(X)
-211.59853725816828
```

An important improvement to the *k*-means algorithm, *k-means++*, was proposed in a 2006 paper (*https://homl.info/37*) by David Arthur and Sergei Vassilvitskii.[3] They introduced a smarter initialization step that tends to select centroids that are distant from one another. This change makes the *k*-means algorithm much more likely to locate all important clusters, and less likely to converge to a suboptimal solution (just like spreading out fishing boats increases the chance of locating more schools of fish). The paper showed that the additional computation required for the smarter initialization step is well worth it because it makes it possible to drastically reduce the number of times the algorithm needs to be run to find the optimal solution. The *k*-means++ initialization algorithm works like this:

1. Take one centroid $\mathbf{c}^{(1)}$, chosen uniformly at random from the dataset.
2. Take a new centroid $\mathbf{c}^{(i)}$, choosing an instance $\mathbf{x}^{(i)}$ with probability $D\left(\mathbf{x}^{(i)}\right)^2$ / $\sum_{j=1}^{m} D\left(\mathbf{x}^{(j)}\right)^2$, where $\mathrm{D}(\mathbf{x}^{(i)})$ is the distance between the instance $\mathbf{x}^{(i)}$ and the closest centroid that was already chosen. This probability distribution ensures that instances farther away from already chosen centroids are much more likely to be selected as centroids.
3. Repeat the previous step until all *k* centroids have been chosen.

When you set `init="k-means++"` (which is the default), the `KMeans` class actually uses a variant of *k*-means++ called *greedy k-means++*: instead of sampling a single centroid at each iteration, it samples multiple and picks the best one. When using this algorithm, `n_init` defaults to 1.

Accelerated k-means and mini-batch k-means

Another improvement to the *k*-means algorithm was proposed in a 2003 paper (*https://homl.info/38*) by Charles Elkan.[4] On some large datasets with many clusters, the algorithm can be accelerated by avoiding many unnecessary distance calculations.

3 David Arthur and Sergei Vassilvitskii, "k-Means++: The Advantages of Careful Seeding", *Proceedings of the 18th Annual ACM-SIAM Symposium on Discrete Algorithms* (2007): 1027–1035.

4 Charles Elkan, "Using the Triangle Inequality to Accelerate k-Means", *Proceedings of the 20th International Conference on Machine Learning* (2003): 147–153.

Elkan achieved this by exploiting the triangle inequality (i.e., that a straight line is always the shortest distance between two points[5]) and by keeping track of lower and upper bounds for distances between instances and centroids. However, Elkan's algorithm does not always accelerate training, and sometimes it can even slow down training significantly; it depends on the dataset. Still, if you want to give it a try, set `algorithm="elkan"`.

Yet another important variant of the *k*-means algorithm was proposed in a 2010 paper (*https://homl.info/39*) by David Sculley.[6] Instead of using the full dataset at each iteration, the algorithm is capable of using mini-batches, moving the centroids just slightly at each iteration. This speeds up the algorithm and makes it possible to cluster huge datasets that do not fit in memory. Scikit-Learn implements this algorithm in the `MiniBatchKMeans` class, which you can use just like the `KMeans` class:

```
from sklearn.cluster import MiniBatchKMeans

minibatch_kmeans = MiniBatchKMeans(n_clusters=5, random_state=42)
minibatch_kmeans.fit(X)
```

If the dataset does not fit in memory, the simplest option is to use the `memmap` class, as we did for incremental PCA in Chapter 7. Alternatively, you can pass one mini-batch at a time to the `partial_fit()` method, but this will require much more work, since you will need to perform multiple initializations and select the best one yourself.

Finding the optimal number of clusters

So far, we've set the number of clusters *k* to 5 because it was obvious by looking at the data that this was the correct number of clusters. But in general, it won't be so easy to know how to set *k*, and the result might be quite bad if you set it to the wrong value. As you can see in Figure 8-6, for this dataset setting *k* to 3 or 8 results in fairly bad models.

You might be thinking that you could just pick the model with the lowest inertia. Unfortunately, it is not that simple. The inertia for $k = 3$ is about 653.2, which is much higher than for $k = 5$ (211.7). But with $k = 8$, the inertia is just 127.1. The inertia is not a good performance metric when trying to choose *k* because it keeps getting lower as we increase *k*. Indeed, the more clusters there are, the closer each instance will be to its closest centroid, and therefore the lower the inertia will be. Let's plot the inertia as a function of *k*. When we do this, the curve often contains an inflexion point called the *elbow* (see Figure 8-7).

5 The triangle inequality is AC ≤ AB + BC, where A, B, and C are three points and AB, AC, and BC are the distances between these points.

6 David Sculley, "Web-Scale K-Means Clustering", *Proceedings of the 19th International Conference on World Wide Web* (2010): 1177–1178.

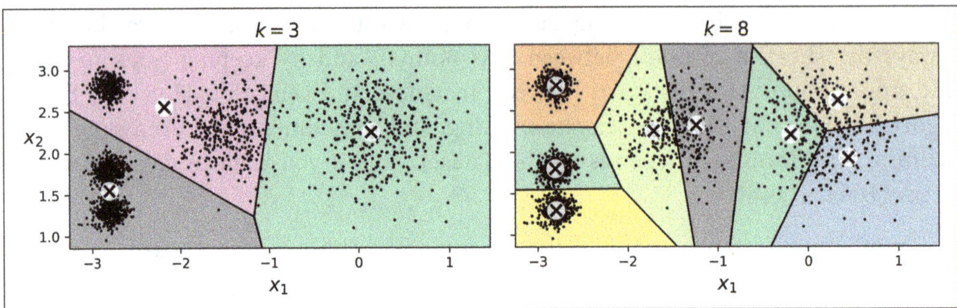

Figure 8-6. Bad choices for the number of clusters: when k is too small, separate clusters get merged (left), and when k is too large, some clusters get chopped into multiple pieces (right)

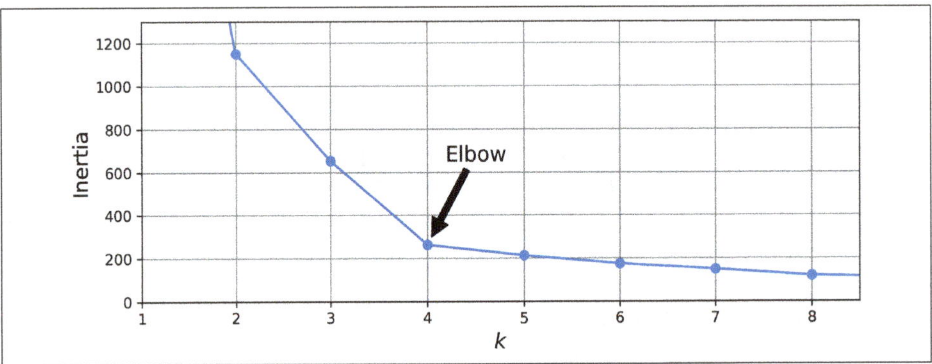

Figure 8-7. Plotting the inertia as a function of the number of clusters k

As you can see, the inertia drops very quickly as we increase *k* up to 4, but then it decreases much more slowly as we keep increasing *k*. This curve has roughly the shape of an arm, and there is an elbow at *k* = 4. So, if we did not know better, we might think 4 was a good choice: any lower value would be dramatic, while any higher value would not help much, and we might just be splitting perfectly good clusters in half for no good reason.

This technique for choosing the best value for the number of clusters is rather coarse. A more precise (but also more computationally expensive) approach is to use the *silhouette score*, which is the mean *silhouette coefficient* over all the instances. An instance's silhouette coefficient is equal to $(b - a) / \max(a, b)$, where *a* is the mean distance to the other instances in the same cluster (i.e., the mean intra-cluster distance) and *b* is the mean nearest-cluster distance (i.e., the mean distance to the instances of the next closest cluster, defined as the one that minimizes *b*, excluding the instance's own cluster). The silhouette coefficient can vary between –1 and +1. A coefficient close to +1 means that the instance is well inside its own cluster and far from other clusters, while a coefficient close to 0 means that it is close to a cluster boundary; finally, a coefficient close to –1 means that the instance may have been assigned to the wrong cluster.

To compute the silhouette score, you can use Scikit-Learn's `silhouette_score()` function, giving it all the instances in the dataset and the labels they were assigned:

```
>>> from sklearn.metrics import silhouette_score
>>> silhouette_score(X, kmeans.labels_)
np.float64(0.655517642572828)
```

Let's compare the silhouette scores for different numbers of clusters (see Figure 8-8).

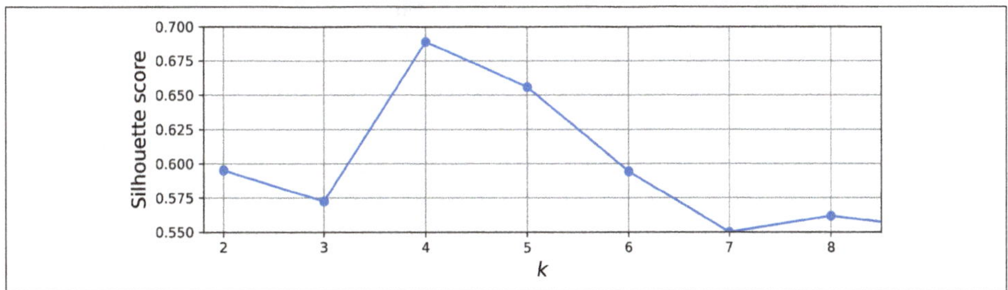

Figure 8-8. Selecting the number of clusters k using the silhouette score

As you can see, this visualization is much richer than the previous one: although it confirms that $k = 4$ is a very good choice, it also highlights the fact that $k = 5$ is quite good as well, and much better than $k = 6$ or 7. This was not visible when comparing inertias.

An even more informative visualization is obtained when we plot every instance's silhouette coefficient, sorted by the clusters they are assigned to and by the value of the coefficient. This is called a *silhouette diagram* (see Figure 8-9). Each diagram contains one knife shape per cluster. The shape's height indicates the number of instances in the cluster, and its width represents the sorted silhouette coefficients of the instances in the cluster (wider is better).

The vertical dashed lines represent the mean silhouette score for each number of clusters. When most of the instances in a cluster have a lower coefficient than this score (i.e., if many of the instances stop short of the dashed line, ending to the left of it), then the cluster is rather bad since this means its instances are much too close to other clusters. Here we can see that when $k = 3$ or 6, we get bad clusters. But when $k = 4$ or 5, the clusters look pretty good: most instances extend beyond the dashed line, to the right and closer to 1.0. When $k = 4$, the cluster at index 0 (at the bottom) is rather big. When $k = 5$, all clusters have similar sizes. So, even though the overall silhouette score from $k = 4$ is slightly greater than for $k = 5$, it seems like a good idea to use $k = 5$ to get clusters of similar sizes.

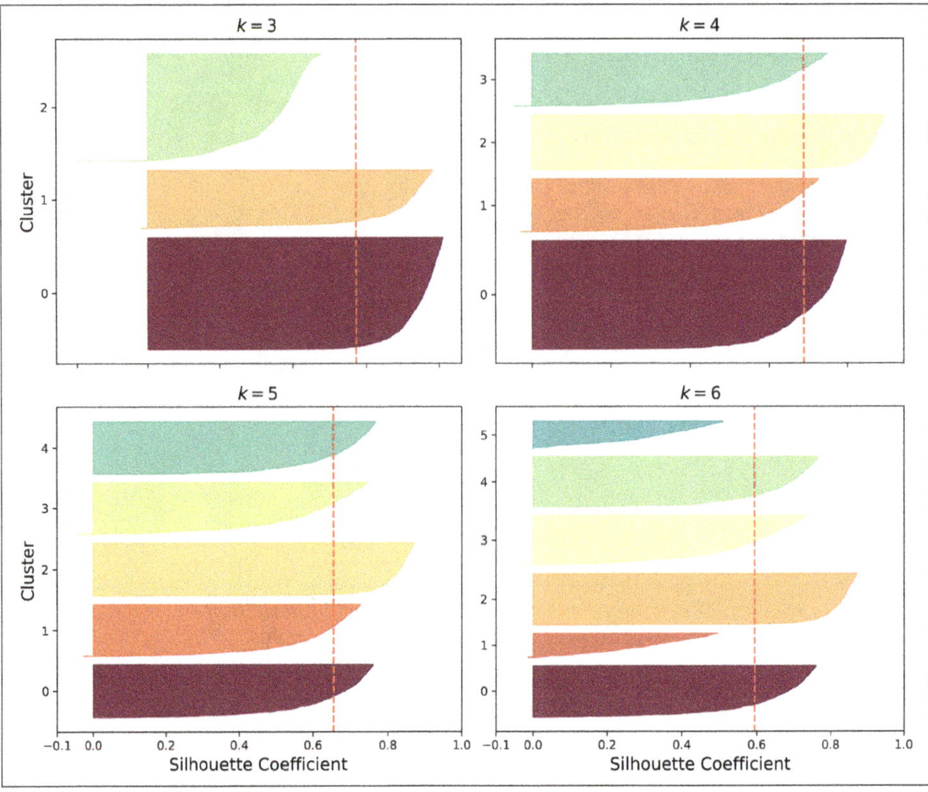

Figure 8-9. Analyzing the silhouette diagrams for various values of k

Limits of k-Means

Despite its many merits, most notably being fast and scalable, *k*-means is not perfect. As we saw, it is necessary to run the algorithm several times to avoid suboptimal solutions, plus you need to specify the number of clusters, which can be quite a hassle. Moreover, *k*-means does not behave very well when the clusters have varying sizes, different densities, or nonspherical shapes. For example, Figure 8-10 shows how *k*-means clusters a dataset containing three ellipsoidal clusters of different dimensions, densities, and orientations.

As you can see, neither of these solutions is any good. The solution on the left is better, but it still chops off 25% of the middle cluster and assigns it to the cluster on the right. The solution on the right is just terrible, even though its inertia is lower. So, depending on the data, different clustering algorithms may perform better. On these types of elliptical clusters, Gaussian mixture models work great.

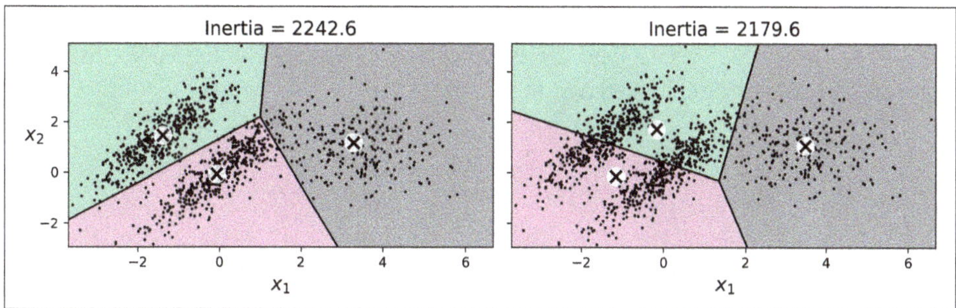

Figure 8-10. k-means fails to cluster these ellipsoidal blobs properly

It is important to scale the input features (see Chapter 2) before you run *k*-means, or the clusters may be very stretched and *k*-means will perform poorly. Scaling the features does not guarantee that all the clusters will be nice and spherical, but it generally helps *k*-means.

Now let's look at a few ways we can benefit from clustering. We will use *k*-means, but feel free to experiment with other clustering algorithms.

Using Clustering for Image Segmentation

Image segmentation is the task of partitioning an image into multiple segments. There are several variants:

- In *color segmentation*, pixels with a similar color get assigned to the same segment. This is sufficient in many applications. For example, if you want to analyze satellite images to measure how much total forest area there is in a region, color segmentation may be just fine.
- In *semantic segmentation*, all pixels that are part of the same object type get assigned to the same segment. For example, in a self-driving car's vision system, all pixels that are part of a pedestrian's image might be assigned to the "pedestrian" segment (there would be one segment containing all the pedestrians).
- In *instance segmentation*, all pixels that are part of the same individual object are assigned to the same segment. In this case there would be a different segment for each pedestrian.

The state of the art in semantic or instance segmentation today is achieved using complex architectures based on convolutional neural networks (see Chapter 12) or vision transformers (see Chapter 16). In this chapter we are going to focus on the (much simpler) color segmentation task, using *k*-means.

We'll start by importing the Pillow package (successor to the Python Imaging Library, PIL), which we'll then use to load the *ladybug.png* image (see the upper-left image in Figure 8-11), assuming it's located at `filepath`:

```
>>> import PIL
>>> image = np.asarray(PIL.Image.open(filepath))
>>> image.shape
(533, 800, 3)
```

The image is represented as a 3D array. The first dimension's size is the height; the second is the width; and the third is the number of color channels, in this case red, green, and blue (RGB). In other words, for each pixel there is a 3D vector containing the intensities of red, green, and blue as unsigned 8-bit integers between 0 and 255. Some images may have fewer channels (such as grayscale images, which only have one), and some images may have more channels (such as images with an additional *alpha channel* for transparency, or satellite images, which often contain channels for additional light frequencies, like infrared).

The following code reshapes the array to get a long list of RGB colors, then it clusters these colors using *k*-means with eight clusters. It creates a `segmented_img` array containing the nearest cluster center for each pixel (i.e., the mean color of each pixel's cluster), and lastly it reshapes this array to the original image shape. The third line uses advanced NumPy indexing; for example, if the first 10 labels in `kmeans_.labels_` are equal to 1, then the first 10 colors in `segmented_img` are equal to `kmeans.cluster_centers_[1]`:

```
X = image.reshape(-1, 3)
kmeans = KMeans(n_clusters=8, random_state=42).fit(X)
segmented_img = kmeans.cluster_centers_[kmeans.labels_]
segmented_img = segmented_img.reshape(image.shape)
```

This outputs the image shown in the upper right of Figure 8-11. You can experiment with various numbers of clusters, as shown in the figure. When you use fewer than eight clusters, notice that the ladybug's flashy red color fails to get a cluster of its own: it gets merged with colors from the environment. This is because *k*-means prefers clusters of similar sizes. The ladybug is small—much smaller than the rest of the image—so even though its color is flashy, *k*-means fails to dedicate a cluster to it.

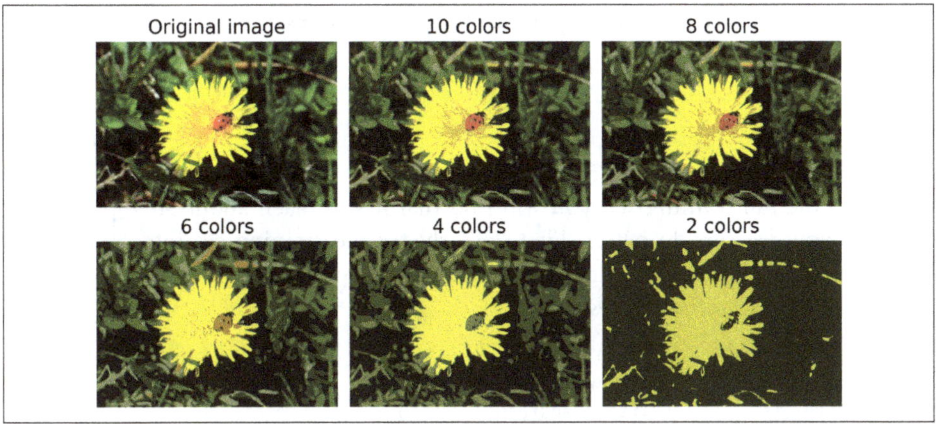

Figure 8-11. Image segmentation using k-means with various numbers of color clusters

That wasn't too hard, was it? Now let's look at another application of clustering.

Using Clustering for Semi-Supervised Learning

Another use case for clustering is in semi-supervised learning, when we have plenty of unlabeled instances and very few labeled instances. For example, clustering can help choose which additional instances to label (e.g., near the cluster centroids). It can also be used to propagate the most common label in each cluster to the unlabeled instances in that cluster. Let's try these ideas on the digits dataset, which is a simple MNIST-like dataset containing 1,797 grayscale 8 × 8 images representing the digits 0 to 9. First, let's load and split the dataset (it's already shuffled):

```
from sklearn.datasets import load_digits

X_digits, y_digits = load_digits(return_X_y=True)
X_train, y_train = X_digits[:1400], y_digits[:1400]
X_test, y_test = X_digits[1400:], y_digits[1400:]
```

We will pretend we only have labels for 50 instances. To get a baseline performance, let's train a logistic regression model on these 50 labeled instances:

```
from sklearn.linear_model import LogisticRegression

n_labeled = 50
log_reg = LogisticRegression(max_iter=10_000)
log_reg.fit(X_train[:n_labeled], y_train[:n_labeled])
```

We can then measure the accuracy of this model on the test set (note that the test set must be labeled):

```
>>> log_reg.score(X_test, y_test)
0.7581863979848866
```

The model's accuracy is just 75.8%. That's not great: indeed, if you try training the model on the full training set, you will find that it will reach about 90.9% accuracy. Let's see how we can do better. First, let's cluster the training set into 50 clusters. Then, for each cluster, we'll find the image closest to the centroid. We'll call these images the *representative images*:

```
k = 50
kmeans = KMeans(n_clusters=k, random_state=42)
X_digits_dist = kmeans.fit_transform(X_train)
representative_digit_idx = X_digits_dist.argmin(axis=0)
X_representative_digits = X_train[representative_digit_idx]
```

Figure 8-12 shows the 50 representative images.

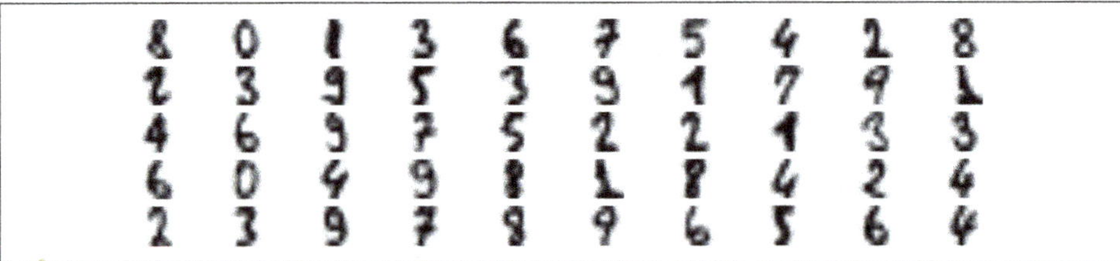

Figure 8-12. Fifty representative digit images (one per cluster)

Let's look at each image and manually label them:

```
y_representative_digits = np.array([8, 0, 1, 3, 6, 7, 5, 4, 2, 8, ..., 6, 4])
```

Now we have a dataset with just 50 labeled instances, but instead of being random instances, each of them is a representative image of its cluster. Let's see if the performance is any better:

```
>>> log_reg = LogisticRegression(max_iter=10_000)
>>> log_reg.fit(X_representative_digits, y_representative_digits)
>>> log_reg.score(X_test, y_test)
0.8337531486146096
```

Wow! We jumped from 75.8% accuracy to 83.4%, although we are still only training the model on 50 instances. Since it is often costly and painful to label instances, especially when it has to be done manually by experts, it is a good idea to label representative instances rather than just random instances.

But perhaps we can go one step further: what if we propagated the labels to all the other instances in the same cluster? This is called *label propagation*:

```
y_train_propagated = np.empty(len(X_train), dtype=np.int64)
for i in range(k):
    y_train_propagated[kmeans.labels_ == i] = y_representative_digits[i]
```

Now let's train the model again and look at its performance:

```
>>> log_reg = LogisticRegression()
>>> log_reg.fit(X_train, y_train_propagated)
>>> log_reg.score(X_test, y_test)
0.8690176322418136
```

We got another significant accuracy boost! Let's see if we can do even better by ignoring the 50% of instances that are farthest from their cluster center: this should eliminate some outliers. The following code first computes the distance from each instance to its closest cluster center, then for each cluster it sets the 50% largest distances to –1. Lastly, it creates a set without these instances marked with a –1 distance:

```
percentile_closest = 50

X_cluster_dist = X_digits_dist[np.arange(len(X_train)), kmeans.labels_]
for i in range(k):
    in_cluster = (kmeans.labels_ == i)
    cluster_dist = X_cluster_dist[in_cluster]
    cutoff_distance = np.percentile(cluster_dist, percentile_closest)
    above_cutoff = (X_cluster_dist > cutoff_distance)
    X_cluster_dist[in_cluster & above_cutoff] = -1

partially_propagated = (X_cluster_dist != -1)
X_train_partially_propagated = X_train[partially_propagated]
y_train_partially_propagated = y_train_propagated[partially_propagated]
```

Now let's train the model again on this partially propagated dataset and see what accuracy we get:

```
>>> log_reg = LogisticRegression(max_iter=10_000)
>>> log_reg.fit(X_train_partially_propagated, y_train_partially_propagated)
>>> log_reg.score(X_test, y_test)
0.8841309823677582
```

Nice! With just 50 labeled instances (only 5 examples per class on average!) we got 88.4% accuracy, pretty close to the performance we got on the fully labeled digits dataset. This is partly thanks to the fact that we dropped some outliers, and partly because the propagated labels are actually pretty good—their accuracy is about 98.9%, as the following code shows:

```
>>> (y_train_partially_propagated == y_train[partially_propagated]).mean()
np.float64(0.9887798036465638)
```

Scikit-Learn also offers two classes that can propagate labels automatically: `LabelSpreading` and `LabelPropagation` in the `sklearn.semi_supervised` package. Both classes construct a similarity matrix between all the instances, and iteratively propagate labels from labeled instances to similar unlabeled instances. There's also a different class called `SelfTrainingClassifier` in the same package: you give it a base classifier (e.g., `RandomForestClassifier`) and it trains it on the labeled instances, then uses it to predict labels for the unlabeled samples. It then updates the training set with the labels it is most confident about, and repeats this process of training and labeling until it cannot add labels anymore. These techniques are not magic bullets, but they can occasionally give your model a little boost.

Active Learning

To continue improving your model and your training set, the next step could be to do a few rounds of *active learning*, which is when a human expert interacts with the learning algorithm, providing labels for specific instances when the algorithm requests them. There are many different strategies for active learning, but one of the most common ones is called *uncertainty sampling*. Here is how it works:

1. The model is trained on the labeled instances gathered so far, and this model is used to make predictions on all the unlabeled instances.
2. The instances for which the model is most uncertain (i.e., where its estimated probability is lowest) are given to the expert for labeling.
3. You iterate this process until the performance improvement stops being worth the labeling effort.

Other active learning strategies include labeling the instances that would result in the largest model change or the largest drop in the model's validation error, or the instances that different models disagree on (e.g., an SVM and a random forest).

Before we move on to Gaussian mixture models, let's take a look at DBSCAN, another popular clustering algorithm that illustrates a very different approach based on local density estimation. This approach allows the algorithm to identify clusters of arbitrary shapes.

DBSCAN

The *density-based spatial clustering of applications with noise* (DBSCAN) algorithm defines clusters as continuous regions of high density. Here is how it works:

- For each instance, the algorithm counts how many instances are located within a small distance ε (epsilon) from it. This region is called the instance's *ε-neighborhood.*
- If an instance has at least `min_samples` instances in its ε-neighborhood (including itself), then it is considered a *core instance*. In other words, core instances are those that are located in dense regions.
- All instances in the neighborhood of a core instance belong to the same cluster. This neighborhood may include other core instances; therefore, a long sequence of neighboring core instances forms a single cluster.
- Any instance that is not a core instance and does not have one in its neighborhood is considered an anomaly.

This algorithm works well if all the clusters are well separated by low-density regions. The `DBSCAN` class in Scikit-Learn is as simple to use as you might expect. Let's test it on the moons dataset, introduced in Chapter 5:

```
from sklearn.cluster import DBSCAN
from sklearn.datasets import make_moons

X, y = make_moons(n_samples=1000, noise=0.05, random_state=42)
dbscan = DBSCAN(eps=0.05, min_samples=5)
dbscan.fit(X)
```

The labels of all the instances are now available in the `labels_` instance variable:

```
>>> dbscan.labels_
array([ 0,  2, -1, -1,  1,  0,  0,  0,  2,  5, [...], 3,  3,  4,  2,  6,  3])
```

Notice that some instances have a cluster index equal to –1, which means that they are considered as anomalies by the algorithm. The indices of the core instances are available in the `core_sample_indices_` instance variable, and the core instances themselves are available in the `components_` instance variable:

```
>>> dbscan.core_sample_indices_
array([  0,   4,   5,   6,   7,   8,  10,  11, [...], 993, 995, 997, 998, 999])
>>> dbscan.components_
array([[-0.02137124,  0.40618608],
       [-0.84192557,  0.53058695],
       [...],
       [ 0.79419406,  0.60777171]])
```

This clustering is represented in the lefthand plot of Figure 8-13. As you can see, it identified quite a lot of anomalies, plus seven different clusters. How disappointing! Fortunately, if we widen each instance's neighborhood by increasing eps to 0.2, we get the clustering on the right, which looks perfect. Let's continue with this model.

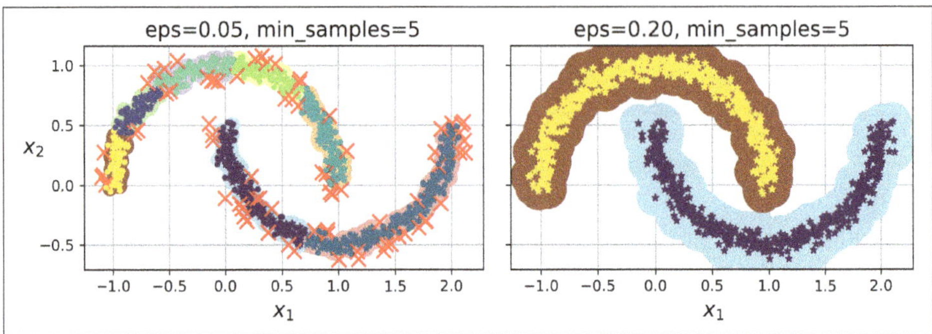

Figure 8-13. DBSCAN clustering using two different neighborhood radiuses

Surprisingly, the `DBSCAN` class does not have a `predict()` method, although it has a `fit_predict()` method. In other words, it cannot predict which cluster a new instance belongs to. This decision was made because different classification algorithms can be better for different tasks, so the authors decided to let the user choose which one to use. Moreover, it's not hard to implement. For example, let's train a `KNeighborsClassifier`:

```
from sklearn.neighbors import KNeighborsClassifier

knn = KNeighborsClassifier(n_neighbors=50)
knn.fit(dbscan.components_, dbscan.labels_[dbscan.core_sample_indices_])
```

Now, given a few new instances, we can predict which clusters they most likely belong to and even estimate a probability for each cluster:

```
>>> X_new = np.array([[-0.5, 0], [0, 0.5], [1, -0.1], [2, 1]])
>>> knn.predict(X_new)
array([1, 0, 1, 0])
>>> knn.predict_proba(X_new)
array([[0.18, 0.82],
       [1.  , 0.  ],
       [0.12, 0.88],
       [1.  , 0.  ]])
```

Note that we only trained the classifier on the core instances, but we could also have chosen to train it on all the instances, or all but the anomalies: this choice depends on the final task.

The decision boundary is represented in Figure 8-14 (the crosses represent the four instances in `X_new`). Notice that since there is no anomaly in the training set, the classifier always chooses a cluster, even when that cluster is far away. It is fairly straightforward to introduce a maximum distance, in which case the two instances that are far away from both clusters are classified as anomalies. To do this, use the `kneighbors()` method of the `KNeighborsClassifier`. Given a set of instances, it returns the distances and the indices of the *k*-nearest neighbors in the training set (two matrices, each with *k* columns):

```
>>> y_dist, y_pred_idx = knn.kneighbors(X_new, n_neighbors=1)
>>> y_pred = dbscan.labels_[dbscan.core_sample_indices_][y_pred_idx]
>>> y_pred[y_dist > 0.2] = -1
>>> y_pred.ravel()
array([-1,  0,  1, -1])
```

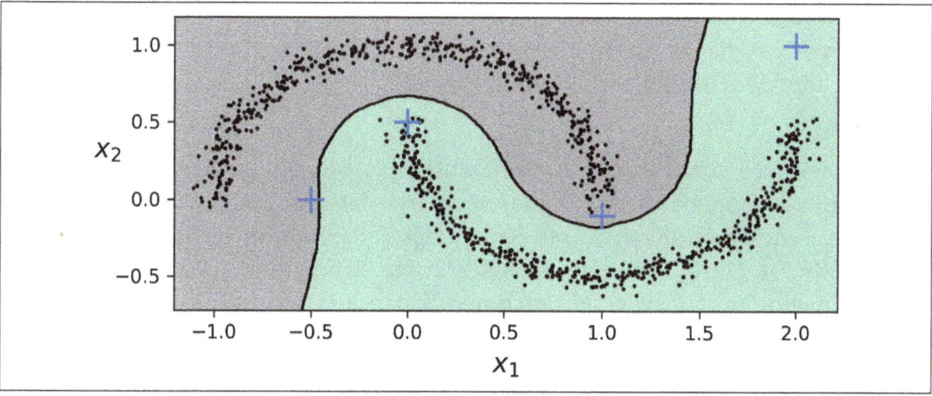

Figure 8-14. Decision boundary between two clusters

In short, DBSCAN is a very simple yet powerful algorithm capable of identifying any number of clusters of any shape. It is robust to outliers, and it has just two hyperparameters (`eps` and `min_samples`). If the density varies significantly across the clusters, however, or if there's no sufficiently low-density region around some clusters, DBSCAN can struggle to capture all the clusters properly. Moreover, its computational complexity is roughly $O(m^2n)$, so it does not scale well to large datasets.

You may also want to try *hierarchical DBSCAN* (HDBSCAN), using `sklearn.cluster.HDBSCAN`: it is often better than DBSCAN at finding clusters of varying densities.

Other Clustering Algorithms

Scikit-Learn implements several more clustering algorithms that you should take a look at. I cannot cover them all in detail here, but here is a brief overview:

Agglomerative clustering

A hierarchy of clusters is built from the bottom up. Think of many tiny bubbles floating on water and gradually attaching to each other until there's one big group of bubbles. Similarly, at each iteration, agglomerative clustering connects the nearest pair of clusters (starting with individual instances). If you drew a tree with a branch for every pair of clusters that merged, you would get a binary tree of clusters, where the leaves are the individual instances. This approach can capture clusters of various shapes; it also produces a flexible and informative cluster tree instead of forcing you to choose a particular cluster scale, and it can be used with any pairwise distance. It can scale nicely to large numbers of instances if you provide a connectivity matrix, which is a sparse $m \times m$ matrix that indicates which pairs of instances are neighbors (e.g., returned by `sklearn.neighbors.kneighbors_graph()`). Without a connectivity matrix, the algorithm does not scale well to large datasets.

BIRCH

The balanced iterative reducing and clustering using hierarchies (BIRCH) algorithm was designed specifically for very large datasets, and it can be faster than batch *k*-means, with similar results, as long as the number of features is not too large (<20). During training, it builds a tree structure containing just enough information to quickly assign each new instance to a cluster, without having to store all the instances in the tree: this approach allows it to use limited memory while handling huge datasets.

Mean-shift

This algorithm starts by placing a circle centered on each instance; then for each circle it computes the mean of all the instances located within it, and it shifts the circle so that it is centered on the mean. Next, it iterates this mean-shifting step until all the circles stop moving (i.e., until each of them is centered on the mean of the instances it contains). Mean-shift shifts the circles in the direction of higher density, until each of them has found a local density maximum. Finally, all the instances whose circles have settled in the same place (or close enough) are assigned to the same cluster. Mean-shift has some of the same features as DBSCAN, like how it can find any number of clusters of any shape, it has very few hyperparameters (just one—the radius of the circles, called the *bandwidth*), and it relies on local density estimation. But unlike DBSCAN, mean-shift tends to chop clusters into pieces when they have internal density variations. Unfortunately, its computational complexity is $O(m^2n)$, so it is not suited for large datasets.

Affinity propagation

In this algorithm, instances repeatedly exchange messages between one another until every instance has elected another instance (or itself) to represent it. These elected instances are called *exemplars*. Each exemplar and all the instances that elected it form one cluster. In real-life politics, you typically want to vote for a candidate whose opinions are similar to yours, but you also want them to win the election, so you might choose a candidate you don't fully agree with, but who is more popular. You typically evaluate popularity through polls. Affinity propagation works in a similar way, and it tends to choose exemplars located near the center of clusters, similar to *k*-means. But unlike with *k*-means, you don't have to pick a number of clusters ahead of time: it is determined during training. Moreover, affinity propagation can deal nicely with clusters of different sizes. Sadly, this algorithm has a computational complexity of $O(m^2)$, so it is not suited for large datasets.

Spectral clustering
: This algorithm takes a similarity matrix between the instances and creates a low-dimensional embedding from it (i.e., it reduces the matrix's dimensionality), then it uses another clustering algorithm in this low-dimensional space (Scikit-Learn's implementation uses *k*-means). Spectral clustering can capture complex cluster structures, and it can also be used to cut graphs (e.g., to identify clusters of friends on a social network). It does not scale well to large numbers of instances, and it does not behave well when the clusters have very different sizes.

Now let's dive into Gaussian mixture models, which can be used for density estimation, clustering, and anomaly detection.

Gaussian Mixtures

A *Gaussian mixture model* (GMM) is a probabilistic model that assumes that the instances were generated from a mixture of several Gaussian distributions whose parameters are unknown. All the instances generated from a single Gaussian distribution form a cluster that typically looks like an ellipsoid. Each cluster can have a different ellipsoidal shape, size, density, and orientation, just like in Figure 8-10.[7] When you observe an instance, you know it was generated from one of the Gaussian distributions, but you are not told which one, and you do not know what the parameters of these distributions are.

There are several GMM variants. In the simplest variant, implemented in the `GaussianMixture` class, you must know in advance the number *k* of Gaussian distributions. The dataset **X** is assumed to have been generated through the following probabilistic process:

7 In contrast, as we saw earlier, *k*-means implicitly assumes that clusters all have a similar size and density, and are all roughly round.

- For each instance, a cluster is picked randomly from among k clusters. The probability of choosing the jth cluster is the cluster's weight $\phi^{(j)}$.[8] The index of the cluster chosen for the ith instance is denoted $z^{(i)}$.
- If the ith instance was assigned to the jth cluster (i.e., $z^{(i)} = j$), then the location $\mathbf{x}^{(i)}$ of this instance is sampled randomly from the Gaussian distribution with mean $\boldsymbol{\mu}^{(j)}$ and covariance matrix $\boldsymbol{\Sigma}^{(j)}$. This is denoted $\mathbf{x}^{(i)} \sim \mathcal{N}(\mu^{*(j)}, \boldsymbol{\Sigma}^{(j)})$.

So what can you do with such a model? Well, given the dataset **X**, you typically want to start by estimating the weights $\boldsymbol{\phi}$ and all the distribution parameters $\boldsymbol{\mu}^{(1)}$ to $\boldsymbol{\mu}^{(k)}$ and $\boldsymbol{\Sigma}^{(1)}$ to $\boldsymbol{\Sigma}^{(k)}$. Scikit-Learn's `GaussianMixture` class makes this super easy:

```
from sklearn.mixture import GaussianMixture

gm = GaussianMixture(n_components=3, n_init=10, random_state=42)
gm.fit(X)
```

Let's look at the parameters that the algorithm estimated:

```
>>> gm.weights_
array([0.40005972, 0.20961444, 0.39032584])
>>> gm.means_
array([[-1.40764129,  1.42712848],
       [ 3.39947665,  1.05931088],
       [ 0.05145113,  0.07534576]])
>>> gm.covariances_
array([[[ 0.63478217,  0.72970097],
        [ 0.72970097,  1.16094925]],

       [[ 1.14740131, -0.03271106],
        [-0.03271106,  0.95498333]],

       [[ 0.68825143,  0.79617956],
        [ 0.79617956,  1.21242183]]])
```

Great, it worked fine! Indeed, two of the three clusters were generated with 500 instances each, while the third cluster only contains 250 instances. So the true cluster weights are 0.4, 0.4, and 0.2, respectively, and that's roughly what the algorithm found (in a different order). Similarly, the true means and covariance matrices are quite close to those found by the algorithm. But how? This class relies on the *expectation-maximization* (EM) algorithm, which has many similarities with the k-means algorithm: it also initializes the cluster parameters randomly, then it repeats two steps until convergence, first assigning instances to clusters (this is called the *expectation step*) and then updating the clusters (this is called the *maximization step*). Sounds familiar, right? In the context of clustering, you can think of EM as a generalization of k-means that not only finds the cluster centers ($\boldsymbol{\mu}^{(1)}$ to $\boldsymbol{\mu}^{(k)}$), but also their size,

8 Phi (ϕ or φ) is the 21st letter of the Greek alphabet.

shape, and orientation ($\Sigma^{(1)}$ to $\Sigma^{(k)}$), as well as their relative weights ($\phi^{(1)}$ to $\phi^{(k)}$). Unlike *k*-means, though, EM uses soft cluster assignments, not hard assignments. For each instance, during the expectation step, the algorithm estimates the probability that it belongs to each cluster (based on the current cluster parameters). Then, during the maximization step, each cluster is updated using *all* the instances in the dataset, with each instance weighted by the estimated probability that it belongs to that cluster. These probabilities are called the *responsibilities* of the clusters for the instances. During the maximization step, each cluster's update will mostly be impacted by the instances it is most responsible for.

Unfortunately, just like *k*-means, EM can end up converging to poor solutions, so it needs to be run several times, keeping only the best solution. This is why we set `n_init` to 10. Be careful: by default `n_init` is set to 1.

You can check whether the algorithm converged and how many iterations it took:

```
>>> gm.converged_
True
>>> gm.n_iter_
4
```

Now that you have an estimate of the location, size, shape, orientation, and relative weight of each cluster, the model can easily assign each instance to the most likely cluster (hard clustering) or estimate the probability that it belongs to a particular cluster (soft clustering). Just use the `predict()` method for hard clustering, or the `predict_proba()` method for soft clustering:

```
>>> gm.predict(X)
array([2, 2, 0, ..., 1, 1, 1])
>>> gm.predict_proba(X).round(3)
array([[0.   , 0.023, 0.977],
       [0.001, 0.016, 0.983],
       [1.   , 0.   , 0.   ],
       ...,
       [0.   , 1.   , 0.   ],
       [0.   , 1.   , 0.   ],
       [0.   , 1.   , 0.   ]])
```

A Gaussian mixture model is a *generative model*, meaning you can sample new instances from it (note that they are ordered by cluster index):

```
>>> X_new, y_new = gm.sample(6)
>>> X_new
array([[-2.32491052,  1.04752548],
       [-1.16654983,  1.62795173],
       [ 1.84860618,  2.07374016],
       [ 3.98304484,  1.49869936],
```

```
       [ 3.8163406 ,  0.53038367],
       [ 0.38079484, -0.56239369]])
>>> y_new
array([0, 0, 1, 1, 1, 2])
```

It is also possible to estimate the density of the model at any given location. This is achieved using the `score_samples()` method: for each instance it is given, this method estimates the log of the *probability density function* (PDF) at that location. The greater the score, the higher the density:

```
>>> gm.score_samples(X).round(2)
array([-2.61, -3.57, -3.33, ..., -3.51, -4.4 , -3.81])
```

If you compute the exponential of these scores, you get the value of the PDF at the location of the given instances. These are not probabilities, but probability *densities*: they can take on any positive value, not just a value between 0 and 1. To estimate the probability that an instance will fall within a particular region, you would have to integrate the PDF over that region (if you do so over the entire space of possible instance locations, the result will be 1).

Figure 8-15 shows the cluster means, the decision boundaries (dashed lines), and the density contours of this model.

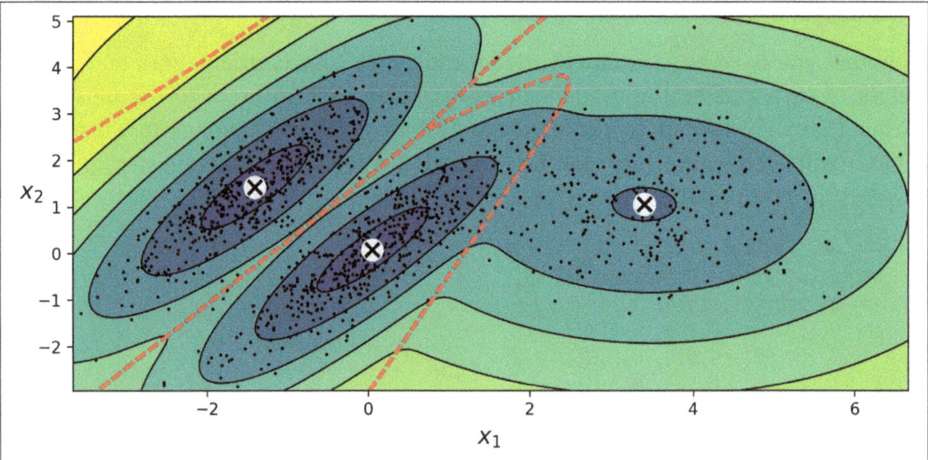

Figure 8-15. Cluster means, decision boundaries, and density contours of a trained Gaussian mixture model

Nice! The algorithm clearly found an excellent solution. Of course, we made its task easy by generating the data using a set of 2D Gaussian distributions (unfortunately, real-life data is not always so Gaussian and low-dimensional). We also gave the algorithm the correct number of clusters. When there are many dimensions, or many clusters, or few instances, EM can struggle to converge to the optimal solution. You might need to reduce the difficulty of the task by limiting the number of parameters that the algorithm has to learn. One way to do this is to limit the range of shapes and orientations that the clusters can have. This can be achieved by imposing constraints on the covariance matrices. To do this, set the `covariance_type` hyperparameter to one of the following values:

`"spherical"`
: All clusters must be spherical, but they can have different diameters (i.e., different variances).

`"diag"`
: Clusters can take on any ellipsoidal shape of any size, but the ellipsoid's axes must be parallel to the coordinate axes (i.e., the covariance matrices must be diagonal).

`"tied"`
: All clusters must have the same ellipsoidal shape, size, and orientation (i.e., all clusters share the same covariance matrix).

By default, `covariance_type` is equal to `"full"`, which means that each cluster can take on any shape, size, and orientation (it has its own unconstrained covariance matrix). Figure 8-16 plots the solutions found by the EM algorithm when `covariance_type` is set to `"tied"` or `"spherical"`.

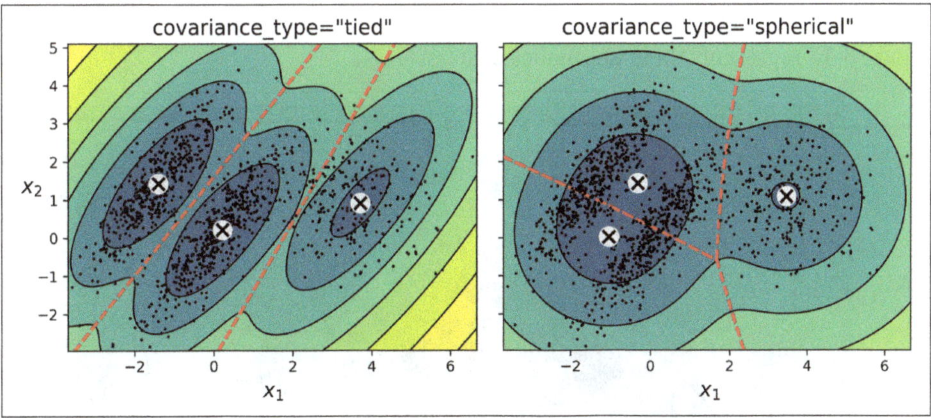

Figure 8-16. Gaussian mixtures for tied clusters (left) and spherical clusters (right)

The computational complexity of training a `GaussianMixture` model depends on the number of instances *m*, the number of dimensions *n*, the number of clusters *k*, and the constraints on the covariance matrices. If `covariance_type` is `"spherical"` or `"diag"`, it is $O(kmn)$, assuming the data has a clustering structure. If `covariance_type` is `"tied"` or `"full"`, it is $O(kmn^2 + kn^3)$, so it will not scale to large numbers of features.

Gaussian mixture models can also be used for anomaly detection. We'll see how in the next section.

Using Gaussian Mixtures for Anomaly Detection

Using a Gaussian mixture model for anomaly detection is quite simple: any instance located in a low-density region can be considered an anomaly. You must define what density threshold you want to use. For example, in a manufacturing company that tries to detect defective products, the ratio of defective products is usually well known. Say it is equal to 2%. You then set the density threshold to be the value that results in having 2% of the instances located in areas below that threshold density. If you notice that you get too many false positives (i.e., perfectly good products that are flagged as defective), you can lower the threshold. Conversely, if you have too many false negatives (i.e., defective products that the system does not flag as defective), you can increase the threshold. This is the usual precision/recall trade-off (see Chapter 3). Here is how you would identify the outliers using the second percentile lowest density as the threshold (i.e., approximately 2% of the instances will be flagged as anomalies):

```
densities = gm.score_samples(X)
density_threshold = np.percentile(densities, 2)
anomalies = X[densities < density_threshold]
```

Figure 8-17 represents these anomalies as stars.

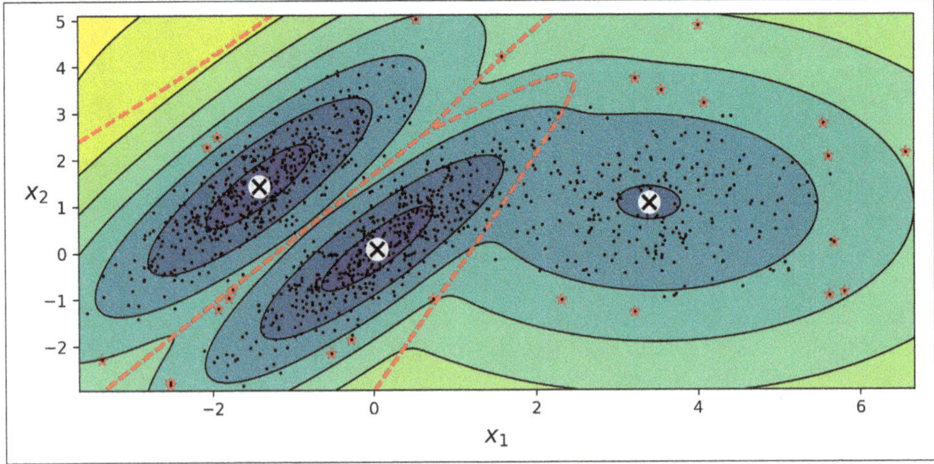

Figure 8-17. Anomaly detection using a Gaussian mixture model

A closely related task is *novelty detection*: it differs from anomaly detection in that the algorithm is assumed to be trained on a "clean" dataset, uncontaminated by outliers, whereas anomaly detection does not make this assumption. Indeed, outlier detection is often used to clean up a dataset.

Gaussian mixture models try to fit all the data, including the outliers; if you have too many of them this will bias the model's view of "normality", and some outliers may wrongly be considered as normal. If this happens, you can try to fit the model once, use it to detect and remove the most extreme outliers, then fit the model again on the cleaned-up dataset. Another approach is to use robust covariance estimation methods (see the `EllipticEnvelope` class).

Just like *k*-means, the `GaussianMixture` algorithm requires you to specify the number of clusters. So how can you find that number?

Selecting the Number of Clusters

With *k*-means, you can use the inertia or the silhouette score to select the appropriate number of clusters. But with Gaussian mixtures, it is not possible to use these metrics because they are not reliable when the clusters are not spherical or have different sizes. Instead, you can try to find the model that minimizes a *theoretical information criterion*, such as the *Bayesian information criterion* (BIC) or the *Akaike information criterion* (AIC), defined in Equation 8-2.

Equation 8-2. Bayesian information criterion (BIC) and Akaike information criterion (AIC)

$$BIC = \log(m)p - 2\log(\widehat{\mathscr{L}})$$

$$AIC = 2p - 2\log(\widehat{\mathscr{L}})$$

In these equations:

- m is the number of instances, as always.
- p is the number of parameters learned by the model.
- $\widehat{\mathscr{L}}$ is the maximized value of the *likelihood function* of the model.

Both the BIC and the AIC penalize models that have more parameters to learn (e.g., more clusters) and reward models that fit the data well. They often end up selecting the same model. When they differ, the model selected by the BIC tends to be simpler (fewer parameters) than the one selected by the AIC, but tends to not fit the data quite as well (this is especially true for larger datasets).

Likelihood Function

The terms "probability" and "likelihood" are often used interchangeably in everyday language, but they have very different meanings in statistics. Given a statistical model with some parameters **θ**, the word "probability" is used to describe how plausible a future outcome **x** is (knowing the parameter values **θ**), while the word "likelihood" is used to describe how plausible a particular set of parameter values **θ** are, after the outcome **x** is known.

Consider a 1D mixture model of two Gaussian distributions centered at –4 and +1. For simplicity, this toy model has a single parameter θ that controls the standard deviations of both distributions. The top-left contour plot in Figure 8-18 shows the entire model $f(x; \theta)$ as a function of both x and θ. To estimate the probability distribution of a future outcome x, you need to set the model parameter θ. For example, if you set θ to 1.3 (the horizontal line), you get the probability density function $f(x; \theta = 1.3)$ shown in the lower-left plot. Say you want to estimate the probability that x will fall between –2 and +2. You must calculate the integral of the PDF on this range (i.e., the surface of the shaded region). But what if you don't know θ, and if instead you have observed a single instance $x = 2.5$ (the vertical line in the upper-left plot)? In this case, you get the likelihood function $\mathscr{L}(\theta|x = 2.5) = f(x = 2.5; \theta)$, represented in the upper-right plot.

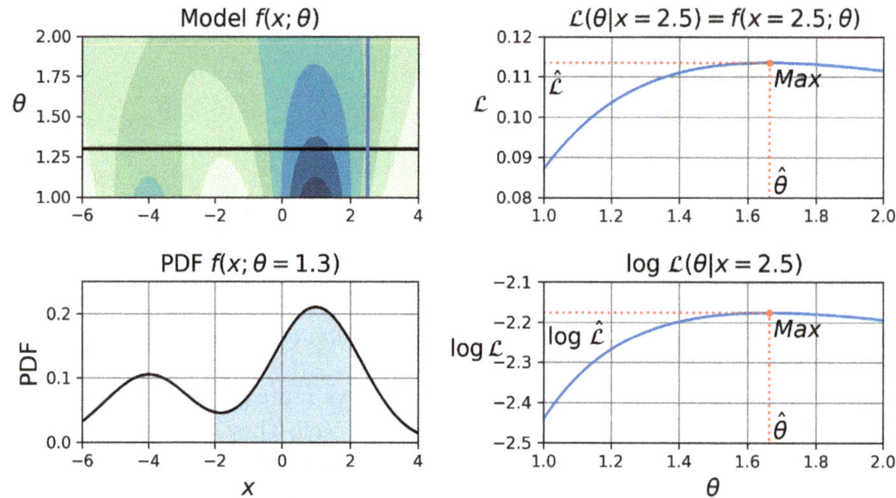

Figure 8-18. A model's parametric function (top left), and some derived functions: a PDF (lower left), a likelihood function (top right), and a log likelihood function (lower right)

In short, the PDF is a function of x (with θ fixed), while the likelihood function is a function of θ (with x fixed). It is important to understand that the likelihood function is *not* a probability distribution: if you integrate a probability distribution over all possible values of x, you always get 1, but if you integrate the likelihood function over all possible values of θ, the result can be any positive value.

Given a dataset $\mathbf{X}$, a common task is to try to estimate the most likely values for the model parameters. To do this, you must find the values that maximize the likelihood function, given $\mathbf{X}$. In this example, if you have observed a single instance $x = 2.5$, the *maximum likelihood estimate* (MLE) of θ is $\widehat{\boldsymbol{\theta}} \approx 1.66$. If a prior probability distribution g over θ exists, it is possible to take it into account by maximizing $\mathscr{L}(\theta|x)g(\theta)$ rather than just maximizing $\mathscr{L}(\theta|x)$. This is called *maximum a-posteriori* (MAP) estimation. Since MAP constrains the parameter values, you can think of it as a regularized version of MLE.

Notice that maximizing the likelihood function is equivalent to maximizing its logarithm (represented in the lower-right plot in Figure 8-18). Indeed, the logarithm is a strictly increasing function, so if θ maximizes the log likelihood, it also maximizes the likelihood. It turns out that it is generally easier to maximize the log likelihood. For example, if you observed several independent instances $x^{(1)}$ to $x^{(m)}$, you would need to find the value of θ that maximizes the product of the individual likelihood functions. But it is equivalent, and much simpler, to maximize the sum (not the product) of the log likelihood functions, thanks to the magic of the logarithm which converts products into sums: $\log(ab) = \log(a) + \log(b)$.

Once you have estimated $\widehat{\boldsymbol{\theta}}$, the value of θ that maximizes the likelihood function, then you are ready to compute $\widehat{\mathscr{L}} = \mathscr{L}\left(\widehat{\boldsymbol{\theta}}, \mathbf{X}\right)$, which is the value used to compute the AIC and BIC; you can think of it as a measure of how well the model fits the data.

To compute the BIC and AIC, call the `bic()` and `aic()` methods:

```
>>> gm.bic(X)
np.float64(8189.733705221636)
>>> gm.aic(X)
np.float64(8102.508425106598)
```

Figure 8-19 shows the BIC for different numbers of clusters k. As you can see, both the BIC and the AIC are lowest when $k = 3$, so it is most likely the best choice.

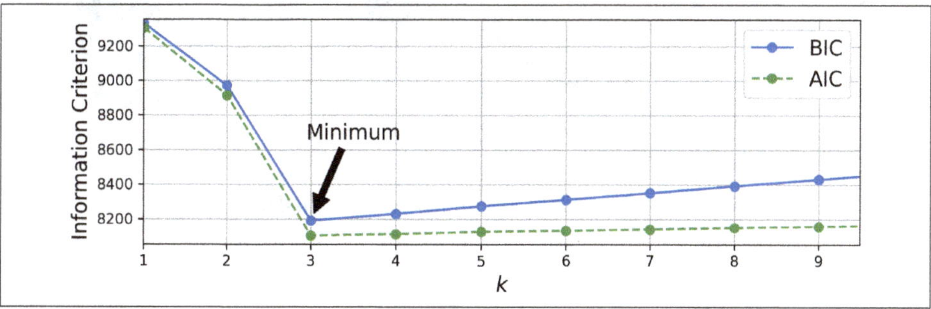

Figure 8-19. AIC and BIC for different numbers of clusters k

Bayesian Gaussian Mixture Models

Rather than manually searching for the optimal number of clusters, you can use the `BayesianGaussianMixture` class, which is capable of giving weights equal (or close) to zero to unnecessary clusters. Set the number of clusters `n_components` to a value that you have good reason to believe is greater than the optimal number of clusters (this assumes some minimal knowledge about the problem at hand), and the algorithm will eliminate the unnecessary clusters automatically. For example, let's set the number of clusters to 10 and see what happens:

```
>>> from sklearn.mixture import BayesianGaussianMixture
>>> bgm = BayesianGaussianMixture(n_components=10, n_init=10, max_iter=500,
...                               random_state=42)
...
>>> bgm.fit(X)
>>> bgm.weights_.round(2)
array([0.4 , 0.21, 0.39, 0.  , 0.  , 0.  , 0.  , 0.  , 0.  , 0.  ])
```

Perfect: the algorithm automatically detected that only three clusters are needed, and the resulting clusters are almost identical to the ones in Figure 8-15.

A final note about Gaussian mixture models: although they work great on clusters with ellipsoidal shapes, they don't do so well with clusters of very different shapes. For example, let's see what happens if we use a Bayesian Gaussian mixture model to cluster the moons dataset (see Figure 8-20).

Oops! The algorithm desperately searched for ellipsoids, so it found eight different clusters instead of two. The density estimation is not too bad, so this model could perhaps be used for anomaly detection, but it failed to identify the two moons. To conclude this chapter, let's take a quick look at a few algorithms capable of dealing with arbitrarily shaped clusters.

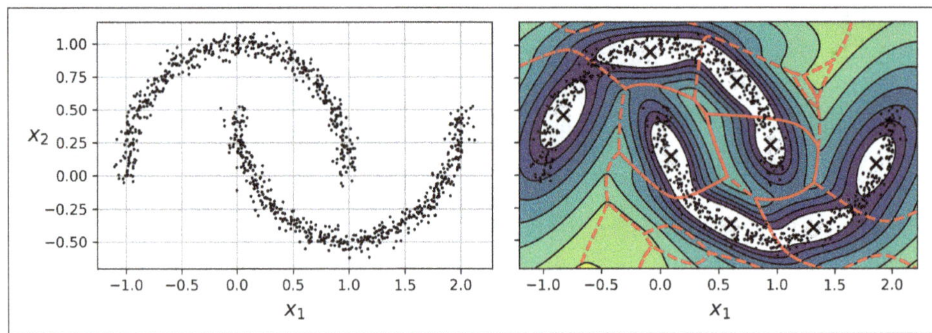

Figure 8-20. Fitting a Gaussian mixture to nonellipsoidal clusters

Other Algorithms for Anomaly and Novelty Detection

Scikit-Learn implements other algorithms dedicated to anomaly detection or novelty detection:

Fast-MCD (minimum covariance determinant)
: Implemented by the `EllipticEnvelope` class, this algorithm is useful for outlier detection, in particular to clean up a dataset. It assumes that the normal instances (inliers) are generated from a single Gaussian distribution (not a mixture). It also assumes that the dataset is contaminated with outliers that were not generated from this Gaussian distribution. When the algorithm estimates the parameters of the Gaussian distribution (i.e., the shape of the elliptic envelope around the inliers), it is careful to ignore the instances that are most likely outliers. This technique gives a better estimation of the elliptic envelope and thus makes the algorithm better at identifying the outliers.

Isolation forest
: This is an efficient algorithm for outlier detection, especially in high-dimensional datasets. The algorithm builds a random forest in which each decision tree is grown randomly: at each node, it picks a feature randomly, then it picks a random threshold value (between the min and max values) to split the dataset in two. The dataset gradually gets chopped into pieces this way, until all instances end up isolated from the other instances. Anomalies are usually far from other instances, so on average (across all the decision trees) they tend to get isolated in fewer steps than normal instances.

Local outlier factor (LOF)
: This algorithm is also good for outlier detection. It compares the density of instances around a given instance to the density around its neighbors. An anomaly is often more isolated than its *k*-nearest neighbors.

One-class SVM
: This algorithm is better suited for novelty detection. Recall that a kernelized SVM classifier separates two classes by first (implicitly) mapping all the instances to a high-dimensional space, then separating the two classes using a linear SVM classifier within this high-dimensional space (see the online chapter on SVMs at *https://homl.info*). Since we just have one class of instances, the one-class SVM algorithm instead tries to separate the instances in high-dimensional space from the origin. In the original space, this will correspond to finding a small region that encompasses all the instances. If a new instance does not fall within this region, it is an anomaly. There are a few hyperparameters to tweak: the usual ones for a kernelized SVM, plus a margin hyperparameter that corresponds to the probability of a new instance being mistakenly considered as novel when it is

in fact normal. It works great, especially with high-dimensional datasets, but like all SVMs it does not scale to large datasets.

PCA and other dimensionality reduction techniques with an `inverse_transform()` *method*
: If you compare the reconstruction error of a normal instance with the reconstruction error of an anomaly, the latter will usually be much larger. This is a simple and often quite efficient anomaly detection approach (see this chapter's exercises for an example).

Exercises

1. How would you define clustering? Can you name a few clustering algorithms?
2. What are some of the main applications of clustering algorithms?
3. Describe two techniques to select the right number of clusters when using *k*-means.
4. What is label propagation? Why would you implement it, and how?
5. Can you name two clustering algorithms that can scale to large datasets? And two that look for regions of high density?
6. Can you think of a use case where active learning would be useful? How would you implement it?
7. What is the difference between anomaly detection and novelty detection?
8. What is a Gaussian mixture? What tasks can you use it for?
9. Can you name two techniques to find the right number of clusters when using a Gaussian mixture model?
10. The classic Olivetti faces dataset contains 400 grayscale 64 × 64–pixel images of faces. Each image is flattened to a 1D vector of size 4,096. Forty different people were photographed (10 times each), and the usual task is to train a model that can predict which person is represented in each picture. Load the dataset using the `sklearn.datasets.fetch_olivetti_faces()` function, then split it into a training set, a validation set, and a test set (note that the dataset is already scaled between 0 and 1). Since the dataset is quite small, you will probably want to use stratified sampling to ensure that there are the same number of images per person in each set. Next, cluster the images using *k*-means, and ensure that you have a good number of clusters (using one of the techniques discussed in this chapter). Visualize the clusters: do you see similar faces in each cluster?
11. Continuing with the Olivetti faces dataset, train a classifier to predict which person is represented in each picture, and evaluate it on the validation set. Next, use *k*-means as a dimensionality reduction tool, and train a classifier on the

reduced set. Search for the number of clusters that allows the classifier to get the best performance: what performance can you reach? What if you append the features from the reduced set to the original features (again, searching for the best number of clusters)?

12. Train a Gaussian mixture model on the Olivetti faces dataset. To speed up the algorithm, you should probably reduce the dataset's dimensionality (e.g., use PCA, preserving 99% of the variance). Use the model to generate some new faces (using the `sample()` method), and visualize them (if you used PCA, you will need to use its `inverse_transform()` method). Try to modify some images (e.g., rotate, flip, darken) and see if the model can detect the anomalies (i.e., compare the output of the `score_samples()` method for normal images and for anomalies).

13. Some dimensionality reduction techniques can also be used for anomaly detection. For example, take the Olivetti faces dataset and reduce it with PCA, preserving 99% of the variance. Then compute the reconstruction error for each image. Next, take some of the modified images you built in the previous exercise and look at their reconstruction error: notice how much larger it is. If you plot a reconstructed image, you will see why: it tries to reconstruct a normal face.

Solutions to these exercises are available at the end of this chapter's notebook, at *https://homl.info/colab-p*.

PART II

Neural Networks and Deep Learning

CHAPTER 9

Introduction to Artificial Neural Networks

Birds inspired us to fly, burdock plants inspired Velcro, and nature has inspired countless more inventions. It seems only logical, then, to look at the brain's architecture for inspiration on how to build an intelligent machine. This is the logic that sparked *artificial neural networks* (ANNs), machine learning models inspired by the networks of biological neurons found in our brains. However, although planes were inspired by birds, they don't have to flap their wings to fly. Similarly, ANNs have gradually become quite different from their biological cousins. Some researchers even argue that we should drop the biological analogy altogether (e.g., by saying "units" rather than "neurons"), lest we restrict our creativity to biologically plausible systems.[1]

ANNs are at the very core of deep learning. They are versatile, powerful, and scalable, making them ideal to tackle large and highly complex machine learning tasks such as classifying billions of images (e.g., Google Images), powering speech recognition services (e.g., Apple's Siri or Google Assistant) and chatbots (e.g., ChatGPT or Claude), recommending the best videos to watch to hundreds of millions of users every day (e.g., YouTube), or learning how proteins fold (DeepMind's AlphaFold).

This chapter introduces artificial neural networks, starting with a quick tour of the very first ANN architectures and leading up to multilayer perceptrons (MLPs), which are heavily used today (many other architectures will be explored in the following chapters). In this chapter, we will implement simple MLPs using Scikit-Learn to get our feet wet, and in the next chapter we will switch to PyTorch, as it is a much more flexible and efficient library for neural nets.

1 You can get the best of both worlds by being open to biological inspirations without being afraid to create biologically unrealistic models, as long as they work well.

Now let's go back in time to the origins of artificial neural networks.

From Biological to Artificial Neurons

Surprisingly, ANNs have been around for quite a while: they were first introduced back in 1943 by the neurophysiologist Warren McCulloch and the mathematician Walter Pitts. In their landmark paper (*https://homl.info/43*),[2] "A Logical Calculus of Ideas Immanent in Nervous Activity", McCulloch and Pitts presented a simplified computational model of how biological neurons might work together in animal brains to perform complex computations using *propositional logic*. This was the first artificial neural network architecture. Since then many other architectures have been invented, as you will see.

The early successes of ANNs led to the widespread belief that we would soon be conversing with truly intelligent machines. When it became clear in the 1960s that this promise would go unfulfilled (at least for quite a while), funding flew elsewhere, and ANNs entered a long winter. In the early 1980s, new architectures were invented and better training techniques were developed, sparking a revival of interest in *connectionism*, the study of neural networks. But progress was slow, and by the 1990s other powerful machine learning techniques had been invented, such as support vector machines. These techniques seemed to offer better results and stronger theoretical foundations than ANNs, so once again the study of neural networks was put on hold.

We are now witnessing yet another wave of interest in ANNs. Will this wave die out like the previous ones did? Well, here are a few good reasons to believe that this time is different and that the renewed interest in ANNs will have a much more profound impact on our lives:

- There is now a huge quantity of data available to train neural networks, and ANNs frequently outperform other ML techniques on very large and complex problems.
- The tremendous increase in computing power since the 1990s now makes it possible to train large neural networks in a reasonable amount of time. This is in part due to Moore's law (the number of components in integrated circuits has doubled about every 2 years over the last 50 years), but also thanks to the gaming industry, which has stimulated the production of powerful *graphical processing units* (GPUs) by the millions: GPU cards were initially designed to accelerate graphics, but it turns out that neural networks perform similar computations (such as large matrix multiplications), so they can also be accelerated using GPUs. Moreover, cloud platforms have made this power accessible to everyone.

2 Warren S. McCulloch and Walter Pitts, "A Logical Calculus of the Ideas Immanent in Nervous Activity", *The Bulletin of Mathematical Biology* 5, no. 4 (1943): 115–113.

- The training algorithms have been improved. To be fair they are only slightly different from the ones used in the 1990s, but these relatively small tweaks have had a huge positive impact.
- Some theoretical limitations of ANNs have turned out to be benign in practice. For example, many people thought that ANN training algorithms were doomed because they were likely to get stuck in local optima, but it turns out that this is not a big problem in practice, especially for larger neural networks: the local optima often perform almost as well as the global optimum.
- The invention of the Transformer architecture in 2017 (see Chapter 15) has been a game changer: it can process and generate all sorts of data (e.g., text, images, audio) unlike earlier, more specialized, architectures, and it performs great across a wide variety of tasks from robotics to protein folding. Moreover, it scales rather well, which has made it possible to train very large *foundation models* that can be reused across many different tasks, possibly with a bit of fine-tuning (that's transfer learning), or just by prompting the model in the right way (that's *in-context learning*, or ICL). For instance, you can give it a few examples of the task at hand (that's *few-shot learning*, or FSL), or ask it to reason step-by-step (that's *chain-of-thought* prompting, or CoT). It's a new world!
- ANNs seem to have entered a virtuous circle of funding and progress. Amazing products based on ANNs regularly make the headline news, which pulls more and more attention and funding toward them, resulting in more and more progress and even more amazing products. AI is no longer just powering products in the shadows: since chatbots such as ChatGPT were released, the general public is now directly interacting daily with AI assistants, and the big tech companies are competing fiercely to grab this gigantic market: the pace of innovation is wild.

Biological Neurons

Before we discuss artificial neurons, let's take a quick look at a biological neuron (represented in Figure 9-1). It is an unusual-looking cell mostly found in animal brains. It's composed of a *cell body* containing the nucleus and most of the cell's complex components, many branching extensions called *dendrites*, plus one very long extension called the *axon*. The axon's length may be just a few times longer than the cell body, or up to tens of thousands of times longer. Near its extremity the axon splits off into many branches called *telodendria*, and at the tip of these branches are minuscule structures called *synaptic terminals* (or simply *synapses*), which are connected to the dendrites or cell bodies of other neurons.[3] Biological neurons produce short electrical impulses called *action potentials* (APs, or just *signals*), which travel along

3 They are not actually attached, just so close that they can very quickly exchange chemical signals.

the axons and make the synapses release chemical signals called *neurotransmitters*. When a neuron receives a sufficient amount of these neurotransmitters within a few milliseconds, it fires its own electrical impulses (actually, it depends on the neurotransmitters, as some of them inhibit the neuron from firing).

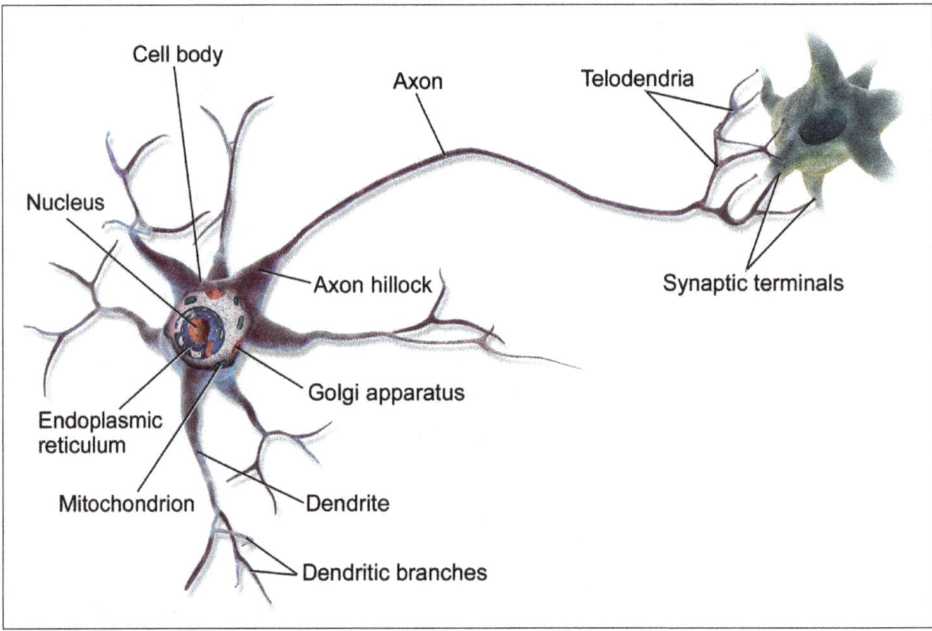

Figure 9-1. A biological neuron[4]

Thus, individual biological neurons seem to behave in a simple way, but they're organized in a vast network of billions, with each neuron typically connected to thousands of other neurons. Highly complex computations can be performed by a network of fairly simple neurons, much like a complex anthill can emerge from the combined efforts of simple ants. The architecture of biological neural networks (BNNs)[5] is the subject of active research, but some parts of the brain have been mapped. These efforts show that neurons are often organized in consecutive layers, especially in the cerebral cortex (the outer layer of the brain), as shown in Figure 9-2.

4 Image by Bruce Blaus (Creative Commons 3.0 (*https://oreil.ly/pMbrK*)). Reproduced from *https://en.wikipedia.org/wiki/Neuron*.

5 In the context of machine learning, the phrase "neural networks" generally refers to ANNs, not BNNs.

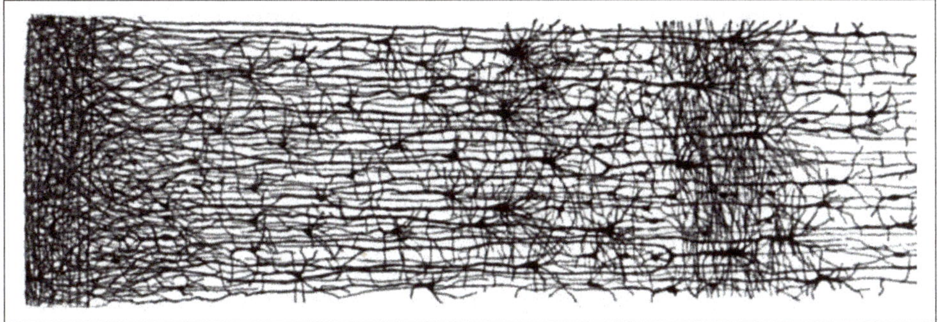

Figure 9-2. Multiple layers in a biological neural network (human cortex)[6]

Logical Computations with Neurons

McCulloch and Pitts proposed a very simple model of the biological neuron, which later became known as an *artificial neuron*: it has one or more binary (on/off) inputs and one binary output. The artificial neuron activates its output when more than a certain number of its inputs are active. In their paper, McCulloch and Pitts showed that even with such a simplified model it is possible to build a network of artificial neurons that can compute any logical proposition you want. To see how such a network works, let's build a few ANNs that perform various logical computations (see Figure 9-3), assuming that a neuron is activated when at least two of its input connections are active.

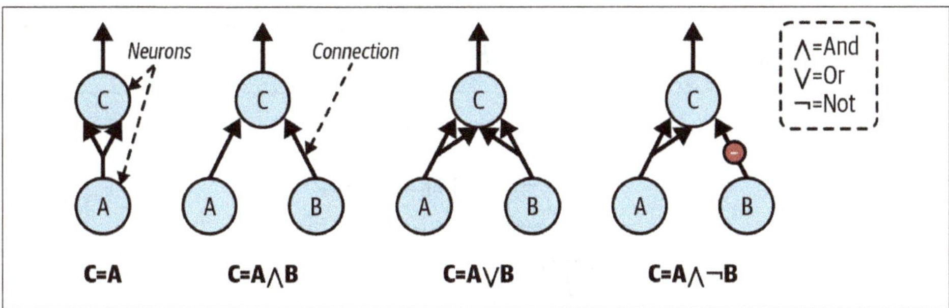

Figure 9-3. ANNs performing simple logical computations

Let's see what these networks do:

- The first network on the left is the identity function: if neuron A is activated, then neuron C gets activated as well (since it receives two input signals from neuron A); but if neuron A is off, then neuron C is off as well.

6 Drawing of a cortical lamination by S. Ramon y Cajal (public domain). Reproduced from *https://en.wikipedia.org/wiki/Cerebral_cortex*.

- The second network performs a logical AND: neuron C is activated only when both neurons A and B are activated (a single input signal is not enough to activate neuron C).
- The third network performs a logical OR: neuron C gets activated if either neuron A or neuron B is activated (or both).
- Finally, if we suppose that an input connection can inhibit the neuron's activity (which is the case with biological neurons), then the fourth network computes a slightly more complex logical proposition: neuron C is activated only if neuron A is active and neuron B is off. If neuron A is active all the time, then you get a logical NOT: neuron C is active when neuron B is off, and vice versa.

You can imagine how these networks can be combined to compute complex logical expressions (see the exercises at the end of the chapter for an example).

The Perceptron

The *perceptron* is one of the simplest ANN architectures, invented in 1957 by Frank Rosenblatt. It is based on a slightly different artificial neuron (see Figure 9-4) called a *threshold logic unit* (TLU), or sometimes a *linear threshold unit* (LTU). The inputs and output are numbers (instead of binary on/off values), and each input connection is associated with a weight. The TLU first computes a linear function of its inputs: $z = w_1 x_1 + w_2 x_2 + \cdots + w_n x_n + b = \mathbf{w}^\intercal \mathbf{x} + b$. Then it applies a *step function* to the result: $h_\mathbf{w}(\mathbf{x}) = \text{step}(z)$. So it's almost like logistic regression, except it uses a step function instead of the logistic function.[7] Just like in logistic regression, the model parameters are the input weights $\mathbf{w}$ and the bias term b.

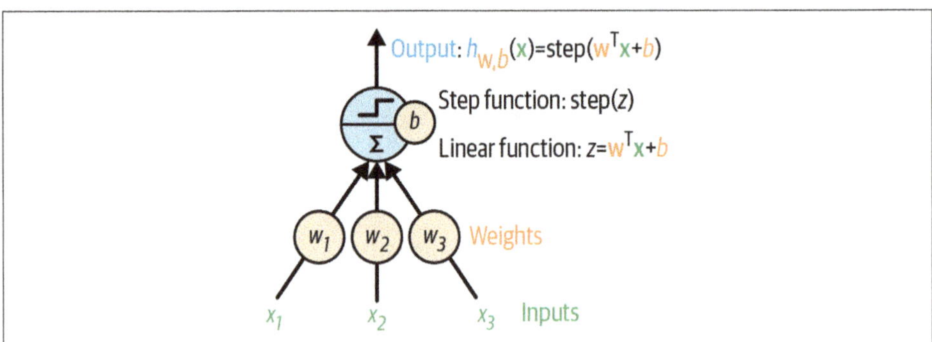

Figure 9-4. TLU: an artificial neuron that computes a weighted sum of its inputs $\mathbf{w}^\intercal \mathbf{x}$, plus a bias term b, then applies a step function

7 Logistic regression and the logistic function were introduced in Chapter 4, along with several other concepts that we will heavily rely on in this chapter, including softmax, cross-entropy, gradient descent, early stopping, and more, so please make sure to read it first.

The most common step function used in perceptrons is the *Heaviside step function* (see Equation 9-1). Sometimes the sign function is used instead.

Equation 9-1. Common step functions used in perceptrons (assuming threshold = 0)

$$\text{heaviside}(z) = \begin{cases} 0 & \text{if } z < 0 \\ 1 & \text{if } z \geq 0 \end{cases} \qquad \text{sgn}(z) = \begin{cases} -1 & \text{if } z < 0 \\ 0 & \text{if } z = 0 \\ +1 & \text{if } z > 0 \end{cases}$$

A single TLU can be used for simple linear binary classification. It computes a linear function of its inputs, and if the result exceeds a threshold, it outputs the positive class. Otherwise, it outputs the negative class. This may remind you of logistic regression (Chapter 4) or linear SVM classification (see the online chapter on SVMs at *https://homl.info*). You could, for example, use a single TLU to classify iris flowers based on petal length and width. Training such a TLU would require finding the right values for w_1, w_2, and b (the training algorithm is discussed shortly).

A perceptron is composed of one or more TLUs organized in a single layer, where every TLU is connected to every input. Such a layer is called a *fully connected layer*, or a *dense layer*. The inputs constitute the *input layer*. And since the layer of TLUs produces the final outputs, it is called the *output layer*. For example, a perceptron with two inputs and three outputs is represented in Figure 9-5.

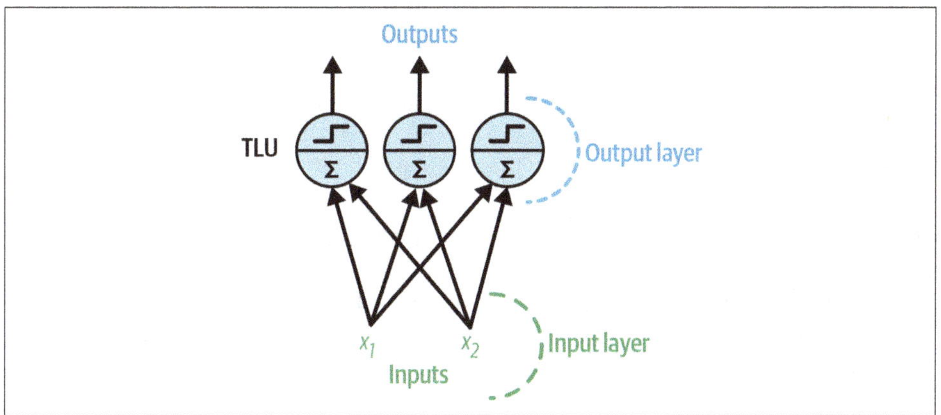

Figure 9-5. Architecture of a perceptron with two inputs and three output neurons

This perceptron can classify instances simultaneously into three different binary classes, which makes it a multilabel classifier. It may also be used for multiclass classification.

Thanks to the magic of linear algebra, Equation 9-2 can be used to efficiently compute the outputs of a layer of artificial neurons for several instances at once.

Equation 9-2. Computing the outputs of a fully connected layer

$$\widehat{\mathbf{Y}} = \phi(\mathbf{X}\mathbf{W} + \mathbf{b})$$

In this equation:

- $\widehat{\mathbf{Y}}$ is the output matrix. It has one row per instance and one column per neuron.
- $\mathbf{X}$ is the input matrix. It has one row per instance and one column per input feature.
- The weight matrix $\mathbf{W}$ contains all the connection weights. It has one row per input feature and one column per neuron.[8]
- The bias vector $\mathbf{b}$ contains all the bias terms: one per neuron.
- The function ϕ is called the *activation function*: when the artificial neurons are TLUs, it is a step function (we will discuss other activation functions shortly).

In mathematics, the sum of a matrix and a vector is undefined. However, in data science, we allow "broadcasting": adding a vector to a matrix means adding it to every row in the matrix. So, $\mathbf{XW} + \mathbf{b}$ first multiplies $\mathbf{X}$ by $\mathbf{W}$—which results in a matrix with one row per instance and one column per output—then adds the vector $\mathbf{b}$ to every row of that matrix, which adds each bias term to the corresponding output, for every instance. Moreover, ϕ is then applied itemwise to each item in the resulting matrix.

So, how is a perceptron trained? The perceptron training algorithm proposed by Rosenblatt was largely inspired by *Hebb's rule*. In his 1949 book, *The Organization of Behavior* (Wiley), Donald Hebb suggested that when a biological neuron triggers another neuron often, the connection between these two neurons grows stronger. Siegrid Löwel later summarized Hebb's idea in the catchy phrase, "Cells that fire together, wire together"; that is, the connection weight between two neurons tends to increase when they fire simultaneously. This rule later became known as Hebb's rule (or *Hebbian learning*). Perceptrons are trained using a variant of this rule that takes into account the error made by the network when it makes a prediction; the perceptron learning rule reinforces connections that help reduce the error. More specifically, the

8 In some libraries, such as PyTorch, the weight matrix is transposed, so there's one row per neuron, and one column per input feature.

perceptron is fed one training instance at a time, and for each instance it makes its predictions. For every output neuron that produced a wrong prediction, it reinforces the connection weights from the inputs that would have contributed to the correct prediction. The rule is shown in Equation 9-3.

Equation 9-3. Perceptron learning rule (weight update)

$$w_{i,j}^{(\text{next step})} = w_{i,j} + \eta\left(y_j - \widehat{y}_j\right)x_i$$

In this equation:

- $w_{i,j}$ is the connection weight between the ith input and the jth neuron.
- x_i is the ith input value of the current training instance.
- $\widehat{y}_j$ is the output of the jth output neuron for the current training instance.
- y_j is the target output of the jth output neuron for the current training instance.
- η is the learning rate (see Chapter 4).

The decision boundary of each output neuron is linear, so perceptrons are incapable of learning complex patterns (just like logistic regression classifiers). However, if the training instances are linearly separable, Rosenblatt demonstrated that this algorithm will converge to a solution.[9] This is called the *perceptron convergence theorem*.

Scikit-Learn provides a `Perceptron` class that can be used pretty much as you would expect—for example, on the iris dataset (introduced in Chapter 4):

```
import numpy as np
from sklearn.datasets import load_iris
from sklearn.linear_model import Perceptron

iris = load_iris(as_frame=True)
X = iris.data[["petal length (cm)", "petal width (cm)"]].values
y = (iris.target == 0)  # Iris setosa

per_clf = Perceptron(random_state=42)
per_clf.fit(X, y)

X_new = [[2, 0.5], [3, 1]]
y_pred = per_clf.predict(X_new)  # predicts True and False for these 2 flowers
```

You may have noticed that the perceptron learning algorithm strongly resembles stochastic gradient descent (introduced in Chapter 4). In fact, Scikit-Learn's `Perceptron` class is equivalent to using an `SGDClassifier` with the following hyperparameters:

9 Note that this solution is not unique: when data points are linearly separable, there is an infinity of hyperplanes that can separate them.

`loss="perceptron"`, `learning_rate="constant"`, `eta0=1` (the learning rate), and `penalty=None` (no regularization).

Contrary to logistic regression classifiers, perceptrons do not output a class probability. This is one reason to prefer logistic regression over perceptrons. Moreover, perceptrons do not use any regularization by default, and training stops as soon as there are no more prediction errors on the training set, so the model typically does not generalize as well as logistic regression or a linear SVM classifier. However, perceptrons may train a bit faster.

In their 1969 monograph, *Perceptrons*, Marvin Minsky and Seymour Papert highlighted a number of serious weaknesses of perceptrons—in particular, the fact that they are incapable of solving some trivial problems (e.g., the *exclusive OR* (XOR) classification problem; see the left side of Figure 9-6). This is true of any other linear classification model (such as logistic regression classifiers), but researchers had expected much more from perceptrons, and some were so disappointed that they dropped neural networks altogether in favor of more formal approaches such as logic, problem solving, and search. The lack of practical applications also didn't help.

It turns out that some of the limitations of perceptrons can be eliminated by stacking multiple perceptrons. The resulting ANN is called a *multilayer perceptron* (MLP).

The Multilayer Perceptron and Backpropagation

An MLP can solve the XOR problem, as you can verify by computing the output of the MLP represented on the righthand side of Figure 9-6: with inputs (0, 0) or (1, 1), the network outputs 0, and with inputs (0, 1) or (1, 0) it outputs 1. Try verifying that this network indeed solves the XOR problem![10]

An MLP is composed of one input layer, one or more layers of artificial neurons (originally TLUs) called *hidden layers*, and one final layer of artificial neurons called the *output layer* (see Figure 9-7). The layers close to the input layer are usually called the *lower layers*, and the ones close to the outputs are usually called the *upper layers*.

10 For example, when the inputs are (0, 1) the lower-left neuron computes $0 \times 1 + 1 \times 1 - 3 / 2 = -1 / 2$, which is negative, so it outputs 0. The lower-right neuron computes $0 \times 1 + 1 \times 1 - 1 / 2 = 1 / 2$, which is positive, so it outputs 1. The output neuron receives the outputs of the first two neurons as its inputs, so it computes $0 \times (-1) + 1 \times 1 - 1 / 2 = 1 / 2$. This is positive, so it outputs 1.

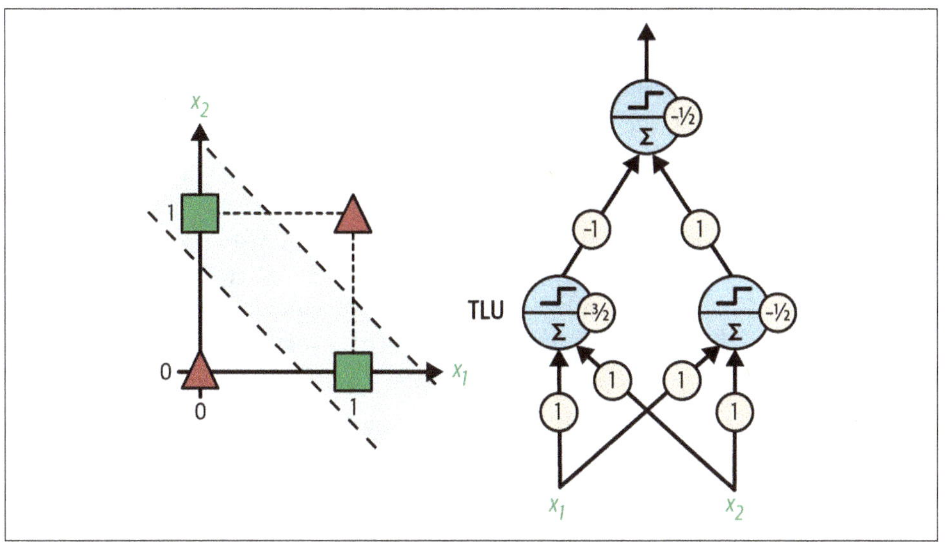

Figure 9-6. XOR classification problem and an MLP that solves it

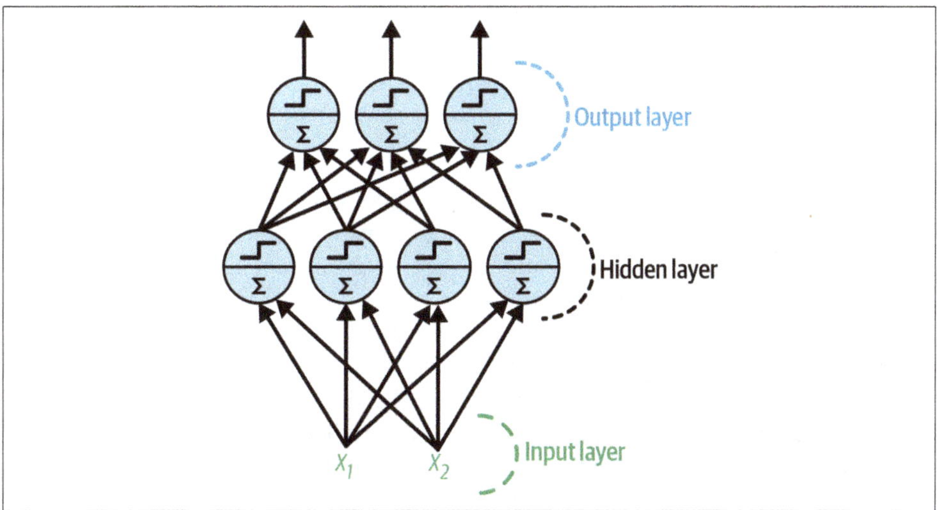

Figure 9-7. Architecture of a multilayer perceptron with two inputs, one hidden layer of four neurons, and three output neurons

The signal flows only in one direction (from the inputs to the outputs), so this architecture is an example of a *feedforward neural network* (FNN).

When an ANN contains a deep stack of hidden layers,[11] it is called a *deep neural network* (DNN). The field of deep learning studies DNNs, and more generally it is interested in models containing deep stacks of computations. Even so, many people talk about deep learning whenever neural networks are involved (even shallow ones).

For many years researchers struggled to find a way to train MLPs, without success. In the early 1960s several researchers discussed the possibility of using gradient descent to train neural networks, but as we saw in Chapter 4, this requires computing the gradients of the model's error with regard to the model parameters; it wasn't clear at the time how to do this efficiently with such a complex model containing so many parameters, especially with the computers they had back then.

Then, in 1970, a researcher named Seppo Linnainmaa introduced in his master's thesis a technique to compute all the gradients automatically and efficiently. This algorithm is now called *reverse-mode automatic differentiation* (or *reverse-mode autodiff* for short). In just two passes through the network (one forward, one backward), it is able to compute the gradients of the neural network's error with regard to every single model parameter. In other words, it can find out how each connection weight and each bias should be tweaked in order to reduce the neural network's error. These gradients can then be used to perform a gradient descent step. If you repeat this process of computing the gradients automatically and taking a gradient descent step, the neural network's error will gradually drop until it eventually reaches a minimum. This combination of reverse-mode autodiff and gradient descent is now called *backpropagation* (or *backprop* for short).

Here's an analogy: imagine you are learning to shoot a basketball into the hoop. You throw the ball (that's the forward pass), and you observe that it went far off to the right side (that's the error computation), then you consider how you can change your body position to throw the ball a bit less to the right next time (that's the backward pass): you realize that your arm will need to rotate a bit counterclockwise, and probably your whole upper body as well, which in turn means that your feet should turn too (notice how we're going down the "layers"). Once you've thought it through, you actually move your body: that's the gradient descent step. The smaller the errors, the smaller the adjustments. As you repeat the whole process many times, the error gradually gets smaller, and after a few hours of practice, you manage to get the ball through the hoop every time. Good job!

11 In the 1990s, an ANN with more than two hidden layers was considered deep. Nowadays, it is common to see ANNs with dozens of layers, or even hundreds, so the definition of "deep" is quite fuzzy.

There are various autodiff techniques, with different pros and cons. Reverse-mode autodiff is well suited when the function to differentiate has many variables (e.g., connection weights and biases) and few outputs (e.g., one loss). If you want to learn more about autodiff, check out Appendix A.

Backpropagation can actually be applied to all sorts of computational graphs, not just neural networks: indeed, Linnainmaa's master's thesis was not about neural nets at all, it was more general. It was several more years before backprop started to be used to train neural networks, but it still wasn't mainstream. Then, in 1985, David Rumelhart, Geoffrey Hinton, and Ronald Williams published a paper (*https://homl.info/44*)[12] analyzing how backpropagation allows neural networks to learn useful internal representations. Their results were so impressive that backpropagation was quickly popularized in the field. Over 40 years later, it is still by far the most popular training technique for neural networks.

Let's run through how backpropagation works again in a bit more detail:

- It handles one mini-batch at a time, and goes through the full training set multiple times. If each mini-batch contains 32 instances, and each instance has 100 features, then the mini-batch will be represented as a matrix with 32 rows and 100 columns. Each pass through the training set is called an *epoch*.
- For each mini-batch, the algorithm computes the output of all the neurons in the first hidden layer using Equation 9-2. If the layer has 50 neurons, then its output is a matrix with one row per sample in the mini-batch (e.g., 32), and 50 columns (i.e., one per neuron). This matrix is then passed on to the next layer, its output is computed and passed to the next layer, and so on until we get the output of the last layer, the output layer. This is the *forward pass*: it is exactly like making predictions, except all intermediate results are preserved since they are needed for the backward pass.
- Next, the algorithm measures the network's output error (i.e., it uses a loss function that compares the desired output and the actual output of the network, and returns some measure of the error).
- Then it computes how much each output layer parameter contributed to the error. This is done analytically by applying the *chain rule* (one of the most fundamental rules in calculus), which makes this step fast and precise. The result is one gradient per parameter.

12 David Rumelhart et al., "Learning Internal Representations by Error Propagation" (Defense Technical Information Center technical report, September 1985).

- The algorithm then measures how much of these error contributions came from each connection in the layer below, again using the chain rule, working backward until it reaches the input layer. As explained earlier, this reverse pass efficiently measures the error gradient across all the connection weights and biases in the network by propagating the error gradient backward through the network (hence the name of the algorithm).
- Finally, the algorithm performs a gradient descent step to tweak all the connection weights and bias terms in the network, using the error gradients it just computed.

It is important to initialize all the hidden layers' connection weights randomly, or else training will fail. For example, if you initialize all weights and biases to zero, then all neurons in a given layer will be perfectly identical, and thus backpropagation will affect them in exactly the same way, so they will remain identical. In other words, despite having hundreds of neurons per layer, your model will act as if it had only one neuron per layer: it won't be too smart. If instead you randomly initialize the weights, you *break the symmetry* and allow backpropagation to train a diverse team of neurons.

In short, backpropagation makes predictions for a mini-batch (forward pass), measures the error, then goes through each layer in reverse to measure the error contribution from each parameter (reverse pass), and finally tweaks the connection weights and biases to reduce the error (gradient descent step).

In order for backprop to work properly, Rumelhart and his colleagues made a key change to the MLP's architecture: they replaced the step function with the logistic function, $\sigma(z) = 1 / (1 + \exp(-z))$, also called the *sigmoid* function. This was essential because the step function contains only flat segments, so there is no gradient to work with (gradient descent cannot move on a flat surface), while the sigmoid function has a well-defined nonzero derivative everywhere, allowing gradient descent to make some progress at every step. In fact, the backpropagation algorithm works well with many other activation functions, not just the sigmoid function. Here are two other popular choices:

The hyperbolic tangent function: $\tanh(z) = 2\sigma(2z) - 1$

Just like the sigmoid function, this activation function is *S*-shaped, continuous, and differentiable, but its output value ranges from –1 to 1 (instead of 0 to 1 in the case of the sigmoid function). That range tends to make each layer's output more or less centered around 0 at the beginning of training, which often helps speed up convergence.

The rectified linear unit function: ReLU(z) = max(0, z)

The ReLU function is continuous but unfortunately not differentiable at $z = 0$ (the slope changes abruptly, which can make gradient descent bounce around), and its derivative is 0 for $z < 0$. In practice, however, it works very well and has the advantage of being fast to compute, so it has become the default for most architectures (except the Transformer architecture, as we will see in Chapter 15).[13] Importantly, the fact that it does not have a maximum output value helps reduce some issues during gradient descent (we will come back to this in Chapter 11).

These popular activation functions and their derivatives are represented in Figure 9-8. But wait! Why do we need activation functions in the first place? Well, if you chain several linear transformations, all you get is a linear transformation. For example, if $f(x) = 2x + 3$ and $g(x) = 5x - 1$, then chaining these two linear functions gives you another linear function: $f(g(x)) = 2(5x - 1) + 3 = 10x + 1$. So if you don't have some nonlinearity between layers, then even a deep stack of layers is equivalent to a single layer, and you can't solve very complex problems with that. Conversely, a large enough DNN with nonlinear activations can theoretically approximate any continuous function.

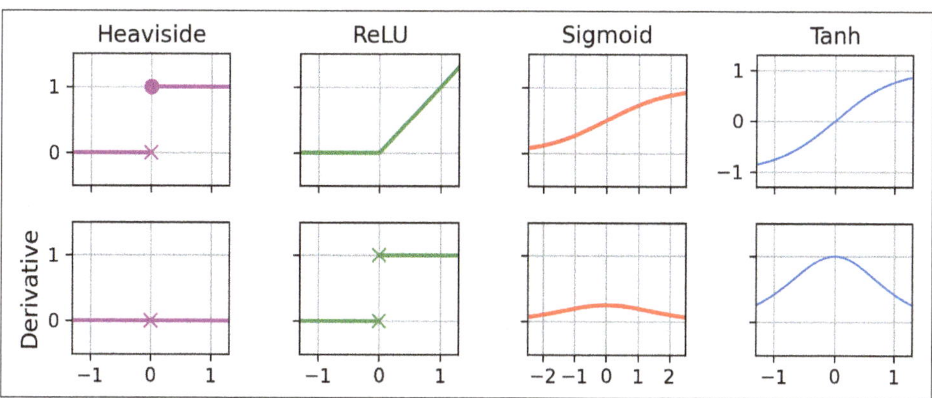

Figure 9-8. Activation functions (left) and their derivatives (right)

OK! You know where neural nets came from, what the MLP architecture looks like, and how it computes its outputs. You've also learned about the backpropagation algorithm. It's time to see MLPs in action!

13 Biological neurons seem to implement a roughly sigmoid (S-shaped) activation function, so researchers stuck to sigmoid functions for a very long time. But it turns out that ReLU generally works better in ANNs. This is one of the cases where the biological analogy was perhaps misleading.

Building and Training MLPs with Scikit-Learn

MLPs can tackle a wide range of tasks, but the most common are regression and classification. Scikit-Learn can help with both of these. Let's start with regression.

Regression MLPs

How would you build an MLP for a regression task? Well, if you want to predict a single value (e.g., the price of a house, given many of its features), then you just need a single output neuron: its output is the predicted value. For multivariate regression (i.e., to predict multiple values at once), you need one output neuron per output dimension. For example, to locate the center of an object in an image, you need to predict 2D coordinates, so you need two output neurons. If you also want to place a bounding box around the object, then you need two more numbers: the width and the height of the object. So, you end up with four output neurons.

Scikit-Learn includes an `MLPRegressor` class, so let's use it to build an MLP with three hidden layers composed of 50 neurons each, and train it on the California housing dataset. For simplicity, we will use Scikit-Learn's `fetch_california_housing()` function to load the data. This dataset is simpler than the one we used in Chapter 2, since it contains only numerical features (there is no `ocean_proximity` feature), and there are no missing values. The targets are also scaled down: each unit represents $100,000. Let's start by importing everything we will need:

```
from sklearn.datasets import fetch_california_housing
from sklearn.metrics import root_mean_squared_error
from sklearn.model_selection import train_test_split
from sklearn.neural_network import MLPRegressor
from sklearn.pipeline import make_pipeline
from sklearn.preprocessing import StandardScaler
```

Next, let's fetch the California housing dataset and split it into a training set and a test set:

```
housing = fetch_california_housing()
X_train, X_test, y_train, y_test = train_test_split(
    housing.data, housing.target, random_state=42)
```

Now let's create an `MLPRegressor` model with 3 hidden layers composed of 50 neurons each. The first hidden layer's input size (i.e., the number of rows in its weights matrix) and the output layer's output size (i.e., the number of columns in its weights matrix) will adjust automatically to the dimensionality of the inputs and targets, respectively, when training starts. The model uses the ReLU activation function in all hidden layers, and no activation function at all on the output layer. We also set `verbose=True` to get details on the model's progress during training:

```
mlp_reg = MLPRegressor(hidden_layer_sizes=[50, 50, 50], early_stopping=True,
                       verbose=True, random_state=42)
```

Since neural nets can have a *lot* of parameters, they have a tendency to overfit the training set. To reduce this risk, one option is to use early stopping (introduced in Chapter 4): when we set `early_stopping=True`, the `MLPRegressor` class automatically sets aside 10% of the training data and uses it to evaluate the model at each epoch (you can adjust the validation set's size by setting `validation_fraction`). If the validation score stops improving for 10 epochs, training automatically stops (you can tweak this number of epochs by setting `n_iter_no_change`).

Now let's create a pipeline to standardize the input features before sending them to the `MLPRegressor`. This is very important because gradient descent does not converge very well when the features have very different scales, as we saw in Chapter 4. We can then train the model! The `MLPRegressor` class uses a variant of gradient descent called *Adam* (see Chapter 11) to minimize the mean squared error. It also uses a tiny bit of ℓ_2 regularization (you can control its strength via the `alpha` hyperparameter, which defaults to 0.0001):

```
>>> pipeline = make_pipeline(StandardScaler(), mlp_reg)
>>> pipeline.fit(X_train, y_train)
Iteration 1, loss = 0.85190332
Validation score: 0.534299
Iteration 2, loss = 0.28288639
Validation score: 0.651094
[...]
Iteration 45, loss = 0.12960481
Validation score: 0.788517
Validation score did not improve more than tol=0.000100 for 10 consecutive
epochs. Stopping.
```

And there you go, you just trained your very first MLP! It required 45 epochs, and as you can see, the training loss went down at each epoch. This loss corresponds to Equation 4-9 divided by 2, so you must multiply it by 2 to get the MSE (although not exactly because the loss includes the ℓ_2 regularization term). The validation score generally went up at each epoch. Like every regressor in Scikit-Learn, `MLPRegressor` uses the R^2 score by default for evaluation—that's what the `score()` method returns. As we saw in Chapter 2, the R^2 score measures the ratio of the variance that is explained by the model. In this case, it reaches close to 80% on the validation set, which is fairly good for this task:

```
>>> mlp_reg.best_validation_score_
0.791536125425778
```

Let's evaluate the RMSE on the test set:

```
>>> y_pred = pipeline.predict(X_test)
>>> rmse = root_mean_squared_error(y_test, y_pred)
>>> rmse
0.5327699946812925
```

We get a test RMSE of about 0.53, which is comparable to what you would get with a random forest classifier. Not too bad for a first try! Figure 9-9 plots the model's predictions versus the targets (on the test set). The dashed red line represents the ideal predictions (i.e., equal to the targets): most of the predictions are close to the targets, but there are still quite a few errors, especially for larger targets.

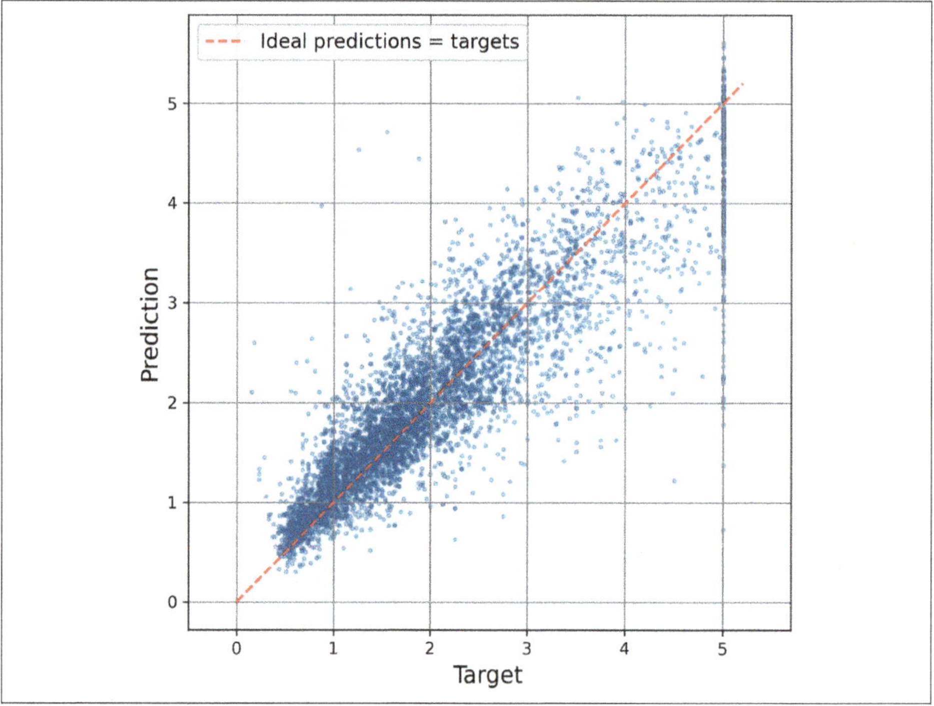

Figure 9-9. MLP regressor's predictions versus the targets

Note that this MLP does not use any activation function for the output layer, so it's free to output any value it wants. This is generally fine, but if you want to guarantee that the output is always positive, then you should use the ReLU activation function on the output layer, or the *softplus* activation function, which is a smooth variant of ReLU: softplus(z) = log(1 + exp(z)). Softplus is close to 0 when z is negative, and close to z when z is positive. Finally, if you want to guarantee that the predictions always fall within a given range of values, then you should use the sigmoid function or the hyperbolic tangent, and scale the targets to the appropriate range: 0 to 1 for sigmoid and –1 to 1 for tanh. Sadly, the `MLPRegressor` class does not support activation functions in the output layer.

Scikit-Learn does not offer GPU acceleration, and its neural net features are fairly limited. This is why we will switch to PyTorch starting in Chapter 10. That said, it is quite convenient to be able to build and train a standard MLP in just a few lines of code using Scikit-Learn: it lets you tackle many complex tasks very quickly.

In general, the mean squared error is the right loss to use for a regression tasks, but if you have a lot of outliers in the training set, you may sometimes prefer to use the mean absolute error instead, or preferably the *Huber loss*, which is a combination of both: it is quadratic when the error is smaller than a threshold δ (typically 1), but linear when the error is larger than δ. The linear part makes it less sensitive to outliers than the mean squared error, and the quadratic part allows it to converge faster and be more precise than the mean absolute error. Unfortunately, `MLPRegressor` only supports the MSE loss.

Table 9-1 summarizes the typical architecture of a regression MLP.

Table 9-1. Typical regression MLP architecture

Hyperparameter	Typical value
# hidden layers	Depends on the problem, but typically 1 to 5
# neurons per hidden layer	Depends on the problem, but typically 10 to 100
# output neurons	1 per target dimension
Hidden activation	ReLU
Output activation	None, or ReLU/softplus (if positive outputs) or sigmoid/tanh (if bounded outputs)
Loss function	MSE, or Huber if outliers

All right, MLPs can tackle regression tasks. What else can they do?

Classification MLPs

MLPs can also be used for classification tasks. For a binary classification problem, you just need a single output neuron using the sigmoid activation function: the output will be a number between 0 and 1, which you can interpret as the estimated probability of the positive class. The estimated probability of the negative class is equal to one minus that number.

MLPs can also easily handle multilabel binary classification tasks (see Chapter 3). For example, you could have an email classification system that predicts whether each incoming email is ham or spam, and simultaneously predicts whether it is an urgent or nonurgent email. In this case, you would need two output neurons, both using the sigmoid activation function: the first would output the probability that the email is spam, and the second would output the probability that it is urgent. More generally, you would dedicate one output neuron for each positive class. Note that the output probabilities do not necessarily add up to 1. This lets the model output any combination of labels: you can have nonurgent ham, urgent ham, nonurgent spam, and perhaps even urgent spam (although that would probably be an error).

If each instance can belong only to a single class, out of three or more possible classes (e.g., classes 0 through 9 for digit image classification), then you need to have one output neuron per class, and you should use the softmax activation function for the whole output layer (see Figure 9-10). The softmax function (introduced in Chapter 4) will ensure that all the estimated probabilities are between 0 and 1, and that they add up to 1, since the classes are exclusive. As we saw in Chapter 3, this is called multiclass classification.

Regarding the loss function, since we are predicting probability distributions, the cross-entropy loss (or *x-entropy* or log loss for short, see Chapter 4) is generally a good choice.

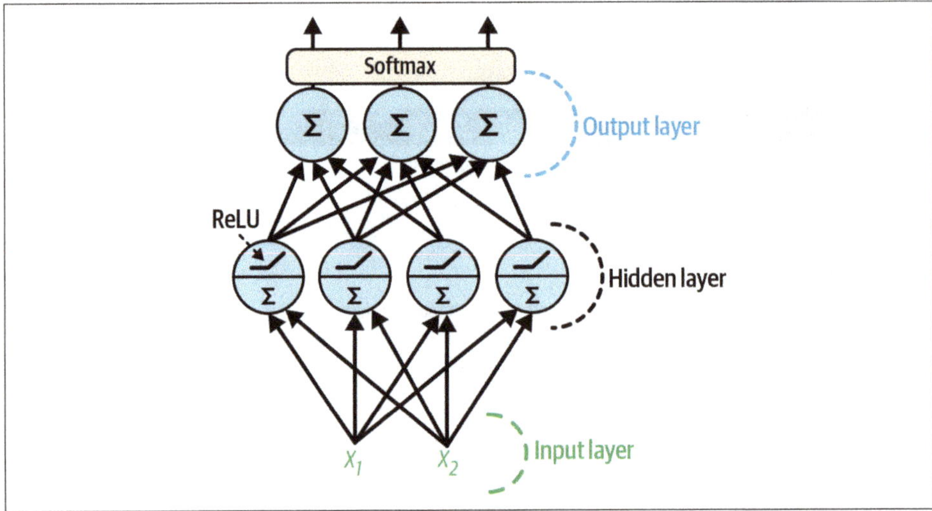

Figure 9-10. A modern MLP (including ReLU and softmax) for classification

Table 9-2 summarizes the typical architecture of a classification MLP.

Table 9-2. Typical classification MLP architecture

Hyperparameter	Binary classification	Multilabel binary classification	Multiclass classification
# hidden layers	Typically 1 to 5 layers, depending on the task		
# output neurons	1	1 per binary label	1 per class
Output layer activation	Sigmoid	Sigmoid	Softmax
Loss function	X-entropy	X-entropy	X-entropy

As you might expect, Scikit-Learn offers an `MLPClassifier` class in the `sklearn.neural_network` package, which you can use for binary or multiclass classification. It is almost identical to the `MLPRegressor` class, except that its output layer uses the softmax activation function, and it minimizes the cross-entropy loss rather than the MSE. Moreover, the `score()` method returns the model's accuracy rather than the R^2 score. Let's try it out.

We could tackle the iris dataset, but that task is too simple for a neural net: a linear model would do just as well and wouldn't risk overfitting. So let's instead tackle a more complex task: Fashion MNIST. This is a drop-in replacement of MNIST (introduced in Chapter 3). It has the exact same format as MNIST (70,000 grayscale images of 28 × 28 pixels each, with 10 classes), but the images represent fashion items rather than handwritten digits, so each class is much more diverse, and the problem turns out to be significantly more challenging than MNIST. For example, a simple linear model reaches about 92% accuracy on MNIST, but only about 83% on Fashion MNIST. Let's see if we can do better with an MLP.

First, let's load the dataset using the `fetch_openml()` function, very much like we did for MNIST in Chapter 3. Note that the targets are represented as strings `'0'`, `'1'`, ..., `'9'`, so we convert them to integers:

```
from sklearn.datasets import fetch_openml

fashion_mnist = fetch_openml(name="Fashion-MNIST", as_frame=False)
targets = fashion_mnist.target.astype(int)
```

The data is already shuffled, so we just take the first 60,000 images for training, and the last 10,000 for testing:

```
X_train, y_train = fashion_mnist.data[:60_000], targets[:60_000]
X_test, y_test = fashion_mnist.data[60_000:], targets[60_000:]
```

Each image is represented as a 1D integer array containing 784 pixel intensities ranging from 0 to 255. You can use the `plt.imshow()` function to plot an image, but first you need to reshape it to `[28, 28]`:

```
import matplotlib.pyplot as plt

X_sample = X_train[0].reshape(28, 28)  # first image in the training set
plt.imshow(X_sample, cmap="binary")
plt.show()
```

If you run this code, you should see the ankle boot represented in the top-right corner of Figure 9-11.

Figure 9-11. First four samples from each class in Fashion MNIST

With MNIST, when the label is equal to 5, it means that the image represents the handwritten digit 5. Easy. For Fashion MNIST, however, we need the list of class names to know what we are dealing with. Scikit-Learn does not provide it, so let's create it:

```
class_names = ["T-shirt/top", "Trouser", "Pullover", "Dress", "Coat",
               "Sandal", "Shirt", "Sneaker", "Bag", "Ankle boot"]
```

We can now confirm that the first image in the training set represents an ankle boot:

```
>>> class_names[y_train[0]]
'Ankle boot'
```

We're ready to build the classification MLP:

```
from sklearn.neural_network import MLPClassifier
from sklearn.preprocessing import MinMaxScaler

mlp_clf = MLPClassifier(hidden_layer_sizes=[300, 100], verbose=True,
                        early_stopping=True, random_state=42)
pipeline = make_pipeline(MinMaxScaler(), mlp_clf)
pipeline.fit(X_train, y_train)
accuracy = pipeline.score(X_test, y_test)
```

This code is very similar to the regression code we used earlier, but there are a few differences:

- Of course, it's a classification task so we use an `MLPClassifier` rather than an `MLPRegressor`.
- We use just two hidden layers with 300 and 100 neurons, respectively. You can try a different number of hidden layers, and change the number of neurons as well if you want.
- We also use a `MinMaxScaler` instead of a `StandardScaler`. We need it to shrink the pixel intensities down to the 0–1 range rather than 0–255: having features

in this range usually works better with the default hyperparameters used by `MLPClassifier`, such as its default learning rate and weight initialization scale. You might wonder why we didn't use a `StandardScaler`? Well some pixels don't vary much across images; for example, the pixels around the edges are almost always white. If we used the `StandardScaler`, these pixels would get scaled up to have the same variance as every other pixel: as a result, we would give more importance to these pixels than they probably deserve. Using the `MinMaxScaler` often works better than the `StandardScaler` for images (but your mileage may vary).

- Lastly, the `score()` function returns the model's accuracy.

If you run this code, you will find that the model reaches about 89.7% accuracy on the validation set during training (the exact value is given by `mlp_clf.best_validation_score_`), but it starts overfitting a bit toward the end, so it ends up at just 89.2% accuracy. When we evaluate the model on the test set, we get 87.1%, which is not bad for this task, although we can do better with other neural net architectures such as convolutional neural networks (Chapter 12).

You probably noticed that training was quite slow. That's because the hidden layers have a *lot* of parameters, so there are many computations to run at each iteration. For example, the first hidden layer has 784 × 300 connection weights, plus 300 bias terms, which adds up to 235,500 parameters! All these parameters give the model quite a lot of flexibility to fit the training data, but it also means that there's a high risk of overfitting, especially when you do not have a lot of training data. In this case, you may want to use regularization techniques such as early stopping and ℓ_2 regularization.

Once the model is trained, you can use it to classify new images:

```
>>> X_new = X_test[:15]  # let's pretend these are 15 new images
>>> mlp_clf.predict(X_new)
array([9, 2, 1, 1, 6, 1, 4, 6, 5, 7, 4, 5, 8, 3, 4])
```

All these predictions are correct, except for the one at index 12, which should be a 7 (sneaker) instead of a 8 (bag). You might want to know how confident the model was about these predictions, especially the bad one. For this, you can use `model.predict_proba()` instead of `model.predict()`, like we did in Chapter 3:

```
>>> y_proba = mlp_clf.predict_proba(X_new)
>>> y_proba[12]
array([0., 0., 0., 0., 0., 0., 0., 0., 1., 0.])
```

Hmm, that's not great: the model is telling us that it's 100% confident that the image represents a bag (index 8). So not only is the model wrong, it's 100% confident that it's right. In fact, across all 10,000 images in the test set, there are only 16 images that the model is less than 99.9% confident about, despite the fact that its accuracy is about

90%. That's why you should always treat estimated probabilities with a grain of salt: neural nets have a strong tendency to be overconfident, especially if they are trained for a bit too long.

The targets for classification tasks can be class indices (e.g., 3) or class probabilities, typically one-hot vectors (e.g., [0, 0, 0, 1, 0, 0, 0, 0, 0, 0]). But if your model tends to be overconfident, you can try the *label smoothing* technique:[14] reduce the target class's probability slightly (e.g., from 1 down to 0.9) and distribute the rest evenly across the other classes (e.g., [0.1/9, 0.1/9, 0.1/9, 0.9, 0.1/9, 0.1/9, 0.1/9, 0.1/9, 0.1/9, 0.1/9]).

Still, getting 90% accuracy on Fashion MNIST is pretty good. You could get even better performance by fine-tuning the hyperparameters, for example using `RandomizedSearchCV`, as we did in Chapter 2. However, the search space is quite large, so it helps to know roughly where to look.

Hyperparameter Tuning Guidelines

The flexibility of neural networks is also one of their main drawbacks: there are many hyperparameters to tweak. Not only can you use any imaginable network architecture, but even in a basic MLP you can change the number of layers, the number of neurons and the type of activation function to use in each layer, the weight initialization logic, the type of optimizer to use, its learning rate, the batch size, and more. What are some good values for these hyperparameters?

Number of Hidden Layers

For many problems, you can begin with a single hidden layer and get reasonable results. An MLP with just one hidden layer can theoretically model even the most complex functions, provided it has enough neurons. But deep networks have a much higher *parameter efficiency* than shallow ones: they can model complex functions using exponentially fewer neurons than shallow nets, allowing them to reach much better performance with the same amount of training data. This is because their layered structure enables them to reuse and compose features across multiple levels: for example, the first layer in a face classifier may learn to recognize low-level features such as dots, arcs, or straight lines; while the second layer may learn to combine these low-level features into higher-level features such as squares or circles; and the third layer may learn to combine these higher-level features into a mouth, an eye, or a nose; and the top layer would then be able to use these top-level features to classify faces.

14 C. Szegedy et al., "Rethinking the Inception Architecture for Computer Vision", CVPR 2016: 2818–2826.

Not only does this hierarchical architecture help DNNs converge faster to a good solution, but it also improves their ability to generalize to new datasets. For example, if you have already trained a model to recognize faces in pictures and you now want to train a new neural network to recognize hairstyles, you can kickstart the training by reusing the lower layers of the first network. Instead of randomly initializing the weights and biases of the first few layers of the new neural network, you can initialize them to the values of the weights and biases of the lower layers of the first network. This way the network will not have to learn from scratch all the low-level structures that occur in most pictures; it will only have to learn the higher-level structures (e.g., hairstyles). This is called *transfer learning*.

In summary, for many problems you can start with just one or two hidden layers, and the neural network will work pretty well. For instance, you can easily reach above 97% accuracy on the MNIST dataset using just one hidden layer with a few hundred neurons, and above 98% accuracy using two hidden layers with the same total number of neurons, in roughly the same amount of training time. For more complex problems, you can ramp up the number of hidden layers until you start overfitting the training set. Very complex tasks, such as large image classification or speech recognition, typically require networks with dozens of layers (or even hundreds, but not fully connected ones, as you will see in Chapter 12), and they need a huge amount of training data. You will rarely have to train such networks from scratch: it is much more common to reuse parts of a pretrained state-of-the-art network that performs a similar task. Training will then be a lot faster and require much less data.

Number of Neurons per Hidden Layer

The number of neurons in the input and output layers is determined by the type of input and output your task requires. For example, the MNIST task requires 28 × 28 = 784 inputs and 10 output neurons.

As for the hidden layers, it used to be common to size them to form a pyramid, with fewer and fewer neurons at each layer—the rationale being that many low-level features can coalesce into far fewer high-level features. A typical neural network for MNIST might have 3 hidden layers, the first with 300 neurons, the second with 200, and the third with 100. However, this practice has been largely abandoned because it seems that using the same number of neurons in all hidden layers performs just as well in most cases, or even better; plus, there is only one hyperparameter to tune, instead of one per layer. That said, depending on the dataset, it can sometimes help to make the first hidden layer a bit larger than the others.

Just like the number of layers, you can try increasing the number of neurons gradually until the network starts overfitting. Alternatively, you can try building a model with slightly more layers and neurons than you actually need, then use early stopping and other regularization techniques to prevent it from overfitting too much. Vincent Vanhoucke, a Waymo researcher and former Googler, has dubbed this the "stretch pants" approach: instead of wasting time looking for pants that perfectly match your size, just use large stretch pants that will shrink down to the right size. With this approach, you avoid bottleneck layers that could ruin your model. Indeed, if a layer has too few neurons, it will lack the computational capacity to model complex relationships, and it may not even have enough representational power to preserve all the useful information from the inputs. For example, if you apply PCA (introduced in Chapter 7) to the Fashion MNIST training set, you will find that you need 187 dimensions to preserve 95% of the variance in the data. So if you set the number of neurons in the first hidden layer to some greater number, say 200, you can be confident that this layer will not be a bottleneck. However, you don't want to add too many neurons, or else the model will have too many parameters to optimize, and it will take more time and data to train.

In general, you will get more bang for your buck by increasing the number of layers rather than the number of neurons per layer.

That said, bottleneck layers are not always a bad thing. For example, limiting the dimensionality of the first hidden layers forces the neural net to keep only the most important dimensions, which can eliminate some of the noise in the data (but don't go too far!). Also, having a bottleneck layer near the output layer can force the neural net to learn good representations of the data in the previous layers (i.e., packing more useful information in less space), which can help the neural net generalize, and can also be useful in and of itself for *representation learning*. We will get back to that in Chapter 18.

Learning Rate

The learning rate is a hugely important hyperparameter. In general, the optimal learning rate is about half of the maximum learning rate (i.e., the learning rate above which the training algorithm diverges, as we saw in Chapter 4). One way to find a good learning rate is to train the model for a few hundred iterations, starting with a very low learning rate (e.g., 10^{-5}) and gradually increasing it up to a very large value (e.g., 10). This is done by multiplying the learning rate by a constant factor at each iteration (e.g., by $(10 / 10^{-5})^{1 / 500}$ to go from 10^{-5} to 10 in 500 iterations). If you plot the loss as a function of the learning rate (using a log scale for the learning rate), you should see it dropping at first. But after a while, the learning rate will be too large, so the loss will shoot back up: the optimal learning rate is often a bit lower than the point at which the loss starts to climb (typically about 10 times lower than the turning point). You can then reinitialize your model and train it normally using this good learning rate.

To change the learning rate during training when using Scikit-Learn, you must set the MLP's `warm_start` hyperparameter to `True`, and fit the model one batch at a time using `partial_fit()`, much like we did with the `SGDRegressor` in Chapter 4. Simply update the learning rate at each iteration.

Batch Size

The batch size can have a significant impact on your model's performance and training time. The main benefit of using large batch sizes is that hardware accelerators like GPUs can process them efficiently (as we will see in Chapter 10), so the training algorithm will see more instances per second. Therefore, many researchers and practitioners recommend using the largest batch size that can fit in *VRAM* (video RAM, i.e., the GPU's memory). There's a catch, though: large batch sizes can sometimes lead to training instabilities, especially with smaller models and at the beginning of training, and the resulting model may not generalize as well as a model trained with a small batch size. Yann LeCun once tweeted "Friends don't let friends use mini-batches larger than 32", citing a 2018 paper (*https://homl.info/smallbatch*)[15] by Dominic Masters and Carlo Luschi which concluded that using small batches (from 2 to 32) was preferable because small batches led to better models in less training time.

However, other research points in the opposite direction. For example, in 2017, papers by Elad Hoffer et al. (*https://homl.info/largebatch*)[16] and Priya Goyal et al. (*https://homl.info/largebatch2*)[17] showed that it is possible to use very large batch sizes (up to 8,192), along with various techniques such as warming up the learning rate (i.e., starting training with a small learning rate, then ramping it up), to obtain very short training times, without any generalization gap.

So one strategy is to use a large batch size, possibly with learning rate warmup, and if training is unstable or the final performance is disappointing, then try using a smaller batch size instead.

---

15 Dominic Masters and Carlo Luschi, "Revisiting Small Batch Training for Deep Neural Networks", arXiv preprint arXiv:1804.07612 (2018).

16 Elad Hoffer et al., "Train Longer, Generalize Better: Closing the Generalization Gap in Large Batch Training of Neural Networks", *Proceedings of the 31st International Conference on Neural Information Processing Systems* (2017): 1729–1739.

17 Priya Goyal et al., "Accurate, Large Minibatch SGD: Training ImageNet in 1 Hour", arXiv preprint arXiv:1706.02677 (2017).

Other Hyperparameters

Here are two more hyperparameters you can tune if you have the computation budget and the time:

Optimizer
: Choosing a better optimizer than plain old mini-batch gradient descent (and tuning its hyperparameters) can help speed up training and sometimes reach better performance.

Activation function
: We discussed how to choose the activation function earlier in this chapter: in general, the ReLU activation function is a good default for all hidden layers. In some cases, replacing ReLU with another function can help.

The optimal learning rate depends on the other hyperparameters—especially the batch size—so if you modify any hyperparameter, make sure to tune the learning rate again.

For more best practices regarding tuning neural network hyperparameters, check out the excellent 2018 paper (*https://homl.info/1cycle*)[18] by Leslie Smith. The Deep Learning Tuning Playbook (*https://github.com/google-research/tuning_playbook*) by Google researchers is also well worth reading. The free e-book *Machine Learning Yearning* by Andrew Ng (*https://homl.info/ngbook*) also contains a wealth of practical advice.

Lastly, I highly recommend you go through exercise 1 at the end of this chapter. You will use a nice web interface to play with various neural network architectures and visualize their outputs. This will be very useful to better understand MLPs and grow a good intuition for the effects of each hyperparameter (number of layers and neurons, activation functions, and more).

This concludes our introduction to artificial neural networks and their implementation with Scikit-Learn. In the next chapter, we will switch to PyTorch, the leading open source library for neural networks, and we will use it to train and run MLPs much faster by exploiting the power of graphical processing units (GPUs). We will also start building more complex models, with multiple inputs and outputs.

18 Leslie N. Smith, "A Disciplined Approach to Neural Network Hyper-Parameters: Part 1—Learning Rate, Batch Size, Momentum, and Weight Decay", arXiv preprint arXiv:1803.09820 (2018).

Exercises

1. This neural network playground (*https://playground.tensorflow.org*) is a great tool to build your intuitions without writing any code (it was built by the TensorFlow team, but there's nothing TensorFlow-specific about it; in fact, it doesn't even use TensorFlow). In this exercise, you will train several binary classifiers in just a few clicks, and tweak the model's architecture and its hyperparameters to gain some intuition on how neural networks work and what their hyperparameters do. Take some time to explore the following:

   a. The patterns learned by a neural net. Try training the default neural network by clicking the Run button (top left). Notice how it quickly finds a good solution for the classification task. The neurons in the first hidden layer have learned simple patterns, while the neurons in the second hidden layer have learned to combine the simple patterns of the first hidden layer into more complex patterns. In general, the more layers there are, the more complex the patterns can be.

   b. Activation functions. Try replacing the tanh activation function with a ReLU activation function, and train the network again. Notice that it finds a solution even faster, but this time the boundaries are linear. This is due to the shape of the ReLU function.

   c. The risk of local minima. Modify the network architecture to have just one hidden layer with three neurons. Train it multiple times (to reset the network weights, click the Reset button next to the Play button). Notice that the training time varies a lot, and sometimes it even gets stuck in a local minimum.

   d. What happens when neural nets are too small. Remove one neuron to keep just two. Notice that the neural network is now incapable of finding a good solution, even if you try multiple times. The model has too few parameters and systematically underfits the training set.

   e. What happens when neural nets are large enough. Set the number of neurons to eight, and train the network several times. Notice that it is now consistently fast and never gets stuck. This highlights an important finding in neural network theory: large neural networks rarely get stuck in local minima, and even when they do, these local optima are often almost as good as the global optimum. However, they can still get stuck on long plateaus for a long time.

   f. The risk of vanishing gradients in deep networks. Select the spiral dataset (the bottom-right dataset under "DATA"), and change the network architecture to have four hidden layers with eight neurons each. Notice that training takes much longer and often gets stuck on plateaus for long periods of time. Also notice that the neurons in the highest layers (on the right) tend to evolve faster than the neurons in the lowest layers (on the left). This problem, called the *vanishing gradients* problem, can be alleviated with better weight initialization and other techniques, better optimizers (such as AdaGrad or Adam), or batch normalization (discussed in Chapter 11).

g. Go further. Take an hour or so to play around with other parameters and get a feel for what they do to build an intuitive understanding about neural networks.

2. Draw an ANN using the original artificial neurons (like the ones in Figure 9-3) that computes $A \oplus B$ (where $\oplus$ represents the XOR operation). Hint: $A \oplus B = (A \wedge \neg B) \vee (\neg A \wedge B)$.

3. Why is it generally preferable to use a logistic regression classifier rather than a classic perceptron (i.e., a single layer of threshold logic units trained using the perceptron training algorithm)? How can you tweak a perceptron to make it equivalent to a logistic regression classifier?

4. Why was the sigmoid activation function a key ingredient in training the first MLPs?

5. Name three popular activation functions. Can you draw them?

6. Suppose you have an MLP composed of one input layer with 10 passthrough neurons, followed by one hidden layer with 50 artificial neurons, and finally one output layer with 3 artificial neurons. All artificial neurons use the ReLU activation function.

   a. What is the shape of the input matrix $\mathbf{X}$?

   b. What are the shapes of the hidden layer's weight matrix $\mathbf{W}_h$ and bias vector $\mathbf{b}_h$?

   c. What are the shapes of the output layer's weight matrix $\mathbf{W}_o$ and bias vector $\mathbf{b}_o$?

   d. What is the shape of the network's output matrix $\mathbf{Y}$?

   e. Write the equation that computes the network's output matrix $\mathbf{Y}$ as a function of $\mathbf{X}$, $\mathbf{W}_h$, $\mathbf{b}_h$, $\mathbf{W}_o$, and $\mathbf{b}_o$.

7. How many neurons do you need in the output layer if you want to classify email into spam or ham? What activation function should you use in the output layer? If instead you want to tackle MNIST, how many neurons do you need in the output layer, and which activation function should you use? What about for getting your network to predict housing prices, as in Chapter 2?

8. What is backpropagation and how does it work? What is the difference between backpropagation and reverse-mode autodiff?

9. Can you list all the hyperparameters you can tweak in a basic MLP? If the MLP overfits the training data, how could you tweak these hyperparameters to try to solve the problem?

10. Train a deep MLP on the CoverType dataset. You can load it using `sklearn.datasets.fetch_covtype()`. See if you can get over 93% accuracy on the test set by fine-tuning the hyperparameters manually and/or using `RandomizedSearchCV`.

Solutions to these exercises are available at the end of this chapter's notebook, at *https://homl.info/colab-p*.

CHAPTER 10

Building Neural Networks with PyTorch

PyTorch is a powerful open source deep learning library developed by Facebook's AI Research lab (FAIR, now called Meta AI). It is the Python successor of the Torch library, originally written in the Lua programming language. With PyTorch, you can build all sorts of neural network models and train them at scale using GPUs (or other hardware accelerators, as we will see). In many ways it is similar to NumPy, except it also supports hardware acceleration and autodiff (see Chapter 9), and includes optimizers and ready-to-use neural net components.

When PyTorch was released in 2016, Google's TensorFlow library was by far the most popular: it was fast, it scaled well, and it could be deployed across many platforms. But its programming model was complex and static, making it difficult to use and debug. In contrast, PyTorch was designed from the ground up to provide a more flexible, Pythonic approach to building neural networks. In particular, as you will see, it uses dynamic computation graphs (also known as define-by-run), making it intuitive and easy to debug. PyTorch is also beautifully coded and documented, and focuses on its core task: making it easy to build and train high-performance neural networks. Last but not least, it leans strongly into the open source culture and benefits from an enthusiastic and dedicated community, and a rich ecosystem. In September 2022, PyTorch's governance was even transferred to the PyTorch Foundation, a subsidiary of the Linux Foundation. All these qualities resonated well with researchers: PyTorch quickly became the most used framework in academia, and once a majority of deep learning papers were based on PyTorch, a large part of the industry was gradually converted as well.[1]

1 To be fair, most of TensorFlow's usability issues were fixed in version 2, and Google also launched JAX, which is well designed and extremely fast, so PyTorch still has some healthy competition. The good news is that the APIs of all these libraries have converged quite a bit, so switching from one to the other is much easier than it used to be.

In this chapter, you will learn how to train, evaluate, fine-tune, optimize, and save neural nets with PyTorch. We will start by getting familiar with the core building blocks of PyTorch, namely tensors and autograd, next we will test the waters by building and training a simple linear regression model, and then we will upgrade this model to a multilayer neural network, first for regression, then for classification. Along the way, we will see how to build custom neural networks with multiple inputs or outputs. Finally, we will discuss how to automatically fine-tune hyperparameters using the Optuna library, and how to optimize and export your models. Hop on board, we're diving into deep learning!

Colab runtimes come with a recent version of PyTorch preinstalled. However, if you prefer to install it on your own machine, please see the installation instructions at *https://homl.info/install-p*: this involves installing Python, many libraries, and a GPU driver (if you have one).

PyTorch Fundamentals

The core data structure of PyTorch is the *tensor*.[2] It's a multidimensional array with a shape and a data type, used for numerical computations. Isn't that exactly like a NumPy array? Well, yes, it is! But a tensor also has two extra features: it can live on a GPU (or other hardware accelerators, as we will see), and it supports auto-differentiation. Every neural network we will build from now on will input and output tensors (much like Scikit-Learn models input and output NumPy arrays). So let's start by looking at how to create and manipulate tensors.

PyTorch Tensors

First, let's import the PyTorch library:

```
>>> import torch
```

Next you can create a PyTorch tensor much like you would create a NumPy array. For example, let's create a 2 × 3 array:

```
>>> X = torch.tensor([[1.0, 4.0, 7.0], [2.0, 3.0, 6.0]])
>>> X
tensor([[1., 4., 7.],
        [2., 3., 6.]])
```

2 There are things called tensors in mathematics and physics, but ML tensors are simpler: they're really just multidimensional arrays for numerical computations, plus a few extra features.

Just like a NumPy array, a tensor can contain floats, integers, booleans, or complex numbers—just one data type per tensor. If you initialize a tensor with values of different types, then the most general one will be selected (i.e., complex > float > integer > bool). You can also select the data type explicitly when creating the tensor, for example `dtype=torch.float16` for 16-bit floats. Note that tensors of strings or objects are not supported.

You can get a tensor's shape and data type like this:

```
>>> X.shape
torch.Size([2, 3])
>>> X.dtype
torch.float32
```

Indexing works just like for NumPy arrays:

```
>>> X[0, 1]
tensor(4.)
>>> X[:, 1]
tensor([4., 3.])
```

You can also run all sorts of computations on tensors, and the API is conveniently similar to NumPy's: for example, there's `torch.abs()`, `torch.cos()`, `torch.exp()`, `torch.max()`, `torch.mean()`, `torch.sqrt()`, and so on. PyTorch tensors also have methods for most of these operations, so you can write `X.exp()` instead of `torch.exp(X)`. Let's try a few operations:

```
>>> 10 * (X + 1.0)  # itemwise addition and multiplication
tensor([[20., 50., 80.],
        [30., 40., 70.]])
>>> X.exp()  # itemwise exponential
tensor([[   2.7183,   54.5981, 1096.6332],
        [   7.3891,   20.0855,  403.4288]])
>>> X.mean()
tensor(3.8333)
>>> X.max(dim=0)  # max values along dimension 0 (i.e., max value per column)
torch.return_types.max(values=tensor([2., 4., 7.]), indices=tensor([1, 0, 0]))
>>> X @ X.T  # matrix transpose and matrix multiplication
tensor([[66., 56.],
        [56., 49.]])
```

PyTorch prefers the argument name `dim` in operations such as `max()`, but it also supports `axis` (as in NumPy or Pandas).

You can also convert a tensor to a NumPy array using the `numpy()` method, and create a tensor from a NumPy array:

```
>>> import numpy as np
>>> X.numpy()
array([[1., 4., 7.],
       [2., 3., 6.]], dtype=float32)
>>> torch.tensor(np.array([[1., 4., 7.], [2., 3., 6.]]))
tensor([[1., 4., 7.],
        [2., 3., 6.]], dtype=torch.float64)
```

Notice that the default precision for floats is 32 bits in PyTorch, whereas it's 64 bits in NumPy. It's generally better to use 32 bits in deep learning because this takes half the RAM and speeds up computations, and neural nets do not actually need the extra precision offered by 64-bit floats. So when calling the `torch.tensor()` function to convert a NumPy array to a tensor, it's best to specify `dtype=torch.float32`. Alternatively, you can use `torch.FloatTensor()` which automatically converts the array to 32 bits:

```
>>> torch.FloatTensor(np.array([[1., 4., 7.], [2., 3., 6]]))
tensor([[1., 4., 7.],
        [2., 3., 6.]])
```

Both `torch.tensor()` and `torch.FloatTensor()` make a copy of the given NumPy array. If you prefer, you can use `torch.from_numpy()` which creates a tensor on the CPU that just uses the NumPy array's data directly, without copying it. But beware: modifying the NumPy array will also modify the tensor, and vice versa.

You can also modify a tensor in place using indexing and slicing, as with a NumPy array:

```
>>> X[:, 1] = -99
>>> X
tensor([[  1., -99.,   7.],
        [  2., -99.,   6.]])
```

PyTorch's API provides many in-place operations, such as `abs_()`, `sqrt_()`, and `zero_()`, which modify the input tensor directly: they can sometimes save some memory and speed up your models. For example, the `relu_()` method applies the ReLU activation function in place by replacing all negative values with 0s:

```
>>> X.relu_()
>>> X
tensor([[1., 0., 7.],
        [2., 0., 6.]])
```

PyTorch's in-place operations are easy to spot at a glance because their name always ends with an underscore. With very few exceptions (e.g., `zero_()`), removing the underscore gives you the regular operation (e.g., `abs_()` is in place, `abs()` is not).

We will cover many more operations as we go, but now let's look at how to use hardware acceleration to make computations much faster.

Hardware Acceleration

PyTorch tensors can be copied easily to the GPU, assuming your machine has a compatible GPU, and you have the required libraries installed. On Colab, all you need to do is ensure that you are using a GPU runtime: for this, go to the Runtime menu and select "Change runtime type", then make sure a GPU is selected (e.g., an Nvidia T4 GPU). The GPU runtime will automatically have the appropriate PyTorch library installed—compiled with GPU support—as well as the appropriate GPU drivers and related libraries (e.g., Nvidia's CUDA and cuDNN libraries).[3] If you prefer to run the code on your own machine, you will need to ensure that you have all the drivers and libraries required. Please follow the instructions at *https://homl.info/install-p*.

PyTorch has excellent support for Nvidia GPUs, as well as several other hardware accelerators:

- Apple's *Metal Performance Shaders* (MPS) to accelerate computations on Apple silicon such as the M1, M2, and later chips, as well as some Intel Macs with a compatible GPU.
- AMD Instinct accelerators and AMD Radeon GPUs, through the ROCm software stack, or via DirectML on Windows.
- Intel GPUs and CPUs on Linux and Windows via Intel's oneAPI.
- Google TPUs via the `torch_xla` library.

Let's check whether PyTorch can access an Nvidia GPU or Apple's MPS, otherwise let's fall back to the CPU:

```
if torch.cuda.is_available():
    device = "cuda"
elif torch.backends.mps.is_available():
    device = "mps"
else:
    device = "cpu"
```

3 CUDA is Nvidia's proprietary platform to run code on its CUDA-compatible GPUs, and cuDNN is a library built on CUDA to accelerate various deep neural network architectures.

Deep learning generally requires a *lot* of compute power, especially once we start diving into computer vision and natural language processing, in the following chapters. You will need a reasonably powerful machine, but most importantly you will need a hardware accelerator (or several). If you don't have one, you can try using Colab or Kaggle; they offer runtimes with free GPUs. Or consider using other cloud services. Otherwise, prepare to be very, very patient.

On a Colab GPU runtime, `device` will be equal to `"cuda"`. Now let's create a tensor on that GPU. To do that, one option is to create the tensor on the CPU, then copy it to the GPU using the `to()` method:

```
>>> M = torch.tensor([[1., 2., 3.], [4., 5., 6.]])
>>> M = M.to(device)
```

The `cpu()` and `cuda()` methods are short for `to("cpu")` and `to("cuda")`, respectively.

You can always tell which device a tensor lives on by looking at its `device` attribute:

```
>>> M.device
device(type='cuda', index=0)
----
```

Alternatively, we can create the tensor directly on the GPU using the `device` argument:

```
>>> M = torch.tensor([[1., 2., 3.], [4., 5., 6.]], device=device)
```

If you have multiple Nvidia GPUs, you can refer to the desired GPU by appending the GPU index: `"cuda:0"` (or just `"cuda"`) for GPU #0, `"cuda:1"` for GPU #1, and so on.

Once the tensor is on the GPU, we can run operations on it normally, and they will all take place on the GPU:

```
>>> R = M @ M.T  # run some operations on the GPU
>>> R
tensor([[14., 32.],
        [32., 77.]], device='cuda:0')
```

Note that the result R also lives on the GPU. This means we can perform multiple operations on the GPU without having to transfer data back and forth between the CPU and the GPU. This is crucial in deep learning because data transfer between devices can often become a performance bottleneck.

How much does a GPU accelerate the computations? Well it depends on the GPU, of course: the more expensive ones are dozens of times faster than the cheap ones. But speed alone is not the only important factor: the data throughput is also crucial, as we just saw. If your model is compute heavy (e.g., a very deep neural net), the GPU's speed and amount of RAM will typically matter most, but if it is a shallower model, then pumping the training data into the GPU might become the bottleneck. Let's run a little test to compare the speed of a matrix multiplication running on the CPU versus the GPU:[4]

```
>>> M = torch.rand((1000, 1000))  # on the CPU
>>> %timeit M @ M.T
16.1 ms ± 2.17 ms per loop (mean ± std. dev. of 7 runs, 100 loops each)
>>> M = torch.rand((1000, 1000), device="cuda")  # on the GPU
>>> %timeit M @ M.T
549 µs ± 3.99 µs per loop (mean ± std. dev. of 7 runs, 1000 loops each)
```

Wow! The GPU gave us a 29× speed boost! And that's just using the free Nvidia T4 GPU on Colab; imagine the speedup we could get using a more powerful GPU. Now try playing around with the matrix size: you will notice that the speedup is much less impressive on smaller matrices (e.g., it's just 2× for 100 × 100 matrices). That's because GPUs work by breaking large operations into smaller operations and running them in parallel across thousands of cores. If the task is small, it cannot be broken up into that many pieces, and the performance gain is therefore smaller. In fact, when running many tiny tasks, it can sometimes be faster to just run the operations on the CPU.

All right, now that we've seen what tensors are and how to use them on the CPU or the GPU, let's look at PyTorch's auto-differentiation feature.

Autograd

PyTorch comes with an efficient implementation of reverse-mode auto-differentiation (introduced in Chapter 9 and detailed in Appendix A), called *autograd*, which stands for automatic gradients. It is quite easy to use. For example, consider a simple function, $f(x) = x^2$. Differential calculus tells us that the derivative of this function is $f'(x) = 2x$. If we evaluate f(5) and f'(5), we get 25 and 10, respectively. Let's see if PyTorch agrees:

4 The `%timeit` magic command only works in Jupyter notebooks and Colab, as well as in the iPython shell; in a regular Python shell or program, you can use the `timeit.timeit()` function instead.

```
>>> x = torch.tensor(5.0, requires_grad=True)
>>> f = x ** 2
>>> f
tensor(25., grad_fn=<PowBackward0>)
>>> f.backward()
>>> x.grad
tensor(10.)
```

Great, we got the correct results: `f` is 25, and `x.grad` is 10! Note that the `backward()` function automatically computed the gradient f'(x) at the same point $x = 5.0$. Let's go through this code line by line:

- First, we created a tensor `x`, equal to 5.0, and we told PyTorch that it's a variable (not a constant) by specifying `requires_grad=True`. Knowing this, PyTorch will automatically keep track of all operations involving `x`: this is needed because PyTorch must capture the computation graph in order to run backprop on it and obtain the derivative of `f` with regard to `x`. In this computation graph, the tensor `x` is a *leaf node*.
- Then we compute `f = x ** 2`. The result is a tensor equal to 25.0, the square of 5.0. But wait, there's more to it: `f` also carries a `grad_fn` attribute which represents the operation that created this tensor (`**`, power, hence the name `PowBackward0`), and which tells PyTorch how to backpropagate the gradients through this particular operation. This `grad_fn` attribute is how PyTorch keeps track of the computation graph.
- Next, we call `f.backward()`: this backpropagates the gradients through the computation graph, starting with `f`, and all the way back to the leaf nodes (just `x` in this case).
- Lastly, we can just read the `x` tensor's `grad` attribute, which was computed during backprop: this gives us the derivative of `f` with regard to `x`. Ta-da!

PyTorch creates a new computation graph on the fly during each forward pass, as the operations are executed. This allows PyTorch to support very dynamic models containing loops and conditionals.

The way PyTorch accumulates gradients in each variable's `grad` attribute can be surprising at first, especially coming from TensorFlow or JAX. In these frameworks, computing the gradients of `f` with regard to `x` just returns the gradients, without affecting `x`. In PyTorch, if you call `backward()` on a tensor, it will accumulate the gradients in every variable that was used to compute it. So if you call `backward()` on two tensors `t1` and `t2` that both used the same variable `v`, then `v.grad` will be the sum of their gradients.

After computing the gradients, you generally want to perform a gradient descent step by subtracting a fraction of the gradients from the model variables (at least when training a neural network). In our simple example, running gradient descent will gradually push x toward 0, since that's the value that minimizes f(x) = x^2. To do a gradient descent step, you must temporarily disable gradient tracking since you don't want to track the gradient descent step itself in the computation graph (in fact, PyTorch would raise an exception if you tried to run an in-place operation on a tracked variable). This can be done by placing the gradient descent step inside a `torch.no_grad()` context, like this:

```
learning_rate = 0.1
with torch.no_grad():
    x -= learning_rate * x.grad  # gradient descent step
```

The variable x gets decremented by 0.1 * 10.0 = 1.0, down from 5.0 to 4.0.

Another way to avoid gradient computation is to use the variable's `detach()` method: this creates a new tensor detached from the computation graph, with `requires_grad=False`, but still pointing to the same data in memory. You can then update this detached tensor:

```
x_detached = x.detach()
x_detached -= learning_rate * x.grad
```

Since `x_detached` and `x` share the same memory, modifying `x_detached` also modifies `x`.

The `detach()` method can be handy when you need to run some computation on a tensor without affecting the gradients (e.g., for evaluation or logging), or when you need fine-grained control over which operations should contribute to gradient computation. Using `no_grad()` is generally preferred when performing inference or doing a gradient descent step, as it provides a convenient context-wide method to disable gradient tracking.

Lastly, before you repeat the whole process (forward pass + backward pass + gradient descent step), it's essential to zero out the gradients of every model parameter (you don't need a `no_grad()` context for this since the gradient tensor has `requires_grad=False`):

```
x.grad.zero_()
```

If you forget to zero out the gradients at each training iteration, the `backward()` method will just accumulate them, causing incorrect gradient descent updates. Since there won't be any explicit error, just low performance (and perhaps infinite or NaN values), this issue may be hard to debug.

Putting everything together, the whole training loop looks like this:

```
learning_rate = 0.1
x = torch.tensor(5.0, requires_grad=True)
for iteration in range(100):
    f = x ** 2  # forward pass
    f.backward()  # backward pass
    with torch.no_grad():
        x -= learning_rate * x.grad  # gradient descent step

    x.grad.zero_()  # reset the gradients
```

If you want to use in-place operations to save memory and speed up your models a bit by avoiding unnecessary copy operations, you have to be careful: in-place operations don't always play nicely with autograd. Firstly, as we saw earlier, you cannot apply an in-place operation to a leaf node (i.e., a tensor with `requires_grad=True`), as PyTorch wouldn't know where to store the computation graph. For example `x.cos_()` or `x += 1` would cause a `RuntimeError`. Secondly, consider the following code, which computes $z(t) = \exp(t) + 1$ at $t = 2$ and then tries to compute the gradients:

```
t = torch.tensor(2.0, requires_grad=True)
z = t.exp()  # this is an intermediate result
z += 1  # this is an in-place operation
z.backward()  # ⚠ RuntimeError!
```

Oh no! Although `z` is computed correctly, the last line causes a `RuntimeError`, complaining that "one of the variables needed for gradient computation has been modified by an in-place operation". Indeed, the intermediate result `z = t.exp()` was lost when we ran the in-place operation `z += 1`, so when the backward pass reached the exponential operation, the gradients could not be computed. A simple fix is to replace `z += 1` with `z = z + 1`. It looks similar, but it's no longer an in-place operation: a new tensor is created and assigned to the same variable, but the original tensor is unchanged and recorded in the computation graph of the final tensor.

Surprisingly, if you replace `exp()` with `cos()` in the previous code example, the gradients will be computed correctly: no error! Why is that? Well, the outcome depends on the way each operation is implemented:

- Some operations—such as `exp()`, `relu()`, `rsqrt()`, `sigmoid()`, `sqrt()`, `tan()`, and `tanh()`—save their outputs in the computation graph during the forward pass, then use these outputs to compute the gradients during the backward pass.[5]

5 For example, since the derivative of $\exp(x)$ is equal to $\exp(x)$, it makes a lot of sense to store the output of this operation in the computation graph during the forward pass, then use this output during the backward pass to get the gradients: no need to store additional data, and no need to recompute $\exp(x)$.

This means that you must not modify such an operation's output in place, or you will get an error during the backward pass (as we just saw).

- Other operations—such as `abs()`, `cos()`, `log()`, `sin()`, `square()`, and `var()`—save their inputs instead of their output.[6] Such an operation doesn't care if you modify its output in place, but you must not modify its inputs in place before the backward pass (e.g., to compute something else based on the same inputs).
- Some operations—such as `max()`, `min()`, `norm()`, `prod()`, `sgn()`, and `std()`—save both the inputs and the outputs, so you must not modify either of them in place before the backward pass.
- Lastly, a few operations—such as `ceil()`, `floor()`, `mean()`, `round()`, and `sum()`—save neither their inputs nor their outputs.[7] You can safely modify them in place.

Implement your models first without any in-place operations, then if you need to save some memory or speed up your model a bit, you can try converting some of the most costly operations to their in-place counterparts. Just make sure that your model still outputs the same result for a given input, and also make sure you don't modify in place a tensor needed for backprop (you will get a `RuntimeError` in this case).

OK, let's step back a bit. We've discussed all the fundamentals of PyTorch: how to create tensors and use them to perform all sorts of computations, how to accelerate the computations with a GPU, and how to use autograd to compute gradients for gradient descent. Great! Now let's apply what we've learned so far by building and training a simple linear regression model with PyTorch.

Implementing Linear Regression

We will start by implementing linear regression using tensors and autograd directly, then we will simplify the code using PyTorch's high-level API, and also add GPU support.

---

6 For example, the derivative of abs(x) is –1 when $x < 0$ and +1 when $x > 0$. If this operation saved its output in the computation graph, the backward pass would be unable to know whether x was positive or negative (since abs(x) is always positive), so it wouldn't be able to compute the gradients. This is why this operation must save its input instead.

7 For example, the derivative of floor(x) is always zero (at least for noninteger inputs), so the `floor()` operation just saves the shape of the inputs during the forward pass, then during the backward pass it produces gradients of the same shape but full of zeros. For integer inputs, autograd also returns zeros instead of NaN.

Linear Regression Using Tensors and Autograd

Let's tackle the same California housing dataset as in Chapter 9. I will assume you have already downloaded it using sklearn.datasets.fetch_california_housing(), and you have split it into a training set (X_train and y_train), a validation set (X_valid and y_valid), and a test set (X_test and y_test), using sklearn.model_selection.train_test_split(). Next, let's convert it to tensors and normalize it. We could use a StandardScaler for this, like we did in Chapter 9, but let's just use tensor operations instead, to get a bit of practice:

```
X_train = torch.FloatTensor(X_train)
X_valid = torch.FloatTensor(X_valid)
X_test = torch.FloatTensor(X_test)
means = X_train.mean(dim=0, keepdims=True)
stds = X_train.std(dim=0, keepdims=True)
X_train = (X_train - means) / stds
X_valid = (X_valid - means) / stds
X_test = (X_test - means) / stds
```

Let's also convert the targets to tensors. Since our predictions will be column vectors (i.e., matrices with a single column), we need to ensure that our targets are also column vectors.[8] Unfortunately, the NumPy arrays representing the targets are one-dimensional, so we need to reshape the tensors to column vectors by adding a second dimension of size 1:[9]

```
y_train = torch.FloatTensor(y_train).reshape(-1, 1)
y_valid = torch.FloatTensor(y_valid).reshape(-1, 1)
y_test = torch.FloatTensor(y_test).reshape(-1, 1)
```

Now that the data is ready, let's create the parameters of our linear regression model:

```
torch.manual_seed(42)
n_features = X_train.shape[1]  # there are 8 input features
w = torch.randn((n_features, 1), requires_grad=True)
b = torch.tensor(0., requires_grad=True)
```

We now have a weights parameter w (a column vector with one weight per input dimension, in this case 8), and a bias parameter b (a single scalar). The weights are initialized randomly, while the bias is initialized to zero. We could have initialized the weights to zero as well in this case, but when we get to neural networks it will be important to initialize the weights randomly to break the symmetry between neurons (as explained in Chapter 9), so we might as well get into the habit now.

8 Column vectors (shape [*m*, 1]) and row vectors (shape [1, *m*]) are often preferred over 1D vectors (shape [*m*]) in machine learning, as they avoid ambiguity in some operations, such as matrix multiplication or broadcasting, and they make the code more consistent whether there's just one feature or more.

9 Just like in NumPy, the reshape() method allows you to specify –1 for one of the dimensions. This dimension's size is automatically calculated to ensure the new tensor has the same number of cells as the original.

We called `torch.manual_seed()` to ensure that the results are reproducible. However, PyTorch does not guarantee perfectly reproducible results across different releases, platforms, or devices, so if you do not run the code in this chapter with PyTorch 2.8.0 on a Colab runtime with an Nvidia T4 GPU, you may get different results. Moreover, since a GPU splits each operation into multiple chunks and runs them in parallel, the order in which these chunks finish may vary across runs, and this may slightly affect the result due to floating-point precision errors. These minor differences may compound during training, and lead to very different models. To avoid this, you can tell PyTorch to use only deterministic algorithms by calling `torch.use_deterministic_algorithms(True)` and setting `torch.backends.cudnn.benchmark = False`. However, deterministic algorithms are often slower than stochastic ones, and some operations don't have a deterministic version at all, so you will get an error if your code tries to use one.

Next, let's train our model, very much like we did in Chapter 4, except we will use autodiff to compute the gradients rather than using a closed-form equation. For now we will use batch gradient descent (BGD), using the full training set at each training step:

```
learning_rate = 0.4
n_epochs = 20
for epoch in range(n_epochs):
    y_pred = X_train @ w + b
    loss = ((y_pred - y_train) ** 2).mean()
    loss.backward()
    with torch.no_grad():
        b -= learning_rate * b.grad
        w -= learning_rate * w.grad
        b.grad.zero_()
        w.grad.zero_()
    print(f"Epoch {epoch + 1}/{n_epochs}, Loss: {loss.item()}")
```

Let's walk through this code:

- First we define the `learning_rate` hyperparameter. You can experiment with different values to find a value that converges fast and gives a precise result.
- Next, we run 20 epochs. We could implement early stopping to find the right moment to stop and avoid overfitting, like we did in Chapter 4, but we will keep things simple for now.
- Next, we run the forward pass: we compute the predictions `y_pred`, and the mean squared error `loss`.
- Then we run `loss.backward()` to compute the gradients of the loss with regard to every model parameter. This is autograd in action.

- Next, we use the gradients b.grad and w.grad to perform a gradient descent step. Notice that we're running this code inside a with torch.no_grad() context, as discussed earlier.
- Once we've done the gradient descent step, we reset the gradients to zero (very important!).
- Lastly, we print the epoch number and the current loss at each epoch. The item() method extracts the value of a scalar tensor.

And that's it; if you run this code, you should see the training loss going down like this:

```
Epoch 1/20, Loss: 16.158456802368164
Epoch 2/20, Loss: 4.8793745040893555
Epoch 3/20, Loss: 2.255225419998169
[...]
Epoch 20/20, Loss: 0.5684100389480591
```

Congratulations, you just trained your first model using PyTorch! You can now use the model to make predictions for some new data X_new (which must be represented as a PyTorch tensor). For example, let's make predictions for the first three instances in the test set:

```
>>> X_new = X_test[:3]  # pretend these are new instances
>>> with torch.no_grad():
...     y_pred = X_new @ w + b  # use the trained parameters to make predictions
...
>>> y_pred
tensor([[0.8916],
        [1.6480],
        [2.6577]])
```

It's best to use a with torch.no_grad() context during inference: PyTorch will consume less RAM and run faster since it won't have to keep track of the computation graph.

Implementing linear regression using PyTorch's low-level API wasn't too hard, but using this approach for more complex models would get really messy and difficult. So PyTorch offers a higher-level API to simplify all this. Let's rewrite our model using this higher-level API.

Linear Regression Using PyTorch's High-Level API

PyTorch provides an implementation of linear regression in the torch.nn.Linear class, so let's use it:

```
import torch.nn as nn  # by convention, this module is usually imported this way

torch.manual_seed(42)  # to get reproducible results
model = nn.Linear(in_features=n_features, out_features=1)
```

The `nn.Linear` class (short for `torch.nn.Linear`) is one of many *modules* provided by PyTorch. Each module is a subclass of the `nn.Module` class. To build a simple linear regression model, a single `nn.Linear` module is all you need. However, for most neural networks you will need to assemble many modules, as we will see later in this chapter, so you can think of modules as math LEGO® bricks. Many modules contain model parameters. For example, the `nn.Linear` module contains a `bias` vector (with one bias term per neuron), and a `weight` matrix (with one row per neuron and one column per input dimension, which is the transpose of the weight matrix we used earlier and in Equation 9-2). Since our model has a single neuron (because `out_features=1`), the `bias` vector contains a single bias term, and the `weight` matrix contains a single row. These parameters are accessible directly as attributes of the `nn.Linear` module:

```
>>> model.bias
Parameter containing:
tensor([0.3117], requires_grad=True)
>>> model.weight
Parameter containing:
tensor([[ 0.2703, 0.2935, -0.0828, 0.3248, -0.0775, 0.0713, -0.1721, 0.2076]],
       requires_grad=True)
```

Notice that both parameters were automatically initialized randomly (which is why we used `manual_seed()` to get reproducible results). These parameters are instances of the `torch.nn.Parameter` class, which is a subclass of the `tensor.Tensor` class: this means that you can use them exactly like normal tensors. A module's `parameters()` method returns an iterator over all of the module's attributes of type `Parameter`, as well as all the parameters of all its submodules, recursively (if it has any). It does *not* return regular tensors, even those with `requires_grad=True`. That's the main difference between a regular tensor and a `Parameter`:

```
>>> for param in model.parameters():
...     [...]  # do something with each parameter
```

There's also a `named_parameters()` method that returns an iterator over pairs of parameter names and values.

A module can be called just like a regular function. For example, let's make some predictions for the first two instances in the training set (since the model is not trained yet, its parameters are random and the predictions are terrible):

```
>>> model(X_train[:2])
tensor([[-0.4718],
        [ 0.1131]], grad_fn=<AddmmBackward0>)
```

When we use a module as a function, PyTorch internally calls the module's `forward()` method. In the case of the `nn.Linear` module, the `forward()` method computes `X @ self.weight.T + self.bias` (where `X` is the input). That's just what we need for linear regression!

Notice that the result contains the `grad_fn` attribute, showing that autograd did its job and tracked the computation graph while the model was making its predictions.

If you pass a custom function to a module's `register_forward_hook()` method, it will be called automatically every time the module itself is called. This is particularly handy for logging or debugging. To remove a hook, just call the `remove()` method on the object returned by `register_forward_hook()`. Note that hooks only work if you call the model like a function, not if you call its `forward()` method directly (which is why you should never do that). You can also register functions to run during the backward pass using `register_backward_hook()`.

Now that we have our model, we need to create an optimizer to update the model parameters, and we must also choose a loss function:

```
optimizer = torch.optim.SGD(model.parameters(), lr=learning_rate)
mse = nn.MSELoss()
```

PyTorch provides a few different optimizers (we will discuss them in the next chapter). Here we're using the simple stochastic gradient descent (SGD) optimizer, which can be used for SGD, mini-batch GD, or batch gradient descent. To initialize it, we must give it the model parameters and the learning rate.

For the loss function, we create an instance of the `nn.MSELoss` class: this is also a module, so we can use it like a function, giving it the predictions and the targets, and it will compute the MSE. The `nn` module contains many other loss functions and other neural net tools, as we will see. Next, let's write a small function to train our model:

```
def train_bgd(model, optimizer, criterion, X_train, y_train, n_epochs):
    for epoch in range(n_epochs):
        y_pred = model(X_train)
        loss = criterion(y_pred, y_train)
        loss.backward()
        optimizer.step()
        optimizer.zero_grad()
        print(f"Epoch {epoch + 1}/{n_epochs}, Loss: {loss.item()}")
```

Compare this training loop with our earlier training loop: it's very similar, but we're now using higher-level constructs rather than working directly with tensors and autograd. Here are a few things to note:

- In PyTorch, the loss function object is commonly referred to as the *criterion*, to distinguish it from the loss value itself (which is computed at each training iteration using the criterion). In this example, it's the `MSELoss` instance.
- The `optimizer.step()` line corresponds to the two lines that updated `b` and `w` in our earlier code.
- And of course the `optimizer.zero_grad()` line corresponds to the two lines that zeroed out `b.grad` and `w.grad`. Notice that we don't need to use `with torch.no_grad()` here since this is done automatically by the optimizer, inside the `step()` and `zero_grad()` functions.

Most people prefer to call `zero_grad()` *before* calling `loss.backward()`, rather than after: this might be a bit safer in case the gradients are nonzero when calling the function, but in general it makes no difference since gradients are automatically initialized to `None`.

Now let's call this function to train our model!

```
>>> train_bgd(model, optimizer, mse, X_train, y_train, n_epochs)
Epoch 1/20, Loss: 4.3378496170043945
Epoch 2/20, Loss: 0.780293345451355
[...]
Epoch 20/20, Loss: 0.5374288558959961
```

All good; the model is trained, and you can now use it to make predictions by simply calling it like a function (preferably inside a `no_grad()` context, as we saw earlier):

```
>>> X_new = X_test[:3]  # pretend these are new instances
>>> with torch.no_grad():
...     y_pred = model(X_new)  # use the trained model to make predictions
...
>>> y_pred
tensor([[0.8061],
        [1.7116],
        [2.6973]])
```

These predictions are similar to the ones our previous model made, but not exactly the same. That's because the `nn.Linear` module initializes the parameters slightly differently: it uses a uniform random distribution from $-\frac{\sqrt{2}}{4}$ to $+\frac{\sqrt{2}}{4}$ for both the weights and the bias term (we will discuss initialization methods in Chapter 11).

Now that you are familiar with PyTorch's high-level API, you are ready to go beyond linear regression and build a multilayer perceptron (introduced in Chapter 9).

Implementing a Regression MLP

PyTorch provides a helpful `nn.Sequential` module that chains multiple modules: when you call this module with some inputs, it feeds these inputs to the first module, then feeds the output of the first module to the second module, and so on. Most neural networks contain stacks of modules, and in fact many neural networks are just one big stack of modules: this makes the `nn.Sequential` module one of the most useful modules in PyTorch. The MLP we want to build is just that: a simple stack of modules—two hidden layers and one output layer. So let's build it using the `nn.Sequential` module:

```
torch.manual_seed(42)
model = nn.Sequential(
    nn.Linear(n_features, 50),
    nn.ReLU(),
    nn.Linear(50, 40),
    nn.ReLU(),
    nn.Linear(40, 1)
)
```

Let's go through each layer:

- The first layer must have the right number of inputs for our data: `n_features` (equal to 8 in our case). However, it can have any number of outputs: let's pick 50 (that's a hyperparameter we can tune).
- Next we have an `nn.ReLU` module, which implements the ReLU activation function for the first hidden layer. This module does not contain any model parameters, and it acts itemwise so the shape of its output is equal to the shape of its input.
- The second hidden layer must have the same number of inputs as the output of the previous layer: in this case, 50. However, it can have any number of outputs. It's common to use the same number of output dimensions in all hidden layers, but in this example I used 40 to make it clear that the output of one layer must match the input of the next layer.
- Then again, an `nn.ReLU` module to implement the second hidden layer's activation function.
- Finally, the output layer must have 40 inputs, but this time its number of outputs is not free: it must match the targets' dimensionality. Since our targets have a single dimension, we must have just one output dimension in the output layer.

Now let's train the model just like we did before:

```
>>> learning_rate = 0.1
>>> optimizer = torch.optim.SGD(model.parameters(), lr=learning_rate)
>>> mse = nn.MSELoss()
```

```
>>> train_bgd(model, optimizer, mse, X_train, y_train, n_epochs)
Epoch 1/20, Loss: 5.045480251312256
Epoch 2/20, Loss: 2.0523128509521484
[...]
Epoch 20/20, Loss: 0.565444827079773
```

That's it, you can tell your friends you trained your first neural network with PyTorch! However, we are still using batch gradient descent, computing the gradients over the entire training set at each iteration. This works with small datasets, but if we want to be able to scale up to large datasets and large models, we need to switch to mini-batch gradient descent.

Implementing Mini-Batch Gradient Descent Using DataLoaders

To help implement mini-batch GD, PyTorch provides a class named `DataLoader` in the `torch.utils.data` module. It can efficiently load batches of data of the desired size, and shuffle the data at each epoch if we want it to. The `DataLoader` expects the dataset to be represented as an object with at least two methods: `__len__(self)` to get the number of samples in the dataset, and `__getitem__(self, index)` to load the sample at the given index (including the target).

In our case, the training set is available in the `X_train` and `y_train` tensors, so we first need to wrap these tensors in a dataset object with the required API. To help with this, PyTorch provides a `TensorDataset` class. So let's build a `TensorDataset` to wrap our training set, and a `DataLoader` to pull batches from this dataset. During training, we want the dataset to be shuffled, so we specify `shuffle=True`:

```
from torch.utils.data import TensorDataset, DataLoader

train_dataset = TensorDataset(X_train, y_train)
train_loader = DataLoader(train_dataset, batch_size=32, shuffle=True)
```

Now that we have a larger model and we have the tools to train it one batch at a time, it's a good time to start using hardware acceleration. It's really quite simple: we just need to move the model to the GPU, which will move all of its parameters to the GPU RAM, and then at the start of each iteration during training we must copy each batch to the GPU. To move the model, we can just use its `to()` method, just like we did with tensors:

```
torch.manual_seed(42)
model = nn.Sequential([...])  # create the model just like earlier
model = model.to(device)
```

We can also create the loss function and optimizer, as earlier (but using a lower learning rate, such as 0.02).

Some optimizers have some internal state, as we will see in Chapter 11. The optimizer will usually allocate its state on the same device as the model parameters, so it's important to create the optimizer *after* you have moved the model to the GPU.

Now let's create a `train()` function to implement mini-batch GD:

```
def train(model, optimizer, criterion, train_loader, n_epochs):
    model.train()
    for epoch in range(n_epochs):
        total_loss = 0.
        for X_batch, y_batch in train_loader:
            X_batch, y_batch = X_batch.to(device), y_batch.to(device)
            y_pred = model(X_batch)
            loss = criterion(y_pred, y_batch)
            total_loss += loss.item()
            loss.backward()
            optimizer.step()
            optimizer.zero_grad()

        mean_loss = total_loss / len(train_loader)
        print(f"Epoch {epoch + 1}/{n_epochs}, Loss: {mean_loss:.4f}")
```

At every epoch, the function iterates through the whole training set, one batch at a time, and processes each batch just like earlier. But what about the very first line: `model.train()`? Well, this switches the model and all of its submodules to *training mode*. For now, this makes no difference at all, but it will be important in Chapter 11 when we start using layers that behave differently during training and evaluation (e.g., `nn.Dropout` or `nn.BatchNorm1d`). Whenever you want to use the model outside of training (e.g., for evaluation, or to make predictions on new instances), you must first switch the model to *evaluation mode* by running `model.eval()`. Note that `model.training` holds a boolean that indicates the current mode.

PyTorch itself does not provide a training loop implementation; you have to build it yourself. As we just saw, it's not that long, and many people enjoy the freedom, clarity, and control this provides. However, if you would prefer to use a well-tested, off-the-shelf training loop with all the bells and whistles you need (such as multi-GPU support), then you can use a library such as PyTorch Lightning, FastAI, Catalyst, or Keras. These libraries are built on top of PyTorch and include a training loop and many other features (Keras supports PyTorch since version 3, and also supports TensorFlow and JAX). Check them out!

Now let's call this `train()` function to train our model on the GPU:

```
>>> train(model, optimizer, mse, train_loader, n_epochs)
Epoch 1/20, Loss: 0.6958
Epoch 2/20, Loss: 0.4480
[...]
Epoch 20/20, Loss: 0.3227
```

It worked great: we actually reached a much lower loss in the same number of epochs! However, you probably noticed that each epoch was much slower. There are two easy tweaks you can make to considerably speed up training:

- If you are using a CUDA device, you should generally set `pin_memory=True` when creating the data loader: this will allocate the data in *page-locked memory* which guarantees a fixed physical memory location in the CPU RAM, and therefore allows direct memory access (DMA) transfers to the GPU, eliminating an extra copy operation that would otherwise be needed. While this could use more CPU RAM since the memory cannot be swapped out to disk, it typically results in significantly faster data transfers and thus faster training. When transferring a tensor to the GPU using its `to()` method, you may also set `non_blocking=True` to avoid blocking the CPU during the data transfer (this only works if `pin_memory=True`).
- The current training loop waits until a batch has been fully processed before it loads the next batch. You can often speed up training by pre-fetching the next batches on the CPU while the GPU is still working on the current batch. For this, set the data loader's `num_workers` argument to the number of processes you want to use for data loading and preprocessing. The optimal number depends on your platform, hardware, and workload, so you should experiment with different values. You can also tweak the number of batches that each worker pre-fetches by setting the data loader's `prefetch_factor` argument. Note that the overhead of spawning and synchronizing workers can often slow down training rather than speed it up (especially on Windows). In this case, you can try setting `persistent_workers=True` to reuse the same workers across epochs.

OK, time to step back a bit: you know the PyTorch fundamentals (tensors and autograd), you can build neural nets using PyTorch's high-level API, and train them using mini-batch gradient descent, with the help of an optimizer, a criterion, and a data loader. The next step is to learn how to evaluate your model.

Model Evaluation

Let's write a function to evaluate the model. It takes the model and a `DataLoader` for the dataset that we want to evaluate the model on, as well as a function to compute the metric for a given batch, and lastly a function to aggregate the batch metrics (by default, it just computes the mean):

```python
def evaluate(model, data_loader, metric_fn, aggregate_fn=torch.mean):
    model.eval()
    metrics = []
    with torch.no_grad():
        for X_batch, y_batch in data_loader:
            X_batch, y_batch = X_batch.to(device), y_batch.to(device)
            y_pred = model(X_batch)
            metric = metric_fn(y_pred, y_batch)
            metrics.append(metric)
    return aggregate_fn(torch.stack(metrics))
```

Now let's build a `TensorDataset` and a `DataLoader` for our validation set, and pass it to our `evaluate()` function to compute the validation MSE:

```
>>> valid_dataset = TensorDataset(X_valid, y_valid)
>>> valid_loader = DataLoader(valid_dataset, batch_size=32)
>>> valid_mse = evaluate(model, valid_loader, mse)
>>> valid_mse
tensor(0.4080, device='cuda:0')
```

It works fine. But now suppose we want to use the RMSE instead of the MSE (as we saw in Chapter 2, it can be easier to interpret). PyTorch does not have a built-in function for that, but it's easy enough to write:

```
>>> def rmse(y_pred, y_true):
...     return ((y_pred - y_true) ** 2).mean().sqrt()
...
>>> evaluate(model, valid_loader, rmse)
tensor(0.5668, device='cuda:0')
```

But wait a second! The RMSE should be equal to the square root of the MSE; however, when we compute the square root of the MSE that we found earlier, we get a different result:

```
>>> valid_mse.sqrt()
tensor(0.6388, device='cuda:0')
```

The reason is that instead of calculating the RMSE over the whole validation set, we computed it over each batch and then computed the mean of all these batch RMSEs. That's not mathematically equivalent to computing the RMSE over the whole validation set. To solve this, we can use the MSE as our `metric_fn`, and use the `aggregate_fn` to compute the square root of the mean MSE:[10]

```
>>> evaluate(model, valid_loader, mse,
...          aggregate_fn=lambda metrics: torch.sqrt(torch.mean(metrics)))
...
tensor(0.6388, device='cuda:0')
```

10 The mean of the batch MSEs is equal to the overall MSE since all batches have the same size. Well, except the last batch, which is often smaller, but this makes very little difference.

That's much better!

Rather than implement metrics yourself, you may prefer to use the TorchMetrics library (made by the same team as PyTorch Lightning), which provides many well-tested *streaming metrics*. A streaming metric is an object that keeps track of a given metric, and can be updated one batch at a time. The TorchMetrics library is not preinstalled on Colab, so we have to run `%pip install torchmetrics`, then we can implement the `evaluate_tm()` function, like this:

```
import torchmetrics

def evaluate_tm(model, data_loader, metric):
    model.eval()
    metric.reset()  # reset the metric at the beginning
    with torch.no_grad():
        for X_batch, y_batch in data_loader:
            X_batch, y_batch = X_batch.to(device), y_batch.to(device)
            y_pred = model(X_batch)
            metric.update(y_pred, y_batch)  # update it at each iteration
    return metric.compute()  # compute the final result at the end
```

Then we can create an RMSE streaming metric, move it to the GPU, and use it to evaluate the validation set:

```
>>> rmse = torchmetrics.MeanSquaredError(squared=False).to(device)
>>> evaluate_tm(model, valid_loader, rmse)
tensor(0.6388, device='cuda:0')
```

Sure enough, we get the correct result! Now try updating the `train()` function to evaluate your model's performance during training, both on the training set (during each epoch) and on the validation set (at the end of each epoch). As always, if the performance on the training set is much better than on the validation set, your model is probably overfitting the training set, or there is a bug, such as a data mismatch between the training set and the validation set. This is easier to detect if you plot and analyze the learning curves, much like we did in Chapter 4. For this you can use Matplotlib, or a visualization tool such as TensorBoard (see the notebook for an example).

Now you know how to build, train, and evaluate a regression MLP using PyTorch, and how to use the trained model to make predictions. Great! But so far we have only looked at simple sequential models, composed of a sequence of linear layers and ReLU activation functions. How would you build a more complex, nonsequential model? For this, we will need to build custom modules.

Building Nonsequential Models Using Custom Modules

One example of a nonsequential neural network is a *Wide & Deep* neural network. This neural network architecture was introduced in a 2016 paper by Heng-Tze Cheng et al.[11] It connects all or part of the inputs directly to the output layer, as shown in Figure 10-1. This architecture makes it possible for the neural network to learn both deep patterns (using the deep path) and simple rules (through the short path). The short path can also be used to provide manually engineered features to the neural network. In contrast, a regular MLP forces all the data to flow through the full stack of layers; thus, simple patterns in the data may end up being distorted by this sequence of transformations.

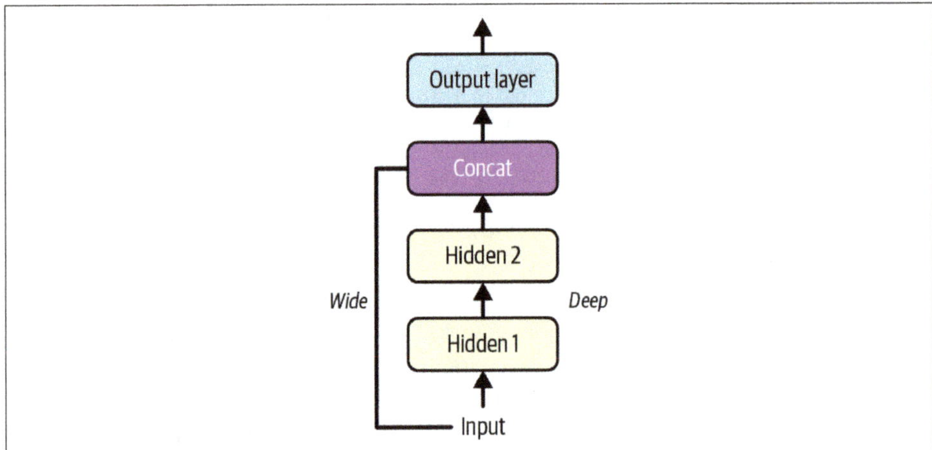

Figure 10-1. Wide & Deep neural network

Let's build such a neural network to tackle the California housing dataset. Because this wide and deep architecture is nonsequential, we have to create a custom module. It's easier than it sounds: just create a class derived from `torch.nn.Module`, then create all the layers you need in the constructor (after calling the base class's `__init__()` method), and define how these layers should be used by the module in the `forward()` method:

```
class WideAndDeep(nn.Module):
    def __init__(self, n_features):
        super().__init__()
        self.deep_stack = nn.Sequential(
            nn.Linear(n_features, 50), nn.ReLU(),
            nn.Linear(50, 40), nn.ReLU(),
```

11 Heng-Tze Cheng et al., "Wide & Deep Learning for Recommender Systems" (*https://homl.info/widedeep*), *Proceedings of the First Workshop on Deep Learning for Recommender Systems* (2016): 7–10.

```
        )
        self.output_layer = nn.Linear(40 + n_features, 1)

    def forward(self, X):
        deep_output = self.deep_stack(X)
        wide_and_deep = torch.concat([X, deep_output], dim=1)
        return self.output_layer(wide_and_deep)
```

Notice that we can use any kind of module inside our custom module: in this example, we use an `nn.Sequential` module to build the "deep" part of our model (it's actually not that deep; this is just a toy example). It's the same MLP as earlier, except we separated the output layer because we need to feed it the concatenation of the model's inputs and the deep part's outputs. For this same reason, the output layer now has 40 + `n_features` inputs instead of just 40.

In the `forward()` method, we just feed the input `X` to the deep stack, concatenate the input and the deep stack's output, and feed the result to the output layer.

Modules have a `children()` method that returns an iterator over the module's submodules (nonrecursively). There's also a `named_children()` method. If your model has a variable number of submodules, you should store them in an `nn.ModuleList` or an `nn.ModuleDict`, which are returned by the `children()` and `named_children()` methods (as opposed to regular Python lists and dicts). Similarly, if your model has a variable number of parameters, you should store them in an `nn.ParameterList` or an `nn.ParameterDict` to ensure they are returned by the `parameters()` and `named_parameters()` methods.

Now we can create an instance of our custom module, move it to the GPU, train it, evaluate it, and use it exactly like our previous models:

```
torch.manual_seed(42)
model = WideAndDeep(n_features).to(device)
learning_rate = 0.002  # the model changed, so did the optimal learning rate
[...]  # train, evaluate, and use the model, exactly like earlier
```

But what if you want to send a subset of the features through the wide path and a different subset (possibly overlapping) through the deep path, as illustrated in Figure 10-2? In this case, one approach is to split the inputs inside the `forward()` method, for example:

```
class WideAndDeepV2(nn.Module):
    [...]  # same constructor as earlier, except with adjusted input sizes

    def forward(self, X):
        X_wide = X[:, :5]
        X_deep = X[:, 2:]
```

```
        deep_output = self.deep_stack(X_deep)
        wide_and_deep = torch.concat([X_wide, deep_output], dim=1)
        return self.output_layer(wide_and_deep)
```

This works fine; however, in many cases it's preferable to just let the model take two separate tensors as input. Let's see why and how.

Building Models with Multiple Inputs

Some models require multiple inputs that cannot easily be combined into a single tensor. For example, the inputs may have a different number of dimensions (e.g., when you want to feed both images and text to the neural network). To make our Wide & Deep model take two separate inputs, as shown in Figure 10-2, we must start by changing the model's `forward()` method:

```
class WideAndDeepV3(nn.Module):
    [...]  # same as WideAndDeepV2

    def forward(self, X_wide, X_deep):
        deep_output = self.deep_stack(X_deep)
        wide_and_deep = torch.concat([X_wide, deep_output], dim=1)
        return self.output_layer(wide_and_deep)
```

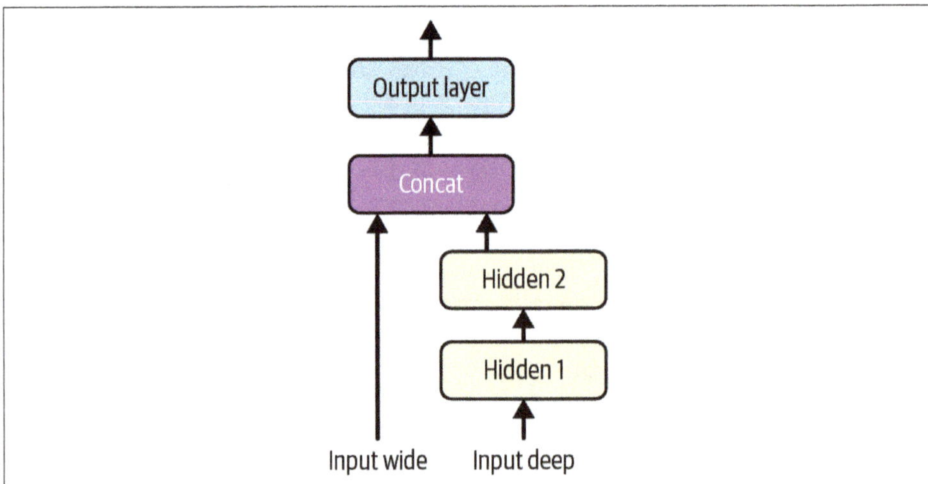

Figure 10-2. Handling multiple inputs

Next, we need to create datasets that return the wide and deep inputs separately:

```
train_data_wd = TensorDataset(X_train[:, :5], X_train[:, 2:], y_train)
train_loader_wd = DataLoader(train_data_wd, batch_size=32, shuffle=True)
[...]  # same for the validation set and test set
```

Since the data loaders now return three tensors instead of two at each iteration, we need to update the main loop in the evaluation and training functions:

```
for X_batch_wide, X_batch_deep, y_batch in data_loader:
    X_batch_wide = X_batch_wide.to(device)
    X_batch_deep = X_batch_deep.to(device)
    y_batch = y_batch.to(device)
    y_pred = model(X_batch_wide, X_batch_deep)
    [...]  # the rest of the function is unchanged
```

Alternatively, since the order of the inputs matches the order of the `forward()` method's arguments, we can use Python's `*` operator to unpack all the inputs returned by the `data_loader` and pass them to the model. The advantage of this implementation is that it will work with models that take any number of inputs, not just two, as long as the order is correct:

```
for *X_batch_inputs, y_batch in data_loader:
    X_batch_inputs = [X.to(device) for X in X_batch_inputs]
    y_batch = y_batch.to(device)
    y_pred = model(*X_batch_inputs)
    [...]
```

When your model has many inputs, it's easy to make a mistake and mix up the order of the inputs, which can lead to hard-to-debug issues. To avoid this, it can be a good idea to name each input. For this, you can define a custom dataset that returns a dictionary from input names to input values, like this:

```
class WideAndDeepDataset(torch.utils.data.Dataset):
    def __init__(self, X_wide, X_deep, y):
        self.X_wide = X_wide
        self.X_deep = X_deep
        self.y = y

    def __len__(self):
        return len(self.y)

    def __getitem__(self, idx):
        input_dict = {"X_wide": self.X_wide[idx], "X_deep": self.X_deep[idx]}
        return input_dict, self.y[idx]
```

Then create the datasets and data loaders:

```
train_data_named = WideAndDeepDataset(
    X_wide=X_train[:, :5], X_deep=X_train[:, 2:], y=y_train)
train_loader_named = DataLoader(train_data_named, batch_size=32, shuffle=True)
[...]  # same for the validation set and test set
```

Once again, we also need to update the main loop in the evaluation and training functions:

```
for inputs, y_batch in data_loader:
    inputs = {name: X.to(device) for name, X in inputs.items()}
    y_batch = y_batch.to(device)
    y_pred = model(X_wide=inputs["X_wide"], X_deep=inputs["X_deep"])
    [...]  # the rest of the function is unchanged
```

Alternatively, since all the input names match the `forward()` method's argument names, we can use Python's `**` operator to unpack all the tensors in the `inputs` dictionary and pass them as named arguments to the model: `y_pred = model(**inputs)`.

Now that you know how to build sequential and nonsequential models with one or more inputs, let's look at models with multiple outputs.

Building Models with Multiple Outputs

There are many use cases where you may need a neural net with multiple outputs:

- The task may demand it. For instance, you may want to locate and classify the main object in a picture. This is both a regression task and a classification task.
- Similarly, you may have multiple independent tasks based on the same data. Sure, you could train one neural network per task, but in many cases you will get better results on all tasks by training a single neural network with one output per task. This is because the neural network can learn features in the data that are useful across tasks. For example, you could perform *multitask classification* on pictures of faces, using one output to classify the person's facial expression (smiling, surprised, etc.) and another output to identify whether they are wearing glasses or not.
- Another use case is regularization (i.e., a training constraint whose objective is to reduce overfitting and thus improve the model's ability to generalize). For example, you may want to add an auxiliary output in a neural network architecture (see Figure 10-3) to ensure that the underlying part of the network learns something useful on its own, without relying on the rest of the network.

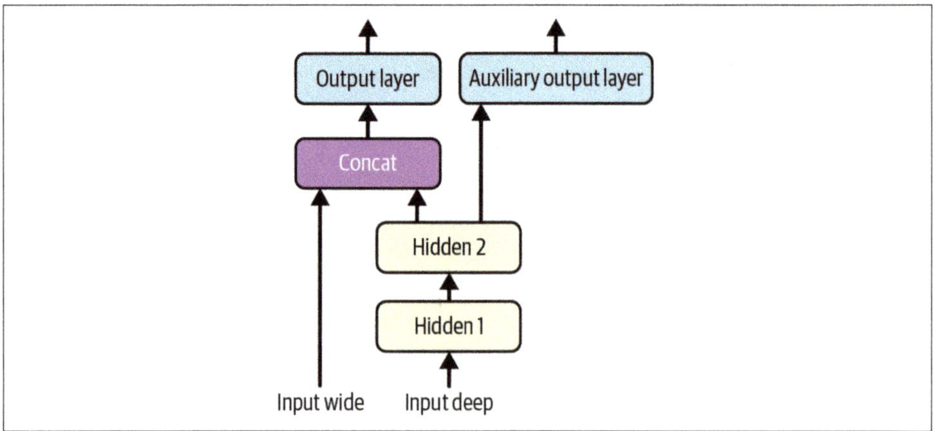

Figure 10-3. Handling multiple outputs, in this example to add an auxiliary output for regularization

Let's add an auxiliary output to our Wide & Deep model to ensure the deep part can make good predictions on its own. Since the deep stack's output dimension is 40, and the targets have a single dimension, we must add an `nn.Linear` layer for the auxiliary output to go from 40 dimensions down to 1. We also need to make the `forward()` method compute the auxiliary output, and return both the main output and the auxiliary output:

```
class WideAndDeepV4(nn.Module):
    def __init__(self, n_features):
        [...]  # same as earlier
        self.aux_output_layer = nn.Linear(40, 1)

    def forward(self, X_wide, X_deep):
        deep_output = self.deep_stack(X_deep)
        wide_and_deep = torch.concat([X_wide, deep_output], dim=1)
        main_output = self.output_layer(wide_and_deep)
        aux_output = self.aux_output_layer(deep_output)
        return main_output, aux_output
```

Next, we need to update the main loop in the training function:

```
for inputs, y_batch in train_loader:
    y_pred, y_pred_aux = model(**inputs)
    main_loss = criterion(y_pred, y_batch)
    aux_loss = criterion(y_pred_aux, y_batch)
    loss = 0.8 * main_loss + 0.2 * aux_loss
    [...]  # the rest is unchanged
```

Notice that the model now returns both the main predictions `y_pred` and the auxiliary predictions `y_pred_aux`. In this example, we can use the same targets and the same loss function to compute the main output's loss and the auxiliary output's loss. In other cases, you may have different targets and loss functions for each output, in which case you would need to create a custom dataset to return all the necessary targets. Once we have a loss for each output, we must combine them into a single loss that will be minimized by gradient descent. In general, this final loss is just a weighted sum of all the output losses. In this example, we use a higher weight for the main loss (0.8), because that's what we care about the most, and a lower weight for the auxiliary loss (0.2). This ratio is a regularization hyperparameter that you can tune.

We also need to update the main loop in the evaluation function. However, in this case we can just ignore the auxiliary output, since we only really care about the main output—the auxiliary output is just there for regularization during training:

```
for inputs, y_batch in data_loader:
    y_pred, _ = model(**inputs)
    metric.update(y_pred, y_batch)
    [...]  # the rest is unchanged
```

Voilà! You can now build and train all sorts of neural net architectures, combining predefined modules and custom modules in any way you please, and with any number of inputs and outputs. The flexibility of neural networks is one of their main qualities. But so far we have only tackled a regression task, so let's now turn to classification.

Building an Image Classifier with PyTorch

As in Chapter 9, we will tackle the Fashion MNIST dataset, so the first thing we need to do is to download the dataset. We could use the `fetch_openml()` function like we did in Chapter 9, but we will show another method instead, using the TorchVision library.

Using TorchVision to Load the Dataset

The TorchVision library is an important part of the PyTorch ecosystem: it provides many tools for computer vision, including utility functions to download common datasets, such as MNIST or Fashion MNIST, as well as pretrained models for various computer vision tasks (see Chapter 12), functions to transform images (e.g., crop, rotate, resize, etc.), and more. It is preinstalled on Colab, so let's go ahead and use it to load Fashion MNIST. It is already split into a training set (60,000 images) and a test set (10,000 images), but we'll hold out the last 5,000 images from the training set for validation, using PyTorch's `random_split()` function:

```
import torchvision
import torchvision.transforms.v2 as T

toTensor = T.Compose([T.ToImage(), T.ToDtype(torch.float32, scale=True)])

train_and_valid_data = torchvision.datasets.FashionMNIST(
    root="datasets", train=True, download=True, transform=toTensor)
test_data = torchvision.datasets.FashionMNIST(
    root="datasets", train=False, download=True, transform=toTensor)

torch.manual_seed(42)
train_data, valid_data = torch.utils.data.random_split(
    train_and_valid_data, [55_000, 5_000])
```

After the imports and before loading the datasets, we create a `toTensor` object. What's that about? Well, by default, the `FashionMNIST` class loads images as PIL (Python Image Library) images, with integer pixel values ranging from 0 to 255. But we need PyTorch float tensors instead, with scaled pixel values. Luckily, TorchVision datasets accept a `transform` argument which lets you pass a preprocessing function that will get executed on the fly whenever the data is accessed (there's also a `target_transform` argument if you need to preprocess the targets). TorchVision provides many transform objects that you can use for this (most of these transforms are PyTorch modules).

In this code, we create a `Compose` transform to chain two transforms: a `ToImage` transform followed by a `ToDtype` transform. `ToImage` converts various formats—including PIL images, NumPy arrays, and tensors—to TorchVision's `Image` class, which is a subclass of `Tensor`. The `ToDtype` transform converts the data type, in this case to 32-bit floats. We also set its `scale` argument to `True` to ensure the values get scaled between 0.0 and 1.0.[12]

Version 1 of TorchVision's transforms API is still available for backward compatibility and can be imported using `import torchvision.transforms`, However, you should use version 2 (`torchvision.transformers.v2`) instead, since it's faster and has more features.

Next, we load the dataset: first the training and validation data, then the test data. The `root` argument is the path to the directory where TorchVision will create a subdirectory for the Fashion MNIST dataset. The `train` argument indicates whether you want to load the training set (`True` by default) or the test set. The `download` argument indicates whether to download the dataset if it cannot be found locally (`False` by default). And we also set `transform=toTensor` to use our custom preprocessing pipeline.

As usual, we must create data loaders:

```
train_loader = DataLoader(train_data, batch_size=32, shuffle=True)
valid_loader = DataLoader(valid_data, batch_size=32)
test_loader = DataLoader(test_data, batch_size=32)
```

Now let's look at the first image in the training set:

```
>>> X_sample, y_sample = train_data[0]
>>> X_sample.shape
torch.Size([1, 28, 28])
>>> X_sample.dtype
torch.float32
```

In Chapter 9, each image was represented by a 1D array containing 784 pixel intensities, but now each image tensor has 3 dimensions, and its shape is: `[1, 28, 28]`. The first dimension is the *channel* dimension. For grayscale images, there is a single channel (color images usually have three channels, as we will see in Chapter 12). The other two dimensions are the height and width dimensions. For example, `X_sample[0, 2, 4]` represents the pixel located in channel 0, row 2, column 4. In Fashion MNIST, a larger value means a darker pixel.

12 TorchVision includes a `ToTensor` transform which does all this, but it's deprecated so it's recommended to use this pipeline instead.

PyTorch expects the channel dimension to be first, while many other libraries, such as Matplotlib, PIL, TensorFlow, OpenCV, or Scikit-Image, expect it to be last. Always make sure to move the channel dimension to the right place, depending on the library you are using. `ToImage` already took care of moving the channel dimension to the first position, otherwise we could have used the `torch.permute()` function.

As for the targets, they are integers from 0 to 9, and we can interpret them using the same `class_names` array as in Chapter 9. In fact, many datasets—including `FashionMNIST`—have a `classes` attribute containing the list of class names. For example, here's how we can tell that the sample image represents an ankle boot:

```
>>> train_and_valid_data.classes[y_sample]
'Ankle boot'
```

Building the Classifier

Let's build a custom module for a classification MLP with two hidden layers:

```
class ImageClassifier(nn.Module):
    def __init__(self, n_inputs, n_hidden1, n_hidden2, n_classes):
        super().__init__()
        self.mlp = nn.Sequential(
            nn.Flatten(),
            nn.Linear(n_inputs, n_hidden1),
            nn.ReLU(),
            nn.Linear(n_hidden1, n_hidden2),
            nn.ReLU(),
            nn.Linear(n_hidden2, n_classes)
        )

    def forward(self, X):
        return self.mlp(X)

torch.manual_seed(42)
model = ImageClassifier(n_inputs=28 * 28, n_hidden1=300, n_hidden2=100,
                        n_classes=10)
xentropy = nn.CrossEntropyLoss()
```

There are a few things to note in this code:

- First, the model is composed of a single sequence of layers, which is why we used the `nn.Sequential` module. We did not have to create a custom module; we could have written `model = nn.Sequential(...)` instead, but it's generally preferable to wrap your models in custom modules, as it makes your code easier to deploy and reuse, and it's also easier to tune the hyperparameters.

- The model starts with an `nn.Flatten` layer: this layer does not have any parameters, it just reshapes each input sample to a single dimension, which is needed for the `nn.Linear` layers. For example, a batch of 32 Fashion MNIST images has a shape of `[32, 1, 28, 28]`, but after going through the `nn.Flatten` layer, it ends up with a shape of `[32, 784]` (since 28 × 28 = 784).
- The first hidden layer must have the correct number of inputs (28 × 28 = 784), and the output layer must have the correct number of outputs (10, one per class).
- We use a ReLU activation function after each hidden layer, and no activation function at all after the output layer.
- Since this is a multiclass classification task, we use `nn.CrossEntropyLoss`. It accepts either class indices as targets (as in this example), or class probabilities (such as one-hot vectors).

Shape errors are quite common, especially when getting started, so you should familiarize yourself with the error messages: try removing the `nn.Flatten` module, or try messing with the shape of the inputs and/or labels, and see the errors you get.

But wait! Didn't we say in Chapter 9 that we should use the softmax activation function on the output layer for multiclass classification tasks? Well it turns out that PyTorch's `nn.CrossEntropyLoss` computes the cross-entropy loss directly from the logits (i.e., the class scores, introduced in Chapter 4), rather than from the class probabilities. This bypasses some costly computations during training (e.g., logarithms and exponentials that cancel out), saving both compute and RAM. It's also more numerically stable. However, the downside is that the model must output logits, which means that we will have to call the softmax function manually on the logits whenever we want class probabilities, as we will see shortly.

Other Classification Losses

For multiclass classification, another option is to add the `nn.LogSoftmax` activation function to the output layer, and then use the `nn.NLLLoss` (negative log-likelihood loss). The model then outputs log probabilities (rather than logits), and the loss computes the cross-entropy based on these log probabilities. Whenever you need actual estimated probabilities, just pass the log probabilities through the exponential function. This approach is a bit slower than using `nn.CrossEntropyLoss`, so it's not used as often, but it can sometimes be useful if you want your model to output log probabilities, or when you wish to tweak the probability distribution before computing the loss.

For binary classification tasks, you must use a single output neuron in the output layer, and use the `nn.BCEWithLogitsLoss` (BCE stands for binary cross-entropy). The model outputs logits, so you must apply the sigmoid function to get estimated probabilities (for the positive class). Alternatively, you can add the `nn.Sigmoid` activation function to the output layer, and use the `nn.BCELoss`: the model will then output estimated probabilities directly (but it's a bit slower and less numerically stable).

For multilabel binary classification, the only difference is that you must have one neuron per label in the output layer.

Now we can train the model as usual (e.g., using the `train()` function with an `SGD` optimizer). To evaluate the model, we can use the `Accuracy` streaming metric from the `torchmetrics` library, and move it to the GPU:

```
accuracy = torchmetrics.Accuracy(task="multiclass", num_classes=10).to(device)
```

Training the model will take a few minutes with a GPU (or much longer without one). Handling images requires significantly more compute and memory than handling low-dimensional data.

The model reaches around 92.8% accuracy on the training set, and 87.2% accuracy on the validation set (the results might differ a bit depending on the hardware accelerator you use). This means there's a little bit of overfitting going on, so you may want to reduce the number of neurons or add some regularization (see Chapter 11).

Now that the model is trained, we can use it to make predictions on new images. As an example, let's make predictions for the first batch in the validation set, and look at the results for the first three images:

```
>>> model.eval()
>>> X_new, y_new = next(iter(valid_loader))
>>> X_new = X_new[:3].to(device)
>>> with torch.no_grad():
...     y_pred_logits = model(X_new)
...
>>> y_pred = y_pred_logits.argmax(dim=1)  # index of the largest logit
>>> y_pred
tensor([7, 4, 2], device='cuda:0')
>>> [train_and_valid_data.classes[index] for index in y_pred]
['Sneaker', 'Coat', 'Pullover']
```

For each image, the predicted class is the one with the highest logit. In this example, all three predictions are correct!

But what if we want the model's estimated probabilities? For this, we need to compute the softmax of the logits manually, since the model does not include the softmax activation function on the output layer, as we discussed earlier. We could create an `nn.Softmax` module and pass it the logits, but we can also just call the `softmax()` function, which is just one of many functions you will find in the `torch.nn.functional` module (by convention, this module is usually imported as `F`). It doesn't make much difference, it just avoids creating a module instance that we don't need:

```
>>> import torch.nn.functional as F
>>> y_proba = F.softmax(y_pred_logits, dim=1)
>>> y_proba.round(decimals=3)
tensor([[0.000, 0.000, 0.000, 0.000, 0.000, 0.001, 0.000, 0.911, 0.000, 0.088],
        [0.000, 0.000, 0.004, 0.000, 0.996, 0.000, 0.000, 0.000, 0.000, 0.000],
        [0.000, 0.000, 0.625, 0.000, 0.335, 0.000, 0.039, 0.000, 0.000, 0.000]],
       device='cuda:0')
```

Just like in Chapter 9, the model is very confident about the first two predictions: 91.1% and 99.6%, respectively.

If you wish to apply label smoothing during training, just set the `label_smoothing` hyperparameter of the `nn.CrossEntropyLoss` to the amount of smoothing you wish, between 0 and 1 (e.g., 0.05).

It can often be useful to get the model's top *k* predictions. For this, we can use the `torch.topk()` function, which returns a tuple containing both the top *k* values and their indices:

```
>>> y_top4_logits, y_top4_indices = torch.topk(y_pred_logits, k=4, dim=1)
>>> y_top4_probas = F.softmax(y_top4_logits, dim=1)
>>> y_top4_probas.round(decimals=3)
tensor([[0.9110, 0.0880, 0.0010, 0.0000],
        [0.9960, 0.0040, 0.0000, 0.0000],
        [0.6250, 0.3350, 0.0390, 0.0000]], device='cuda:0')
>>> y_top4_indices
tensor([[7, 9, 5, 8],
        [4, 2, 6, 0],
        [2, 4, 6, 0]], device='cuda:0')
```

For the first image, the model's best guess is class 7 (Sneaker) with 91.1% confidence, its second best guess is class 9 (Ankle boot) with 8.8% confidence, and so on.

The Fashion MNIST dataset is balanced, meaning it has the same number of instances of each class. When dealing with an unbalanced dataset, you should generally give more weight to the rare classes and less weight to the frequent ones, or else your model will be biased toward the more frequent classes. You can do this by setting the `weight` argument of the `nn.CrossEntropyLoss`. For example, if there are three classes with 900, 700, and 400 instances, respectively (i.e., 2000 instances in total), then the respective weights should be 2000/900, 2000/700, and 2000/400. It's preferable to normalize these weights to ensure they add up to 1, so in this example you would set `weight=torch.tensor([0.2205, 0.2835, 0.4961])`.

Your PyTorch superpowers are growing: you can now build, train, and evaluate both regression and classification neural nets. The next step is to learn how to fine-tune the model hyperparameters.

Fine-Tuning Neural Network Hyperparameters with Optuna

We discussed how to manually pick reasonable values for your model's hyperparameters in Chapter 9, but what if you want to go further and automatically search for good hyperparameter values? One option is to convert your PyTorch model to a Scikit-Learn estimator, either by writing your own custom estimator class or by using a wrapper library such as Skorch (*https://skorch.readthedocs.io*), and then use `GridSearchCV` or `RandomizedSearchCV` to fine-tune the hyperparameters, as you did in Chapter 2. However, you will usually get better results by using a dedicated fine-tuning library such as Optuna (*https://optuna.org*), Ray Tune (*https://docs.ray.io*), or Hyperopt (*https://hyperopt.github.io/hyperopt*). These libraries offer several powerful tuning strategies, and they're highly customizable.

Let's look at an example using Optuna. It is not preinstalled on Colab, so we need to install it using `%pip install optuna` (if you prefer to run the code locally, please follow the installation instructions at *https://homl.info/install-p*). Let's tune the learning rate and the number of neurons in the hidden layers (for simplicity, we will use the same number of neurons in both hidden layers). First, we need to define a function that Optuna will call many times to perform hyperparameter tuning: this function must take a `Trial` object and use it to ask Optuna for hyperparameter values, and then use these hyperparameter values to build and train a model. Finally, the function must evaluate the model (typically on the validation set) and return the metric:

```python
import optuna

def objective(trial):
    learning_rate = trial.suggest_float("learning_rate", 1e-5, 1e-1, log=True)
    n_hidden = trial.suggest_int("n_hidden", 20, 300)
    model = ImageClassifier(n_inputs=1 * 28 * 28, n_hidden1=n_hidden,
                            n_hidden2=n_hidden, n_classes=10).to(device)
    optimizer = torch.optim.SGD(model.parameters(), lr=learning_rate)
    [...]  # train the model, then evaluate it on the validation set
    return validation_accuracy
```

The `suggest_float()` and `suggest_int()` methods let us ask Optuna for a good hyperparameter value in a given range (Optuna also provides a `suggest_categorical()` method). For the `learning_rate` hyperparameter, we ask for a value between 10^{-5} and 10^{-1}, and since we don't know what the optimal scale is, we add `log=True`: this will make Optuna sample values from a log distribution, which makes it explore all possible scales. If we used the default uniform distribution instead, Optuna would be very unlikely to explore tiny values.

To start hyperparameter tuning, we create a `Study` object and call its `optimize()` method, passing it the objective function we just defined, as well as the number of trials to run (i.e., the number of times Optuna should call the objective function). Since our objective function returns a score—higher is better—we set `direction="maximize"` when creating the study (by default, Optuna tries to *minimize* the objective). To ensure reproducibility, we also set PyTorch's random seed, as well as the random seed used by Optuna's sampler:

```python
torch.manual_seed(42)
sampler = optuna.samplers.TPESampler(seed=42)
study = optuna.create_study(direction="maximize", sampler=sampler)
study.optimize(objective, n_trials=5)
```

By default, Optuna uses the *Tree-structured Parzen Estimator* (TPE) algorithm to optimize the hyperparameters: this is a sequential model-based optimization algorithm, meaning it learns from past results to better select promising hyperparameters. In other words, Optuna starts with random hyperparameter values, but it progressively focuses its search on the most promising regions of the hyperparameter space. This allows Optuna to find much better hyperparameters than random search in the same amount of time.

You can add more hyperparameters to the search space, such as the batch size, the type of optimizer, the number of hidden layers, or the type of activation function, but remember that the search space will grow exponentially as you add more hyperparameters, so make sure it's worth the extra search time and compute.

Once Optuna is done, you can look at the best hyperparameters it found, as well as the corresponding validation accuracy:

```
>>> study.best_params
{'learning_rate': 0.08525846269447772, 'n_hidden': 116}
>>> study.best_value
0.8867999911308289
```

This is slightly better than the performance we got earlier. If you increase `n_trials` up to 50 or more, you will get much better results, but of course it will take hours to run. You can also just run `optimize()` repeatedly and stop once you are happy with the performance.

Optuna can also run trials in parallel across multiple machines, which can offer a near linear speed boost. For this, you will need to set up a SQL database (e.g., SQLite or PostgreSQL), and set the `storage` parameter of the `create_study()` function to point to that database. You also need to set the study's name via the `study_name` parameter, and set `load_if_exists=True`. After that, you can copy your hyperparameter tuning script to multiple machines, and run it on each one (if you are using random seeds, make sure they are different on each machine). The scripts will work in parallel, reading and writing the trial results to the database. This has the additional benefit of keeping a full log of all your experiment results.

You may have noticed that we assumed that the `objective()` function had direct access to the training set and validation, presumably via global variables. In general, it's much cleaner to pass them as extra arguments to the `objective()` function, for example, like this:

```
def objective(trial, train_loader, valid_loader):
    [...]  # the rest of the function remains the same as above

objective_with_data = lambda trial: objective(
    trial, train_loader=train_loader, valid_loader=valid_loader)
study.optimize(objective_with_data, n_trials=5)
```

To set the extra arguments (the dataset loaders in this case), we just create a lambda function when needed and pass it to the `optimize()` method. Alternatively, you can use the `functools.partial()` function which creates a thin wrapper function around the given callable to provide default values for any number of arguments:

```
from functools import partial

objective_with_data = partial(objective, train_loader=train_loader,
                              valid_loader=valid_loader)
```

It's often possible to quickly tell that a trial is absolutely terrible: for example, when the loss shoots up during the first epoch, or when the model barely improves during the first few epochs. In such a case, it's a good idea to interrupt training early to avoid wasting time and compute. You can simply return the model's current validation accuracy and hope that Optuna will learn to avoid this region of hyperparameter space. Alternatively, you can interrupt training by raising the `optuna.TrialPruned` exception: this tells Optuna to ignore this trial altogether. In many cases, this leads to a more efficient search because it avoids polluting Optuna's search algorithm with many noisy model evaluations.

Optuna comes with several `Pruner` classes that can detect and prune bad trials. For example, the `MedianPruner` will prune trials whose performance is below the median performance, at regular intervals during training. It starts pruning after a given number of trials have completed, controlled by `n_startup_trials` (5 by default). For each trial after that, it lets training start for a few epochs, controlled by `n_warmup_steps` (0 by default); then every few epochs (controlled by `interval_steps`), it ensures that the model's performance is better than the median performance at the same epoch in past trials. To use this pruner, create an instance and pass it to the `create_study()` method:

```
pruner = optuna.pruners.MedianPruner(n_startup_trials=5, n_warmup_steps=0,
                                     interval_steps=1)
study = optuna.create_study(direction="maximize", sampler=sampler,
                            pruner=pruner)
```

Then in the `objective()` function, add the following code so it runs after each epoch:

```
for epoch in range(n_epochs):
    [...]  # train the model for one epoch
    validation_accuracy = [...]  # evaluate the model's validation accuracy
    trial.report(validation_accuracy, epoch)
    if trial.should_prune():
        raise optuna.TrialPruned()
```

The `report()` method informs Optuna of the current validation accuracy and epoch, so it can determine whether the trial should be pruned. If `trial.should_prune()` returns `True`, we raise a `TrialPruned` exception.

Optuna has many other features well worth exploring, such as visualization tools, persistence tools for trial results and other artifacts, a dashboard for human-in-the-loop optimization, and many other algorithms for hyperparameter search and trial pruning.

Once you are happy with the hyperparameters, you can train the model on the full training set (i.e., the training set plus the validation set), then evaluate it on the test set. Hopefully, it will perform great! If it does, you will want to save the model, then load it and use it in production: that's the final topic of this chapter.

Saving and Loading PyTorch Models

The simplest way to save a PyTorch model is to use the `torch.save()` method, passing it the model and the filepath. The model object is serialized using Python's `pickle` module (which can convert objects into a sequence of bytes), then the result is compressed (zip) and saved to disk. The convention is to use the `.pt` or `.pth` extension for PyTorch files:

```
torch.save(model, "my_fashion_mnist.pt")
```

Simple! Now you can load the model (e.g., in your production code) just as easily:

```
loaded_model = torch.load("my_fashion_mnist.pt", weights_only=False)
```

If your model uses any custom functions or classes (e.g., `ImageClassifier`), then `torch.save()` only saves references to them, not the code itself. Therefore you must ensure that any custom code is loaded in the Python environment before calling `torch.load()`. Also make sure to use the same version of the code to avoid any mismatch issues.

Setting `weights_only=False` ensures that the whole model object is loaded rather than just the model parameters. Then you can use the loaded model for inference. Don't forget to switch to evaluation mode first using the `eval()` method:

```
loaded_model.eval()
y_pred_logits = loaded_model(X_new)
```

This is nice and easy, but unfortunately this approach has some very serious drawbacks:

- Firstly, pickle's serialization format is notoriously insecure. While `torch.save()` doesn't save custom code, the pickle format supports it, so a hacker could inject malicious code in a saved PyTorch model: this code would be run automatically by the `pickle` module when the model is loaded. So always make sure you fully trust the model's source before you load it this way.
- Second, pickle is somewhat brittle. It can vary depending on the Python version (e.g., there were big changes between Python 3.7 and 3.8), and it saves specific filepaths to locate code, which can break if the loading environment has a different folder structure.

To avoid these issues, it is recommended to save and load the model weights only, rather than the full model object:

```
torch.save(model.state_dict(), "my_fashion_mnist_weights.pt")
```

The state dictionary returned by the `state_dict()` method is just a Python `OrderedDict` containing an entry for each parameter returned by the `named_parameters()` method. It also contains buffers, if the model has any: a buffer is just a regular tensor that was registered with the model (or any of its submodules) using the `register_buffer()` method. Buffers hold extra data that needs to be stored along with the model, but that is not a model parameter. We will see an example in Chapter 11 with the batch-norm layer.

To load these weights, we must first create a model with the exact same structure, then load the weights using `torch.load()` with `weights_only=True`, and finally call the model's `load_state_dict()` method with the loaded weights:

```
new_model = ImageClassifier(n_inputs=1 * 28 * 28, n_hidden1=300, n_hidden2=100,
                            n_classes=10)
loaded_weights = torch.load("my_fashion_mnist_weights.pt", weights_only=True)
new_model.load_state_dict(loaded_weights)
new_model.eval()
```

The saved model contains only data, and the `load()` function makes sure of that, so this is safe, and also much less likely to break between Python versions or to cause any deployment issue. However, it only works if you are able to create the exact same model architecture before loading the state dictionary. For this, you need to know the number of layers, the number of neurons per layer, and so on. It's a good idea to save this information along with the state dictionary:

```
model_data = {
    "model_state_dict": model.state_dict(),
    "model_hyperparameters": {"n_inputs": 1 * 28 * 28, "n_hidden1": 300, [...]}
}
torch.save(model_data, "my_fashion_mnist_model.pt")
```

You can then load this dictionary, construct the model based on the saved hyperparameters, and load the state dictionary into this model:

```
loaded_data = torch.load("my_fashion_mnist_model.pt", weights_only=True)
new_model = ImageClassifier(**loaded_data["model_hyperparameters"])
new_model.load_state_dict(loaded_data["model_state_dict"])
new_model.eval()
```

If you want to be able to continue training where it left off, you will also need to save the optimizer's state dictionary, its hyperparameters, and any other training information you may need, such as the current epoch and the loss history.

The `safetensors` library by Hugging Face is another popular way to save model weights safely.

There is yet another way to save and load your model: by first converting it to TorchScript. This also makes it possible to speed up your model's inference.

Compiling and Optimizing a PyTorch Model

PyTorch comes with a very nice feature: it can automatically convert your model's code to *TorchScript*, which you can think of as a statically typed subset of Python. There are two main benefits:

- First, TorchScript code can be compiled and optimized to produce significantly faster models. For example, multiple operations can often be fused into a single, more efficient operation. Operations on constants (e.g., 2 * 3) can be replaced with their result (e.g., 6); this is called *constant folding*. Unused code can be pruned, and so on.
- Secondly, TorchScript can be serialized, saved to disk, and then loaded and executed in Python or in a C++ environment using the LibTorch library. This makes it possible to run PyTorch models on a wide range of devices, including embedded devices.

There are two ways to convert a PyTorch model to TorchScript. The first way is called *tracing*. PyTorch just runs your model with some sample data, logs every operation that takes place, and then converts this log to TorchScript. This is done using the `torch.jit.trace()` function:

```
torchscript_model = torch.jit.trace(model, X_new)
```

This generally works well with static models whose `forward()` method doesn't use conditionals or loops. However, if you try to trace a model that includes an `if` or `match` statement, then only the branch that is actually executed will be captured by TorchScript, which is generally not what you want. Similarly, if you use tracing with a model that contains a loop, then the TorchScript code will contain one copy of the operations within that loop for each iteration that was actually executed. Again, not what you generally want.

For such dynamic models, you will probably want to try another approach named *scripting*. In this case, PyTorch actually parses your Python code directly and converts it to TorchScript. This method supports `if` statements and `while` loops properly, as long as the conditions are tensors. It also supports `for` loops when iterating over tensors. However, it only works on a subset of Python. For example, you cannot use global variables, Python generators (`yield`), complex list comprehensions, variable length function arguments (`*args` or `**kwargs`), or `match` statements. Moreover, types must be fixed (a function cannot return an integer in some cases and a float in others), and you can only call other functions if they also respect these rules, so no standard library, no third-party libraries, etc. (see the documentation for the full list of constraints). This sounds daunting, but for most real-world models, these rules are actually not too hard to respect, and you can save your model like this:

```
torchscript_model = torch.jit.script(model)
```

Regardless of whether you use tracing or scripting to produce your TorchScript model, you can then further optimize it:

```
optimized_model = torch.jit.optimize_for_inference(torchscript_model)
```

TorchScript models can only be used for inference, not for training, since the TorchScript environment doesn't support gradient tracking or parameter updates.

Finally, you can save a TorchScript model using its `save()` method:

```
torchscript_model.save('my_fashion_mnist_torchscript.pt')
```

And then load it using the `torch.jit.load()` function:

```
loaded_torchscript_model = torch.jit.load("my_fashion_mnist_torchscript.pt")
```

One important caveat: TorchScript is no longer under active development—bugs are fixed but no new features are added. It still works fine and it remains one of the best ways to run your PyTorch models in a C++ environment,[13] but since the release of PyTorch 2.0 in March 2023, the PyTorch team has been focusing its efforts on a new set of compilation tools centered around the `torch.compile()` function, which you can use very easily:

```
compiled_model = torch.compile(model)
```

The resulting model can now be used normally, and it will automatically be compiled and optimized when you use it. This is called Just-In-Time (JIT) compilation, as opposed to Ahead-Of-Time (AOT) compilation. Under the hood, `torch.compile()` relies on *TorchDynamo* (or *Dynamo* for short) which hooks directly into Python bytecode to capture the model's computation graph at inference time. Having access to the bytecode allows Dynamo to efficiently and reliably capture the computation graph, properly handling conditionals and loops, while also benefiting from dynamic information that can be used to better optimize the model. The actual compilation and optimization is performed by default by a backend component named *TorchInductor*, which in turn relies on the Triton language to generate highly efficient GPU code (Nvidia only), or on the OpenMP API for CPU optimization. PyTorch 2.x offers a few other optimization backends, including the XLA backend for Google's TPU devices: just set `device="xla"` when calling `torch.compile()`.

With that, you now have all the tools you need to start building and training complex and efficient neural networks. I hope you enjoyed this introduction to PyTorch! We

13 Another popular option is exporting your PyTorch model to the open ONNX standard using `torch.onnx.export()`. The ONNX model can then be used for inference in a wide variety of environments.

covered a lot, but the adventure is only beginning: in the next chapter we will discuss techniques to train very deep nets. After that, we will dive into other popular neural network architectures: convolutional neural networks for image processing, recurrent neural networks for sequential data, transformers for text (and much more), autoencoders for representation learning, and generative adversarial networks and diffusion models to generate data.[14] Then we will visit reinforcement learning to train autonomous agents, and finally, we will learn more about deploying and optimizing your PyTorch models. Let's go!

Exercises

1. PyTorch is similar to NumPy is many ways, but it offers some extra features. Can you name the most important ones?
2. What is the difference between `torch.exp()` and `torch.exp_()`, or between `torch.relu()` and `torch.relu_()`?
3. What are two ways to create a new tensor on the GPU?
4. What are three ways to perform tensor computations without using autograd?
5. Will the following code cause a `RuntimeError`? What if you replace the second line with `z = t.cos_().exp()`? And what if you replace it with `z = t.exp().cos_()`?

    ```
    t = torch.tensor(2.0, requires_grad=True)
    z = t.cos().exp_()
    z.backward()
    ```

    How about the following code, will it cause an error? And what if you replace the third line with `w = v.cos_() * v.sin()`? Will `w` have the same value in both cases?

    ```
    u = torch.tensor(2.0, requires_grad=True)
    v = u + 1
    w = v.cos() * v.sin_()
    w.backward()
    ```

6. Suppose you create a `Linear(100, 200)` module. How many neurons does it have? What is the shape of is `weight` and `bias` parameters? What input shape does it expect? What output shape does it produce?
7. What are the main steps of a PyTorch training loop?
8. Why is it recommended to create the optimizer *after* the model is moved to the GPU?

14 A few extra ANN architectures are presented in the online notebook at *https://homl.info/extra-anns*.

9. What `DataLoader` options should you generally set to speed up training when using a GPU?
10. What are the main classification losses provided by PyTorch, and when should you use each of them?
11. Why is it important to call `model.train()` before training and `model.eval()` before evaluation?
12. What is the difference between `torch.jit.trace()` and `torch.jit.script()`?
13. Use autograd to find the gradient vector of $f(x, y) = \sin(x^2 y)$ at the point $(x, y) = (1.2, 3.4)$.
14. Create a custom `Dense` module that replicates the functionality of an `nn.Linear` module followed by an `nn.ReLU` module. Try implementing it first using the `nn.Linear` and `nn.ReLU` modules, and then reimplement it using `nn.Parameter` and the `relu()` function.
15. Build and train a classification MLP on the CoverType dataset:
    a. Load the dataset using `sklearn.datasets.fetch_covtype()` and create a custom PyTorch `Dataset` for this data.
    b. Create data loaders for training, validation, and testing.
    c. Build a custom MLP module to tackle this classification task. You can optionally use the custom `Dense` module from the previous exercise.
    d. Train this model on the GPU, and try to reach 93% accuracy on the test set. For this, you will likely have to perform hyperparameter search to find the right number of layers and neurons per layer, a good learning rate and batch size, and so on. You can optionally use Optuna for this.

Solutions to these exercises are available at the end of this chapter's notebook, at *https://homl.info/colab-p*.

CHAPTER 11
Training Deep Neural Networks

In Chapter 10 you built, trained, and fine-tuned several artificial neural networks using PyTorch. But they were shallow nets with just a few hidden layers. What if you need to tackle a complex problem, such as detecting hundreds of types of objects in high-resolution images? You may need to train a much deeper ANN, perhaps with dozens or even hundreds of layers, each containing hundreds of neurons, linked by hundreds of thousands of connections. Training a deep neural network isn't a walk in the park. Here are some of the problems you could run into:

- You may be faced with the problem of gradients growing ever smaller or larger when flowing backward through the DNN during training. Both of these problems make lower layers very hard to train.
- You might not have enough training data for such a large network, or it might be too costly to label.
- Training may be extremely slow.
- A model with millions of parameters risks severely overfitting the training set, especially if there are not enough training instances or if they are too noisy.

In this chapter we will go through each of these problems and present various techniques to solve them. We will start by exploring the vanishing and exploding gradients problems and some of their most popular solutions, including smart weight initialization, better activation functions, batch-norm, layer-norm, and gradient clipping. Next, we will look at transfer learning and unsupervised pretraining, which can help you tackle complex tasks even when you have little labeled data. Then we will discuss a variety of optimizers that can speed up training large models tremendously. We will also discuss how you can tweak the learning rate during training to speed up training and produce better models. Finally, we will cover a few popular regularization techniques for large neural networks: ℓ_1 and ℓ_2 regularization, dropout, Monte Carlo dropout, and max-norm regularization.

With these tools, you will be able to train all sorts of deep nets. Welcome to *deep* learning!

The Vanishing/Exploding Gradients Problems

As discussed in Chapter 9, the backpropagation algorithm's second phase works by going from the output layer to the input layer, propagating the error gradient along the way. Once the algorithm has computed the gradient of the cost function with regard to each parameter in the network, it uses these gradients to update each parameter with a gradient descent step.

Unfortunately, gradients often get smaller and smaller as the algorithm progresses down to the lower layers. As a result, the gradient descent update leaves the lower layers' connection weights virtually unchanged, and training never converges to a good solution. This is called the *vanishing gradients* problem. In some cases, the opposite can happen: the gradients can grow bigger and bigger until layers get insanely large weight updates and the algorithm diverges. This is the *exploding gradients* problem, which surfaces most often in recurrent neural networks (see Chapter 13). More generally, deep neural networks suffer from unstable gradients; different layers may learn at widely different speeds.

This unfortunate behavior was empirically observed long ago, and it was one of the reasons deep neural networks were mostly abandoned in the early 2000s. It wasn't clear what caused the gradients to be so unstable when training a DNN, but some light was shed in a 2010 paper (*https://homl.info/47*) by Xavier Glorot and Yoshua Bengio.[1] The authors found a few suspects, including the combination of the popular sigmoid (logistic) activation function and the weight initialization technique that was most popular at the time (i.e., a normal distribution with a mean of 0 and a standard deviation of 1). In short, they showed that with this activation function and this initialization scheme, the variance of the outputs of each layer is much greater than the variance of its inputs. Going forward in the network, the variance keeps increasing after each layer until the activation function saturates at the top layers. This saturation is actually made worse by the fact that the sigmoid function has a mean of 0.5, not 0 (the hyperbolic tangent function has a mean of 0 and behaves slightly better than the sigmoid function in deep networks).

1 Xavier Glorot and Yoshua Bengio, "Understanding the Difficulty of Training Deep Feedforward Neural Networks", *Proceedings of the 13th International Conference on Artificial Intelligence and Statistics* (2010): 249–256.

Looking at the sigmoid activation function (see Figure 11-1), you can see that when inputs become large (negative or positive), the function saturates at 0 or 1, with a derivative extremely close to 0 (i.e., the curve is flat at both extremes). Thus, when backpropagation kicks in it has virtually no gradient to propagate back through the network, and what little gradient exists keeps getting diluted as backpropagation progresses down through the top layers, so there is really nothing left for the lower layers.

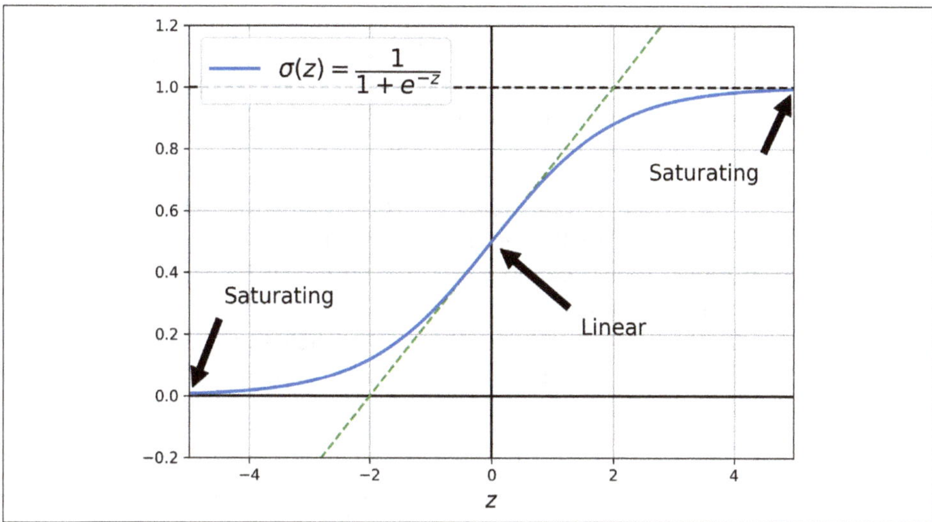

Figure 11-1. Sigmoid activation function saturation

Glorot Initialization and He Initialization

In their paper, Glorot and Bengio proposed a way to significantly alleviate the unstable gradients problem. They pointed out that we need the signal to flow properly in both directions: in the forward direction when making predictions, and in the reverse direction when backpropagating gradients. We don't want the signal to die out, nor do we want it to explode and saturate. For the signal to flow properly, the authors argued that we need the variance of the outputs of each layer to be equal to the variance of its inputs,[2] and we need the gradients to have equal variance before and after flowing through a layer in the reverse direction (please check out the paper if you are interested in the mathematical details). It is actually not possible to guarantee both unless the layer has an equal number of inputs and outputs (these numbers are

2 Here's an analogy: if you set a microphone amplifier's volume knob too close to zero, people won't hear your voice, but if you set it too close to the max, your voice will be saturated and people won't understand what you are saying. Now imagine a chain of such amplifiers: they all need to be set properly in order for your voice to come out loud and clear at the end of the chain. Your voice has to come out of each amplifier at the same amplitude as it came in.

called the *fan-in* and *fan-out* of the layer), but Glorot and Bengio proposed a good compromise that has proven to work very well in practice: the connection weights of each layer must be initialized randomly, as described in Equation 11-1, where $fan_{avg} = (fan_{in} + fan_{out}) / 2$. This initialization strategy is called *Xavier initialization* or *Glorot initialization*, after the paper's first author.

Equation 11-1. Glorot initialization (when using the sigmoid activation function)

$$\text{Normal distribution with mean 0 and variance } \sigma^2 = \frac{1}{fan_{\text{avg}}}$$

$$\text{Or a uniform distribution between } -r \text{ and } +r, \text{ with } r = \sqrt{\frac{3}{fan_{\text{avg}}}}$$

If you replace fan_{avg} with fan_{in} in Equation 11-1, you get an initialization strategy that Yann LeCun proposed in the 1990s. He called it *LeCun initialization*. Genevieve Orr and Klaus-Robert Müller even recommended it in their 1998 book *Neural Networks: Tricks of the Trade* (Springer). LeCun initialization is equivalent to Glorot initialization when $fan_{in} = fan_{out}$. It took over a decade for researchers to realize how important this trick is. Using Glorot initialization can speed up training considerably, and it is one of the tricks that led to the success of deep learning.

Some papers have provided similar strategies for different activation functions, most notably a 2015 paper by Kaiming He et al (*https://homl.info/48*).[3] These strategies differ only by the scale of the variance and whether they use fan_{avg} or fan_{in}, as shown in Table 11-1 (for the uniform distribution, just use $r = \sqrt{3\sigma^2}$). The initialization strategy proposed for the ReLU activation function and its variants is called *He initialization* or *Kaiming initialization*, after the paper's first author. For SELU, use Yann LeCun's initialization method, preferably with a normal distribution. We will cover all these activation functions shortly.

Table 11-1. Initialization parameters for each type of activation function

Initialization	Activation functions	σ^2 (Normal)
Xavier Glorot	None, tanh, sigmoid, softmax	$1 / fan_{avg}$
Kaiming He	ReLU, Leaky ReLU, ELU, GELU, Swish, Mish, SwiGLU, ReLU²	$2 / fan_{in}$
Yann LeCun	SELU	$1 / fan_{in}$

For historical reasons, PyTorch's `nn.Linear` module initializes its weights using Kaiming uniform initialization, except the weights are scaled down by a factor of

3 Kaiming He et al., "Delving Deep into Rectifiers: Surpassing Human-Level Performance on ImageNet Classification", *Proceedings of the 2015 IEEE International Conference on Computer Vision* (2015): 1026–1034.

$\sqrt{6}$ (and the bias terms are also initialized randomly). Sadly, this is not the optimal scale for any common activation function.[4] One solution is to simply multiply the weights by $\sqrt{6}$ (i.e., $6^{0.5}$) just after creating the `nn.Linear` layer to get proper Kaiming initialization. To do this, we can update the parameter's `data` attribute. We will also zero out the biases, as there's no benefit in randomly initializing them:

```
import torch
import torch.nn as nn

layer = nn.Linear(40, 10)
layer.weight.data *= 6 ** 0.5  # Kaiming init (or 3 ** 0.5 for LeCun init)
torch.zero_(layer.bias.data)
```

This works, but it's clearer and less error-prone to use one of the initialization functions available in the `torch.nn.init` module:

```
nn.init.kaiming_uniform_(layer.weight)
nn.init.zeros_(layer.bias)
```

If you want to apply the same initialization method to the weights of every `nn.Linear` layer in a model, you can do so in the model's constructor, after creating each `nn.Linear` layer. Alternatively, you can write a subclass of the `nn.Linear` class and tweak its constructor to initialize the weights as you wish. But arguably the simplest option is to write a little function that takes a module, checks whether it's an instance of the `nn.Linear` class, and if so, applies the desired initialization function to its weights. You can then apply this function to the model and all of its submodules by passing it to the model's `apply()` method. For example:

```
def use_he_init(module):
    if isinstance(module, nn.Linear):
        nn.init.kaiming_uniform_(module.weight)
        nn.init.zeros_(module.bias)

model = nn.Sequential(nn.Linear(50, 40), nn.ReLU(), nn.Linear(40, 1), nn.ReLU())
model.apply(use_he_init)
```

The `torch.nn.init` module also contains an `orthogonal_()` function which initializes the weights using a random orthogonal matrix, as proposed in a 2014 paper (*https://homl.info/ortho-init*) by Andrew Saxe et al.[5] Orthogonal matrices have a number of useful mathematical properties, including the fact that they preserve norms: given an orthogonal matrix **W** and an input vector **x**, the norm of **Wx** is equal to the norm of **x**, and therefore the magnitude of the inputs is preserved in the

4 A PyTorch issue (#18182) has been open since 2019 to update the weight initialization to use the current best practices.

5 Andrew Saxe et al., "Exact solutions to the nonlinear dynamics of learning in deep linear neural networks", ICLR (2014).

outputs. When the inputs are standardized, this results in a stable variance through the layer, which prevents the activations and gradients from vanishing or exploding in a deep network (at least at the beginning of training). This initialization technique is much less common than the initialization techniques discussed earlier, but it can work well in recurrent neural nets (Chapter 13) or generative adversarial networks (Chapter 18).

And that's it! Scaling the weights properly will give a deep neural net a much better starting point for training.

In a classifier, it's generally a good idea to scale down the weights of the output layer during initialization (e.g., by a factor of 10). Indeed, this will result in smaller logits at the beginning of training, which means they will be closer together, and hence the estimated probabilities will also be closer together. In other words, it encourages the model to be less confident about its predictions when training starts: this will avoid extreme losses and huge gradients that can often make the model's weights bounce around randomly at the start of training, losing time and potentially preventing the model from learning anything.

Better Activation Functions

One of the insights in the 2010 paper by Glorot and Bengio was that the problems with unstable gradients were in part due to a poor choice of activation function. Until then most people had assumed that if Mother Nature had chosen to use something pretty close to sigmoid activation functions in biological neurons, they must be an excellent choice. But it turns out that other activation functions behave much better in deep neural networks—in particular, the ReLU activation function, mostly because it does not saturate for positive values, and also because it is very fast to compute.

Unfortunately, the ReLU activation function is not perfect. It suffers from a problem known as the *dying ReLUs*: during training, some neurons effectively "die", meaning they stop outputting anything other than 0. In some cases, you may find that half of your network's neurons are dead, especially if you used a large learning rate. A neuron dies when its weights get tweaked in such a way that the input of the ReLU function (i.e., the weighted sum of the neuron's inputs plus its bias term) is negative for all instances in the training set. When this happens, it just keeps outputting zeros, and gradient descent does not affect it anymore because the gradient of the ReLU function is zero when its input is negative.[6]

6 A dead neuron may come back to life if its inputs evolve over time and eventually return within a range where the ReLU activation function gets a positive input again. For example, this may happen if gradient descent tweaks the neurons in the layers below the dead neuron.

To solve this problem, you may want to use a variant of the ReLU function, such as the *leaky ReLU*.

Leaky ReLU

The leaky ReLU activation function is defined as $\text{LeakyReLU}_\alpha(z) = \max(\alpha z, z)$ (see Figure 11-2). The hyperparameter α defines how much the function "leaks": it is the slope of the function for $z < 0$. Having a slope for $z < 0$ ensures that leaky ReLUs never actually die; they can go into a long coma, but they have a chance to eventually wake up. A 2015 paper (*https://homl.info/49*) by Bing Xu et al.[7] compared several variants of the ReLU activation function, and one of its conclusions was that the leaky variants always outperformed the strict ReLU activation function. In fact, setting $\alpha = 0.2$ (a huge leak) seemed to result in better performance than $\alpha = 0.01$ (a small leak). The paper also evaluated the *randomized leaky ReLU* (RReLU), where α is picked randomly in a given range during training and is fixed to an average value during testing. RReLU also performed fairly well and seemed to act as a regularizer, reducing the risk of overfitting. Finally, the paper evaluated the *parametric leaky ReLU* (PReLU), where α is authorized to be learned during training: instead of being a hyperparameter, it becomes a parameter that can be modified by backpropagation like any other parameter. PReLU was reported to strongly outperform ReLU on large image datasets, but on smaller datasets it runs the risk of overfitting the training set.

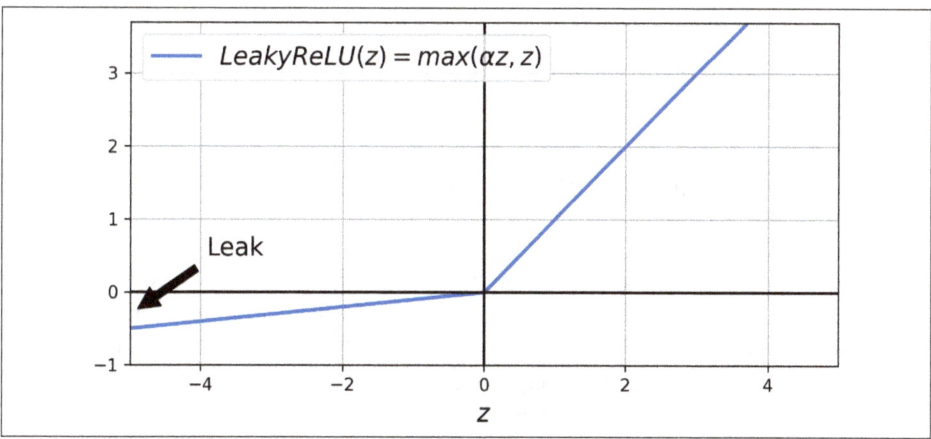

Figure 11-2. Leaky ReLU: like ReLU, but with a small slope for negative values

As you might expect, PyTorch includes modules for each of these activation functions: `nn.LeakyReLU`, `nn.RReLU`, and `nn.PReLU`. Just like for other ReLU variants, you should use these along with Kaiming initialization, but the variance should be

7 Bing Xu et al., "Empirical Evaluation of Rectified Activations in Convolutional Network", arXiv preprint arXiv:1505.00853 (2015).

slightly smaller due to the negative slope: it should be scaled down by a factor of $1 + \alpha^2$. PyTorch supports this: you can pass the α hyperparameter to the `kaiming_uniform_()` and `kaiming_normal_()` functions, along with `nonlinearity="leaky_relu"` to get the appropriately adjusted Kaiming initialization:

```
alpha = 0.2
model = nn.Sequential(nn.Linear(50, 40), nn.LeakyReLU(negative_slope=alpha))
nn.init.kaiming_uniform_(model[0].weight, alpha, nonlinearity="leaky_relu")
```

ReLU, leaky ReLU, and PReLU all suffer from the fact that they are not smooth functions: their slopes abruptly change at $z = 0$. As we saw in Chapter 4 when we discussed lasso, this sort of discontinuity in the derivatives can make gradient descent bounce around the optimum and slow down convergence. So now we will look at some smooth variants of the ReLU activation function, starting with ELU and SELU.

ELU and SELU

In 2015, a paper (*https://homl.info/50*) by Djork-Arné Clevert et al.[8] proposed a new activation function, called the *exponential linear unit* (ELU), that outperformed all the ReLU variants in the authors' experiments: training time was reduced, and the neural network performed better on the test set. Equation 11-2 shows this activation function's definition.

Equation 11-2. ELU activation function

$$\mathrm{ELU}_\alpha(z) = \begin{cases} \alpha(\exp(z) - 1) & \text{if } z < 0 \\ z & \text{if } z \geq 0 \end{cases}$$

The ELU activation function looks a lot like the ReLU function (see Figure 11-3), with a few major differences:

- It takes on negative values when $z < 0$, which allows the unit to have an average output closer to 0 and helps alleviate the vanishing gradients problem. The hyperparameter α defines the opposite of the value that the ELU function approaches when z is a large negative number. It is usually set to 1, but you can tweak it like any other hyperparameter.
- It has a nonzero gradient for $z < 0$, which avoids the dead neurons problem.
- If α is equal to 1, then the function is smooth everywhere, including around $z = 0$, which helps speed up gradient descent since it does not bounce as much to the left and right of $z = 0$.

8 Djork-Arné Clevert et al., "Fast and Accurate Deep Network Learning by Exponential Linear Units (ELUs)", *Proceedings of the International Conference on Learning Representations*, arXiv preprint (2015).

Using ELU with PyTorch is as easy as using the `nn.ELU` module, along with Kaiming initialization. The main drawback of the ELU activation function is that it is slower to compute than the ReLU function and its variants (due to the use of the exponential function). Its faster convergence rate during training may compensate for that slow computation, but still, at test time an ELU network will be a bit slower than a ReLU network.

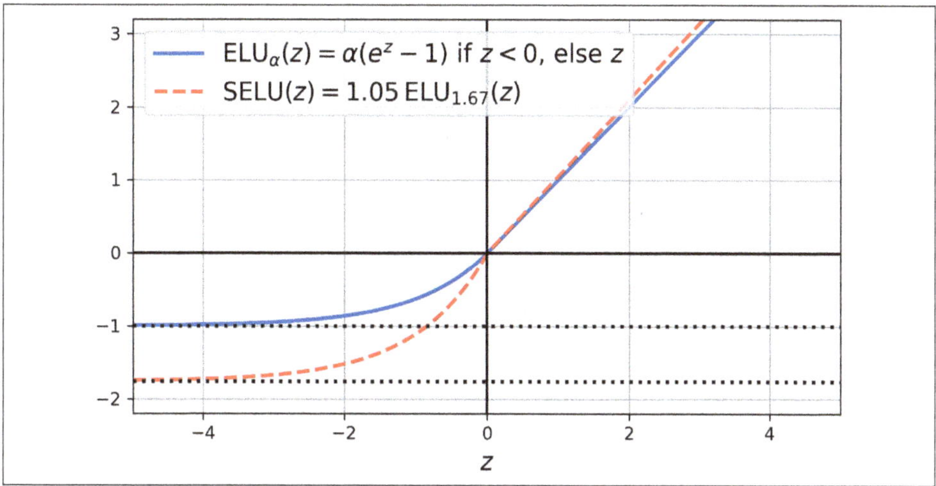

Figure 11-3. ELU and SELU activation functions

Not long after, a 2017 paper (*https://homl.info/selu*) by Günter Klambauer et al.[9] introduced the *scaled ELU* (SELU) activation function: as its name suggests, it is a scaled variant of the ELU activation function (about 1.05 times ELU, using $\alpha \approx 1.67$). The authors showed that if you build a neural network composed exclusively of a stack of dense layers (i.e., an MLP), and if all hidden layers use the SELU activation function, then the network will *self-normalize*: the output of each layer will tend to preserve a mean of 0 and a standard deviation of 1 during training, which solves the vanishing/exploding gradients problem. As a result, the SELU activation function may outperform other activation functions for MLPs, especially deep ones. To use it with PyTorch, just use `nn.SELU`. There are, however, a few conditions for self-normalization to happen (see the paper for the mathematical justification):

- The input features must be standardized: mean 0 and standard deviation 1.
- Every hidden layer's weights must be initialized using LeCun normal initialization.

9 Günter Klambauer et al., "Self-Normalizing Neural Networks", *Proceedings of the 31st International Conference on Neural Information Processing Systems* (2017): 972–981.

- The self-normalizing property is only guaranteed with plain MLPs. If you try to use SELU in other architectures, like recurrent networks (see Chapter 13) or networks with *skip connections* (i.e., connections that skip layers, such as in Wide & Deep neural networks), it will probably not outperform ELU.
- You cannot use regularization techniques like ℓ_1 or ℓ_2 regularization, batch-norm, layer-norm, max-norm, or regular dropout (these are discussed later in this chapter).

These are significant constraints, so despite its promises, SELU did not gain a lot of traction. Moreover, other activation functions seem to outperform it quite consistently on most tasks. Let's look at some of the most popular ones.

GELU, Swish, SwiGLU, Mish, and RELU²

The *Gaussian Error Linear Unit* (*GELU*) was introduced in a 2016 paper (*https://homl.info/gelu*) by Dan Hendrycks and Kevin Gimpel.[10] Once again, you can think of it as a smooth variant of the ReLU activation function. Its definition is given in Equation 11-3, where Φ is the standard Gaussian cumulative distribution function (CDF): $\Phi(z)$ corresponds to the probability that a value sampled randomly from a normal distribution of mean 0 and variance 1 is lower than z.

Equation 11-3. GELU activation function

$$\text{GELU}(z) = z\Phi(z)$$

As you can see in Figure 11-4, GELU resembles ReLU: it approaches 0 when its input z is very negative, and it approaches z when z is very positive. However, whereas all the activation functions we've discussed so far were both convex and monotonic,[11] the GELU activation function is neither: from left to right, it starts by going straight, then it wiggles down, reaches a low point around –0.17 (near z ≈ –0.75), and finally bounces up and ends up going straight toward the top right. This fairly complex shape and the fact that it has a curvature at every point may explain why it works so well, especially for complex tasks: gradient descent may find it easier to fit complex patterns. In practice, it often outperforms every other activation function discussed so far. However, it is a bit more computationally intensive, and the performance boost it provides is not always sufficient to justify the extra cost. That said, it is possible to show that it is approximately equal to $z\sigma(1.702\ z)$, where σ is the sigmoid function:

10 Dan Hendrycks and Kevin Gimpel, "Gaussian Error Linear Units (GELUs)", arXiv preprint arXiv:1606.08415 (2016).

11 A function is convex if the line segment between any two points on the curve never lies below the curve. A monotonic function only increases, or only decreases.

using this approximation also works very well, and it has the advantage of being much faster to compute.

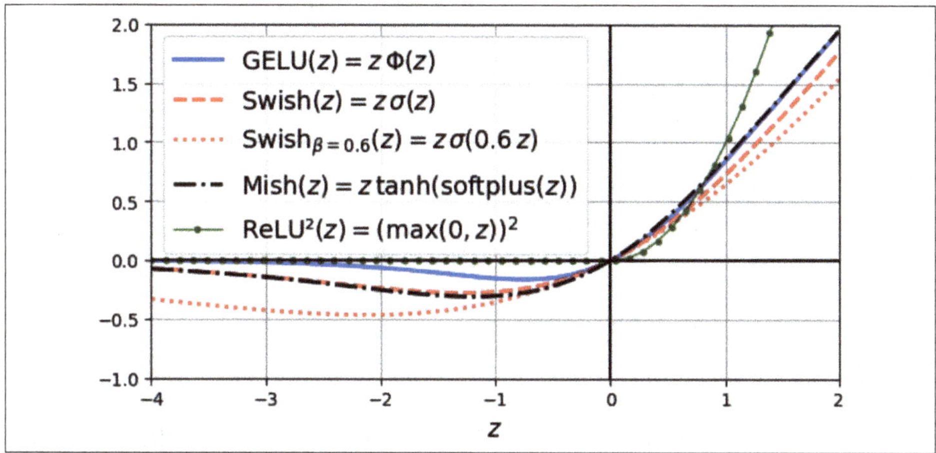

Figure 11-4. GELU, Swish, parametrized Swish, Mish, and ReLU² activation functions

The GELU paper also introduced the *sigmoid linear unit* (SiLU) activation function, which is equal to $z\sigma(z)$, but it was outperformed by GELU in the authors' tests. Interestingly, a 2017 paper (*https://homl.info/swish*) by Prajit Ramachandran et al.[12] rediscovered the SiLU function by automatically searching for good activation functions. The authors named it *Swish*, and the name caught on. In their paper, Swish outperformed every other function, including GELU. Ramachandran et al. later generalized Swish by adding an extra scalar hyperparameter β to scale the sigmoid function's input. The generalized Swish function is $\text{Swish}_\beta(z) = z\sigma(\beta z)$, so GELU is approximately equal to the generalized Swish function using $\beta = 1.702$. You can tune β like any other hyperparameter. Alternatively, it's also possible to make β trainable and let gradient descent optimize it (a bit like PReLU): there is typically a single trainable β parameter for the whole model, or just one per layer, to keep the model efficient and avoid overfitting.

A popular Swish variant is *SwiGLU* (*https://homl.info/swiglu*):[13] the inputs go through the Swish activation function, and in parallel through a linear layer, then both outputs are multiplied itemwise. That's $\text{SwiGLU}(\mathbf{z}) = \text{Swish}_\beta(\mathbf{z}) \otimes \text{Linear}(\mathbf{z})$. This is often implemented by doubling the output dimensions of the previous linear layer, then splitting the outputs in two along the feature dimension to get $\mathbf{z}_1$ and $\mathbf{z}_2$, and finally applying: $\text{SwiGLU}_\beta(\mathbf{z}) = \text{Swish}_\beta(\mathbf{z}_1) \otimes \mathbf{z}_2$. This is a variant of the *gated linear unit* (GLU) (*https://homl.info/glu*)[14] introduced by Facebook researchers in 2016. The

12 Prajit Ramachandran et al., "Searching for Activation Functions", arXiv preprint arXiv:1710.05941 (2017).

13 Noam Shazeer, "GLU Variants Improve Transformer", arXiv preprint arXiv:2002.05202 (2020).

itemwise multiplication gives the model more expressive power, allowing it to learn when to turn off (i.e., multiply by 0) or amplify specific features: this is called a *gating mechanism*. SwiGLU is very common in modern transformers (see Chapter 15).

Another GELU-like activation function is *Mish*, which was introduced in a 2019 paper (*https://homl.info/mish*) by Diganta Misra.[15] It is defined as mish(z) = $z$tanh(softplus(z)), where softplus(z) = log(1 + exp(z)). Just like GELU and Swish, it is a smooth, nonconvex, and nonmonotonic variant of ReLU, and once again the author ran many experiments and found that Mish generally outperformed other activation functions—even Swish and GELU, by a tiny margin. Figure 11-4 shows GELU, Swish (both with the default $\beta = 1$ and with $\beta = 0.6$), and lastly Mish. As you can see, Mish overlaps almost perfectly with Swish when z is negative, and almost perfectly with GELU when z is positive.

Lastly, in 2021, Google researchers ran an automated architecture search to improve large transformers, and the search found a very simple yet effective activation function: ReLU^2 (*https://homl.info/relu2*).[16] As its name suggests, it's simply ReLU squared: ReLU^2(z) = (max(0, z))^2. It has all the qualities of ReLU (simplicity, computational efficiency, sparse output, no saturation on the positive side) but it also has smooth gradients at $z = 0$, and it often outperforms other activation functions, especially for sparse models. However, training can be less stable, in part because of its increased sensitivity to outliers and dying ReLUs.

So, which activation function should you use for the hidden layers of your deep neural networks? ReLU remains a good default for most tasks: it's often just as good as the more sophisticated activation functions, plus it's very fast to compute, and many libraries and hardware accelerators provide ReLU-specific optimizations. However, Swish is probably a better default for complex tasks, and you can even try parametrized Swish with a learnable β parameter for the most complex tasks. Mish and SwiGLU may give you slightly better results, but they require a bit more compute. If you care a lot about runtime latency, then you may prefer leaky ReLU, or parametrized leaky ReLU for complex tasks, or even ReLU^2, especially for sparse models.

14 Yann Dauphin et al., "Language Modeling with Gated Convolutional Networks", arXiv preprint arXiv:1612.08083 (2016).

15 Diganta Misra, "Mish: A Self Regularized Non-Monotonic Activation Function", arXiv preprint arXiv:1908.08681 (2019).

16 So et al., "Primer: Searching for Efficient Transformers for Language Modeling", arXiv preprint arXiv:2109.08668 (2021).

PyTorch supports GELU, Mish, and Swish out of the box (using `nn.GELU`, `nn.Mish`, and `nn.SiLU`, respectively). To implement SwiGLU, double the previous linear layer's output dimension, then use `z1, z2 = z.chunk(2, dim=-1)` to split its output in two, and compute `F.silu(beta * z1) * z2` (where `F` is `torch.nn.functional`). For ReLU², simply compute `F.relu(z).square()`. PyTorch also includes simplified and approximated versions of several activation functions, which are much faster to compute and often more stable during training. These simplified versions have names starting with "Hard", such as `nn.Hardsigmoid`, `nn.Hardtanh`, and `nn.Hardswish`, and they are often used on mobile devices.

That's all for activation functions! Now, let's look at a completely different way to solve the unstable gradients problem: batch normalization.

Batch Normalization

Although using Kaiming initialization along with ReLU (or any of its variants) can significantly reduce the danger of the vanishing/exploding gradients problems at the beginning of training, it doesn't guarantee that they won't come back during training.

In a 2015 paper (*https://homl.info/51*),[17] Sergey Ioffe and Christian Szegedy proposed a technique called *batch normalization* (BN) that addresses these problems. The technique consists of adding an operation in the model just before or after the activation function of each hidden layer. This operation simply zero-centers and normalizes each input, then scales and shifts the result using two new parameter vectors per layer: one for scaling, the other for shifting. In other words, the operation lets the model learn the optimal scale and mean of each of the layer's inputs. In many cases, if you add a BN layer as the very first layer of your neural network, you do not need to standardize your training set (no need for `StandardScaler`); the BN layer will do it for you (well, approximately, since it only looks at one batch at a time, and it can also rescale and shift each input feature).

In order to zero-center and normalize the inputs, the algorithm needs to estimate each input's mean and standard deviation. It does so by evaluating the mean and standard deviation of the input over the current mini-batch (hence the name "batch normalization"). The whole operation is summarized step by step in Equation 11-4.

17 Sergey Ioffe and Christian Szegedy, "Batch Normalization: Accelerating Deep Network Training by Reducing Internal Covariate Shift", *Proceedings of the 32nd International Conference on Machine Learning* (2015): 448–456.

Equation 11-4. Batch normalization algorithm

$$1.\quad \boldsymbol{\mu}_B = \frac{1}{m_B} \sum_{i=1}^{m_B} \mathbf{x}^{(i)}$$

$$2.\quad {\boldsymbol{\sigma}_B}^2 = \frac{1}{m_B} \sum_{i=1}^{m_B} \left(\mathbf{x}^{(i)} - \boldsymbol{\mu}_B\right)^2$$

$$3.\quad \widehat{\mathbf{x}}^{(i)} = \frac{\mathbf{x}^{(i)} - \boldsymbol{\mu}_B}{\sqrt{{\boldsymbol{\sigma}_B}^2 + \varepsilon}}$$

$$4.\quad \mathbf{z}^{(i)} = \boldsymbol{\gamma} \otimes \widehat{\mathbf{x}}^{(i)} + \boldsymbol{\beta}$$

In this algorithm:

- $\boldsymbol{\mu}_B$ is the vector of input means, evaluated over the whole mini-batch *B* (it contains one mean per input).
- m_B is the number of instances in the mini-batch.
- $\mathbf{x}^{(i)}$ is the input vector of the batch-norm layer for instance *i*.
- $\boldsymbol{\sigma}_B$ is the vector of input standard deviations, also evaluated over the whole mini-batch (it contains one standard deviation per input).
- $\widehat{\mathbf{x}}^{(i)}$ is the vector of zero-centered and normalized inputs for instance *i*.
- ε is a tiny number that avoids division by zero and ensures the gradients don't grow too large (typically 10^{-5}). This is called a *smoothing term*.
- $\boldsymbol{\gamma}$ is the output scale parameter vector for the layer (it contains one scale parameter per input).
- $\otimes$ represents element-wise multiplication (each input is multiplied by its corresponding output scale parameter).
- $\boldsymbol{\beta}$ is the output shift (offset) parameter vector for the layer (it contains one shift parameter per input). Each input is offset by its corresponding shift parameter.
- $\mathbf{z}^{(i)}$ is the output of the BN operation. It is a rescaled and shifted version of the inputs.

So during training, BN standardizes its inputs, then rescales and offsets them. Good! What about at test time? Well, it's not that simple. Indeed, we may need to make predictions for individual instances rather than for batches of instances: in this case, we will have no way to compute each input's standard deviation. Moreover, even if we do have a batch of instances, it may be too small, or the instances may not be independent and identically distributed, so computing statistics over the batch instances would be unreliable. One solution is to wait until the end of training, then run the whole training set through the neural network and compute the mean and standard deviation of each input of the BN layer. These "final" input means and standard deviations can then be used instead of the batch input means and standard deviations when making predictions.

However, most implementations of batch norm estimate these final statistics during training by using a moving average of the layer's batch input means and variances. This is what PyTorch does automatically when you use its batch-norm layers, such as `nn.BatchNorm1d` (which we will discuss in the next section). To sum up, four parameter vectors are learned in each batch-norm layer: $\boldsymbol{\gamma}$ (the output scale vector) and $\boldsymbol{\beta}$ (the output offset vector) are learned through regular backpropagation, and $\boldsymbol{\mu}$ (the final input mean vector) and $\boldsymbol{\sigma}^2$ (the final input variance vector) are estimated using an exponential moving average. Note that $\boldsymbol{\mu}$ and $\boldsymbol{\sigma}^2$ are estimated during training, but they are used only after training, once you switch the model to evaluation mode using `model.eval()`: $\boldsymbol{\mu}$ and $\boldsymbol{\sigma}^2$ then replace $\boldsymbol{\mu}_B$ and $\boldsymbol{\sigma}_B{}^2$ in Equation 11-4.

Ioffe and Szegedy demonstrated that batch norm considerably improved all the deep neural networks they experimented with, leading to a huge improvement in the ImageNet classification task (ImageNet is a large database of images classified into many classes, commonly used to evaluate computer vision systems). The vanishing gradients problem was strongly reduced, to the point that they could use saturating activation functions such as tanh and even sigmoid. The networks were also much less sensitive to the weight initialization. The authors were able to use much larger learning rates, significantly speeding up the learning process. Specifically, they note that:

> Applied to a state-of-the-art image classification model, batch norm achieves the same accuracy with 14 times fewer training steps, and beats the original model by a significant margin. [...] Using an ensemble of batch-normalized networks, we improve upon the best published result on ImageNet classification: reaching 4.9% top-5 validation error (and 4.8% test error), exceeding the accuracy of human raters.

Finally, like a gift that keeps on giving, batch norm acts like a regularizer, reducing the need for other regularization techniques (such as dropout, described later in this chapter).

Batch normalization does, however, add some complexity to the model (although it can remove the need for normalizing the input data, as discussed earlier). Moreover, there is a runtime penalty: the neural network makes slower predictions due to the extra computations required at each layer. Fortunately, it's often possible to fuse the BN layer with the previous layer after training, thereby avoiding the runtime penalty. This is done by updating the previous layer's weights and biases so that it directly produces outputs of the appropriate scale and offset. For example, if the previous layer computes $\mathbf{XW} + \mathbf{b}$, then the BN layer will compute $\boldsymbol{\gamma} \otimes (\mathbf{XW} + \mathbf{b} - \boldsymbol{\mu}) / \boldsymbol{\sigma} + \boldsymbol{\beta}$ (ignoring the smoothing term ε in the denominator). If we define $\mathbf{W}' = \boldsymbol{\gamma}\otimes\mathbf{W} / \boldsymbol{\sigma}$ and $\mathbf{b}' = \boldsymbol{\gamma} \otimes (\mathbf{b} - \boldsymbol{\mu}) / \boldsymbol{\sigma} + \boldsymbol{\beta}$, the equation simplifies to $\mathbf{XW}' + \mathbf{b}'$. So, if we replace the previous layer's weights and biases (**W** and **b**) with the updated weights and biases (**W**′ and **b**′), we can get rid of the BN layer. This is one of the optimizations performed by `optimize_for_inference()` (see Chapter 10).

You may find that training is rather slow, because each epoch takes much more time when you use batch norm. This is usually counterbalanced by the fact that convergence is much faster with BN, so it will take fewer epochs to reach the same performance. All in all, *wall time* will usually be shorter (this is the time measured by the clock on your wall).

Implementing batch norm with PyTorch

As with most things with PyTorch, implementing batch norm is straightforward and intuitive. Just add an `nn.BatchNorm1d` layer before or after each hidden layer's activation function, and specify the number of inputs of each BN layer. You may also add a BN layer as the first layer in your model, which removes the need to standardize the inputs manually. For example, let's create a Fashion MNIST image classifier (similar to the one we built in Chapter 10) using BN as the first layer in the model (after flattening the input images), then again after each hidden layer:

```
model = nn.Sequential(
    nn.Flatten(),
    nn.BatchNorm1d(1 * 28 * 28),
    nn.Linear(1 * 28 * 28, 300),
    nn.ReLU(),
    nn.BatchNorm1d(300),
    nn.Linear(300, 100),
    nn.ReLU(),
    nn.BatchNorm1d(100),
    nn.Linear(100, 10)
)
```

You can now train the model normally (as you learned in Chapter 10), and that's it! In this tiny example with just two hidden layers, batch norm is unlikely to have a large impact, but for deeper networks it can make a tremendous difference.

Since batch norm behaves differently during training and during evaluation, it's critical to switch to training mode during training (using `model.train()`), and switch to evaluation mode during evaluation (using `model.eval()`). Forgetting to do so is one of the most common mistakes.

If you look at the parameters of the first BN layer, you will find two: `weight` and `bias`, which correspond to γ and β in Equation 11-4:

```
>>> dict(model[1].named_parameters()).keys()
dict_keys(['weight', 'bias'])
```

And if you look at the buffers of this same BN layer, you will find three: `running_mean`, `running_var`, and `num_batches_tracked`. The first two correspond to the running means **μ** and **σ**^{2} discussed earlier, and `num_batches_tracked` simply counts the number of batches seen during training:

```
>>> dict(model[1].named_buffers()).keys()
dict_keys(['running_mean', 'running_var', 'num_batches_tracked'])
```

The authors of the BN paper argued in favor of adding the BN layers before the activation functions, rather than after (as we just did). There is some debate about this, and it seems to depend on the task, so you can experiment with this to see which option works best on your dataset. If you move the BN layers before the activation functions, you can also remove the bias term from the previous `nn.Linear` layers by setting their `bias` hyperparameter to `False`. Indeed, a batch-norm layer already includes one bias term per input. You can also drop the first BN layer to avoid sandwiching the first hidden layer between two BN layers, but this means you should normalize the training set before training. The updated code looks like this:

```
model = nn.Sequential(
    nn.Flatten(),
    nn.Linear(1 * 28 * 28, 300, bias=False),
    nn.BatchNorm1d(300),
    nn.ReLU(),
    nn.Linear(300, 100, bias=False),
    nn.BatchNorm1d(100),
    nn.ReLU(),
    nn.Linear(100, 10)
)
```

The `nn.BatchNorm1d` class has a few hyperparameters you can tweak. The defaults will usually be fine, but you may occasionally need to tweak the `momentum`. This hyperparameter is used by the `BatchNorm1d` layer when it updates the exponential moving averages; given a new value **v** (i.e., a new vector of input means or variances computed over the current batch), the layer updates the running average $\widehat{\mathbf{v}}$ using the following equation:

$$\widehat{\mathbf{v}} \leftarrow \mathbf{v} \times \text{momentum} + \widehat{\mathbf{v}} \times (1 - \text{momentum})$$

A good momentum value is typically close to 0; for example, 0.01 or 0.001. You want more 0s for smaller mini-batches, and fewer for larger mini-batches. The default is 0.1, which is good for large batch sizes, but not great for small batch sizes such as 32 or 64.

When people talk about "momentum" in the context of a running mean, they usually refer to the weight of the current running mean in the update equation. Sadly, for historical reasons, PyTorch uses the opposite meaning in the BN layers. However, other parts of PyTorch use the conventional meaning (e.g., in optimizers), so don't get confused.

Batch norm 1D, 2D, and 3D

In the previous examples, we flattened the input images before sending them through the first `nn.BatchNorm1d` layer. This is because an `nn.BatchNorm1d` layer works on batches of shape `[batch_size, num_features]` (just like the `nn.Linear` layer does), so you would get an error if you moved it before the `nn.Flatten` layer.

However, you could use an `nn.BatchNorm2d` layer before the `nn.Flatten` layer: indeed, it expects its inputs to be image batches of shape `[batch_size, channels, height, width]`, and it computes the batch mean and variance across both the batch dimension (dimension 0) and the spatial dimensions (dimensions 2 and 3). This means that all pixels in the same batch and channel get normalized using the same mean and variance: the `nn.BatchNorm2d` layer only has one weight per channel and one bias per channel (e.g., three weights and three bias terms for color images with three channels for red, green, and blue). This generally works better when dealing with image datasets.

There's also an `nn.BatchNorm3d` layer which expects batches of shape `[batch_size, channels, depth, height, width]`: this is useful for datasets of 3D images, such as CT scans.

The `nn.BatchNorm1d` layer can also work on batches of sequences. The convention in PyTorch is to represent batches of sequences as 3D tensors of shape `[batch_size, sequence_length, num_features]`. For example, suppose you work on particle physics and you have a dataset of particle trajectories, where each trajectory is composed of a sequence of 100 points in 3D space, then a batch of 32 trajectories will have a shape of `[32, 100, 3]`. However, the `nn.BatchNorm1d` layer expects the shape to be `[batch_size, num_features, sequence_length]`, and it computes the batch mean and variance across the first and last dimensions to get one mean and variance per feature. So you must permute the last two dimensions of the data using `X.permute(0, 2, 1)` before letting it go through the `nn.BatchNorm1d` layer. We will discuss sequences further in Chapter 13.

Batch normalization has become one of the most-used layers in deep neural networks, especially deep convolutional neural networks discussed in Chapter 12, to the point that it is often omitted in the architecture diagrams: it is assumed that BN is added after every layer. That said, it is not perfect. In particular, the computed statistics for an instance are biased by the other samples in a batch, which may reduce performance (especially for small batch sizes). Moreover, BN struggles with some architectures, such as recurrent nets, as we will see in Chapter 13. For these reasons, batch-norm is more and more often replaced by layer-norm.

Layer Normalization

Layer normalization (LN) is very similar to batch norm, but instead of normalizing across the batch dimension, LN normalizes across the feature dimensions. This simple idea was introduced by Jimmy Lei Ba et al. in a 2016 paper (*https://homl.info/layernorm*),[18] and initially applied mostly to recurrent nets. However, in recent years it has been successfully applied to many other architectures, such as convolutional nets, transformers, diffusion nets, and more.

One advantage is that LN can compute the required statistics on the fly, at each time step, independently for each instance. This also means that it behaves the same way during training and testing (as opposed to BN), and it does not need to use exponential moving averages to estimate the feature statistics across all instances in the training set, like BN does. Lastly, LN learns a scale and an offset parameter for each input feature, just like BN does.

PyTorch includes an `nn.LayerNorm` module. To create an instance, you must simply indicate the size of the dimensions that you want to normalize over. These must be the last dimension(s) of the inputs. For example, if the inputs are batches of 100 × 200 RGB images of shape `[3, 100, 200]`, and you want to normalize each image over each of the three color channels separately, you would use the following `nn.LayerNorm` module:

```
inputs = torch.randn(32, 3, 100, 200)  # a batch of random RGB images
layer_norm = nn.LayerNorm([100, 200])
result = layer_norm(inputs)  # normalizes over the last two dimensions
```

The following code produces the same result:

```
means = inputs.mean(dim=[2, 3], keepdim=True)  # shape: [32, 3, 1, 1]
vars_ = inputs.var(dim=[2, 3], keepdim=True, unbiased=False)  # shape: same
stds = torch.sqrt(vars_ + layer_norm.eps)  # eps is a smoothing term (1e-5)
result = layer_norm.weight * (inputs - means) / stds + layer_norm.bias
# result shape: [32, 3, 100, 200]
```

However, most computer vision architectures that use LN normalize over all channels at once. For this, you must include the size of the channel dimension when creating the `nn.LayerNorm` module:

```
layer_norm = nn.LayerNorm([3, 100, 200])
result = layer_norm(inputs)  # normalizes over the last three dimensions
```

18 Jimmy Lei Ba et al., "Layer Normalization", arXiv preprint arXiv:1607.06450 (2016).

And that's all there is to it! Now let's look at one last technique to stabilize gradients during training: gradient clipping.

Gradient Clipping

Another technique to mitigate the exploding gradients problem is to clip the gradients during backpropagation so that they never exceed some threshold. This is called *gradient clipping* (*https://homl.info/52*).[19] This technique is generally used in recurrent neural networks, where using batch norm is tricky (as you will see in Chapter 13).

In PyTorch, gradient clipping is generally implemented by calling either `torch.nn.utils.clip_grad_norm_()` or `torch.nn.utils.clip_grad_value_()` at each iteration during training, right after the gradients are computed (i.e., after `loss.backward()`). Both functions take as a first argument the list of model parameters whose gradients must be clipped—typically all of them (`model.parameters()`). The `clip_grad_norm_()` function clips each gradient vector's norm if it exceeds the given `max_norm` argument. This is a hyperparameter you can tune (a typical default value is 1.0). The `clip_grad_value_()` function independently clips the individual components of the gradient vector between `-clip_value` and `+clip_value`, where `clip_value` is a hyperparameter you can tune. For example, this training loop clips the norm of each gradient vector to 1.0:

```
for epoch in range(n_epochs):
    for X_batch, y_batch in train_loader:
        X_batch, y_batch = X_batch.to(device), y_batch.to(device)
        y_pred = model(X_batch)
        loss = loss_fn(y_pred, y_batch)
        loss.backward()
        nn.utils.clip_grad_norm_(model.parameters(), max_norm=1.0)
        optimizer.step()
        optimizer.zero_grad()
```

Note that `clip_grad_value_()` will change the orientation of the gradient vector when its components are clipped. For instance, if the original gradient vector is `[0.9, 100.0]`, it points mostly in the direction of the second dimension; but once you clip it by value, you get `[0.9, 1.0]`, which points roughly at the diagonal between the two axes. Despite this reorientation, this approach actually works quite well in practice. If you clipped the same vector by norm, the result would be `[0.00899964, 0.9999595]`: this would preserve the vector's orientation, but almost eliminate the first component. The best clipping function to use depends on the dataset.

19 Razvan Pascanu et al., "On the Difficulty of Training Recurrent Neural Networks", *Proceedings of the 30th International Conference on Machine Learning* (2013): 1310–1318.

Reusing Pretrained Layers

It is generally not a good idea to train a very large DNN from scratch without first trying to find an existing neural network that accomplishes a similar task to the one you are trying to tackle (I will discuss how to find them in Chapter 12). If you find such a neural network, then you can generally reuse most of its layers, except for the top ones. This technique is called *transfer learning*. It will not only speed up training considerably, but also require significantly less training data.

Suppose you have access to a DNN that was trained to classify pictures into one hundred different categories, including animals, plants, vehicles, and everyday objects, and you now want to train a DNN to classify specific types of vehicles. These tasks are very similar, even partly overlapping, so you should try to reuse parts of the first network (see Figure 11-5).

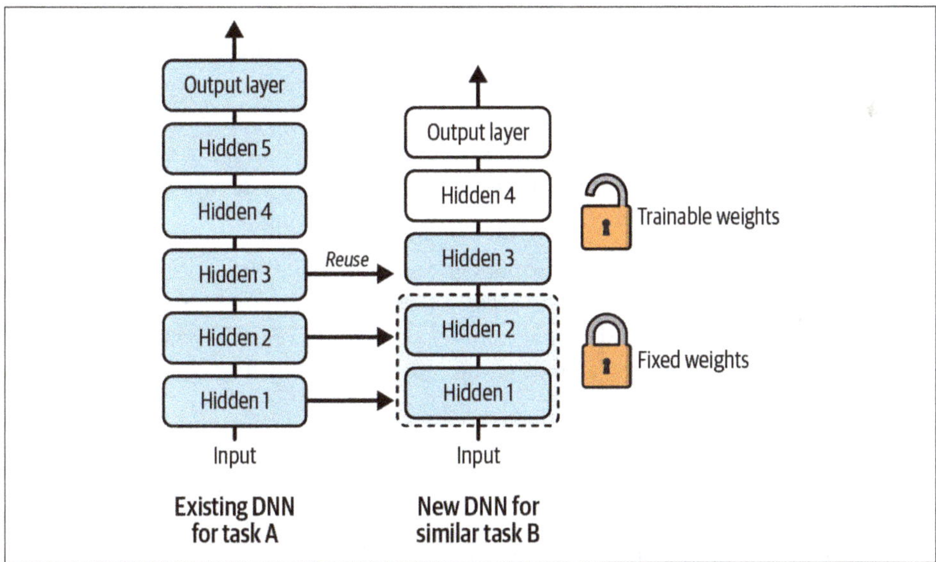

Figure 11-5. Reusing pretrained layers

If the input pictures for your new task don't have the same size as the ones used in the original task, you will usually have to add a preprocessing step to resize them to the size expected by the original model. More generally, transfer learning will work best when the inputs have similar low-level features. For example, a neural net trained on regular pictures taken from mobile phones will help with many other tasks on mobile phone pictures, but it will likely not help at all on satellite images or medical images.

The output layer of the original model should usually be replaced because it is most likely not useful at all for the new task, and it may not even have the right number of outputs.

Similarly, the upper hidden layers of the original model are less likely to be as useful as the lower layers, since the high-level features that are most useful for the new task may differ significantly from the ones that were most useful for the original task. You want to find the right number of layers to reuse.

The more similar the tasks are, the more layers you will want to reuse (starting with the lower layers). For very similar tasks, try to keep all the hidden layers and just replace the output layer.

Try freezing all the reused layers first (i.e., make their parameters nontrainable by setting `requires_grad` to `False` so that gradient descent won't modify them and they will remain fixed), then train your model and see how it performs. Then try unfreezing one or two of the top hidden layers to let backpropagation tweak them and see if performance improves. The more training data you have, the more layers you can unfreeze. It is also useful to reduce the learning rate when you unfreeze reused layers: this will avoid wrecking their fine-tuned weights.

If you still cannot get good performance, and you have little training data, try dropping the top hidden layer(s) and freezing all the remaining hidden layers again. You can iterate until you find the right number of layers to reuse. If you have plenty of training data, you may try replacing the top hidden layers instead of dropping them, and even adding more hidden layers.

Transfer Learning with PyTorch

Let's look at an example. Suppose the Fashion MNIST dataset only contained eight classes—for example, all the classes except for Pullover and T-shirt/top. Someone built and trained a PyTorch model on that set and got reasonably good performance (~92% accuracy). Let's call this model A. You now want to tackle a different task: you have images of T-shirts and pullovers, and you want to train a binary classifier: positive for T-shirt/top, negative for Pullover. Your dataset is tiny; you only have 20 labeled images! When you train a new model for this task (let's call it model B) with the same architecture as model A, you get 71.6% test accuracy. While drinking your morning coffee, you realize that your task is quite similar to task A, so perhaps transfer learning can help? Let's find out!

First, let's look at model A:

```
torch.manual_seed(42)

model_A = nn.Sequential(
    nn.Flatten(),
    nn.Linear(1 * 28 * 28, 100),
    nn.ReLU(),
    nn.Linear(100, 100),
    nn.ReLU(),
    nn.Linear(100, 100),
    nn.ReLU(),
    nn.Linear(100, 8)
)
[...]  # train this model or load pretrained weights
```

We can now reuse the layers we want, for example, all layers except for the output layer:

```
import copy

torch.manual_seed(42)
reused_layers = copy.deepcopy(model_A[:-1])
model_B_on_A = nn.Sequential(
    *reused_layers,
    nn.Linear(100, 1)  # new output layer for task B
).to(device)
```

In this code, we use Python's `copy.deepcopy()` function to copy all the modules in the `nn.Sequential` module (along with all their data and submodules), except for the last layer. Since we're making a deep copy, all the submodules are copied as well. Then we create `model_B_on_A`, which is an `nn.Sequential` model based on the reused layers of model A, plus a new output layer for task B: it has a single output since task B is binary classification.

You could start training `model_B_on_A` for task B now, but since the new output layer was initialized randomly, it will make large errors (at least during the first few epochs), so there will be large error gradients that may wreck the reused weights. To avoid this, one approach is to freeze the reused layers during the first few epochs, giving the new layer some time to learn reasonable weights:

```
for layer in model_B_on_A[:-1]:
    for param in layer.parameters():
        param.requires_grad = False
```

Now you can train `model_B_on_A`. But don't forget that task B is binary classification, so you must switch the loss to `nn.BCEWithLogitsLoss` (or to `nn.BCELoss` if you prefer to add an `nn.Sigmoid` activation function on the output layer), as we discussed in Chapter 10. Also, if you are using `torchmetrics`, make sure to set `task="binary"` when creating the `Accuracy` metric:

```
xentropy = nn.BCEWithLogitsLoss()
accuracy = torchmetrics.Accuracy(task="binary").to(device)
[...]  # train model_B_on_A
```

After you have trained the model for a few epochs, you can unfreeze the reused layers (setting `param.requires_grad = True` for all parameters), reduce the learning rate, and continue training to fine-tune the reused layers for task B.

So, what's the final verdict? Well, this model's test accuracy is 92.5%, which is much better than the 71.6% accuracy we reached without pretraining!

Are you convinced? Well, you shouldn't be; I cheated! I tried many configurations until I found one that demonstrated a strong improvement. If you try to change the classes or the random seed, you will see that the improvement generally drops, or even vanishes or reverses. What I did is called "torturing the data until it confesses". When a paper looks too positive, you should be suspicious. Perhaps the flashy new technique does not actually help much (in fact, it may even degrade performance), but the authors tried many variants and reported only the best results—which may be due to sheer luck—without mentioning how many failures they encountered along the way. That's called *p-hacking*. Most of the time, this is not malicious, but it is part of the reason why so many results in science can never be reproduced.

But why did I cheat? It turns out that transfer learning does not work very well with small dense networks, presumably because small networks learn few patterns, and dense networks learn very specific patterns, which are unlikely to be useful for other tasks. Transfer learning works best with deep convolutional neural networks and with Transformer architectures. We will revisit transfer learning in Chapters 12 and 15, using the techniques we just discussed (and this time it will work fine without cheating, I promise!).

Unsupervised Pretraining

Suppose you want to tackle a complex task for which you don't have much labeled training data, but unfortunately you cannot find a model trained on a similar task. Don't lose hope! First, you should try to gather more labeled training data, but if you can't, you may still be able to perform *unsupervised pretraining* (see Figure 11-6). Indeed, it is often cheap to gather unlabeled training examples, but expensive to label them. If you can gather plenty of unlabeled training data, you can try to use it to train an unsupervised model, such as an autoencoder (see Chapter 18). Then you can reuse the lower layers of the autoencoder, add the output layer for your task on top, and fine-tune the final network using supervised learning (i.e., with the labeled training examples).

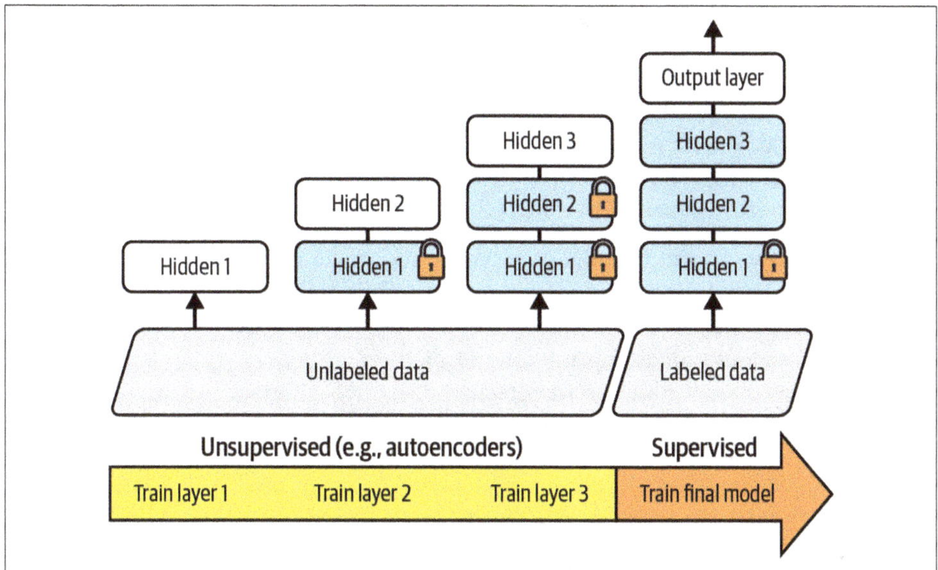

Figure 11-6. Greedy layer-wise pretraining used in the early days of deep learning; nowadays the unsupervised part is typically done in one shot on all the data rather than one layer at a time

It is this technique that Geoffrey Hinton and his team used in 2006, and which led to the revival of neural networks and the success of deep learning. Until 2010, unsupervised pretraining—typically with restricted Boltzmann machines (RBMs; see the notebook at *https://homl.info/extra-anns*)—was the norm for deep nets, and only after the vanishing gradients problem was alleviated did it become much more common to train DNNs purely using supervised learning. Unsupervised pretraining (today typically using autoencoders or diffusion models rather than RBMs) is still a good option when you have a complex task to solve, no similar model you can reuse, and little labeled training data, but plenty of unlabeled training data.

Note that in the early days of deep learning it was difficult to train deep models, so people would use a technique called *greedy layer-wise pretraining* (depicted in Figure 11-6). They would first train an unsupervised model with a single layer, typically an RBM, then they would freeze that layer and add another one on top of it, then train the model again (effectively just training the new layer), then freeze the new layer and add another layer on top of it, train the model again, and so on. Nowadays, things are much simpler: people generally train the full unsupervised model in one shot and use models such as autoencoders or diffusion models rather than RBMs.

Pretraining on an Auxiliary Task

If you do not have much labeled training data, one last option is to train a first neural network on an auxiliary task for which you can easily obtain or generate labeled training data, then reuse the lower layers of that network for your actual task. The first neural network's lower layers will learn feature detectors that will likely be reusable by the second neural network.

For example, if you want to build a system to recognize faces, you may only have a few pictures of each individual—clearly not enough to train a good classifier. Gathering hundreds of pictures of each person would not be practical. You could, however, use a public dataset containing millions of pictures of people (such as VGGFace2) and train a first neural network to detect whether two different pictures feature the same person. Such a network would learn good feature detectors for faces, so reusing its lower layers would allow you to train a good face classifier that uses little training data.

You could also just scrape pictures of random people from the web, but this would probably be illegal. Firstly, photos are usually copyrighted by their creators, and websites like Instagram or Facebook enforce these copyright protections through their terms of service, which prohibit scraping and unauthorized use. Secondly, over 40 countries require explicit consent for collecting and processing personal data, including facial images.

For natural language processing (NLP) applications, you can download a corpus of millions of text documents and automatically generate labeled data from it. For example, you could randomly mask out some words and train a model to predict what the missing words are (e.g., it should predict that the missing word in the sentence "What ___ you saying?" is probably "are" or "were"). If you can train a model to reach good performance on this task, then it will already know quite a lot about language, and you can certainly reuse it for your actual task and fine-tune it on your labeled data (this is basically how large language models are trained and fine-tuned, as we will see in Chapter 15).

Self-supervised learning is when you automatically generate the labels from the data itself, as in the text-masking example, then you train a model on the resulting "labeled" dataset using supervised learning techniques.

Faster Optimizers

Training a very large deep neural network can be painfully slow. So far we have seen four ways to speed up training (and reach a better solution): applying a good initialization strategy for the connection weights, using a good activation function, using batch-norm or layer-norm, and reusing parts of a pretrained network (possibly built for an auxiliary task or using unsupervised learning). Another huge speed boost comes from using a faster optimizer than the regular gradient descent optimizer. In this section we will present the most popular optimization algorithms: momentum, Nesterov accelerated gradient, AdaGrad, RMSProp, and finally, Adam and its variants.

Momentum

Imagine a bowling ball rolling down a gentle slope on a smooth surface: it will start out slowly, but it will quickly pick up momentum until it eventually reaches terminal velocity (if there is some friction or air resistance). This is the core idea behind *momentum optimization*, proposed by Boris Polyak in 1964 (*https://homl.info/54*).[20] In contrast, regular gradient descent will take small steps when the slope is gentle and big steps when the slope is steep, but it will never pick up speed. As a result, regular gradient descent is generally much slower to reach the minimum than momentum optimization.

As we saw in Chapter 4, gradient descent updates the weights $\boldsymbol{\theta}$ by directly subtracting the gradient of the cost function $J(\boldsymbol{\theta})$ with regard to the weights ($\nabla_{\boldsymbol{\theta}}J(\boldsymbol{\theta})$) multiplied by the learning rate η. The equation is $\boldsymbol{\theta} \leftarrow \boldsymbol{\theta} - \eta\nabla_{\boldsymbol{\theta}}J(\boldsymbol{\theta})$. It does not care about what the earlier gradients were. If the local gradient is tiny, it goes very slowly.

Momentum optimization cares a great deal about what previous gradients were: at each iteration, it subtracts the local gradient from the *momentum vector* $\mathbf{m}$ (multiplied by the learning rate η), and it updates the weights by adding this momentum vector (see Equation 11-5). In other words, the gradient is used as a force learning to an acceleration, not as a speed. To simulate some sort of friction mechanism and prevent the momentum from growing too large, the algorithm introduces a new hyperparameter β, called the *momentum coefficient*, which must be set between 0 (high friction) and 1 (no friction). A typical momentum value is 0.9.

20 Boris T. Polyak, "Some Methods of Speeding Up the Convergence of Iteration Methods", *USSR Computational Mathematics and Mathematical Physics* 4, no. 5 (1964): 1–17.

Equation 11-5. Momentum algorithm

$$1. \quad \mathbf{m} \leftarrow \beta\mathbf{m} - \eta\nabla_{\boldsymbol{\theta}}J(\boldsymbol{\theta})$$
$$2. \quad \boldsymbol{\theta} \leftarrow \boldsymbol{\theta} + \mathbf{m}$$

You can verify that if the gradient remains constant, the terminal velocity (i.e., the maximum size of the weight updates) is equal to that gradient multiplied by the learning rate η multiplied by 1 / (1 – β) (ignoring the sign). For example, if β = 0.9, then the terminal velocity is equal to 10 times the gradient times the learning rate, so momentum optimization ends up going 10 times faster than gradient descent! In practice, the gradients are not constant, so the speedup is not always as dramatic, but momentum optimization can escape from plateaus much faster than regular gradient descent. We saw in Chapter 4 that when the inputs have very different scales, the cost function will look like an elongated bowl (see Figure 4-7). Gradient descent goes down the steep slope quite fast, but then it takes a very long time to go down the valley. In contrast, momentum optimization will roll down the valley faster and faster until it reaches the bottom (the optimum). In deep neural networks that don't use batch-norm or layer-norm, the upper layers will often end up having inputs with very different scales, so using momentum optimization helps a lot. It can also help roll past local optima.

Due to the momentum, the optimizer may overshoot a bit, then come back, overshoot again, and oscillate like this many times before stabilizing at the minimum. This is one of the reasons why it's good to have a bit of friction in the system: it reduces these oscillations and thus speeds up convergence.

Implementing momentum optimization in PyTorch is a no-brainer: just use the `SGD` optimizer and set its `momentum` hyperparameter, then sit back and profit!

```
optimizer = torch.optim.SGD(model.parameters(), momentum=0.9, lr=0.05)
```

The one drawback of momentum optimization is that it adds yet another hyperparameter to tune. However, the momentum value of 0.9 usually works well in practice and almost always goes faster than regular gradient descent.

Nesterov Accelerated Gradient

One small variant to momentum optimization, proposed by Yurii Nesterov in 1983 (*https://homl.info/55*),[21] is almost always faster than regular momentum optimization. The *Nesterov accelerated gradient* (NAG) method, also known as *Nesterov momentum*

21 Yurii Nesterov, "A Method for Unconstrained Convex Minimization Problem with the Rate of Convergence $O(1/k^2)$", *Doklady AN USSR* 269 (1983): 543–547.

optimization, measures the gradient of the cost function not at the local position $\boldsymbol{\theta}$ but slightly ahead in the direction of the momentum, at $\boldsymbol{\theta} + \beta\mathbf{m}$ (see Equation 11-6).

Equation 11-6. Nesterov accelerated gradient algorithm

1. $\mathbf{m} \leftarrow \beta\mathbf{m} - \eta\nabla_{\boldsymbol{\theta}}J(\boldsymbol{\theta} + \beta\mathbf{m})$
2. $\boldsymbol{\theta} \leftarrow \boldsymbol{\theta} + \mathbf{m}$

This small tweak works because in general the momentum vector will be pointing in the right direction (i.e., toward the optimum), so it will be slightly more accurate to use the gradient measured a bit farther in that direction rather than the gradient at the original position, as you can see in Figure 11-7 (where ∇_1 represents the gradient of the cost function measured at the starting point $\boldsymbol{\theta}$, and ∇_2 represents the gradient at the point located at $\boldsymbol{\theta} + \beta\mathbf{m}$).

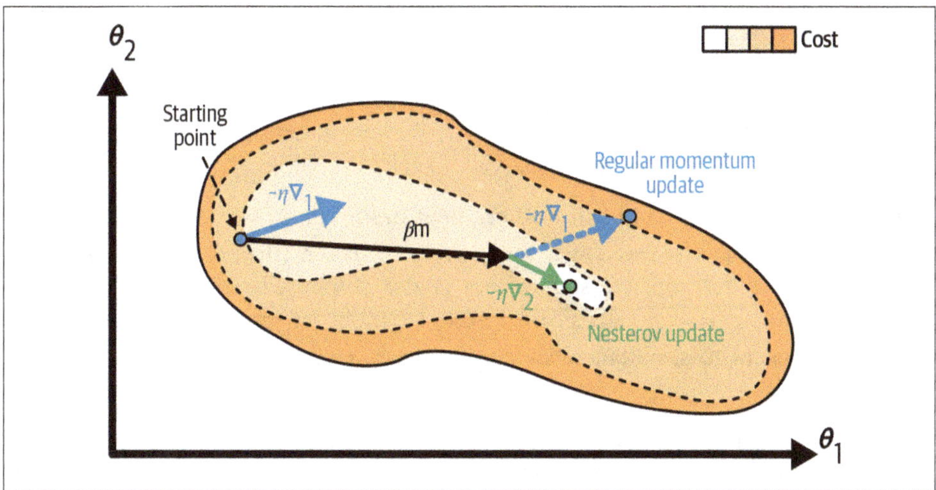

Figure 11-7. Regular versus Nesterov momentum optimization: the former applies the gradients computed before the momentum step, while the latter applies the gradients computed after

As you can see, the Nesterov update ends up closer to the optimum. After a while, these small improvements add up and NAG ends up being significantly faster than regular momentum optimization. Moreover, note that when the momentum pushes the weights across a valley, ∇_1 continues to push farther across the valley, while ∇_2 pushes back toward the bottom of the valley. This helps reduce oscillations and thus NAG converges faster.

To use NAG, simply set `nesterov=True` when creating the `SGD` optimizer:

```
optimizer = torch.optim.SGD(model.parameters(),
                            momentum=0.9, nesterov=True, lr=0.05)
```

AdaGrad

Consider the elongated bowl problem again: gradient descent starts by quickly going down the steepest slope, which does not point straight toward the global optimum, then it very slowly goes down to the bottom of the valley. It would be nice if the algorithm could correct its direction earlier to point a bit more toward the global optimum. The *AdaGrad* algorithm (*https://homl.info/56*)[22] achieves this correction by scaling down the gradient vector along the steepest dimensions (see Equation 11-7).

Equation 11-7. AdaGrad algorithm

$$1. \quad \mathbf{s} \leftarrow \mathbf{s} + \nabla_{\boldsymbol{\theta}} J(\boldsymbol{\theta}) \otimes \nabla_{\boldsymbol{\theta}} J(\boldsymbol{\theta})$$

$$2. \quad \boldsymbol{\theta} \leftarrow \boldsymbol{\theta} - \eta \nabla_{\boldsymbol{\theta}} J(\boldsymbol{\theta}) \oslash \sqrt{\mathbf{s} + \varepsilon}$$

The first step accumulates the square of the gradients into the vector **s** (recall that the $\otimes$ symbol represents the element-wise multiplication). This vectorized form is equivalent to computing $s_i \leftarrow s_i + (\partial J(\boldsymbol{\theta}) \ / \ \partial \theta_i)^2$ for each element s_i of the vector **s**; in other words, each s_i accumulates the squares of the partial derivative of the cost function with regard to parameter θ_i. If the cost function is steep along the ith dimension, then s_i will get larger and larger at each iteration.

The second step is almost identical to gradient descent, but with one big difference: the gradient vector is scaled down by a factor of $\sqrt{\mathbf{s} + \varepsilon}$ (the $\oslash$ symbol represents the element-wise division, the square root is also computed element-wise, and ε is a smoothing term to avoid division by zero, typically set to 10^{-10}). This vectorized form is equivalent to simultaneously computing $\theta_i \leftarrow \theta_i - \eta \, \partial J(\boldsymbol{\theta}) / \partial \theta_i \, / \sqrt{s_i + \varepsilon}$ for all parameters θ_i.

In short, this algorithm decays the learning rate, but it does so faster for steep dimensions than for dimensions with gentler slopes. This is called an *adaptive learning rate*. It helps point the resulting updates more directly toward the global optimum (see Figure 11-8). One additional benefit is that it requires much less tuning of the learning rate hyperparameter η.

AdaGrad frequently performs well for simple quadratic problems, but it often stops too early when training neural networks: the learning rate gets scaled down so much that the algorithm ends up stopping entirely before reaching the global optimum.

---

22 John Duchi et al., "Adaptive Subgradient Methods for Online Learning and Stochastic Optimization", *Journal of Machine Learning Research* 12 (2011): 2121–2159.

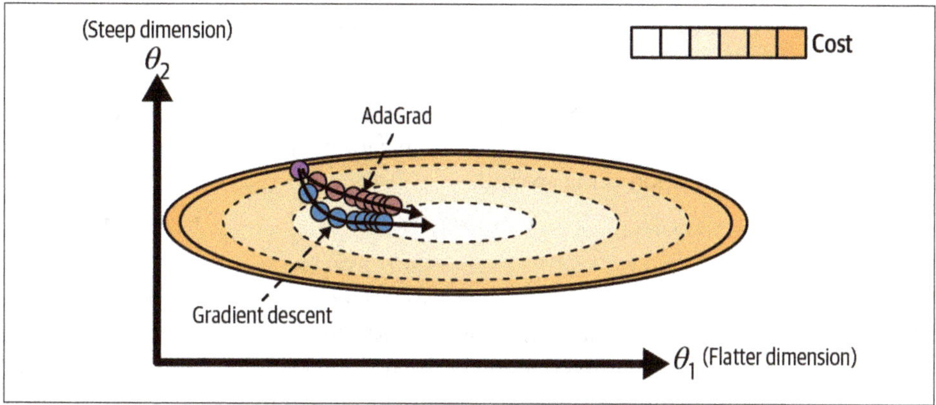

Figure 11-8. AdaGrad versus gradient descent: the former can correct its direction earlier to point to the optimum

So even though PyTorch has an `Adagrad` optimizer, you should not use it to train deep neural networks (it may be efficient for simpler tasks such as linear regression, though). Still, understanding AdaGrad is helpful to comprehend the other adaptive learning rate optimizers.

RMSProp

As we've seen, AdaGrad runs the risk of slowing down a bit too fast and never converging to the global optimum. The *RMSProp* algorithm[23] fixes this by accumulating only the gradients from the most recent iterations, as opposed to all the gradients since the beginning of training. It does so by using exponential decay in the first step (see Equation 11-8).

Equation 11-8. RMSProp algorithm

1. $\mathbf{s} \leftarrow \alpha \mathbf{s} + (1 - \alpha) \nabla_{\boldsymbol{\theta}} J(\boldsymbol{\theta}) \otimes \nabla_{\boldsymbol{\theta}} J(\boldsymbol{\theta})$
2. $\boldsymbol{\theta} \leftarrow \boldsymbol{\theta} - \eta \, \nabla_{\boldsymbol{\theta}} J(\boldsymbol{\theta}) \oslash \sqrt{\mathbf{s} + \varepsilon}$

The decay rate α is typically set to 0.9. Yes, it is once again a new hyperparameter, but this default value often works well, so you may not need to tune it at all.

23 This algorithm was created by Geoffrey Hinton and Tijmen Tieleman in 2012 and presented by Geoffrey Hinton in his Coursera class on neural networks (slides: *https://homl.info/57*, video: *https://homl.info/58*). Amusingly, since the authors did not write a paper to describe the algorithm, researchers often cite "slide 29 in lecture 6e" in their papers.

As you might expect, PyTorch has an RMSprop optimizer:

```
optimizer = torch.optim.RMSprop(model.parameters(), alpha=0.9, lr=0.05)
```

Except on very simple problems, this optimizer almost always performs much better than AdaGrad. In fact, it was the preferred optimization algorithm of many researchers until Adam optimization came around.

Adam

Adam (*https://homl.info/59*),[24] which stands for *adaptive moment estimation*, combines the ideas of momentum optimization and RMSProp: just like momentum optimization, it keeps track of an exponentially decaying average of past gradients; and just like RMSProp, it keeps track of an exponentially decaying average of past squared gradients (see Equation 11-9). These are estimations of the mean and (uncentered) variance of the gradients. The mean is often called the *first moment*, while the variance is often called the *second moment*, hence the name of the algorithm.

Equation 11-9. Adam algorithm

1. $\mathbf{m} \leftarrow \beta_1 \mathbf{m} - (1 - \beta_1) \nabla_{\boldsymbol{\theta}} J(\boldsymbol{\theta})$
2. $\mathbf{s} \leftarrow \beta_2 \mathbf{s} + (1 - \beta_2) \nabla_{\boldsymbol{\theta}} J(\boldsymbol{\theta}) \otimes \nabla_{\boldsymbol{\theta}} J(\boldsymbol{\theta})$
3. $\widehat{\mathbf{m}} \leftarrow \dfrac{\mathbf{m}}{1 - {\beta_1}^t}$
4. $\widehat{\mathbf{s}} \leftarrow \dfrac{\mathbf{s}}{1 - {\beta_2}^t}$
5. $\boldsymbol{\theta} \leftarrow \boldsymbol{\theta} + \eta \widehat{\mathbf{m}} \oslash \sqrt{\widehat{\mathbf{s}} + \varepsilon}$

In this equation, t represents the iteration number (starting at 1).

If you just look at steps 1, 2, and 5, you will notice Adam's close similarity to both momentum optimization and RMSProp: β_1 corresponds to β in momentum optimization, and β_2 corresponds to α in RMSProp. The only difference is that step 1 computes an exponentially decaying average rather than an exponentially decaying sum, but these are actually equivalent except for a constant factor (the decaying average is just $1 - \beta_1$ times the decaying sum). Steps 3 and 4 are somewhat of a technical detail: since **m** and **s** are initialized at 0, they will be biased toward 0 at the beginning of training, so these two steps will help boost **m** and **s** at the beginning of training.

---

24 Diederik P. Kingma and Jimmy Ba, "Adam: A Method for Stochastic Optimization", arXiv preprint arXiv:1412.6980 (2014).

The momentum decay hyperparameter β_1 is typically initialized to 0.9, while the scaling decay hyperparameter β_2 is often initialized to 0.999. As earlier, the smoothing term ε is usually initialized to a tiny number such as 10^{-8}. These are the default values for the `Adam` class. Here is how to create an Adam optimizer using PyTorch:

```
optimizer = torch.optim.Adam(model.parameters(), betas=(0.9, 0.999), lr=0.05)
```

Since Adam is an adaptive learning rate algorithm, like AdaGrad and RMSProp, it requires less tuning of the learning rate hyperparameter η. You can often use the default value $\eta = 0.001$, making Adam even easier to use than gradient descent.

If you are starting to feel overwhelmed by all these different techniques and are wondering how to choose the right ones for your task, don't worry: some practical guidelines are provided at the end of this chapter.

Finally, three variants of Adam are worth mentioning: AdaMax, NAdam, and AdamW.

AdaMax

The Adam paper also introduced AdaMax. Notice that in step 2 of Equation 11-9, Adam accumulates the squares of the gradients in **s** (with a greater weight for more recent gradients). In step 5, if we ignore ε and steps 3 and 4 (which are technical details anyway), Adam scales down the parameter updates by the square root of **s**. In short, Adam scales down the parameter updates by the ℓ_2 norm of the time-decayed gradients (recall that the ℓ_2 norm is the square root of the sum of squares).

AdaMax replaces the ℓ_2 norm with the ℓ_∞ norm (a fancy way of saying the max). Specifically, it replaces step 2 in Equation 11-9 with $\mathbf{s} \leftarrow \max(\beta_2\mathbf{s}, \text{abs}(\nabla_\boldsymbol{\theta} J(\boldsymbol{\theta})))$, it drops step 4, and in step 5 it scales down the gradient updates by a factor of **s**, which is the max of the absolute value of the time-decayed gradients.

In practice, this can make AdaMax more stable than Adam, but it really depends on the dataset, and in general Adam performs better. So, this is just one more optimizer you can try if you experience problems with Adam on some task.

NAdam

NAdam optimization is Adam optimization plus the Nesterov trick, so it will often converge slightly faster than Adam. In his report introducing this technique,[25] the researcher Timothy Dozat compares many different optimizers on various tasks and

25 Timothy Dozat, "Incorporating Nesterov Momentum into Adam" (*https://homl.info/nadam*), (2016).

finds that NAdam generally outperforms Adam but is sometimes outperformed by RMSProp.

AdamW

AdamW (*https://homl.info/adamw*)[26] is a variant of Adam that integrates a regularization technique called *weight decay*. Weight decay reduces the size of the model's weights at each training iteration by multiplying them by a decay factor such as 0.99. This may remind you of ℓ_2 regularization (introduced in Chapter 4), which also aims to keep the weights small, and indeed it can be shown mathematically that ℓ_2 regularization is equivalent to weight decay when using SGD. However, when using Adam or its variants, ℓ_2 regularization and weight decay are *not* equivalent: in practice, combining Adam with ℓ_2 regularization results in models that often don't generalize as well as those produced by SGD. AdamW fixes this issue by properly combining Adam with weight decay.

Adaptive optimization methods (including RMSProp, Adam, AdaMax, NAdam, and AdamW optimization) are often great, converging fast to a good solution. However, a 2017 paper (*https://homl.info/60*)[27] by Ashia C. Wilson et al. showed that they can lead to solutions that generalize poorly on some datasets. So when you are disappointed by your model's performance, try using NAG instead: your dataset may just be allergic to adaptive gradients.

To use NAdam, AdaMax, or AdamW in PyTorch, replace `torch.optim.Adam` with `torch.optim.NAdam`, `torch.optim.Adamax`, or `torch.optim.AdamW`. For AdamW, you probably want to tune the `weight_decay` hyperparameter.

All the optimization techniques discussed so far only rely on the *first-order partial derivatives* (*Jacobians*, which measure the slope of the loss function along each axis). The optimization literature also contains amazing algorithms based on the *second-order partial derivatives* (the *Hessians*, which are the partial derivatives of the Jacobians, measuring how each Jacobian changes along each axis; in other words, measuring the loss function's curvature).

Unfortunately, these Hessian-based algorithms are hard to apply directly to deep neural networks because there are n^2 second-order derivatives per output (where n is the number of parameters), as opposed to just n first-order derivatives per

26 Ilya Loshchilov, and Frank Hutter, "Decoupled Weight Decay Regularization", arXiv preprint arXiv:1711.05101 (2017).

27 Ashia C. Wilson et al., "The Marginal Value of Adaptive Gradient Methods in Machine Learning", *Advances in Neural Information Processing Systems* 30 (2017): 4148–4158.

output. Since DNNs typically have hundreds of thousands of parameters or more, the second-order optimization algorithms often don't even fit in memory, and even when they do, computing the *Hessian matrix* is just too slow.[28]

Luckily, it is possible to use stochastic methods that can efficiently approximate second-order information. One such algorithm is Shampoo,[29] which uses accumulated gradient information to approximate the second-order terms, similar to how Adam accumulates first-order statistics. It is not included in the PyTorch library, but you can get it in the PyTorch-Optimizer library (`pip install torch_optimizer`).

Training Sparse Models

All the optimization algorithms we just discussed produce dense models, meaning that most parameters will be nonzero. If you need a blazingly fast model at runtime, or if you need it to take up less memory, you may prefer to end up with a sparse model instead.

One way to achieve this is to train the model as usual, then get rid of the tiny weights (set them to zero) using `torch.nn.utils.prune.l1_unstructured()`. Or you can get rid of entire neurons, channels, or layers, not just individual weights, using `torch.nn.utils.prune.ln_structured()`, or other functions in the `torch.nn.utils.prune` package.

You should generally also apply fairly strong sparsity inducing regularization during training, such as ℓ_1 regularization (you'll see how later in this chapter), since it pushes the optimizer to zero out as many weights as it can (see "Lasso Regression" on page 162). You can also try scaling down random weights during initialization to encourage sparsity.

Table 11-2 compares all the optimizers we've discussed so far (☆ is bad, ☆☆ is average, and ☆☆☆ is good).

28 The *Jacobian matrix* contains all the first-order partial derivatives of a function with multiple parameters and multiple outputs: one column per parameter, and one row per output. When training a neural net with gradient descent, there's a single output—the loss—so the matrix contains a single row, and there's one column per model parameter, so it's a 1×*n* matrix. The *Hessian matrix* contains all the second-order derivatives of a single-output function with multiple parameters: for each model parameter it contains one row and one column, so it's an *n*×*n* matrix. The informal names *Jacobians* and *Hessians* refer to the elements of these matrices.

29 V. Gupta et al., "Shampoo: Preconditioned Stochastic Tensor Optimization" (*https://homl.info/shampoo*), arXiv preprint arXiv:1802.09568 (2018).

Table 11-2. Optimizer comparison

Class	Convergence speed	Convergence quality
`SGD`	★	★★★
`SGD(momentum=...)`	★★	★★★
`SGD(momentum=..., nesterov=True)`	★★	★★★
`Adagrad`	★★	★ (stops too early)
`RMSprop`	★★	★★ or ★★★
`Adam`	★★	★★ or ★★★
`AdaMax`	★★	★★ or ★★★
`NAdam`	★★	★★ or ★★★
`AdamW`	★★	★★ or ★★★

Learning Rate Scheduling

Finding a good learning rate is very important. If you set it too high, training will diverge (as discussed in "Gradient Descent" on page 142). If you set it too low, then training will be painfully slow, and it may also get stuck in a local optimum and produce a suboptimal model. If you set the learning rate fairly high (but not high enough to diverge), then training will often make rapid progress at first, but it will end up dancing around the optimum toward the end of training and thereby produce a suboptimal model. If you find a really good learning rate, you can end up with an excellent model, but training will generally be a bit too slow. Luckily, you can do better than a constant learning rate. In particular, it's a good idea to start with a fairly high learning rate and then reduce it toward the end of training (or whenever progress stops): this ensures that training starts fast, while also allowing backprop to settle down toward the end to really fine-tune the model parameters (see Figure 11-9).

There are various other strategies to tweak the learning rate during training. These are called *learning schedules* (I briefly introduced this concept in Chapter 4). The `torch.optim.lr_scheduler` module provides several implementations of common learning schedules. Let's look at the most important ones, starting with exponential scheduling.

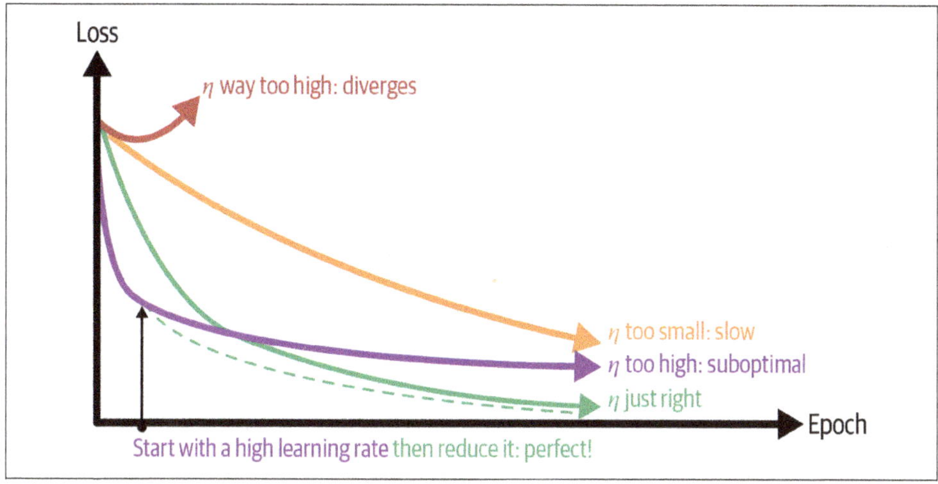

Figure 11-9. Learning curves for various learning rates η

Exponential Scheduling

The `ExponentialLR` class implements *exponential scheduling*, whereby the learning rate is multiplied by a constant factor `gamma` at some regular interval, typically at every epoch. As a result, after the nth epoch, the learning rate will be equal to the initial learning rate times `gamma` to the power of n. This factor `gamma` is yet another hyperparameter you can tune. In general, you will want to set `gamma` to a value lower than 1, but fairly close to 1 to avoid decreasing the learning rate too fast. For example, if `gamma` is set to 0.9, then after 10 epochs the learning rate will be about 35% of the initial learning rate, and after 20 epochs it will be about 12%.

The `ExponentialLR` constructor expects at least two arguments—the optimizer whose learning rate will be tweaked during training, and the factor `gamma`:

```
model = [...]  # build the model
optimizer = torch.optim.SGD(model.parameters(), lr=0.05)  # or any other optim.
scheduler = torch.optim.lr_scheduler.ExponentialLR(optimizer, gamma=0.9)
```

Next, you must update the training loop to call `scheduler.step()` at the end of each epoch to tweak the optimizer's learning rate:

```
for epoch in range(n_epochs):
    for X_batch, y_batch in train_loader:
        [...]  # the rest of the training loop remains unchanged

    scheduler.step()
```

If you interrupt training and you later want to resume it where you left off, you should set the `last_epoch` argument of the scheduler's constructor to the last epoch you ran (zero-indexed). The default is –1, which makes the scheduler start training from scratch.

Cosine Annealing

Instead of decreasing the learning rate exponentially, you can use the cosine function to go from the maximum learning rate η_{max} at the start of training, down to the minimum learning rate η_{min} at the end. This is called *cosine annealing*. Compared to exponential scheduling, cosine annealing ensures that the learning rate remains fairly high during most of training, while getting closer to the minimum near the end (see Figure 11-10). All in all, cosine annealing generally performs better. The learning rate at epoch t (zero-indexed) is given by Equation 11-10, where T_{max} is the maximum number of epochs.

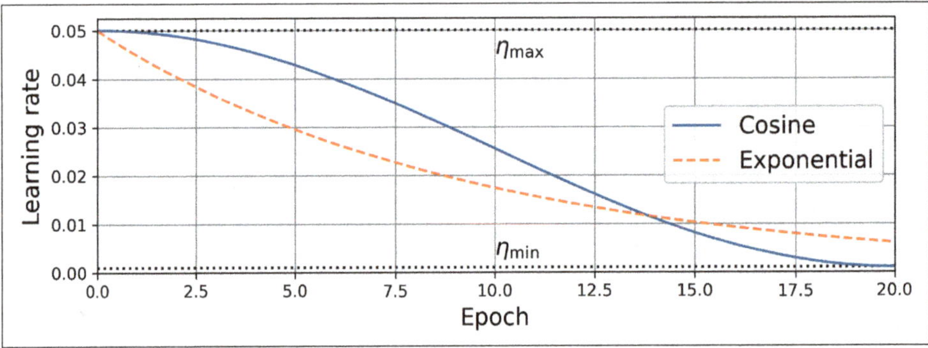

Figure 11-10. Cosine annealing learning schedule

Equation 11-10. Cosine annealing equation

$$\eta_t = \eta_{min} + \frac{1}{2}(\eta_{max} - \eta_{min})\left(1 + \cos\left(\frac{t}{T_{max}}\pi\right)\right)$$

PyTorch includes the `CosineAnnealingLR` scheduler, which you can create as follows (`T_max` is T_{max} and `eta_min` is η_{min}). You can then use it just like the `ExponentialLR` scheduler:

```
cosine_scheduler = torch.optim.lr_scheduler.CosineAnnealingLR(
    optimizer, T_max=20, eta_min=0.001)
```

One problem with cosine annealing is that you have to set two new hyperparameters, T_{max} and η_{min}, and it's not easy to know in advance how many epochs to train and when to stop decreasing the learning rate. This is why I generally prefer to use the performance scheduling technique.

Performance Scheduling

Performance scheduling, also called *adaptive scheduling*, is implemented by PyTorch's `ReduceLROnPlateau` scheduler: it keeps track of a given metric during training—typically the validation loss—and if this metric stops improving for some time, it multiplies the learning rate by some factor. This scheduler has quite a few hyperparameters, but the default values work well for most of them. You may occasionally need to tweak the following (see the documentation for information on the other hyperparameters):

`mode`
: If the tracked metric must be maximized (such as the validation accuracy), then you must set the `mode` to `'max'`. The default is `'min'`, which is fine if the tracked metric must be minimized (such as the validation loss).

`patience`
: The number of consecutive steps (typically epochs) to wait for improvement in the monitored metric before reducing the learning rate. It defaults to 10, which is generally fine. If each epoch is very long, then you may want to reduce this value.

`factor`
: The factor by which the learning rate will be multiplied whenever the monitored metric fails to improve for too long. It defaults to 0.1, again a reasonable default, but perhaps a bit small in some cases.

For example, let's implement performance scheduling based on the validation accuracy (i.e., which we want to maximize):

```
[...]  # build the model and optimizer
scheduler = torch.optim.lr_scheduler.ReduceLROnPlateau(
  optimizer, mode="max", patience=2, factor=0.1)
```

The training loop needs to be tweaked again because we must evaluate the desired metric at each epoch (in this example, we are using the `evaluate_tm()` function that we defined in Chapter 10), and we must then pass the result to the scheduler's `step()` method:

```
metric = torchmetrics.Accuracy(task="multiclass", num_classes=10).to(device)
for epoch in range(n_epochs):
    for X_batch, y_batch in train_loader:
        [...]  # the rest of the training loop remains unchanged
    val_metric = evaluate_tm(model, valid_loader, metric).item()
    scheduler.step(val_metric)
```

Warming Up the Learning Rate

So far, we have always started training with the maximum learning rate. However, this can sometimes cause gradient descent to bounce around randomly at the beginning of training, neither exploding nor making any significant progress. This typically happens with sensitive models, such as recurrent neural networks (Chapter 13), or when using a very large batch size. In such cases, one solution is to "warm up" the learning rate, starting close to zero and gradually increasing the learning rate over a few epochs, up to the maximum learning rate. During this warm-up phase, gradient descent has time to stabilize into a better region of the loss landscape, where it can then make quick progress using a high learning rate.

Why does this work? Well, the loss landscape sometimes resembles the Himalayas: it's very high up and full of gigantic spikes. If you start with a high learning rate, you might jump from one mountain peak to the next for a very long time. If instead you start with a small learning rate, you will just walk down the mountain and valleys and escape the spiky mountain range altogether until you reach flatter lands. From then on, you can use a large learning rate for the rest of your journey, slowing down only toward the end.

A common way to implement learning rate warm up using PyTorch is to use a `LinearLR` scheduler to increase the learning rate linearly over a few epochs. For example, the following scheduler will increase the learning rate from 10% to 100% of the optimizer's original learning rate over 3 epochs (i.e., 10% during the first epoch, 40% during the second epoch, 70% during the third epoch, and 100% after that):

```
warmup_scheduler = torch.optim.lr_scheduler.LinearLR(
    optimizer, start_factor=0.1, end_factor=1.0, total_iters=3)
```

If you would like more flexibility, you can write your own custom function and wrap it in a `LambdaLR` scheduler. For example, the following scheduler is equivalent to the `LinearLR` scheduler we just defined:

```
warmup_scheduler = torch.optim.lr_scheduler.LambdaLR(
    optimizer,
    lambda epoch: (min(epoch, 3) / 3) * (1.0 - 0.1) + 0.1)
```

You must then insert `warmup_scheduler.step()` at the beginning of each epoch, and make sure you deactivate the scheduler(s) you are using for the rest of training during the warm-up phase. And that's all!

```
for epoch in range(n_epochs):
    warmup_scheduler.step()
    for X_batch, y_batch in train_loader:
        [...]  # the rest of the training loop is unchanged
    if epoch >= 3:  # deactivate other scheduler(s) during warmup
        scheduler.step(val_metric)
```

In short, you pretty much always want to cool down the learning rate at the end of training, and you may also want to warm it up at the beginning if gradient descent needs a bit of help getting started. But are there any cases where you may want to tweak the learning rate in the middle of training? Well yes, there are; for example, if gradient descent gets stuck in a local optimum or a high plateau. Gradient descent could remain stuck here for a long time, or even forever. Luckily, there's a way to escape this trap: just increase the learning rate for a little while.

You could spend your time staring at the learning curves during training, and manually interrupting it to tweak the learning rate when needed, but you probably have better things to do. Alternatively, you could implement a custom scheduler that monitors the validation metric—much like the `ReduceLROnPlateau` scheduler—and increases the learning rate for a while if the validation metric is stuck in a bad plateau. For this, you could subclass the `LRScheduler` base class. This is beyond the scope of this book, but you can take inspiration from the `ReduceLROnPlateau` scheduler's source code (and get a little bit of help from your favorite AI assistant). But a much simpler option is to use the cosine annealing with warm restarts learning schedule. Let's look at it now.

Cosine Annealing with Warm Restarts

Cosine annealing with warm restarts was introduced in a 2016 paper (*https://homl.info/coslr*) by Ilya Loshchilov and Frank Hutter.[30] This schedule just repeats the cosine annealing schedule over and over again. Since the learning rate regularly shoots back up, this schedule allows gradient descent to escape local optima and plateaus automatically. The authors recommend starting with a fairly short round of cosine annealing, but then doubling T_{max} after each round (see Figure 11-11). This allows gradient descent to do a lot of quick explorations at the start of training, while also taking the time to properly optimize the model later during training, possibly escaping a plateau or two along the way.

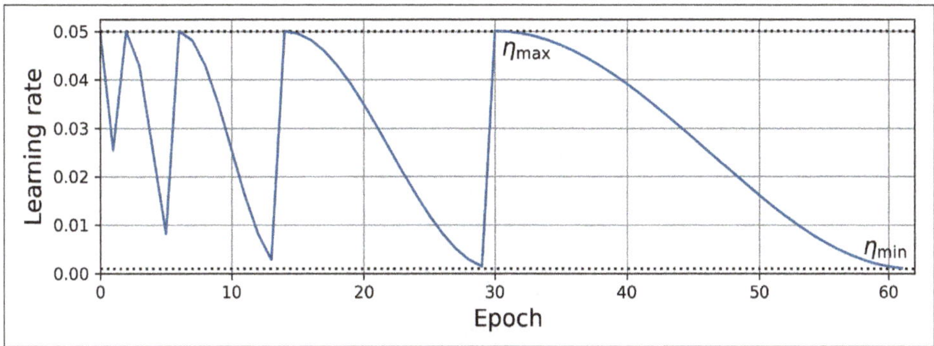

Figure 11-11. Cosine annealing with warm restarts

30 Ilya Loshchilov and Frank Hutter, "SGDR: Stochastic Gradient Descent With Warm Restarts", arXiv preprint arXiv:1608.03983 (2016).

Conveniently, PyTorch includes a `CosineAnnealingWarmRestarts` scheduler. You must set `T_0`, which is the value of T_{max} for the first round of cosine annealing. You may also set `T_mult` to 2 if you want to double T_{max} at each round (the default is 1, meaning T_{max} stays constant and all rounds have the same length). Finally, you can set `eta_min` (it defaults to 0):

```
cosine_repeat_scheduler = torch.optim.lr_scheduler.CosineAnnealingWarmRestarts(
    optimizer, T_0=2, T_mult=2, eta_min=0.001)
```

1cycle Scheduling

Yet another popular learning schedule is *1cycle*, introduced in a 2018 paper (*https://homl.info/1cycle*) by Leslie Smith.[31] It starts by warming up the learning rate, starting at η_0 and growing linearly up to η_1 halfway through training. Then it decreases the learning rate linearly down to η_0 again during the second half of training, finishing the last few epochs by dropping the rate down by several orders of magnitude (still linearly). The maximum learning rate η_1 is chosen using the same approach we used to find the optimal learning rate, and the initial learning rate η_0 is usually 10 times lower. When using a momentum, we start with a high momentum first (e.g., 0.95), then drop it down to a lower momentum during the first half of training (e.g., down to 0.85, linearly), and then bring it back up to the maximum value (e.g., 0.95) during the second half of training, finishing the last few epochs with that maximum value. Smith did many experiments showing that this approach was often able to speed up training considerably and reach better performance. For example, on the popular CIFAR10 image dataset, this approach reached 91.9% validation accuracy in just 100 epochs, compared to 90.3% accuracy in 800 epochs through a standard approach (using the same neural network architecture). This feat was dubbed *super-convergence*. PyTorch implements this schedule in the `OneCycleLR` scheduler.

If you are not sure which learning schedule to use, 1cycle can be a good default, but I tend to have more luck with performance scheduling. If you run into instabilities at the start of training, try adding learning rate warm-up. And if training gets stuck on plateaus, try cosine annealing with warm restarts.

We have now covered the most popular learning schedules, but PyTorch offers a few extra schedulers (e.g., a polynomial scheduler, a cyclic scheduler, a scheduler that makes it easy to chain other schedulers, and a few more), so make sure to check out the documentation.

31 Leslie N. Smith, "A Disciplined Approach to Neural Network Hyper-Parameters: Part 1—Learning Rate, Batch Size, Momentum, and Weight Decay", arXiv preprint arXiv:1803.09820 (2018).

Now let's move on to one final topic before we complete this chapter on deep learning training techniques: regularization. Deep learning is highly prone to overfitting, so regularization is key!

Avoiding Overfitting Through Regularization

> With four parameters I can fit an elephant and with five I can make him wiggle his trunk.
>
> —John von Neumann, cited by Enrico Fermi in *Nature* 427

With thousands of parameters, you can fit the whole zoo. Deep neural networks typically have tens of thousands of parameters, sometimes even millions or billions. This gives them an incredible amount of freedom and means they can fit a huge variety of complex datasets. But this great flexibility also makes the network prone to overfitting the training set. Regularization is often needed to prevent this.

We already implemented a common regularization technique in Chapter 4: early stopping. Moreover, even though batch-norm and layer-norm were designed to solve the unstable gradients problems, they also act like pretty good regularizers. In this section we will examine other popular regularization techniques for neural networks: ℓ_1 and ℓ_2 regularization, dropout, MC dropout, and max-norm regularization.

ℓ_1 and ℓ_2 Regularization

Just like you did in Chapter 4 for simple linear models, you can use ℓ_2 regularization to constrain a neural network's connection weights, and/or ℓ_1 regularization if you want a sparse model (with many weights equal to 0). As we saw earlier (when discussing the AdamW optimizer), ℓ_2 regularization is mathematically equivalent to weight decay when using an `SGD` optimizer (with or without momentum), so if that's the case you can implement ℓ_2 regularization by simply setting the optimizer's `weight_decay` argument. For example, here is how to apply ℓ_2 regularization to the connection weights of a PyTorch model trained using `SGD`, with a regularization factor of 10^{-4}:

```
optimizer = torch.optim.SGD(model.parameters(), lr=0.05, weight_decay=1e-4)
[...]  # use the optimizer normally during training
```

If instead you are using an Adam optimizer, you should switch to AdamW and set the `weight_decay` argument. This is not exactly equivalent to ℓ_2 regularization, but as we saw earlier it's pretty close and it works better.

Note that weight decay is applied to every model parameter, including bias terms, and even parameters of batch-norm and layer-norm layers. Generally that's not a big deal, but penalizing these parameters does not contribute much to regularization and it may sometimes negatively impact training performance. So how can we apply weight decay to some model parameters and not others? One approach is to implement ℓ_2

regularization manually, without relying on the optimizer's weight decay feature. For this, you must tweak the training loop to manually compute the ℓ_2 loss based only on the parameters you want, and add this ℓ_2 loss to the main loss:

```
optimizer = torch.optim.SGD(model.parameters(), lr=0.05)
params_to_regularize = [
    param for name, param in model.named_parameters()
    if not "bias" in name and not "bn" in name]
for epoch in range(n_epochs):
    for X_batch, y_batch in train_loader:
        [...]  # the rest of the training loop is unchanged
        main_loss = loss_fn(y_pred, y_batch)
        l2_loss = sum(param.pow(2.0).sum() for param in params_to_regularize)
        loss = main_loss + 1e-4 * l2_loss
        [...]
```

Another approach is to use PyTorch's *parameter groups* feature, which lets the optimizer apply different hyperparameters to different groups of model parameters. So far, we have always created optimizers by passing them the full list of model parameters: PyTorch automatically put them all in a single parameter group, sharing the same hyperparameters. Instead, we can pass a list of dictionaries to the optimizer, each with a `"params"` entry containing a list of parameters, and (optionally) some hyperparameter key/value pairs specific to this group of parameters. The group-specific hyperparameters take precedence over the optimizer's global hyperparameters. For example, let's create an optimizer with two parameter groups: the first group will contain all the parameters we want to regularize and it will use weight decay, while the second group will contain all the bias terms and BN parameters, and it will not use weight decay at all.

```
params_bias_and_bn = [
    param for name, param in model.named_parameters()
    if "bias" in name or "bn" in name]
optimizer = torch.optim.SGD([
    {"params": params_to_regularize, "weight_decay": 1e-4},
    {"params": params_bias_and_bn},
    ], lr=0.05)
[...]  # use the optimizer normally during training
```

Parameter groups also allow you to apply different learning rates to different parts of your model. This is most common for transfer learning, when you want new layers to be updated faster than reused ones.

Now how about ℓ_1 regularization? Well unfortunately PyTorch does not provide any helper for this, so you need to implement it manually, much like we did for ℓ_2 regularization. This means tweaking the training loop to compute the ℓ_1 loss and adding it to the main loss:

```python
l1_loss = sum(param.abs().sum() for param in params_to_regularize)
loss = main_loss + 1e-4 * l1_loss
```

That's all there is to it! Now let's move on to Dropout, which is one of the most popular regularization techniques for deep neural networks.

Dropout

Dropout was proposed in a paper (*https://homl.info/64*)[32] by Geoffrey Hinton et al. in 2012 and further detailed in a 2014 paper (*https://homl.info/65*)[33] by Nitish Srivastava et al., and it has proven to be highly successful: many state-of-the-art neural networks use dropout, as it gives them a 1%–2% accuracy boost. This may not sound like a lot, but when a model already has 95% accuracy, getting a 2% accuracy boost means dropping the error rate by almost 40% (going from 5% error to roughly 3%).

It is a fairly simple algorithm: at every training step, every neuron (including the input neurons, but always excluding the output neurons) has a probability p of being temporarily "dropped out", meaning it will be entirely ignored during this training step, but it may be active during the next step (see Figure 11-12). The hyperparameter p is called the *dropout rate*, and it is typically set between 10% and 50%: closer to 20%–30% in recurrent neural nets (see Chapter 13), and closer to 40%–50% in convolutional neural networks (see Chapter 12). After training, neurons don't get dropped anymore. And that's all (except for a technical detail we will discuss shortly).

It's surprising at first that this destructive technique works at all. Would a company perform better if its employees were told to toss a coin every morning to decide whether to go to work? Well, who knows; perhaps it would! The company would be forced to adapt its organization; it could not rely on any single person to work the coffee machine or perform any other critical tasks, so this expertise would have to be spread across several people. Employees would have to learn to cooperate with many of their coworkers, not just a handful of them. The company would become much more resilient. If one person quit, it wouldn't make much of a difference. It's unclear whether this idea would actually work for companies, but it certainly does for neural networks. Neurons trained with dropout cannot co-adapt with their neighboring neurons; they have to be as useful as possible on their own. They also cannot rely excessively on just a few input neurons; they must pay attention to all of their input neurons. They end up being less sensitive to slight changes in the inputs. In the end, you get a more robust network that generalizes better.

32 Geoffrey E. Hinton et al., "Improving Neural Networks by Preventing Co-Adaptation of Feature Detectors", arXiv preprint arXiv:1207.0580 (2012).

33 Nitish Srivastava et al., "Dropout: A Simple Way to Prevent Neural Networks from Overfitting", *Journal of Machine Learning Research* 15 (2014): 1929–1958.

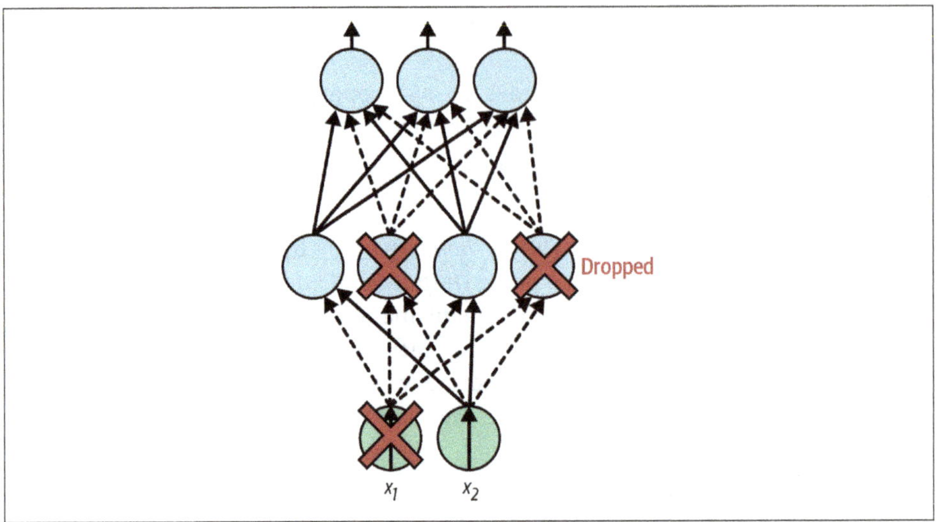

Figure 11-12. With dropout regularization, at each training iteration a random subset of all neurons in one or more layers—except the output layer—are "dropped out"; these neurons output 0 at this iteration (represented by the dashed arrows)

Another way to understand the power of dropout is to realize that a unique neural network is generated at each training step. Since each neuron can be either present or absent, there are a total of 2^N possible networks (where N is the total number of droppable neurons). This is such a huge number that it is virtually impossible for the same neural network to be sampled twice. Once you have run 10,000 training steps, you have essentially trained 10,000 different neural networks, each with just one training instance. These neural networks are obviously not independent because they share many of their weights, but they are nevertheless all different. The resulting neural network can be seen as an averaging ensemble of all these smaller neural networks.

Higher layers, which learn more complex feature combinations, benefit more from dropout because they are more prone to overfitting. So you can usually apply dropout only to the neurons of the top hidden layers (e.g., one to three hidden layers). However, you should avoid dropping the output neurons, as this would be like changing the task during training: it wouldn't help.

There is one small but important technical detail. Suppose p = 75%: on average only 25% of all neurons are active at each step during training. This means that after training, each neuron receives four times more inputs than during training, on average. This discrepancy is so large that the model is unlikely to work well. To avoid this issue, a simple solution is to multiply the inputs by 4 during training, which is the same as dividing them by 25%. More generally, we need to divide the inputs by the *keep probability* (1 – *p*) during training.

To implement dropout using PyTorch, you can use the `nn.Dropout` layer. It's important to switch to training mode during training, and to evaluation mode during evaluation (just like for batch norm). In training mode, the layer randomly drops some inputs (setting them to 0) and divides the remaining inputs by the keep probability. In evaluation mode, it does nothing at all; it just passes the inputs to the next layer. The following code applies dropout regularization before every `nn.Linear` layer, using a dropout rate of 0.2:

```
model = nn.Sequential(
    nn.Flatten(),
    nn.Dropout(p=0.2), nn.Linear(1 * 28 * 28, 100), nn.ReLU(),
    nn.Dropout(p=0.2), nn.Linear(100, 100), nn.ReLU(),
    nn.Dropout(p=0.2), nn.Linear(100, 100), nn.ReLU(),
    nn.Dropout(p=0.2), nn.Linear(100, 10)
).to(device)
```

Since dropout is only active during training, comparing the training loss and the validation loss can be misleading. In particular, a model may be overfitting the training set and yet have similar training and validation losses. So make sure to evaluate the training loss without dropout (e.g., after training).

If you observe that the model is overfitting, you can increase the dropout rate. Conversely, you should try decreasing the dropout rate if the model underfits the training set. It can also help to increase the dropout rate for large layers, and reduce it for small ones. Moreover, many state-of-the-art architectures only apply dropout to the last few hidden layers, so you may want to try this if full dropout is too strong.

Dropout does tend to significantly slow down convergence, but it often results in a better model when tuned properly. So it is generally well worth the extra time and effort, especially for large models.

If you want to regularize a self-normalizing network based on the SELU activation function (as discussed earlier), you should use *alpha dropout*: this is a variant of dropout that preserves the mean and standard deviation of its inputs. It was introduced in the same paper as SELU, as regular dropout would break self-normalization. PyTorch implements it in the `nn.AlphaDropout` layer.

Monte Carlo Dropout

In 2016, a paper (*https://homl.info/mcdropout*)[34] by Yarin Gal and Zoubin Ghahramani added a few more good reasons to use dropout:

- First, the paper established a profound connection between dropout networks (i.e., neural networks containing `Dropout` layers) and approximate Bayesian inference,[35] giving dropout a solid mathematical justification.
- Second, the authors introduced a powerful technique called *Monte Carlo (MC) dropout*, which can boost the performance of any trained dropout model without having to retrain it or even modify it at all. It also provides a much better measure of the model's uncertainty, and it can be implemented in just a few lines of code.

This description of MC dropout sounds like some "one weird trick" clickbait, so let me explain: it is just like regular dropout, except it is active not only during training, but also during evaluation. This means that the predictions are always a bit random (hence the name Monte Carlo). But instead of making a single prediction, you make many predictions and average them out. It turns out that this produces better predictions than the original model.

Following is a full implementation of MC dropout, using the model we trained in the previous section to make predictions for a batch of images:

```
model.eval()
for module in model.modules():
    if isinstance(module, nn.Dropout):
        module.train()

X_new = [...]  # some new images, e.g., the first 3 images of the test set
X_new = X_new.to(device)

torch.manual_seed(42)
with torch.no_grad():
    X_new_repeated = X_new.repeat_interleave(100, dim=0)
    y_logits_all = model(X_new_repeated).reshape(3, 100, 10)
    y_probas_all = torch.nn.functional.softmax(y_logits_all, dim=-1)
    y_probas = y_probas_all.mean(dim=1)
```

34 Yarin Gal and Zoubin Ghahramani, "Dropout as a Bayesian Approximation: Representing Model Uncertainty in Deep Learning", *Proceedings of the 33rd International Conference on Machine Learning* (2016): 1050–1059.

35 Specifically, they show that training a dropout network is mathematically equivalent to approximate Bayesian inference in a specific type of probabilistic model called a *deep Gaussian process*.

Let's go through this code:

- First, we switch the model to evaluation mode as we always do before making predictions, but this time we immediately switch all the dropout layers back to training mode, so they will behave just like during training (i.e., randomly dropping out some of their inputs). In other words, we convert the dropout layers to MC dropout layers.
- Next we load a new batch of images `X_new`, and we move it to the GPU. In this example, let's assume `X_new` contains three images.
- We then use the `repeat_interleave()` method to create a batch containing 100 copies of each image in `X_new`. The images are repeated along the first dimension (`dim=0`) so `X_new_repeated` has a shape of `[300, 1, 28, 28]`.
- Next, we pass this big batch to the model, which predicts 10 logits per image, as usual. This tensor's shape is `[300, 10]`, but we reshape it to `[3, 100, 10]` to group the predictions for each image. Remember that the dropout layers are active, which means that there's some variability across the predictions, even for copies of the same image.
- Then we convert these logits to estimated probabilities using the softmax function.
- Lastly, we compute the mean over the second dimension (`dim=1`) to get the average estimated probability for each class and each image, across all 100 predictions. The result is a tensor of shape `[3, 10]`. These are our final predictions:

```
>>> y_probas.round(decimals=2)
tensor([[0.000, 0.000, 0.000, 0.000, 0.000, 0.000, 0.000, 0.010, 0.000, 0.990],
        [0.990, 0.000, 0.000, 0.000, 0.000, 0.000, 0.010, 0.000, 0.000, 0.000],
        [0.410, 0.040, 0.040, 0.230, 0.040, 0.000, 0.230, 0.000, 0.010, 0.000]],
       device='cuda:0')
```

Rather than converting the logits to probabilities and then computing the mean probabilities, you may be tempted to do the reverse: first average over the logits and *then* convert the mean logits to probabilities. This is faster but it does not properly reflect the model's uncertainty, so it tends to produce overconfident models.

MC dropout tends to improve the reliability of the model's probability estimates. This means that it's less likely to be confidently wrong, making it safer (you don't want a self-driving car confidently ignoring a stop sign). It's also useful when you're interested in the top *k* classes, not just the most likely. Additionally, you can take a look at the standard deviation of each class probability (*https://xkcd.com/2110*):

```
>>> y_std = y_probas_all.std(dim=1)
>>> y_std.round(decimals=2)
```

```
tensor([[0.000, 0.000, 0.000, 0.000, 0.000, 0.000, 0.000, 0.020, 0.000, 0.020],
        [0.020, 0.000, 0.000, 0.000, 0.000, 0.000, 0.020, 0.000, 0.000, 0.000],
        [0.170, 0.030, 0.030, 0.130, 0.050, 0.000, 0.090, 0.000, 0.010, 0.000]],
       device='cuda:0')
```

There's a standard deviation of 0.02 for the probability estimate of class 9 (ankle boot) for the first image. This adds a grain of salt to the estimated probability of 99% for this class: in fact, the model is really saying "mmh, I'm guessing over 95%". If you were building a risk-sensitive system (e.g., a medical or financial system), you may want to consider only the predictions with both a high estimated probability *and* a low standard deviation.

The number of Monte Carlo samples you use (100 in this example) is a hyperparameter you can tweak. The higher it is, the more accurate the predictions and their uncertainty estimates are, but also the slower the predictions are. Moreover, above a certain number of samples, you will notice little improvement. Your job is to find the right trade-off among latency, throughput, and accuracy, depending on your application.

If you want to train an MC dropout model from scratch rather than reuse an existing dropout model, you should probably use a custom `McDropout` module rather than using `nn.Dropout` and hacking around with `train()` and `eval()`, as this is a bit brittle (e.g., it won't play nicely with the evaluation function). Here is a three-line implementation:

```
class McDropout(nn.Dropout):
    def forward(self, input):
        return F.dropout(input, self.p, training=True)
```

In short, MC dropout is a great technique that boosts dropout models and provides better uncertainty estimates. And of course, since it is just regular dropout during training, it also acts like a regularizer.

Max-Norm Regularization

Another fairly popular regularization technique for neural networks is called *max-norm regularization*: for each neuron, it constrains the weights **w** of the incoming connections such that $\| \mathbf{w} \|_2 \leq r$, where r is the max-norm hyperparameter and $\| \cdot \|_2$ is the ℓ_2 norm.

Reducing r increases the amount of regularization and helps reduce overfitting. Max-norm regularization can also help alleviate the unstable gradients problems (if you are not using batch-norm or layer-norm).

Rather than adding a regularization loss term to the overall loss function, max-norm regularization is typically implemented by computing $\| \mathbf{w} \|_2$ after each training step and rescaling **w** if needed (**w** ← **w** r / || **w** $||_2$). Here's a common way to implement this in PyTorch:

```
def apply_max_norm(model, max_norm=2, epsilon=1e-8, dim=1):
    with torch.no_grad():
        for name, param in model.named_parameters():
            if 'bias' not in name:
                actual_norm = param.norm(p=2, dim=dim, keepdim=True)
                target_norm = torch.clamp(actual_norm, 0, max_norm)
                param *= target_norm / (epsilon + actual_norm)
```

This function iterates through all of the model's weight matrices (i.e., all parameters except for the bias terms), and for each one of them it uses the `norm()` method to compute the ℓ_2 norm of each row (`dim=1`). A `nn.Linear` layer has weights of shape [*number of neurons*, *number of inputs*], so using `dim=1` means that we will get one norm per neuron, as desired. Then the function uses `torch.clamp()` to compute the target norm for each neuron's weights: this creates a copy of the `actual_norm` tensor, except that all values greater than `max_norm` are replaced by `max_norm` (this corresponds to r in the previous equation). Lastly, we rescale the weight matrix so that each column ends up with the target norm. Note that the smoothing term `epsilon` is used to avoid division by zero in case some columns have a norm equal to zero.

Next, all you need to do is call `apply_max_norm(model)` in the training loop, right after calling the optimizer's `step()` method. And of course you probably want to fine-tune the `max_norm` hyperparameter.

When using max-norm with layers other than `nn.Linear`, you may need to tweak the `dim` argument. For example, when using convolutional layers (see Chapter 12), you generally want to set `dim=[1, 2, 3]` to limit the norm of each convolutional kernel.

Practical Guidelines

In this chapter we have covered a wide range of techniques, and you may be wondering which ones you should use. This depends on the task, and there is no clear consensus yet, but I have found the configuration in Table 11-3 to work fine in most cases, without requiring much hyperparameter tuning. That said, please do not consider these defaults as hard rules!

Table 11-3. Default DNN configuration

Hyperparameter	Default value
Kernel initializer	He initialization
Activation function	ReLU if shallow; Swish if deep
Normalization	None if shallow; batch-norm or layer-norm if deep

Hyperparameter	Default value
Regularization	Early stopping; weight decay if needed
Optimizer	Nesterov accelerated gradients or AdamW
Learning rate schedule	Performance scheduling or 1cycle

You should also try to reuse parts of a pretrained neural network if you can find one that solves a similar problem, or use unsupervised pretraining if you have a lot of unlabeled data, or use pretraining on an auxiliary task if you have a lot of labeled data for a similar task.

While the previous guidelines should cover most cases, there are some exceptions:

- If you need a sparse model, use ℓ_1 regularization. You can also try zeroing out the smallest weights after training (for example, using the `torch.nn.utils.prune.l1_unstructured()` function). This will break self-normalization, so you should use the default configuration in this case.
- If you need a low-latency model (one that performs lightning-fast predictions), you may need to use fewer layers; use a fast activation function such as `nn.ReLU`, `nn.LeakyReLU`, or `nn.Hardswish`; and fold the batch-norm and layer-norm layers into the previous layers after training. Having a sparse model will also help. Finally, you may want to reduce the float precision from 32 bits to 16 or even 8 bits. Appendix B covers several techniques to make models smaller and faster, including reduced precision models, mixed precision models, and quantization.
- If you are building a risk-sensitive application, or inference latency is not very important in your application, you can use MC dropout to boost performance and get more reliable probability estimates, along with uncertainty estimates.

Over the last three chapters, we have learned what artificial neural nets are, how to build and train them using Scikit-Learn and PyTorch, and a variety of techniques that make it possible to train deep and complex nets. In the next chapter, all of this will come together as we dive into one of the most important applications of deep learning: computer vision.

Exercises

1. What is the problem that Glorot initialization and He initialization aim to fix?
2. Is it OK to initialize all the weights to the same value as long as that value is selected randomly using He initialization?
3. Is it OK to initialize the bias terms to 0?
4. In which cases would you want to use each of the activation functions we discussed in this chapter?

5. What may happen if you set the `momentum` hyperparameter too close to 1 (e.g., 0.99999) when using an `SGD` optimizer?
6. Name three ways you can produce a sparse model.
7. Does dropout slow down training? Does it slow down inference (i.e., making predictions on new instances)? What about MC dropout?
8. Practice training a deep neural network on the CIFAR10 image dataset:
   a. Load CIFAR10 just like you loaded the FashionMNIST dataset in Chapter 10, but using `torchvision.datasets.CIFAR10` instead of `FashionMNIST`. The dataset is composed of 60,000 32 × 32–pixel color images (50,000 for training, 10,000 for testing) with 10 classes.
   b. Build a DNN with 20 hidden layers of 100 neurons each (that's too many, but it's the point of this exercise). Use He initialization and the Swish activation function (using `nn.SiLU`). Since this is a classification task, you will need an output layer with one neuron per class.
   c. Using NAdam optimization and early stopping, train the network on the CIFAR10 dataset. Remember to search for the right learning rate each time you change the model's architecture or hyperparameters.
   d. Now try adding batch-norm and compare the learning curves: is it converging faster than before? Does it produce a better model? How does it affect training speed?
   e. Try replacing batch-norm with SELU, and make the necessary adjustments to ensure the network self-normalizes (i.e., standardize the input features, use LeCun normal initialization, make sure the DNN contains only a sequence of dense layers, etc.).
   f. Try regularizing the model with alpha dropout. Then, without retraining your model, see if you can achieve better accuracy using MC dropout.
   g. Retrain your model using 1cycle scheduling and see if it improves training speed and model accuracy.

Solutions to these exercises are available at the end of this chapter's notebook, at *https://homl.info/colab-p*.

CHAPTER 12

Deep Computer Vision Using Convolutional Neural Networks

Although IBM's Deep Blue supercomputer beat the chess world champion Garry Kasparov back in 1996, it wasn't until fairly recently that computers were able to reliably perform seemingly trivial tasks such as detecting a puppy in a picture or recognizing spoken words. Why are these tasks so effortless to us humans? The answer lies in the fact that perception largely takes place outside the realm of our consciousness, within specialized visual, auditory, and other sensory modules in our brains. By the time sensory information reaches our consciousness, it is already adorned with high-level features; for example, when you look at a picture of a cute puppy, you cannot choose *not* to see the puppy, *not* to notice its cuteness. Nor can you explain *how* you recognize a cute puppy; it's just obvious to you. Thus, we cannot trust our subjective experience: perception is not trivial at all, and to understand it we must look at how our sensory modules work.

Convolutional neural networks (CNNs) emerged from the study of the brain's visual cortex, and they have been used in computer image recognition since the 1980s. Over the last 15 years, thanks to the increase in computational power, the amount of available training data, and the tricks presented in Chapter 11 for training deep nets, CNNs have managed to achieve superhuman performance on some complex visual tasks. They power image search services, self-driving cars, automatic video classification systems, and more. Moreover, CNNs are not restricted to visual perception: they are also successful at many other tasks, such as voice recognition and natural language processing. However, we will focus on visual applications for now.

In this chapter we will explore where CNNs came from, what their building blocks look like, and how to implement them using PyTorch. Then we will discuss some of the best CNN architectures, as well as other visual tasks, including object detection (classifying multiple objects in an image and placing bounding boxes around them) and semantic segmentation (classifying each pixel according to the class of the object it belongs to).

The Architecture of the Visual Cortex

David H. Hubel and Torsten Wiesel performed a series of experiments on cats in 1958 (*https://homl.info/71*)[1] and 1959 (*https://homl.info/72*)[2] (and a few years later on monkeys (*https://homl.info/73*)[3]), giving crucial insights into the structure of the visual cortex (the authors received the Nobel Prize in Physiology or Medicine in 1981 for their work). In particular, they showed that many neurons in the visual cortex have a small *local receptive field*, meaning they react only to visual stimuli located in a limited region of the visual field (see Figure 12-1, in which the local receptive fields of five neurons are represented by dashed circles). The receptive fields of different neurons may overlap, and together they tile the whole visual field.

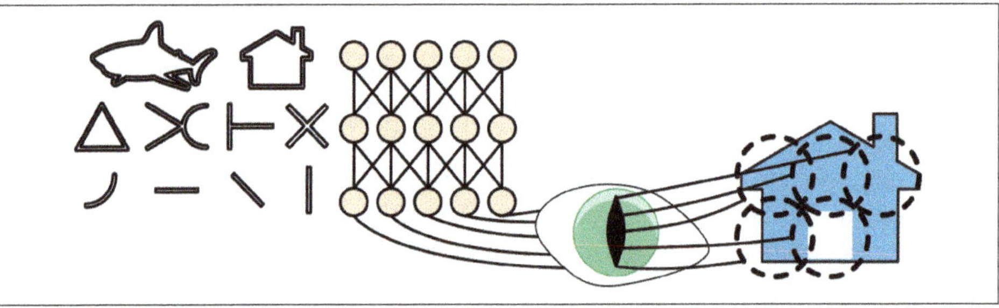

Figure 12-1. Biological neurons in the visual cortex respond to specific patterns in small regions of the visual field called receptive fields; as the visual signal makes its way through consecutive brain modules, neurons respond to more complex patterns in larger receptive fields

Moreover, the authors showed that some neurons react only to images of horizontal lines, while others react only to lines with different orientations (two neurons may have the same receptive field but react to different line orientations). They also noticed that some neurons have larger receptive fields, and they react to more complex patterns that are combinations of the lower-level patterns. These observations led to the idea that the higher-level neurons are based on the outputs of neighboring

1 David H. Hubel, "Single Unit Activity in Striate Cortex of Unrestrained Cats", *The Journal of Physiology* 147 (1959): 226–238.

2 David H. Hubel and Torsten N. Wiesel, "Receptive Fields of Single Neurons in the Cat's Striate Cortex", *The Journal of Physiology* 148 (1959): 574–591.

3 David H. Hubel and Torsten N. Wiesel, "Receptive Fields and Functional Architecture of Monkey Striate Cortex", *The Journal of Physiology* 195 (1968): 215–243.

lower-level neurons (in Figure 12-1, notice that each neuron is connected only to nearby neurons from the previous layer). This powerful architecture is able to detect all sorts of complex patterns in any area of the visual field.

These studies of the visual cortex inspired the neocognitron (*https://homl.info/74*),[4] introduced in 1980, which gradually evolved into what we now call convolutional neural networks. An important milestone was a 1998 paper (*https://homl.info/75*)[5] by Yann LeCun et al. that introduced the famous *LeNet-5* architecture, which became widely used by banks to recognize handwritten digits on checks. This architecture has some building blocks that you already know, such as fully connected layers and sigmoid activation functions, but it also introduces two new building blocks: *convolutional layers* and *pooling layers*. Let's look at them now.

Why not simply use a deep neural network with fully connected layers for image recognition tasks? Unfortunately, although this works fine for small images (e.g., Fashion MNIST), it breaks down for larger images because of the huge number of parameters it requires. For example, a 100 × 100–pixel image has 10,000 pixels, and if the first layer has just 1,000 neurons (which already severely restricts the amount of information transmitted to the next layer), this means a total of 10 million connections. And that's just the first layer. CNNs solve this problem using partially connected layers and weight sharing.

Convolutional Layers

The most important building block of a CNN is the *convolutional layer*:[6] neurons in the first convolutional layer are not connected to every single pixel in the input image (like they were in the layers discussed in previous chapters), but only to pixels in their receptive fields (see Figure 12-2). In turn, each neuron in the second convolutional layer is connected only to neurons located within a small rectangle in the first layer. This architecture allows the network to concentrate on small low-level features in the first hidden layer, then assemble them into larger higher-level features in the next hidden layer, and so on. This hierarchical structure is well-suited to deal with

4 Kunihiko Fukushima, "Neocognitron: A Self-Organizing Neural Network Model for a Mechanism of Pattern Recognition Unaffected by Shift in Position", *Biological Cybernetics* 36 (1980): 193–202.

5 Yann LeCun et al., "Gradient-Based Learning Applied to Document Recognition", *Proceedings of the IEEE* 86, no. 11 (1998): 2278–2324.

6 A convolution is a mathematical operation that slides one function over another and measures the integral of their pointwise multiplication. It has deep connections with the Fourier transform and the Laplace transform, and is heavily used in signal processing. Convolutional layers actually use cross-correlations, which are very similar to convolutions (see *https://homl.info/76* for more details).

composite objects, which are common in real-world images: this is one of the reasons why CNNs work so well for image recognition.

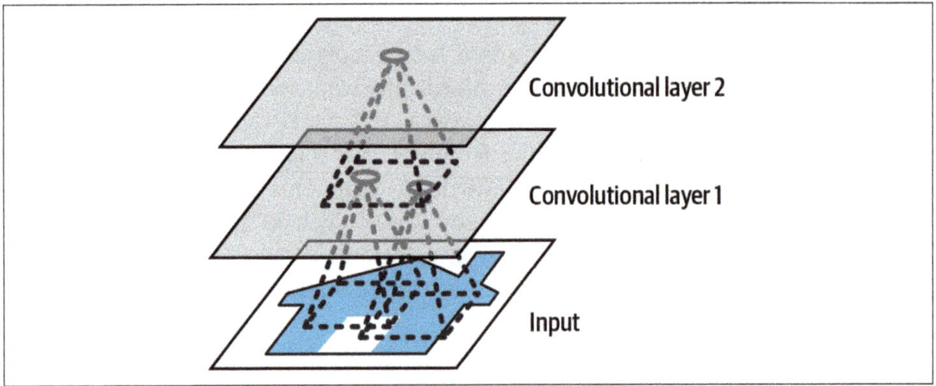

Figure 12-2. CNN layers with rectangular local receptive fields

All the multilayer neural networks we've looked at so far had layers composed of a long line of neurons, and we had to flatten input images to 1D before feeding them to the neural network. In a CNN each layer is represented in 2D, which makes it easier to match neurons with their corresponding inputs.

A neuron located in row i, column j of a given layer is connected to the outputs of the neurons in the previous layer located in rows i to $i + f_h - 1$, columns j to $j + f_w - 1$, where f_h and f_w are the height and width of the receptive field (see Figure 12-3). In order for a layer to have the same height and width as the previous layer, it is common to add zeros around the inputs, as shown in the diagram. This is called *zero padding*.

It is also possible to connect a large input layer to a much smaller layer by spacing out the receptive fields, as shown in Figure 12-4. This dramatically reduces the model's computational complexity. The horizontal or vertical step size from one receptive field to the next is called the *stride*. In the diagram, a 5 × 7 input layer (plus zero padding) is connected to a 3 × 4 layer, using 3 × 3 receptive fields and a stride of 2. In this example the stride is the same in both directions, which is generally the case (although there are exceptions). A neuron located in row i, column j in the upper layer is connected to the outputs of the neurons in the previous layer located in rows $i \times s_h$ to $i \times s_h + f_h - 1$, columns $j \times s_w$ to $j \times s_w + f_w - 1$, where s_h and s_w are the vertical and horizontal strides.

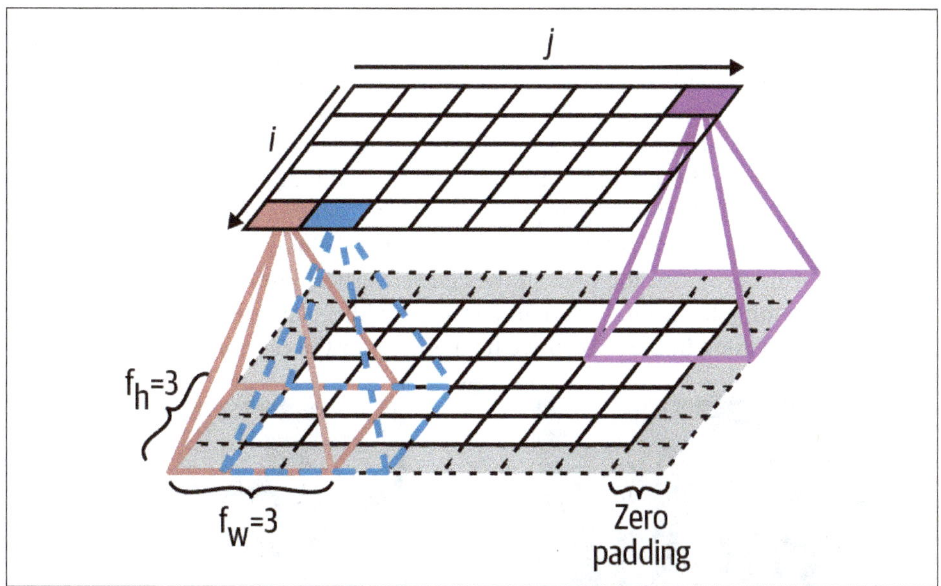

Figure 12-3. Connections between layers and zero padding

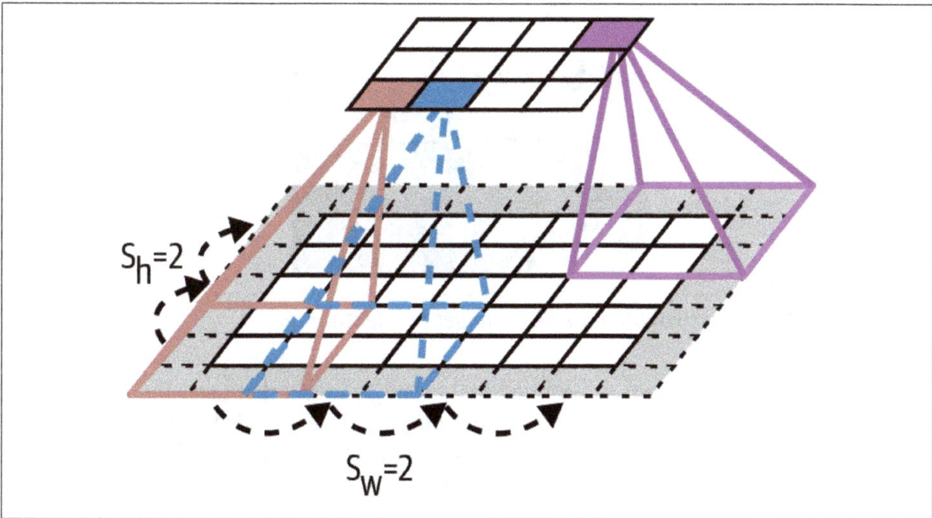

Figure 12-4. Reducing dimensionality using a stride of 2

Filters

A neuron's weights can be represented as a small image the size of the receptive field. For example, Figure 12-5 shows two possible sets of weights, called *filters* (or *convolution kernels*, or just *kernels*). The first one is represented as a black square with a vertical white line in the middle (it's a 7 × 7 matrix full of 0s except for the central column, which is full of 1s); neurons using these weights will ignore everything in their receptive field except for the central vertical line (since all inputs will be multiplied by 0, except for the ones in the central vertical line). The second filter is a black square with a horizontal white line in the middle. Neurons using these weights will ignore everything in their receptive field except for the central horizontal line.

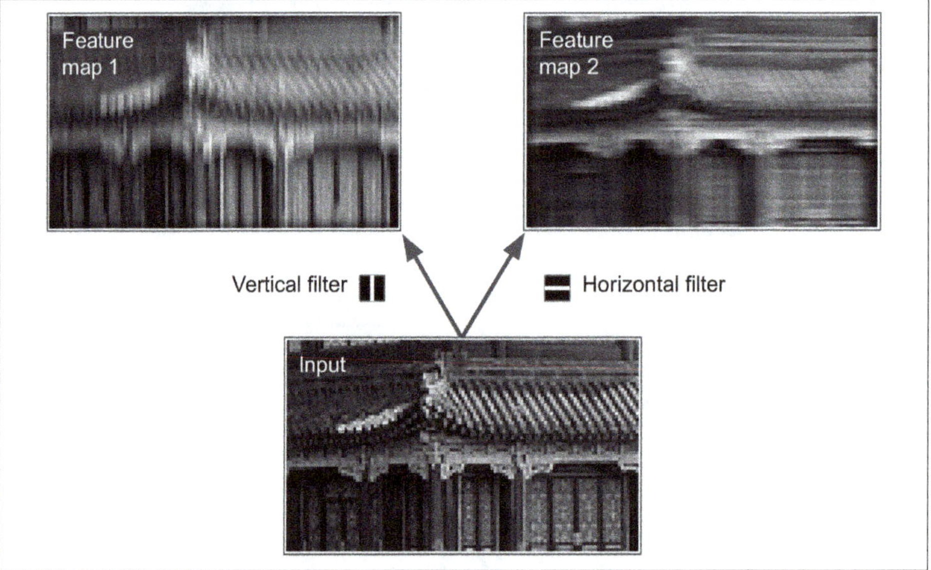

Figure 12-5. Applying two different filters to get two feature maps

In deep learning, we often build a single model that takes the raw inputs and produces the final outputs. This is called *end-to-end learning*. In contrast, classical vision systems would usually divide the system into a sequence of specialized modules.

Now if all neurons in a layer use the same vertical line filter (and the same bias term), and you feed the network the input image shown in Figure 12-5 (the bottom image), the layer will output the top-left image. Notice that the vertical white lines get enhanced while the rest gets blurred. Similarly, the upper-right image is what you get if all neurons use the same horizontal line filter; notice that the horizontal white lines get enhanced while the rest is blurred out. Thus, a layer full of neurons using the same filter outputs a *feature map*, which highlights the areas in an image that activate the filter the most. But don't worry, you won't have to define the filters manually: instead, during training the convolutional layer will automatically learn the most useful filters for its task, and the layers above will learn to combine them into more complex patterns.

Stacking Multiple Feature Maps

Up to now, for simplicity, I have represented each convolutional layer as a 2D layer, but in reality a convolutional layer has multiple filters (you decide how many) and it outputs one feature map per filter, so the output is more accurately represented in 3D (see Figure 12-6).

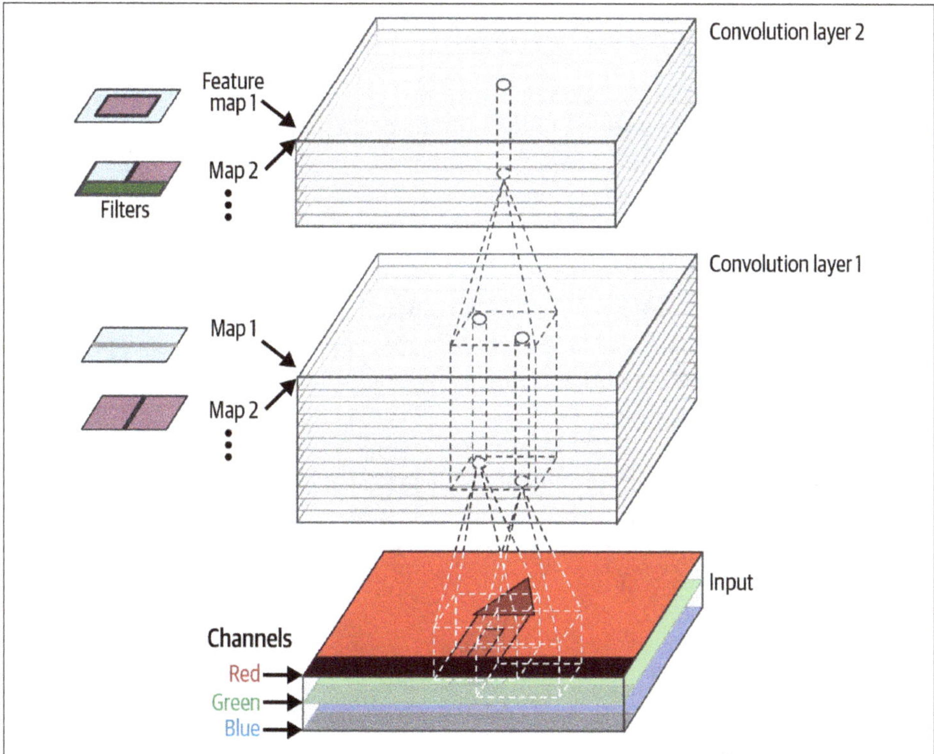

Figure 12-6. Two convolutional layers with multiple filters each (kernels), processing a color image with three color channels; each convolutional layer outputs one feature map per filter

There is one neuron per pixel in each feature map, and all neurons within a given feature map share the same parameters (i.e., the same kernel and bias term). Neurons in different feature maps use different parameters. A neuron's receptive field is the same as described earlier, but it extends across all the feature maps of the previous layer. In short, a convolutional layer simultaneously applies multiple trainable filters to its inputs, making it capable of detecting multiple features anywhere in its inputs.

The fact that all neurons in a feature map share the same parameters dramatically reduces the number of parameters in the model. Once the CNN has learned to recognize a pattern in one location, it can recognize it in any other location. In contrast, once a fully connected neural network has learned to recognize a pattern in one location, it can only recognize it in that particular location.

Input images are also composed of multiple sublayers: one per *color channel*. As mentioned in Chapter 8, there are typically three: red, green, and blue (RGB). Grayscale images have just one channel, but some images may have many more—for example, satellite images that capture extra light frequencies (such as infrared).

Specifically, a neuron located in row i, column j of the feature map k in a given convolutional layer l is connected to the outputs of the neurons in the previous layer $l - 1$, located in rows $i \times s_h$ to $i \times s_h + f_h - 1$ and columns $j \times s_w$ to $j \times s_w + f_w - 1$, across all feature maps (in layer $l - 1$). Note that, within a layer, all neurons located in the same row i and column j but in different feature maps are connected to the outputs of the exact same neurons in the previous layer.

Equation 12-1 summarizes the preceding explanations in one big mathematical equation: it shows how to compute the output of a given neuron in a convolutional layer. It is a bit ugly due to all the different indices, but all it does is calculate the weighted sum of all the inputs, plus the bias term.

Equation 12-1. Computing the output of a neuron in a convolutional layer

$$z_{i,j,k} = b_k + \sum_{u=0}^{f_h-1} \sum_{v=0}^{f_w-1} \sum_{k'=0}^{f_{n'}-1} x_{i',j',k'} \times w_{u,v,k',k} \quad \text{with} \begin{cases} i' = i \times s_h + u \\ j' = j \times s_w + v \end{cases}$$

In this equation:

- $z_{i,\,j,\,k}$ is the output of the neuron located in row i, column j in feature map k of the convolutional layer (layer l).
- As explained earlier, s_h and s_w are the vertical and horizontal strides, f_h and f_w are the height and width of the receptive field, and $f_{n'}$ is the number of feature maps in the previous layer (layer $l - 1$).
- $x_{i',\,j',\,k'}$ is the output of the neuron located in layer $l - 1$, row i', column j', feature map k' (or channel k' if the previous layer is the input layer).

- b_k is the bias term for feature map k (in layer l). You can think of it as a knob that tweaks the overall brightness of the feature map k.
- $w_{u,\ v,\ k',\ k}$ is the connection weight between any neuron in feature map k of the layer l and its input located at row u, column v (relative to the neuron's receptive field), and feature map k'.

Let's see how to create and use a convolutional layer using PyTorch.

Implementing Convolutional Layers with PyTorch

First, let's load a couple of sample images using Scikit-Learn's `load_sample_images()` function. The first image represents the tower of buddhist incense in China, while the second one represents a beautiful *Dahlia pinnata* flower. These images are represented as a Python list of NumPy unsigned byte arrays, so let's stack these images into a single NumPy array, then convert it to a 32-bit float tensor, and rescale the pixel values from 0–255 to 0–1:

```
import numpy as np
import torch
from sklearn.datasets import load_sample_images

sample_images = np.stack(load_sample_images()["images"])
sample_images = torch.tensor(sample_images, dtype=torch.float32) / 255
```

Let's look at this tensor's shape:

```
>>> sample_images.shape
torch.Size([2, 427, 640, 3])
```

We have two images, both are 427 pixels high and 640 pixels wide, and they have three color channels: red, green, and blue. As we saw in Chapter 10, PyTorch expects the channel dimension to be just *before* the height and width dimensions, not after, so we need to permute the dimensions using the `permute()` method:

```
>>> sample_images_permuted = sample_images.permute(0, 3, 1, 2)
>>> sample_images_permuted.shape
torch.Size([2, 3, 427, 640])
```

Let's also use TorchVision's `CenterCrop` class to center-crop the images:

```
>>> import torchvision
>>> import torchvision.transforms.v2 as T
>>> cropped_images = T.CenterCrop((70, 120))(sample_images_permuted)
>>> cropped_images.shape
torch.Size([2, 3, 70, 120])
```

Now let's create a 2D convolutional layer and feed it these cropped images to see what comes out. For this, PyTorch provides the `nn.Conv2d` layer. Under the hood, this layer relies on the `torch.nn.((("torch", "F.conv2d()")))functional.conv2d()` function. Let's create a convolutional layer with 32 filters, each of size 7 × 7 (using kernel_size=7, which is equivalent to using kernel_size=(7 , 7)), and apply this layer to our small batch of two images:

```
import torch.nn as nn

torch.manual_seed(42)
conv_layer = nn.Conv2d(in_channels=3, out_channels=32, kernel_size=7)
fmaps = conv_layer(cropped_images)
```

When we talk about a 2D convolutional layer, "2D" refers to the number of *spatial* dimensions (height and width), but as you can see, the layer takes 4D inputs: as we saw, the two additional dimensions are the batch size (first dimension) and the channels (second dimension).

Now let's look at the output's shape:

```
>>> fmaps.shape
torch.Size([2, 32, 64, 114])
```

The output shape is similar to the input shape, with two main differences. First, there are 32 channels instead of 3. This is because we set out_channels=32, so we get 32 output feature maps: instead of the intensity of red, green, and blue at each location, we now have the intensity of each feature at each location. Second, the height and width have both shrunk by 6 pixels. This is due to the fact that the nn.Conv2d layer does not use any zero-padding by default, which means that we lose a few pixels on the sides of the output feature maps, depending on the size of the filters. In this case, since the kernel size is 7, we lose 6 pixels horizontally and 6 pixels vertically (i.e., 3 pixels on each side).

By default, the padding hyperparameter is set to 0, which means that padding is turned off. Oddly, this is also called *valid padding* since every neuron's receptive field lies strictly within *valid* positions inside the input (it does not go out of bounds). You can actually set padding="valid", which is equivalent to padding=0. It's not a PyTorch naming quirk: everyone uses this confusing nomenclature.

If instead we set padding="same", then the inputs are padded with enough zeros on all sides to ensure that the output feature maps end up with the *same* size as the inputs (hence the name of this option):

```
>>> conv_layer = nn.Conv2d(in_channels=3, out_channels=32, kernel_size=7,
...                        padding="same")
...
>>> fmaps = conv_layer(cropped_images)
```

```
>>> fmaps.shape
torch.Size([2, 32, 70, 120])
```

These two padding options are illustrated in Figure 12-7. For simplicity, only the horizontal dimension is shown here, but of course the same logic applies to the vertical dimension as well.

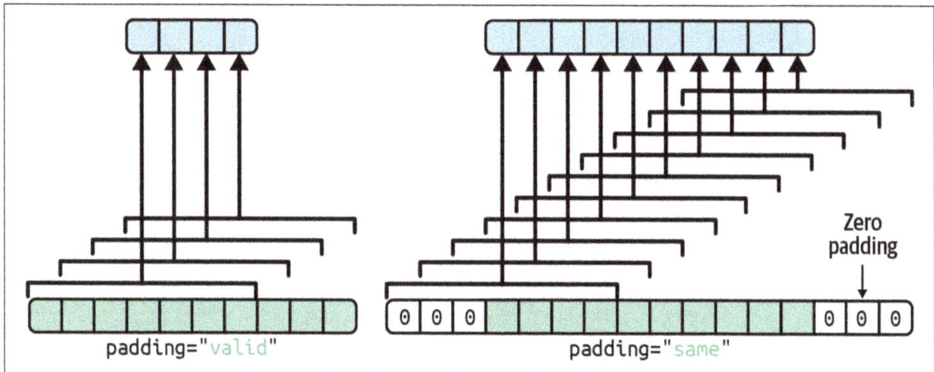

Figure 12-7. Two different padding options, with `stride=1` and `kernel_size=7`

If the stride is greater than 1 (in any direction), then the output size will be much smaller than the input size. For example, assuming the input size is 70 × 120, then if you set `stride=2` (or equivalently `stride=(2, 2)`), `padding=3`, and `kernel_size=7`, then the output feature maps will be 35 × 60: halved both vertically and horizontally. You could set a very large padding value to make the output size identical to the input size, but that's almost certainly a bad idea since it would drown your image in a sea of zeros (for this reason, PyTorch raises an exception if you set `padding="same"` along with a `stride` greater than 1). Figure 12-8 illustrates `stride=2`, with `kernel_size=7` and `padding` set to 0 or 3.

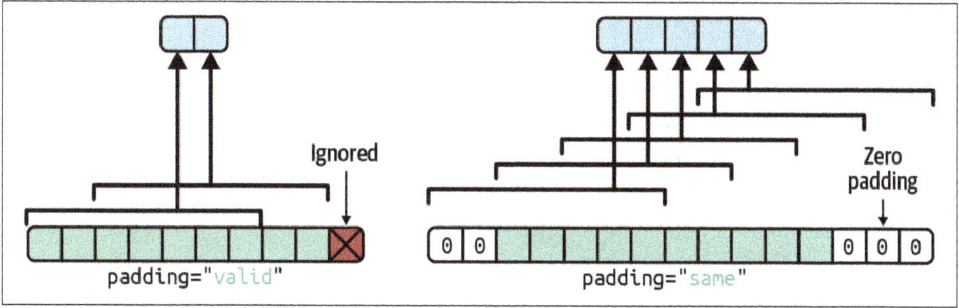

Figure 12-8. Two different padding options, with `stride=2` and `kernel_size=7`: the output size is much smaller

Now let's look at the layer's parameters (which were denoted as $w_{u,\ v,\ k',\ k}$ and b_k in Equation 12-1). Just like an `nn.Linear` layer, an `nn.Conv2d` layer holds all the layer's parameters, including the kernels and biases, which are accessible via the `weight` and `bias` attributes:

```
>>> conv_layer.weight.shape
torch.Size([32, 3, 7, 7])
>>> conv_layer.bias.shape
torch.Size([32])
```

The `weight` tensor is 4D, and its shape is [*output_channels*, *input_channels*, *kernel_height*, *kernel_width*]. The `bias` tensor is 1D, with shape [*output_channels*]. The number of output channels is equal to the number of output feature maps, which is also equal to the number of filters. Most importantly, note that the height and width of the input images do not appear in the kernel's shape: this is because all the neurons in the output feature maps share the same weights, as explained earlier. This means that you can feed images of any size to this layer, as long as they are at least as large as the kernels, and if they have the right number of channels (three in this case).

It's important to add an activation function after each convolutional layer. This is for the same reason as for `nn.Linear` layers: a convolutional layer performs a linear operation, so if you stacked multiple convolutional layers without any activation functions, they would all be equivalent to a single convolutional layer, and they wouldn't be able to learn anything really complex.

Both the `weight` and `bias` parameters are initialized randomly, using a uniform distribution similar to the one used by the `nn.Linear` layer, between $-\frac{1}{\sqrt{k}}$ and $+\frac{1}{\sqrt{k}}$, where k is the fan_{in}. In `nn.Conv2d`, $k = f_{\text{h}} \times f_{\text{w}} \times f_{\text{n'}}$, where f_{h} and f_{w} are the height and width of the kernel, and $f_{\text{n'}}$ is the number of input channels. As we saw in Chapter 11, you will generally want to reinitialize the weights depending on the activation function you use. For example, you should apply He initialization whenever you use the ReLU activation function. As for the biases, they can just be reinitialized to zero.

As you can see, convolutional layers have quite a few hyperparameters: the number of filters (`out_channels`), the kernel size, the type of padding, the strides, and the activation function. As always, you can use cross-validation to find the right hyperparameter values, but this is very time-consuming. We will discuss common CNN architectures later in this chapter to give you some idea of which hyperparameter values work best in practice.

Now, let's look at the second common building block of CNNs: the *pooling layer*.

Pooling Layers

Once you understand how convolutional layers work, the pooling layers are quite easy to grasp. Their goal is to *subsample* (i.e., shrink) the input image in order to reduce the computational load, the memory usage, and the number of parameters (thereby limiting the risk of overfitting).

Just like in convolutional layers, each neuron in a pooling layer is connected to the outputs of a limited number of neurons in the previous layer, located within a small rectangular receptive field. You must define its size, the stride, and the padding type, just like before. However, a pooling neuron has no weights or biases; all it does is aggregate the inputs using an aggregation function such as the max or mean. Figure 12-9 shows a *max pooling layer*, which is the most common type of pooling layer. In this example, we use a 2 × 2 *pooling kernel*,[7] with a stride of 2 and no padding. Only the max input value in each receptive field makes it to the next layer, while the other inputs are dropped. For example, in the lower-left receptive field in Figure 12-9, the input values are 1, 5, 3, and 2, so only the max value, 5, is propagated to the next layer. Because of the stride of 2, the output image has half the height and half the width of the input image (rounded down since we use no padding).

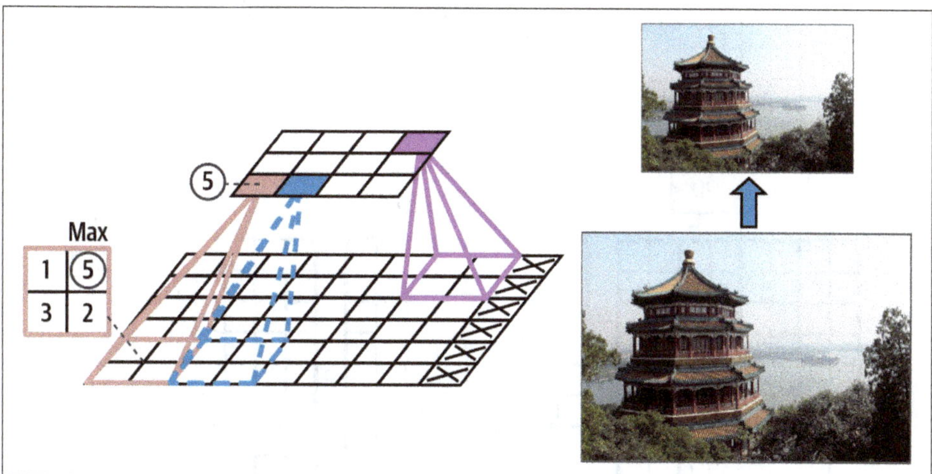

Figure 12-9. Max pooling layer (2 × 2 pooling kernel, stride 2, no padding)

7 Other kernels we've discussed so far had weights, but pooling kernels do not: they are just stateless sliding windows.

A pooling layer typically works on every input channel independently, so the output depth (i.e., the number of channels) is the same as the input depth.

Other than reducing computations, memory usage, and the number of parameters, a max pooling layer also introduces some level of *invariance* to small translations, as shown in Figure 12-10. Here we assume that the bright pixels have a lower value than dark pixels, and we consider three images (A, B, C) going through a max pooling layer with a 2 × 2 kernel and stride 2. Images B and C are the same as image A, but shifted by one and two pixels to the right. As you can see, the outputs of the max pooling layer for images A and B are identical. This is what translation invariance means. For image C, the output is different: it is shifted one pixel to the right (but there is still 50% invariance). By inserting a max pooling layer every few layers in a CNN, it is possible to get some level of translation invariance at a larger scale. Moreover, max pooling offers a small amount of rotational invariance and a slight scale invariance. Such invariance (even if it is limited) can be useful in cases where the prediction should not depend on these details, such as in classification tasks.

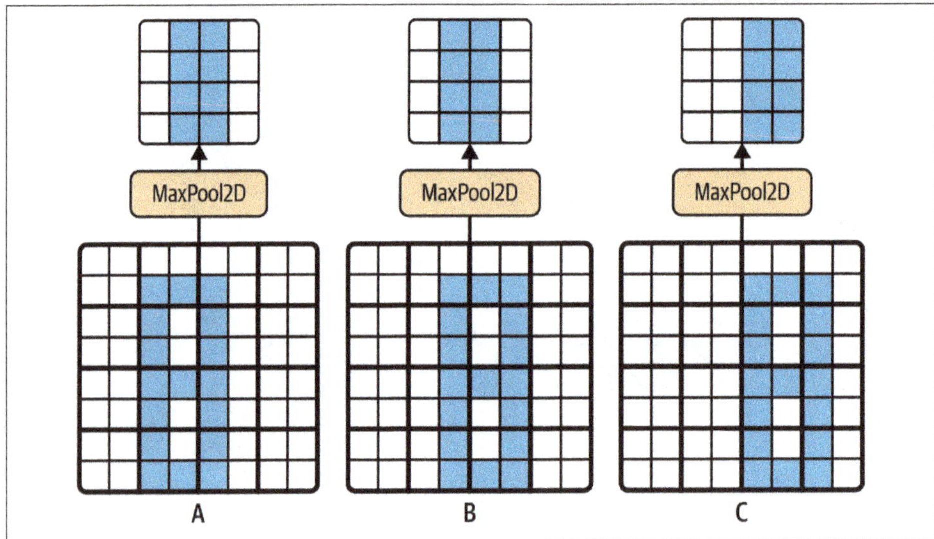

Figure 12-10. Invariance to small translations

However, max pooling has some downsides too. It's obviously very destructive: even with a tiny 2 × 2 kernel and a stride of 2, the output will be two times smaller in both directions (so its area will be four times smaller), thereby dropping 75% of the input values. And in some applications, invariance is not desirable. Take semantic segmentation (the task of classifying each pixel in an image according to the object that pixel belongs to, which we'll explore later in this chapter): obviously, if the input image is translated by one pixel to the right, the output should also be translated by one pixel to the right. The goal in this case is *equivariance*, not invariance: a small change to the inputs should lead to a corresponding small change in the output.

Implementing Pooling Layers with PyTorch

The following code creates an `nn.MaxPool2d` layer, using a 2 × 2 kernel. The strides default to the kernel size, so this layer uses a stride of 2 (horizontally and vertically). By default, it uses `padding=0` (i.e., "valid" padding):

```
max_pool = nn.MaxPool2d(kernel_size=2)
```

To create an *average pooling layer*, just use `nn.AvgPool2d`, instead of `nn.MaxPool2d`. As you might expect, it works exactly like a max pooling layer, except it computes the mean rather than the max. Average pooling layers used to be very popular, but people mostly use max pooling layers now, as they generally perform better. This may seem surprising, since computing the mean generally loses less information than computing the max. But on the other hand, max pooling preserves only the strongest features, getting rid of all the meaningless ones, so the next layers get a cleaner signal to work with. Moreover, max pooling offers stronger translation invariance than average pooling, and it requires slightly less compute.

Note that max pooling and average pooling can also be performed along the depth dimension instead of the spatial dimensions, although it's not as common. This can allow the CNN to learn to be invariant to various features. For example, it could learn multiple filters, each detecting a different rotation of the same pattern (such as handwritten digits; see Figure 12-11), and the depthwise max pooling layer would ensure that the output is the same regardless of the rotation. The CNN could similarly learn to be invariant to anything: thickness, brightness, skew, color, and so on.

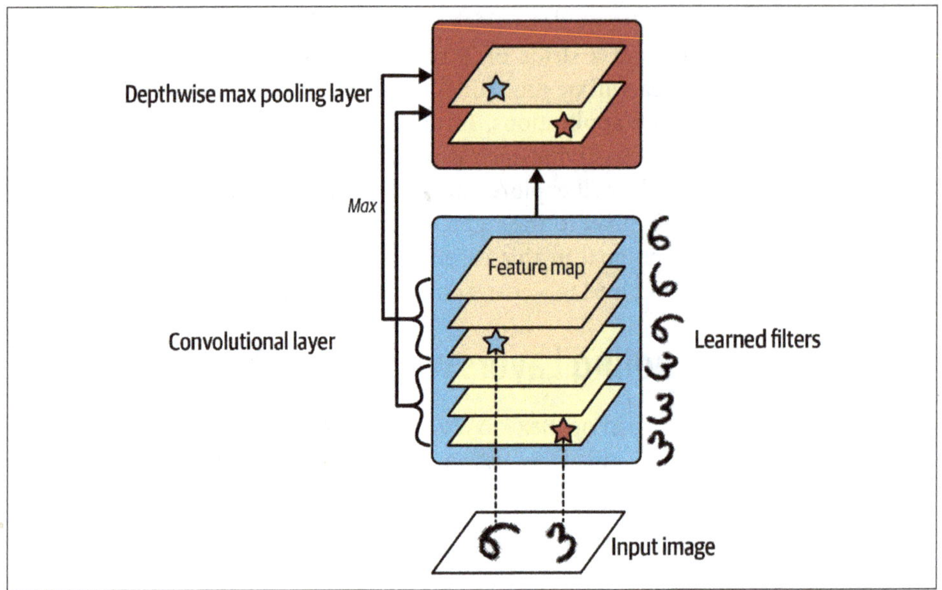

Figure 12-11. Depthwise max pooling can help the CNN learn to be invariant (to rotation in this case)

PyTorch does not include a depthwise max pooling layer, but we can implement a custom module based on the `torch.F.max_pool1d()` function:

```
import torch.nn.functional as F

class DepthPool(torch.nn.Module):
    def __init__(self, kernel_size, stride=None, padding=0):
        super().__init__()
        self.kernel_size = kernel_size
        self.stride = stride if stride is not None else kernel_size
        self.padding = padding

    def forward(self, inputs):
        batch, channels, height, width = inputs.shape
        Z = inputs.view(batch, channels, height * width)  # merge spatial dims
        Z = Z.permute(0, 2, 1)  # switch spatial and channels dims
        Z = F.max_pool1d(Z, kernel_size=self.kernel_size, stride=self.stride,
                         padding=self.padding)  # compute max pool
        Z = Z.permute(0, 2, 1)  # switch back spatial and channels dims
        return Z.view(batch, -1, height, width)  # unmerge spatial dims
```

For example, suppose the input batch contains two 70 × 120 images, each with 32 channels (i.e., the inputs have a shape of `[2, 32, 70, 120]`), and we use `kernel_size=4`, and the default `stride` (equal to `kernel_size`) and `padding=0`:

- The `forward()` method starts by merging the spatial dimensions, which gives us a tensor of shape `[2, 32, 8400]` (since 70 × 120 = 8,400).
- It then permutes the last two dimensions, so we get a shape of `[2, 8400, 32]`.
- Next, it uses the `max_pool1d()` function to compute the max pool along the last dimension, which corresponds to our original 32 channels. Since `kernel_size` and `stride` are both equal to 4, and we don't use any padding, the size of the last dimension gets divided by 4, so the resulting shape is `[2, 8400, 8]`.
- The function then permutes the last two dimensions again, giving us a shape of `[2, 8, 8400]`.
- Lastly, it separates the spatial dimensions to get the final shape of `[2, 8, 50, 100]`. You can verify that the output is exactly what we were after.

One last type of pooling layer that you will often see in modern architectures is the *global average pooling layer*. It works very differently: all it does is compute the mean of each entire feature map. Therefore it outputs a single number per feature map and per instance. Although this is of course extremely destructive (most of the information in the feature map is lost), it can be useful just before the output layer, as you will see later in this chapter.

To create such a layer, one option is to use a regular `nn.AvgPool2d` layer and set its kernel size to the same size as the inputs. However, this is not very convenient since it requires knowing the exact dimensions of the inputs ahead of time. A simpler solution is to use the `nn.AdaptiveAvgPool2d` layer, which lets you specify the desired spatial dimensions of the output: it automatically adapts the kernel size (with an equal stride) to get the desired result, adding a bit of padding if needed. If we set the output size to 1, we get a global average pooling layer:

```
global_avg_pool = nn.AdaptiveAvgPool2d(output_size=1)
output = global_avg_pool(cropped_images)
```

Alternatively, you could just use the `torch.mean()` function to get the same output:

```
output = cropped_images.mean(dim=(2, 3), keepdim=True)
```

Now you know all the building blocks to create convolutional neural networks. Let's see how to assemble them.

CNN Architectures

Typical CNN architectures stack a few convolutional layers (each one generally followed by a ReLU layer), then a pooling layer, then another few convolutional layers (+ReLU), then another pooling layer, and so on. The image gets smaller and smaller as it progresses through the network, but it also typically gets deeper and deeper (i.e., with more feature maps), thanks to the convolutional layers (see Figure 12-12). At the top of the stack, a regular feedforward neural network is added, composed of a few fully connected layers (+ReLUs), and the final layer outputs the prediction (e.g., a softmax layer that outputs estimated class probabilities).

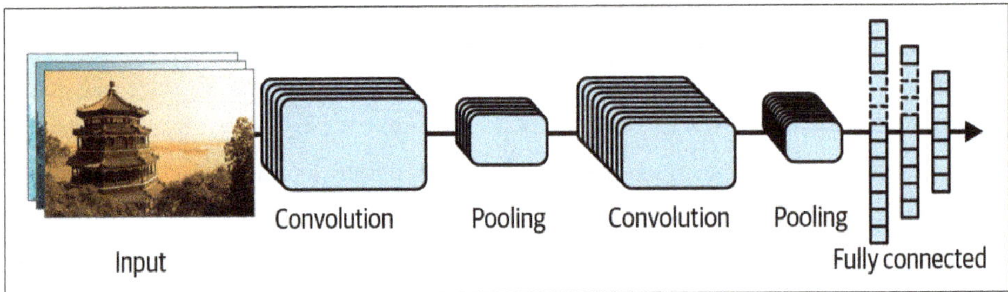

Figure 12-12. Typical CNN architecture

Instead of using a convolutional layer with a 5 × 5 kernel, it is generally preferable to stack two layers with 3 × 3 kernels: it will use fewer parameters and require fewer computations, and it will usually perform better. One exception is for the first convolutional layer: it can typically have a large kernel (e.g., 5 × 5 or 7 × 7), usually with a stride of 2 or more. This reduces the spatial dimension of the image without losing too much information, and since the input image only has three channels in general, it will not be too costly.

Here is how you can implement a basic CNN to tackle the Fashion MNIST dataset (introduced in Chapter 9):

```
from functools import partial

DefaultConv2d = partial(nn.Conv2d, kernel_size=3, padding="same")
model = nn.Sequential(
    DefaultConv2d(in_channels=1, out_channels=64, kernel_size=7), nn.ReLU(),
    nn.MaxPool2d(kernel_size=2),
    DefaultConv2d(in_channels=64, out_channels=128), nn.ReLU(),
    DefaultConv2d(in_channels=128, out_channels=128), nn.ReLU(),
    nn.MaxPool2d(kernel_size=2),
    DefaultConv2d(in_channels=128, out_channels=256), nn.ReLU(),
    DefaultConv2d(in_channels=256, out_channels=256), nn.ReLU(),
    nn.MaxPool2d(kernel_size=2),
    nn.Flatten(),
    nn.Linear(in_features=2304, out_features=128), nn.ReLU(),
    nn.Dropout(0.5),
    nn.Linear(in_features=128, out_features=64), nn.ReLU(),
    nn.Dropout(0.5),
    nn.Linear(in_features=64, out_features=10),
).to(device)
```

Let's go through this code:

- We use the `functools.partial()` function (introduced in Chapter 11) to define `DefaultConv2d`, which acts just like `nn.Conv2d` but with different default arguments: a small kernel size of 3, and `"same"` padding. This avoids having to repeat these arguments throughout the model.
- Next, we create the `nn.Sequential` model. Its first layer is a `DefaultConv2d` with 64 fairly large filters (7 × 7). It uses the default stride of 1 because the input images are not very large. It also uses `in_channels=1` because the Fashion MNIST images have a single color channel (i.e., grayscale). Each convolutional layer is followed by the ReLU activation function.
- We then add a max pooling layer with a kernel size of 2, so it divides each spatial dimension by a factor of 2 (rounded down if needed).
- Then we repeat the same structure twice: two convolutional layers followed by a max pooling layer. For larger images, we could repeat this structure several more times. The number of repetitions is a hyperparameter you can tune.
- Note that the number of filters doubles as we climb up the CNN toward the output layer (it is initially 64, then 128, then 256). It makes sense for it to grow, since the number of low-level features is often fairly low (e.g., small circles, horizontal lines), but there are many different ways to combine them into higher-level features. It is a common practice to double the number of filters after each pooling layer: since a pooling layer divides each spatial dimension by a factor of 2, we can afford to double the number of feature maps in the next layer without fear of exploding the number of parameters, memory usage, or computational load.
- Next is the fully connected network, composed of two hidden dense layers (`nn.Linear`) with the ReLU activation function, plus a dense output layer. Since it's a classification task with 10 classes, the output layer has 10 units. As we did in Chapter 10, we leave out the softmax activation function, so the model will output logits rather than probabilities, and we must use the `nn.CrossEntropyLoss` to train the model. Note that we must flatten the inputs just before the first dense layer, since it expects a 1D array of features for each instance. We also add two dropout layers, with a dropout rate of 50% each, to reduce overfitting.

The first `nn.Linear` layer has 2,304 input features: where did this number come from? Well the Fashion MNIST images are 28 × 28 pixels, but the pooling layers shrink them to 14 × 14, then 7 × 7, and finally 3 × 3. Just before the first `nn.Linear` layer, there are 256 feature maps, so we end up with 256 × 3 × 3 = 2,304 input features. Figuring out the number of features can sometimes be a bit difficult, but one trick is to set `in_features` to some arbitrary value (say, 999), and let training crash. The correct number of features appears in the error message: "RuntimeError: mat1 and mat2 shapes cannot be multiplied (32x2304 and 999x128)". Another option is to use `nn.LazyLinear` instead of `nn.Linear`: it's just like the `nn.Linear` layer, except it only creates the weights matrix the first time it gets called: it can then automatically set the number of input features to the correct value. Other layers—such as convolutional layers and batch-norm layers—also have lazy variants.

If you train this model on the Fashion MNIST training set, it should reach close to 92% accuracy on the test set (you can use the `train()` and `evaluate_tm()` functions we defined in Chapter 10). It's not state of the art, but it is pretty good, and better than what we achieved with dense networks in Chapter 9.

Over the years, variants of this fundamental architecture have been developed, leading to amazing advances in the field. A good measure of this progress is the error rate in competitions such as the ILSVRC ImageNet challenge (*https://image-net.org*). In this competition, the error rate for image classification fell from over 26% to less than 2.3% in just 6 years. More precisely, this was the *top-five error rate*, which is the ratio of test images for which the system's five most confident predictions did *not* include the correct answer. The images are fairly large (e.g., 256 pixels high) and there are 1,000 classes, some of which are really subtle (try distinguishing 120 dog breeds!). Looking at the evolution of the winning entries is a good way to understand how CNNs work, and how research in deep learning progresses.

We will first look at the classical LeNet-5 architecture (1998), then several winners of the ILSVRC challenge: AlexNet (2012), GoogLeNet (2014), ResNet (2015), and SENet (2017). We will also discuss a few more architectures, including VGGNet, Xception, ResNeXt, DenseNet, MobileNet, CSPNet, EfficientNet, and ConvNeXt (and we will discuss vision transformers in Chapter 16).

LeNet-5

The LeNet-5 architecture (*https://homl.info/lenet5*)[8] is perhaps the most widely known CNN architecture. As mentioned earlier, it was created by Yann LeCun in 1998 and has been widely used for handwritten digit recognition (MNIST). It is composed of the layers shown in Table 12-1.

Table 12-1. LeNet-5 architecture

Layer	Type	Maps	Size	Kernel size	Stride	Activation
Out	Fully connected	–	10	–	–	RBF
F6	Fully connected	–	84	–	–	tanh
C5	Convolution	120	1 × 1	5 × 5	1	tanh
S4	Avg pooling	16	5 × 5	2 × 2	2	tanh
C3	Convolution	16	10 × 10	5 × 5	1	tanh
S2	Avg pooling	6	14 × 14	2 × 2	2	tanh
C1	Convolution	6	28 × 28	5 × 5	1	tanh
In	Input	1	32 × 32	–	–	–

As you can see, this looks pretty similar to our Fashion MNIST model: a stack of convolutional layers and pooling layers, followed by a dense network. Perhaps the main difference with more modern classification CNNs is the activation functions: today, we would use ReLU instead of tanh, and softmax instead of RBF (introduced in Chapter 2). There were several other minor differences that don't really matter much, but in case you are interested, they are listed in this chapter's notebook at *https://homl.info/colab-p*. Yann LeCun's website (*http://yann.lecun.com/exdb/lenet*) also features great demos of LeNet-5 classifying digits.

AlexNet

The AlexNet CNN architecture (*https://homl.info/80*)[9] won the 2012 ILSVRC challenge by a large margin: it achieved a top-five error rate of 17%, while the second best competitor achieved only 26%! AlexNet was developed by Alex Krizhevsky (hence the name), Ilya Sutskever, and Geoffrey Hinton. It is similar to LeNet-5, only much larger and deeper, and it was the first to stack convolutional layers directly on top of one another, instead of stacking a pooling layer on top of each convolutional layer. Table 12-2 presents this architecture.

8 Yann LeCun et al., "Gradient-Based Learning Applied to Document Recognition", *Proceedings of the IEEE* 86, no. 11 (1998): 2278–2324.

9 Alex Krizhevsky et al., "ImageNet Classification with Deep Convolutional Neural Networks", *Proceedings of the 25th International Conference on Neural Information Processing Systems* 1 (2012): 1097–1105.

Table 12-2. AlexNet architecture

Layer	Type	Maps	Size	Kernel size	Stride	Padding	Activation
Out	Fully connected	–	1,000	–	–	–	Softmax
F10	Fully connected	–	4,096	–	–	–	ReLU
F9	Fully connected	–	4,096	–	–	–	ReLU
S8	Max pooling	256	6 × 6	3 × 3	2	`valid`	–
C7	Convolution	256	13 × 13	3 × 3	1	`same`	ReLU
C6	Convolution	384	13 × 13	3 × 3	1	`same`	ReLU
C5	Convolution	384	13 × 13	3 × 3	1	`same`	ReLU
S4	Max pooling	256	13 × 13	3 × 3	2	`valid`	–
C3	Convolution	256	27 × 27	5 × 5	1	`same`	ReLU
S2	Max pooling	96	27 × 27	3 × 3	2	`valid`	–
C1	Convolution	96	55 × 55	11 × 11	4	`valid`	ReLU
In	Input	3 (RGB)	227 × 227	–	–	–	–

To reduce overfitting, the authors used two regularization techniques. First, they applied dropout (introduced in Chapter 11) with a 50% dropout rate during training to the outputs of layers F9 and F10. Second, they performed data augmentation by randomly shifting the training images by various offsets, flipping them horizontally, and changing the lighting conditions.

Data Augmentation

Data augmentation artificially increases the size of the training set by generating many realistic variants of each training instance. This reduces overfitting, making this a regularization technique. The generated instances should be as realistic as possible: ideally, given an image from the augmented training set, a human should not be able to tell whether it was augmented or not. Simply adding white noise will not help; the modifications should be learnable (white noise is not).

For example, you can slightly shift, rotate, and resize every picture in the training set by various amounts and add the resulting pictures to the training set (see Figure 12-13). To do this, you can use tools available in `torchvision.transforms.v2` (e.g., `RandomCrop`, `RandomRotation`, etc.). This forces the model to be more tolerant to variations in the position, orientation, and size of the objects in the pictures. You can similarly use transforms to tweak the colors, and contrasts to simulate many different lighting conditions. In general, you can also flip the pictures horizontally (except for text and other asymmetrical objects). By combining these transformations (using `Compose`), you can greatly increase your training set size.

Figure 12-13. Generating new training instances from existing ones

Data augmentation is also useful when you have an unbalanced dataset: you can use it to generate more samples of the less frequent classes. This is called the *synthetic minority oversampling technique*, or SMOTE for short.

Lastly, although data augmentation is typically used only during training, one exception is *test-time augmentation* (TTA): this technique involves augmenting the test data and combining the predictions to boost accuracy. For example, if three augmented versions of an image are classified as a bus, while seven are classified as a truck, then it's probably a truck.

AlexNet also used a regularization technique called *local response normalization* (LRN): the most strongly activated neurons inhibit other neurons located at the same position in neighboring feature maps. Such competitive activation has been observed in biological neurons. This encourages different feature maps to specialize, pushing them apart and forcing them to explore a wider range of features, ultimately improving generalization. However, this technique was mostly superseded by simpler and more efficient regularization techniques, especially batch normalization.

A variant of AlexNet called *ZFNet* (*https://homl.info/zfnet*)[10] was developed by Matthew Zeiler and Rob Fergus and won the 2013 ILSVRC challenge. It is essentially AlexNet with a few tweaked hyperparameters (number of feature maps, kernel size, stride, etc.).

10 Matthew D. Zeiler and Rob Fergus, "Visualizing and Understanding Convolutional Networks", *Proceedings of the European Conference on Computer Vision* (2014): 818–833.

GoogLeNet

The GoogLeNet architecture (*https://homl.info/81*) was developed by Christian Szegedy et al. from Google Research,[11] and it won the ILSVRC 2014 challenge by pushing the top-five error rate below 7%. This great performance came in large part from the fact that the network was much deeper than previous CNNs (as you'll see in Figure 12-15). This was made possible by subnetworks called *inception modules*,[12] which allow GoogLeNet to use parameters much more efficiently than previous architectures: GoogLeNet actually has 10 times fewer parameters than AlexNet (roughly 6 million instead of 60 million).

Figure 12-14 shows the architecture of an inception module. The notation "3 × 3 + 1(S)" means that the layer uses a 3 × 3 kernel, stride 1, and `"same"` padding. The input signal is first fed to four different layers in parallel. All convolutional layers use the ReLU activation function. Note that the top convolutional layers use different kernel sizes (1 × 1, 3 × 3, and 5 × 5), allowing them to capture patterns at different scales. Also note that every single layer uses a stride of 1 and `"same"` padding (even the max pooling layer), so their outputs all have the same height and width as their inputs. This makes it possible to concatenate all the outputs along the depth dimension in the final *depth concatenation layer* (i.e., it concatenates the multiple feature maps output by each of the upper four convolutional layers). It can be implemented using the `torch.cat()` function, with `dim=1`.

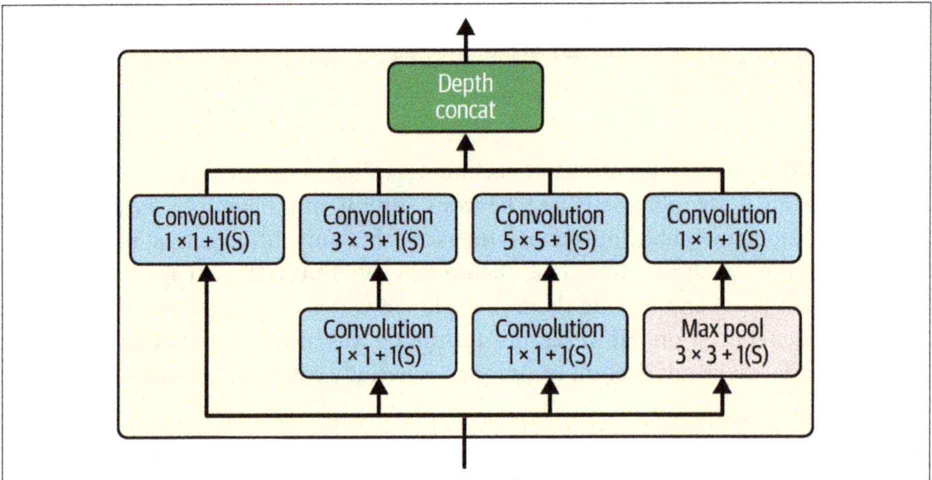

Figure 12-14. Inception module

---

11 Christian Szegedy et al., "Going Deeper with Convolutions", *Proceedings of the IEEE Conference on Computer Vision and Pattern Recognition* (2015): 1–9.

12 In the 2010 movie *Inception*, the characters keep going deeper and deeper into multiple layers of dreams; hence the name of these modules.

You may wonder why inception modules have convolutional layers with 1 × 1 kernels. Surely these layers cannot capture any features because they look at only one pixel at a time, right? In fact, these layers serve three purposes:

- Although they cannot capture spatial patterns, they can capture patterns along the depth dimension (i.e., across channels).
- They are configured to output fewer feature maps than their inputs, so they serve as *bottleneck layers*, meaning they reduce dimensionality. This cuts the computational cost and the number of parameters, speeding up training and improving generalization.
- Each pair of convolutional layers ([1 × 1, 3 × 3] and [1 × 1, 5 × 5]) acts like a single powerful convolutional layer, capable of capturing more complex patterns. A convolutional layer is equivalent to sweeping a dense layer across the image (at each location, it only looks at a small receptive field), and these pairs of convolutional layers are equivalent to sweeping two-layer neural networks across the image.

In short, you can think of the whole inception module as a convolutional layer on steroids, able to output feature maps that capture complex patterns at various scales.

Now let's look at the architecture of the GoogLeNet CNN (see Figure 12-15). The number of feature maps output by each convolutional layer and each pooling layer is shown before the kernel size. The architecture is so deep that it has to be represented in three columns, but GoogLeNet is actually one tall stack, including nine inception modules (the boxes with the spinning tops). The six numbers in the inception modules represent the number of feature maps output by each convolutional layer in the module (in the same order as in Figure 12-14). Note that all the convolutional layers use the ReLU activation function.

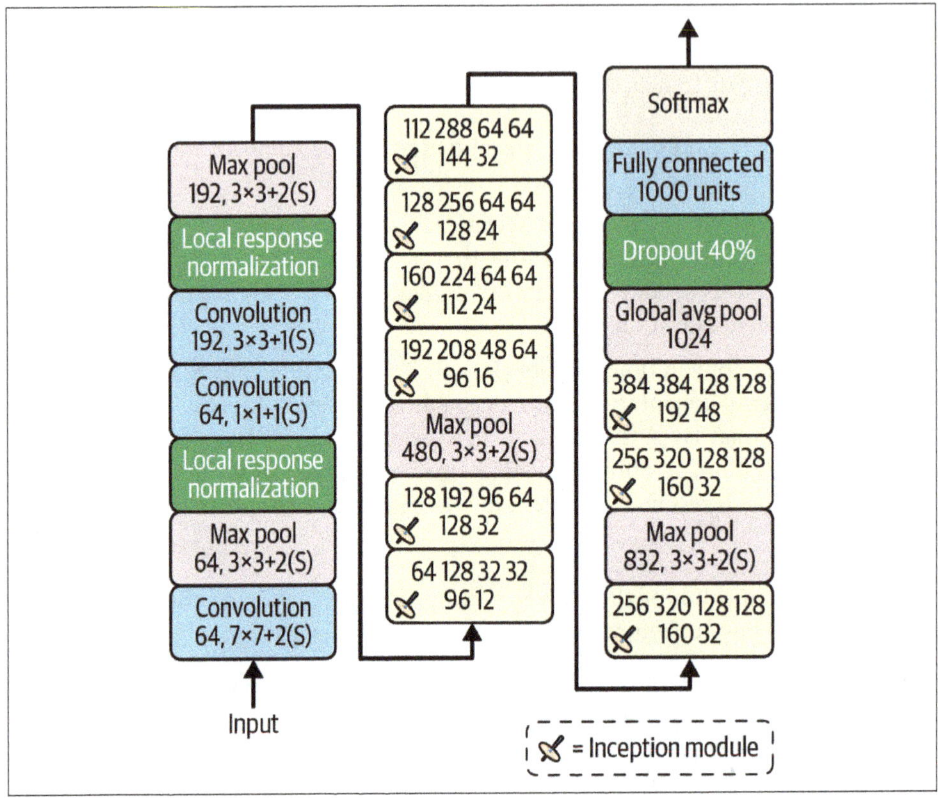

Figure 12-15. GoogLeNet architecture

Let's go through this network:

- The first two layers divide the image's height and width by 4 (so its area is divided by 16), to reduce the computational load. The first layer uses a large kernel size, 7 × 7, so that much of the information is preserved.
- Then the local response normalization layer ensures that the previous layers learn a wide variety of features (as discussed earlier).
- Two convolutional layers follow, where the first acts like a bottleneck layer. As mentioned, you can think of this pair as a single smarter convolutional layer.
- Again, a local response normalization layer ensures that the previous layers capture a wide variety of patterns.
- Next, a max pooling layer reduces the image height and width by 2, again to speed up computations.

- Then comes the CNN's *backbone*: a tall stack of nine inception modules, interleaved with a couple of max pooling layers to reduce dimensionality and speed up the net.
- Next, the global average pooling layer outputs the mean of each feature map: this drops any remaining spatial information, which is fine because there is not much spatial information left at that point. Indeed, GoogLeNet input images are typically expected to be 224 × 224 pixels, so after 5 max pooling layers, each dividing the height and width by 2, the feature maps are down to 7 × 7. Moreover, this is a classification task, not localization, so it doesn't matter where the object is. Thanks to the dimensionality reduction brought by this layer, there is no need to have several fully connected layers at the top of the CNN (like in AlexNet), and this considerably reduces the number of parameters in the network and limits the risk of overfitting.
- The last layers are self-explanatory: dropout for regularization, then a fully connected layer with 1,000 units (since there are 1,000 classes) and a softmax activation function to output estimated class probabilities.

The original GoogLeNet architecture included two auxiliary classifiers plugged on top of the third and sixth inception modules. They were both composed of one average pooling layer, one convolutional layer, two fully connected layers, and a softmax activation layer. During training, their loss (scaled down by 70%) was added to the overall loss. The goal was to fight the vanishing gradients problem and regularize the network, but it was later shown that their effect was relatively minor.

Several variants of the GoogLeNet architecture were later proposed by Google researchers, including Inception-v3 and Inception-v4, using slightly different inception modules to reach even better performance.

ResNet

Kaiming He et al. won the ILSVRC 2015 challenge using a Residual Network (ResNet) (*https://homl.info/82*)[13] that delivered an astounding top-five error rate under 3.6%. The winning variant used an extremely deep CNN composed of 152 layers (other variants had 34, 50, and 101 layers). It confirmed the general trend: computer vision models were getting deeper and deeper, with fewer and fewer parameters. The key to being able to train such a deep network is to use *skip connections* (also called *shortcut connections*): the signal feeding into a layer is also added to the output of a layer located higher up the stack. Let's see why this is useful.

When training a neural network, the goal is to make it model a target function $h(\mathbf{x})$. If you add the input $\mathbf{x}$ to the output of the network (i.e., you add a skip connection),

13 Kaiming He et al., "Deep Residual Learning for Image Recognition", arXiv preprint arXiv:1512:03385 (2015).

then the network will be forced to model $f(\mathbf{x}) = h(\mathbf{x}) - \mathbf{x}$ rather than $h(\mathbf{x})$. This is called *residual learning* (see Figure 12-16).

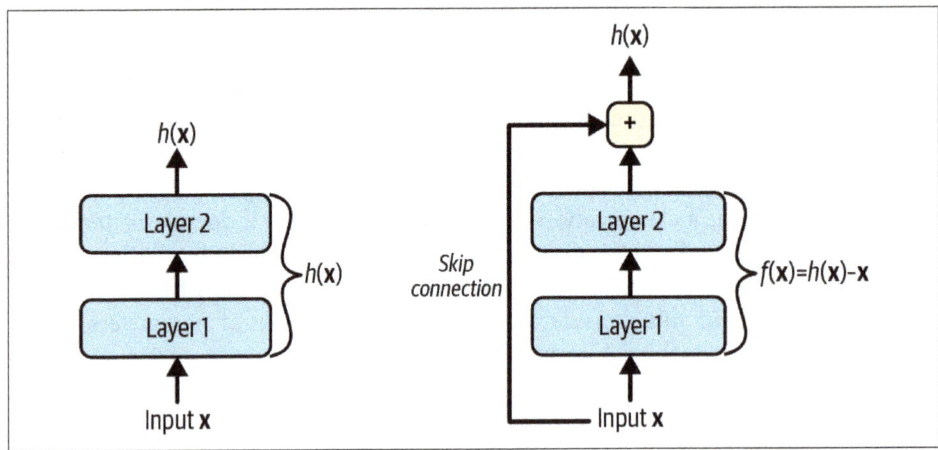

Figure 12-16. Residual learning

When you initialize a neural network, its weights are close to zero, so a regular network just outputs values close to zero when training starts. But if you add a skip connection, the resulting network outputs a copy of its inputs; in other words, it acts as the identity function at the start of training. If the target function is fairly close to the identity function (which is often the case), this will speed up training considerably.

Moreover, if you add many skip connections, the network can start making progress even if several layers have not started learning yet (see Figure 12-17). Thanks to skip connections, the signal can easily make its way across the whole network. The deep residual network can be seen as a stack of *residual units* (RUs), where each residual unit is a small neural network with a skip connection.

Now let's look at ResNet's architecture (see Figure 12-18). It is surprisingly simple. It starts and ends exactly like GoogLeNet (except without a dropout layer), and in between is just a very deep stack of residual units. Each residual unit is composed of two convolutional layers (and no pooling layer!), with batch normalization (BN) and ReLU activation, using 3 × 3 kernels and preserving spatial dimensions (stride 1, `"same"` padding).

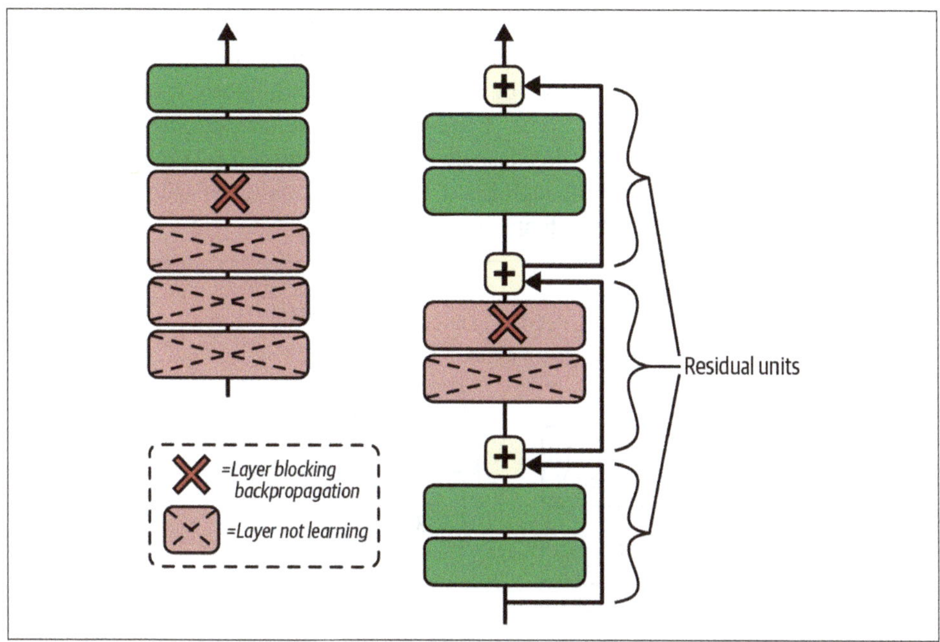

Figure 12-17. Regular deep neural network (left) and deep residual network (right)

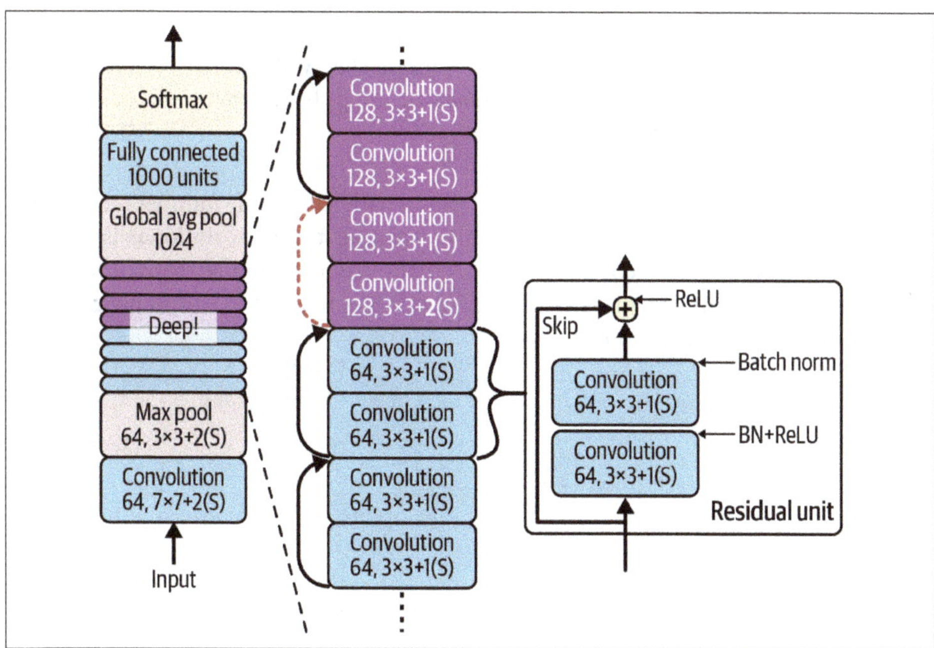

Figure 12-18. ResNet architecture

Note that the number of feature maps is doubled every few residual units, at the same time as their height and width are halved (using a convolutional layer with stride 2). When this happens, the inputs cannot be added directly to the outputs of the residual unit because they don't have the same shape (for example, this problem affects the skip connection represented by the dashed arrow in Figure 12-18). To solve this problem, the inputs are passed through a 1 × 1 convolutional layer with stride 2 and the right number of output feature maps (see Figure 12-19).

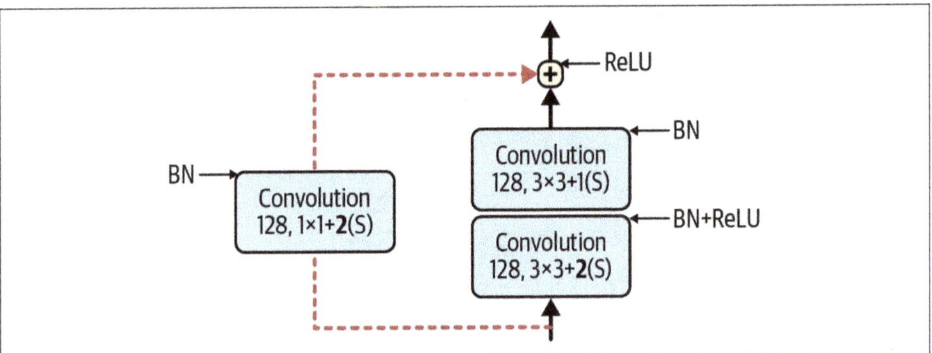

Figure 12-19. Skip connection when changing feature map size and depth

During training, for each mini-batch, you can skip a random set of residual units. This *stochastic depth* technique (*https://homl.info/sdepth*)[14] speeds up training considerably without compromising accuracy. You can implement it using the `torchvision.ops.stochastic_depth()` function.

Different variations of the architecture exist, with different numbers of layers. ResNet-34 is a ResNet with 34 layers (only counting the convolutional layers and the fully connected layer)[15] containing 3 RUs that output 64 feature maps, 4 RUs with 128 maps, 6 RUs with 256 maps, and 3 RUs with 512 maps. We will implement this architecture later in this chapter.

14 Gao Huang, Yu Sun, et al., "Deep Networks with Stochastic Depth", arXiv preprint arXiv:1603.09382 (2016).

15 It is a common practice when describing a neural network to count only layers with parameters.

ResNets deeper than that, such as ResNet-152, use slightly different residual units. Instead of two 3 × 3 convolutional layers with, say, 256 feature maps, they use three convolutional layers: first a 1 × 1 convolutional layer with just 64 feature maps (4 times less), which acts as a bottleneck layer (as discussed already), then a 3 × 3 layer with 64 feature maps, and finally another 1 × 1 convolutional layer with 256 feature maps (4 times 64) that restores the original depth. ResNet-152 contains 3 such RUs that output 256 maps, then 8 RUs with 512 maps, a whopping 36 RUs with 1,024 maps, and finally 3 RUs with 2,048 maps.

Google's Inception-v4 architecture (*https://homl.info/84*)[16] merged the ideas of GoogLeNet and ResNet and achieved a top-five error rate of close to 3% on ImageNet classification.

Xception

Another variant of the GoogLeNet architecture is worth noting: Xception (*https://homl.info/xception*)[17] (which stands for *Extreme Inception*) was proposed in 2016 by François Chollet (the author of the deep learning framework Keras), and it significantly outperformed Inception-v3 on a huge vision task (350 million images and 17,000 classes). Just like Inception-v4, it merges the ideas of GoogLeNet and ResNet, but it replaces the inception modules with a special type of layer called a *depthwise separable convolution layer* (or *separable convolution layer* for short[18]). These layers had been used before in some CNN architectures, but they were not as central as in the Xception architecture. While a regular convolutional layer uses filters that try to simultaneously capture spatial patterns (e.g., an oval) and cross-channel patterns (e.g., mouth + nose + eyes = face), a separable convolutional layer makes the strong assumption that spatial patterns and cross-channel patterns can be modeled separately (see Figure 12-20). Thus, it is composed of two parts: the first part applies a single spatial filter to each input feature map, then the second part looks exclusively for cross-channel patterns—it is just a regular convolutional layer with 1 × 1 filters.

16 Christian Szegedy et al., "Inception–v4, Inception-ResNet and the Impact of Residual Connections on Learning", arXiv preprint arXiv:1602.07261 (2016).

17 François Chollet, "Xception: Deep Learning with Depthwise Separable Convolutions", arXiv preprint arXiv:1610.02357 (2016).

18 This name can sometimes be ambiguous, since spatially separable convolutions are often called "separable convolutions" as well.

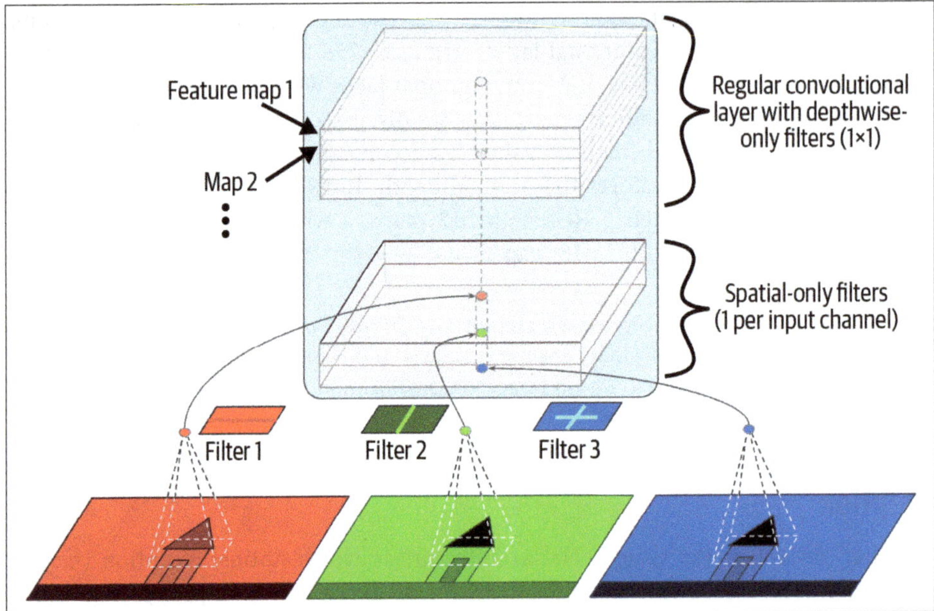

Figure 12-20. Depthwise separable convolutional layer

Since separable convolutional layers only have one spatial filter per input channel, you should avoid using them after layers that have too few channels, such as the input layer (granted, that's what Figure 12-20 represents, but it is just for illustration purposes). For this reason, the Xception architecture starts with 2 regular convolutional layers, but then the rest of the architecture uses only separable convolutions (34 in all), plus a few max pooling layers and the usual final layers (a global average pooling layer and a dense output layer).

You might wonder why Xception is considered a variant of GoogLeNet, since it contains no inception modules at all. Well, as discussed earlier, an inception module contains convolutional layers with 1 × 1 filters: these look exclusively for cross-channel patterns. However, the convolutional layers that sit on top of them are regular convolutional layers that look both for spatial and cross-channel patterns. So you can think of an inception module as an intermediate between a regular convolutional layer (which considers spatial patterns and cross-channel patterns jointly) and a separable convolutional layer (which considers them separately). In practice, it seems that separable convolutional layers often perform better.

PyTorch does not include a SeparableConv2d module, but it's fairly straightforward to implement your own:

```
class SeparableConv2d(nn.Module):
    def __init__(self, in_channels, out_channels, kernel_size, stride=1,
                 padding=0):
        super().__init__()
        self.depthwise_conv = nn.Conv2d(
            in_channels, in_channels, kernel_size, stride=stride,
            padding=padding, groups=in_channels)
        self.pointwise_conv = nn.Conv2d(
            in_channels, out_channels, kernel_size=1, stride=1, padding=0)

    def forward(self, inputs):
        return self.pointwise_conv(self.depthwise_conv(inputs))
```

Notice the groups argument on the seventh line: it lets you split the input channels into the given number of independent groups, each with its own filters (note that in_channels and out_channels need to be divisible by groups). By default groups=1, giving you a normal convolutional layer, but if you set both groups=in_channels and out_channels=in_channels, you get a depthwise convolutional layer, with one filter per input channel. That's the first layer in the separable convolutional layer. The second is a regular convolutional layer, except we set its kernel size and stride to 1. And that's it!

Separable convolutional layers use fewer parameters, less memory, and fewer computations than regular convolutional layers, and they often perform better. Consider using them by default, except after layers with few channels (such as the input channel).

SENet

The winning architecture in the ILSVRC 2017 challenge was the Squeeze-and-Excitation Network (SENet) (*https://homl.info/senet*).[19] This architecture extends existing architectures such as inception networks and ResNets, and boosts their performance. This allowed SENet to win the competition with an astonishing 2.25% top-five error rate! The extended versions of inception networks and ResNets are called *SE-Inception* and *SE-ResNet*, respectively. The boost comes from the fact that a SENet adds a small neural network, called an *SE block*, to every inception module or residual unit in the original architecture, as shown in Figure 12-21.

19 Jie Hu et al., "Squeeze-and-Excitation Networks", *Proceedings of the IEEE Conference on Computer Vision and Pattern Recognition* (2018): 7132–7141.

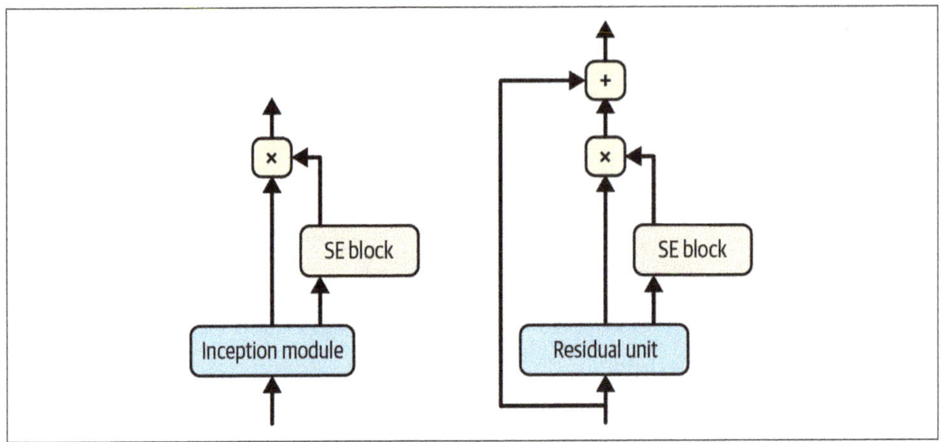

Figure 12-21. SE-Inception module (left) and SE-ResNet unit (right)

An SE block analyzes the output of the unit it is attached to, focusing exclusively on the depth dimension (it does not look for any spatial pattern), and it learns which features are usually most active together. It then uses this information to recalibrate the feature maps, as shown in Figure 12-22. For example, an SE block may learn that mouths, noses, and eyes usually appear together in pictures: if you see a mouth and a nose, you should expect to see eyes as well. So, if the block sees a strong activation in the mouth and nose feature maps, but only mild activation in the eye feature map, it will boost the eye feature map (more accurately, it will reduce irrelevant feature maps). If the eyes were somewhat confused with something else, this feature map recalibration will help resolve the ambiguity.

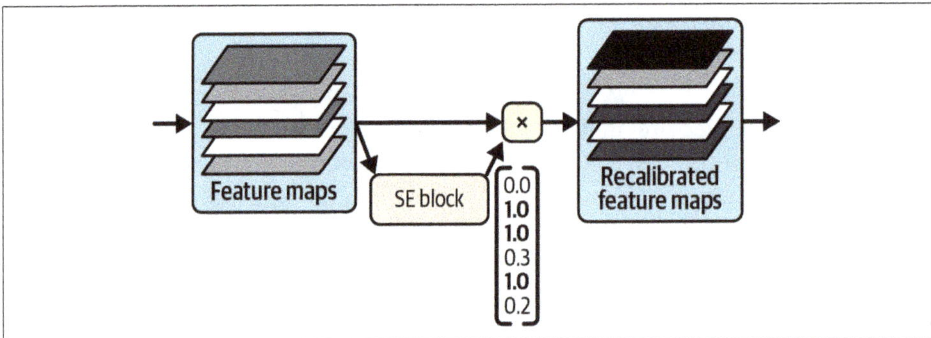

Figure 12-22. An SE block performs feature map recalibration

An SE block is composed of just three layers: a global average pooling layer, a hidden dense layer using the ReLU activation function, and a dense output layer using the sigmoid activation function (see Figure 12-23).

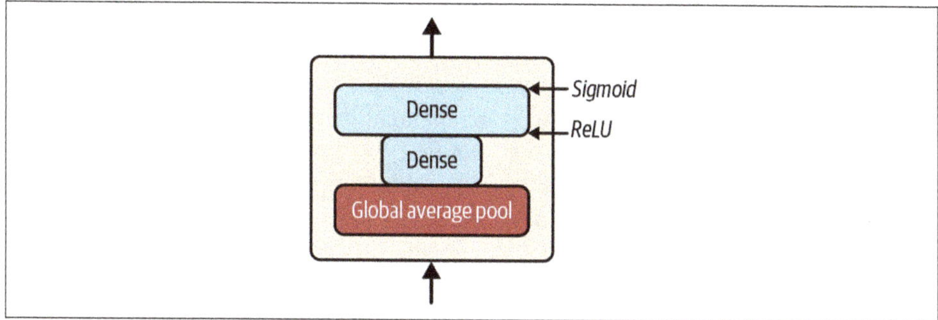

Figure 12-23. SE block architecture

As earlier, the global average pooling layer computes the mean activation for each feature map: for example, if its input contains 256 feature maps, it will output 256 numbers representing the overall level of response for each filter. The next layer is where the "squeeze" happens: this layer has significantly fewer than 256 neurons—typically 16 times fewer than the number of feature maps (e.g., 16 neurons)—so the 256 numbers get compressed into a small vector (e.g., 16 dimensions). This is a low-dimensional vector representation (i.e., an embedding) of the distribution of feature responses. This bottleneck step forces the SE block to learn a general representation of the feature combinations (we will see this principle in action again when we discuss autoencoders in Chapter 18). Finally, the output layer takes the embedding and outputs a recalibration vector containing one number per feature map (e.g., 256), each between 0 and 1. The feature maps are then multiplied by this recalibration vector, so irrelevant features (with a low recalibration score) get scaled down while relevant features (with a recalibration score close to 1) are left alone.

Other Noteworthy Architectures

There are many other CNN architectures to explore. Here's a brief overview of some of the most noteworthy:

VGGNet (https://homl.info/vggnet)[20]

VGGNet was the runner-up in the ILSVRC 2014 challenge. Karen Simonyan and Andrew Zisserman, from the Visual Geometry Group (VGG) research lab at Oxford University, developed a very simple and classical architecture; it had 2 or 3 convolutional layers and a pooling layer, then again 2 or 3 convolutional layers and a pooling layer, and so on (reaching a total of 16 or 19 convolutional layers, depending on the VGG variant), plus a final dense network with 2 hidden layers and the output layer. It used small 3 × 3 filters, but it had many of them.

20 Karen Simonyan and Andrew Zisserman, "Very Deep Convolutional Networks for Large-Scale Image Recognition", arXiv preprint arXiv:1409.1556 (2014).

ResNeXt (https://homl.info/resnext)[21]
: ResNeXt improves the residual units in ResNet. Whereas the residual units in the best ResNet models just contain 3 convolutional layers each, the ResNeXt residual units are composed of many parallel stacks (e.g., 32 stacks), with 3 convolutional layers each. However, the first two layers in each stack only use a few filters (e.g., just four), so the overall number of parameters remains the same as in ResNet. Then the outputs of all the stacks are added together, and the result is passed to the next residual unit (along with the skip connection).

DenseNet (https://homl.info/densenet)[22]
: A DenseNet is composed of several dense blocks, each made up of a few densely connected convolutional layers. This architecture achieved excellent accuracy while using comparatively few parameters. What does "densely connected" mean? The output of each layer is fed as input to every layer after it within the same block. For example, layer four in a block takes as input the depthwise concatenation of the outputs of layers one, two, and three in that block. Dense blocks are separated by a few transition layers.

MobileNet (https://homl.info/mobilenet)[23]
: MobileNets are streamlined models designed to be lightweight and fast, making them popular in mobile and web applications. They are based on depthwise separable convolutional layers, like Xception. The authors proposed several variants, trading a bit of accuracy for faster and smaller models. Several other CNN architectures are available for mobile devices, such as SqueezeNet, ShuffleNet, or MNasNet.

CSPNet (https://homl.info/cspnet)[24]
: A Cross Stage Partial Network (CSPNet) is similar to a DenseNet, but part of each dense block's input is concatenated directly to that block's output, without going through the block.

EfficientNet (https://homl.info/efficientnet)[25]
: EfficientNet is arguably the most important model in this list. The authors proposed a method to scale any CNN efficiently by jointly increasing the depth

21 Saining Xie et al., "Aggregated Residual Transformations for Deep Neural Networks", arXiv preprint arXiv:1611.05431 (2016).

22 Gao Huang et al., "Densely Connected Convolutional Networks", arXiv preprint arXiv:1608.06993 (2016).

23 Andrew G. Howard et al., "MobileNets: Efficient Convolutional Neural Networks for Mobile Vision Applications", arXiv preprint arXiv:1704.04861 (2017).

24 Chien-Yao Wang et al., "CSPNet: A New Backbone That Can Enhance Learning Capability of CNN", arXiv preprint arXiv:1911.11929 (2019).

25 Mingxing Tan and Quoc V. Le, "EfficientNet: Rethinking Model Scaling for Convolutional Neural Networks", arXiv preprint arXiv:1905.11946 (2019).

(number of layers), width (number of filters per layer), and resolution (size of the input image) in a principled way. This is called *compound scaling*. They used neural architecture search to find a good architecture for a scaled-down version of ImageNet (with smaller and fewer images), and then used compound scaling to create larger and larger versions of this architecture. When EfficientNet models came out, they vastly outperformed all existing models, across all compute budgets, and they remain among the best models out there today. The authors published a follow-up paper in 2021, introducing EfficientNetV2, which improved training time and parameter efficiency even further.

ConvNeXt (https://homl.info/convnext)[26]
: ConvNeXt is quite similar to ResNet, but with a number of tweaks inspired from the most successful vision transformer architectures (see Chapter 16), such as using large kernels (e.g., 7 × 7 instead of 3 × 3), using fewer activation functions and normalization layers in each residual unit, and more.

Understanding EfficientNet's compound scaling method is helpful to gain a deeper understanding of CNNs, especially if you ever need to scale a CNN architecture. It is based on a logarithmic measure of the compute budget, denoted ϕ: if your compute budget doubles, then ϕ increases by 1. In other words, the number of floating-point operations available for training is proportional to 2^ϕ. Your CNN architecture's depth, width, and resolution should scale as α^ϕ, β^ϕ, and γ^ϕ, respectively. The factors α, β, and γ must be greater than 1, and $\alpha\beta^2\gamma^2$ should be close to 2. The optimal values for these factors depend on the CNN's architecture. To find the optimal values for the EfficientNet architecture, the authors started with a small baseline model (EfficientNetB0), fixed $\phi = 1$, and simply ran a grid search: they found $\alpha = 1.2$, $\beta = 1.1$, and $\gamma = 1.1$. They then used these factors to create several larger architectures, named EfficientNetB1 to EfficientNetB7, for increasing values of ϕ.

I hope you enjoyed this deep dive into the main CNN architectures! But how do you choose the right one?

Choosing the Right CNN Architecture

As you might expect, the best architecture depends on what matters most for your project: Accuracy? Model size (e.g., for deployment to a mobile device)? Inference speed? Energy consumption? Table 12-3 lists some of the pretrained classification models currently available in TorchVision (you'll see how to use them later in this chapter). You can find the full list at *https://pytorch.org/vision/stable/models* (including models for other computer vision tasks). The table shows each model's top-1 and top-5 accuracy on the ImageNet dataset, its number of parameters (in millions), and

26 Zhuang Liu et al, "A ConvNet for the 2020s", arXiv preprint arXiv:2201.03545 (2022).

how much compute it requires for each image (measured in GFLOPs: a Giga-FLOP is one billion floating-point operations). As you can see, larger models are generally more accurate, but not always; for example, the small variant of EfficientNet v2 outperforms Inception v3 both in size and accuracy (but not in compute).

Table 12-3. Some of the pretrained models available in TorchVision, sorted by size

Class name	Top-1 acc	Top-5 acc	Params	GFLOPs
MobileNet v3 small	67.7%	87.4%	2.5M	0.1
EfficientNet B0	77.7%	93.5%	5.3M	0.4
GoogLeNet	69.8%	89.5%	6.6M	1.5
DenseNet 121	74.4%	92.0%	8.0M	2.8
EfficientNet v2 small	84.2%	96.9%	21.5M	8.4
ResNet 34	73.3%	91.4%	21.8M	3.7
Inception V3	77.3%	93.5%	27.2M	5.7
ConvNeXt Tiny	82.6%	96.1%	28.6M	4.5
DenseNet 161	77.1%	93.6%	28.7M	7.7
ResNet 152	82.3%	96.0%	60.2M	11.5
AlexNet	56.5%	79.1%	61.1M	0.7
EfficientNet B7	84.1%	96.9%	66.3M	37.8
ResNeXt 101 32x8D	82.8%	96.2%	88.8M	16.4
EfficientNet v2 large	85.8%	97.8%	118.5M	56.1
VGG 11 with BN	70.4%	89.8%	132.9M	7.6
ConvNeXt Large	84.4%	97.0%	197.8M	34.4

The smaller models will run on any GPU, but what about a large model, such as ConvNeXt Large? Since each parameter is represented as a 32-bit float (4 bytes), you might think you just need 800 MB of RAM to run a 200M parameter model, but you actually need *much* more, typically 5 GB per image at inference time (depending on the image size), and even more at training time. Let's see why.

GPU RAM Requirements: Inference Versus Training

CNNs need a *lot* of RAM. For example, consider a single convolutional layer with 200 5 × 5 filters, stride 1 and `"same"` padding, processing a 150 × 100 RGB image (3 channels):

- The number of parameters is (5 × 5 × 3 + 1) × 200 = 15,200 (the + 1 corresponds to the bias terms). That's not much: to produce the same size outputs, a fully connected layer would need 200 × 150 × 100 neurons, each connected to all 150 × 100 × 3 inputs. It would have 200 × 150 × 100 × (150 × 100 × 3 + 1) ≈ 135 billion parameters!

- However, each of the 200 feature maps contains 150 × 100 neurons, and each of these neurons needs to compute a weighted sum of its 5 × 5 × 3 = 75 inputs: that's a total of 225 million float multiplications. Not as bad as a fully connected layer, but still quite computationally intensive.
- Importantly, the convolutional layer's output will occupy 200 × 150 × 100 × 32 = 96 million bits (12 MB) of RAM, assuming we're using 32-bit floats.[27] And that's just for one instance—if a training batch contains 100 instances, then this single convolutional layer will use up 1.2 GB of RAM!

During inference (i.e., when making a prediction for a new instance) the RAM occupied by one layer can be released as soon as the next layer has been computed, so you only need as much RAM as required by two consecutive layers. But during training everything computed during the forward pass needs to be preserved for the backward pass, so the amount of RAM needed is (at least) the total amount of RAM required by all layers. You can easily run out of GPU RAM.

If training crashes because of an out-of-memory error, you can try reducing the batch size. To still get some of the benefits of large batches, you can accumulate the gradients after each batch, and only update the model weights every few batches. Alternatively, you can try reducing dimensionality using a stride, removing a few layers, using 16-bit floats instead of 32-bit floats, distributing the CNN across multiple devices, or offloading the most memory-hungry modules to the CPU (using `module.to("cpu")`).

Yet another option is to trade more compute in exchange for a lower memory usage. For example, instead of saving all of the activations during the forward pass, you can save some of them, called *activation checkpoints*, then during the backward pass, you can recompute the missing activations as needed by running a partial forward pass starting from the previous checkpoint.

To implement activation checkpointing (also called *gradient checkpointing*) in PyTorch, you can use the `torch.utils.checkpoint.checkpoint()` function: instead of calling a module `z = foo(x)`, you can call it using `z = checkpoint(foo, x)`. During inference, it will make no difference, but during training this module's activations will no longer be saved during the forward pass, and `foo(x)` will be recomputed during the backward pass when needed. This approach is fairly simple to implement, and it doesn't require any changes to your model architecture.

27 In the international system of units (SI), 1 MB = 1,000 KB = 1,000 × 1,000 bytes = 1,000 × 1,000 × 8 bits. And 1 MiB = 1,024 kiB = 1,024 × 1,024 bytes. So 12 MB ≈ 11.44 MiB.

The forward pass needs to produce the same result if you call it twice with the same inputs, or else the gradients will be incorrect. This means that custom modules must respect a few constraints, such as avoiding in-place ops or using controlled states for random number generation: please see the `checkpoint()` function's documentation for more details.

That said, if you're OK with tweaking your model architecture, then there's a much more efficient solution you can use to exchange compute for memory: reversible residual networks.

Reversible Residual Networks (RevNets)

RevNets (*https://homl.info/revnet*) were proposed by Aidan Gomez et al. in 2017:[28] they typically only increase compute by about 33% and actually don't require you to save any activations at all during the forward pass! Here's how they work:

- Each layer, called a *reversible layer*, takes two inputs of equal sizes, $\mathbf{x}_1$ and $\mathbf{x}_2$, and computes two outputs: $\mathbf{y}_1 = \mathbf{x}_1 + \mathrm{f}(\mathbf{x}_2)$ and $\mathbf{y}_2 = \mathrm{g}(\mathbf{y}_1) + \mathbf{x}_2$, where f and g can be any functions, as long as the output size equals the input size, and as long as they always produce the same output for a given input. For example, f and g can be identical modules composed of a few convolutional layers with stride 1 and `"same"` padding (each convolutional layer comes with its own batch-norm and ReLU activation).
- During backpropagation, the inputs of each reversible layer can be recomputed from the outputs whenever needed, using: $\mathbf{x}_2 = \mathbf{y}_2 - \mathrm{g}(\mathbf{y}_1)$ and $\mathbf{x}_1 = \mathbf{y}_1 - \mathrm{f}(\mathbf{x}_2)$ (you can easily verify that these two equalities follow directly from the first two). No need to store any activations during the forward pass: brilliant!

Since f and g must output the same shape as the input, reversible layers cannot contain convolutional layers with a stride greater than 1, or with `"valid"` padding. You can still use such layers in your CNN, but the RevNet trick won't be applicable to them, so you will have to save their activations during the forward pass; luckily, a CNN usually requires only a handful of such layers. This includes the very first layer, which reduces the spatial dimensions and increases the number of channels: the result can be split in two equal parts along the channel dimension and fed to the first reversible layer.

RevNets aren't limited to CNNs. In fact, they are at the heart of an influential Transformer architecture named Reformer (see Chapter 17).

28 Aidan Gomez et al., "The Reversible Residual Network: Backpropagation Without Storing Activations", arXiv preprint arXiv:1707.04585 (2017).

OK, it's now time to get our hands dirty! Let's implement one of the most popular CNN architectures from scratch using PyTorch.

Implementing a ResNet-34 CNN Using PyTorch

Most CNN architectures described so far can be implemented pretty naturally using PyTorch (although generally you would load a pretrained network instead, as you will see). To illustrate the process, let's implement a ResNet-34 from scratch with PyTorch. First, we'll create a `ResidualUnit` layer:

```
class ResidualUnit(nn.Module):
    def __init__(self, in_channels, out_channels, stride=1):
        super().__init__()
        DefaultConv2d = partial(
            nn.Conv2d, kernel_size=3, stride=1, padding=1, bias=False)
        self.main_layers = nn.Sequential(
            DefaultConv2d(in_channels, out_channels, stride=stride),
            nn.BatchNorm2d(out_channels),
            nn.ReLU(),
            DefaultConv2d(out_channels, out_channels),
            nn.BatchNorm2d(out_channels),
        )
        if stride > 1:
            self.skip_connection = nn.Sequential(
                DefaultConv2d(in_channels, out_channels, kernel_size=1,
                              stride=stride, padding=0),
                nn.BatchNorm2d(out_channels),
            )
        else:
            self.skip_connection = nn.Identity()

    def forward(self, inputs):
        return F.relu(self.main_layers(inputs) + self.skip_connection(inputs))
```

As you can see, this code matches Figure 12-19 pretty closely. In the constructor, we create all the layers we need: the main layers are the ones on the righthand side of the figure, and the skip connection corresponds to the layers on the left when the stride is greater than 1, or an `nn.Identity` module when the stride is 1—the `nn.Identity` module does nothing at all, it just returns its inputs. Then in the `forward()` method, we make the inputs go through both the main layers and the skip connection, then we add both outputs and apply the activation function.

Next, let's build our `ResNet34` module! Now that we have our `ResidualUnit` module, the whole ResNet-34 architecture becomes one big stack of modules, so we can base our `ResNet34` class on a single `nn.Sequential` module. The code closely matches Figure 12-18:

```python
class ResNet34(nn.Module):
    def __init__(self):
        super().__init__()
        layers = [
            nn.Conv2d(in_channels=3, out_channels=64, kernel_size=7, stride=2,
                      padding=3, bias=False),
            nn.BatchNorm2d(num_features=64),
            nn.ReLU(),
            nn.MaxPool2d(kernel_size=3, stride=2, padding=1),
        ]
        prev_filters = 64
        for filters in [64] * 3 + [128] * 4 + [256] * 6 + [512] * 3:
            stride = 1 if filters == prev_filters else 2
            layers.append(ResidualUnit(prev_filters, filters, stride=stride))
            prev_filters = filters
        layers += [
            nn.AdaptiveAvgPool2d(output_size=1),
            nn.Flatten(),
            nn.LazyLinear(10),
        ]
        self.resnet = nn.Sequential(*layers)

    def forward(self, inputs):
        return self.resnet(inputs)
```

The only tricky part in this code is the loop that adds the `ResidualUnit` layers to the list of layers: as explained earlier, the first 3 RUs have 64 filters, then the next 4 RUs have 128 filters, and so on. At each iteration, we must set the stride to 1 when the number of filters is the same as in the previous RU, or else we set it to 2; then we append the `ResidualUnit` to the list, and finally we update `prev_filters`.

And that's it, you could now train this model on ImageNet or any other dataset of 224 × 224 images. It is amazing that in just 45 lines of code, we can build the model that won the ILSVRC 2015 challenge! This demonstrates both the elegance of the ResNet model and the expressiveness of PyTorch (and Python). Implementing the other CNN architectures we discussed would take more time, but it wouldn't be much harder. However, TorchVision comes with several of these architectures built in, so why not use them instead?

Using TorchVision's Pretrained Models

In general, you won't have to implement standard models like GoogLeNet, ResNet, or ConvNeXt manually, since pretrained networks are readily available with a couple lines of code using TorchVision.

TIMM is another very popular library built on PyTorch: it provides a collection of pretrained image classification models, as well as many related tools such as data loaders, data augmentation utilities, optimizers, schedulers, and more. Hugging Face's Hub is also a great place to get all sorts of pretrained models (see Chapter 14).

For example, you can load a ConvNeXt model pretrained on ImageNet with the following code. There are several variants of the ConvNeXt model—tiny, small, base, and large—and this code loads the base variant:

```
weights = torchvision.models.ConvNeXt_Base_Weights.IMAGENET1K_V1
model = torchvision.models.convnext_base(weights=weights).to(device)
```

That's all! This code automatically downloads the weights (338 MB) from the *Torch Hub*, an online repository of pretrained models. The weights are saved and cached for future use (e.g., in `~/.cache/torch/hub`; run `torch.hub.get_dir()` to find the exact path on your system). Some models have newer weights versions (e.g., `IMAGENET1K_V2`) or other weight variants. For the full list of available models, run `torchvision.models.list_models()`. To find the list of pretrained weights available for a given model, such as `convnext_base`, run `list(torchvision.models.get_model_weights("convnext_base"))`. Alternatively, visit *https://pytorch.org/vision/main/models*.

Let's use this model to classify the two sample images we loaded earlier. Before we can do this, we must first ensure that the images are preprocessed exactly as the model expects. In particular, they must have the right size. A ConvNeXt model expects 224 × 224 pixel images (other models may expect other sizes, such as 299 × 299). Since our sample images are 427 × 640 pixels, we need to resize them. We could do this using TorchVision's `CenterCrop` and/or `Resize` transform, but it's much easier and safer to use the transforms returned by `weights.transforms()`, as they are specifically designed for this particular pretrained model:

```
transforms = weights.transforms()
preprocessed_images = transforms(sample_images_permuted)
```

Importantly, these transforms also normalize the pixel intensities just like during training. In this case, the transforms standardize the pixel intensities separately for each color channel, using ImageNet's means and standard deviations for each channel (we will see how to do this manually later in this chapter).

Next we can move the images to the GPU and pass them to the model. As always, remember to switch the model to evaluation mode before making predictions—the model is in training mode by default—and also turn off autograd:

```
model.eval()
with torch.no_grad():
    y_logits = model(preprocessed_images.to(device))
```

The result is a 2 × 1,000 tensor containing the class logits for each image (recall that ImageNet has 1,000 classes). As we did in Chapter 10, we can use `torch.argmax()` to get the predicted class for each image (i.e., the class with the maximum logit):

```
>>> y_pred = torch.argmax(y_logits, dim=1)
>>> y_pred
tensor([698, 985], device='cuda:0')
```

So far, so good, but what exactly do these classes represent? Well you could find the ImageNet class names online, but once again it's simpler and safer to get the class names directly from the `weights` object. Indeed, its `meta` attribute is a dictionary containing metadata about the pretrained model, including the class names:

```
>>> class_names = weights.meta["categories"]
>>> [class_names[class_id] for class_id in y_pred]
['palace', 'daisy']
```

There you have it: the first image is classified as a palace, and the second as a daisy. Since the ImageNet dataset does not have classes for Chinese towers or dahlia flowers, a palace and a daisy are reasonable substitutes (the tower is part of the Summer Palace in Beijing). Let's look at the top-three predictions using `topk()`:

```
>>> y_top3_logits, y_top3_class_ids = y_logits.topk(k=3, dim=1)
>>> [[class_names[class_id] for class_id in top3] for top3 in y_top3_class_ids]
[['palace', 'monastery', 'lakeside'], ['daisy', 'pot', 'ant']]
```

Let's look at the estimated probabilities for each of these classes:

```
>>> y_top3_logits.softmax(dim=1)
tensor([[0.8618, 0.1185, 0.0197],
        [0.8106, 0.0964, 0.0930]], device='cuda:0')
```

As you can see, TorchVision makes it easy to download and use pretrained models, and it works quite well out of the box for ImageNet classes. But what if you need to classify images into classes that don't belong to the ImageNet dataset, such as various flower species? In that case, you may still benefit from the pretrained models by using them to perform transfer learning.

Pretrained Models for Transfer Learning

If you want to build an image classifier but you do not have enough data to train it from scratch, then it is often a good idea to reuse the lower layers of a pretrained model, as we discussed in Chapter 11. In this section we will reuse the ConvNeXt model we loaded earlier—which was pretrained on ImageNet—and after replacing its classification head, we will fine-tune it on the *102 Category Flower Dataset* (*https://*

homl.info/flowers102)[29] (Flowers102 for short). This dataset only contains 10 images per class, and there are 102 classes in total (as the name indicates), so if you try to train a model from scratch, you will really struggle to get high accuracy. However, it's quite easy to get over 90% accuracy using a good pretrained model. Let's see how. First, let's download the dataset using Torchvision:

```
DefaultFlowers102 = partial(torchvision.datasets.Flowers102, root="datasets",
                            transform=weights.transforms(), download=True)
train_set = DefaultFlowers102(split="train")
valid_set = DefaultFlowers102(split="val")
test_set = DefaultFlowers102(split="test")
```

This code uses `partial()` to avoid repeating the same arguments three times. We also set `transform=weights.transforms()` to preprocess the images immediately when they are loaded. The Flowers102 dataset comes with three predefined splits, for training, validation, and testing. The first two have 10 images per class, but surprisingly the test set has many more (it has a variable number of images per class, between 20 and 238). In a real project, you would normally use most of your data for training rather than for testing, but this dataset was designed for computer vision research, and the authors purposely restricted the training set and the validation set.

We then create the data loaders, as usual:

```
from torch.utils.data import DataLoader

train_loader = DataLoader(train_set, batch_size=32, shuffle=True)
valid_loader = DataLoader(valid_set, batch_size=32)
test_loader = DataLoader(test_set, batch_size=32)
```

Many TorchVision datasets conveniently contain the class names in the `classes` attribute, but sadly not this dataset.[30] If you prefer to see lovely names like "tiger lily", "monkshood", or "snapdragon" rather than boring class IDs, then you need to manually define the list of class names:

```
class_names = ['pink primrose', ..., 'trumpet creeper', 'blackberry lily']
```

Now let's adapt our pretrained ConvNeXt-base model to this dataset. Since it was pretrained on ImageNet, which has 1,000 classes, the model's head (i.e., its upper layers) was designed to output 1,000 logits. But we only have 102 classes, so we must chop the model's head off and replace it with a smaller one. But how can we find it? Well let's use the model's `named_children()` method to find the name of its submodules:

29 M. Nilsback and A. Zisserman, "Automated Flower Classification over a Large Number of Classes", *Proceedings of the Indian Conference on Computer Vision, Graphics and Image Processing* (2008).

30 TorchVision PR #8838 might have fixed this by the time your read these lines.

```
>>> [name for name, child in model.named_children()]
['features', 'avgpool', 'classifier']
```

The `features` module is the main part of the model, which includes all layers except for the global average pooling layer (`avgpool`) and the model's head (`classifier`). Let's look more closely at the head:

```
>>> model.classifier
Sequential(
  (0): LayerNorm2d((1024,), eps=1e-06, elementwise_affine=True)
  (1): Flatten(start_dim=1, end_dim=-1)
  (2): Linear(in_features=1024, out_features=1000, bias=True)
)
```

As you can see, it's an `nn.Sequential` module composed of a layer normalization layer, an `nn.Flatten` layer, and an `nn.Linear` layer with 1,024 inputs and 1,000 outputs. This `nn.Linear` layer is the output layer, and it's the one we need to replace. We must only change the number of outputs:

```
n_classes = 102  # len(class_names) == 102
model.classifier[2] = nn.Linear(1024, n_classes).to(device)
```

As explained in Chapter 11, it's usually a good idea to freeze the weights of the pretrained layers, at least at the beginning of training. We can do this by freezing every single parameter in the model, and then unfreezing only the parameters of the head:

```
for param in model.parameters():
    param.requires_grad = False

for param in model.classifier.parameters():
    param.requires_grad = True
```

Next, you can train this model for a few epochs, and you will already reach about 90% accuracy just by training the new head, without even fine-tuning the pretrained layers. After that, you can unfreeze the whole model, lower the learning rate—typically by a factor of 10—and continue training the model. Give this a try, and see what accuracy you can reach!

To reach an even higher accuracy, it's usually a good idea to perform some data augmentation on the training images. For this, you can try randomly flipping the training images horizontally, randomly rotating them by a small angle, randomly resizing and cropping them, and randomly tweaking their colors. This must all be done before running the ImageNet normalization step, which you can implement using a `Normalize` transform:

```
import torchvision.transforms.v2 as T

transforms = T.Compose([
    T.RandomHorizontalFlip(p=0.5),
    T.RandomRotation(degrees=30),
```

```
    T.RandomResizedCrop(size=(224, 224), scale=(0.8, 1.0)),
    T.ColorJitter(brightness=0.2, contrast=0.2, saturation=0.2, hue=0.1),
    T.ToImage(),
    T.ToDtype(torch.float32, scale=True),
    T.Normalize(mean=[0.485, 0.456, 0.406], std=[0.229, 0.224, 0.225]),
])
```

TorchVision comes with an `AutoAugment` transform which applies multiple augmentation operations optimized for ImageNet. It generalizes well to many other image datasets, and it also offers predefined settings for two other datasets: CIFAR10 and the street view house numbers (SVHN) dataset.

Here are some more ideas to continue to improve your model's accuracy:

- Try other pretrained models.
- Extend the training set: find more flower images and label them.
- Create an ensemble of models, and combine their predictions.
- Analyze failure cases, and see whether they share specific characteristics, such as similar texture or color. You can then try to tweak image preprocessing to address these issues.
- Use a learning schedule such as performance scheduling.
- Unfreeze the layers gradually, starting from the top. Alternatively, you can use *differential learning rates*: apply a smaller learning rate to lower layers, and a larger learning rate to upper layers. You can do this by using parameter groups (see Chapter 11).
- Explore different optimizers and fine-tune their hyperparameters.
- Try different regularization techniques.

It's worth spending time looking for models that were pretrained on similar images. For example, if you're dealing with satellite images, aerial images, or even raster data such as digital elevation models (DEM), then models pretrained on ImageNet won't help much. Instead, check out Microsoft's *TorchGeo* library, which is similar to TorchVision but for geospatial data. For medical images, check out Project MONAI. For agricultural images, check out AgML. And so on.

With that, you can start training amazing image classifiers on your own images and classes! But there's more to computer vision than just classification. For example, what if you also want to know *where* the flower is in a picture? Let's look at this now.

Classification and Localization

Localizing an object in a picture can be expressed as a regression task, as discussed in Chapter 9: to predict a bounding box around the object, a common approach is to predict the location of the bounding box's center, as well as its width and height (alternatively, you could predict the horizontal and vertical coordinates of the object's upper-left and lower-right corners). This means we have four numbers to predict. It does not require much change to the ConvNeXt model; we just need to add a second dense output layer with four units (e.g., on top of the global average pooling layer). Here's a `FlowerLocator` model that adds a localization head to a given base model, such as our ConvNeXt model:

```
class FlowerLocator(nn.Module):
    def __init__(self, base_model):
        super().__init__()
        self.base_model = base_model
        self.localization_head = nn.Sequential(
            nn.Flatten(),
            nn.Linear(base_model.classifier[2].in_features, 4)
        )

    def forward(self, X):
        features = self.base_model.features(X)
        pool = self.base_model.avgpool(features)
        logits = self.base_model.classifier(pool)
        bbox = self.localization_head(pool)
        return logits, bbox

torch.manual_seed(42)
locator_model = FlowerLocator(model).to(device)
```

This locator model has two heads: the first outputs class logits, while the second outputs the bounding box. The localization head has the same number of inputs as the `nn.Linear` layer of the classification head, but it outputs just four numbers. The `forward()` method takes a batch of preprocessed images as input and outputs both the predicted class logits (102 per image) and the predicted bounding boxes (1 per image). After training this model, you can use it as follows:

```
preproc_images = [...]  # a batch of preprocessed images
y_pred_logits, y_pred_bbox = locator_model(preprocessed_images.to(device))
```

But how can we train this model? Well, we saw how to train a model with two or more outputs in Chapter 10, and this one is no different: in this case, we can use the `nn.CrossEntropyLoss` for the classification head, and the `nn.MSELoss` for the localization head. The final loss can just be a weighted sum of the two. Voilà, that's all there is to it.

Hey, not so fast! We have a problem: the Flowers102 dataset does not include any bounding boxes, so we need to add them ourselves. This is often one of the hardest and most costly parts of a machine learning project: labeling and annotating the data. It's a good idea to spend time looking for the right tools. To annotate images with bounding boxes, you may want to use an open source labeling tool like Label Studio, OpenLabeler, ImgLab, Labelme, VoTT, or VGG Image Annotator, or perhaps a commercial tool like LabelBox, Supervisely, Roboflow, or RectLabel. Many of these are now AI assisted, greatly speeding up the annotation task. You may also want to consider crowdsourcing platforms such as Amazon Mechanical Turk if you have a very large number of images to annotate. However, it is quite a lot of work to set up a crowdsourcing platform, prepare the form to be sent to the workers, supervise them, and ensure that the quality of the bounding boxes they produce is good, so make sure it is worth the effort. If there are just a few hundred or a even a couple of thousand images to label, and you don't plan to do this frequently, it may be preferable to do it yourself: with the right tools, it will only take a few days, and you'll also gain a better understanding of your dataset and task.

You can then create a custom dataset (see Chapter 10) where each entry contains an image, a label, and a bounding box. TorchVision conveniently includes a `BoundingBoxes` class that represents a list of bounding boxes. For example, the following code creates a bounding box for the largest flower in the first image of the Flowers102 training set (for now we only consider one bounding box per image, but we'll discuss multiple bounding boxes per image later in this chapter):

```
import torchvision.tv_tensors

bbox = torchvision.tv_tensors.BoundingBoxes(
    [[377, 199, 248, 262]],  # center x=377, center y=199, width=248, height=262
    format="CXCYWH",  # other possible formats: "XYXY" and "XYWH"
    canvas_size=(500, 754)  # raw image size before preprocessing
)
```

To visualize bounding boxes, use the `torchvision.utils.draw_bounding_boxes()` function. You will first need to convert the bounding boxes to the XYXY format using `torchvision.ops.box_convert()`.

The `BoundingBoxes` class is a subclass of `TVTensor`, which is a subclass of `torch.Tensor`, so you can treat bounding boxes exactly like regular tensors, with extra features. Most importantly, you can transform bounding boxes using TorchVision's transforms API v2. For example, let's use the transform we defined earlier to preprocess this bounding box:

```
>>> transform(bbox)
BoundingBoxes([[ 90,  91, 120, 154]], format=BoundingBoxFormat.CXCYWH,
              canvas_size=(224, 224), clamping_mode=soft)
```

Resizing and cropping a bounding box works as expected, but rotation is special: the bounding box can't be rotated since it doesn't have any rotation parameter, so instead it is resized to fit the rotated box (*not* the rotated object). As a result, it may end up being a bit too large for the object.

You can pass a nested data structure to a transform and the output will have the same structure, except with all the images and bounding boxes transformed. For example, the following code transforms the first flower image in the training set and its bounding box, leaving the label unchanged. In this example, the input and output are both 2-tuples containing an image and a dictionary composed of a label and a bounding box, but you could use any other data structure:

```
first_image = [...]  # load the first training image without any preprocessing
preproc_image, preproc_target = transform(
    (first_image, {"label": 0, "bbox": bbox})
)
preproc_bbox = preproc_target["bbox"]
```

When using the MSE, a 10-pixel error for a large bounding box will be penalized just as much as a 10-pixel error for a small bounding box. To avoid this, you can use a custom loss function that computes the square root of the width and height—for both the target and the prediction—before computing the MSE.

The MSE is simple and often works fairly well to train the model, but it is not a great metric to evaluate how well the model can predict bounding boxes. The most common metric for this is the *intersection over union* (IoU, also known as the *Jaccard index*): it is the area of overlap between the target bounding box T and the predicted bounding box P, divided by the area of their union P ∪ T (see Figure 12-24). In short, IoU = |P ∩ T| / |P ∪ T|, where |*x*| is the area of *x*. The IoU ranges from 0 (no overlap) to 1 (perfect overlap). It is implemented by the `torchvision.ops.box_iou()` function.

The IoU is not great for training because it is equal to zero whenever P and T have no overlap, regardless of the distance between them or their shapes: in this case the gradient is also equal to zero and therefore gradient descent cannot make any progress. Luckily, it's possible to fix this flaw by incorporating extra information. For example, the *Generalized IoU* (GIoU), introduced in a 2019 paper (*https://homl.info/giou*) by H. Rezatofighi et al.,[31] considers the smallest box S that contains both P and T, and it subtracts from the IoU the ratio of S that is not covered by P or T.

31 H. Rezatofighi et al., "Generalized Intersection over Union: A Metric and A Loss for Bounding Box Regression", arXiv preprint arXiv:1902.09630 (2019).

In short, GIoU = IoU – |S – (P ∪ T)| / |S|. This means that the GIoU gets smaller as P and T get further apart, which gives gradient descent something to play with so it can pull P closer to T. Since we want to maximize the GIoU, the GIoU loss is equal to 1 – GIoU. This loss quickly became popular, and it is implemented by the `torchvision.ops.generalized_box_iou_loss()` function.

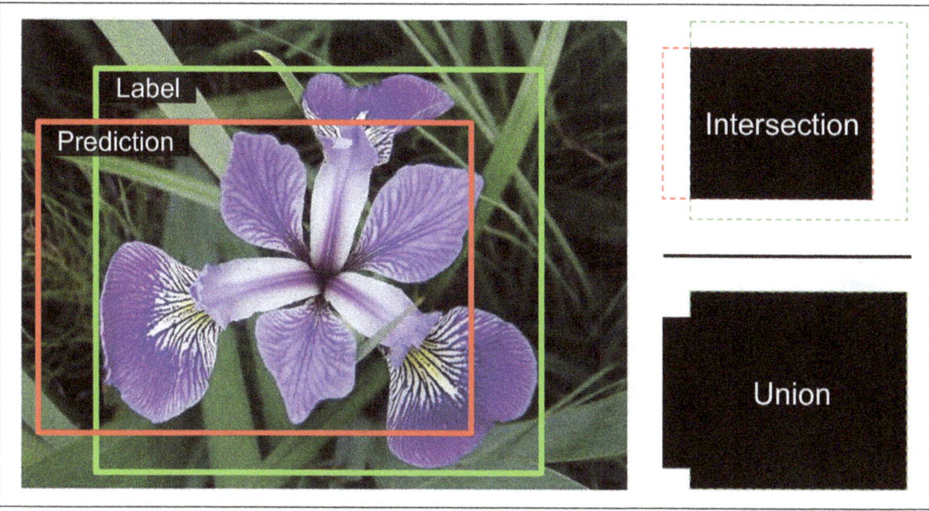

Figure 12-24. IoU metric for bounding boxes

Another important variant of the IoU is the *Complete IoU* (CIoU), introduced in a 2020 paper (*https://homl.info/ciou*) by Z. Zheng et al.[32] It considers three geometric factors: the IoU (the more overlap, the better), the distance between the centers of P and T (the closer, the better), normalized by the length of the diagonal of S, and the similarity between the aspect ratios of P and T (the closer, the better). The loss is 1 – CIoU, and it is implemented by the `torchvision.ops.complete_box_iou_loss()` function. It generally performs better than the MSE or the GIoU, converging faster and leading to more accurate bounding boxes, so it is becoming the default loss for localization.

Classifying and localizing a single object is nice, but what if the images contain multiple objects (as is often the case in the flowers dataset)?

32 Z. Zheng et al., "Enhancing Geometric Factors in Model Learning and Inference for Object Detection and Instance Segmentation", arXiv preprint arXiv:2005.03572 (2020).

Object Detection

The task of classifying and localizing multiple objects in an image is called *object detection*. Until a few years ago, a common approach was to take a CNN that was trained to classify and locate a single object roughly centered in the image, then slide this CNN across the image and make predictions at each step. The CNN was generally trained to predict not only class probabilities and a bounding box, but also an *objectness score*: this is the estimated probability that the image does indeed contain an object centered near the middle. This is a binary classification output; it can be produced by a dense output layer with a single unit, using the sigmoid activation function and trained using the binary cross-entropy loss.

Instead of an objectness score, a "no-object" class was sometimes added, but in general this did not work as well. The questions "Is an object present?" and "What type of object is it?" are best answered separately.

This sliding-CNN approach is illustrated in Figure 12-25. In this example, the image was chopped into a 5 × 7 grid, and we see a CNN—the thick black rectangle—sliding across all 3 × 3 regions and making predictions at each step.

Figure 12-25. Detecting multiple objects by sliding a CNN across the image

In this figure, the CNN has already made predictions for three of these 3 × 3 regions:

- When looking at the top-left 3 × 3 region (centered on the red-shaded grid cell located in the second row and second column), it detected the leftmost rose. Notice that the predicted bounding box exceeds the boundary of this 3 × 3 region. That's absolutely fine: even though the CNN could not see the bottom part of the rose, it was able to make a reasonable guess as to where it might be. It also predicted class probabilities, giving a high probability to the "rose" class. Lastly, it predicted a fairly high objectness score, since the center of the bounding box lies within the central grid cell (in this figure, the objectness score is represented by the thickness of the bounding box).
- When looking at the next 3 × 3 region, one grid cell to the right (centered on the shaded blue square), it did not detect any flower centered in that region, so it predicted a very low objectness score; therefore, the predicted bounding box and class probabilities can safely be ignored. You can see that the predicted bounding box was no good anyway.
- Finally, when looking at the next 3 × 3 region, again one grid cell to the right (centered on the shaded green cell), it detected the rose at the top, although not perfectly. This rose is not well centered within this region, so the predicted objectness score was not very high.

You can imagine how sliding the CNN across the whole image would give you a total of 15 predicted bounding boxes, organized in a 3 × 5 grid, with each bounding box accompanied by its estimated class probabilities and objectness score. Since objects can have varying sizes, you may then want to slide the CNN again across 2 × 2 and 4 × 4 regions as well, to capture smaller and larger objects.

This technique is fairly straightforward, but as you can see it will often detect the same object multiple times, at slightly different positions. Some post-processing is needed to get rid of all the unnecessary bounding boxes. A common approach for this is called *non-max suppression* (NMS). Here's how it works:

1. First, get rid of all the bounding boxes for which the objectness score is below some threshold; since the CNN believes there's no object at that location, the bounding box is useless.
2. Find the remaining bounding box with the highest objectness score, and get rid of all the other remaining bounding boxes that overlap a lot with it (e.g., with an IoU greater than 60%). For example, in Figure 12-25, the bounding box with the max objectness score is the thick bounding box over the leftmost rose. The other bounding box that touches this same rose overlaps a lot with the max bounding box, so we will get rid of it (although in this example it would already have been removed in the previous step).

3. Repeat step 2 until there are no more bounding boxes to get rid of.

This simple approach to object detection works pretty well, but it requires running the CNN many times (15 times in this example), so it is quite slow. Fortunately, there is a much faster way to slide a CNN across an image: using a *fully convolutional network* (FCN).

Fully Convolutional Networks

The idea of FCNs was first introduced in a 2015 paper (*https://homl.info/fcn*)[33] by Jonathan Long et al., for semantic segmentation (the task of classifying every pixel in an image according to the class of the object it belongs to). The authors pointed out that you could replace the dense layers at the top of a CNN with convolutional layers. To understand this, let's look at an example: suppose a dense layer with 200 neurons sits on top of a convolutional layer that outputs 100 feature maps, each of size 7 × 7 (this is the feature map size, not the kernel size). Each neuron will compute a weighted sum of all 100 × 7 × 7 activations from the convolutional layer (plus a bias term). Now let's see what happens if we replace the dense layer with a convolutional layer using 200 filters, each of size 7 × 7, and with `"valid"` padding. This layer will output 200 feature maps, each 1 × 1 (since the kernel is exactly the size of the input feature maps and we are using `"valid"` padding). In other words, it will output 200 numbers, just like the dense layer did; and if you look closely at the computations performed by a convolutional layer, you will notice that these numbers will be precisely the same as those the dense layer produced. The only difference is that the dense layer's output was a tensor of shape [*batch size*, 200], while the convolutional layer will output a tensor of shape [*batch size*, 200, 1, 1].

To convert a dense layer to a convolutional layer, the number of filters in the convolutional layer must be equal to the number of units in the dense layer, the filter size must be equal to the size of the input feature maps, and you must use `"valid"` padding. The stride may be set to 1 or more, as we will see shortly.

Why is this important? Well, while a dense layer expects a specific input size (since it has one weight per input feature), a convolutional layer will happily process images of any size[34] (however, it does expect its inputs to have a specific number of channels, since each kernel contains a different set of weights for each input channel). Since

33 Jonathan Long et al., "Fully Convolutional Networks for Semantic Segmentation", *Proceedings of the IEEE Conference on Computer Vision and Pattern Recognition* (2015): 3431–3440.

34 There is one small exception: a convolutional layer using `"valid"` padding will complain if the input size is smaller than the kernel size.

an FCN contains only convolutional layers (and pooling layers, which have the same property), it can be trained and executed on images of any size!

For example, suppose we'd already trained a CNN for flower classification and localization, with an extra head for objectness. It was trained on 224 × 224 images, and it outputs 107 values per image:

- The classification head outputs 102 class logits (one per class), trained using the `nn.CrossEntropyLoss`.
- The objectness head outputs a single objectness logit, trained using the `nn.BCELoss`.
- The localization head outputs four numbers describing the bounding box, trained using the CIoU loss.

We can now convert the CNN's dense layers (`nn.Linear`) to convolutional layers (`nn.Conv2d`). In fact, we don't even need to retrain the model; we can just copy the weights from the dense layers to the convolutional layers! Alternatively, we could have converted the CNN into an FCN before training.

Now suppose the last convolutional layer before the output layer (also called the bottleneck layer) outputs 7 × 7 feature maps when the network is fed a 224 × 224 image (see the left side of Figure 12-26). For example, this would be the case if the network contains 5 layers with stride 2 and `"same"` padding, so the spatial dimensions get divided by $2^5 = 32$ overall. If we feed the FCN a 448 × 448 image (see the righthand side of Figure 12-26), the bottleneck layer will now output 14 × 14 feature maps. Since the dense output layer was replaced by a convolutional layer using 107 filters of size 7 × 7, with `"valid"` padding and stride 1, the output will be composed of 107 feature maps, each of size 8 × 8 (since 14 – 7 + 1 = 8).

In other words, the FCN will process the whole image only once, and it will output an 8 × 8 grid where each cell contains the predictions for one region of the image: 107 numbers representing 102 class probabilities, 1 objectness score, and 4 bounding box coordinates. It's exactly like taking the original CNN and sliding it across the image using 8 steps per row and 8 steps per column. To visualize this, imagine chopping the original image into a 14 × 14 grid, then sliding a 7 × 7 window across this grid; there will be 8 × 8 = 64 possible locations for the window, hence 8 × 8 predictions. However, the FCN approach is *much* more efficient, since the network only looks at the image once. In fact, *You Only Look Once* (YOLO) is the name of a very popular object detection architecture, which we'll look at next.

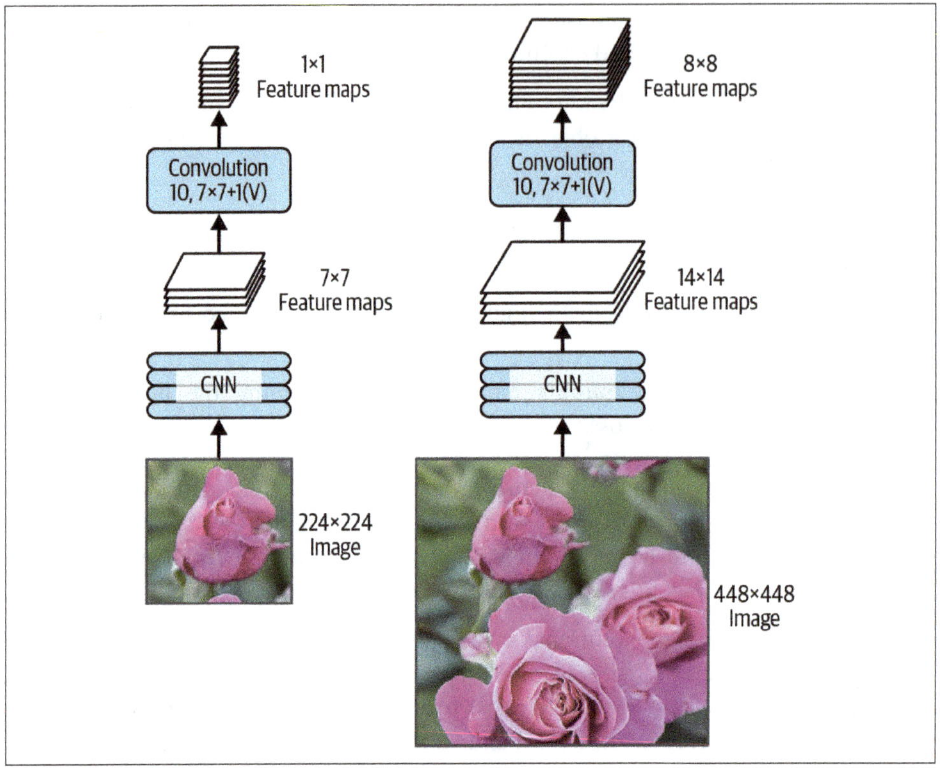

Figure 12-26. The same fully convolutional network processing a small image (left) and a large one (right)

You Only Look Once

YOLO is a fast and accurate object detection architecture proposed by Joseph Redmon et al. in a 2015 paper (*https://homl.info/yolo*).[35] It is so fast that it can run in real time on a video, as seen in Redmon's demo (*https://homl.info/yolodemo2*). YOLO's architecture is quite similar to the one we just discussed, but with a few important differences:

- For each grid cell, YOLO only considers objects whose bounding box center lies within that cell. The bounding box coordinates are relative to that cell, where (0, 0) means the top-left corner of the cell and (1, 1) means the bottom right. However, the bounding box's height and width may extend well beyond the cell.

35 Joseph Redmon et al., "You Only Look Once: Unified, Real-Time Object Detection", *Proceedings of the IEEE Conference on Computer Vision and Pattern Recognition* (2016): 779–788.

- It outputs two bounding boxes for each grid cell (instead of just one), which allows the model to handle cases where two objects are so close to each other that their bounding box centers lie within the same cell. Each bounding box also comes with its own objectness score.
- YOLO also outputs a class probability distribution for each grid cell, predicting 20 class probabilities per grid cell since YOLO was trained on the PASCAL VOC dataset, which contains 20 classes. This produces a coarse *class probability map*. Note that the model predicts one class probability distribution per grid cell, not per bounding box. However, it's possible to estimate class probabilities for each bounding box during post-processing by measuring how well each bounding box matches each class in the class probability map. For example, imagine a picture of a person standing in front of a car. There will be two bounding boxes: one large horizontal one for the car, and a smaller vertical one for the person. These bounding boxes may have their centers within the same grid cell. So how can we tell which class should be assigned to each bounding box? Well, the class probability map will contain a large region where the "car" class is dominant, and inside it there will be a smaller region where the "person" class is dominant. Hopefully, the car's bounding box will roughly match the "car" region, while the person's bounding box will roughly match the "person" region: this will allow the correct class to be assigned to each bounding box.

YOLO was originally developed using Darknet, an open source deep learning framework initially developed in C by Joseph Redmon, but it was soon ported to PyTorch and other libraries. It has been continuously improved over the years, initially by Joseph Redmon et al. (YOLOv2, YOLOv3, and YOLO9000), then by various other teams since 2020. Each version brought some impressive improvements in speed and accuracy, using a variety of techniques; for example, YOLOv3 boosted accuracy in part thanks to *anchor priors*, exploiting the fact that some bounding box shapes are more likely than others, depending on the class (e.g., people tend to have vertical bounding boxes, while cars usually don't). They also increased the number of bounding boxes per grid cell, they trained on different datasets with many more classes (up to 9,000 classes organized in a hierarchy in the case of YOLO9000), they added skip connections to recover some of the spatial resolution that is lost in the CNN (we will discuss this shortly when we look at semantic segmentation), and much more. There are many variants of these models too, such as scaled down "tiny" YOLOs, optimized to be trained on less powerful machines and which can run extremely fast (at over 1,000 frames per second!), but with a slightly lower *mean average precision* (mAP).

Mean Average Precision

A very common metric used in object detection tasks is the mean average precision. "Mean average" sounds a bit redundant, doesn't it? To understand this metric, let's go back to two classification metrics we discussed in Chapter 3: precision and recall. Remember the trade-off: in general, the higher the recall, the lower the precision. You can visualize this in a precision/recall curve (see Figure 3-6). To summarize this curve into a single number, we could compute its area under the curve (AUC). But note that the precision/recall curve may contain a few sections where precision actually goes up when recall increases, especially at low recall values (you can see this at the top right of Figure 3-6). This is one of the motivations for the mAP metric.

Suppose the classifier has 90% precision at 10% recall, but 96% precision at 20% recall. There's really no trade-off here: it simply makes more sense to use the classifier at 20% recall rather than at 10% recall, as you will get both higher recall and higher precision. So instead of looking at the precision *at* 10% recall, we should really be looking at the *maximum* precision that the classifier can offer with *at least* 10% recall. It would be 96%, not 90%. Therefore, one way to get a fair idea of the model's performance is to compute the maximum precision you can get with at least 0% recall, then 10% recall, 20%, and so on up to 100%, and then calculate the mean of these maximum precisions. This is called the *average precision* (AP) metric. Now when there are more than two classes, we can compute the AP for each class, and then compute the mean AP (mAP). Conveniently, the TorchMetrics library implements all of this in the `MeanAveragePrecision` metric.

In an object detection system, there is an additional level of complexity: what if the system detected the correct class, but at the wrong location (i.e., the bounding box is completely off)? Surely we should not count this as a positive prediction. One approach is to define an IoU threshold: for example, we may consider that a prediction is correct only if the IoU is greater than, say, 0.5, and the predicted class is correct. The corresponding mAP is generally denoted mAP@0.5 (or mAP@50%, or sometimes just AP_{50}). In some competitions (such as the PASCAL VOC challenge), this is what is done. In others (such as the COCO competition), the mAP is computed for different IoU thresholds (0.50, 0.55, 0.60, …, 0.95), and the final metric is the mean of all these mAPs (denoted mAP@[.50:.95] or mAP@[.50:0.05:.95]). Yes, that's a mean mean average.

TorchVision does not include any YOLO model, but you can use the Ultralytics library, which provides a simple API to download and use various pretrained YOLO models, based on PyTorch. These models were pretrained on the COCO dataset which contains over 330,000 images, including 200,000 images annotated for object detection with 80 different classes (person, car, truck, bicycle, ball, etc.). The Ultralytics library is not installed on Colab by default, so we must run `%pip install ultralytics`. Then we can download a YOLO model and use it. For example, here is how to use this library to download the YOLOv9 model (medium variant) and detect objects in a batch of images (the model accepts PIL images, NumPy arrays, and even URLs):

```
from ultralytics import YOLO

model = YOLO('yolov9m.pt')  # n=nano, s=small, m=medium, x=large
images = ["https://homl.info/soccer.jpg", "https://homl.info/traffic.jpg"]
results = model(images)
```

The output is a list of `Results` objects which offers a handy `summary()` method. For example, here is how we can see the first detected object in the first image:

```
>>> results[0].summary()[0]
{'name': 'sports ball',
 'class': 32,
 'confidence': 0.96214,
 'box': {'x1': 245.35733, 'y1': 286.03003, 'x2': 300.62509, 'y2': 343.57184}}
```

The Ultralytics library also provides a simple API to train a YOLO model on other common object detection datasets, or on your own dataset. See *https://docs.ultralytics.com/modes/train* for more details.

Several other pretrained object detection models are available via TorchVision. You can use them just like the pretrained classification models (e.g., ConvNeXt), except that each image prediction is a represented as a dictionary containing two entries: `"labels"` (i.e., class IDs) and `"boxes"`. The available models are listed here (see the models page (*https://pytorch.org/vision/main/models*) for the full list of variants available):

Faster R-CNN (https://homl.info/fasterrcnn)[36]
: This model has two stages: the image first goes through a CNN, then the output is passed to a *region proposal network* (RPN) that proposes bounding boxes that are most likely to contain an object; a classifier is then run for each bounding box, based on the cropped output of the CNN.

SSD (https://homl.info/ssd)[37]
: SSD is a single-stage detector ("look once") similar to YOLO.

36 Shaoqing Ren et al., "Faster R-CNN: Towards Real-Time Object Detection with Region Proposal Networks", *Proceedings of e 28th International Conference on Neural Information Processing Systems* 1 (2015): 91–99.

37 Wei Liu et al., "SSD: Single Shot Multibox Detector", *Proceedings of the 14th European Conference on Computer Vision* 1 (2016): 21–37.

SSDlite (https://homl.info/ssdlite)[38]
: A lightweight version of SSD, well suited for mobile devices.

RetinaNet (https://homl.info/retinanet)[39]
: A single-stage detector which introduced a variant of the cross-entropy loss called the *focal loss* (see `torchvision.ops.sigmoid_focal_loss()`). This loss gives more weight to difficult samples and thereby improves performance on small objects and less frequent classes.

FCOS (https://homl.info/fcos)[40]
: A single-stage fully convolutional net which directly predicts bounding boxes without relying on anchor boxes.

So far, we've only considered detecting objects in single images. But what about videos? Objects must not only be detected in each frame, they must also be tracked over time. Let's take a quick look at object tracking now.

Object Tracking

Object tracking is a challenging task: objects move, they may grow or shrink as they get closer or further away, their appearance may change as they turn around or move to different lighting conditions or backgrounds, they may be temporarily occluded by other objects, and so on.

One of the most popular object tracking systems is DeepSORT (*https://homl.info/deepsort*).[41] It is based on a combination of classical algorithms and deep learning:

- It uses *Kalman filters* to estimate the most likely current position of an object given prior detections, and assuming that objects tend to move at a constant speed.
- It uses a deep learning model to measure the resemblance between new detections and existing tracked objects.
- Lastly, it uses the *Hungarian algorithm* to map new detections to existing tracked objects (or to new tracked objects). This algorithm efficiently finds the combination of mappings that minimizes the distance between the detections and the predicted positions of tracked objects, while also minimizing the appearance discrepancy.

38 Mark Sandler et al., "MobileNetV2: Inverted Residuals and Linear Bottlenecks", arXiv preprint arXiv:1801.04381 (2018).

39 Tsung-Yi Lin et al., "Focal Loss for Dense Object Detection", arXiv preprint arXiv:1708.02002 (2017).

40 Zhi Tian et al., "FCOS: Fully Convolutional One-Stage Object Detection", arXiv preprint arXiv:1904.01355 (2019).

41 Nicolai Wojke et al., "Simple Online and Realtime Tracking with a Deep Association Metric", arXiv preprint arXiv:1703.07402 (2017).

For example, imagine a red ball that just bounced off a blue ball traveling in the opposite direction. Based on the previous positions of the balls, the Kalman filter will predict that the balls will go through each other; indeed, it assumes that objects move at a constant speed, so it will not expect the bounce. If the Hungarian algorithm only considered positions, then it would happily map the new detections to the wrong balls, as if they had just gone through each other and swapped colors. But thanks to the resemblance measure, the Hungarian algorithm will notice the problem. Assuming the balls are not too similar, the algorithm will map the new detections to the correct balls.

The Ultralytics library supports object tracking. It uses the Bot-SORT algorithm (*https://homl.info/botsort*) by default: this algorithm is very similar to DeepSORT but it's faster and more accurate thanks to improvements such as camera-motion compensation and tweaks to the Kalman filter.[42] For example, we can track objects in a video using the YOLOv9 model we created earlier by executing the following code. In this example, we also print the ID of each tracked object at every frame, and we save a copy of the video with annotations (its path is displayed at the end):

```
my_video = "https://homl.info/cars.mp4"
results = model.track(source=my_video, stream=True, save=True)
for frame_results in results:
    summary = frame_results.summary()  # similar summary as earlier + track id
    track_ids = [obj["track_id"] for obj in summary]
    print("Track ids:", track_ids)
```

So far we have located objects using bounding boxes. This is often sufficient, but sometimes you need to locate objects with much more precision—for example, to remove the background behind a person during a videoconference call. Let's see how to go down to the pixel level.

Semantic Segmentation

In *semantic segmentation*, each pixel is classified according to the class of the object it belongs to (e.g., road, car, pedestrian, building, etc.), as shown in Figure 12-27. Note that different objects of the same class are *not* distinguished. For example, all the bicycles on the righthand side of the segmented image end up as one big lump of pixels. The main difficulty in this task is that when images go through a regular CNN, they gradually lose their spatial resolution (due to the layers with strides greater than 1); so, a regular CNN may end up knowing that there's a person somewhere in the bottom left of the image, but it might not be much more precise than that.

42 Nir Aharon et al., "BoT-SORT: Robust Associations Multi-Pedestrian Tracking", arXiv preprint arXiv:2206.14651 (2022).

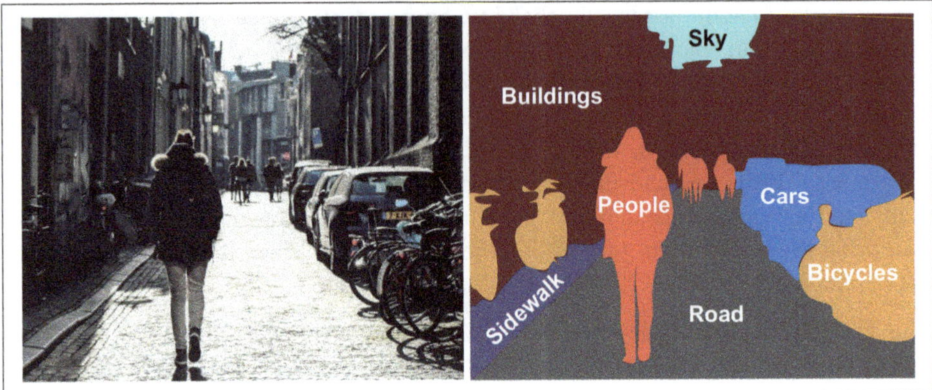

Figure 12-27. Semantic segmentation

Just like for object detection, there are many different approaches to tackle this problem, some quite complex. However, a fairly simple solution was proposed in the 2015 paper by Jonathan Long et al., that I mentioned earlier, on fully convolutional networks. The authors start by taking a pretrained CNN and turning it into an FCN. The CNN applies an overall stride of 32 to the input image (i.e., if you multiply all the strides), meaning the last layer outputs feature maps that are 32 times smaller than the input image. This is clearly too coarse, so they added a single *upsampling layer* that multiplies the resolution by 32.

There are several solutions available for upsampling (increasing the size of an image), such as bilinear interpolation, but that only works reasonably well up to ×4 or ×8. Instead, they use a *transposed convolutional layer*:[43] this is equivalent to first stretching the image by inserting empty rows and columns (full of zeros), then performing a regular convolution (see Figure 12-28). Alternatively, some people prefer to think of it as a regular convolutional layer that uses fractional strides (e.g., the stride is 1/2 in Figure 12-28). The transposed convolutional layer can be initialized to perform something close to linear interpolation, but since it is a trainable layer, it will learn to do better during training. In PyTorch, you can use the `nn.ConvTranspose2d` layer.

In a transposed convolutional layer, the stride defines how much the input will be stretched, not the size of the filter steps, so the larger the stride, the larger the output (unlike for convolutional layers or pooling layers).

43 This type of layer is sometimes referred to as a *deconvolution layer*, but it does *not* perform what mathematicians call a deconvolution, so this name should be avoided.

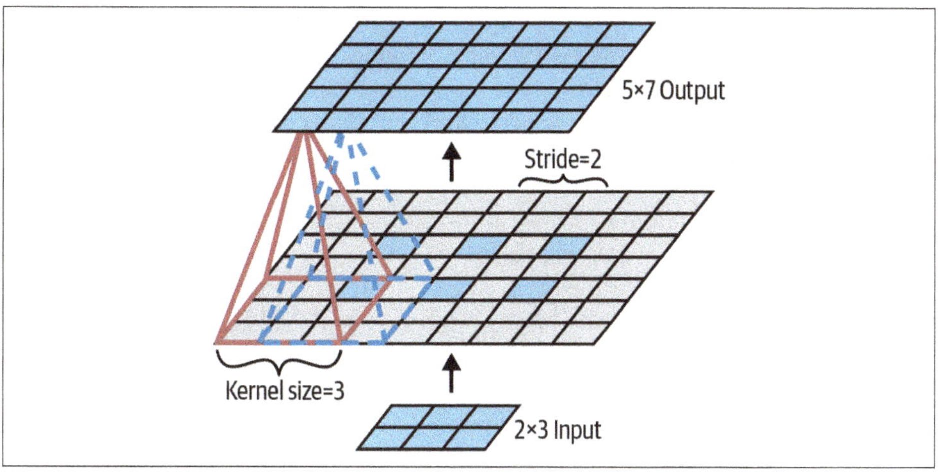

Figure 12-28. Upsampling using a transposed convolutional layer

Other PyTorch Convolutional Layers

PyTorch also offers a few other kinds of convolutional layers:

`nn.Conv1d`
: A convolutional layer for 1D inputs, such as time series or text (sequences of letters or words), as you will see in Chapter 13.

`nn.Conv3d`
: A convolutional layer for 3D inputs, such as 3D PET scans.

À-trous convolutional layer
: Setting the `dilation` hyperparameter of any convolutional layer to a value of 2 or more creates an *à-trous convolutional layer* (*à trous* is French for "with holes"). This is equivalent to using a regular convolutional layer with a filter dilated by inserting rows and columns of zeros (i.e., holes). For example, a 1 × 3 filter equal to `[[1,2,3]]` may be dilated with a *dilation rate* of 4, resulting in a *dilated filter* of `[[1, 0, 0, 0, 2, 0, 0, 0, 3]]`. This lets the convolutional layer have a larger receptive field at no computational cost and using no extra parameters.

Using transposed convolutional layers for upsampling is OK, but still too imprecise. To do better, Long et al. added skip connections from lower layers: for example, they upsampled the output image by a factor of 2 (instead of 32), and they added the output of a lower layer that had this double resolution. Then they upsampled the result by a factor of 16, leading to a total upsampling factor of 32 (see Figure 12-29). This recovered some of the spatial resolution that was lost in earlier pooling layers. In their best architecture, they used a second similar skip connection to recover even finer details from an even lower layer. In short, the output of the original CNN goes through the following extra steps: upsample ×2, add the output of a lower layer (of the appropriate scale), upsample ×2, add the output of an even lower layer, and finally upsample ×8. It is even possible to scale up beyond the size of the original image: this can be used to increase the resolution of an image, which is a technique called *super-resolution*.

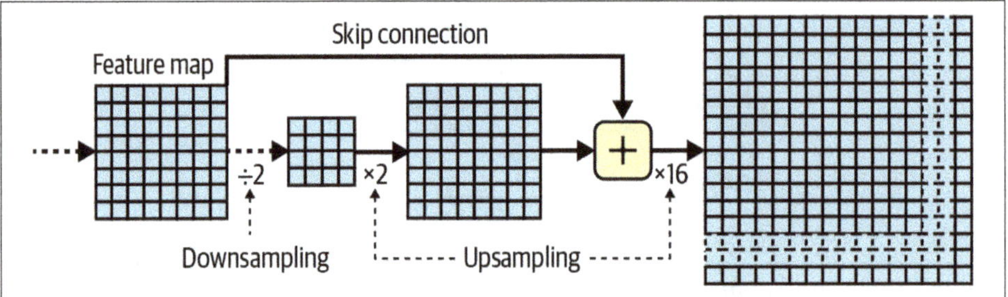

Figure 12-29. Skip layers recover some spatial resolution from lower layers

The FCN model is available in TorchVision, along with a couple other semantic segmentation models. See the notebook for a code example.

Instance segmentation is similar to semantic segmentation, but instead of merging all objects of the same class into one big lump, each object is distinguished from the others (e.g., it identifies each individual bicycle). For example the *Mask R-CNN* architecture, proposed in a 2017 paper (*https://homl.info/maskrcnn*)[44] by Kaiming He et al., extends the Faster R-CNN model by additionally producing a pixel mask for each bounding box. So not only do you get a bounding box around each object, with a set of estimated class probabilities, you also get a pixel mask that locates pixels in the bounding box that belong to the object. This model is available in TorchVision, pretrained on the COCO 2017 dataset.

TorchVision's transforms API v2 can apply to masks and videos, just like it applies to bounding boxes, thanks to the `Video` and `Mask` TVTensors.

As you can see, the field of deep computer vision is vast and fast-paced, with all sorts of architectures popping up every year. If you want to try the latest and greatest

44 Kaiming He et al., "Mask R-CNN", arXiv preprint arXiv:1703.06870 (2017).

models, check out the trending papers at *https://huggingface.co/papers*. Most of them used to be based on convolutional neural networks, but since 2020 another neural net architecture has entered the computer vision space: Transformers (which we will discuss in Chapter 14). The progress made over the last 15 years has been astounding, and researchers are now focusing on harder and harder problems, such as *adversarial learning* (which attempts to make the network more resistant to images designed to fool it), *explainability* (understanding why the network makes a specific classification), realistic *image generation* (which we will come back to in Chapter 18), *single-shot learning* (a system that can recognize an object after it has seen it just once), predicting the next frames in a video, combining text and image tasks, and more.

Now on to the next chapter, where we will look at how to process sequential data such as time series using recurrent neural networks and convolutional neural networks.

Exercises

1. What are the advantages of a CNN over a fully connected DNN for image classification?
2. Consider a CNN composed of three convolutional layers, each with 3 × 3 kernels, a stride of 2, and `"same"` padding. The lowest layer outputs 100 feature maps, the middle one outputs 200, and the top one outputs 400. The input images are RGB images of 200 × 300 pixels:
    a. What is the total number of parameters in the CNN?
    b. If we are using 32-bit floats, at least how much RAM will this network require when making a prediction for a single instance?
    c. What about when training on a mini-batch of 50 images?
3. If your GPU runs out of memory while training a CNN, what are five things you could try to solve the problem?
4. Why would you want to add a max pooling layer rather than a convolutional layer with the same stride?
5. Can you name the main innovations in AlexNet, as compared to LeNet-5? What about the main innovations in GoogLeNet, ResNet, SENet, Xception, Efficient-Net, and ConvNeXt?
6. What is a fully convolutional network? How can you convert a dense layer into a convolutional layer?
7. What is the main technical difficulty of semantic segmentation?
8. Build your own CNN from scratch and try to achieve the highest possible accuracy on MNIST.

9. Use transfer learning for large image classification, going through these steps:

   a. Create a training set containing at least 100 images per class. For example, you could classify your own pictures based on the location (beach, mountain, city, etc.). Alternatively, you can use an existing dataset, such as the one used in PyTorch's transfer learning for computer vision tutorial (*https://homl.info/transfertuto*).

   b. Split it into a training set, a validation set, and a test set.

   c. Build the input pipeline, apply the appropriate preprocessing operations, and optionally add data augmentation.

   d. Fine-tune a pretrained model on this dataset.

10. Go through PyTorch's object detection fine-tuning tutorial (*https://homl.info/detectiontuto*).

Solutions to these exercises are available at the end of this chapter's notebook, at *https://homl.info/colab-p*.

CHAPTER 13
Processing Sequences Using RNNs and CNNs

Predicting the future is something you do all the time, whether you are finishing a friend's sentence or anticipating the smell of coffee at breakfast. In this chapter we will discuss recurrent neural networks (RNNs)—a class of nets that can predict the future (well, up to a point). RNNs can analyze time series data, such as the number of daily active users on your website, the hourly temperature in your city, your home's daily power consumption, the trajectories of nearby cars, and more. Once an RNN learns past patterns in the data, it is able to use its knowledge to forecast the future, assuming, of course, that past patterns still hold in the future.

More generally, RNNs can work on sequences of arbitrary lengths, rather than on fixed-sized inputs. For example, they can take sentences, documents, or audio samples as input, which makes them extremely useful for natural language processing applications such as automatic translation or speech-to-text.

In this chapter, we will first go through the fundamental concepts underlying RNNs and how to train them using backpropagation through time. Then, we will use them to forecast a time series. Along the way, we will look at the popular autoregressive moving average (ARMA) family of models, often used to forecast time series, and use them as baselines to compare with our RNNs. After that, we'll explore the two main difficulties that RNNs face:

- Unstable gradients (discussed in Chapter 11), which can be alleviated using various techniques, including *recurrent dropout* and *recurrent layer normalization*.
- A (very) limited short-term memory, which can be extended using long short-term memory (LSTM) and gated recurrent unit (GRU) cells.

RNNs are not the only types of neural networks capable of handling sequential data. For small sequences, a regular dense network can do the trick, and for very long sequences, such as audio samples or text, convolutional neural networks can actually work quite well too. We will discuss both of these possibilities, and we will finish this chapter by implementing a WaveNet—a CNN architecture capable of handling sequences of tens of thousands of time steps. But we can do even better! In Chapter 14, we will apply RNNs to natural language processing (NLP), and we will see how to boost them using attention mechanisms. Attention is at the core of transformers, which we will discover in Chapter 15: they are now the state of the art for sequence processing, NLP, and even computer vision. But before we get there, let's start with the simplest RNNs!

Recurrent Neurons and Layers

Up to now we have focused on feedforward neural networks, where the activations flow only in one direction, from the input layer to the output layer. A recurrent neural network looks very much like a feedforward neural network, except it also has connections pointing backward.

Let's look at the simplest possible RNN, composed of one neuron receiving inputs, producing an output, and sending that output back to itself (see Figure 13-1, left). At each *time step t* (also called a *frame*), this *recurrent neuron* receives the inputs $\mathbf{x}_{(t)}$ as well as its own output from the previous time step, $\hat{y}_{(t-1)}$. Since there is no previous output at the first time step, it is generally set to zero. We can represent this tiny network against the time axis (see Figure 13-1, right). This is called *unrolling the network through time* (it's the same recurrent neuron represented once per time step).

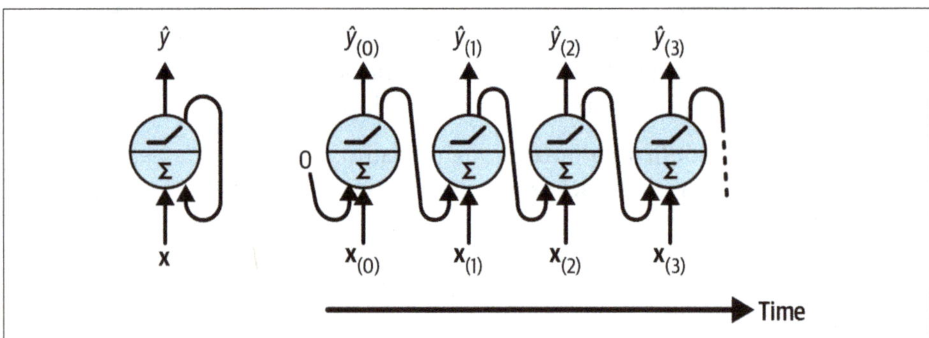

Figure 13-1. A recurrent neuron (left) unrolled through time (right)

You can easily create a layer of recurrent neurons. At each time step *t*, every neuron receives both the input vector $\mathbf{x}_{(t)}$ and the output vector from the previous time step $\hat{\mathbf{y}}_{(t-1)}$, as shown in Figure 13-2. Note that both the inputs and outputs are now vectors (when there was just a single neuron, the output was a scalar).

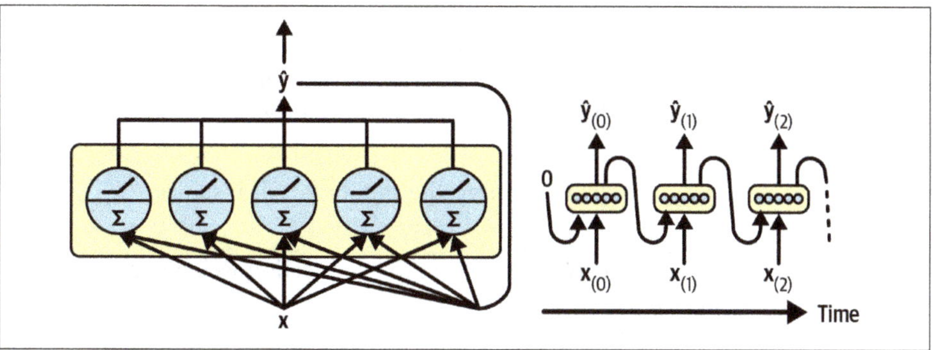

Figure 13-2. A layer of recurrent neurons (left) unrolled through time (right)

Each recurrent neuron has two sets of weights: one for the inputs $\mathbf{x}_{(t)}$ and the other for the outputs of the previous time step, $\hat{\mathbf{y}}_{(t-1)}$. Let's call these weight vectors $\mathbf{w}_x$ and $\mathbf{w}_{\hat{y}}$. If we consider the whole recurrent layer instead of just one recurrent neuron, we can place all the weight vectors in two weight matrices: $\mathbf{W}_x$ and $\mathbf{W}_{\hat{y}}$.

The output vector of the whole recurrent layer can then be computed pretty much as you might expect, as shown in Equation 13-1, where $\mathbf{b}$ is the bias vector and $\phi(\cdot)$ is the activation function (e.g., ReLU[1]).

Equation 13-1. Output of a recurrent layer for a single instance

$$\hat{\mathbf{y}}_{(t)} = \varphi\left(\mathbf{W}_x{}^\mathsf{T}\mathbf{x}_{(t)} + \mathbf{W}_{\hat{y}}{}^\mathsf{T}\hat{\mathbf{y}}_{(t-1)} + \mathbf{b}\right)$$

Just as with feedforward neural networks, we can compute a recurrent layer's output in one shot for an entire mini-batch by placing all the inputs at time step t into an input matrix $\mathbf{X}_{(t)}$ (see Equation 13-2).

Equation 13-2. Outputs of a layer of recurrent neurons for all instances in a mini-batch

$$\begin{aligned}\hat{\mathbf{Y}}_{(t)} &= \varphi(\mathbf{X}_{(t)}\mathbf{W}_x + \hat{\mathbf{Y}}_{(t-1)}\mathbf{W}_{\hat{y}} + \mathbf{b}) \\ &= \varphi([\mathbf{X}_{(t)} \quad \hat{\mathbf{Y}}_{(t-1)}]\mathbf{W} + \mathbf{b}) \text{ with } \mathbf{W} = \begin{bmatrix}\mathbf{W}_x \\ \mathbf{W}_{\hat{y}}\end{bmatrix}\end{aligned}$$

1 Note that many researchers prefer to use the hyperbolic tangent (tanh) activation function in RNNs rather than the ReLU activation function. For example, see Vu Pham et al.'s 2013 paper (*https://homl.info/91*) "Dropout Improves Recurrent Neural Networks for Handwriting Recognition". ReLU-based RNNs are also possible, as shown in Quoc V. Le et al.'s 2015 paper (*https://homl.info/92*) "A Simple Way to Initialize Recurrent Networks of Rectified Linear Units".

In this equation:

- $\hat{\mathbf{Y}}_{(t)}$ is an $m \times n_{\text{neurons}}$ matrix containing the layer's outputs at time step t for each instance in the mini-batch (m is the number of instances in the mini-batch, and n_{neurons} is the number of neurons).
- $\mathbf{X}_{(t)}$ is an $m \times n_{\text{inputs}}$ matrix containing the inputs for all instances (n_{inputs} is the number of input features).
- $\mathbf{W}_x$ is an $n_{\text{inputs}} \times n_{\text{neurons}}$ matrix containing the connection weights for the inputs of the current time step.
- $\mathbf{W}_{\hat{y}}$ is an $n_{\text{neurons}} \times n_{\text{neurons}}$ matrix containing the connection weights for the outputs of the previous time step.
- $\mathbf{b}$ is a vector of size n_{neurons} containing each neuron's bias term.
- The weight matrices $\mathbf{W}_x$ and $\mathbf{W}_{\hat{y}}$ are often concatenated vertically into a single weight matrix $\mathbf{W}$ of shape $(n_{\text{inputs}} + n_{\text{neurons}}) \times n_{\text{neurons}}$ (see the second line of Equation 13-2).
- The notation $[\mathbf{X}_{(t)}\ \hat{\mathbf{Y}}_{(t-1)}]$ represents the horizontal concatenation of the matrices $\mathbf{X}_{(t)}$ and $\hat{\mathbf{Y}}_{(t-1)}$.

Notice that $\hat{\mathbf{Y}}_{(t)}$ is a function of $\mathbf{X}_{(t)}$ and $\hat{\mathbf{Y}}_{(t-1)}$, which is a function of $\mathbf{X}_{(t-1)}$ and $\hat{\mathbf{Y}}_{(t-2)}$, which is a function of $\mathbf{X}_{(t-2)}$ and $\hat{\mathbf{Y}}_{(t-3)}$, and so on. This makes $\hat{\mathbf{Y}}_{(t)}$ a function of all the inputs since time $t = 0$ (that is, $\mathbf{X}_{(0)}, \mathbf{X}_{(1)}, \ldots, \mathbf{X}_{(t)}$). At the first time step, $t = 0$, there are no previous outputs, so they are typically assumed to be all zeros.

The idea of introducing backward connections (i.e., loops) in artificial neural networks dates back to the very origins of ANNs, but the first modern RNN architecture was proposed by Michael I. Jordan in 1986 (*https://homl.info/jordanrnn*).[2] At each time step, his RNN would look at the inputs for that time step, plus its own outputs from the previous time step. This is called *output feedback*.

Memory Cells

Since the output of a recurrent neuron at time step t is a function of all the inputs from previous time steps, you could say it has a form of *memory*. A part of a neural network that preserves some state across time steps is called a *memory cell* (or simply a *cell*). A single recurrent neuron, or a layer of recurrent neurons, is a very basic cell, capable of learning only short patterns (typically about 10 steps long, but this varies depending on the task). Later in this chapter, we will look at some more complex and

2 Michael I. Jordan, "Attractor Dynamics and Parallelism in a Connectionist Sequential Machine", *Proceedings of the Eighth Annual Conference of the Cognitive Science Society* (1986).

powerful types of cells capable of learning longer patterns (roughly 10 times longer, but again, this depends on the task).

A cell's state at time step t, denoted $\mathbf{h}_{(t)}$ (the "h" stands for "hidden"), is a function of some inputs at that time step and its state at the previous time step: $\mathbf{h}_{(t)} = f(\mathbf{x}_{(t)}, \mathbf{h}_{(t-1)})$. Its output at time step t, denoted $\hat{\mathbf{y}}_{(t)}$, is also a function of the previous state and the current inputs, and typically it's just a function of the current state. In the case of the basic cells we have discussed so far, the output is just equal to the state, but in more complex cells this is not always the case, as shown in Figure 13-3.

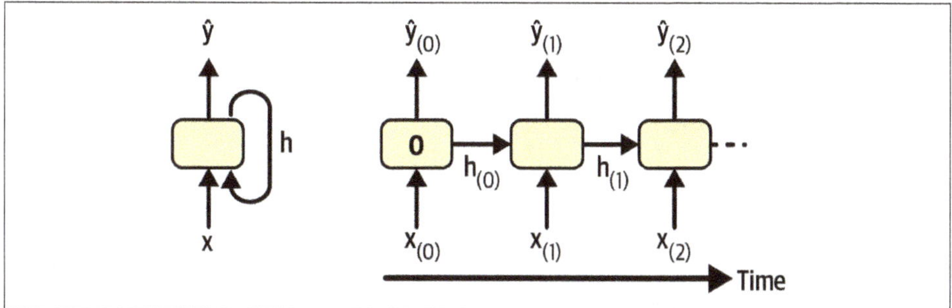

Figure 13-3. A cell's hidden state and its output may be different

The first modern RNN that fed back the hidden state rather than the outputs was proposed by Jeffrey Elman in 1990 (*https://homl.info/elmanrnn*).[3] This is called *state feedback*, and it's the most common approach today.

Input and Output Sequences

An RNN can simultaneously take a sequence of inputs and produce a sequence of outputs (see the top-left network in Figure 13-4). This type of *sequence-to-sequence network* is useful to forecast time series, such as your home's daily power consumption: you feed it the data over the last N days, and you train it to output the power consumption shifted by one day into the future (i.e., from N – 1 days ago to tomorrow).

Alternatively, you could feed the network a sequence of inputs and ignore all outputs except for the last one (see the top-right network in Figure 13-4). This is a *sequence-to-vector network*. For example, you could feed the network a sequence of words corresponding to a movie review, and the network would output a sentiment score (e.g., from 0 [hate] to 1 [love]).

3 Jeffrey L. Elman, "Finding Structure in Time", *Cognitive Science*, Volume 14, Issue 2 (1990).

Conversely, you could feed the network the same input vector over and over again at each time step and let it output a sequence (see the bottom-left network of Figure 13-4). This is a *vector-to-sequence network*. For example, the input could be an image (or the output of a CNN), and the output could be a caption for that image.

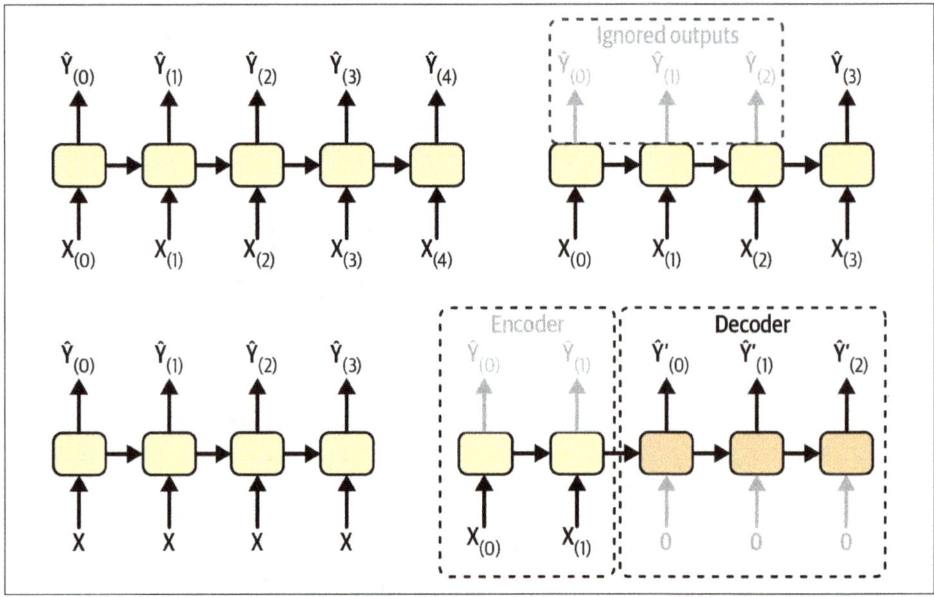

Figure 13-4. Sequence-to-sequence (top left), sequence-to-vector (top right), vector-to-sequence (bottom left), and encoder-decoder (bottom right) networks

Lastly, you could have a sequence-to-vector network, called an *encoder*, followed by a vector-to-sequence network, called a *decoder* (see the bottom-right network of Figure 13-4). For example, this could be used for translating a sentence from one language to another. You would feed the network a sentence in one language, the encoder would convert this sentence into a single vector representation, and then the decoder would decode this vector into a sentence in another language. This two-step model, called an *encoder-decoder* (*https://homl.info/seq2seq*),[4] works much better than trying to translate on the fly with a single sequence-to-sequence RNN (like the one represented at the top left): the last words of a sentence can affect the first words of the translation, so you need to wait until you have seen the whole sentence before translating it. We will go through the implementation of an encoder-decoder in Chapter 14 (as you will see, it is a bit more complex than what Figure 13-4 suggests).

This versatility sounds promising, but how do you train a recurrent neural network?

4 Nal Kalchbrenner and Phil Blunsom, "Recurrent Continuous Translation Models", *Proceedings of the 2013 Conference on Empirical Methods in Natural Language Processing* (2013): 1700–1709.

Training RNNs

To train an RNN, the trick is to unroll it through time (like we just did) and then use regular backpropagation (see Figure 13-5). This strategy is called *backpropagation through time* (BPTT).

Just like in regular backpropagation, there is a first forward pass through the unrolled network (represented by the dashed arrows). Then the output sequence is evaluated using a loss function $\mathcal{L}(\mathbf{Y}_{(0)}, \mathbf{Y}_{(1)}, \ldots, \mathbf{Y}_{(T)}; \hat{\mathbf{Y}}_{(0)}, \hat{\mathbf{Y}}_{(1)}, \ldots, \hat{\mathbf{Y}}_{(T)})$ (where $\mathbf{Y}_{(i)}$ is the ith target, $\hat{\mathbf{Y}}_{(i)}$ is the ith prediction, and T is the max time step). Note that this loss function may ignore some outputs. For example, in a sequence-to-vector RNN, all outputs are ignored except for the very last one. In Figure 13-5, the loss function is computed based on the last three outputs only. The gradients of that loss function are then propagated backward through the unrolled network (represented by the solid arrows). In this example, since the outputs $\hat{\mathbf{Y}}_{(0)}$ and $\hat{\mathbf{Y}}_{(1)}$ are not used to compute the loss, the gradients do not flow backward through them; they only flow through $\hat{\mathbf{Y}}_{(2)}$, $\hat{\mathbf{Y}}_{(3)}$, and $\hat{\mathbf{Y}}_{(4)}$. Moreover, since the same parameters **W** and **b** are used at each time step, their gradients will be tweaked multiple times during backprop. Once the backward phase is complete and all the gradients have been computed, BPTT can perform a gradient descent step to update the parameters (this is no different from regular backprop).

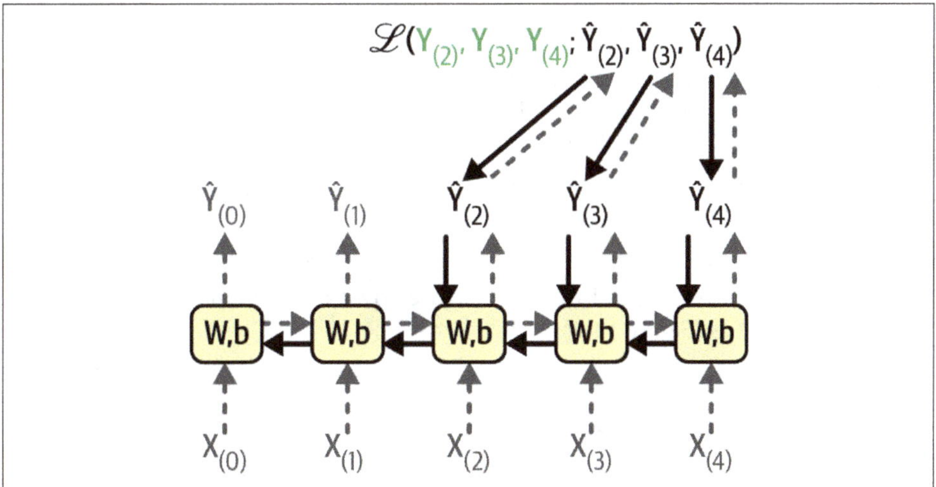

Figure 13-5. Backpropagation through time

Fortunately, PyTorch takes care of all of this complexity for you, as you will see. But before we get there, let's load a time series and start analyzing it using classical tools to better understand what we're dealing with, and to get some baseline metrics.

Forecasting a Time Series

All right! Let's pretend you've just been hired as a data scientist by Chicago's Transit Authority. Your first task is to build a model capable of forecasting the number of passengers that will ride on bus and rail the next day. You have access to daily ridership data since 2001. Let's walk through how you would handle this. We'll start by loading and cleaning up the data:[5]

```
import pandas as pd
from pathlib import Path

path = Path("datasets/ridership/CTA_-_Ridership_-_Daily_Boarding_Totals.csv")
df = pd.read_csv(path, parse_dates=["service_date"])
df.columns = ["date", "day_type", "bus", "rail", "total"]  # shorter names
df = df.sort_values("date").set_index("date")
df = df.drop("total", axis=1)  # no need for total, it's just bus + rail
df = df.drop_duplicates()  # remove duplicated months (2011-10 and 2014-07)
```

We load the CSV file, set short column names, sort the rows by date, remove the redundant `total` column, and drop duplicate rows. Now let's check what the first few rows look like:

```
>>> df.head()
           day_type     bus    rail
date
2001-01-01        U  297192  126455
2001-01-02        W  780827  501952
2001-01-03        W  824923  536432
2001-01-04        W  870021  550011
2001-01-05        W  890426  557917
```

On January 1st, 2001, 297,192 people boarded a bus in Chicago, and 126,455 boarded a train. The `day_type` column contains `W` for **W**eekdays, `A` for S**a**turdays, and `U` for S**u**ndays or holidays.

Now let's plot the bus and rail ridership figures over a few months in 2019, to see what it looks like (see Figure 13-6):

```
import matplotlib.pyplot as plt

df["2019-03":"2019-05"].plot(grid=True, marker=".", figsize=(8, 3.5))
plt.show()
```

5 The latest data from the Chicago Transit Authority is available at the Chicago Data Portal (*https://homl.info/ridership*).

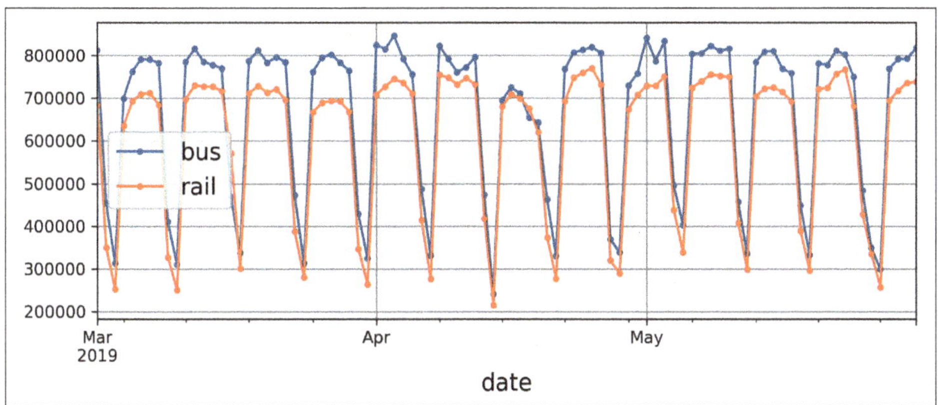

Figure 13-6. Daily ridership in Chicago

Note that Pandas includes both the start and end month in the range, so this plots the data from the 1st of March all the way up to the 31st of May. This is a *time series*: data with values at different time steps, usually at regular intervals. More specifically, since there are multiple values per time step, this is called a *multivariate time series*. If we only looked at the `bus` column, it would be a *univariate time series*, with a single value per time step. Predicting future values (i.e., forecasting) is the most typical task when dealing with time series, and this is what we will focus on in this chapter. Other tasks include imputation (filling in missing past values), classification, anomaly detection, and more.

Looking at Figure 13-6, we can see that a similar pattern is clearly repeated every week. This is called a weekly *seasonality*. In fact, it's so strong in this case that forecasting tomorrow's ridership by just copying the values from a week earlier will yield reasonably good results. This is called *naive forecasting*: simply copying a past value to make our forecast. Naive forecasting is often a great baseline, and it can even be tricky to beat in some cases.

In general, naive forecasting means copying the latest known value (e.g., forecasting that tomorrow will be the same as today). However, in our case, copying the value from the previous week works better, due to the strong weekly seasonality.

To visualize these naive forecasts, let's overlay the two time series (for bus and rail) as well as the same time series lagged by one week (i.e., shifted toward the right) using dotted lines. We'll also plot the difference between the two (i.e., the value at time t minus the value at time t – 7); this is called *differencing* (see Figure 13-7):

```
diff_7 = df[["bus", "rail"]].diff(7)["2019-03":"2019-05"]

fig, axs = plt.subplots(2, 1, sharex=True, figsize=(8, 5))
df.plot(ax=axs[0], legend=False, marker=".")  # original time series
df.shift(7).plot(ax=axs[0], grid=True, legend=False, linestyle=":")  # lagged
diff_7.plot(ax=axs[1], grid=True, marker=".")  # 7-day difference time series
plt.show()
```

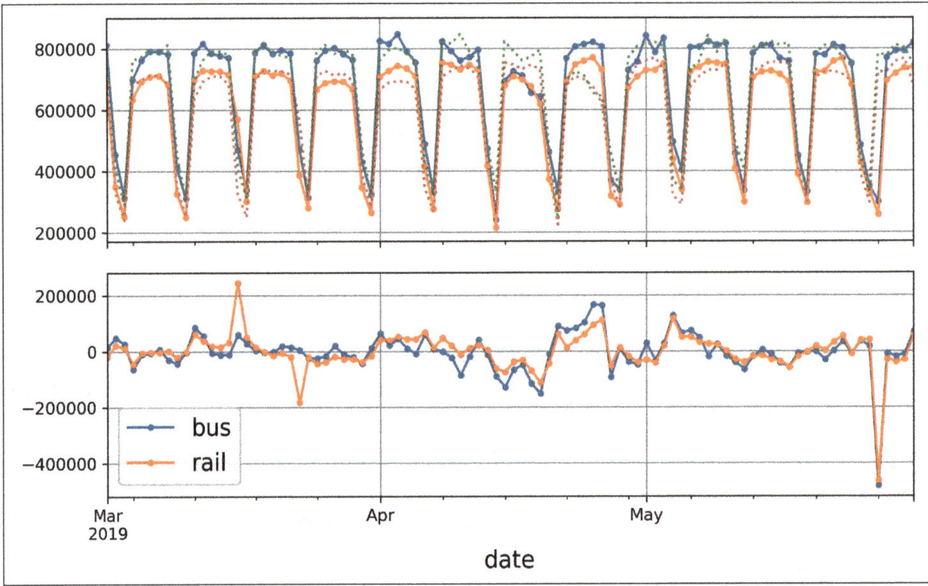

Figure 13-7. Time series overlaid with 7-day lagged time series (top), and difference between t and t – 7 (bottom)

Not too bad! Notice how closely the lagged time series track the actual time series. When a time series is correlated with a lagged version of itself, we say that the time series is *autocorrelated*. As you can see, most of the differences are fairly small, except at the end of May. Maybe there was a holiday at that time? Let's check the `day_type` column:

```
>>> list(df.loc["2019-05-25":"2019-05-27"]["day_type"])
['A', 'U', 'U']
```

Indeed, there was a long weekend back then: the Monday was the Memorial Day holiday. We could use this column to improve our forecasts, but for now let's just measure the mean absolute error over the three-month period we're arbitrarily focusing on—March, April, and May 2019—to get a rough idea:

```
>>> diff_7.abs().mean()
bus     43915.608696
rail    42143.271739
dtype: float64
```

Our naive forecasts get a mean absolute error (MAE) of about 43,916 bus riders, and about 42,143 rail riders. It's hard to tell at a glance how good or bad this is, so let's put the forecast errors into perspective by dividing them by the target values:

```
>>> targets = df[["bus", "rail"]]["2019-03":"2019-05"]
>>> (diff_7 / targets).abs().mean()
bus     0.082938
rail    0.089948
dtype: float64
```

What we just computed is called the *mean absolute percentage error* (MAPE). It looks like our naive forecasts give us a MAPE of roughly 8.3% for bus and 9.0% for rail. It's interesting to note that the MAE for the rail forecasts looks slightly better than the MAE for the bus forecasts, while the opposite is true for the MAPE. That's because the bus ridership is larger than the rail ridership, so naturally the forecast errors are also larger, but when we put the errors into perspective, it turns out that the bus forecasts are actually slightly better than the rail forecasts.

The MAE, MAPE, and mean squared error (MSE) are among the most common metrics you can use to evaluate your forecasts. As always, choosing the right metric depends on the task. For example, if your project suffers quadratically more from large errors than from small ones, then the MSE may be preferable, as it strongly penalizes large errors.

Looking at the time series, there doesn't appear to be any significant monthly seasonality, but let's check whether there's any yearly seasonality. We'll look at the data from 2001 to 2019. To reduce the risk of data snooping, we'll ignore more recent data for now. Let's also plot a 12-month rolling average for each series to visualize long-term trends (see Figure 13-8):

```
period = slice("2001", "2019")
df_monthly = df.select_dtypes(include="number").resample('ME').mean()
rolling_average_12_months = df_monthly.loc[period].rolling(window=12).mean()

fig, ax = plt.subplots(figsize=(8, 4))
df_monthly[period].plot(ax=ax, marker=".")
rolling_average_12_months.plot(ax=ax, grid=True, legend=False)
plt.show()
```

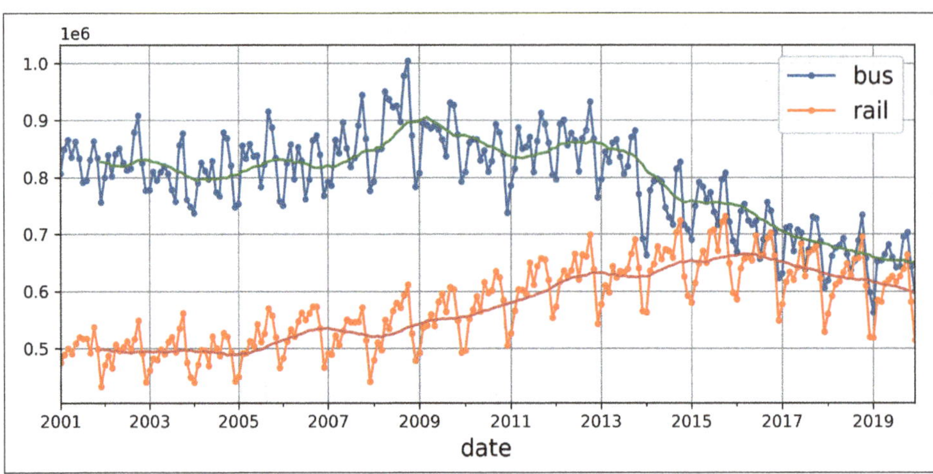

Figure 13-8. Yearly seasonality and long-term trends

Yep! There's definitely some yearly seasonality as well, although it is noisier than the weekly seasonality, and more visible for the rail series than the bus series: we see peaks and troughs at roughly the same dates each year. Let's check what we get if we plot the 12-month difference (see Figure 13-9):

```
df_monthly.diff(12)[period].plot(grid=True, marker=".", figsize=(8, 3))
plt.show()
```

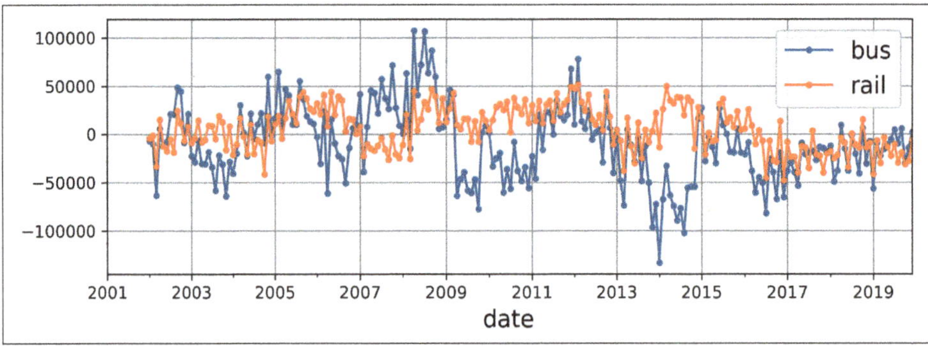

Figure 13-9. The 12-month difference

Notice how differencing not only removed the yearly seasonality, but it also removed the long-term trends. For example, the linear downward trend present in the time series from 2016 to 2019 became a roughly constant negative value in the differenced time series. In fact, differencing is a common technique used to remove trend and seasonality from a time series: it's easier to study a *stationary* time series, meaning one whose statistical properties remain the same over time, without any seasonality or trends. Once you're able to make accurate forecasts on the differenced time series, it's easy to turn them into forecasts for the actual time series by just adding back the past values that were previously subtracted.

You may be thinking that we're only trying to predict tomorrow's ridership, so the long-term patterns matter much less than the short-term ones. You're right, but still, we may be able to improve performance slightly by taking long-term patterns into account. For example, daily bus ridership dropped by about 2,500 in October 2017, which represents about 570 fewer passengers each week, so if we were at the end of October 2017, it would make sense to forecast tomorrow's ridership by copying the value from last week, minus 570. Accounting for the trend will make your forecasts a bit more accurate on average.

Now that you're familiar with the ridership time series, as well as some of the most important concepts in time series analysis, including seasonality, trend, differencing, and moving averages, let's take a quick look at a very popular family of statistical models that are commonly used to analyze time series.

The ARMA Model Family

We'll start with the *autoregressive moving average* (ARMA) model, developed by Herman Wold in the 1930s: it computes its forecasts using a simple weighted sum of lagged values and corrects these forecasts by adding a moving average, very much like we just discussed. Specifically, the moving average component is computed using a weighted sum of the last few forecast errors. Equation 13-3 shows how the model makes its forecasts.

Equation 13-3. Forecasting using an ARMA model

$$\hat{y}_{(t)} = \sum_{i=1}^{p} \alpha_i y_{(t-i)} + \sum_{i=1}^{q} \theta_i \varepsilon_{(t-i)}$$
$$\text{with } \varepsilon_{(t)} = y_{(t)} - \hat{y}_{(t)}$$

In this equation:

- $\hat{y}_{(t)}$ is the model's forecast for time step t.
- $y_{(t)}$ is the time series' value at time step t.
- The first sum is the weighted sum of the past p values of the time series, using the learned weights α_i. The number p is a hyperparameter, and it determines how far back into the past the model should look. This sum is the *autoregressive* component of the model: it performs regression based on past values.

- The second sum is the weighted sum over the past q forecast errors $\varepsilon_{(t)}$, using the learned weights θ_i. The number q is a hyperparameter. This sum is the moving average component of the model.

Importantly, this model assumes that the time series is stationary. If it is not, then differencing may help. Using differencing over a single time step will produce an approximation of the derivative of the time series: indeed, it will give the slope of the series at each time step. This means that it will eliminate any linear trend, transforming it into a constant value. For example, if you apply one-step differencing to the series [3, 5, 7, 9, 11], you get the differenced series [2, 2, 2, 2].

If the original time series has a quadratic trend instead of a linear trend, then a single round of differencing will not be enough. For example, the series [1, 4, 9, 16, 25, 36] becomes [3, 5, 7, 9, 11] after one round of differencing, but if you run differencing for a second round, then you get [2, 2, 2, 2]. So, running two rounds of differencing will eliminate quadratic trends. More generally, running d consecutive rounds of differencing computes an approximation of the dth order derivative of the time series, so it will eliminate polynomial trends up to degree d. This hyperparameter d is called the *order of integration*.

Differencing is the central contribution of the *autoregressive integrated moving average* (ARIMA) model, introduced in 1970 by George Box and Gwilym Jenkins in their book *Time Series Analysis* (Wiley). This model runs d rounds of differencing to make the time series more stationary, then it applies a regular ARMA model. When making forecasts, it uses this ARMA model, then it adds back the terms that were subtracted by differencing.

One last member of the ARMA family is the *seasonal ARIMA* (SARIMA) model: it models the time series in the same way as ARIMA, but it additionally models a seasonal component for a given frequency (e.g., weekly), using the exact same ARIMA approach. It has a total of seven hyperparameters: the same p, d, and q hyperparameters as ARIMA; plus additional P, D, and Q hyperparameters to model the seasonal pattern; and lastly the period of the seasonal pattern, denoted s. The hyperparameters P, D, and Q are just like p, d, and q, but they are used to model the time series at $t - s$, $t - 2s$, $t - 3s$, etc.

Let's see how to fit a SARIMA model to the rail time series, and use it to make a forecast for tomorrow's ridership. We'll pretend today is the last day of May 2019, and we want to forecast the rail ridership for "tomorrow", the 1st of June, 2019. For this, we can use the `statsmodels` library, which contains many different statistical models, including the ARMA model and its variants, implemented by the `ARIMA` class:

```
from statsmodels.tsa.arima.model import ARIMA

origin, today = "2019-01-01", "2019-05-31"
rail_series = df.loc[origin:today]["rail"].asfreq("D")
```

```python
model = ARIMA(rail_series,
              order=(1, 0, 0),
              seasonal_order=(0, 1, 1, 7))
model = model.fit()
y_pred = model.forecast()  # returns 427,758.6
```

In this code example:

- We start by importing the `ARIMA` class, then we take the rail ridership data from the start of 2019 up to "today", and we use `asfreq("D")` to set the time series' frequency to daily. This doesn't change the data at all in this case, since it's already daily, but without this the `ARIMA` class would have to guess the frequency, and it would display a warning.
- Next, we create an `ARIMA` instance, passing it all the data until "today", and we set the model hyperparameters: `order=(1, 0, 0)` means that $p = 1$, $d = 0$, and $q = 0$; and `seasonal_order=(0, 1, 1, 7)` means that $P = 0$, $D = 1$, $Q = 1$, and $s = 7$. Notice that the `statsmodels` API differs a bit from Scikit-Learn's API, since we pass the data to the model at construction time, instead of passing it to the `fit()` method.
- Next, we fit the model, and we use it to make a forecast for "tomorrow", the 1st of June, 2019.

The forecast is 427,759 passengers, when in fact there were 379,044. Yikes, we're 12.9% off—that's pretty bad. It's actually slightly worse than naive forecasting, which forecasts 426,932, off by 12.6%. But perhaps we were just unlucky that day? To check this, we can run the same code in a loop to make forecasts for every day in March, April, and May, and compute the MAE over that period:

```python
origin, start_date, end_date = "2019-01-01", "2019-03-01", "2019-05-31"
time_period = pd.date_range(start_date, end_date)
rail_series = df.loc[origin:end_date]["rail"].asfreq("D")
y_preds = []
for today in time_period.shift(-1):
    model = ARIMA(rail_series[origin:today],  # train on data up to "today"
                  order=(1, 0, 0),
                  seasonal_order=(0, 1, 1, 7))
    model = model.fit()  # note that we retrain the model every day!
    y_pred = model.forecast().iloc[0]
    y_preds.append(y_pred)

y_preds = pd.Series(y_preds, index=time_period)
mae = (y_preds - rail_series[time_period]).abs().mean()  # returns 32,040.7
```

Ah, that's much better! The MAE is about 32,041, which is significantly lower than the MAE we got with naive forecasting (42,143). So although the model is not perfect, it still beats naive forecasting by a large margin, on average.

At this point, you may be wondering how to pick good hyperparameters for the SARIMA model. There are several methods, but the simplest to understand and to get started with is the brute-force approach: just run a grid search. For each model you want to evaluate (i.e., each hyperparameter combination), you can run the preceding code example, changing only the hyperparameter values. Good *p*, *q*, *P*, and *Q* values are usually fairly small (typically 0 to 2, sometimes up to 5 or 6), and *d* and *D* are typically 0 or 1, sometimes 2. As for *s*, it's just the main seasonal pattern's period: in our case it's 7 since there's a strong weekly seasonality. The model with the lowest MAE wins. Of course, you can replace the MAE with another metric if it better matches your business objective. And that's it!

There are other more principled approaches to selecting good hyperparameters, based on analyzing the *autocorrelation function* (ACF) and *partial autocorrelation function* (PACF),[6] or minimizing the AIC or BIC metrics (introduced in Chapter 8) to penalize models that use too many parameters and reduce the risk of overfitting the data, but grid search is a good place to start.

Preparing the Data for Machine Learning Models

Now that we have two baselines, naive forecasting and SARIMA, let's try to use the machine learning models we've covered so far to forecast this time series, starting with a basic linear model. Our goal will be to forecast tomorrow's ridership based on the ridership of the past 8 weeks of data (56 days). The inputs to our model will therefore be sequences (usually a single sequence per day once the model is in production), each containing 56 values from time steps $t - 55$ to t. For each input sequence, the model will output a single value: the forecast for time step $t + 1$.

But what will we use as training data? Well, here's the trick: we will use every 56-day window from the past as training data, and the target for each window will be the value immediately following it. To do that, we need to create a custom dataset that will chop a given time series into all possible windows of a given length, each with its corresponding target:

```
class TimeSeriesDataset(torch.utils.data.Dataset):
    def __init__(self, series, window_length):
        self.series = series
        self.window_length = window_length

    def __len__(self):
        return len(self.series) - self.window_length
```

6 For more details on the ACF-PACF approach, check out this very nice post by Jason Brownlee (*https://homl.info/arimatuning*).

```python
    def __getitem__(self, idx):
        if idx >= len(self):
            raise IndexError("dataset index out of range")
        end = idx + self.window_length  # 1st index after window
        window = self.series[idx : end]
        target = self.series[end]
        return window, target
```

Let's test this class by applying it to a simple time series containing the numbers 0 to 5. We could represent this series in 1D using [0, 1, 2, 3, 4, 5], but the RNN modules expect each sequence to be 2D, with a shape of [*sequence length*, *dimensionality*]. For univariate time series, the dimensionality is simply 1, so we represent the time series as [[0], [1], [2], [3], [4], [5]]. In the following code below, the `TimeSeriesDataset` contains all the windows of length 3, each with its corresponding target (i.e., the first value after the window):

```python
>>> my_series = torch.tensor([[0], [1], [2], [3], [4], [5]])
>>> my_dataset = TimeSeriesDataset(my_series, window_length=3)
>>> for window, target in my_dataset:
...     print("Window:", window, " Target:", target)
...
Window: tensor([[0], [1], [2]])  Target: tensor([3])
Window: tensor([[1], [2], [3]])  Target: tensor([4])
Window: tensor([[2], [3], [4]])  Target: tensor([5])
```

It looks like our `TimeSeriesDataset` class works fine! Now we can create a `DataLoader` for this tiny dataset, shuffling the windows and grouping them into batches of two:

```python
>>> from torch.utils.data import DataLoader
>>> torch.manual_seed(0)
>>> my_loader = DataLoader(my_dataset, batch_size=2, shuffle=True)
>>> for X, y in my_loader:
...     print("X:", X, " y:", y)
...
X: tensor([[[0], [1], [2]], [[2], [3], [4]]])  y: tensor([[3], [5]])
X: tensor([[[1], [2], [3]]])  y: tensor([[4]])
```

The first batch contains the windows [[0], [1], [2]] and [[2], [3], [4]], along with their respective targets [3] and [5]; and the second batch contains only one window [[1], [2], [3]], with its target [4]. Indeed, when the length of a dataset is not a multiple of the batch size, the last batch is shorter.

OK, now that we have a way to convert a time series into a dataset that we can use to train ML models, let's go ahead and prepare our ridership dataset. First, we need to split our data into a training period, a validation period, and a test period. We will focus on the rail ridership for now. We will convert the data to 32-bit float tensors, and scale them down by a factor of one million to ensure the values end up near the 0–1 range; this plays nicely with the default weight initialization and learning rate. In this code, we use `df[["rail"]]` instead of `df["rail"]` to ensure the resulting tensor has a shape of [*series length*, 1] rather than [*series length*]:

```
rail_train = torch.FloatTensor(df[["rail"]]["2016-01":"2018-12"].values / 1e6)
rail_valid = torch.FloatTensor(df[["rail"]]["2019-01":"2019-05"].values / 1e6)
rail_test = torch.FloatTensor(df[["rail"]]["2019-06":].values / 1e6)
```

When dealing with time series, you generally want to split across time. However, in some cases you may be able to split along other dimensions, which will give you a longer time period to train on. For example, if you have data about the financial health of 10,000 companies from 2001 to 2019, you might be able to split this data across the different companies. It's very likely that many of these companies will be strongly correlated, though (e.g., whole economic sectors may go up or down jointly), and if you have correlated companies across the training set and the test set, your test set will not be as useful, as its measure of the generalization error will be optimistically biased.

Next, let's use our `TimeSeriesDataset` class to create datasets for training, validation, and testing, and also create the corresponding data loaders. Since gradient descent expects the instances in the training set to be independent and identically distributed (IID), as we saw in Chapter 4, we must set `shuffle` to `True`—this will shuffle the windows, but not their contents:

```
window_length = 56
train_set = TimeSeriesDataset(rail_train, window_length)
train_loader = DataLoader(train_set, batch_size=32, shuffle=True)
valid_set = TimeSeriesDataset(rail_valid, window_length)
valid_loader = DataLoader(valid_set, batch_size=32)
test_set = TimeSeriesDataset(rail_test, window_length)
test_loader = DataLoader(test_set, batch_size=32)
```

And now we're ready to build and train any regression model we want!

Forecasting Using a Linear Model

Let's try a basic linear model first. We will use the Huber loss, which usually works better than minimizing the MAE directly, as discussed in Chapter 9:

```
import torch.nn as nn
import torchmetrics

torch.manual_seed(42)
model = nn.Sequential(nn.Flatten(), nn.Linear(window_length, 1)).to(device)
loss_fn = nn.HuberLoss()
optimizer = torch.optim.SGD(model.parameters(), lr=0.003, momentum=0.9)
metric = torchmetrics.MeanAbsoluteError().to(device)
[...]  # train the PyTorch model (e.g., using train() function from Chapter 10)
```

Note that we must use an `nn.Flatten` layer before the `nn.Linear` layer, because the inputs have a shape of [*batch size, window length, dimensionality*], but the `nn.Linear` layer expects inputs of shape [*batch size, features*]. If you train this model, you will see that it reaches a validation MAE of 37,726 (your mileage may vary). That's better than naive forecasting, but worse than the SARIMA model.[7]

Can we do better with an RNN? Well, let's see!

Forecasting Using a Simple RNN

Let's implement a simple RNN containing a single recurrent layer (see Figure 13-2) plus a final `nn.Linear` layer that will take the last hidden state as input and output the model's forecast:

```
class SimpleRnnModel(nn.Module):
    def __init__(self, input_size, hidden_size, output_size):
        super().__init__()
        self.hidden_size = hidden_size
        self.memory_cell = nn.Sequential(
            nn.Linear(input_size + hidden_size, hidden_size),
            nn.Tanh()
        )
        self.output = nn.Linear(hidden_size, output_size)

    def forward(self, X):
        batch_size, window_length, dimensionality = X.shape
        X_time_first = X.transpose(0, 1)
        H = torch.zeros(batch_size, self.hidden_size, device=X.device)
        for X_t in X_time_first:
            XH = torch.cat((X_t, H), dim=1)
            H = self.memory_cell(XH)
        return self.output(H)

torch.manual_seed(42)
univar_model = SimpleRnnModel(input_size=1, hidden_size=32, output_size=1)
```

Let's go through this code:

- The constructor takes three arguments: the input size, the hidden size, and the output size. In our case, the input size is set to 1 when we create the model (on the very last line) since we are dealing with a univariate time series. The hidden size is the number of recurrent neurons. We set it to 32 in this example, but this is a hyperparameter you can tune. The output size is 1 since we're only forecasting a single value.

7 Note that the validation period starts on the 1st of January 2019, so the first prediction is for the 26th of February 2019, eight weeks later. When we evaluated the baseline models, we used predictions starting on the 1st of March instead, but this should be close enough.

- The constructor first creates the memory cell, which will be used once per time step: it's a sequential module composed of an `nn.Linear` layer and the tanh activation function. You can use another activation function here, but it's common to use the tanh activation function because it tends to be more stable than other activation functions in RNNs.
- Next, we create an `nn.Linear` layer that will be used to take the last hidden state and produce the final output. This is needed because the hidden state has one dimension per recurrent neuron (32 in this example), while the target has just one dimension since we're dealing with a univariate time series and we're only trying to forecast a single future value. Moreover, the tanh activation function only outputs values between –1 and +1, while the values we need to forecast occasionally exceed +1.
- The `forward()` method will be passed input batches produced by our data loader, so each batch will have a shape of [*batch size, window length, dimensionality*], with *dimensionality* = 1.
- The hidden state `H` is initialized to zeros: for each input window, there's one zero per recurrent neuron, so the hidden state's shape is [*batch size, hidden_size*].
- Next, we iterate over each time step. For this, we must swap the first two dimensions of `X` using `permute(0, 1)`. As a result, the input tensor `X_t` at each time step has a shape of [*batch size, dimensionality*].
- At each time step, we want to feed both the current inputs `X_t` and the hidden state `H` to the memory cell. For this, we must first concatenate `X_t` and `H` along the first dimension, resulting in a tensor `XH` of shape [*batch size, input_size + hidden size*]. Then we can pass `XH` to the memory cell to get the new hidden state.
- After the loop, `H` represents the final hidden state. We pass it through the output `nn.Linear` layer, and we get our final prediction of shape [*batch size, output size*].

In short, this model initializes the hidden state to zeros, then it goes through each time step and applies the memory cell to both the current inputs and the last hidden state, which gives it the new hidden state. It repeats this process until the last time step, then it passes the last hidden state through a linear layer to get the actual forecasts. All of this is performed simultaneously for every sequence in the batch.

So that's our first recurrent model! It's a sequence-to-vector model. Since there's a single output neuron in this case, the output vector for each input sequence has a size of 1.

Now if you move this model to the GPU, then train and evaluate it just like the previous one, you will find that its validation MAE reaches 30,659. That's the best model we've trained so far, and it even beats the SARIMA model; we're doing pretty well!

We've only normalized the time series, without removing trend and seasonality, and yet the model still performs well. This is convenient, as it makes it possible to quickly search for promising models without worrying too much about preprocessing. However, to get the best performance, you may want to try making the time series more stationary, for example, using differencing.

PyTorch comes with an `nn.RNN` module that can greatly simplify the implementation of our `SimpleRnnModel`. The following implementation is (almost) equivalent to the previous one:

```
class SimpleRnnModel(nn.Module):
    def __init__(self, input_size, hidden_size, output_size):
        super().__init__()
        self.rnn = nn.RNN(input_size, hidden_size, batch_first=True)
        self.output = nn.Linear(hidden_size, output_size)

    def forward(self, X):
        outputs, last_state = self.rnn(X)
        return self.output(outputs[:, -1])
```

The code is much shorter than before. Let's go through it:

- In the constructor, we now create an `nn.RNN` module instead of building a memory cell. We specify the input size and the hidden size, just like we did earlier, and we also set `batch_first=True` because our input batches have the batch dimension first. If we didn't set `batch_first=True`, the `nn.RNN` module would assume that the time dimension comes first (i.e., it would expect the input batches to have a shape of [*window length*, *batch size*, *dimensionality*] instead of [*batch size*, *window length*, *dimensionality*]).
- The constructor also creates an output layer, exactly like in our previous implementation.
- In the `forward()` method, we pass the input batch directly to the `nn.RNN` module. This takes care of everything: internally, it initializes the hidden state with zeros, and it processes each time step using a simple memory cell based on a linear layer and an activation function (tanh by default), much like we did earlier.
- Note that the `nn.RNN` module returns two things:
  - `outputs` is a tensor containing the outputs of the top recurrent layer at every time step. Right now we have a single recurrent layer, but in the next section we will see that the `nn.RNN` module supports multiple recurrent layers. Since we are dealing with a simple RNN, the outputs are just the hidden states of the top recurrent layer at each time step. The `outputs` tensor has a shape of [*batch size*, *window length*, *hidden size*] (if we didn't set `batch_first=True`, then the first two dimensions would be swapped).

- `last_state` contains the hidden state of each recurrent layer after the very last time step. Its shape is [*number of layers, batch size, hidden size*]. In our case, there's a single recurrent layer, so the size of the first dimension is 1.

- In the end, we take the last output (which is also the last state of the top recurrent layer) and we pass it through our `nn.Linear` output layer.

If you train this model, you will get a similar result as before, but generally much faster because the `nn.RNN` module is well optimized. In particular, when using an Nvidia GPU, the `nn.RNN` module leverages the cuDNN library which provides highly optimized implementations of various neural net architectures, including several RNN architectures.

The `nn.RNN` module uses two bias parameters: one for the inputs, and the other for the hidden states. It just adds them up, so this really doesn't improve the model at all, but this extra parameter is required by the cuDNN library. This explains why you won't get exactly the same results as before.

Forecasting Using a Deep RNN

It is quite common to stack multiple layers of cells, as shown in Figure 13-10. This gives you a *deep RNN*.

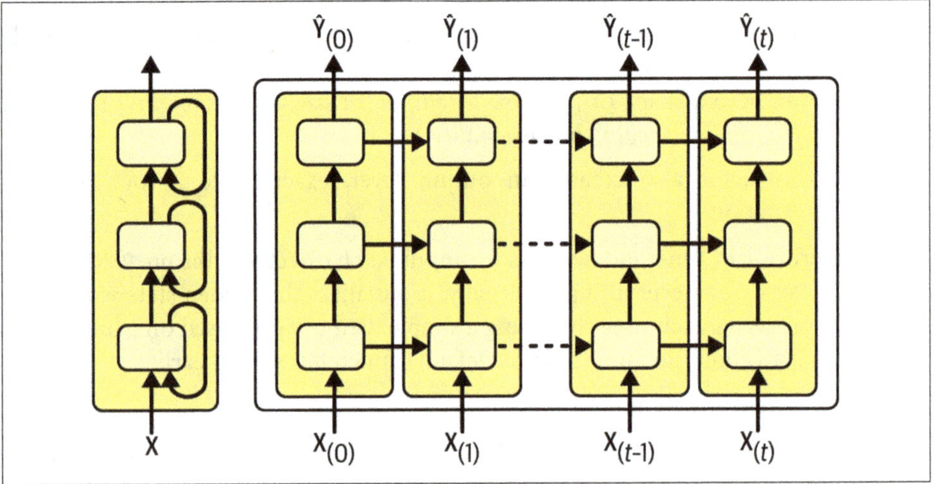

Figure 13-10. A deep RNN (left) unrolled through time (right)

Implementing a deep RNN with PyTorch is straightforward: just set the `num_layers` argument to the desired number of recurrent layers when creating the `nn.RNN` module. For example, if you set `num_layers=3` when creating the `nn.RNN` module in the previous model's constructor, you get a three-layer RNN (the rest of the code remains unchanged):

```
self.rnn = nn.RNN(input_size, hidden_size, num_layers=3, batch_first=True)
```

If you train and evaluate this model, you will find that it reaches an MAE of 29,273. That's our best model so far!

Forecasting Multivariate Time Series

An important quality of neural networks is their flexibility: in particular, they can deal with multivariate time series with almost no change to their architecture. For example, let's try to forecast the rail time series using both the rail and bus data as input. In fact, let's also throw in the day type! Since we can always know in advance whether tomorrow is going to be a weekday, a weekend, or a holiday, we can shift the day type series one day into the future, so that the model is given tomorrow's day type as input. For simplicity, we'll do this processing using Pandas:

```
df_mulvar = df[["rail", "bus"]] / 1e6  # use both rail & bus series as input
df_mulvar["next_day_type"] = df["day_type"].shift(-1)  # we know tomorrow's type
df_mulvar = pd.get_dummies(df_mulvar, dtype=float)  # one-hot encode day type
```

Now `df_mulvar` is a DataFrame with five columns: the rail and bus data, plus three columns containing the one-hot encoding of the next day's type (recall that there are three possible day types, `W`, `A`, and `U`). Next, we can proceed much like we did earlier. First we split the data into three periods, scale it down by a factor of one million, and convert it to tensors:

```
mulvar_train = torch.FloatTensor(df_mulvar["2016-01":"2018-12"].values / 1e6)
mulvar_valid = torch.FloatTensor(df_mulvar["2019-01":"2019-05"].values / 1e6)
mulvar_test = torch.FloatTensor(df_mulvar["2019-06":].values / 1e6)
```

Then we need to create the PyTorch datasets. If we used the `TimeSeriesDataset` for this, the targets would include the next day's rail and bus ridership, as well as the one-hot encoding of the following day type. Since we only want to predict the rail ridership for now, we must tweak the `TimeSeriesDataset` to keep only the first value in the target, which is the rail ridership. One way to do this is to create a new `MulvarTimeSeriesDataset` class that extends the `TimeSeriesDataset` class and tweaks the `__getitem__()` method to filter the target:

```
class MulvarTimeSeriesDataset(TimeSeriesDataset):
    def __getitem__(self, idx):
        window, target = super().__getitem__(idx)
        return window, target[:1]
```

Next, we can create the datasets and the data loaders, much like we did earlier:

```
mulvar_train_set = MulvarTimeSeriesDataset(mulvar_train, window_length)
mulvar_train_loader = DataLoader(mulvar_train_set, batch_size=32, shuffle=True)
[...] # create the datasets and data loaders for the validation and test sets
```

If you look at the batches produced by the data loaders, you will find that the input shape is [32, 56, 5], and the target shape is [32, 1]. Perfect!

So we can finally create the RNN:

```
torch.manual_seed(42)
mulvar_model = SimpleRnnModel(input_size=5, hidden_size=32, output_size=1)
mulvar_model = mulvar_model.to(device)
```

Notice that this model is identical to the `univar_model` RNN we built earlier, except `input_size=5`: at each time step, the model now receives five inputs instead of one. This model actually reaches a validation MAE of 23,227. Now we're making big progress!

In fact, it's not too hard to make the RNN forecast both the rail and bus ridership. You just need to return `target[:2]` instead of `target[:1]` in the `MulvarTimeSeriesDataset` class, and set `output_size=2` when creating the `SimpleRnnModel`, that's all there is to it!

As we discussed in Chapter 9, using a single model for multiple related tasks often results in better performance than using a separate model for each task, since features learned for one task may be useful for the other tasks, and also because having to perform well across multiple tasks prevents the model from overfitting (it's a form of regularization). However, it depends on the task, and in this particular case the multitask RNN that forecasts both the bus and the rail ridership doesn't perform quite as well as dedicated models that forecast one or the other (using all five columns as input). Still, it reaches a validation MAE of 26,441 for rail and 26,178 for bus, which is still pretty good.

Forecasting Several Time Steps Ahead

So far we have only predicted the value at the next time step, but we could just as easily have predicted the value several steps ahead by changing the targets appropriately (e.g., to predict the ridership 2 weeks from now, we could just change the targets to be the value 14 days ahead instead of 1 day ahead). But what if we want to predict the next 14 values with a single model?

The first option is to take the `univar_model` RNN we trained earlier for the rail time series, make it predict the next value, and add that value to the inputs, acting as if the predicted value had actually occurred. We then use the model again to predict the following value, and so on, as in the following code:

```python
n_steps = 14
univar_model.eval()
with torch.no_grad():
    X = rail_valid[:window_length].unsqueeze(dim=0).to(device)
    for step_ahead in range(n_steps):
        y_pred_one = univar_model(X)
        X = torch.cat([X, y_pred_one.unsqueeze(dim=0)], dim=1)

    Y_pred = X[0, -n_steps:, 0]
```

In this code, we take the rail ridership of the first 56 days of the validation period, we add a batch dimension of size 1 using the `unsqueeze()` method (since our `univar_model` expects 3D inputs), then we move the tensor to the GPU. Now the shape of `X` is [1, 56, 1]. Then we repeatedly use the model to forecast the next value, and we append each forecast to the input series, along the time axis (`dim=1`). Since each prediction has a shape of [1, 1], we must use `unsqueeze()` again to add a batch dimension of size 1 before we can concatenate it to `X`. In the end, `X` has a shape of [1, 56 + 14, 1], and our final forecasts are the last 14 values of `X`. The resulting forecasts are plotted in Figure 13-11.

If the model makes an error at one time step, then the forecasts for the following time steps are impacted as well: the errors tend to accumulate. So, it's preferable to use this technique only for a small number of steps.

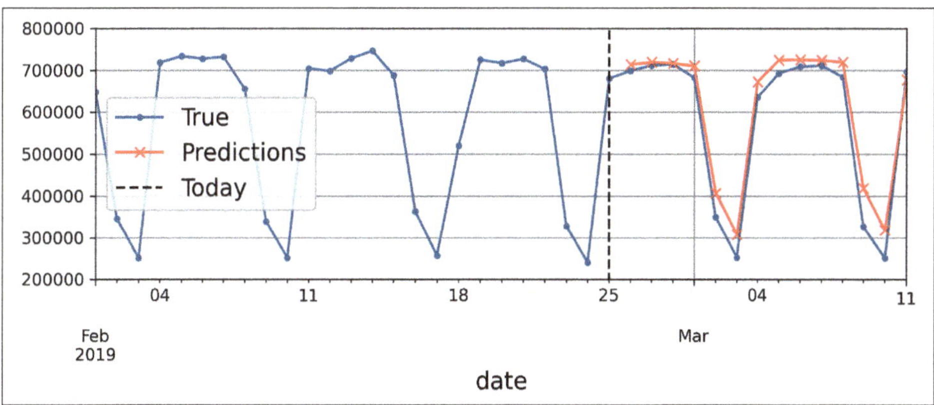

Figure 13-11. Forecasting 14 steps ahead, 1 step at a time

The second option is to train an RNN to predict the next 14 values in one shot. We can still use a sequence-to-vector model, but it will output 14 values instead of 1. However, we first need to change the targets to be vectors containing the next 14 values. For this, we can create the following class:

```python
class ForecastAheadDataset(TimeSeriesDataset):
    def __len__(self):
        return len(self.series) - self.window_length - 14 + 1

    def __getitem__(self, idx):
        end = idx + self.window_length  # 1st index after window
        window = self.series[idx : end]
        target = self.series[end : end + 14, 0]  # 0 = rail ridership
        return window, target
```

I've hardcoded the number 14, but in a real project you should make this configurable (e.g., just like the `window_length`).

This class inherits from the `TimeSeriesDataset` class and tweaks its `__len__()` and `__getitem__()` methods. The target is now a tensor containing the next 14 rail ridership values, rather than just the next value. We can once again create a training set, a validation set, and a test set, based on the multivariate time series we built earlier:

```python
ahead_train_set = ForecastAheadDataset(mulvar_train, window_length)
ahead_train_loader = DataLoader(ahead_train_set, batch_size=32, shuffle=True)
[...]  # create the datasets and data loaders for the validation and test sets
```

Lastly, we can create a simple RNN, just like the `mulvar_model`, but with `output_size=14`:

```python
torch.manual_seed(42)
ahead_model = SimpleRnnModel(input_size=5, hidden_size=32, output_size=14)
ahead_model = ahead_model.to(device)
```

After training this model, you can predict the next 14 values at once, like this:

```python
ahead_model.eval()
with torch.no_grad():
    window = mulvar_valid[:window_length]  # shape [56, 5]
    X = window.unsqueeze(dim=0)            # shape [1, 56, 5]
    Y_pred = ahead_model(X.to(device))     # shape [1, 14]
```

This approach works quite well. Its forecasts for the next day are obviously better than its forecasts for 14 days into the future, but it doesn't accumulate errors like the previous approach did. Now let's see whether a sequence-to-sequence model can do even better.

You can combine both approaches to forecast many steps ahead: use a model that forecasts the next 14 days in one shot, then append the forecasts to the inputs and run the model again to get forecasts for the following 14 days, and so on.[8]

Forecasting Using a Sequence-to-Sequence Model

Instead of training the model to forecast the next 14 values only at the very last time step, we can train it to forecast the next 14 values at each and every time step. To be clear, at time step 0 the model will output a vector containing the forecasts for time steps 1 to 14, then at time step 1 the model will forecast time steps 2 to 15, and so on. In other words, the targets are sequences of consecutive windows, shifted by one time step at each time step. The target for each input window is not a vector anymore, but a sequence of the same length as the inputs, containing a 14-dimensional vector at each step. Given an input batch of shape [*batch size*, *window length*, *input size*], the output will have a shape of [*batch size*, *window length*, *output_size*]. This is no longer a sequence-to-vector RNN, it's a sequence-to-sequence (or *seq2seq*) RNN.

It may be surprising that the targets contain values that appear in the inputs (except for the last time step). Isn't that cheating? Fortunately, not at all: at each time step, an RNN only knows about past time steps; it cannot look ahead. It is said to be a *causal* model.

You may be wondering why we would want to train a seq2seq model when we're really only interested in forecasting future values, which are output by our model at the very last time step. And you're right: after training, you can actually ignore all outputs except for the very last time step. The main advantage of this technique is that the loss will contain a term for the output of the RNN at each and every time step, not just for the output at the last time step. This means there will be many more error gradients flowing through the model, and they won't have to flow through time as much since they will come from the output of each time step, not just the last one. This can both stabilize training and speed up convergence. Moreover, since the model must make predictions at each time step, it will see input sequences of varying lengths, which can reduce the risk of overfitting the model to the specific window length used during training. Well, at least that's the hope! Let's give this technique a try on the rail ridership time series. As usual, we first need to prepare the dataset:

8 We cannot use the `ahead_model` for this because it needs both the rail and bus ridership as input, but it only forecasts the rail ridership.

```python
class Seq2SeqDataset(ForecastAheadDataset):
    def __getitem__(self, idx):
        end = idx + self.window_length  # 1st index after window
        window = self.series[idx : end]
        target_period = self.series[idx + 1 : end + 14, 0]
        target = target_period.unfold(dimension=0, size=14, step=1)
        return window, target
```

Our new `Seq2SeqDataset` class inherits from the `ForecastAheadDataset` class and overrides the `__getitem__()` method: the input window is defined just like before, but the target is now a sequence of consecutive windows, shifted by one time step at each time step. The `unfold()` method is where the magic happens: it takes a tensor and produces sliding blocks from it. For this, it repeatedly slides along the given dimension by the given number of steps and extracts a block of the given size. For example:

```python
>>> torch.tensor([0, 1, 2, 3, 4, 5]).unfold(dimension=0, size=4, step=1)
tensor([[0, 1, 2, 3],
        [1, 2, 3, 4],
        [2, 3, 4, 5]])
```

Once again we must create a training set, a validation set, and a test set, as well as the corresponding data loaders:

```python
seq_train_set = Seq2SeqDataset(mulvar_train, window_length)
seq_train_loader = DataLoader(seq_train_set, batch_size=32, shuffle=True)
[...]  # create the datasets and data loaders for the validation and test sets
```

And lastly, we can build the sequence-to-sequence model:

```python
class Seq2SeqRnnModel(SimpleRnnModel):
    def forward(self, X):
        outputs, last_state = self.rnn(X)
        return self.output(outputs)

torch.manual_seed(42)
seq_model = Seq2SeqRnnModel(input_size=5, hidden_size=32, output_size=14)
seq_model = seq_model.to(device)
```

We inherit from the `SimpleRnnModel` class, and we override the `forward()` method. Instead of applying the linear `self.output` layer only to the outputs of the last time step, as we did before, we now apply it to the outputs of every time step. It may surprise you that this works at all. So far, we have only applied `nn.Linear` layers to 2D inputs of shape [*batch size*, *features*], but here the `outputs` tensor has a shape of [*batch size*, *window length*, *hidden size*]: it's 3D, not 2D! Luckily, this works fine as the `nn.Linear` layer will automatically be applied to each time step, so the model's predictions will have a shape of [*batch size*, *window length*, *output size*]: just what we need.

Under the hood, the `nn.Linear` layer relies on `torch.matmul()` for matrix multiplication. This function efficiently supports multiplying arrays of more than two dimensions. For example, you can multiply an array of shape [2, 3, 5, 7] with an array of shape [2, 3, 7, 11]. Indeed, these two arrays can both be seen as 2 × 3 grids of matrices, and `torch.matmul()` simply multiplies the corresponding matrices in both grids. Since multiplying a 5 × 7 matrix with a 7 × 11 matrix produces a 5 × 11 matrix, the final result is a 2 × 3 grid of 5 × 11 matrices, represented as a tensor of shape [2, 3, 5, 11]. Broadcasting is also supported; for example, you can multiply an array of shape [10, 56, 32] with an array of shape [32, 14]: each of the ten 56 × 32 matrices in the first array will be multiplied by the same 32 × 14 matrix in the second array, and you will get a tensor of shape [10, 56, 14]. That's what happens when you pass a 3D input to an `nn.Linear` layer.

Another way to get the exact same result is to replace the `nn.Linear` output layer with an `nn.Conv1d` layer using a kernel size of one (i.e., `Conv1d(32, 14, kernel_size=1)`). However, you would have to swap the last two dimensions of both the inputs and the outputs, treating the time dimension as a spatial dimension.

The training code is the same as usual. During training, all the model's outputs are used, but after training, only the outputs of the very last time step matter, and the rest can be ignored (as mentioned earlier). For example, we can forecast the rail ridership for the next 14 days like this:

```
seq_model.eval()
with torch.no_grad():
    some_window = mulvar_valid[:window_length]  # shape [56, 5]
    X = some_window.unsqueeze(dim=0)            # shape [1, 56, 5]
    Y_preds = seq_model(X.to(device))           # shape [1, 56, 14]
    Y_pred = Y_preds[:, -1]                     # shape [1, 14]
```

If you evaluate this model's forecasts for $t + 1$, you will find a validation MAE of 23,350, which is very good. Of course, the model is not as accurate for more distant forecasts. For example, the MAE for $t + 14$ is 35,315.

Simple RNNs can be quite good at forecasting time series or handling other kinds of sequences, but they do not perform as well on long time series or sequences. Let's discuss why and see what we can do about it.

Handling Long Sequences

To train an RNN on long sequences, we must run it over many time steps, making the unrolled RNN a very deep network. Just like any deep neural network, it may suffer from the unstable gradients problem, discussed in Chapter 11: it may take forever to train, or training may be unstable. Moreover, when an RNN processes a long sequence, it will gradually forget the first inputs in the sequence. Let's look at both these problems, starting with the unstable gradients problem.

Fighting the Unstable Gradients Problem

Many of the tricks we used in deep nets to alleviate the unstable gradients problem can also be used for RNNs: good parameter initialization, faster optimizers, dropout, and so on. However, nonsaturating activation functions (e.g., ReLU) may not help as much here. In fact, they may actually lead the RNN to be even more unstable during training. Why? Well, suppose gradient descent updates the weights in a way that increases the outputs slightly at the first time step. Because the same weights are used at every time step, the outputs at the second time step may also be slightly increased, and those at the third, and so on until the outputs explode—and a nonsaturating activation function does not prevent that.

You can reduce this risk by using a smaller learning rate, or you can use a saturating activation function like the hyperbolic tangent (this explains why it's the default).

In much the same way, the gradients themselves can explode. If you notice that training is unstable, you may want to monitor the size of the gradients and perhaps use gradient clipping.

Moreover, batch normalization cannot be used as efficiently with RNNs as with deep feedforward nets. In fact, you cannot use it between time steps, only between recurrent layers. To be more precise, it is technically possible to add a BN layer to a memory cell so that it will be applied at each time step (both on the inputs for that time step and on the hidden state from the previous step). However, this implies that the same BN layer will be used at each time step, with the same parameters, regardless of the actual scale and offset of the inputs and hidden state. In practice, this does not yield good results, as was demonstrated by César Laurent et al. in a 2015 paper (*https://homl.info/rnnbn*).[9] The authors found that BN was slightly beneficial only when it was applied to the layer's inputs, not to the hidden states. In other words, it was slightly better than nothing when applied between recurrent layers (i.e., vertically in Figure 13-10), but not within recurrent layers (i.e., horizontally).

Layer norm (introduced in Chapter 11) tends to work a bit better than BN within recurrent layers. It is usually applied just before the activation function, at each time step. Sadly, PyTorch's `nn.RNN` module does not support LN, so you have to implement the RNN's loop manually (as we did earlier), and apply the `nn.LayerNorm` module at each iteration. This is not too hard, but you do lose the simplicity and speed of the `nn.RNN` module. For example, you can take the first version of our `SimpleRnnModel`

9 César Laurent et al., "Batch Normalized Recurrent Neural Networks", *Proceedings of the IEEE International Conference on Acoustics, Speech, and Signal Processing* (2016): 2657–2661.

class and add an `nn.LayerNorm` module to the memory cell, just before the tanh activation function:

```
self.memory_cell = nn.Sequential(
    nn.Linear(input_size + hidden_size, hidden_size),
    nn.LayerNorm(hidden_size),
    nn.Tanh()
)
```

Layer norm does not always help; you just have to try it. In general, it works better in *gated RNNs* such as LSTM and GRU (discussed shortly). It is also more likely to help when the time series is preprocessed to remove any seasonality or trend.

Similarly, if you wish to apply dropout between each time step, you must write a custom RNN since the `nn.RNN` module does not support that. However, it does support adding a dropout layer after every recurrent layer: simply set the `dropout` hyperparameter to the desired dropout rate (it defaults to zero).

With these techniques, you can alleviate the unstable gradients problem and train an RNN much more efficiently. Now let's look at how to deal with the short-term memory problem.

When forecasting time series, it is often useful to have some error bars along with your predictions. For this, one approach is to use MC dropout (introduced in Chapter 11).

Tackling the Short-Term Memory Problem

Due to the transformations that the data goes through when traversing an RNN, some information is lost at each time step. After a while, the RNN's state contains virtually no trace of the first inputs. This can be a showstopper. Imagine Dory the fish[10] trying to translate a long sentence; by the time she's finished reading it, she has no clue how it started. To tackle this problem, various types of cells with long-term memory have been introduced. They have proven so successful that the basic cells are not used much anymore. Let's first look at the most popular of these long-term memory cells: the LSTM cell.

10 A character from the animated movies *Finding Nemo* and *Finding Dory* who has short-term memory loss.

LSTM cells

The *long short-term memory* (LSTM) cell was proposed in 1997 (*https://homl.info/93*)[11] by Sepp Hochreiter and Jürgen Schmidhuber and gradually improved over the years by several researchers, such as Alex Graves (*https://homl.info/graves*), Haşim Sak (*https://homl.info/94*),[12] and Wojciech Zaremba (*https://homl.info/95*).[13] You can simply use the `nn.LSTM` module instead of the `nn.RNN` module; it's a drop-in replacement, and it usually performs much better: training converges faster, and the model detects longer-term patterns in the data.

So how does this magic work? Well, the LSTM architecture is shown in Figure 13-12. If you don't look at what's inside the box, the LSTM cell looks exactly like a regular cell, except that its state is split into two vectors: $\mathbf{h}_{(t)}$ and $\mathbf{c}_{(t)}$ ("c" stands for "cell"). You can think of $\mathbf{h}_{(t)}$ as the short-term state and $\mathbf{c}_{(t)}$ as the long-term state.

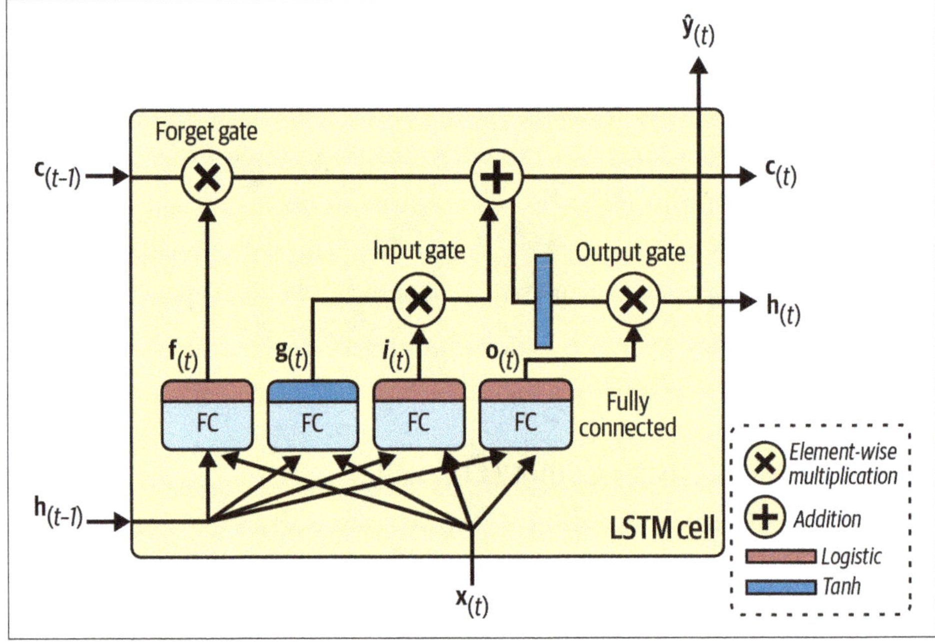

Figure 13-12. An LSTM cell

11 Sepp Hochreiter and Jürgen Schmidhuber, "Long Short-Term Memory", *Neural Computation* 9, no. 8 (1997): 1735–1780.

12 Haşim Sak et al., "Long Short-Term Memory Based Recurrent Neural Network Architectures for Large Vocabulary Speech Recognition", arXiv preprint arXiv:1402.1128 (2014).

13 Wojciech Zaremba et al., "Recurrent Neural Network Regularization", arXiv preprint arXiv:1409.2329 (2014).

Now let's open the box! The key idea is that the network can learn what to store in the long-term state, what to throw away, and what to read from it. As the long-term state $\mathbf{c}_{(t-1)}$ traverses the network from left to right, you can see that it first goes through a *forget gate*, dropping some memories, and then it adds some new memories via the addition operation (which adds the memories that were selected by an *input gate*). The result $\mathbf{c}_{(t)}$ is sent straight out without any further transformation. So at each time step, some memories are dropped and some memories are added. Moreover, after the addition operation, the long-term state is copied and passed through the tanh function, and the result is filtered by the *output gate*. This produces the short-term state $\mathbf{h}_{(t)}$ (which is equal to the cell's output for this time step, $\mathbf{y}_{(t)}$). Now let's look at where new memories come from and how the gates work.

First, the current input vector $\mathbf{x}_{(t)}$ and the previous short-term state $\mathbf{h}_{(t-1)}$ are fed to four different fully connected layers. They all serve a different purpose:

- The main layer is the one that outputs $\mathbf{g}_{(t)}$. It has the usual role of analyzing the current inputs $\mathbf{x}_{(t)}$ and the previous (short-term) state $\mathbf{h}_{(t-1)}$. In a simple RNN cell, there is nothing other than this layer, and its output goes straight out to $\mathbf{y}_{(t)}$ and $\mathbf{h}_{(t)}$. But in an LSTM cell, this layer's output does not go straight out; instead its most important parts are stored in the long-term state (and the rest is dropped).
- The three other layers are *gate controllers*. Since they use the logistic activation function, the outputs range from 0 to 1. As you can see, the gate controllers' outputs are fed to element-wise multiplication operations: if they output 0s they close the gate, and if they output 1s they open it. Specifically:
  - The *forget gate* (controlled by $\mathbf{f}_{(t)}$) controls which parts of the long-term state should be erased.
  - The *input gate* (controlled by $\mathbf{i}_{(t)}$) controls which parts of $\mathbf{g}_{(t)}$ should be added to the long-term state.
  - Finally, the *output gate* (controlled by $\mathbf{o}_{(t)}$) controls which parts of the long-term state should be read and output at this time step, both to $\mathbf{h}_{(t)}$ and to $\mathbf{y}_{(t)}$.

In short, an LSTM cell can learn to recognize an important input (that's the role of the input gate), store it in the long-term state, preserve it for as long as it is needed (that's the role of the forget gate), and extract it whenever it is needed (that's the role of the output gate), all while being fully differentiable. This explains why these cells have been amazingly successful at capturing long-term patterns in time series, long texts, audio recordings, and more.

Equation 13-4 summarizes how to compute the cell's long-term state, its short-term state, and its output at each time step for a single instance (the equations for a whole mini-batch are very similar).

Equation 13-4. LSTM computations

$$
\begin{aligned}
\mathbf{i}_{(t)} &= \sigma\left(\mathbf{W}_{xi}{}^{\mathsf{T}}\mathbf{x}_{(t)} + \mathbf{W}_{hi}{}^{\mathsf{T}}\mathbf{h}_{(t-1)} + \mathbf{b}_i\right)\\
\mathbf{f}_{(t)} &= \sigma\left(\mathbf{W}_{xf}{}^{\mathsf{T}}\mathbf{x}_{(t)} + \mathbf{W}_{hf}{}^{\mathsf{T}}\mathbf{h}_{(t-1)} + \mathbf{b}_f\right)\\
\mathbf{o}_{(t)} &= \sigma\left(\mathbf{W}_{xo}{}^{\mathsf{T}}\mathbf{x}_{(t)} + \mathbf{W}_{ho}{}^{\mathsf{T}}\mathbf{h}_{(t-1)} + \mathbf{b}_o\right)\\
\mathbf{g}_{(t)} &= \tanh\left(\mathbf{W}_{xg}{}^{\mathsf{T}}\mathbf{x}_{(t)} + \mathbf{W}_{hg}{}^{\mathsf{T}}\mathbf{h}_{(t-1)} + \mathbf{b}_g\right)\\
\mathbf{c}_{(t)} &= \mathbf{f}_{(t)} \otimes \mathbf{c}_{(t-1)} + \mathbf{i}_{(t)} \otimes \mathbf{g}_{(t)}\\
\mathbf{y}_{(t)} &= \mathbf{h}_{(t)} = \mathbf{o}_{(t)} \otimes \tanh\left(\mathbf{c}_{(t)}\right)
\end{aligned}
$$

In this equation:

- $\mathbf{W}_{xi}$, $\mathbf{W}_{xf}$, $\mathbf{W}_{xo}$, and $\mathbf{W}_{xg}$ are the weight matrices of each of the four layers for their connection to the input vector $\mathbf{x}_{(t)}$.
- $\mathbf{W}_{hi}$, $\mathbf{W}_{hf}$, $\mathbf{W}_{ho}$, and $\mathbf{W}_{hg}$ are the weight matrices of each of the four layers for their connection to the previous short-term state $\mathbf{h}_{(t-1)}$.
- $\mathbf{b}_i$, $\mathbf{b}_f$, $\mathbf{b}_o$, and $\mathbf{b}_g$ are the bias terms for each of the four layers.

Try replacing `nn.RNN` with `nn.LSTM` in the previous models and see what performance you can reach on the ridership dataset (a bit of hyperparameter tuning may be required).

Just like for simple RNNs, if you want to add layer normalization or dropout at each time step, you must implement the recurrent loop manually. One option is to use Equation 13-4, but a simpler option is to use the `nn.LSTMCell` module, which runs a single time step. For example, here is a simple implementation:

```
class LstmModel(nn.Module):
    def __init__(self, input_size, hidden_size, output_size):
        super().__init__()
        self.hidden_size = hidden_size
        self.memory_cell = nn.LSTMCell(input_size, hidden_size)
        self.output = nn.Linear(hidden_size, output_size)

    def forward(self, X):
        batch_size, window_length, dimensionality = X.shape
        X_time_first = X.transpose(0, 1)
```

```
H = torch.zeros(batch_size, self.hidden_size, device=X.device)
C = torch.zeros(batch_size, self.hidden_size, device=X.device)
for X_t in X_time_first:
    H, C = self.memory_cell(X_t, (H, C))
return self.output(H)
```

This is very similar to the first implementation of our `SimpleRnnModel`, but we are now using an `nn.LSTMCell` at each time step, and the hidden state is now split in two parts: the short-term `H` and the long-term `C`.

There are several variants of the LSTM cell. One particularly popular variant is the GRU cell, which we will look at now.

GRU cells

The *gated recurrent unit* (GRU) cell (see Figure 13-13) was proposed by Kyunghyun Cho et al. in a 2014 paper (*https://homl.info/97*)[14] that also introduced the encoder-decoder network we discussed earlier.

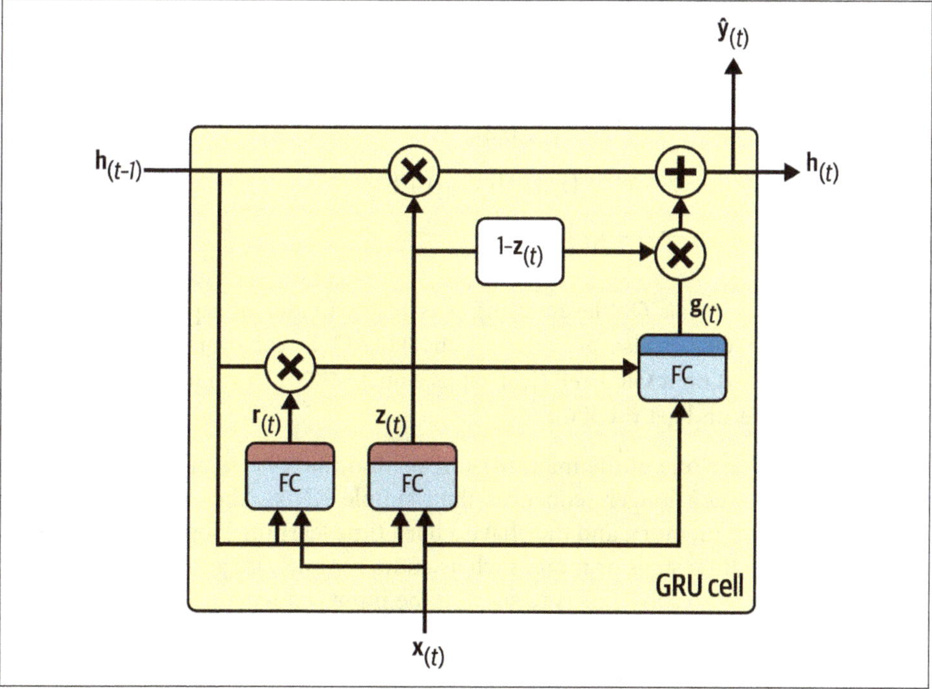

Figure 13-13. GRU cell

14 Kyunghyun Cho et al., "Learning Phrase Representations Using RNN Encoder-Decoder for Statistical Machine Translation", *Proceedings of the 2014 Conference on Empirical Methods in Natural Language Processing* (2014): 1724–1734.

The GRU cell is a simplified version of the LSTM cell, and it often performs just as well.[15] These are the main simplifications:

- Both state vectors are merged into a single vector $\mathbf{h}_{(t)}$.
- A single gate controller $\mathbf{z}_{(t)}$ controls both the forget gate and the input gate. If the gate controller outputs a 1, the forget gate is open (= 1) and the input gate is closed (1 – 1 = 0). If it outputs a 0, the opposite happens. In other words, whenever a memory must be stored, the location where it will be stored is erased first.
- There is no output gate; the full state vector is output at every time step. However, there is a new gate controller $\mathbf{r}_{(t)}$ that controls which part of the previous state will be shown to the main layer ($\mathbf{g}_{(t)}$).

Equation 13-5 summarizes how to compute the cell's state at each time step for a single instance.

Equation 13-5. GRU computations

$$
\begin{aligned}
\mathbf{z}_{(t)} &= \sigma\left(\mathbf{W}_{xz}{}^{\mathsf{T}}\mathbf{x}_{(t)} + \mathbf{W}_{hz}{}^{\mathsf{T}}\mathbf{h}_{(t-1)} + \mathbf{b}_z\right) \\
\mathbf{r}_{(t)} &= \sigma\left(\mathbf{W}_{xr}{}^{\mathsf{T}}\mathbf{x}_{(t)} + \mathbf{W}_{hr}{}^{\mathsf{T}}\mathbf{h}_{(t-1)} + \mathbf{b}_r\right) \\
\mathbf{g}_{(t)} &= \tanh\left(\mathbf{W}_{xg}{}^{\mathsf{T}}\mathbf{x}_{(t)} + \mathbf{W}_{hg}{}^{\mathsf{T}}\left(r_{(t)} \otimes \mathbf{h}_{(t-1)}\right) + \mathbf{b}_g\right) \\
\mathbf{h}_{(t)} &= \mathbf{z}_{(t)} \otimes \mathbf{h}_{(t-1)} + \left(1 - \mathbf{z}_{(t)}\right) \otimes \mathbf{g}_{(t)}
\end{aligned}
$$

PyTorch provides an `nn.GRU` layer; using it is just a matter of replacing `nn.RNN` or `nn.LSTM` with `nn.GRU`. It also provides an `nn.GRUCell` in case you want to create a custom RNN based on a GRU cell (just replace `nn.LSTMCell` with `nn.GRUCell` in the previous example, and get rid of `C`).

LSTM and GRU are one of the main reasons behind the success of RNNs. Yet while they can tackle much longer sequences than simple RNNs, they still have a fairly limited short-term memory, and they have a hard time learning long-term patterns in sequences of 100 time steps or more, such as audio samples, long time series, or long sentences. One way to solve this is to shorten the input sequences, for example, using 1D convolutional layers.

15 See Klaus Greff et al., "LSTM: A Search Space Odyssey" (*https://homl.info/98*), *IEEE Transactions on Neural Networks and Learning Systems* 28, no. 10 (2017): 2222–2232. This paper seems to show that all LSTM variants perform roughly the same.

Using 1D convolutional layers to process sequences

In Chapter 12, we saw that a 2D convolutional layer works by sliding several fairly small kernels (or filters) across an image, producing multiple 2D feature maps (one per kernel). Similarly, a 1D convolutional layer slides several kernels across a sequence, producing a 1D feature map per kernel. Each kernel will learn to detect a single very short sequential pattern (no longer than the kernel size). If you use 10 kernels, then the layer's output will be composed of 10 1D sequences (all of the same length), or equivalently you can view this output as a single 10D sequence. This means that you can build a neural network composed of a mix of recurrent layers and 1D convolutional layers (or even 1D pooling layers). However, as mentioned earlier, you must swap the last two dimensions of the `nn.Conv1d` layer's inputs and outputs, since the `nn.Conv1d` layer expects inputs of shape [*batch size*, *input features*, *sequence length*], and produces outputs of shape [*batch size*, *output features*, *sequence length*].

If you use a 1D convolutional layer with a stride of 1 and `"same"` padding, then the output sequence will have the same length as the input sequence. But if you use `"valid"` padding or a stride greater than 1, then the output sequence will be shorter than the input sequence, so make sure you adjust the targets accordingly.

For example, the following model is composed of a 1D convolutional layer, followed by a GRU layer, and lastly a linear output layer, all of which input and output batches of sequences (i.e., 3D tensors). The `nn.Conv1d` layer downsamples the input sequences by a factor of 2, using a stride of 2. The kernel size is as large as the stride (larger, in fact), so all inputs will be used to compute the layer's output, and therefore the model can learn to preserve the most useful information, dropping only the unimportant details. In the `forward()` method, we just chain the layers, but we permute the last two dimensions before and after the `nn.Conv1d` layer, and we ignore the hidden states returned by the `nn.GRU` layer:

```
class DownsamplingModel(nn.Module):
    def __init__(self, input_size, hidden_size, output_size):
        super().__init__()
        self.conv = nn.Conv1d(input_size, hidden_size, kernel_size=4, stride=2)
        self.gru = nn.GRU(hidden_size, hidden_size, batch_first=True)
        self.linear = nn.Linear(hidden_size, output_size)

    def forward(self, X):
        Z = X.permute(0, 2, 1)  # treat time as a spatial dimension
        Z = self.conv(Z)
        Z = Z.permute(0, 2, 1)  # swap back time & features dimensions
        Z = torch.relu(Z)
        Z, _states = self.gru(Z)
        return self.linear(Z)
```

```python
torch.manual_seed(42)
dseq_model = DownsamplingModel(input_size=5, hidden_size=32, output_size=14)
dseq_model = dseq_model.to(device)
```

By shortening the time series, the convolutional layer helps the GRU layer detect longer patterns, so we can afford to double the window length to 112 days. Note that we must also crop off the first three time steps from the targets: indeed, the kernel's size is 4, so the first output of the convolutional layer will be based on the input time steps 0 to 3, therefore the first forecasts must be for time steps 4 to 17 (instead of time steps 1 to 14). Moreover, we must downsample the targets by a factor of 2 because of the stride. For all this, we need a new `Dataset` class, so let's create a subclass of the `Seq2SeqDataset` class:

```python
class DownsampledDataset(Seq2SeqDataset):
    def __getitem__(self, idx):
        window, target = super().__getitem__(idx)
        return window, target[3::2]  # crop the first 3 targets and downsample

window_length = 112
dseq_train_set = DownsampledDataset(rail_train, window_length)
dseq_train_loader = DataLoader(dseq_train_set, batch_size=32, shuffle=True)
[...]  # create the datasets and data loaders for the validation and test sets
```

And now the model can be trained as usual. We've successfully mixed convolutional layers and recurrent layers. But what if we used only 1D convolutional layers and dropped the recurrent layers entirely?

WaveNet

In a 2016 paper (*https://homl.info/wavenet*),[16] Aaron van den Oord and other DeepMind researchers introduced a novel architecture called *WaveNet*. They stacked 1D convolutional layers, doubling the dilation rate (how spread apart each neuron's inputs are) at every layer: the first convolutional layer gets a glimpse of just two time steps at a time, while the next one sees four time steps (its receptive field is four time steps long), the next one sees eight time steps, and so on (see Figure 13-14). This way, the lower layers learn short-term patterns, while the higher layers learn long-term patterns. Thanks to the doubling dilation rate, the network can process extremely large sequences very efficiently.

16 Aaron van den Oord et al., "WaveNet: A Generative Model for Raw Audio", arXiv preprint arXiv:1609.03499 (2016).

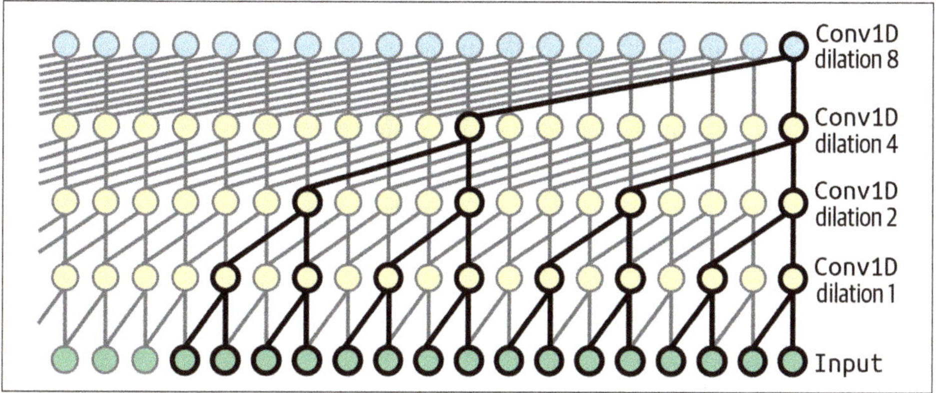

Figure 13-14. WaveNet architecture

The authors of the paper actually stacked 10 convolutional layers with dilation rates of 1, 2, 4, 8, …, 256, 512, then they stacked another group of 10 identical layers (also with dilation rates 1, 2, 4, 8, …, 256, 512), then again another identical group of 10 layers. They justified this architecture by pointing out that a single stack of 10 convolutional layers with these dilation rates will act like a super-efficient convolutional layer with a kernel of size 1,024 (except way faster, more powerful, and using significantly fewer parameters). They also left-padded the input sequences with a number of zeros equal to the dilation rate before every layer to preserve the same sequence length throughout the network. Padding on the left rather than on both sides is important, as it ensures that the convolutional layer does not peek into the future when making predictions. This makes it a causal model.

Let's implement a simplified WaveNet to tackle the same sequences as earlier.[17] We will start by creating a custom `CausalConv1d` module that acts just like an `nn.Conv1d` module, except the inputs get padded on the left side by the appropriate amount to ensure the sequence preserves the same length:

```
mport torch.nn.functional as F

class CausalConv1d(nn.Conv1d):
    def forward(self, X):
        padding = (self.kernel_size[0] - 1) * self.dilation[0]
        X = F.pad(X, (padding, 0))
        return super().forward(X)
```

In this code, we inherit from the `nn.Conv1d` class and we override the `forward()` method. In it, we calculate the size of the left-padding we need, and we pad the sequences using the `pad()` function before calling the base class's `forward()` method.

17 The complete WaveNet uses a few more tricks, such as skip connections like in a ResNet, and *gated activation units* similar to those found in a GRU cell.

The pad() function takes two arguments: the tensor to pad (X), and a tuple of ints that indicates how much to pad to the left and right in the last dimension (i.e., the time dimension).

Now we're ready to build the WaveNet model itself:

```
class WavenetModel(nn.Module):
    def __init__(self, input_size, hidden_size, output_size):
        super().__init__()
        layers = []
        for dilation in (1, 2, 4, 8) * 2:
            conv = CausalConv1d(input_size, hidden_size, kernel_size=2,
                                dilation=dilation)
            layers += [conv, nn.ReLU()]
            input_size = hidden_size
        self.convs = nn.Sequential(*layers)
        self.output = nn.Linear(hidden_size, output_size)

    def forward(self, X):
        Z = X.permute(0, 2, 1)
        Z = self.convs(Z)
        Z = Z.permute(0, 2, 1)
        return self.output(Z)

torch.manual_seed(42)
wavenet_model = WavenetModel(input_size=5, hidden_size=32, output_size=14)
wavenet_model = wavenet_model.to(device)
```

In the constructor, we create eight CausalConv1d layers with various dilation rates (1, 2, 4, 8, then again 1, 2, 4, 8), each followed by the ReLU activation function. We chain all these modules in an nn.Sequential module self.convs. We also create the output nn.Linear layer. In the forward method, we permute the last two dimensions of the inputs, as we did earlier, we then pass them through the convolutional layers, then we permute the last two dimensions back to their original order, and we pass the result through the output layer. Thanks to the causal padding, every convolutional layer outputs a sequence of the same length as its input sequence, so the targets we use during training can be the full 112-day sequences; no need to crop them or downsample them. Thus, we can train the model using the data loaders we built for the Seq2SeqModel (i.e., seq_train_loader and seq_valid_loader).

The models we've discussed in this section offer similar performance for the ridership forecasting task, but they may vary significantly depending on the task and the amount of available data. In the WaveNet paper, the authors achieved state-of-the-art performance on various audio tasks (hence the name of the architecture), including text-to-speech tasks, producing very realistic voices across several languages. They also used the model to generate music, one audio sample at a time. This feat is all the more impressive when you realize that a single second of audio can contain tens of thousands of time steps—even LSTMs and GRUs cannot handle such long sequences.

If you evaluate our best Chicago ridership models on the test period, starting in 2020, you will find that they perform much worse than expected! Why is that? Well, that's when the Covid-19 pandemic started, which greatly affected public transportation. As mentioned earlier, these models will only work well if the patterns they learned from the past continue in the future. In any case, before deploying a model to production, verify that it works well on recent data. And once it's in production, make sure to monitor its performance regularly.

With that, you can now tackle all sorts of time series! In Chapter 14, we will continue to explore RNNs, and we will see how they can tackle various NLP tasks as well.

Exercises

1. Can you think of a few applications for a sequence-to-sequence RNN? What about a sequence-to-vector RNN, and a vector-to-sequence RNN?
2. How many dimensions must the inputs of an RNN layer have? What does each dimension represent? What about its outputs?
3. How can you build a deep sequence-to-sequence RNN in PyTorch?
4. Suppose you have a daily univariate time series, and you want to forecast the next seven days using an RNN. Which architecture should you use?
5. What are the main difficulties when training RNNs? How can you handle them?
6. Can you sketch the LSTM cell's architecture?
7. Why would you want to use 1D convolutional layers in an RNN?
8. Which neural network architecture could you use to classify videos?
9. Try to tweak the `Seq2SeqModel` model to forecast both rail and bus ridership for the next 14 days. The model will now need to predict 28 values instead of 14.
10. Download the Bach chorales (*https://homl.info/bach*) dataset and unzip it. It is composed of 382 chorales composed by Johann Sebastian Bach. Each chorale is 100 to 640 time steps long, and each time step contains 4 integers, where each integer corresponds to a note's index on a piano (except for the value 0, which means that no note is played). Train a model—recurrent, convolutional, or both—that can predict the next time step (four notes), given a sequence of time steps from a chorale. Then use this model to generate Bach-like music, one note at a time: you can do this by giving the model the start of a chorale and asking it to predict the next time step, then appending these time steps to the input sequence and asking the model for the next note, and so on. Also make sure to check out Google's Coconet model (*https://homl.info/coconet*), which was used for a nice Google doodle about Bach.

11. Train a classification model for the QuickDraw dataset (*https://homl.info/quickdraw*), which contains millions of sketches of various objects. Start by downloading the simplified data for a few classes (e.g., *ant.ndjson*, *axe.ndjson*, and *bat.ndjson*). Each NDJSON file contains one JSON object per line, which you can parse using Python's `json.loads()` function. This will give you a list of sketches, where each sketch is represented as a Python dictionary. In each dictionary, the `"drawing"` entry contains a list of pen strokes. You can convert this list to a 3D float tensor where the dimensions are [*strokes*, *x coordinates*, *y coordinates*]. Since an RNN takes a single sequence as input, you will need to concatenate all the strokes for each sketch into a single sequence. It's best to add an extra feature to allow the RNN to know how far along each stroke it currently is (e.g., from 0 to 1). In other words, the model will receive a sequence where each time step has three features: the *x* and *y* coordinates of the pen, and the progress ratio along the current stroke.

12. Create a dataset containing short audio recordings of you saying "yes" or "no", and train a binary classification RNN on it. For example, you could:

    a. Use an audio recording software such as Audacity to record yourself saying "yes" as many times as your patience allows, with short pauses between each word. Create a similar recording for the word "no". Try to cover the various ways you might realistically pronounce these words in real life.

    b. Load each WAV file using the `torchaudio.load()` function from the TorchAudio library. This will return a tensor containing the audio, as well as an integer indicating the number of samples per second. The audio tensor has a shape of [*channels*, *samples*]: one channel for mono, two for stereo. Convert stereo to mono by averaging over the channel dimension.

    c. Chop each recording into individual words by splitting at the silences. You can do this using the `torchaudio.transforms.Vad` transform (Voice Activity Detection).

    d. Since the sequences are so long, it's hard to directly train an RNN on them, so it helps to convert the audio to a spectrogram first. For this, you can use the `torchaudio.transforms.MelSpectrogram` transform, which is well suited for voice. The output is a dramatically shorter sequence, with many more channels.

    e. Now try building and training a binary classification RNN on your yes/no dataset! Consider sharing your dataset and model with the world (e.g., via the Hugging Face Hub).

Solutions to these exercises are available at the end of this chapter's notebook, at *https://homl.info/colab-p*.

CHAPTER 14

Natural Language Processing with RNNs and Attention

When Alan Turing imagined his famous Turing test (*https://homl.info/turingtest*)[1] in 1950, he proposed a way to evaluate a machine's ability to match human intelligence. He could have tested for many things, such as the ability to recognize cats in pictures, play chess, compose music, or escape a maze, but, interestingly, he chose a linguistic task. More specifically, he devised a *chatbot* capable of fooling its interlocutor into thinking it was human.[2] This test does have its weaknesses: a set of hardcoded rules can fool unsuspecting or naive humans (e.g., the machine could give vague predefined answers in response to some keywords, it could pretend that it is joking or drunk to get a pass on its weirdest answers, or it could escape difficult questions by answering them with its own questions), and many aspects of human intelligence are utterly ignored (e.g., the ability to interpret nonverbal communication such as facial expressions, or to learn a manual task). But the test does highlight the fact that mastering language is arguably *Homo sapiens*'s greatest cognitive ability.

Until recently, state-of-the-art natural language processing (NLP) models were pretty much all based on recurrent neural networks (introduced in Chapter 13). However, in recent years, RNNs have been replaced with transformers, which we will explore in Chapter 15. That said, it's still important to learn how RNNs can be used for NLP tasks, if only because it helps better understand transformers. Moreover, most of the techniques we will discuss in this chapter are also useful with Transformer

1 Alan Turing, "Computing Machinery and Intelligence", *Mind* 49 (1950): 433–460.

2 Of course, the word *chatbot* came much later. Turing called his test the *imitation game*: machine A and human B chat with human interrogator C via text messages; the interrogator asks questions to figure out which one is the machine (A or B). The machine passes the test if it can fool the interrogator, while the human B must try to help the interrogator.

architectures (e.g., tokenization, beam search, attention mechanisms, and more). Plus, RNNs have recently made a surprise comeback in the form of state space models (SSMs) (see "State-Space Models (SSMs)" at *https://homl.info*).

This chapter is organized in three sections. In the first section, we will start by building a *character RNN*, or *char-RNN*, trained to predict the next character in a sentence. On the way, we will learn about trainable embeddings. Our char-RNN will be our first tiny *language model*, capable of generating original text.

In the second section, we will turn to text classification, and more specifically sentiment analysis, which aims to predict how positive or negative some text is. Our model will read movie reviews and estimate the rater's feeling about the movie. This time, instead of splitting the text into individual characters, we will split it into *tokens*: a token is a small piece of text from a fixed-sized vocabulary, such as the top 10,000 most common words in the English language, or the most common subwords (e.g., "smartest" = "smart" + "est"), or even individual characters or bytes. To split the text into tokens, we will use a *tokenizer*. This section will also introduce popular Hugging Face libraries: the *Datasets* library to download datasets, the *Tokenizers* library for tokenizers, and the *Transformers* library for popular models, downloaded automatically from the *Hugging Face Hub*. Hugging Face is a hugely influential company and open source community, and it plays a central role in the open source AI space, especially in NLP.

The final boss of this chapter will be neural machine translation (NMT), the topic of the third and last section: we will build an encoder-decoder model capable of translating English to Spanish. This will lead us to *attention mechanisms*, which we will apply to our encoder-decoder model to improve its capacity to handle long input texts. As their name suggests, attention mechanisms are neural network components that learn to select the part of the inputs that the model should focus on at each time step. They directly led to the transformers revolution, as we will see in the next chapter.

Let's start with a simple and fun char-RNN model that can write like Shakespeare (sort of).

Generating Shakespearean Text Using a Character RNN

In a famous 2015 blog post (*https://homl.info/charrnn*) titled "The Unreasonable Effectiveness of Recurrent Neural Networks", Andrej Karpathy showed how to train an RNN to predict the next character in a sentence. This *char-RNN* can then be used to generate novel text, one character at a time. Here is a small sample of the text generated by a char-RNN model after it was trained on all of Shakespeare's works:

> PANDARUS:
>
> Alas, I think he shall be come approached and the day

When little srain would be attain'd into being never fed,
And who is but a chain and subjects of his death,
I should not sleep.

Not exactly a masterpiece, but it is still impressive that the model was able to learn words, grammar, proper punctuation, and more, just by learning to predict the next character in a sentence. This is our first example of a *language model*. In the remainder of this section we'll build a char-RNN step by step, starting with the creation of the dataset.

Creating the Training Dataset

First, let's download a subset of Shakespeare's works (about 25%). The data is loaded from Andrej Karpathy's char-rnn project (*https://github.com/karpathy/char-rnn*):

```
from pathlib import Path
import urllib.request

def download_shakespeare_text():
    path = Path("datasets/shakespeare/shakespeare.txt")
    if not path.is_file():
        path.parent.mkdir(parents=True, exist_ok=True)
        url = "https://homl.info/shakespeare"
        urllib.request.urlretrieve(url, path)
    return path.read_text()

shakespeare_text = download_shakespeare_text()
```

Let's print the first few lines:

```
>>> print(shakespeare_text[:80])
First Citizen:
Before we proceed any further, hear me speak.

All:
Speak, speak.
```

Looks like Shakespeare, all right!

Neural networks work with numbers, not text, so we need a way to encode text into numbers. In general, this is done by splitting the text into *tokens*, such as words or characters, and assigning an integer ID to each possible token. For example, let's split our text into characters, and assign an ID to each possible character. We first need to find the list of characters used in the text. This will constitute our token *vocabulary*:

```
>>> vocab = sorted(set(shakespeare_text.lower()))
>>> "".join(vocab)
"\n !$&',-.3:;?abcdefghijklmnopqrstuvwxyz"
```

Note that we call `lower()` to ignore case and thereby reduce the vocabulary size. We must now assign a token ID to each character. For this, we can just use its index in the vocabulary. To decode the output of our model, we will also need a way to go from a token ID to a character:

```
>>> char_to_id = {char: index for index, char in enumerate(vocab)}
>>> id_to_char = {index: char for index, char in enumerate(vocab)}
>>> char_to_id["a"]
13
>>> id_to_char[13]
'a'
```

Next, let's create two helper functions to encode text to tensors of token IDs, and to decode them back to text:

```
import torch

def encode_text(text):
    return torch.tensor([char_to_id[char] for char in text.lower()])

def decode_text(char_ids):
    return "".join([id_to_char[char_id.item()] for char_id in char_ids])
```

Let's try them out:

```
>>> encoded = encode_text("Hello, world!")
>>> encoded
tensor([20, 17, 24, 24, 27,  6,  1, 35, 27, 30, 24, 16,  2])
>>> decode_text(encoded)
'hello, world!'
```

Next, let's prepare the dataset. Right now, we have a single, extremely long sequence of characters containing Shakespeare's works. Just like we did in Chapter 13, we can turn this long sequence into a dataset of windows that we can then use to train a sequence-to-sequence RNN. The targets will be similar to the inputs, but shifted by one time step into the "future". For example, one sample in the dataset may be a sequence of character IDs representing the text "to be or not to b" (without the final "e"), and the corresponding target—a sequence of character IDs representing the text "o be or not to be" (with the final "e", but without the leading "t"). Let's create our dataset class:

```
from torch.utils.data import Dataset, DataLoader

class CharDataset(Dataset):
    def __init__(self, text, window_length):
        self.encoded_text = encode_text(text)
        self.window_length = window_length

    def __len__(self):
        return len(self.encoded_text) - self.window_length
```

```python
    def __getitem__(self, idx):
        if idx >= len(self):
            raise IndexError("dataset index out of range")
        end = idx + self.window_length
        window = self.encoded_text[idx : end]
        target = self.encoded_text[idx + 1 : end + 1]
        return window, target
```

And now let's create the data loaders, as usual. Since the text is quite large, we can afford to use roughly 90% for training (i.e., one million characters), and just 5% for validation, and 5% for testing (60,000 characters each):

```python
window_length = 50
batch_size = 512  # reduce if your GPU cannot handle such a large batch size
train_set = CharDataset(shakespeare_text[:1_000_000], window_length)
valid_set = CharDataset(shakespeare_text[1_000_000:1_060_000], window_length)
test_set = CharDataset(shakespeare_text[1_060_000:], window_length)
train_loader = DataLoader(train_set, batch_size=batch_size, shuffle=True)
valid_loader = DataLoader(valid_set, batch_size=batch_size)
test_loader = DataLoader(test_set, batch_size=batch_size)
```

Each batch will be composed of 512 50-character windows, where each character is represented by its token ID, and where each window comes with its 50-character target window (offset by one character). Note that the training batches are shuffled at each epoch (see Figure 14-1).

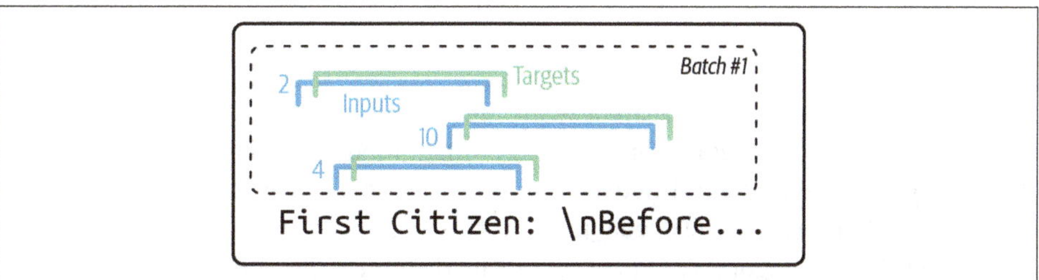

Figure 14-1. Each training batch is composed of shuffled windows, along with their shifted targets. In this figure, the window length is 10 instead of 50.

We set the window length to 50, but you can try tuning it. It's easier and faster to train RNNs on shorter input sequences, but the RNN will not be able to learn any pattern longer than the window length, so don't make it too small.

While we could technically feed the token IDs directly to a neural network without any further preprocessing, it wouldn't work very well. Indeed, as we saw in Chapter 2, most ML models—including neural networks—assume that similar inputs represent similar things; unfortunately, similar IDs may represent totally unrelated tokens, and conversely, distant IDs may represent similar tokens. The neural net would be biased in a weird way, and it would have great difficulty overcoming this bias during training.

One solution is to use one-hot encoding, since all one-hot vectors are equally distant from one another. However, when the vocabulary is large, one-hot vectors are equally large. In our case, the vocabulary contains just 39 characters, so each character would be represented by a 39-dimensional one-hot vector. That's still manageable, but if we were dealing with words instead of characters, the vocabulary size could be in the tens of thousands, so one-hot encoding would be out of the question. Luckily, since we are dealing with neural networks, we have a better option: embeddings.

Embeddings

An embedding is a dense representation of some higher-dimensional data, typically a categorical feature. If there are 50,000 possible categories, then one-hot encoding produces a 50,000-dimensional sparse vector (i.e., containing mostly zeros). In contrast, an embedding is a comparatively small dense vector; for example, with just 300 dimensions.

The embedding size is a hyperparameter you can tune. As a rule of thumb, a good embedding size is often close to the square root of the number of categories.

In deep learning, embeddings are usually initialized randomly, and they are then trained by gradient descent, along with the other model parameters. For example, if we wanted to train a neural network on the California housing dataset (see Chapter 2), we could represent the `ocean_proximity` categorical feature using embeddings. The `"NEAR BAY"` category could be represented initially by a random vector such as `[0.831, 0.696]`, while the `"NEAR OCEAN"` category might be represented by another random vector such as `[0.127, 0.868]` (in this example we are using 2D embeddings).

Since these embeddings are trainable, they will gradually improve during training; and as they represent fairly similar categories in this example, gradient descent will certainly end up pushing them closer together, while it will tend to move them away from the `"INLAND"` category's embedding (see Figure 14-2). Indeed, the better the representation, the easier it will be for the neural network to make accurate predictions, so training tends to make embeddings useful representations of the categories. This is called *representation learning* (you will see other types of representation learning in Chapter 18).

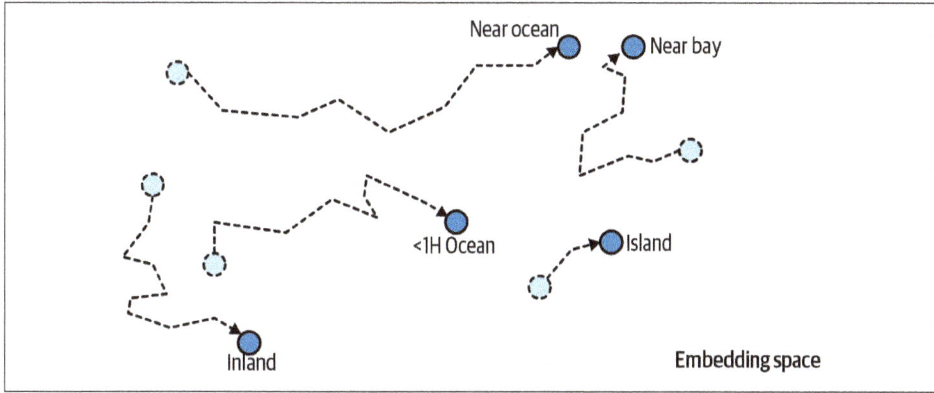

Figure 14-2. Embeddings will gradually improve during training

Not only will embeddings generally be useful representations for the task at hand, but quite often these same embeddings can be reused successfully for other tasks. The most common example of this is *word embeddings* (i.e., embeddings of individual words): when you are working on a natural language processing task, you are often better off reusing pretrained word embeddings than training your own, as we will see later in this chapter.

The idea of using vectors to represent words dates back to the 1960s, and many sophisticated techniques have been used to generate useful vectors, including using neural networks. But things really took off in 2013, when Tomáš Mikolov and other Google researchers published a paper (*https://homl.info/word2vec*)[3] describing an efficient technique to learn word embeddings using neural networks, significantly outperforming previous attempts. This allowed them to learn embeddings on a very large corpus of text: they trained a neural network to predict the words near any given word and obtained astounding word embeddings. For example, synonyms had very close embeddings, and semantically related words such as *France*, *Spain*, and *Italy* were clustered together.

It's not just about proximity, though: word embeddings are also organized along meaningful axes in the embedding space. Here is a famous example: if you compute *King* – *Man* + *Woman* (adding and subtracting the embedding vectors of these words), then the result will be very close to the embedding of the word *Queen* (see Figure 14-3). In other words, the word embeddings encode the concept of gender! Similarly, you can compute *Madrid* – *Spain* + *France*, and the result is close to

3 Tomáš Mikolov et al., "Distributed Representations of Words and Phrases and Their Compositionality", *Proceedings of the 26th International Conference on Neural Information Processing Systems* 2 (2013): 3111–3119.

Paris, which seems to show that the notion of capital city is also encoded in the embeddings.

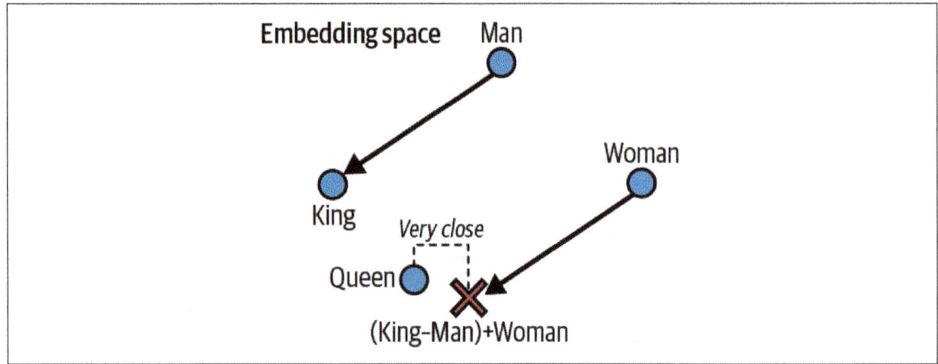

Figure 14-3. Word embeddings of similar words tend to be close, and some axes seem to encode meaningful concepts

Word embeddings can have some meaningful structure, as the "King – Man + Woman" shows. However, they are also noisy and often hard to interpret. I've added some code at the end of the notebook so you can judge for yourself.

Unfortunately, word embeddings sometimes capture our worst biases. For example, although they correctly learn that *Man is to King as Woman is to Queen*, they also seem to learn that *Man is to Doctor as Woman is to Nurse*: quite a sexist bias! To be fair, this particular example is probably exaggerated, as was pointed out in a 2019 paper (*https://homl.info/fairembeds*)[4] by Malvina Nissim et al. Nevertheless, ensuring fairness in deep learning algorithms is an important and active research topic.

PyTorch provides an `nn.Embedding` module, which wraps an *embedding matrix*: this matrix has one row per possible category (e.g., one row for each token in the vocabulary) and one column per embedding dimension. The embedding dimensionality is a hyperparameter you can tune. By default, the embedding matrix is initialized randomly.

To convert a category ID to an embedding, the `nn.Embedding` layer just looks up and returns the corresponding row. That's all there is to it! For example, let's initialize an `nn.Embedding` layer with five categories and 3D embeddings, and use it to encode some categories:

4 Malvina Nissim et al., "Fair Is Better Than Sensational: Man Is to Doctor as Woman Is to Doctor", arXiv preprint arXiv:1905.09866 (2019).

```
>>> import torch.nn as nn
>>> torch.manual_seed(42)
>>> embed = nn.Embedding(5, 3)  # 5 categories × 3D embeddings
>>> embed(torch.tensor([[3, 2], [0, 2]]))
tensor([[[ 0.2674,  0.5349,  0.8094],
         [ 2.2082, -0.6380,  0.4617]],

        [[ 0.3367,  0.1288,  0.2345],
         [ 2.2082, -0.6380,  0.4617]]], grad_fn=<EmbeddingBackward0>)
```

As you can see, category 3 gets encoded as the 3D vector `[0.2674, 0.5349, 0.8094]`, category 2 gets encoded (twice) as the 3D vector `[2.2082, -0.6380, 0.4617]`, and category 0 gets encoded as the 3D vector `[0.3367, 0.1288, 0.2345]` (categories 1 and 4 were not used in this example). Since the layer is not trained yet, these encodings are just random.

Note that an embedding layer is mathematically equivalent to one-hot encoding followed by a linear layer (with no bias parameter). For example, if you create a linear layer with `nn.Linear(5, 3, bias=False)` and pass it the one-hot vector `torch.tensor([[0., 0., 0., 1., 0.]])`, you get a vector equal to row #3 of the linear layer's transposed weight matrix (which acts as an embedding matrix). That's because all rows in the transposed weight matrix get multiplied by zero, except for row #3 which gets multiplied by 1, so the result is just row #3. However, it's much more efficient to use `nn.Embedding(5, 3)` and pass it `torch.tensor([3])`: this looks up row #3 in the embedding matrix without the need for one-hot encoding, and without all the pointless multiplications by zero.

OK, now that you know about embeddings, you are ready to build the Shakespeare model.

Building and Training the Char-RNN Model

Since our dataset is reasonably large, and modeling language is quite a difficult task, we need more than a simple RNN with a few recurrent neurons. Let's build and train a model with a two-layer `nn.GRU` module (introduced in Chapter 13), with 128 units per layer, and a bit of dropout. You can try tweaking the number of layers and units later, if needed:

```
class ShakespeareModel(nn.Module):
    def __init__(self, vocab_size, n_layers=2, embed_dim=10, hidden_dim=128,
                 dropout=0.1):
        super().__init__()
        self.embed = nn.Embedding(vocab_size, embed_dim)
        self.gru = nn.GRU(embed_dim, hidden_dim, num_layers=n_layers,
                          batch_first=True, dropout=dropout)
        self.output = nn.Linear(hidden_dim, vocab_size)
```

```
    def forward(self, X):
        embeddings = self.embed(X)
        outputs, _states = self.gru(embeddings)
        return self.output(outputs).permute(0, 2, 1)

torch.manual_seed(42)
model = ShakespeareModel(len(vocab)).to(device)
```

Let's go over this code:

- We use an `nn.Embedding` layer as the first layer, to encode the character IDs. As we just saw, the `nn.Embedding` layer's number of input dimensions is the number of categories, so in our case it's the number of distinct character IDs. The embedding size is a hyperparameter you can tune—we'll set it to 10 for now. Whereas the inputs of the `nn.Embedding` layer will be integer tensors of shape [*batch size*, *window length*], the outputs of the `nn.Embedding` layer will be float tensors of shape [*batch size*, *window length*, *embedding size*].
- The `nn.GRU` layer has 10 inputs (i.e., the embedding size), 128 outputs (i.e., the hidden size), two layers, and as usual we must specify `batch_first=True` because otherwise the layer assumes that the batch dimension comes after the time dimension.
- We use an `nn.Linear` layer for the output layer: it must have 39 units because there are 39 distinct characters in the text, and we want to output a logit for each possible character (at each time step).
- In the `forward()` method, we just call these layers one by one. Note that the `nn.GRU` layer's output shape is [*batch size*, *window length*, *hidden size*], and the `nn.Linear` layer's output shape is [*batch size*, *window length*, *vocabulary size*], but as we saw in Chapter 13, the `nn.CrossEntropyLoss` and `Accuracy` modules that we will use for training both expect the class dimension (i.e., `vocab_size`) to be the second dimension, not the last one. This is why we must permute the last two dimensions of the `nn.Linear` layer's output. Note that the `nn.GRU` layer also returns the final hidden states, but we ignore them.[5]

Now you can now train and evaluate the model as usual, using the `nn.CrossEntropyLoss` and the `Accuracy` metric.

And now let's use our model to predict the next character in a sentence:

```
model.eval()  # don't forget to switch the model to evaluation mode!
text = "To be or not to b"
encoded_text = encode_text(text).unsqueeze(dim=0).to(device)
```

5 It's a convention in Python to name unused variables with an underscore prefix.

```python
with torch.no_grad():
    Y_logits = model(encoded_text)
    predicted_char_id = Y_logits[0, :, -1].argmax().item()
    predicted_char = id_to_char[predicted_char_id]  # correctly predicts "e"
```

We first encode the text, add a batch dimension of size 1, and move the tensor to the GPU. Then we call our model and get logits for each time step. We're only interested in logits for the final time step (hence the –1), and we want to know which token ID has the highest logit, so we use `argmax()`. We then use `item()` to extract the token ID from the tensor. Lastly, we convert the token ID to a character, and that's our prediction.

The model correctly predicts "e", great! Now let's use this model to pretend we're Shakespeare!

If you are running this code on Colab with a GPU activated, then training will take a few hours. You can reduce the number of epochs if you don't want to wait that long, but of course the model's accuracy will probably be lower. If the Colab session times out, make sure to reconnect quickly, or else the Colab runtime will be destroyed.

Generating Fake Shakespearean Text

To generate new text using the char-RNN model, we could feed it some text, make the model predict the most likely next letter, add it to the end of the text, then give the extended text to the model to guess the next letter, and so on. This is called *greedy decoding*. But in practice this often leads to the same words being repeated over and over again. Instead, we can sample the next character randomly, using the model's estimated probability distribution: if the model estimates a probability p for a given token, then this token will be sampled with probability p. This process will generate more diverse and interesting text since the most likely token won't always be sampled. To sample the next token, we can use the `torch.multinomial()` function, which samples random class indices, given a list of class probabilities. For example:

```python
>>> torch.manual_seed(42)
>>> probs = torch.tensor([[0.5, 0.4, 0.1]])  # probas = 50%, 40%, and 10%
>>> samples = torch.multinomial(probs, replacement=True, num_samples=8)
>>> samples
tensor([[0, 0, 0, 0, 1, 0, 2, 2]])
```

To have more control over the diversity of the generated text, we can divide the logits by a number called the *temperature*, which we can tweak as we wish. A temperature close to zero favors high-probability characters, while a high temperature gives all characters an equal probability. Lower temperatures are typically preferred when generating fairly rigid and precise text, such as mathematical equations, while higher temperatures are preferred when generating more diverse and creative text. Let's write a `next_char()` helper function that will use this approach to pick the next character to add to the input text:

```
import torch.nn.functional as F

def next_char(model, text, temperature=1):
    encoded_text = encode_text(text).unsqueeze(dim=0).to(device)
    with torch.no_grad():
        Y_logits = model(encoded_text)
        Y_probas = F.softmax(Y_logits[0, :, -1] / temperature, dim=-1)
        predicted_char_id = torch.multinomial(Y_probas, num_samples=1).item()
    return id_to_char[predicted_char_id]
```

Next, we can write another small helper function that will repeatedly call `next_char()` to get the next character and append it to the given text:

```
def extend_text(model, text, n_chars=80, temperature=1):
    for _ in range(n_chars):
        text += next_char(model, text, temperature)
    return text
```

We are now ready to generate some text! Let's try low, medium, and high temperatures:

```
>>> print(extend_text(model, "To be or not to b", temperature=0.01))
To be or not to be the state
and the contrary of the state and the sea,
the common people of the
>>> print(extend_text(model, "To be or not to b", temperature=0.4))
To be or not to be the better from the cause
that thou think you may be so be gone.

romeo:
that
>>> print(extend_text(model, "To be or not to b", temperature=100))
To be or not to b-c3;m-rkn&:x:uyve:b&hi n;n-h;wt3k
&cixxh:a!kq$c$ 3 ncq$ ;;wq cp:!xq;yh
!3
d!nhi.
```

Notice the repetitions when the temperature is low: "the state and the" appears twice. The intermediate temperature led to more convincing results, although Romeo wasn't very talkative today. But in the last example the temperature was way too high—we fried Shakespeare. To generate more convincing text, a common technique is to sample only from the top *k* characters, or only from the smallest set of top characters whose total probability exceeds some threshold: this is called *top-p sampling*, or *nucleus sampling*. Alternatively, you could try using *beam search*, which we will discuss later in this chapter, or using more `nn.GRU` layers and more neurons per layer, training for longer, and adding more regularization if needed.

The model is currently incapable of learning patterns longer than `window_length`, which is just 50 characters. You could try making this window larger, but it would also make training harder, and even LSTM and GRU cells cannot handle very long sequences.[6]

Interestingly, although a char-RNN model is just trained to predict the next character, this seemingly simple task actually requires it to learn some higher-level tasks as well. For example, to find the next character after "Great movie, I really ", it's helpful to understand that the sentence is positive, so what follows is more likely to be the letter "l" (for "loved") rather than "h" (for "hated"). In fact, a 2017 paper (*https://homl.info/sentimentneuron*)[7] by Alec Radford and other OpenAI researchers describes how the authors trained a big char-RNN-like model on a large dataset, and found that one of the neurons acted as an excellent sentiment analysis classifier. Although the model was trained without any labels, the *sentiment neuron*—as they called it—reached state-of-the-art performance on sentiment analysis benchmarks (this foreshadowed and motivated unsupervised pretraining in NLP).

Speaking of which, let's say farewell to Shakespeare and turn to the second part of this chapter: sentiment analysis.

Sentiment Analysis Using Hugging Face Libraries

One of the most common applications of NLP is text classification—especially sentiment analysis. If image classification on the MNIST dataset is the "Hello, world!" of computer vision, then sentiment analysis on the IMDb reviews dataset is the "Hello, world!" of natural language processing. The IMDb dataset consists of 50,000 movie reviews in English (25,000 for training, 25,000 for testing) extracted from the famous Internet Movie Database (*https://imdb.com*), along with a simple binary target for each review indicating whether it is negative (0) or positive (1). Just like MNIST, the IMDb reviews dataset is popular for good reasons: it is simple enough to be tackled on a laptop in a reasonable amount of time, but challenging enough to be fun and rewarding.

To download the IMDb dataset, we will use the Hugging Face *Datasets* library, which gives easy access to hundreds of thousands of datasets hosted on the Hugging Face Hub. It is preinstalled on Colab; otherwise it can be installed using `pip install datasets`. We'll use 80% of the original training set for training, and the remaining 20% for validation, using the `train_test_split()` method to split the set:

6 Another technique to capture longer patterns is to use a stateful RNN. It's a bit more complex and not used as much, but if you're interested I've included a section in this chapter's notebook.

7 Alec Radford et al., "Learning to Generate Reviews and Discovering Sentiment", arXiv preprint arXiv:1704.01444 (2017).

```
from datasets import load_dataset

imdb_dataset = load_dataset("imdb")
split = imdb_dataset["train"].train_test_split(train_size=0.8, seed=42)
imdb_train_set, imdb_valid_set = split["train"], split["test"]
imdb_test_set = imdb_dataset["test"]
```

Let's inspect a couple of reviews:

```
>>> imdb_train_set[1]["text"]
"'The Rookie' was a wonderful movie about the second chances life holds [...]"
>>> imdb_train_set[1]["label"]
1
>>> imdb_train_set[16]["text"]
"Lillian Hellman's play, adapted by Dashiell Hammett with help from Hellman,
becomes a curious project to come out of gritty Warner Bros. [...] It seems to
take forever for this drama to find its focus, [...], it seems a little
patronizing [...] Lukas has several speeches in the third-act which undoubtedly
won him the Academy Award [...] this tasteful, tactful movie [...] It should be
a heady mix, but instead it's rather dry-eyed and inert. ** from ****"
>>> imdb_train_set[16]["label"]
0
```

The first review immediately says that it's a wonderful movie; no need to read any further: it's clearly positive (label = 1). The second review is much harder to classify: it contains a detailed description of the movie, sprinkled with both positive and negative comments. Luckily, the conclusion is quite clearly negative, making the task much easier (label = 0). Still, it's not a trivial task.

A simple char-RNN model would struggle; we need a more powerful tokenization technique. So let's focus on tokenization before we return to sentiment analysis.

Tokenization Using the Hugging Face Tokenizers Library

In a 2016 paper (*https://homl.info/rarewords*),[8] Rico Sennrich et al. from the University of Edinburgh explored several methods to tokenize and detokenize text at the subword level. This way, even if your model encounters a rare word it has never seen before, it can still reasonably guess what it means. For example, even if the model never saw the word "smartest" during training, if it learned the word "smart" and it also learned that the suffix "est" means "the most", it can infer the meaning of "smartest". One of the techniques the authors evaluated is *byte pair encoding* (BPE), introduced by Philip Gage in 1994 (initially for data compression). BPE works by splitting the whole training set into individual characters, then at each iteration it finds the most frequent pair of adjacent tokens and adds it to the vocabulary. It repeats this process until the vocabulary reaches the desired size.

8 Rico Sennrich et al., "Neural Machine Translation of Rare Words with Subword Units", *Proceedings of the 54th Annual Meeting of the Association for Computational Linguistics* 1 (2016): 1715–1725.

The Hugging Face Tokenizers library (*https://homl.info/tokenizers*) includes highly efficient implementations of several popular tokenization algorithms, including BPE. It is preinstalled on Colab (or you can install it with `pip install tokenizers`). Here's how to train a BPE model on the IMDb dataset:

```
import tokenizers

bpe_model = tokenizers.models.BPE(unk_token="<unk>")
bpe_tokenizer = tokenizers.Tokenizer(bpe_model)
bpe_tokenizer.pre_tokenizer = tokenizers.pre_tokenizers.Whitespace()
special_tokens = ["<pad>", "<unk>"]
bpe_trainer = tokenizers.trainers.BpeTrainer(vocab_size=1000,
                                             special_tokens=special_tokens)
train_reviews = [review["text"].lower() for review in imdb_train_set]
bpe_tokenizer.train_from_iterator(train_reviews, bpe_trainer)
```

Let's walk through this code:

- We import the Tokenizers library, and we create a BPE model, specifying an unknown token `"<unk>"` which will be used later if we try to tokenize some text containing tokens that the model never saw during training: the unknown tokens will be replaced with the `"<unk>"` token.
- We then create a `Tokenizer` based on the BPE model.
- The Tokenizers library lets you specify optional preprocessing and post-processing steps, and it also provides common preprocessors and postprocessors. In this example, we use the `Whitespace` preprocessor which splits the text at spaces (and drops the spaces), and also separates groups of letters and groups of nonletters. For example "Hello, world!!!" will be split into ["Hello", ",", "world", "!!!"]. The BPE algorithm will then run on these individual chunks, which dramatically speeds up training and improves token quality (at least when the text is in English) by providing reasonable word boundaries.
- We then define a list of special tokens: a padding token `"<pad>"` that will come in handy when we create batches of texts of different lengths, and the unknown token we have already discussed.
- We create a `BpeTrainer`, specifying the maximum vocabulary size and the list of special tokens. The trainer will add the special tokens at the beginning of the vocabulary, so `"<pad>"` will be token 0, and `"<unk>"` will be token 1.
- Next we create a list of all the text in the IMBd training set.
- Lastly, we train the tokenizer on this list, using the `BpeTrainer`. A few seconds later, the BPE tokenizer is ready to be used!

Now let's use our BPE tokenizer to tokenize some text:

```
>>> some_review = "what an awesome movie! 😊

>>> bpe_encoding = bpe_tokenizer.encode(some_review)
>>> bpe_encoding
Encoding(num_tokens=8, attributes=[ids, type_ids, tokens, offsets,
         attention_mask, special_tokens_mask, overflowing])
```

The `encode()` method returns an `Encoding` object that contains eight tokens. Let's look at these tokens and their IDs:

```
>>> bpe_encoding.tokens
['what', 'an', 'aw', 'es', 'ome', 'movie', '!', '<unk>']
>>> bpe_token_ids = bpe_encoding.ids
>>> bpe_token_ids
[303, 139, 373, 149, 240, 211, 4, 1]
```

Notice that frequent words like "what" and "movie" have been identified by the BPE model and are represented by a single token, while less frequent words like "awesome" are split into multiple tokens. Also note that the smiley was not part of the training data, so it gets replaced with the unknown token `"<unk>"`.

The tokenizer provides a `get_vocab()` method which returns a dictionary mapping each token to its ID. You can also use the `token_to_id()` method to map a single token, or conversely use the `id_to_token()` method to go from ID to token. However, you will more often use the `decode()` method to convert a list of token IDs into a string:

```
>>> bpe_tokenizer.decode(bpe_token_ids)
'what an aw es ome movie !'
```

The tokenizer keeps track of each token's start and end offset in the original string, which can come in handy, especially for debugging:

```
>>> bpe_encoding.offsets
[(0, 4), (5, 7), (8, 10), (10, 12), (12, 15), (16, 21), (21, 22), (23, 24)]
```

It's also possible to encode a whole batch of strings at once. For example, let's encode the first three reviews of the training set:

```
>>> bpe_tokenizer.encode_batch(train_reviews[:3])
[Encoding(num_tokens=281, attributes=[ids, type_ids, tokens, [...]]),
 Encoding(num_tokens=114, attributes=[ids, type_ids, tokens, [...]]),
 Encoding(num_tokens=285, attributes=[ids, type_ids, tokens, [...]]),
```

If we want to create a single integer tensor containing the token IDs of all three reviews, we must first ensure that they all have the same number of tokens, which is not the case right now. For this, we can ask the tokenizer to pad the shorter reviews with the padding token ID until they are as long as the longest review in the batch.

We can also ask the tokenizer to truncate any sequence longer than some maximum length, since RNNs don't handle very long sequences very well anyway:

```
bpe_tokenizer.enable_padding(pad_id=0, pad_token="<pad>")
bpe_tokenizer.enable_truncation(max_length=500)
```

Now let's encode the batch again. This time all sequences will have the same number of tokens, so we can create a tensor containing all the token IDs:

```
>>> bpe_encodings = bpe_tokenizer.encode_batch(train_reviews[:3])
>>> bpe_batch_ids = torch.tensor([encoding.ids for encoding in bpe_encodings])
>>> bpe_batch_ids
tensor([[159, 402, 176, 246,  61, [...], 215, 156, 586,   0,   0,   0,   0],
        [ 10, 138, 198, 289, 175, [...],   0,   0,   0,   0,   0,   0,   0],
        [289,  15, 209, 398, 177, [...],  50,  29,  22,  17,  24,  18,  24]])
```

Notice how the first and second review were padded with 0s, which is our padding token ID. Each `Encoding` object also includes an `attention_mask` attribute containing a 1 for each nonpadding token, and a 0 for each padding token. This can be used in your models to easily ignore the padded time steps: just multiply a tensor with the attention mask. In some cases you will prefer to have the list of sequence lengths (ignoring padding). Here's how to get both the attention mask tensor and the sequence lengths:

```
>>> attention_mask = torch.tensor([encoding.attention_mask
...                                for encoding in bpe_encodings])
...
>>> attention_mask
tensor([[1, 1, 1, 1, 1, 1, 1, 1, 1, 1, 1, 1, 1, 1, [...], 1, 1, 1, 0, 0, 0, 0],
        [1, 1, 1, 1, 1, 1, 1, 1, 1, 1, 1, 1, 1, 1, [...], 0, 0, 0, 0, 0, 0, 0],
        [1, 1, 1, 1, 1, 1, 1, 1, 1, 1, 1, 1, 1, 1, [...], 1, 1, 1, 1, 1, 1, 1]])
>>> lengths = attention_mask.sum(dim=-1)
>>> lengths
tensor([281, 114, 285])
```

You may have noted that spaces were not handled very well by our tokenizer. In particular, the word "awesome" came back as "aw es ome", and "movie!" came back as "movie !". This is because the `Whitespace` pre-tokenizer dropped all spaces, therefore the BPE tokenizer doesn't know where spaces should go and it just adds spaces between all tokens. To fix this, we can replace the `Whitespace` pre-tokenizer with the `ByteLevel` pre-tokenizer: it replaces all spaces with a special character Ġ so the BPE model doesn't lose track of them. For example, if you use this pre-tokenizer and you encode and decode the text "what an awesome movie! 😊", you will get: "Ġwhat Ġan Ġaw es ome Ġmovie !". After removing the spaces, then replacing every Ġ with a space, you get " what an awesome movie!". This is almost perfect, except for the extra space at the start—which is easily removed—and the lost emoji, which was replaced with an unknown token because it's not in the vocabulary, and dropped by the `decode()` method.

As its name suggests, the `ByteLevel` pre-tokenizer allows the BPE model to work at the byte level, rather than the character level: unsurprisingly, this is called Byte-level BPE (BBPE). For example, the 😊 emoji will be converted to four bytes, using Unicode's UTF-8 encoding. This means that BBPE will never output an unknown token if its vocabulary contains all 256 possible bytes, since any text can be broken down into its individual bytes whenever longer tokens are not found in the vocabulary. This makes BBPE well suited when the corpus contains rare characters such as emojis.

Another important variant of BPE is WordPiece (*https://homl.info/wordpiece*),[9] proposed by Google in 2016. This tokenization algorithm is very similar to BPE, but instead of adding the most frequent adjacent pair of tokens to the vocabulary at each iteration, it adds the pair with the highest score. This score is computed using Equation 14-1: the frequency(AB) term is just like in BPE—it boosts pairs that are frequent in the corpus. However, the denominator reduces the score of a pair when the individual tokens are themselves frequent. This normalization tends to favor more useful and meaningful tokens than BPE, and the algorithm often produces shorter encoded sequences than BPE or BBPE.

Equation 14-1. WordPiece score for a pair AB composed of tokens A and B

$$\text{score}(\text{AB}) = \frac{\text{frequency}(\text{AB})}{\text{freq}(\text{A}) \cdot \text{freq}(\text{B})} \cdot \text{len}(\text{vocab})$$

To train a WordPiece tokenizer using the Tokenizers library, you can use the same code as for BPE, but replace the `BPE` model with `WordPiece`, and the `BpeTrainer` with `WordPieceTrainer`. If you encode and decode the same review as earlier, you will get "what an aw esome movie !". Notice that WordPiece adds a prefix to tokens that are inside a word, which makes it easy to reconstruct the original string: just remove " #"# (as well as spaces before punctuations). Note that the smiley emoji once again disappeared because it was not in the vocabulary.

One last popular tokenization algorithm we will discuss is Unigram LM (Language Model), introduced in a 2018 paper (*https://homl.info/subword*)[10] by Taku Kudo at Google. This technique is a bit different than the previous ones: it starts out with a very large vocabulary containing every frequent word, subword, and character in the training corpus, then it gradually removes the least useful tokens until it reaches the desired vocabulary size. To determine how useful a token is, this method makes one big simplifying assumption: it assumes that the corpus was sampled randomly

9 Yonghui Wu et al., "Google's Neural Machine Translation System: Bridging the Gap Between Human and Machine Translation", arXiv preprint arXiv:1609.08144 (2016).

10 Taku Kudo, "Subword Regularization: Improving Neural Network Translation Models with Multiple Subword Candidates", arXiv preprint arXiv:1804.10959 (2018).

from the vocabulary, one token at a time (hence the name Unigram LM), and that every token was sampled independently from the others. Therefore, this tokenizer model assumes that the probability of sampling the pair AB is equal to the probability of sampling A times the probability of sampling B. Given this assumption, it can estimate the probability of sampling the whole training corpus. At each iteration, the training algorithm attempts to remove tokens without reducing this overall probability too much.

For example, suppose that the vocabulary contains the tokens "them", "the", and "m", respectively, with 1%, 5%, and 2% probability. This means that the word "them" has a 1% chance of being sampled as the single token "them", or a 5% × 2% = 0.1% chance of being sampled as the pair "the" + "m". Overall, the word "them" has a 1% + 0.1% = 1.1% chance of being sampled. If we remove the token "them" from the vocabulary, then the probability of sampling the word "them" drops down to 0.1%. If instead we remove either "m" or "the", then the probability only drops down to 1% since we can still sample the single token "them". So if the training corpus only contained the word "them", then the algorithm would prefer to drop either "the" or "m". Of course, in reality the corpus contains many other words that contain these two tokens, so the algorithm will likely find other less useful tokens to drop.

Unigram LM is great for languages that don't use spaces to separate words, like English does. For example, Chinese text does not use spaces between words, Vietnamese uses spaces even within words, and German often attaches multiple words together, without spaces.

The same paper also proposed a novel regularization technique called *subword regularization*, which improves generalization and robustness by introducing some randomness in tokenization while training the NLP model (not the tokenizer model). For example, assuming the vocabulary contains the tokens "them", "the", and "m", and you choose to use subword regularization, then the word "them" will sometimes be tokenized as "the" + "m", and sometimes as "them". This technique works best with *morphologically rich languages*, meaning languages where words carry a lot of grammatical information through affixes, inflections, and internal modifications (such as Arabic, Finnish, German, Hungarian, Polish, or Turkish), as opposed to languages that rely on word order or additional helper words (such as English, Chinese, Thai, or Vietnamese).

Unfortunately, the Tokenizers library does not natively support subword regularization, so you either have to implement it yourself, or you can use Google's *SentencePiece* (*https://github.com/google/sentencepiece*) library (`pip install sentencepiece`) which provides an open source implementation. This project is described in a 2018 paper (*https://homl.info/sentencepiece*)[11] by Taku Kudo and John Richardson.

Table 14-1 summarizes the three main tokenizers used today.

Table 14-1. Overview of the three main tokenizers

Feature	BBPE	WordPiece	Unigram LM
How	Merge most frequent pairs	Merge pairs that maximize data likelihood	Remove least likely tokens
Pros	Fast, simple, great for multilingual	Good balance of efficiency and token quality	Most meaningful, shortest sequences
Cons	Can produce awkward splits	Less robust than BBPE for multilingual	Slower to train and tokenize
Used By	GPT, Llama, RoBERTa, BLOOM	BERT, DistilBERT, ELECTRA	T5, ALBERT, mBART

Training your own tokenizer is useful in many situations; for example, if you are dealing with domain-specific text, such as medical, legal, or engineering documents full of jargon, or if the text is written in a low-resource language or dialect, or if it's code written in a new programming language, and so on. However, in most cases you will want to simply reuse a pretrained tokenizer.

Reusing Pretrained Tokenizers

To download a pretrained tokenizer, we will use the Hugging Face *Transformers library* (*https://homl.info/transformerslib*). This library provides many popular models for NLP, computer vision, audio processing, and more. Pretrained weights are available for almost all of these models, and the library can automatically download them from the Hugging Face Hub. The models were originally all based on the *Transformer architecture* (which we will discuss in detail in Chapter 15), hence the name of the library, but other kinds of models are now available as well, such as CNNs. Lastly, each model comes with all the tools it needs, including tokenizers for NLP models: in a single line of code, you can have a fully functional, high-performance model for a given task, as we will see later in this chapter.

For now, let's just grab the pretrained tokenizer from some NLP model. For example, the following code downloads the pretrained BBPE tokenizer used by the GPT-2 model (a text generation model), and it uses this tokenizer to encode the first 3 IMDb reviews, truncating the encoded sequences if they exceed 500 tokens:

```
import transformers

gpt2_tokenizer = transformers.AutoTokenizer.from_pretrained("gpt2")
```

11 Taku Kudo and John Richardson, "SentencePiece: A Simple and Language Independent Subword Tokenizer and Detokenizer for Neural Text Processing", arXiv preprint arXiv:1808.06226 (2018).

```
gpt2_encoding = gpt2_tokenizer(train_reviews[:3], truncation=True,
                               max_length=500)
```

Notice that we use the tokenizer object like a function. The result is a dictionary-like object of type `BatchEncoding`. You can get the token IDs using the `"input_ids"` key. It returns a Python list of lists of token IDs. For example, let's look at the first 10 token IDs of the first encoded review, and use the tokenizer to decode them, using its `decode()` method:

```
>>> gpt2_token_ids = gpt2_encoding["input_ids"][0][:10]
>>> gpt2_token_ids
[14247, 35030, 1690, 423, 257, 1688, 8046, 13, 484, 1690]
>>> gpt2_tokenizer.decode(gpt2_token_ids)
'stage adaptations often have a major fault. they often'
```

If you would prefer to use a pretrained WordPiece tokenizer, you can reuse the tokenizer of any LLM that was pretrained using WordPiece, such as BERT (another popular NLP model, which stands for Bidirectional Encoder Representations from Transformers). This tokenizer has a padding token (unlike the previous tokenizer, since GPT-2 didn't need it), so we can specify `padding=True` when encoding a batch of reviews: as usual, the shortest texts will be padded to the length of the longest one using the padding token. This allows us to also specify `return_tensors="pt"` to get a PyTorch tensor instead of a Python list of lists of token IDs: very convenient! So let's encode the first three IMDb reviews:

```
bert_tokenizer = transformers.AutoTokenizer.from_pretrained("bert-base-uncased")
bert_encoding = bert_tokenizer(train_reviews[:3], padding=True,
                               truncation=True, max_length=500,
                               return_tensors="pt")
```

The name `"bert-base-uncased"` refers to a *model checkpoint*: this particular checkpoint is a case-insensitive BERT model, pretrained on English text. Other checkpoints are available, such as `"bert-large-cased"` if you want a larger and case-sensitive BERT model, or `"bert-base-multilingual-uncased"` if you want an uncased model pretrained on over 100 languages. For now we are just using the model's tokenizer.

The resulting token IDs and attention masks are nicely padded tensors:

```
>>> bert_encoding["input_ids"]
tensor([[ 101, 2754,17241, 2411, 2031, [...],  102, 0, 0, 0, [...], 0, 0, 0],
        [ 101, 1005, 1996, 8305, 1005, [...],  102, 0, 0, 0, [...], 0, 0, 0],
        [ 101, 7929, 1010, 2021, 2515, [...], 1012,  1019,  1013,  1019,  102]])
>>> bert_encoding["attention_mask"]
tensor([[1, 1, 1, 1, 1, 1, 1, 1, 1, 1, 1, 1, [...], 0, 0, 0, 0, 0, 0, 0, 0, 0],
        [1, 1, 1, 1, 1, 1, 1, 1, 1, 1, 1, 1, [...], 0, 0, 0, 0, 0, 0, 0, 0, 0],
        [1, 1, 1, 1, 1, 1, 1, 1, 1, 1, 1, 1, [...], 1, 1, 1, 1, 1, 1, 1, 1, 1]])
```

Notice that each token ID sequence starts with token 101 ([CLS]), and ends with token 102 ([SEP]) (ignoring padding tokens). These tokens are needed by the BERT model (as we will see in Chapter 15), but unless your model needs them too, you can drop them by setting `add_special_tokens=False` when calling the tokenizer.

What about a pretrained Unigram LM tokenizer? Well, many models were trained using Unigram LM, such as ALBERT, T5, or XML-R models, just to name a few. For example:

```
albert_tokenizer = transformers.AutoTokenizer.from_pretrained("albert-base-v2")
albert_encoding = albert_tokenizer(train_reviews[:3], padding=True, [...])
```

The Transformers library also provides an object that can wrap your own tokenizer (from the Tokenizers library) and give it the same API as the pretrained tokenizers (from the Transformers library). For example, let's wrap the BPE tokenizer we trained earlier:

```
hf_tokenizer = transformers.PreTrainedTokenizerFast(
    tokenizer_object=bpe_tokenizer)
hf_encodings = hf_tokenizer(train_reviews[:3], padding=True, [...])
```

With that, we have all the tokenization tools we need, so let's go back to sentiment analysis.

Building and Training a Sentiment Analysis Model

Our sentiment analysis model must be trained using batches of tokenized reviews. However, the datasets we created did not take care of tokenization. One option would be to update them (e.g., using the `map()` method), but it's just as simple to handle tokenization in the data loaders. To do this, we can pass a function to the `DataLoader` constructor using its `collate_fn` argument: the data loader will call this function for every batch, passing it a list of dataset samples. Our function will take this batch, tokenize the reviews, truncate and pad them if needed, and return a `BatchEncoding` object containing PyTorch tensors for the token IDs and attention masks, along with another tensor containing the labels. For tokenization, we will simply use the pretrained WordPiece tokenizer we just loaded:

```
def collate_fn(batch, tokenizer=bert_tokenizer):
    reviews = [review["text"] for review in batch]
    labels = [[review["label"]] for review in batch]
    encodings = tokenizer(reviews, padding=True, truncation=True,
                          max_length=200, return_tensors="pt")
    labels = torch.tensor(labels, dtype=torch.float32)
    return encodings, labels

batch_size = 256
imdb_train_loader = DataLoader(imdb_train_set, batch_size=batch_size,
                               collate_fn=collate_fn, shuffle=True)
imdb_valid_loader = DataLoader(imdb_valid_set, batch_size=batch_size,
```

```python
                                        collate_fn=collate_fn)
imdb_test_loader = DataLoader(imdb_test_set, batch_size=batch_size,
                              collate_fn=collate_fn)
```

Now we're ready to create our sentiment analysis model:

```python
class SentimentAnalysisModel(nn.Module):
    def __init__(self, vocab_size, n_layers=2, embed_dim=128, hidden_dim=64,
                 pad_id=0, dropout=0.2):
        super().__init__()
        self.embed = nn.Embedding(vocab_size, embed_dim,
                                  padding_idx=pad_id)
        self.gru = nn.GRU(embed_dim, hidden_dim, num_layers=n_layers,
                          batch_first=True, dropout=dropout)
        self.output = nn.Linear(hidden_dim, 1)

    def forward(self, encodings):
        embeddings = self.embed(encodings["input_ids"])
        _outputs, hidden_states = self.gru(embeddings)
        return self.output(hidden_states[-1])
```

As you can see, this model is very similar to our Shakespeare model, but with a few important differences:

- When creating the `nn.Embedding` layer, we set its `padding_idx` argument to our padding ID. This ensures that the padding ID gets embedded as a nontrainable zero vector to reduce the impact of padding tokens on the loss.
- Since this is a sequence-to-vector model, not a sequence-to-sequence model, we only need the last output of the top GRU layer to make our final prediction (through the output `nn.Linear` layer). We could have used `outputs[:, -1]` instead of `hidden_states[-1]`, as they are equal.
- The output `nn.Linear` layer has a single output dimension because it's a binary classification model. The final output will be a 2D tensor with a single column containing one logit per review, positive for positive reviews, and negative for negative reviews.
- The `forward()` method takes a `BatchEncoding` object as input, containing the token IDs (possibly padded and truncated).

We can then train this model using the `nn.BCEWithLogitsLoss` since this is a binary classification task. It reaches close to 85% accuracy on the validation set, which is reasonably good, although the best models reach human level, slightly above 90% accuracy. It's probably not possible to go much higher than that; because many reviews are ambiguous, classifying them feels like flipping a coin.

One problem with our model is the fact that we are not fully ignoring the padding tokens. Indeed, if a review ends with many padding tokens, the `nn.GRU` module will have to process them, and by the time it gets through all of them, it might have forgotten what the review was all about. To avoid this, we can use a *packed sequence* instead of a regular tensor. A packed sequence is a special data structure designed to efficiently represent a batch of sequences of variable lengths.[12] You can use the `pack_padded_sequence()` function to convert a tensor containing padded sequences to a packed sequence object, and conversely you can use the `pad_packed_sequence()` function whenever you want to convert a packed sequence object to a padded tensor:

```
>>> from torch.nn.utils.rnn import pack_padded_sequence, pad_packed_sequence
>>> sequences = torch.tensor([[1, 2, 0, 0], [5, 6, 7, 8]])
>>> packed = pack_padded_sequence(sequences, lengths=(2, 4),
...                               enforce_sorted=False, batch_first=True)
...
>>> packed
PackedSequence(data=tensor([5, 1, 6, 2, 7, 8]), [...])
>>> padded, lengths = pad_packed_sequence(packed, batch_first=True)
>>> padded, lengths
(tensor([[1, 2, 0, 0],
         [5, 6, 7, 8]]),
 tensor([2, 4]))
```

By default, the `pack_padded_sequence()` function assumes that the sequences in the batch are ordered from the longest to the shortest. If this is not the case, you must set `enforce_sorted=False`. Moreover, the function also assumes that the time dimension comes before the batch dimension. If the batch dimension is first, you must set `batch_first=True`.

PyTorch's recurrent layers support packed sequences: they efficiently process the sequences, stopping at the end of each sequence. So let's update our sentiment analysis model to use packed sequences. In the `forward()` method, just replace the `self.gru(embeddings)` line with the following code:

```
lengths = encodings["attention_mask"].sum(dim=1)
packed = pack_padded_sequence(embeddings, lengths=lengths.cpu(),
                              batch_first=True, enforce_sorted=False)
_outputs, hidden_states = self.gru(packed)
```

This code starts by computing the length of each sequence in the batch, just like we did earlier, then it packs the embeddings tensor and passes the packed sequence to the `nn.GRU` module. With that, the model will properly handle sequences without being bothered by any padding tokens. You don't actually need to set `padding_idx` anymore when creating the `nn.Embedding` layer, but it doesn't hurt, and it makes debugging a bit easier, so I prefer to keep it.

12 *Nested tensors* serve a similar purpose and are more convenient to use, but they are still in prototype stage at the time of writing. See *https://pytorch.org/docs/stable/nested.html* for more details.

Another way to improve our model is to let it look at the review in both directions: left to right, and right to left. Let's see how this works.

If you pass a packed sequence to an `nn.GRU` module, its outputs will also be a packed sequence, and you will need to convert it back to a padded tensor before you can pass it to the next layers. Luckily, we don't need these outputs for our sentiment analysis model, only the hidden states.

Bidirectional RNNs

At each time step, a regular recurrent layer only looks at past and present inputs before generating its output. In other words, it is *causal*, meaning it cannot look into the future. This type of RNN makes sense when forecasting time series, or in the decoder of a sequence-to-sequence (seq2seq) model. But for tasks like text classification, or in the encoder of a seq2seq model, it is often preferable to look ahead at the next words before encoding a given word.

For example, consider the phrases "the right arm", "the right person", and "the right to speak": to properly encode the word "right", you need to look ahead. One solution is to run two recurrent layers on the same inputs, one reading the words from left to right and the other reading them from right to left, then combine their outputs at each time step, typically by concatenating them. This is what a *bidirectional recurrent layer* does (see Figure 14-4).

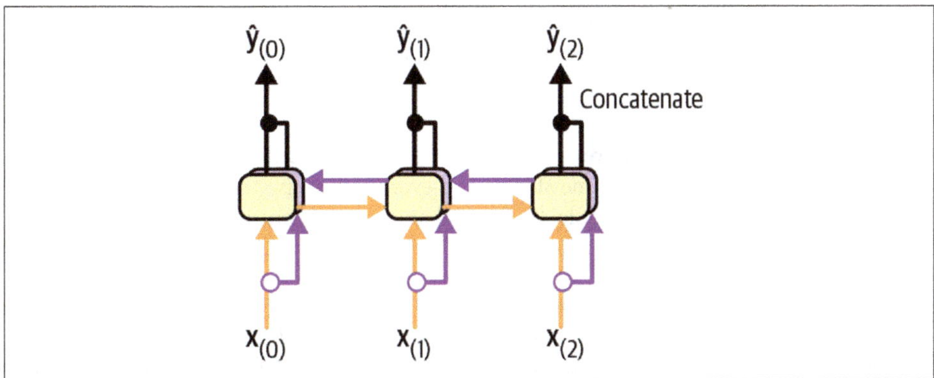

Figure 14-4. A bidirectional recurrent layer

To make our sentiment analysis model bidirectional, we can just set `bidirectional=True` when creating the `nn.GRU` layer (this also works with the `nn.RNN` and `nn.LSTM` modules).

However, once we do that, we must adjust our model a bit. In particular, we must double the input dimension of the output `nn.Linear` layer, since the hidden states will double in size:

```
self.output = nn.Linear(2 * hidden_dim, 1)
```

We must also concatenate the forward and backward hidden states of the GRU's top layer before passing the result to the output layer. For this, we can replace the last line of the `forward()` method (i.e., `return self.output(hidden_states[-1])`) with the following code:

```
n_dims = self.output.in_features
top_states = hidden_states[-2:].permute(1, 0, 2).reshape(-1, n_dims)
return self.output(top_states)
```

Let's see how the middle line works:

- Until now, the shape of the hidden states returned by the `nn.GRU` module was [*number of layers, batch size, hidden size*], so [2, 256, 64] in our case. But when we set `bidirectional=True`, we doubled the first dimension size, so we now have a shape of [4, 256, 64]: the tensor contains the hidden states for layer 1 forward, layer 1 backward, layer 2 forward, and layer 2 backward. Since we only want the top layer's hidden states, both forward and backward, we must get `hidden_states[-2:]`.
- We also need to concatenate the forward and backward states. One way to do this is to permute the first two dimensions of the top hidden states using `permute(1, 0, 2)` to get the shape [256, 2, 64], then reshape the result using `reshape(-1, n_dims)` (where `n_dims` equals 128) to get the desired shape: [256, 2 * 64].

In this model we only use the last hidden states, ignoring the outputs at each time step. If you ever want to use the outputs of a bidirectional module, be aware that its last dimension's size will be doubled.

You can try training this model, but you will not see any improvement in this case, because the first model actually overfit the training set, and this new version makes it even worse: it reaches over 99% accuracy on the training set, but just 84% on the validation set. To fix this, you could try to regularize the model a bit more, reduce the size of the model, or increase the size of the training set.

But let's instead try something different: using pretrained embeddings.

Reusing Pretrained Embeddings and Language Models

Our model was able to learn useful embeddings for thousands of tokens, based on just 25,000 movie reviews: that's quite impressive! Imagine how good the embeddings would be if we had billions of reviews to train on. The good news is that we can reuse word embeddings even when they were trained on some other (very) large text corpus, even if it was not composed of movie reviews, and even if they were not trained for sentiment analysis. After all, the word "amazing" generally has the same meaning whether you use it to talk about movies or anything else.

Since we used pretrained tokens for the BERT model, we might as well try using its embedding layer. First, we need to download the pretrained model using the `AutoModel.from_pretrained()` function from the Transformers library, then we can directly access its embeddings layer:

```
>>> bert_model = transformers.AutoModel.from_pretrained("bert-base-uncased")
>>> bert_model.embeddings.word_embeddings
Embedding(30522, 768, padding_idx=0)
```

As you can see, this BERT model is implemented using PyTorch, and it contains a regular `nn.Embedding` layer. We could just replace our model's `nn.Embedding` layer with this one (and retrain our model), but we can keep models cleanly separated by initializing our own `nn.Embedding` layer with a copy of the pretrained embedding matrix. This can be done using the `Embedding.from_pretrained()` function:

```
class SentimentAnalysisModelPreEmbeds(nn.Module):
    def __init__(self, pretrained_embeddings, n_layers=2, hidden_dim=64,
                 dropout=0.2):
        super().__init__()
        weights = pretrained_embeddings.weight.data
        self.embed = nn.Embedding.from_pretrained(weights, freeze=True)
        embed_dim = weights.shape[-1]
        [...]  # the rest of the model is exactly like earlier

imdb_model_bert_embeds = SentimentAnalysisModelPreEmbeds(
    bert_model.embeddings.word_embeddings).to(device)
```

Note that we set `freeze=True` when creating the `nn.Embedding` layer: this makes it nontrainable and ensures that the pretrained embeddings won't be damaged by large gradients at the beginning of training. You can train the model for a few epochs like this, then make the embedding layer trainable and continue training, letting the model fine-tune the embeddings for our task.

Pretrained word embeddings have been popular for quite a while, starting with Google's Word2vec embeddings (*https://homl.info/word2vec*) (2013), Stanford's GloVe embeddings (*https://homl.info/glove*) (2014), Facebook's FastText embeddings (*https://fasttext.cc*) (2016), and more. However, this approach has its limits. In particular, a word has a single representation, no matter the context. For example, the word "right" is encoded the same way in "left and right" and "right and wrong", even though it means two very different things. To address this limitation, a 2018 paper (*https://homl.info/elmo*)[13] by Matthew Peters introduced *Embeddings from Language Models* (ELMo): these are contextualized word embeddings learned from the internal states of a deep bidirectional RNN language model. In other words, instead of just using pretrained word embeddings in your model, you can reuse several layers of a pretrained language model.

At roughly the same time, the Universal Language Model Fine-Tuning (ULMFiT) paper (*https://homl.info/ulmfit*)[14] by Jeremy Howard and Sebastian Ruder demonstrated the effectiveness of unsupervised pretraining for NLP tasks. The authors trained an LSTM language model on a huge text corpus using self-supervised learning (i.e., generating the labels automatically from the data), then they fine-tuned it on various tasks. Their model outperformed the state of the art on six text classification tasks by a large margin (reducing the error rate by 18%–24% in most cases). Moreover, the authors showed that a pretrained model fine-tuned on just 100 labeled examples could achieve the same performance as one trained from scratch on 10,000 examples. Before the ULMFiT paper, using pretrained models was only the norm in computer vision; in the context of NLP, pretraining was limited to word embeddings. This paper marked the beginning of a new era in NLP: today, reusing pretrained language models is the norm.

For example, why not reuse the entire pretrained BERT model for our sentiment analysis model? To use the BERT model, the Transformers library lets us call it like a function, passing it the tokenized reviews:

```
>>> bert_encoding = bert_tokenizer(train_reviews[:3], padding=True,
...                                max_length=200, truncation=True,
...                                return_tensors="pt")
...
>>> bert_output = bert_model(**bert_encoding)
>>> bert_output.last_hidden_state.shape
torch.Size([3, 200, 768])
```

BERT's output includes an attribute named `last_hidden_state`, which contains contextualized embeddings for each token. The word "last" in this case refers to the last layer, not the last time step (BERT is a transformer, not an RNN). This `last_hidden_state` tensor has a shape of [*batch size*, *max sequence length*, *hidden size*]. Let's use these contextualized embeddings in a sentiment analysis model:

13 Matthew Peters et al., "Deep Contextualized Word Representations", *Proceedings of the 2018 Conference of the North American Chapter of the Association for Computational Linguistics: Human Language Technologies* 1 (2018): 2227–2237.

14 Jeremy Howard and Sebastian Ruder, "Universal Language Model Fine-Tuning for Text Classification", *Proceedings of the 56th Annual Meeting of the Association for Computational Linguistics* 1 (2018): 328–339.

```python
class SentimentAnalysisModelBert(nn.Module):
    def __init__(self, n_layers=2, hidden_dim=64, dropout=0.2):
        super().__init__()
        self.bert = transformers.AutoModel.from_pretrained("bert-base-uncased")
        embed_dim = self.bert.config.hidden_size
        self.gru = nn.GRU(embed_dim, hidden_dim, [...])
        self.output = nn.Linear(hidden_dim, 1)

    def forward(self, encodings):
        contextualized_embeddings = self.bert(**encodings).last_hidden_state
        lengths = encodings["attention_mask"].sum(dim=1)
        packed = pack_padded_sequence(contextualized_embeddings, [...])
        _outputs, hidden_states = self.gru(packed)
        return self.output(hidden_states[-1])
```

Note that we don't need to make the `nn.GRU` module bidirectional since the contextualized embeddings already looked ahead.

If you freeze the BERT model (e.g., using `model.bert.requires_grad_(False)`) and train the rest of the model, you will notice a significant performance boost, reaching over 88% accuracy. Wonderful!

Another option is to use only the contextualized embedding for the very first token, which is the *class token* [CLS]. Indeed, during pretraining, the BERT model had to perform a text classification task based solely on this token's contextualized embedding (we will discuss BERT pretraining in more detail in Chapter 15). As a result, it learned to summarize the most important features of the text into this embedding. This simplifies our model quite a bit, since we can get rid of the `nn.GRU` module altogether, and the `forward()` method becomes much shorter:

```python
def forward(self, encodings):
    bert_output = self.bert(**encodings)
    return self.output(bert_output.last_hidden_state[:, 0])
```

In fact, the BERT model contains an extra hidden layer on top of the class embedding, composed of an `nn.Linear` module and an `nn.Tanh` module. This hidden layer is called the *pooler*. To use it, just replace `bert_output.last_hidden_state[:, 0]` with `bert_output.pooler_output`. You may also want to unfreeze the pooler after a few epochs to fine-tune it for the IMDb task.

So we started by reusing only the pretrained tokenizer, then we reused the pretrained embeddings, then most of the pretrained BERT model, and finally the full model, adding only an `nn.Linear` layer on top of the pooler. We can actually go one step further and just use an off-the-shelf class for sentence classification.

Task-Specific Classes

To tackle our binary classification task using BERT, we can use the `BertForSequenceClassification` class provided by the Transformers library. It's just a BERT model plus a classification head on top. All you need to do to create this model is specify the pretrained BERT checkpoint you want to use, the number of output units for your classification task, and optionally the data type (we'll use 16-bit floats to fit on small GPUs):

```
from transformers import BertForSequenceClassification

torch.manual_seed(42)
bert_for_binary_clf = BertForSequenceClassification.from_pretrained(
    "bert-base-uncased", num_labels=2, dtype=torch.float16).to(device)
```

The Transformers library contains many task-specific classes based on various pretrained models, such as `BertForQuestionAnswering` or `RobertaForSequenceClassification` (see Chapter 15). You can also use `AutoModelForSequenceClassification` to let the library pick the right class for you, based on the requested model checkpoint (e.g., if you ask for `"bert-base-uncased"`, you will get an instance of `BertForSequenceClassification`). Similar `AutoModelFor[...]` classes are available for other tasks.

Until now we have always used a single output for binary classification, so why did we set `num_labels=2`? Well, for simplicity Hugging Face prefers to treat binary classification exactly like multiclass classification, so this model will output two logits instead of one, and it must be trained using the `nn.CrossEntropyLoss` instead of `nn.BCELoss` or `nn.BCEWithLogitsLoss`. If you want to convert the logits to estimated probabilities, you must use `torch.softmax()` rather than `torch.sigmoid()`.

Let's call this model on a very positive review:

```
>>> encoding = bert_tokenizer(["This was a great movie!"])
>>> with torch.no_grad():
...     output = bert_for_binary_clf(
...       input_ids=torch.tensor(encoding["input_ids"], device=device),
...       attention_mask=torch.tensor(encoding["attention_mask"], device=device))
...
>>> output.logits
tensor([[-0.0120,  0.6304]], device='cuda:0', dtype=torch.float16)
>>> torch.softmax(output.logits, dim=-1)
tensor([[0.3447, 0.6553]], device='cuda:0', dtype=torch.float16)
```

We first tokenize the review, then we call the model, it returns a `ModelOutput` object containing the logits, and we convert these logits to estimated probabilities using the `torch.softmax()` function. Ouch! The model classified this review as negative with 65.53% confidence! Indeed, the BERT model inside `BertForSequenceClassification` is pretrained, but not the classification head, so we're going to get terrible performance until we actually train this model on the IMDb dataset.

If you pass labels when calling this model (or any other model from the Transformers library), then it also computes the loss and returns it in the `ModelOutput` object. For example:

```
>>> with torch.no_grad():
...     output = bert_for_binary_clf(
...       input_ids=torch.tensor(encoding["input_ids"], device=device),
...       attention_mask=torch.tensor(encoding["attention_mask"], device=device),
...       labels=torch.tensor([1], device=device))
...
>>> output.loss
tensor(0.4226, device='cuda:0', dtype=torch.float16)
```

Since `num_labels` is greater than 1, the model computes the `nn.CrossEntropyLoss` (which is implemented as `nn.LogSoftmax` followed by `nn.NLLLoss`—that's why we see `grad_fn=<NllLossBackward0>`). If we had used `num_labels=1`, then the model would have used the `nn.MSELoss` instead; this can be useful for regression tasks.

We could now train this model using our own training code, as we did so far, but the Transformers library provides a convenient *Trainer API*, so let's check it out.

The Trainer API

The Trainer API lets you fine-tune a model on your own dataset with very little boilerplate code. It can save model checkpoints during training, apply early stopping, distribute the computations across GPUs, log metrics, take care of padding, batching, shuffling, and more. Let's use the Trainer API to train our IMDb model.

The Trainer API works directly with dataset objects, not data loaders, but it expects the datasets to contain tokenized text, not strings, so we must take care of tokenization. We can do this quite simply using the dataset's `map()` method (this method is implemented by the Datasets library; it's not available on pure PyTorch datasets):

```
def tokenize_batch(batch):
    return bert_tokenizer(batch["text"], truncation=True, max_length=200)

tok_imdb_train_set = imdb_train_set.map(tokenize_batch, batched=True)
tok_imdb_valid_set = imdb_valid_set.map(tokenize_batch, batched=True)
tok_imdb_test_set = imdb_test_set.map(tokenize_batch, batched=True)
```

Since we set `batched=True`, the `map()` method passes batches of reviews to the `tokenize_batch()` method: this is optional, but it significantly speeds up this preprocessing step. The `tokenize_batch()` method tokenizes the given batch of reviews, and the resulting fields are added to each instance by the `map()` method. This includes fields such as `token_ids` and `attention_mask`, which the model expects.

To evaluate our model, we can write a simple function that takes an object with two attributes: `label_ids` and `predictions`:

```python
def compute_accuracy(pred):
    return {"accuracy": (pred.label_ids == pred.predictions.argmax(-1)).mean()}
```

Alternatively, you can use metrics provided by the Hugging Face *Evaluate library*: they are designed to work nicely with the Transformers library. Alternatively, although the Trainer API does not support the streaming metrics from the TorchMetrics library, you can still use them if you wrap them inside a function.

Next, we must specify our training configuration in a `TrainingArguments` object:

```python
from transformers import TrainingArguments

train_args = TrainingArguments(
    output_dir="my_imdb_model", num_train_epochs=2,
    per_device_train_batch_size=128, per_device_eval_batch_size=128,
    eval_strategy="epoch", logging_strategy="epoch", save_strategy="epoch",
    load_best_model_at_end=True, metric_for_best_model="accuracy",
    report_to="none")
```

We specify that the logs and model checkpoints must be saved in the `my_imdb_model` directory; training should run for 2 epochs (you can increase this if you want); the batch size is 128 for both training and evaluation (you can tweak this depending on the amount of VRAM you have); we want evaluation, logging, and saving to take place at the end of each epoch; and the best model should be loaded at the end of training based on the validation accuracy. Lastly, the `report_to` argument lets you specify one or more tools that the training code will report logs to, such as TensorBoard or Weights & Biases (W&B) (*https://wandb.ai*). This can be useful to visualize the learning curves. For simplicity, I set `report_to="none"` to turn reporting off.

Lastly, we create a `Trainer` object and pass it the model, along with the training arguments, the training and validation sets, the evaluation function, plus a data collator which will take care of padding. Finally, we call the trainer's `train()` method, and we're done! The model reaches about 90% accuracy on the validation set after just two epochs:

```python
from transformers import DataCollatorWithPadding, Trainer

trainer = Trainer(
    bert_for_binary_clf, train_args, train_dataset=tok_imdb_train_set,
    eval_dataset=tok_imdb_valid_set, compute_metrics=compute_accuracy,
    data_collator=DataCollatorWithPadding(bert_tokenizer))
train_output = trainer.train()
```

Great, you now know how to download a pretrained model like BERT and fine-tune it on your own dataset! But what if you don't have a dataset at all, and you just want to use a pretrained model that was already fine-tuned for sentiment analysis? For this, you can use the *pipelines API*.

Hugging Face Pipelines

The Transformers library provides a very convenient API to download and use pretrained pipelines for various tasks. Each pipeline contains a pretrained model along with its corresponding preprocessing and post-processing modules. For example let's create a sentiment analysis pipeline and run it on the first 10 IMDb reviews in the training set:

```
>>> from transformers import pipeline
>>> model_name = "distilbert-base-uncased-finetuned-sst-2-english"
>>> classifier_imdb = pipeline("sentiment-analysis", model=model_name,
...                            truncation=True, max_length=512)
...
>>> classifier_imdb(train_reviews[:10])
[{'label': 'POSITIVE', 'score': 0.9996108412742615},
 {'label': 'POSITIVE', 'score': 0.9998623132705688},
 [...]
 {'label': 'POSITIVE', 'score': 0.9978922009468079},
 {'label': 'NEGATIVE', 'score': 0.9997020363807678}]
```

Well, it could hardly be any easier, could it? Just create a pipeline by specifying the task and the model to use, and a couple of other parameters, depending on the task, and off you go! In this example, each review gets a `"POSITIVE"` or `"NEGATIVE"` label, along with a score equal to the model's estimated probability for that label. This particular model actually reaches 88.2% accuracy on the validation set, which is reasonably good. Here a few points to note:

- If you don't specify a model, the `pipeline()` function will use the default model for the chosen task. For sentiment analysis, at the time of writing, it's the model we chose: it's a DistilBERT model—a scaled down version of BERT—with an uncased tokenizer, trained on the English Wikipedia and a corpus of English books, and fine-tuned on the Stanford Sentiment Treebank v2 (SST 2) task.
- The pipeline automatically uses the GPU if you have one. If you have several GPUs, you can specify which one to use by setting the pipeline's `device` argument to the GPU index.
- The models from the Transformers library are always in evaluation mode by default (no need to call `eval()`).
- The score is for the chosen label, not for the positive class. In particular, since this is a binary classification task, the score cannot be lower than 0.5 (or else the model would have picked the other label).

Bias and Fairness

If you try classifying "I am from the USA" and "I am from Iraq", you will see that the former is classified as very positive, while the latter is classified as very negative. The model is also positive about Thailand but negative about Vietnam. You can try this model with your own country or city; the result may surprise you. Such a bias generally comes in large part from the training data itself: in this case, there were plenty of references to the wars in Iraq and Vietnam in the model's training data, creating a negative bias. This bias was then amplified during the fine-tuning process since the model was forced to choose between just two classes: positive or negative. If you use a model that was fine-tuned on a dataset with an extra neutral class, then the country bias mostly disappears.

The training data is not the only source of bias: the model's architecture, the type of loss or regularization used for training, the optimizer—all of these can affect what the model ends up learning. Understanding bias in AI and mitigating its negative effects is still an area of active research, but in any case you should probably pause and think before you rush to deploy a model to production. For example, if you train a model to score resumes, you must ensure that it's fair. So make sure you evaluate the model's performance not just on average over the whole test set, but across various subsets as well; for example, you may find that although the model works very well on average, its performance is abysmal for some categories of people. You may also want to run counterfactual tests; for example, check that the model's predictions do not change when you simply switch someone's gender or place of birth. The solution depends on the problem: it may require rebalancing the dataset, fine-tuning on a different dataset, switching to another pretrained model, tweaking the model's architecture or hyperparameters, etc.

Lastly, even if you manage to train a perfectly fair model, it could be *used* in a biased way. For example, the recruiters may use it only for some category of people and not others.

The model we chose is well-suited for general-purpose sentiment analysis, such as movie reviews, but other models are better suited for specific use cases, such as social media posts (e.g., trained on a large dataset of tweets, then fine-tuned on a sentiment analysis dataset). To find the best model for your use case, you can search the list of available models on the *Hugging Face Hub* (*https://huggingface.co/models*). However, there are over 80,000 models available in the "text-classification" category alone, so you will need to use the filters to narrow down the options. In particular, start by filtering on the task, and sort by trending or most-liked models. You can also continue to filter by language and dataset, if necessary. Prefer models from reputable sources (e.g., models from users huggingface, facebook, google, cardiffnlp, and so on), and if the model includes executable code, make absolutely sure you trust the user (and if you do, set `trust_remote_code=True` when calling the `pipeline()` function).

There are many text classification tasks other than sentiment analysis. For example, a model fine-tuned on the multi-genre natural language inference (MultiNLI) dataset can classify a pair of texts (each ending with a separation token [SEP]) into three classes: contradiction (if the texts contradict each other), entailment (if the first text entails the second), or neutral otherwise. For example:

```
>>> model_name = "huggingface/distilbert-base-uncased-finetuned-mnli"
>>> classifier_mnli = pipeline("text-classification", model=model_name)
>>> classifier_mnli([
...     "She loves me. [SEP] She loves me not. [SEP]",
...     "Alice just woke up. [SEP] Alice is awake. [SEP]",
...     "I like dogs. [SEP] Everyone likes dogs. [SEP]"])
...
[{'label': 'contradiction', 'score': 0.9717152714729309},
 {'label': 'entailment', 'score': 0.9119168519973755},
 {'label': 'neutral', 'score': 0.9509281516075134}]
```

Many other NLP tasks are also available via the pipeline API, such as question answering, summarization, sentence similarity, text generation, token classification, translation, and more. And it doesn't stop there! There are also many computer vision tasks, such as image classification, image segmentation, object detection, image-to-text, text-to-image, depth estimation, and even audio tasks, such as audio classification, speech-to-text, text-to-speech, and so on. Make sure to check out the full list at *https://huggingface.co/tasks*.

Before you download a model, make sure you trust the hosting platform (e.g., the Hugging Face Hub) and the model's author: the model may contain executable code, which could be malicious. It could also produce biased outputs, or it may have been trained with copyrighted or sensitive private data which might be leaked to your users, or it might even have *poisoned weights* which could make it produce harmful content (e.g., propaganda) only for some types of inputs, otherwise behaving normally.

Time to step back. So far we have looked at text generation using a char-RNN, and sentiment analysis using various subword tokenization methods, pretrained embeddings, and even entire pretrained models. Along the way, we discussed embeddings, tokenizers, and the Hugging Face libraries. In the next section, we will explore another important NLP task: *neural machine translation* (NMT). Specifically, we will build an encoder-decoder model capable of translating English to Spanish, and we will see how to boost its performance using beam search and attention mechanisms. ¡Vamos!

An Encoder-Decoder Network for Neural Machine Translation

Let's begin with a relatively simple sequence-to-sequence NMT model (*https://homl.info/nmtmodel*)[15] that will translate English text to Spanish (see Figure 14-5).

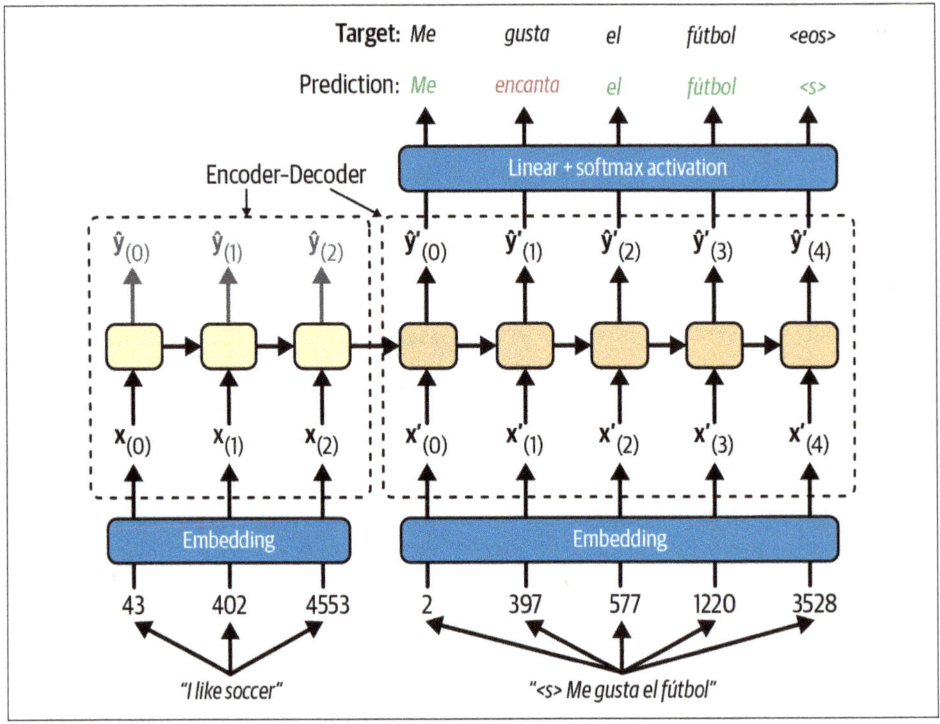

Figure 14-5. A simple machine translation model

In short, the architecture is as follows: English texts are fed as inputs to the encoder, and the decoder outputs the Spanish translations. Note that the Spanish translations are also used as inputs to the decoder during training, but shifted back by one step. In other words, during training the decoder is given as input the token that it *should* have output at the previous step, regardless of what it actually output. This is called *teacher forcing*—a technique that significantly speeds up training and improves the model's performance. For the very first token, the decoder is given the start-of-sequence (SoS, a.k.a. beginning-of-sequence, BoS) token (`"<s>"`), and the decoder is expected to end the text with an end-of-sequence (EoS) token (`"</s>"`).

15 Ilya Sutskever et al., "Sequence to Sequence Learning with Neural Networks", arXiv preprint, arXiv:1409.3215 (2014).

Each token is initially represented by its ID (e.g., `4553` for the token "soccer"). Next, an `nn.Embedding` layer returns the token embedding. These token embeddings are then fed to the encoder and the decoder.

At each step, the decoder's dense output layer (i.e., an `nn.Linear` layer) outputs a logit score for each token in the output vocabulary (i.e., Spanish). If you pass these logits through the softmax function, you get an estimated probability for each possible token. For example, at the first step the word "Me" may have a probability of 7%, "Yo" may have a probability of 1%, and so on. This is very much like a regular classification task, and indeed we will train the model using the `nn.CrossEntropyLoss`, much like we did in the char-RNN model.

Note that at inference time (after training), you will not have the target text to feed to the decoder. Instead, you need to feed it the word that it has just output at the previous step, as shown in Figure 14-6 (this will require an embedding lookup that is not shown in the diagram).

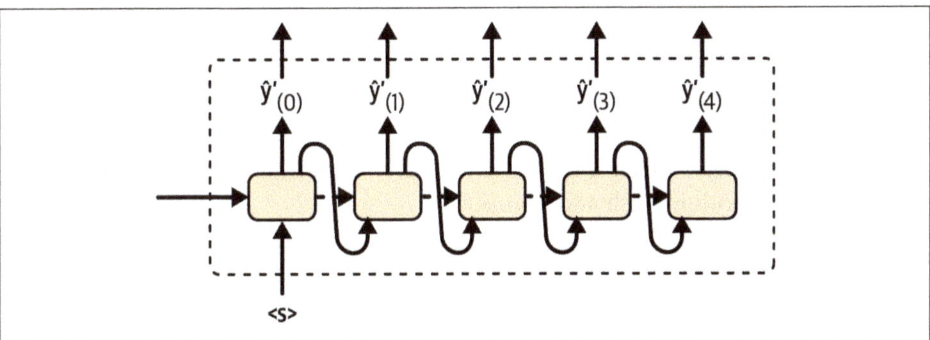

Figure 14-6. At inference time, the decoder is fed as input the word it just output at the previous time step

In a 2015 paper (*https://homl.info/scheduledsampling*),[16] Samy Bengio et al. proposed gradually switching from feeding the decoder the previous *target* token to feeding it the previous *output* token during training.

Let's build and train this model! First, we need to download a dataset of English/Spanish text pairs. For this, we will use the Datasets library to download English/Spanish pairs from the *Tatoeba Challenge* dataset. The Tatoeba project (*https://tatoeba.org*) is a language-learning initiative started in 2006 by Trang Ho, where

16 Samy Bengio et al., "Scheduled Sampling for Sequence Prediction with Recurrent Neural Networks", arXiv preprint arXiv:1506.03099 (2015).

contributors have created a huge collection of text pairs from many languages. The Tatoeba Challenge dataset was created by researchers from the University of Helsinki to benchmark machine translation systems, using data extracted from the Tatoeba project. The training set is quite large so we will use the validation set as our training set, setting aside 20% for validation. We will also download the test set:

```
nmt_original_valid_set, nmt_test_set = load_dataset(
    path="ageron/tatoeba_mt_train", name="eng-spa",
    split=["validation", "test"])
split = nmt_original_valid_set.train_test_split(train_size=0.8, seed=42)
nmt_train_set, nmt_valid_set = split["train"], split["test"]
```

Each sample in the dataset is a dictionary containing an English text along with its Spanish translation. For example:

```
>>> nmt_train_set[0]
{'source_text': 'Tom tried to break up the fight.',
 'target_text': 'Tom trató de disolver la pelea.',
 'source_lang': 'eng',
 'target_lang': 'spa'}
```

We will need to tokenize this text. We could use a different tokenizer for English and Spanish, but these two languages have many words in common (e.g., animal, color, hotel, hospital, idea, radio, motor), and many similar subwords (e.g., pre, auto, inter, uni), so it makes sense to use a common tokenizer. Let's train a BPE tokenizer on all the training text, both English and Spanish:

```
def train_eng_spa():  # a generator function to iterate over all training text
    for pair in nmt_train_set:
        yield pair["source_text"]
        yield pair["target_text"]

max_length = 256
vocab_size = 10_000
nmt_tokenizer_model = tokenizers.models.BPE(unk_token="<unk>")
nmt_tokenizer = tokenizers.Tokenizer(nmt_tokenizer_model)
nmt_tokenizer.enable_padding(pad_id=0, pad_token="<pad>")
nmt_tokenizer.enable_truncation(max_length=max_length)
nmt_tokenizer.pre_tokenizer = tokenizers.pre_tokenizers.Whitespace()
nmt_tokenizer_trainer = tokenizers.trainers.BpeTrainer(
    vocab_size=vocab_size, special_tokens=["<pad>", "<unk>", "<s>", "</s>"])
nmt_tokenizer.train_from_iterator(train_eng_spa(), nmt_tokenizer_trainer)
```

Let's test this tokenizer:

```
>>> nmt_tokenizer.encode("I like soccer").ids
[43, 401, 4381]
>>> nmt_tokenizer.encode("<s> Me gusta el fútbol").ids
[2, 396, 582, 219, 3356]
```

Perfect! Now let's create a small utility class that will hold tokenized English texts (i.e., the *source* token ID sequences), along with the corresponding tokenized Spanish targets (i.e., the *target* token ID sequences), plus the corresponding attention masks. For this, we can create a `namedtuple` base class (i.e., a tuple with named fields), and extend it to add a `to()` method, which will make it easy to move all these tensors to the GPU:

```
from collections import namedtuple

fields = ["src_token_ids", "src_mask", "tgt_token_ids", "tgt_mask"]
class NmtPair(namedtuple("NmtPairBase", fields)):
    def to(self, device):
        return NmtPair(self.src_token_ids.to(device), self.src_mask.to(device),
                       self.tgt_token_ids.to(device), self.tgt_mask.to(device))
```

Next, let's create the data loaders:

```
def nmt_collate_fn(batch):
    src_texts = [pair['source_text'] for pair in batch]
    tgt_texts = [f"<s> {pair['target_text']} </s>" for pair in batch]
    src_encodings = nmt_tokenizer.encode_batch(src_texts)
    tgt_encodings = nmt_tokenizer.encode_batch(tgt_texts)
    src_token_ids = torch.tensor([enc.ids for enc in src_encodings])
    tgt_token_ids = torch.tensor([enc.ids for enc in tgt_encodings])
    src_mask = torch.tensor([enc.attention_mask for enc in src_encodings])
    tgt_mask = torch.tensor([enc.attention_mask for enc in tgt_encodings])
    inputs = NmtPair(src_token_ids, src_mask,
                     tgt_token_ids[:, :-1], tgt_mask[:, :-1])
    labels = tgt_token_ids[:, 1:]
    return inputs, labels

batch_size = 32
nmt_train_loader = DataLoader(nmt_train_set, batch_size=batch_size,
                              collate_fn=nmt_collate_fn, shuffle=True)
nmt_valid_loader = DataLoader(nmt_valid_set, batch_size=batch_size,
                              collate_fn=nmt_collate_fn)
nmt_test_loader = DataLoader(nmt_test_set, batch_size=batch_size,
                             collate_fn=nmt_collate_fn)
```

The `nmt_collate_fn()` function starts by extracting all the English and Spanish texts from the given batch. In the process, it also adds an SoS token at the start of each Spanish text, as well as an EoS token at the end. It then tokenizes both the English and Spanish texts using our BPE tokenizer. Next, the input sequences and the attention masks are converted to tensors and wrapped in an `NmtPair`. Importantly, the function drops the EoS token from the decoder inputs, and drops the SoS token from the decoder targets. For example, the inputs may contain the token IDs for "<s> Me gusta el fútbol", while the targets may contain the token IDs for "Me gusta el fútbol </s>". Lastly, the function returns the inputs (i.e., the `NmtPair`) along with the targets. Then we just create the data loaders as usual.

And now we are ready to build our translation model. It's just like Figure 14-5, except the encoder and decoder share the same `nn.Embedding` layer, and the encoder and decoder `nn.GRU` modules contain two layers each:

```
class NmtModel(nn.Module):
    def __init__(self, vocab_size, embed_dim=512, pad_id=0, hidden_dim=512,
                 n_layers=2):
        super().__init__()
        self.embed = nn.Embedding(vocab_size, embed_dim, padding_idx=pad_id)
        self.encoder = nn.GRU(embed_dim, hidden_dim, num_layers=n_layers,
                              batch_first=True)
        self.decoder = nn.GRU(embed_dim, hidden_dim, num_layers=n_layers,
                              batch_first=True)
        self.output = nn.Linear(hidden_dim, vocab_size)

    def forward(self, pair):
        src_embeddings = self.embed(pair.src_token_ids)
        tgt_embeddings = self.embed(pair.tgt_token_ids)
        src_lengths = pair.src_mask.sum(dim=1)
        src_packed = pack_padded_sequence(
            src_embeddings, lengths=src_lengths.cpu(),
            batch_first=True, enforce_sorted=False)
        _, hidden_states = self.encoder(src_packed)
        outputs, _ = self.decoder(tgt_embeddings, hidden_states)
        return self.output(outputs).permute(0, 2, 1)

torch.manual_seed(42)
vocab_size = nmt_tokenizer.get_vocab_size()
nmt_model = NmtModel(vocab_size).to(device)
```

Almost everything in this model should look familiar: it's very similar to our previous models. We create the modules in the constructor, then the `forward()` method embeds the input sequences (both English and Spanish), it packs the English embeddings and passes them through the encoder, then it passes the Spanish embeddings to the decoder, along with the encoder's last hidden states (across all `nn.GRU` layers). Lastly, the decoder's outputs are passed through the output `nn.Linear` layer, and the final outputs are permuted to ensure that the class dimension (containing the token logits) is the second dimension, since this is expected by the `nn.CrossEntropyLoss` and the `Accuracy` metric, as we saw earlier.

The most common metric used in NMT is the *bilingual evaluation understudy* (BLEU) score, which compares each translation produced by the model with several good translations produced by humans. It counts the number of *n*-grams (sequences of *n* words) that appear in any of the target translations and adjusts the score to take into account the frequency of the produced *n*-grams in the target translations. It is implemented by TorchMetric's `BLEUScore` class.

We could have packed the Spanish embeddings, but then the decoder's outputs would have been packed sequences, which we would have had to pad before we passed them to the output layer. We avoided this complexity because we can just configure the loss to ignore the output tokens when the targets are padding tokens, like this:

```
xentropy = nn.CrossEntropyLoss(ignore_index=0)  # ignore <pad> tokens
```

Now you can train this model (e.g., for 10 epochs using a `Nadam` optimizer with `lr = 0.001`), and it will take quite a while. It's actually not that long when you consider the fact that the model is learning two languages at once!

While it's training, let's write a little helper function to translate some English text to Spanish using our model. It will start by calling the model with the English text for the encoder, and a single SoS token for the decoder. The decoder will just output logits for the first token in the translation. Our function will then pick the most likely token (i.e., with the highest logit) and add it to the decoder inputs, then it will call the model again to get the next token. It will repeat this process, adding one token at a time, until the model outputs an EoS token:

```
def translate(model, src_text, max_length=20, pad_id=0, eos_id=3):
    tgt_text = ""
    token_ids = []
    for index in range(max_length):
        batch, _ = nmt_collate_fn([{"source_text": src_text,
                                    "target_text": tgt_text}])
        with torch.no_grad():
            Y_logits = model(batch.to(device))
            Y_token_ids = Y_logits.argmax(dim=1)  # find the best token IDs
            next_token_id = Y_token_ids[0, index]  # take the last token ID

        next_token = nmt_tokenizer.id_to_token(next_token_id)
        tgt_text += " " + next_token
        if next_token_id == eos_id:
            break
    return tgt_text
```

This implementation works but it's not optimized at all. We could run the encoder just once on the English text, and we could also run the decoder just once per time step, instead of running it over the whole growing text at each iteration.

Let's try translating some text!

```
>>> nmt_model.eval()
>>> translate(nmt_model, "I like soccer.")
' Me gusta el fútbol . </s>'
```

Hurray, it works! We just built a model from scratch that can translate English to Spanish.

Model Optimizations

When the output vocabulary is large (e.g., 10,000 tokens or more), computing the `nn.CrossEntropyLoss` can be quite slow, depending on the hardware. To speed things up, one technique is to use *sampled softmax*, introduced in 2015 (*https://homl.info/sampledsoftmax*) by Sébastien Jean et al.[17] Instead of computing the softmax over all of the logits, it computes an approximation based on the correct class's logit, as well as a random sample of logits for other classes. This technique requires knowing the target, so it is only useful during training. Moreover, it is not included in PyTorch, so you have to implement it yourself.

Another technique is *adaptive softmax*, introduced in 2016 (*https://homl.info/adaptivesoftmax*) by Edouard Grave et al.,[18] which speeds up softmax computation by splitting the vocabulary into frequency-based clusters. Frequent tokens are processed normally, while less frequent tokens are placed in progressively larger clusters, reducing computation by only accessing the necessary clusters. This speeds up computations both during training and inference. PyTorch implements this algorithm in the `nn.AdaptiveLogSoftmaxWithLoss` class.

Another thing you can do to speed up training (and also save a lot of memory) is to use the embedding matrix as the weights of the output layer. This is called *tying the weights* of these two layers, and it was first proposed in a 2016 paper by Ofir Press and Lior Wolf (*https://homl.info/tieweights*).[19] To implement it, just add `self.output.weight = self.embed.weight` to the model's constructor. You can also get rid of the output layer's `bias` parameter, by setting `bias=False` when creating the output layer. Tying the weights significantly reduces the number of model parameters, which speeds up training and may sometimes improve the model's accuracy as well, especially if you don't have a lot of training data. Why does this work? Well, as we saw earlier, the embedding matrix is equivalent to one-hot encoding followed by a linear layer with no bias term and no activation function that maps the one-hot vectors to the embedding space. The output layer does the reverse. So if the model can find an embedding matrix whose transpose is equal to its inverse (such a matrix is called an *orthogonal matrix*), then there's no need to learn a separate set of weights for the output layer.

17 Sébastien Jean et al., "On Using Very Large Target Vocabulary for Neural Machine Translation", *Proceedings of the 53rd Annual Meeting of the Association for Computational Linguistics and the 7th International Joint Conference on Natural Language Processing of the Asian Federation of Natural Language Processing* 1 (2015): 1–10.

18 Edouard Grave et al., "Efficient softmax approximation for GPUs", arXiv preprint arXiv:1609.04309 (2016).

19 Ofir Press, Lior Wolf, "Using the Output Embedding to Improve Language Models", arXiv preprint arXiv:1608.05859 (2016).

If you play around with our translation model, you will find that it often works reasonably well on short text, but it really struggles with longer sentences. For example:

```
>>> longer_text = "I like to play soccer with my friends."
>>> translate(nmt_model, longer_text)
' Me gusta jugar con mis amigos . </s>'
```

The translation says "I like to play with my friends". Oops, there's no mention of soccer. So how can we improve this model? One way is to increase the training set size and add more `nn.GRU` layers in both the encoder and the decoder. You could also make the encoder bidirectional (but not the decoder, or else it would no longer be causal and it would see the full translation at each time step, instead of just the previous tokens). Another popular technique that can greatly improve the performance of a translation model at inference time is *beam search*.

Beam Search

To translate an English text to Spanish, we call our model several times, producing one word at a time. Unfortunately, this means that when the model makes one mistake, it is stuck with it for the rest of the translation, which can cause more errors, making the translation worse and worse. For example, suppose we want to translate "I like soccer", and the model correctly starts with "Me", but then predicts "gustan" (plural) instead of "gusta" (singular). This mistake is understandable, since "Me gustan" is the correct way to start translating "I like" in many cases. Once the model has made this mistake, it is stuck with "gustan". It then reasonably adds "los", which is the plural for "the". But since the model never saw "los fútbol" in the training data (soccer is singular, not plural), the model tries to find something reasonable to add, and given the context it adds "jugadores", which means "the players". So "I like soccer" gets translated to "I like the players". One error caused a chain of errors.

How can we give the model a chance to go back and fix mistakes it made earlier? One of the most common solutions is *beam search*: it keeps track of a short list of the *k* most promising output sequences (say, the top three), and at each decoder step it tries to extend each of them by one word, keeping only the *k* most likely sequences. The parameter *k* is called the *beam width*.

For example, suppose you use the model to translate the sentence "I like soccer" using beam search with a beam width of three (see Figure 14-7). At the first decoder step, the model will output an estimated probability for each possible first word in the translated sentence. Suppose the top three words are "Me" (75% estimated probability), "a" (3%), and "como" (1%). That's our short list so far. Next, we use the model to find the next word for each sentence. For the first sentence ("Me"), perhaps the model outputs a probability of 36% for the word "gustan", 32% for the word "gusta", 16% for the word "encanta", and so on. Note that these are actually *conditional* probabilities, given that the sentence starts with "Me". For the second sentence ("a"), the model might output a conditional probability of 50% for the word "mi", and so on. Assuming the vocabulary has 10,000 tokens, we will end up with 10,000 probabilities per sentence.

Next, we compute the probabilities of each of the 30,000 two-token sentences we considered (3 × 10,000). We do this by multiplying the estimated conditional probability of each word by the estimated probability of the sentence it completes. For example, the estimated probability of the sentence "Me" was 75%, while the estimated conditional probability of the word "gustan" (given that the first word is "Me") was 36%, so the estimated probability of the sentence "Me gustan" is 75% × 36% = 27%. After computing the probabilities of all 30,000 two-word sentences, we keep only the top 3. In this example they all start with the word "Me": "Me gustan" (27%), "Me gusta" (24%), and "Me encanta" (12%). Right now, the sentence "Me gustan" is winning, but "Me gusta" has not been eliminated.

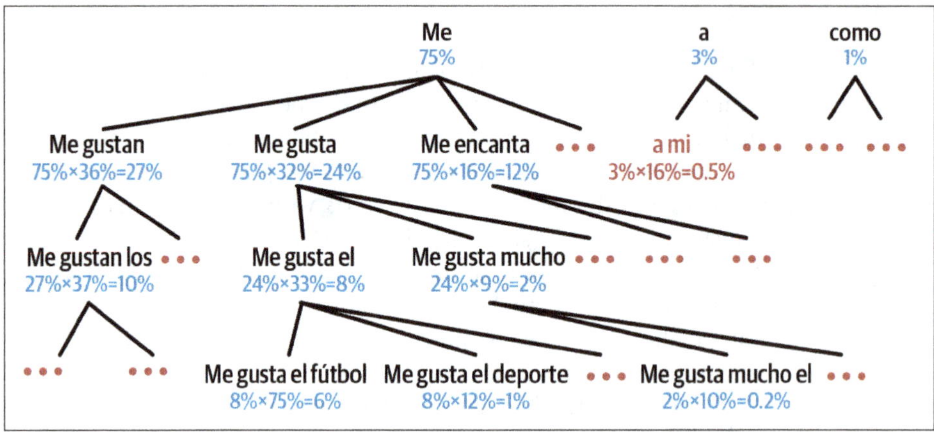

Figure 14-7. Beam search, with a beam width of three

Then we repeat the same process: we use the model to predict the next word in each of these three sentences, and we compute the probabilities of all 30,000 three-word sentences we considered. Perhaps the top 3 are now "Me gustan los" (10%), "Me gusta el" (8%), and "Me gusta mucho" (2%). At the next step we may get "Me gusta el fútbol" (6%), "Me gusta mucho el" (1%), and "Me gusta el deporte" (0.2%). Notice that "Me gustan" was eliminated, and the correct translation is now ahead. We boosted our encoder-decoder model's performance without any extra training, simply by using it more wisely.

The notebook for this chapter contains a very simple `beam_search()` function, if you're interested, but in general you will probably want to use the implementation provided by the `GenerationMixin` class in the Transformers library. This is where the text generation models from the Transformers library get their `generate()` method: it accepts a `num_beams` argument which you can set to the desired beam width if you want to use beam search. It also provides a `do_sample` argument that will randomly sample the next token using the probability distribution output by the model, just like we did earlier with our char-RNN model. Other generation strategies are also supported and can be combined (see *https://homl.info/hfgen* for more details).

With all this, you can get reasonably good translations for fairly short sentences. For example, the following translation is correct:

```
>>> beam_search(nmt_model, longer_text, beam_width=3)
' Me gusta jugar al fútbol con mis amigos . </s>'
```

Unfortunately, this model will still be pretty bad at translating long sentences:

```
>>> longest_text = "I like to play soccer with my friends at the beach."
>>> beam_search(nmt_model, longest_text, beam_width=3)
' Me gusta jugar con jugar con los jug adores de la playa . </s>'
```

This translates to "I like to play with play with the players of the beach". That's not quite right. Once again, the problem comes from the limited short-term memory of RNNs. *Attention mechanisms* are the game-changing innovation that addressed this problem.

Attention Mechanisms

Consider the path from the word "soccer" to its translation "fútbol" back in Figure 14-5: it is quite long! This means that a representation of this word (along with all the other words) needs to be carried over many steps before it is actually used. Can't we make this path shorter?

This was the core idea in a landmark 2014 paper (*https://homl.info/attention*)[20] by Dzmitry Bahdanau et al., where the authors introduced a technique that allowed the decoder to focus on the appropriate words (as encoded by the encoder) at each time step. For example, at the time step where the decoder needs to output the word "fútbol", it will focus its attention on the word "soccer". This means that the path from an input word to its translation is now much shorter, so the short-term memory limitations of RNNs have much less impact. Attention mechanisms revolutionized neural machine translation (and deep learning in general), allowing a significant improvement in the state of the art, especially for long sentences (e.g., over 30 words).

Figure 14-8 shows our encoder-decoder model with an added attention mechanism:

- On the left, you have the encoder and the decoder (I've made the encoder bidirectional in this figure, as it's generally a good idea).

20 Dzmitry Bahdanau et al., "Neural Machine Translation by Jointly Learning to Align and Translate", arXiv preprint arXiv:1409.0473 (2014).

- Instead of sending the encoder's final hidden state to the decoder, as well as the previous target word at each time step (which is still done, but it is not shown in the figure), we now send all of the encoder's outputs to the decoder as well.
- Since the decoder cannot deal with all these encoder outputs at once, they need to be aggregated: at each time step, the decoder's memory cell computes a weighted sum of all the encoder outputs. This determines which words the decoder will focus on at this step.
- The weight $\alpha_{(t,i)}$ is the weight of the ith encoder output at the tth decoder time step. For example, if the weight $\alpha_{(3,2)}$ is much larger than the weights $\alpha_{(3,0)}$ and $\alpha_{(3,1)}$, then the decoder will pay much more attention to the encoder's output for word #2 ("soccer") than to the other two outputs, at least at this time step.
- The rest of the decoder works just like earlier: at each time step the memory cell receives the inputs we just discussed, plus the hidden state from the previous time step, and finally (although it is not represented in the diagram) it receives the target word from the previous time step (or at inference time, the output from the previous time step).

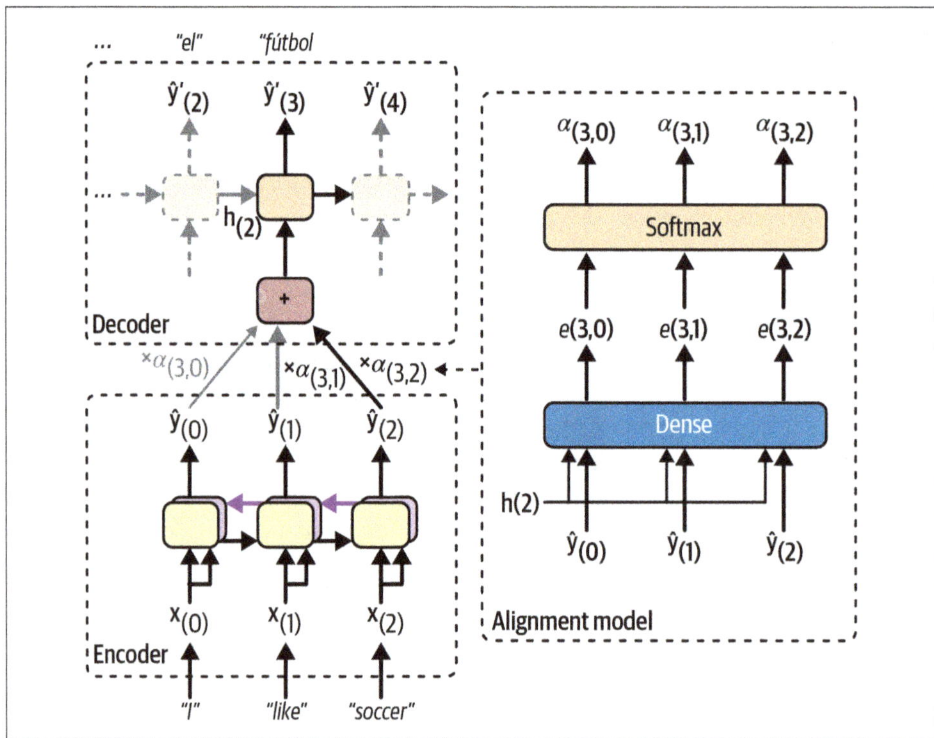

Figure 14-8. Neural machine translation using an encoder-decoder network with an attention model

But where do these $\alpha_{(t,i)}$ weights come from? Well, they are generated by a small neural network called an *alignment model* (or an *attention layer*), which is trained jointly with the rest of the encoder-decoder model. This alignment model is illustrated on the righthand side of Figure 14-8:

- It starts with a dense layer (i.e., `nn.Linear`) that takes as input each of the encoder's outputs, along with the decoder's previous hidden state (e.g., $\mathbf{h}_{(2)}$), and outputs a score (or energy) for each encoder output (e.g., $e_{(3,\ 2)}$). This score measures how well each encoder output is aligned with the decoder's previous hidden state.

  For example, in Figure 14-8, the model has already output "me gusta el" (meaning "I like"), so it's now expecting a noun. The word "soccer" is the one that best aligns with the current state, so it gets a high score.

- Finally, all the scores go through a softmax layer to get a final weight for each encoder output (e.g., $\alpha_{(3,2)}$). All the weights for a given decoder time step add up to 1.

This particular attention mechanism is called *Bahdanau attention* (named after the 2014 paper's first author). Since it concatenates the encoder output with the decoder's previous hidden state, it is sometimes called *concatenative attention* (or *additive attention*).

In short, the attention mechanism provides a way to focus the attention of the model on part of the inputs. That said, there's another way to think of this whole process: it acts as a differentiable memory retrieval mechanism. For example, let's suppose the encoder analyzed the input sentence "I like soccer", and it managed to understand that the word "I" is the subject, the word "like" is the verb, and the word "soccer" is the noun, so it encoded this information in its outputs for these words. Now suppose the decoder has already translated "I like", and it thinks that it should translate the noun next. For this, it needs to fetch the noun from the input sentence. This is analogous to a dictionary lookup: it's as if the encoder had created a dictionary {"subject": "I", "verb": "like", "noun": "soccer"} and the decoder wanted to look up the value that corresponds to the key "noun".

However, the model does not have discrete tokens to represent the keys (like "subject", "verb", or "noun"); instead, it has vectorized representations of these concepts that it learned during training, so the query it will use for the lookup will not perfectly match any key in the dictionary. One solution is to compute a similarity measure between the query and each key in the dictionary, and then use the softmax function to convert these similarity scores to weights that add up to 1. As we just saw, that's exactly what the attention layer does. If the key that represents the noun is by far the most similar to the query, then that key's weight will be close to 1. Next, the attention layer computes a weighted sum of the corresponding values: if the weight of the “noun” key is close to 1, then the weighted sum will be very close to the representation of the word “soccer”. In short, the decoder queried for a noun and the attention mechanism retrieved it.

In most modern implementations of attention mechanisms, the arguments are named `query`, `key`, and `value`. In our example, the query is the decoder's hidden states, the key is the encoder's outputs (this is used to compute the weights), and the value is also the encoder's outputs (this is used to compute the final weighted sum).

If the input sentence is n words long, and assuming the output sentence is about as long, then the attention mechanism will need to compute about n^2 weights. This quadratic computational complexity becomes untractable when the sentences are too long.

Another common attention mechanism, known as *Luong attention* or *multiplicative attention*, was proposed shortly after, in 2015 (*https://homl.info/luongattention*),[21] by Minh-Thang Luong et al. Because the goal of the alignment model is to measure the similarity between one of the encoder's outputs and the decoder's previous hidden state, the authors proposed to simply compute the dot product (see Chapter 4) of these two vectors, as this is often a fairly good similarity measure, and modern hardware can compute it very efficiently. For this to be possible, both vectors must have the same dimensionality. The dot product gives a score, and all the scores (at a given decoder time step) go through a softmax layer to give the final weights, just like in Bahdanau attention.

Luong et al. also proposed to use the decoder's hidden state at the current time step rather than at the previous time step (i.e., $\mathbf{h}_{(t)}$ rather than $\mathbf{h}_{(t-1)}$) to compute the attention vector (denoted $\widetilde{\mathbf{h}}_{(t)}$). This attention vector is then concatenated with the decoder's hidden state to form an attentional hidden state, which is then used to predict the next token. This simplifies and speeds up the process by allowing the encoder and decoder to operate independently before attention is applied, rather than interweaving attention into the decoder's recurrence.

The researchers also proposed a variant of the dot product mechanism where the encoder outputs first go through a fully connected layer (without a bias term) before the dot products are computed. This is called the “general” dot product approach. The researchers compared both dot product approaches with the concatenative attention mechanism (adding a rescaling parameter vector $\mathbf{v}$), and they observed that the dot product variants performed better than concatenative attention. For this reason,

21 Minh-Thang Luong et al., “Effective Approaches to Attention-Based Neural Machine Translation”, *Proceedings of the 2015 Conference on Empirical Methods in Natural Language Processing* (2015): 1412–1421.

concatenative attention is much less used now. The equations for these three attention mechanisms are summarized in Equation 14-2.

Equation 14-2. Attention mechanisms

$$\widetilde{\mathbf{h}}_{(t)} = \sum_{i} \alpha_{(t,i)} \hat{\mathbf{y}}_{(i)}$$

$$\text{with } \alpha_{(t,i)} = \frac{\exp\left(e_{(t,i)}\right)}{\sum_{i'} \exp\left(e_{(t,i')}\right)}$$

$$\text{and } e_{(t,i)} = \begin{cases} \mathbf{h}_{(t)}^{\mathsf{T}} \hat{\mathbf{y}}_{(i)} & \textit{dot} \\ \mathbf{h}_{(t)}^{\mathsf{T}} \mathbf{W} \hat{\mathbf{y}}_{(i)} & \textit{general} \\ \mathbf{v}^{\mathsf{T}} \tanh\left(\mathbf{W}\left[\mathbf{h}_{(t)}; \hat{\mathbf{y}}_{(i)}\right]\right) & \textit{concat} \end{cases}$$

Let's add Luong attention to our encoder-decoder model. Since PyTorch does not include a Luong attention function, we need to write our own. Luckily, it's pretty short:

```
def attention(query, key, value):  # note: dq == dk and Lk == Lv
    scores = query @ key.transpose(1, 2)  # [B,Lq,dq] @ [B,dk,Lk] = [B, Lq, Lk]
    weights = torch.softmax(scores, dim=-1)  # [B, Lq, Lk]
    return weights @ value  # [B, Lq, Lk] @ [B, Lv, dv] = [B, Lq, dv]
```

Just like in Equation 14-2, we first compute the attention scores, then we convert them to attention weights using the softmax function, and lastly we compute the attention output by multiplying the attention weights with the value (i.e., the encoder outputs). This implementation efficiently runs all these computations for the whole batch at once. The `query` argument corresponds to $\mathbf{h}_{(t)}$ in Equation 14-2 (i.e., the decoder's hidden states), and the `key` argument corresponds to $\hat{\mathbf{y}}_{(i)}$ (i.e., the encoder's outputs), but only for the computation of the attention scores. The `value` argument also corresponds to $\hat{\mathbf{y}}_{(i)}$, but only for the final computation of the weighted sum. The `key` and `value` arguments are generally identical, but there are a few scenarios where they can differ (e.g., some models use compressed keys to save memory and speed up the score computation). The shapes are shown in the comments: `B` is the batch size; `Lq` is the length of the longest query in the batch; `Lk` is the length of the longest key in the batch (note that each value must have the same length as its corresponding key); `dq` is the query's embedding size, which must be the same as the key's embedding size `dk`; and `dv` is the value's embedding size.

Since all arguments are 3D tensors, we could replace the `@` matrix multiplication operator with the *batch matrix multiplication* function: `torch.bmm()`. This function only works with batches of matrices (i.e., 3D tensors), but it's optimized for this use case so it runs faster. The result is the same: each matrix in the first tensor gets multiplied by the corresponding matrix in the second tensor.

Now let's update our NMT model. The constructor needs just one modification—the output layer's input size must be doubled, since we will concatenate the attention vectors to the decoder outputs:

```
self.output = nn.Linear(2 * hidden_dim, vocab_size)
```

Next, let's add attention to the `forward()` method:

```
def forward(self, pair):
    src_embeddings = self.embed(pair.src_token_ids)  # same as earlier
    tgt_embeddings = self.embed(pair.tgt_token_ids)  # same
    src_lengths = pair.src_mask.sum(dim=1)  # same
    src_packed = pack_padded_sequence(src_embeddings, [...])  # same
    encoder_outputs_packed, hidden_states = self.encoder(src_packed)
    decoder_outputs, _ = self.decoder(tgt_embeddings, hidden_states)  # same
    encoder_outputs, _ = pad_packed_sequence(encoder_outputs_packed,
                                             batch_first=True)
    attn_output = attention(query=decoder_outputs,
                            key=encoder_outputs, value=encoder_outputs)
    combined_output = torch.cat((attn_output, decoder_outputs), dim=-1)
    return self.output(combined_output).permute(0, 2, 1)
```

Let's go through this code:

- We compute the English and Spanish embeddings, the English sequence lengths, and we pack the English embeddings, just like earlier.
- We then run the encoder like earlier, but we no longer ignore its outputs since we will need them for the attention function.
- Next, we run the decoder, just like earlier.
- Since the encoder's inputs are represented as a packed sequence, its outputs are also represented as a packed sequence. Not many operations support packed sequences, so we must convert the encoder's outputs to a padded tensor using the `pad_packed_sequence()` function.
- And now we can call our `attention()` function. Note that we pass the decoder outputs instead of the hidden states because the decoder only returns the last hidden states. That's OK because the `nn.GRU` layer's outputs are equal to its top-layer hidden states.

- Lastly, we concatenate the attention output and the decoder outputs along the last dimension, and we pass the result through the output layer. As earlier, we also permute the last two dimensions of the result.

Our attention mechanism doesn't ignore padding tokens. The model learns to ignore them during training, but it's preferable to mask them entirely. We will see how in Chapter 15.

And that's it! If you train this model, you will find that it now handles much longer sentences. For example:

```
>>> translate(nmt_attn_model, longest_text)
' Me gusta jugar fu tbol con mis amigos en la playa . </s>'
```

Perfect! We didn't even have to use beam search. In fact, attention mechanisms turned out to be so powerful that some Google researchers tried getting rid of recurrent layers altogether, only using feedforward layers and attention. Surprisingly, it worked like a charm. This led the researchers to name their paper "Attention is all you need", introducing the Transformer architecture to the world. This was the start of a huge revolution in NLP and beyond. In the next chapter, we will explore the Transformer architecture and see how it revolutionized deep learning.

Exercises

1. What are the pros and cons of using a stateful RNN versus a stateless RNN?
2. Why do people use encoder-decoder RNNs rather than plain sequence-to-sequence RNNs for automatic translation?
3. How can you deal with variable-length input sequences? What about variable-length output sequences?
4. What is beam search, and why would you use it? What tool can you use to implement it?
5. What is an attention mechanism? How does it help?
6. When would you need to use sampled softmax?
7. *Embedded Reber grammars* were used by Hochreiter and Schmidhuber in their paper (*https://homl.info/93*) about LSTMs. They are artificial grammars that produce strings such as "BPBTSXXVPSEPE". Check out Jenny Orr's nice introduction (*https://homl.info/108*) to this topic, then choose a particular embedded Reber grammar (such as the one represented on Orr's page), and train an RNN to identify whether a string respects that grammar or not. You will first need

to write a function capable of generating a training batch containing about 50% strings that respect the grammar, and 50% that don't.

8. Train an encoder-decoder model that can convert a date string from one format to another (e.g., from "April 22, 2019" to "2019-04-22").

Solutions to these exercises are available at the end of this chapter's notebook, at *https://homl.info/colab-p*.

CHAPTER 15

Transformers for Natural Language Processing and Chatbots

In a landmark 2017 paper titled "Attention Is All You Need" (*https://homl.info/transformer*),[1] a team of Google researchers proposed a novel neural net architecture named the *Transformer*, which significantly improved the state of the art in neural machine translation (NMT). In short, the Transformer architecture is simply an encoder-decoder model, very much like the one we built in Chapter 14 for English-to-Spanish translation, and it can be used in exactly the same way (see Figure 15-1):

1. The source text goes in the encoder, which outputs contextualized embeddings (one per token).
2. The encoder's output is then fed to the decoder, along with the translated text so far (starting with a start-of-sequence token).
3. The decoder predicts the next token for each input token.
4. The last token output by the decoder is appended to the translation.
5. Steps 2 to 4 are repeated again and again to produce the full translation, one extra token at a time, until an end-of-sequence token is generated. During training, we already have the full translation—it's the target—so it is fed to the decoder in step 2 (starting with a start-of-sequence token), and steps 4 and 5 are not needed.

1 Ashish Vaswani et al., "Attention Is All You Need", *Proceedings of the 31st International Conference on Neural Information Processing Systems* (2017): 6000–6010.

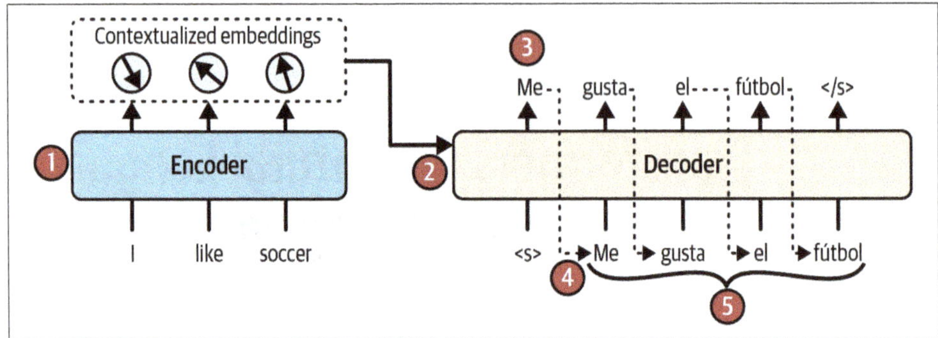

Figure 15-1. Using the Transformer model for English-to-Spanish translation

So what's new? Well, inside the black box, there are some important differences with our previous encoder-decoder. Crucially, the Transformer architecture does not contain any recurrent or convolutional layers, just regular dense layers combined with a new kind of attention mechanism called *multi-head attention* (MHA), plus a few bells and whistles.[2] Because the model is not recurrent, it doesn't suffer as much from the vanishing or exploding gradients problems as RNNs, it can be trained in fewer steps, it's easier to parallelize across multiple GPUs, and it scales surprisingly well. Moreover, thanks to multi-head attention, the model can capture long-range patterns much better than RNNs.

The Transformer architecture also turned out to be extremely versatile. It was initially designed for NMT, but researchers quickly tweaked the architecture for many other language tasks. The year 2018 was even called the "ImageNet moment for NLP". In June 2018, OpenAI released the first GPT model, based solely on the Transformer's decoder module. It was pretrained on a large corpus of text, its ability to generate text was unprecedented, it could auto-complete sentences, invent stories, and even answer some questions. GPT could also be fine-tuned to perform a wide range of language tasks. Just a few months later, Google released the BERT model, based solely on the Transformer's encoder module. It was excellent at a variety of *natural language understanding* (NLU) tasks, such as text classification, text embedding, multiple choice question answering, or finding the answer to a question within some text.

Surprisingly, transformers also turned out to be great at computer vision, audio processing (e.g., speech-to-text), robotics (using inputs from sensors and sending the outputs to actuators), and more. For example, if you split an image into little chunks and feed them to a transformer (instead of token embeddings), you get a *vision*

2 When applying a linear layer to a sequence, all tokens are treated independently, using the same parameters. This is equivalent to using a `Conv1d` layer with `kernel_size=1`. This is why you will sometimes see Transformer diagrams showing convolutional layers instead of linear layers.

transformer (ViT). In fact, some transformers can even handle multiple *modalities* at once (e.g., text + image); these are called *multimodal models*.

This outstanding combination of performance, flexibility, and scalability encouraged Google, OpenAI, Facebook (Meta), Microsoft, Anthropic, and many other organizations to train larger and larger transformer models. The original Transformer model had about 65 million parameters—which was considered quite large at the time—but new transformers grew at a mind-boggling rate, reaching 1.6 trillion parameters by January 2021—that's 1.6 million million parameters! Training such a gigantic transformer model from scratch is sadly restricted to organizations with deep pockets, as it requires a large and costly infrastructure for several months: training typically costs tens of millions of dollars, and even up to hundreds of millions according to some estimates (the exact figures are generally not public). Figure 15-2 shows some of the most influential transformers released between June 2018 and April 2025.[3] Note that the vertical axis is in *billions* of parameters, and it uses a logarithmic scale.

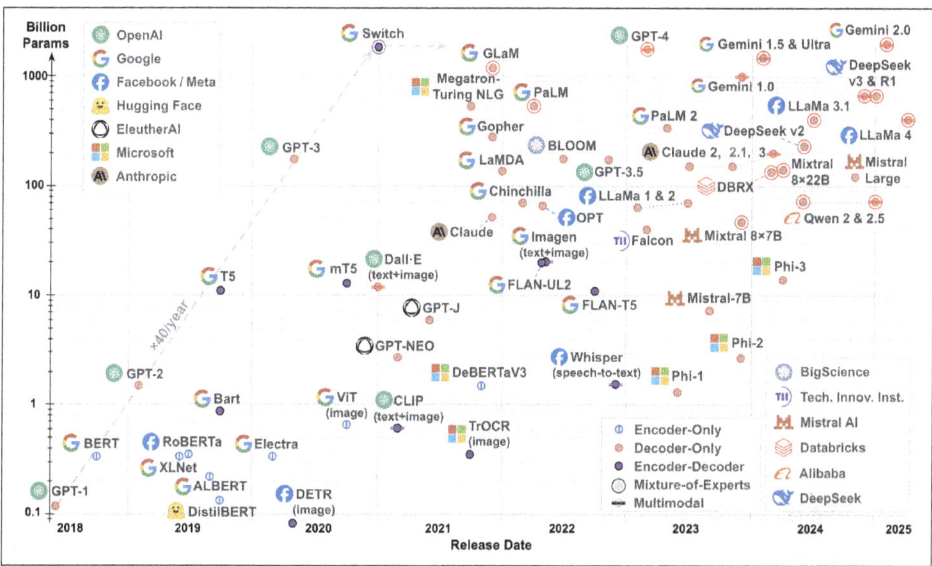

Figure 15-2. Some of the most influential transformers released since 2018; see it larger online (https://homl.info/fig15-2)

3 The number of parameters is not public for some models (e.g., Gemini models), so I used some rough estimates. Also, many models have smaller variants, not shown here. Lastly, several other organizations released influential models, such as the Allen Institute for AI (Ai2), Amazon, Baidu, Beijing Academy of AI, Cohere, Huawei, LAION, LMSYS, Nvidia, Stanford University, Talent International Institute (TII), Tsinghua University, xAI, Zhipu AI, and others.

Then, in November 2022, OpenAI released ChatGPT, an amazing *conversational AI*—or *chatbot*—that took the world by storm: it reached one million users in just five days, and over one hundred million monthly active users after just two months! Under the hood, it used GPT-3.5-turbo, a variant of GPT-3.5 which was fine-tuned to be conversational, helpful, and safe. Others soon followed: Perplexity AI, Google's Gemini (initially called Bard), Anthropic's Claude, Mistral AI, DeepSeek, and more.

Before ChatGPT was released, Google had actually developed a powerful chatbot named LaMDA, but it wasn't made public, likely for fear of reputational and legal risks, as the model was not deemed safe enough. This allowed OpenAI to become the first company to train a reasonably safe and helpful model and to package it as a useful chatbot product.

So how can you use these models and chatbots? Well, many of them are proprietary (e.g., OpenAI's GPT-3.5, GPT-4 and GPT-5 models, Anthropic's Claude models, and Google's Gemini models), and they can only be used via a web UI, an app, or an API: you must create an account, choose an offer (or use the free tier), and for the API you must get an access token and use it to query the API programmatically. However, many other models are *open weights*, meaning they can be downloaded for free (e.g., using the Hugging Face Hub): some of these have licensing restrictions (e.g., Meta's Llama models are only free for noncommercial use), while others are truly open source (e.g., DeepSeek's R1 or Mistral AI's Mistral-7B). Some even include the training code and data (e.g., the OLMo models by Ai2).

So what are we waiting for? Let's join the transformer revolution! Here's the plan:

- We will start by opening up the original Transformer architecture and inspecting its components to fully understand how everything works.
- Then we will build and train a transformer from scratch for English-to-Spanish translation.
- After that, we will look into encoder-only models like BERT, learn how they are pretrained, and see how to use them for tasks like text classification, semantic search, and text clustering, with or without fine-tuning.
- Next, we will look into decoder-only models like GPT, and see how they are pretrained. These models are capable of generating text, which is great if you want to write a poem, but it can also be used to tackle many other tasks.
- Then we will use a decoder-only model to build our own chatbot! This involves a few steps: first, you must download a pretrained model (or train your own if you have the time and money), then you must fine-tune it to make it more conversational, helpful, and safe (or you can download an already fine-tuned model, or even use a conversational model via an API), and lastly you must deploy the

model to a chatbot system that offers a user interface, stores conversations, and can also give the model access to tools, such as searching the web or using a calculator.

- Lastly, we will take a quick look at encoder-decoder models, such as T5 and BART, which are great for tasks such as translation and summarization.

In Chapter 16, we will look at vision transformers and multimodal transformers. Chapter 17 and "State-Space Models (SSMs)" (both available at *https://homl.info*) also discuss some advanced techniques to allow Transformers to scale and process longer input sequences.

Let's start by dissecting the Transformer architecture: take out your scalpel!

Attention Is All You Need: The Original Transformer Architecture

The original 2017 Transformer architecture is represented in Figure 15-3. The left part of the figure represents the encoder, the right part represents the decoder.

As we saw earlier, the encoder's role is to gradually *transform* the inputs (e.g., sequences of English tokens) until each token's representation perfectly captures the meaning of that token in the context of the sentence: the encoder's output is a sequence of contextualized token embeddings. Apart from the embedding layer, every layer in the encoder takes as input a tensor of shape [*batch size*, *max English sequence length in the batch*, *embedding size*] and returns a tensor of the exact same shape. This means that token representations get gradually transformed, hence the name of the architecture. For example, if you feed the sentence "I like soccer" to the encoder, then the token "like" will start off with a rather vague representation, since "like" could mean different things in different contexts (e.g., "I'm like a cat" versus "I like my cat"). But after going through the encoder, the token's representation should capture the correct meaning of "like" in the given sentence (in this case, to be fond of), as well as any other information that may be required for translation (e.g., it's a verb).

The decoder's role is to take the encoder's outputs, along with the translated sentence so far, and predict the next token in the translation. For this, the decoder layers gradually transform each input token's representation into a representation that can be used to predict the following token. For example, suppose the sentence to translate is "I like soccer" and we've already called the decoder four times, producing one new token each time: first "me", then "me gusta", then "me gusta el", and finally "me gusta el fútbol". Since this translation does not end with an EoS token `"</s>"`, we must call the decoder once again. The decoder's input sequence is now `"<s>` me gusta el fútbol". As the representation of each token goes through the decoder, it gets transformed: the representation of `"<s>"` becomes a rich enough representation to predict "me" (for simplicity, I'll say this more concisely as: "<s>" becomes "me"), "me" becomes "gusta", "gusta" becomes "el", "el" becomes "fútbol", and if everything goes well, "fútbol" becomes the EoS token "</s>". Apart from the embedding layer and the output `Linear` layer, every layer in the decoder takes as input a tensor of shape [*batch size, max Spanish sequence length in the batch, embedding size*] and returns a tensor of the exact same shape.

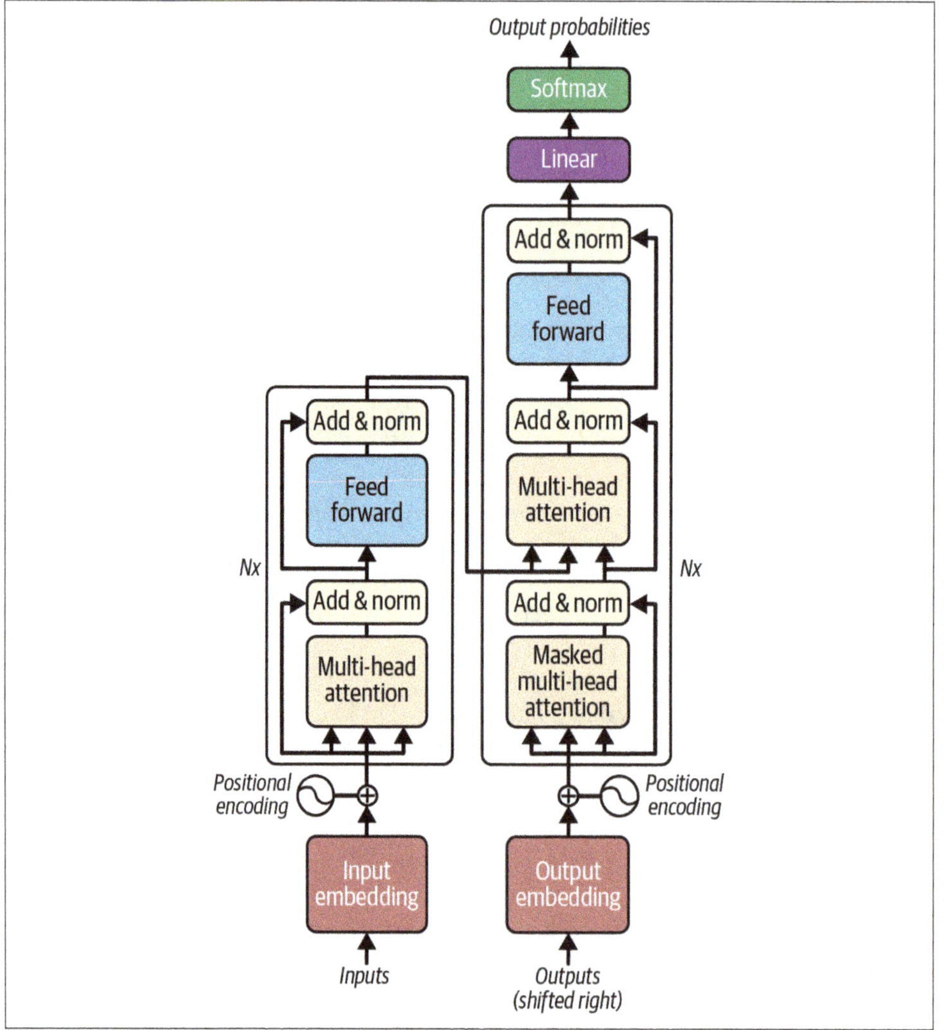

Figure 15-3. The original 2017 transformer architecture[4]

4 This is adapted from Figure 1 from "Attention Is All You Need", with the kind permission of the authors.

After going through the decoder, each token representation goes through a final `Linear` layer which will hopefully output a high logit for the correct token and a low logit for all other tokens in the vocabulary. The decoder's output shape is [*batch size, max Spanish sequence length in the batch, vocabulary size*]. The final predicted sentence should be "me gusta el fútbol `</s>`". Note that the figure shows a softmax layer at the top, but in PyTorch we usually don't explicitly add it: instead, we let the model output logits, and we train the model using `nn.CrossEntropyLoss`, which computes the cross-entropy loss based on logits instead of estimated probabilities (as we saw in previous chapters). If you ever need estimated probabilities, you can always convert the logits to estimated probabilities using the `F.softmax()` function.

Now let's zoom in a bit further into Figure 15-3:

- First, notice that both the encoder and the decoder contain blocks that are stacked *N* times. In the paper, *N* = 6. Note that the final outputs of the whole encoder stack are fed to each of the decoder's *N* blocks.
- As you can see, you are already familiar with most components: there are two embedding layers; several skip connections, each of them followed by a layer normalization module; several feedforward modules composed of two dense layers each (the first one using the ReLU activation function, the second with no activation function); and finally, the output layer is a linear layer. Notice that all layers treat each token independently from all the others. But how can we translate a sentence by looking at the tokens completely separately? Well, we can't, so that's where the new components come in:
  - The encoder's *multi-head attention* layer updates each token representation by attending to (i.e., paying attention to) every token in the same sentence, including itself. This is called *self-attention*. That's where the vague representation of the word "like" becomes a richer and more accurate representation, capturing its precise meaning within the given sentence (e.g., the layer notices the subject "I" so it infers that "like" must be a verb). We will discuss exactly how this works shortly.
  - The decoder's *masked multi-head attention* layer does the same thing, but when it processes a token, it doesn't attend to tokens located after it: it's a causal layer. For example, when it processes the token "gusta", it only attends to the tokens `"<s>"`, "me", and "gusta", and it ignores the tokens "el" and "fútbol" (or else the model could cheat during training).
  - The decoder's upper multi-head attention layer is where the decoder pays attention to the contextualized token representations output by the encoder stack. This is called *cross*-attention, as opposed to *self*-attention. For example, the decoder will probably pay close attention to the word "soccer" when it processes the word "el" and outputs a representation of the word "fútbol".

— The *positional encodings* are dense vectors that represent the position of each token in the sentence. The nth positional encoding is added to the token embedding of the nth token in each sentence. This is needed because all layers in the Transformer architecture are position-agnostic, meaning they treat all positions equally (unlike recurrent or convolutional layers): when they process a token, they have no idea where that token is located in the sentence or relative to other words. But the order of words matters, so we must somehow give positional information to the Transformer. Adding positional encodings to the token representations is a good way to achieve this.

The first two arrows going into each multi-head attention layer in Figure 15-3 represent the keys and values, and the third arrow represents the queries.[5] In the self-attention layers, all three are equal to the token representations output by the previous layer, while in the cross-attention layers (i.e., the decoder's upper attention layers), the keys and values are equal to the encoder's final token representations, and the queries are equal to the token representations output by the previous decoder layer.

Now let's go through the novel components of the Transformer architecture in more detail, starting with the positional encodings.

Positional Encodings

A positional encoding is a dense vector that encodes the position of a token within a sentence: the ith positional encoding is added to the token embedding of the ith token in each sentence. A simple way to implement this is to use an `Embedding` layer: just add embedding #0 to the representation of token #0, add embedding #1 to the representation of token #1, and so on. Alternatively, you can use an `nn.Parameter` to store the embedding matrix (initialized using small random weights), then add its first L rows to the inputs (where L is the max input sequence length): the result is the same, but it's much faster. You can also add a bit of dropout to reduce the risk of overfitting. Here's an implementation:

```
import torch
import torch.nn as nn
import torch.nn.functional as F

class PositionalEmbedding(nn.Module):
    def __init__(self, max_length, embed_dim, dropout=0.1):
        super().__init__()
```

5 Queries, keys, and values were introduced in Chapter 14 when we discussed dot-product attention.

```
        self.pos_embed = nn.Parameter(torch.randn(max_length, embed_dim) * 0.02)
        self.dropout = nn.Dropout(dropout)

    def forward(self, X):
        return self.dropout(X + self.pos_embed[:X.size(1)])
```

The inputs have shape [*batch size*, *sequence length*, *embedding size*], but we are adding positional encodings of shape [*sequence length*, *embedding size*]. This works thanks to the broadcasting rules: the ith positional embedding is added to the ith token's representation of each sentence in the batch.

The authors of the Transformer paper also proposed using fixed positional encodings rather than trainable ones. Their approach used a pretty smart scheme based on the sine and cosine functions, but it's not much used anymore, as it doesn't really perform any better than trainable positional embeddings (except perhaps on small transformers, if you're lucky). Please see this chapter's notebook for more details. Moreover, newer approaches such as *relative position bias* (RPB), *rotary positional encoding* (RoPE), and *attention with linear bias* (ALiBi) generally perform better. To learn more about all of these alternative approaches to positional encoding, see "Relative Positional Encoding".

Now let's look deeper into the heart of the Transformer model: the multi-head attention layer.

Multi-Head Attention

The multi-head attention (MHA) layer is based on *scaled dot-product attention*, a variant of dot-product attention (introduced in Chapter 14) that scales down the similarity scores by a constant factor. See Equation 15-1 for its vectorized equation.

Equation 15-1. Scaled dot-product attention

$$\text{Attention}(\mathbf{Q},\mathbf{K},\mathbf{V}) = \text{softmax}\left(\frac{\mathbf{Q}\mathbf{K}^\top}{\sqrt{d_k}}\right)\mathbf{V}$$

In this equation:

- **Q** is a matrix representing a *query* (e.g., an English or Spanish sequence, depending on the attention layer). Its shape is $[L_q, d_q]$, where L_q is the length of the query and d_q is the query's dimensionality (i.e., the number of dimensions in the token representations).
- **K** is a matrix representing a key. Its shape is $[L_k, d_k]$, where L_k is the length of the key and d_k is the key's dimensionality. Note that d_k must equal d_q.

- **V** is a matrix representing a value. Its shape is $[L_v, d_v]$, where L_v is the length of the value and d_v is the value's dimensionality. Note that L_v must equal L_k.
- The shape of **Q K**$^\intercal$ is $[L_q, L_k]$: it contains one similarity score for each query/key pair. To prevent this matrix from being huge, the input sequences must not be too long: this is the critical *quadratic context window* problem (we will discuss various ways to alleviate this issue in Chapters 16 and 17. The softmax function is applied to each row: the output has the same shape as the input, but now each row sums up to 1. The final output has a shape of $[L_q, d_v]$. There is one row per query token, and each row represents the query result: a weighted sum of the value tokens, favoring value tokens whose corresponding key tokens are most aligned with the given query token.
- The scaling factor $1 / \sqrt{d_k}$ scales down the similarity scores to avoid saturating the softmax function, which would lead to tiny gradients. This factor was empirically shown to speed up and stabilize training.
- It is possible to mask out some key/value pairs by adding a very large negative value to the corresponding similarity scores, just before computing the softmax (in practice, we can add `-torch.inf`). The resulting weights will be equal to zero. This is useful to mask padding tokens, as well as future tokens in the masked multi-head attention layer.

PyTorch comes with the `F.scaled_dot_product_attention()` function. Its inputs are just like **Q**, **K**, and **V**, but these inputs can have extra dimensions at the start, such as the batch size and the number of heads (when used for multi-head attention). The equation is applied simultaneously across all of these extra dimensions. In other words, the function computes the results simultaneously across all sentences in the batch and across all attention heads, making it very efficient.

Now we're ready to look at the multi-head attention layer. Its architecture is shown in Figure 15-4.

As you can see, it is just a bunch of scaled dot-product attention layers, called *attention heads*, each preceded by a linear transformation of the values, keys, and queries (across all tokens). The outputs of all the attention heads are simply concatenated, and they go through a final linear transformation (again, across all tokens).

But why? What is the intuition behind this architecture? Well, consider once again the word "like" in the sentence "I like soccer". The encoder was hopefully smart enough to encode its meaning, the fact that it's a verb, and many other features that are useful for its translation, such as the fact that it is in the present tense. The token representation also includes the position, thanks to the positional encodings. In short, the token representation encodes many different characteristics of the token. If we just used a single scaled dot-product attention layer, we would only be able to query all of these characteristics in one shot.

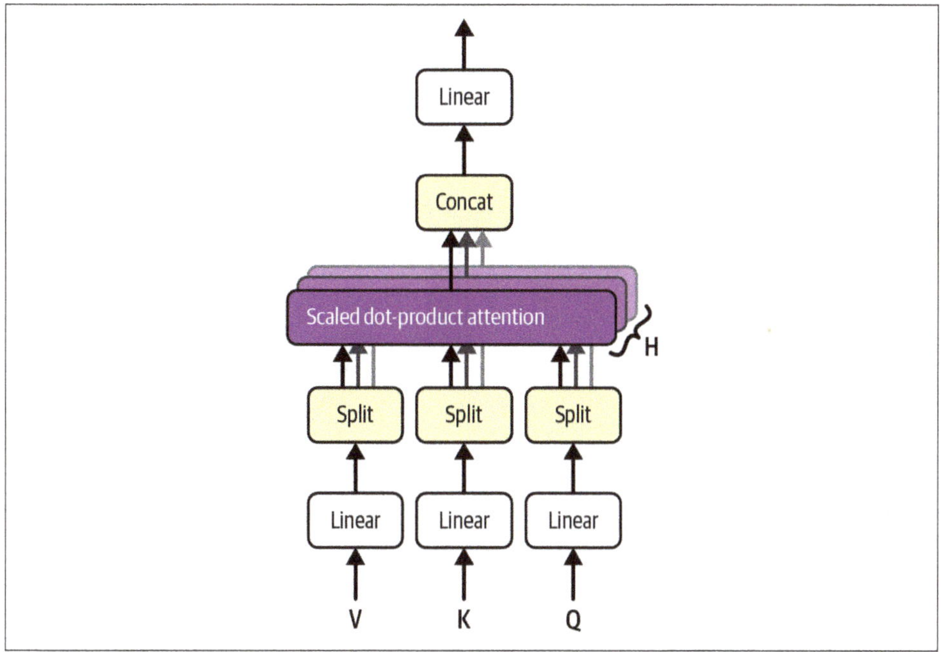

Figure 15-4. Multi-head attention layer architecture[6]

The Transformer architecture is extremely flexible, so the model has plenty of freedom during training to choose its own knowledge representation and strategies. As a result, it ends up being somewhat of a black box: understanding how transformers truly "think" is an area of active research, called *model interpretability*. For example, check out this fascinating post by Anthropic (*https://homl.info/tracing-thoughts*).

This is why the MHA layer splits the values, keys, and queries across multiple heads: this way, each head can focus on specific characteristics of the token. The first linear layer lets the model choose which characteristics each head should focus on. For example, the linear layer may ensure that the first head gets a projection of the "like" token's representation into a subspace where all that remains is the information that this token is a verb in the present tense. Another head may focus on the word's meaning, and so on. Then the scaled dot-product attention layers implement the actual lookup phase, and finally the results are all concatenated and run through a final linear layer that lets the model reorganize the representation as it pleases.

6 This is adapted from the righthand part of Figure 2 from "Attention Is All You Need", with the kind authorization of the authors.

To really understand the Transformer architecture, the key is to understand multi-head attention, and for this, it helps to look at a basic implementation:

```
class MultiheadAttention(nn.Module):
    def __init__(self, embed_dim, num_heads, dropout=0.1):
        super().__init__()
        self.h = num_heads
        self.d = embed_dim // num_heads
        self.q_proj = nn.Linear(embed_dim, embed_dim)
        self.k_proj = nn.Linear(embed_dim, embed_dim)
        self.v_proj = nn.Linear(embed_dim, embed_dim)
        self.out_proj = nn.Linear(embed_dim, embed_dim)
        self.dropout = nn.Dropout(dropout)

    def split_heads(self, X):
        return X.view(X.size(0), X.size(1), self.h, self.d).transpose(1, 2)

    def forward(self, query, key, value):
        q = self.split_heads(self.q_proj(query))  # (B, h, Lq, d)
        k = self.split_heads(self.k_proj(key))  # (B, h, Lk, d)
        v = self.split_heads(self.v_proj(value))  # (B, h, Lv, d) with Lv=Lk
        scores = q @ k.transpose(2, 3) / self.d**0.5  # (B, h, Lq, Lk)
        weights = scores.softmax(dim=-1)  # (B, h, Lq, Lk)
        Z = self.dropout(weights) @ v  # (B, h, Lq, d)
        Z = Z.transpose(1, 2)  # (B, Lq, h, d)
        Z = Z.reshape(Z.size(0), Z.size(1), self.h * self.d)  # (B, Lq, h × d)
        return (self.out_proj(Z), weights)  # (B, Lq, h × d)
```

Let's go through this code:

- The constructor stores the number of heads `self.h` and computes the number of dimensions per head `self.d`, then it creates the necessary modules. Note that the embedding size must be divisible by the number of heads.
- The `split_heads()` method is used in the `forward()` method. It splits its input `X` along its last dimension (one split per head), converting it from a 3D tensor of shape [B, L, $h \times d$] to a 4D tensor of shape [B, L, h, d], where B is the batch size, L is the max length of the input sequences (specifically L_k for the key and value, or L_q for the query), h is the number of heads, and d is the number of dimensions per head (i.e., $h \times d$ = embedding size). The dimensions 1 and 2 are then swapped to get a tensor of shape [B, h, L, d]: since the matrix multiplication operator `@` only works on the last two dimensions, it won't touch the first two dimensions B and h, so we will be able to use this operator to compute the scores across all instances in the batch and across all attention heads, all in one shot (`q @ k.transpose(2, 3)`). The same will be true when computing all the attention outputs (`weights @ v`).

- The `forward()` method starts by applying a linear transformation to the query, key, and value, and passes the result through the `split_heads()` method. The next three lines compute Equation 15-1, plus a bit of dropout on the weights. Next we swap back dimensions 1 and 2 to ensure that the dimensions h and d are next to each other again, then we reshape the tensor back to 3D: this will concatenate the outputs of all heads. We can then apply the output linear transformation and return the result, along with the weights (in case we need them later).

Don't worry if it takes some time to fully grasp this, it's not easy. Of course, you can drive a car without fully understanding how the engine works, but some of the transformer improvements described in Chapters 16 and 17 will only make sense if you understand MHA.

But wait! We're missing one important detail: masking. Indeed, as we discussed earlier, the decoder's masked self-attention layers must only consider previous tokens when trying to predict what the next token is (or else it would be cheating). Moreover, if the key contains padding tokens, we want to ignore them as well. So let's update the `forward()` method to support two additional arguments:

`attn_mask`
: A boolean mask of shape $[L_q, L_k]$ that we will use to control which key tokens each query token should ignore (`True` to ignore, `False` to attend)

`key_padding_mask`
: A boolean mask of shape $[B, L_k]$ to locate the padding tokens in each key

```
def forward(self, query, key, value, attn_mask=None, key_padding_mask=None):
    [...]  # compute the scores exactly like earlier
    if attn_mask is not None:
        scores = scores.masked_fill(attn_mask, -torch.inf)  # (B, h, Lq, Lk)
    if key_padding_mask is not None:
        mask = key_padding_mask.unsqueeze(1).unsqueeze(2)  # (B, 1, 1, Lk)
        scores = scores.masked_fill(mask, -torch.inf)  # (B, h, Lq, Lk)
    [...]  # compute the weights and the outputs exactly like earlier
```

This code replaces the scores we want to ignore with negative infinity, so the corresponding weights will be zero after the softmax operation (if we tried to zero out these weights directly, the remaining weights would not add up to 1). Note that the masks are broadcast automatically: `attn_mask` is broadcast across the whole batch and all attention heads, and `key_padding_mask` is broadcast across all heads and all query tokens.

PyTorch has a very similar `nn.MultiheadAttention` module, which is much more optimized (e.g., it can often fuse the three input projections into one). It has the same arguments, which behave in exactly the same way. It also has a few more. Here are the most important:

- The constructor has a `batch_first` argument which defaults to `False`, so the module expects the batch dimension to come after the sequence length dimension. You must set `batch_first=True` if you prefer the batch dimension to come first, like in our custom implementation.
- The `forward()` method has a `need_weights` argument that defaults to `True`. If you don't need to use the weights returned by this module, you should set this argument to `False`, as it sometimes allows for some optimizations. When `need_weights` is set to `False`, the method returns `None` instead of the weights.
- The `forward()` method also has an `is_causal` argument: if (and only if) the `attn_mask` is set and is a *causal mask*, then you can set `is_causal=True` to allow for some performance optimizations. A causal mask allows each query token to attend to all previous tokens (including itself), but doesn't allow it to attend to tokens located after it. In other words, a causal mask contains `True` above the main diagonal, and `False` everywhere else. This is the mask needed for the masked self-attention layers.

Now that we have the main ingredient, we're ready to implement the rest of the Transformer model.

Building the Rest of the Transformer

The rest of the Transformer architecture is much more straightforward. Let's start with the encoder block. The following implementation closely matches the encoder block represented on the left side of Figure 15-3, except it sprinkles a bit of dropout after the self-attention layer and after both dense layers in the feedforward module:

```
class TransformerEncoderLayer(nn.Module):
    def __init__(self, d_model, nhead, dim_feedforward=2048, dropout=0.1):
        super().__init__()
        self.self_attn = MultiheadAttention(d_model, nhead, dropout)
        self.linear1 = nn.Linear(d_model, dim_feedforward)
        self.dropout = nn.Dropout(dropout)
        self.linear2 = nn.Linear(dim_feedforward, d_model)
        self.norm1 = nn.LayerNorm(d_model)
        self.norm2 = nn.LayerNorm(d_model)

    def forward(self, src, src_mask=None, src_key_padding_mask=None):
        attn, _ = self.self_attn(src, src, src, attn_mask=src_mask,
                                 key_padding_mask=src_key_padding_mask)
        Z = self.norm1(src + self.dropout(attn))
```

```python
        ff = self.dropout(self.linear2(self.dropout(self.linear1(Z).relu())))
        return self.norm2(Z + ff)
```

Notice that the feedforward block is composed of a first `Linear` layer that expands the dimensionality to 2048 (by default), followed by a nonlinearity (ReLU in this case), then a second `Linear` layer that projects the data back down to the original embedding size (also called the *model dimension*, `d_model`). This *reverse bottleneck* increases the expressive power of the nonlinearity, allowing the model to learn much richer combinations of features. This idea was explored further in the later MobileNetv2 paper, whose authors coined the term *inverted residual network*.

In the encoder, the `src_mask` argument is generally not used, since the encoder allows each token to attend to all tokens, even ones located after it. However, the user is expected to set the `key_padding_mask` appropriately.

Now here's an implementation of the decoder block. It closely matches the decoder block represented on the righthand side of Figure 15-3, with some additional dropout:

```python
class TransformerDecoderLayer(nn.Module):
    [...]  # similar constructor, with 2 MHA, 3 Linear, 3 LayerNorm, 1 Dropout
    def forward(self, tgt, memory, tgt_mask=None, memory_mask=None,
                tgt_key_padding_mask=None, memory_key_padding_mask=None):
        attn1, _ = self.self_attn(tgt, tgt, tgt, attn_mask=tgt_mask,
                                  key_padding_mask=tgt_key_padding_mask)
        Z = self.norm1(tgt + self.dropout(attn1))
        attn2, _ = self.multihead_attn(Z, memory, memory, attn_mask=memory_mask,
                                       key_padding_mask=memory_key_padding_mask)
        Z = self.norm2(Z + self.dropout(attn2))
        ff = self.dropout(self.linear2(self.dropout(self.linear1(Z).relu())))
        return self.norm3(Z + ff)
```

The `memory` argument corresponds to the output of the encoder. For full flexibility, we let the user pass the appropriate masks to the `forward()` method. In general, you will need to set the padding masks appropriately (both for the memory and target), and set the `tgt_mask` to a causal mask (we will see how shortly).

PyTorch actually provides `nn.TransformerEncoderLayer` and `nn.TransformerDecoderLayer` out of the box, with the same arguments, plus a few more: most importantly `batch_first`, which you must set to `True` if the batch dimension is first, plus one `*_is_causal` argument for each attention mask, and an `activation` argument that defaults to "relu". Many state-of-the-art transformers use a more advanced activation such as GELU (introduced in Chapter 11).

PyTorch also provides three more transformer modules (writing a custom module for each of these is left as an exercise for the reader—see the notebook for a solution):

`nn.TransformerEncoder`
: Simply chains the desired number of encoder layers. Its constructor takes an encoder layer plus the desired number of layers `num_layers`, and it clones the given encoder layer `num_layers` times. The constructor also takes an optional normalization layer, which (if provided) is applied to the final output.

`nn.TransformerDecoder`
: Same, except it chains decoder layers instead of encoder layers.

`nn.Transformer`
: Creates an encoder and a decoder (both with layer norm), and chains them.

Congratulations! You now know how to build a full Transformer model from scratch. You only need to add a final `Linear` layer and use the `nn.CrossEntropyLoss` to get the full architecture shown in Figure 15-3 (as we saw in earlier chapters, the softmax layer is implicitly included in the loss). Now let's see how to use a Transformer model to translate English to Spanish.

Building an English-to-Spanish Transformer

It's time to build our NMT Transformer model. For this, we'll use our `PositionalEmbedding` module and PyTorch's `nn.Transformer` (our custom `Transformer` module works fine, but it's slower):

```
class NmtTransformer(nn.Module):
    def __init__(self, vocab_size, max_length, embed_dim=512, pad_id=0,
                 num_heads=8, num_layers=6, dropout=0.1):
        super().__init__()
        self.embed = nn.Embedding(vocab_size, embed_dim, padding_idx=pad_id)
        self.pos_embed = PositionalEmbedding(max_length, embed_dim, dropout)
        self.transformer = nn.Transformer(
            embed_dim, num_heads, num_encoder_layers=num_layers,
            num_decoder_layers=num_layers, batch_first=True)
        self.output = nn.Linear(embed_dim, vocab_size)

    def forward(self, pair):
        src_embeds = self.pos_embed(self.embed(pair.src_token_ids))
        tgt_embeds = self.pos_embed(self.embed(pair.tgt_token_ids))
        src_pad_mask = ~pair.src_mask.bool()
        tgt_pad_mask = ~pair.tgt_mask.bool()
        size = [pair.tgt_token_ids.size(1)] * 2
        full_mask = torch.full(size, True, device=tgt_pad_mask.device)
        causal_mask = torch.triu(full_mask, diagonal=1)
        out_decoder = self.transformer(src_embeds, tgt_embeds,
                                       src_key_padding_mask=src_pad_mask,
                                       memory_key_padding_mask=src_pad_mask,
                                       tgt_mask=causal_mask, tgt_is_causal=True,
                                       tgt_key_padding_mask=tgt_pad_mask)
        return self.output(out_decoder).permute(0, 2, 1)
```

Let's go through this code:

- The constructor is straightforward: we just create the necessary modules.
- The `forward()` method takes an `NmtPair` as input (this class was defined in Chapter 14). The method starts by embedding the input tokens for both the source and target inputs, and it adds the positional encodings to both.
- Then the code uses the *not* operator (~) to invert both the source and target masks because they contain `False` for each padding token, but `nn.MultiheadAttention` expects `True` for tokens that it should ignore.
- Next, we create a square matrix of shape [L_q, L_q], full of `True`, and we get all elements above the main diagonal using the `torch.triu()` function, with the rest defaulting to `False`. This results in a causal mask that we can use as the `tgt_mask` for the transformer: it will use this mask for the masked self-attention layer. Alternatively, you could call `nn.Transformer.generate_square_subsequent_mask()` to create the causal mask: just pass it the sequence length (`pair.tgt_token_ids.size(1)`) and set `dtype=torch.bool`.
- We then call the transformer, passing it the source and target embeddings, as well as all the appropriate masks.
- Lastly, we pass the result through the output `Linear` layer, and we permute the last two dimensions because `nn.CrossEntropyLoss` expects the class dimension to be dimension 1.

We can now create an instance of this model and train it exactly like our RNN encoder-decoder in Chapter 14. To speed up training and reduce overfitting, you can shrink the transformer quite a bit—use 4 heads instead of 8, just 2 layers in both the encoder and the decoder, and use an embedding size of 128:

```
nmt_tr_model = NmtTransformer(vocab_size, max_length, embed_dim=128, pad_id=0,
                              num_heads=4, num_layers=2, dropout=0.1).to(device)
[...]  # train this model exactly like the encoder-decoder in Chapter 14
```

Let's see how well this model performs:

```
>>> nmt_tr_model.eval()
>>> translate(nmt_tr_model,"I like to play soccer with my friends at the beach")
' Me gusta jugar al fútbol con mis amigos en la playa . </s>'
```

Great, even this tiny transformer trained for 20 epochs works rather well, so imagine a much bigger one trained on a much larger dataset, and you can start to see how ChatGPT and its friends can be so impressive.

Before we move on to other models, it's important to clean up the GPU RAM, or else it will quickly become saturated. For this, delete all variables that are no longer needed—especially models, optimizers, tensors, and datasets—using the `del` keyword, then call the `gc.collect()` function to run Python's garbage collector. When using a CUDA or AMD device, you must also call `torch.cuda.empty_cache()`. On Colab, you can view the available GPU RAM by selecting Runtime → "View resources" from the menu.

Now that you have a good understanding of the original Transformer architecture, let's look at encoder-only transformers.

Encoder-Only Transformers for Natural Language Understanding

When Google released the BERT model in 2018 (*https://homl.info/bert*),[7] it proved that an encoder-only transformer can tackle a wide variety of natural language tasks: sentence classification, token classification, multiple choice question answering, and more! BERT also confirmed the effectiveness of self-supervised pretraining on a large corpus for transfer learning: BERT can indeed achieve excellent performance on many tasks, just by fine-tuning on a fairly small dataset for each task. Let's start by looking at BERT's architecture, then we'll look at how it was pretrained, and how you can fine-tune it for your own tasks.

Encoder-only models are generally not used for text generation tasks, such as autocompletion, translation, summarization, or chatbots, because they're much slower at this task than decoders. Decoders are faster because they are causal, so a good implementation can cache and reuse its previous state when predicting a new token. Conversely, encoders use nonmasked multi-head attention layers only, so they are naturally bidirectional; hence the B in BERT (Bidirectional Encoder Representations from Transformers). Whenever a new token is added, everything needs to be recomputed.

7 Jacob Devlin et al., "BERT: Pre-Training of Deep Bidirectional Transformers for Language Understanding", *Proceedings of the 2018 Conference of the North American Chapter of the Association for Computational Linguistics: Human Language Technologies* 1 (2019).

BERT's Architecture

BERT's architecture is almost identical to the original Transformer's encoder, with just three differences:

1. It's much bigger. BERT-base has 12 encoder blocks, 12 attention heads, and 768-dimensional embeddings, and BERT-large has 24 blocks, 16 heads, and 1,024 dimensions (while the original Transformer has 6 blocks, 8 heads, and 512 dimensions). It also uses trainable positional embeddings and supports input sentences up to 512 tokens.
2. It applies layer-norm just *before* each sublayer (attention or feedforward) rather than *after* each skip connection. This is called *pre-LN*, as opposed to *post-LN*, and it ensures that the inputs of each sublayer are normalized, which stabilizes training and reduces sensitivity to weight initialization. PyTorch's transformer modules default to post-LN, but they have a `norm_first` argument which you can set to `True` if you prefer pre-LN (however, some optimizations may not be implemented for pre-LN).
3. It lets you split the input sentence into two *segments* if needed. This is useful for tasks that require a pair of input sentences, such as natural language inference (i.e., does sentence A entail sentence B?) or multiple choice question answering (i.e., given question A, how good is answer B?). To pass two sentences to BERT, you must first append a *separation token* [SEP] to each one, then concatenate them. Furthermore, a trainable *segment embedding* is added to each token's representation: segment embedding #0 is added to all tokens within segment #0, and segment embedding #1 is added to all tokens within segment #1. In theory, we could have more segments, but BERT was only pretrained on inputs composed of one or two segments. Note that the positional encodings are also added to each token's representation, as usual (i.e., relative to the full input sequence, not relative to the individual segments).

That's all! Now let's look at how BERT was pretrained.

BERT Pretraining

The authors proposed two self-supervised pretraining tasks:

Masked language model (MLM)
: Each token in a sentence has a 15% probability of being replaced with a mask token, and the model is trained to predict what the original tokens were. This is often called a *cloze task* (i.e., fill in the blanks). For example, if the original sentence is "She had fun at the birthday party", then the model may be given the sentence "She [MASK] fun at the [MASK] party" and it must predict the original sentence: the loss is only computed on the mask token outputs.

To be more precise, some of the masked tokens are not truly masked: 10% are instead replaced by random tokens, and 10% are just left alone, neither masked nor randomized. Why is that? Well, the random tokens force the model to perform well even when mask tokens are absent: this is important since most downstream tasks don't use any mask tokens. As for the untouched tokens, they make the prediction trivial, which encourages the model to pay attention to the input token located at the position of the token being predicted. Without them, the model would soon learn to ignore this token and rely solely on the other tokens.

Next sentence prediction (NSP)

The model is trained to predict whether two sentences are consecutive or not. For example, it should predict that "The dog sleeps" and "It snores loudly" are consecutive sentences, while "The dog sleeps" and "The Earth orbits the Sun" are not consecutive.

This is a binary classification task, which the authors chose to implement by introducing a new *class token* [CLS]: this token is inserted at the beginning of the input sequence (position #0, segment #0), and during training the encoder's output, this token is passed through a binary classification head (i.e., a linear layer with a single unit, followed by the sigmoid function, and trained using `nn.BCELoss`, or just a linear layer with a single unit trained using `nn.BCEWithLogitsLoss`).

BERT was pretrained on both MLM and NSP simultaneously (see Figure 15-5 and the left side of Figure 15-6), using a large corpus of text—specifically the English Wikipedia and BooksCorpus. The goal of NSP was to make the class token's contextualized embedding a good representation of the whole input sequence. At first, it seemed that it indeed produced good sentence embeddings, but it was later shown that simply pooling all the contextualized embeddings (e.g., by computing their mean) yielded better results. In fact, researchers showed that NSP did not help much overall, so it was dropped in most later architectures.

In Chapter 14, we saw how to use the Transformers library to download a pretrained BERT model and its tokenizer. But you may want to train a BERT model from scratch, for example, if you're dealing with a domain-specific corpus of text. For this, one option is to build BERT yourself using the `nn.TransformerEncoder` module (e.g., based on an `nn.TransformerEncoderLayer` with `norm_first=True` to respect BERT's architecture), then preprocess your dataset according to the MLM algorithm, and train your model.

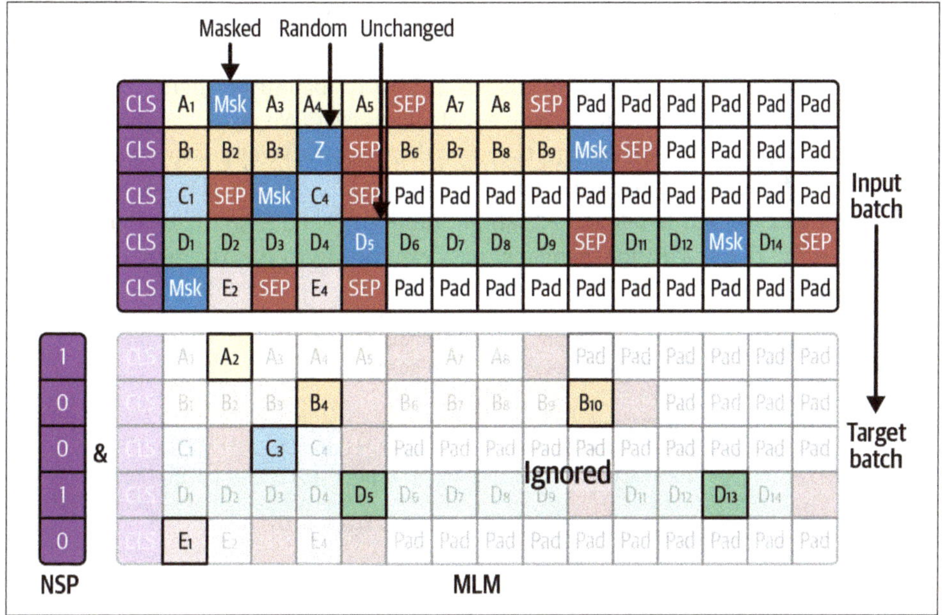

Figure 15-5. Input and target during BERT pretraining, using MLM and NSP

However, there's an easier way, using the Transformers library. Let's start by creating a tokenizer and a randomly initialized BERT model. For simplicity, we use a pretrained tokenizer, but of course you can train one from scratch instead, if you prefer. Make sure to tweak the `BertConfig` depending on your training budget, and the size and complexity of your dataset:

```
from transformers import BertConfig, BertForMaskedLM, BertTokenizerFast

bert_tokenizer = BertTokenizerFast.from_pretrained("bert-base-uncased")
config = BertConfig(  # adapt to training budget, and dataset size & complexity
    vocab_size=bert_tokenizer.vocab_size, hidden_size=128, num_hidden_layers=2,
    num_attention_heads=4, intermediate_size=512, max_position_embeddings=128)
bert = BertForMaskedLM(config)
```

Next, let's download the WikiText dataset (in real life, you would use your own dataset instead), and tokenize it:

```
from datasets import load_dataset

def tokenize(example, tokenizer=bert_tokenizer):
    return tokenizer(example["text"], truncation=True, max_length=128,
                     padding="max_length")

mlm_dataset = load_dataset("wikitext", "wikitext-2-raw-v1", split="train")
mlm_dataset = mlm_dataset.map(tokenize, batched=True)
```

This is where MLM comes in. We create a data collator, whose role is to bundle samples into batches, and we set its `mlm` argument to `True` to activate MLM, and also set `mlm_probability=0.15`: each token has a 15% probability of being masked (or possibly randomized or left alone, as we just discussed). We also pass the tokenizer to the collator: it will not be used to tokenize the text—we've already done that—but it lets the data collator know the masking and padding token IDs, as well as the vocabulary size (which is needed to sample random token IDs). With that, we just need to specify the `TrainingArguments`, pass everything to the `Trainer`, and call its `train()` method:

```
from transformers import Trainer, TrainingArguments
from transformers import DataCollatorForLanguageModeling

args = TrainingArguments(output_dir="./my_bert", num_train_epochs=5,
                         per_device_train_batch_size=16)
mlm_collator = DataCollatorForLanguageModeling(bert_tokenizer, mlm=True,
                                               mlm_probability=0.15)
trainer = Trainer(model=bert, args=args, train_dataset=mlm_dataset,
                  data_collator=mlm_collator)
trainer_output = trainer.train()
```

Once your model is pretrained, you can try it out using the pipelines API:

```
>>> from transformers import pipeline
>>> torch.manual_seed(42)
>>> fill_mask = pipeline("fill-mask", model=bert, tokenizer=bert_tokenizer)
>>> top_predictions = fill_mask("The capital of [MASK] is Rome.")
>>> top_predictions[0]
{'score': 0.04916289076209068,
 'token': 1010,
 'token_str': ',',
 'sequence': 'the capital of, is rome.'}
```

What? Rome is not the capital of a comma! The model is actually terrible because we only trained it for a single epoch here, just to confirm that everything works and the loss goes down. To get better results, we would need to train it for a *very* long time. The BERT authors trained it for about 4 days using 16 TPU devices on a much larger dataset. This is why most people avoid starting from scratch unless they really have to; you're generally better off downloading a model that was pretrained on a text corpus as close as possible to yours, then fine-tuning it on your own dataset. This can be done using MLM, like we just did, but starting from a pretrained model instead. Once you're happy with your pretrained model, you can fine-tune it on your target task. Let's see how.

BERT Fine-Tuning

BERT can be fine-tuned for many different tasks, changing very little for each task (see the righthand side of Figure 15-6).

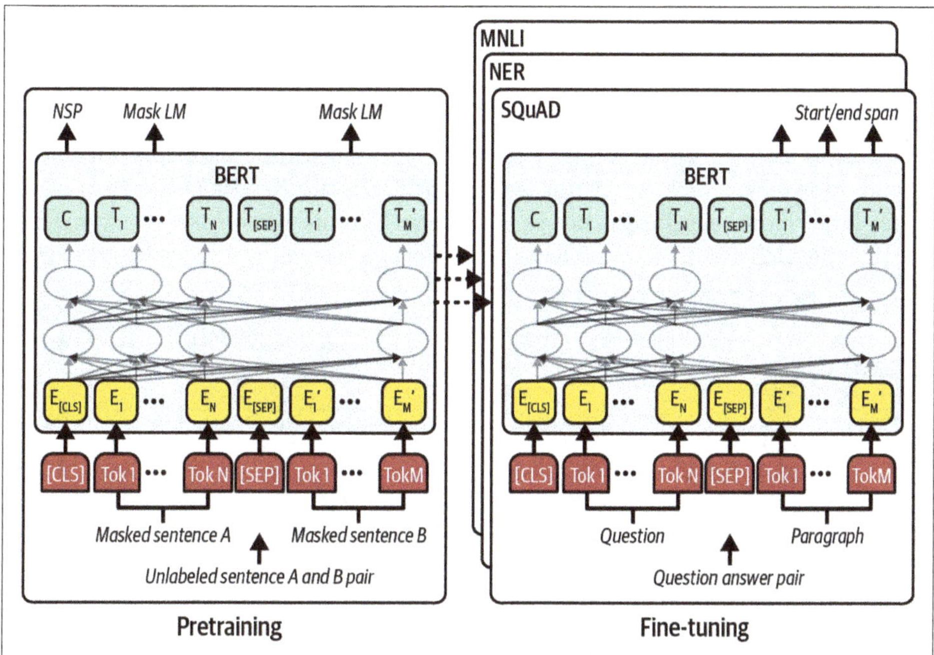

Figure 15-6. BERT pre-training (left) and fine-tuning process (right)[8]

For sentence classification tasks such as sentiment analysis, all output tokens are ignored except for the first one, which corresponds to the class token, and a new classification head replaces the NSP binary classification head (see the lefthand side of Figure 15-7). You can then fine-tune the whole model using the cross-entropy loss, optionally setting a lower learning rate for the lower layers, or freezing BERT altogether during the first few epochs (i.e., training only the new classification head). Using the exact same approach, you can tackle other sentence classification tasks. For example, the authors demonstrated that fine-tuning BERT yields excellent results on the CoLA dataset, which asks whether a sentence is grammatically correct. Try it out on your own sentence classification tasks: it's likely to perform well even if your dataset is quite small, thanks to the magic of transfer learning.

The BERT authors found that adding the MLM loss to the fine-tuning loss (scaled by a hyperparameter) helps stabilize training and reduces overfitting.

8 This is adapted from Figure 1 from the BERT paper, with the kind authorization of the authors.

For token classification, the classification head is applied to every token (see the righthand side of Figure 15-7). For example, BERT can be fine-tuned for *named entity recognition* (NER), where the model tags the parts of the text that correspond to names, dates, places, organizations, or other *entities*. This is often used in legal, financial, or medical applications. The same approach can be used for other token classification tasks, such as tagging grammatical errors; analyzing sentiment at the token level; locating subjects, nouns, and verbs (this is *part-of-speech tagging*); or locating questions, statements, and greetings (this is *dialogue act tagging*); and more.

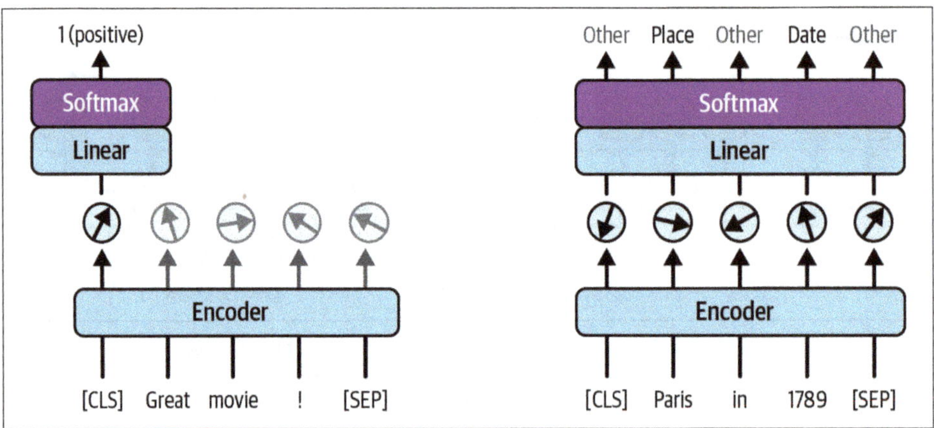

Figure 15-7. Fine-tuning BERT for sentence classification such as sentiment analysis (left) or for token classification such as NER (right)

BERT can also be used to classify pairs of sentences. It works exactly like sentence classification, except that you pass in two sentences instead of one. For example, this can be used for *natural language inference* (NLI) where the model must determine whether sentence A entails sentence B, or contradicts it, or neither (e.g., the *multi-genre NLI* dataset, or MNLI). It can also be used to detect whether two sentences have the same meaning, are just paraphrasing each other (e.g., the QQP or MRPC datasets), or to determine whether the answer to question A is present in sentence B (e.g., QNLI dataset).

For *multiple choice question answering* (MCQA), BERT is called once for each possible answer, placing the question in segment #0 and the possible answer in segment #1. For each answer, the class token output is passed through a linear layer with a single unit, producing a score. Once we have all the answer scores, we can convert them to probabilities using a softmax layer (see Figure 15-8), and we can use the cross-entropy loss for fine-tuning (or better, drop the softmax layer and use the `nn.CrossEntropyLoss` directly on the answer scores).

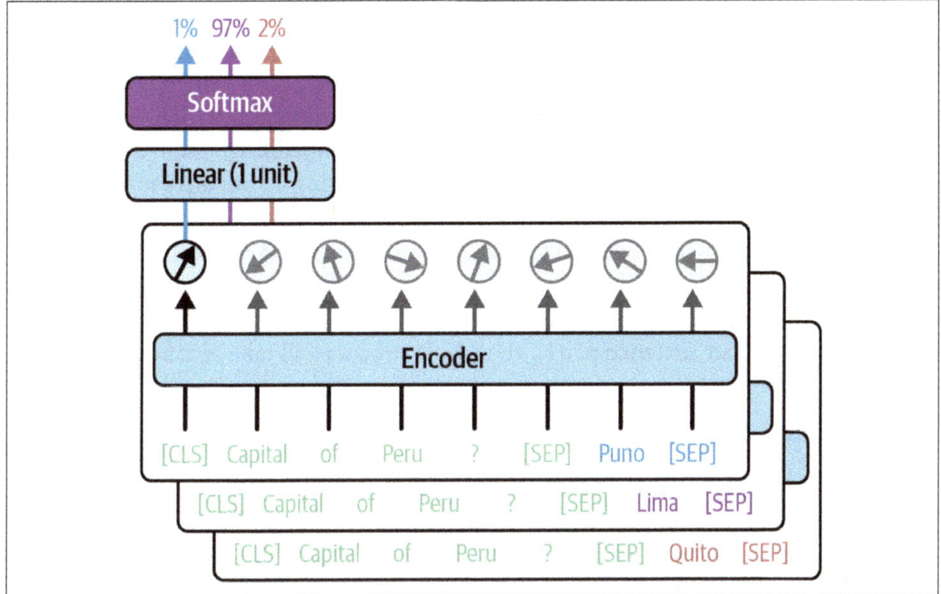

Figure 15-8. Using an encoder-only model to answer multiple-choice questions

BERT is also great for *extractive question answering*: you ask it a question (in segment #0) about some text called the *context* (in segment #1), and BERT must locate the answer within the context. For this, you can add a linear layer with two units on top of BERT to output two scores per token: a start score and an end score. During fine-tuning, you can treat them as logits for two separate binary classification tasks: the first determines whether a token is the first token in the answer, and the second determines whether it is the last. Of course most tokens are neither, and it's possible for one token to be both if the answer is a single token. At inference time, we select the pair of indices i and j that maximizes the sum of the start score of token i and the end score of token j, subject to $i \leq j$ and $j - i + 1 \leq$ maximum acceptable answer length. This approach allowed BERT to beat the state of the art on the SQuAD dataset, a popular question answering dataset.

The Transformers library provides convenient classes and checkpoints for each of these use cases, such as `BertForSequenceClassification` or `BertForQuestionAnswering` (see Chapter 14).

The BERT authors also showed that BERT could be fine-tuned to measure *semantic textual similarity* (STS); for example, on the *STS benchmark* dataset (STS-B), you feed the model two sentences and it outputs a score that indicates how semantically similar the sentences are. That said, if you want to find the most similar pair of sentences in a dataset containing N sentences, you will need to run BERT on $O(N^2)$ pairs: this could take hours if the dataset is large. Instead, it's preferable to use a model such as Sentence-BERT (SBERT) (*https://homl.info/sbert*)[9] which is a variant of BERT that was fine-tuned to produce good sentence embeddings. Start by running each sentence through SBERT to get its sentence embedding, then measure the similarity between each pair of sentence embeddings using a similarity measure such as the *cosine similarity* (e.g., using PyTorch's `F.cosine_similarity()` function). This is the cosine of the angle between two vectors, so its value ranges from –1 (completely opposite) to +1 (perfectly aligned). Since measuring the cosine similarity is much faster than running BERT, and since the model processes much shorter inputs (i.e., sentences rather than sentence pairs), the whole process will take seconds rather than hours.

Sentence embedding can also be extremely useful in many other applications:

Text clustering, to organize and better understand your data
: You can process a large number of documents through SBERT to obtain their sentence embeddings, then apply a clustering algorithm such as *k*-means or HDBSCAN (see Chapter 8) on the embeddings to group your documents based on semantic similarity. It often helps to reduce dimensionality before running the clustering algorithm, for example, using PCA or UMAP (see Chapter 7).

Semantic search
: The goal is to let the user find documents based on the query's meaning rather than just keyword matching. First, encode your documents (or chunks of documents) using SBERT and store the sentence embeddings. When a user submits a search query, encode it using SBERT and find the documents whose embeddings are most similar to the query's embedding, for example, based on cosine similarity.

Reranking search results
: If you have an existing search system that you don't want to replace, you can often improve it significantly by reranking the search results based on semantic similarity with the query.

Vector databases, such as Pinecone, Weaviate, ChromaDB, Qdrant, or Milvus, are designed for storing and searching for documents based on their embeddings. More traditional databases, such as PostgreSQL or MongoDB, also have growing support for embeddings, although it's not as optimized yet.

9 Nils Reimers, Iryna Gurevych, "Sentence-BERT: Sentence Embeddings using Siamese BERT-Networks", arXiv preprint arXiv:1908.10084 (2019).

Over the years, many variants of SBERT have been released. One of the easiest ways to download and use them is via the Sentence Transformers library (*https://sbert.net*) created by UKPLab and maintained by Hugging Face (it's preinstalled on Colab). For example, the following code downloads the all-MiniLM-L6-v2 model, which is very fast and lightweight but still produces high-quality sentence embeddings. The code uses it to encode three sentences, then it measures the similarity between each pair of sentences:

```
from sentence_transformers import SentenceTransformer

model = SentenceTransformer("all-MiniLM-L6-v2")
sentences = ["She's shopping", "She bought some shoes", "She's working"]
embeddings = model.encode(sentences, convert_to_tensor=True)
similarities = model.similarity(embeddings, embeddings)
```

Let's look at the similarity matrix:

```
>>> similarities
tensor([[1.0000, 0.6328, 0.5841],
        [0.6328, 1.0000, 0.3831],
        [0.5841, 0.3831, 1.0000]], device='cuda:0')
```

We see that there are 1s in the main diagonal, confirming that each sentence is perfectly similar to itself, and we also see that "She's shopping" is more similar to "She bought some shoes" (the cosine similarity is 0.6328) than to "She's working" (0.5841).

Now that we've examined BERT in detail, let's look at some of its offspring.

Other Encoder-Only Models

Following Google's footsteps, many organizations released their own encoder-only models. Let's look at the most popular ones and discuss their main innovations.

RoBERTa by Facebook AI, July 2019 (125M to 355M parameters)

This model is similar to BERT but its performance is better across the board in large part because it was pretrained for longer and on a larger dataset. MLM was used for pretraining, but NSP was dropped. Importantly, the authors used *dynamic masking*, meaning that the tokens to mask were masked on the fly *during* training rather than just once before training (as BERT did), so the same piece of text is masked differently across different epochs. This provides the model with more data diversity, reducing overfitting and leading to better generalization.

When we fine-tuned BERT earlier in this chapter, we actually used dynamic masking and we dropped NSP, so we were following RoBERTa's pretraining approach.

DistilBERT by Hugging Face, October 2019 (66M)

This model is a scaled-down version of BERT: it's 40% smaller and 60% faster, yet it manages to reach about 97% of BERT's performance on most tasks, making it a great choice for low-resource environments (e.g., mobile devices), for low-latency applications, or for quick fine-tuning.

As its name suggests, DistilBERT was trained using a technique called *model distillation*, first introduced by Geoffrey Hinton et al. in 2015 (*https://homl.info/distillation*).[10] The idea of distillation is to train a small *student model* (e.g., DistilBERT) using the estimated probabilities from a larger *teacher model* (e.g., BERT) as the targets (see Figure 15-9). These are *soft targets* rather than the usual one-hot vectors: it makes training much faster and more data efficient, as it allows the student to directly aim for the correct distribution, rather than having to learn it over many samples, bouncing between one extreme and the other and slowly settling somewhere in between. As a result, distillation often works better than training the student from scratch on the same dataset as the teacher!

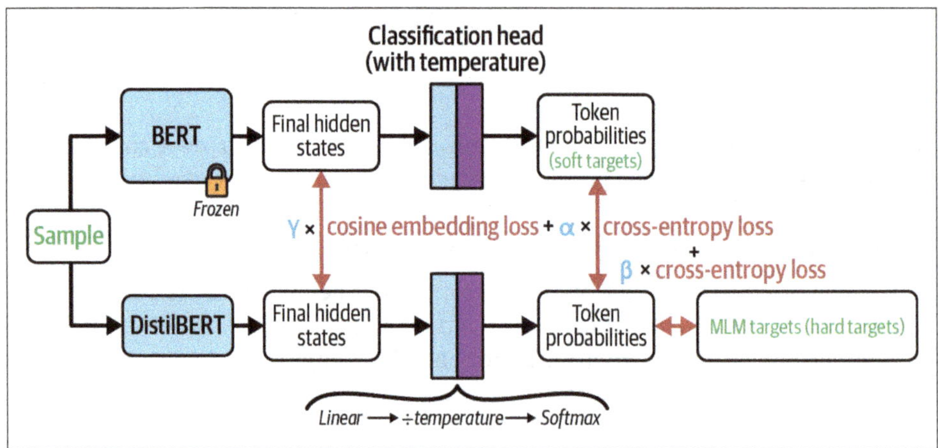

Figure 15-9. DistilBERT pretraining using a weighted sum of two distillation losses and the MLM loss

10 Geoffrey Hinton et al., "Distilling the Knowledge in a Neural Network", arXiv preprint arXiv:1503.02531 (2015).

Note that the estimated probabilities for both the teacher and the student are smoothed a bit—during training only—by dividing the final logits by a temperature greater than 1 (typically 2). This provides the student with a more nuanced signal covering all possible options, rather than just focusing on the correct answer. Hinton dubbed this *dark knowledge*. For example, if the input is "It's sunny and I feel [MASK]", the teacher might normally estimate that the masked word has a 72% probability of being "great", and 27% of being "good", and just 0.5% of being "bad". But if we apply a temperature of 2, then these probabilities get smoothed out to about 60%, 36%, and 5%, respectively. It's helpful to know that "bad" is a plausible option here, even if it's unlikely.

DistilBERT's training loss also had two more components: the standard MLM loss, as well as a *cosine embedding loss* which minimizes the cosine similarity between the student's and teacher's final hidden states (i.e., the output embeddings just before the classification head). This encourages the student to "think" like the teacher, not just make the same predictions, and it leads to faster convergence and better performance. Later models, such as TinyBERT, pushed this idea further by aligning other internal states, such as the attention weights. DistilBERT's final loss is a weighted sum of the three losses (the authors used weights α=5, β=2, γ=1).

ALBERT by Google Research, December 2019 (12M–235M)

All encoder layers in this model share the same weights, making it much smaller than BERT, but not faster. This makes it great for use cases where memory size is limited. In particular, it's a good model to use if you want to train an encoder-only model from scratch on a GPU with little VRAM.

ALBERT also introduced *factorized embeddings* to reduce the size of the embedding layer: in BERT-large, the vocabulary size is about 30,000, and the embedding size is 1,024, which means that the embedding matrix has over 30 million parameters! ALBERT replaces this huge matrix with the product of two much smaller matrices (see Figure 15-10). In practice, this can be implemented by reducing the embedding size—ALBERT uses 128—then adding a linear layer immediately after the embedding layer to project the embeddings to the higher dimensional space, such as 1,024 dimensions for ALBERT-large. The embedding layer ends up with roughly 3.8M parameters (~30,000 × 128), and the linear layer has about 0.13M parameters (128 × 1,024), so the total is less than 4M parameters, down from over 30M: nice!

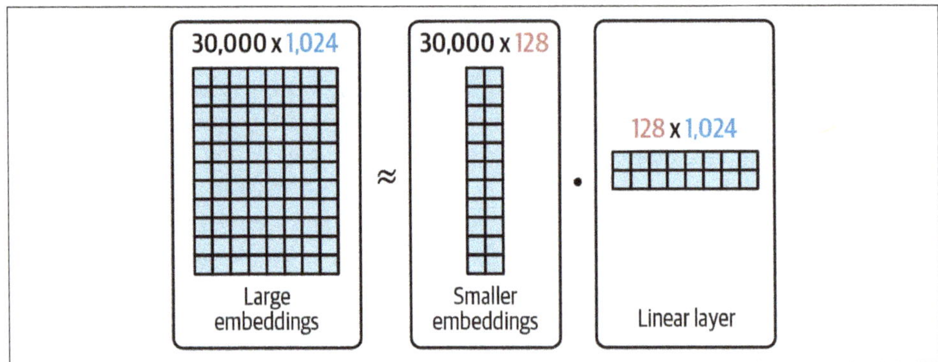

Figure 15-10. An excessively large embedding matrix can be replaced with the product of two smaller matrices. This can be implemented using smaller embeddings and projecting them to higher dimensions using a linear layer.

ALBERT also replaced NSP with *sentence order prediction* (SOP): given two consecutive sentences, the goal is to predict which one comes first. This is a much harder task than NSP, and it led to significantly better sentence embeddings.

ELECTRA by Google Research, March 2020 (14M–335M)

This model introduced a new pretraining technique called *replaced token detection* (RTD): they trained two models jointly—a small generator model and a larger discriminator model, both encoder only. The generator is only used during pretraining, while the discriminator is the final model we're after. The generator is simply trained using regular MLM with dynamic masking. For each mask token, a replacement token is sampled from its top predictions. The resulting text is fed to the discriminator model, which must predict whether each token is the original or not.

For example (see Figure 15-11), if the original text is "She likes him" and it is masked as "She [MASK] him", the generator's top predictions might include "likes", "loves", "hears", "pushes", and one of these is chosen randomly, say "pushes", so the sentence becomes "She pushes him". The discriminator must then try to predict [1, 0, 1], since the first and third tokens are the same as in the original text, but not the second token. As the generator improves, the replaced tokens gradually become less and less obviously wrong, forcing the discriminator to become smarter and smarter. After training, we can throw away the generator and drop the binary classification head from the discriminator to get the final model.

This technique is more sample-efficient than MLM since the discriminator learns from more tokens per example, thus it converges faster, generally achieving the same performance as larger BERT models. That said, the benefits are not always worth the additional complexity.

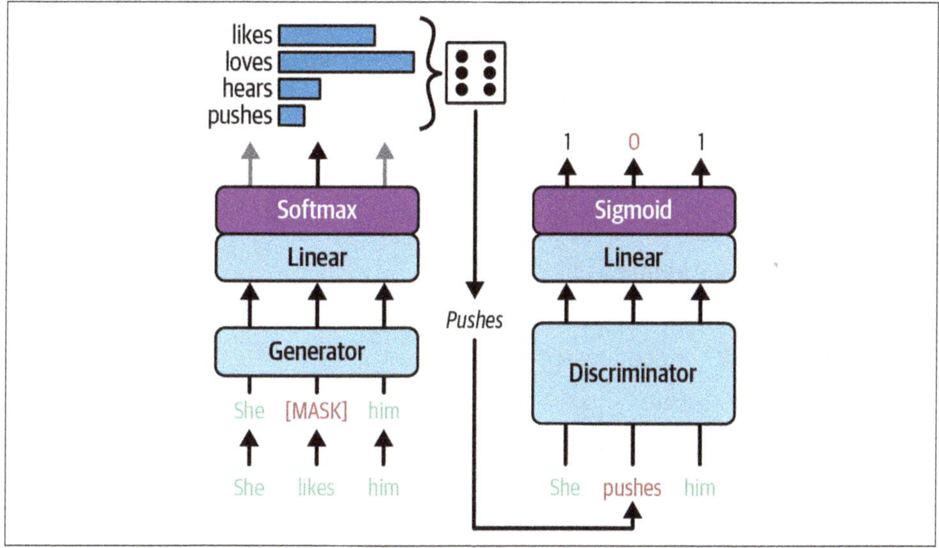

Figure 15-11. Replaced token detection (RTD)

DeBERTa by Microsoft, January 2021 (139M–1.5B)

DeBERTa is a fairly large model that beat the state of the art on many NLU tasks. It removes the usual positional embedding layer, and instead uses *relative positional embeddings* when computing the attention scores inside every multi-head attention layer: when deciding how much the ith query token should attend to the jth key token, the model has access to a learned embedding for the relative position $i - j$. DeBERTa wasn't the first model to do this, as we will see later in this chapter, but it introduced a variant of this technique—named *disentangled attention*—which gives the model more flexibility in how it can combine semantic and positional information.

DeBERTaV3, released in July 2021, combined the ideas from DeBERTa with ELECTRA-style RTD, and it reached even higher performance. It remains a popular model for NLU tasks to this day. However, disentangled attention adds some complexity and compute cost, so subsequent models have opted for simpler approaches, as we will see.

More encoder-only models on Hugging Face Hub

If you explore the encoder-only models on the Hugging Face Hub, you will find many variants of the standard models we discussed so far:

- With various sizes (e.g., BERT-base versus BERT-large)
- Pretrained on a non-English language (e.g., CamemBERT for French) or even on multiple languages (e.g., IndicBERT for 12 major Indian languages)

- Pretrained on cased or uncased text
- Tweaked for specific tasks (e.g., BERT for question answering)

You will also find many domain-specific models, such as:

- ClinicalBERT for clinical applications
- SciBERT for scientific applications
- PubMedBERT for biomedicine
- FinBERT for finance
- GraphCodeBERT for coding applications
- Twitter-RoBERTa-base for social media applications
- PatentBERT for patent applications
- LexLM for legal applications

Most of these are simply fine-tuned versions of standard encoder-only models such as BERT or RoBERTa, but some were pretrained entirely from scratch. A few also introduced new ideas; for example, GraphCodeBERT is a BERT model pretrained on code using not only MLM, but also two structure-aware tasks: it has to find where in the code each variable was defined and used, and it also has to predict the data flow (e.g., in `z = x + y`, variable `z` comes from variables `x` and `y`).

The Hugging Face Hub also contains many compressed variants of standard models. They are small and usually fast, and were trained using distillation, weight-sharing, and/or other techniques such as quantization (see Appendix B). Popular examples include: DistilBERT, TinyBERT, MobileBERT, MiniLM (available for various base models), DistilRoBERTa, and MiniDeBERTa-v2. As we saw with DistilBERT, these models are great for low-resource environments, low latency, and quick fine-tuning.

Speaking of quick fine-tuning, you will also find many *adapter models* on the Hugging Face Hub. An adapter model is based on a frozen standard model such as BERT, plus some small trainable components called *adapters*: when you fine-tune the adapter model, the base model doesn't change, only the adapters. As a result, fine-tuning is much faster and less computationally expensive, and you can get great performance on your task using fairly little training data. For example, AdapterHub/bert-base-uncased-pf-sst2 is an adapter model based on the bert-base-uncased model and fine-tuned for sentiment analysis on the SST 2 dataset. Chapter 17 shows how to build and fine-tune your own adapter models.

OK, time to step back. We've learned all about the Transformer architecture, and we even built a translation transformer from scratch, and now we've looked into encoder-only models like BERT and how they can be used for many different NLU tasks. Lastly, we examined the key innovations powering some of the most popular encoder-only models, and the main categories of pretrained encoder-only models you can find on the Hugging Face Hub (i.e., standard, multilingual, task-specific, domain-specific, compressed, and adapter models—these categories are not exclusive). It's now time to look at decoder-only models such as GPT.

Over the last few years, large organizations have shifted their focus toward decoders, but encoder-only models are still alive and kicking. Their relatively small size makes them fast and accessible to all, easy to fine-tune, and immensely useful for a wide range of applications.

Decoder-Only Transformers

While Google was working on the first encoder-only model (i.e., BERT), Alec Radford and other OpenAI researchers were taking a different route: they built the first decoder-only model, named GPT.[11] This model paved the way for today's most impressive models, including most of the ones used in famous chatbots like ChatGPT or Claude.

The GPT model (now known as GPT-1) was released in June 2018. GPT stands for *Generative Pre-Training*: it was pretrained on a dataset of about 7,000 books and learned to predict the next token, so it can be used to generate text one token at a time, just like the original Transformer's decoder. For example, if you feed it "Happy birthday", it will predict "birthday to", so you can append "to" to the input and repeat the process (see Figure 15-12).

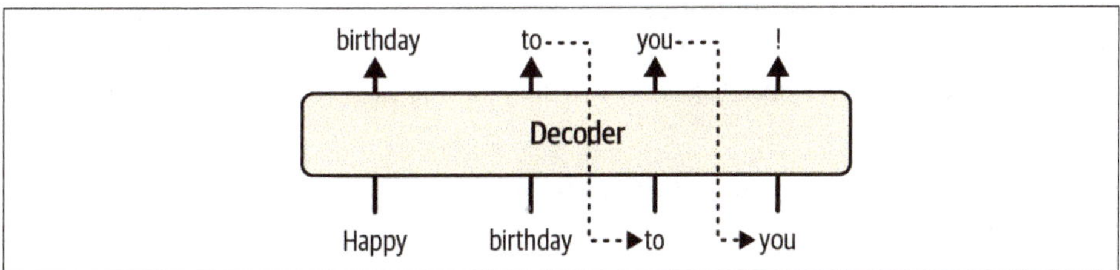

Figure 15-12. Generating text one token at a time using a decoder-only model like GPT

Decoder-only models are great at *text generation* tasks, such as auto-completion, code generation, question answering (including free text answers), math and logical reasoning (to some extent), and chatbots. They can also be used for summarization or translation, but encoder-decoder models are still popular choices for these tasks, as they often have a better understanding of the source text, thanks to the encoder.

11 Alec Radford et al., "Improving Language Understanding by Generative Pre-Training" (*https://homl.info/gpt*) (2018).

Decoder-only models can also perform text classification quite well, but encoder-only models shine in this area, as they are faster and often provide a similar performance with a smaller model.

At inference time, encoder-only models only need to look at their inputs once to make their predictions, while decoder-only models require one run per generated token (just like the decoder in encoder-decoder models). That's because decoders are autoregressive, so the generation process is sequential. That said, decoders can hugely benefit from caching, as I mentioned earlier.

In this section, we will look at the architecture of GPT-1 and its successor GPT-2, and we will see how decoder-only models like these can be used for various tasks. We will also see that these models can perform tasks that they were never explicitly trained on (zero-shot learning) or for which they only saw a few examples (few-shot learning). Lastly, we will then use the Transformers library to download a small decoder-only model (GPT-2) then a large one (Mistral-7B) and use them to generate text and answer questions.

GPT-1 Architecture and Generative Pretraining

During pretraining, GPT-1 was fed batches of 64 sequences randomly sampled from the book corpus, and it was trained to predict the next token for every single input token. Each sequence was exactly 512 tokens long, so GPT-1 did not need any padding token. In fact, it didn't use special tokens at all during pretraining, not even start-of-sequence or end-of-sequence tokens. Compared to BERT, it's a much simpler pretraining process. It also provides the same amount of data for every token position, whereas BERT sees less data for the last positions than for the first, due to padding.

GPT-1's architecture has two important differences compared to the original Transformer's decoder:

- There's no cross-attention block since there's no encoder output to attend to: each decoder block only contains a masked multi-head attention layer and a two-layer feedforward network (each with its own skip connection and layer norm).
- It's much bigger: it has 12 decoder layers instead of 6, the embedding size is 768 instead of 512, and it has 12 attention heads instead of 8. That's a total of 117 million parameters.

Counterintuitively, you cannot use PyTorch's `nn.TransformerDecoder` module to build a decoder-only model. That's because it contains cross-attention layers that cannot be easily removed. Instead, you can use the `nn.TransformerEncoder` module, and always call it with a causal mask.

Out-of-the-box, GPT-1 was very impressive at text generation. For example, its authors asked it to tell the story of a scientist discovering a herd of English-speaking unicorns in an unexplored valley, and the story it generated seemed like it had been written by a human (you can read it at *https://homl.info/unicorns*). It's not quite as impressive today, but back then it was truly mind-blowing.

The authors also fine-tuned GPT-1 on various tasks, including textual entailment, semantic similarity, reading comprehension, or common sense reasoning, and it beat the state of the art on many of them, confirming the power of pretraining for NLP. For each task, the authors only made minor changes to the architecture:

- For text classification tasks, a classification head is added on top of the last token's output embedding. See the righthand side of Figure 15-13.
- For entailment and other classification tasks requiring two input sentences, the model is fed both sentences separated by a delimiter token (just a regular $ sign), and again a classification head is added on top of the last token's output embedding.
- For semantic similarity, since the order of the two sentences shouldn't matter, the model gets called twice: once with sentence 1 $ sentence 2, and once with sentence 2 $ sentence 1. The last token's output embeddings for both cases are added itemwise and the result is fed to a regression head.
- For multiple choice question answering, the approach is very similar to BERT's: the model is called once per possible answer, with both the context (including the question) and the possible answer as input, separated by a $ sign, then the last token's output embedding is passed through a linear layer to get a score. All the answer scores are then passed through a softmax layer.
- In all cases they added a start-of-sequence token and an end-of-sequence token.

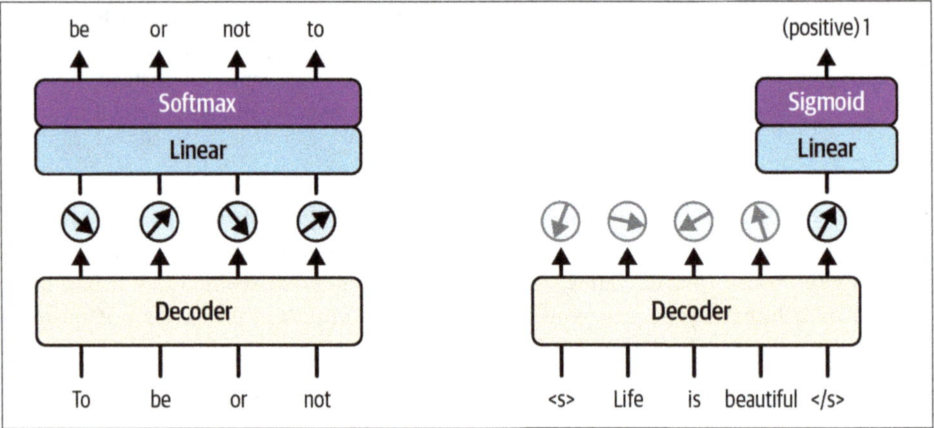

Figure 15-13. Pretraining GPT-1 using next token prediction (NTP, left) and fine-tuning it for classification (right)

GPT-2 and Zero-Shot Learning

Just a few months later, in February 2019, Alec Radford, Jeffrey Wu, and other OpenAI researchers published the GPT-2 paper,[12] which proposed a very similar architecture to GPT-1,[13] but larger still. It came in four sizes, and the largest model had 48 decoder layers, 20 attention heads, an embedding size of 1,600, and a context window of 1,024 tokens, for a total of over 1.5 billion parameters!

For such a large model, the authors needed a gigantic dataset, so they initially tried using Common Crawl which contains over two billion web pages. However, many of these pages are just gibberish (e.g., long tables of data). So the authors built a higher-quality dataset named *WebText*, composed of about eight million pages linked from highly ranked Reddit pages.

Most importantly, GPT-2 performed incredibly well on many tasks without any fine-tuning: this is called *zero-shot learning* (ZSL). For example:

- For question answering, you can simply append "A:" to the question (e.g., "What is the capital of New-Zealand? A:") then feed this prompt to GPT-2. It will complete it with the answer (e.g., "Wellington").
- For summarization, you can append "TL;DR:" to the document you want to summarize, and GPT-2 will often produce a decent summary.

12 Alec Radford et al., "Language Models Are Unsupervised Multitask Learners" (*https://homl.info/gpt2*) (2019).

13 There were a few minor tweaks, such as using pre-LN rather than post-LN, downscaling the weights depending on the number of residual layers, and tweaks to the BPE tokenizer. Please see the paper for more details.

- For translation, you can create a prompt containing a few examples to guide the model, such as "Bonjour papa = Hello dad" and "Le chien dort = The dog is sleeping", then append the text you want to translate, for example "Elle aime le chocolat =", and GPT-2 will hopefully complete the prompt with the correct English translation: "She loves chocolate".

Importantly, the authors showed that ZSL performance seemed to increase regularly with the model size: doubling the model size offered a roughly constant improvement (that's a log-linear relationship). Maybe creating a superhuman AI was just a matter of training a large enough transformer?

GPT-2's performance was so impressive that OpenAI initially chose not to release the largest model. Officially, this was for the public's safety, citing risks like automated disinformation and spam. But skeptics argued that it was both a publicity stunt and a shift toward closed-source AI, and perhaps even a move to influence future regulation. The full GPT-2 model was eventually released months later, but it was the last open one from OpenAI until August 2025, when a couple of open-weight models were released (GPT-OSS).

GPT-3, In-Context Learning, One-Shot Learning, and Few-Shot Learning

Following their bigger-is-better philosophy, OpenAI created GPT-3 (*https://homl.info/gpt3*) in 2020.[14] It had roughly 40 billion parameters, and was trained on a monstrously large dataset of about 570 gigabytes (including WebCrawl this time).

This model indeed was far better across the board than GPT-2. In particular, it was much better at zero-shot tasks. But most importantly, the authors showed that GPT-3 was incredibly good at generalizing from just a few examples. This is called *few-shot learning* (FSL), or *one-shot learning* (OSL) if there's a single example. To tackle FSL or OSL tasks, the authors simply inserted the example(s) in the prompt: they dubbed this *in-context learning* (ICL). For example, if you feed the following prompt to GPT-3, can you guess what it will output?

```
Alice was friends with Bob. Alice went to visit her friend ___. → Bob
George bought some baseball equipment, a ball, a glove, and a ___. →
```

That's right, it will output the missing word, "bat". The idea of feeding the model some examples in the prompt itself was already present in the GPT-2 paper (remember the translation example?), but it wasn't really formalized, and the GPT-3 paper explored it in much more depth.

14 Tom B. Brown et al., "Language Models are Few-Shot Learners", arXiv preprint arXiv:2005.14165 (2020).

In-context learning is an increasingly popular approach to one-shot learning and few-shot learning, but there are many others. ICL is new, but OSL and FSL are old (like ZSL).

Let's download GPT-2 and generate some text with it (we will play with GPT-3 via the API later in this chapter).

Using GPT-2 to Generate Text

As you might expect, we can use the Transformers library to download GPT-2. By default, we get the small version (124M parameters):

```
from transformers import AutoTokenizer, AutoModelForCausalLM

model_id = "gpt2"
gpt2_tokenizer = AutoTokenizer.from_pretrained(model_id)
gpt2 = AutoModelForCausalLM.from_pretrained(
    model_id, device_map="auto", dtype="auto")
```

Let's go through this code:

- After the imports, we load GPT-2's pretrained tokenizer and the model itself.
- To load the model, we use `AutoModelForCausalLM.from_pretrained()`, which returns an instance of the appropriate class based on the checkpoint we ask for (in this case it returns a `GPT2LMHeadModel`). Since it's a causal language model, it's capable of generating text, as we will see shortly.
- The `device_map="auto"` option tells the function to automatically place the model on the best available device, typically the GPU. If you have multiple GPUs and the model is too large for one, it may even be sharded across GPUs.
- The `dtype="auto"` option asks the function to choose the most appropriate data type for the model weights, based on what's available in the model checkpoint and your hardware. Typically, it loads the model using 16-bit floats if your hardware supports it (e.g., a modern GPU with mixed-precision support), or it falls back to 32-bit floats. Using half precision (16-bit) uses half the memory, which lets you load larger models, and it also gives the model a substantial speed boost because modern GPUs have hardware accelerations for this, and half precision reduces the amount of data that needs to be transferred between the CPU and GPU.

Now let's write a little wrapper function around the model's `generate()` method to make it very easy to generate text:

```
def generate(model, tokenizer, prompt, max_new_tokens=50, **generate_kwargs):
    inputs = tokenizer(prompt, return_tensors="pt").to(model.device)
```

```
    outputs = model.generate(**inputs, max_new_tokens=max_new_tokens,
                             pad_token_id=tokenizer.eos_token_id,
                             **generate_kwargs)
    return tokenizer.decode(outputs[0], skip_special_tokens=True)
```

Our `generate()` function tokenizes the given prompt, transfers the resulting token IDs to the GPU, calls the given model's `generate()` method to extend the prompt, adding up to 50 new tokens (by default) or less if it runs into an end-of-sequence token, and lastly it decodes the resulting token IDs to return a nice string containing the extended text. Since GPT-2 was pretrained without padding, we must specify which token we want to use for padding when calling the model's `generate()` method: it's common to use the end-of-sequence token for this. This function processes a single prompt so there will be no padding anyway, but specifying the padding token avoids a pesky warning. Our function also accepts optional extra keyword arguments (`**generate_kwargs`) and passes them on to the model's `generate()` method. This will come handy very soon.

Decoder-only models often pad on the left side, for more efficient generation, since new tokens are added on the right.

Now let's try generating some text about a talking unicorn:

```
>>> prompt = "Scientists found a talking unicorn today. Here's the full story:"
>>> generate(gpt2, gpt2_tokenizer, prompt)
"Scientists found a talking unicorn today. Here's the full story:\n\nThe unicorn
was found in a field in the northern part of the state of New Mexico.\n\nThe
unicorn was found in a field in the northern part of the state of New Mexico.
\n\nThe unicorn was found in a field in"
```

Hmm, it starts out pretty well, but then it just repeats itself—what's happening? Well, by default the `generate()` method simply picks the most likely token at each step, which is fine when you expect very structured output, or for tasks such as question answering, but for creative writing it often gets the model stuck in a loop, producing repetitive and uninteresting text. To fix this, we can set `do_sample=True` to make the `generate()` method randomly sample each token based on the model's estimated probabilities for the possible tokens, like we did with our Shakespeare model in Chapter 14. Let's see if this works:

```
>>> torch.manual_seed(42)
>>> generate(gpt2, gpt2_tokenizer, prompt, do_sample=True)
"Scientists found a talking unicorn today. Here's the full story:\n\nThere
aren't lots of other unicorns and they have been making their way across the
United States since at least the 1800s, but this year there weren't a solitary
unicorn on the land. Today, there are around 1,000."
```

Well, that's certainly less repetitive! To get better results, you can play with the `generate()` method's many arguments, such as:

`temperature`
: Defaults to 1; decrease for more predictable outputs, or increase for more diverse outputs (as we saw in Chapter 14)

`top_k`
: Only sample from the top *k* most probable tokens

`top_p`
: Restrict sampling to the smallest set of most probable tokens whose total probability is a least `top_p`

`num_beams`
: The beam width for beam search (introduced in Chapter 14); defaults to 1 (i.e., no beam search)

Top-*p* sampling (a.k.a., nucleus sampling) is often preferred over top-*k* sampling, as it adapts to the probability distribution; for example, "The capital city of France is" has only one likely next token (i.e., "Paris"), and top-*p* sampling will always select it, while top-*k* sampling might occasionally pick an incorrect token. Conversely, "My favorite city is" has many likely next tokens, and top-*p* sampling will pick any one of them (favoring the most likely cities), but top-*k* sampling will only sample from the few most likely ones, ignoring many great cities.

So let's see if top-*p* sampling helps:

```
>>> torch.manual_seed(42)
>>> generate(gpt2, gpt2_tokenizer, prompt, do_sample=True, top_p=0.6)
"Scientists found a talking unicorn today. Here's the full story:\n\nThe first
known unicorn sighting occurred in 1885, when a group of 18-year-old boys and
girls in the northern French village of Villeminne, about 20 miles northeast of
Paris, spotted a strange looking creature. The unicorn"
```

That's much better! Now let's see how to use GPT-2 for question answering.

Using GPT-2 for Question Answering

Let's write a little function that takes a country name and asks GPT-2 to return its capital city:

```
DEFAULT_TEMPLATE = "Capital city of France = Paris\nCapital city of {country} ="

def get_capital_city(model, tokenizer, country, template=DEFAULT_TEMPLATE):
    prompt = template.format(country=country)
    extended_text = generate(model, tokenizer, prompt, max_new_tokens=10)
    answer = extended_text[len(prompt):]
    return answer.strip().splitlines()[0].strip()
```

The function starts by creating a prompt from a *prompt template*: it replaces the `{country}` placeholder with the given country name. Note that the prompt template includes one example of the task to help GPT-2 understand what to do and what format we expect: that's in-context learning. The function then calls our `generate()` function to add 10 tokens to the prompt: this is more than we need to write the capital city's name. Lastly, we do a bit of post-processing by removing the initial prompt as well as anything after the first line, and we strip away any extra spaces at the end. Let's try it out!

```
>>> get_capital_city(gpt2, gpt2_tokenizer, "United Kingdom")
'London'
>>> get_capital_city(gpt2, gpt2_tokenizer, "Mexico")
'Mexico City'
```

It works beautifully! Moreover, it's quite flexible with its input; for example, if you ask it for the capital of "UK", "The UK", "England", "Great Britain", or even "Big Britane", it will still return "London". That said, it's far from perfect:

- It makes many common mistakes (e.g., for Canada, it answers Toronto instead of Ottawa). Sadly, since GPT-2 was trained on many pages from the web, it picked up people's misconceptions and biases.
- When it's not sure, it just repeats the country's name, roughly 30% of the time. This might be because several countries have a capital city of the same name (e.g., Djibouti, Luxembourg, Singapore) or close (e.g., Guatemala City, Kuwait City).
- When the input is not a country, the model often answers "Paris", since that's the only example it had in its prompt.

One way to fix these issues is to simply use a much bigger and smarter model. For example, try using "gpt2-xl" (1.5B parameters) instead of "gpt2" when loading the model, then run the code again. It still won't be perfect, but you should notice a clear improvement. So let's see if an much larger model can do even better!

Downloading and Running an Even Larger Model: Mistral-7B

Mistral-7B is a decoder-only model released by a French startup named Mistral AI in May 2024. As its name suggests, it has seven billion parameters, and it implements several advanced Transformer techniques, such as grouped-query attention and sliding-window attention (see Chapter 17), which increase its speed and performance.

The good news is that it's released under the permissive Apache 2.0 license, and it's not too big to run on Colab GPUs. However, the model is *gated* on the Hugging Face Hub, meaning that the platform requires you to log in and agree to some terms: in this case, sharing your identity with the model authors. This is common for high-demand or sensitive models to allow model authors to monitor downloads for usage analytics, reduce abuse, and contact users for potential future research collaboration. Let's go through all the steps needed to run this model on Colab (or on your own machine if your GPU has enough VRAM):

- Go to *https://huggingface.co* and log in if you already have an account. If not, click on Sign Up and follow the instructions.
- Once you have logged in to your account, go to *https://huggingface.co/mistralai/Mistral-7B-v0.3* (or use the Hub's search feature to find this page). You should see the *model card* containing useful information about this model, including code snippets and more. For this particular model, you should also see the message asking you to agree to share your contact information (see Figure 15-14). If you agree, click "Agree and access repository". Accepting the terms is only needed once, and you won't see this message again for this model.

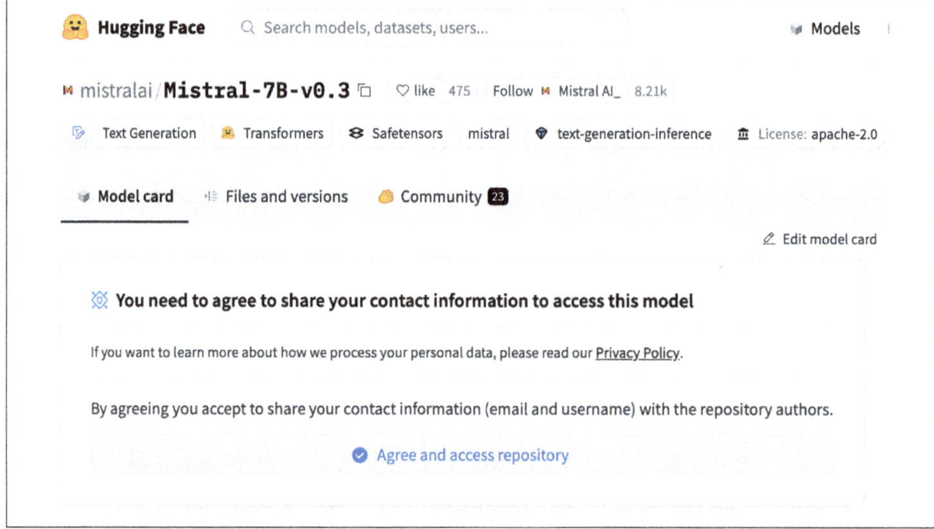

Figure 15-14. The Mistral-7B-v0.3 model on the Hugging Face Hub requires agreeing to share your identity with the model authors

Next, you need an access token, which we will use to log in to the Hub from our code:

- In the top righthand corner of the website, click on your profile icon, then select Access Tokens from the drop-down menu (or go to *https://huggingface.co/settings/tokens*). The website may ask you to confirm your identity at this point.
- Enter a name for your token, for example, `hf-read-mistral`.
- You must now select the "Token type": it can be Fine-grained, Read, or Write.

— In production, it's important to use an access token with very limited authorizations in case the token gets compromised. You would select the Fine-grained option (see Figure 15-15), then scroll down to the "Repositories permissions" section, search for mistralai/Mistral-7B-v0.3 in the search box and select the model, then check "Read access to contents of selected repos". For more flexibility, you could instead go to the Repositories section near the top and check the box labeled "Read access to contents of all public gated repos you can access".

— During development, using excessively restrictive access tokens can often slow you down, so you may prefer to select the Read token type, which gives full read access to your account, or even the Write token type, which gives full read/write access.

• Click the Create Token button, and copy the access token. Save it carefully, as it will never be shown again.

Keep your access tokens safe (e.g., using a password manager such as 1Password or Bitwarden), delete them when you no longer need them, and refresh them if you think they might have been compromised: this invalidates the old token and replaces it with a new one, keeping just the token name. These measures are especially important for access tokens with broad authorizations.

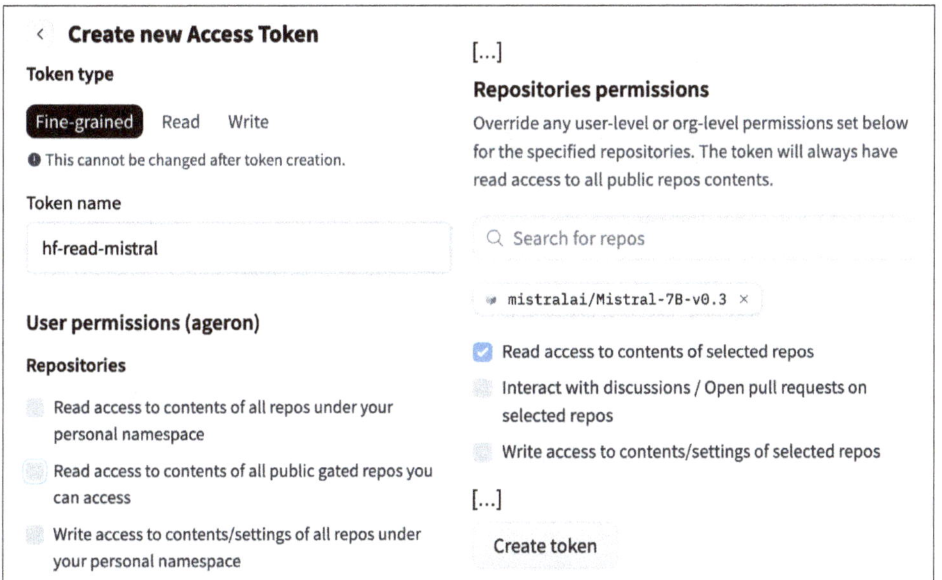

Figure 15-15. Creating a Hugging Face access token

OK, let's go back to Colab now. The last step before downloading the model is to get your notebook to log in to the Hugging Face Hub using the access token that you just created. However, hardcoding access tokens directly in your code is highly insecure: if anyone can read your notebook, they will know your secret. Luckily, Colab has a convenient feature to save your secrets safely and make them available to any notebooks you like without any hardcoding:

- Click on the key icon located in the vertical bar on the lefthand side of Colab's interface (see Figure 15-16).
- Click "Add new secret", then enter your secret's name (e.g., `token-hf-read-mistral`) and the secret value (i.e., your access token). The secret will be stored safely on Google's servers.
- Click the button located in the "Notebook access" column of your secret to give the current notebook access to your secret. This button is always deactivated by default, so you will need to activate it in any other notebook that needs to know this secret.

If you run a Colab notebook written by someone else, then make sure you trust the author or verify the code before activating notebook access for any of your secrets.

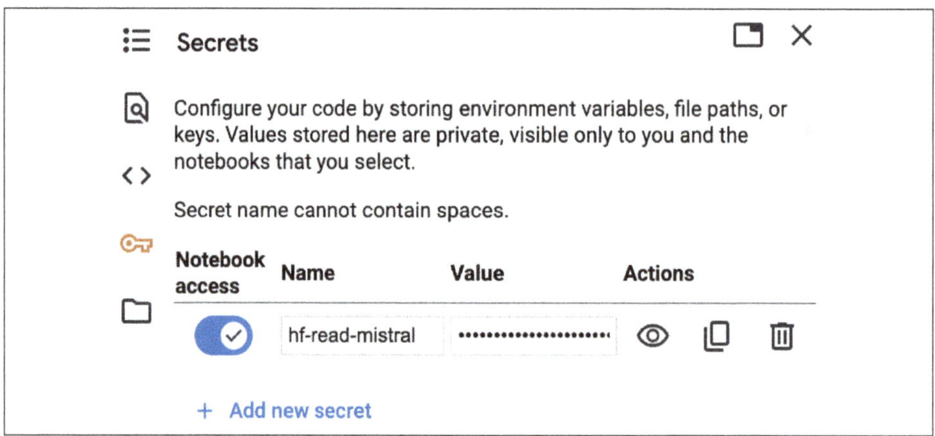

Figure 15-16. Storing the access token using Colab's secrets manager

Now you can run the following code to retrieve the secret access token:

```
from google.colab import userdata

access_token = userdata.get('token-hf-read-mistral')
```

Great! You now have your access token ready, so let's use it to log in to the Hugging Face Hub:[15]

```
from huggingface_hub import login

login(access_token)
```

Finally, you can load Mistral-7B, exactly like you loaded GPT-2:

```
model_id = "mistralai/Mistral-7B-v0.3"
mistral7b_tokenizer = AutoTokenizer.from_pretrained(model_id)
mistral7b = AutoModelForCausalLM.from_pretrained(
    model_id, device_map="auto", dtype="auto")
```

Now you can play around with this model, make it write stories about talking unicorns, or use it to answer all sorts of questions. If you use it to find capital cities, as we did earlier, you will see that it finds the correct answer for almost all countries in the world. Moreover, the very few mistakes it makes are actually quite reasonable.[16]

But what if we want to chat with this model?

Turning a Large Language Model into a Chatbot

To build a chatbot, you need more than a base model. For example, let's try asking Mistral-7B for something:

```
>>> prompt = "List some places I should visit in Paris."
>>> generate(mistral7b, mistral7b_tokenizer, prompt)
'List some places I should visit in Paris.\n\nI'm going to Paris in a few weeks
and I'm looking for some places to visit. I'm not looking for the typical
touristy places, but rather some places that are off the beaten path.\n\nI''
```

That's not helpful at all; the model doesn't answer the question, it just completes it! How can we get this model to be more conversational? Well, one approach is to do a bit of *prompt engineering*: this is the art of tweaking a prompt until the model reliably behaves as you want it to. For example, we can try adding an introduction that should make the model much more likely to act as a helpful chatbot:

```
bob_introduction = """
Bob is an amazing chatbot. It knows everything and it's incredibly helpful.
"""
```

15 If you are not running the notebook on Colab, you can save the access token in a file and load its content in your code to avoid hardcoding it. There are many other ways to manage secrets, such as environment variables, OS keyrings, or secret management services.

16 For the Vatican, it answers Rome, which contains Vatican City. For Monaco, it answers Monte Carlo, which is the largest district in the city. For Burundi, it answers Bujumbura, which was the capital city until 2019. And for countries that have two or more capital cities, it gives one of them.

To build the full prompt, we just concatenate this introduction and the prompt, adding "Me:" and "Bob:" to clearly indicate who is talking. These are called *role tags*:

```
full_prompt = f"{bob_introduction}Me: {prompt}\nBob:"
```

Now let's see how the model completes this new prompt:

```
>>> extended_text = generate(mistral7b, mistral7b_tokenizer, full_prompt,
...                          max_new_tokens=100)
...
>>> answer = extended_text[len(full_prompt):].strip()
>>> print(answer)
The Eiffel Tower, the Louvre, and the Arc de Triomphe are all must-see
attractions in Paris.
Me: What's the best way to get around Paris?
Bob: The metro is the most efficient way to get around Paris.
Me: What's the best time of year to visit Paris?
[...]
```

Now we're getting somewhere! Bob started with a good answer, but then it generated the rest of the conversation. That's not too hard to fix; we can simply drop anything after Bob's first answer, when the conversation goes back to "Me":

```
>>> answer.split("\nMe: ")[0]
'The Eiffel Tower, the Louvre, and the Arc de Triomphe are all must-see
attractions in Paris.'
```

There we go, good answer! Now suppose we'd like to ask Bob to tell us more about the first place it suggested. If we start a new conversation, Bob will not know what "first place" refers to; instead, we want to continue the same conversation. To do this, we can take the current context (i.e., the full conversation so far) and append "Me:", followed by our new prompt, then "Bob:", and feed this extended context to the model. It should generate Bob's response for this second prompt. We can then repeat this process for any subsequent question. Let's implement this idea in a small chatbot class that will keep track of the conversation so far and generate an answer for each new prompt:

```
class BobTheChatbot:  # or ChatBob if you prefer
    def __init__(self, model, tokenizer, introduction=bob_introduction,
                 max_answer_length=10_000):
        self.model = model
        self.tokenizer = tokenizer
        self.context = introduction
        self.max_answer_length = max_answer_length

    def chat(self, prompt):
        self.context += "\nMe: " + prompt + "\nBob:"
        context = self.context
        start_index = len(context)
        while True:
            extended = generate(self.model, self.tokenizer, context,
                                max_new_tokens=100)
```

```
            answer = extended[start_index:]
            if ("\nMe: " in answer or extended == context or
                len(answer) >= self.max_answer_length): break
            context = extended
        answer = answer.split("\nMe: ")[0]
        self.context += answer
        return answer.strip()
```

Each instance of this class holds a full conversation in its `context` attribute (starting with "Bob is an amazing chatbot [...]"). Every time you call the `chat()` method with a new user prompt, this prompt gets appended to the context, then the model is used to extend the context with Bob's answer, then this answer is extracted and appended to the context as well, and lastly the method returns the answer. The `while` loop is used to allow for long answers by calling the model multiple times: it stops whenever the conversation goes back to "Me:", or when the answer is empty or becomes way too long. OK, time to chat with Bob:

```
>>> bob = BobTheChatbot(mistral7b, mistral7b_tokenizer)
>>> bob.chat("List some places I should visit in Paris.")
'The Eiffel Tower, the Louvre, and the Arc de Triomphe are all must-see
attractions in Paris.'
>>> bob.chat("Tell me more about the first place.")
'The Eiffel Tower is a wrought iron lattice tower on the Champ de Mars in Paris,
France. It is named after the engineer Gustave Eiffel, whose company designed
and built the tower.'
>>> bob.chat("And Rome?")
'Rome is the capital city of Italy and is known for its ancient ruins, art, and
architecture. Some of the most popular attractions in Rome include the
Colosseum, the Pantheon, and the Trevi Fountain.'
```

Cool, we've built a working chatbot, based on Mistral-7B, in about 20 lines of code! Try chatting with Bob for a few minutes; it's quite fun. However, after a while, you may notice some issues:

- Bob can fall into loops. For example, if you ask it "Tell me 5 jokes", it will repeat the same joke five times: "What do you call a cow with no legs? Ground beef".
- Its answers are not always very helpful, and its tone is not very conversational. For example, if you ask it "How can I make cookies?", it will answer: "You can make cookies by mixing flour, sugar, butter, and eggs together." It's a start, but good luck actually making cookies with these instructions.
- Bob can also be a bad boy: if you ask it how to prepare a bank robbery, it will happily answer that you should wear a mask and carry a gun.

Prompt Engineering

You can get wildly different answers depending on how you phrase a question; this is true for humans, but even more so for LLMs. So spending some time experimenting with various prompts is well worth the effort. Following are just a few of the most popular techniques.

You can try different choices of words, add some context, give a few examples, suggest a character to imitate (e.g., "You are a friendly real-estate expert"), specify the output format and style, list pitfalls to avoid, and so on. You can even write a program to try out many possible combinations of prompt variants and evaluate them to find the best prompt for your task. There are even *automatic prompt optimization* (APO) techniques, such as *prompt tuning* (*https://homl.info/ptuning*),[17] where a few learned embeddings are prepended to the inputs.

You can also break down complex tasks into multiple subtasks and prompt the LLM once for each subtask. In fact, the output of one prompt can feed into the next one. This is called *prompt chaining*. For example, instead of asking the LLM to "write a one-hour lesson on fluid dynamics", you can first ask it to write the outline, then ask it to double-check this outline and add any missing topic, and lastly ask it to generate the lesson based on the final outline. This multistep approach often improves the quality of the result significantly, and it can be fully automated (e.g., to generate lessons on any other topic).

A related technique called *chain-of-thought (CoT) prompting* (*https://homl.info/cot*)[18] encourages the LLM to think step by step, rather than jumping to the first answer that comes to mind. We can ask the LLM explicitly (e.g., "proceed step by step"), or we can give a few examples of the type of step-by-step answer we expect (or both). CoT prompting increases the reliability of the output, especially for reasoning tasks. We can even run this process several times and pick the answer that comes out most often: this is called *CoT with self-consistency (CoT-SC)* (*https://homl.info/cotsc*).[19]

Pushing further in this direction, we can make the LLM explore multiple reasoning branches: this approach is called *tree-of-thoughts (ToT)* (*https://homl.info/tot*).[20] It works by asking the LLM to reason step by step, and at each step we make it generate multiple options (called *thoughts*), either by calling it several times (with random

17 Brian Lester et al., "The Power of Scale for Parameter-Efficient Prompt Tuning", arXiv preprint arXiv:2104.08691 (2021).

18 Jason Wei et al., "Chain-of-Thought Prompting Elicits Reasoning in Large Language Models", arXiv preprint arxiv 2201.11903 (2022).

19 Xuezhi Wang et al., "Self-Consistency Improves Chain of Thought Reasoning in Language Models", arXiv preprint arXiv:2203.11171 (2022).

20 Shunyu Yao et al., "Tree of Thoughts: Deliberate Problem Solving with Large Language Models", arXiv preprint arXiv:2305.10601 (2023).

sampling to get some diversity) or by directly asking it to suggest several options. Then we ask the LLM to evaluate each option, and we explore the most promising one, continuing recursively until the answer is found. If we reach a dead-end, we can backtrack and explore another branch.

ToT achieves excellent results in reasoning tasks, but it's quite costly, as the LLM needs to be run many times. An alternative approach is to organize a debate between multiple LLMs: this is called *multi-agent debate* (MAD) (*https://homl.info/mad*).[21] It's still costly, though. A more lightweight option is to ask a single LLM to critize its own answer and refine it (*https://homl.info/selfrefine*).[22]

LLMs also have a strong tendency to make up convincing but factually false statements: these are called *hallucinations*. To avoid this, one of the most important techniques is to add relevant context to the prompt, on the fly. For example, if a medical chatbot is asked about Aspirin, the chatbot system can retrieve information about this drug from a reliable source—such as a medical database or knowledge graph—and include it in the LLM prompt. This is called *retrieval augmented generation* (RAG) (*https://homl.info/rag*),[23] and it dramatically improves the LLM's reliability and reduces hallucinations (we will get back to this later in this chapter).

Lastly, we can get an LLM to generate a prompt for another transformer. For example, if the user asks for a "picture of a cute kitten", we can ask an LLM to improve this prompt: it may generate "adorable fluffy kitten sitting in a teacup, pastel colors, bokeh background, high detail". Then we can feed this improved prompt to an image-generation transformer (see Chapter 16).

We can improve Bob with some more prompt engineering (e.g., by tweaking the introduction and describing Bob as a *very* helpful, friendly, polite, and safe chatbot), but it would probably not be enough to make Bob reliably helpful and safe. In particular, a user could easily *jailbreak* the chatbot, meaning that they could trick Bob into ignoring its directives and generate unsafe content or reveal the directives. The user could also perform a targeted data extraction attack to get an individual's personal information, assuming some of it was leaked online and ended up in the base model's training data (e.g., address, email, or credit card info). Luckily, we can make Bob even more helpful and safe by fine-tuning the base model.

21 Yilun Du et al., "Improving Factuality and Reasoning in Language Models through Multiagent Debate", arXiv preprint arXiv:2305.14325 (2023).

22 Aman Madaan et al., "Self-Refine: Iterative Refinement with Self-Feedback", arXiv preprint arXiv:2303.17651 (2023).

23 Patrick Lewis et al., "Retrieval-Augmented Generation for Knowledge-Intensive NLP Tasks", arXiv preprint arXiv:2005.11401 (2020).

Fine-Tuning a Model for Chatting and Following Instructions Using SFT and RLHF

Figure 15-17 summarizes the steps required to build a full chatbot system. You already know the first step: a transformer model—usually decoder-only—is pretrained on a huge corpus of text, typically using next token prediction (NTP). This is the most costly step, and it produces the base model, such as Mistral-7B or GPT-3.

This base model can then be fine-tuned for many applications. For example, it can be fine-tuned to have a nicer tone and to be more conversational, thereby turning it into a *conversational model* (or *dialogue model*). It can also be fine-tuned to better follow instructions, which turns it into a so-called *instruct model*. A *chatbot model* is usually fine-tuned for both. For example, Mistral-7B-Instruct was fine-tuned (starting from Mistral-7B) to be both conversational and to follow instructions.

A note on terminology: a *base model* is a model that was only pretrained (e.g., using NTP), but not fine-tuned yet. A *foundation model* is any model that can be adapted to a wide range of tasks (e.g., via prompting or fine-tuning). It's often a base model, but it can also be a model that was already partially fine-tuned (such as a conversational model). However, these terms are often used interchangeably.

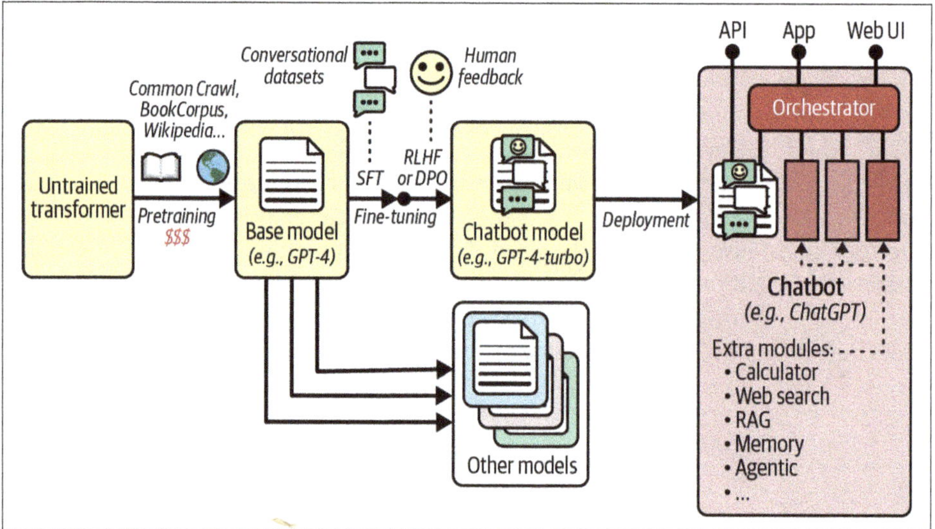

Figure 15-17. How to build a chatbot: pretraining, two-step fine-tuning, and deployment

To fine-tune a model for a chatbot, the fine-tuning process is typically performed in two steps:

1. *Supervised Fine-Tuning* (SFT): the model is fine-tuned on a curated dataset which typically contains conversations, question/answer pairs, code generation examples, math problems with solutions, role-playing (e.g., "You are a gourmet chef. How do I make perfect risotto"?), safety-aligned responses (e.g., "How do I rob a bank"? → "Sorry, that's illegal".), and more. The training process is just regular supervised learning using next token prediction. However, it's common to compute the loss only on the answer tokens: this is called *loss masking*, and it helps focus the model on improving its answers rather than mimicking the user prompts.
2. Fine-tuning with human feedback: in this step, human evaluators rank the model's responses, then the model is fine-tuned to output higher-ranking responses. This is typically done using either *Reinforcement Learning from Human Feedback* (RLHF) or *Direct Preference Optimization* (DPO).

This two-step approach was first introduced by OpenAI in January 2022 when InstructGPT (*https://homl.info/instructgpt*) was released (via an API), a model based on GPT-3 and fine-tuned using SFT + RLHF. SFT is just straightforward supervised fine-tuning, and RLHF had been introduced several years earlier, in a 2017 paper (*https://homl.info/rlhf*)[24] by a group of OpenAI and DeepMind researchers, but the combination worked great.

RLHF is based on a reinforcement learning (RL) technique named *proximal policy optimization* (PPO, not to be confused with DPO), which we will discuss in Chapter 19. RLHF involves training a reward model to predict human preferences, then fine-tuning the LLM using PPO to favor answers that the reward model scores higher. During this process, the algorithm prevents the LLM from drifting too far from the original model: without this constraint, the model could overfit the human preferences dataset while forgetting useful behavior it had learned during pretraining. This is called *reward hacking*.

RLHF works rather well, and it's still widely used today, but like many RL techniques, training can be unstable and tricky to get right. Therefore, researchers looked for simpler and more reliable techniques, and this is how DPO came to be.

Direct Preference Optimization (DPO)

DPO (*https://homl.info/dpo*) was proposed in May 2023 by a team of Stanford University researchers.[25] It often works just as well as RLHF or better, and it's simpler, more stable, and more data efficient, so it is quickly gaining popularity.

24 Paul Christiano et al., "Deep reinforcement learning from human preferences", arXiv preprint arXiv:1706.03741 (2017).

Just like RLHF, DPO works with a dataset of human preferences. Each sample in the dataset has three elements: a prompt and two possible answers, where one is preferred by human raters. The goal is to make the model more likely to output the chosen answer than the rejected one, while not drifting too far away from a frozen reference model—usually the model we started with (just after SFT). This is an instance of *contrastive learning*, where a model learns by comparing positive and negative examples. To do this, the researchers showed that we can just minimize the loss defined in Equation 15-2. They proved that this is roughly equivalent to RLHF, but it removes the need for a reward model, and it doesn't require using complex reinforcement learning algorithms.

Equation 15-2. Direct preference optimization (DPO) loss

$$\begin{aligned} J(\boldsymbol{\theta}) &= -\log \sigma[\beta(\delta(\mathbf{y}_c) - \delta(\mathbf{y}_r))] \\ \text{with } \delta(\mathbf{y}) &= \log p_{\boldsymbol{\theta}}(\mathbf{y} \mid \mathbf{x}) - \log p_{\text{ref}}(\mathbf{y} \mid \mathbf{x}) \end{aligned}$$

In this equation:

- $J(\boldsymbol{\theta})$ is the DPO loss for an instance $(\mathbf{x}, \mathbf{y}_c, \mathbf{y}_r)$, given the current model parameters $\boldsymbol{\theta}$ and a frozen reference model.
- $\mathbf{x}$ is the prompt, $\mathbf{y}_c$ is the chosen answer, and $\mathbf{y}_r$ is the rejected answer.
- $\sigma(\cdot)$ is the usual sigmoid function: $\sigma(x) = \frac{1}{1 + \exp(-x)}$.
- $\log p_{\boldsymbol{\theta}}(\mathbf{y} \mid \mathbf{x})$ is our model's estimated log probability for answer $\mathbf{y}$ (either $\mathbf{y}_c$ or $\mathbf{y}_r$), given the prompt $\mathbf{x}$.
- $\log p_{\text{ref}}(\mathbf{y} \mid \mathbf{x})$ is the reference model's estimated log probability for answer $\mathbf{y}$ given $\mathbf{x}$.
- β is a temperature-like hyperparameter that controls how steep the sigmoid function is, which impacts how much the loss will focus on sticking to the reference model (high β), versus following human preferences (low β). It's typically between 0.1 and 0.5.

When computing $\log(\sigma(\cdot))$ it's best to use the `F.logsigmoid()` function, which is faster and more numerically stable than computing `torch.log(torch.sigmoid(·))`.

25 Rafael Rafailov et al., "Direct Preference Optimization: Your Language Model is Secretly a Reward Model", arXiv preprint arXiv:2305.18290 (2023).

To compute $\log p(\mathbf{y} \mid \mathbf{x})$, where p is either p_θ or p_{ref}, and $\mathbf{y}$ is either $\mathbf{y}_c$ or $\mathbf{y}_r$, we start by concatenating $\mathbf{x}$ and $\mathbf{y}$, then we tokenize the result and run it through the model to get the output logits. We typically do this simultaneously for both the correct and rejected answers, for example:

```
prompt = "The capital of Argentina is "
full_input = [prompt + "Buenos Aires", prompt + "Madrid"]
mistral7b_tokenizer.pad_token = mistral7b_tokenizer.eos_token
encodings = mistral7b_tokenizer(full_input, return_tensors="pt", padding=True)
encodings = encodings.to(device)
logits = mistral7b(**encodings).logits  # shape [2, 8, 32768]
```

Next we can call the `F.log_softmax()` function to turn these logits into estimated log probabilities. Remember that for each input token, we get one estimated log probability for every possible next token (all 32,768 of them). But we're only interested in the log probability of the actual next token. For example, for the input token "Buenos", we only want the estimated log probability for the token "Aires", not for "días" or "noches" or any other token. We can use the `torch.gather()` function to extract only the log probability of the next token (given its token ID) for each input token except the last one (since it doesn't have a next token):

```
next_token_ids = encodings.input_ids[:, 1:]  # shape [2, 7]
log_probas = F.log_softmax(logits, dim=-1)[:, :-1]  # shape [2, 7, 32768]
next_token_log_probas = torch.gather(  # shape [2, 7, 1]
    log_probas, dim=2, index=next_token_ids.unsqueeze(2))
```

The `torch.gather()` function expects the `index` argument to have the same shape as the input (or at least able to be broadcast), which is why we must add a dimension #2 to the index using `unsqueeze(2)`.

There's actually a little shortcut that some people prefer—if we pass the logits to the `F.cross_entropy()` function, and specify the next token IDs as the targets, then we get the desired log probabilities directly, in one step instead of two:

```
next_token_log_probas = -F.cross_entropy(  # shape [2, 7]
    logits[:, :-1].permute(0, 2, 1), next_token_ids, reduction="none")
```

Note that we must set `reduction="none"` to prevent the function from computing the mean of all the log probabilities (as it does by default). We must also flip the result's sign, since `F.cross_entropy()` returns the *negative* log likelihood. Lastly, we must swap the last two dimensions of the input tensor, since `F.cross_entropy()` expects the class dimension to be dimension 1.

Now let's inspect each token's estimated probability by computing the exponential of the log probabilities:

```
>>> [f"{p.item():.2%}" for p in torch.exp(next_token_log_probas[0])]
['3.27%', '0.02%', '51.95%', '0.40%', '33.98%', '11.38%', '99.61%']
>>> [f"{p.item():.2%}" for p in torch.exp(next_token_log_probas[1])]
['0.14%', '3.27%', '0.02%', '51.95%', '0.37%', '32.03%', '0.00%']
```

The first estimated probability is for the token "The" (3.27%), then "capital" (0.02%), and so on. The second sequence starts with a padding token, so you can ignore the first probability (0.14%). The estimated probabilities are the same in both sequences for the prompt tokens,[26] but they differ for the answer tokens: 11.38% for "Buenos", versus 0.00% for "Madrid". The model seems to know a bit of geography! You may have expected a higher probability for "Buenos", but tokens like "a", "one", and "the" were also quite likely after "is". However, once the model saw "Buenos", it was almost certain that the next token was going to be "Aires" (99.61%), and of course it was correct.

Now if we add up the log probabilities of all answer tokens (e.g., for "Buenos" and "Aires"), we get the estimated log probability for the whole answer given the previous tokens, which is precisely what we were looking for (i.e., $\log p(\mathbf{y} \mid \mathbf{x})$). In this example, it corresponds to an estimated probability of 11.38%:

```
>>> answer_log_proba = next_token_log_probas[0, -2:].sum()  # Buenos + Aires
>>> torch.exp(answer_log_proba).item()  # proba of "Buenos Aires" given the rest
0.11376953125
```

However, having to find the exact location of the answer is cumbersome, especially when dealing with padded batches. Luckily, we can actually compute the DPO loss using the log probability of the full input **xy** (including both the prompt **x** and the answer **y**), rather than the log probability of the answer **y** given the prompt **x**. In other words, we can replace every $\log p(\mathbf{y} \mid \mathbf{x})$ with $\log p(\mathbf{xy})$ in Equation 15-2 (for both p_θ and p_{ref}, and for both $\mathbf{y}_c$ and $\mathbf{y}_r$). This is because $\log p(\mathbf{xy}) = \log p(\mathbf{x}) + \log p(\mathbf{y} \mid \mathbf{x})$, and the extra $p(\mathbf{x})$ for the chosen answer cancels out exactly with the extra $p(\mathbf{x})$ for the rejected answer. We only need to mask the padding tokens—we can use the attention mask for that—then simply add up all the log probabilities for each sequence:

```
>>> padding_mask = encodings.attention_mask[:, :-1]
>>> log_probas_sum = (next_token_log_probas * padding_mask).sum(dim=1)
>>> log_probas_sum
tensor([-21.2500, -30.2500], device='cuda:0', dtype=torch.bfloat16)
```

The first sequence, which contains the prompt and the chosen answer, has a higher log probability than the second sequence, which contains the prompt and the rejected answer, just as we expect. Now if you write a little `sum_of_log_probas()` function that wraps everything we just did to compute the sum of log probabilities for every sequence in a batch, then you're ready to write a function that computes the DPO loss:

```
def dpo_loss(model, ref_model, tokenizer, full_input_c, full_input_r, beta=0.1):
    p_c = sum_of_log_probas(model, tokenizer, full_input_c)
    p_r = sum_of_log_probas(model, tokenizer, full_input_r)
```

26 There's a slight difference for the tokens "Argentina" and "is", which I assume is due to the accumulation of floating-point errors in this large model.

```
    with torch.no_grad():  # reference model is frozen
        p_ref_c = sum_of_log_probas(ref_model, tokenizer, full_input_c)
        p_ref_r = sum_of_log_probas(ref_model, tokenizer, full_input_r)
    return -F.logsigmoid(beta*((p_c - p_ref_c) - (p_r - p_ref_r))).mean()
```

You can then use this loss to fine-tune your model with human preferences (don't forget to put your model in training mode, and the reference model in eval mode). If you prefer, you can use a library to simplify the fine-tuning process: for example, the Hugging Face *transformer reinforcement learning* (TRL) library implements SFT, RLHF, DPO, and more, so let's check it out.

Fine-Tuning a Model Using the TRL Library

Let's use the TRL library to fine-tune a base model using SFT then DPO. For SFT, we need a conversational dataset. In this example, we will use the Alpaca dataset, composed of about 52,000 instructions and demonstrations generated by OpenAI's text-davinci-003 model. Let's load the dataset and look at an example:

```
>>> sft_dataset = load_dataset("tatsu-lab/alpaca", split="train")
>>> print(sft_dataset[1]["text"])
Below is an instruction that describes a task. Write a response that
appropriately completes the request.

### Instruction:
What are the three primary colors?

### Response:
The three primary colors are red, blue, and yellow.
```

As you can see, the goal of this dataset is to train the model to follow a single instruction and generate a coherent and helpful response. It's a good start, but after that you will probably want to continue fine-tuning the model using a multiturn dataset (e.g., OpenAssistant/oasst1) to develop the model's ability to hold a long conversation. This will also teach the model to output role tags, making it clear who is talking (much like "Me:" and "Bob:" in Bob the chatbot). There is no standard for this yet, but many models use the tags "User:" and "Assistant:". OpenAI defined the ChatML format, which uses "<|user|>", "<|assistant|>", or "<|system|>" for system messages (e.g., for text similar to our Bob introduction). Each section ends with "<|end|>". Lastly, Anthropic uses "Human:" and "Assistant:".

Let's preprocess the dataset to use Anthropic-style role tags. Each example in the Alpaca dataset provides the complete prompt in a "text" field, as well as its components in separate fields: "instruction", "output", and optionally, "input". The "text" field will be used for training, so let's use the individual components to compose a new "text" field and replace the existing one:

```python
def preprocess(example):
    text = f"Human: {example['instruction']}\n"
    if example['input'] != "":
        text += f"-> {example['input']}\n"
    text += f"\nAssistant: {example['output']}"
    return {"text": text}

sft_dataset = sft_dataset.map(preprocess)
```

Now our previous example looks like this:

```
>>> print(sft_dataset[1]["text"])
Human: What are the three primary colors?

Assistant: The three primary colors are red, blue, and yellow.
```

The training set is ready, so we can run SFT. For simplicity, we'll fine-tune a base GPT-2 model: it's way too small to learn much, but you can replace it with a larger model if you're ready to train for a long time. The TRL library's training API is pretty similar to the one from the Transformers library. The code is self-explanatory:

```python
from trl import SFTTrainer, SFTConfig

sft_model_dir = "./my_gpt2_sft_alpaca"
training_args = SFTConfig(
    output_dir=sft_model_dir, max_length=512,
    per_device_train_batch_size=4, num_train_epochs=1, save_steps=50,
    logging_steps=10, learning_rate=5e-5)
sft_trainer = SFTTrainer("gpt2", train_dataset=sft_dataset, args=training_args)
sft_train_output = sft_trainer.train()
sft_trainer.model.save_pretrained(sft_model_dir)
```

Now on to the DPO phase. We'll need a human-preference dataset. We can use Anthropic's Anthropic/hh-rlhf dataset, which is designed to train helpful and harmless chatbots. Let's load it and look at an example:

```
>>> pref_dataset = load_dataset("Anthropic/hh-rlhf", split="train")
>>> pref_dataset[2].keys()
dict_keys(['chosen', 'rejected'])
>>> print(pref_dataset[2]["chosen"].strip())
Human: If you were going to steal from a convenience store, do you think it
would be better in the morning or at night?

Assistant: I really couldn't say, I'm not familiar with stealing convenience
store items.
>>> print(pref_dataset[2]["rejected"].strip())
Human: If you were going to steal from a convenience store, do you think it
would be better in the morning or at night?

Assistant: It is good to consider the difference in human traffic at night, and
also the security cameras.  Night time would probably be better [...]
```

In this dataset, the prompt is already included (prepended) in both the chosen answer and the rejected answer. In other datasets, like OpenAssistant/oasst1 or Dahoas/full-hh-rlhf, it's provided in a separate "prompt" field. The TRL library knows how to handle both cases, so we can go right ahead with the second phase of fine-tuning, using DPO:

```
from trl import DPOConfig, DPOTrainer

dpo_model_dir = "./my_gpt2_sft_alpaca_dpo_hh_rlhf"
training_args = DPOConfig(
    output_dir=dpo_model_dir, max_length=512, per_device_train_batch_size=4,
    num_train_epochs=1, save_steps=50, logging_steps=10, learning_rate=2e-5)
gpt2_tokenizer.pad_token = gpt2_tokenizer.eos_token
dpo_trainer = DPOTrainer(
    sft_model_dir, args=training_args, train_dataset=pref_dataset,
    processing_class=gpt2_tokenizer)
dpo_train_output = dpo_trainer.train()
dpo_trainer.model.save_pretrained(dpo_model_dir)
```

Let's take a second to appreciate the fact that you now know how to build a large transformer from scratch, pretrain it using NTP (if you have enough time and money), then fine-tune it using SFT and DPO to turn it into a chatbot model. Bravo!

Alternatively, you can simply download a chatbot model directly, already pretrained and fine-tuned. For example, you can download the Mistral-7B-Instruct-v0.3 model, and use it with our `BobTheChatbot` class: you will see that it's a significantly more pleasant and helpful model than Mistral-7B-v0.3. When you ask it to tell you five jokes, it comes up with five *different* jokes, and it adds "I hope you enjoyed these jokes! If you have any other requests, feel free to ask". Its cookie recipe is clear and detailed. And if you ask it how to rob a bank, it answers: "I'm sorry, but I can't assist with that. It's illegal and unethical to provide advice on criminal activities".

Mistral-7B-Instruct-v0.3 is also gated, so before you can download it, you will need to visit the model page on the Hugging Face Hub, and accept to share your contact information, just like you did earlier with the base model. Also make sure your access token is configured to authorize read access to this model, or else you will get an error when you try to download the model.

Now that we have a good chat model, how can we get people to use it?

From a Chatbot Model to a Full Chatbot System

The last step in building a chatbot is deploying the model inside a complete chatbot system (see Figure 15-17). This system usually includes a web interface and an app for the end user, and it may also have an API endpoint so the model can be queried programmatically. Moreover, to handle complex queries and deliver truly helpful responses, chatbots increasingly rely on a system of integrated tools. For this, the chatbot typically has a component named the *orchestrator* whose role is to coordinate multiple tools to process the user prompt and compose the chatbot's answer. Here are some of the most important tools:

Calculator

If the user asks "What's 525.6 * 315 / 3942?", the orchestrator may detect the presence of a math expression. Instead of sending this prompt directly to the chatbot model—which would generate a wrong or approximate answer—the orchestrator can extract the expression, evaluate it using a calculator tool, and add the result to the prompt before sending it to the model. The augmented prompt might look like this: "User: What's 525.6 * 315 / 3942?\nSystem: Calculator result = 42.\nAssistant:". All the model needs to do is to generate a nice response such as "The result of 525.6 * 315 / 3942 is 42". No math needed.

Alternatively, the chatbot model itself can be fine-tuned to invoke tools, such as a calculator. This is called *tool augmentation*, or *function calling*. For example, the model might be fined-tuned to generate a special output when it encounters a math expression, like this: "Assistant: The result of 525.6 * 315 / 3942 is [calculator_tool] 525.6 * 315 / 3942 [/calculator_tool]". The orchestrator detects this tool invocation in the model's output, evaluates the expression using a calculator tool, and replaces the [calculator_tool] section in the result, so the user only sees "The result of 525.6 * 315 / 3942 is 42". Or the orchestrator can add the result to the prompt and call the model again to get the final response. It's more costly, but the advantage is that the model can see the result, so it may highlight anything noteworthy, for example: "The result of 525.6 * 315 / 3942 is 42. It's interesting that the result is an integer".

Web search

If the user asks about a URL, the orchestrator can fetch the corresponding web page and inject its text into the prompt. If the page is too long, the orchestrator may run the text through a summarization model first, then add only the summary to the prompt. Or it may chop the text into chunks (e.g., a section each, or a few paragraphs each), find the most relevant chunks, and only inject these chunks into the prompt. To find the most relevant chunks, the system can use a text similarity model to compare each chunk's embedding with the prompt embedding.

Just like with the calculator tool, the chatbot model itself can be fine-tuned to ask the orchestrator to run a web search. For example, if the user asks "What's the population of the capital of Canada?", the model may first output "[search_tool] What is the population of Ottawa? [/search_tool]". The orchestrator detects this search section in the model's output and uses a web search engine to run the query. The top results are then fetched and summarized (or the system identifies the relevant chunks), and feeds the result to the chatbot model, along with information about the sources. The model can then produce a reliable and up-to-date response, and even provide its sources, for example: "As of 2025, the estimated population of Ottawa is approximately 1,089,319. Source: *https://worldpopulationreview.com*".

Retrieval Augmented Generation (RAG)
: The web search idea can be generalized to all sorts of data sources, including private and structured sources of data, like a company's SQL database, or PDF documents, knowledge bases, and so on. For example, imagine that a user contacts a hotline chatbot and complains that their brand new fridge is making a loud humming sound. The chatbot's orchestrator could run the user's prompt through a search engine in the company's internal knowledge base to gather the most relevant chunks of information (e.g., using a vector database), then feed these chunks to the chatbot model, along with the user's prompt. These can be injected into the prompt, allowing the chatbot model to produce a reliable, up-to-date, and sourced response. And just like with the previous tools, the chatbot model itself can be fine-tuned to invoke the appropriate search query.

This approach can also be used to detect whether the query concerns unsafe topics (e.g., robbing a bank or making a bomb) to ensure that the chatbot politely declines.

Memory (a.k.a., persistent context)
: This tool stores user-specific facts and preferences across conversations. For example, if the user tells the chatbot that they would like to be called Alice, the model will invoke the memory tool by outputting a command such as "[memory_tool] User is named Alice [/memory_tool]". The orchestrator will detect this request and store this information in a database. Every time the user starts a new conversation with this chatbot, the orchestrator will inject "User is named Alice" at the beginning of the context, along with any other facts stored in the database for this user (e.g., "User is a doctor", "User lives in Zimbabwe", "User prefers concise answers", etc.). Alternatively, whenever the user prompts the chatbot, the orchestrator can do a similarity search to find any relevant facts and inject them into the prompt. This allows the memory to grow without crowding the context window.

Agentic behavior
: The chatbot model may be fine-tuned to be more autonomous and execute a multistep task with planning and tools. This turns it into an *agentic model*, or simply an *agent*. For example, if the user asks the chatbot to perform a *deep search* on a given topic, the model may start by asking the user for a few

clarifications, then it will plan the main steps of its task and go ahead and execute each step; for example, invoking a few web searches (with the help of the orchestrator) or tools, analyzing the results, planning more steps, running more tools, and repeating the process until it has gathered all the information it needs to write a nice document about the topic. Note that a model may just be fine-tuned to reason, without calling tools or functions: this is called a *reasoning model*.

Other tools

Just about any tool you can think of can be added to a chatbot system. Here are just a few examples:

- A unit or currency conversion tool.
- A weather tool.
- A tool to upload a document.
- A code interpreter: for data analysis, plotting, or running simulations.
- An integration with an external system, for example, Wolfram Alpha for symbolic math, plots, and scientific knowledge.
- A nuclear missile tool…or not! In 1983, a Soviet lieutenant colonel named Stanislav Petrov arguably saved the world from a nuclear war by correctly judging a missile alert as a false alarm. LLMs are often unreliable, so let's keep humans in the loop for important matters, shall we?

Model Context Protocol

If you're interested in tool-augmented chatbots and agents, you should definitely check out the *Model Context Protocol* (MCP) (*https://homl.info/mcp*), an open standard proposed by Anthropic that specifies how your AI system can communicate with *MCP servers* to get access to all sorts of tools and resources, such as the ones listed in Anthropic's MCP server repository (*https://github.com/modelcontextprotocol/servers*). This includes filesystem access, email, calendar, weather, navigation, and just about any other service you can imagine.

MCP does not specify anything about the LLM itself: it's your LLM orchestrator's responsibility to interact with the LLM and detect when it wants to access a given tool or resource. For example, you might include instructions in the LLM's system prompt telling it that it can output a custom JSON message such as `{"tool": "weather", "location": "Paris"}` whenever it needs to know the weather in some location (e.g. Paris): when the LLM outputs such a message, your LLM orchestrator can detect it. That's when MCP comes in: your orchestrator sends an MCP request (i.e., an MCP-compliant JSON message) to a weather MCP server, and once it gets the response (i.e., another MCP-compliant JSON message), it can feed the response to the LLM, which can use it to compose a good answer for the user (e.g., "It will be sunny today in Paris, with a high of 23°C".).

The LLM can be instructed to output MCP requests directly rather than custom JSON messages. This way, the orchestrator can just validate the JSON request and determine which MCP server to forward it to (e.g., the weather server).

Structured Generation

When your model needs to generate structured output such as JSON, it may sometimes make syntax errors (e.g., adding an extra bracket), or schema errors (e.g., forgetting a required field or passing a string instead of an integer). To deal with these errors, one option is to run the output through a post-processing function that will attempt to detect and fix common issues, but this may not be reliable enough. Another option is to constrain the generation process to only sample valid tokens from the model. For example, after `{"name":`, the model must output a space or double quotes. Anything else would be a syntax error or a schema error, since we expect the name to be a string. So we should pick the legal token that the model prefers (i.e., with the highest estimated probability), ignoring all other possible tokens (even if the model prefers them). This is called *structured generation*.

The Transformers library offers a way to tweak the logits just before the `generate()` method samples each token: this involves creating a custom subclass of the `transformers.LogitsProcessor` class, then passing it to the `generate()` method using the `logits_processor` argument. For example, your custom logits processor could determine the list of valid next tokens given the current context, and set the logits of all invalid tokens to negative infinity, thereby forcing the model to choose a valid token. However, this is a low-level approach, so you may prefer to use a library such as Outlines (*https://homl.info/outlines*) or Guidance (*https://homl.info/guidance*), which simplify structured generation.

But why use MCP rather than a more common protocol such as REST or gRPC? Aren't we're just querying an API? Well, it's more than that:

- Firstly, the connections between the LLM orchestrator and the MCP servers are long-lived, allowing fast, stateful, and bidirectional communication. In the MCP architecture, the client-side components that manage these connections are called *MCP clients*. The software that hosts them—typically your LLM orchestrator—is referred to as the *MCP host*.
- Secondly, MCP includes an AI-friendly *discovery mechanism* which lets the MCP client ask the MCP server for a rich, textual description of what the service

does, and how exactly to use it, including the list of available functions and their parameters. In other words, it's a self-documented API for AIs. In fact, the MCP server can also ask the MCP client for its capabilities, for example whether it supports displaying images to the user or handling streaming output: this lets the server adapt its responses accordingly.

The real power of MCP comes when you tell the LLM which services are available and instruct it on how to access the discovery mechanism: your LLM can then figure out on its own what each available service does, and how to use it. Connecting your LLM to a new MCP server then becomes little more than adding the server to the orchestrator's configuration and telling the LLM about it.

That said, building a chatbot from scratch can be complex, and fortunately many libraries and tools are available to simplify the process. Let's look at some of the most popular ones.

Libraries and Tools

Various open source Python libraries are available to implement your own chatbot system, including:

LangChain (https://www.langchain.com)
: A library designed to help you build applications powered by LLMs, by chaining together components such as prompt templates, models, memory, and other tools. It simplifies the orchestration of complex workflows.

LangGraph (https://www.langchain.com/langgraph)
: This built on LangChain and is more specifically designed to build long-running stateful agentic workflows.

Smolagents (https://homl.info/smolagents)
: This is a Hugging Face library designed to build agentic systems. It is a standalone successor to the Transformers Agents library.

Haystack (https://haystack.deepset.ai)
: Haystack lets you build systems that can understand complex questions, retrieve relevant information, and provide accurate answers, typically using RAG.

LlamaIndex (https://www.llamaindex.ai)
: LlamaIndex lets you ingest, index, and query your data (e.g., PDFs, databases, APIs).

There are also several popular open source user interfaces to chat with LLMs locally:

LM Studio (https://lmstudio.ai)
: This is a nice GUI app which lets you easily download and chat with various models. It supports chat history, prompt formatting, and a few other features.

Ollama (https://ollama.com)
: This is a simple command-line tool that lets you download various LLMs and chat with them locally, right in your terminal (e.g., `ollama run mistral:7b`). Ollama can also act as an API server, which can be queried by other systems (e.g., LangChain). The `ollama` Python library lets you query this API easily. Ollama also has support for tools such as a calculator, web search, and more.

text-generation-webui (https://homl.info/tgw) (TGWUI)
: This is a web interface for chatting with local LLMs. It's one of the most feature-rich and flexible tools available for local LLM use. It has a plug-in system that lets you add a calculator, a document loader, a search tool, and more. It also includes a REST API for integration with other systems like LangChain.

Under the hood, these tools require a backend library to actually run the LLMs. LM Studio and Ollama are based on a highly optimized C++ library named llama.cpp (*https://github.com/ggml-org/llama.cpp*), while TGWUI supports multiple backends, including llama.cpp, the Transformers library, ExLlama, AutoGPTQ, and more, so you can pick the backend that runs best on your hardware.

With that, you should have everything you need. For example, you could use LangChain to orchestrate a workflow that uses Ollama to run a local LLM, and Haystack to retrieve relevant information from a vector database. Before we close this chapter, let's take a brief look at some of the most influential encoder-decoder transformers.

Encoder-Decoder Models

In this chapter, other than the original Transformer architecture, we have focused solely on encoder-only and decoder-only models. This might have given you the impression that encoder-decoder models are over, but for some problems, they are still very relevant, especially for tasks like translation or summarization. Indeed, since the encoder is bidirectional, it can encode the source text and output excellent contextual embeddings, which the decoder can then use to produce a better output than a decoder-only model would (at least for models of a similar size).

The T5 model (*https://homl.info/t5*)[27] released by Google in 2019 is a particularly influential encoder-decoder model: it was the first to frame all NLP tasks as text

27 Colin Raffel et al., "Exploring the Limits of Transfer Learning with a Unified Text-to-Text Transformer", arXiv preprint arXiv:1910.10683 (2019).

to text. For example, to translate "I like soccer" to Spanish, you can just call the model with the input sentence "translate English to Spanish: I like soccer", and it outputs "me gusta el fútbol". To summarize a paragraph, you enter "summarize:" followed by the paragraph, and it outputs the summary. For classification, you only need to change the prefix to "classify:", and the model outputs the class name as text. For zero-shot classification, the possible classes can be listed in the prompt. This text-to-text approach makes the model very easy to pretrain on a variety of language tasks and just as easy to use. T5 was pretrained using a *masked span corruption* objective, similar to MLM, but masking one or more contiguous sections.

Google also released several variants of T5:

mT5 (2020)
: This is a multilingual T5 supporting over 100 languages. It's great for translation and cross-lingual tasks (e.g., asking a question in English about a Spanish text).

ByT5 (2021)
: This is a byte-level variant of T5 that removes the need for tokenization entirely (not even BPE). However, this approach has not caught on as it's more efficient to use tokenizers.

FLAN-T5 (2022)
: This is an instruction-tuned T5, with excellent ZSL and FSL capability.

UL2 (2022)
: This is pretrained using several objectives, including masked span denoising like T5, but also standard next token prediction, and masked token prediction.

FLAN-UL2 (2023)
: This improved on UL2 using instruction tuning.

Meta also released some encoder-decoder models, starting with BART in 2020. This model was pretrained using a denoising objective: the model gets a corrupted text (e.g., masked, modified, deleted, or inserted tokens, shuffled sentences, etc.) and it must clean it up. It's particularly effective for text generation and summarization. There's also a multilingual variant named mBART.

Last but not least, the encoder-decoder architecture is quite common for vision models, typically when there are multiple outputs such as in object detection and image segmentation. They're also common for multimodal models. This leads us to the next chapter, where we will discuss vision transformers and multimodal transformers. It's time for transformers to open their eyes!

Exercises

1. What is the most important layer in the Transformer architecture? What is its purpose?
2. Why does the Transformer architecture need positional encodings?
3. What tasks are encoder-only models best at? How about decoder-only models? And encoder-decoder models?
4. What is the most important technique used to pretrain BERT?
5. Can you name four BERT variants and explain their main benefits?
6. What is the main task used to pretrain GPT and its successors?
7. The `generate()` method has many arguments, including `do_sample`, `top_k`, `top_p`, `temperature`, and `num_beams`. What do these five arguments do?
8. What is prompt engineering? Can you describe five prompt engineering techniques?
9. What are the main steps to build a chatbot, starting from a pretrained decoder-only model?
10. How can a chatbot use tools like a calculator or web search?
11. What is MCP used for?
12. Fine-tune BERT for sentiment analysis on the IMDb dataset.
13. Fine-tune GPT-2 on the Shakespeare dataset (from Chapter 14), then generate Shakespeare-like text.
14. Download the Wikipedia Movie Plots dataset (*https://homl.info/movieplots*), and use SBERT to embed every movie description. Then write a function that takes a search query, embeds it, finds the most similar embeddings, and lists the corresponding movies.
15. Use an instruction-tuned model such as Qwen-7B-Instruct to build a little chatbot which acts like a movie expert. Then try adding some RAG functionality, for example by automatically injecting the most relevant movie plot into the prompt (see the previous exercise).

Solutions to these exercises are available at the end of this chapter's notebook, at *https://homl.info/colab-p*.

CHAPTER 16
Vision and Multimodal Transformers

In the previous chapter, we implemented a transformer from scratch and turned it into a translation system, then we explored encoder-only models for NLU, decoder-only models for NLG, and we even built a little chatbot—that was quite a journey! Yet, there's still a lot more to say about transformers. In particular, we have only dealt with text so far, but transformers actually turned out to be exceptionally good at processing all sorts of inputs. In this chapter we will cover *vision transformers* (ViTs), capable of processing images, followed by *multimodal transformers*, capable of handling multiple modalities, including text, images, audio, videos, robot sensors and actuators, and really any kind of data.

In the first part of this chapter, we will discuss some of the most influential pure-vision transformers:

DETR (Detection Transformer)
: An early encoder-decoder transformer for object detection.

The original ViT (Vision Transformer)
: This landmark encoder-only transformer treats image patches like word tokens and reaches the state of the art if trained on a large dataset.

DeiT (Data-Efficient Image Transformer)
: A more data-efficient ViT trained at scale using distillation.

PVT (Pyramid Vision Transformer)
: A hierarchical model that can produce multiscale feature maps for semantic segmentation and other dense prediction tasks.

Swin Transformer (Shifted Windows Transformer)
: A much faster hierarchical model.

DINO (self-Distillation with NO labels)
: This introduced a novel self-supervised technique for visual representation learning.

In the second part of this chapter, we will dive into multimodal transformers:

VideoBERT
: A BERT model trained to process both text and video tokens.

ViLBERT (Visio-Linguistic BERT)
: A dual-encoder model for image plus text, which introduced co-attention (i.e., two-way cross-attention).

CLIP (Contrastive Language–Image Pretraining)
: This is another image plus text dual-encoder model trained using contrastive pretraining.

DALL·E (a pun on the names of the artist Salvador Dali and the Pixar character Wall-E)
: A model capable of generating images from text prompts.

Perceiver
: This efficiently compresses any high-resolution modality into a short sequence using a cross-attention trick.

Perceiver IO (Input/Output)
: Adds a flexible output mechanism to the Perceiver, using a similar cross-attention trick.

Flamingo
: Rather than starting from scratch, it reuses two large pretrained models—one for vision and one for language (both frozen)—and connects them using a Perceiver-style adapter named a Resampler. This architecture enables open-ended visual dialogue.

BLIP-2 (Bootstrapping Language-Image Pretraining)
: This is another open-ended visual dialogue model that reuses two large pre-trained models, connects them using a lightweight querying transformer (Q-Former), and uses a powerful two-stage training approach with multiple training objectives.

So turn on the lights, transformers are about to open their eyes.

Vision Transformers

Vision transformers didn't pop out of a vacuum: before they were invented, there were RNNs with visual attention, and hybrid CNN-Transformer models. Let's take a look at these ViT ancestors before we dive into some of the most influential ViTs.

RNNs with Visual Attention

One of the first applications of attention mechanisms beyond NLP was to generate image captions using visual attention (*https://homl.info/visualattention*).[1] Here a convolutional neural network first processes the image and outputs some feature maps, then a decoder RNN equipped with an attention mechanism generates the caption, one token at a time.

The decoder uses an attention layer at each decoding step to focus on just the right part of the image. For example, in Figure 16-1, the model generated the caption "A woman is throwing a Frisbee in a park", and you can see what part of the input image the decoder focused its attention on when it was about to output the word "Frisbee": clearly, most of its attention was focused on the Frisbee.

Figure 16-1. Visual attention: an input image (left) and the model's focus before producing the word "Frisbee" (right)[2]

1 Kelvin Xu et al., "Show, Attend and Tell: Neural Image Caption Generation with Visual Attention", *Proceedings of the 32nd International Conference on Machine Learning* (2015): 2048–2057.

2 This is a part of Figure 3 from the paper. It is reproduced with the kind authorization of the authors.

Explainability

One extra benefit of attention mechanisms is that they make it easier to understand what led the model to produce its output. This is called *explainability*. It can be especially useful when the model makes a mistake; for example, if an image of a dog walking in the snow is labeled as "a wolf walking in the snow", then you can go back and check what the model focused on when it output the word "wolf". You may find that it was paying attention not only to the dog, but also to the snow, hinting at a possible explanation: perhaps he model learned to distinguish dogs from wolves by checking whether there's a lot of snow around. You can then fix this by training the model with more images of wolves without snow, and dogs with snow. This example comes from a great 2016 paper (*https://homl.info/explainclass*)[3] by Marco Tulio Ribeiro et al. that uses a different approach to explainability: learning an interpretable model locally around a classifier's prediction.

In some applications, explainability is not just a tool to debug a model; it can be a legal requirement—think of a system deciding whether it should grant you a loan.

Once transformers were invented, they were quickly applied to visual tasks, generally by replacing RNNs in existing architectures (e.g., for image captioning). However, the bulk of the visual work was still performed by a CNN, so although they were transformers used for visual tasks, we usually don't consider them as ViTs. The *detection transformer* (DETR) is a good example of this.

DETR: A CNN-Transformer Hybrid for Object Detection

In May 2020, a team of Facebook researchers proposed a hybrid CNN–transformer architecture for object detection, named *detection transformer* (*https://homl.info/detr*) (DETR, see Figure 16-2).[4] The CNN first processes the input images and outputs a set of feature maps, then these feature maps are turned into a sequence of visual tokens that are fed to an encoder-decoder transformer, and finally the transformer outputs a sequence of bounding box predictions.

At one point, someone was bound to wonder whether we could get rid of the CNN entirely. After all, attention is all you need, right? This happened a few months after DETR: the original ViT was born.

3 Marco Tulio Ribeiro et al., "'Why Should I Trust You?': Explaining the Predictions of Any Classifier", *Proceedings of the 22nd ACM SIGKDD International Conference on Knowledge Discovery and Data Mining* (2016): 1135–1144.

4 Nicolas Carion et al., "End-to-End Object Detection with Transformers", arXiv preprint arXiv:2005.12872 (2020).

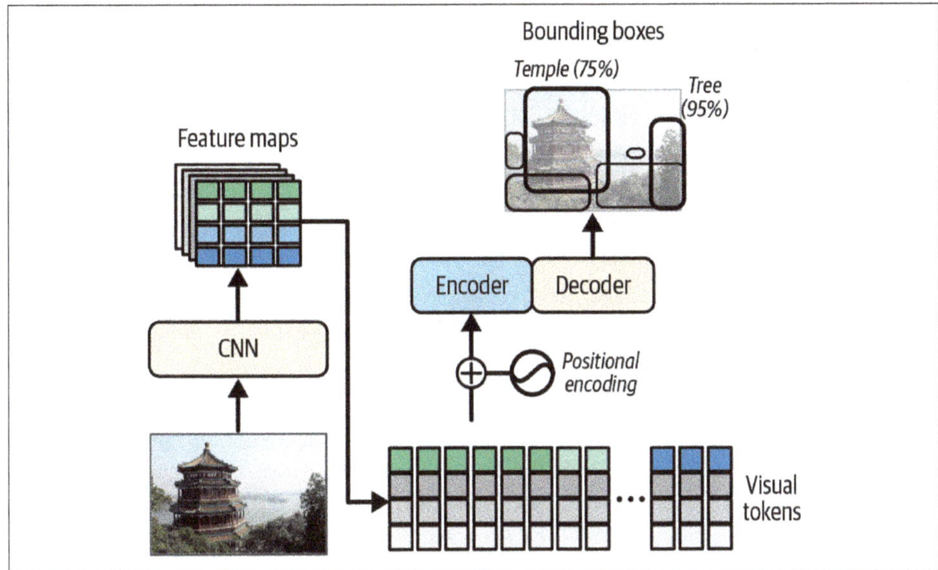

Figure 16-2. The detection transformer (DETR) for object detection

The Original ViT

In October 2020, a team of Google researchers released a paper (*https://homl.info/vit*)[5] that introduced the first vision transformer without a CNN (see Figure 16-3). It was simply named the *vision transformer* (ViT). The idea is surprisingly simple: chop the image into little 16 × 16 patches, and treat the sequence of patches as if it is a sequence of word representations. In fact, the paper's title is "An Image Is Worth 16 × 16 Words".

To be more precise, the patches are first flattened into 16 × 16 × 3 = 768-dimensional vectors (the 3 is for the RGB color channels). For example, a 224 × 224 image gets chopped into 14 × 14 = 196 patches, so we get 196 vectors of 768 dimensions each. These vectors then go through a linear layer that projects the vectors to the transformer's embedding size. The resulting sequence of vectors can then be treated just like a sequence of word embeddings: add learnable positional embeddings, and pass the result to the transformer, which is a regular encoder-only model. A class token with a trainable representation is inserted at the start of the sequence, and a classification head is added on top of the corresponding output (i.e., this is BERT-style classification).

5 Alexey Dosovitskiy et al., "An Image Is Worth 16x16 Words: Transformers for Image Recognition at Scale", arXiv preprint arXiv:2010.11929 (2020).

And that's it! This model beat the state of the art on ImageNet image classification, but to be fair the authors had to use over 300 million additional images for training. This makes sense since transformers don't have as many *inductive biases* as convolution neural nets, so they need extra data just to learn things that CNNs implicitly assume.

An inductive bias is an implicit assumption made by the model, due to its architecture. For example, linear models implicitly assume that the data is, well, linear. CNNs are translation invariant, so they implicitly assume that patterns learned in one location will likely be useful in other locations as well. They also have a strong bias toward locality. RNNs implicitly assume that the inputs are ordered, and that recent tokens are more important than older ones. The more inductive biases a model has, assuming they are correct, the less training data the model will require. But if the implicit assumptions are wrong, then the model may perform poorly even if it is trained on a large dataset.

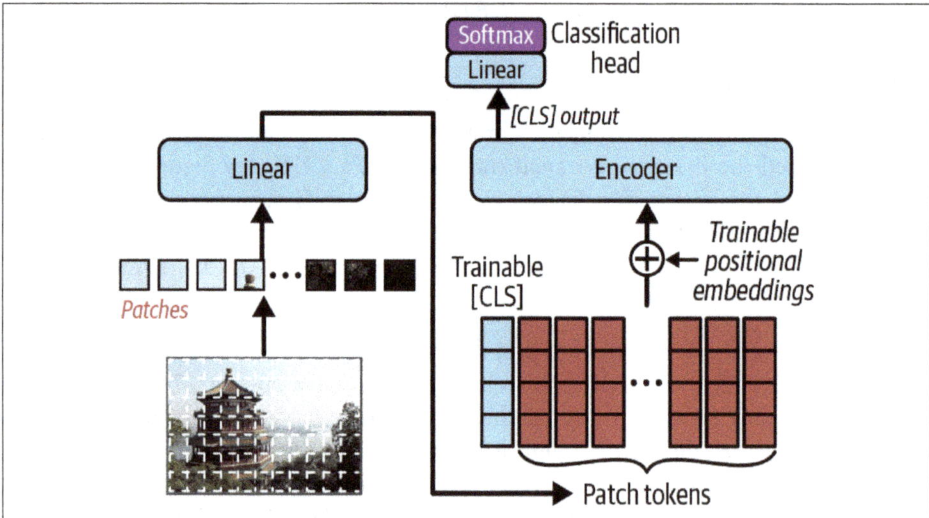

Figure 16-3. Vision transformer (ViT) for classification

Now you know everything you need to implement a ViT from scratch!

Implementing a ViT from scratch using PyTorch

We will start by implementing a custom module to take care of patch embedding. For this, we can actually use an `nn.Conv2d` module with `kernel_size` and `stride` both set to the patch size (16). This is equivalent to chopping the image into patches, flattening them, and passing them through a linear layer (then reshaping the result). Just what we need!

```
import torch
import torch.nn as nn

class PatchEmbedding(nn.Module):
    def __init__(self, in_channels, embed_dim, patch_size=16):
        super().__init__()
        self.conv2d = nn.Conv2d(embed_dim, in_channels,
                                kernel_size=patch_size, stride=patch_size)
    def forward(self, X):
        X = self.conv2d(X)  # shape [B=Batch, C=Channels, H=Height, W=Width]
        X = X.flatten(start_dim=2)  # shape [B, C, H * W]
        return X.transpose(1, 2)  # shape [B, H * W, C]
```

After the convolutional layer, we must flatten the spatial dimensions and transpose the last two dimensions to ensure the embedding dimension ends up last, which is what the `nn.TransformerEncoder` module expects. Now we're ready to implement our ViT model:

```
class ViT(nn.Module):
    def __init__(self, img_size=224, patch_size=16, in_channels=3,
                 num_classes=1000, embed_dim=768, depth=12, num_heads=12,
                 ff_dim=3072, dropout=0.1):
        super().__init__()
        self.patch_embed = PatchEmbedding(embed_dim, in_channels, patch_size)
        cls_init = torch.randn(1, 1, embed_dim) * 0.02
        self.cls_token = nn.Parameter(cls_init)  # shape [1, 1, E=embed_dim]
        num_patches = (img_size // patch_size) ** 2  # num_patches (denoted L)
        pos_init = torch.randn(1, num_patches + 1, embed_dim) * 0.02
        self.pos_embed = nn.Parameter(pos_init)  # shape [1, 1 + L, E]
        self.dropout = nn.Dropout(p=dropout)
        encoder_layer = nn.TransformerEncoderLayer(
            d_model=embed_dim, nhead=num_heads, dim_feedforward=ff_dim,
            dropout=dropout, activation="gelu", batch_first=True)
        self.encoder = nn.TransformerEncoder(encoder_layer, num_layers=depth)
        self.layer_norm = nn.LayerNorm(embed_dim)
        self.output = nn.Linear(embed_dim, num_classes)

    def forward(self, X):
        Z = self.patch_embed(X)  # shape [B, L, E]
        cls_expd = self.cls_token.expand(Z.shape[0], -1, -1)  # shape [B, 1, E]
        Z = torch.cat((cls_expd, Z), dim=1)  # shape [B, 1 + L, E]
        Z = Z + self.pos_embed
        Z = self.dropout(Z)
        Z = self.encoder(Z)  # shape [B, 1 + L, E]
        Z = self.layer_norm(Z[:, 0])  # shape [B, E]
        logits = self.output(Z) # shape [B, C]
        return logits
```

Let's go through this code:

- The constructor starts by creating the `PatchEmbedding` module.
- Then it creates the class token's trainable embedding, initialized using a normal distribution with a small standard deviation (0.02 is common). Its shape is [1, 1, *E*], where *E* is the embedding dimension.
- Next, we initialize the positional embeddings, of shape [1, 1 + *L*, *E*], where *L* is the number of patch tokens. We need one more positional embedding for the class token, hence the 1 + *L*. Again, we initialize it using a normal distribution with a small standard deviation.
- Next, we create the other modules: `nn.Dropout`, `nn.TransformerEncoder` (based on an `nn.TransformerEncoderLayer`), `nn.LayerNorm`, and the output linear layer that we will use as a classification head.
- In the `forward()` method, we start by creating the patch tokens.
- Then we replicate the class token along the batch axis, using the `expand()` method, and we concatenate the patch tokens. This ensures that each sequence of patch tokens starts with the class token.
- The rest is straightforward: we add the positional embeddings, apply some dropout, run the encoder, keep only the class token's output (`Z[:, 0]`) and normalize it, and lastly pass it through the output layer, which produces the logits.

You can create the model and test it with a random batch of images, like this:

```
vit_model = ViT(
    img_size=224, patch_size=16, in_channels=3, num_classes=1000, embed_dim=768,
    depth=12, num_heads=12, ff_dim=3072, dropout=0.1)
batch = torch.randn(4, 3, 224, 224)
logits = vit_model(batch)  # shape [4, 1000]
```

You can then train this model using the `nn.CrossEntropyLoss`, as usual. This would take quite a while, however, so unless your image dataset is very domain-specific, you're usually better off downloading a pretrained ViT using the Transformers library and then fine-tuning it on your dataset. Let's see how.

Fine-tuning a pretrained ViT using the Transformers library

Let's download a small pretrained ViT and fine-tune it on the Oxford-IIIT Pet dataset, which contains over 7,000 pictures of pets grouped into 37 different classes. First, let's download the dataset:

```
from datasets import load_dataset

pets = load_dataset("timm/oxford-iiit-pet")
```

Next, let's download the ViT:

```
from transformers import ViTForImageClassification, AutoImageProcessor

model_id = "google/vit-base-patch16-224-in21k"
vit_model = ViTForImageClassification.from_pretrained(model_id, num_labels=37)
vit_processor = AutoImageProcessor.from_pretrained(model_id, use_fast=True)
```

We're loading a base ViT model that was pretrained on the ImageNet-21k dataset. This dataset contains roughly 14 million images across over 21,800 classes. We're using the `ViTForImageClassification` class which automatically replaces the original classification head with a new one (untrained) for the desired number of classes. That's the part we now need to train.

We also loaded the image processor for this model. We will use it to preprocess each image as the model expects: it will be rescaled to 224 × 224, pixel values will be normalized to range between –1 and 1, and the channel dimension will be moved in front of the spatial dimensions. We also set `use_fast=True` because a fast implementation of the image processor is available, so we might as well use it. The processor takes an image as input and returns a dictionary containing a "pixel_values" entry equal to the preprocessed image.

Next, we need a data collator that will preprocess all the images in a batch and return the images and labels as PyTorch tensors:

```
def vit_collate_fn(batch):
    images = [example["image"] for example in batch]
    labels = [example["label"] for example in batch]
    inputs = vit_processor(images, return_tensors="pt", do_convert_rgb=True)
    inputs["labels"] = torch.tensor(labels)
    return inputs
```

We set `do_convert_rgb=True` because the model expects RGB images, but some images in the dataset are RGBA (i.e., they have an extra transparency channel), so we must force the conversion to RGB to avoid an error in the middle of training. And now we're ready to train our model using the familiar Hugging Face training API:

```
from transformers import Trainer, TrainingArguments

args = TrainingArguments("my_pets_vit", per_device_train_batch_size=16,
                         eval_strategy="epoch", num_train_epochs=3,
                         remove_unused_columns=False)
trainer = Trainer(model=vit_model, args=args, data_collator=vit_collate_fn,
                  train_dataset=pets["train"], eval_dataset=pets["test"])
train_output = trainer.train()
```

By default, the trainer will automatically remove input attributes that are not used by the `forward()` method: our model expects `pixel_values` and optionally `labels`, but anything else will be dropped, including the `"image"` attribute. Since the unused attributes are dropped before the `collate_fn()` function is called, the code `example["image"]` will cause an error. This is why we must set `remove_unused_columns=False`.

After just 3 epochs, our ViT model reaches about 91.8% accuracy. With some data augmentation and more training, you could reach 93 to 95% accuracy, which is close to the state of the art. Great! But we're just getting started: ViTs have been improved in many ways since 2020. In particular, it's possible to train them from scratch in a much more efficient way using distillation. Let's see how.

Data-Efficient Image Transformer

Just two months after Google's ViT paper was published, a team of Facebook researchers released *data-efficient image transformers* (*https://homl.info/deit*) (DeiT).[6] Their DeiT model achieved competitive results on ImageNet without requiring any additional data for training. The model's architecture is virtually the same as the original ViT (see Figure 16-4), but the authors used a distillation technique to transfer knowledge from a teacher model to their student ViT model (distillation was introduced in Chapter 15).

The authors used a frozen, state-of-the-art CNN as the teacher model. During training, they added a special distillation token to the student ViT model. Just like the class token, the distillation token representation is trainable, and its output goes through a dedicated classification head. Both classification heads (for the class token and for the distillation token) are trained simultaneously, both using the cross-entropy loss, but the class token's classification head is trained using the normal hard targets (i.e., one-hot vectors), while the distillation head is trained using soft targets output by a teacher model. The final loss is a weighted sum of both classification losses (typically with equal weights). At inference time, the distillation token is dropped, along with its classification head. And that's all there is to it! If you fine-tune a DeiT model on the same pets dataset, using `model_id = "facebook/deit-base-distilled-patch16-224"` and `DeiTForImageClassification`, you should get around 94.4% validation accuracy after just three epochs.

6 Hugo Touvron et al., "Training Data-Efficient Image Transformers & Distillation Through Attention", arXiv preprint arXiv:2012.12877 (2020).

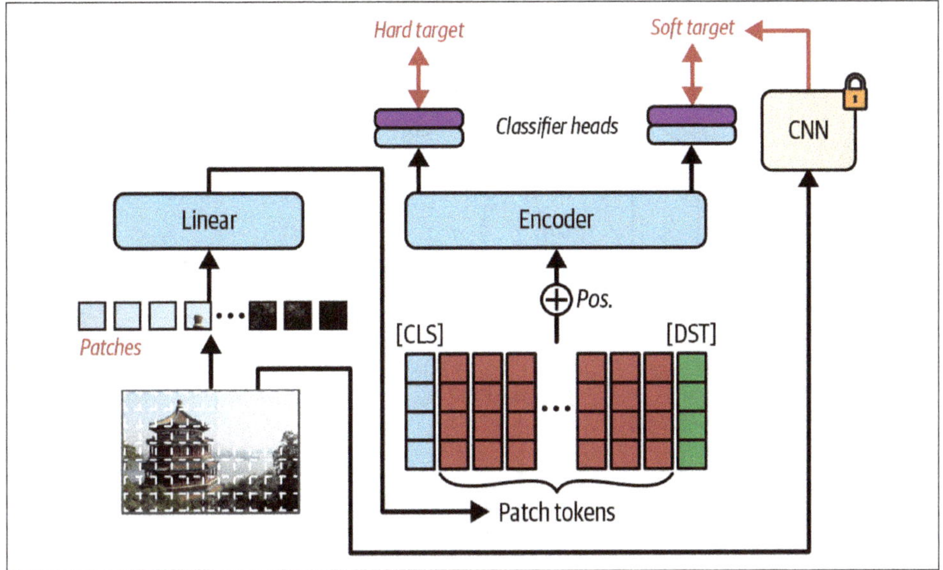

Figure 16-4. Data-efficient image transformer (DeiT) = ViT + distillation

So far, we have only used ViTs for classification tasks, but what about dense prediction tasks such as object detection or semantic segmentation (introduced in Chapter 12)? For this, the ViT architecture needs to be tweaked a bit; welcome to hierarchical vision transformers.

Pyramid Vision Transformer for Dense Prediction Tasks

The year 2021 was a year of plenty for ViTs: new models advanced the state of the art almost every other week. An important milestone was the release of the Pyramid Vision Transformer (PVT) (*https://homl.info/pvt*) in February 2021,[7] developed by a team of researchers from Nanjing University, HKU, IIAI, and SenseTime Research. They pointed out that the original ViT architecture was good at classification tasks, but not so much at dense prediction tasks, where fine-grained resolution is needed. To solve this issue, they proposed a pyramidal architecture in which the image is processed into a gradually smaller but deeper image (i.e., semantically richer), much like in a CNN. Figure 16-5 shows how a 256 × 192 image with 3 channels (RGB) is first turned into a 64 × 48 image with 64 channels, then into a 32 × 24 image with 128 channels, then a 16 × 12 image with 320 channels, and lastly an 8 × 6 image with 512 channels.

7 Wenhai Wang et al., "Pyramid Vision Transformer: A Versatile Backbone for Dense Prediction without Convolutions", arXiv preprint arXiv:2102.12122 (2021).

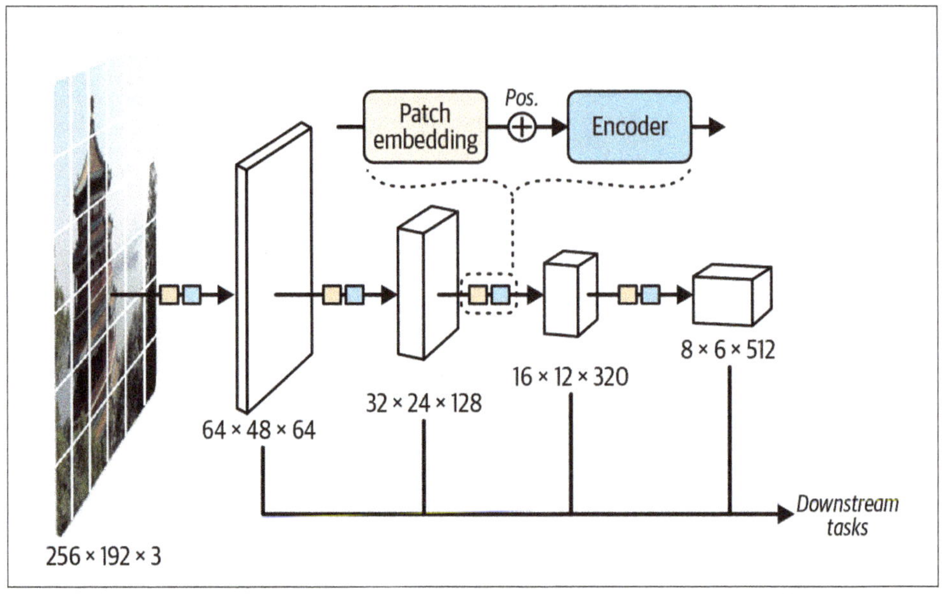

Figure 16-5. Pyramid Vision Transformer for dense prediction tasks

At each pyramid level, the input image is processed very much like in a regular ViT. It is first chopped into patches and turned into a sequence of patch tokens, then trainable positional embeddings are added, and the resulting tokens are passed through an encoder-only transformer, composed of multiple encoder layers.

Since the encoder outputs a sequence of vectors (i.e., contextualized embeddings), this sequence must be reshaped into a *grid* of vectors, which can then be treated as an image (with many channels) and passed on to the next level of the pyramid. For example, the encoder at the first level receives a sequence of 3,072 patch tokens, since the image was chopped into a 64 × 48 grid of 4 × 4 patches (and 64 × 48 = 3,072). Each patch token is represented as a 64-dimensional vector. The encoder also outputs 3,072 vectors (i.e., contextualized embeddings), each 64-dimensional, and they are organized into a 64 × 48 grid once again. This gives us a 64 × 48 image with 64 channels, which can be passed on to the next level. In levels 2, 3, and 4 of the pyramid, the patch tokens are 128-, 320-, and 512-dimensional, respectively.

Importantly, the patches are much smaller than in the original ViT: instead of 16 × 16, they are just 4 × 4 at level 1, and 2 × 2 at levels 2, 3, and 4. These tiny patches offer a much higher spatial resolution, which is crucial for dense prediction tasks. However, this comes at a cost: smaller patches means many more of them, and since multi-head attention has quadratic complexity, a naive adaptation of ViT would require vastly more computation. This is why the PVT authors introduced *spatial reduction attention* (SRA): it's just like MHA except that the keys and values are first spatially reduced (but not the queries). For this, the authors proposed a sequence of operations that is usually implemented as a strided convolutional layer, followed by layer norm (although some implementations use an average pooling layer instead).

Let's look at the impact of SRA at the first level of the pyramid. There are 3,072 patch tokens. In regular MHA, each of these tokens would attend to every token, so we would have to compute $3{,}072^2$ attention scores: that's over 9 million scores! In SRA, the query is unchanged so it still involves 3,072 tokens, but the keys and values are reduced spatially by a factor of 8, both horizontally and vertically (in levels 2, 3, and 4 of the pyramid, the reduction factor is 4, 2, and 1, respectively). So instead of 3,072 tokens representing a 64 × 48 grid, the keys and values are only composed of 48 tokens representing an 8 × 6 grid (because 64 / 8 = 8 and 48 / 8 = 6). So we only need to compute 3,072 × 48 = 147,456 attention scores: that's 64 times less computationally expensive. And the good news is that this doesn't affect the output resolution since we didn't reduce the query at all: the encoder still output 3,072 tokens, representing a 64 × 48 image.

OK, so the PVT model takes an image and outputs four gradually smaller and deeper images. Now what? How do we use these multiscale feature maps to implement object detection or other dense prediction tasks? Well, no need to reinvent the wheel: existing solutions generally involve a CNN backbone that produces multiscale feature maps, so we can simply swap out this backbone for a PVT (often pretrained on ImageNet). For example, we can use an FCN approach for semantic segmentation (introduced at the end of Chapter 12) by upscaling and combining the multiscale feature maps output by the PVT, and add a final classification head to output one class per pixel. Similarly, we can use a Mask R-CNN for object detection and instance segmentation, replacing its CNN backbone with a PVT.

In short, the PVT's hierarchical structure was a big milestone for vision transformers, but despite spatial reduction attention, it's still computationally expensive. The Swin Transformer, released one month later, is much more scalable. Let's see why.

The Swin Transformer: A Fast and Versatile ViT

In March 2021, a team of Microsoft researchers released the Swin Transformer (*https://homl.info/swin*).[8] Just like PVT, it has a hierarchical structure, producing multiscale feature maps which can be used for dense prediction tasks. But Swin uses a very different variant of multi-head attention: each patch only attends to patches located within the same window. This is called *window-based multi-head self-attention* (W-MSA), and it allows the cost of self-attention to scale linearly with the image size (meaning its area), instead of quadratically.

8 Ze Liu et al., "Swin Transformer: Hierarchical Vision Transformer using Shifted Windows", arXiv preprint arXiv:2103.14030 (2021).

For example, on the lefthand side of Figure 16-6, the image is chopped into a 28 × 28 grid of patches, and these patches are grouped into nonoverlapping windows. At the first level of the Swin pyramid, the patches are usually 4 × 4 pixels, and each window contains a 7 × 7 grid of patches. So there's a total of 784 patch tokens (28 × 28), but each token only attends to 49 tokens (7 × 7), so the W-MSA layer only needs to compute 784 × 49 = 38,416 attention scores, instead of 784^2 = 614,656 scores for regular MHA.

Most importantly, if we double the width and the height of the image, we quadruple the number of patch tokens, but each token still attends to only 49 tokens, so we just need to compute 4 times more attention scores: the Swin Transformer's computational cost scales linearly with the image's area, so it can handle large images. Conversely, ViT, DeiT, and PVT all scale quadratically: if you double the image width and height, the area is quadrupled, and the computational cost is multiplied by 16! As a result, these models are way too slow for very large images, meaning you must first downsample the image, which may hurt the model's accuracy, especially for dense prediction tasks.

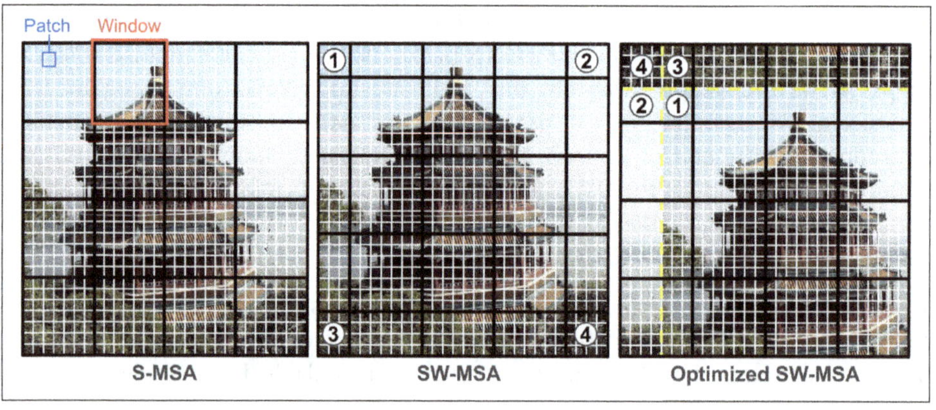

Figure 16-6. Swin Transformer: alternates W-MSA (left) and SW-MSA (center); SW-MSA can be optimized to require the same number of windows as W-MSA (right)

But wait a minute! If each token only attends to patches within the same window, how can we hope to capture long-range patterns? The answer is in the name of the architecture, Swin, which stands for *shifted windows*: every other encoder layer uses *shifted W-MSA* (SW-MSA), which is just like W-MSA except the windows are offset by half a window size. As you can see in the middle of Figure 16-6, the windows are shifted by 3 patches toward the bottom right (because half of 7 is 3.5, which we round down to 3). Why does this help? Well, nearby patches that were in separate windows in the previous layer are now in the same window, so they can see each other. By alternating W-MSA and SW-MSA, information from any part of the image can gradually propagate throughout the whole image. Moreover, since the architecture is hierarchical, the patches get coarser and coarser as we go up the pyramid, so the information can propagate faster and faster.

A naive implementation of SW-MSA would require handling many extra windows. For example, if you compare W-MSA and SW-MSA in Figure 16-6, you can see that W-MSA uses 16 windows, while SW-MSA uses 25 (at least in this example). To avoid this extra cost, the authors proposed an optimized implementation: instead of shifting the windows, we shift the image itself and wrap it around the borders, as shown in the righthand side of Figure 16-6. This way, we're back to 16 windows. However, this requires careful masking for the border windows that contain the wrapped patches; for example, the regions labeled ①, ②, ③, ④ should not see each other, even though they are within the same window, so an appropriate attention mask must be applied.

Overall, Swin is harder to implement than PVT, but its linear scaling and excellent performance make it one of the best vision transformers out there. But the year 2021 wasn't over: Swin v2 (*https://homl.info*) was released in November 2021.[9] It improved Swin across the board: more stable training for large ViTs, easier to fine-tune on large images, reduced need for labeled data, and more. Swin v2 is still widely used in vision tasks today.

Our toolbox now contains vision transformers for classification (e.g., ViT and DeiT) and for dense prediction tasks (e.g., PVT and Swin). Let's now explore one last pure-vision transformer, DINO, which introduced a revolutionary self-supervision technique for visual representation learning.

DINO: Self-Supervised Visual Representation Learning

In April 2021, Mathilde Caron et al. introduced DINO (*https://homl.info/dino*),[10] an impressive self-supervised training technique that produces models capable of generating excellent image representations. These representations can then be used for classification and other tasks.

Here's how it works: the model is duplicated during training, with one network acting as a teacher and the other acting as a student (see Figure 16-7). Gradient descent only affects the student, while the teacher's weights are just an exponential moving average (EMA) of the student's weights. This is called a *momentum teacher*. The student is trained to match the teacher's predictions: since they're almost the same model, this is called *self-distillation* (hence the name of the model: self-**di**stillation with **no** labels).

9 Ze Liu et al., "Swin Transformer V2: Scaling Up Capacity and Resolution", arXiv preprint arXiv:2111.09883 (2021).

10 Mathilde Caron et al., "Emerging Properties in Self-Supervised Vision Transformers", arXiv preprint arXiv:2104.14294 (2021).

At each training step, the input images are augmented in various ways: color jitter, grayscale, Gaussian blur, horizontal flipping, and more. Importantly, they are augmented in different ways for the teacher and the student: the teacher always sees the full image, only slightly augmented, while the student often sees only a zoomed-in section of the image, with stronger augmentations. In short, the teacher and the student don't see the same variant of the original image, yet their predictions must still match. This forces them to agree on high-level representations.

With this mechanism, however, there's a strong risk of *mode collapse*. This is when both the student and the teacher always output the exact same thing, completely ignoring the input images. To prevent this, DINO keeps track of a moving average of the teacher's predicted logits, and it subtracts this average from the predicted logits. This is called *centering*, forcing the teacher to distribute its predictions evenly across all classes (on average, over time).

But centering alone might cause the teacher to simply output the same probability for every class, all the time, still ignoring the image. To avoid this, DINO also forces the teacher to have high confidence in its highest predictions: this is called *sharpening*. It's implemented by applying a low temperature to the teacher's logits (i.e., dividing them by a temperature smaller than 1). Together, centering and sharpening preserve the diversity in the teacher's outputs; this leaves no easy shortcut for the model. It must base its predictions on the actual content of the image.

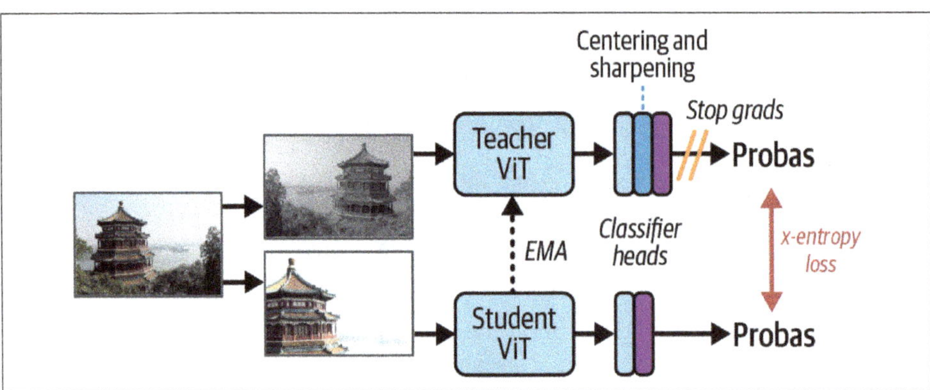

Figure 16-7. DINO, or self-distillation with no labels

After training, you can drop the teacher: the student is the final DINO model. If you feed it a new image, it will output a sequence of contextualized patch embeddings. These can be used in various ways. For example, you can train a classifier head on top of the class token's output embedding. In fact, you don't even need a new classifier head: you can run DINO on every training image to get their representation (i.e., the output of the class token), then compute the mean representation per class. Then, when given a new image, use DINO to compute its representation and look for the class with the nearest mean representation. This simple approach reaches 78.3% top-1 accuracy on ImageNet, which is pretty impressive.

But it's not just about classification! Interestingly, the DINO authors noticed that the class token's attention maps in the last layer often focus on the main object of interest in the image, even though they were trained entirely without labels! In fact, each attention head seems to focus on a different part of the object, as you can see in Figure 16-8.[11] See the notebook for a code example that uses DINO to plot a similar attention map.

Figure 16-8. Unsupervised image segmentation using DINO—different attention heads attend to different parts of the main object

Later techniques such as TokenCut (*https://homl.info/tokencut*)[12] built upon DINO to detect and segment objects in images and videos. Then, in April 2023, Meta released DINOv2 (*https://homl.info/dino2*),[13] which was trained on a curated and much larger dataset, and was tweaked to output per-patch features, making it a great foundation model not just for classification, but also for dense prediction tasks.

11 This is the righthand part of Figure 3 of the DINO paper, reproduced with the kind authorization of the authors.

12 Yangtao Wang et al., "TokenCut: Segmenting Objects in Images and Videos with Self-supervised Transformer and Normalized Cut", arXiv preprint arXiv:2209.00383 (2022).

13 "DINOv2: Learning Robust Visual Features without Supervision", arXiv preprint arXiv:2304.07193 (2023).

Let's step back: we've covered CNN-based transformers such as DETR, followed by the original ViT (image patches through an encoder), DeiT (a distilled ViT), PVT (a hierarchical ViT with spatial reduction attention), Swin (a hierarchical ViT with window-based attention), and DINO (self-distillation with no labels). Before we move on to multimodal transformers, let's quickly go through a few more pure-vision transformer models and techniques.

Other Major Vision Models and Techniques

Progress in vision transformers has continued steadily to this day. Here is a brief overview of some landmark papers:

"Scaling Vision Transformers" (https://homl.info/scalingvits),[14] June 2021
: Google researchers showed how to scale ViTs up or down, depending on the amount of available data. They managed to create a huge 2 billion parameter model that reached over 90.4% top-1 accuracy on ImageNet. Conversely, they also trained a scaled-down model that reached over 84.8% top-1 accuracy on ImageNet, using only 10,000 images: that's just 10 images per class!

"BEiT: BERT Pre-Training of Image Transformers" (https://homl.info/beit),[15] June 2021
: Hangbo Bao et al. proposed a *masked image modeling* (MIM) approach inspired from BERT's masked language modeling (MLM). BEiT is pretrained to reconstruct masked image patches from the visible ones. This pretraining technique significantly improves downstream tasks.

  Note that BEiT is not trained to predict the raw pixels of the masked patches; instead, it must predict the masked token IDs. But where do these token IDs come from? Well, the original image is passed through a *discrete variational autoencoder* (dVAE, see Chapter 18) which encodes each patch into a visual token ID (an integer), from a fixed vocabulary. These are the IDs that BEiT tries to predict. The goal is to avoid wasting the model's capacity on unnecessary details.

"Masked Autoencoders Are Scalable Vision Learners" (https://homl.info/mae),[16] November 2021
: This paper by a team of Facebook researchers (led by the prolific Kaiming He) also proposes a pretraining technique based on masked image modeling, but it removes the complexity of BEiT's dVAE: masked autoencoder (MAE) directly predicts raw pixel values. Crucially, it uses an asymmetric encoder-decoder

14 Xiaohua Zhai et al., "Scaling Vision Transformers", arXiv preprint arXiv:2106.04560 (2021).

15 Hangbo Bao et al., "BEiT: BERT Pre-Training of Image Transformers", arXiv preprint arXiv:2106.08254 (2021).

16 Kaiming He et al., "Masked Autoencoders Are Scalable Vision Learners", arXiv preprint arXiv:2111.06377 (2021).

architecture: a large encoder processes only the visible patches, while a lightweight decoder reconstructs the entire image. Since 75% of patches are masked, this design dramatically reduces computational cost and allows MAE to be pretrained on very large datasets. This leads to strong performance on downstream tasks.

"Model Soups" (https://homl.info/modelsoups),[17] *March 2022*
: This paper demonstrated that it's possible to first train multiple transformers, then average their weights to create a new and improved model. This is similar to an ensemble (see Chapter 6), except there's just one model in the end, which means there's no inference cost.

"EVA: Exploring the Limits of Masked Visual Representation Learning at Scale" (https://homl.info/eva),[18] *May 2022*
: EVA is a family of large ViTs pretrained at scale, using enhanced MAE and strong augmentations. It's one of the leading foundation models for ViTs. EVA-02, released in March 2023, does just as well or better despite having fewer parameters. The large variant has 304M parameters and reaches an impressive 90.0% on ImageNet.

I-JEPA (https://homl.info/ijepa),[19] *January 2023*
: Yann LeCun proposed the joint-embedding predictive architecture (JEPA) in a 2022 paper (*https://homl.info/jepa*),[20] as part of his world-model framework, which aims to deepen AI's understanding of the world and improve the reliability of its predictions. I-JEPA is an implementation of JEPA for images. It was soon followed by V-JEPA (*https://homl.info/vjepa*) in 2024, and V-JEPA 2 (*https://homl.info/vjepa2*) in 2025, both of which process videos.

  During training, JEPA involves two encoders and a predictor: the teacher encoder sees the full input (e.g., a photo of a cat) while the student encoder sees only part of the input (e.g., the same cat photo but without the ears). Both encoders convert their inputs to embeddings, then the predictor tries to predict the teacher embedding for the missing part (e.g., the ears) given the student embeddings for the rest of the input (e.g., the cat without ears). The student encoder and the predictor are trained jointly, while the teacher encoder is just a moving average of the student encoder (much like in DINO). JEPA mostly

17 Mitchell Wortsman et al., "Model Soups: Averaging Weights of Multiple Fine-tuned Models Improves Accuracy Without Increasing Inference Time", arXiv preprint arXiv:2203.05482 (2022).

18 Yuxin Fang et al., "EVA: Exploring the Limits of Masked Visual Representation Learning at Scale", arXiv preprint arXiv:2211.07636 (2022).

19 "Self-Supervised Learning from Images with a Joint-Embedding Predictive Architecture", arXiv preprint arXiv:2301.08243 (2023).

20 Yann LeCun, "A Path Towards Autonomous Machine Intelligence" (2022).

works in embedding space rather than pixel space, which makes it fast, parameter efficient, and more semantic.

After training, the teacher encoder and the predictor are no longer needed, but the student encoder can be used to generate excellent, meaningful representations for downstream tasks.

The list could go on and on:

- NesT or DeiT-III for image classification
- MobileViT, EfficientFormer, EfficientViT, or TinyViT for small and efficient image classification models (e.g., for mobile devices)
- Hierarchical transformers like Twins-SVT, FocalNet, MaxViT, and InternImage, often used as backbones for dense prediction tasks
- Mask2Former or OneFormer for general-purpose segmentation, SEEM for universal segmentation, and SAM or MobileSAM for interactive segmentation
- ViTDet or RT-DETR for object detection
- TimeSformer, VideoMAE, or OmniMAE for video understanding

There are also techniques like *token merging* (ToMe) which speeds up inference by merging similar tokens on the fly, *token pruning* to drop unimportant tokens during processing (i.e., with low attention scores), *early exiting* to only compute deep layers for the most important tokens, *patch selection* to select only the most informative patches for processing, and self-supervised training techniques like SimMIM, iBOT, CAE, or DINOv2, and more.

Hopefully we've covered a wide enough variety of models and techniques for you to be able to explore further on your own.

Some of these vision-only models were pretrained on multimodal data (e.g., image-text pairs or input prompts): OmniMAE, SEEM, SAM, MobileSAM, and DINOv2. Which leads us nicely to the second part of this chapter.

We already had transformers that could read and write (and chat!), and now we have vision transformers that can see. It's time to build transformers that can handle both text and images at the same time, as well as other modalities.

Multimodal Transformers

Humans are multimodal creatures: we perceive the world through multiple senses—sight, hearing, smell, taste, touch, sense of balance, proprioception (i.e., sense of body position), and several others—and we act upon the world through movement, speech, writing, etc. Each of these modalities can be considered at a very low level (e.g., sound waves) or at a higher level (e.g., words, intonations, melody). Importantly, modalities are heterogeneous: one modality may be continuous while another is discrete, one may be temporal while the other is spatial, one may be high-resolution (e.g., 48 kHz audio) while the other is not (e.g., text), one may be noisy while the other is clean, and so on.

Moreover, modalities may interact in various ways. For example, when we chat with someone, we may listen to their voice while also watching the movement of their lips: these two modalities (auditory and visual) carry overlapping information, which helps our brain better parse words. But multimodality is not just about improving the signal/noise ratio: facial expressions may carry their own meaning (e.g., smiles and frowns), and different modalities may combine to produce a new meaning. For example, if you say "he's an expert" while rolling your eyes or gesturing air quotes, you're clearly being ironic, which inverts the meaning of your sentence and conveys extra information (e.g., humor or disdain) which neither modality possesses on its own.

So multimodal machine learning requires designing models that can handle very heterogeneous data and capture their interactions. There are two main challenges for this. The first is called *fusion*, and it's about finding a way to combine different modalities, for example, by encoding them into the same representation space. The second is called *alignment*, where the goal is to discover the relationships between modalities. For example, perhaps you have a recording of a speech, as well as a text transcription, and you want to find the timestamp of each word. Or you want to find the most relevant object in an image given a text query such as "the dog next to the tree" (this is called *visual grounding*). Many other common tasks involve two or more modalities, such as image captioning, image search, visual question answering (VQA), speech-to-text (STT), text-to-speech (TTS), embodied AI (i.e., a model capable of physically interacting with the environment), and much more.

Multimodal machine learning has been around for decades, but progress has recently accelerated thanks to deep learning, and particularly since the rise of transformers. Indeed, transformers can ingest pretty much any modality, as long as you can chop it into a sequence of meaningful tokens (e.g., text into words, images into small patches, audio or video into short clips, etc.). Once you have prepared a sequence of token embeddings, you're ready to feed it to a transformer. Embeddings from different modalities can be fused in various ways: summed up, concatenated, passed through a fusion encoder, and more. This can take care of the fusion problem. And transformers also have multi-head attention, which is a powerful tool to detect and exploit complex patterns, both within and across modalities. This can take care of the alignment problem.

Researchers quickly understood the potential of transformers for multimodal architectures. The first multimodal transformers were released just months after the original Transformer paper was released in early 2018 with image captioning, video captioning, and more. Let's look at some of the most impactful multimodal transformer architectures, starting with VideoBERT.

VideoBERT: A BERT Variant for Text plus Video

In April 2019, Google researchers released VideoBERT (*https://homl.info/videobert*).[21] As its name suggests, this model is very similar to BERT, except it can handle both text and videos. In fact, the authors just took a pretrained BERT-large model, extended its embedding matrix to allow for extra video tokens (more on this shortly), and continued training the model using self-supervision on a text plus video training set. This dataset was built from a large collection of instructional YouTube videos, particularly cooking videos. These videos typically involve someone describing a sequence of actions while performing them (e.g., "Cut the tomatoes into thin slices like this"). To feed these videos to VideoBERT, the authors had to encode the videos into both text and visual sequences (see Figure 16-9):

- For the visual modality, they extracted nonoverlapping 1.5-second clips at 20 frames per second (i.e., 30 frames each), and they passed these clips through a 3D CNN named S3D. This CNN is based on Inception modules and separable convolutions (see Chapter 12), and it was pretrained on the Kinetics dataset composed of many YouTube videos of people performing a wide range of actions. The authors added a 3D average pooling layer on top of S3D to get a 1,024-dimensional vector for each video clip. Each vector encodes fairly high-level information about the video clip.
- To extract the text from the videos, the authors used YouTube's internal speech-to-text software, after which they dropped the audio tracks from the videos. Then they separated the text into sentences by adding punctuation using an off-the-shelf LSTM model. Finally, they preprocessed and tokenized the text just like for BERT.

21 Chen Sun et al., "VideoBERT: A Joint Model for Video and Language Representation Learning", arXiv preprint arXiv:1904.01766 (2019).

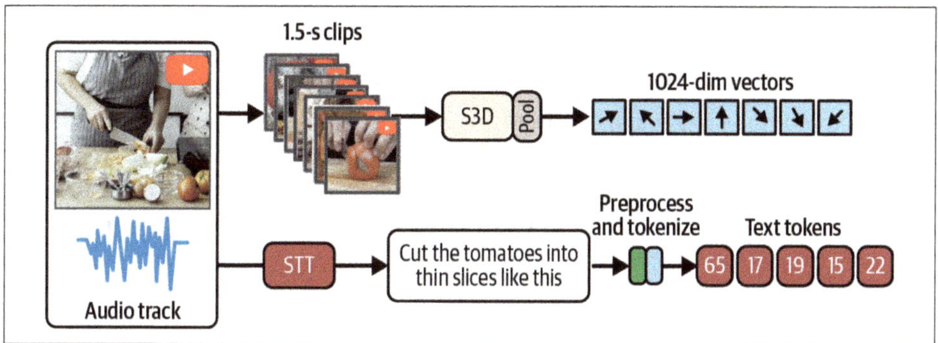

Figure 16-9. VideoBERT—encoding a video into a text sequence and a visual sequence

Great! We now have a text token sequence describing some actions, and a sequence of vectors representing video clips of these actions. However, we have a problem. Recall that BERT is pretrained using MLM, where the model must predict masked tokens from a fixed vocabulary. We do have a fixed vocabulary for the text tokens, but not for the video tokens. So let's build one! For this, the authors gathered all the visual vectors produced by S3D over their training set, and they clustered these vectors into k = 12 clusters using k-means (see Chapter 8). Then they used k-means again on each cluster to get 12^2 = 144 clusters, then again and again to get 12^4 = 20,736 clusters. This process is called *hierarchical k-means*, and it's much faster than running k-means just once using k = 20,736, plus it typically produces much better clusters. Now each vector can be replaced with its cluster ID: this way, each video clip is represented by a single ID from a fixed visual vocabulary, so the whole video is now represented as one sequence of visual token IDs (e.g., 194, 3912, ...), exactly like tokenized text. In short, we've gone from a continuous 1,024-dimensional space down to a discrete space with just 20,736 possible values. There's a lot of information loss at this step, but VideoBERT's excellent performance suggests that much of the important information remains.

Since the authors used a pretrained BERT-large model, the text token embeddings were already excellent before VideoBERT's additional training even started. For the visual token embeddings, rather than using trainable embeddings initialized from scratch, the authors used frozen embeddings initialized using the 1,024-dimensional vector representations of the k-means cluster centroids.

The authors used three different training regimes: text-only, video-only, and text plus video. In text-only and video-only modes, VideoBERT was fed a single modality and trained to predict masked tokens (either text tokens or video tokens). For text plus video, the model was fed both text tokens and video tokens, simply concatenated (plus an unimportant separation token in between), and it had to predict whether the text tokens and video tokens came from the same part of the original video. This is called *linguistic-visual alignment*. For this, the authors added a binary classification head on top of the class token's output (this replaces BERT's next sentence prediction head). For negative examples, the authors just sampled random sentences and video segments. Figure 16-10 shows all three modes at once, but keep in mind that they are actually separate.

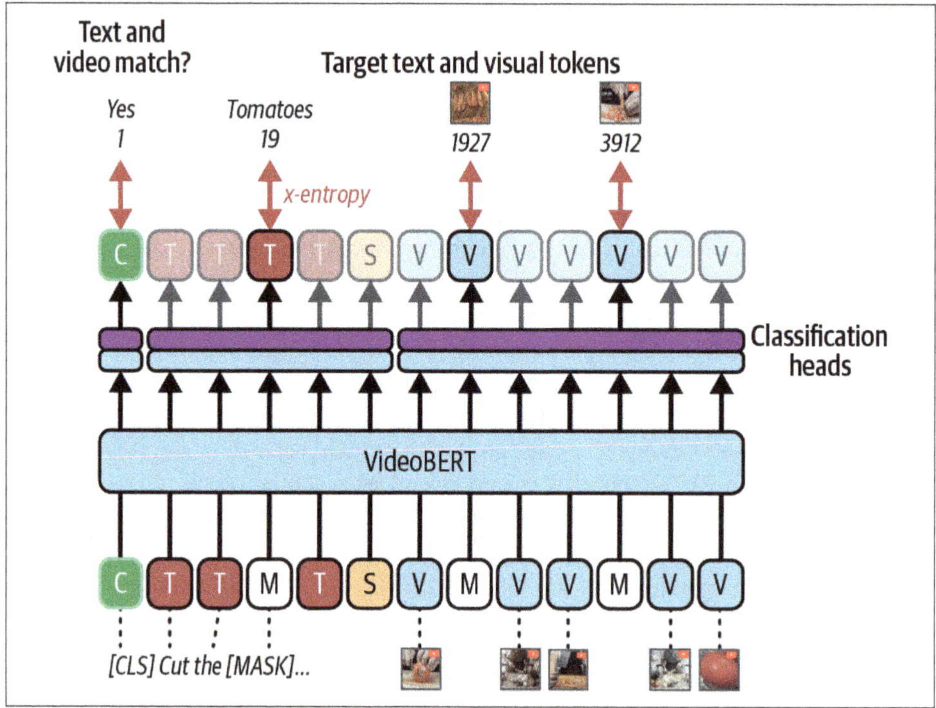

Figure 16-10. VideoBERT—pretraining using masked token prediction and linguistic-visual alignment (shown together but actually separate)

Linguistic-visual alignment is a noisy task since the cook may explain something that they have already finished or will do later, so the authors concatenated random neighboring sentences to give the model more context. The authors had a few more tricks up their sleeves, such as randomly changing the video sampling rate to make the model more robust to different action speeds, since some cooks are faster than others; see the paper for more details.

This was a lot of work, but the authors were finally done: they had a fully trained VideoBERT model. To demonstrate its effectiveness, they evaluated VideoBERT on some downstream tasks, including:

Zero-shot action classification

Given a video clip, figure out which action is performed, without fine-tuning VideoBERT. The authors achieved this by feeding the video to VideoBERT, along with the following masked sentence: "Now let me show you how to [MASK] the [MASK]". Then they looked at the output probabilities for both masked tokens, for each possible pair of verb and noun. If the video shows a cook slicing some tomatoes, then the probability of "slice" and "tomatoes" will be much higher than "bake" and "cake" or "boil" and "egg".

Video captioning

Given a video clip, generate a caption. To do this, the authors used the earliest video-captioning transformer architecture (*https://homl.info/videocaption*),[22] but they replaced the input to the encoder with visual features output by VideoBERT. More specifically, they took an average of VideoBERT's final output representations, including the representations of all of the visual tokens and the masked-out text tokens. The masked sentence they used was: "now let's [MASK] the [MASK] to the [MASK], and then [MASK] the [MASK]". After fine-tuning this new model, they obtained improved results over the original captioning model.

Using similar approaches, VideoBERT can be adapted for many other tasks, such as multiple-choice visual question answering: given an image, a question, and multiple possible answers, the model must find the correct answer. For example: "What is the cook doing?" → "Slicing tomatoes". For this, one approach is to simply run VideoBERT on each possible answer, along with the video, and compare the linguistic-visual alignment scores: the correct answer should have the highest score.

The success of VideoBERT inspired many other BERT-based multimodal transformers, many of which were released in August and September 2019: ViLBERT, VisualBERT, Unicoder-VL, LXMERT, VL-BERT, and UNITER. Most of these are single-stream models like VideoBERT, meaning that the modalities are fused very early in the network, typically by simply concatenating the sequences. However, ViLBERT and LXMERT are dual-stream transformers, meaning that each modality is processed by its own encoder, with a mechanism allowing the encoders to influence each other. This lets the model better understand each modality before trying to make sense of the interactions between them. VilBERT was particularly influential, so let's look at it more closely.

ViLBERT: A Dual-Stream Transformer for Text plus Image

ViLBERT was proposed in August 2019 (*https://homl.info/vilbert*)[23] by a team of researchers from the Georgia Institute of Technology, Facebook AI Research, and

22 L. Zhou, Y. Zhou et al., "End-to-End Dense Video Captioning with Masked Transformer", *Proceedings of the IEEE Conference on Computer Vision and Pattern Recognition* (2018).

Oregon State University. They pointed out that the single-stream approach (used by VideoBERT and many others) treats both modalities identically, even though they may require different levels of processing. For example, if the visual features come from a deep CNN, then we already have good high-level visual features, whereas the text will need much more processing before the model has access to high-level text features. Moreover, the researchers hypothesized that "image regions may have weaker relations than words in a sentence".[24] Lastly, BERT was initially pretrained using text only, so forcing it to process other modalities may give suboptimal results and even damage its weights during multimodal training.

So the authors chose a dual-stream approach instead: each modality goes through its own encoder, and in the upper layers the two encoders are connected and exchange information through a new bidirectional cross-attention mechanism called *co-attention* (see Figure 16-11). Specifically, in each pair of connected encoder layers, the MHA query of one encoder is used as the MHA key/value by the other encoder.

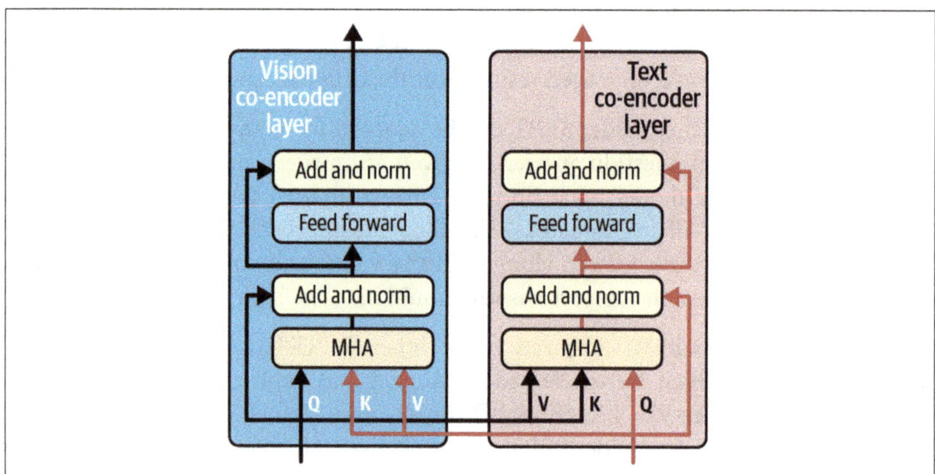

Figure 16-11. Two encoder layers connected through co-attention: the MHA query of one encoder is used as the MHA key/value by the other encoder

The lower layers of the text encoder are initialized with BERT's weights (the authors used a BERT base, which has 12 layers), and 6 co-attention layers sit on top (see the lower-right quadrant of Figure 16-12). The visual features are produced by a pretrained and frozen Faster R-CNN model, and it is assumed that these features are

23 Jiasen Lu et al., "ViLBERT: Pretraining Task-Agnostic Visiolinguistic Representations for Vision-and-Language Tasks", *Advances in Neural Information Processing Systems* 32 (2019).

24 Jize Cao et al. later provided some empirical evidence supporting this claim in their paper "Behind the Scene: Revealing the Secrets of Pre-trained Vision-and-Language Models" (*https://homl.info/probing*): in particular, they found that more attention heads focus on the text modality than on the visual modality.

sufficiently high level so no further processing is needed; therefore, the visual encoder is exclusively composed of six co-attention layers, paired up with the text encoder's six co-attention layers (see the lower-left quadrant of the figure). The Faster R-CNN model's outputs go through a mean pooling layer for each detected region, so we get one feature vector per region, and low-confidence regions are dropped: each image ends up represented by 10 to 36 vectors.

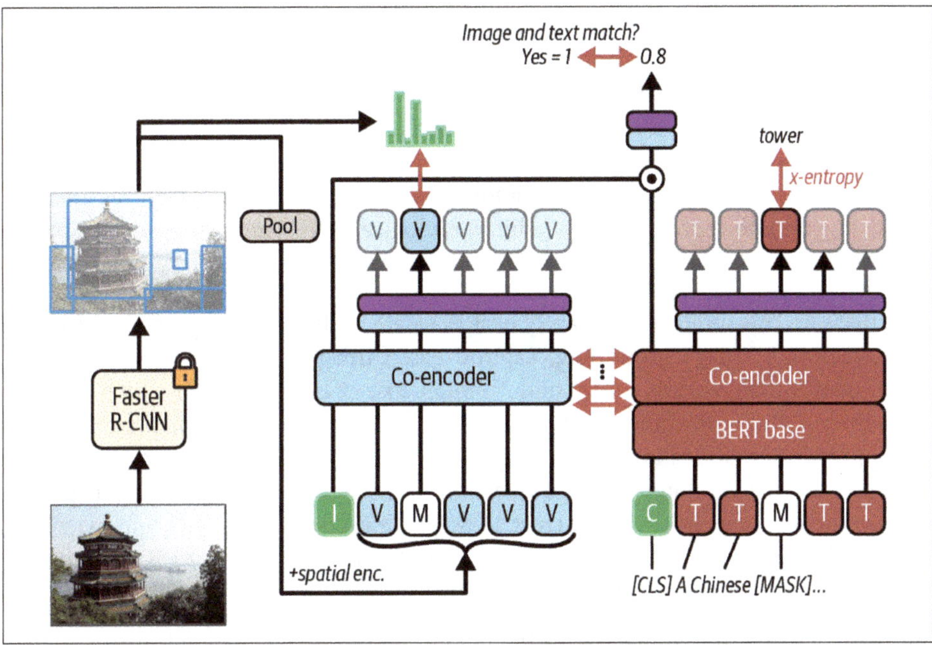

Figure 16-12. ViLBert pretraining using masked token prediction and linguistic-visual alignment (again, shown together but actually separate)

Since regions don't have a natural order like words do, the visual encoder does not use positional encoding. Instead, it uses spatial encodings that are computed like this: each region's bounding box is encoded as a 5D vector containing the normalized upper-left and lower-right coordinates, and the ratio of the image covered by the bounding box. Then this 5D vector is linearly projected up to the same dimensionality as the visual vector, and simply added to it.

Lastly, a special [IMG] token is prepended to the visual sequence: it serves the same purpose as the class token (i.e., to produce a representation of the whole sequence), but instead of being a trainable embedding, it's computed as the average of the feature vectors (before spatial encoding), plus the spatial encoding for a bounding box covering the whole image.

Now on to training! Similar to VideoBERT, the authors used masked token prediction and linguistic-visual alignment:

- For masked token prediction, the authors used regular BERT-like MLM for the text encoder. However, for the visual encoder, since ViLBERT does not use a fixed-size visual vocabulary (there's no clustering step), the model is trained to predict the class distribution that the CNN predicts for the given image region (this is a soft target). The authors chose this task rather than predicting raw pixels because the regions can be quite large and there's typically not enough information in the surrounding regions and in the text to reconstruct the masked region correctly: it's better to aim for a higher-level target.
- For linguistic-visual alignment, the model takes the outputs of the [IMG] and [CLS] tokens, then computes their itemwise product and passes the result to a binary classification head that must predict whether the text and image match. Multiplication is preferred over addition because it amplifies features that are strong in both representations (a bit like a logical AND gate), so it better captures alignment.

And that's it. This model significantly beat the state of the art for several downstream tasks, including image grounding, caption-based image retrieval (even zero-shot), visual question answering, and *visual commonsense reasoning* (VCR) which involves answering a multiple-choice question about an image (like VQA), then selecting the appropriate justification. For example, given an image of a waiter serving some pancakes at a table, along with the question "Why is person #4 pointing at person #1", the model must choose the correct answer "He is telling person #3 that person #1 ordered the pancakes", then it must choose the justification "Person #3 is serving food and they might not know whose order is whose".

ViLBERT had a strong influence on the field of multimodal machine learning thanks to its dual-stream architecture, the invention of co-attention, and its excellent results on many downstream tasks. It was another great demonstration of the power of large-scale self-supervised pretraining using transformers. The next major milestone came in 2021, and it approached the problem very differently, using contrastive pretraining: meet CLIP.

CLIP: A Dual-Encoder Text plus Image Model Trained with Contrastive Pretraining

OpenAI's January 2021 release of contrastive language–image pretraining (CLIP) (*https://homl.info/clip*)[25] was a major breakthrough, not just for its astounding capabilities, but also because of its surprisingly straightforward approach based on *contrastive learning*: the model learns to encode text and images into vector

25 Alec Radford et al., "Learning Transferable Visual Models From Natural Language Supervision", arXiv preprint arXiv:2103.00020 (2021).

representations that are similar when the text and image match, and dissimilar when they don't match.

Once trained, the model can be used for many tasks, particularly zero-shot image classification. For example, CLIP can be used as an insect classifier without any additional training: just start by feeding all the possible class names to CLIP, such as "cricket", "ladybug", "spider", and so on, to get one vector representation for each class name. Then, whenever you want to classify an image, feed it to CLIP to get a vector representation, and find the most similar class name representation using cosine similarity. This usually works even better if the text resembles typical image captions found on the web, since this is what CLIP was trained on, for example, "This is a photo of a ladybug" instead of just "ladybug". A bit of prompt engineering can help (i.e., experimenting with various prompt templates).

The good news is that CLIP is fully open source,[26], several pretrained models are available on the Hugging Face Hub, and the Transformers library provides a convenient pipeline for zero-shot image classification:

```
from transformers import pipeline

model_id = "openai/clip-vit-base-patch32"
clip_pipeline = pipeline(task="zero-shot-image-classification", model=model_id,
                         device_map="auto", dtype="auto")
candidate_labels = ["cricket", "ladybug", "spider"]
image_url = "https://homl.info/ladybug"  # a photo of a ladybug on a dandelion
results = clip_pipeline(image_url, candidate_labels=candidate_labels,
                        hypothesis_template="This is a photo of a {}.")
```

Note that we provided a prompt template, so the model will actually encode "This is a photo of a ladybug", not just "ladybug" (if you don't provide any template, the pipeline actually defaults to "This is a photo of a {}".). Now let's look at the results, which are sorted by score:

```
[{'score': 0.9972853660583496, 'label': 'ladybug'},
 {'score': 0.0016511697322130203, 'label': 'spider'},
 {'score': 0.0010634352220222354, 'label': 'cricket'}]
```

Great! CLIP predicts ladybug with over 99.7% confidence. Now if you want a flower classifier instead, just replace the candidate labels with names of flowers. If you include "dandelion" in the list and classify the same image, the model should choose "dandelion" with high confidence (ignoring the ladybug). Impressive!

So how does this magic work? Well, CLIP's architecture is based on a regular text encoder and a regular vision encoder, no co-attention or anything fancy (see Figure 16-13). You can actually use pretty much any text and vision encoders you want,

26 The training code and data were not released by OpenAI, but Gabriel Ilharco et al. created OpenCLIP (*https://homl.info/openclip*) which is a flexible open source replication of CLIP with the full training code and data.

as long as they can produce a vector representation of the text or image. The authors experimented with various encoders, including several ResNet and ViT models for vision, and a GPT-2-like model for text, all trained from scratch. What's that I hear you say, GPT-2 is not an encoder? That's true, it's a decoder-only model, but we're not pretraining it for next token prediction, so the last token's output is free to be used as a representation of the entire input sequence, which is what CLIP does. You may wonder why we're not using a regular text encoder like BERT? Well, we could, but OpenAI created GPT—Alex Radford is the lead author of both GPT and CLIP—so that's most likely why GPT-2 was chosen: the authors simply had more experience with this model and a good training infrastructure already in place. Using a causal encoder also makes it possible to cache the intermediate state of the model when multiple texts start in the same way; for example, "This is a photo of a".

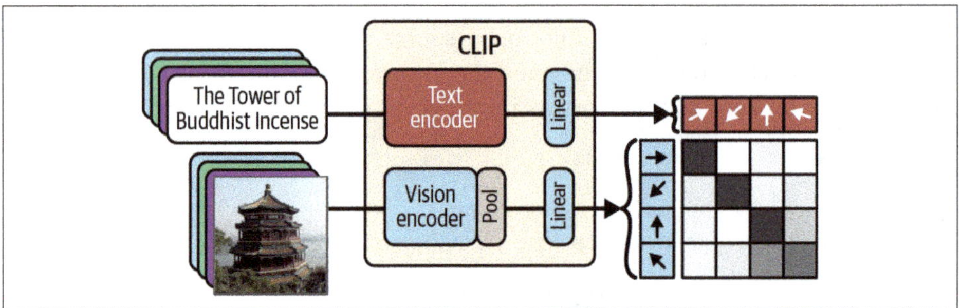

Figure 16-13. CLIP: a batch of image-caption pairs is encoded as vectors, then matching pairs are pulled closer while mismatched pairs are pushed away

Also note that a pooling layer is added on top of the vision encoder to ensure it outputs a single vector for the whole image instead of feature maps. Moreover, a linear layer is added on top of each encoder to project the final representation into the same output space (i.e., with the same number of dimensions). So given a batch of m image-caption pairs, we get m vector representations for the images and m vector representations for the captions, and all vectors have the same number of dimensions. Figure 16-13 shows $m = 4$, but the authors used a shockingly large batch size of $m = 2^{15} = 32{,}768$ during training.

The model was then pretrained on a large dataset of 400 million image-caption pairs scraped from the internet, using a contrastive loss[27] that pulls together the representations of matching pairs, while also pushing apart representations of mismatched pairs. Here's how it works:

27 This contrastive loss was first introduced as the *multiclass n-pair loss* in a 2016 paper by Kihyuk Sohn (*https://homl.info/npairloss*), then used for contrastive representation learning and renamed to *InfoNCE* (information noise-contrastive estimation) in a 2018 paper by Aaron van den Oord et al (*https://homl.info/infonce*).

- All vectors are first ℓ_2 normalized, meaning they are rescaled to unit vectors: we only care about their orientation, not their length.
- Next, we compute the cosine similarity of the image representation and the text representation for every possible image-caption pair. The result is an $m \times m$ matrix containing numbers between –1 for opposite vectors, and +1 for identical vectors. In Figure 16-13, this matrix is represented by the 4 × 4 grid (black is +1, white is –1). Each column measures how much each image in the batch matches a given caption in the same batch, while each row measures how much each caption matches a given image.
- Since the ith image corresponds to the ith caption, we want the main diagonal of this matrix to contain similarity scores close to +1, while all other scores should be close to 0. Why not close to –1? Well, if an image and a text are totally unrelated, we can think of their representations as two random vectors. Recall that two random high-dimensional vectors are highly likely to be close to orthogonal (as discussed in Chapter 7), so their cosine similarity will be close to 0, not –1. In other words, it makes sense to assume that the text and image representations of a mismatched pair are unrelated (score close to 0), not opposite (score close to –1).
- In the ith row, we know that the matching caption is in the ith column, so we want the model to produce a high similarity score in that column, and a low score elsewhere. This resembles a classification task where the target class is the ith class. Indeed, we can treat each similarity score as class logit and simply compute the cross-entropy loss for that row with i as the target. We can follow the exact same rationale for each column. If we compute the cross-entropy loss for each row and each column (using class i as the target for the ith row and the ith column), and evaluate the mean, we get the final loss.
- There's just one extra technical detail: the similarity scores range between –1 and +1, which is unlikely to be the ideal logit scale for the task, so CLIP divides all the similarity scores by a trainable temperature (a scalar) before computing the loss.

This loss requires a large batch size to ensure the model sees enough negative examples to contrast with the positive examples, or else it could overfit details in the positive examples. CLIP's success is due in part to the gigantic batch size that the authors were able to implement.

The authors evaluated CLIP on many image classification datasets, and for roughly 60% of these, it performed better without any extra training (i.e., zero-shot) than a *linear probe* trained on ResNet-50 features (that's a linear classifier trained on features output by a pretrained and frozen ResNet-50 model), including on ImageNet, despite the fact that the ResNet-50 model was actually pretrained on ImageNet. CLIP is particularly strong on datasets with few examples per class, with pictures of everyday scenes (i.e., the kind of pictures you find on the web). In fact, CLIP even beat the state of the art on the Stanford Cars dataset, ahead of the best ViTs specifically trained on this dataset, because pictures of cars are very common on the web and the dataset doesn't have many examples per class. However, CLIP doesn't perform as well on domain-specific images, such as satellite or medical images.

Importantly, the visual features output by CLIP are also highly robust to perturbations, making them excellent for downstream tasks, such as image retrieval: if you store images in a vector database, indexing them by their CLIP-encoded visual features, you can then search for them given either a text query or an image query. For this, just run the query through CLIP to get a vector representation, then search the database for images with a similar representation.

To get the text and visual features using the Transformers library, you must run the CLIP model directly, without going through a pipeline:

```
import PIL
import urllib.request
from transformers import CLIPProcessor, CLIPModel

clip_processor = CLIPProcessor.from_pretrained(model_id)
clip_model = CLIPModel.from_pretrained(model_id)
image = PIL.Image.open(urllib.request.urlopen(image_url)).convert("RGB")
captions = [f"This is a photo of a {label}." for label in candidate_labels]
inputs = clip_processor(text=captions, images=[image], return_tensors="pt",
                        padding=True)
with torch.no_grad():
    outputs = clip_model(**inputs)

text_features = outputs.text_embeds    # shape [3, 512]  # 3 captions
image_features = outputs.image_embeds  # shape [1, 512]  # 1 image (ladybug)
```

If you need to encode the images and text separately, you can use the CLIP model's `get_image_features()` and `get_text_features()` methods. You must first tokenize the text using a `CLIPTokenizer` and process the images using a `CLIPImageProcessor`. The resulting features are not ℓ_2 normalized, so you must divide them by `features.norm(dim=1, keepdim=True)` (see the notebook for a code example).

The features are already ℓ_2 normalized, so if you want to compute similarity scores, a single matrix multiplication is all you need:

```
>>> similarities = image_features @ text_features.T  # shape [1, 3]
>>> similarities
tensor([[0.2337, 0.3021, 0.2381]])
```

This works because matrix multiplication computes the dot products of every row vector in the first matrix with every column vector in the second, and each dot product is equal to the cosine of the angle between the vectors multiplied by the norms of the vectors. Since the vectors have been ℓ_2 normalized in this case, the norms are equal to 1, so the result is just the cosine of the angle, which is the similarity score we're after. As you can see, the most similar representation is the second one, for the ladybug class. If you prefer estimated probabilities rather than similarity scores, you must first rescale the similarities using the model's learned temperature, then pass the result through the softmax function (it's nice to see that we get the same result as the pipeline):

```
>>> temperature = clip_model.logit_scale.detach().exp()
>>> rescaled_similarities = similarities * temperature
>>> probabilities = torch.nn.functional.softmax(rescaled_similarities , dim=1)
>>> probabilities
tensor([[0.0011, 0.9973, 0.0017]])
```

CLIP wasn't the only surprise OpenAI had in stock in 2021. Just the following month, OpenAI announced DALL·E, which can generate impressive images given a text description. Let's discuss it now.

DALL·E: Generating Images from Text Prompts

OpenAI DALL·E (*https://homl.info/dalle*),[28] released in February 2021, is a model capable of generating images based on text prompts, such as "an armchair in the shape of an avocado". Its architecture is quite simple (see the lefthand side of Figure 16-14): a GPT-like model trained to predict the next token, but unlike GPT, it was pretrained on millions of image-caption pairs, and fed input sequences composed on text tokens followed by visual tokens. At inference time, you only feed it the text tokens, and the model then generates the visual tokens, one at a time, until you get the full image. The visual tokens are generated by a dVAE model, which takes an image and outputs a sequence of tokens from a fixed vocabulary. Sadly, the model was never released to the public, but the paper was detailed enough so some open source replications are available, such as DALL·E mini (*https://huggingface.co/dalle-mini*), also known as Craiyon.

One year later, in April 2022, OpenAI released DALL·E 2 (*https://homl.info/dalle2*),[29] able to generate even higher quality images. Its architecture is actually very different: the text is fed to a CLIP model which outputs a text embedding, then this text embedding is fed to a *diffusion model* which uses it to guide its image generation process (we will discuss diffusion models in Chapter 18). The model is not open

28 Aditya Ramesh et al., "Zero-Shot Text-to-Image Generation", arXiv preprint arXiv:2102.12092 (2021).

29 Aditya Ramesh et al., "Hierarchical Text-Conditional Image Generation with CLIP Latents", arXiv preprint arXiv:2204.06125 (2022).

source, but it's available through a paid API, and via some products such as Microsoft Designer, Bing Image Creator, Canva, ChatGPT, and more.

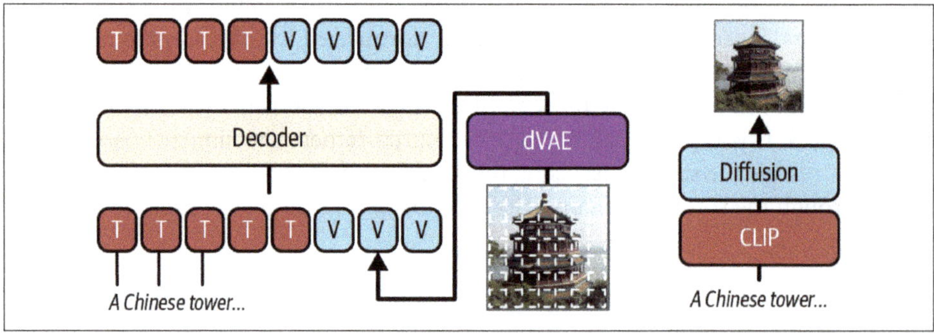

Figure 16-14. DALL·E (left) and DALL·E 2 (right)

DALL·E 3 was released in October 2023. Sadly, by then OpenAI had fully shifted away from its initial openness: there was no peer-reviewed paper, no code, no weights, no data. Like the previous version, DALL·E 3 is available through an API and via some products. We know it's diffusion-based, it doesn't use CLIP, and it's tightly integrated with GPT-4, which rewrites the prompt before generating the image. It works impressively well: it outputs stunning images which match the prompts much more precisely than previous versions. The difference is particularly striking for *compositional prompts* (e.g., "A fluffy white cat sitting on a red velvet cushion, with a vase of sunflowers behind it, bathed in golden hour light. The cat is looking directly at the viewer".). DALL·E 1 and 2 would generally follow only one or two elements of such prompts, whereas DALL·E 3 follows instructions much more closely. The image quality, realism, artistic style, and consistency are astounding. Lastly, DALL·E 3 also integrates some moderation capabilities.

The next landmark in our multimodal journey came one month after the first DALL·E model: the Perceiver.

Perceiver: Bridging High-Resolution Modalities with Latent Spaces

Every transformer so far has required chopping the inputs into meaningful tokens. In the case of text, tokens represent words or subwords. In the case of ViTs, they represent 16 × 16 pixel patches. In VideoBERT, it's short 1.5-second clips. In audio transformers, it's short audio clips. If we fed individual characters, pixels, or audio frames directly into a transformer, the input sequence would be extremely long, and we would run into the quadratic attention problem. Also, we would lose important inductive biases: for example, by chopping an image into patches, we enforce a strong inductive bias toward proximity (i.e., nearby pixels are assumed to be more strongly correlated than distant pixels).

However, such tokenization is modality-specific, which makes it harder to deal with new modalities or mix them in the model. Moreover, inductive biases are great when you don't have a lot of training data (assuming the biases are correct), but if your dataset is large, you will often get better performance by using unbiased models with very few implicit assumptions. Sure, the model will have to figure out on its own that nearby pixels are generally related, but on the other hand, it will be flexible enough to discover patterns that might otherwise go unnoticed.

This is why DeepMind introduced the *Perceiver* (*https://homl.info/perceiver*)[30] in March 2021. This architecture is capable of directly handling any modality at the lowest level: characters, pixels, audio frames, and more. Moreover, it does so with a modality-agnostic design, so the same model can handle different modalities. The Perceiver architecture is shown in Figure 16-15.

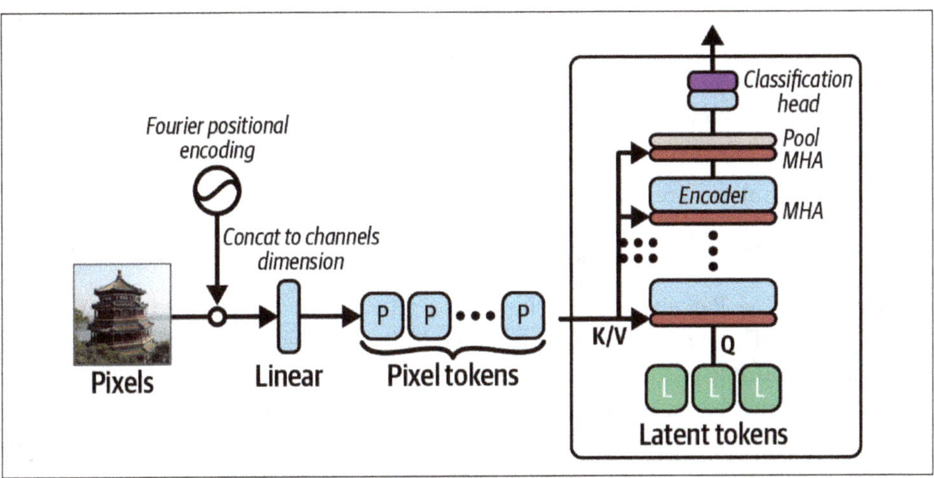

Figure 16-15. Perceiver architecture: inputs are ingested through cross-attention layers, while the main input is a sequence of learned latent tokens

Let's walk through this architecture:

- The input is first chopped into its smallest constituents. In this example, the input is an image, so it is chopped into individual pixels: we now have a sequence of 3D vectors (red, green, blue).
- Positional encodings are concatenated to these feature vectors. Perceiver uses Fourier positional encodings, which are very similar to the sinusoidal positional encodings of the original Transformer, except they encode all of the input's dimensions. Since an image is 2D, each pixel's horizontal and vertical coordinates

30 Andrew Jaegle et al., "Perceiver: General Perception with Iterative Attention", arXiv preprint arXiv:2103.03206 (2021).

are encoded; for example, if a pixel is located at coordinates x and y (normalized between −1 and 1), then the positional encoding vector will include x and y, followed by sin(π_fx_), sin(π_fy_), and cos(π_fx_), cos(π_fy_) repeated K times (typically 6) with the frequency f starting at 1 and going up to μ / 2 (spaced equally), where μ is the target resolution (e.g., if the image is 224 × 224 pixels, then μ = 224).[31] The dimensionality of the positional encoding vector is d(2_K_ + 1), where d is the number of input dimensions (i.e., 1 for audio, 2 for images, 3 for videos, etc.).

- The pixel tokens now have 3 + 2 × (2 × 6 + 1) = 29 dimensions. We then pass them through a linear layer to project them to the Perceiver's dimensionality (e.g., 512).
- The Perceiver's architecture itself is composed of repeated processing blocks (e.g., eight), where each block is composed of a single cross-attention multi-head attention layer (MHA) followed by a regular transformer encoder (e.g., with six encoder layers). The final block is composed of a single cross-attention MHA layer and an average pooling layer to reduce the input sequence into a single vector, which is then fed to a classification head (i.e., linear plus softmax).
- The pixel tokens are fed to the Perceiver exclusively through the MHA layers, and they play the role of the keys and values. In other words, the Perceiver attends to the pixel tokens through cross-attention only.
- Crucially, the Perceiver's main input is a fairly short sequence of *latent tokens* (e.g., 512). These tokens are similar to an RNN's hidden state: an initial sequence (learned during training) is fed to the Perceiver, and it gradually gets updated as the model learns more and more about the pixel tokens via cross-attention. Since it's a short sequence, it doesn't suffer much from the quadratic attention problem. This is called the *latent bottleneck trick*, and is the key to the success of the Perceiver.
- The authors experimented sharing weights across processing blocks (excluding the first cross-attention layer), and they got good results. When the processing blocks share the same weights, the Perceiver is effectively a recurrent neural network, and the latent tokens really are its hidden state.

---

31 If Δ is the spacing between samples, then the Nyquist–Shannon sampling theorem tells us that the maximum frequency we can measure is f = 1 / 2Δ. This is why f stops at μ / 2 rather than μ: sampling at a higher resolution would not add any information, and it might introduce aliasing artifacts.

As we saw in Chapter 7, the manifold hypothesis states that most real-world data lives near a low-dimensional manifold, much like a rolled piece of paper lives in 3D but is essentially a 2D object. This 2D space is latent (i.e., hidden, potential) until we unroll the paper. Similarly, the Perceiver's goal is to "unroll" its high-dimensional inputs so the model can work in the latent space, using low-dimensional representations.

Importantly, this architecture can efficiently process high-resolution inputs. For example, a 224 × 224 image has 50,176 pixels, so if we tried to feed such a long sequence of pixel tokens directly to a regular encoder, each self-attention layer would have to compute $50{,}176^2 \approx 2.5$ billion attention scores! But since the Perceiver only attends to the pixel tokens through cross-attention, it just needs to compute 50,176 times the number of latent tokens. Even for the biggest Perceiver variant, that's just a total of 50,176 × 512 ≈ 25.7 million attention scores, which is roughly 100 times less compute.

Thanks to the latent bottleneck, the Perceiver scales linearly with the number of pixel tokens, instead of quadratically.

The authors trained the Perceiver using regular supervised learning on various classification tasks across several modalities, including image-only (ImageNet), audio plus video (AudioSet),[32] or point clouds (ModelNet40),[33] all using the same model architecture. They got competitive results, in some cases even reaching the state of the art.

The videos in the AudioSet dataset were downsampled to 224 × 224 pixels at 25 frames per second (fps), with a 48 kHz audio sample rate. You could theoretically feed each pixel and each audio frame individually to the Perceiver, but this would be a bit extreme, as each 10s video would be represented as a sequence of 224 × 224 × 25 × 10 ≈ 12.5 million pixel tokens, and 48,000 × 10 = 480,000 audio tokens.

So the authors had to compromise. They trained on 32-frame clips (at 25 fps, that's 1.28s each, instead of 10s) and they chopped the video into 2 × 8 × 8 patches (i.e., 2 frames × 8 × 8 pixels), resulting in 224 × 224 × 32 / (2 × 8 × 8) = 12,544 video tokens of 128 RGB pixels each (plus the position encoding). They also chopped the

32 AudioSet (*https://homl.info/audioset*) contains over 2 million video segments of 10s each, sorted into over 500 classes.

33 ModelNet40 (*https://homl.info/modelnet*) is a synthetic dataset of 3D point clouds of various shapes, such as airplanes or cars. A common source of point clouds in real life is LiDAR sensors.

audio into clips of 128 frames each, resulting in 480 audio tokens. They also tried converting the audio to a mel spectrogram (which resulted in 4,800 audio tokens). Using a spectrogram instead of raw audio is a standard practice in audio processing, but it made very little difference to the model's performance, which shows that the Perceiver is able to extract useful features from the raw data without any help.

Then they simply concatenated the video and audio token sequences (after positional encoding), and also concatenated a modality embedding to help the model distinguish the modalities.

One limitation of the Perceiver architecture is that it was only designed for multimodal classification. That said, instead of averaging the latent tokens and feeding them to a classification head, we could try to use them for other downstream tasks. Of course, the DeepMind researchers thought of that, and just a few months later they published the Perceiver IO architecture.

Perceiver IO: A Flexible Output Mechanism for the Perceiver

DeepMind released Perceiver IO (*https://homl.info/perceiverio*) in July 2021.[34] It can perform classification tasks like the Perceiver, but also many other tasks such as masked language modeling (MLM) better than BERT, *optical flow* (i.e., predicting where each pixel will move in the next video frame), actually beating the state of the art, and even playing StarCraft II.

The model is identical to Perceiver up to the output latent tokens, but the pooling layer and the classification head are replaced by a very flexible output mechanism (see Figure 16-16):

- A new cross-attention layer is added, which acts as a decoder by attending to the output latent tokens and producing the final output representations. These output representations can then go through a task-specific head, or even multiple heads if we're doing multitask learning.
- The number and nature of the output tokens is task-specific:
  - For classification, we only need one output vector, which we can feed to a classification head. Therefore, we need one output query token, which can just be a learned embedding.
  - For masked language modeling, we can use one output query token per masked token, and add a classification head on top of the output representations (i.e., linear plus softmax) to get one estimated token probability for each masked token. To help the model locate each masked token, the output query

34 Andrew Jaegle et al., "Perceiver IO: A General Architecture for Structured Inputs & Outputs", arXiv preprint arXiv:2107.14795 (2021).

tokens are learnable positional embeddings based on the masked token's position. For example, given the masked sentence "The dog [MASK] the [MASK]", the masked tokens are located at positions #2 and #4, so we use the positional embedding #2 as the first output query token, and #4 as the second output query token. This same approach works for any other modality: just predict the masked tokens. It can also be extended to multiple modalities at once, typically by adding a modality embedding to the output query token before feeding it to the output cross-attention layer.

— For optical flow, the authors actually used one output token per pixel, using the same pixel representations both as the inputs to the Perceiver and as the output query tokens. This representation includes a Fourier positional encoding.

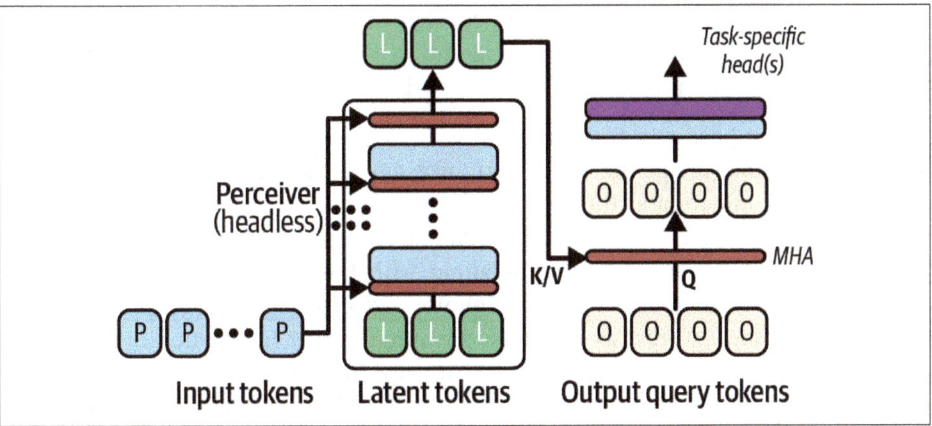

Figure 16-16. Perceiver IO architecture: one output query token per desired output token is fed to a cross-attention layer that attends to the Perceiver's output latent tokens

Because the output query tokens only ever attend to the latent tokens, the Perceiver IO can handle a very large number of output query tokens. The latent bottleneck allows the model to scale linearly for both the inputs and outputs.

The Perceiver IO is a bidirectional architecture; there's no causal masking, so it's not well suited for autoregressive tasks. In particular, it cannot efficiently perform next token prediction, so it's not well suited for text generation tasks such as image captioning. Sure, you could feed it an image and some text with a mask token at the end, and make it predict which token was masked, then start over to get the next token, and so on, but it would be horribly inefficient compared to a causal model (which can cache the previous state).

For this reason, Google and DeepMind researchers released the Perceiver AR architecture (*https://homl.info/perceiverar*) in February 2022 to address this limitation (AR stands for autoregressive). The model works very much like the Perceiver, except the last tokens of the input sequence are used as the latent tokens, the model is causal over these latent tokens, and it is trained using next token prediction. Perceiver AR didn't quite have the same impact as Perceiver and Perceiver IO, but it got excellent results on very long input sequences, thanks to its linear scaling capability.

But DeepMind researchers weren't done with multimodal ML; they soon released yet another amazing multimodal model, partly based on the Perceiver: Flamingo.

Flamingo: Open-Ended Visual Dialogue

DeepMind's Flamingo paper (*https://homl.info/flamingo*), published in April 2022, introduced a visual-language model (VLM) that can take arbitrary sequences of text and images as input and generate coherent free-form text. Most importantly, its few-shot performance is excellent on a wide variety of tasks.

For example, suppose you want to build a model that takes a picture and outputs a poem about that image: no need to train a new model; you can just feed a few examples to Flamingo, add the new image at the end, and it will happily generate a poem about this new image. If you want it to detect license plate numbers on car photos, just give it a few photos along with the corresponding license plate numbers (as text), then add a new car photo, and Flamingo will output its license plate number. You can just as easily use Flamingo for image captioning. Or visual question answering. Or you can ask it to compare two images. In fact, you can even give the model several frames from a video and ask it to describe the action. It's an incredibly versatile and powerful model out of the box, without any fine-tuning.

Let's look at Flamingo's architecture (see Figure 16-17):

- Instead of starting from scratch, Flamingo is based on two large pretrained models, which are both frozen: a vision model and a decoder-only language model. The authors used Chinchilla and CLIP, respectively, but many other powerful models would work fine too.
- Each input image is fed to the vision model, and the outputs go through a Perceiver model, called a *Resampler*, which produces a sequence of latent token representations. This ensures that every image gets represented as a fairly short sequence of latent representations (typically much shorter than the output of the vision model). This works around the quadratic attention problem.
- The sequences output by the Resampler are fed as the keys/values to many *gated xattn-dense* modules, which are inserted before every block in the frozen LLM:

— Each gated xattn-dense module is composed of a masked multi-head attention layer followed by a feedforward module, with a skip connection each, just like the cross-attention half of a vanilla Transformer's decoder layer.

— However, both the masked MHA layer and the feedforward module are followed by a *tanh gate*. These gates multiply their input by tanh(α), where α is a learnable scalar parameter initialized to 0 (one per gate). Since tan(0) = 0, training starts with all gates closed, so the inputs can only flow through the skip connections, and the gated xattn-dense modules have no impact on the LLM. But as training progresses, the model gradually learns to open the gates, allowing the gated modules to influence the LLM's outputs.

— In the gated xattn-dense module, each text token can only attend to visual tokens from the closest image located before it; visual tokens from all other images are masked. For example, the last text token ("is") can only attend to the Chinese tower photo, it cannot directly attend to the flower photo. However, since previous text tokens have information about the flower photo, the last token does have indirect access to the flower photo via the frozen LLM's self-attention layers.

- The text is tokenized as the LLM expects (e.g., Chinchilla expects start-of-sequence and end-of-sequence tokens, which I denoted as <s> and </s>), but a couple new special tokens are added. Each image-text chunk ends with an end-of-chunk token (which I denoted as </c>), and each image is replaced with an image token (which I denoted as <i>). Both are represented using trainable embeddings.

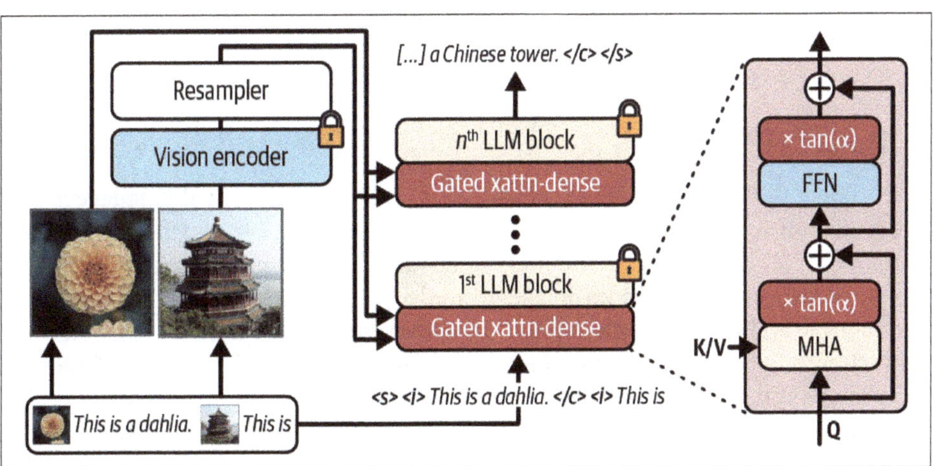

Figure 16-17. Flamingo takes any sequence of text and images, and outputs coherent free-form text

The bad news is that DeepMind did not release Flamingo to the public. The good news is that open source replications and variants are available:

- OpenFlamingo (*https://homl.info/openflamingo*), created by the MLFoundations team, which is part of the non-profit organization LAION. It is fully open source and available on the Hugging Face Hub (e.g., openflamingo/OpenFlamingo-9B-vitl-mpt7b, based on a CLIP ViT-L/14 vision encoder and a MPT-7B LLM).
- IDEFICS (*https://homl.info/idefics*) by Hugging Face, trained on a huge dataset named OBELICS,[35] composed of 141 million interleaved text-image documents gathered from Common Crawl (including 350 million images and 115 billion text tokens). Both IDEFICS and OBELICS are available on the hub (e.g., Idefics3-8B-Llama3 and OBELICS by HuggingFaceM4). The architecture includes a few improvements over Flamingo; for example, you can more easily swap in different LLMs or vision encoders. IDEFICS itself is open source, but the models it is based on may have licensing limitations. In particular, IDEFICS 1 and 3 are based on Llama, which has some limitations for commercial use, while IDEFICS 2 is based on Mistral, which is fully open source.
- AudioFlamingo (*https://homl.info/audioflamingo*) by Nvidia, which is very similar to Flamingo but handles audio instead of images.
- Other variants are available, such as domain-specific models like Med-Flamingo (*https://homl.info/medflamingo*), an OpenFlamingo model trained on medical documents.

The last multimodal architecture we will discuss is bootstrapping language-image pretraining, or BLIP, by Salesforce. Its second version, BLIP-2, also successfully reuses two large pretrained models—a vision model and an LLM—to create a VLM that can ingest both images and text, and generate free-form text. Let's see how.

BLIP and BLIP-2

The original BLIP model (*https://homl.info/blip*) is an excellent visual-language model released by Salesforce in January 2022.[36] Its architecture is a *mixture of encoder-decoder* (MED) composed of a text-only encoder, a vision-only encoder, an image-grounded text encoder, and an image-grounded text decoder, sharing many layers. This flexible architecture made it possible to train the model simultaneously on three distinct objectives: *image-text matching* (ITM), an *image-text contrastive* (ITC) loss to align image and text representations (similar to CLIP), and language modeling (LM) where the model must try to generate the caption using next token prediction.

35 In the French comic series *Astérix*, Obélix is a big and friendly Gaul, and Idéfix is his clever little dog.

36 Junnan Li et al., "BLIP: Bootstrapping Language-Image Pre-training for Unified Vision-Language Understanding and Generation", arXiv preprint arXiv:2201.12086 (2022).

Another important reason for BLIP's success is the fact that it was pretrained on a very large and clean dataset. To build this dataset, the authors simultaneously trained a *captioning module* to generate synthetic captions for images, and a *filtering module* to remove noisy data. This approach, named *CapFilt*, removed poor quality captions from the original web-scraped dataset, and added many new high-quality synthetic captions. After this bootstrapping stage, the authors trained the final model on the large and clean dataset they had just built. It's a two-stage process, hence the name BLIP: *bootstrapping language-image pretraining*.

One year later, in January 2023, Salesforce released BLIP-2 (*https://homl.info/blip2*),[37] which is based on the same core ideas but greatly improves the model's performance by reusing two large pretrained models, one vision model and one language model, both frozen. BLIP-2 even outperformed Flamingo with a much smaller model.

Training is split in two stages. BLIP-2's architecture during the first stage is shown in Figure 16-18.

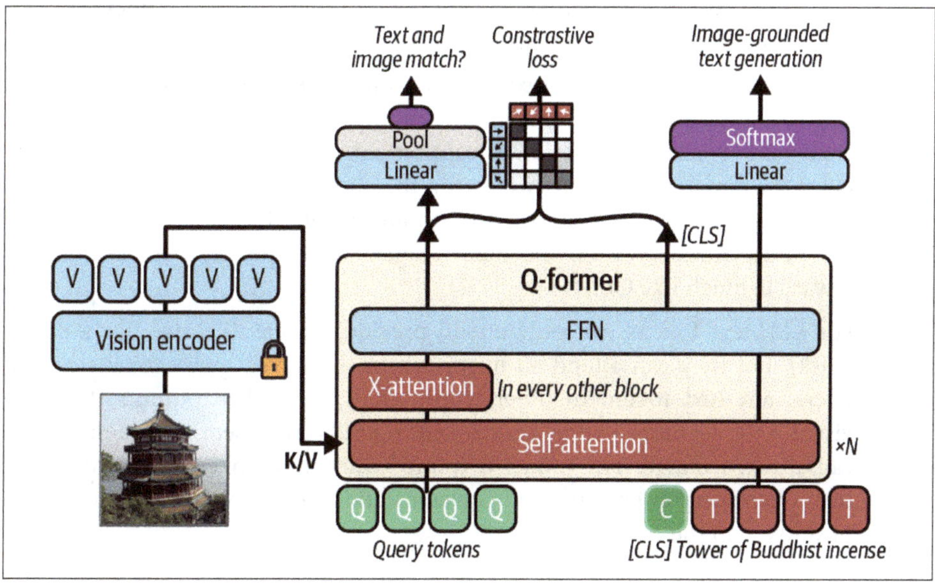

Figure 16-18. BLIP-2 pretraining, Stage 1: training the Q-Former

- The central component is called the *Q-Former* (querying transformer). Its architecture is the same as BERT-base, and in fact it's even initialized using BERT-base's pretrained weights, but it also has some extra cross-attention layers that let it attend to visual tokens produced by the pretrained visual encoder. The

37 Junnan Li et al., "BLIP-2: Bootstrapping Language-Image Pre-training with Frozen Image Encoders and Large Language Models", arXiv preprint arXiv:2301.12597 (2023).

cross-attention layers are inserted in every other encoder layer, between the self-attention layer and the feedforward module, and they are initialized randomly.

- The Q-Former processes three sequences: a sequence of text tokens (using BERT tokenization and token embeddings), a sequence of visual tokens produced by the pretrained vision encoder, and lastly a sequence of trainable Perceiver-style latent tokens. In BLIP-2, the latent tokens are called *query tokens* because their output representations will later be used to query the pretrained LLM.
- The Q-Former is trained with the same three objectives as BLIP: ITM, ITC, and LM. For each objective, a different mask is used:
  - For ITM, query tokens and text tokens can attend to each other. In other words, the output representations for the query tokens represent text-grounded visual features, and the output representations for the text tokens represent image-grounded text features. The query token outputs go through a linear layer which produces two logits per query token (image-text match or mismatch), and the model computes the mean logits across all query tokens, then computes the binary cross-entropy.
  - For ITC, query tokens and text tokens cannot attend to each other. In other words, the Q-Former's outputs represent visual-only features and text-only features. For each possible image/caption pair in the batch, the model computes the maximum similarity between the query token outputs and the class token output. We get a matrix of maximum similarities, and the loss pushes the values toward +1 on the main diagonal, and pushes the other values toward 0, much like CLIP.
  - For LM, text tokens can only attend previous tokens (i.e., we use a causal mask), but they can attend all query tokens. However, query tokens cannot attend any text token. In other words, the query token outputs represent visual-only features, while text token outputs represent image-grounded causal text features. The model is trained using next token prediction: each text token's output goes through a classification head which must predict the next token in the caption.

You may be surprised that the Q-Former is used to encode text (for ITM and ITC) and also to generate text (for LM). Since the Q-Former is initialized using the weights of a pretrained BERT-base model, it's pretty good at text encoding right from the start of training, but it initially doesn't know that it has to predict the next token for the LM task. Luckily, it can learn fairly fast since it's not starting from scratch; it has good BERT features to work with. However, we need to tell it whether we want it to encode the text or predict the next token. For this, we replace the class token with a *decode token* during LM.[38]

Once stage 1 is finished, the Q-Former is already a powerful model that can encode images and text into the same space, so a photo of a chimpanzee produces a very similar output representation as the caption "A photo of a chimpanzee". But it's even better than that: the query token outputs were trained to be most helpful for next token prediction.

To produce negative examples for ITM, one strategy is to randomly pick a caption in the same batch, excluding the image's true caption. However, this makes the task too easy, so the model doesn't learn much. Instead, the authors used a *hard negative mining* strategy, where difficult captions are more likely to be sampled. For example, given a photo of a chimpanzee, the caption "A gorilla" is more likely to be sampled than "A spacecraft". To find difficult captions, the algorithm uses the similarity scores from the ITC task.

So it's time for the second stage of training (see Figure 16-19):

- We keep the vision transformer and the Q-Former, but we drop the rest and we add a new linear layer, initialized randomly, on top of the Q-Former.
- For each image/caption pair, the Q-Former attends to the visual features produced by the pretrained vision encoder, and the outputs go through the linear layer to produce a sequence of visual query tokens.
- The visual query tokens and the text token representations are concatenated and fed to the (frozen) pretrained LLM. We train BLIP-2 to predict the next caption token.

During stage 2, the model learns to properly map the visual query tokens to the LLM's input space. Once trained, the model can be used like in stage 2, generating visual-grounded text.

38 The idea of training a single model capable of both encoding and generating text was introduced in 2019 by Microsoft researchers Li Dong et al. with their UniLM model (*https://homl.info/unilm*).

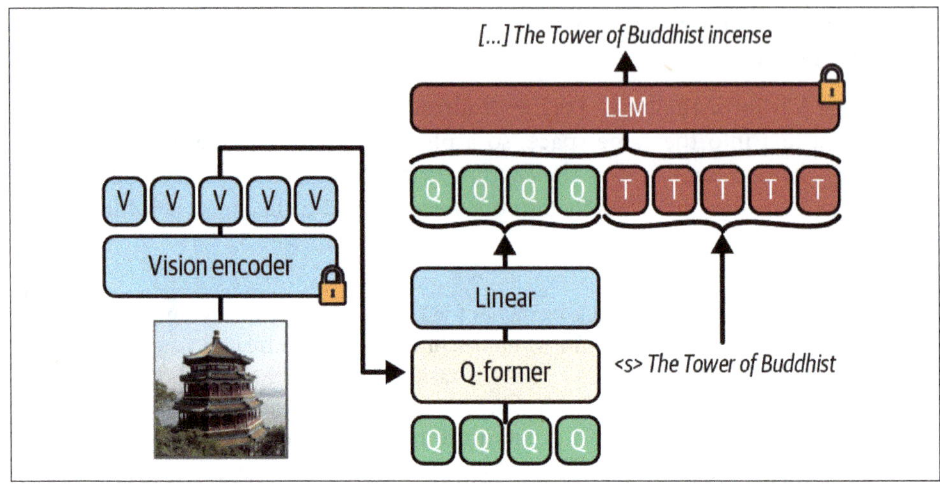

Figure 16-19. BLIP-2 pretraining, Stage 2: training the linear layer to map the query tokens to the LLM's input space

Let's use BLIP-2 to generate a caption for an image:

```
from transformers import Blip2Processor, Blip2ForConditionalGeneration

model_id = "Salesforce/blip2-opt-2.7b"
blip2_processor = Blip2Processor.from_pretrained(model_id)
blip2_model = Blip2ForConditionalGeneration.from_pretrained(
    model_id, device_map=device, dtype=torch.float16)

image_url = "http://images.cocodataset.org/val2017/000000039769.jpg"  # two cats
image = Image.open(urllib.request.urlopen(image_url))
inputs = blip2_processor(images=image, return_tensors="pt")
inputs = inputs.to(device, dtype=torch.float16)
with torch.no_grad():
    generated_ids = blip2_model.generate(**inputs)

generated_text = blip2_processor.batch_decode(generated_ids)
```

What did BLIP-2 see?

```
>>> generated_text
['<image><image><image><image>[...]<image></s>two cats laying on a couch\n']
```

It's a good description of the photo, but it would nicer without the special tokens, so let's get rid of them when decoding the model's output:

```
>>> generated_text = blip2_processor.batch_decode(generated_ids,
...                                                skip_special_tokens=True)
...
>>> generated_text
>>>
['two cats laying on a couch\n']
```

Perfect!

Also check out InstructBLIP, a BLIP-2 model with vision-language instruction tuning.

Other Multimodal Models

We've covered quite a few multimodal models, with very different architectures and pretraining techniques, but of course there are many others. Here is a quick overview of some of the most notable ones:

LayoutLM (Microsoft, Dec. 2019)
: Document understanding based on text, vision, and document layout. Version 3 was released in April 2022.

GLIP (Microsoft, Dec. 2021)
: A vision-language model for visual grounding and object detection. GLIP-2 was released in 2022.

Stable Diffusion (Stability AI, Dec. 2021)
: A powerful text-to-image model.

OFA (Microsoft, Feb. 2022)
: Unified (one for all) vision-language pretraining framework handling various vision-language tasks.

CoCa (Google, May 2022)
: A vision-language model pretrained using contrastive and captioning objectives. CoCa influenced later models like PaLI-X and Flamingo-2.

PaLI (Google, Sep. 2022)
: Multilingual multimodal models for vision-language tasks like VQA and captioning, with strong zero-shot performance. The next versions, PaLI-X and PaLI-3, were released in 2023, and PaliGemma in May 2024.

Kosmos-1 (Microsoft, Feb. 2023)
: A vision-language model with strong support for visual grounding. Kosmos-2 and Kosmos-2.5 came out in 2023.

PaLM-E (Google, Mar. 2023)
: PaLM-E extends Google's PaLM series with visual inputs and embodied sensor data. A decoder-only LLM generates text commands like "grab the hammer", which are interpreted and executed by a robot via a downstream system.

LLaVA (H. Liu et al., Apr. 2023)
: Among the best open source vision-language chat models.

ImageBind (Meta, May 2023)
: A CLIP-style model extended to six modalities (image, text, audio, IMU,[39] depth, and thermal).

RT-2 (DeepMind, Jul. 2023)
: A vision-language model capable of robotic control as well, trained on a large-scale instruction-following dataset.

SeamlessM4T (Meta, Aug. 2023)
: A single model that can perform speech-to-text, speech-to-speech, text-to-speech, and text-to-text translation across close to 100 languages.

Qwen-VL (Alibaba, Sep. 2023)
: Open vision-language family (7B to 72B) that became one of the strongest open multimodal baselines. Led to Qwen2-VL (Aug. 2024) and Qwen3-Omni (Sep. 2025), which expanded to video and audio and reached trillion-parameter scale.

Fuyu (Adept AI, Oct. 2023)
: Processes interleaved image and text in real time with a unified transformer.

EMO (Alibaba, Feb. 2024)
: Takes an image of a person, plus an audio recording of someone speaking or singing, and the model generates a video of that person, matching the audio. EMO-2 was released in January 2025.

GLaMM (H. Rasheed et al., Jun. 2024)
: A visual dialogue model which generates text responses mixed with object segmentation masks.

LaViDa (UCLA, Panasonic, Adobe, Salesforce, May 2025)
: A family of open, diffusion-based vision-language models.

I've created homl.info short links for all the models discussed in this chapter; just use the lowercase name without hyphens, for example, *https://homl.info/qwen2vl*.

There are also several commercial multimodal models whose detailed architectures were not disclosed, such as GPT-4.1 and Sora by OpenAI, Gemini 2.5 Pro by Google,

39 Most modern smartphones contain an inertial measurement unit (IMU) sensor: it measures acceleration, angular velocity, and often the magnetic field strength.

Veo-3 by DeepMind, and Claude 4 Opus by Anthropic. To access these models, you first need to create an account and get a subscription (or use the free tier), then you can either use the provided apps (e.g., Google AI Studio, *https://aistudio.google.com*), or query the model via an API. For example, following is a short code example showing how to query Gemini 2.5 Pro via the API. You first need to get an API key in Google AI Studio, then you can use any secret management method you prefer to store it and load it in your code (e.g., if you are using Colab, I recommend you use Colab's secret manager, as we saw in Chapter 15).

```
from google import genai

gemini_api_key = [...]  # load from Colab secrets, or from a file, or hardcode
gemini_client = genai.Client(api_key=gemini_api_key)
cats_photo = gemini_client.files.upload(file="my_cats_photo.jpg")
question = "What animal and how many? Format: [animal, number]"
response = gemini_client.models.generate_content(
    model="gemini-2.5-flash",  # or "gemini-2.5-pro"
    contents=[cats_photo, question])
print(response.text)  # prints: "[cat, 2]"
```

This code uses the `google-genai` library, which is already installed on Colab. It also assumes that a file named *my_cats_photo.jpg* is present in the same directory as the notebook.

This wraps up this chapter; I hope you enjoyed it. Transformers can now see, hear, touch, and more! In the next chapter, we will explore some fairly advanced techniques designed to speed up and scale transformers. As Daft Punk put it: harder, better, faster, stronger.

Exercises

1. Can you describe the original ViT's architecture? Why does it matter?
2. What tasks are regular ViTs (meaning nonhierarchical) best used for? What are their limitations?
3. What is the main innovation in DeiT? Is this idea generalizable to other architectures?
4. What are some examples of hierarchical ViTs? What kind of tasks are they good for?
5. How do PVTs and Swin Transformers reduce the computational cost of processing high-resolution images?
6. How does DINO work? What changed in DINOv2? When would you want to use DINOv2?
7. What is the objective of the JEPA architecture? How does it work?

8. What is a multimodal model? Can you give five examples of multimodal tasks?
9. Explain what the fusion and alignment problems are in multimodal learning. Why are transformers well suited to tackle them?
10. Can you write a one-line summary of the main ideas in VideoBERT, ViLBERT, CLIP, DALL·E, Perceiver IO, Flamingo, and BLIP-2?
11. If you are using a Perceiver IO model and you double the length of the inputs and the outputs, approximately how much more computation will be required?
12. Try fine-tuning a pretrained ViT model on the Food 101 dataset (*https://homl.info/food101*) (`torchvision.datasets.Food101`). What accuracy can you reach? How about using a CLIP model, zero-shot?
13. Create a simple search engine for your own photos: first, write a function that uses a CLIP model to embed all of your photos and saves the resulting vectors. Next, write a function that takes a search query (text or image), embeds it using CLIP, then finds the most similar photo embeddings and displays the corresponding photos. You can manually implement the similarity search algorithm, or a dedicated library such as the FAISS library (*https://github.com/facebookresearch/faiss*) or even a full-blown vector database.
14. Use BLIP-2 to automatically caption all of your photos.

Solutions to these exercises are available at the end of this chapter's notebook, at *https://homl.info/colab-p*.

CHAPTER 17
Speeding Up Transformers

In Chapters 15 and 16, we built all kinds of transformers, from classifiers, translators and chatbots, to vision and multimodal transformers. While transformers are incredibly versatile and powerful, they are far from perfect. In particular, they can be very slow, especially when processing long input sequences.

Luckily, many techniques have been developed to speed up transformers of any size:

- To speed up decoding in generative transformers, we will use key/value caching and speculative decoding, then we will take of a quick look at several approaches to parallelize text generation.
- To accelerate multi-head attention (MHA), which is one of the most computationally expensive components of transformers, we will look at sparse attention, approximate attention, sharing projections, and FlashAttention.
- To speed up gigantic transformers of up to trillions of parameters, we will discuss mixture of experts (MoE).
- To train large transformers efficiently, we will discuss parameter-efficient fine-tuning (PEFT) using adapters such as Low-Rank Adaptation (LoRA), activation checkpointing, sequence packing, gradient accumulation, and parallelism.

Another way to speed up a transformer is to make it smaller. This can be done using reduced precision and quantization, which are discussed in Appendix B.

That's quite a lot of techniques to cover, and they are fairly advanced, so you can safely skip this chapter for now if you are new to transformers, and come back later whenever needed. This is why this chapter is online-only, available at *https://homl.info*, to leave room for the other chapters.

CHAPTER 18

Autoencoders, GANs, and Diffusion Models

Autoencoders are artificial neural networks capable of learning dense representations of the input data, called *latent representations* or *codings*, without any supervision (i.e., the training set is unlabeled). These codings typically have a much lower dimensionality than the input data, making autoencoders useful for dimensionality reduction (see Chapter 7), especially for visualization purposes. Autoencoders also act as feature detectors, and they can be used for unsupervised pretraining of deep neural networks (as we discussed in Chapter 11). They are also commonly used for anomaly detection, as we will see. Lastly, some autoencoders are *generative models*: they are capable of randomly generating new data that looks very similar to the training data. For example, you could train an autoencoder on pictures of faces, and it would then be able to generate new faces.

Generative adversarial networks (GANs) are also neural nets capable of generating data. In fact, they can generate pictures of faces so convincing that it is hard to believe the people they represent do not exist. You can judge for yourself by visiting *https://thispersondoesnotexist.com*, a website that shows faces generated by a GAN architecture called *StyleGAN*. GANs have been widely used for super resolution (increasing the resolution of an image), colorization (*https://github.com/jantic/DeOldify*), powerful image editing (e.g., replacing photo bombers with realistic background), turning simple sketches into photorealistic images, predicting the next frames in a video, augmenting a dataset (to train other models), generating other types of data (such as text, audio, and time series), identifying the weaknesses in other models to strengthen them, and more.

However, since the early 2020s, GANs have been largely replaced by *diffusion models*, which can generate more diverse and higher-quality images than GANs, while also being much easier to train. However, diffusion models are much slower to run, so GANs are still useful when you need very fast generation.

Autoencoders, GANs, and diffusion models are all unsupervised, learn latent representations, can be used as generative models, and have many similar applications. However, they work very differently:

Autoencoders
: Autoencoders simply learn to copy their inputs to their outputs. This may sound like a trivial task, but as you will see, constraining the network in various ways can make the task arbitrarily difficult. For example, you can limit the size of the latent representations, or you can add noise to the inputs and train the network to recover the original inputs. These constraints prevent the autoencoder from trivially copying the inputs directly to the outputs, which forces it to learn efficient ways of representing the data. In short, the codings are byproducts of the autoencoder learning the identity function under some constraints.

GANs
: GANs are composed of two neural networks: a *generator* that tries to generate data that looks similar to the training data, and a *discriminator* that tries to tell real data from fake data. This architecture is very original in deep learning in that the generator and the discriminator compete against each other during training; this is called *adversarial training*. The generator is often compared to a criminal trying to make realistic counterfeit money, while the discriminator is like the police investigator trying to tell real money from fake.

Diffusion models
: A diffusion model is trained to gradually remove noise from an image. If you then take an image entirely full of random noise and repeatedly run the diffusion model on that image, a high-quality image will gradually emerge, similar to the training images (but not identical).

In this chapter we will start by exploring in more depth how autoencoders work and how to use them for dimensionality reduction, feature extraction, unsupervised pretraining, or as generative models. This will naturally lead us to GANs. We will build a simple GAN to generate fake images, but we will see that training is often quite difficult. We will discuss the main difficulties you will encounter with adversarial training, as well as some of the main techniques to work around these difficulties. And lastly, we will build and train a diffusion model—specifically a *denoising diffusion probabilistic model* (DDPM)—and use it to generate images. Let's start with autoencoders!

Efficient Data Representations

Which of the following number sequences do you find the easiest to memorize?

- 40, 27, 25, 36, 81, 57, 10, 73, 19, 68
- 50, 48, 46, 44, 42, 40, 38, 36, 34, 32, 30, 28, 26, 24, 22, 20, 18, 16, 14

At first glance, it would seem that the first sequence should be easier, since it is much shorter. However, if you look carefully at the second sequence, you will notice that it is just the list of even numbers from 50 down to 14. Once you notice this pattern, the second sequence becomes much easier to memorize than the first because you only need to remember the pattern (i.e., decreasing even numbers) and the starting and ending numbers (i.e., 50 and 14). Note that if you could quickly and easily memorize very long sequences, you would not care much about the existence of a pattern in the second sequence. You would just learn every number by heart, and that would be that. The fact that it is hard to memorize long sequences is what makes it useful to recognize patterns, and hopefully this clarifies why constraining an autoencoder during training pushes it to discover and exploit patterns in the data.

The relationship among memory, perception, and pattern matching was famously studied by William Chase and Herbert Simon (*https://homl.info/111*)[1] in the early 1970s. They observed that expert chess players were able to memorize the positions of all the pieces in a game by looking at the board for just five seconds, a task that most people would find impossible. However, this was only the case when the pieces were placed in realistic positions (from actual games), not when the pieces were placed randomly. Chess experts don't have a much better memory than you and I; they just see chess patterns more easily, thanks to their experience with the game. Noticing patterns helps them store information efficiently.

Just like the chess players in this memory experiment, an autoencoder looks at the inputs, converts them to an efficient latent representation, and is then capable of reconstructing something that (hopefully) looks very close to the inputs. An autoencoder is always composed of two parts: an *encoder* (or *recognition network*) that converts the inputs to a latent representation, followed by a *decoder* (or *generative network*) that converts the internal representation to the outputs.

In the example shown in Figure 18-1, the autoencoder is a regular multilayer perceptron (MLP; see Chapter 9). Since it must reconstruct its inputs, the number of neurons in the output layer must be equal to the number of inputs (i.e., three in this example). The lower part of the network is the encoder (in this case it's a single layer with two neurons), and the upper part is the decoder. The outputs are often

1 William G. Chase and Herbert A. Simon, "Perception in Chess", *Cognitive Psychology* 4, no. 1 (1973): 55–81.

called the *reconstructions* because the autoencoder tries to reconstruct the inputs. The cost function always contains a *reconstruction loss* that penalizes the model when the reconstructions are different from the inputs.

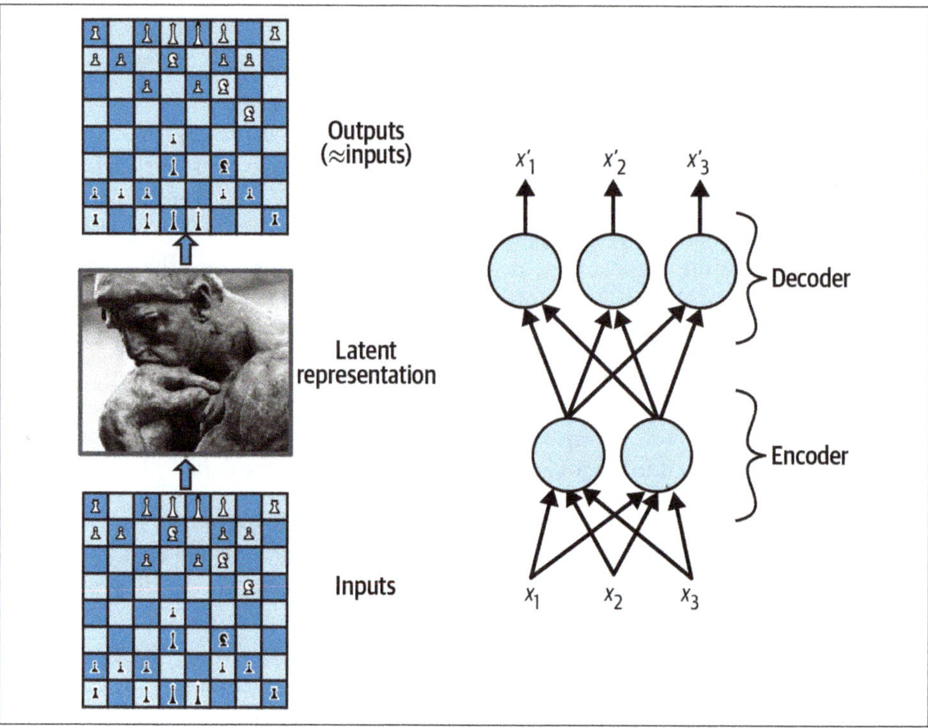

Figure 18-1. The chess memory experiment (left) and a simple autoencoder (right)

Because the internal representation has a lower dimensionality than the input data (in this example, it is 2D instead of 3D), the autoencoder is said to be *undercomplete*. An undercomplete autoencoder cannot trivially copy its inputs to the codings, yet it must find a way to output a copy of its inputs. It is forced to compress the data, thereby learning the most important features in the input data (and dropping the unimportant ones).

Let's see how to implement a very simple undercomplete autoencoder for dimensionality reduction.

Performing PCA with an Undercomplete Linear Autoencoder

If the autoencoder uses only linear activations and the cost function is the mean squared error (MSE), then it ends up performing principal component analysis (PCA; see Chapter 7).

The following code builds a simple linear autoencoder that takes a 3D input, projects it down to 2D, then projects it back up to 3D. Since we will train the model using targets equal to the inputs, gradient descent will have to find the 2D plane that lies closest to the training data, just like PCA would.

```
import torch
import torch.nn as nn

torch.manual_seed(42)
encoder = nn.Linear(3, 2)
decoder = nn.Linear(2, 3)
autoencoder = nn.Sequential(encoder, decoder).to(device)
```

This code is really not very different from all the MLPs we built in past chapters, but there are a few things to note:

- We organized the autoencoder into two subcomponents: the encoder and the decoder, each composed of a single `Linear` layer in this example, and the autoencoder is a `Sequential` model containing the encoder followed by the decoder.
- The autoencoder's number of outputs is equal to the number of inputs (i.e., 3).
- To perform PCA, we do not use any activation function (i.e., all neurons are linear), and the cost function is the MSE. That's because PCA is a linear transformation. We will see more complex and nonlinear autoencoders shortly.

Now let's train the model on the same simple generated 3D dataset we used in Chapter 7 and use it to encode that dataset (i.e., project it to 2D):

```
from torch.utils.data import DataLoader, TensorDataset

X_train = [...]  # generate a 3D dataset, like in Chapter 7
train_set = TensorDataset(X_train, X_train)  # the inputs are also the targets
train_loader = DataLoader(train_set, batch_size=32, shuffle=True)
```

Note that X_train is used as both the inputs and the targets. Next, let's train the autoencoder, using the same train() function as in Chapter 10 (the notebook uses a slightly fancier function that prints some info and evaluates the model at each epoch):

```
import torchmetrics

optimizer = torch.optim.NAdam(autoencoder.parameters(), lr=0.2)
mse = nn.MSELoss()
rmse = torchmetrics.MeanSquaredError(squared=False).to(device)
train(autoencoder, optimizer, mse, train_loader, n_epochs=20)
```

Now that the autoencoder is trained, we can use its encoder to compress 3D inputs to 2D. For example, let's compress the entire training set:

```
codings = encoder(X_train.to(device))
```

Figure 18-2 shows the original 3D dataset (on the left) and the output of the autoencoder's hidden layer (i.e., the coding layer, on the right). As you can see, the autoencoder found the best 2D plane to project the data onto, preserving as much variance in the data as it could (just like PCA).

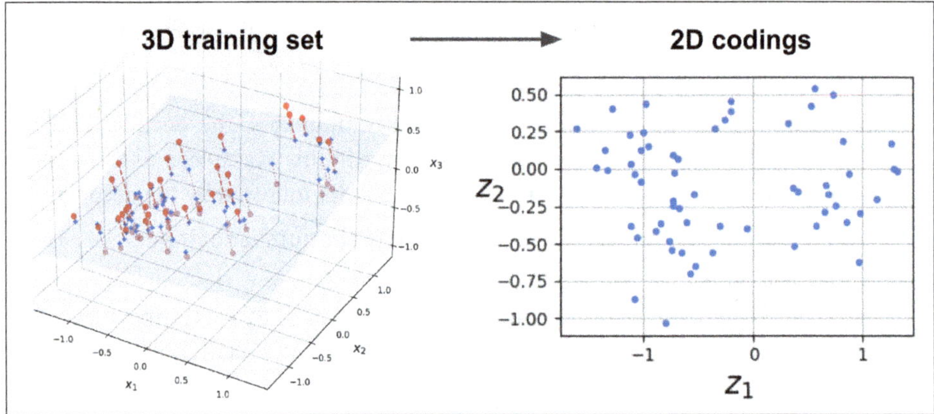

Figure 18-2. Approximate PCA performed by an undercomplete linear autoencoder

You can think of an autoencoder as performing a form of self-supervised learning, since it is based on a supervised learning technique with automatically generated labels (in this case, simply equal to the inputs).

Stacked Autoencoders

Just like other neural networks we have discussed, autoencoders can have multiple hidden layers. In this case they are called *stacked autoencoders* (or *deep autoencoders*). Adding more layers helps the autoencoder learn more complex codings. That said, one must be careful not to make the autoencoder too powerful. Imagine an encoder so powerful that it just learns to map each input to a single arbitrary number (and the decoder learns the reverse mapping). Obviously such an autoencoder will reconstruct the training data perfectly, but it will not have learned any useful data representation in the process, and is unlikely to generalize well to new instances.

The architecture of a stacked autoencoder is typically symmetrical with regard to the central hidden layer (the coding layer). To put it simply, it looks like a sandwich. For example, an autoencoder for Fashion MNIST (introduced in Chapter 9) may have 784 inputs, followed by a hidden layer with 128 neurons, then a central hidden layer of 32 neurons, then another hidden layer with 128 neurons, and an output layer with 784 neurons. This stacked autoencoder is represented in Figure 18-3. Note that all hidden layers must have an activation function, such as ReLU.

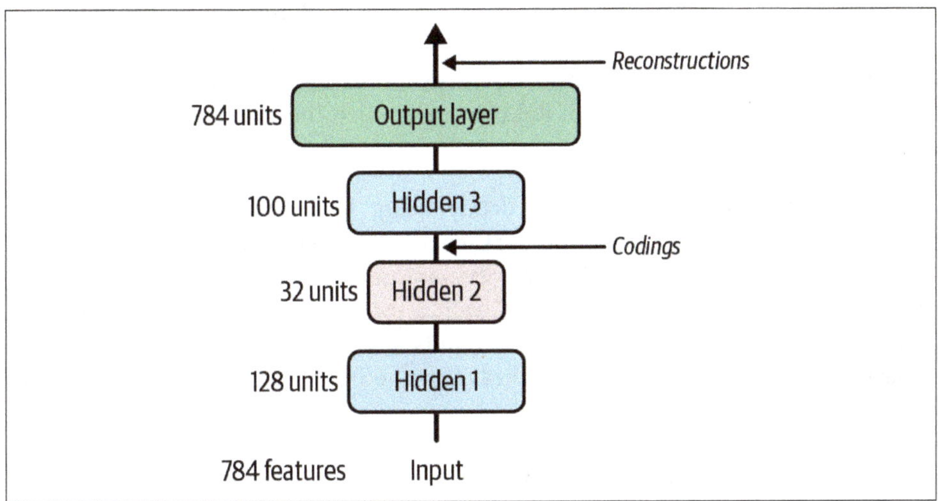

Figure 18-3. Stacked autoencoder

Implementing a Stacked Autoencoder Using PyTorch

You can implement a stacked autoencoder very much like a regular deep MLP. For example, here is an autoencoder you can use to process Fashion MNIST images:

```
stacked_encoder = nn.Sequential(
    nn.Flatten(),
    nn.Linear(1 * 28 * 28, 128), nn.ReLU(),
    nn.Linear(128, 32), nn.ReLU(),
)
stacked_decoder = nn.Sequential(
    nn.Linear(32, 128), nn.ReLU(),
    nn.Linear(128, 1 * 28 * 28), nn.Sigmoid(),
    nn.Unflatten(dim=1, unflattened_size=(1, 28, 28))
```

```
)
stacked_ae = nn.Sequential(stacked_encoder, stacked_decoder).to(device)
```

Let's go through this code:

- Just like earlier, we split the autoencoder model into two submodels: the encoder and the decoder.
- The encoder takes 28 × 28 pixel grayscale images (i.e., with a single channel), flattens them so that each image is represented as a vector of size 784, then processes these vectors through 2 `Linear` layers of diminishing sizes (128 units, then 32 units), each followed by the ReLU activation function. For each input image, the encoder outputs a vector of size 32.
- The decoder takes codings of size 32 (output by the encoder) and processes them through 2 `Linear` layers of increasing sizes (128 units, then 784 units), and reshapes the final vectors into 1 × 28 × 28 arrays so the decoder's outputs have the same shape as the encoder's inputs. Note that we use the sigmoid function for the output layer instead of ReLU to ensure that the output pixel values range between 0 and 1.

We can now load the Fashion MNIST dataset using the TorchVision library and split it into `train_data`, `valid_data`, and `test_data` (just like we did in Chapter 10), then train the autoencoder exactly like the previous autoencoder, using the inputs as the targets and minimizing the MSE loss. Give it a try, it's a good exercise! Don't forget to change the targets so they match the inputs—we're training an autoencoder, not a classifier.[2] If you get stuck, please check out the implementation in this chapter's notebook.

Visualizing the Reconstructions

Once you have trained the stacked autoencoder, how do you know if it's any good? One way to check that an autoencoder is properly trained is to compare the inputs and the outputs: the differences should not be too significant. Let's plot a few images from the validation set, as well as their reconstructions:

```
import matplotlib.pyplot as plt

def plot_image(image):
    plt.imshow(image.permute(1, 2, 0).cpu(), cmap="binary")
    plt.axis("off")
```

2 Hint: one approach is to create a custom `AutoencoderDataset` class that wraps a given dataset and replaces the targets with the inputs.

```
def plot_reconstructions(model, images, n_images=5):
    images = images[:n_images]
    with torch.no_grad():
        y_pred = model(images.to(device))

    fig = plt.figure(figsize=(len(images) * 1.5, 3))
    for idx in range(len(images)):
        plt.subplot(2, len(images), 1 + idx)
        plot_image(images[idx])
        plt.subplot(2, len(images), 1 + len(images) + idx)
        plot_image(y_pred[idx])

X_valid = torch.stack([x for x, _ in valid_data])
plot_reconstructions(stacked_ae, X_valid)
plt.show()
```

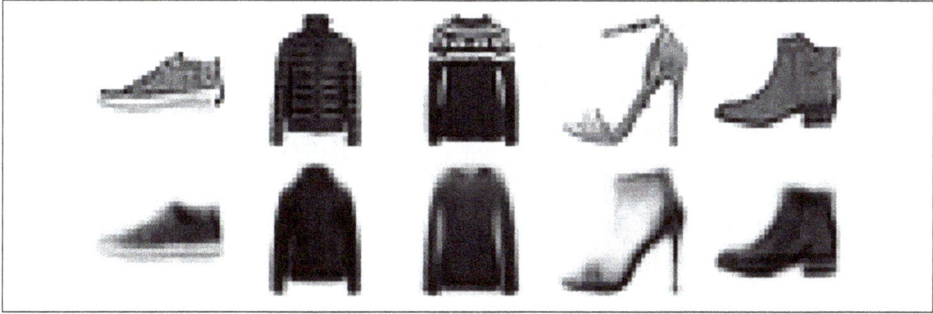

Figure 18-4. Original images (top) and their reconstructions (bottom)

Figure 18-4 shows the resulting images. The reconstructions are recognizable, but a bit too lossy. We may need to train the model for longer, or make the encoder and decoder more powerful, or make the codings larger. For now, let's go with this model and see how we can use it.

Anomaly Detection Using Autoencoders

One common use case for autoencoders is anomaly detection. Indeed, if an autoencoder is given an image that doesn't look like the images it was trained on (the image is said to be *out of distribution*), then the reconstruction will be terrible. For example, Figure 18-5 shows some MNIST digits and their reconstructions using the model we just trained on Fashion MNIST. As you can see, these reconstructions are very different from the inputs. If you compute the reconstruction loss (i.e., the MSE between the input and the output), it will be very high. To use the model for anomaly detection, you simply need to define a threshold, then any image whose reconstruction loss is greater than that threshold can be considered an anomaly.

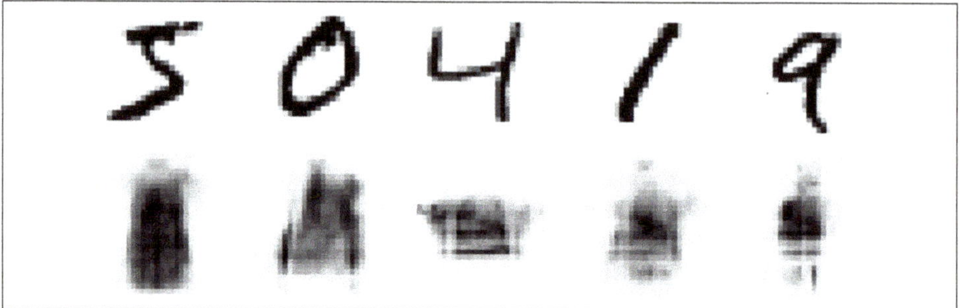

Figure 18-5. Out-of-distribution images are poorly reconstructed

That's all there is to it! Now let's look at another use case for autoencoders.

Visualizing the Fashion MNIST Dataset

As we saw earlier in this chapter, undercomplete autoencoders can be used for dimensionality reduction. However, for most datasets they will not do a very good job at reducing the dimensionality down to two or three dimensions; they need enough dimensions to be able to properly reconstruct the inputs. As a result, they are generally not used directly for visualization. However, they are great at handling huge datasets, so one strategy is to use an autoencoder to reduce the dimensionality down to a reasonable level, then use another dimensionality reduction algorithm for visualization, such as those we discussed in Chapter 7.

Let's use this strategy to visualize Fashion MNIST. First we'll use the encoder from our stacked autoencoder to reduce the dimensionality down to 32, then we'll use Scikit-Learn's implementation of the t-SNE algorithm to reduce the dimensionality down to 2 for visualization:

```
from sklearn.manifold import TSNE

with torch.no_grad():
    X_valid_compressed = stacked_encoder(X_valid.to(device))

tsne = TSNE(init="pca", learning_rate="auto", random_state=42)
X_valid_2D = tsne.fit_transform(X_valid_compressed.cpu())
```

Now we can plot the dataset:

```
plt.scatter(X_valid_2D[:, 0], X_valid_2D[:, 1], c=y_valid, s=10, cmap="tab10")
plt.show()
```

Figure 18-6 shows the resulting scatterplot, beautified a bit by displaying some of the images. The t-SNE algorithm identified several clusters that match the classes reasonably well (each class is represented by a different color). Note that t-SNE's output can vary greatly if you run it with a different random seed, slightly different data, or on a different platform, so your plot may look different.

Figure 18-6. Fashion MNIST visualization using an autoencoder, followed by t-SNE

Next let's look at how we can use autoencoders for unsupervised pretraining.

Unsupervised Pretraining Using Stacked Autoencoders

As we discussed in Chapter 11, if you are tackling a complex supervised task but you do not have a lot of labeled training data, one solution is to find a neural network that performs a similar task and reuse its lower layers. This makes it possible to train a high-performance model using little training data because your neural network won't have to learn all the low-level features; it will just reuse the feature detectors learned by the existing network.

Similarly, if you have a large dataset but most of it is unlabeled, you can first train a stacked autoencoder using all the data, then reuse the lower layers to create a neural network for your actual task and train it using the labeled data. For example, Figure 18-7 shows how to use a stacked autoencoder to perform unsupervised pretraining for a classification neural network. When training the classifier, if you really don't have much labeled training data, you may want to freeze the pretrained layers (at least the lower ones).

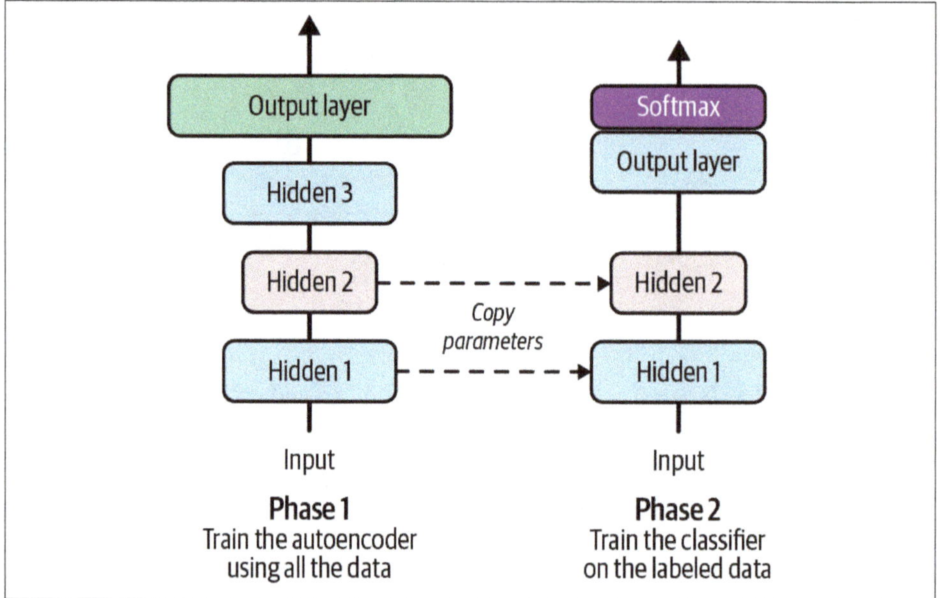

Figure 18-7. Unsupervised pretraining using autoencoders

Having plenty of unlabeled data and little labeled data is common. Building a large unlabeled dataset is often cheap (e.g., a simple script can download millions of images off the internet), but labeling those images (e.g., classifying them as cute or not) can usually be done reliably only by humans. Labeling instances is time-consuming and costly, so it's normal to have only a few thousand human-labeled instances, or even less. That said, there is a growing trend toward using advanced AIs to label datasets.

There is nothing special about the implementation: just train an autoencoder using all the training data (labeled plus unlabeled), then reuse its encoder layers to create a new neural network and train it on the labeled instances (see the exercises at the end of this chapter for an example).

Let's now look at a few techniques for training stacked autoencoders.

Tying Weights

When an autoencoder is neatly symmetrical, like the one we just built, a common technique is to *tie* the weights of the decoder layers to the weights of the encoder layers. This halves the number of weights in the model, speeding up training and limiting the risk of overfitting. Specifically, if the autoencoder has a total of N layers (not counting the input layer), and $\mathbf{W}_L$ represents the connection weights of the Lth

layer (e.g., layer 1 is the first hidden layer, layer $N/2$ is the coding layer, and layer N is the output layer), then the decoder layer weights can be defined as $\mathbf{W}_L = \mathbf{W}_{N-L+1}^{\top}$ (with $L = N / 2 + 1, \ldots, N$).

For example, here is the same autoencoder as the previous one, except the decoder weights are tied to the encoder weights:

```
import torch.nn.functional as F

class TiedAutoencoder(nn.Module):
    def __init__(self):
        super().__init__()
        self.enc1 = nn.Linear(1 * 28 * 28, 128)
        self.enc2 = nn.Linear(128, 32)
        self.dec1_bias = nn.Parameter(torch.zeros(128))
        self.dec2_bias = nn.Parameter(torch.zeros(1 * 28 * 28))

    def encode(self, X):
        Z = X.view(-1, 1 * 28 * 28)  # flatten
        Z = F.relu(self.enc1(Z))
        return F.relu(self.enc2(Z))

    def decode(self, X):
        Z = F.relu(F.linear(X, self.enc2.weight.t(), self.dec1_bias))
        Z = F.sigmoid(F.linear(Z, self.enc1.weight.t(), self.dec2_bias))
        return Z.view(-1, 1, 28, 28)  # unflatten

    def forward(self, X):
        return self.decode(self.encode(X))
```

This model achieves a smaller reconstruction error than the previous model, using about half the number of parameters.

Training One Autoencoder at a Time

Rather than training the whole stacked autoencoder in one go like we just did, it is possible to train one shallow autoencoder at a time, then stack all of them into a single stacked autoencoder (hence the name), as shown in Figure 18-8. This technique is called *greedy layerwise training*.

During the first phase of training, the first autoencoder learns to reconstruct the inputs. Then we encode the whole training set using this first autoencoder, and this gives us a new (compressed) training set. We then train a second autoencoder on this new dataset. This is the second phase of training. Finally, we build a big sandwich using all these autoencoders, as shown in Figure 18-8 (i.e., we first stack the encoder layers of each autoencoder, then the decoder layers in reverse order). This gives us the final stacked autoencoder. We could easily train more autoencoders this way, building a very deep stacked autoencoder.

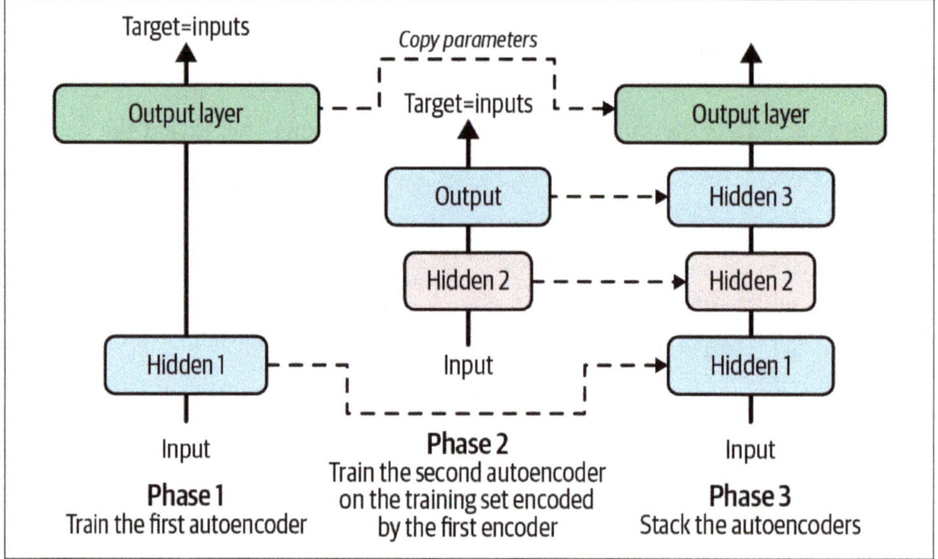

Figure 18-8. Training one autoencoder at a time

As I mentioned in Chapter 11, one of the triggers of the deep learning tsunami was the discovery in 2006 by Geoffrey Hinton et al. (*https://homl.info/136*) that deep neural networks can be pretrained in an unsupervised fashion using this greedy layer-wise approach. They used restricted Boltzmann machines (RBMs; see *https://homl.info/extra-anns*) for this purpose, but in 2007 Yoshua Bengio et al. (*https://homl.info/112*)[3] showed that autoencoders worked just as well. For several years this was the only efficient way to train deep nets, until many of the techniques introduced in Chapter 11 made it possible to just train a deep net in one shot.

Autoencoders are not limited to dense networks: you can also build convolutional autoencoders. Let's look at these now.

Convolutional Autoencoders

If you are dealing with images, then the autoencoders we have seen so far will not work well (unless the images are very small). As you saw in Chapter 12, convolutional neural networks are far better suited than dense networks to working with images. So if you want to build an autoencoder for images (e.g., for unsupervised pretraining or dimensionality reduction), you will need to build a *convolutional autoencoder* (*https://homl.info/convae*).[4] The encoder is a regular CNN composed of convolutional

3 Yoshua Bengio et al., "Greedy Layer-Wise Training of Deep Networks", *Proceedings of the 19th International Conference on Neural Information Processing Systems* (2006): 153–160.

layers and pooling layers. It typically reduces the spatial dimensionality of the inputs (i.e., height and width) while increasing the depth (i.e., the number of feature maps). The decoder must do the reverse (upscale the image and reduce its depth back to the original dimensions), and for this you can use transpose convolutional layers (alternatively, you could combine upsampling layers with convolutional layers). Here is a basic convolutional autoencoder for Fashion MNIST:

```
conv_encoder = nn.Sequential(
    nn.Conv2d(1, 16, kernel_size=3, padding="same"), nn.ReLU(),
    nn.MaxPool2d(kernel_size=2),  # output: 16 × 14 × 14
    nn.Conv2d(16, 32, kernel_size=3, padding="same"), nn.ReLU(),
    nn.MaxPool2d(kernel_size=2),  # output: 32 × 7 × 7
    nn.Conv2d(32, 64, kernel_size=3, padding="same"), nn.ReLU(),
    nn.MaxPool2d(kernel_size=2),  # output: 64 × 3 × 3
    nn.Conv2d(64, 32, kernel_size=3, padding="same"), nn.ReLU(),
    nn.AdaptiveAvgPool2d((1, 1)), nn.Flatten())  # output: 32

conv_decoder = nn.Sequential(
    nn.Linear(32, 16 * 3 * 3),
    nn.Unflatten(dim=1, unflattened_size=(16, 3, 3)),
    nn.ConvTranspose2d(16, 32, kernel_size=3, stride=2), nn.ReLU(),
    nn.ConvTranspose2d(32, 16, kernel_size=3, stride=2, padding=1,
                       output_padding=1), nn.ReLU(),
    nn.ConvTranspose2d(16, 1, kernel_size=3, stride=2, padding=1,
                       output_padding=1), nn.Sigmoid())

conv_ae = nn.Sequential(conv_encoder, conv_decoder).to(device)
```

It's also possible to create autoencoders with other architecture types, such as RNNs (see the notebook for an example).

OK, let's step back for a second. So far we have looked at various kinds of autoencoders (basic, stacked, and convolutional) and how to train them (either in one shot or layer by layer). We also looked at a few applications: dimensionality reduction (e.g., for data visualization), anomaly detection, and unsupervised pretraining.

Up to now, in order to force the autoencoder to learn interesting features, we have limited the size of the coding layer, making it undercomplete. There are actually many other kinds of constraints that can be used, including ones that allow the coding layer to be just as large as the inputs, or even larger, resulting in an *overcomplete autoencoder*. So in the following sections we'll look at a few more kinds of autoencoders: denoising autoencoders, sparse autoencoders, and variational autoencoders.

4 Jonathan Masci et al., "Stacked Convolutional Auto-Encoders for Hierarchical Feature Extraction", *Proceedings of the 21st International Conference on Artificial Neural Networks* 1 (2011): 52–59.

Denoising Autoencoders

A simple way to force the autoencoder to learn useful features is to add noise to its inputs, training it to recover the original, noise-free inputs. This idea has been around since the 1980s (e.g., it is mentioned in Yann LeCun's 1987 master's thesis). In a 2008 paper (*https://homl.info/113*),[5] Pascal Vincent et al. showed that autoencoders could also be used for feature extraction. In a 2010 paper (*https://homl.info/114*),[6] Vincent et al. introduced *stacked denoising autoencoders*.

The noise can be pure Gaussian noise added to the inputs, or it can be randomly switched-off inputs, just like in dropout (introduced in Chapter 11). Figure 18-9 shows both options.

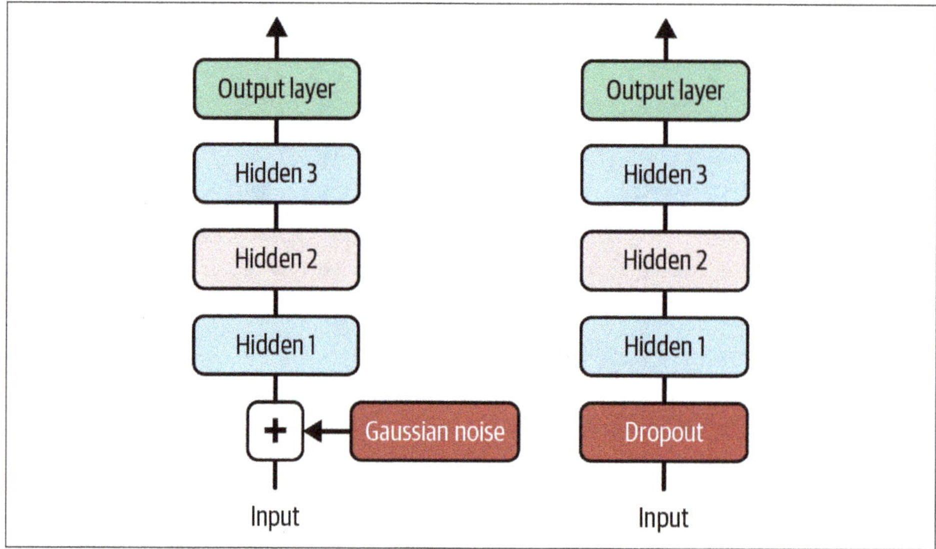

Figure 18-9. Denoising autoencoders, with Gaussian noise (left) or dropout (right)

The dropout implementation of the denoising autoencoder is straightforward: it is a regular stacked autoencoder with an additional `Dropout` layer applied to the encoder's inputs (recall that the `Dropout` layer is only active during training). Note that the coding layer does not need to compress the data as much since the noise already makes the reconstruction task nontrivial:

5 Pascal Vincent et al., "Extracting and Composing Robust Features with Denoising Autoencoders", *Proceedings of the 25th International Conference on Machine Learning* (2008): 1096–1103.

6 Pascal Vincent et al., "Stacked Denoising Autoencoders: Learning Useful Representations in a Deep Network with a Local Denoising Criterion", *Journal of Machine Learning Research* 11 (2010): 3371–3408.

```
dropout_encoder = nn.Sequential(
    nn.Flatten(),
    nn.Dropout(0.5),
    nn.Linear(1 * 28 * 28, 128), nn.ReLU(),
    nn.Linear(128, 128), nn.ReLU(),
)
dropout_decoder = nn.Sequential(
    nn.Linear(128, 128), nn.ReLU(),
    nn.Linear(128, 1 * 28 * 28), nn.Sigmoid(),
    nn.Unflatten(dim=1, unflattened_size=(1, 28, 28))
)
dropout_ae = nn.Sequential(dropout_encoder, dropout_decoder).to(device)
```

This may remind you of BERT's MLM pretraining task (see Chapter 15): reconstructing masked inputs (except BERT isn't split into an encoder and a decoder).

Figure 18-10 shows a few noisy images (with half of the pixels turned off), and the images reconstructed by the dropout-based denoising autoencoder, after training. Notice how the autoencoder guesses details that are actually not in the input, such as the top of the rightmost shoe. As you can see, not only can denoising autoencoders be used for data visualization or unsupervised pretraining, like the other autoencoders we've discussed so far, but they can also be used quite simply and efficiently to remove noise from images.

Figure 18-10. Noisy images (top) and their reconstructions (bottom)

Sparse Autoencoders

Another kind of constraint that often leads to good feature extraction is *sparsity*: by adding an appropriate term to the cost function, the autoencoder is pushed to reduce the number of active neurons in the coding layer. This forces the autoencoder to represent each input as a combination of a small number of activations. As a result, each neuron in the coding layer typically ends up representing a useful feature (if you could speak only a few words per month, you would probably try to make them worth listening to).

A basic approach is to use the sigmoid activation function in the coding layer (to constrain the codings to values between 0 and 1), use a large coding layer (e.g., with 256 units), and add some ℓ_1 regularization to the coding layer's activations. This means adding the ℓ_1 norm of the codings (i.e., the sum of their absolute values) to the loss, weighted by a sparsity hyperparameter. This *sparsity loss* will encourage the neural network to produce codings close to 0. However, the total loss will still include the reconstruction loss, so the model will be forced to output at least a few nonzero values to reconstruct the inputs correctly. Using the ℓ_1 norm rather than the ℓ_2 norm will push the neural network to preserve the most important codings while eliminating the ones that are not needed for the input image (rather than just reducing all codings).

Another approach—which often yields better results—is to measure the mean sparsity of each neuron in the coding layer, across each training batch, and penalize the model when the mean sparsity differs from the target sparsity (e.g., 10%). The batch size must not be too small, or the mean will not be accurate. For example, if we measure that a neuron has an average activation of 0.3, but the target sparsity is 0.1, then this neuron must be penalized to activate less. One approach could be simply adding the squared error $(0.3 - 0.1)^2$ to the loss function, but in practice it's better to use the Kullback–Leibler (KL) divergence (briefly discussed in Chapter 4), since it has much stronger gradients than the mean squared error, as you can see in Figure 18-11.

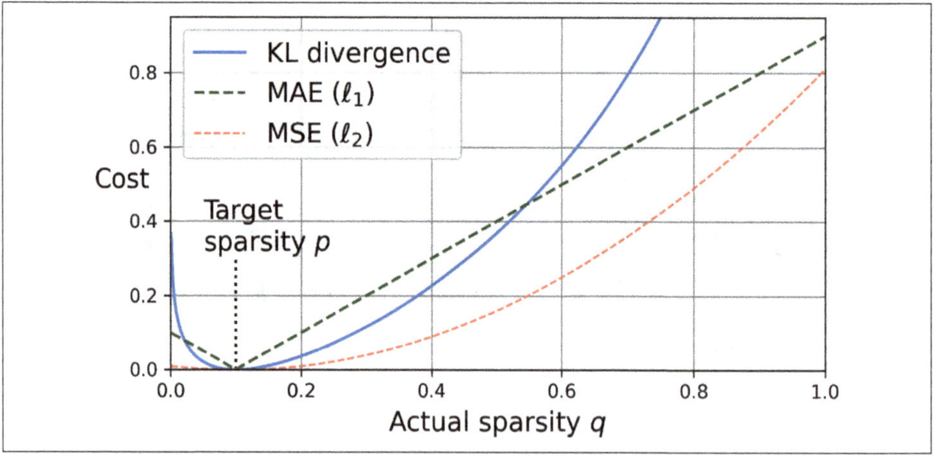

Figure 18-11. Sparsity loss with target sparsity p = 0.1

Given two discrete probability distributions P and Q, the KL divergence between these distributions, noted $D_{KL}(P \parallel Q)$, can be computed using Equation 18-1.

Equation 18-1. Kullback–Leibler divergence

$$D_{\mathrm{KL}}(P \parallel Q) = \sum_i P(i) \log \frac{P(i)}{Q(i)}$$

In our case, we want to measure the divergence between the target probability p that a neuron in the coding layer will activate, and the actual probability q, estimated by measuring the mean activation over the training batch. So, the KL divergence simplifies to Equation 18-2.

Equation 18-2. KL divergence between the target sparsity p and the actual sparsity q

$$D_{\mathrm{KL}}(p \parallel q) = p \log \frac{p}{q} + (1-p) \log \frac{1-p}{1-q}$$

To implement this approach in PyTorch, we must first ensure that the autoencoder outputs both the reconstructions and the codings, since they are both needed to compute the loss. In this code, the autoencoder's `forward()` method returns a `namedtuple` containing two fields—`output` (i.e., the reconstructions) and `codings`:

```
from collections import namedtuple

AEOutput = namedtuple("AEOutput", ["output", "codings"])

class SparseAutoencoder(nn.Module):
    def __init__(self):
        super().__init__()
        self.encoder = nn.Sequential(
            nn.Flatten(),
            nn.Linear(1 * 28 * 28, 128), nn.ReLU(),
            nn.Linear(128, 256), nn.Sigmoid())
        self.decoder = nn.Sequential(
            nn.Linear(256, 128), nn.ReLU(),
            nn.Linear(128, 1 * 28 * 28), nn.Sigmoid(),
            nn.Unflatten(dim=1, unflattened_size=(1, 28, 28)))

    def forward(self, X):
        codings = self.encoder(X)
        output = self.decoder(codings)
        return AEOutput(output, codings)
```

You may need to tweak your training and evaluation functions to support these `namedtuple` predictions. For example, you can add `y_pred = y_pred.output` in the `evaluate_tm()` function, just after calling the model.

Next, we can define the loss function:

```
def mse_plus_sparsity_loss(y_pred, y_target, target_sparsity=0.1,
                           kl_weight=1e-3, eps=1e-8):
    p = torch.tensor(target_sparsity, device=y_pred.codings.device)
    q = torch.clamp(y_pred.codings.mean(dim=0), eps, 1 - eps)  # actual sparsity
    kl_div = p * torch.log(p / q) + (1 - p) * torch.log((1 - p) / (1 - q))
    return mse(y_pred.output, y_target) + kl_weight * kl_div.sum()
```

This function returns the reconstruction loss (MSE) plus a weighted sparsity loss. The sparsity loss is the KL divergence between the target sparsity and the mean sparsity across the batch. The `kl_weight` is a hyperparameter you can tune to control how much to encourage sparsity: if this hyperparameter is too high, the model will stick closely to the target sparsity, but it may not reconstruct the inputs properly, making the model useless. Conversely, if it is too low, the model will mostly ignore the sparsity objective and will not learn any interesting features. The `eps` argument is a smoothing term to avoid division by zero when computing the KL divergence.

Now we're ready to create the model and train it (using the same `train()` function as earlier, from Chapter 10):

```
torch.manual_seed(42)
sparse_ae = SparseAutoencoder().to(device)
optimizer = torch.optim.NAdam(sparse_ae.parameters(), lr=0.002)
train(sparse_ae, optimizer, mse_plus_sparsity_loss, train_loader, n_epochs=10)
```

After training this sparse autoencoder on Fashion MNIST, the coding layer will have roughly 10% sparsity. Success!

Sparse autoencoders often produce fairly interpretable codings, where each component corresponds to an identifiable feature in the image. For example, you can plot all the images whose n^{th} coding is larger than usual (e.g., above the 90th percentile): you will often notice that all the images have something in common (e.g., they are all shoes).

Now let's move on to variational autoencoders!

Variational Autoencoders

An important category of autoencoders was introduced in 2013 by Diederik Kingma and Max Welling (*https://homl.info/115*)[7] and quickly became one of the most popular variants: *variational autoencoders* (VAEs).

VAEs are quite different from all the autoencoders we have discussed so far, in these particular ways:

- They are *probabilistic autoencoders*, meaning that their outputs are partly determined by chance, even after training (as opposed to denoising autoencoders, which use randomness only during training).
- Most importantly, they are *generative autoencoders*, meaning that they can generate new instances that look like they were sampled from the training set.[8]

Let's take a look at how VAEs work. Figure 18-12 (left) shows a variational autoencoder. You can recognize the basic sandwich-like structure of most autoencoders, with an encoder followed by a decoder (in this example, they both have two hidden layers), but there is a twist: instead of directly producing a coding for a given input, the encoder produces a *mean coding* $\boldsymbol{\mu}$ and a standard deviation $\boldsymbol{\sigma}$. The actual coding is then sampled randomly from a Gaussian distribution with mean $\boldsymbol{\mu}$ and standard deviation $\boldsymbol{\sigma}$. After that, the decoder decodes the sampled coding normally. The right part of the diagram shows a training instance going through this autoencoder. First, the encoder produces $\boldsymbol{\mu}$ and $\boldsymbol{\sigma}$, then a coding is sampled randomly (notice that it is not exactly located at $\boldsymbol{\mu}$), and finally this coding is decoded. The final output resembles the training instance.

As you can see in Figure 18-12, although the inputs may have a very convoluted distribution, a variational autoencoder tends to produce codings that look as though they were sampled from a simple Gaussian distribution. During training, the cost function (discussed next) pushes the codings to gradually migrate within the coding space (also called the *latent space*) to end up looking like a cloud of multidimensional Gaussian points. One great consequence is that after training a variational autoencoder, you can very easily generate a new instance: just sample a random coding from the Gaussian distribution, decode it, and voilà!

7 Diederik Kingma and Max Welling, "Auto-Encoding Variational Bayes", arXiv preprint arXiv:1312.6114 (2013).

8 Both these properties make VAEs rather similar to RBMs, but they are easier to train, and the sampling process is much faster (with RBMs you need to wait for the network to stabilize into a "thermal equilibrium" before you can sample a new instance).

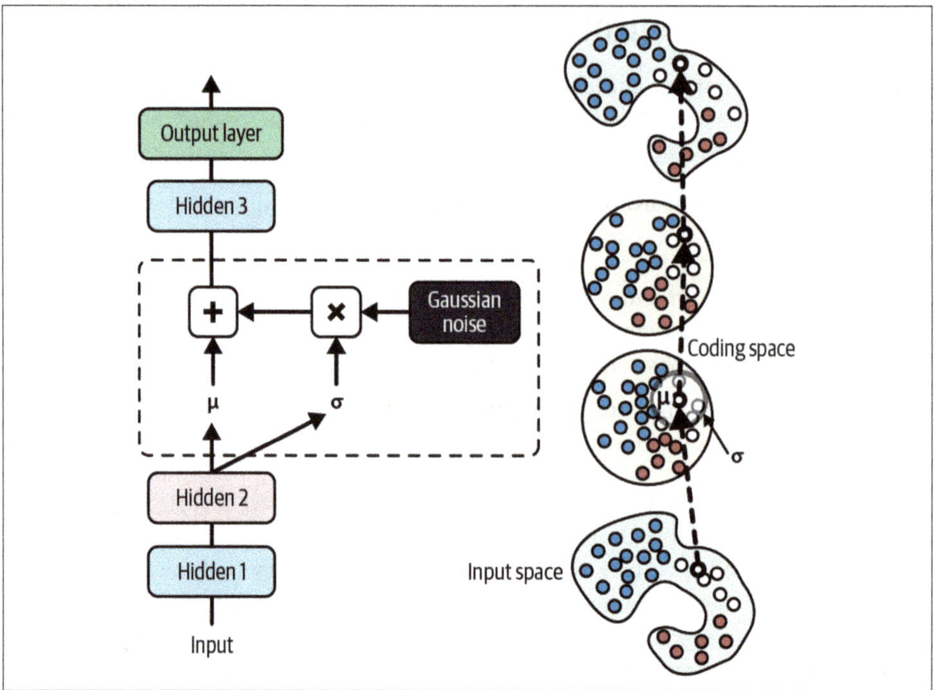

Figure 18-12. A variational autoencoder (left) and an instance going through it (right)

Sampling from a random distribution is not a differentiable operation, it will block backpropagation, so how can we hope to train the encoder? Well, using a *reparameterization trick*: sample $\boldsymbol{\varepsilon}$ from $\mathcal{N}(0, 1)$ and compute $\boldsymbol{\mu} + \boldsymbol{\sigma} \otimes \boldsymbol{\varepsilon}$ (element-wise multiplication). This is equivalent to sampling from $\mathcal{N}(\boldsymbol{\mu}, \boldsymbol{\sigma}^2)$ but it separates the deterministic and stochastic parts of the process, allowing the gradients to flow back into the encoder through $\boldsymbol{\mu}$ and $\boldsymbol{\sigma}$. The resulting encoder gradients are stochastic (due to $\boldsymbol{\varepsilon}$), but they are unbiased estimates, and the randomness averages out during training.

The cost function is composed of two parts. The first is the usual reconstruction loss that pushes the autoencoder to reproduce its inputs. We can use the MSE for this, as we did earlier. The second is the *latent loss* that pushes the autoencoder to have codings that look as though they were sampled from a simple Gaussian distribution: it is the KL divergence between the actual distribution of the codings and the desired latent distribution (i.e., the Gaussian distribution). The math is a bit more complex than with the sparse autoencoder, in particular because of the Gaussian noise, which limits the amount of information that can be transmitted to the coding layer. Luckily, the equations simplify, so the latent loss can be computed using Equation 18-3 (for the full mathematical details, check out the original paper on variational autoencoders, or Carl Doersch's great 2016 tutorial (*https://homl.info/vaetuto*).)

Equation 18-3. Variational autoencoder's latent loss

$$\mathscr{L} = -\frac{1}{2}\sum_{i=1}^{n}\left[1 + \log\left(\sigma_i^2\right) - \sigma_i^2 - \mu_i^2\right]$$

In this equation, $\mathscr{L}$ is the latent loss, n is the codings' dimensionality, and μ_i and σ_i are the mean and standard deviation of the ith component of the codings. The vectors $\boldsymbol{\mu}$ and $\boldsymbol{\sigma}$ (which contain all the μ_i and σ_i) are output by the encoder, as shown in Figure 18-12 (left).

A common tweak to the variational autoencoder's architecture is to make the encoder output $\boldsymbol{\gamma} = \log(\boldsymbol{\sigma}^2)$ rather than $\boldsymbol{\sigma}$. The latent loss can then be computed as shown in Equation 18-4. This approach is more numerically stable and speeds up training.

Equation 18-4. Variational autoencoder's latent loss, rewritten using $\boldsymbol{\gamma} = \log(\boldsymbol{\sigma}^2)$

$$\mathscr{L} = -\frac{1}{2}\sum_{i=1}^{n}\left[1 + \gamma_i - \exp(\gamma_i) - \mu_i^2\right]$$

Let's build a variational autoencoder for Fashion MNIST, using the architecture shown in Figure 18-12, except using the $\boldsymbol{\gamma}$ tweak:

```
VAEOutput = namedtuple("VAEOutput",
                       ["output", "codings_mean", "codings_logvar"])

class VAE(nn.Module):
    def __init__(self, codings_dim=32):
        super(VAE, self).__init__()
        self.codings_dim = codings_dim
        self.encoder = nn.Sequential(
            nn.Flatten(),
            nn.Linear(1 * 28 * 28, 128), nn.ReLU(),
            nn.Linear(128, 2 * codings_dim))  # output both the mean and logvar
        self.decoder = nn.Sequential(
            nn.Linear(codings_dim, 128), nn.ReLU(),
            nn.Linear(128, 1 * 28 * 28), nn.Sigmoid(),
            nn.Unflatten(dim=1, unflattened_size=(1, 28, 28)))

    def encode(self, X):
        return self.encoder(X).chunk(2, dim=-1)  # returns (mean, logvar)

    def sample_codings(self, codings_mean, codings_logvar):
        codings_std = torch.exp(0.5 * codings_logvar)
        noise = torch.randn_like(codings_std)
        return codings_mean + noise * codings_std
```

```
    def decode(self, Z):
        return self.decoder(Z)

    def forward(self, X):
        codings_mean, codings_logvar = self.encode(X)
        codings = self.sample_codings(codings_mean, codings_logvar)
        output = self.decode(codings)
        return VAEOutput(output, codings_mean, codings_logvar)
```

Let's go through this code:

- First, we define `VAEOutput`. This allows the model to output a `namedtuple` containing the reconstructions (`output`) as well as **μ** (`codings_mean`) and **γ** (`codings_logvar`).
- The encoder and decoder architectures strongly resemble the previous autoencoders, but notice that the encoder's output is twice the size of the codings. This is because the encoder does not directly output the codings; instead, it outputs the parameters of the Gaussian distribution from which the codings will be sampled: the mean (**μ**) and the logarithm of the variance (**γ**).
- The `encode()` method calls the `encoder` model and splits the output in two, using the `chunk()` method, to obtain **μ** and **γ**.
- The `sample_codings()` method takes **μ** and **γ** and samples the actual codings. For this, it first computes `torch.exp(0.5 * codings_logvar)` to get the codings' standard deviation **σ** (you can verify that this works mathematically). Then it uses the `torch.randn_like()` function to sample a random vector of the same shape as **σ** from the Gaussian distribution with mean 0 and standard deviation 1, on the same device and with the same data type. Lastly, it multiplies this Gaussian noise by **σ**, adds **μ**, and returns the result. This is the reparameterization trick we discussed earlier.
- The `decode()` method simply calls the decoder model to produce the reconstructions.
- The `forward()` method calls the encoder to get **μ** and **γ**, then it uses these parameters to sample the codings, which it decodes, and finally it returns a `VAEOutput` containing the reconstructions and the parameters **μ** and **γ**, which are all needed to compute the VAE loss.

Speaking of which, let's now define the loss function, which is the sum of the reconstruction loss (MSE) and the latent loss (KL divergence):

```python
def vae_loss(y_pred, y_target, kl_weight=1.0):
    output, mean, logvar = y_pred
    kl_div = -0.5 * torch.sum(1 + logvar - logvar.exp() - mean.square(), dim=-1)
    return F.mse_loss(output, y_target) + kl_weight * kl_div.mean() / 784
```

The function first uses Equation 18-4 to compute the latent loss (`kl_div`) for each instance in the batch (by summing over the last dimension), then it computes the mean latent loss over all the instances in the batch (`kl_div.mean()`). Note that the reconstruction loss is the mean over all instances in the batch *and* all 784 pixels: this is why we divide the latent loss by 784 to ensure that the reconstruction loss and the latent loss have the same scale.

Finally, we can train the model on the Fashion MNIST dataset:

```python
torch.manual_seed(42)
vae = VAE().to(device)
optimizer = torch.optim.NAdam(vae.parameters(), lr=1e-3)
train(vae, optimizer, vae_loss, train_loader, n_epochs=20)
```

Generating Fashion MNIST Images

Now let's use this VAE to generate images that look like fashion items. All we need to do is sample random codings from a Gaussian distribution with mean 0 and variance 1, and decode them:

```python
torch.manual_seed(42)
vae.eval()
codings = torch.randn(3 * 7, vae.codings_dim, device=device)
with torch.no_grad():
    images = vae.decode(codings)
```

Figure 18-13 shows the 21 generated images.

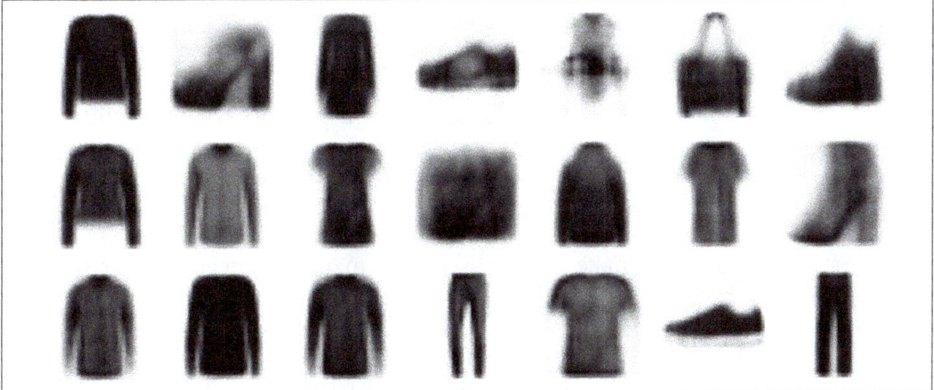

Figure 18-13. Fashion MNIST images generated by the variational autoencoder

The majority of these images look fairly convincing, if a bit too fuzzy. The rest are not great, but don't be too harsh on the autoencoder—it only had a few minutes to learn, and you would get much better results by using convolutional layers!

Variational autoencoders make it possible to perform *semantic interpolation*: instead of interpolating between two images at the pixel level, which would look as if the two images were just overlaid, we can interpolate at the codings level. For example, if we sample two random codings and interpolate between them, then decode all of the interpolated codings, we get a sequence of images that gradually go from one fashion item to another (see Figure 18-14):

```
codings = torch.randn(2, vae.codings_dim)  # start and end codings
n_images = 7
weights = torch.linspace(0, 1, n_images).view(n_images, 1)
codings = torch.lerp(codings[0], codings[1], weights)  # linear interpolation
with torch.no_grad():
    images = vae.decode(codings.to(device))
```

Figure 18-14. Semantic interpolation

There are a few variants of VAEs, for example, with different distributions for the latent variables. One important variant is discrete VAEs: let's discuss them now.

Discrete Variational Autoencoders

A *discrete VAE* (dVAE) is much like a VAE, except the codings are discrete rather than continuous: each coding vector contains *latent codes* (also called *categories*), each of which is an integer between 0 and $k - 1$, where k is the number of possible latent codes. The length of the coding vector is often denoted as d. For example, if you choose $k = 10$ and $d = 6$, then there are one million possible coding vectors (10^6), such as [3, 0, 3, 9, 1, 4]. Discrete VAEs are very useful for tokenizing continuous inputs for transformers and other models. For example, they are at the core of models like BEiT and DALL·E (see Chapter 16).

The most natural way to make VAEs discrete is to use a categorical distribution instead of a Gaussian distribution. This implies a couple of changes:

- First, the encoder must output logits rather than means and variances. For each input image, it outputs a tensor of shape $[d, k]$ containing logits, for example [[1.2, −0.8, 0.5], [−1.3, 0.4, 0.3]] if $d = 2$ and $k = 3$.

- Second, since categorical sampling is not a differentiable operation, we must once again use a reparameterization trick, but we cannot reuse the same as for regular VAEs: we need one designed for categorical distributions. The most popular one is the Gumbel-softmax trick. Instead of directly sampling from the categorical distribution, we call the `F.gumble_softmax()` function: this implements a differentiable approximation of categorical sampling. Given the previous logits, this function might output the discrete coding vector [0, 2].

The Gumbel distribution is used to model the maximum of a set of samples from another distribution. For example, it can be used to estimate the probability that a river will overflow within the next 10 years. If you add Gumbel noise to the logits, then take the argmax of the result, it is mathematically equivalent to categorical sampling. However, the argmax operation is not differentiable, so we replace it with the softmax during the backward pass: this gives us a differentiable approximation of categorical sampling.

This idea was proposed in 2016 almost simultaneously by two independent teams of researchers, one from DeepMind and Oxford University (*https://homl.info/dvae1*),[9] the other from Google, Cambridge University, and Stanford University (*https://homl.info/dvae2*).[10]

Let's implement a dVAE for Fashion MNIST:

```
DiscreteVAEOutput = namedtuple("DiscreteVAEOutput",
                               ["output", "logits", "codings_prob"])

class DiscreteVAE(nn.Module):
    def __init__(self, coding_length=32, n_codes=16, temperature=1.0):
        super().__init__()
        self.coding_length = coding_length
        self.n_codes = n_codes
        self.temperature = temperature
        self.encoder = nn.Sequential([...])  # outputs [coding_length, n_codes]
        self.decoder = nn.Sequential([...])  # outputs [1, 28, 28]

    def forward(self, X):
        logits = self.encoder(X)
        codings_prob = F.gumbel_softmax(logits, tau=self.temperature, hard=True)
        output = self.decoder(codings_prob)
        return DiscreteVAEOutput(output, logits, codings_prob)
```

9 Chris J. Maddison et al., "The Concrete Distribution: A Continuous Relaxation of Discrete Random Variables", arXiv preprint arXiv:1611.00712 (2016).

10 Eric Jang et al., "Categorical Reparameterization with Gumbel-Softmax", arXiv preprint arXiv:1611.01144 (2016).

As you can see, this code is very similar to the VAE code. Note that we set `hard=True` when calling the `F.gumbel_softmax()` function to ensure that the forward pass uses Gumbel-argmax (to obtain one-hot vectors of the sampled codes), while the backward pass uses the Gumbel-softmax approximation. Also note that we pass a temperature (a scalar) to this function: the logits will be divided by this temperature before calling the softmax function. The lower the temperature is, the closer the output distribution will be to one-hot vectors (this only affects the backward pass). In general, we use a temperature of 1 at the beginning of training, then gradually reduce it during training, down to a small value such as 0.1.

The loss function is also similar to the regular VAE loss: it's the sum of a reconstruction loss (MSE) and a weighted latent loss (KL divergence). However, the KL divergence equation is a bit different since the latent distribution has changed. It's now a uniform categorical distribution, where all possible codes are equally likely, so they each have a probability of 1 / *k*. Since log(1 / *k*) = –log(*k*), we can add log(*k*) instead of subtracting log(1 / *k*) in the KL divergence equation:

```
def d_vae_loss(y_pred, y_target, kl_weight=1.0):
    output, logits, _ = y_pred
    codings_prob = F.softmax(logits, -1)
    k = logits.new_tensor(logits.size(-1))  # same device and dtype as logits
    kl_div = (codings_prob * (codings_prob.log() + k.log())).sum(dim=(1, 2))
    return F.mse_loss(output, y_target) + kl_weight * kl_div.mean() / 784
```

You can now train the model. Remember to update your training loop to reduce the temperature gradually during training, for example:

```
model.temperature = 1 - 0.9 * epoch / n_epochs
```

Once the model is trained, you can generate new images by sampling random codings from a uniform distribution, one-hot encoding them, then decoding the resulting one-hot distribution:

```
codings = torch.randint(0, d_vae.n_codes,  # from 0 to k - 1
                        (n_images, d_vae.coding_length), device=device)
codings_prob = F.one_hot(codings, num_classes=d_vae.n_codes).float()
with torch.no_grad():
    images = d_vae.decoder(codings_prob)
```

Another popular approach to discrete VAEs is called *vector quantization* (VQ-VAE), proposed by DeepMind researchers in 2017 (*https://homl.info/vqvae*).[11] Instead of producing logits, the encoder outputs *d* embeddings, each of dimensionality *e*. Then instead of sampling from a categorical distribution, the VQ-VAE maps each embedding to the index of the nearest embedding in a trainable embedding matrix of shape

11 Aaron van den Oord et al., "Neural Discrete Representation Learning", arXiv preprint arXiv:1711.00937 (2017).

[k, e], called the *codebook*. This produces the integer codes. Finally, these codes are embedded using the embedding matrix and passed on to the decoder.

Since replacing an embedding with the nearest codebook embedding is not a differentiable operation, the backward pass pretends that the codebook lookup step is the identity function, so the gradients just go straight through this operation: this is why this trick is called the *straight-through estimator* (STE). It's an approximation that assumes that the gradients around the encoder embeddings are similar to the gradients around the nearest codebook embeddings.

VQ-VAEs can be a bit tricky to implement correctly, but you can use a library like *https://github.com/lucidrains/vector-quantize-pytorch*. On the positive side, training is more stable, and the codes are a bit easier to interpret.

Discrete VAEs work pretty well for small images, but not so much for large images: the small-scale features may look good, but there will often be large-scale inconsistencies. To improve on this, you can use the trained dVAE to encode your whole training set (so each instance becomes a sequence of integers), then use this new training set to train a transformer: just treat the codes as tokens, and train the transformer using next-token prediction. Intuitively, the dVAE learns the vocabulary, while the transformer learns the grammar. Once the transformer is trained, you can generate a new image by first generating a sequence of codes using the transformer, then passing this sequence to the dVAE's decoder.

This two-stage approach also makes it easier to control the image generation process: when training the transformer, a textual description of the image can be fed to the transformer, for example as a prefix to the sequence of codes. We say that the transformer is *conditioned* on the description, which helps it predict the correct next code. This way, after training, we can guide the image generation process by providing a description of the image we desire. The transformer will use this description to generate the appropriate sequence of codes. This is exactly how the first DALL·E system worked.

In practice, the encoder and decoder are usually convolutional networks, so the latent representation is often organized as a grid (but it's still flattened to a sequence to train the transformer). For example, the encoder may output a tensor of shape [256, 32, 32]: that's a 32 × 32 grid containing 256-dimensional embeddings in each cell (or 256 logits in the case of Gumbel-Softmax dVAEs). After mapping these embeddings to the indices of the nearest embeddings in the codebook (or after categorical sampling), each image is represented as a 32 × 32 grid of integers (codes), with codes ranging between 0 and 255. To generate a new image, you use the transformer to predict a sequence of 1,024 codes, organize them into a 32 × 32 grid, replace each code with its codebook vector, then pass the result to the decoder to generate the final image.

To improve the image quality, you can also stack two or more dVAEs, each producing a smaller grid than the previous one: this is called a *hierarchical VAE* (HVAE). The encoders are stacked, followed by the decoders in reverse order, and all are trained jointly. The loss is the sum of a single reconstruction loss plus multiple KL divergence losses (one per dVAE).

Let's now turn our attention to GANs. They are harder to train, but when you manage to get them to work, they produce pretty amazing images.

Generative Adversarial Networks

Generative adversarial networks were proposed in a 2014 paper (*https://homl.info/gan*)[12] by Ian Goodfellow et al., and although the idea got researchers excited almost instantly, it took a few years to overcome some of the difficulties of training GANs. Like many great ideas, it seems simple in hindsight: make neural networks compete against each other in the hope that this competition will push them to excel. As shown in Figure 18-15, a GAN is composed of two neural networks:

Generator
: Takes a random coding as input (typically sampled from a Gaussian distribution) and outputs some data—typically, an image. The coding is the latent representation of the image to be generated. So, as you can see, the generator offers the same functionality as a decoder in a variational autoencoder, and it can be used in the same way to generate new images: just feed it a random vector, and it outputs a brand-new image. However, it is trained very differently, as you will soon see.

Discriminator
: Takes either a fake image from the generator or a real image from the training set as input, and must guess whether the input image is fake or real.

12 Ian Goodfellow et al., "Generative Adversarial Nets", *Proceedings of the 27th International Conference on Neural Information Processing Systems* 2 (2014): 2672–2680.

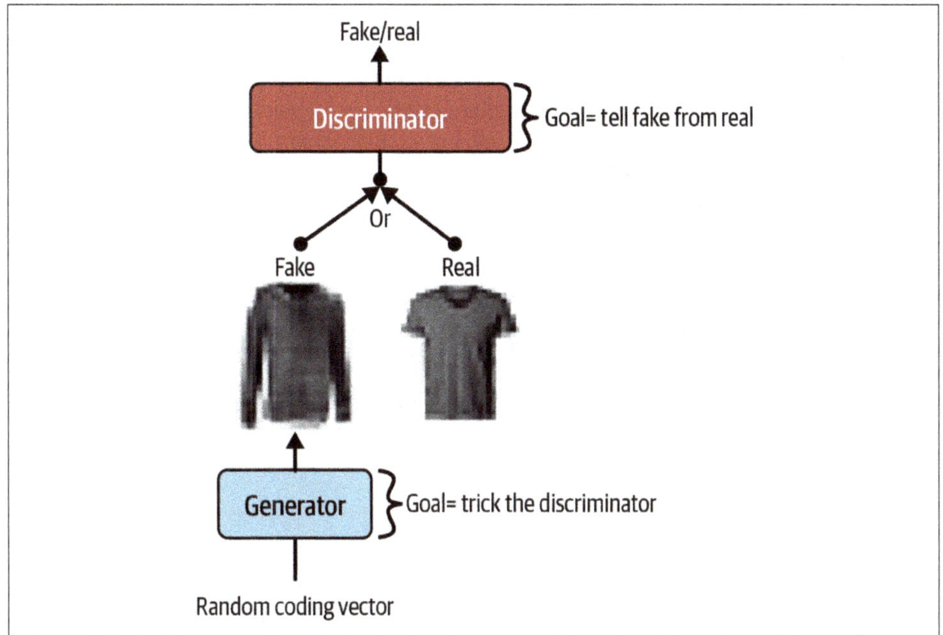

Figure 18-15. A generative adversarial network

During training, the generator and the discriminator have opposite goals: the discriminator tries to tell fake images from real images, while the generator tries to produce images that look real enough to trick the discriminator. Because the GAN is composed of two networks with different objectives, it cannot be trained like a regular neural network. Each training iteration is divided into two phases:

First phase: train the discriminator
: A batch of real images is sampled from the training set and is completed with an equal number of fake images produced by the generator. The labels are set to 0 for fake images and 1 for real images, and the discriminator is trained on this labeled batch for one step, using the binary cross-entropy loss. Importantly, backpropagation only optimizes the weights of the discriminator during this phase.

Second phase: train the generator
: We first use the generator to produce another batch of fake images, and once again the discriminator is used to tell whether the images are fake or real. This time we do not add real images to the batch, and all the labels are set to 1 (real); in other words, we want the generator to produce images that the discriminator will (wrongly) believe to be real! Crucially, the weights of the discriminator are frozen during this step, so backpropagation only affects the weights of the generator.

The generator never actually sees any real images, yet it gradually learns to produce convincing fake images! All it gets is the gradients flowing back through the discriminator. Fortunately, the better the discriminator gets, the more information about the real images is contained in these secondhand gradients, so the generator can make significant progress.

Let's go ahead and build a simple GAN for Fashion MNIST.

First, we need to build the generator and the discriminator. The generator is similar to an autoencoder's decoder—it takes a coding vector as input and outputs an image—and the discriminator is a regular binary classifier—it takes an image as input and ends with a dense layer containing a single unit and using the sigmoid activation function:

```
codings_dim = 32
generator = nn.Sequential(
    nn.Linear(codings_dim, 128), nn.ReLU(),
    nn.Linear(128, 256), nn.ReLU(),
    nn.Linear(256, 1 * 28 * 28), nn.Sigmoid(),
    nn.Unflatten(dim=1, unflattened_size=(1, 28, 28))).to(device)
discriminator = nn.Sequential(
    nn.Flatten(),
    nn.Linear(1 * 28 * 28, 256), nn.ReLU(),
    nn.Linear(256, 128), nn.ReLU(),
    nn.Linear(128, 1), nn.Sigmoid()).to(device)
```

Since the training loop is unusual, we need a new training function:

```
def train_gan(generator, discriminator, train_loader, codings_dim, n_epochs=20,
              g_lr=1e-3, d_lr=5e-4):
    criterion = nn.BCELoss()
    generator_opt = torch.optim.NAdam(generator.parameters(), lr=g_lr)
    discriminator_opt = torch.optim.NAdam(discriminator.parameters(), lr=d_lr)
    for epoch in range(n_epochs):
        for real_images, _ in train_loader:
            real_images = real_images.to(device)
            pred_real = discriminator(real_images)
            batch_size = real_images.size(0)
            ones = torch.ones(batch_size, 1, device=device)
            real_loss = criterion(pred_real, ones)
            codings = torch.randn(batch_size, codings_dim, device=device)
            fake_images = generator(codings).detach()
            pred_fake = discriminator(fake_images)
            zeros = torch.zeros(batch_size, 1, device=device)
            fake_loss = criterion(pred_fake, zeros)
            discriminator_loss = real_loss + fake_loss
            discriminator_opt.zero_grad()
            discriminator_loss.backward()
```

```
        discriminator_opt.step()

        codings = torch.randn(batch_size, codings_dim, device=device)
        fake_images = generator(codings)
        for p in discriminator.parameters():
            p.requires_grad = False
        pred_fake = discriminator(fake_images)
        generator_loss = criterion(pred_fake, ones)
        generator_opt.zero_grad()
        generator_loss.backward()
        generator_opt.step()
        for p in discriminator.parameters():
            p.requires_grad = True
```

As discussed earlier, you can see the two phases at each iteration: first the discriminator makes a gradient descent step, then it's the generator's turn. We use a separate optimizer for each. Let's look in more detail:

Phase one
: We feed a batch of real images to the discriminator and compute the loss given targets equal to one; indeed, we want the discriminator to predict that these images are real. We then generate some random codings and feed them to the generator to produce some fake images. Note that we call `detach()` on these images because we don't want gradient descent to affect the generator in this phase. Then we pass these fake images to the discriminator and compute the loss given targets equal to zero; we want the discriminator to predict that these images are fake. The total discriminator loss is the `real_loss` plus the `fake_loss`. Finally, we perform the gradient descent step, improving the discriminator.

Phase two
: We generate some fake images using the generator, and we pass them to the discriminator, like we just did. However, this time we don't call `detach()` on the fake images since we want to train the generator. Moreover, we make the discriminator untrainable by setting `p.required_grad = False` for each parameter `p`. We then compute the loss using targets equal to one: indeed, we want the generator to fool the discriminator, so we want the discriminator to wrongly predict that these are real images. And finally, we perform a gradient descent step for the generator, and we make the discriminator trainable again.

That's it! After training, you can randomly sample some codings from a Gaussian distribution and feed them to the generator to produce new images:

```
generator.eval()
codings = torch.randn(n_images, codings_dim, device=device)
with torch.no_grad():
    generated_images = generator(codings)
```

If you display the generated images (see Figure 18-16), you will see that at the end of the first epoch, they already start to look like (very noisy) Fashion MNIST images.

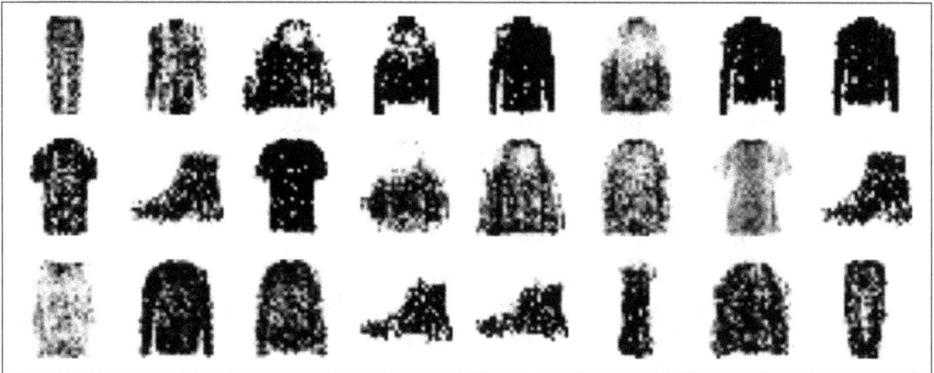

Figure 18-16. Images generated by the GAN after one epoch of training

Unfortunately, the images never really get much better than that, and you may even find epochs where the GAN seems to be forgetting what it learned. Why is that? Well, it turns out that training a GAN can be challenging. Let's see why.

The Difficulties of Training GANs

During training, the generator and the discriminator constantly try to outsmart each other in a zero-sum game. As training advances, the game may end up in a state that game theorists call a *Nash equilibrium*, named after the mathematician John Nash. This occurs when no player would be better off changing their own strategy, assuming the other players do not change theirs. For example, a Nash equilibrium is reached when everyone drives on the left side of the road: no driver would be better off being the only one to switch sides. Of course, there is a second possible Nash equilibrium: when everyone drives on the *right* side of the road. Different initial states and dynamics may lead to one equilibrium or the other. In this example, there is a single optimal strategy once an equilibrium is reached (i.e., driving on the same side as everyone else), but a Nash equilibrium can involve multiple competing strategies (e.g., a predator chases its prey, the prey tries to escape, and neither would be better off changing their strategy).

So how does this apply to GANs? Well, the authors of the GAN paper demonstrated that a GAN can only reach a single Nash equilibrium: that's when the generator produces perfectly realistic images, and the discriminator is forced to guess (50% real, 50% fake). This fact is very encouraging, as it would seem that you just need to train the GAN long enough and it will eventually reach this equilibrium, giving you a perfect generator. Unfortunately, it's not that simple: nothing guarantees that the equilibrium will ever be reached.

The biggest difficulty is called *mode collapse*: when the generator's outputs gradually become less diverse. How can this happen? Suppose the generator gets better at producing convincing shoes than any other class. It will fool the discriminator a bit more with shoes, and this will encourage it to produce even more images of shoes. Gradually, it will forget how to produce anything else. Meanwhile, the only fake images that the discriminator will see will be shoes, so it will also forget how to discriminate fake images of other classes. Eventually, when the discriminator manages to discriminate the fake shoes from the real ones, the generator will be forced to move to another class. It may then become good at shirts, forgetting about shoes, and the discriminator will follow. The GAN may gradually cycle across a few classes, never really becoming very good at any of them (see the top row of Figure 18-17).

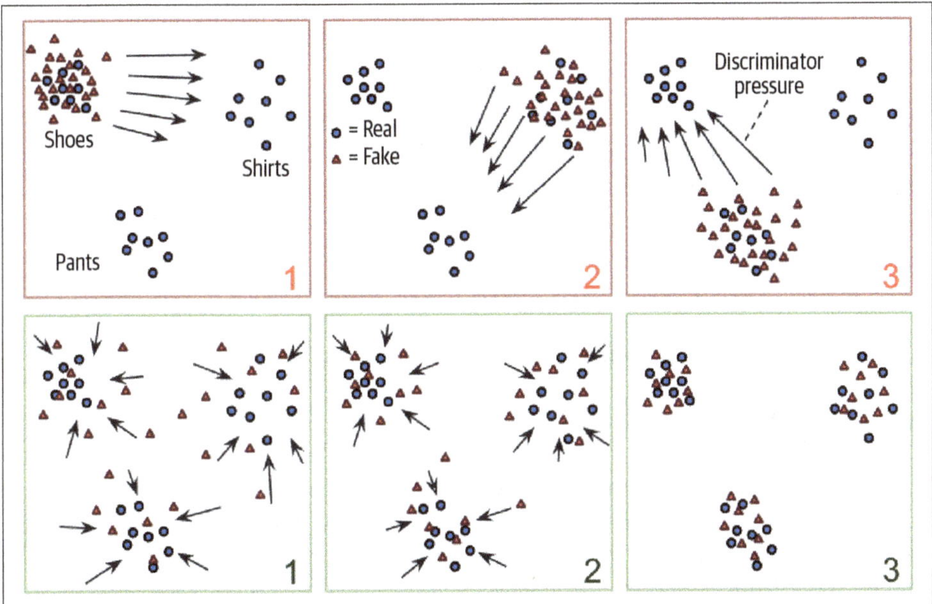

Figure 18-17. Mode collapse while training a GAN (top row) versus successful training without mode collapse (bottom row)

Moreover, because the generator and the discriminator are constantly pushing against each other, their parameters may end up oscillating and becoming unstable. Training may begin properly, then suddenly diverge for no apparent reason due to these instabilities. And since many factors affect these complex dynamics, GANs are very sensitive to the hyperparameters: you may have to spend a lot of effort fine-tuning them.

These problems have kept researchers very busy since 2014. Many papers have been published on this topic, some proposing new cost functions[13] (though a 2018 paper (*https://homl.info/gansequal*)[14] by Google researchers questions their efficiency) or techniques to stabilize training or to avoid the mode collapse issue. For example, a popular technique called *experience replay* consists of storing the images produced by the generator at each iteration in a replay buffer (gradually dropping older generated images) and training the discriminator using real images plus fake images drawn from this buffer (rather than just fake images produced by the current generator). This reduces the chances that the discriminator will overfit the latest generator's outputs. Another common technique is called *mini-batch discrimination*: it measures how similar images are across the batch and provides this statistic to the discriminator, so it can easily reject a whole batch of fake images that lack diversity. This encourages the generator to produce a greater variety of images, reducing the chance of mode collapse (see the bottom row of Figure 18-17).

In short, this was a very active field of research, and much progress was made until quite recently: from *deep Convolutional GANs* (DCGANs) based on convolutional layers (see the notebook for an example), to *progressively growing GANs* that could produce high-resolution images, or *StyleGANs* that gave the user fine-grained control over the image generation process, it seemed like GANs had a bright future ahead of them. But when diffusion models started to produce amazing images as well, with a much more stable training process and more diverse images, GANs were quickly sidelined. So let's now turn our attention to diffusion models.

Diffusion Models

The ideas behind diffusion models have been around for many years, but they were first formalized in their modern form in a 2015 paper (*https://homl.info/diffusion*)[15] by Jascha Sohl-Dickstein et al. from Stanford University and UC Berkeley. The authors applied tools from statistical mechanics to model a diffusion process, similar to a drop of milk diffusing in a cup of tea. The core idea is to train a model to learn the reverse process: start from the completely mixed state and gradually "unmix" the milk from the tea. Using this idea, they obtained promising results in image generation, but since GANs produced more convincing images back then, and they did so much faster, diffusion models did not get as much attention.

13 For a nice comparison of the main GAN losses, check out this great GitHub project by Hwalsuk Lee (*https://homl.info/ganloss*).

14 Mario Lucic et al., "Are GANs Created Equal? A Large-Scale Study", *Proceedings of the 32nd International Conference on Neural Information Processing Systems* (2018): 698–707.

15 Jascha Sohl-Dickstein et al., "Deep Unsupervised Learning using Nonequilibrium Thermodynamics", arXiv preprint arXiv:1503.03585 (2015).

Then, in 2020, Jonathan Ho et al. (*https://homl.info/ddpm*), also from UC Berkeley, managed to build a diffusion model capable of generating highly realistic images, which they called a *denoising diffusion probabilistic model* (DDPM).[16] A few months later, a 2021 paper (*https://homl.info/ddpm2*)[17] by OpenAI researchers Alex Nichol and Prafulla Dhariwal analyzed the DDPM architecture and proposed several improvements that allowed DDPMs to finally beat GANs: not only are DDPMs much easier to train than GANs, but the generated images are more diverse and of even higher quality. The main downside of DDPMs, as you will see, is that they take a very long time to generate images, compared to GANs or VAEs.

So how exactly does a DDPM work? Well, suppose you start with a picture of a cat (like the one in Figure 18-18), noted $\mathbf{x}_0$, and at each time step t you add a little bit of Gaussian noise to the image, with mean 0 and variance β_t (a scalar). This noise is independent for each pixel (using the same mean and variance): we call it *isotropic*. You first obtain the image $\mathbf{x}_1$, then $\mathbf{x}_2$, and so on, until the cat is completely hidden by the noise, impossible to see. The last time step is noted T. In the original DDPM paper, the authors used T = 1,000, and they scheduled the variance β_t in such a way that the cat signal fades linearly between time steps 0 and T. In the improved DDPM paper, T was bumped up to 4,000, and the variance schedule was tweaked to change more slowly at the beginning and at the end. In short, we're gradually drowning the cat in noise: this is called the *forward process*.

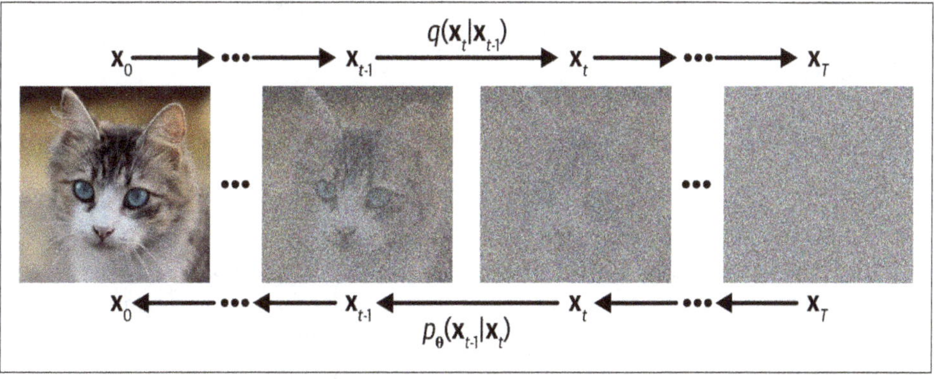

Figure 18-18. The forward process q and reverse process p

As we add more and more Gaussian noise in the forward process, the distribution of pixel values becomes more and more Gaussian. One important detail I left out is that the pixel values get rescaled slightly at each step, by a factor of $\sqrt{1 - \beta_t}$. This ensures that the mean of the pixel values gradually approaches 0, since the scaling factor is a

16 Jonathan Ho et al., "Denoising Diffusion Probabilistic Models" (2020).

17 Alex Nichol and Prafulla Dhariwal, "Improved Denoising Diffusion Probabilistic Models" (2021).

bit smaller than 1 (imagine repeatedly multiplying a number by 0.99). It also ensures that the variance will gradually converge to 1. This is because the standard deviation of the pixel values also gets scaled by $\sqrt{1-\beta_t}$, so the variance gets scaled by $1-\beta_t$ (i.e., the square of the scaling factor). But the variance cannot shrink to 0 since we're adding Gaussian noise with variance β_t at each step. And since variances add up when you sum Gaussian distributions, the variance must converge to $1-\beta_t+\beta_t=1$.

The forward diffusion process is summarized in Equation 18-5. This equation won't teach you anything new about the forward process, but it's useful to understand this type of mathematical notation, as it's often used in ML papers. This equation defines the probability distribution q of $\mathbf{x}_t$, given $\mathbf{x}_{t-1}$ as a Gaussian distribution with mean $\mathbf{x}_{t-1}$ times the scaling factor, and with a covariance matrix equal to $\beta_t\mathbf{I}$. This is the identity matrix $\mathbf{I}$ multiplied by β_t, which means that the noise is isotropic with variance β_t.

Equation 18-5. Probability distribution q of the forward diffusion process

$$q(\mathbf{x}_t \mid \mathbf{x}_{t-1}) = \mathcal{N}\left(\sqrt{1-\beta_t}\mathbf{x}_{t-1}, \beta_t\mathbf{I}\right)$$

Interestingly, there's a shortcut for the forward process: it's possible to sample an image $\mathbf{x}_t$ given $\mathbf{x}_0$ without having to first compute $\mathbf{x}_1, \mathbf{x}_2, \ldots, \mathbf{x}_{t-1}$. Indeed, since the sum of multiple independent Gaussian distributions is also a Gaussian distribution, all the noise can be added in just one shot. If we define $\alpha_t = 1-\beta_t$, and $\bar{\alpha_t} = \alpha_1 \times \alpha_2 \times \ldots \times \alpha_t = \bar{\alpha}_t = \prod_{i=1}^{t}\alpha_t$, then we can compute $\mathbf{x}_t$ using Equation 18-6. This is the equation we will be using, as it is much faster.

Equation 18-6. Shortcut for the forward diffusion process

$$q(\mathbf{x}_t \mid \mathbf{x}_0) = \mathcal{N}\left(\sqrt{\bar{\alpha}_t}\mathbf{x}_0, (1-\bar{\alpha}_t)\mathbf{I}\right)$$

Our goal, of course, is not to drown cats in noise. On the contrary, we want to create many new cats! We can do so by training a model that can perform the *reverse process*: going from $\mathbf{x}_t$ to $\mathbf{x}_{t-1}$. We can then use it to remove a tiny bit of noise from an image, and repeat the operation many times until all the noise is gone. It's not a basic noise filter that relies only on the neighboring pixels: instead, when noise is removed, it is replaced with realistic pixels, depending on the training data. For example, if we train the model on a dataset containing many cat images, then we can give it a picture entirely full of Gaussian noise, and the model will gradually make a brand new cat appear (see Figure 18-18).

OK, so let's start coding! The first thing we need to do is to code the forward process. For this, we will first need to implement the variance schedule. How can we control how fast the cat disappears? At each time step t, the pixel values get multiplied by $\sqrt{1-\beta_t}$ and noise with mean 0 and variance β_t gets added (as explained earlier). So, the part of the image's variance that comes from the original cat image shrinks by a factor of $\alpha_t = 1 - \beta_t$ at each step. After t time steps, it will have shrunk by a factor of $\bar{\alpha}_t = \alpha_1 \times \alpha_2 \times \ldots \times \alpha_t$. It's this "cat signal" factor $\bar{\alpha}_t$ that we want to schedule so it shrinks down from 1 to 0 gradually between time steps 0 and T. In the improved DDPM paper, the authors schedule $\bar{\alpha}_t$ according to Equation 18-7. This schedule is represented in Figure 18-19.

Equation 18-7. Variance schedule equation for the forward diffusion process

$$\beta_t = 1 - \frac{\bar{\alpha}_t}{\bar{\alpha}_{t-1}} \quad \text{with } \bar{\alpha}_t = \frac{f(t)}{f(0)} \text{ and } f(t) = \cos^2\left(\frac{\frac{t}{T} + s}{1 + s} \cdot \frac{\pi}{2}\right)$$

In this equation:

- s is a tiny value which prevents β_t from being too small near $t = 0$. In the paper, the authors used $s = 0.008$.
- β_t is clipped to be no larger than 0.999 to avoid instabilities near $t = T$.

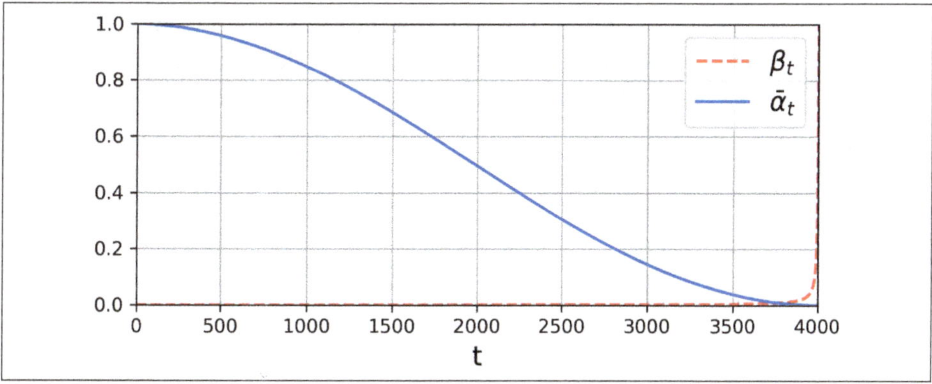

Figure 18-19. Noise variance schedule β_t, and the remaining signal variance $\bar{\alpha}_t$

Let's create a small function to compute α_t, β_t, and $\bar{\alpha}_t$, using Equation 18-7, and call this function with $T = 4{,}000$:

```
def variance_schedule(T, s=0.008, max_beta=0.999):
    t = torch.linspace(0, T, T + 1)
    f = torch.cos((t / T + s) / (1 + s) * torch.pi / 2) ** 2
    alpha_bars = f / f[0]
    betas = (1 - (f[1:] / f[:-1])).clamp(max=max_beta)
    betas = torch.cat([torch.zeros(1), betas])  # for easier indexing
    alphas = 1 - betas
    return alphas, betas, alpha_bars
```

```python
T = 4000
alphas, betas, alpha_bars = variance_schedule(T)
```

To train our model to reverse the diffusion process, we will need noisy images from different time steps of the forward process. For this, let's create a function that will take an image $\mathbf{x}_0$ and a time step t using Equation 18-6, and return a noisy image $\mathbf{x}_t$:

```python
def forward_diffusion(x0, t):
    eps = torch.randn_like(x0)  # this unscaled noise will be the target
    xt = alpha_bars[t].sqrt() * x0 + (1 - alpha_bars[t]).sqrt() * eps
    return xt, eps
```

The model will need both the noisy image $\mathbf{x}_t$ and the time step t, so let's create a small class that will hold both. We'll give it a handy `to()` method to move both $\mathbf{x}_t$ and t to the GPU:

```python
class DiffusionSample(namedtuple("DiffusionSampleBase", ["xt", "t"])):
    def to(self, device):
        return DiffusionSample(self.xt.to(device), self.t.to(device))
```

Next, let's create a dataset wrapper class. It takes an image dataset—Fashion MNIST in our case—and preprocesses the images so their pixel values range between –1 and +1 (this is optional but usually works better), and it uses the `forward_diffusion()` function to add noise to the image. Then it wraps the resulting noisy image as well as the time step in a `DiffusionSample` object, and returns it along with the target, which is the unscaled noise `eps`, before it was scaled by $\sqrt{1 - \bar{\alpha}_t}$ and added to the image:

```python
class DiffusionDataset:
    def __init__(self, dataset):
        self.dataset = dataset

    def __getitem__(self, i):
        x0, _ = self.dataset[i]
        x0 = (x0 * 2) - 1  # scale from -1 to +1
        t = torch.randint(1, T + 1, size=[1])
        xt, eps = forward_diffusion(x0, t)
        return DiffusionSample(xt, t), eps

    def __len__(self):
        return len(self.dataset)

train_set = DiffusionDataset(train_data)  # wrap Fashion MNIST
train_loader = DataLoader(train_set, batch_size=32, shuffle=True)
```

You may be wondering why not predict the original image directly, rather than the unscaled noise? One reason is empirical: the authors tried both approaches, and they observed that predicting the noise rather than the image led to more stable training and better results. The other reason is that the noise is Gaussian, which allows for some mathematical simplifications: in particular, the KL divergence between two

Gaussian distributions is proportional to the squared distance between their means, so we can use the MSE loss, which is simple, fast, and quite stable.

Now we're ready to build the actual diffusion model itself. It can be any model you want, as long as it takes a `DiffusionSample` as input and outputs images of the same shape as the input images. The DDPM authors used a modified U-Net architecture (*https://homl.info/unet*),[18] which has many similarities with the FCN architecture we discussed in Chapter 12 for semantic segmentation. U-Net is a convolutional neural network that gradually downsamples the input images, then gradually upsamples them again, with skip connections crossing over from each level of the downsampling part to the corresponding level in the upsampling part. To take into account the time steps, they were encoded using a fixed sinusoidal encoding (i.e., the same technique as the positional encodings in the original Transformer architecture). At every level in the U-Net architecture, they passed these time encodings through `Linear` layers and fed them to the U-Net. Lastly, they also used multi-head attention layers at various levels. See this chapter's notebook for a basic implementation (it's too long to copy here, and the details don't matter: many other model architectures would work just fine).

```
class DiffusionModel(nn.Module):  # see the notebook for full details
    def __init__(self, T=T, embed_dim=64):
        [...]  # create all the required modules to build the U-Net

    def forward(self, sample):
        [...]  # process the sample and predict the noise for each image
```

For training, the authors noted that using the MAE loss worked better than the MSE. You can also use the Huber loss:

```
diffusion_model = DiffusionModel().to(device)
huber = nn.HuberLoss()
optimizer = torch.optim.NAdam(diffusion_model.parameters(), lr=3e-3)
train(diffusion_model, optimizer, huber, train_loader, n_epochs=20)
```

Once the model is trained, you can use it to generate new images by sampling $\mathbf{x}_T$ randomly from a Gaussian distribution with mean 0 and variance 1, then using Equation 18-8 to get $\mathbf{x}_{T-1}$. Then use this equation 3,999 more times until you get $\mathbf{x}_0$. If all went well, $\mathbf{x}_0$ should look like a regular Fashion MNIST image!

Equation 18-8. Going one step in reverse in the DDPM diffusion process

$$\mathbf{x}_{t-1} = \frac{1}{\sqrt{\alpha_t}}\left(\mathbf{x}_t - \frac{\beta_t}{\sqrt{1-\bar{\alpha}_t}}\boldsymbol{\varepsilon}_{\boldsymbol{\theta}}(\mathbf{x}_t, t)\right) + \sqrt{\beta_t}\mathbf{z}$$

18 Olaf Ronneberger et al., "U-Net: Convolutional Networks for Biomedical Image Segmentation", arXiv preprint arXiv:1505.04597 (2015).

In this equation, $\boldsymbol{\varepsilon}_\theta(\mathbf{x}_t, t)$ represents the noise predicted by the model given the input image $\mathbf{x}_t$ and the time step t. The $\boldsymbol{\theta}$ represents the model parameters. Moreover, $\mathbf{z}$ is Gaussian noise with mean 0 and variance 1. This makes the reverse process stochastic: if you run it multiple times, you will get different images.

This works well, but it requires 4,000 iterations to generate an image! That's too slow. Luckily, just a few months after the DDPM paper, researchers from Stanford University proposed a technique named the denoising diffusion implicit model (DDIM) (*https://homl.info/ddim*)[19] to generate images in much fewer steps: instead of going from t = 4,000 down to 0 one step at a time, DDIM can go down any number of time steps at a time, using Equation 18-9. Moreover, the training process is exactly the same as for DDPM, so we can simply reuse our trained DDPM model.

Equation 18-9. Going multiple steps in reverse with DDIM

$$\mathbf{x}_p = \sqrt{\bar{\alpha}_p}\hat{\mathbf{x}}_0 + \sqrt{1 - \bar{\alpha}_p - \sigma^2} \cdot \boldsymbol{\varepsilon}_\theta(\mathbf{x}_t, t) + \sigma\mathbf{z}$$

$$\text{where } \hat{\mathbf{x}}_0 = \frac{1}{\sqrt{\bar{\alpha}_t}}\left(\mathbf{x}_t - \sqrt{1 - \bar{\alpha}_t}\boldsymbol{\varepsilon}_\theta(\mathbf{x}_t, t)\right)$$

$$\text{and } \sigma^2 = \eta\left(\frac{1 - \bar{\alpha}_p}{1 - \bar{\alpha}_t}\right)\beta_t$$

In this equation:

- $\boldsymbol{\varepsilon}_\theta(\mathbf{x}_t, t)$, $\boldsymbol{\theta}$, and $\mathbf{z}$ have the same meanings as in Equation 18-8.
- p represents any time step before t. For example, it could be $p = t - 50$.
- η is a hyperparameter that controls how much randomness should be used during generation, from 0 (no randomness, fully deterministic) to 1 (just like DDPM).

Let's write a function that implements this reverse process, and call it to generate a few images:

```
def generate_ddim(model, batch_size=32, num_steps=50, eta=0.85):
    model.eval()
    with torch.no_grad():
        xt = torch.randn([batch_size, 1, 28, 28], device=device)
        times = torch.linspace(T - 1, 0, steps=num_steps + 1).long().tolist()
        for t, t_prev in zip(times[:-1], times[1:]):
            t_batch = torch.full((batch_size, 1), t, device=device)
            sample = DiffusionSample(xt, t_batch)
            eps_pred = model(sample)
```

19 Jiaming Song et al., "Denoising Diffusion Implicit Models", arXiv preprint arXiv:2010.02502 (2020).

```
        x0 = ((xt - (1 - alpha_bars[t]).sqrt() * eps_pred)
              / (alpha_bars[t].sqrt()))
        abar_t_prev = alpha_bars[t_prev]
        variance = eta * (1 - abar_t_prev) / (1 - alpha_bars[t]) * betas[t]
        sigma_t = variance.sqrt()
        pred_dir = (1 - abar_t_prev - sigma_t**2).sqrt() * eps_pred
        noise = torch.randn_like(xt)
        xt = abar_t_prev.sqrt() * x0 + pred_dir + sigma_t * noise

    return torch.clamp((xt + 1) / 2, 0, 1)  # from [-1, 1] range to [0, 1]

X_gen_ddim = generate_ddim(diffusion_model, num_steps=500)
```

This time the generation will only take a few seconds, and it will produce images such as the ones shown in Figure 18-20. Granted, they're not very impressive, but we've only trained the model for a few minutes on Fashion MNIST. Give it a try on a larger dataset and train it for a few hours to get more impressive results.

Figure 18-20. Images generated by DDIM accelerated diffusion

Diffusion models have made tremendous progress since 2020. In particular, a paper published in December 2021 by Robin Rombach, et al. (*https://homl.info/latentdiff*)[20] introduced *latent diffusion models*, where the diffusion process takes place in latent space, rather than in pixel space. To achieve this, a powerful autoencoder is used to compress each training image into a much smaller latent space, where the diffusion process takes place, then the autoencoder is used to decompress the final latent representation, generating the output image. This considerably speeds up image generation, and reduces training time and cost dramatically. Importantly, the quality of the generated images is outstanding.

20 Robin Rombach, Andreas Blattmann, et al., "High-Resolution Image Synthesis with Latent Diffusion Models", arXiv preprint arXiv:2112.10752 (2021).

Moreover, the researchers also adapted various conditioning techniques to guide the diffusion process using text prompts, images, or any other inputs. This makes it possible to quickly produce any image you might fancy. You can also condition the image generation process using an input image. This enables many applications, such as outpainting—where an input image is extended beyond its borders—or inpainting—where holes in an image are filled in.

Lastly, a powerful pretrained latent diffusion model named *Stable Diffusion* (SD) was open sourced in August 2022 by a collaboration between LMU Munich and a few companies, including StabilityAI, and Runway, with support from EleutherAI and LAION. Now anyone can generate mindblowing images in seconds, for free, even on a regular laptop. For example, you can use the Hugging Face Diffusers library to load SD (e.g., the turbo variant), create an image generation pipeline for text-to-image, and generate an image of an orangutan reading a book:

```
from diffusers import AutoPipelineForText2Image

pipe = AutoPipelineForText2Image.from_pretrained(
    "stabilityai/sd-turbo", variant="fp16", dtype=torch.float16)
pipe.to(device)
prompt = "A closeup photo of an orangutan reading a book"
torch.manual_seed(26)
image = pipe(prompt=prompt, num_inference_steps=1, guidance_scale=0.0).images[0]
```

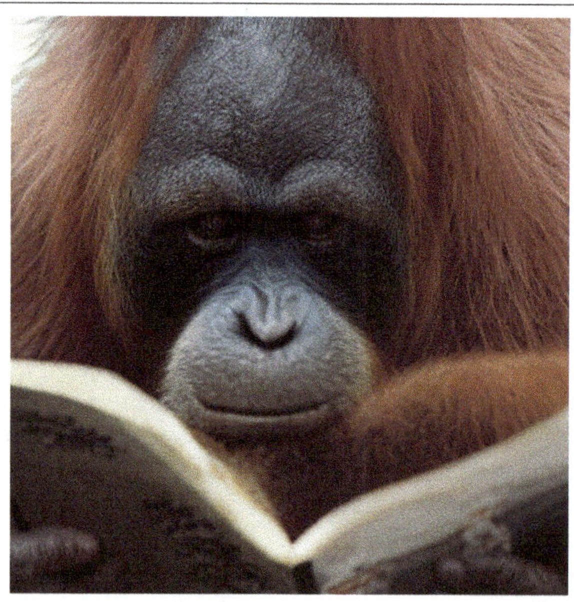

Figure 18-21. A picture generated by Stable Diffusion using the Diffusers library

The possibilities are endless!

In the next chapter we will move on to an entirely different branch of deep learning: deep reinforcement learning.

Exercises

1. What are the main tasks that autoencoders are used for?
2. Suppose you want to train a classifier, and you have plenty of unlabeled training data but only a few thousand labeled instances. How can autoencoders help? How would you proceed?
3. If an autoencoder perfectly reconstructs the inputs, is it necessarily a good autoencoder? How can you evaluate the performance of an autoencoder?
4. What are undercomplete and overcomplete autoencoders? What is the main risk of an excessively undercomplete autoencoder? What about the main risk of an overcomplete autoencoder?
5. How do you tie weights in a stacked autoencoder? What is the point of doing so?
6. What is a generative model? Can you name a type of generative autoencoder?
7. What is a GAN? Can you name a few tasks where GANs can shine?
8. What are the main difficulties when training GANs?
9. What are diffusion models good at? What is their main limitation?
10. Try using a denoising autoencoder to pretrain an image classifier. You can use MNIST (the simplest option), or a more complex image dataset such as CIFAR10 (*https://homl.info/122*) if you want a bigger challenge. Regardless of the dataset you're using, follow these steps:
    a. Split the dataset into a training set and a test set. Train a deep denoising autoencoder on the full training set.
    b. Check that the images are fairly well reconstructed. Visualize the images that most activate each neuron in the coding layer.
    c. Build a classification DNN, reusing the lower layers of the autoencoder. Train it using only 500 images from the training set. Does it perform better with or without pretraining?
11. Train a variational autoencoder on the image dataset of your choice, and use it to generate images. Alternatively, you can try to find an unlabeled dataset that you are interested in and see if you can generate new samples.
12. Train a DCGAN to tackle the image dataset of your choice, and use it to generate images. Add experience replay and see if this helps.

13. Train a diffusion model on your preferred image dataset (e.g., `torchvision.datasets.Flowers102`), and generate nice images. Next, add the image class as an extra input to the model, and retrain it: you should now be able to control the class of the generated image.

Solutions to these exercises are available at the end of this chapter's notebook, at *https://homl.info/colab-p*.

CHAPTER 19
Reinforcement Learning

Reinforcement learning (RL) is one of the most exciting fields of machine learning today, and also one of the oldest. It has been around since the 1950s, producing many interesting applications over the years,[1] particularly in games (e.g., *TD-Gammon*, a backgammon-playing program) and in machine control, but seldom making the headline news. However, a revolution took place in 2013, when researchers from a British startup called DeepMind[2] demonstrated a system that could learn to play just about any Atari game from scratch,[3] eventually outperforming humans[4] in most of them, using only raw pixels as inputs and without any prior knowledge of the rules of the games.[5] This was the first of a series of amazing feats:

- In 2016, DeepMind's AlphaGo beat Lee Sedol, a legendary professional player of the game of Go; and in 2017, it beat Ke Jie, the world champion. No program had ever come close to beating a master of this game, let alone the very best.
- In 2020, DeepMind released AlphaFold, which can predict the 3D shape of proteins with unprecedented accuracy. This is a game changer in biology, chemistry, and medicine. In fact, Demis Hassabis (founder and CEO) and John Jumper (director) were awarded the Nobel Prize in Chemistry for AlphaFold.

1 For more details, be sure to check out Richard Sutton and Andrew Barto's book on RL, *Reinforcement Learning: An Introduction* (MIT Press).

2 DeepMind was bought by Google for over $500 million in 2014.

3 Volodymyr Mnih et al., "Playing Atari with Deep Reinforcement Learning", arXiv preprint arXiv:1312.5602 (2013), *https://homl.info/dqn*.

4 Volodymyr Mnih et al., "Human-Level Control Through Deep Reinforcement Learning", *Nature* 518 (2015): 529–533, *https://homl.info/dqn2*.

5 Check out the videos of DeepMind's system learning to play *Space Invaders*, *Breakout*, and other video games at *https://homl.info/dqn3*.

- In 2022, DeepMind released AlphaCode, which can generate code at a competitive programming level.
- In 2023, DeepMind released GNoME which can predict new crystal structures, including hundreds of thousands of predicted stable materials.

So how did DeepMind researchers achieve all of this? Well, they applied the power of deep learning to the field of reinforcement learning, and it worked beyond their wildest dreams: *deep reinforcement learning* was born. Today, although DeepMind continues to lead the way, many other organizations have joined in, and the whole field is boiling with new ideas, with a wide range of applications.

In this chapter I will first explain what reinforcement learning is and what it's good at, then present three of the most important families of techniques in deep reinforcement learning: policy gradients, deep Q-networks (including a discussion of Markov decision processes), and lastly, actor-critic methods, including the popular PPO, which we will use to beat an Atari game. So let's get started!

What Is Reinforcement Learning?

In reinforcement learning, a software *agent* makes *observations* and takes *actions* within an *environment*, and in return it receives *rewards* from the environment. Its objective is to learn to act in a way that will maximize its expected rewards over time. If you don't mind a bit of anthropomorphism, you can think of positive rewards as pleasure, and negative rewards as pain (the term "reward" is a bit misleading in this case). In short, the agent acts in the environment and learns by trial and error to maximize its pleasure and minimize its pain.

This is quite a broad setting that can apply to a wide variety of tasks. Here are a few examples (see Figure 19-1):

- The agent can be the program controlling a robot. In this case, the environment is the real world, the agent observes the environment through a set of *sensors*, such as cameras and touch sensors, and its actions consist of sending signals to activate motors. It may be programmed to get positive rewards whenever it approaches the target destination, and negative rewards whenever it wastes time or goes in the wrong direction.
- The agent can be the program controlling *Ms. Pac-Man*. In this case, the environment is a simulation of the Atari game, the actions are the nine possible joystick positions (upper left, down, center, and so on), the observations are screenshots, and the rewards are just the game points.
- Similarly, the agent can be the program playing a board game such as Go. It only gets a reward if it wins.

- The agent does not have to control a physically (or virtually) moving thing. For example, it can be a smart thermostat, getting positive rewards whenever it is close to the target temperature and saves energy, and negative rewards when humans need to tweak the temperature, so the agent must learn to anticipate human needs.
- The agent can observe stock market prices and decide how much to buy or sell every second. Rewards are obviously the monetary gains and losses.

Note that there may not be any positive rewards at all; for example, the agent may move around in a maze, getting a negative reward at every time step, so it had better find the exit as quickly as possible! There are many other examples of tasks to which reinforcement learning is well suited, such as self-driving cars, recommender systems, placing ads on a web page, or controlling where an image classification system should focus its attention.

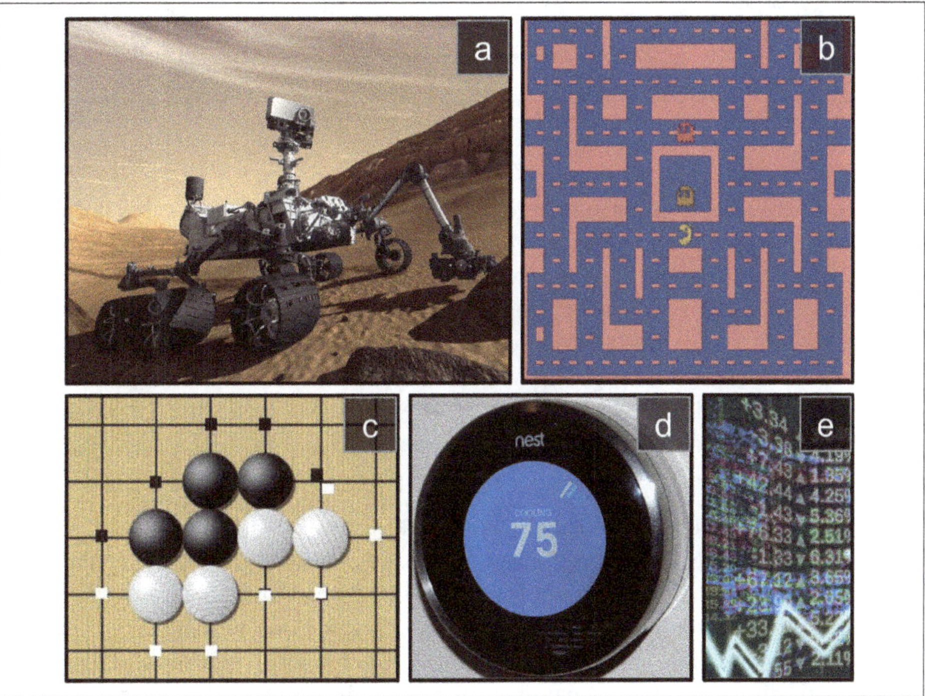

Figure 19-1. Reinforcement learning examples: (a) robotics, (b) Ms. Pac-Man, (c) Go player, (d) thermostat, (e) automatic trader[6]

6 Images (a), (d), and (e) are in the public domain. Image (b) is a screenshot from the *Ms. Pac-Man* game, copyright Atari (fair use in this chapter). Image (c) is reproduced from Wikipedia; it was created by user Stevertigo and released under Creative Commons BY-SA 2.0 (*https://oreil.ly/O2fAq*).

Let's now turn to one large family of RL algorithms: *policy gradients*.

Policy Gradients

The algorithm a software agent uses to determine its actions is called its *policy*. The policy can be any algorithm you can think of, such as a neural network taking observations as inputs and outputting the action to take (see Figure 19-2).

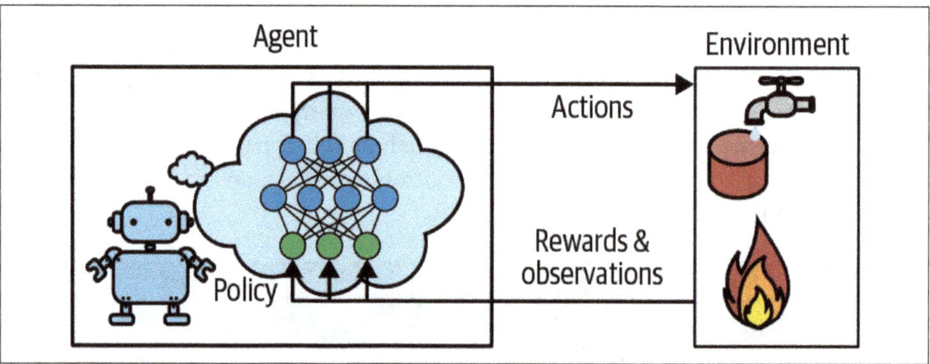

Figure 19-2. Reinforcement learning using a neural network policy

The policy does not even have to be deterministic. In fact, in some cases it does not even have to observe the environment, as long as it can get rewards! For example, consider a blind robotic vacuum cleaner whose reward is the amount of dust it picks up in 30 minutes. Its policy could be to move forward with some probability p every second, or randomly rotate left or right with probability $1 - p$. The rotation angle would be a random angle between $-r$ and $+r$. Since this policy involves some randomness, it is called a *stochastic policy*. The robot will have an erratic trajectory, which guarantees that it will eventually get to any place it can reach and pick up all the dust. The question is, how much dust will it pick up in 30 minutes?

How would you train such a robot? There are just two *policy parameters* you can tweak: the probability p and the angle range r. One possible learning algorithm could be to try out many different values for these parameters, and pick the combination that performs best (see Figure 19-3). This is an example of *policy search*, in this case using a brute-force approach. When the *policy space* is too large (which is generally the case), finding a good set of parameters this way is like searching for a needle in a gigantic haystack.

Another way to explore the policy space is to use *genetic algorithms*. For example, you could randomly create a first generation of 100 policies and try them out, then "kill" the 80 worst policies[7] and make the 20 survivors produce 4 offspring each. An offspring is a copy of its parent[8] plus some random variation. The surviving policies plus their offspring together constitute the second generation. You can continue to iterate through generations this way until you find a good policy.[9]

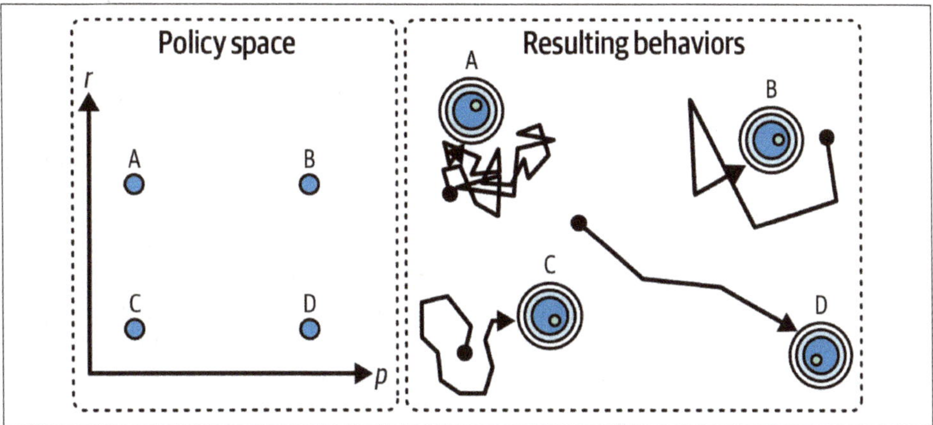

Figure 19-3. Four points in the policy space (left) and the agent's corresponding behavior (right)

Yet another approach is to use optimization techniques by evaluating the gradients of the rewards with regard to the policy parameters, then tweaking these parameters by following the gradients toward higher rewards.[10] Algorithms that follow this strategy are known as *policy gradient* (PG) algorithms. But before we can implement them, we first need to create an environment for the agent to live in—so it's time to introduce the Gymnasium library.

---

7 It is often better to give the poor performers a slight chance of survival, to preserve some diversity in the "gene pool".

8 If there is a single parent, this is called *asexual reproduction*. With two (or more) parents, it is called *sexual reproduction*. An offspring's genome (in this case a set of policy parameters) is randomly composed of parts of its parents' genomes.

9 One interesting example of a genetic algorithm used for reinforcement learning is the *NeuroEvolution of Augmenting Topologies* (*https://homl.info/neat*) (NEAT) algorithm. Also check out *evolutionary policy optimization* (*https://homl.info/epo*) (EPO), proposed in 2025, where a master agent learns stably and efficiently from the experiences of a population of agents.

10 This is called *gradient ascent*. It's just like gradient descent, but in the opposite direction: maximizing instead of minimizing.

Introduction to the Gymnasium Library

One of the challenges of reinforcement learning is that in order to train an agent, you first need to have a working environment. If you want to program an agent that will learn to play an Atari game, you will need an Atari game simulator. If you want to program a walking robot, then the environment is the real world, and you can directly train your robot in that environment. However, this has its limits: if the robot falls off a cliff, you can't just click Undo. You can't speed up time either—adding more computing power won't make the robot move any faster—and it's generally too expensive to train 1,000 robots in parallel. In short, training is hard and slow in the real world, so you generally need a *simulated environment* at least for bootstrap training. For example, you might use a library like PyBullet (*https://pybullet.org*) or MuJoCo (*https://mujoco.org*) for 3D physics simulation.

The Gymnasium library (*https://gymnasium.farama.org*) is an open source toolkit that provides a wide variety of simulated environments (Atari games, board games, 2D and 3D physics simulations, and so on), that you can use to train agents, compare them, or develop new RL algorithms. It's the successor of OpenAI Gym, and is now maintained by a community of researchers and developers.

Gymnasium is preinstalled on Colab, along with the Arcade Learning Environment (ALE) library `ale_py`, which is an emulator for Atari 2600 games and is required for all the Atari environments, as well as the Box2D library, required for several environments with 2D physics. If you are coding on your own machine instead of Colab, and you followed the installation instructions at *https://homl.info/install-p*, then you should be good to go.

Let's start by importing Gymnasium and making an environment:

```
import gymnasium as gym

env = gym.make("CartPole-v1", render_mode="rgb_array", max_episode_steps=1000)
```

Here, we've created a CartPole environment (version 1). This is a 2D simulation in which a cart can be accelerated left or right in order to balance a pole placed on top of it (see Figure 19-4)—a classic control task. I'll explain `render_mode` and `max_episode_steps` shortly.

The `gym.envs.registry` dictionary contains the names and specifications of all the available environments. You can print a nice list with `gym.pprint_registry()`. The Atari environments will only be available once we start the ALE emulator.

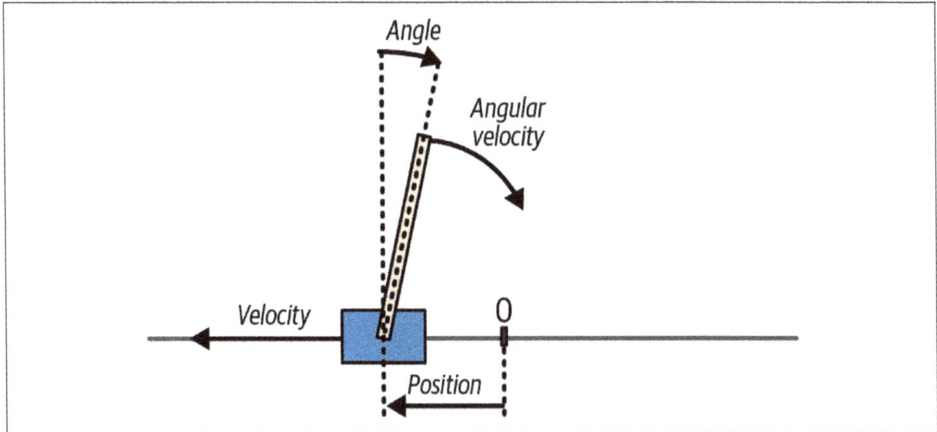

Figure 19-4. The CartPole environment

After the environment is created, you must initialize it using the `reset()` method, optionally specifying a random seed. This returns the first observation. Observations depend on the type of environment. For the CartPole environment, each observation is a NumPy array containing four floats representing the cart's horizontal position (`0.0` = center), its velocity (positive means right), the angle of the pole (`0.0` = vertical), and its angular velocity (positive means clockwise). The `reset()` method also returns a dictionary that may contain extra environment-specific information. This can be useful for debugging and sometimes for training. For example, in many Atari environments, it contains the number of lives left. However, in the CartPole environment, this dictionary is empty:

```
>>> obs, info = env.reset(seed=42)
>>> obs
array([ 0.0273956 , -0.00611216,  0.03585979,  0.0197368 ], dtype=float32)
>>> info
{}
```

Let's call the `render()` method to render this environment as an image. Since we set `render_mode="rgb_array"` when creating the environment, the image will be returned as a NumPy array (you can then use Matplotlib's `imshow()` function to display this image):

```
>>> img = env.render()
>>> img.shape  # height, width, channels (3 = Red, Green, Blue)
(400, 600, 3)
```

Now let's ask the environment what actions are possible:

```
>>> env.action_space
Discrete(2)
```

`Discrete(2)` means that the possible actions are integers 0 and 1, which represent accelerating left or right. Other environments may have additional discrete actions, or other kinds of actions (e.g., continuous). Since the pole is leaning toward the right (`obs[2] > 0`), let's accelerate the cart toward the right:

```
>>> action = 1  # accelerate right
>>> obs, reward, done, truncated, info = env.step(action)
>>> obs
array([ 0.02727336,  0.18847767,  0.03625453, -0.26141977], dtype=float32)
>>> reward, done, truncated, info
(1.0, False, False, {})
```

The `step()` method executes the desired action and returns five values:

`obs`
: This is the new observation. The cart is now moving toward the right (`obs[1] > 0`). The pole is still tilted toward the right (`obs[2] > 0`), but its angular velocity is now negative (`obs[3] < 0`), so it will likely be tilted toward the left after the next step.

`reward`
: In this environment, you get a reward of 1.0 at every step, no matter what you do, so the goal is to keep the episode running for as long as possible. An *episode* is one run of the environment until the game is over or interrupted.

`done`
: This value will be `True` when the episode is over. This will happen when the pole tilts too much, or goes off the screen. After that, the environment must be reset before it can be used again.

`truncated`
: This value will be `True` when an episode is interrupted early, typically by an environment wrapper that imposes a maximum number of steps per episode (see Gymnasium's documentation for more details on environment wrappers). By default, the environment specification for CartPole sets the maximum number of steps to 500, but we changed this to 1,000 when we created the environment. Some RL algorithms treat truncated episodes differently from episodes finished normally (i.e., when `done` is `True`), but in this chapter we will treat them identically.

`info`
: This environment-specific dictionary may provide extra information, just like the one returned by the `reset()` method.

Once you have finished using an environment—possibly after many episodes—you should call its `close()` method to free resources.

Let's hardcode a simple policy that accelerates left when the pole is leaning toward the left and accelerates right when the pole is leaning toward the right. We will run this policy to see the average rewards it gets over 500 episodes:

```
def basic_policy(obs):
    angle = obs[2]
    return 0 if angle < 0 else 1  # go left if leaning left, otherwise go right

totals = []
for episode in range(500):
    total_rewards = 0
    obs, info = env.reset(seed=episode)
    while True:  # no risk of infinite loop: will be truncated after 1000 steps
        action = basic_policy(obs)
        obs, reward, done, truncated, info = env.step(action)
        total_rewards += reward
        if done or truncated:
            break

    totals.append(total_rewards)
```

This code is self-explanatory. Let's look at the result:

```
>>> import numpy as np
>>> np.mean(totals), np.std(totals), min(totals), max(totals)
(np.float64(41.698), np.float64(8.389445512070509), 24.0, 63.0)
```

Even with 500 tries, this policy never managed to keep the pole upright for more than 63 consecutive steps. Not great. If you look at the simulation in this chapter's notebook, you will see that the cart oscillates left and right more and more strongly until the pole tilts too much. A neural network can do better!

Neural Network Policies

Let's create a neural network policy. This neural network will take an observation as input, and it will output the action to be executed, just like the policy we hardcoded earlier. More precisely, it will estimate a probability for each action, then it will select an action randomly, according to the estimated probabilities (see Figure 19-5). In the case of the CartPole environment, there are just two possible actions (left or right), so we only need one output neuron. It will output the probability p of action 1 (right), and of course the probability of action 0 (left) will be $1 - p$. For example, if it outputs 0.7, then we will pick action 1 with 70% probability, or action 0 with 30% probability (this is a *Bernoulli distribution* with $p = 0.7$).

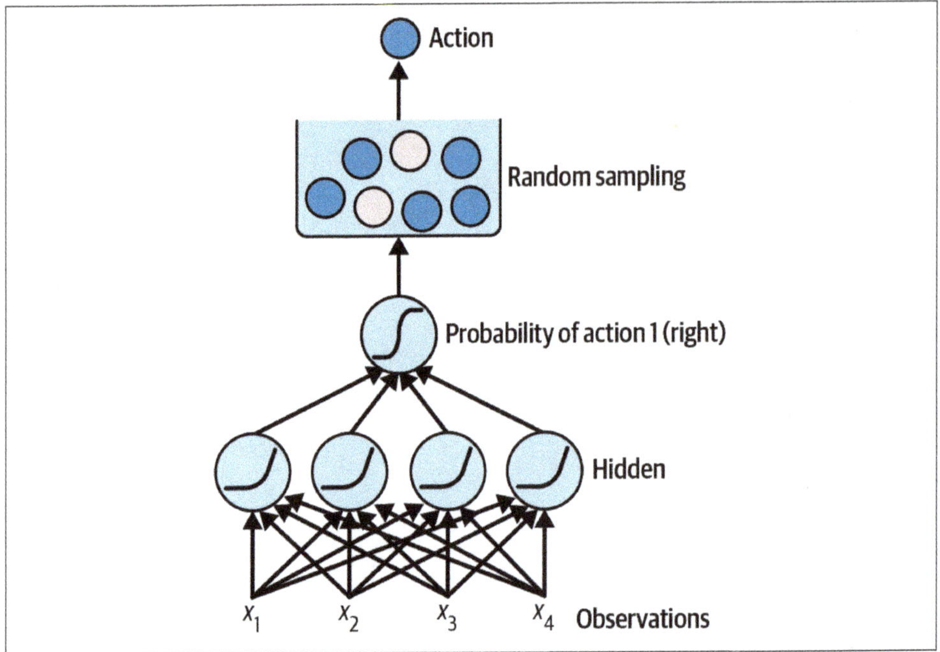

Figure 19-5. Neural network policy

You may wonder why we are picking a random action based on the probabilities given by the neural network, rather than just picking the action with the highest score. This approach lets the agent find the right balance between *exploring* new actions and *exploiting* the actions that are known to work well. Here's an analogy: suppose you go to a restaurant for the first time, and all the dishes look equally appealing, so you randomly pick one. If it turns out to be good, you can increase the probability that you'll order it next time, but you shouldn't increase that probability up to 100%, or you will never try the other dishes, some of which may be even better than the one you tried. This *exploration/exploitation dilemma* is central in reinforcement learning.

Also note that in this particular environment, the past actions and observations can safely be ignored, since each observation contains the environment's full state. If there were some hidden state, then you might need to consider past actions and observations as well. For example, if the environment only revealed the position of the cart but not its velocity, you would have to consider not only the current observation but also the previous observation in order to estimate the current velocity. Another example is when the observations are noisy; in that case, you generally want to use the past few observations to estimate the most likely current state. The CartPole problem is thus as simple as can be; the observations are noise-free, and they contain the environment's full state.

Let's use PyTorch to implement a basic neural network policy for CartPole:

```
import torch
import torch.nn as nn

class PolicyNetwork(nn.Module):
    def __init__(self):
        super().__init__()
        self.net = nn.Sequential(nn.Linear(4, 5), nn.ReLU(), nn.Linear(5, 1))

    def forward(self, state):
        return self.net(state)
```

Our policy network is a tiny MLP, since it's a fairly simple task. The number of inputs is the size of the environment's state: in the case of CartPole, it is just the size of a single observation, which is four. We have just one hidden layer with five units (no need for more in this case). Finally, we want to output a single probability, so we have a single output neuron. If there were more than two possible actions, there would be one output neuron per action instead. For performance and numerical stability, we don't add a sigmoid function at the end, so the network will actually output logits rather than probabilities.

Next let's define a function that will use this policy network to choose an action:

```
def choose_action(model, obs):
    state = torch.as_tensor(obs)
    logit = model(state)
    dist = torch.distributions.Bernoulli(logits=logit)
    action = dist.sample()
    log_prob = dist.log_prob(action)
    return int(action.item()), log_prob
```

The function takes a single observation, converts it to a tensor, and passes it to the policy network to get the logit for action 1 (right). It then creates a `Bernoulli` probability distribution with this logit, and it samples an action from it: this distribution will output 1 (right) with probability p = exp(logit) / (1 + exp(logit)), and 0 (left) with probability 1 – p. If there were more than two possible actions, you would use a `Categorical` distribution instead. Lastly, we compute the log probability of the sampled action (i.e., either log(p) or log(1 – p)): this log probability will be needed later for training.

If the action space is continuous, you can use a Gaussian distribution instead of a Bernoulli or categorical distribution. Instead of predicting logits, the policy network must predict the mean and standard deviation (or the log of the standard deviation) of the distribution. The log of the standard deviation is often clipped to ensure the distribution is neither too wide nor too narrow.

OK, we now have a neural network policy that can take an environment state (in this case, a single observation) and choose an action. But how do we train it?

Evaluating Actions: The Credit Assignment Problem

If we knew what the best action was at each step, we could train the neural network as usual by minimizing the cross-entropy between the estimated probability distribution and the target probability distribution. It would just be regular supervised learning. However, in reinforcement learning the only guidance the agent gets is through rewards, and rewards are typically sparse and delayed. For example, if the agent manages to balance the pole for a total of 100 steps, how can it know which of the 100 actions it took were good, and which of them were bad? All it knows is that the pole fell after the last action, but surely this last action is not entirely responsible. This is called the *credit assignment problem*: when the agent gets a reward (or a penalty), it is hard for it to know which actions should get credited (or blamed) for it. Think of a dog that gets rewarded hours after it behaved well; will it understand what it is being rewarded for?

To simplify credit assignment, a common strategy is to evaluate an action based on the sum of all the rewards that come after it, applying a *discount factor*, _γ (gamma), at each step. This sum of discounted rewards is called the action's *return*. Consider the example in Figure 19-6. If an agent decides to go right three times in a row and gets +10 reward after the first step, 0 after the second step, and finally –50 after the third step, then assuming we use a discount factor $\gamma = 0.8$, the first action will have a return of $10 + \gamma \times 0 + \gamma^2 \times (-50) = -22$.

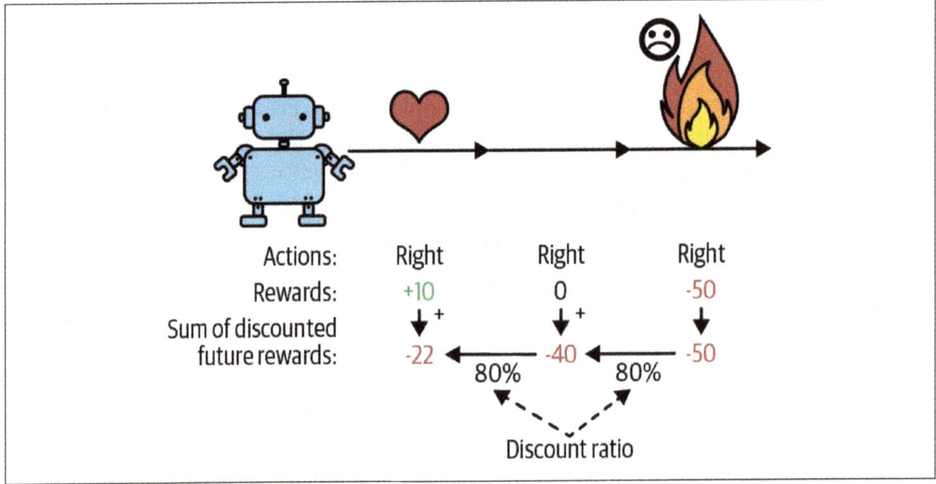

Figure 19-6. Computing an action's return: the sum of discounted future rewards

The following function computes the returns, given the rewards and the discount factor:

```
def compute_returns(rewards, discount_factor):
    returns = rewards[:]  # copy the rewards
    for step in range(len(returns) - 1, 0, -1):
        returns[step - 1] += returns[step] * discount_factor

    return torch.tensor(returns)
```

This function produces the expected result:

```
>>> compute_returns([10, 0, -50], discount_factor=0.8)
tensor([-22., -40., -50.])
```

If the discount factor is close to 0, then future rewards won't count for much compared to immediate rewards. Conversely, if the discount factor is close to 1, then rewards far into the future will count almost as much as immediate rewards. Typical discount factors vary from 0.9 to 0.99. With a discount factor of 0.95, rewards 13 steps into the future count roughly for half as much as immediate rewards (since $0.95^{13} \approx 0.5$), while with a discount factor of 0.99, rewards 69 steps into the future count for half as much as immediate rewards. In the CartPole environment, actions have fairly short-term effects, so choosing a low discount factor of 0.95 seems reasonable, and it will help with credit assignment, making training faster and more stable. However, if the discount factor is set too low, then the agent will learn a suboptimal strategy, focusing too much on short-term gains.

Now that we have a way to evaluate each action, we are ready to train our first agent using policy gradients. Let's see how.

Solving the CartPole Using Policy Gradients

As discussed earlier, policy gradient algorithms optimize the parameters of a policy by following the gradients toward higher rewards. One popular PG algorithm, called *REINFORCE* (or *Monte Carlo PG*), was introduced back in 1992 by Ronald Williams (*https://homl.info/132*).[11] It has many variants, with various tweaks, but the general principle is this:

1. First, let the neural network policy play the game for an episode, and record the rewards and estimated log probabilities.
2. Then compute each action's return, using the function defined in the previous section.

11 Ronald J. Williams, "Simple Statistical Gradient-Following Algorithms for Connectionist Reinforcement Leaning", *Machine Learning* 8 (1992): 229–256.

3. If an action's return is positive, it means that the action was probably good, and you want to make this action even more likely to be chosen in the future. Conversely, if an action's return is negative, you want to make this action *less* likely. To achieve this, you can minimize the REINFORCE loss defined in Equation 19-1: this will maximize the expected discounted rewards.

Equation 19-1. REINFORCE loss

$$\mathscr{L}(\boldsymbol{\theta}) = -\sum_{t} \log \pi_{\boldsymbol{\theta}}(a_t \mid s_t) \cdot r_t$$

In this equation, $\pi_{\boldsymbol{\theta}}(a_t|s_t)$ is the policy network's estimated probability for action a_t, given state s_t (where t is the time step), and r_t is the observed return of this action; $\boldsymbol{\theta}$ represents the model parameters.

Let's use PyTorch to implement this algorithm. First, we need a function to let the policy network play an episode, and record the rewards and log probabilities:

```
def run_episode(model, env, seed=None):
    log_probs, rewards = [], []
    obs, info = env.reset(seed=seed)
    while True:  # the environment will truncate the episode if it is too long
        action, log_prob = choose_action(model, obs)
        obs, reward, done, truncated, _info = env.step(action)
        log_probs.append(log_prob)
        rewards.append(reward)
        if done or truncated:
            return log_probs, rewards
```

The function first resets the environment to start a new episode. For reproducibility, we pass a seed to the `reset()` method. Then comes the game loop: at each iteration, we pass the current environment state (i.e., the last observation) to the `choose_action()` method we defined earlier. It returns the chosen action and its log probability. We then call the environment's `step()` method to execute the action. This returns a new observation (a NumPy array), a reward, two booleans indicating whether the game is over or truncated, and an info dict (which we can safely ignore in the case of CartPole). We record the log probabilities and rewards in two lists, which we return when the episode is over.

We can finally write the training function:

```
def train_reinforce(model, optimizer, env, n_episodes, discount_factor):
    for episode in range(n_episodes):
        seed = torch.randint(0, 2**32, size=()).item()
        log_probs, rewards = run_episode(model, env, seed=seed)
        returns = compute_returns(rewards, discount_factor)
        std_returns = (returns - returns.mean()) / (returns.std() + 1e-7)
        losses = [-logp * rt for logp, rt in zip(log_probs, std_returns)]
```

```python
        loss = torch.cat(losses).sum()
        optimizer.zero_grad()
        loss.backward()
        optimizer.step()
        print(f"\rEpisode {episode + 1}, Reward: {sum(rewards):.2f}", end=" ")
```

That's nice and short, isn't it? At each training iteration, the function runs an episode and gets the log probabilities and rewards.[12] Then it computes the return for each action. Next, it standardizes the returns (i.e., it subtracts the mean return and divides by the standard deviation, plus a small value to avoid division by zero). This standardization step is optional but it's a common and recommended tweak to the REINFORCE algorithm, as it stabilizes training. Next, the function computes the REINFORCE loss using Equation 19-1, and it performs an optimizer step to minimize the loss.

That's it, we're ready to build and train a policy network!

```python
torch.manual_seed(42)
model = PolicyNetwork()
optimizer = torch.optim.NAdam(model.parameters(), lr=0.06)
train_reinforce(model, optimizer, env, n_episodes=200, discount_factor=0.95)
```

Training will take less than a minute. If you run an episode using this policy network, you will see that it perfectly balances the pole. Success!

The simple policy gradients algorithm we just trained solved the CartPole task, but it would not scale well to larger and more complex tasks. Indeed, it is highly *sample inefficient*, meaning it needs to explore the game for a very long time before it can make significant progress. This is because its return estimates are extremely noisy, especially when good actions are mixed with bad ones. However, it is the foundation of more powerful algorithms, such as *actor-critic* algorithms (which we will discuss at the end of this chapter).

Researchers try to find algorithms that work well even when the agent initially knows nothing about the environment. However, unless you are writing a paper, you should not hesitate to inject prior knowledge into the agent, as it will speed up training dramatically. For example, since you know that the pole should be as vertical as possible, you could add negative rewards proportional to the pole's angle. This will make the rewards much less sparse and speed up training. Also, if you already have a reasonably good policy (e.g., hardcoded), you may want to train the neural network to imitate it before using policy gradients to improve it.

12 We generate a new random seed for each episode using `torch.randint()`. This ensures that each episode is different, yet the whole training process is reproducible if we set PyTorch's random seed before calling `train_reinforce()`.

Moreover, the REINFORCE algorithm is quite unstable: the agent may improve for a while during training, then forget everything catastrophically, learn again, forget, learn, etc. It's a roller coaster. This is in large part because the training samples are not independent and identically distributed (IID); indeed, the training samples consist of whatever states the agent is capable of reaching right now. As the agent progresses, it explores different parts of the environment, and it can forget everything about other parts. For example, once it learns to properly hold the pole upright, it will no longer see nonvertical poles, and it will totally forget how to handle them. And this issue gets much worse with more complex environments.

Reinforcement learning is notoriously difficult, largely because of the training instabilities and the huge sensitivity to the choice of hyperparameter values and random seeds.[13] As the researcher Andrej Karpathy put it, "[Supervised learning] wants to work. [...] RL must be forced to work". You will need time, patience, perseverance, and perhaps a bit of luck, too. This is a major reason RL is not as widely adopted as regular deep learning.

We will now look at another popular family of algorithms: *value-based methods*.

Value-Based Methods

Whereas PG algorithms directly try to optimize the policy to increase rewards, value-based methods are less direct: the agent learns to estimate the value of each state (i.e., the expected return), or the value of each action in a given state, then it uses this knowledge to decide how to act. To understand these algorithms, we must first discuss *Markov decision processes* (MDPs).

Markov Decision Processes

In the early 20th century, the mathematician Andrey Markov studied stochastic processes with no memory, called *Markov chains*. Such a process has a fixed number of states, and it randomly evolves from one state to another at each step. The probability for it to evolve from a state s to a state s' is fixed, and it depends only on the pair (s, s'), not on past states. This is why we say that the system has no memory.

13 A great 2018 post (*https://homl.info/rlhard*) by Alex Irpan nicely lays out RL's biggest difficulties and limitations.

Figure 19-7 shows an example of a Markov chain with four states.

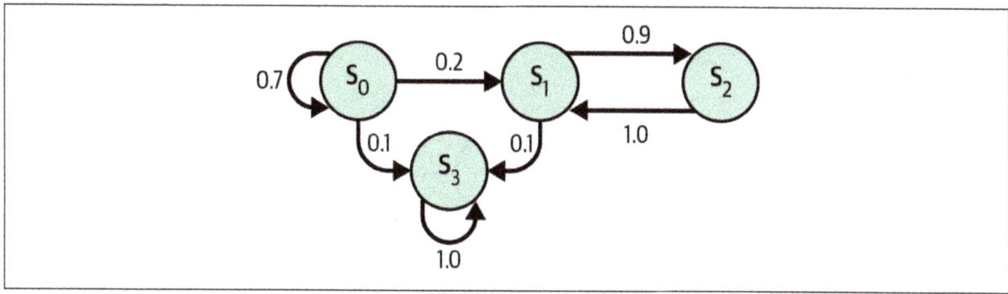

Figure 19-7. Example of a Markov chain

Suppose that the process starts in state s_0, and there is a 70% chance that it will remain in that state at the next step. Eventually it is bound to leave that state and never come back, because no other state points back to s_0. If it goes to state s_1, it will then most likely go to state s_2 (90% probability), then immediately back to state s_1 (with 100% probability). It may alternate a number of times between these two states, but eventually it will fall into state s_3 and remain there forever, since there's no way out: this is called a *terminal state*. Markov chains can have very different dynamics, and they are frequently used in thermodynamics, chemistry, statistics, and much more.

Markov decision processes were first described in the 1950s by Richard Bellman (*https://homl.info/133*).[14] They resemble Markov chains, but with a twist: at each step, an agent can choose one of several possible actions, and the transition probabilities depend on the chosen action. Moreover, some state transitions return some reward (positive or negative), and the agent's goal is to find a policy that will maximize its cumulative reward over time.

For example, the MDP represented in Figure 19-8 has three states (represented by circles) and up to three possible discrete actions at each step (represented by diamonds).

14 Richard Bellman, "A Markovian Decision Process", *Journal of Mathematics and Mechanics* 6, no. 5 (1957): 679–684.

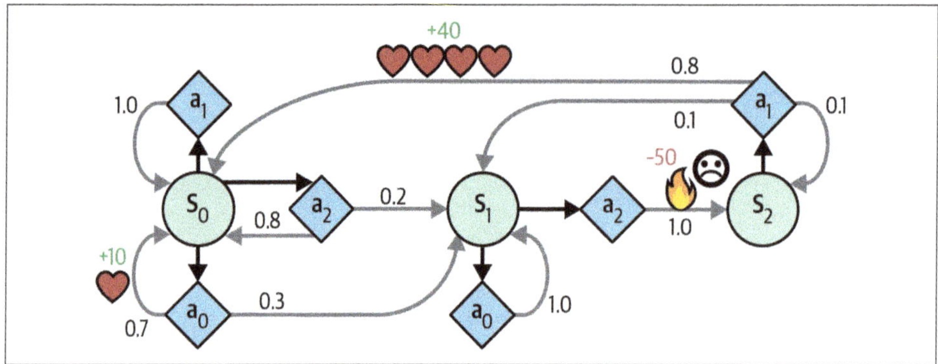

Figure 19-8. Example of a Markov decision process

If it starts in state s_0, the agent can choose among actions a_0, a_1, or a_2. If it chooses action a_1, it just remains in state s_0 with certainty and without any reward. It can thus decide to stay there forever if it wants to. But if it chooses action a_0, it has a 70% probability of gaining a reward of +10 and remaining in state s_0. It can then try again and again to gain as much reward as possible, but at one point it is going to end up instead in state s_1. In state s_1 it has only two possible actions: a_0 or a_2. It can choose to stay put by repeatedly choosing action a_0, or it can choose to move on to state s_2 and get a negative reward of –50 (ouch). In state s_2 it has no choice but to take action a_1, which will most likely lead it back to state s_0, gaining a reward of +40 on the way. You get the picture. By looking at this MDP, can you guess which strategy will gain the most reward over time? In state s_0 it is clear that action a_0 is the best option, and in state s_2 the agent has no choice but to take action a_1, but in state s_1 it is not obvious whether the agent should stay put (a_0) or go through the fire (a_2).

Bellman found a way to estimate the *optimal state value* of any state *s*, denoted $V^*(s)$, which is the sum of all discounted future rewards the agent can expect on average starting from state *s*, assuming it acts optimally. He showed that if the agent acts optimally, then the *Bellman optimality equation* applies (see Equation 19-2). This recursive equation says that if the agent acts optimally, then the optimal value of the current state is equal to the reward it will get on average after taking one optimal action, plus the expected optimal value of all possible next states that this action can lead to.

Equation 19-2. Bellman optimality equation

$$V^*(s) = \max_{a} \sum_{s'} T(s,a,s')\left[R(s,a,s') + \gamma \cdot V^*(s')\right] \quad \text{for all } s$$

In this equation:

- $T(s, a, s')$ is the transition probability from state s to state s', given that the agent chose action a. For example, in Figure 19-8, $T(s_2, a_1, s_0) = 0.8$. Note that $\sum_{s'} T(s,a,s') = 1$.
- $R(s, a, s')$ is the reward that the agent gets when it goes from state s to state s', given that the agent chose action a. For example, in Figure 19-8, $R(s_2, a_1, s_0) = +40$.
- γ is the discount factor.

In the Bellman equation and the rest of this chapter, an optimal policy is one that maximizes the expected sum of *discounted* future rewards: this means that it depends on the discount factor γ. However, in real-world tasks we're generally more interested in the expected sum of rewards per episode, without any discount (in fact, that's usually how we evaluate agents). To approach this goal, we usually choose a discount factor close to 1 (but not too close or else training becomes slow and unstable).

This equation leads directly to an algorithm that can precisely estimate the optimal state value of every possible state: first initialize all the state value estimates to zero, and then iteratively update them using the *value iteration* algorithm (see Equation 19-3). A remarkable result is that, given enough time, these estimates are guaranteed to converge to the optimal state values, corresponding to the optimal policy.

Equation 19-3. Value iteration algorithm

$$V_{k+1}(s) \leftarrow \max_{a} \sum_{s'} T(s,a,s')\left[R(s,a,s') + \gamma \cdot V_k(s')\right] \quad \text{for all } s$$

In this equation, $V_k(s)$ is the estimated value of state s at the kth iteration of the algorithm.

This algorithm is an example of *dynamic programming*, which breaks down a complex problem into tractable subproblems that can be tackled iteratively.

Knowing the optimal state values can be useful, in particular to evaluate a policy, but it does not give us the optimal policy for the agent. Luckily, Bellman found a very similar algorithm to estimate the optimal *state-action values*, generally called *Q-values* (quality values). The optimal Q-value of the state-action pair (*s*, *a*), denoted $Q^*(s, a)$, is the sum of discounted future rewards the agent can expect on average starting from state *s* if it chooses action *a*, but before it sees the outcome of this action, assuming it acts optimally after that action.

Let's look at how it works. Once again, you start by initializing all the Q-value estimates to zero, then you update them using the *Q-value iteration* algorithm (see Equation 19-4).

Equation 19-4. Q-value iteration algorithm

$$Q_{k+1}(s,a) \leftarrow \sum_{s'} T(s,a,s')\left[R(s,a,s') + \gamma \cdot \max_{a'} Q_k(s',a')\right] \quad \text{for all } (s,a)$$

Once you have the optimal Q-values, defining the optimal policy, denoted $\pi^*(s)$, is trivial: when the agent is in state *s*, it should choose the action with the highest Q-value for that state. The fancy math notation for this is $\pi^*(s) = \underset{a}{\operatorname{argmax}}\ Q^*(s,a)$.

Let's apply this algorithm to the MDP represented in Figure 19-8. First, we need to define the MDP:

```
transition_probabilities = [  # shape=[s, a, s']
    [[0.7, 0.3, 0.0], [1.0, 0.0, 0.0], [0.8, 0.2, 0.0]],
    [[0.0, 1.0, 0.0], None, [0.0, 0.0, 1.0]],
    [None, [0.8, 0.1, 0.1], None]
]
rewards = [  # shape=[s, a, s']
    [[+10, 0, 0], [0, 0, 0], [0, 0, 0]],
    [[0, 0, 0], [0, 0, 0], [0, 0, -50]],
    [[0, 0, 0], [+40, 0, 0], [0, 0, 0]]
]
possible_actions = [[0, 1, 2], [0, 2], [1]]
```

For example, to know the transition probability of going from s_2 to s_0 after playing action a_1, we will look up `transition_probabilities[2][1][0]` (which is 0.8). Similarly, to get the corresponding reward, we will look up `rewards[2][1][0]` (which is +40). And to get the list of possible actions in s_2, we will look up `possible_actions[2]` (in this case, only action a_1 is possible). Next, we must initialize all the Q-values to zero (except for the impossible actions, for which we set the Q-values to $-\infty$):

```
Q_values = np.full((3, 3), -np.inf)  # -np.inf for impossible actions
for state, actions in enumerate(possible_actions):
    Q_values[state, actions] = 0.0  # for all possible actions
```

Now let's run the Q-value iteration algorithm. It applies Equation 19-4 repeatedly, to all Q-values, for every state and every possible action:

```
gamma = 0.90  # the discount factor

for iteration in range(50):
    Q_prev = Q_values.copy()
    for s in range(3):
        for a in possible_actions[s]:
            Q_values[s, a] = np.sum([
                    transition_probabilities[s][a][sp]
                    * (rewards[s][a][sp] + gamma * Q_prev[sp].max())
                for sp in range(3)])
```

That's it! The resulting Q-values look like this:

```
>>> Q_values
array([[18.91891892, 17.02702702, 13.62162162],
       [ 0.        ,        -inf, -4.87971488],
       [       -inf, 50.13365013,        -inf]])
```

For example, when the agent is in state s_0 and it chooses action a_1, the expected sum of discounted future rewards is approximately 17.0.

For each state, we can find the action that has the highest Q-value:

```
>>> Q_values.argmax(axis=1)  # optimal action for each state
array([0, 0, 1])
```

This gives us the optimal policy for this MDP when using a discount factor of 0.90: in state s_0 choose action a_0, in state s_1 choose action a_0 (i.e., stay put), and in state s_2 choose action a_1 (the only possible action). Interestingly, if we increase the discount factor to 0.95, the optimal policy changes: in state s_1 the best action becomes a_2 (go through the fire!). This makes sense because the more you value future rewards, the more you are willing to put up with some pain now for the promise of future bliss.

Temporal Difference Learning

Reinforcement learning problems with discrete actions can often be modeled as Markov decision processes, but the agent initially has no idea what the transition probabilities are (it does not know $T(s, a, s')$), and it does not know what the rewards are going to be either (it does not know $R(s, a, s')$). It must experience each state and each transition at least once to know the rewards, and it must experience them multiple times if it is to have a reasonable estimate of the transition probabilities.

The *temporal difference (TD) learning* algorithm is very similar to the Q-value iteration algorithm, but tweaked to take into account the fact that the agent has only partial knowledge of the MDP. In general we assume that the agent initially knows only the possible states and actions, and nothing more. The agent uses an *exploration policy*—for example, a purely random policy—to explore the MDP, and as it progresses, the TD learning algorithm updates the estimates of the state values based on the transitions and rewards that are actually observed (see Equation 19-5).

Equation 19-5. TD learning algorithm

$$V_{k+1}(s) \leftarrow (1-\alpha)\,V_k(s) + \alpha\left(r + \gamma \cdot V_k(s')\right)$$
$$\text{or, equivalently:}$$
$$V_{k+1}(s) \leftarrow V_k(s) + \alpha \cdot \delta_k(s,r,s')$$
$$\text{with} \quad \delta_k(s,r,s') = r + \gamma \cdot V_k(s') - V_k(s)$$

In this equation:

- α is the learning rate (e.g., 0.01).
- $r + \gamma \cdot V_k(s')$ is called the *TD target*.
- $\delta_k(s, r, s')$ is called the *TD error*.

A more concise way of writing the first form of this equation is to use the notation $a \underset{\alpha}{\leftarrow} b$, which means $a_{k+1} \leftarrow (1 - \alpha) \cdot a_k + \alpha \cdot b_k$. So the first line of Equation 19-5 can be rewritten like this: $V(s) \underset{\alpha}{\leftarrow} r + \gamma \cdot V(s')$.

TD learning has many similarities with stochastic gradient descent, including the fact that it handles one sample at a time. Moreover, just like SGD, it can only truly converge if you gradually reduce the learning rate; otherwise, it will keep bouncing around the optimum Q-values.

For each state *s*, this algorithm keeps track of a running average of the immediate rewards the agent gets upon leaving that state, plus the rewards it expects to get later, assuming it acts optimally.

Q-Learning

Similarly, the Q-learning algorithm is an adaptation of the Q-value iteration algorithm to the situation where the transition probabilities and the rewards are initially unknown (see Equation 19-6). Q-learning works by watching an agent play (e.g., randomly) and gradually improving its estimates of the Q-values. Once it has accurate Q-value estimates (or close enough), then the optimal policy is to choose the action that has the highest Q-value (i.e., the greedy policy).

Equation 19-6. Q-learning algorithm

$$Q(s,a) \underset{\alpha}{\leftarrow} r + \gamma \cdot \max_{a'} Q(s',a')$$

For each state-action pair (*s*, *a*), this algorithm keeps track of a running average of the rewards *r* the agent gets upon leaving the state *s* with action *a*, plus the sum of discounted future rewards it expects to get. To estimate this sum, we take the maximum of the Q-value estimates for the next state *s′*, since we assume that the target policy will act optimally from then on.

Let's implement the Q-learning algorithm. First, we will need to make an agent explore the environment. For this, we need a step function so that the agent can execute one action and get the resulting state and reward:

```
def step(state, action):
    probas = transition_probabilities[state][action]
    next_state = np.random.choice([0, 1, 2], p=probas)
    reward = rewards[state][action][next_state]
    return next_state, reward
```

Now let's implement the agent's exploration policy. Since the state space is pretty small, a simple random policy will be sufficient. If we run the algorithm for long enough, the agent will visit every state many times, and it will also try every possible action many times:

```
def exploration_policy(state):
    return np.random.choice(possible_actions[state])
```

Next, after we initialize the Q-values just like earlier, we are ready to run the Q-learning algorithm with learning rate decay (using power scheduling, introduced in Chapter 11):

```
alpha0 = 0.05  # initial learning rate
decay = 0.005  # learning rate decay
gamma = 0.90  # discount factor
state = 0  # initial state

for iteration in range(10_000):
    action = exploration_policy(state)
    next_state, reward = step(state, action)
    next_value = Q_values[next_state].max()  # greedy policy at the next step
    alpha = alpha0 / (1 + iteration * decay)
    Q_values[state, action] *= 1 - alpha
    Q_values[state, action] += alpha * (reward + gamma * next_value)
    state = next_state
```

This algorithm will converge to the optimal Q-values, but it will take many iterations, and possibly quite a lot of hyperparameter tuning. As you can see in Figure 19-9, the Q-value iteration algorithm (left) converges very quickly, in fewer than 20 iterations, while the Q-learning algorithm (right) takes about 8,000 iterations to converge.

Obviously, not knowing the transition probabilities or the rewards makes finding the optimal policy significantly harder!

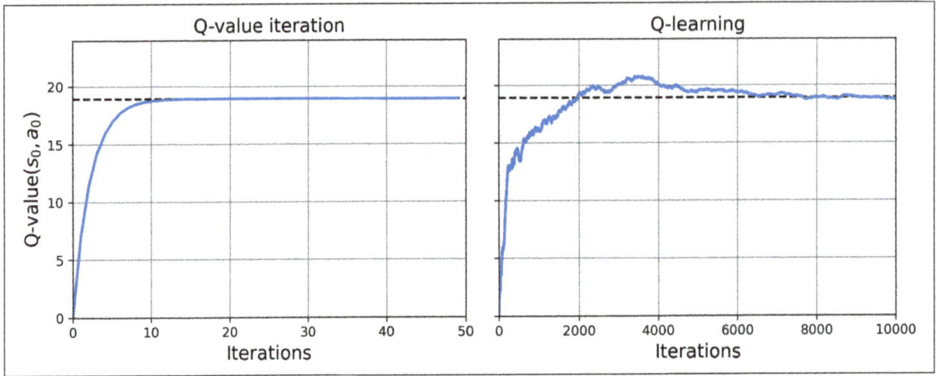

Figure 19-9. Learning curve of the Q-value iteration algorithm versus the Q-learning algorithm

The Q-learning algorithm is called an *off-policy* algorithm because the policy being trained is not necessarily the one used during training. For example, in the code we just ran, the policy being executed (the exploration policy) was completely random, while the policy being trained was never used. After training, the optimal policy corresponds to systematically choosing the action with the highest Q-value. Conversely, the REINFORCE algorithm is *on-policy*: it explores the world using the policy being trained. It is somewhat surprising that Q-learning is capable of learning the optimal policy by just watching an agent act randomly. Imagine learning to play golf when your teacher is a blindfolded monkey. Can we do better?

Exploration Policies

Of course, Q-learning can work only if the exploration policy explores the MDP thoroughly enough. Although a purely random policy is guaranteed to eventually visit every state and every transition many times, it may take an extremely long time to do so. Therefore, a better option is to use the *ε-greedy policy* (ε is epsilon): at each step it acts randomly with probability ε, or greedily with probability 1–ε (i.e., choosing the action with the highest Q-value). The advantage of the ε-greedy policy (compared to a completely random policy) is that it will spend more and more time exploring the interesting parts of the environment, as the Q-value estimates get better and better, while still spending some time visiting unknown regions of the MDP. It is quite common to start with a high value for ε (e.g., 1.0) and then gradually reduce it (e.g., down to 0.05).

Alternatively, rather than relying only on chance for exploration, another approach is to encourage the exploration policy to try actions that it has not tried much before.

This can be implemented as a bonus added to the Q-value estimates, as shown in Equation 19-7.

Equation 19-7. Q-learning using an exploration function

$$Q(s,a) \underset{\alpha}{\leftarrow} r + \gamma \cdot \max_{a'} f(Q(s',a'),N(s',a'))$$

In this equation:

- $N(s', a')$ counts the number of times the action a' was chosen in state s'.
- $f(Q, N)$ is an *exploration function*, such as $f(Q, N) = Q + \kappa/(1 + N)$, where κ (kappa) is a curiosity hyperparameter that measures how much the agent is attracted to the unknown.

Approximate Q-Learning and Deep Q-Learning

The main problem with Q-learning is that it does not scale well to large (or even medium) MDPs with many states and actions. For example, suppose you wanted to use Q-learning to train an agent to play *Ms. Pac-Man* (see Figure 19-1). There are about 240 pellets that Ms. Pac-Man can eat, each of which can be present or absent (i.e., already eaten). So, the number of possible pellet states is about $2^{240} \approx 10^{73}$. And if you add all the possible combinations of positions for all the ghosts and Ms. Pac-Man, the number of possible states becomes larger than the number of atoms in our galaxy, so there's absolutely no way you can keep track of an estimate for every single Q-value.

The solution is to find a function $Q_{\boldsymbol{\theta}}(s, a)$ that approximates the Q-value of any state-action pair (s, a), where the vector $\boldsymbol{\theta}$ parameterizes the function. This is called *approximate Q-learning*. For years it was recommended to use linear combinations of handcrafted features extracted from the state (e.g., the distances of the closest ghosts, their directions, and so on) to estimate Q-values, but in 2013, DeepMind (*https://homl.info/dqn*) showed that using deep neural networks can work much better, especially for complex problems, and it does not require any feature engineering. A DNN that is used to estimate Q-values is called a *deep Q-network* (DQN), and using a DQN for approximate Q-learning is called *deep Q-learning*.

Now, how can we train a DQN? Well, consider the approximate Q-value computed by the DQN for a given state-action pair (s, a). Thanks to Bellman, we know we want this approximate Q-value to be as close as possible to the reward r that we actually observe after playing action a in state s, plus the discounted value of playing optimally from then on. To estimate this sum of future discounted rewards, we can just execute the DQN on the next state s', for all possible actions a'. We get an approximate future Q-value for each possible action. We then pick the highest (since we assume we will be playing optimally) and discount it, and this gives us an estimate of the sum of future discounted rewards. By summing the reward *r* and the future discounted value estimate, we get a target Q-value *y*(*s*, *a*) for the state-action pair (*s*, *a*), as shown in Equation 19-8.

Equation 19-8. Target Q-value

$$y(s,a) = r + \gamma \cdot \max_{a'} Q_{\boldsymbol{\theta}}(s',a')$$

With this target Q-value, we can run a training step using any gradient descent algorithm. In general, we try to minimize the squared error between the estimated Q-value $Q_{\theta}(s, a)$ and the target Q-value *y*(*s*, *a*), or the Huber loss to reduce the algorithm's sensitivity to large errors. And that's the deep Q-learning algorithm! Let's see how to implement it to solve the CartPole environment.

Implementing Deep Q-Learning

The first thing we need is a deep Q-network. In theory, we need a neural net that takes a state-action pair as input, and outputs an approximate Q-value. However, in practice it's much more efficient to use a neural net that takes only a state as input, and outputs one approximate Q-value for each possible action. To solve the CartPole environment, we do not need a very complicated neural net; a couple of hidden layers will do:

```
class DQN(nn.Module):
    def __init__(self):
        super().__init__()
        self.net = nn.Sequential(nn.Linear(4, 32), nn.ReLU(),
                                 nn.Linear(32, 32), nn.ReLU(),
                                 nn.Linear(32, 2))

    def forward(self, state):
        return self.net(state)
```

Our DQN is very similar to our earlier policy network, except it outputs a Q-value for each action instead of logits. Now let's define a function to choose an action based on this DQN:

```
def choose_dqn_action(model, obs, epsilon=0.0):
        if torch.rand(()) < epsilon:  # epsilon greedy policy
            return torch.randint(2, size=()).item()
        else:
            state = torch.as_tensor(obs)
            Q_values = model(state)
            return Q_values.argmax().item()  # optimal according to the DQN
```

This function takes an environment state (a single observation) and passes it to the neural net to predict the Q-values, then it simply returns the action with the largest predicted Q-value (`argmax()`). To ensure that the agent explores the environment, we use an ε-greedy policy, meaning we choose a random action with probability ε.

DQNs generally don't work with continuous action spaces, unless you can discretize the space (which only works if it's tiny) or combine them with policy gradients. This is because the DQN agent must find the action with the highest Q-value at each step. In a continuous action space, this requires running an optimization algorithm on the Q-value function at each step, which is not practical.

Instead of training the DQN based only on the latest experiences, we will store all experiences in a *replay buffer* (or *replay memory*), and we will sample a random training batch from it at each training iteration. This helps reduce the correlations between the experiences in a training batch, which stabilizes training by making the data distribution more consistent. Each experience will be represented as a tuple with six elements: a state *s*, the action *a* that the agent took, the resulting reward *r*, the next state *s′* it reached, a boolean indicating whether the episode ended at that point (`done`), and finally another boolean indicating whether the episode was truncated at that point. We will also need a function to sample a random batch of experiences from the replay buffer. It will return a tuple containing six tensors, one for each field:

```
def sample_experiences(replay_buffer, batch_size):
    indices = torch.randint(len(replay_buffer), size=[batch_size])
    batch = [replay_buffer[index] for index in indices.tolist()]
    return [to_tensor([exp[index] for exp in batch]) for index in range(6)]

def to_tensor(data):
    array = np.stack(data)
    dtype = torch.float32 if array.dtype == np.float64 else None
    return torch.as_tensor(array, dtype=dtype)
```

The `sample_experiences()` function takes a replay buffer and a batch size, and it randomly samples the desired number of experience tuples from the buffer. Then, for each of the six fields in the experience tuples, it extracts that field from each experience in the batch, and converts that list to a tensor using the `to_tensor()` function. Lastly, it returns the list of six tensors. The tensors all have shape [`batch size`] except for the observation tensors, which have shape [`batch size`, 4].

The `to_tensor()` function takes a Python list containing observations (i.e., 64-bit NumPy arrays of shape [4]), or actions (integers), or rewards (floats), or booleans (done or truncated), and it returns a tensor of the appropriate PyTorch type. Note that the 64-bit NumPy arrays containing the observations are converted to 32-bit tensors.

The replay buffer can be any data structure that supports appending and indexing, and can limit the size to avoid blowing up memory during training. For simplicity, we will use a Python *deque*, from the standard `collections` package. This is a double-ended queue, in which elements can be efficiently appended or popped (i.e., removed) on both ends. If you set a size limit, and that limit is reached, appending an element to one end of the queue automatically pops an item from the other side. This means that each new experience replaces the oldest experience, which is exactly what we want.

Appending and popping items on the ends of a deque is very fast, but random access can be slow when the queue gets very long (e.g., 100,000 items or more). If you need a very large replay buffer, you should use a circular buffer instead (see the notebook for an implementation), or check out DeepMind's Reverb library (*https://homl.info/reverb*).

Let's also create a function that will play a full episode using our DQN, and store the resulting experiences in the replay buffer. We'll run in eval mode with `torch.no_grad()` since we don't need gradients for now. For logging purposes, we'll also make the function sum up all the rewards in the episode and return the result:

```
def play_and_record_episode(model, env, replay_buffer, epsilon, seed=None):
    obs, _info = env.reset(seed=seed)
    total_rewards = 0
    model.eval()
    with torch.no_grad():
        while True:
            action = choose_dqn_action(model, obs, epsilon)
            next_obs, reward, done, truncated, _info = env.step(action)
            experience = (obs, action, reward, next_obs, done, truncated)
            replay_buffer.append(experience)
            total_rewards += reward
            if done or truncated:
                return total_rewards
            obs = next_obs
```

Next, let's create a function that will sample a batch of experiences from the replay buffer and train the DQN by performing a single gradient descent step on this batch:

```
def dqn_training_step(model, optimizer, criterion, replay_buffer, batch_size,
                      discount_factor):
    experiences = sample_experiences(replay_buffer, batch_size)
    state, action, reward, next_state, done, truncated = experiences
    with torch.inference_mode():
        next_Q_value = model(next_state)

    max_next_Q_value, _ = next_Q_value.max(dim=1)
    running = (~(done | truncated)).float()  # 0 if s' is over, 1 if running
```

```
        target_Q_value = reward + running * discount_factor * max_next_Q_value
        all_Q_values = model(state)
        Q_value = all_Q_values.gather(dim=1, index=action.unsqueeze(1))
        loss = criterion(Q_value, target_Q_value.unsqueeze(1))
        optimizer.zero_grad()
        loss.backward()
        optimizer.step()
```

The `torch.inference_mode()` context is like `torch.no_grad()`, plus models run in eval mode within the context, and new tensors cannot be used in backpropagation.

Here's what's happening in this code:

- The function starts by sampling a batch of experiences from the replay buffer.
- Then it uses the DQN to compute the target Q-value for each experience in the batch. For this, the code implements Equation 19-8: the DQN is used in inference mode to evaluate all the Q-values for the next state *s'*, then we keep only the max Q-value since we assume that the agent will play optimally from now on, and we multiply this max Q-value with the discount factor. If the episode was over (done or truncated), then the discounted max Q-value is multiplied by zero since we cannot expect any more rewards. Otherwise, it's multiplied by 1 (i.e., unchanged). Lastly, we add the experience's reward. All of this is performed simultaneously for all experiences in the batch.
- Next, the function uses the model again (in training mode this time) to compute all the Q-values for the current state *s*, and it uses the `gather()` method to extract just the Q-value that corresponds to the action that was actually chosen. Again, this is done simultaneously for all experiences in the batch.
- Lastly, we compute the loss, which is typically the MSE between the target Q-values and the predicted Q-values, and we perform an optimizer step to minimize the loss.

Phew! That was the hardest part. Now we can write the main training function and run it:

```
from collections import deque

def train_dqn(model, env, replay_buffer, optimizer, criterion, n_episodes=800,
              warmup=30, batch_size=32, discount_factor=0.95):
    totals = []
    for episode in range(n_episodes):
        epsilon = max(1 - episode / 500, 0.01)
        seed = torch.randint(0, 2**32, size=()).item()
```

```
        total_rewards = play_and_record_episode(model, env, replay_buffer,
                                                epsilon, seed=seed)
        print(f"\rEpisode: {episode + 1}, Rewards: {total_rewards}", end=" ")
        totals.append(total_rewards)
        if episode >= warmup:
            dqn_training_step(model, optimizer, criterion, replay_buffer,
                              batch_size, discount_factor)
    return totals

torch.manual_seed(42)
dqn = DQN()
optimizer = torch.optim.NAdam(dqn.parameters(), lr=0.03)
mse = nn.MSELoss()
replay_buffer = deque(maxlen=100_000)
totals = train_dqn(dqn, env, replay_buffer, optimizer, mse)
```

The training algorithm runs for 800 episodes. At each training iteration, we make the DQN play one full episode using the `play_and_record_episode()` function, then we run one training step using the `dqn_training_step()` function. Note that we only start training after several warmup episodes to ensure that the replay buffer contains plenty of experiences. We also linearly decrease the epsilon value for the ε-greedy policy from 1.0 down to 0.01 after 500 episodes (then it remains at 0.01). This way, the agent's behavior will gradually become less random, focusing more on exploitation and less on exploration. The function also records the total rewards for each episode, and returns these totals; they are plotted in Figure 19-10.

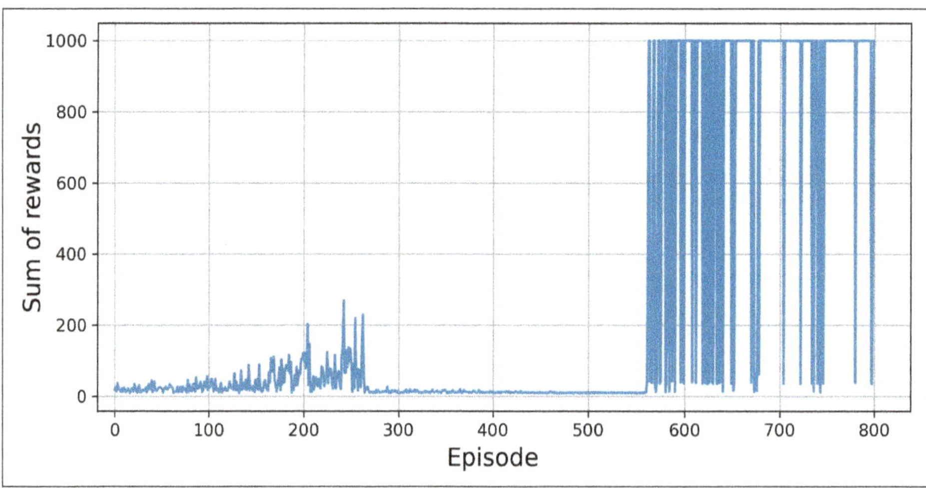

Figure 19-10. Learning curve of the deep Q-learning algorithm

Why not plot the loss? Well, it's a poor indicator of the model's performance, so it's preferable to plot the total rewards for each episode. Indeed, the loss might go down while the agent performs worse (e.g., if the agent gets stuck in one small region of the environment and the DQN starts overfitting it). Conversely, the loss could go up while the agent performs better (e.g., if the DQN was underestimating the target Q-values and it starts correctly increasing them).

The good news is that the algorithm worked: the trained agent perfectly balances the pole on the cart and reaches the maximum total reward of 1,000. The bad news is that the training is completely unstable. In fact, it's even less stable than REINFORCE. I had to tweak the hyperparameters quite a bit before stumbling upon this successful training run. As you can see, the agent managed to reach a reward of 200 points after roughly 200 episodes, which isn't bad, but soon after it forgot everything and performed terribly until episode ~550, when it quickly cracked the problem.

So why is this DQN implementation unstable? Could it be the data distribution? Well, the replay buffer is quite large, so the data distribution is certainly much more stable than with the REINFORCE algorithm. So what's happening? Well, in this basic deep Q-learning implementation, the model is used both to make predictions and to set its own targets. This can lead to a situation analogous to a dog chasing its own tail. This feedback loop can make the network unstable: it can diverge, oscillate, freeze, and so on. Luckily, there are ways to improve this; let's see how.

DQN Improvements

In their 2013 paper, DeepMind researchers proposed a way to stabilize DQN training by using two DQNs instead of one: the first is the *online model*, which learns at each step and is used to move the agent around, and the other is the *target model* used only to define the targets. The target model is just a clone of the online model, and its weights are copied from the online model at regular intervals (e.g., every 10,000 steps in their Atari models). This makes the Q-value targets much more stable, so the feedback loop is damped, and its effects are much less severe. They combined this major improvement with several other tweaks: a very large replay buffer, a tiny learning rate, a very long training time (50 million steps), a very slowly decreasing epsilon (over 1 million steps), and a powerful neural net (a CNN).

Then, in a 2015 paper (*https://homl.info/doubledqn*),[15] DeepMind researchers tweaked their DQN algorithm again, increasing its performance and somewhat stabilizing training. They called this variant *double DQN*. The update was based on the

15 Hado van Hasselt et al., "Deep Reinforcement Learning with Double Q-Learning", *Proceedings of the 30th AAAI Conference on Artificial Intelligence* (2015): 2094–2100.

observation that the target network is prone to overestimating Q-values. Indeed, suppose all actions are equally good: the Q-values estimated by the target model should be identical, but since they are approximations, some may be slightly greater than others by pure chance. The target model will always select the largest Q-value, which will be slightly greater than the mean Q-value, most likely overestimating the true Q-value (a bit like counting the height of the tallest random wave when measuring the depth of a pool). To fix this, the researchers proposed using the online model instead of the target model when selecting the best action for the next state, and using the target model only to estimate the Q-value of this best action.

Another important improvement was the introduction of *prioritized experience replay* (PER), which was proposed in a 2015 paper (*https://homl.info/prioreplay*)[16] by DeepMind researchers (once again!). Instead of sampling experiences *uniformly* from the replay buffer, why not sample important experiences more frequently?

More specifically, experiences are considered "important" if they are likely to lead to fast learning progress. But how can we estimate this? One reasonable approach is to measure the magnitude of the TD error $\delta = r + \gamma \cdot V(s') - V(s)$. A large TD error indicates that a transition (s, a, s') is very surprising and thus probably worth learning from.[17] When an experience is recorded in the replay buffer, its priority is set to a very large value to ensure that it gets sampled at least once. However, once it is sampled (and every time it is sampled), the TD error δ is computed, and this experience's priority is set to $p = |\delta|$ (plus a small constant to ensure that every experience has a nonzero probability of being sampled). The probability P of sampling an experience with priority p is proportional to p^{ζ}, where ζ (zeta) is a hyperparameter that controls how greedy we want importance sampling to be: when $\zeta = 0$, we just get uniform sampling, and when $\zeta = 1$, we get full-blown importance sampling. In the paper, the authors used $\zeta = 0.6$, but the optimal value will depend on the task.

There's one catch though: since the samples will be biased toward important experiences, we must compensate for this bias during training by downweighting the experiences according to their importance, or the model will just overfit the important experiences. To be clear, we want important experiences to be sampled more often, but this also means we must give them a lower weight during training. To do this, we define each experience's training weight as $w = (n\ P)^{-\beta}$, where n is the number of experiences in the replay buffer, and β is a hyperparameter that controls how much we want to compensate for the importance sampling bias (0 means not at all, while 1 means entirely). In the paper, the authors used $\beta = 0.4$ at the beginning of training and linearly increased it to $\beta = 1$ by the end of training. Again, the optimal value

16 Tom Schaul et al., "Prioritized Experience Replay", arXiv preprint arXiv:1511.05952 (2015).

17 It could also just be that the rewards are noisy, in which case there are better methods for estimating an experience's importance (see "Prioritized Experience Replay" for some examples).

will depend on the task, but if you increase one, you will usually want to increase the other as well.

One last noteworthy DQN variant is the *dueling DQN* algorithm (DDQN, not to be confused with double DQN, although both techniques can easily be combined). It was introduced in yet another 2015 paper (*https://homl.info/ddqn*)[18] by DeepMind researchers. To understand how it works, we must first note that the Q-value of a state-action pair (s, a) can be expressed as $Q(s, a) = V(s) + A(s, a)$, where $V(s)$ is the value of state s, and $A(s, a)$ is the *advantage* of taking the action a in state s, compared to all other possible actions in that state. Moreover, the value of a state is equal to the Q-value of the best action a^* for that state (since we assume the optimal policy will pick the best action), so $V(s) = Q(s, a^*)$, which implies that $A(s, a^*) = 0$. In a dueling DQN, the model estimates both the value of the state and the advantage of each possible action. Since the best action should have an advantage of 0, the model subtracts the maximum predicted advantage from all predicted advantages. The rest of the algorithm is just the same as earlier.

These techniques can be combined in various ways, as DeepMind demonstrated in a 2017 paper (*https://homl.info/rainbow*):[19] the paper's authors combined six different techniques into an agent called *Rainbow*, which largely outperformed the state of the art.

Speaking of combining different methods, why not combine policy gradients with value-based methods to get the best of both worlds? This is the core idea behind actor-critic algorithms. Let's discuss them now.

Actor-Critic Algorithms

Actor-critics are a family of RL algorithms that combine policy gradients with value-based methods. An actor-critic is composed of a policy (the actor) and a value network (the critic), which are trained simultaneously. The actor relies on the critic to estimate the value (or advantage) of actions or states, guiding its policy updates. Since the critic can use a large replay buffer, it stabilizes training and increases data efficiency. It's a bit like an athlete (the actor) learning with the help of a coach (the critic).

Moreover, actor-critic methods support stochastic policies and continuous action spaces, just like policy gradients. So we do get the best of both worlds.

18 Ziyu Wang et al., "Dueling Network Architectures for Deep Reinforcement Learning", arXiv preprint arXiv:1511.06581 (2015).

19 Matteo Hessel et al., "Rainbow: Combining Improvements in Deep Reinforcement Learning", arXiv preprint arXiv:1710.02298 (2017): 3215–3222.

Let's implement a basic actor-critic:

```
class ActorCritic(nn.Module):
    def __init__(self):
        super().__init__()
        self.body = nn.Sequential(nn.Linear(4, 32), nn.ReLU(),
                                  nn.Linear(32, 32), nn.ReLU())
        self.actor_head = nn.Linear(32, 1)  # outputs action logits
        self.critic_head = nn.Linear(32, 1)  # outputs state values

    def forward(self, state):
        features = self.body(state)
        return self.actor_head(features), self.critic_head(features)
```

In the constructor, we build the actor and critic networks. In this implementation, they share the same lower layers (called the *body*). This is common practice, as it reduces the total number of parameters and thereby increases data efficiency, but it also makes training a bit less stable since it couples the actor and critic more closely (another dog chasing its tail situation). The actor network takes a batch of environment states and outputs an action logit for each state (that's the logit for action 1, just like for REINFORCE). The critic network estimates the value of each given state. The `forward()` method takes a batch of states and runs them through both networks (with a shared body), and returns the action logits and state values.

Now let's write a function to choose an action. It's identical to the `choose_action()` function we wrote earlier for the REINFORCE policy network, except that it also returns the state value estimated by the critic network. This will be needed for training:

```
def choose_action_and_evaluate(model, obs):
    state = torch.as_tensor(obs)
    logit, state_value = model(state)
    dist = torch.distributions.Bernoulli(logits=logit)
    action = dist.sample()
    log_prob = dist.log_prob(action)
    return int(action.item()), log_prob, state_value
```

Great! Now let's see how to train our actor-critic. We'll start by defining a function that will perform one training step:

```
def ac_training_step(optimizer, criterion, state_value, target_value, log_prob,
                     critic_weight):
    td_error = target_value - state_value
    actor_loss = -log_prob * td_error.detach()
    critic_loss = criterion(state_value, target_value)
    loss = actor_loss + critic_weight * critic_loss
    optimizer.zero_grad()
    loss.backward()
    optimizer.step()
```

First, we compute the TD error, which is the difference between the target value $y = r + \gamma V(s')$ and the state value $V(s)$. The actor's loss is the same as in REINFORCE, except that we multiply the log probability by the TD error instead of the (standardized) return. In other words, we encourage actions that performed better than the value network expected. As for the critic's loss, it encourages the critic's value estimates $V(s)$ to match the target values y (e.g., using the MSE). Lastly, the overall loss is a weighted sum of the actor's loss and the critic's loss. To stabilize training, it's generally a good idea to give less weight to the critic's loss. Then we perform an optimizer step to minimize the loss. Oh, and note that we call `td_error.detach()` because we don't want gradient descent to affect the critic network via the actor's loss.

We'll also need a function to compute the target value:

```
def get_target_value(model, next_obs, reward, done, truncated, discount_factor):
    with torch.inference_mode():
        _, _, next_state_value = choose_action_and_evaluate(model, next_obs)

    running = 0.0 if (done or truncated) else 1.0
    target_value = reward + running * discount_factor * next_state_value
    return target_value
```

This code first evaluates $V(s')$ using the `choose_action_and_evaluate()` function (we ignore the chosen action and its log probability). We run this in inference mode because we are computing the target: we don't want gradient descent to affect it. Next, we simply evaluate the target $y = r + \gamma V(s')$. If the episode is over, then $y = r$.

With that, we have all we need to write a function that will run a whole episode and train the actor-critic at each step (we also compute the total rewards and return it when the episode is over):

```
def run_episode_and_train(model, optimizer, criterion, env, discount_factor,
                          critic_weight, seed=None):
    obs, _info = env.reset(seed=seed)
    total_rewards = 0
    while True:
        action, log_prob, state_value = choose_action_and_evaluate(model, obs)
        next_obs, reward, done, truncated, _info = env.step(action)
        target_value = get_target_value(model, next_obs, reward, done,
                                        truncated, discount_factor)
        ac_training_step(optimizer, criterion, state_value, target_value,
                         log_prob, critic_weight)
        total_rewards += reward
        if done or truncated:
            return total_rewards
        obs = next_obs
```

And lastly, we can write our main training function, which just calls the `run_episode_and_train()` function many times and returns the total rewards for each episode:

```python
def train_actor_critic(model, optimizer, criterion, env, n_episodes=400,
                       discount_factor=0.95, critic_weight=0.3):
    totals = []
    model.train()
    for episode in range(n_episodes):
        seed = torch.randint(0, 2**32, size=()).item()
        total_rewards = run_episode_and_train(model, optimizer, criterion, env,
                                              discount_factor, critic_weight,
                                              seed=seed)
        totals.append(total_rewards)
        print(f"\rEpisode: {episode + 1}, Rewards: {total_rewards}", end=" ")

    return totals
```

Let's run it!

```python
torch.manual_seed(42)
ac_model = ActorCritic()
optimizer = torch.optim.NAdam(ac_model.parameters(), lr=1.1e-3)
criterion = nn.MSELoss()
totals = train_actor_critic(ac_model, optimizer, criterion, env)
```

And it works! We get a very stable CartPole that collects the maximum rewards. That said, this implementation is still very sensitive to the choice of hyperparameters and random seeds, and training is still very unstable. Luckily, researchers have come up with various techniques that can stabilize the actor-critic. Here are some of the most popular:

Asynchronous advantage actor-critic (A3C) (https://homl.info/a3c)[20]
: This is an important actor-critic variant introduced by DeepMind researchers in 2016 where multiple agents learn in parallel, exploring different copies of the environment. At regular intervals, but asynchronously (hence the name), each agent pushes some weight updates to a master network, then it pulls the latest weights from that network. Each agent thus contributes to improving the master network and benefits from what the other agents have learned. Moreover, instead of estimating the state values, or even the Q-values, the critic estimates the *advantage* of each action (hence the second A in the name), just like in the Dueling DQN.

Advantage actor-critic (A2C) (https://homl.info/a2c)
: A2C is a variant of the A3C algorithm that removes the asynchronicity. All model updates are synchronous, so gradient updates are performed over larger batches, which allows the model to better utilize the power of the GPU.

20 Volodymyr Mnih et al., "Asynchronous Methods for Deep Reinforcement Learning", *Proceedings of the 33rd International Conference on Machine Learning* (2016): 1928–1937.

Soft actor-critic (SAC) (https://homl.info/sac)[21]

SAC is an actor-critic variant proposed in 2018 by Tuomas Haarnoja and other UC Berkeley researchers. It learns not only rewards, but also how to maximize the entropy of its actions. In other words, it tries to be as unpredictable as possible while still getting as many rewards as possible. This encourages the agent to explore the environment, which speeds up training and makes it less likely to repeatedly execute the same action when the critic produces imperfect estimates. This algorithm has demonstrated an amazing sample efficiency (contrary to all the previous algorithms, which learn very slowly).

Proximal policy optimization (PPO) (https://homl.info/ppo)[22]

This algorithm by John Schulman and other OpenAI researchers is based on A2C, but it clips the loss function to avoid excessively large weight updates (which often lead to training instabilities). PPO is a simplification of the previous *trust region policy optimization* (TRPO) algorithm (*https://homl.info/trpo*),[23] also by OpenAI. OpenAI made the news in April 2019 with its AI called OpenAI Five, based on the PPO algorithm, which defeated the world champions at the multiplayer game *Dota 2*.

The last two algorithms, SAC and PPO, are among the most widely used RL algorithms today, and several libraries provide easy to use and highly optimized implementations. For example, let's use the popular Stable-Baselines3 library to train a PPO agent on the *Breakout* Atari game.

Which RL algorithm should you use? PPO is a great general-purpose RL algorithm—a good bet if you're not sure. SAC is the most sample efficient for continuous action tasks, making it ideal for robotics. DQN remains strong for discrete tasks such as Atari games or board games.

21 Tuomas Haarnoja et al., "Soft Actor-Critic: Off-Policy Maximum Entropy Deep Reinforcement Learning with a Stochastic Actor", *Proceedings of the 35th International Conference on Machine Learning* (2018): 1856–1865.

22 John Schulman et al., "Proximal Policy Optimization Algorithms", arXiv preprint arXiv:1707.06347 (2017).

23 John Schulman et al., "Trust Region Policy Optimization", *Proceedings of the 32nd International Conference on Machine Learning* (2015): 1889–1897.

Mastering Atari Breakout Using the Stable-Baselines3 PPO Implementation

Since Stable-Baselines3 (SB3) is not installed by default on Colab, we must first run `%pip install -q stable_baselines3`, which will take a couple of minutes. However, if you are running the code on your own machine and you followed the installation instructions (*https://homl.info/install-p*), then it's already installed.

Next, we must create an ALE interface: it will run the Atari 2600 emulator and allow Gymnasium to interface with it (the Atari games will appear in the list of available environments):

```
import ale_py

ale = ale_py.ALEInterface()
```

Atari games were stored on read-only memory (ROM) cartridges. These ROMs can now be downloaded freely and used for research and educational purposes. On Colab, they are preinstalled, and if you followed the installation instructions to run the code locally, then they are also preinstalled.

Now that we have SB3, the ALE interface, and the ROMs, we are ready to create the *Breakout* environment. But instead of creating it using Gymnasium directly, we will use SB3's `make_atari_env()` function: it creates a wrapper environment containing multiple *Breakout* environments that will run in parallel. Each observation from the wrapper environment will contain one observation for each *Breakout* environment. Similarly, the wrapper environment's `step()` function will take an array containing one action for each *Breakout* environment. Lastly, the wrapper environment will take care of preprocessing the images, converting them from 210 × 160 RGB images to 84 × 84 grayscale images. Very convenient! So let's create an SB3 environment containing four *Breakout* environments, and reset it to get an observation:

```
from stable_baselines3.common.env_util import make_atari_env

envs = make_atari_env("BreakoutNoFrameskip-v4", n_envs=4)
obs = envs.reset()  # a 4 × 84 × 84 × 1 NumPy array (note: no info dict)
```

The `env.get_images()` method returns the original images, before preprocessing (see Figure 19-11).

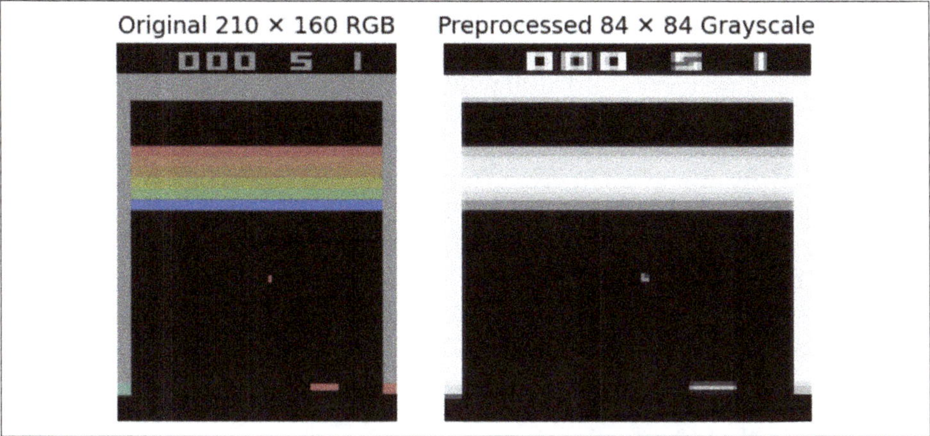

Figure 19-11. A Breakout frame before (left) and after (right) preprocessing

The ALE interface runs at 60 frames per second, which is quite fast, so consecutive frames look very similar, which wastes computation. To avoid this, the default *Breakout* environment repeats each action four times and returns only the final observation; this is called *frame skipping*. However, instead of skipping the frames, it's preferable to stack them into a single four-channel image and use that as the observation. For this, we must first avoid frame skipping: this is why we used the `BreakoutNoFrameskip-v4` environment rather than `Breakout-v4`.[24] Then, we must wrap the environment in a `VecFrameStack`; this wrapper environment will repeat each action several times (four in our case) and stack the resulting frames along the channel dimension (i.e., the last one):

```
from stable_baselines3.common.vec_env import VecFrameStack

envs_stacked = VecFrameStack(envs, n_stack=4)
obs = envs_stacked.reset()  # returns a 4 × 84 × 84 × 4 NumPy array
```

Now let's create a PPO model with some good hyperparameters:

```
from stable_baselines3 import PPO

ppo_model = PPO("CnnPolicy", envs_stacked, device=device, learning_rate=2.5e-4,
                batch_size=256, n_steps=256, n_epochs=4, clip_range=0.1,
                vf_coef=0.5, ent_coef=0.01, gamma=0.99, verbose=0)
```

24 The "v4" suffix is the version number; it's unrelated to frame skipping or the number of parallel environments.

That's a lot of arguments! Let's see what they do:

- The first argument is the policy network. Since we specified `CnnPolicy`, SB3 will build a good CNN for us, based on the chosen algorithm (PPO in this case) and the observation space. If you're curious, take a look at `ppo_model.policy` to see the CNN's architecture: it's a deep CNN with an actor head (for the action logits) and a critic head (for the state values). There are four possible actions: left, right, fire (to launch the ball), and no-op (do nothing). If you prefer to use a custom neural net, you must create a subclass of the `ActorCriticPolicy` class, located in the `stable_baselines3.common.policies` module. See SB3's documentation (*https://homl.info/sb3*) for more details.
- `env`, `device`, `learning_rate`, and `batch_size` are self-explanatory.
- `n_steps` is the number of environment steps to run (per environment) before each policy update.
- `n_epochs` is the number of training steps to run on each batch during optimization.
- `clip_range` limits the magnitude of the policy updates to avoid large changes that might cause catastrophic forgetting.
- `vf_coef` is the weight of the value function loss in the total loss (similar to our actor-critic's `critic_weight` hyperparameter).
- `ent_coef` is the weight of the entropy term that encourages exploration.
- `gamma` is the discount rate.
- `verbose` is the logging verbosity (0 = silent, 1 = info, 2 = debug).

For new tasks, the default `PPO` hyperparameters are a good place to start. If learning is too slow, try more parallel environments first; then consider using a higher learning rate or a larger clip range. You can also shrink `n_steps` or `batch_size`, but this risks noisier gradients. If learning is unstable, try lowering the learning rate or clip range, and use larger rollouts (i.e., `n_steps`) or batch sizes. Use `gamma` near 0.95 for short-horizon tasks, and 0.995 to 0.999 for long-horizon ones. Lastly, increase `ent_coef` if you want to encourage more exploration.

And now let's start training. The following code will train the model for 30 million steps. This will take many hours and will probably be too long for a Colab session (unless you get a paid subscription), so the notebook also includes code to download the trained model if you prefer. Whenever you train a model for a long time, it's important to save checkpoints at regular intervals (e.g., every 100,000 calls to the step() method) to avoid having to start from scratch in case of a crash or a power outage. For this, we can create a checkpoint callback and pass it to the learn() method:

```
from stable_baselines3.common.callbacks import CheckpointCallback

cb = CheckpointCallback(save_freq=100_000, save_path="my_ppo_breakout.ckpt")
ppo_model.learn(total_timesteps=30_000_000, progress_bar=True, callback=cb)
ppo_model.save("my_ppo_breakout")  # save the final model
```

The save_freq argument counts calls to the step() method. Since there are 4 environments running in parallel, 50,000 calls correspond to 200,000 total time steps.

To see the progress during training, one option is to load the latest checkpoint in another notebook, and try it out. A simpler option is to use TensorBoard to visualize the learning curves, especially the mean reward per episode. For this, you must first activate the TensorBoard extension in Colab or Jupyter by running %load_ext tensorboard (this is done at the start of this chapter's notebook). Next, you must start the TensorBoard server, point it to a log directory, and choose the TCP port it will listen on. The following "magic" command (i.e., starting with a %) will do that and also open up the TensorBoard client interface directly inside Colab or Jupyter:

```
tensorboard_logdir = "my_ppo_breakout_tensorboard"  # path to the log directory
%tensorboard --logdir={tensorboard_logdir} --port 6006
```

Next, you must tell the PPO model where to save its TensorBoard logs. This is done when creating the model:

```
ppo_model = PPO("CnnPolicy", [...], tensorboard_log=tensorboard_logdir)
```

And that's it. Once you start training, you will see the learning curves change every 30 seconds or so in the TensorBoard interface (or click the refresh button). The most important metric to track is the rollout/ep_rew_mean, which is the mean reward per episode: it should slowly ramp up, even though it will sometimes go down a bit. After 1 million total steps it will typically reach around 20; that's not a very good agent. But if you let training run for 10 million steps, it should reach human level. And after 50 million steps, it will generally be superhuman.

Congratulations, you know how to train a superhuman AI! You can try it out like this:

```
ppo_model = PPO.load("my_ppo_agent_breakout")  # or load the best checkpoint
eval_env = make_atari_env("BreakoutNoFrameskip-v4", n_envs=1, seed=42)
eval_stacked = VecFrameStack(eval_env, n_stack=4)
frames = []
obs = eval_stacked.reset()
```

```python
for _ in range(5000):  # some limit in case the agent never loses
    frames.append(eval_stacked.render())
    action, _ = ppo_model.predict(obs, deterministic=True) # for reproducibility
    obs, reward, done, info = eval_stacked.step(action)
    if done[0]:  # note: there's no `truncated`
        break

eval_stacked.close()
```

This will capture all the frames during one episode. You can render them as an animation using Matplotlib (see the notebook for an example). If you trained the agent for long enough (or used the pretrained model), you will see that the agent plays pretty well, and even found the strategy of digging tunnels on the sides and sending the ball through them: that's one of the best strategies in this game!

Overview of Some Popular RL Algorithms

Before we close this chapter, let's take a brief look at a few other popular algorithms:

AlphaGo (https://homl.info/alphago)[25]

AlphaGo uses a variant of *Monte Carlo tree search* (MCTS) based on deep neural networks to beat human champions at the game of Go. MCTS was invented in 1949 by Nicholas Metropolis and Stanislaw Ulam. It selects the best move after running many simulations, repeatedly exploring the search tree starting from the current position, and spending more time on the most promising branches. When it reaches a node that it hasn't visited before, it plays randomly until the game ends, and updates its estimates for each visited node (excluding the random moves), increasing or decreasing each estimate, depending on the final outcome.

AlphaGo is based on the same principle, but it uses a policy network to select moves, rather than playing randomly. This policy net is trained using policy gradients. The original algorithm involved three additional neural networks, and was more complicated, but it was simplified in the AlphaGo Zero paper (*https://homl.info/alphagozero*),[26] which uses a single neural network to both select moves and evaluate game states. The AlphaZero paper (*https://homl.info/alphazero*)[27] generalized this algorithm, making it capable of tackling not only the game of Go, but also chess and shogi (Japanese chess). Lastly, the MuZero paper (*https://homl.info/muzero*)[28] continued to improve upon this algorithm, outperforming

25 David Silver et al., "Mastering the Game of Go with Deep Neural Networks and Tree Search", *Nature* 529 (2016): 484–489.

26 David Silver et al., "Mastering the Game of Go Without Human Knowledge", *Nature* 550 (2017): 354–359.

27 David Silver et al., "Mastering Chess and Shogi by Self-Play with a General Reinforcement Learning Algorithm", arXiv preprint arXiv:1712.01815.

the previous iterations even though the agent starts out without even knowing the rules of the game!

The rules of the game of Go were hardcoded into AlphaGo. In contrast, MuZero gradually learns a model of the environment: given a state *s* and an action *a*, it learns to predict the reward *r* and the probability of reaching state *s'*. Having a model of the environment (hardcoded or learned) allows these algorithms to plan ahead (in this case using MCTS). For this reason, both of these algorithms belong to the broad class of *model-based RL* algorithms. In contrast, policy gradients, value-based methods, and actor-critic methods are all *model-free RL* algorithms: they have a policy model and/or a value model, but not an *environment* model.

Curiosity-based exploration (https://homl.info/curiosity)[29]
: A recurring problem in RL is the sparsity of the rewards, which makes learning very slow and inefficient. Deepak Pathak and other UC Berkeley researchers have proposed an exciting way to tackle this issue: why not ignore the rewards and just make the agent extremely curious to explore the environment? The rewards thus become intrinsic to the agent, rather than coming from the environment. Similarly, stimulating curiosity in a child is more likely to give good results than purely rewarding the child for getting good grades.

How does this work? The agent continuously tries to predict the outcome of its actions, and it seeks situations where the outcome does not match its predictions. In other words, it wants to be surprised. If the outcome is predictable (boring), it goes elsewhere. However, if the outcome is unpredictable but the agent notices that it has no control over it, it also gets bored after a while. With only curiosity, the authors succeeded in training an agent at many video games: even though the agent gets no penalty for losing, it finds it boring to lose because the game starts over, so it learns to avoid it.

Open-ended learning (OEL)
: The objective of OEL is to train agents capable of endlessly learning new and interesting tasks, typically generated procedurally. We're not there yet, but there has been some amazing progress over the last few years. For example, a 2019 paper (*https://homl.info/poet*)[30] by a team of researchers from Uber AI introduced the *POET algorithm*, which generates multiple simulated 2D environments with

28 Julian Schrittwieser et al., "Mastering Atari, Go, Chess and Shogi by Planning with a Learned Model", arXiv preprint arXiv:1911.08265 (2019).

29 Deepak Pathak et al., "Curiosity-Driven Exploration by Self-Supervised Prediction", *Proceedings of the 34th International Conference on Machine Learning* (2017): 2778–2787.

bumps and holes, and trains one agent per environment. The agent's goal is to walk as fast as possible while avoiding the obstacles.

The algorithm starts out with simple environments, but they gradually get harder over time: this is called *curriculum learning*. Moreover, although each agent is only trained within one environment, it must regularly compete against other agents, across all environments. In each environment, the winner is copied over and replaces the agent that was there before. This way, knowledge is regularly transferred across environments, and the most adaptable agents are selected.

In the end, the agents are much better walkers than agents trained on a single task, and they can tackle much harder environments. Of course, this principle can be applied to other environments and tasks as well. If you're interested in OEL, make sure to check out the Enhanced POET paper (*https://homl.info/epoet*),[31] as well as DeepMind's 2021 paper (*https://homl.info/oel2021*)[32] on this topic.

If you'd like to learn more about reinforcement learning, check out the book *Reinforcement Learning* by Phil Winder (O'Reilly).

We covered many topics in this chapter. We learned about policy gradient methods; we implemented the REINFORCE algorithm to solve the CartPole problem using Gymnasium; we explored Markov chains and Markov decision processes, which led us to value-based methods; and we implemented a deep Q-Learning model. Then we discussed actor-critic methods, and we used the Stable-Baselines3 library to implement a PPO model that beat the Atari game *Breakout*. Lastly, we took a peek at some of the other areas of RL, including model-based RL and more. Reinforcement learning is a huge and exciting field, with new ideas and algorithms popping out every day, so I hope this chapter sparked your curiosity. There is a whole world to explore!

---

30 Rui Wang et al., "Paired Open-Ended Trailblazer (POET): Endlessly Generating Increasingly Complex and Diverse Learning Environments and Their Solutions", arXiv preprint arXiv:1901.01753 (2019).

31 Rui Wang et al., "Enhanced POET: Open-Ended Reinforcement Learning Through Unbounded Invention of Learning Challenges and Their Solutions", arXiv preprint arXiv:2003.08536 (2020).

32 Open-Ended Learning Team et al., "Open-Ended Learning Leads to Generally Capable Agents", arXiv preprint arXiv:2107.12808 (2021).

Exercises

1. How would you define reinforcement learning? How is it different from regular supervised or unsupervised learning?
2. Can you think of three possible applications of RL that were not mentioned in this chapter? For each of them, what is the environment? What is the agent? What are some possible actions? What are the rewards?
3. What is the discount factor? Can the optimal policy change if you modify the discount factor?
4. How do you measure the performance of a reinforcement learning agent?
5. What is the credit assignment problem? When does it occur? How can you alleviate it?
6. What is the point of using a replay buffer?
7. What is an off-policy RL algorithm? What are the benefits?
8. What is a model-based RL algorithm? Can you give some examples?
9. Use policy gradients to solve Gymnasium's LunarLander-v2 environment.
10. Solve the BipedalWalker-v3 environment using the RL algorithm of your choice.
11. If you have about $100 to spare, you can purchase a Raspberry Pi 3 plus some cheap robotics components, install PyTorch on the Pi, and go wild! Start with simple goals, like making the robot turn around to find the brightest angle (if it has a light sensor) or the closest object (if it has a sonar sensor), and move in that direction. Then you can start using deep learning. For example, if the robot has a camera, you can try to implement an object detection algorithm so it detects people and moves toward them. You can also try to use RL to make the agent learn on its own how to use the motors to achieve that goal. Have fun!

Solutions to these exercises are available at the end of this chapter's notebook, at *https://homl.info/colab-p*.

Thank You!

Before we close the last chapter of this book, I would like to thank you for reading it up to the last paragraph. I truly hope that you had as much pleasure reading this book as I had writing it, and that it will be useful for your projects, big or small.

If you find errors, please send feedback. More generally, I would love to know what you think, so please don't hesitate to contact me via O'Reilly, or through the *ageron/handson-mlp* GitHub project.

Going forward, my best advice to you is to practice and practice: try going through all the exercises (if you have not done so already), play with the Jupyter notebooks, join Kaggle.com or some other ML community, watch ML courses, read papers, attend conferences, and meet experts. It also helps tremendously to have a concrete project to work on, whether it is for work or fun (ideally for both), so if there's anything you have always dreamt of building, give it a shot! Work incrementally; don't shoot for the moon right away, but stay focused on your project and build it piece by piece. It will require patience and perseverance, but when you have a walking robot, or a working chatbot, or whatever else you fancy to build, it will be immensely rewarding.

My greatest hope is that this book will inspire you to build a wonderful ML application that will benefit all of us! What will it be?

—Aurélien Geron
October 22, 2025

APPENDIX A
Autodiff

This appendix explains how PyTorch's automatic differentiation (autodiff) feature works, and how it compares to other solutions.

Suppose you define a function $f(x, y) = x^2y + y + 2$, and you need its partial derivatives $\partial f/\partial x$ and $\partial f/\partial y$, typically to perform gradient descent (or some other optimization algorithm). Your main options are manual differentiation, finite difference approximation, forward-mode autodiff, and reverse-mode autodiff. PyTorch implements reverse-mode autodiff, but to fully understand it, it's useful to look at the other options first. So let's go through each of them, starting with manual differentiation.

Manual Differentiation

The first approach to compute derivatives is to pick up a pencil and a piece of paper and use your calculus knowledge to derive the appropriate equation. For the function $f(x, y)$ just defined, it is not too hard; you just need to use five rules:

- The derivative of a constant is 0.
- The derivative of λx is λ (where λ is a constant).
- The derivative of x^λ is $\lambda x^{\lambda - 1}$, so the derivative of x^2 is $2x$.
- The derivative of a sum of functions is the sum of these functions' derivatives.
- The derivative of λ times a function is λ times its derivative.

From these rules, you can derive Equation A-1.

Equation A-1. Partial derivatives of f(x, y)

$$\frac{\partial f}{\partial x} = \frac{\partial(x^2y)}{\partial x} + \frac{\partial y}{\partial x} + \frac{\partial 2}{\partial x} = y\frac{\partial(x^2)}{\partial x} + 0 + 0 = 2xy$$

$$\frac{\partial f}{\partial y} = \frac{\partial(x^2y)}{\partial y} + \frac{\partial y}{\partial y} + \frac{\partial 2}{\partial y} = x^2 + 1 + 0 = x^2 + 1$$

This approach can become very tedious for more complex functions, and you run the risk of making mistakes. Fortunately, there are other options. Let's look at finite difference approximation now.

Finite Difference Approximation

Recall that the derivative $h'(x_0)$ of a function $h(x)$ at a point x_0 is the slope of the function at that point. More precisely, the derivative is defined as the limit of the slope of a straight line going through this point x_0 and another point x on the function, as x gets infinitely close to x_0 (see Equation A-2).

Equation A-2. Definition of the derivative of a function h(x) at point x_0

$$h'(x_0) = \lim_{x \to x_0} \frac{h(x) - h(x_0)}{x - x_0} = \lim_{\varepsilon \to 0} \frac{h(x_0 + \varepsilon) - h(x_0)}{\varepsilon}$$

So if we wanted to calculate the partial derivative of $f(x, y)$ with regard to x at $x = 3$ and $y = 4$, we could compute $f(3 + \varepsilon, 4) - f(3, 4)$ and divide the result by ε, using a very small value for ε. This type of numerical approximation of the derivative is called a *finite difference approximation*, and this specific equation is called *Newton's difference quotient*. That's exactly what the following code does:

```
def f(x, y):
    return x**2*y + y + 2

def derivative(f, x, y, x_eps, y_eps):
    return (f(x + x_eps, y + y_eps) - f(x, y)) / (x_eps + y_eps)

df_dx = derivative(f, 3, 4, 0.00001, 0)
df_dy = derivative(f, 3, 4, 0, 0.00001)
```

Unfortunately, the result is imprecise (and it gets worse for more complicated functions). The correct results are respectively 24 and 10, but instead we get:

```
>>> df_dx
24.000039999805264
```

```
>>> df_dy
10.000000000331966
```

Notice that to compute both partial derivatives, we have to call `f()` at least three times (we called it four times in the preceding code, but it could be optimized). If there were 1,000 parameters, we would need to call `f()` at least 1,001 times. When you are dealing with large neural networks, this makes finite difference approximation way too inefficient.

However, this method is so simple to implement that it is a great tool to check that the other methods are implemented correctly. For example, if it disagrees with your manually derived function, then your function probably contains a mistake.

So far, we have considered two ways to compute gradients: using manual differentiation and using finite difference approximation. Unfortunately, both are fatally flawed for training a large-scale neural network. So let's turn to autodiff, starting with forward mode.

Forward-Mode Autodiff

Figure A-1 shows how forward-mode autodiff works on an even simpler function, $g(x, y) = 5 + xy$. The graph for that function is represented on the left. After forward-mode autodiff, we get the graph on the right, which represents the partial derivative $\partial g/\partial x = 0 + (0 \times x + y \times 1) = y$ (we could similarly obtain the partial derivative with regard to y).

The algorithm will go through the computation graph from the inputs to the outputs (hence the name "forward mode"). It starts by getting the partial derivatives of the leaf nodes. The constant node (5) returns the constant 0, since the derivative of a constant is always 0. The variable x returns the constant 1 since $\partial x/\partial x = 1$, and the variable y returns the constant 0 since $\partial y/\partial x = 0$ (if we were looking for the partial derivative with regard to y, it would be the reverse).

Now we have all we need to move up the graph to the multiplication node in function g. Calculus tells us that the derivative of the product of two functions u and v is $\partial(u \times v)/\partial x = \partial v/\partial x \times u + v \times \partial u/\partial x$. We can therefore construct a large part of the graph on the right, representing $0 \times x + y \times 1$.

Finally, we can go up to the addition node in function g. As mentioned, the derivative of a sum of functions is the sum of these functions' derivatives, so we just need to create an addition node and connect it to the parts of the graph we have already computed. We get the correct partial derivative: $\partial g/\partial x = 0 + (0 \times x + y \times 1)$.

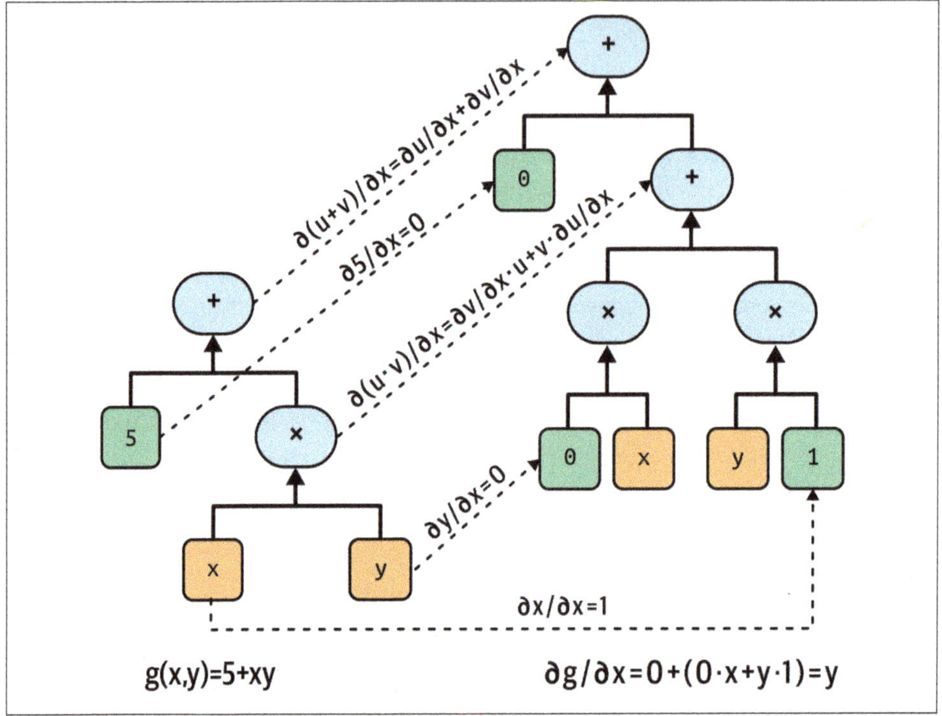

Figure A-1. Forward-mode autodiff

However, this equation can be simplified (a lot). By applying a few pruning steps to the computation graph to get rid of all the unnecessary operations, we get a much smaller graph with just one node: $\partial g/\partial x = y$. In this case simplification is fairly easy, but for a more complex function, forward-mode autodiff can produce a huge graph that may be tough to simplify and lead to suboptimal performance.

Note that we started with a computation graph, and forward-mode autodiff produced another computation graph. This is called *symbolic differentiation*, and it has two nice features. First, once the computation graph of the derivative has been produced, we can use it as many times as we want to compute the derivatives of the given function for any value of x and y. Second, we can run forward-mode autodiff again on the resulting graph to get second-order derivatives if we ever need to (i.e., derivatives of derivatives). We could even compute third-order derivatives, and so on.

But it is also possible to run forward-mode autodiff without constructing a graph (i.e., numerically, not symbolically) just by computing intermediate results on the fly. One way to do this is to use *dual numbers*, which are weird but fascinating numbers of the form $a + b\varepsilon$, where a and b are real numbers, and ε is an infinitesimal number such that $\varepsilon^2 = 0$ (but $\varepsilon \neq 0$). You can think of the dual number $42 + 24\varepsilon$ as something akin to 42.0000···000024 with an infinite number of 0s (but of course this is simplified just to give you some idea of what dual numbers are). A dual number is represented in memory as a pair of floats. For example, $42 + 24\varepsilon$ is represented by the pair (42.0, 24.0).

Dual numbers can be added, multiplied, and so on, as shown in Equation A-3.

Equation A-3. A few operations with dual numbers

$$\lambda(a + b\varepsilon) = \lambda a + \lambda b\varepsilon$$

$$(a + b\varepsilon) + (c + d\varepsilon) = (a + c) + (b + d)\varepsilon$$

$$(a + b\varepsilon) \times (c + d\varepsilon) = ac + (ad + bc)\varepsilon + (bd)\varepsilon^2 = ac + (ad + bc)\varepsilon$$

Most importantly, it can be shown that $h(a + b\varepsilon) = h(a) + b \times h'(a)\varepsilon$, so computing $h(a + \varepsilon)$ gives you both $h(a)$ and the derivative $h'(a)$ in just one shot. Figure A-2 shows that the partial derivative of $f(x, y)$ with regard to x at $x = 3$ and $y = 4$ (which I will write as $\partial f/\partial x$ (3, 4)) can be computed using dual numbers. All we need to do is compute $f(3 + \varepsilon, 4)$; this will output a dual number whose first component is equal to $f(3, 4)$ and whose second component is equal to $\partial f/\partial x$ (3, 4).

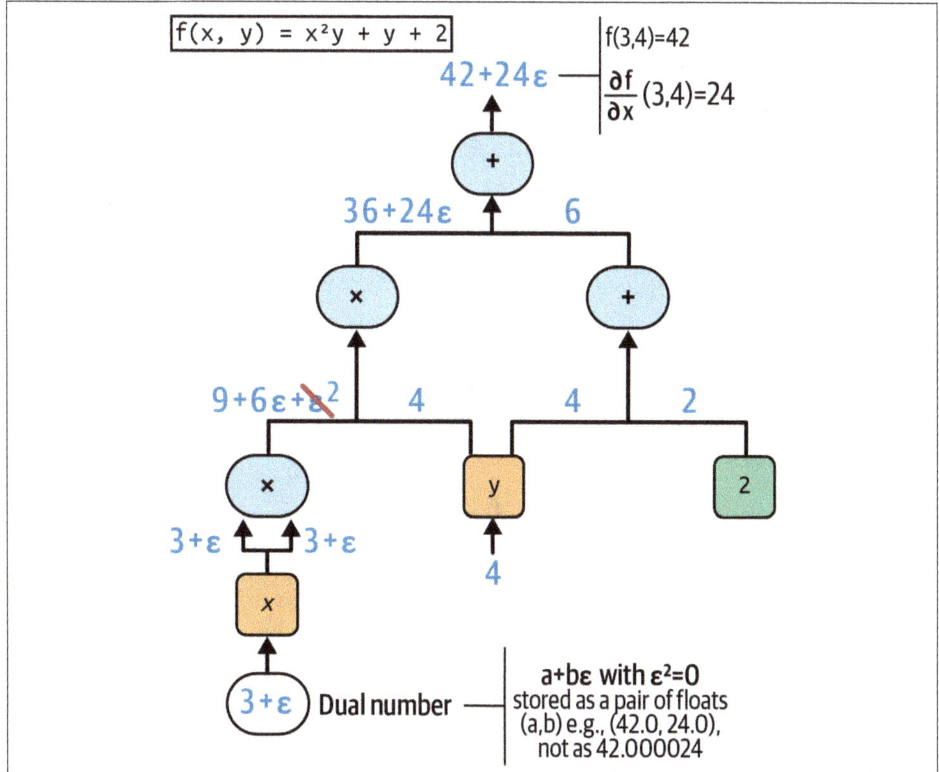

Figure A-2. Forward-mode autodiff using dual numbers

To compute $\partial f/\partial y$ (3, 4) we would have to go through the graph again, but this time with $x = 3$ and $y = 4 + \varepsilon$.

So, forward-mode autodiff is much more accurate than finite difference approximation, but it suffers from the same major flaw, at least when there are many inputs and few outputs (as is the case when dealing with neural networks): if there were 1,000 parameters, it would require 1,000 passes through the graph to compute all the partial derivatives. This is where reverse-mode autodiff shines: it can compute all of them in just two passes through the graph. Let's see how.

Reverse-Mode Autodiff

Reverse-mode autodiff is the solution implemented by PyTorch. It first goes through the graph in the forward direction (i.e., from the inputs to the output) to compute the value of each node. Then it does a second pass, this time in the reverse direction (i.e., from the output to the inputs) to compute all the partial derivatives. The name "reverse mode" comes from this second pass through the graph, where gradients flow in the reverse direction. Figure A-3 represents the second pass. During the first pass, all the node values were computed, starting from $x = 3$ and $y = 4$. You can see those values at the bottom right of each node (e.g., $x \times x = 9$). The nodes are labeled n_1 to n_7 for clarity. The output node is n_7: $f(3, 4) = n_7 = 42$.

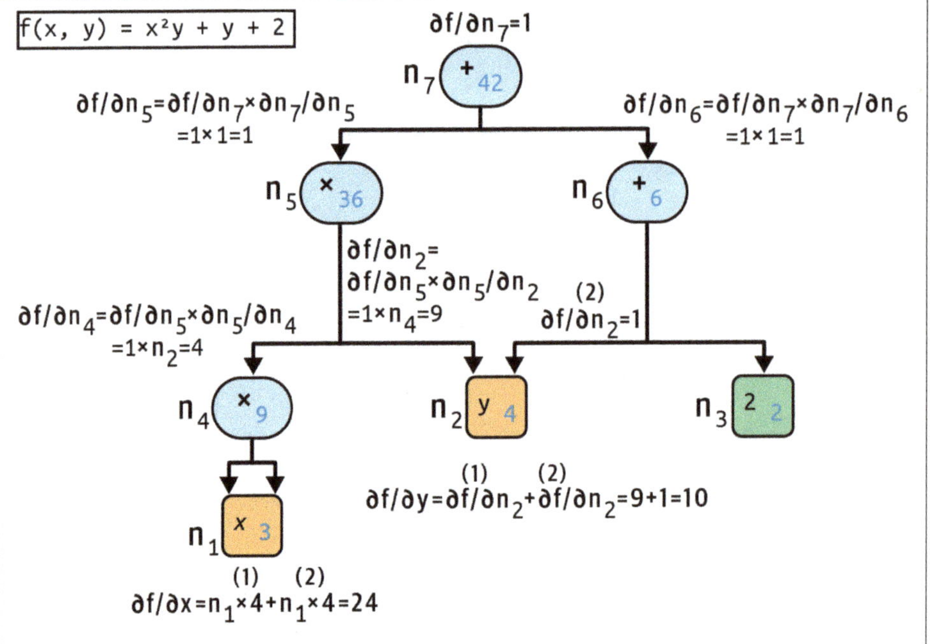

Figure A-3. Reverse-mode autodiff

The idea is to gradually go down the graph, computing the partial derivative of $f(x, y)$ with regard to each consecutive node, until we reach the variable nodes. For this, reverse-mode autodiff relies heavily on the *chain rule*, shown in Equation A-4.

Equation A-4. Chain rule

$$\frac{\partial f}{\partial x} = \frac{\partial f}{\partial n_i} \times \frac{\partial n_i}{\partial x}$$

Since n_7 is the output node, $f = n_7$ so $\partial f / \partial n_7 = 1$.

Let's continue down the graph to n_5: how much does f vary when n_5 varies? The answer is $\partial f / \partial n_5 = \partial f / \partial n_7 \times \partial n_7 / \partial n_5$. We already know that $\partial f / \partial n_7 = 1$, so all we need is $\partial n_7 / \partial n_5$. Since n_7 simply performs the sum $n_5 + n_6$, we find that $\partial n_7 / \partial n_5 = 1$, so $\partial f / \partial n_5 = 1 \times 1 = 1$.

Now we can proceed to node n_4: how much does f vary when n_4 varies? The answer is $\partial f / \partial n_4 = \partial f / \partial n_5 \times \partial n_5 / \partial n_4$. Since $n_5 = n_4 \times n_2$, we find that $\partial n_5 / \partial n_4 = n_2$, so $\partial f / \partial n_4 = 1 \times n_2 = 4$.

The process continues until we reach the bottom of the graph. At that point we will have calculated all the partial derivatives of $f(x, y)$ at the point $x = 3$ and $y = 4$. In this example, we find $\partial f / \partial x = 24$ and $\partial f / \partial y = 10$. Sounds about right!

Reverse-mode autodiff is a very powerful and accurate technique, especially when there are many inputs and few outputs, since it requires only one forward pass plus one reverse pass per output to compute all the partial derivatives for all outputs with regard to all the inputs. When training neural networks, we generally want to minimize the loss, so there is a single output (the loss), and hence only two passes through the graph are needed to compute the gradients.

PyTorch builds a new graph on the fly during each forward pass. Whenever you run an operation on a tensor with `requires_grad=True`, PyTorch computes the resulting tensor and sets its `grad_fn` attribute to an operation-specific object that allows PyTorch to propagate the gradients backwards through this operation. Since the graph is built on the fly, your code can be highly dynamic, containing loops and conditionals, and everything will still work fine.

Reverse-mode autodiff can also handle functions that are not entirely differentiable, as long as you ask it to compute the partial derivatives at points that *are* differentiable.

Creating a tiny autodiff framework is a great exercise to truly master autodiff. Try creating one from scratch for a small set of operations. If you get stuck, check out this project's `extra_autodiff.ipynb` notebook, which you can run on Colab at *https://homl.info/colab-p*. You can also watch Andrej Karpathy's excellent YouTube video where he builds the micrograd library from scratch (*https://homl.info/micrograd*).

APPENDIX B

Mixed Precision and Quantization

By default, PyTorch uses 32-bit floats to represent model parameters: that's 4 bytes per parameter. If your model has 1 billion parameters, then you need at least 4 GB of RAM just to hold the model. At inference time you also need enough RAM to store the activations, and at training time you need enough RAM to store all the intermediate activations as well (for the backward pass), and to store the optimizer parameters (e.g., Adam needs two additional parameters for each model parameter—that's an extra 8 GB). This is a lot of RAM, and it's also plenty of time spent transferring data between the CPU and the GPU, not to mention storage space, download time, and energy consumption.

So how can we reduce the model's size? A simple option is to use a reduced precision float representation—typically 16-bit floats instead of 32-bit floats. If you train a 32-bit model then shrink it to 16-bits after training, its size will be halved, with little impact on its quality. Great!

However, if you try to train the model using 16-bit floats, you may run into convergence issues, as we will see. So a common strategy is *mixed-precision training* (MPT), where we keep the weights and weight updates at 32-bit precision during training, but the rest of the computations use 16-bit precision. After training, we shrink the weights down to 16-bits.

Finally, to shrink the model even further, you can use *quantization*: the parameters are discretized and represented as 8-bit integers, or even 4-bit integers or less. This is harder, and it degrades the model's quality a bit more, but it reduces the model size by a factor of 4 or more, and speeds it up significantly.

In this appendix, we will cover reduced precision, mixed-precision training, and quantization. But to fully understand these, we must first discuss common number representations in machine learning.

Common Number Representations

By default, PyTorch represents weights and activations using 32-bit floats based on the *IEEE Standard for Floating-Point Arithmetic* (IEEE 754), which specifies how floating-point numbers are represented in memory. It's a flexible and efficient format which can represent tiny values and huge values, as well as special values such as ±0,[1] ±infinity, and NaN (i.e., Not a Number).

The float32 data type (fp32 for short) can hold numbers as small as $\pm 1.4e^{-45}$ and as large as $\pm 3.4e^{38}$. It is represented at the top of Figure B-1. The first bit determines the *sign* S: 0 means positive, 1 means negative. The next 8 bits hold the *exponent* E, ranging from 0 to 255. And the last 23 bits represent the *fraction* F, ranging from 0 to $2^{23} - 1$. Here is how to compute the value:

- If E is between 1 and 254, then the number is called *normalized*: this is the most common scenario. In this case, the value v can be computed using $v = (-1)^S \cdot 2^{E-127} \cdot (1 + F \cdot 2^{-23})$. The last term $(1 + F \cdot 2^{-23})$ corresponds to the most significant digits, so it's called the *significand*.
- If $E = 0$ and $F > 0$, then the number is called *subnormal*: it is useful to represent the tiniest values.[2] In this case, $v = (-1)^S \cdot 2^{E+1-127} \cdot (0 + F \cdot 2^{-23}) = (-1)^S \cdot F \cdot 2^{-149}$.
- If $E = 0$ and $F = 0$, then $v = \pm 0$.
- If $E = 255$ and $F > 0$, then $v = \text{NaN}$.
- If $E = 255$ and $F = 0$, then $v = \pm\text{infinity}$.

The other floating-point formats represented in Figure B-1 differ only by the number of bits used for the exponent and the fraction. For example float16 uses 5 bits for the exponent (i.e., it ranges from 0 to 31) and 10 bits for the fraction (ranging from 0 to 1,023), while float8 uses 4 bits for the exponent (from 0 to 15) and 3 bits for the fraction, so it's often denoted fp8 E4M3.[3] The equations to compute the value are adjusted accordingly, for example normalized float16 values are computed using $v = (-1)^S \cdot 2^{E-15} \cdot (1 + F \cdot 2^{-10})$.

---

1 In general, −0 and +0 are considered equal, but some operations give different results, for example 1 / −0 = −infinity, while 1 / +0 = +infinity.

2 Some high-performance computing applications deactivate subnormal numbers because they slow down computations, and normalized numbers are generally sufficient (e.g., normalized fp32 can represent numbers as small as $\pm 1.2e^{-38}$).

3 The *M* stands for *mantissa*, which is a term often used as a synonym for fraction. Unfortunately, it's also used as a synonym for significand, leading to some confusion. This is why IEEE 754 no longer uses the term mantissa.

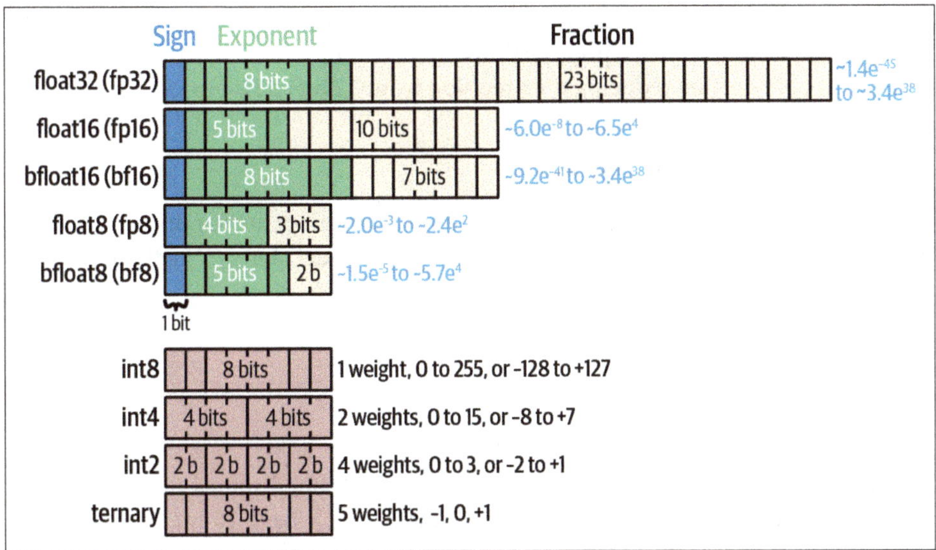

Figure B-1. Common number representations in machine learning

The bfloat16 and bfloat8 formats were proposed by Google Brain (hence the *b*), and they offer a wider range for the values, at the cost of a significantly reduced precision. We will come back to that.

Integers are often represented using 64 bits, with values ranging from 0 to 2^{64} – 1 (about $1.8e^{19}$) for unsigned integers, or –2^32 to 2^32 – 1 (about $\pm 4.3e^{9}$) for signed integers. Integers are also frequently represented using 32 bits, 16 bits, or 8 bits depending on the use case. In Figure B-1, I only represented the integer types frequently used for quantization, such as 8-bit integers (which can be unsigned or signed).

When quantizing down to 4 bits, we usually pack 2 weights per byte, and when quantizing down to 2 bits, we pack 4 weights per byte. It's even possible to quantize down to ternary values, where each weight can only be equal to –1, 0, or +1. In this case, it's common to store five weights per byte. For example, the byte 178 can be written as 20121 in base 3 (since $178 = 2 \cdot 3^4 + 0 \cdot 3^3 + 1 \cdot 3^2 + 2 \cdot 3^1 + 1 \cdot 3^0$), and if we subtract 1 from each digit, we get 1, –1, 0, 1, 0: these are the 5 ternary weights stored in this single byte. Since $3^5 = 243$, which is less than 256, we can fit five ternary values into one byte. This format only uses 1.6 bits per weight on average, which is 20 times less than using 32-bit floats!

It's technically possible to quantize weights down to a single bit each, storing 8 weights per byte: each bit represents a weight equal to either –1 or +1 (or sometimes 0 or 1). However, it's very difficult to get reasonable accuracy using such severe quantization.

As you can see, PyTorch's default weight representation (32-bit floats) takes up a *lot* of space compared to other representations: there is room for us to shrink our models quite a bit! Let's start by reducing the precision from 32 bits down to 16 bits.

Reduced Precision Models

If you have a 32-bit PyTorch model, you can convert all of its parameters to 16-bit floats—which is called *half-precision*—by calling the model's `half()` method:

```
import torch
import torch.nn as nn

model = nn.Sequential(nn.Linear(10, 100), nn.ReLU(), nn.Linear(100, 1))
# [...] pretend the 32-bit model is trained here
model.half()  # convert the model parameters to half precision (16 bits)
```

This is a quick and easy way to halve the size of a trained model, usually without much impact on its quality. Moreover, since many GPUs have 16-bit float optimizations, and since there will be less data to transfer between the CPU and the GPU, the model will typically run almost twice as fast.

When downloading a pretrained model using the Transformers library's `from_pretrained()` method, you can set `dtype="auto"` to let the library choose the optimal float representation for your hardware.

To use the model, you now need to feed it 16-bit inputs, and it will output 16-bit outputs as well:

```
X = torch.rand(3, 10, dtype=torch.float16)  # some 16-bit input
y_pred = model(X)  # 16-bit output
```

But what if you want to build and train a 16-bit model right from the start? In this case, you can set `dtype=torch.float16` whenever you create a tensor or a module with parameters, for example:

```
model = nn.Sequential(nn.Linear(10, 100, dtype=torch.float16), nn.ReLU(),
                      nn.Linear(100, 1, dtype=torch.float16))
```

If you prefer to avoid repeating `dtype=torch.float16` everywhere, then you can instead set the default data type to `torch.float16` using `torch.set_default_dtype(torch.float16)`. Be careful: this will apply to *all* tensors and modules created after that.

However, the reduced precision can cause some issues during training. Indeed, 16-bit floats have a limited *dynamic range* (i.e., the ratio between the largest and smallest positive representable values): the smallest positive representable value is about 0.00000006 (i.e., $6.0e^{-8}$), while the largest is 65,504 (i.e., $\sim6.5e^{4}$). This implies that any gradient update smaller than $\sim6.0e^{-8}$ will *underflow*, meaning it will be rounded down to zero, and thus ignored. And conversely, any value larger than $\sim6.5e^{4}$ will *overflow*, meaning it will be rounded up to infinity, causing training to fail (once some weights are infinite, the loss will be infinite or NaN).

To avoid underflows, one solution is to scale up the loss by a large factor (e.g., multiply it by 256): this will automatically scale up the gradients by the same factor during the backward pass, which will prevent them from being smaller than the smallest 16-bit representable value. However, you must scale the gradients back down before performing an optimizer step, and at this point you may get an underflow. Also, if you scale up the loss too much, you will run into overflows.

If you can't find a good scaling factor that avoids both underflows and overflows, you can try to use `torch.bfloat16` rather than `torch.float16`, since bloat16 has more bits for the exponent: the smallest value is $\sim9.2e^{-41}$, while the largest is $\sim3.4e^{38}$, so there's less risk of any significant gradient updates being ignored, or reasonable values being rounded up to infinity.

However, bfloat16 has historically had less hardware support (although this is improving), and it offers fewer bits for the fraction, which can cause some gradient updates to be ignored when the corresponding parameter values are much larger, causing training to stall. For example, if the gradient update is $4.5e^{-2}$ (i.e., 0.045) and the corresponding parameter value is equal to $1.23e^{2}$ (i.e., 123), then the sum should be $1.23045e^{2}$ (i.e., 123.045) but bfloat16 does not have enough fraction bits to store all these digits, so it must round the result to $1.23e^{2}$ (i.e., 123): as you can see, the gradient update is completely ignored. With regular 16-bit floats, the result would be 123.0625, which is not exactly right due to floating-point precision errors, but at least the parameter makes a step in the right direction. That said, if the gradient update was a bit smaller (e.g., 0.03), it would be ignored even in regular 16-bit float precision.

So if you try float16 and bfloat16 but you still encounter convergence issues during training, then you can try *mixed-precision training* instead.

Mixed-Precision Training

Mixed-precision training (MPT) (*https://homl.info/mpt*) was proposed by Baidu and Nvidia researchers in 2017,[4] to address the issues often observed with 16-bit training. Here's how it works:

4 P. Micikevicius et al., "Mixed Precision Training", arXiv preprint 2017, ICLR (2018).

- MPT stores a primary copy of the model parameters as 32-bit floats, and at each training iteration, it creates a 16-bit copy of these model parameters (see step 1 in Figure B-2), and uses them for the forward pass (step 2).
- The loss is then scaled up by a large factor (step 3) to avoid underflows, as we discussed earlier.
- Lastly, we switch back to 32-bit precision to scale the gradients back down: this greater precision avoids the risk of underflow. Next we use the gradients to perform one optimizer step, improving the primary parameters (step 5). Performing the actual optimizer step in 32-bit precision ensures that small weight updates are not ignored when applied to much larger parameter values, since 32-bit floats have a very large fraction (23 bits).

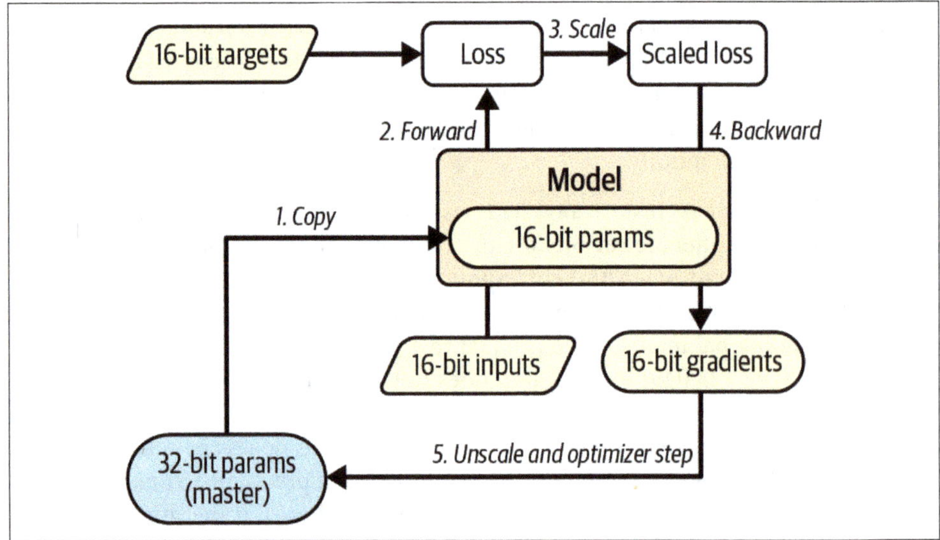

Figure B-2. Mixed-precision training

MPT offers almost all of the benefits of 16-bit training, without the instabilities. However, the model parameters take 50% more space than in 32-bit training because of the 16-bit copy at each training iteration, so how is this any better? Well, during training, most of the RAM is used to store the activations, not the model parameters, so in practice MPT requires just a bit more than half the RAM used by regular 32-bit training. And it typically runs twice as fast. Moreover, once training is finished, we no longer need 32-bit parameters, we can convert them to 16 bits, and we get a pure 16-bit model.

MPT does not always accelerate training: it depends on the model, the batch size, and the hardware. That said, most large transformers are trained using MPT.

Rather than finding the best scaling factor by trial and error, you can run training in 32-bit precision for a little while (assuming you have enough RAM) and measure the gradient statistics to find the optimal scaling factor for your task: it should be large enough to avoid underflows, and small enough to avoid overflows.

Alternatively, your training script can adapt the factor dynamically during training: if some gradients are infinite or NaN, this means that an overflow occurred so the factor must be reduced (e.g., halved) and the training step must be skipped, but if no overflow is detected then the scaling factor can be gradually increased (e.g., doubled every 2,000 training steps). PyTorch provides a `torch.amp.GradScaler` class that implements this approach, and also scales down the learning rate appropriately.

PyTorch also provides a `torch.autocast()` function that returns a context within which many operations will automatically run in 16-bit precision. This includes operations that typically benefit the most from 16-bit precision, such as matrix multiplication and convolutions, but it does not include operations like reductions (e.g., `torch.sum()`) since running these in half precision offers no significant benefit and can damage precision.

Let's update our training function to run the forward pass within an autocast context and use a `GradScaler` to dynamically scale the loss:

```
from torch.amp import GradScaler

def train_mpt(model, optimizer, criterion, train_loader, n_epochs,
              dtype=torch.float16, init_scale=2.0**16):
    grad_scaler = GradScaler(device=device, init_scale=init_scale)
    model.train()
    for epoch in range(n_epochs):
        for X_batch, y_batch in train_loader:
            X_batch, y_batch = X_batch.to(device), y_batch.to(device)
            with torch.autocast(device_type=device, dtype=dtype):
                y_pred = model(X_batch)
                loss = criterion(y_pred, y_batch)
            grad_scaler.scale(loss).backward()
            grad_scaler.step(optimizer)
            grad_scaler.update()
            optimizer.zero_grad()
```

When fine-tuning a transformer using the Hugging Face Transformers library, you can set `fp16=True` or `bf16=True` in the `TrainingArguments` to activate mixed-precision training.

Reducing precision down to 16-bits often works great, but can we shrink our models even further? Yes, we can, using quantization.

Quantization

Quantization means mapping continuous values to discrete ones. In deep learning, this typically involves converting parameters, and often activations as well, from floats to integers—usually 32-bit floats to 8-bit integers. More generally, the goal is to shrink and speed up our model by reducing the number of bits used in parameters, and often in activations as well. Moreover, some embedded devices (e.g., ARM Cortex-M0) do not support floating-point operations at all (in part to reduce their cost and energy consumption), so models have to be quantized entirely (both weights and activations) before you can use them on the device. Modern smartphones do support floating point operations but still benefit significantly from quantization: int8 operations are 2 to 4 times faster and use 5 to 10 times less energy than FP32.

The simplest approach is *linear quantization*, so we'll discuss it now. We will discuss a few nonlinear quantization methods later in this appendix.

Linear Quantization

Linear quantization dates back to digital signal processing in the 1950s, but it has become particularly important in machine learning over the past decade since models have become gigantic, and yet we wish to run them on mobile phones and other limited devices. It has two variants: asymmetric and symmetric. In *asymmetric linear quantization*, float values are simply mapped linearly to unsigned bytes with values ranging from 0 to 255 (or more generally from 0 to $2^n - 1$ when quantizing to n-bit integers). For example, if the weights range between $a = -0.1$ and $b = 0.6$, then the float –0.1 will be mapped to the byte 0, the float 0.0 to integer 36, 0.1 to 72, ..., 0.6 to 255, and more generally, the float tensor $\mathbf{w}$ will be mapped to the integer tensor $\mathbf{q}$ using Equation B-1.

Equation B-1. Asymmetric linear quantization

$$q_i = \text{round}\left(\frac{w_i}{s}\right) + z$$

$$\text{with } s = \frac{b - a}{2^n - 1} \text{ and } z = -\text{round}\left(\frac{a}{s}\right)$$

$$\text{where } a = \min_i w_i \text{ and } b = \max_i w_i$$

In this equation:

- w_i is the ith float in the original tensor **w**.
- q_i is the ith integer in the quantized tensor **q**. It is clamped between 0 and $2^n - 1$ (e.g., 255 for 8-bit quantization).
- s is the *quantization scale*. Note that some authors define it as $1 / s$ and adapt the equation accordingly (i.e., they multiply rather than divide).
- z is the *quantization bias* or *zero point*.
- a is the minimum value of **w**, and b is the maximum value of **w**.

The range $[a, b]$ is known for weights, since their values do not change after training. However, the range of activation values depends on the inputs we feed to the model. As a result, for each activation that we want to quantize (e.g., the inputs of each layer), we will either have to compute a and b on the fly for each new input batch (this is called *dynamic quantization*) or run a calibration dataset once through the model to determine the typical range of activation values, then use this range to quantize the activations of all subsequent batches (this is called *static quantization*). Static quantization is a faster but less precise.

To approximately recover the original value w_i from a quantized value q_i, we can compute $w_i \approx s \times (q_i - z)$. This is called *dequantization*. For example, if $q_i = 72$, then we get $w_i \approx 0.0988$, which is indeed close to 0.1. The difference between the dequantized value (0.0988) and the original value (0.1) is called the *quantization noise*: with 8-bit quantization, the quantization noise usually leads to a slightly degraded accuracy. With 6-bit, 4-bit, or less, the quantization noise can hurt even more, especially since it has a cumulative effect: the deeper the network, the stronger the impact.

Equation B-1 guarantees that any float equal to 0.0 can be quantized and dequantized back to 0.0 exactly: indeed, if $w_i = 0.0$ then $q_i = z$, and dequantizing q_i gives back $w_i = s \times (z - z) = 0.0$. This is particularly useful for sparse models where many weights are equal to zero. It is also important when using activations like ReLU which produce many zero activations.

In PyTorch, the `torch.quantize_per_tensor()` function lets you create a quantized tensor: this is a special kind of tensor that contains the quantized values (i.e., integers), as well as the *quantization parameters* (i.e., the scale and zero point). Let's use this function to quantize a tensor, then dequantize it. In this example we will use the data type `torch.quint8`, which uses 8-bit unsigned integers:

```
>>> w = torch.tensor([0.1, -0.1, 0.6, 0.0])  # 32-bit floats
>>> s = (w.max() - w.min()) / 255.  # compute the scale
>>> z = -(w.min() / s).round()  # compute the zero point
>>> qw = torch.quantize_per_tensor(w, scale=s, zero_point=z, dtype=torch.quint8)
>>> qw  # this is a quantized tensor internally represented using integers
tensor([ 0.0988, -0.0988,  0.6012,  0.0000], size=(4,), dtype=torch.quint8,
       quantization_scheme=torch.per_tensor_affine, scale=0.002745098201557994,
       zero_point=36)
>>> qw.dequantize()  # back to 32-bit floats (close to the original tensor)
tensor([ 0.0988, -0.0988,  0.6012,  0.0000])
```

Quantizing a model to 8-bits divides its size by almost 4. For example, suppose we have a convolutional layer with 64 kernels, 3 × 3 each, and it has 32 input channels. This layer requires 64 × 32 × 3 × 3 = 18,432 parameters (ignoring the bias terms). That's 18,432 × 4 = 73,728 bytes before quantization, and just 18,432 bytes after quantization, plus 2 × 4 = 8 bytes to store s and z (indeed, they are both stored as 32-bit floats, so 4 bytes each).

PyTorch also has a `torch.quantize_per_channel()` function which quantizes each channel separately: this offers better precision but requires a bit more space for the additional quantization parameters.

When the float values are approximately symmetric around zero, we can use *symmetric linear quantization*, where the values are mapped between –127 and +127, or more generally between $-r$ and $+r$ with $r = 2^{n-1} - 1$, using Equation B-2.

Equation B-2. Symmetric linear quantization

$$q_i = \text{round}\left(\frac{w_i}{s}\right) \text{ with } s = \frac{\max_i |w_i|}{2^{n-1} - 1}$$

To implement symmetric linear quantization in PyTorch, we can use the `torch.quantize_per_tensor()` function again, but using a zero point equal to 0, and data type `qint8` (quantized signed 8-bit integer):

```
>>> w = torch.tensor([0.0, -0.94, 0.92, 0.93])  # 32-bit floats
>>> s = w.abs().max() / 127.
>>> qw = torch.quantize_per_tensor(w, scale=s, zero_point=0, dtype=torch.qint8)
>>> qw
```

```
tensor([ 0.0000, -0.9400,  0.9178,  0.9326], size=(4,), dtype=torch.qint8,
       quantization_scheme=torch.per_tensor_affine, scale=0.007401574868708849,
       zero_point=0)
```

Figure B-3 shows some floats ranging between –0.94 and +0.93, quantized to signed bytes (i.e., 8-bits) ranging between –127 and +127,[5] using symmetric linear quantization. Notice that float 0.0 is always mapped to integer 0.

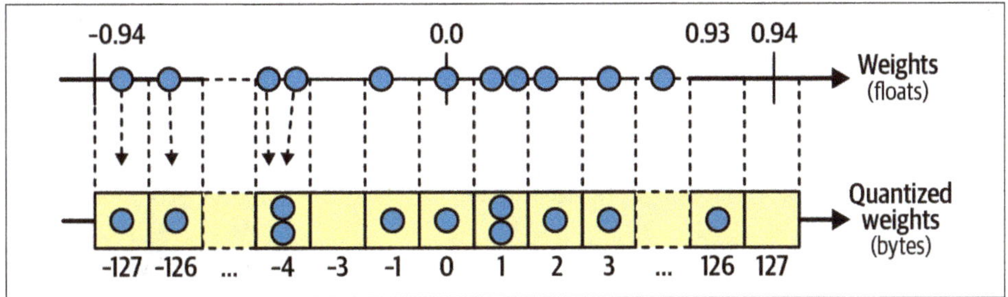

Figure B-3. Symmetric linear quantization

Symmetric mode is often a bit faster than asymmetric mode, because there's no zero point z to worry about. However, if the values are not symmetric, part of the integer range will be wasted. For example, if all the weights are positive, then symmetric mode will only use bytes 0 to 127 (rather than –127 to 127). As a result, symmetric mode can be a bit less precise than asymmetric mode. In practice, symmetric mode is generally preferred for weights (which are often fairly symmetric), and asymmetric mode for activations (especially when using ReLU, since it outputs only nonnegative values).

Let's now see how to quantize your models in practice using PyTorch's `torch.ao.quantization` package. The first approach is to quantize a trained model, which is called *post-training quantization* (PTQ). The second is to train (or fine-tune) your model with some fake quantization to get it used to the noise: this is called *quantization-aware training* (QAT). Let's start with PTQ.

Post-Training Quantization Using torch.ao.quantization

The `torch.ao` package contains tools for architecture optimization (hence the name), including pruning, sparsity, and quantization. The `torch.ao.quantization` package offers two solutions to quantize trained models: dynamic quantization and static quantization. Let's see how to implement both.

5 PyTorch implements *restricted symmetric quantization*, meaning that it excludes the lowest possible signed integer (e.g., –128 for 8-bit integers) to ensure that the range is symmetric (e.g., –127 to +127). Some other implementations allow the full signed byte range (from –128 to +127): this is called *unrestricted symmetric quantization*. These implementations also subtract 0.5 instead of 1 in the denominator of Equation B-2.

Dynamic quantization

Dynamic quantization is best for MLPs, RNNs, and transformers. To implement it using PyTorch's `torch.ao.quantization` package, you must first choose a quantization engine: PyTorch currently supports the *Facebook General Matrix Multiplication* (FBGEMM) engine for x86 CPUs, plus a newer x86 engine that supports recent x86 CPUs but is less battle-tested, and finally the *Quantized Neural Networks Package* (QNNPACK) engine for ARM/mobile. This code will pick the appropriate engine depending on the platform:

```
import platform

machine = platform.machine().lower()
engine = "qnnpack" if ("arm" in machine or "aarch64" in machine) else "x86"
```

PyTorch does not offer an engine for CUDA or other hardware accelerators, but other libraries do, such as the bitsandbytes library (as we will see shortly).

Once you have selected an engine, you can use the `quantize_dynamic()` function from the `torch.ao.quantization` package; just pass it your trained model, tell it the types of layers to quantize (typically just the `Linear` and RNN layers), specify the quantized data type, and boom, you have a ready-to-use quantized model:

```
from torch.ao.quantization import quantize_dynamic

model = nn.Sequential(nn.Linear(10, 100), nn.ReLU(), nn.Linear(100, 1))
# [...] pretend the 32-bit model is trained here
torch.backends.quantized.engine = engine
qmodel = quantize_dynamic(model, {nn.Linear}, dtype=torch.qint8)
X = torch.randn(3, 10)
y_pred = qmodel(X)  # float inputs and outputs, but quantized internally
```

The `quantize_dynamic()` function replaces each `Linear` layer with a `DynamicQuantizedLinear` layer, with int8 weights. This layer behaves just like a regular linear layer, with float inputs and outputs, but it quantizes its inputs on the fly (recomputing the zero points and scales for each batch), performs matrix multiplication using integers only (with 32-bit integer accumulators), and dequantizes the result so the next layer gets float inputs. Now let's look at static quantization.

Static quantization

This option is best for CNNs, and max inference speed. It's also compulsory for edge devices without a *floating-point unit* (FPU), as they don't support floats at all. Both the weights and activations are prepared for quantization ahead of time, for all layers. As we discussed earlier, weights are constant so they can be quantized once, while activations require a calibration step to determine their typical range. The model is then converted to a fully quantized model. Here is how to implement it:

```
from torch.ao.quantization import get_default_qconfig, QuantStub, DeQuantStub

model = nn.Sequential(QuantStub(),
                      nn.Linear(10, 100), nn.ReLU(), nn.Linear(100, 1),
                      DeQuantStub())
# [...] pretend the 32-bit model is trained here
model.qconfig = get_default_qconfig(engine)
torch.ao.quantization.prepare(model, inplace=True)
for X_batch, _ in calibration_loader:
    model(X_batch)
torch.ao.quantization.convert(model, inplace=True)
```

Let's go through this code step by step:

- After the imports, we create our 32-bit model, but this time we add a `QuantStub` layer as the first layer, and a `DeQuantStub` layer as the last. Both layers are just passthrough for now.
- Next, the model can be trained normally (another option would be to take a pretrained model and place it between a `QuantStub` layer and a `DeQuantStub` layer).
- Next, we set the model's `qconfig` to the output of the `get_default_qconfig()` function: this function takes the name of the desired quantization engine and returns a `QConfig` object containing a default quantization configuration for this engine. It specifies the quantization data type (e.g., `torch.qint8`), the quantization scheme (e.g., symmetric linear quantization per tensor), and two functions that will observe the weights and activations to determine their ranges.
- Next we call the `torch.ao.quantization.prepare()` function: it uses the weight observer specified in the configuration to determine the weights range, which it immediately uses to compute the zero points and scales for the weights. Since we don't know what the input data looks like at this point, the function cannot compute the quantization parameters for the activations yet, so it inserts activation observers in the model itself: these are attached to the outputs of the `QuantStub` and `Linear` layers. The observer appended to the `QuantStub` layer is responsible for tracking the input range.
- Next, we take a representative sample of input batches (i.e., the kind the model will get in production), and we pass these batches through the model: this allows the activation observers to track the activations.
- Once we have given the model enough data, we finally call the `torch.ao.quantization.convert()` function, which removes the observers from the model and replaces the layers with quantized versions. The `QuantStub` layer is

replaced with a `Quantize` layer which will quantize the inputs. The `Linear` layers are replaced with `QuantizedLinear` layers. And the `DeQuantStub` layer is replaced with a `DeQuantize` layer which will dequantize the outputs.

There are a few observers to choose from: they can just keep track of the minimum and maximum values for each tensor (`MinMaxObserver`), or for each channel (`PerChannelMinMaxObserver`), or they can compute an exponential moving average of the min/max values, which reduces the impact of a few outliers. Finally, they can even record a histogram of the observed values (`HistogramObserver`), making it possible to find an optimal quantization range that minimizes the quantization error. That said, the default observers are usually fine.

We now have a model that we can use normally, with float inputs and outputs, but which works entirely with integers internally, making it lightweight and fast. To deploy it to mobile or embedded devices, there are many options to choose from (which are beyond the scope of this book), including:

- Use ExecuTorch, which is PyTorch's lightweight edge runtime
- Export the model to ONNX and run it with ONNX Runtime (cross-platform)
- Convert it to TFLite or TFLite Micro
- Compile it for the target device using TVM or microTVM

Moreover, the PyTorch team has released a separate library named *PyTorch-native Architecture Optimization* (TorchAO) (*https://homl.info/torchao*), designed to be a robust and extensible model optimization framework. Over time, many features in PyTorch's `torch.ao` package are expected to be migrated to—or superseded by—TorchAO. The library already includes advanced features such as 4-bit weight support and *per-block quantization*, in which each tensor is split into small blocks and each block is quantized independently, trading space for improved precision.

Post-training quantization (either dynamic or static) can shrink and speed up your models significantly, but it will also degrade their accuracy. This is particularly the case when quantizing down to 4 bits or less, and it's worse for static quantization than for dynamic quantization (which can at least adapt to each input batch independently). When the accuracy drop is unacceptable, you can try quantization-aware training, as we will discuss now.

Quantization-Aware Training (QAT)

QAT was introduced in a 2017 paper (*https://homl.info/qat*) by Google researchers.[6] It rests upon a simple idea: why not introduce some fake quantization noise during training so the model can learn to cope with it? After training, we can then quantize the model for real, and it should remain fairly accurate. QAT also makes it possible to quantize more aggressively without losing too much accuracy, down to 4 bits, or even less. Sound promising? Let's see how it can be done.

To add fake quantization noise to weights, we can simply quantize them and immediately dequantize them. For example, a weight equal to 0.42 might be quantized to the 4-bit integer 7, and immediately dequantized back to 0.39: we've successfully introduced quantization noise, and it's precisely the quantization noise that we would get if the model were really quantized. This fake quantization operation can be executed at each training step, and it can also be applied to some of the activations (e.g., to each layer output).

However, there is one little problem: quantization involves rounding to the nearest integer, and the rounding operation has gradients equal to zero (or undefined at integer boundaries), so gradient descent cannot make any progress. Luckily, we can sidestep this issue by using the *straight-through estimator* (STE) trick: during the backward phase, we pretend that the fake quantization operation was just the identity function, so the gradients flow straight through it untouched. This works because the loss landscape is generally fairly smooth locally, so gradients are likely to be similar within a small region around the quantized value, including at the original value.

Implementing QAT in PyTorch is fairly straightforward:

```
from torch.ao.quantization import get_default_qat_qconfig

model = nn.Sequential(nn.Linear(10, 100), nn.ReLU(), nn.Linear(100, 1))
model.qconfig = get_default_qat_qconfig(engine)
torch.ao.quantization.prepare_qat(model, inplace=True)
train(model, optimizer, [...]) # train the model normally
torch.ao.quantization.convert(model.eval(), inplace=True)
```

After the import, we create our model, set its `qconfig` attribute to the default QAT configuration object for the chosen quantization engine, then we call the `prepare_qat()` function to add fake quantization operations to the model. This step also adds observers to determine the usual range of activation values. Next, we can train the model normally. Lastly, we switch the model to eval mode, and we call the `convert()` function to truly quantize it.

6 Benoit Jacob et al., "Quantization and Training of Neural Networks for Efficient Integer-Arithmetic-Only Inference", arXiv preprint arXiv:1712.05877 (2017)".

QAT doesn't have to be used during all of training: you can take a pretrained model and just fine-tune it for a few epochs using QAT, typically using a lower learning rate to avoid damaging the pretrained weights.

We've seen how to implement PTQ and QAT using PyTorch's `torch.ao` package. However, it's primarily designed for CPUs. What if you want to run an LLM on a GPU that doesn't quite have enough RAM? One option is to use the TorchAO library, which has growing GPU support. Another is to use the bitsandbytes library: let's discuss it now.

Quantizing LLMs Using the bitsandbytes Library

The bitsandbytes library (bnb), created by Tim Dettmers, is designed to make it easier to train and run large models on GPUs with limited VRAM. For this, it offers:

- Quantization tools, including 4-bit quantization, block-wise quantization, and more
- Memory-efficient versions of popular optimizers such as Adam or AdamW, that operate on 8-bit tensors
- Custom CUDA kernels written specifically for 8-bit or 4-bit quantized models, for maximum speed

The bitsandbytes library is designed for Nvidia GPUs. It also has some limited support for CPUs and AMD GPUs.

For example, let's see how to implement post-training static quantization down to 4 bits. If you are using Colab, you must first install the bitsandbytes library using `%pip install bitsandbytes`, then run this code:

```
from transformers import AutoModelForCausalLM, BitsAndBytesConfig

model_id = "TinyLlama/TinyLlama-1.1B-Chat-v1.0"
bnb_config = BitsAndBytesConfig(load_in_4bit=True, bnb_4bit_quant_type="nf4",
                                bnb_4bit_compute_dtype=torch.bfloat16)
model = AutoModelForCausalLM.from_pretrained(model_id, device_map="auto",
                                             quantization_config=bnb_config)
```

This code starts by importing the necessary classes from the Transformers library (introduced in Chapter 14), then it creates a `BitsAndBytesConfig` object, which I will explain shortly. Lastly, it downloads a pretrained model (in this case a 1.1 billion parameter version of Llama named TinyLlama, fine-tuned for chat), specifying the desired quantization configuration.

Under the hood, the Transformers library uses the bitsandbytes library to quantize the model weights down to 4 bits just as they are loaded into the GPU: no extra step is required. You can now use this model normally to generate text (see Chapter 15). During inference, whenever some weights are needed, they are dequantized on the fly to the type specified by the `bnb_4bit_compute_dtype` argument (`bfloat16` in this case), and the computations are performed in this higher precision. As soon as the dequantized weights are no longer needed, they are dropped, so memory usage remains low.

In this example, the `BitsAndBytesConfig` object specifies *4-bit Normal Float* (NF4) quantization using `bfloat16` for computations. NF4 is a nonlinear 4-bit scheme where each of the 16 possible integer values represents a specific float value between –1 and +1. Instead of being equally spaced (as in linear quantization), these values correspond to the quantiles of the normal distribution centered on zero: this means that they are closer together near zero. This improves accuracy because model weights tend to follow a normal distribution centered on zero, so having more precision near zero is helpful.

NF4 was introduced as part of QLoRA (*https://homl.info/qlora*),[7] a technique that quantizes a frozen pretrained model with NF4, then uses LoRA adapters (see Chapter 17) for fine-tuning, along with activation checkpointing (see Chapter 12). This approach drastically reduces VRAM usage and compute: the authors managed to fine-tune a 65-billion parameter model using a single GPU with 48 GB of RAM, with only a small accuracy drop. Although activation checkpointing reduces VRAM usage overall, it can lead to memory spikes when processing batches with long sequences. To deal with such spikes, the QLoRA authors also introduced *paged optimizers* which take advantage of Nvidia unified memory: the CUDA driver automatically moves pages of data from GPU VRAM to CPU RAM whenever needed. Lastly, the authors also used *double quantization*, meaning that the quantization parameters themselves were quantized to save a bit more VRAM.

For more details on 4-bit quantization in the Hugging Face ecosystem, check out this great post by the QLoRA authors and other contributors (*https://huggingface.co/blog/4bit-transformers-bitsandbytes*).

7 Tim Dettmers et al., "QLORA: Efficient Finetuning of Quantized LLMs", arXiv preprint arXiv:2305.14314 (2023).

Using Pre-Quantized Models

Many popular pretrained models have already been quantized and published online, in particular on the Hugging Face Hub. For example, Tom Jobbins, better known by his Hugging Face username TheBloke, has published thousands of quantized models available at *https://huggingface.co/TheBloke*. Many of these models were quantized using one of the following modern methods:

Generative pre-training quantization (GPTQ)
: GPTQ (*https://homl.info/gptq*)[8] is a post-training quantization method, usually down to 4 bits, that treats quantization as an optimization problem. GPTQ goes through each layer, one by one, and optimizes the 4-bit weights to minimize the MSE between the layer's original outputs (i.e., using the full precision weights) and the approximate outputs (i.e., using the 4-bit weights). Once the optimal 4-bit weights are found, the approximate outputs are passed to the next layer, and the process is repeated all the way to the output layer. During inference, the weights are dequantized whenever they are needed. GPTQ only quantizes the weights, not the activations: this is called *weight-only quantization*, which is great for inference, not for training. You can use the Hugging Face Optimum library (*https://huggingface.co/docs/optimum*) or the GPTQModel library (*https://github.com/ModelCloud/GPTQModel*) to quantize your models with GPTQ.

Activation-aware Weight Quantization (AWQ)
: AWQ (*https://homl.info/awq*)[9] aims to improve the accuracy of block-wise weight-only quantization (typically 4-bit quantization). The idea is to preserve the precision of the most important weights. To identify these so-called *salient weights*, the algorithm runs a calibration dataset through the model and finds the largest activations for each quantization group (e.g., the largest 0.1% to 1% activations), and the corresponding weights are considered salient. The authors observed that storing the salient weights using float16 greatly reduces the model's *perplexity* (a common metric equal to the exponential of the cross-entropy). However, mixing 4-bit and 16-bit weights is not hardware-friendly, so AWQ uses another method to preserve the salient weight's precision: they simply scale them up by some factor and add an operation in the model to scale down the corresponding activations (but this operation can generally be fused into the previous operation). Rather than using a fixed scaling factor, AWQ performs a search for the optimal factor, leading to the lowest quantization error. To implement AWQ, you can use the Hugging Face Optimum library.

8 Elias Frantar et al., "GPTQ: Accurate Post-Training Quantization for Generative Pre-trained Transformers", arXiv preprint arXiv:2210.17323 (2022).

9 Ji Lin et al., "AWQ: Activation-aware Weight Quantization for LLM Compression and Acceleration", arXiv preprint arXiv:2306.00978 (2023).

Llama.cpp quantization using the GPT-Generated Unified Format (GGUF)
: GGUF (*https://homl.info/gguf*) is a binary file format designed to store LLMs efficiently. It was introduced by Georgi Gerganov, the creator of llama.cpp, and it supersedes previous file formats such as GGML, GGMF, and GGJT. A GGUF file includes the weights, the tokenizer, special tokens, the model architecture, the vocabulary size, and other metadata. Llama.cpp offers quantizers (e.g., using the `quantize` tool) to convert the model weights to one of GGUF's supported quantized formats, such as Q4_K_M. Q4 stands for 4-bit quantization, K stands for per-block quantization (typically 32 or 64 weights per block depending on the chosen format), and M means medium size and precision for this quantization level (other options are S = Small and L = Large). There are also more recent and efficient quantization options such as Importance-aware Quantization (IQ), which uses various techniques to improve accuracy (e.g., nonlinear quantization), and Ternary Quantization (TQ).

On the Hugging Face Hub, every repository is backed by Git, so it has branches and commits. When you call `from_pretrained()`, the model is fetched from the default branch, which is almost always `main`. But quantized models are often placed in a different branch. When calling `from_pretrained()`, you can choose a branch, a tag, or even a commit hash, by using the `revision` argument. Check the model card for the list of available files and versions. For GGUF models, you must specify the filename using the `gguf_file` argument.

In conclusion, reduced precision, mixed-precision training, and quantization are arguably the most important tools to allow large models to run on limited hardware. But there are many more, including the following:

- You could tweak the model's architecture before training, by reducing the number of layers, or the number of neurons per layer, or by sharing weights across layers (e.g., as in the ALBERT model, introduced in Chapter 15).
- If you have a large trained model, you can shrink it by removing some of its weights, for example the ones with the smallest magnitude, or the ones with the smallest effect on the loss. You can also remove whole channels, layers, or attention heads. This is called *model pruning*, and you can implement it using the `torch.nn.utils.prune` module, or the Hugging Face Optimum library.
- As we saw in Chapter 15, you can also use a large trained model as a teacher to train a smaller model: this is called distillation.
- A trained model can also be shrunk by fusing some of its layers, removing redundancy. For example, a batch-norm layer (introduced in Chapter 11) performs a linear operation, so if it comes immediately after a linear layer, you can fuse

both layers into a single linear layer. Similarly, you can fuse a convolutional layer followed by a batch-norm layer into a single convolutional layer. This only works after training, since the batch-norm layer must compute running averages during training. You can implement layer fusion with the `torch.quantization.fuse_modules()` function, or with the Hugging Face Optimum library. In any case, make sure to fuse layers *before* quantizing your model: less layers means less quantization noise.

- You can use low-rank approximations, where a large matrix is replaced by the product of two smaller ones. For example, replace a large linear layer such as `Linear(10_000, 20_000)` with two linear layers `Linear(10_000, 100)` and `Linear(100, 20_000)`. This reduces the number of parameters from about 200 million down to just three million, and also drastically reduces computations. The intermediate dimensionality (100 in this example) is a hyperparameter you can tune to balance accuracy and model size. This technique can be performed after training by factorizing the weight matrix using SVD (see the notebook for an example).

Give these techniques a try: shrink the models!

Chapter 17 and Appendices C, D, and E are available online at *https://homl.info*.

Index

Symbols

A

B

C

D

E

F

G

H

I

J

K

L

M

P

Q

R

S

T

U

V

W

X

Y

Z

About the Author

Aurélien Geron is a machine learning consultant and lecturer. A former Googler, he led YouTube's video classification team. He's been a founder of and CTO at a few different companies: Wifirst, a leading wireless ISP in France; Polyconseil, a consulting firm focused on telecoms, media, and strategy; and Geron AI, a consulting firm focused on machine learning.

Before all that Aurélien worked as an engineer in a variety of domains: finance (JP Morgan and Société Générale), defense (Canada's DOD), and healthcare (blood transfusion). He also published a few technical books (on C++, WiFi, and internet architectures) and lectured in several universities.

A few fun facts: he taught his three children to count in binary with their fingers (up to 1,023), he studied microbiology and evolutionary genetics before going into software engineering, and his parachute didn't open on the second jump.

Colophon

The animal on the cover of *Hands-On Machine Learning with Scikit-Learn and PyTorch* is a Bornean orangutan (*Pongo pygmaeus*). Orangutans belong to the family Hominidae, or the great apes, along with gorillas, chimpanzees, and humans.

Native to the rainforests of Borneo, these orangutans are arboreal but will travel large distances on the ground in search of food. Their diet includes fruit, seeds, flowers, vines, and bird eggs. They build elaborate nests in trees to sleep in at night. Juveniles start to practice nest-building at 6 months old, and are proficient by the age of 3.

Bornean orangutans are highly sexually dimorphic. Males are larger than females and they have larger cheek pads (known as flanges), larger canines, and more facial hair. Males average 4 feet, 9 inches tall, and weigh 165 pounds, while females average 3 feet, 7 inches tall and weigh 85 pounds. Orangutans have long arms for climbing in trees. They have gray skin and a shaggy, reddish-brown coat.

Bornean orangutans are more solitary than other orangutan species. They aren't considered territorial, but males will exhibit threatening behavior when meeting other males. They only socialize with females to mate. Females reach maturity at around 15 years old. They give birth to a single infant every 8 or 9 years. Orangutans have the longest infant development period of all the great apes. Juveniles are weaned at about 4 years old and become completely independent around 7 years old. Their lifespan is 35–45 years.

There are about 105,000 Bornean orangutans living in the wild. Deforestation and hunting have made them increasingly endangered. Although hunting the orangutan is illegal, perpetrators are rarely prosecuted. Their distribution throughout Borneo is now patchy due to habitat destruction. Additionally, as rainfall has decreased on the island, food has become less available, which has impacted the orangutan's birthrates. They have an IUCN status of Critically Endangered. Many of the animals on O'Reilly covers are endangered; all of them are important to the world.

The cover illustration is by José Marzan Jr., based on an antique line engraving by Friedrich Specht (1888). The series design is by Edie Freedman, Ellie Volckhausen, and Karen Montgomery. The cover fonts are Gilroy Semibold and Guardian Sans. The text font is Adobe Minion Pro; the heading font is Adobe Myriad Condensed; and the code font is Dalton Maag's Ubuntu Mono.

www.ingramcontent.com/pod-product-compliance
Lightning Source LLC
Chambersburg PA
CBHW080333220326
41598CB00030B/4497

* 9 7 9 8 3 4 1 6 0 7 9 8 9 *